COMPA

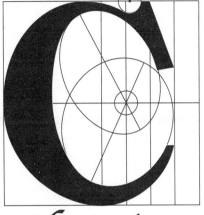

Classics®

YOUR PERSONAL PORTABLE LIBRARY

VOLUME III

Compact Classics, Inc.
1994

COMPACT

Classics®

First Printing, October 1994

Lan C. England, Publisher
Stevens W. Anderson, Editor

Compact Classics, Inc.
P.O. Box 526145
Salt Lake City, Utah
84152-6145

ISBN 1-880184-25-7

Printed in the United States of America

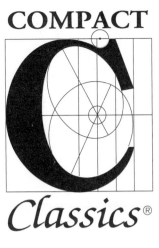

COMPACT
Classics®

VOLUME III

■ **INTRODUCTION**: *Compact Classics Volume III*

Get ready. . . because Volume III of *Compact Classics* has *more*. More great classics, more unforgettable quotes, more eye-opening facts and trivia, and more captivating chronicles and creations. And, like Volumes I and II, *Compact Classics* III is available in *more* formats: *Compact Classics* hardcover, softcover and binder editions, and new **LARGE PRINT, CD-ROM** and **Diskette** versions so that you can enjoy *Compact Classics'* summaries and facts anywhere, anytime.

Volume III takes the exploration of the human mind and spirit in new exciting directions—from fantastic **"Dreamscapes"** of mystery and myth to the sometimes harsh and brutal **"Realityscapes"** of our world. Volume III also includes three dynamic new libraries: **"People, Places and Times"**, **"Issues and Insights"**, and **"They Made a Difference"** where you'll encounter the issues and people who have created our history, and continue to shape our world.

And, you'll find still more of the best children's classics, fiction and non-fiction. . . as well as **"Thought Collections"** and **"Fantastic Facts and Inquiries"** to entertain and enlighten for many years to come.

■ Invest in Yourself. Read even more *Classics*.

INVITATION: We want to hear from you. **(See back page)**

Since *Compact Classics* is read by people around the world, our best suggestions for future inclusions come from *you*, the reader. If you have run across a particularly significant book, let us know about it. If we use your original suggestion in a future volume, we'll pay you for it. In the event that several people suggest the same title, we'll pay the first person who sent it in. So don't delay. Write or call toll-free **1-800-755-9777**.

INDEX: A Table of Contents

LIBRARY #2: Realityscapes   **77**

confronting the waking world

Changing Backdrops—in search of the "best of times"

Immortal Voices—words from history that live on

COMPACT

Classics®

LIBRARY #1: Dreamscapes
exploring the worlds within

Get ready for a heady plunge into the endless, life-giving oceans of the human mind and spirit.

Our **Dreamscapes** library will carry you through realms of myth, mystery, and allegory; of nightmare and visionary hope. And there you will dream, dare, despair, and triumph with such richly diverse characters as Malory's legendary Sir Lancelot, tragically rash and supremely chivalrous; the heroically poignant Charlie of Daniel Keyes' Flowers for Algernon, who retains his purity of soul throughout a devastating round-trip journey between imbecility and genius; and Madeleine L'Engle's wrinkled-in-time young adventuress Meg Murry, who worries about failing school even while she leads a company of children to rescue her physicist father from doom on a distant planet.

"I am all," says the Overmind—the vast, creative spirtual force in Childhood's End who ultimately transforms the children of Earth. So immerse yourself in these Dreamscapes—and connect with the sourcewaters of all that is best and worst—and all that is truly creative—in the soul of humankind.

THE JUNGLE BOOK

by
Rudyard Kipling
(1865 - 1936)

Type of work: Children's fantasy tales
Setting: 19th-century colonial India

It is not by accident that Mowgli and Rikki-tikki-tavi, protagonists of the following *Jungle Book* excerpts, are both orphans. Though born in India, Rudyard Kipling was himself separated from his parents at a young age when they took him back to England and left him in "The House of Desolation"—the name young Rudyard gave to his foster-home lodgings. Perhaps his later return to India as a journalist and his lifelong fascination with issues of East vs. West expressed, in part, his richly productive struggle to define and reclaim "home."

While he was still a young man, Kipling earned literary fame in a variety of genres, and in 1907 he became the first English recipient of the Nobel Prize for Literature.

Mowgli's Brothers

On a warm evening in the Seeonee Hills, as Father Wolf made ready to hunt, Tabaqui the jackal breathlessly arrived to warn him that the sinister tiger Shere Khan had been spotted in the area. This angered Father Wolf. Listening carefully, he could hear the throaty cough of the tiger rumbling through the jungle, and he knew that much of the game would be scared off.

A short time later, Mother Wolf spied a strange figure climbing up toward their cave. "Is that a man's cub?" she asked Father Wolf. "I have never seen one. Bring it here." At first she was disgusted by the smell and sight of the clumsy, naked creature that her mate deposited in front of her, but as the cub pushed his furless little body awkwardly in amongst her own and began to feed, Mother Wolf's heart softened. She resolved to keep the helpless foundling—and to protect him from Shere Khan's constant threat.

And so the seasons passed. The man-cub, called Mowgli by Mother Wolf, did not grow as fast as his wolf brothers, but in many ways he was far wiser. As time went on, Akela, the leader of the wolf pack—and Mowgli's protector—slowly grew weaker and his authority waned. Finally the day came when Akela missed his kill, a sign that he could no longer be trusted to reign over the wolves. Bagheera the Panther had warned Mowgli that this day would come, and Mowgli had prepared by creeping into the nearby village to steal The Red Flower that Man called "fire," which he now tended carefully with sticks and twigs.

Akela was called to the Council Rock and stripped of his dominion. Then the council turned to banish Mowgli, arguing that a man-cub had no place in the pack. Alone, the outcast made his way through the jungle—until he met up with Shere Khan and a marauding band of outlaw wolves which the tiger had lured to his side. As the animals closed in around him, Mowgli produced a torch, bright red fire blooming at one end. He pushed the fire-stick forward, singeing Shere Khan's whiskers—and the great cat whimpered in fright before bounding off, with his wolf soldiers scurrying after him.

Now at last Mowgli knew that he must go and live amongst Man. He was no longer a wolf; like Man, he had The Red Flower.

Tiger-Tiger!

After seeking shelter amongst Men in the village by the river, the eleven-year-old Mowgli was taken in by Messua, a woman whose son had been stolen years earlier by Shere Khan. He learned the speech of Man and was made a herd boy in charge of the water buffalo. One day while he tended the buffalo, he spied Grey Brother, the eldest of his old wolf-cub siblings. After that, Grey Brother would come to Mowgli every day with news from the jungle. And finally the day came when Grey Brother announced that Shere Khan—Mowgli's mortal enemy—had returned. The tiger, Grey Brother said, had crept close to the village, intent on ambushing Mowgli at a nearby ravine. Mowgli thought quickly; then he asked Grey Brother if he could divide the buffalo herd in two. No, he did not have the skill to cut the heard, said Grey Brother—but he had brought one who could. And Mowgli was much pleased to see his old friend Akela raise his head out of the grass.

Akela deftly raced into the herd, dividing the cows from the bulls. Then, while Grey Brother drove the cows to the base of the ravine to keep Shere Khan from escaping up the walls, Mowgli and Akela maneuvered the bulls to the top of the ravine and stampeded them down toward Shere Khan. The tiger, sluggish after a heavy meal, was trampled by the oncoming herd.

At first, Buldeo, the village hunter, tried to take away the skin of Shere Khan to claim the reward of 100 rupees, but Mowgli had Akela frighten the false claimant off. Sadly, however, Buldeo sought revenge; and his spiteful stories soon set the villagers against Mowgli. Once more the boy became an outcast.

And once more the man-cub returned to the Council Rock in the Seeonee Hills, where he laid Shere Khan's tawny hide. The cry, "Look well! Look well, O Wolves!" rang through the hills again, and Akela once again took up his place as the pack leader.

Then, with order restored in the jungle, Mowgli retired forever from the pack. No longer Wolf and no longer welcomed by Man, he would live out his life in the forest, independent of both.

Rikki-Tikki-Tavi

One day Rikki-tikki-tavi, a young mongoose, was washed out of his family burrow by a spring flood. Bedraggled and half-drowned, he was found and rescued by a boy who lived in a nearby bungalow. After resting and being dried off inside the house, the mongoose felt much better. He ran about exploring throughout the day, and that evening, he slept with the boy, Teddy.

The next morning, the curious Rikki-tikki set off to investigate his splendid new hunting-ground—the bungalow garden. There he soon encountered Nag and Nagaina, the evil and cunning cobras who ruled the garden—and sought to rule the bungalow as well. Knowing that mongooses are deadly and formidable snake fighters, Nagaina, the she-cobra, began laying traps for the hated newcomer.

At mid-day, the mongoose had his first clash in the garden—with a wicked little dust-colored snake named Karait, whose bite is more deadly than that of ten cobras. Waiting until the enemy lashed out, Rikki-tikki darted in like a whiplash to seize the snake high behind the head; and in short order the menacing little devil became a tasty meal.

That night, the stealthy Nag lay in wait for the "big man" in the bungalow's bathroom. But the mongoose had been warned of this plan by Chuchundra the muskrat, and now he silently moved in for the kill. Locking his powerful jaws onto the back of Nag's head just below the hood, Rikki held on as the huge snake thrashed about. Tighter and tighter the mongoose clenched his jaw as he felt himself banged against the floor; "for the honour of his family, he preferred to be found with his teeth locked." He was sure now that he would die, but suddenly something went off like a thunderclap, and a hot wind knocked him senseless. "The big man had been awakened by the noise, and had fired both barrels of a shot-gun into Nag . . ."

The following day, Rikki-tikki, sore but unintimidated by his ordeal, found Darzee, the "feather-brained" tailor-bird, singing for joy. Never again would Nag come to eat his hatchlings. Rikki, however, knew that Nag's brooding mate still remained to be dealt with. And there was no way of knowing when Nagaina's eggs—said by Darzee to be hidden in the melon patch—would hatch, leaving Rikki to fend off an entire nest of cobras.

So, in concert with Darzee's wife—a bird as sensible as Darzee was foolish—Rikki set his plan in motion. First, Darzee's mate coaxed Nagaina away from the melon-bed by fluttering in front of the snake and crying that the boy had broken her wing. Then Rikki-tikki raced in to crush the twenty-five cobra eggs lining Nagaina's nest. As he was finishing, Darzee's wife reappeared to warn him that Nagaina had gone to the veranda, and "she means killing!" Gently snatching up the last uncrushed egg in his mouth, the wily mongoose scuttled to the veranda. There he found the human family at the breakfast table—but no one was eating. Their faces ashen white, "they sat stone-still" as Nagaina swayed to and fro within easy striking distance of Teddy's bare leg. " . . . Oh, foolish people, who killed my Nag," she hissed.

Rikki-tikki challenged the taunting cobra to turn and fight. But Nagaina hissed back that she would settle her account with Rikki-tikki after disposing of the humans. "Look at your eggs," wheedled the mongoose. Go and look, Nagaina." Then, producing the remaining cobra egg, Rikki shouted, "What price for . . . the last,

the very last of the brood?" At this, the snake "spun clear around" to face her adversary, while Teddy's father caught the boy by the shoulder and dragged him to safety. "Tricked . . . Rikk-tck-tck!" chuckled Rikki. "The boy is safe, and it was I—I—I that caught Nag by the hood last night . . . Come and fight with me. You shall not be a widow long."

" . . . Give me the last of my eggs," Nagaina implored, lowering her hood, "and I will go away and never come back." But Rikki-tikki knew better. His eyes glowing like hot coals, he danced around the writhing cobra. Then, suddenly, like lightning, Nagaina lunged out to seize the unguarded egg in her mouth and flashed away. But Rikki was after her; and just as the snake disappeared into her rat-hole den, the mongoose latched his fierce jaws onto her tail.

Watching his friend drawn into the black den of Nagaina, Darzee launched into a mournful song; surely now the brave mongoose was dead. Just at "the most touching part" of the dirge, however, the grass quivered, "and Rikki-tikki, covered with dirt, dragged himself out of the hole leg by leg, licking his whiskers."

"It is all over," he said. "The widow will never come out again." And as the frogs and birds of the garden frolicked, the exhausted hero "curled himself up in the grass and slept where he was . . . for he had done a hard day's work."

That night Rikki-tikki ate all that his human family gave him, then went proudly to bed on Teddy's shoulder. Why, "he had a right to be proud of himself." And from that night on, Rikki-tikki-tavi "kept that garden as a mongoose should keep it, with tooth and jump and spring and bite, till never a cobra dared show its head inside the walls."

Commentary:

Rudyard Kipling's many poems, novels and tales—including *Kim, Gunga Din,* and the ever-popular "Just So Stories" series for children ("How the Camel Got His Hump," "The Elephant's Child," etc.)—quickly propelled him into the most elite circles of Victorian-era world writers. Over the years his writing has been accused of exhibiting imperialist sympathies and of biases which run through most of our contemporary blacklist of "isms," including racism, chauvinism, ethnocentrism and sexism.

In *The Jungle Book,* however, there are few such "isms" with which to castigate its author: If the Indian villagers appear simple and superstitious in their dealings with Mowgli, then it is Mowgli, an Indian child, who becomes elevated at their expense. (And incidentally, it is the Wolf *Mother* who chooses to rear and protect him.) And though it is true that Rikki-tikki-tavi receives a home with an English family who employs Indian domestics, it is also true that the naive vulnerability exhibited by Teddy and his parents in their foreign post reveals colonial *weakness* rather than strength.

But whether one considers the author as a propagandist of Victorian imperialism or as a storyteller mimicking his times, there is no denying the excitement and sheer originality of Rudyard Kipling's amazing body of work.

THE WIND IN THE WILLOWS

by Kenneth Grahame
(1859 - 1932)

Type of work: Children's fantasy novel

Setting: The English countryside; early 1900s

Principal characters:

> *The Mole*, a level-headed, considerate animal
>
> *The Water Rat*, the Mole's brave, intelligent, and water-loving friend
>
> *Mr. Toad*, the generous, conceited, although good-hearted resident of Toad Hall
>
> *The Badger*, a stern, unsociable but completely loyal friend of the other animals

Commentary:

Published in 1908, *The Wind in the Willows*, has remained a favorite children's classic throughout the Twentieth Century. From generation to generation, children have delighted in Kenneth Grahame's fanciful renderings of life among the little animals that are hidden from view in the rivers, woods, and fields around us.

Grahame endows his creatures with such endearing and human characters that it is not hard to imagine Mr. Toad throwing himself a banquet in the palatial Toad Hall, or Rat and Mole enjoying a day of boating on the river. And the world which frames their adventures is painted in such vivid and cozy tints that Nature, too, becomes one of the most beloved characters in the stories. The good humor and spirit of the animals and the beauty of the countryside that surrounds them blend to create a tale of magic which calls to the child in all of us, no matter what our age.

Story Overview:

Mole was busily spring-cleaning his little underground home when he suddenly found himself beset by the warming season's "spirit of divine discontent and longing."

"Hang Spring-cleaning!" he said, and throwing down his brush, "he bolted out of the den without even waiting to put on his coat." Down through the meadows to the water's edge ran Mole—in awe at the first river he had ever seen. And there he stopped to gape. "This sleek, sinuous, full-bodied animal, chasing and chuckling, gripping things with a gurgle and leaving them with a laugh . . . All was a-shake and a-shiver—glints and gleams and sparkles, rustle and swirl, chatter and bubble."

There on the river bank Mole met the Water Rat, who introduced him to the wonderful world of "messing about in boats." And all that summer, Rat taught Mole about the ways of The River. Mole learned how to swim and row and how to avoid the dangers of the Wild Wood. Rat also introduced his new friend to Mr. Toad, the wealthy, light-hearted, and sometimes recklessly adventurous master of Toad Hall. Against their better judgment, in fact, Toad soon convinced Mole and Rat to accompany him on a road trip in the latest object to have captivated his fancy—a canary-yellow gypsy cart. "There's real life for you embodied in that little cart," Toad promised. "The open road, the dusty highway, the heath, the common, the hedgerows, the rolling downs . . . the whole world before you, and a horizon that's always changing!"

But before the little group had got very far from home, disaster struck: a motor-car sped past them on the road "at incredible speed, while from out the dust a faint 'poop-poop' wailed like an uneasy animal in pain." The automobile startled the adventurers' old grey horse, which reared up, pitching their lovely cart into a ditch.

The gypsy cart was now "an irredeemable wreck." But Toad didn't seem to care; he "sat straight down in the middle of the dusty road, his legs stretched out before him, and stared fixedly in the direction of the disappearing motor-car. He breathed short, his face wore a placid, satisfied expression, and at intervals he faintly murmured 'Poop-poop!'" Toad's new obsession had been born: the very next day he went to town and ordered a large and very expensive motor-car.

The seasons changed, and a snowy winter's afternoon found Mole and Rat warm and comfortably situated in Badger's den, where the three animals discussed all the trouble Toad had been getting into with his motor-cars, already having smashed seven automobiles, landed in the hospital three times, and paid countless fines for his recklessness. Toad's friends decided then and there that, come spring, they would take silly Toad in hand and "make him be a sensible Toad."

So the winter faded, and once again summer drew near. And one day, sure enough, Badger appeared at Rat's door and brazenly announced that the time had come to march over to Toad Hall and show wild-driving Toad the error of his ways. Toad's friends found him to be hopelessly stubborn, however; he refused to admit that he had been foolish when it came to his motor-cars. As a result, Rat and Badger found themselves obliged to send back Toad's new, bright-red motor-car and put him under house arrest until he changed his ways.

But Toad would not be routed so easily from his obsession. One day, when the Badger and the Mole were away from Toad Hall, Toad tricked Rat into believing he was deathly ill. While Rat ran to fetch the doctor, Toad used his bed sheets to lower himself out the window.

Filled with conceit at the cleverness of his escape, Toad stopped at a local inn to eat—and suddenly he heard an all-too-familiar sound that "made him start and fall a-trembling all over. The poop-poop! drew nearer and nearer, the car could be heard to turn into the inn-yard and come to a stop, and Toad had to hold on to the leg of the table to conceal his overmastering emotion." He slipped outside to take a look—only a look—at the car; but somehow he found himself first climbing inside, and then starting the machine up and driving off! "He increased his pace, and as the car devoured the street and leapt forth on the high road through the open country, he was only conscious that he was Toad once more, Toad at his best and highest, Toad the terror, the traffic-queller, the Lord of the lone trail, before whom all must give way or be smitten into nothingness and everlasting night."

This last brief, glorious reign of terror on the roads landed Toad a 20-year sentence in the "remotest dungeon of the best-guarded keep of the stoutest castle in all the length and breadth of Merry England." Fortunately, he was befriended by the jailer's tender-hearted young daughter, who helped keep his spirits up. In fact, the sharp-witted girl finally came up with a plan for Toad's deliverance: Her aunt, a washer-woman, had free access to all of the castle, and would agree—for a price!—to let Toad dress in her own clothes so that he could walk out of the castle unimpeded; if she should be discovered, the aunt would pretend that Toad had overpowered her and taken her clothes by force.

This plan worked wonderfully, and soon Toad was outside the castle, again extremely proud of his own poise and intelligence. But when he arrived at the train station to complete his escape, he realized to his horror that he had left all his money in the prison cell. And so it happened that a very *distressed* washerwoman threw herself on the mercies of the conductor—finally finagling a ride by promising to wash some of his shirts.

The battle had not been won yet, however—Toad soon found his train being hotly pursued by another train filled with guards and soldiers. In desperation, he finally revealed his plight and his true identity. The conductor, who was rather annoyed about being chased by another train, decided to help poor Toad. Close to the woods, where hiding places were as abundant as the shadows, he dropped the fugitive off.

After several more rash and reckless adventures, Toad—assisted by Rat and still dressed as a washerwoman—sauntered cockily along the road, very much puffed up by the accomplishment of his Grand Escape. Inspired to melody, he triumphantly began to croon. Of course, the song centered around himself:

The clever men at Oxford
Know all that there is to be knowed.
But they none of them know one half as much
As intelligent Mr. Toad! . . .

All at once Toad heard the familiar hum and sputter of a motor-car. Intending to hitch a ride with its driver and arrive home in glory, he turned to flag it down. To his horror, however, he saw that the approaching vehicle was the very same motor-car which he himself had stolen not long before! Certain that he was about to be recognized and imprisoned again, Toad cowered down in the dust to await his fate. The motor-car's genteel occupants, however, saw only a poor washerwoman who had fainted in the road. Tenderly, they "lifted Toad into the motor-car . . . and proceeded on their way."

It didn't take long for the incorrigible Toad to persuade these kind gentlemen to let the "washerwoman" take the wheel of their car. Of course he "tried to beat down the tremors, the yearnings, the old cravings that rose up and beset him." But once again he failed completely. Speeding in frantic delight down the roadway, he announced to his astonished passengers that he was really "Toad the motor-car snatcher, the prison-breaker, the Toad who always escapes!" Naturally, the gentlemen moved to seize him—causing Toad to steer the motor-car straight into a pond.

Giggling as he fled the sinking vehicle, Toad scrambled under a hedge and launched into another stirring anthem to his own great prowess. He abruptly lost his voice, however, at the approach of the dunked and irate gentlemen, accompanied by two policemen. Running blindly, he fell headlong into the river. As luck would have it, he surfaced, sputtering, right on the bank where Rat had dug his home.

Of course, the rat took Toad in, but he had some horrible news for his renegade friend: The Wild Wooders—the forest's stoats, weasels, and ferrets—had taken over Toad Hall. In Toad's absence, Mole and Badger had been watching over his property, but they reported that the premises had now been thoroughly overrun by guards who wouldn't let anyone near it.

Not long after this, Mole and Badger themselves arrived at Rat's dwelling, and the reunited comrades began formulating a plan to recapture Toad Hall. Badger was privy to a secret tunnel that led into the Hall—a secret which Toad's own father had not entrusted him with!—and, with this advantage, the friends designed their strategy: Brandishing sticks, they would attack the Wild Wooders in the midst of one of their vulgar banquets.

Well, this plan of attack worked wonderfully: "In five minutes the room was cleared. Through the broken windows the shrieks of terrified weasels escaping across the lawn were borne faintly to their ears . . . " And now the friends, having purged Toad Hall of the wicked scoundrels, "finished their supper in great joy and contentment, and presently retired to rest between clean sheets, safe in Toad's ancestral home, won back by matchless valour, consummate strategy, and a proper handling of sticks."

Toad orchestrated a grand banquet to celebrate his return. And there, with heroic self-mastery, he honored one of several promises he had made to his friends. As a first gesture towards turning over a new leaf, he resisted singing even one self-congratulatory ballad or making one boast about his cleverness and daring in the face of disaster. Mole and Rat were simply amazed at Toad's change of heart. "He was indeed an altered Toad!"

A WRINKLE IN TIME

by Madeleine L'Engle, Farrar, Strauss, Giroux, New York, N.Y., 1962

Type of work: Young adult fantasy

Setting: Earth and various dimensions and planets; 1960s

Principal characters:
Mr. Murry, a prominent physicist
Mrs. Murry, an equally brilliant research biologist
Meg, their daughter
Charles Wallace, their son
Calvin O'Keefe, a boy from Meg's school
Mrs. Whatsit, Mrs. Who, and *Mrs. Which*, dead stars who appear in the form of strange old ladies
IT, the evil overmind of Camazotz

Commentary:

In accepting the 1963 Newbery Award for *A Wrinkle in Time*, Madeleine L'Engle wrote: "What a child doesn't realize until he is grown is that in responding to fantasy, fairy tale, and myth he is responding to what Erich Fromm calls the one universal language . . . that cuts across all barriers of time, place, race, and culture."

Story Overview:

It was a dark and stormy night. . . . Wrapped in her quilt, Meg shook. She wasn't usually afraid of weather, she thought. It's the weather on top of everything else . . . on top of Meg Murry doing everything wrong. School had been going badly for some time, and for the daughter of two brilliant research scientists, that was indeed a humiliating thing—as her teachers took every occasion to remind her.

"I'll make myself some cocoa," Meg decided. "That'll cheer me up." The light in the kitchen was already on, and Charles Wallace, her little brother, was seated at the table with milk and bread and jam. "Hi," he said cheerfully, " . . . I put some milk on the stove for you. It ought to be hot by now." For some reason, Charles Wallace was always able to tell when Meg was perturbed. "You've put in more than twice enough . . . " Meg muttered. "I thought that Mother might like some," Charles replied serenely. And sure enough, Meg looked up at that moment to see her mother in the doorway.

As the three Murrys sat drinking cocoa and eating sandwiches, suddenly, through the door stepped a strange old woman "bundled up in scarves, wearing a felt hat, rubber boots, and a "shocking pink stole knotted about a rough overcoat."

"Mrs. Whatsit," Charles Wallace intoned. Charles knew the bizarre Mrs. Whatsit, who lived with two equally odd companions, Mrs. Who and Mrs. Which, in the creepy house across the field. So tonight when she found herself "blown off course" by the wind, as she put it, she had headed for his house. "I shall just sit down for a moment and pop off my boots," she announced, "and then I'll be on my way." Turning to Mrs. Murry, the old woman added casually, "Speaking of ways, pet, by the way, there *is* such a thing as a tesseract."

"The tesseract—" Mrs. Murry whispered as the odd old woman vanished back into the night. "How could she have known?"

When Meg awakened the next morning, the preceding night's events seemed like a bizarre dream. "What *is* a tesseract?" she asked her mother at breakfast. "It's a concept," Mrs. Murry replied. Beyond this, Meg could glean only that her parents had been working together on the "tesseract" just before her father's disappearance.

When Meg returned home from school that afternoon, Charles was waiting for her. "Come on," he commanded, "let's go." Mrs. Whatsit's mysterious remark the night before about "that tesseract thing" had intrigued him and he wanted to pay the woman a visit. Along the way, Charles and Meg ran into Calvin O'Keefe, star of the basketball team at Meg's school and a top student. As they walked on together, chatting, it occurred to Charles that Calvin might be gifted like himself and the three old ladies, with superhuman access to the vibrations of other minds, and to the rhythms of time and space. He decided to present Calvin for Mrs. Whatsit's appraisal. "If he's not okay," Charles told Meg, "she'll know."

The house, which stood shaded by a clump of elms, looked vaguely haunted. The three visitors first entered into a darkened kitchen, where they found Mrs. Who. The old lady generously used quotes from famous writers and historic personalities: "It's getting near time, Charlsie. *Ab honesto virum bonum nihil deterret . . .* 'Nothing deters a good man from doing what is honorable.'"

That evening after dinner, while Meg, Charles, and Calvin sat talking in the Murry yard, Mrs. Whatsit, Mrs. Who, and Mrs. Which suddenly appeared. And before they quite realized what was happening, the children were dissolved "in a fragment of nothingness" and rematerialized in a sunlit field on the planet Uriel, "the third planet of the star Malak in the spiral nebula, Messier 101."

"Well!" enthused Charles, quite flabbergasted. "That was quite a trip!" Mrs. Whatsit explained: the children had just emerged from the fifth dimension—a "tesseract"; she had essentially whisked them through a "wrinkle in time" that allowed such movement. The three witches revealed their true identities as very old, long-dead stars. Indeed, Mrs. Whatsit continued, tesseracts had been the subject of Mr. Murry's top-secret government research project when he disappeared—and now they had taken on the task of finding him. The ladies insisted that the children see first hand the grim obstacle before them.

First, Mrs. Whatsit transformed herself into a Pegasus and conveyed the children to a mountaintop where a dark, looming shadow chilled them to the core. This darkness, the old ladies explained, was the very essence against which Mr. Murry was grappling. He was at that very moment trapped on a planet surrounded by the Dark.

Suddenly the children were "tessered" once more, to rematerialize on a gray-skied planet in Orion's belt. There, through a crystal ball, they again beheld "the sickness of the shadow," which now "darkened the beauty of Earth."

"We know that it's evil," Calvin shouted, "but what is it?"

"Yyouu hhave ssaid itt!" suddenly reverberated the voice of Mrs. Which. "Itt is Eevill." Then she explained its source: A grand and exciting battle had once been waged against evil, a battle that had spanned the entire cosmos. Planet Earth had produced many great and noble "fighters"; Jesus, Buddha, da Vinci, Gandhi and others had been sent to defeat the darkness. And now, she told them, Mr. Murry was engaged in a similar campaign to save another planet, Camazotz. But somehow he had been swallowed up—and no one knew his present location or condition.

At this, Meg broke down and sobbed. "My child," Mrs. Whatsit crooned, "Do you think that we would have brought you here if there were no hope . . . ? For his children he may be able to do what he cannot do for himself . . . "

"Wee wwill cconnttinnue tto ffightt!" promised Mrs. Which, and with that, the children, again "swept into nothingness," came to rest on the planet Camazotz. "Ggo ddownn innttoo thee ttownn," Mrs. Which commanded, pointing to the valley below. "Bbee sstrongg." Mrs. Who handed Meg a pair of spectacles, instructing her to use them only as "a last resort." Then, after arming the other children with similar gifts, she charged them to be brave and warned them to avoid pride.

Hand in hand, the children descended. *Below them the town was laid out in harsh angular patterns. The houses . . . were all exactly alike, small square boxes painted gray . . . [Though] children were playing ball . . . Meg felt vaguely that something was wrong with their play.* "Look," cried Charles Wallace. "They're skipping and bouncing in rhythm! Everyone's doing it at exactly the same moment."

One building in town stood out from the rest: the "CENTRAL Central Intelligence." It seemed certain, the children reasoned, that someone in CENTRAL Central Intelligence must know where Mr. Murry was. Clutching one another tightly, they entered.

"How do we see whoever's in authority?" Charles anxiously asked a seated figure. The man escorted them to a blank wall and announced that "IT" was inside. Then, merely by placing a card against the marble facing, the wall disappeared and the travellers found themselves on the other side. A man sat at the far end of the room. *Meg stared at the man in horrified fascination. His eyes were bright and had a reddish glow. Above his head was a light, and it glowed in the same manner as the eyes, pulsing, throbbing, in steady rhythm.* Obviously, this was the source of the evil shadow they had witnessed. Charles Wallace instinctively ordered the others to avert their eyes to avoid being hypnotized. The man responded that though it would be easier if their eyes were focused, it made little difference. In no time, the evil being, who had the power both to understand their thoughts and to project his own thoughts into their heads, had challenged Charles to let him into his mind. "If you come—not to stay, you understand— . . . will you tell us where Father is?" Charles asked. "Yes," the man answered.

But the second Charles let Camazotz's red-eyed "Prime Coordinator" into his thoughts, this overmind IT took him as a puppet-master would a puppet. Meg and Calvin could only look on in helpless horror.

"Come," said IT through the hypnotized Charles. "Now see this." At the command, Meg's father, imprisoned inside some sort of transparent column, materialized from behind another wall. Meg rushed at the column, but bounced off its invisible surface. Thinking this certainly constituted a "last resort," Meg put on Mrs. Who's spectacles—and passed through the column unscathed. Then she gave the glasses—and their power—to her astonished father. He put them on, and together they passed back through the column. "IT is not pleased," Charles greeted them, tapping his foot impatiently. Then he led the children into his master's presence.

IT, Meg saw, was nothing more than an oversized "disembodied brain" under a glass dome. As the lights surrounding the brain pulsed, Mr. Murry and the children "had trouble breathing, thinking, or doing anything out of sync with IT's rhythm." Finally, Mr. Murry, fearing the worst, tessered the group out of Camazotz into a new wrinkle of time.

Mr. Murry, however, proved to be a rather inexperienced tesseract traveler. As they tessered onto a freezing-cold planet called Ixchel, Meg was badly injured. To further complicate matters, they had somehow left Charles behind—to fall even deeper into the dark power of IT.

Luckily, these accidents were offset by the fact that Ixchel was inhabited by a gentle species of furry, tentacled "beasts" who took the children into their care and tenderly nursed Meg back to health.

In the meantime, Mrs. Whatsit, Mrs. Who, and Mrs. Which arrived on Ixchel to convince Meg that since she was closest to Charles, she was the one to redeem him from IT's grasp. *"Yyou hhave ssomethiinngg thatt ITT hhass nnott,"* Mrs. Which told Meg. "Thiss ssomethinngg iss yyourr onlly wweapponn. Bbutt yyou mmusstt ffinndd itt fforr yyourrsellf."

When Mrs. Which's voice had faded away, Meg, alone on Camazotz, again entered CENTRAL Central Intelligence and made her way to the domed shrine where IT pulsed out its dark power. What was it that she possessed that IT did not, Meg ardently asked herself. Immediately, IT read her mind and responded through the voice of Charles Wallace: "Nonsense. You have nothing that IT doesn't have . . . Mrs. Whatsit hates you." Meg replied reflexively, "Mrs. Whatsit loves me . . . " and in that moment she knew what great gift she had: it was *love*. "Charles, Charles, I love you," she cried. " . . . I love you . . . Come away from IT, come back, come home."

"Meg," sobbed Charles, restored to himself, as he ran to embrace his sister. And suddenly Meg found herself back in her own home with her mother, looking on as her father, Charles, and Calvin were tessered down through the darkness toward her. Then Mrs. Whatsit's voice rang out. "Oh, my darlings," she chirped. "I'm sorry we don't have time to say good-bye to you properly. You see, we have to—" Then, as if on a puff of wind, all three long-burnt-out stars were gone.

THE SECRET GARDEN

by Frances Hodgson Burnett, Lippincott, Philadelphia, Pennsylvania, 1911

Type of work: Juvenile folk fiction

Setting: An old, dark manor in turn-of-the-century England

Principal characters:

Mary Lennox, a young orphan girl

Colin Craven, Mary's invalid cousin

Lord Archibald Craven, Mary's uncle and Colin's father

Dickon, a young boy in love with nature

Story Overview:

Orphaned Mary Lennox thought the wintry English moors looked dreary from the train window. In fact, everything looked dreary to Mary; it always had. Even in India, before her parents had died in the cholera epidemic, Mary had been unhappy. Perhaps it had begun with her mother, who had not wanted a child at all; when Mary was born, her mother had looked down at the "sickly, fretful, ugly baby" and frowned. Later, as Mary grew into a "sickly, fretful, toddling thing," her mother's main concern was to keep her "out of the way." Thus scorned and neglected by her socialite parents, Mary had been raised by her Indian Amah and the other household servants. To avoid the fits of temper that erupted so often from her small body, Mary's caretakers had learned to cater immediately to her every whim.

The ten-year-old girl, then, who sat staring obliquely out the window on the last leg of her long journey from India was a lonely and rebellious young tyrant. On that particular day, in fact, Mistress Mary had "never felt quite so contrary in all her life." She braced herself for her arrival at her final destination: Misselthwaite Manor, the mysterious "house with a hundred rooms" where she was to live under the guardianship of an uncle she had never seen.

At the station, Mary was met with grim propriety by Mrs. Medlock, the housekeeper at Misselthwaite. They rode on by coach to the manorhouse in a silence broken by one precaution from the housekeeper: Mary must not expect to see her uncle soon. Lord Archibald Craven often was away from Misselthwaite for weeks and months at a time; and when he was home, he allowed few intrusions upon his solitude.

Misselthwaite, a mansion that had seen six hundred years of sadness, was vast and dark, its walls adorned throughout by a sullen wood paneling. The rows of closed rooms flanking its shadowy hallways beckoned Mary temptingly, but her roamings were restricted to one or two wings. She was allowed, however, to explore or play in any of the gardens around the manor—except for one particular garden, walled and hedged in secrecy, which no one had been allowed to enter for over ten years. This, Mary learned, had been the special garden of Archibald Craven's dead wife. After her burial, the Master of the Manor had ordered the wooden door bolted—and then buried the key.

In the beginning Mary did not want to go outside; she preferred to sulk alone in the silent mansion, nursing her resentment of the forbidding hunchbacked uncle whom she had still not met. However, with the passage of time, the secret garden lured her own walled-in and rebellious heart. Envisioning the scene of her uncle burying a piece of metal in a bid to forget his dead wife, she determined to unearth the key.

Outdoors in the gardens, the once-frail Mary grew stronger. Day after day, the fresh, rough air blew over her and filled her lungs with sweetness, gradually whipping color into her cheeks and brightening her dull eyes and hair. Most surprisingly, her disposition became more and more agreeable.

But one thing continued to disturb her. At night in the manorhouse Mary sometimes awoke to hear distant crying sounds. When she asked the servant-girl Martha about it, she was told it was only the night wind, blowing across the moor.

Martha was more forthcoming about other mysteries. There was a tree in the secret garden, she told Mary, from which a branch had protruded, bent like a seat. Letting wild roses canopy over the branch, Mrs. Craven had made this her special retreat. But one day, as she sat perched in her favorite seat, the branch broke—and Mary's aunt had fallen to her death.

Upon hearing this extraordinary story, Mary thought of her solitary, hunchbacked uncle. For the first time she understood what it meant to feel sorry for someone.

The very next day, as she played in the yard, Mary was led by a robin to the spot where the key was buried. Finding her way to the forbidden door, she entered the secret garden.

The plot was a sweet, strange, silent place, its high walls covered by the thick, leafless stems of climbing rosebushes. Some green bulb points were already trying to poke their way up through the ground; Mary dug gently around them to give them space. For the remainder of the day she gave the same loving care to other portions of the garden. At last, as the sun began to set on the horizon, Mary left; but she knew she would return there many times over, determined to bring the secret garden back to life.

Shortly after discovering the secret garden, Mary met Dickon, the young brother of her servant-friend Martha. Dickon knew nature intimately; in fact, he could communicate with animals. As the boy and girl became friends, Mary shared her wonderful secret garden with Dickon. They met together whenever possible to tend its emerging new buds and greenery.

Meanwhile, in the depths of night, Mary continued to be awakened by the mysterious crying. One night she decided to uncover its source. The sound led her at last to a door in one of the manor's forbidden corridors. Behind the door was a boy, crying in his bed. He had a sharp, delicate face, the color of ivory. Mary crept closer—and as she did so her candlelight attracted the crier's attention.

"Are you a ghost?" the boy whispered in fear.

"No, I am not," Mary answered, in a frightened whisper of her own. "Are you one?" Still staring fixedly at Mary, the boy finally stammered that he was Colin Craven, Lord Archibald Craven's son. All these nights, then, Mary had been haunted by the night-wails of her own cousin!

Like Mary, Colin had always been a sickly child, forbidden to walk by himself or to leave his room. He cried at night, he told Mary, because he was sure both he and his hunchbacked father were dying. Mary was both depressed and intrigued by her fragile newfound cousin. Before returning to her bed, she promised Colin that she would come and see him again the next day.

During their second visit, Mary told Colin about his dead mother's secret garden—but did not reveal that she had found the key. Colin was thrilled to hear about his mother's love for nature—a world which he himself had never experienced.

As their visits continued, Mary soon realized that Colin was a very spoiled boy. He gave the servants fits, making them run to his aid every time he screamed. In fact, the only person he couldn't dominate was the strong-willed Mary. When Mrs. Medlock discovered the visitations, she cautiously allowed them to continue, mainly because Colin's behavior had improved under the girl's ministrations.

One afternoon as Mary returned to the house from the secret garden, she noticed the servants were running about in a frenzy. It seemed that Colin had thrown a tantrum because Mary had gone to the gardens that morning instead of visiting him. Indignant, Mary stalked in to Colin's room. When her cousin started wailing about the lump on his back, Mary leapt up onto the bed, turned Colin over onto his stomach, and probed his back with her fingers. "There's not a lump as big as a pin!" she scoffed. The only thing wrong with him, she said, was that he never left his dreary room.

"I'll-I'll go out with you, Mary," Colin finally sheepishly conceded. "I shan't hate fresh air if we can find . . . the secret garden." Delighted, Mary at last took her cousin into her confidence. She told him about Dickon, the animal charmer, and about the key and their work in the secret garden. Indeed, she reported, "the garden had reached the time when every day and every night it seemed as if Magicians were passing through it drawing loveliness out of the earth and the boughs with wands."

Not long afterwards, Mary and Dickon were allowed to take Colin outside in his wheelchair to play. It was not hard to steal him away unnoticed to the secret garden; and as soon as he set eyes on the beautifully manicured lawn and flowers, Colin's cheeks took on a pink glow of color. As the warm sun fell on his face, Mary and Dickon marvelled at the change that had come upon him. "Mary, Dickon," he yelled out. "I shall get well! And I shall live forever and

ever and ever!"

The children visited the garden every day thereafter. Colin, like Mary before him, grew steadily stronger and hardier. He learned to walk, then to run. To allay the servants' suspicion, however, he still pretended to be a hysterical invalid. *He* wanted to be the one to confront his father with the splendid news—if only Archibald Craven would return from his travels.

Meanwhile, as the children at Misselthwaite ran and played and worked in the secret garden, Lord Craven had been experiencing curious dreams about the dead wife who had once brought light to his existence. It was almost as if she were calling him out of darkness back into light. Then one day he received a letter from a servant requesting that he return to Misselthwaite. Fearful that his son might be dying, he prepared himself for the worst.

As Lord Craven stepped from his coach at Misselthwaite and approached the house, he was startled by laughter coming from the direction of the secret garden. He followed the sounds to the ivy-covered wall; and there he stopped, astounded. Flinging open the door, he saw "a boy burst through it at full speed and, without seeing the outsider, dashed almost into his arms."

For a long moment the man stood back and stared at this apparition. "Father," the boy finally said, "I'm Colin. You can't believe it. I scarcely can myself. I'm Colin."

And while his stunned father gazed down at him, Colin excitedly explained how the visions of Mary and Dickon and the magic wonders of the garden had transformed him. Still speechless, Archibald Craven entered the garden with his son and sat down under the tree, which, for so long, had symbolized the great tragedy of his life.

Later, when the house servants saw the Master of Misselthwaite striding across the manor lawn followed by Mary and Dickon, they looked on in disbelief. Then came the most miraculous sight of all: close by his father's side, "with his head up in the air and his eyes full of laughter walked as strongly and steadily as any boy in Yorkshire—Master Colin!"

Commentary:

Written by Frances Hodgson Burnett (1849 - 1924), *The Secret Garden* is a classic story of rebirth. Its plot parallels the seasons and the cycle of renewal as winter turns to spring. Burnett, however, wishes her readers to see this renewal on two levels and at two "secret" sites. The first renewal, of course, is the literal one which takes place in the secret garden. The second and more meaningful renewal is a symbolic one, and its site is the secret garden of the heart.

The parallels between garden sites and renewals are striking. Like the locked and abandoned garden where Mrs. Craven died, the hearts of Mary, Colin, and Lord Craven are similarly marked by family deaths. In a sense, these deaths have cast the lives of each character into a kind of spiritual winter. It is only by unlocking the heart, Burnett seems to say, by revisiting its "magic," that we can hope to renew our lives.

THE WONDERFUL WIZARD OF OZ

by
L. Frank Baum
(1856-1919)

Type of work: Classic fantasy

Setting: Turn-of-the-century Kansas and the marvelous Land of Oz

Principal characters:

Dorothy, an orphan who lives with her aunt and uncle

The Scarecrow, one of Dorothy's companions, a light-hearted fellow who wishes for a brain

The Tin Woodman, another traveler, one who wants a heart

The Lion, yet another pilgrim, on a quest for courage

The Wizard, the Emerald City ruler of Oz

Story Overview:

"Run for the cellar!" Dorothy's Aunt Em shouted over the wailing wind. Holding her beloved dog Toto, Dorothy scrambled towards the trap door, but she tripped and fell. Moments later the cyclone struck: the house whirled up into the air, drifting for hours, until it finally landed on the ground with a thud.

Dorothy picked herself up, opened the front door, and stared in wonder at a marvelously beautiful landscape, alive with "birds [of] rare and brilliant plumage . . . stately trees . . . and gorgeous flowers." Suddenly, she noticed four tiny people approaching: three middle-aged men wearing pointed blue hats and an old woman in a glistening white gown embossed with stars. "You are welcome, most noble Sorceress, to the land of the Munchkins," the woman greeted Dorothy. "We are so grateful to you for having killed the Wicked Witch of the East, and for setting our people free from bondage."

Dorothy, of course, was quite bewildered. Then the woman pointed to two feet encased in beautiful silver shoes sticking out from beneath the house, and explained that the feet—and the shoes—belonged to a Wicked Witch—who had been neatly crushed by the falling farmhouse.

The old woman then introduced herself as the Witch of the North. She was one of two good witches in the Land of Oz—a country "cut off from all the rest of the world." In fact, if Dorothy and Toto wished to return again to Kansas, said the witch, they would have to go all the way to the City of Emeralds and see the ruler of Oz, the Great Wizard himself.

Although Dorothy was reluctant to begin such a long and perilous journey, she *did* want to get back home. And she *did* feel much braver after the Good Witch gave her the Wicked Witch's magical silver shoes and a special kiss to protect her from danger. Then suddenly the Good Witch and the Munchkins disappeared.

Cautiously, Dorothy slipped on the silver shoes—which fit perfectly—and together the girl and her dog headed off down "the road of yellow brick" to the City of Emeralds.

On the second day the little girl spotted a Scarecrow in blue overalls and a pointed blue hat. "Good day," he saluted, winking. "How do you do?" sputtered the astonished Dorothy. As the Scarecrow explained, he was not doing well at all: when the cloth of his head had been restitched just two days previously, he found that his new straw lacked any brains. Dorothy suggested that he accompany her to the City of Emeralds to ask the Wizard's help. The Scarecrow happily accepted this offer, and together the three companions continued down the yellow-brick road.

On their second day's journey, the travelers heard a "deep groan" coming from nearby. Hurrying to investigate, they found "a man made entirely of tin" standing, rain-rusted, with an "uplifted ax in his hands." Dorothy found an oil can and oiled his joints, and the Woodman was enormously grateful. When his new friends told him of their journey to see the great Oz, he politely asked, "Do you suppose Oz could give me a heart?" He had once been a flesh-and-blood woodman, he continued, in love with a beautiful Munchkin maiden—until the Wicked Witch of the West intervened to prevent their marriage. The Witch had brewed up a stew of repeated "ax-idents" that would have left him headless, armless, legless, and eventually bodiless, except for the mercies of a kind tinsmith who patched him up with new parts. But even the tinsmith had not been able to give him a new heart. So, the hopeful Woodman joined the pilgrimage to Oz.

After walking for awhile longer, the group heard a loud roar, and before they could move, "a great lion bounded into the road." Toto lunged at the beast, and as the lion bared his fangs, Dorothy shrieked, "Don't you dare bite Toto!" To her surprise, the lion recoiled in fright. "You are nothing but a big coward," she scolded—and the huge animal burst into tears. Indeed, he admitted, he did not feel one bit like "The King of Beasts." So it was soon decided that the cowardly Lion would accompany the others to the Emerald City—to request "a bit of courage" from the Great Wizard.

Back on the yellow-brick road, the friends journeyed on—until the path was interrupted by the waters of a wide ditch. "I think I could jump over it," bravely volunteered the Lion, and, indeed, one by one he eased his friends onto his back, then leapt across the expanse.

Once on the other side of the ditch, the travelers hurried through a dark and gloomy forest, only to be stopped in their tracks again at the brink of a chasm too broad for even the Lion's maneuvers. But here the Scarecrow came up with a splendid idea: the Woodman, with his ax, could fell a tree to make a bridge across the abyss. The clever plan worked perfectly!

Later, their progress was once again stymied—this time by a broad river cutting across the road. Once again the Woodman went to work, fashioning a fine raft to carry his dear friends to the other shore. No one recognized the courage, brain and heart, however, each displayed as these three challenges were overcome.

As the travelers neared the Emerald City, they waded through vast fields of intoxicating poppies. Dorothy, Toto, and the Lion, whose veins ran with blood that absorbed the poison, quickly fell asleep. The Woodman and the Scarecrow moved the girl and her dog away from the flowers, but they could not budge the Lion. Fortunately, thousands of forest mice appeared and pulled the drowsy lion away to safety on a cart fashioned by the Woodman.

When the pilgrims at last arrived at the Emerald City, the "greenish" guard who appeared at the gate was flabbergasted by their request to see "the great Oz." But finally they were admitted, one by one, into the Throne Room. Dorothy, who went first, cowered to see "an enormous Head, without a body" resting on a huge throne. "What do you wish me to do?" the great head thundered. When Dorothy explained that she longed to go back to Kansas, the voice boomed out its reply: first she would have to kill the Wicked Witch of the West. "I never killed anything, willingly," Dorothy whimpered. But Oz had no sympathy for tears. "Now go," he roared, "and do not ask to see me again until you have done your task."

Next the Scarecrow pleaded for a brain. Now in the form of a "lovely lady" with glorious wings, the Wizard deferred this request also—until the scarecrow had killed the terrible Wicked Witch. To the Woodman Oz appeared in "the shape of a most terrifying Beast"; to the Lion as a glowing "Ball of Fire." But of each he demanded the same price: the death of the powerful Wicked Witch.

The travelers knew they had no choice. Together they followed the sunset to seek the Witch of the West. They could not know that the Witch, through her single eye, "as powerful as a telescope," was tracking their every move. Donning her magical Golden Cap, she dispatched a band of Winged Monkeys, who swooped down on the Woodman and the Scarecrow, dashing their bodies against trees and rocks. Then they seized Dorothy, Toto and the Lion and flew off to the Witch's castle. The Witch cackled with delight—until she saw the imprint of the Good Witch's magical kiss on Dorothy's forehead. Now the evil witch did not "dare hurt the girl," so she put her to hard and tedious work in her castle.

Dorothy complied meekly. Then one day she caught the Witch trying to steal her silver shoes. "You are a wicked creature!" the girl shouted, dumping a pale of water over the Witch's head. "See what you've done!" screeched the Witch. "I shall melt away." And indeed, she did promptly melt into a brown, steamy puddle—which Dorothy quickly mopped up.

Free at last of the Wicked Witch of the West, the grateful slaves in the castle took Dorothy and the Lion to find the Scarecrow and the Woodman, whose "battered and bent" bodies were soon tenderly restored. Dorothy then put on the Witch's Golden Cap and uttered the magic words she had heard the witch use to summon the Winged Monkeys. Now the hideous creatures politely conveyed the travelers to the Emerald City.

After many days, Oz finally admitted the company back into the Throne Room. The grand Wizard was now completely invisible; only a voice demanded the cause of their intrusion. "We have come to claim our promises, O Oz," Dorothy shuddered. But just then Toto sprang forward, knocking over a screen to expose "a little old man with a bald head."

"I am Oz the Great and Terrible," he confessed, his voice now reduced to a trembling whisper. "I have been making believe," he added sheepishly. Once he had been a talented Omaha ventriloquist, he explained; he had arrived in Oz years ago on a runaway circus balloon. "I'm really a very good man," he finished. "But I'm a very bad Wizard, I must admit."

The wizard *was* truly a sincere, good-hearted man, and he provided the Scarecrow with brains—made from "bran . . . mixed with . . . pins and needles"; to the Woodman, he gave a "heart, made . . . of silk and . . . sawdust"; and the Lion drank down a draught of courage, poured into an exquisite bowl. But Dorothy's wish would not be as easy to grant: He would have to escort her back to Kansas himself—in the same gas balloon that had carried him to Oz.

But just as the balloon cables were loosened, Toto darted off, and as Dorothy ran to retrieve him, alas, the wizard rose into the air alone, and floated away.

Now there was only one help left for Dorothy: Glinda, the Good Witch of the South. More perils—and more wonders—confronted the determined girl and her loyal companions on their journey southward, but at last they met the beautiful, radiant Glinda, who confided a wonderful secret to Dorothy: All she had ever needed to return home were the silver slippers that were on her feet.

Dorothy thus bade a tearful goodbye to all her dear friends from Oz. Then she thanked Glinda, clutched Toto to her breast, and "clapped the heels of her shoes together three times." Instantly, she and Toto were back on the Kansas prairie, gazing at their own farmhouse. "My darling child!" cried Aunt Em, catching sight of them. "Where in the world did you come from?"

"From the Land of Oz," said Dorothy gravely. "And . . . oh, Aunt Em! I'm so glad to be at home again!"

Commentary:

When Lyman Frank Baum approached publishers with his story of *The Wonderful Wizard of Oz* in 1899, it was universally rejected; the story of a Kansas farm girl swept away by a tornado to a dreamland under the rule of a 19th-century carnival con man from Omaha was a radical departure from conventional Victorian children's literature. But once it was finally published in 1900—at the sole expense of the debt-ridden author and his devoted illustrator—it swept into the worldwide public imagination with all the energy of an American prairie fire.

THE GOLDEN ASS

by
Lucius Apuleius
(c. A.D. 120)

Type of work: Ancient Roman adventure-satire

Setting: 2nd-century Thessaly, a Roman-ruled city in Greece

Principal characters:
   Lucius, a young merchant who travels to Thessaly
   An assortment of travelers, servants, sorceresses, thieves and nobles

Story Overview:

Enroute to Thessaly on business, Lucius introduced himself to two passing travelers: "Excuse me, but I should like to know what you are discussing—not because I mean to pry, but because I want to know everything in the world . . . or at least a good part of it."

Lucius' curiosity was quickly rewarded. One of his new companions, a retailer named Aristomenes, immediately launched into a tale about a previous trip to Thessaly, where he had witnessed a horrifying feat of magic: A witch had broken into the room Aristomenes shared with his destitute friend, Socrates, slashed Socrates' throat, then ripped out his heart. Miraculously, however, the next morning, Socrates had awakened, resurrected—and in quite a chipper mood. The two friends decided to enjoy their breakfast in the countryside, where Socrates went to the river for a drink; but no sooner had Socrates put the water to his lips than the wound on his neck reopened in a "sudden gush of blood." Moments later, the poor man died.

"I consider nothing impossible," Lucius said in response to Aristomenes' tale. Then the travelers bade each other farewell and parted company; neither suspected that fate would soon provide Lucius with an experience as strange as that of Socrates.

In Thessaly, Lucius looked up a man named Milo, with whom he had a mutual acquaintance. A usurer, well known for his "miserliness and dirty griping ways," Milo nevertheless took an instant liking to Lucius and generously invited the weary sojourner to stay in his home. Although he judged Milo to be no more than a "nasty old man," Lucius accepted. He did, after all, need a place to stay—and he had also noticed the "supple body" of Milo's servant-girl, Fotis.

Lucius easily acclimated himself to life in Thessaly. He passed his days in the marketplaces and public baths—and his nights in the arms of the voluptuous Fotis, "without a sigh of sleep."

He was rather irritated to have this pleasant routine interrupted by an invitation to a dinner party at the house of his cousin Byrrhaena, whom he had chanced to meet on the street. Drinking liberally at his cousin's festive affair, Lucius listened to strange tales of corpses stolen by witches and offerings made to the God of Laughter. As the night wore on, he became thoroughly "wine-soused," and only with the most

"tottering steps" did he find his way through the dark back to Milo's house. There he discovered three men "of the most violent brand" trying to break down the front door. Brandishing his sword, he slashed at the men until they lay at his feet "riddled thickly with gaping wounds."

No sooner had Lucius arisen the next morning from his drunken slumber, than he was arrested and led away to the tribunal at the Forum. Desperately he tried to explain to the magistrates that the three felled had been "villainous brigands" and that he had merely tried to protect the public safety. When he saw instruments for torture brought in, however, Lucius lost all hope for exoneration. Before receiving his punishment, he was instructed to peel back the shrouds of the three dead men. "Good Gods! What a sight was there!" Lucius could not believe what lay beneath the shrouds: three human-shaped winebladders! The court immediately erupted in an "irrepressible roar" of laughter, for the whole trial had simply been a hoax in honor of the God of Laughter.

Freed, Lucius returned to Milo's house, and, once more enfolded in Fotis' arms, he listened as she revealed a tantalizing fact: Milo's wife, Pamphile, was a sorceress who possessed "wonderful secret powers."

"Help me to spy upon your mistress," Lucius entreated. Fotis agreed, and at nightfall they crept upstairs so Lucius could peer through the keyhole into Pamphile's room. He watched as Pamphile smeared oil on her body. To his amazement, "down plumes began to sputter out" of her skin and the woman was transformed into an owl. A moment later, she "swooped wide-winged out of the house." Turning to Fotis, Lucius pleaded, "Get me a little of that same ointment." At once Fotis led her eager lover into her mistress' room and gave him some of the magical oil. Lucius lost no time in spreading the ointment across his flesh, trying very hard "to feel birdlike." He waited—"but no down appeared; no wings burst out."

Instead, he felt his skin begin to roughen; bristles sprouted from his pores, and his "toes and fingers clotted into solid hoofs." Next, a long tail whisked out from his spine, and his face became enormous. Finally his "lips grew pendulous" as his "ears shot hairily aloft." Lucius had become an ass!

"I'm done for," exclaimed Fotis, realizing what a terrible mistake she had made. Lucius could no longer speak; he could only stare at her with great "watering eyes." To his relief, however, Fotis remembered that there was a remedy: if he chewed on rose petals, he would be restored to human form. But since Fotis could not procure the rose petals until daybreak, Lucius would have to spend the night in the stable.

That night, however, fate played another cruel trick on Lucius: robbers ransacked Milo's house and stole all his possessions—including the beasts in his stable. Lucius was led away and forced to carry a great weight of booty on his back. When the robbers beat his wretched hide unmercifully, he felt "little better than a dead donkey." Spotting some rose petals during the long journey, Lucius restrained himself from eating them—surely if he transformed into a man at this point, the brutal bandits would kill him.

At last they reached the robbers' cave, a hideout tended by an old crone. This witch was soon joined by a beautiful young noblewoman named Charite who bitterly lamented her fate. "How can I manage to keep living at all?" she mourned. Why, why had she been snatched from the midst of her wedding ceremony by the evil robbers? To soothe her, the old hag told Charite the story of Cupid and Psyche.

"Once upon a time," the woman began, there lived a king and queen who had three remarkably beautiful daughters. Of the three, the beauty of the youngest, Psyche, was "so glorious, so victorious" that people came from all over to see her. The wonder of Psyche's beauty, however, enraged the goddess Venus, Queen of Beauty, who fumed, "I am degraded to sharing my empire with a mere wench." Venus decided to enlist the help of her son Cupid, the God of Love, who was to arrange for Psyche to fall in love with some "vile" creature. But Psyche kindled even Cupid's passion, and instead he took her for his own wife. He warned her, however, that she must never look upon him.

One day, Psyche's sisters came to visit her in her new "house of gold." Overcome by envy, the two girls tried to destroy their sister's happiness by convincing her that it was in her best interest to see what her mysterious husband looked like. So one night the gullible Psyche lit a candle and stared in wonder at Cupid as he lay sleeping. She saw "the gay lovelocks of his golden head, drenched with ambrosia; the curls gracefully drifting over his milky breasts and ruddy cheeks . . . while the very lamp-flame guttered before the flashing splendour." Mad with desire, Psyche embraced him—and inadvertently overturned the lamp. As the burning oil dripped onto Cupid's skin, he leapt out of bed and flew away.

Psyche, now expecting a child, searched far and wide for her beloved husband. Eventually she came to the palace of Venus, who sent the girl on three seemingly impossible tasks. Psyche, though, completed the tasks, including a perilous journey to "the depths of hell" to bring back for Venus a "scrap of Proserpine's beauty" in a box. But overcome by curiosity, Psyche opened the box and immediately fell into the "Sleep of Innermost Darkness." But alas, Cupid could no longer endure being separated from his wife. He flew to her side and awakened her "with a charming prick of his arrow." Jove, the god of heaven, was so moved by Cupid's love that he brought Psyche to his home, where she bore Cupid a daughter named Joy. Thus ended the tale of Cupid and Psyche.

The happy narrative, however, did not buoy Charite's spirits for long; the robbers were plotting a diabolical end for her—and for Lucius.

Their plan was to slit open the ass' body, remove its entrails, then place Charite inside, "imprisoned in this beastly embrace." Fortunately, Charite's bridegroom, Tlepolemus, arrived to rescue her before the robbers could carry out their vile plan; as they lay in a drunken sleep, Tlepolemus bound each with a strong cord, then placed Charite on Lucius' back for the journey home.

Notwithstanding their reunion in love, all did not end happily for Charite and Tlepolemus. Shortly after their return home, one of Charite's former suitors became intent on winning her back. One day this evil man joined Tlepolemus on a hunt, and during the chase he slashed his rival's horse so that Tlepolemus fell and was gored to death by a boar. In revenge, Charite later invited the man to her bedroom and, after providing him with drugged wine, stabbed out both his eyes with her hairpin. Finally, hurrying to her husband's tomb, she plunged a sword deep into her own breast.

Lucius, though, did not have much opportunity to reflect on the couple's sad fate. He had his own miserable destiny to contend with: Charite's family had turned him over to a cruel herdsman. Lucius escaped, was recaptured, and then sold or stolen repeatedly, serving under a number of different masters. Finally, one day Lucius was brought out by his last owner to woo a murderess in the gladiatorial arena; disgusted, he wrenched free, broke into a full gallop, and made his way to the seashore, where he drifted into sleep. When he awakened, Venus stood before him, wearing a pitch black cloak sprinkled with burning stars. The Goddess promised to change him back into a man.

The next morning, a priest of Venus offered a wreath of roses to Lucius' eager lips. The ass munched the petals greedily, and, restored to human form, dedicated his remaining days to serving the great Goddess who had liberated him from his beastly prison.

Commentary:

Lucius Apuleius grew up in Madura, a Roman colony in North Africa. The son of one of the town's most prominent men, he became known early in life as a traveling lecturer. As his fame spread, he often found himself in circumstances almost as bizarre as those of his characters in *The Golden Ass*. For instance, as a young man he married an older widow whose family brought a suit against him, charging that he had won his wife by magical means and that he had murdered the woman's son. The outcome of the trial is unknown, but presumably he was acquitted because he continued his travels—his wife at his side—and circulated his own account of the trial, known as the *Apologia*. Later, he became a priest of Isis, the Egyptian goddess whose cult was a popular "mystery" sect in classical Rome. Apparently this devotion to Isis—and to Venus, as a manifestation of Isis—inspired *The Golden Ass*, the only surviving complete Roman novel.

For all of its brutal and macabre allusions, romantic turns of phrase, and wry humor, the book culminates in the sincere spiritual conversion of Lucius to the service of the Good Goddess who had redeemed him from his curse.

THE PILGRIM'S PROGRESS

by John Bunyan
(1628 - 1688)

Commentary:

Translated into eighty-four languages and dialects, *The Pilgrim's Progress* has become a religious classic deemed by many second only to the Bible in terms of Christian enlightenment. Its author, John Bunyan, was one of the most noteworthy products of Puritan England. Although he made his daily living with the down-to-earth arts of a tinker and mender, his highly sensitive and creative disposition left him profoundly vulnerable, even as a small child, to the extraordinary religious fervor of his day; and his conversion to the Baptist faith as a young bachelor transported him to the verge of religious mania.

Finally, after serving in Cromwell's army and marrying a woman "as poor as himself," he could no longer resist the call: he went west out into the streets as a roving evangelist. In 1660 he was imprisoned for preaching without a license, and it was in jail that he wrote the first part of his imaginative allegory *Pilgrim's Progress*. In lucid but majestic prose, the book traces the good Christian's journey from the "City of Destruction" to the "Celestial City."

In Bunyan's prefatory "Author's Apology," a cheery and gentle defense written in doggerel verse, he offers an explanation of his allegorical approach to moral edification: *May I not write in such a style as this? / In such a method too, and yet not miss / My end, thy good? / Why may it not be done? / Dark clouds bring waters, when the bright bring none.* He then goes on to explain the moral purposes of his allegory: *This book it chalketh out before thine eyes / The man that seeks the everlasting prize: / It shews you whence he comes, whither he goes: / What he leaves undone; also what he does: / It also shews you how he runs and runs / Til he unto the gate of glory comes.*

Story Overview:

Part I

Bunyan begins by describing a marvelous dream he had: *As I walked through the wilderness of this world, I lighted down on a certain place where was a den; and I laid me down in that place to sleep: and as I slept I dreamed a dream. . . . I saw a man clothed with rags, standing in a certain place, with his face from his own house, a book in his hand, and a great burden upon his back.*

This oppressed figure was Christian, shouldering the burden of his sins, and the book which he held bore horrifying revelations. "I am certainly informed that this our city will be burned with fire from heaven," Christian lamented, speaking to his family, "in which . . . both myself, with thee my wife, and you my sweet babes shall miserably come to ruin." Walking through his fields with a prayer in his heart, Christian sought some remedy to his distress.

Suddenly the figure of Evangelist strode through the fields towards Christian. *Then he gave him a parchment roll; and there was written within, "Flee from the wrath to come."* Confused, Christian asked where he might flee to. *Said Evangelist, "Do you see yonder shining light? . . . Keep that light in your eye, and go up directly thereto, so thou shalt see the [wicket] gate; at which when thou knockest, it shall be told thee what to do."*

Unable to convince his wife and children to follow him, Christian set out alone, running toward the light—a solitary man, a pilgrim seeking truth. His family called after him, begging him to return. But Christian put his fingers in his ears and ran on, crying, "Life! life! eternal life!" Watching his flight, some neighbors mocked him, while others tried to deliver him back to the City of Destruction.

Two of the neighbors who sought to dissuade Christian were called Obstinate and Pliable. When his attempts failed, Obstinate turned back. Pliable, however, swayed by Christian's determination, agreed to accompany him to the Celestial City and to see it for himself.

Unfortunately, the two pilgrims soon slipped and fell into the dank and murky Slough of Despond, where they "wallowed for a time, being grievously bedaubed with the dirt." Unnerved and disgusted, Pliable finally pulled himself out of the trough and raced for home, leaving Christian, still weighted by the burden of sin on his back, to sink in the mire.

By and by, a man named Help came to pull Christian out of the trough; and, weary yet determined, the traveler continued his journey—a solitary pilgrim in pursuit of truth. Nearly diverted from his path by the enticing words of a Worldly Wiseman, Christian was saved by the intervention of Evangelist. At last, with great difficulty he reached the wicket gate and entered onto the Straight and Narrow path.

Up this way therefore did the burdened Christian run, but not without a great deal of difficulty because of the load on his back. He ran thus until he came at a place somewhat ascending and upon that place stood a cross, and a little below in the bottom a sepulchre. So I saw in my dream, that just as Christian came up with the cross, his burden loosed from his shoulders, and fell from off his back, and began to tumble, and so continued to do till it came to the mouth of the sepulchre where it fell in, and I saw it no more. At last free of his heavy load, Christian now moved more quickly.

After a long and arduous journey of ascent, the fatigued Christian finally stopped to rest at the stately Palace Beautiful, where he was fed and fitted with armor and a sword by three damsels, Prudence, Piety, and Charity. Indeed, he would soon need this protection, for the straight and narrow path next led him down into the valley of Humiliation, where he confronted the ill-tempered lion-mouthed, bear-footed monster Apollyon. This terrible beast besieged the traveler, savagely wounding him. Bleeding profusely, Christian gathered the last of his strength to slay the fiend with his sword. A hand then appeared bearing leaves from the tree of life, instantly healing Christian's wounds.

Ahead lay even graver peril. In the Valley of the Shadow of Death, Christian found his sword useless against the myriad demons and dragons who lined his path. Only fervent prayer and supplication carried him past the mouth of Hell and the terrible creatures and sights of the valley. Emerging at last on the other side, Christian met Faithful, a fellow pilgrim. Cheered and strengthened by the companionship, the two continued on.

While crossing the plain of Ease, Christian and Faithful passed through the town of Vanity, and there in its center they came upon Vanity Fair—a large open-air market in which was peddled all manner of ostentatious commodity. When the pilgrims refused to buy and denounced the wicked fair, an angry mob seized them. Faithful, the more vocal of the two, was tried and condemned for his stern denunciations and thrown to the mob, who *scourged him . . . buffeted him . . . lanced his flesh with knives . . . stoned him with stones . . . pricked him with their swords [and, finally,] burned him to ashes at the stake.*

Heartened by a vision of the martyred Faithful carried to the Celestial City in a fiery chariot, Christian escaped the brutal mob. He soon joined forces with Hopeful, a believer who had also witnessed Faithful's execution. Distracted by their discourse, the pair soon wandered onto the property of the Giant Despair, who cast them "into a very dark dungeon, nasty and stinking." Deprived of food and water, the prisoners were flogged by the Giant and at last ordered to take their own lives. But Christian unexpectedly found a key called Promise in his bosom, with which he unlocked the dungeon. Before fleeing the spot, however, the pilgrims erected a sign to warn others of the danger.

Next they forded the deep river of tribulation, whose waters washed over their heads as they strained against the roiling currents. Overwhelmed, Christian cried out, *Jesus Christ . . . tells me, "When thou passest through the waters, I will be with thee!" . . . Wherefore Christian presently found ground to stand upon, and so it followed that the rest of the river was but shallow . . .*

Emerging from the river, the valiant travelers were met by two shining angels, "sent forth to minister to them who shall be heirs of salvation." These emissaries ushered them to the gates of the Celestial City, where *a company of heavenly hosts came out to meet them; to whom it was said by the other two shining ones, "These are the men that have loved our Lord while they were in the world, and have left all for his holy name, and he hath sent us to fetch them, and we have brought them thus far on their desired jour-ney, that they may go in and look their Redeemer in the face with joy."*

Upon entering the glorious gate, Christian and Hopeful were presented with "raiment . . . that shone like gold" and harps and crowns. Thus supplied, they walked down the city's "streets paved with gold" to meet their beloved Lord.

Part II

Bunyan now reports a second dream: After refusing her husband's entreaties to follow him through the fields towards the light, Christiana, Christian's wife, is eventually moved to remorse. *Then said she to her children . . . "I have sinned away your father, and he is gone: he would have had us with him, but I would not go myself: I also have hindered you of life." With that the boys fell into tears and cried to go after their father . . .*

The next night, Christiana also had a dream: *And behold she saw as if a broad parchment was opened before her, in which was recorded the sum of her ways; and the crimes, as she thought, looked very black upon her . . . and then she thought she saw Christian her husband in a place of bliss among many immortals, with a harp in his hand, standing and playing upon it before one that sat upon a throne, with a rainbow about his head . . .*

At her door the following morning stood a messenger named Secret, who handed her an invitation. "Here . . . is a letter for thee," the messenger said, "which I have brought from thy Husband's king: *So she took it and opened it; but it smelt after the manner of the best perfume. Also it was written in letters of gold. The contents of the letter were these: that the King would have her do as did Christian her husband; for that was the only way to come to his City, and to dwell in his presence with joy forever.*

And so it was that Christiana and her children, accompanied by the comforting personage of Mercy, set out on their quest—again over the objections of two neighbors, Mrs. Inconsiderate and Madame Wanton.

Fleeing the City of Destruction and boldly facing a multitude of trials and tribulations as threatening as those which her husband had endured, Christiana sped on towards the light. At last she stood on the far shores of the river which bordered the Celestial City. *. . . All the banks beyond the river were full of horses and chariots, which were come down from above, to accompany her to the city-gate. So she came forth, and entered the river with a beckon of farewell to those that followed her . . . The last words that she was heard to say were, "I come, Lord, to be with thee, and bless thee . . . " So she went and called, and entered in at the gate, with all the ceremonies of joy that her husband Christian had entered with before her.*

And though Bunyan's book gives no account of it, we may safely assume that the reunion of Christian and Christiana was a joyous one, each having braved many perils to achieve sure and ceaseless happiness together in the service of their Lord.

MY LIFE IN THE BUSH OF GHOSTS

by Amos Tutuola, Grove Press, New York, N.Y., 1954

Type of work: Mythological fantasy

Setting: Nigeria and "the Bush of Ghosts"; 19th and 20th centuries

Principal characters:

A nameless seven-year-old boy who grows up in "the Bush of Ghosts"

His older brother, who is captured by slave traders

Their mother, who works in the marketplace

Ghosts, lively spirits who live in the Bush of Ghosts

Introduction:

Amos Tutuola evokes a savage and incandescent dreamscape in *My Life in the Bush of Ghosts.* Tutuola's unnamed narrator and protagonist uses innovative diction to remind us that his pilgrimage to the spirit world is indeed extraordinary. Despite his unique circumstances and syntax, however, there is much in his predicament that strikes us as universal. His exile could be our own. Allegorically, Tutuola seems to suggest that, as children, we all might have found ourselves abandoned under the Tree of the Future Sign.

Story Overview:

The seven-year-old Yoruban boy spent long days alone near the hut with his brother while their mother went to trade wares in the market. She left cooked yams for her sons, hidden so that their father's other two wives—who were jealous because they had only daughters and no sons—would not poison the food. Already the boy had come to understand "the meaning of 'bad' because of hatred"; the "meaning of 'good,'" however, as yet eluded him.

Many wars raged at that time throughout the Yoruban villages. One day as the two brothers sat eating their yams, gunshots suddenly rang out. As bullets rained down all around, the boys' stepmothers immediately snatched up their own children and fled into the bush, leaving the two youngsters dashing wildly through the village, pursued by hordes of panic-stricken "monkeys, wolves, deer, and lions" that had been routed from the bush.

Although the elder brother had lifted the slow-running seven-year-old onto his shoulders, the weight caused the older boy to stumble. The child screamed to his brother that he must go on and save himself, for their mother's sake. Heartbroken, the older youth agreed. As soon as he bolted, however, he was captured and enslaved.

The younger child watched this horrible scene from under a fruit tree. Aware that from now on his life would be wholly different, the boy regarded the tree as *"THE FUTURE SIGN".* In fact, from this tree he would begin his journey, a journey to eliminate war and hate. Plunging headlong into the bush, the boy was too young to know the danger he was in or to understand that he had found the Bush of Ghosts—a place "so dreadful that no superior earthly person [had ever] entered it" before.

He met his first ghosts almost immediately. At the hollowed-out base of a hill, the boy found three rooms: one outfitted in radiant gold, one in copper, and one in silver. He was quite alarmed when three "old and weary" ghosts—each matching the decor of its room—appeared before him, beckoning him to enter. Each hoping to win his favor, the ghosts began to battle amongst themselves. The boy soon found himself paralyzed in their great, glaring flashes of copperish, golden, and silver light.

The battle of lights became so intense that a delegation of ghosts arrived to settle the matter. Among them was "king of all the smelling ghosts," whose stench—of "excretia, urine," and the "rotten blood" of animals—and equally foul appearance disgusted the boy. And much to his horror, the smelling ghost king suddenly swooped him up and put him in his bag. After three days, he was finally set loose in "the 7th town of ghosts," home to all the smelling ghosts.

The child's ordeal had not ended, however; the ghost king now used his "juju" charm to change the boy into a horse. Not only did he have to suffer the indignity of being mounted and ridden by the smelling ghosts, but the boy-horse was also regularly flogged and left unfed.

His life as a horse ended one day when the king inadvertently turned him into a camel. To change his mount back to a horse, the king had to take the camel to the top of a high mountain; here the boy-camel managed to steal the king's juju. But the child did not know the powers of the juju: unexpectedly, it transformed him into a cow.

Although he tried to make himself at home among a herd of "cow-men" ghosts, they despised the weak and idle boy-cow, whom they eventually sold to a woman who wanted a cow to sacrifice. Luckily, the boy-cow soon managed to elude her by dipping himself into a Changing Pond that turned him back into a boy.

For a while, the boy was cared for by a kindly "homeless ghost." Soon, however, the boy again took to the bush, until he came to a town of "burglar ghosts," whose practice it was to rob infants from their mothers' wombs, then crawl into the wombs themselves. Charmed by the "earthly" boy, one ghost-mother decided to adopt him—and the boy was quite happy; he even met "a very beautiful young ghostess" whom he chose to marry.

With his ghostess bride, the boy settled down to live in his in-laws' town. Before long, though, he began to miss his childhood home, and one night he "went round the town and bade goodbye to the prominent ghosts."

But no sooner had the boy left his wife's village than he was captured in the "9th town of ghosts," where he was imprisoned in a dark underground chamber with a thousand snakes. Suddenly, one of the serpents "vomited a kind of coloured light from his mouth," and immediately the snakes vanished. The room then shrank into a "pitcher" from which the boy's head, now greatly enlarged, protruded.

Soon a multitude of ghosts and ghostesses appeared and began sacrificing animals and pouring the sacrificial blood on the boy's immense head. He then realized that they were worshipping him: he had become their god.

After the fame of the god-boy had spread, he was transported in his pitcher to the King of the Bush Gods. The king, however, was not impressed with this new deity. A most terrifying presence, the king showed his guests the bodies of over twenty thousand children whom he had ordered to be "smashed to death." Unnerved by the spectacle, the boy's fears were lessened when the pitcher encasing him broke on the ground and he was able to escape once again into the bush.

Now, however, the dense growth struck him as quite strange: whenever he took a step, the ground cried out, "Don't smash me!" In his haste to evade the voice of the earth, he fell into a "spider web bush." Ensnared like a chrysalis in the web, the boy could not move until a spider-eating ghost arrived hours later to devour him; but instead, thinking the boy was his dead father, he decided to bury him.

The boy didn't stay buried for long, however; another ghost soon dug him up to eat. But as luck would have it, when the ghost burned away the thick web surrounding the human's body, the boy was able to escape into what he thought was a refuse heap of dried leaves— which turned out to be the inside of a "big pouch" of an animal which was trying to elude a band of "Short Ghost" hunters. When they caught the animal, the ghosts cut the boy from its pouch and presented him to their ruler, "the Flash-eyed Mother."

The grotesque Flash-eyed Mother had millions of heads covering her body, and affixed to each head was a pair of "short hands," used for eating. Nevertheless, the boy soon became inured to her fearsome appearance and dwelt in her land for a long time.

At last, when he had been in the Bush of Ghosts for about eighteen years, the boy—who had long since become a man—decided once more to return home. En route he happened upon an antelope which, just as he began to shoot it, suddenly transformed itself into "the super lady," an angelic-faced ghostess, who immediately proposed marriage to him. After some hesitation, the wayfarer agreed, settling in his new wife's luxurious house. A year later the Super Lady bore him a son, whom he called "OKOLE-BAMIDELE"—meaning "you cannot follow me."

Whenever Okole's parents tried to plan for his future, they argued: his mother wanted their remarkable child—who, at only six months old already stood four-and-a-half feet tall—to behave like a "full ghost," while his father wanted him to act like a "full earthly person." Finally, after one particularly heated argument, the traveler decided to leave.

This time on the way home the traveler was arrested as a burglar and imprisoned in an enormous oven, where the king came to visit him. "I am your son," the king announced, to the traveler's astonishment. " . . . Your wife who is Super Lady is my mother." Indeed little Okole

had quickly grown into a man.

Years passed, and even though he was installed in his son's palace, the traveler's longing for home resurfaced. Again he set off into the Bush of Ghosts. Before long he came to a town where he was delighted to meet his dead cousin, an industrious fellow who not only had established "THE METHODIST CHURCH OF THE BUSH OF GHOSTS," but had also taught other ghosts the rudiments of "sanitary work, surveying buildings, first aid, [and] nursery work." Impressed, the traveler decided to remain for a while in his cousin's town.

The day came, however, when the traveler began to dream ever more vividly of his own village. So he said a sad "Bad-Bye" to his new friends; then he resumed the long trek home.

Along his way, the traveler met up with a dreadful looking ghostess, covered with sores and maggots. Weeping bitterly, she begged him to heal the sore on her hand by licking it. Repelled by this request, the traveler was nevertheless intrigued to learn that she was a "television-handed ghostess"; her festering palms, she promised, glowed with scenes from his home village. Compromising, the traveler moistened a plant with his tongue and rubbed it against the sore, which immediately healed. In gratitude, the ghostess opened her palm for him—and, miraculously, he saw *himself* standing under the "Future Sign."

After these many years the traveler had finally escaped the "Bush of Ghosts." Yet, heading home, he was again captured by slave-traders, who sold him to a man bent on sacrificing him to his god; but to the traveler's joy, his new master turned out to be none other than his long-lost elder brother. Although he did not immediately reveal his identity, the day came when he decided to sing a song for his master, who, hearing the familiar melody, was moved to "shout with gladness." The traveler was soon reunited also with his mother—who sternly urged him never again to set foot in the Bush of Ghosts.

Home at last, the weary wanderer concluded that "hatred" had caused him to flee to the ghosts. Still, not all his memories of the ghosts were unpleasant; and from time to time he considered a return visit to their strange realm.

Commentary:

While Western critics have praised *My Life in the Bush of Ghosts,* many of Tutuola's fellow Nigerians have faulted him for taking liberties with the Yoruban folktales that weave through his narrative. Clearly, however, the mission of Tutuola's pilgrim is not to resurrect tribal past; he enters the Bush of Ghosts under the *Future* Sign, with an unmapped, dangerous— and ultimately unfulfilled—calling: to invoke the flawed and powerful spirits of hatred in order to engage and transform them.

When the pilgrim reemerges from the Bush, his mission has changed its focus. If he has been unable to put an end to animosity or warfare, he has nevertheless maintained his humor and discovered the strength of his family, both among the living and the dead.

LOVE IN THE TIME OF CHOLERA

by Gabriel Garcia Marquez (translated by Edith Grossman), Knopf Publishing, New York, N.Y., 1988

Type of work: Magical realism

Setting: Columbia, South America; late 19th, early 20th centuries

Principal characters:
Dr. Juvenal Urbino de la Calle, a respected doctor
Fermina Daza, de la Calle's beautiful and headstrong wife
Florentino Ariza, a romantic who adores Fermina
America Vicuna, Florentino's young relative and lover

Commentary:

In *Love in the Time of Cholera* Nobel prize-winning novelist Gabriel Garcia Marquez displays the same narrative skills that marked his earlier masterpiece *One Hundred Years of Solitude*. In a style critics have dubbed "magical realism," Garcia Marquez constructs a novel in which the characters and landscapes are more reminiscent of mythology than of contemporary fiction. Yet despite its disregard for chronicle and description, *Love in the Time of Cholera* is remarkably accessible: its story of aging, disease, and death is a testament to human nature and to the powers of love. No matter how eccentric Marquez's characters may be, at heart they are simple, home-spun philosophers who bask in their ability to dream and to love.

Story Overview:

Dr. Urbino was thinking of changing his clothes for the funeral of his chess partner Jeremiah Saint Amour, who, at the age of seventy, had committed suicide. Outside, Dr. Urbino could hear his wife's parrot chattering in the mango tree. "You scoundrel!" he shouted at the bothersome bird. "You're even more of a scoundrel, Doctor," the bird replied. With that, Dr. Urbino marched over to the tree, climbed the ladder that rested beside it, and ascended to the fourth rung, where he reached to seize the parrot in a death grip. Clutching the bird triumphantly, however, Dr. Urbino lost his balance and fell to his own death.

While Dr. Urbino's demise was "memorable," his life had been even more so. Everyone in town recalled that the doctor's "drastic new methods" of hygiene and treatment had put an end to "the last cholera epidemic suffered by the province." He also had been responsible for the restoration of the Dramatic Theater, and had even taken a test ride in the "aerostatic balloon" that provided the first airmail service to a nearby Colombian town. Certainly he had always appeared to be an exemplary citizen.

Only Urbino's wife Fermina knew anything of his shortcomings. And the most grievous of these—at least from her point of view—was that the doctor had once had an affair, an affair which he had confessed to his priest. As incensed by her husband's confession as she was by the affair itself, Fermina had shrieked, "You might as well have told the snake charmer in the market." Then,

to avoid the gossip that certainly would be spread, she left Urbino.

Fermina, however, "thought she would die of joy" when her forsaken husband had come to bring her home two years later. After all, she loved him: not only had they raised two children together, traveled to Europe, and taken part in the wondrous balloon expedition, but they had also grown accustomed to each other.

Lately, after so many years of marriage, seventy-two-year-old Fermina had begun to treat her eighty-year-old husband like "a senile baby" and to realize that "they were not capable of living for even an instant without each other." So it was with profound shock and horror that she watched him fall off the ladder by the mango tree. Mustering all her courage, Fermina insisted that a "vigil" be held in the doctor's home, "with mountain coffee and fritters and everyone free to weep for him in any way they chose."

It was at this vigil that Fermina learned that someone had been praying for her husband's death for more than fifty years. This person was Florentino Ariza—the man to whom, as a headstrong and beautiful adolescent, Fermina had once scribbled a note on a sheet of paper from her notebook: "Very well, I will marry you if you promise not to make me eat eggplant." Receiving Fermina's acceptance, the shy Florentino had developed a new "confidence and strength." But despite his ardor, he had still acquiesced to his mother's wishes that the wedding be postponed for two years so that the two would be "very certain of their affections."

Perhaps, then, it was inevitable that Fermina, following her return from an extended vacation, had suffered a change of heart. She had become—or so she thought—"more polished and intense, her beauty purified by the restraint of maturity." Accordingly, after seeing Florentino again, she summarily dismissed him from her life with another note: "Today, when I saw you, I realized that what is between us is no more than an illusion."

Naturally, Florentino had been crushed. And his despair mounted when he learned a few months later that Fermina had decided to marry "the most desirable of bachelors," Dr. Juvenal Urbino. Brokenhearted, Florentino embarked on a "curative journey" aboard one of the boats in his uncle's fleet. The voyage, while it didn't erase the image of Fermina's wedding and honeymoon, did offer one consolation: a mysterious female passenger pulled him into a dark cabin one night "and stripped him, without glory, of his virginity." Thus began Florentino's lifelong obsession with the pleasures of the flesh.

Soon after this shipboard encounter, Florentino came to the conclusion that his love for Fermina Daza could be replaced by an "earthly passion"; and all too happy to oblige him was a certain Widow Nazaret who, upon first meeting Florentino, "removed her widow's weeds and tossed them in the air until she was not even wearing her wedding ring." From this experience, Florentino learned that although he was timid and delicate and "dressed like an old man from another time," he possessed the power to make women "yield without conditions, without asking him for anything, without hoping for anything from him except the tranquility of knowing that they had done him a favor."

Shortly after his affair with the widow Nazaret had ended, he moved on to "the abandoned little birds of the night" and then to Ausencia Santender, who was "almost fifty years old and looked it," but loved him with a lust that was intoxicating.

It was not until he was an old man and had met America Vicuna, that Florentino again fell in love. As a distant relative, he had been appointed guardian of the fourteen-year-old America, who, owning a passion matching his own was, "ready to learn about life" from the venerable Florentino.

For two years Florentino and America reveled in each other. Then one Pentecost Sunday their love-making was interrupted by the tolling of the Cathedral bells. When Florentino learned that the bells were ringing because of Dr. Urbino's death, he at once deserted America and dashed to the widow's house. For even the past fifty years of flesh-filled passions had not been able to eradicate the love of his youth. Try as he might, he had never been able to surrender "the throb of longing in his heart" for Fermina Daza.

Now, viewing the remains of his rival stretched out on the "conjugal bed" in the master bedroom of the couple's house, Florentino noted that finally Urbino was "wallowing in the indignity of death." Eagerly he pushed through the throng of mourners to speak to Fermina Daza.

"Fermina," Florentino said, "I have waited for this opportunity for more than half a century, to repeat to you once again my vow of eternal fidelity and everlasting love." Caught up both in grief and arrogance, Fermina could barely contain her fury. "Get out of here," she roared. "And don't show your face again for the years of life that are left to you."

Florentino, unfazed, retreated from his beloved. Fermina, for her part, tried to forget the impropriety of this man, who, despite his baldness and his false teeth, looked quite fit for his age. True, she had occasionally thought of him over the years—and sometimes fondly—but she was not a sentimentalist by nature.

Nevertheless, on her first night as a widow, Fermina dreamt not of her dead husband, but of Florentino.

As the days passed, Florentino became more determined than ever to win Fermina's love. Consequently, he began to avoid America and to devote all of his time to agonizing over Dr. Urbino's widow.

To his surprise, three weeks after their confrontation, he received a letter from Fermina. Although her words were inspired by "blind rage," Florentino was delighted, and, in answer, he typed her a letter with a "rational and measured" tone. Fermina then sent a second letter, this time obliquely apologizing for her first note. So it was that Florentino began to write her daily.

Fermina received these letters warmly. When they finally met again, she confessed that he had provided her with "serious and thoughtful" reasons to go on living. They began to see each other frequently, chatting or playing cards, and eventually they decided "to take a pleasure cruise along the river" on one of the boats in the fleet that Florentino now owned.

It was on this journey that Fermina fell in love with Florentino. They did not, however, feel like "belated lovers." Instead—lounging on the river, smoking, sipping anisette, or lying in each other's withered arms—they felt "beyond the pitfalls of passion," as if they had discovered the very "heart of love." During their cruise, Fermina often mourned her husband; and on the same cruise Florentino learned that America had committed suicide. Even in their times of sadness, the grieving lovers held true to one another; such pain only intensified their ardor for one another.

As the voyage neared its end, Florentino and Fermina decided that returning home would "be like dying," and so they resolved to remain afloat on the river. It was their aim to keep "going, going, going"—forever.

Commentary:

As *Love in the Time of Cholera* opens, we learn that Jeremiah de Saint Amour has taken his own life. To quell "the torments of memory," the seventy-year-old Saint Amour has inhaled "aromatic fumes of gold cyanide" so that he will "never be old." Indeed, on "the night before Pentecost" he had stretched out on his cot and had bade his lover, "Remember me with a rose." While they are very minor characters in the novel, Saint Amour and his lover serve as important points of reference because, clearly, theirs is a love unable to endure the "ravages of time."

In contrast, Dr. Juvenal Urbino and his wife Fermina Daza sustain their love for over fifty years. Theirs never has been a passionate attachment, but rather a relationship based on tolerance and a somewhat grudging respect. In fact, it is only upon her husband's death that Fermina fully realizes how much she loves him.

After the funeral, however, Fermina makes the firm decision to go on with life. Rather than simply endure the ravages of age, she flourishes. It is, of course, Florentino who strengthens her resolve. Through her new companion's patient courtship, she emerges "glorified," "beautified," restored with "the untamed character she had displayed at the age of twenty."

Fermina and Florentino, however, do not attempt to recapture their youthful infatuation; when Florentino regales Fermina on the boat, he is not leading them on a voyage into the past, but instead is propelling them into a more profound, ageless future, "beyond the pitfalls of passion, beyond the brutal mockery of hope and the phantoms of disillusion," and toward a love "more solid the closer it came to death."

This love endures far beyond the attachments of youth—as poor America Vicuna, who dies for love, must finally acknowledge—and revels even in "the sour smell of old age." It is a love engendering a life "that has no limits."

DREAMING IN CUBAN

by Cristina Garcia, Alfred A. Knopf, New York, N.Y., 1992

Type of work: Contemporary/magic realist/epistolary novel

Setting: Cuba and New York City; mid 1930s through 1980

Principal characters:
> *Celia del Pino,* Cuban matriarch and pillar of the Cuban revolutionary order
> *Jorge,* her husband
> *Felicia,* Celia's insane younger daughter, a dabbler in the occult
> *Lourdes Puente,* Celia's expatriated daughter, a U.S. entrepreneur Pilar, Lourdes' daughter

Introduction:

Cuban-American Cristina Garcia's first novel compresses nearly half a century of history into less than a decade of actual plot time. This blurring of the boundary between past and present mirrors the porous membrane between waking consciousness and dreaming—and between the living and the dead for the del Pino family.

The "dreaming" referred to in the title is the veiled gift of young Pilar, who dream-talks with her Cuban grandmother. To highlight the importance of this connection, Garcia presents Pilar's point of view in the first person.

Story Overview:

It was 1972, and Celia del Pino sat on her porch swing, watching the sea—and dream-talking with Pilar, her granddaughter in America. As dawn spread out over the horizon, a gargantuan figure approached, "walking on water in his white summer suit and Panama hat." It was her husband Jorge, who had left for medical treatment in the United States four years ago. Seemingly unable to converse, the apparition faded away.

When Celia's daughter Felicia arrived the next morning bearing news of Jorge's death, she found her mother still seated on the porch. Celia shared with Felicia an account of Jorge's "visit" the night before, whereupon Felicia's grief turned to annoyance with her deceased father: "You mean he was in the neighborhood and didn't even stop by?"

Early that morning in Brooklyn, Lourdes was preparing for the day's business when a call from an excited nun informed her of her father's demise—or rather his departure. The nun had entered Jorge del Pino's hospital room to find him standing "erect and healthy, except that his head and hands glowed as if lit from within . . . He put on his hat, passed through the window, and headed south, leaving a trail of phosphorous along the East River." Lourdes immediately closed shop and walked over to the hospital morgue to see her dead father.

That night Lourdes' precocious thirteen-year-old daughter Pilar didn't come home. Born eleven days after the revolution, Pilar had been a difficult infant who frightened her nursemaids. "The child is bewitched," one of them had insisted. Indeed, the girl often spoke of conversing with her Grandmother Celia late at night. "She tells me stories about her life," she would ingenuously remark. But ever since her invalid grandfather had come to stay with her family in America, Pilar's ability to hear the voice of her grandmother had begun to fade. Now Pilar was running away, on a bus for Miami en route to Cuba—back to Celia's home.

In 1934, Celia was working as a shopgirl in a prestigious Havana department store. When Gustavo, a "married Spanish lawyer from Grenada" came to look over the cameras, it was the beginning of a passionate affair symbolized for Celia by Gustavo's gift to her: a matching pair of beautiful pearl-drop earrings. As she knew he must, Gustavo eventually returned to Spain, and Celia took to her bed: her life had lost all meaning.

At this, Celia's lowest point, Jorge had stopped by to woo her, saying, "Write to that fool . . . If he doesn't answer, you will marry me." And so she wrote:
> *Mi querido Gustavo,*
> *A fish swims in my lung. Without you, what is there to celebrate? I am yours always,*
> > *Celia*

For the next 25 years, on the eleventh day of each month, Celia wrote—but never mailed—a letter to her first love, Gustavo.

Celia's Letters: 1935-1940 (a composite)

> *Mi querido Gustavo,*
> *In two weeks I will marry Jorge del Pino. He's a good man . . . He tells me to forget you . . .*
> *A fat wax grows inside me. It's looting my veins . . . If it's a boy, I'll leave [Jorge]. I'll sail to Spain, to Grenada, to your kiss, Gustavo . . .*
> *The baby is porous. She has no shadow . . . I've named [her] Felicia . . . Lourdes is two and a half years old . . .*
> *Jorge is a good man, Gustavo . . . I discovered that I loved him . . . Not a passion like ours, Gustavo, but love just the same . . . Yours,*
> > *Celia*

Meanwhile, Pilar arrived in Miami and sought refuge with a cousin whom she trusted not to send her back to New York. His home, however, teemed with family. Afraid to go in until after the relatives left, Pilar finally fell asleep by the pool. Early the next morning, her aunt woke her—she had been discovered! "It's back to Brooklyn for me . . . Back to my . . . crazy mother."

"Lourdes, I'm back . . . Don't be afraid," sounded the voice of her father forty days after Lourdes had seen him buried. "Where are you, Papi?" she asked, for there wasn't a soul to be seen on the street. "Nearby," came the reply, followed by an expression of thanks to his daughter for burying him with his hat and cigars. "Listen for me at twilight," he instructed her, and was gone.

A week later, Jorge returned. "Have you forgotten me?" he teased. But Lourdes only wept, on account of Pilar's running away. "Pilar doesn't hate you," Jorge consoled his daughter. "She just hasn't learned to love you yet."

Felicia, Celia's younger daughter, gradually grew despondent. As her mental state worsened, she relived her relationship with her first husband, from the wild abandon of their earliest encounter to the day when she tried to kill him with a fiery oil-soaked rag dropped blithely onto his sleeping face: "The fire ate the flesh on [his] face and hands, and the stench remained on Palmas Street for many months." She never saw him again.

A concerned Celia removed Felicia's young twin girls from their deteriorating mother, but the smallest child, a boy, refused to leave. Later, when Felicia attempted to kill both herself and her son with an overdose of "pink tablets," it was Celia, warned in a dream of their peril, who had averted the disaster.

Celia's Letters: 1942—1949 (a composite)

Querido Gustavo,
The Civil War came and went and now there are dictatorships in both our countries . . .
I still love you, Gustavo, but it's a habitual love . . . I don't even know if you're alive and whom you love now . . .
Jorge says my smile frightens him . . . I've been . . . wondering what separates suffering from imagination. Do you know? My love,

Celia

A year later, in spite of immersing herself in activities such as presiding as a civilian judge over petty squabbles in her community, Celia was feeling lonely. Her dream-link with Pilar had died; " . . . a cycle between them had ended, and a new one had not yet begun."

Now a volunteer policewoman patrolling the streets of Brooklyn, Celia's first child, Lourdes maintained regular contact with her deceased father. But he would not chat with her while she was making her rounds: he didn't want to "interfere with her work."

It was the year 1976, and Pilar had come to the realization, while attending a Lou Reed gig, that "the family is hostile to the individual." Soon afterwards came an invitation from her mother to present an original piece of artwork during a Bicentennial celebration. When it was unveiled to the public, Pilar's painting of a punk Statue of Liberty precipitated a hostile response. Unaware beforehand of her daughter's stunt, Lourdes nevertheless defended the painting from an offended celebrant who brandished a pocketknife.

Over the next seven years, Jorge's visits became less frequent. His time in this transition state, he said, was drawing to a close: " . . . We can see and understand everything just as well alive as dead, only when we're alive we don't have the time . . . We're too busy rushing to our graves." And then, referring to his wife's departed Spanish lover when he had first courted her 45 years earlier, Jorge del Pino made a startling confession: "A part of me wanted to punish her . . . I wanted to kill her . . . Please return and tell . . . her I'm sorry."

In 1980, Felicia, still struggling to achieve stability, underwent the rites of initiation into *santeria*—a witchcraft of African origin. Her wish to be a priestess, however, went awry when "her eyes dried out like an old woman's and her fingers curled like claws." She gradually grew weaker instead of stronger. The gods, when consulted, confirmed her fate—she died with her mother "rocking and rocking her in the blue gypsy dusk."

Pilar, who had never lost the resolve to return to be with her grandmother, consulted her own specialist in santeria. The omens were clear: she and her mother had to make the journey to Cuba.

That same year, in Celia's rural home, Lourdes and Pilar finally completed the reunion of three generations. After putting the finishing touches to Celia's portrait, Pilar and her grandmother sat together on the swing, talking for hours—this time face to face. At times the old woman's suffering overwhelmed the younger: "My thoughts feel like broken glass in my head. I can't understand what my grandmother tells me. All I hear is her voice, thickened with pain."

After her daughter and granddaughter's stay had ended, Celia left her home for the last time and walked to the beach, where she marched into the surf like a "soldier on a mission," submerging herself. Reaching up, she unfastened and released the left pearl drop earring. Closing her eyes, she repeated the action with the right, envisioning the fading light striking the metal as they sank, a "firefly through the darkened seas . . . its slow extinguishing."

My dearest Gustavo,
The revolution is eleven days old. My granddaughter, Pilar Puente del Pino, was born today. It is also my birthday. I am fifty years old. I will no longer write to you, mi amor. She will remember everything. My love always.

Celia

Commentary:

More than merely recording memories, *Dreaming in Cuban* examines gradations of pain and passion and the power wielded by past events to influence the course of a life. A disjointed narrative structure reflects the dynamic reality of human life: in day-to-day existence, people live as much in the past—as Celia's letters to Gustavo suggest—as they do in the present.

The middle and younger generations in *Dreaming in Cuban* naturally point to the future. Through the pain, passion, suffering and trial of a life as long as Celia's, successive generations are the bitter-sweet solace to whom the burden of love is passed along.

ILLUSIONS: THE ADVENTURES OF A RELUCTANT MESSIAH and JONATHAN LIVINGSTON SEAGULL

by Richard D. Bach, Delacorte Press, New York, N.Y., 1977

Illusions: The Adventures of a Reluctant Messiah

There was a Master come into the earth, born in the holy land of Indiana, raised in the mystical hills east of Fort Wayne. Reared in the Midwest, Donald Shimoda became an auto mechanic—a Master whose memories of his previous lives grew stronger with age, as did his reputation for wisdom. Many people sought his counsel so that they, too, might learn self-reliance. According to the Master's teachings, all human beings were children of the *Is*, the source of all things, and hence all people had the capacity to discover the special purpose the *Is* had devised for them in the world.

As his following grew, the Master had no time to work as a mechanic. Yet as he went about sharing his message of self-reliance and self-discovery, he soon became disgruntled. His students had continually resisted his message and instead had continued to hope that he would solve their problems for them. Disillusioned, the Master prayed to the *Is* so that he might be restored to his former life: *[And] a voice spoke to him on the hilltop, a voice neither male nor female, loud nor soft, a voice infinitely kind: "Not my will, but thine be done, for what is thy will is mine for thee. Go thy way as other men, and be thou happy on the earth."* And hearing, the Master was glad, and gave thanks, and came down from the hilltop humming a little mechanic's song.

As his followers rushed toward him, "he smiled upon the multitudes and said pleasantly, 'I quit.'" Then he pushed his way through the crowd and disappeared.

That summer a young pilot named Richard met up with the Master. The first thing Richard noticed about this most unusual man was the complete *absence* of any dirt, grass or smudges anywhere on his outfit or his plane. As the pilot of an old and dirty aircraft, Richard knew that it was impossible to remain that clean. Over the next few months, however, he discovered that few things were impossible for Donald.

One day, as they worked together on Richard's plane, Donald said, *For the love of God, if you want freedom and joy so much, can't you see it's not anywhere outside of you? Say you have it, and you have it! Act as if it's yours, and it is! Richard, what is so damned hard about that? But they didn't . . . hear, most of them. Miracles—like going to auto races to see the crashes, they came to me to see miracles. First it's frustrating and then after a while it just gets dull. I have no idea how the other messiahs could stand it.*

Suddenly Richard understood. "You put it that way, it does lose some of its charm," he nodded. Then he asked, "Where are we headed today?" Donald passed his hand over the splattered bugs on the windshield of Richard's cockpit and the revived creatures flew away. "I don't know," Donald said, sadly. "I don't know where we're headed." Richard later recalled: *Common sense shouted at me to turn south after takeoff and get as far away from the man as I could get. But as I said, it gets lonely. . . . After takeoff I stayed with him and we flew north and east into that future that he tried not to think about.*

Richard wondered where Donald had acquired so much knowledge and wisdom, and one day he summoned the nerve to ask. Donald simply handed Richard a book titled *Messiah's Handbook—Reminders for the Advanced Soul.* That the book had no page numbers fascinated Richard. Even more fascinating, however, was the book's uncanny ability to anticipate at the appropriate moment the information Richard most needed. He also noticed that Donald, whose very *existence* seemed to be predicated on the book's teachings, no longer seemed to consult its pages—and never asked Richard to return it.

Richard soon understood that Donald could accomplish the impossible on a regular basis. One day, for instance, he landed his plane on an unusually small field and then repeated the feat many times that day—as if landing and airspeed were only whims of nature. Amazed, Richard shook his head and consulted the handbook: *There is no such thing as a problem without a gift for you in its hands. You seek problems because you need their gifts.*

Eventually Richard approached Donald and asked the question that had most perplexed him: Why were people put on earth? Donald didn't answer, and when Richard repeated the question he began to have the faintest glimmering that everyone's life was an illusion; that people enhance their enjoyment of their particular illusions by choosing which of many lives to lead.

Richard's summer with Donald ended abruptly after Donald appeared on a local radio program. Several callers wanted to know how he could just fly around the countryside while the world went down the drain. Calmly, Donald replied that the world's fate was the world's fate, that people were all "divinely selfish souls," and that we all live for our own best interest. One hostile caller likened Donald to the Anti-Christ and threatened to shoot him in the head. Unruffled, Donald replied that the caller was free to do as he pleased.

The next day Donald announced to Richard an important discovery: *it didn't matter whether he communicated or not.* Donald laughed, but Richard discerned an unmistakable tinge of sadness in his friend's voice.

The following day Richard realized that Donald's sadness had been in reaction to a premonition of his own fate: he found Donald in the cockpit of his plane drenched in blood. "Are you OK?" Richard asked foolishly. Donald opened his eyes and smiled. "Richard, what does it look like?" he asked, referring to the gunshot wound to his head. Not knowing what else to say, Richard replied simply, "I'd say you had a bit of a problem." When he inquired if it was meant to end like this, Donald said, "No . . . But I think . . . I like the drama."

"There was a roaring in my ears," Richard recalled. "The world tilted, and I slid down the side of the torn fuselage into the wet red grass." He wondered if "everything a master says is just pretty words that can't save him from the first attack of some mad dog in a farmer's field." Then he opened the book and read the page three times before he believed its words: *Everything in this book may be wrong.*

Jonathan Livingston Seagull

As the morning sky gradually filled with sunlight, the Flock awoke and began its search for food. One gull, however, flew far out over the waters, alone. Jonathan Livingston Seagull stalled in mid-air, trying to perfect his diving curve. His parents and friends in the Flock had not understood Jonathan's turmoil and had often asked him why he could not simply stay with the Flock and feed. After awhile, though, they finally stopped asking and left him to pursue the secrets of high-speed flight.

Having determined that his elongated wings caused his frequent crashes, Jonathan experimented by tucking his wings in during a dive as a falcon might. Suddenly, as Jonathan was in mid-dive, his Flock veered into the practice area: *Jonathan Livingston Seagull fired directly through the center of Breakfast Flock [at] two hundred twelve miles per hour, eyes closed, in a great roaring shriek of wind and feathers. The Gull of Fortune smiled upon him this once, and no one was killed . . .*

When Jonathan Seagull joined the Flock [that night], he was dizzy and terribly tired. Yet in delight he flew a loop to landing, with a snap roll just before touchdown. When they hear of it, he thought, of the Breakthrough, they'll be wild with joy . . . We can lift ourselves out of ignorance . . . We can be free!

Jonathan triumphant news, however, was greeted with scorn: "Jonathan Livingston Seagull! Stand to Center!" the Elder's voice boomed. "Stand to Center for Shame in the sight of your fellow gulls!" Defiant, Jonathan replied, *"Irresponsibility? My Brothers! Who is more responsible than a gull who finds and follows a meaning, a higher purpose for life? For a thousand years we have scrabbled after fish heads, but now we have a reason to live—to learn, to discover, to be free! Give me one chance, let me show you what I've found . . . "* But the other gulls had had enough of Jonathan's foolishness. "The Brotherhood is broken," the gulls announced before banishing Jonathan and turning their backs on him.

Having given up hope on the Flock, Jonathan flew to the Far Cliffs where he continued to experiment with the intricacies of Flight. Over time, he discovered how to ride high winds miles inland, sleep in the air, and dive from great heights to find food below the surface of the water.

Then one night, two perfect gulls appeared at Jonathan's side. After putting them through a flight test no other gull could have matched, they asked him to come Home with them to Heaven.

Heaven's Flock was small, but extremely daring and inventive. No longer alone, Jonathan set out with his companions to master new and more difficult forms of Flight. Finally, one night Jonathan approached the Elder Gull. "Chiang, this world isn't heaven at all, is it?" he asked. "You are learning again, Jonathan Seagull," replied the Elder Gull. "Well, where is it?" Jonathan questioned. "Is there no such place as Heaven?" "No, Jonathan," Chiang replied. "Heaven is not a place, and it is not a time. Heaven is being perfect. You will begin to touch Heaven, Jonathan, the moment that you touch perfect speed. And that isn't flying a thousand miles an hour . . . Because any number is a limit, and perfection doesn't have limits. Perfect speed, my son, is being there." Then, without warning, Chiang vanished and, in an instant, appeared at the water's edge fifty feet away and then vanished again before reappearing at Jonathan's shoulder. "It's kind of fun," Chiang said.

Eventually Chiang's message made sense to Jonathan: he was a perfect Gull, living in all places simultaneously across time and space. Thus, when Chiang disappeared one day to a higher plane, Jonathan was inspired to return to his former Flock on Earth. Perhaps he could teach the Outcasts and bring them to perfection. After all, he reasoned, "the gull sees farthest who flies highest."

After succeeding in his work with the expatriate gulls, Jonathan proudly led his Outcasts back to the Flock. Although the Elder Gull warned that "those who speak with the Outcasts are themselves Outcast," younger gulls soon began to drift over into Jonathan's circle. Jonathan called on his followers to excel, encouraging each to understand his inner self in a search for perfection.

One day, as Chiang had done, Jonathan quite suddenly attained a higher plane. Growing increasingly transparent, he ultimately vanished in thin air, leaving Fletcher Lynd Seagull, one of his most advanced pupils, to teach the expanding flock.

Fletcher Lynd vowed to one day appear on his teacher's beach and show Jonathan a thing or two about Flight.

Commentary:

Bach's work emphasizes the importance of self-discovery and self-empowerment in the quest for truth. In **Illusions**, "Master" Donald Shimoda's search for personal truth leads him to abandon his followers, who, instead of emulating his example of self-reliance, want their Master to solve all of their problems. In Jonathan Livingston Seagull an ostracized gull first finds peace in solitude, then returns, briefly, to share with a flock of outcasts all he has learned. In his "messiah" portraits, Bach suggests that the road to perfection is indeed a highly individualistic one.

WATERSHIP DOWN

by Richard Adams, Avon Books, New York, N.Y., 1972

Type of work: Dramatic fantasy

Setting: A countryside

Principal characters:

A hutch of rabbits, including . . .

Hazel, the rabbit warren's natural leader

Fiver, Hazel's tiny brother who is a "seer"

Bigwig, a strong, courageous rabbit

Blackberry, a clever and insightful young buck

Story Overview:

Two rabbits, Hazel and his small brother Fiver, came upon a sign that had recently been erected by humans. Scanning the bold white letters against the bright red background, Fiver began to shake with fear. "Look!" he cried, his eyes widening. "The field! It's covered with blood!"

Although Hazel wasn't alarmed, he knew that his brother had always been quite prescient. Thus they went to see the Chief Rabbit. However, when Fiver predicted an apocalypse and suggested that all the rabbits flee for their lives, the Chief politely dismissed them.

The brothers, however, were still determined to save everyone they could. Scampering out of the underground warren, they bumped into a brawny rabbit named Bigwig. Because he had just withdrawn from the Owsla—the military group comprised of the warren's strongest males—Bigwig decided to join the brothers. That night the three rabbits would alert the warren to the danger, and then flee.

As the rabbits gathered to make their final plans, Captain Holly suddenly approached with two guards. "You are under arrest [for] spreading dissension and inciting to mutiny," he barked, pointing to Bigwig. Bigwig, however, resisted. Soon other rabbits joined in the fray. In the end there were ten rebellious rabbits who fled from the warren after repelling the guards.

The fugitives, fording rivers and scurrying past forests and fields, continued their journey into the following day, when they came across an unusually large and robust rabbit named Cowslip, who invited all of them to come join his warren. Although Cowslip's warren was quite impressive, and the inhabitants looked healthy and well-fed, for some reason they seemed uneasy and down-hearted. Little Fiver sensed "something unnatural and evil twisted all round this place"; he would have nothing to do with Cowslip's rabbits. Bigwig, however, was now fed up with Fiver's portents of doom. After reprimanding the small rabbit, he went off into the underbrush—only to be caught in a snare.

It was only thanks to fellow fugitive Blackberry's superior intellect that Bigwig was freed from the trap before he lost his life. Indeed Fiver *had* been right. Apparently the farmer had been using this warren as a natural larder: the well-fed rabbits all eventually disappeared—only to reappear on the farmer's plate.

With this revelation, the band of refugees once again set off. After two wet and miserable days of travel, at last they reached the undulating hillside known as Watership Down. The three abandoned rabbit holes there could serve at least as temporary dwellings.

Soon the Watership-Down rabbits were joined by two more refugees—a badly wounded Captain Holly, and Bluebell—who brought with them devastating news: Fiver's prophecy had proved true; men had come to the warren home to flood it with poison gas. Only Holly and Bluebell had survived the attack and the long journey to Watership Down.

One day not long after the arrival of the two survivors, Hazel rescued a mouse from a predator. Gratefully, the mouse vowed, "You 'elp a mouse. One time a mouse 'elp a you." Later, Hazel declared, "I think we ought to do all we can to make these creatures friendly. It might turn out to be well worth the trouble."

Then, just a few days later, the rabbits found a wounded black-headed gull, which they cared for until its wing healed. Intent upon finding doe rabbits for mates, they asked the gull, Keehar, to fly over the countryside in search of a neighboring warren. Keehar returned a few days later to report that he had seen four rabbits at a nearby farm, and also a "town of rabbits" to the south. Holly led the Watership-Down rabbits to visit the warren at the farm, and met a few adventurous does there who agreed to return with them to the Down.

Shortly afterward, Hazel—now the leader of the Watership warren—went south with young Pipkin, a friend of Fiver's, to recruit still more mates. The "town of rabbits" they found there, however, was actually a dozen or so wire hutches. The penned rabbits eagerly agreed to go home with their visitors—assuming that Hazel could free them. Just then, however, a cat approached, its ears laid ominously back. "Why, you pop-eyed, back-door saucer scraper," Hazel sneered—whereupon the cat pounced. But the two rabbits easily outran the enemy and hurried back to Watership Down.

The next night a squadron of rescuers, led by Hazel, returned stealthily to the farm. As they began freeing the penned rabbits, however, the commotion aroused the guard dog into a volley of barks, and two men came running straight for the hutches. Acting as a decoy, Hazel scurried toward the field. Suddenly a bullet tore into his leg. In agony, he dragged himself into a drain, where he soon "passed into a dreaming inert stupor."

Meanwhile, Hazel's little brother Fiver had managed to escape with a few others into a burrow. Grief-stricken over Hazel's fate, Fiver eventually managed to fall asleep, only to reawaken suddenly: His brother was alive—he knew it! Fiver grabbed Blackberry, and the two rabbits raced to Hazel's rescue.

In the meantime, the Watership rabbits came straggling home—without the does they had so gallantly freed. Unfortunately, the does had been apprehended by another rabbit group, the Efafra warren. Commanded by a tyrannical rabbit called General Woundwort, this warren had forced the does into the most oppressive labor.

Before long, Hazel came hobbling triumphantly home, between Blackberry and Fiver.

Now, however, the warren was faced with another, more complicated problem: now that Watership had recently acquired two does, *everyone* wanted a doe. They simply must invade Efafra and rescue the captive does. "I'm afraid," Holly said, "I can't have given you a very clear description of Efafra." "Oh yes," replied Hazel, "you have—the whole idea scares me stiff . . . It can't be done by fighting or fair words, no. So it will have to be done by means of a trick." And so the assignment to design a ruse fell upon the clever Blackberry.

At this point, Fiver revealed that he had no dire premonitions about Efafra. It was then determined that Bigwig would play the most dangerous role, while the gull Keehar would serve as scout, guide, and messenger. Then all but six of the Watership rabbits set off for Efafra.

The trek took only a few days. Keehar performed his job well, correcting the rabbits' course when necessary and keeping them apprised of Efafran patrols. When a camp was established near a river south of Efafra, Blackberry's plan was presented: after freeing the does, the Watership rabbits would flee, evading the Efafrans to vanish in makeshift boats.

According to plan, Bigwig set off leading the way—only to be captured almost immediately by an Efafran patrol. Thinking quickly, he told his captors that he was fleeing to join their warren. Although suspicious, Woundwort, the Efafran general, viewed the large and self-assured Bigwig as a "distinctly useful rabbit," and he made him an officer.

Efafra, Bigwig soon discovered, had "a depressingly efficient system" abundantly staffed by police, spies, and sentries. He would be forced to use all his cunning in order to bring off the escape.

Clearly the plan required careful timing: Bigwig would lead the slave-does out of their work areas and Keehar would attack the sentries, while Hazel and the other rabbits waited for them at the woodline.

Soon Bigwig received news that one of the does had been arrested and was being interrogated. They would have to set their plan in motion immediately. Attracting the guards' attention, Bigwig sent the does creeping out of the warren. But where was Keehar? Where was Hazel? Then, glancing behind him, Bigwig saw General Woundwort himself approaching—leading countless troops of grimly determined Efafrans.

Just as the Efafrans closed in on Bigwig, however, Keehar screeched out his battle cry and descended on the frightened soldiers—who quickly dispersed.

When Bigwig and his allies along with Hazel and the does finally reached the woodline, they leapt into their boat. And Woundwort's rabbits—who had by then regrouped—also piled from the bank and into the boat to join them. While the Efafran leader stared in amazement, the boat, filled to overflowing with refugees, launched off into the water.

As the rabbits sailed back to Watership Down, Hazel summed up the adventure by quoting a rabbit proverb: "Our children's children will hear a good story."

For weeks afterwards, everything at Watership Down went smoothly. Then one day Hazel's loyal mouse friend brought news that a new group of rabbits had arrived on the Down. Cautiously investigating, Hazel found Woundwort and twenty-six other Efafrans encamped not far off. At once, he ordered all the warren's rabbit-holes closed—then he prepared for the siege.

Though Woundwort could no longer count on a surprise attack, he was still determined to have his revenge. The Efafrans thus began digging straight down into the warren. But when the Watership rabbits heard the digging, they concocted a delaying tactic: They would abandon the central chamber, crowd into a large side burrow, and seal up the connecting passages.

As the Efafrans closed in on them, Hazel suddenly remembered the dog at the farm, and in a desperate burst of inspiration burrowed back to the surface and scurried off with Blackberry and Dandelion to the south.

Before dawn the rabbits had reached the farm. While the others waited in the field as decoys, Hazel climbed atop the kennel, bit through the sleeping dog's rope, and stamped his foot to awaken the creature. When the hound opened his eyes to see Dandelion, he lunged, jerking the whole kennel as the rope went taut, then broke, bringing Hazel tumbling to the ground. The dog raced after Dandelion. Then, as Hazel arose, dazed, he felt the raking claws of the pouncing cat.

At Watership Down, meanwhile, Woundwort's soldiers had broken into the main chamber, only to find it empty. Now the general stormed the wall and was soon face to face with Bigwig in the tight tunnel. Immediately bloodied, Woundwort backed out of the passage. None of his followers dared to pursue the hulking, grim Bigwig either, so they followed their General out into the open air—and almost into the teeth of the looming dog. "Dogs aren't dangerous!" shouted Woundwort to his scattering troops. "Come back and fight!" They were the last words he was ever to utter.

The racket outside had awakened the little girl who lived in the farmhouse. She immediately ran outside—just in time to save the poor little bunny from the brutish cat. Later, the doctor came to check on the girl's convalescent mother, and she showed him the injured rabbit. The wound wasn't serious, and the doctor advised her to let the rabbit go: it was a wild animal, he told her, happier in the fields. Then he took the animal to his car. And, taking the girl along for the ride, they drove out to a beautiful meadow and freed the frightened animal.

That was how Hazel returned to a victorious Watership Down, where everyone wanted to know just what had happened to him. "A man brought me in a [car]," said Hazel, "nearly all the way." And they believed him.

Commentary:

Although *Watership Down's* characters are animals, the novel is definitely not a fairy tale. Indeed reading the book is somewhat like viewing a nature program in which the camera crew has somehow induced the creatures to enact their own, less time-honored version of the Trojan War.

THE SHORT STORIES OF WILLIAM FAULKNER

(taken from *Selected Short Stories of William Faulkner*, Random House, New York, N.Y., 1932)

Commentary:

Throughout his career, William Faulkner populated his fictional Mississippian microcosm, Yoknapatawpha county, with a rich assortment of characters, some morose, some bewildered, some unmerciful, and others living in illusion.

The myriad voices of these characters—and especially of Faulkner's varied first-person narrators—present simultaneously one of the great pleasures and one of the great challenges to Faulknerian prose: the use of unrefined dialects. Usage can convey the most subtle of nuances (as with the uncouth omission of the apostrophe in the *donts, cants* and *aints* of the dialogue in *Dry September*) or the broad narrative sweep of an unfamiliar colloquial jargon, as found in *Race at Morning* (not summarized here): "Then the lot, home; and up yonder in the dark, not no piece akchully, close enough to hear us unsaddling and shucking corn prob'ly . . . that old buck in his brake in the bayou." On a par with Mark Twain, Faulkner stands as an American master in the literary use of vernacular.

A Rose for Emily

Miss Emily Grierson had posed a delicate problem for the town authorities since the day in 1894 when, upon the death of her father, then-mayor Colonel Sartoris absolved her of paying taxes. When the succeeding mayor and aldermen attempted to undo this arrangement, Miss Emily genteely ignored their tax notices. And thus the years went by, until at last a deputation was duly assembled to call on the elderly maiden.

As the first visitors to enter the Grierson house since Miss Emily had "ceased giving china-painting lessons eight or ten years earlier," the officials noticed a scent of "dust and disuse—a close, dank smell." Aside from the fetid odor and the closed-in aspect of the house, Miss Emily herself "looked bloated, like a body long submerged in motionless water, and of that [same] pallid hue." She dismissed them curtly with instructions to take up the matter with Colonel Sartoris, who had by this time been dead for over ten years.

"So she vanquished them, horse and foot, just as she had vanquished their fathers thirty years before about the smell." This episode had occurred some time after her father's death and Miss Emily's abandonment by her suitor, a Northerner named Homer Barron. Ever since then, neighbors had reported a powerful stench emanating from the Grierson residence. To one disgruntled neighbor Judge Stevens snapped, "Dammit, sir, will you accuse a lady to her face of smelling bad?"

It was around this time that people began to feel genuinely sorry for Miss Emily. While alive, her father had deemed none of Jefferson's young men equal to his Emily and put off each and every one of those displaying an interest. With his passing no one any longer deigned to avail himself of the opportunity—except for the brash Yankee, Barron.

A gregarious, cigar-chomping merchant, Homer Barron took Miss Emily for rides on Sundays. This was enough to thoroughly upset the town citizenry, who found riding out on the Sabbath a poor example to set for their sons and daughters. However, their indignation was suddenly arrested one day by the abrupt departure of Homer Barron, his business in town having concluded. Afterward, Miss Emily herself was rarely seen.

And then the smell came, followed by the sympathy of the townsfolk for miserable Miss Emily, suspected now of dementia as well as lax sanitary practices. For even after the odor had dispersed, Miss Emily continued in the habits of a recluse, employing one black servant and seeing nobody, save the girls who came to her china-painting classes. Then, when china-painting passed out of vogue and the students stopped coming, she had simply "passed from generation to generation—dear, inescapable, impervious, tranquil, and perverse."

Following Miss Emily's death, the aged manservant showed the ladies who had come to arrange for burial into the parlor, then "walked right through the house and out the back and was not seen again." Not until after her internment was Miss Emily's locked bedroom broken into; and there on the bed, bearing a "profound and fleshless grin," lay Homer Barron. "What was left of him, rotted beneath what was left of the nightshirt, had become inextricable" from the bedclothes which enmeshed him. "Then [it was] noticed that in the second pillow was the indentation of a head."

Dry September

Sixty-two days without rain—and now this. Talk in the barber shop that evening turned on nothing else. "I dont believe Will Mayes did it," the barber announced. "I know Will Mayes." But the barber's innocent remark struck deeply into a seated youth, who leapt from his chair. "Do you accuse a white woman of lying?" he chided. "You damn niggerlover!"

Another speaker tried to quiet the young man: "Shut up, Butch. We got plenty of time." At this chastisement, Butch appeared utterly astounded. "Well, by God!" he exclaimed. "Damn if I'm going to let a white woman—"

All at once someone else spoke up, siding with Butch—to be followed in the next instant by the vigorous entrance of one John McClendon. McClendon had fought with distinction in France, and now his "hot, bold glance swept the group." And the weight of his views was more than enough to tip the scales. "Well," McClendon snapped, "are you going to sit there and let a black son rape a white woman on the streets of Jefferson?"

"Did it really happen?" another man asked.

"Happen?" McClendon growled. "What the hell difference does it make. Are you going to let the black sons get away with it until one really does it?" Then he made a savage, encompassing gesture with his arms. "All that're with me get up from there," he challenged. "The ones that aint—"

The men—some eagerly, others in painful reluctance—made to leave with McClendon. "Boys, dont do that," the barber repeated. "Will Mayes never done it. I know." But paying him no heed, one by one the mob filed out into the street. After a moment's reflection, the barber grabbed his hat and left the shop on a dead run.

The barber caught up with the mob just as McClendon and three others were climbing into a car. He got in and they raced away, bound for the ice plant where Will Mayes worked as night watchman.

"Listen here, boys," the barber spoke up, still hoping to head off trouble. "If he's here, dont that prove he never done it? Dont it? If it was him, he would run." But his pleas fell on deaf ears.

"Cut the lights off!" McClendon ordered. They had arrived. McClendon and Butch exited the car and disappeared into the dark, McClendon calling, "Will! . . . Will!" When three figures returned to the cars, someone muttered, "Kill him, kill the son."

"Not here," said McClendon. "Get him into the car."

"What is it, captains?" Will Mayes said, a perplexed look on his face as he was pushed into the back seat. "I aint done nothing, 'Fore God, Mr. John." With Butch on the running board and Will Mayes sitting between his two captors, McClendon steered the car away from the ice plant—away from town.

"Let me out, John," said the barber. McClendon replied immediately: "Jump out, niggerlover." It was then that Will Mayes spoke the barber's name; repeated it in fact. In a burst of motion, the barber threw open the door, perched on the running board, and vaulted into the swathe of black alongside the country road. "Dust puffed about him, and in a thin, vicious crackling of sapless stems he lay choking and retching."

McClendon arrived home around midnight. Removing his shirt, he wiped the sweat from his torso and leaned against the screen door, beyond which "the dark world seemed to lie stricken beneath the cold moon and the lidless stars."

Beyond

" . . . The hard round ear of the stethoscope was cold and unpleasant against his naked chest." But what bothered the Judge even more was to have his bedroom jammed with people—neighbors, distant business acquaintances. When the doctor removed the offending instrument, the Judge relaxed for a moment—but only for a moment; just then his housekeeper let go with a tremendous, sustained shrieking.

"Chlory!" he bellowed. "Stop that!" Yet she seemed not to hear. The Judge appealed to others around him to remove the woman, yet none so much as turned in her direction. "Then he flung the covers back and rose from the bed and hurried furiously from the room and from the house."

Still in his pajamas, the Judge buttoned his overcoat, noted with relief the shoes on his feet, and entered the throng of passersby. Then he

was through the mass of humanity, standing apart, his face reflecting "quizzical bemusement."

A young man stood nearby, observantly scanning the crowd. When he spied the pajama-clad elderly man, the youth confronted the Judge, asking if he had seen his wife. "I came here to escape someone; not to find anyone," the Judge admitted. "If I were looking for anybody, it would probably be my son."

"Oh. A son. I see," said the other. "Look for him here." At this the Judge laughed rudely. "You mean you don't believe?" the young man said. "Look for him here," he repeated.

The Judge thanked the young man and turned away, only to receive a shock that, for an instant, paralyzed him. He was looking into the irascible features of Mothershed, his grating, cursing utterances filling his ears. "I thought that you were dead . . . " the Judge said stupidly, staring at his former business partner. "I remember raising the pistol . . . " Mothershed glared with contempt at the Judge. Then he intoned, " . . . I know why you are here. You came here looking for that boy."

"No," said the Judge softly. "We never thought, sitting in my office on those afternoons, discussing Voltaire and Ingersoll, that we should ever be brought to this, did we?" Mothershed cursed once more; then he suggested that the Judge meet these very historical characters. The Judge could not control the gasp that emanated from his throat. Were they here, too?

"Sure," Mothershed assured him. "Ingersoll. Paine. Every bastard one of them that I use to waste my time reading when I had been better sitting on the sunny side of a log."

Now heeding Mothershed's directions, the Judge located a "shapeless, gray, sedentary, almost nondescript" figure sitting upon a park bench. This was Ingersoll, the sage lawyer and convincing orator—the man he had worshiped in life.

The Judge took out a picture of his boy and explained how his only son—his only family, his wife having died by then—had a pony that he rode everywhere. "One day they telephoned me at my office," he told the seated form. "He had been found dragging from the stirrups." Should he, the Judge continued, have hope or not in this afterlife? "Give me your word. I will believe."

"Go seek your son," Ingersoll grunted in reply. "Go seek him."

"No," protested the Judge. "I do not require that. To lie beside him will be sufficient for me. There will be a wall of dust between us: that is true, and he is already dust these twenty years. But some day I shall be dust too. And who is he who will affirm that there must be a web of flesh and bone to hold the shape of love?" These final words the Judge spoke "firmly, quietly, with a kind of triumph." Then he hastened home.

Passing the many motor cars lined in front of his estate, the Judge entered the house directly, made his way to the bedroom, and, with great satisfaction, settled himself upon the soft mattress. "Then he heard or felt the decorous scuffing of feet about him, and he lay in the close dark, his hands folded upon his breast as he slept."

THE SHORT STORIES OF WASHINGTON IRVING

(taken from *The Sketch Book*, based upon the Author's Revised Edition, 1848)

These three fantasy pieces, taken from Irving's *The Sketch Book* (first published in 1819), are considered by many to be the best Gothic horror he ever wrote, and are commonly regarded as early-American classics. They demonstrate Irving's innate ability to fascinate readers by combining a witty insight into human nature with remarkable control of the English language.

The Legend of Sleepy Hollow

East of the Hudson River In New York lay a rustic little village of Dutch settlers named Sleepy Hollow, whose local school board employed as schoolmaster an exceedingly lank fellow by the name of Ichabod Crane. Ichabod was also well-known as a man totally absorbed in the study of local folklore, especially ghost tales, and no tale was too gruesome for him. "His appetite for the marvelous, and his powers of digesting it, were equally extraordinary; and both had been increased by his residence in this spell bound region." He had even come to regard the tales as actual events, and when he heard the moan of the whippoorwill or saw the sparks of fire flies, he would work himself into such a genuine frenzy that he himself "was ready to give up the ghost."

There was one thing, however, that could take Ichabod away from his studies—and that was young Katrina Van Tassel. The local beauty had a number of other admirers, the most formidable of whom was Brom Van Brunt, the leader of the local gang of delinquents.

One evening Ichabod put on his best suit of clothes and borrowed a horse from a neighbor to attend a harvest party at the Van Tassel estate. There he joined a group of fellows who were engaged in telling their best ghost stories. Soon the tales focused on a famous local specter, the headless horseman, who kept nightly vigil in the woods and cemetery near town. First Old Brouwer told of how he had met the horseman on the road one night, and had even raced him—until the devilish rider had come along side and butted him into the river. Brom Bones then interrupted to tell of an occasion when the specter, unable to catch him, had disappeared in a flash of light.

After the party's end, the schoolmaster began his lonely ride home through the dark woods. The ebony trees creaked in the winds as he neared the crossing where the apparition had first appeared to Old Brouwer and Brom Bones. Then, suddenly, Ichabod became aware of a presence. "Who are you?" Ichabod demanded, his voice trembling and hoarse—but there was no answer. Then he saw it: a headless horseman "of large dimensions . . . mounted on a black horse of powerful frame." Ichabod urged his steed to quicken its gate, but his horrifying companion kept time with him. His panic peaked when he realized that the dark horseman was carrying his own head in his lap!

Ichabod desperately kicked at his horse, hoping to outrun the demon and cross the bridge before it could reach him. But when he cast a backward glance, he "saw the goblin rising in his stirrups, and in the very act of hurling his head at him."

Ichabod Crane never returned home, although his borrowed steed arrived without him the following day. His disappearance started quite a stir of gossip in Sleepy Hollow. Some said that Ichabod had been spirited away; others rumored that he had changed residence because of the ghost. And in time Brom Bones was able to win the hand of Katrina. Strangely, though, whenever anyone brought up the bizarre disappearance of Ichabod Crane, Brom would grin with a certain sense of knowing. Some believe the ghost of Ichabod still haunts the "tranquil solitudes of Sleepy Hollow."

The Specter Bridegroom

Long after most of the German nobility had abandoned their drafty castles for more convenient housing, the Baron Von Landshort proudly and peacefully remained in his beloved Katzenellenbogen castle. There was one thing, however, that the Baron cherished nearly as much as his "little fortress": feuding with his neighbors. One particularly deep-seated quarrel yet lingered between the Baron and the nearby Von Starkenfaust family.

The nobleman also had one daughter, who had been nurtured by two maiden aunts into "a miracle of accomplishments." The manners and education of the Heiress were equalled only by her extraordinary beauty.

The rhythm of daily life at Katzenellenbogen castle quickened with the news of the imminent arrival of Count Von Altenburg of Bavaria, to whom the Heiress had been betrothed many years earlier, sight unseen. All the Baron's relatives arrived to celebrate the occasion; "the fatted calf had been killed; the forests had rung with the clamor of the huntsmen; the kitchen was crowded with good cheer—indeed, all things were prepared in the true spirit of German hospitality."

Meanwhile, the young Count was making his way through the forest accompanied by an old companion of arms, Herman Von Starkenfaust, who was returning home from the army—the very same Von Starkenfaust who was the Baron's traditional rival. When the two comrades were attacked by robbers, they defended themselves valiantly, but the Count received a mortal wound. With his dying breath he pleaded with Von Starkenfaust to "repair instantly to the Castle of Landshort, and explain the fatal cause of his not keeping his appointment with his bride." Despite the family feud, Von Starkenfaust vowed to honor his friend's last wish.

Upon his arrival at the castle, Von Starkenfaust was instantly mistaken for the Count. He was so overwhelmed by the abundant hospitality offered him and by the beauty and grace of the bride that he was scarcely able to speak. Heiress Landshort was likewise captivated by the man whom she supposed to be her bridegroom, and despaired when he suddenly excused himself, claiming that he had an appointment at the cathedral. ". . . My engagement is with no bride," he stammered, but with "the worms! The worms expect me! I am a dead man—I have been slain by robbers—my body lies at Wurtzburg—at midnight I am to be buried—the grave is waiting for me—I must keep my appointment!" After making this astounding announcement, the cavalier departed.

When the Landshorts learned that the real Count had truly died, a melancholy dread swept over the castle. The Baron's daughter, horrified and heartbroken, retired to her chamber, accompanied by one of her doting aunts. The old woman fell asleep, but her niece stole to the window and gazed into the night. To her surprise, "a tall figure stood among the shadows of the trees. As it raised its head, a beam of moonlight fell upon the countenance . . . the Specter Bridegroom!" A scream shook the castle as the aunt awoke and saw the apparition. But for some vague reason the Heiress found something endearing in him, and made her aunt promise not to reveal her infatuation.

When the Heiress was found missing the next morning, the aunt realized that she had to break her promise and relate the terrifying story of the Specter Bridegroom's return. Baron Von Landshort was shocked by the thought of his daughter being carried off by some goblin; the very suggestion of goblin grandchildren was too much to bear! But the mysterious disappearance was soon solved when his daughter and Herman Von Starkenfaust—a real man of flesh and blood—arrived to announce that they had eloped. The Baron forgave his old enemy and their feud was readily forgotten.

Rip Van Winkle

At the foot of the Catskill Mountains, smoke from a little village could be seen curling upwards. In one of its antique houses lived a man by the name of Rip Van Winkle, the descendant of a gallant line of Van Winkles. "He was a simple good natured man; he was, moreover, a kind neighbor, and an obedient, henpecked husband." His temperament made him a favorite among the townsfolk, but his mildness left him under the rule of his wife's sharp-tongued temper. Unfortunately, "a tart temper never mellows with age; and a sharp tongue is the only edged tool that grows keener with constant use." On occasion Dame Van Winkle even drove Rip and his dog Wolf from home into the mountains.

On one such day the pair hiked to a very high spot and engaged in some squirrel shooting. As Rip and his dog were hurrying for home, he heard a voice calling his name. At first he thought he had only imagined it, but then, very faintly, he heard it again: "Rip Van Winkle! Rip Van Winkle"—and there near the path he spied a "short, square-built old fellow,

with bushy hair and a grizzled beard." The strange man was trying to carry a heavy keg and obviously needed assistance.

At the stranger's request, Rip helped him haul the keg down a rugged path which led through a ravine into a small amphitheater-shaped clearing, where he discovered many other small people. After sitting down to rest, Rip helped serve the beverage in the keg to them. When he tasted it himself, he found it much to his liking, and drank more and more, until "his eyes swam in his head—his head gradually declined and he fell into a deep sleep."

When Rip awoke, it was morning, and there was no sign of his dog, the clearing, or the little people. A rusted old rifle lay where his gun had rested when he had begun his slumber. He fingered his chin and found, to his surprise, that his beard had grown long. Shrugging his shoulders, he started once more down the mountain, dreading with each step his impending encounter with his shrewish wife.

When he reached his house, it was in shambles. There on the porch sat Wolf, growling at him. "My very dog has forgotten me," Rip lamented. Finding no one at home, he went into the village—which he found very unlike the place he had left the day before! What was more, among the passersby he could not recognize a single face. "Where's Nicholas Vedder?" he asked one old man. Vedder died years ago, was the reply. Rip seemed alone in a world of strangers!

Next he heard a woman speaking to her child: "Hush Rip," she was saying. Rip Van Winkle asked her name: "Judith Gardenier," was the answer. "And your father's name?" he queried next. "Ah, poor man, Rip Van Winkle was his name, but it's twenty years now since he went away from home with his gun and has never been heard of since." Soon afterward, the woman said, her mother had died.

Rip was comforted to know that the Dame Van Winkle was dead. He revealed his identity to his daughter, and to the whole town. The story of his twenty-year sleep spread quickly. But finally the clamor died down and Rip, "his neck out of the yoke of matrimony," resumed a leisurely life with his children and grandchildren.

Commentary:

In the 18th and early 19th centuries, all "great" literature was thought to originate in Europe. Finally, American writer Washington Irving's came out with his *Sketch Book* collection—impressing his readership and greatly advancing the short story as an original and accepted literary genre. Indeed, many writers since have discovered America to be a country uniquely suited to the Gothic form, having spawned a host of regional superstitions and being abundantly endowed with a rich Native American folklore. Irving's short fiction and that of other early writers of American Gothic, allowed the United States to gain recognition as a country with a culture and history all its own.

TEN LITTLE INDIANS

(also published as *And Then There Were None*)
by
Agatha Christie
(1891-1975)

Type of work: Murder mystery

Setting: Indian Island, a remote island off the English coast; c. 1930

Story Overview:

A mixed lot, the island's guests included medical doctor George Armstrong; spinster Emily Brent; African colonel William Blore; Captain Philip Lombard; former governess Vera Claythorne; World War I veteran General John Macarthur; handsome young Anthony Marston; and Judge Lawrence Wargrave. Given Indian Island's mysterious name and their anonymous wealthy host, the guests had envisioned opulence, a private pleasure resort "crowned with a beautiful white house." Instead, they found a barren and vaguely sinister-looking rock jutting up out of the water like a "giant Indian head" rising up from the sea.

That evening after dinner, a shrill, disembodied voice suddenly pierced the room: *Ladies and gentlemen! Silence, please!* Then, one by one, the guests and house servants Thomas and Ethel Rogers alike were charged with sundry acts of "deliberate murder." At first mute with terror, the guests finally began discussing the accusations—and in each case found them to be true; at various points in their lives, all of them had been responsible for the death of others.

Later, the manservant Rogers—whom their absent host, U.N. Owen, had hired sight unseen—admitted that it was he who had played the gramophone record of the voice. "I was just obeying orders," he explained to his overwrought guests, adding that he had assumed the record was "just a piece of music," because it bore the title *Swan Song*.

Unnerved by Rogers' "disgraceful and heartless" joke, their mysterious host, and the news that a storm would prevent the next day's supply boat from coming, Wargrave suggested that they escape the island immediately. However, Tony Marston, a young, bronzed god-like fellow disagreed. "Ought to ferret out the mystery before we go," he urged. Then, raising his glass "to crime!" he "drank it off at a gulp." Suddenly, he began to choke and, with contorted face, he fell to the ground. Dr. Armstrong rushed to his side. "My God! he's dead," he gasped. Finally, after investigating all possible causes of the tragedy, the group said good-night and each drifted off to a fitful sleep.

Upon awakening the next morning, they discovered that Mrs. Rogers had apparently died in her sleep—poisoned. Because everyone had trouble absorbing this latest shock, Captain Lombard finally suggested that they needed to find a proper theory to explain the two successive deaths. He then revealed that on the previous night there had been ten "china Indian figures" placed like a centerpiece on the table; now, he counted only eight. Vera Claythorne suddenly recalled that each bedroom contained a framed copy of the old nursery rhyme *Ten Little Indians*, which, as if on cue, Armstrong began to recite:

Ten little Indian boys going out to dine;
One went and choked himself and then there were nine.
Nine little Indian boys sat up late;
One overslept and then there were eight.

Their host, U. N. Owen, Armstrong concluded, "must be a raving maniac!"

As the stormy—and deadly—week progressed, the survivors added new pieces to the puzzle. After General Macarthur was found bludgeoned to death on the beach, Wargrave deduced that their host must be in the house, posing as one of the guests. Indeed, "U.N. Owen"—simply a pun on "Unknown"—was using the nursery rhyme both to forecast how each murder would be accomplished and, in the process, to frighten and divide them:

Eight little Indian boys traveling in Devon;
One said he'd stay and then there were seven.
Seven little Indian boys chopping up sticks;
One chopped himself in halves and then there were six.
Six little Indian boys playing with a hive;
A bumblebee stung one and then there were five.
Five little Indian boys going in for law;
One got in Chancery and then there were four.
Four little Indian boys going out to sea;
A red herring swallowed one and then there were three.
Three little Indian boys walking in the Zoo;
A big bear hugged one and then there were two.
Two little Indian boys sitting in the sun;
One got frizzled up and then there was one.
One little Indian boy left all alone;
He went and hanged himself and then there were none.

Like clockwork, the deaths proceeded—and the Indian figures on the dining room table continued to disappear: Rogers, earlier seen chopping kindling for the fire, was found with a "deep wound" in his head; Emily Brent, poisoned, had a syringe mark on her neck resembling a bee sting; Wargrave, discovered in the dining room, was shot in the back and seated in a highback chair "robed in scarlet with a judge's wig upon his head"; Armstrong simply vanished "clean off the island"; and Blore, "crushed and mangled by a great block of white marble" falling from the terrace, was found with a bear-shaped mantle clock beside his body.

To the two survivors Philip Lombard and Vera Claythorne, Blore's death solved the mystery: Armstrong, the only victim whose body had not been found, was the heinous U.N. Owen. Just as they had begun to trust each other, however, they discovered Armstrong's body on the beach, "flung there by the tide earlier in the day."

In what seemed an odd gesture of pity, Vera suggested they move the body to the house to "get him out of the reach of the sea." Lombard agreed, and while they tugged at the man's bulk, Vera managed to lift Captain Lombard's gun from his pocket and point it at him. "Now look here, dear girl," Lombard puffed, "you just listen—" Then he sprang at her—and Vera, in a flash, shot him "through the heart."

Vera, at once flooded by a sense of panic and "enormous, exquisite relief," returned to the house and started up the stairs. The house, though, "didn't seem like an empty house." She was trying to remember the last line of the rhyme—something about "One little Indian boy left all alone"—when she forced open her bedroom door. There, in the center of the room above a chair, was a hook with a noose tied around it. "Of course," she thought to herself: "He went and hanged himself and then there were none . . . " Obeying the bizarre command, she walked slowly over to the chair and climbed upon it. Then, with her "eyes staring in front of her like a sleepwalker's," she placed the noose around her neck and "kicked away the chair . . . "

When Chief Inspector Maine of Scotland Yard filed his report with Assistant Commissioner Legge, his theory regarding the murders remained incomplete. Ten people on an island and not a living soul left. Maine's suspects, consisted of everyone who had stepped foot on the wind-swept speck of land:

- Dr. Armstrong, a drinker and a convenient dispenser of sedatives—and, perhaps, poison, as he had once been accused and convicted.

- The spinster Emily Brent, who, implicated in the death of one of her servants, had written in her rambling diary of "troubled dreams."

- Ex-C.I.D. man Mr. Blore who amused himself by suspecting everyone else's motives—and who, by committing perjury while testifying in a murder trial, had been responsible for the death of another man.

- Vera Claythorne, an ex-governess with a Coroner's Inquest in her past, had been completely absolved of all guilt; why, even the boy's mother hadn't blamed her for the drowning!

- The life of Captain Philip Lombard didn't bear serious examination, though he was the only one who thought it necessary to carry along a gun.

- General Macarthur, a retired WWI veteran once convicted for the death of his wife's lover, had gruffly admitted to anyone who would listen, "I'll never leave Indian Island alive."

- Anthony "Tony" Marston, as handsome as a Norse god, had hit and killed two college students with his car.

- Justice Wargrave, a reptilian old man once known in the press and in the courts as the "hanging judge," and a man with the blood of countless prisoners—including innocents, perhaps—on his hands.

- And the servants Mr. and Mrs. Rogers, the stammering butler and bloodless cook—said to have induced a heart attack in their former employer—may have needed to fend for themselves when circumstances turned grim.

From the crime scene, Inspector Maine had been able to reconstruct the sequence of the murders, the means by which they were committed, and the apparent motives for each. What he could not explain, however, was the fact that Vera Claythorne's chair "wasn't found kicked over. It was," he told Legge, "like all the other chairs, neatly put back against the wall. That was done *after Vera Claythorne's death—by someone else.*"

Scotland Yard's solution to this seemingly insoluble puzzle would only come later—and then quite by chance—after a trawler fished a bottle from the sea containing a detailed confession, written by the deranged Justice Wargrave, as to how—and why—the murders had taken place:

. . . For some years past I have been aware of a change within myself, a lessening of control—a desire to act instead of to judge . . . to commit a murder myself . . . no ordinary murder . . . but murder on a grand scale. A childish rhyme of my infancy came back into my mind—the rhyme of the ten little Indian boys. It had fascinated me as a child of two . . . the sense of inevitability . . .

I slipped some potassium cyanide into Marston's drink, and . . . chloral hydrate into the brandy that Mr. Rogers later gave Mrs. Rogers. I killed General Macarthur the next day. About this time suspicion started to grow, and my plan called for an ally. I selected Dr. Armstrong for the part. I killed Rogers [and] in the confusion . . . I slipped into Lombard's room and [stole] his revolver. Then at breakfast I slipped my last dose of chloral into Miss Brent's coffee . . .

It was then that I intimated to Armstrong that we must carry our plan into effect. Miss Claythorne screamed the house down when she found the seaweed that I had thoughtfully arranged in her room. They all rushed up, and I took the pose of a murdered man. [Later] I took [Armstrong] behind the house on the edge of the cliff. A quick vigorous push sent him off his balance and . . . into the heaving sea below. I returned the revolver to Lombard's room. And now came the moment I had anticipated—three people who were so frightened of each other that anything might happen—and one of them had a revolver.

I watched them from the windows of the house. When Blore came up alone I had the big marble block poised ready. Exit Blore. From my window I saw Vera Claythorne shoot Lombard. As soon as that happened I set the stage in her bedroom. Vera Claythorne hanged herself before my eyes where I stood in the shadow of the wardrobe. After entrusting my bottle to the sea I shall go to my room and lay myself down on the bed. I shall be found, laid neatly on my bed, shot through the forehead in accordance with the record kept by my fellow victims. When the sea goes down, there will come from the mainland boats and men. And they will find ten dead bodies and an unsolved problem on Indian Island.

(Signed) Lawrence Wargrave

Commentary:

Many critics believe **Ten Little Indians** (1939) to be Agatha Christie's greatest, most clever mystery; the baffling, impossible, and bizarre intrigue it offers remain unsurpassed. The book's enthusiastic reception may be largely due to the fact that the mystery's solution depends upon the reader's *interpretation* of *actual* facts, and not upon unexpected turns of plot.

Many readers, however, simply take pleasure in the novel's artifice and style. But regardless of one's interests, **Ten Little Indians** will likely capture a most deep-seated, spine tingling curiosity.

A STRANGER IS WATCHING

by Mary Higgins Clark, Dell Publishing, New York, N.Y., 1988

Type of work: Suspense novel

Setting: Contemporary Manhattan and Carley, Connecticut

Principal characters:

Arty "Foxy" Taggart, a deranged auto mechanic

Steve Peterson, a widower, editor of *Events* magazine

Neil Peterson, Steve's first-grade son

Sharon Martin, a journalist and social activist

Hugh Taylor, an FBI agent

Story Overview:

Arty Taggart sat watching the "Today" show in his Biltmore Hotel suite, intensity etched on his face. Sharon Martin, author of the best-selling book *The Crime of Capital Punishment*, was debating the case of 19-year-old Ronald Thompson with Steve Peterson, the editor of *Events* magazine. Thompson was scheduled to die the following Wednesday at 11:30 A.M. for the murder of Peterson's wife Nina two and a half years earlier. Sharon was on the program vehemently arguing that capital punishment was "brutalizing," while Steve maintained, just as vehemently, that the death penalty was imposed only "after exhaustive consideration of extenuating circumstances," and was a just and necessary sentence.

Arty was not paying much attention to what either party said; he was far more interested in simply observing Sharon. The expression in her beautiful eyes made him think "that when she looked directly into the camera she had been looking at him." Incredibly, the deranged man became convinced that this woman, whom he had never met, loved him; that "she wanted him to come for her"—which he intended to do. Arty's plan was to kidnap Sharon, and then—precisely at the moment of Ronald Thompson's electrocution—kill her.

Steve and Sharon finished their television appearance. "Can I count on you for tonight?" Steve asked when they found a minute alone. Ironically, he and Sharon had been carrying on a six-month-long romance, even as she fought tirelessly to prevent the execution of his wife's killer. And now, as she nodded to confirm their date, Steve smiled inwardly. At his house that night, he intended to discuss marriage with her. He knew that he loved Sharon, and he was not the least bit angry at her passionate opposition to capital punishment. In fact, he felt that Sharon's crusade was a testament to her vitality and her commitment to her own ethics—two attributes that Steve deeply respected.

That evening, however, when Steve returned home, he was surprised to find neither Sharon nor his young son Neil. On a table he noticed "an untouched cup of cocoa and a glass of sherry"; nearby lay Sharon's suitcase, purse and cape. But the house was silent.

Then, stepping into the kitchen, Steve suddenly froze: on the memo board, written in chalk with uneven lettering, a message stared out at him: *If you want your kid and girlfriend alive, wait for instructions . . . Don't call police.* Scrawled beneath this warning was the name "Foxy."

Later that evening, "Foxy" made contact again, this time through a phone call to Steve's neighbor: Steve was to go to a phone booth at a certain Exxon gas station to receive instructions about a ransom.

Despite the kidnapper's warning, Steve made an urgent stop on his way to the gas station to talk with Hugh Taylor, an FBI agent who had worked on his wife's murder case. Then he drove on to wait in the phone booth; the kidnapper's call soon came through. "I want eighty-two thousand dollars," demanded a male voice. Steve was directed to appear with the money at a street corner in Manhattan—alone. In turn, Steve insisted on proof that Sharon and Neil were still alive. The voice on the phone agreed to produce an audio tape—and hung up.

Within hours, Arty had taped his hostages' voices, wrapped the cassette in brown paper, and left it, just as he had promised, on the altar of a Catholic church. Shortly afterward Steve and Taylor heard Sharon's voice repeating the ransom terms, followed by Neil's young chirp of assurance: "Dad, I'm all right. Sharon is taking care of me." But Steve's new relief was almost instantly shattered. "Why how nice of you," sang out another voice from the tape. "Do come in."

"Oh Christ . . . oh Christ," Steve moaned, "that's my wife, that's Nina!" The voices of the hostages had been taped from an earlier recording. The kidnapper must have known Nina and spoken with her before her death!

Taylor, skeptical, was at first more inclined to believe that Sharon herself had masterminded the kidnapping as a desperate hoax to postpone Thompson's execution. He believed that she was trying to imitate the voice of Steve's wife on tape as "a cheap clumsy way to link the abduction to Nina Peterson's death." But an expert examination soon confirmed that the voice was indeed Nina's. Now it became only too obvious to both Steve and Taylor that Ronald Thompson was not Nina's killer; the man who now held Neil and Sharon at his mercy was the same man who had murdered Steve's wife.

It was now over twenty-four hours since Arty, toting a gun, had forced his way into Steve's house, bound the terrified occupants, stuffed little Neil into a duffel bag, and taken both of them away in a stolen car. After driving along the icy streets into Manhattan, the kidnapper had pulled into a parking lot and reached into the back seat to untie Sharon's feet and removed her gag. "If one scream comes out of you, the boy dies," he threatened as he led her down the stairs of Grand Central Station's lower terminal and into an isolated room. Then, pushing Sharon to the floor, he re-tied her bindings, set down the duffel bag and unzipped it, then turned and left the room, closing the door behind him.

Sharon recognized at once that Neil, who suffered from asthma, was having an attack. "Breathe slowly, Neil," she said, trying to comfort him. "You're brave." Soon the boy drifted off to sleep. But before long, he awoke with a start. "Sharon, that man, the bad man who tied us up," his voice quavered, "that's the man who killed my Mommy."

Early on the morning of Thompson's scheduled execution, Steve made the lonely trip to deliver the ransom. "Did you have anything to do with my wife's death?" he asked the kidnapper point-blank. But the disguised abductor gave no reply; he simply removed the $82,000 from Steve's suitcase—correctly guessing that the luggage was equipped with an FBI "tracer"—and left, with one terse declaration: "If I'm not followed and the money is all here, you'll be told where to pick up your son and Sharon at eleven-thirty this morning."

After Arty had ascertained that he wasn't being shadowed, he returned to the grimy little room in Grand Central Station to pay Sharon and Neil a final visit. "I'm going to set the clock now," he told them quietly, referring to the timer on his lovingly assembled bomb. Then, re-checking the pair's bindings and putting gags in their mouths, he jeered, "You won't feel anything, Sharon. You'll just be gone and Neil will be gone and Ronald Thompson will be gone." Then, leaning over his beautiful hostage, Arty offered a parting line: "I could have loved you very much, Sharon, as I think you could have loved me." As the door closed behind her kidnapper, Sharon looked "at the glowing face of the clock. It was 8:36." The timer had been set for 11:30; in less than three hours she and Neil would be dead.

While Arty was bending to set the timer for his bomb in Grand Central Station, Steve and Taylor were finally piecing together his identity. One of Neil's after-school baby-sitters, it turned out, remembered a bar-buddy, an auto mechanic, who had been casually questioning him about the Peterson household. The name of the mechanic was Arty Taggert. But once again Steve's hopes were quickly dampened, when another message came through from "Foxy": At 11:30 that morning, "during an explosion in New York State"—an allusion to the Thompson execution—Neil and Sharon would also be "executed" at an unnamed major transportation center somewhere in New York City.

With less than two hours to act, Steve and Taylor almost succumbed to despair. Then, miraculously, more information came in: another bar customer had recalled hearing Taggert talk about "going to Arizona." More important, they learned that Taggert had stolen the car he was driving from a parking place in front of the Biltmore Hotel—where he was soon confirmed as a "recent guest." After making a frantic call to notify the Governor of Connecticut that her state was about to execute an innocent man, Taylor and Steve boarded a police helicopter and headed for the "largest New York City transportation center" located near the Biltmore: Grand Central Station.

Meanwhile, Taggert was already waiting at La Guardia Airport to board a plane for Arizona. Just as his flight was announced, he saw the police closing in. With the cunning of a trapped animal, he managed to elude them—but the suitcase full of ransom money was lost. Enraged, Arty decided that Sharon must be punished for his defeat. "A bomb was too good for her" at this point; she would have to die—"look up at him" and "feel his hands on her throat" just as Nina and his other victims had died.

The killer arrived at Grand Central—now evacuated and echoing with silence—at "exactly 11:26." Downstairs waited Sharon, alone and terrified, behind the secret door. In a spasm of orgastic frenzy, his hands gripped her throat—and began to twist and squeeze. At that moment, Steve and Taylor burst into the room. With Sharon's help, Neil had somehow managed to make his way upstairs to alert his frantic father.

After one frozen moment, Taggert bolted into a restroom, locking the door behind him. Steve snatched Sharon's motionless body up in his arms and dashed up the stairs behind Taylor. Together they cleared the station—just as Taggart glimpsed the "blinding flash" of the explosion that "hurtled him into eternity."

At 11:42 A.M., Ronald Thompson's mother looked up from her prayers to find her son's lawyer standing at the back of the church. "Is it over?" she asked. Yes, explained the lawyer, but not in the way she had expected. Instead, at the last minute, it had been absolutely proven that her son was not the murderer of Nina Peterson. Ronald would be coming home.

Sharon, who was just regaining consciousness in a nearby hospital, would be delighted to hear all about Thompson's release later on. But for now all she wanted was to feel "Steve's lips on her cheeks, her forehead, her lips."

Commentary:

An immensely popular novelist, Mary Higgins Clark deftly modulates plot with pacing in her suspense tales. In *A Stranger Is Watching* the early narrative unfolds slowly—alternating its focus from the viewpoints of various characters—then picks up momentum as it moves toward the dramatic final pages.

Born in 1931, Clark began writing professionally to support herself and her children after the death of her husband. She started out by composing short stories for magazines and soon followed with a biography of George Washington, *Aspire to the Heavens,* published in 1969. However, it was not until the release of her third book, *A Stranger Is Watching,* in 1977, that Clark became widely read. After the novel's publication, she emerged as one of the most popular authors in the United States.

"I write for the mainstream," Clark once said in an interview for the *Washington Post.* "I write about nice people not looking for trouble. They invite evil in their own car, home, everyday life." Within this civilized, familiar context, of course, terror, when it comes, seems all the more nightmarish and stark.

THE ADVENTURES OF SHERLOCK HOLMES

by Sir Arthur Conan Doyle, The Reader's Digest Association, Pleasantville, N.Y., 1987

Perhaps no other fictional character in the history of literature has enjoyed the phenomenal celebrity of Conan Doyle's Sherlock Holmes. Whether readers refer to the sleuth as the embodiment of Victorian eccentricity, hyperrationalism, or brooding romanticism, they do more than merely confer on him the status of a cultural icon: they imbue him with reality. Through his combined passions of forensics and deductive logic, Holmes—along with his assistant, John H. Watson, M.D., the chronicler of the cases of Sherlock Holmes—is still considered, after over century of sleuthing fame, the greatest private detective in the world.

The Red-headed League

When Watson arrived at the Baker Street apartment of Sherlock Holmes one fine October morning he found his friend already engrossed in conversation with a Mr. Jabez Wilson, an elderly pawnbroker with fiery red hair. "You could not have possibly come at a better time, my dear Watson," Holmes enthused. Then, because he knew that Watson "shared his love of all that is bizarre," Holmes asked Mr. Jabez Wilson to restate his narrative; it was, Holmes promised, "one of the most singular" he had ever heard.

Wilson explained that the whole affair had begun months earlier when a clever assistant, Mr. Vincent Spaulding, had drawn his attention to a newspaper ad which bore the curious headline "TO THE RED-HEADED LEAGUE." The ad, Wilson said, announced a "vacancy" in the League for a red-headed man over the age of twenty-one. Moreover, the position would pay a handsome salary of £4 a week "for purely nominal services."

Acting, then, on Spaulding's advice, and on the reflection that his own pawnbroker's business was mostly conducted in the evenings, Wilson had applied and gained admittance to the League. The "conditions" of employment were as simple as they were peculiar: each weekday from 10:00 a.m. to 2:00 p.m., he was to come to the League's office and copy by hand the Encyclopedia Britannica. There was one caveat, however: he could not "budge from the office during that time"; if he did, he would forfeit his position forever.

"Eight weeks passed away like this," said Wilson. He had nearly copied the A's and was anticipating moving on to the B's, when "suddenly the whole business came to an end." This morning, he said, when he arrived at work, he had found the office locked and a note tacked to the door: "THE RED-HEADED LEAGUE IS DISSOLVED." He had come to Holmes because he wanted to find out why the League had played this exotic "prank" on him.

At once Holmes and Watson "burst out into a roar of laughter." As Holmes noted, apart from having been the object of a prank, Wilson had no real grievance. Indeed, he was "richer by some £30," to say nothing of his newly acquired mastery over "every subject which comes under the letter A." Nonetheless, because the tale was so "refreshingly unusual," Holmes agreed to take the case. Before Wilson left, he obtained additional information about Spaulding, who, Holmes reasoned, undoubtedly counted "for a good deal in this mystery of the Red-headed League." Most notably, Holmes learned that Spaulding had come to work at "half wages" and that he spent his idle time in the pawnshop's cellar, ostensibly developing photographs.

The pair took the underground railway to Saxe-Coburg Square, the location of Wilson's pawnshop. Holmes tapped the pavement in front of the shop with his cane two or three times and then knocked at the door. Instantly, he pronounced his deduction that Spaulding was, in reality, the notorious criminal John Clay. Holmes then surveyed the surrounding streets, noting that the Coburg Bank abutted the square. "A considerable crime is in contemplation," he informed Watson. "But today being Saturday rather complicates matters. I shall want your help tonight."

At ten o'clock that evening, Holmes and Watson returned to the bank to meet Mr. Merryweather, its director, and Mr. Jones of Scotland Yard. Merryweather escorted the party into the bank vault and explained that according to rumor an attempt might soon be made on the bank's reserve of gold bullion. Holmes nodded presciently. "Matters," he said, would soon "come to a head."

They waited, and after an hour a "gash" of light appeared in the floor; then, through a gaping hole, John Clay lifted himself into the vault, where Holmes immediately seized him "by the collar." His accomplice was caught soon afterward.

"You see, Watson," Holmes later explained, "it was perfectly obvious" that it was Clay who had placed the newspaper ad in order to lure Wilson from the pawnshop in the mornings. Then, while Wilson toiled for the bogus "League of Red-headed Men," Clay had tunnelled from the pawnshop's cellar to the bank's vault. The note announcing the dissolution of the League, Holmes reasoned, confirmed not only that the tunnel had been completed, but that Clay would immediately put it to use.

"You reasoned it out beautifully," Watson exclaimed. "It saved me from ennui," Holmes yawned, adding as an afterthought that solving these "little problems" helped him in his lifelong "effort to escape the commonplaces of existence."

The Adventure of the Speckled Band

The case "associated with the well-known Surrey family of the Roylotts of Stoke Moran" began, as Watson remembered it, "early in April in the year '83." Holmes had awakened Watson that morning with news that a client, a "young lady . . . in a state of excitement," was waiting downstairs.

Watson quickly dressed, and together they descended to the sitting-room where the young woman, "dressed in black and heavily veiled," sat shivering in fear. Her name, she began, was Helen Stoner, and she lived at Stoke Moran with her stepfather Dr. Grimesby Roylott, "the last survivor of one of the oldest Saxon families in England." The Roylott family had long since fallen into ruin when, thirty years earlier in India, Roylott had met and married Miss Stoner's widowed mother. Her mother, she continued, possessed "a considerable sum of money" which she had bequeathed to Roylott with one provision: that an "annual sum" be given to Miss Stoner and her twin sister Julia if either girl should marry.

Eight years later Miss Stoner's mother had died, and Roylott moved the family to his ancestral estate at Stoke Moran. It was then that "a terrible change" came over him. He became reclusive, quarrelsome, and violent; he installed "gypsies" on his estate; and he began to collect "Indian animals," which he let roam "freely over his grounds." Their lives, Miss Stoner reported, quickly degenerated: no servant would stay with them, and Julia's hair had already begun to whiten when she died at thirty, two years ago—only a fortnight before she was to marry.

Miss Stoner then described how, on the night of her sister's death, Julia had come to her room and asked if she had "ever heard anyone whistle in the dead of the night." Miss Stoner replied that she hadn't, but later that night, after a storm began "beating and splashing against the windows," she had heard a "low whistle" and a metallic "clang," followed by Julia's scream. When she arrived at her sister's room, she found Julia writhing in terrible pain on the floor. "Oh, my God! Helen!" she shrieked. "It was the band! The speckled band!"

The reason for her visit now, Miss Stoner apprised Holmes, was that she herself was about to marry, and for the past few nights at about three in the morning, she had heard a low, clear whistle. "You have done wisely," Holmes told her, and then promised that he and Watson would meet her at Stoke Moran later that day.

Some minutes later, the two men were treated to an abrupt visit from Dr. Roylott. He had traced his stepdaughter there, Roylott said. Then snatching up a poker from the fireplace, he bent it in half and warned Holmes not to "meddle" in his affairs.

Holmes and Watson were met at Stoke Moran by Miss Stoner, who allowed them to examine her room. It was a typical "homely" bedroom, except for two details: first, the bell-rope hanging beside the bed was a "dummy"; and second, the rope had been fastened to a ventilator on the ceiling. Holmes then asked to see Roylott's bedroom, and, before leaving, instructed Helen precisely on what to do: that night, professing to have a headache, she would retire early; then when she heard Roylott enter his room, she would signal Holmes and Watson with a lamp.

That evening, after Helen's signal, the sleuths slipped into her room and began their "dreadful vigil." The parish clock had struck twelve when, inside the ventilator, they saw a "momentary gleam of light." A half hour later they heard "a very gentle, soothing sound, like

that of a small jet stream escaping continually from a kettle." Instantly, Holmes sprang to his feet. "You see it, Watson?" he shouted, striking a light and lashing at the rope with his cane. Then Holmes stopped and looked up at the ventilator. Momentarily, they heard a "horrible cry" in Roylott's room. Entering, they found him dead, staring at a corner of the ceiling. "The band! the speckled band!" Holmes pointed as the "strange headgear began to move" on Roylott's head. It was, Holmes explained, a swamp adder, "the deadliest snake in India."

Initially, Holmes told Watson, he had been distracted by the presence of gypsies and the "use of the word *band*." It wasn't until he saw the dummy bell-rope, which he surmised was a "bridge" to allow something to pass from the ventilator to the bed, that the "idea of a snake" occurred to him. That knowledge, in addition to the whistle and Roylott's ready "supply of creatures from India," had led him to conclude that he "was probably on the right track." Thus, when the snake descended the bell-rope and Holmes attacked it with his cane, he knew that he had "roused its snakish temper" and that, as it returned through the ventilator, it would attack "the first person it saw"—its master. "In this way," Holmes concluded, "I am no doubt indirectly responsible for Dr. Grimesby Roylott's death, and I cannot say that it is likely to weigh very heavily upon my conscience."

Commentary:

We may find it hard to bear in mind as we read Sir Arthur Conan Doyle's elegantly crafted stories that most were composed hastily for magazine sale and were initially targeted at passengers and commuters traveling by train. Perhaps the peculiar constraints of writing for this audience, however, help explain two important features of the prose. First, because he wanted each "adventure" to provide his audience with a complete narrative experience, Conan Doyle (1859 - 1930) decided against using a serial format. Instead, he fashioned his plots so that they could be read independently of each other. Second, to allow for some complexity of plot without sacrificing clarity, he devised a narrative form wherein each story could be told, as it were, as a variation on a theme.

Thus, apart from the fact all the adventures are narrated by Watson, each of the plots unfolds in essentially the same way. That is, Holmes receives a communication—usually a letter or telegram—followed by a visit from the client. The client in turn recounts a story that requires some action of Holmes, and, prior to that action, an exercise of his brilliant deductive skills in order to solve the case. Once these elements are established, the action ensues, and then, as the adventure concludes, Holmes explains the process by which he arrived at the solution.

In all, Conan Doyle wrote fifty-six adventures and four detective novels featuring Holmes and Watson, an *oeuvre* which, by the standards of any other reading public, might be considered rather large. For Holmes aficionados, however, the number is regrettably small.

'ROUND THE FIRE STORIES

by Sir Arthur Conan Doyle, Chronicle Books, San Francisco, California, 1991

'Round the Fire Stories is a collection of chilling English tales intended, as Arthur Conan Doyle's title implies, "to be read 'round the fire." In the grand tradition of his better-known Sherlock Holmes mysteries, Doyle (1859 - 1930) interweaves cryptic events, plot twists, surprise endings, and characters as diverse as a disgraced banker, an expatriate gourmet, and a ship's captain all into intriguing arabesques of adventure, suspense, and lush Victorian horror.

The Pot of Caviar

When the Boxer insurrection incited pandemonium throughout northern China, resident Europeans gathered in any safe place they could find. One unfortunate group was huddled together under siege in a little garrison fifty miles from the coast. A nurse, a professor, a priest, a few railworkers, a mother with her teen-age daughter, and a German colonel anxiously watched their food supply dwindle as they awaited the arrival of British reinforcements.

On Thursday, the faint echo of gunshots raised the party's spirits; the distant booms, fired by their own troops, marked the almost certain rout of the rebels. This called for a celebration. "The pot of caviar!" exhorted Ainslie, one of the railworkers; and the others joined in: "The pot!" But Professor Mercer, who had produced the delicacy from his own luggage, demurred. "Better wait," he cautioned. "They still have far to come."

Finally the group agreed to save the luxurious fare for dinner, and the conversation turned to bracing anecdotes of past dangers surmounted. When the professor was asked to recount the tale of his own spectacular encounter with death during a battle in another Asian uprising, he seemed strangely disturbed; nevertheless, his eyes burning with the horror of old memories, he reached into the recesses of his mind to retrieve the past.

Years earlier, Mercer had been trapped in another garrison at Sung-Tong, with another group of civilians, including a number of women. The little fort eventually fell to the enemy, but because Mercer was a doctor, his life was spared. But what about the others? pressed the colonel. "It is wiser not to ask," the professor warned. "It is better not to speak about such things at all."

At this point the professor's story was interrupted. The gunshots were suddenly getting closer, and the company ran outside to judge how long it would be before relief arrived. Only the professor remained behind, as if rooted to his chair, still haunted by vapors from the past. Soon the colonel returned to report the news to him: all was well. Ainslie had gone to the church to await the relief forces and would send a signal of three gunshots as reinforcements approached. Then, still riveted by the story of the Sung-Tong garrison, the German asked, "Could it have been saved?"

"No, everything possible was done—save only one thing," Mercer replied. "No one—above all, no woman—should have been allowed to fall alive into the hands of the Chinese."

The colonel agreed readily on that point, but what, asked the colonel, was the "one thing" that could have been done? Glancing up, the professor slowly replied: "I have seen the death of the hot eggs. I have seen the death of the boiling kettle; I was strapped to a stake with thorns in my eyelids to keep them open, and my grief at their torture was . . . less than my self-reproach when I thought that I could with one tube of tasteless tablets have snatched them at the last instant from the hands of their tormentors."

Suddenly, all was quiet around the garrison; the guns had fallen silent. The colonel again went outside to see why Ainslie had not fired his signal, only to return moments later with a ghastly look on his face. A wounded man outside the gate had informed him that reinforcements could not get through; the garrison, he said, was sure to fall.

The colonel and the professor kept this grim news from the others. At supper the company celebrated their imminent deliverance by opening and eating the caviar. Only one young girl refused the exotic treat.

Soon, one of the group, a railworker, was slumbering peacefully on the table. He was followed in short order by the nurse, and then by the priest. One by one each of the hideaways drifted into sweet oblivion—until only the girl who had not partaken of the caviar remained awake. Not until then did the professor turn to her with a terrible revelation: This time the "one thing" necessary to save them all from a fate worse than death had been done; the professor had mixed cyanide into the caviar. Now he begged the terrified girl also to partake of the poisonous delicacy, but by then she had collapsed in helpless shock. And it was just at that moment, as the professor felt himself falling into his own death-sleep, that the shouts of British soldiers sounded outside the walls. "What have I done?" cried the professor as the gallant reinforcements burst through the door to their hideaway. *"What have I done?"*

The Sealed Room

The Stanniford house was long since denuded of all furnishings; its only ornaments were layers of cobwebs and dust. At the end of the hallway a large door stood closed and sealed, as it had remained for nearly a decade. Felix's father, Stanislaus, had been one of the most successful bankers in all England. However, after a few hapless ventures, he was left owing so much money to his investors that he had simply decided to vanish, leaving his wife and son to fend for themselves.

In the first months after Stanniford's disappearance, Felix and his mother had received two letters from him, the first directing that a seal be immediately placed on the door to the darkroom which Stanislaus had used for his photography, to be removed only by his son Felix upon Felix's twenty-first birthday; until then, the house must remain unrented and unsold. The second letter pronounced that Mrs. Stanniford would see her husband soon, though she had long been an invalid and was now considered on the threshold of death. No further communications were received from the fugitive.

Shortly thereafter, Mrs. Stanniford did, in fact, die, leaving young Felix alone in the blighted house. As years went by, he was forced to sell the furnishings to stay alive. Still, Felix never opened the sealed door.

Finally, on his twenty-first birthday, Felix, as directed, summoned his father's aged clerk Perceval and asked him to turn over the key. "Mr. Stanniford, I hope you will prepare yourself in case any shock should be awaiting you," cautioned Perceval. With many forebodings, the clerk stood by as Felix manipulated the lock—his heart still filled with memories of his master's final confidences. Stanislaus had admitted that his first resolve was to escape disgrace by taking his own life; in the end, he had only hesitated because of the anguish this might cause to his wife. Finally, he had entrusted Perceval with two letters to be mailed soon thereafter; then, voicing his yearning to somehow remain close to them, he had secreted himself to prepare for his disappearance.

The door to the darkroom at last creaked open and a cry of horror escaped Felix Stanniford's throat: seated at the dust-covered desk before him was a shrivelled, lemon-colored corpse.

Thus, Stanniford's last promise to his wife—that she would meet him soon—had been fulfilled after all, on the day when the two were rejoined forever in death. And now, as Felix, utterly stricken, sank to the floor, the old clerk reached forward to extract a final letter from the dead man's hand. "I have taken the poison," read Perceval aloud, "and I feel it working in my veins . . . When these words are read I shall, if my wishes have been faithfully carried out, have been dead many years. Surely no one who had lost money through me will still bear me animosity. And you, Felix, you will forgive me this family scandal. May God find rest for a sorely wearied spirit!"

The Fiend of the Cooperage

The *Gamecock* touched shore. Captain Meldrum, the owner of the small yacht, stepped onto a small tropical island and was greeted by Doctor Severall and Mr. Walker, two business associates who had invited the captain to visit them on the island.

After touring a few points of interest, the three men sat down to dine in a large building with white wooden walls, an iron roof, and an earthen floor. This was the cooperage, a place which the natives were now avoiding in ter-

ror. The specific object of their dread was a harmless-looking bed standing against the far wall of the room. Six days earlier, the watchman who slept in that bed had mysteriously vanished. Since no canoe had been seen and the river surrounding the cooperage was infested by crocodiles, there was no explanation for his disappearance. Then, just three days after that, the new watchman had also come up missing, again leaving behind no clues—no bloodstains and no signs of any violent struggle. The natives were convinced that voodoo was responsible; but this had only left Doctor Severall more determined to solve the mystery. In fact, he had resolved to spend a night in the cooperage himself.

As they discussed this, Mr. Walker was suddenly struck by an attack of a fever common to the islands, and began to sink into delirium. The doctor steered the poor man up to the house, gave him a sedative, and put him to bed. Meanwhile, Meldrum decided to stay the night in the cooperage to keep watch with Severall. The men would take turns sleeping.

After dark, a storm hit the island. Outside the cooperage, the rain and the flooding river roared together turbulently, but inside all remained calm. Once, during a lull in the storm, Severall did rouse to a faint, satiny, slithering noise outside the window, but when he got up to investigate, there was nothing to be seen.

When daylight finally came, the mystery was still unresolved. Severall was happy enough, however, because they had both obviously survived. Then, eager for breakfast, the two men went to check on Walker. Upon reaching the house, however, they were met by a ghastly scene: Walker, still in his pajamas, lay dead on the floor. And it soon became obvious that he had not died of the fever. "The breast bone is gone," said Severall in bewilderment. He looked at Meldrum, shaken; what could have caused such harm?

As the two men raced outside toward the waterfront, they were greeted by another eerie sight: a massive tree trunk, uprooted by the flood, floated by them, and on it lay a human body. The head was flattened, the terrified face stared hideously out at them; and wound around the neck and torso were thick yellow and black coils. "What is it?" cried the captain. "It is our fiend of the cooperage," Severall answered. "The great python of the Gaboon."

Indeed, it must have been the python that Severall had heard slithering past the cooperage during the night. Then, frightened by Severall's movements, the snake had changed course and crawled to the house. There, the sedated Walker was no doubt crushed almost instantly, but before the snake could carry him away, the renewed fury of the storm had frightened it off—to search for still another victim. And after the serpent had fastened onto its prey, the flood had swept the assassin, along with its final victim, to its own watery death.

ALFRED HITCHCOCK'S SUPERNATURAL TALES OF HORROR AND SUSPENSE

edited by Alfred Hitchcock, Random House, New York, N.Y., 1973

In this anthology of supernatural tales, the master of suspense and one of history's great film directors selects his "favorite stories about strange and fantastic occurrences."

The Strange Valley
by T.V. Olsen

Young Elk, Blue Goose, and the shaman's son rode to the hilltop and stared down at the prairie—just another Dakota Valley about a mile across with only a few small oaks and a sparse lacing of buffalo grass enhancing its sandy monotony.

"Is this what you wished us to see, Blue Goose?" Young Elk asked, his voice pricked by annoyance. "Yes," Blue Goose replied. The shaman's son then intervened. "Now that we're here, tell us what you saw the other night." Intently, Blue Goose related how, after hunting, he'd fallen asleep in the valley: "I came awake all at once, and I don't know why. I heard a strange sound, a kind of growl that was very low and steady, and it was a long way off. But it was running very fast in my direction, and I sat in my blanket and waited . . . Then I saw it . . . a huge beast, as big as a small hill, black in the night and running very close to the ground, and its two eyes were yellow and glaring . . . It was bellowing as loud as a hundred bull buffaloes if they all bellowed at once. Suddenly it was gone."

"You should be more careful about what you eat," Young Elk mocked his friend; nevertheless, he "felt a crawl of gooseflesh on his bare shoulders."

Everything had started, he reflected, "early this same summer, on the river of the Greasy Grass that the white men called Little Big Horn, [when] the long haired General Custer had gone down to defeat and death with his troops." In the weeks after the battle, there were those who claimed to have seen dead men "walking the prairie with bloody arrows protruding from them" and to have heard dead voices moaning in the night wind.

"This valley is a strange place," the shaman's son now intoned. "Many strange things happened here in the old days. Men known to be long dead would be seen walking—not as spirits, but in the flesh." Young Elk could not contain his laughter.

"Young Elk does not believe in such things," said the shaman's son. "Why then did he come with us tonight?" Young Elk's reply split the air like a well-flung arrow: "Because, otherwise, for the next moon I would hear nothing from you and Blue Goose but mad stories about what you saw tonight. I'd prefer to see it for myself." And with that, he "kneed his pony forward, down the long grassy dip of hill," his companions following cautiously. But when their ponies "turned skittish" they hesitated. This was a bad omen, the shaman's son warned. "We've come this far," Young Elk countered angrily, "and now we'll see what there is to see, if anything."

Finally, the young braves came to a moonlit stretch of sand. "Here is the place," Blue Goose announced—and at that moment the ponies again began shuffling uneasily beneath their riders. Young Elk drew his throwing ax from his belt and toyed nervously with it. Was that low, swelling growl anything more than a figment of his own fear? Then, all at once, as if the young skeptic had suddenly entered into a dream or a delirium, "the two yellow eyes of which Blue Goose had spoken came boring out of night" towards him, and, transfixed, Young Elk "flung the ax with all his strength . . ."

"I tell you I saw him," the man named Johnny Antelope said, after braking his truck to a tire-screeching stop. "A real old-time Sioux buck on a spotted pony" had attacked the truck. Joe, his trucking buddy, who had been abruptly awakened from his nap, only grunted, "You been on the road too long, kid."

"You white men don't know it all, Joe," Johnny shot back. "This has been our country for a long, long time, and I could tell you some things . . . " Indeed, as Blue Goose's grandson, Johnny had heard many stories about the days when the Sioux dominated the landscape.

Stepping out of the truck, the men directed their flashlights onto an object resting on the sand at the highway's shoulder. Johnny ambled over and picked it up: "A Sioux throwing ax," he said. Then, all at once, as the men looked on, spellbound, the wooden ax handle began dissolving and the leather fastenings crumbled into brittle fragments. *Only the stone blade remained in Johnny's hand, as old and flinty and weathered as if it had lain there by the road for an untold number of years . . .*

Miss Pinkerton's Apocalypse
by Muriel Spark

As usual, Miss Laura Pinkerton had spent the evening in heated disagreement with her dear friend, Mr. George Lake. But when "something flew in at the window," she screeched, "George! Come here! Come quickly!" Still irritated, George trudged in to gaze upon a small, roundish, flying object. "It's a saucer," said Miss Pinkerton, "an antique piece. You can tell by the shape"—an opinion George immediately countered. "It can't be an antique, that's absolutely certain," he stated flatly.

"I should hope I know my facts," rejoined Miss Pinkerton. "I've been in antique china for twenty-three years . . . " Even as she spoke, the "little saucer was cavorting around the lamp." Then it took a dive at George's head. "The thing might be radioactive," he howled, ducking. "It might be dangerous."

"It is not radioactive," Miss Pinkerton rebutted, "it is Spode ware." George dodged the saucer again. "Don't be so damn silly," he spat back. But Miss Pinkerton would not be outdone: "I was only judging by the pattern," she explained with professional aplomb.

Later, when a reporter arrived, he took out a note pad and glanced around the room. "Did the apparition make this mess?" he inquired. "Well, indirectly," replied George. "It struck me that there was some sort of Mind behind it, operating from outer space. It tried to attack me, in fact."

"Mr. Lake was not attacked," Miss Pinkerton corrected. "There was no danger at all. I saw the expression on the pilot's face. He was having a game with Mr. Lake, grinning all over his face . . . " And the quarrel began anew.

Finally, the reporter offered another possible explanation for the sighting: "The lady may have been subject to some sort of hallucination . . . " At this, Miss Pinkerton's voice was stilled. Then suddenly she looked around. "Oh what a mess!" she giggled uncomfortably. "What an evening! We aren't accustomed to drink, you see . . . We really oughtn't have done this . . . I can't keep it up, George."

Although George sputtered and protested that they had indeed witnessed an "extraordinary phenomenon" that night, the reporter promptly left. Although George would not disown his story, Miss Pinkerton simply "smiled tolerably" when anyone asked about it. "Flying saucer? George is very artistic," she would invariably respond.

Yet at least one of the neighbors professed absolute faith in Miss Pinkerton's original report. "I have reason to believe this version," the neighbor explained, "because, not long afterwards, I too received a flying visitation from a saucer. The little pilot, in my case, was shy and inquisitive. He pedaled with all his might. My saucer was Royal Worcester, fake or not I can't say."

The Pram
by A.W. Bennett

Chorn the undertaker "was a man full of meanness." As such, he had always avoided Old Sam when he saw him tramping through the streets in "his ragged clothes, tattered trilby, beard, [and] oversized shoes." Even the hard-spirited undertaker, however, regarded the old man's oversized baby carriage with a certain amount of respect: "That pram had seen life—and death. It had carried lively, lovely kiddies, scrap metal, a gramophone, fruit, manure, firewood, and a corpse—Barmey Betty. In fact, Barmey Betty had her last and probably only ride in that pram. To Chorn's funeral parlor, Old Sam pushing her."

Simple-minded Old Sam and his beloved Betty "were already full of years when they joined forces," and so they never married, though they lived together in a dilapidated brewhouse, each taking on odd jobs—and constantly dragging the old pram after them.

Betty was always chatting about how much she loved the pram, how it served so well for fetching coal and such—and in taking the kiddies for rides. So when she died, Old Sam had fetched Chorn and offered to pay him twenty-one pounds to perform the burial. And Chorn "agreed to tuck her under for that, provided Sam delivered the cadaver to his parlor." But after loading her remains into the precious pram and wheeling them over to Chorn's, Sam paused to reflect on something: "She told me to look after [this] old pram . . . Said I should burn it when I died. She wants the ashes on our grave. Worries me that: burn it when I die. Not before I die, but when. Takes some thinking about, dunnit?"

"Take your heartbreakings somewhere else," Chorn replied when he heard the old man's request. In fact, the only reason he agreed to tend to Old Sam at all was because he "wanted one thing—the fifty-pound fee . . . "

After standing next to Betty's coffin during the brief service and whispering a few tearful words down to the stilled body, Sam went away to prepare in earnest for his own burial. "Got to save fifty at least for when I die," he'd say. "Got to have enough for me *and* the old pram . . . "

Sam departed this life unexpectedly. Trying to save a drowning toddler, he "walked into a flooded river, although he couldn't swim a stroke." Both victims were rescued, but afterwards Sam contracted pneumonia and died.

After a few words were uttered over the burial plot, Sam "was lowered into the same grave as Betty." Yet, in spite of Old Sam's wishes, the unscrupulous Chorn declined to "burn the old pram on his grave then and there." Rather, he declared, "he'd keep it in his warehouse and burn it later."

One night not long thereafter, as a policeman looked on, mesmerized, "Chorn's warehouse doors slowly slid open [and] out came the old pram and set off—uphill. Nobody pushing it, nobody with it."

The policeman followed the pram as it "rocked on, straight to [Sam's and Betty's] grave." At the site, the pram stopped and the policeman "saw a heap of rags in the pram: a moment later they burst into flame. Evidently the heavy body of the pram was made of wood, dry, for soon it was a mass of flames." As the blaze grew more intense, fiery sparks streaked past the policeman, igniting Chorn's warehouse. And the undertaker, rushing forward in an attempt to save his property, was quickly engulfed in the inferno.

Commentary:

With the same inimitable style that he displayed in the selection and production of his screenplays, Alfred Hitchcock (1899-1980) compiled this anthology of ghost stories tinged with both pathos and macabre humor. In fact, the authors here, working in the hallmark tradition of Hitchcock's own movies, have managed to commingle these two strikingly disparate elements in the creation of utterly surreal and unbelievable situations—and yet, somehow, to make us utterly believe in them.

The secret lies to a great extent in the characters they give us. Vividly painted yet wonderfully commonplace, endearingly and very humanly heroic, a rebellious Sioux teenager rides out to confront a ghost truck from the future, a feisty old couple spar with each other for dignity and dominance over the issue of a literal flying saucer, and a chivalrous vagrant exacts the fulfillment of a promise to his beloved—along with an incidental but terrible revenge—from the grave. They provide the reader with a voyage through the many virtual realities of Hitchcock's entertaining, anything-can-happen universe.

TALES OF KING ARTHUR

by
Sir Thomas Malory
(c.1400 - 1471)

Type of work: Tragic chivalric mythology

Setting: Sixth-century Britain

Principal characters:

Arthur, King of England and legendary leader of the Knights of the Round Table

Guinevere, Arthur's queen

Merlin, a worldly magician and a "devil's son"

Lancelot, friend of Arthur, and Guinevere's lover

Galahad, Lancelot's son, finder of the Holy Grail

Mordred, Arthur's illegitimate son

Story Overview:

King Uther Pendragon lusted after Igraine, the Duke of Tintagel's wife. His advances spurned, Uther waged war against Tintagel and besieged his castle. "I am sick for anger and for love of fair Igraine that I may not be whole," he cried. Beholding his king's grief, Ulfius, one of Uther's knights, summoned Merlin.

The wizened magician cast a spell upon Uther that gave him the appearance of Igraine's husband, the Duke; and, so disguised, Uther laid with Igraine and she conceived. But Merlin had required a payment in return: "When [the child] is born . . . it shall be delivered to me to nourish."

Soon after, the Duke died and Uther married Igraine. When the child, Arthur, was born, Merlin claimed him as agreed, and gave him to Sir Ector's wife to nurse. Several years later, when Uther fell sick and died, Arthur became next in line to the throne. The young man, however, had yet to prove his worthiness.

One day Merlin advised the Archbishop to summon all the lords of Britain to a church in London. In the courtyard was a great stone, upon which stood an anvil, "and therein was stuck a fair sword, naked by the point," and inscribed as follows: "WHOSO PULLETH OUT THIS SWORD OF THIS STONE AND ANVIL, IS RIGHTWISE BORN KING OF ENGLAND." Inasmuch as none of the knights gathered there could dislodge the sword, a tournament was called to mollify their indignation.

As it happened, Arthur's guardian, Sir Ector, had a son, Kay, who was to participate in the jousting contest. Kay, however, had left his sword at home and asked Arthur to retrieve it. Unable to find the sword, Arthur decided to "ride to the churchyard and take the sword with me that sticketh in the stone . . . "

When the lad returned to Sir Kay, the knight, seeing the inscription on the hilt, sought to claim kingship for himself—but Ector knew it was Arthur who had fetched the sword. The assembly of lords traveled to the churchyard where Arthur replaced the sword in the stone. Again none could pull it from its place but

Arthur himself, and he was crowned King of England. However, angered that one so young would rule them, three of the lesser kings declared war on Arthur, but he defeated them with his wondrous sword.

One of the defeated kings, Lot, sent his wife Morgawse to spy on Arthur. Arthur, who did not know that Morgawse was in fact his own sister, seduced her, and she bore him an illegitimate son, Mordred.

Merlin, seeing Arthur's plight, disguised himself and went to him as the son of Uther Pendragon. There, he prophesied that Mordred would one day murder Arthur. To circumvent this, Merlin counseled Arthur to gather all the sons of nobles born on May Day—Mordred included—and dispatch them on a ship. Complying with this advice, Arthur later heard that the ship had been smashed on the rocks, with Mordred as the only survivor. Enraged by the loss of their sons, the nobles plotted revenge.

In a skirmish with Pellanor, a gallant knight, Arthur was defeated and lost his sword. Appealing to Merlin to reveal how he might get another, they went to a lake where, in the middle, Arthur saw a woman, as well as a hand, which held a sword and scabbard above the water. The King asked this Lady of the Lake, "Damsel, what sword is that yonder that the arm holdeth above the water? I would it were mine, for I have no sword." Answering that it was his, she took it and laid it in his hand. "While you have the scabbard upon you," Merlin later promised, referring to *Excaliber*, "ye shall lose no blood be ye never so sore wounded."

Merlin, who counseled Arthur in all of his decisions, especially warned him against marrying the lovely Guinevere. Nevertheless, Arthur ignored Merlin's advice, and, after his marriage, he received as dowry the Round Table. From that time forward, Arthur and his Knights of the Round Table devoted themselves to the chivalric code, defending the right and engaging themselves in many acts of valor and mercy.

On one occasion, King Arthur, having declined to pay Roman tribute, sent an invading army, led by Sir Lancelot, into the heart of Italy. In the midst of the battle, Arthur, in hand to hand combat, killed the Emperor, thrusting his sword into Lucius "from the crest of his helm unto the bare paps . . . " Ultimately, the Britons routed the Romans, winning glory for the Round Table and a crown for Arthur in Rome.

Lancelot, determined to gain even greater fame for himself, embarked on a series of triumphant contests against all challengers. As a result, Queen Guinevere favored him above all the knights—and soon Lancelot began to love her more than he loved Arthur.

Unbeknownst to Lancelot, he was destined to become the father of the great Sir Galahad. Thus, in order that fate might be meted out the brave Lancelot would have to be outwitted—and this would be achieved by a woman. Dame Brisen, an enchantress, gave Lancelot a cup of wine that muddled his senses. Asking where Guinevere was, he was directed to the room where Elaine, daughter of a king, lay waiting for him. Believing she was the fair Guinevere, Lancelot laid with her and she conceived Galahad. When he found out that he had been deceived, Lancelot said to Elaine, "Thou traitress, thou shalt die right here of my hands." But when she revealed her identity as King Pelles' daughter and he saw how beautiful she was, he promptly forgave her.

Galahad, son of Lancelot, grew to be the noblest knight in the land. He alone was worthy to remove a sword lodged in red marble that floated on a river. "NEVER SHALL MAN TAKE ME HENCE," the sword's inscription read, "BUT ONLY HE BY WHOSE SIDE I OUGHT TO HANG, AND HE SHALL BE THE BEST KNIGHT OF THE WORLD."

In due time, Galahad and the other knights of the Round Table set out on their quest of the Holy Grail. But the vain and worldly knights were unsuccessful at obtaining the Grail; only humble, brave, and merciful lieges, who did not seek their own fame but followed the teachings of Christ, were deserving of honor.

Lancelot, therefore, having committed adultery with Guinevere, was unworthy to complete the quest. Shaken by this flaw, Lancelot promised to forsake his love of Guinevere and never to see her again.

After many adventures, Galahad, Percival, and Bors obtained the Grail. Even though they were captured and locked in a dungeon, the magic of the Grail fed them great feasts. After Joseph, the son of Joseph of Arimathea, appeared and placed the Grail into Galahad's hands, Galahad beheld a vision of Christ and prayed to be with Him. His prayer offered, he immediately died, and his soul rose to heaven, accompanied by a throng of heavenly angels.

Lancelot, meanwhile, returning from his own, unsuccessful pilgrimage, soon "forgat" his promise and returned to Guinevere. Sir Aggravain, one of Arthur's knights, took note of their renewed affair and spoke of it openly in court. Once again, Lancelot parted with the queen, this time intent on honoring his promise and on defending other maids in jousts.

But Guinevere became inflamed by her beloved's apparent snub and banished him from the kingdom. "Now I well understand that thou art a false recreant knight," she spoke, weeping, "a common lecher [who] lovest and holdest other ladies and of me thou hast disdain and scorn." Accordingly, Lancelot took his leave, deeply saddened.

After a time, Lancelot and Guinevere once more rekindled their romance, but this time Mordred set a trap for them. In the end, Lancelot was caught with the queen. In the bloody battle that ensued, Lancelot wounded Mordred and escaped.

Meanwhile, Guinevere had been swiftly—and falsely—accused of poisoning a knight and was sentenced to burn. Lancelot, hearing of the court's rulings, launched a daring rescue, carrying her off to his castle. The King, in retaliation, besieged Lancelot, who finally returned Guinevere. Arthur, though, would not be appeased, and he began a full-scale assault on Lancelot's domain, leaving all of England in Mordred's sinister power.

In Arthur's absence Mordred usurped his father's throne and took Guinevere—his own mother—to wife. Hearing of this, Arthur immediately returned to England to meet Mordred in battle. Although Arthur was victorious, Mordred fled the field and gathered the many lords who sought vengeance on Arthur.

Once more Mordred came against Arthur at Salisbury, a skirmish that led to an all-day campaign. Spying him on the battlefield, Arthur rushed Mordred and impaled him with a spear, crying, "Traitor, now is thy death day come." In his last breath, however, Mordred struck Arthur in the helmet, mortally wounding his father-king.

Seeing the destruction his sword had caused, the dying king ordered Sir Bedevere to cast Excaliber into the lake from whence it came. As he threw the sword, the hand rose up from the lake's surface and, grasping its hilt, brandished the blade three times before sinking back into the water. Arthur then asked to be placed on a boat accompanied by three queens adorned in black. "I must [go] into the vale of Avilon to heal me of my wound," he sighed.

Arthur was never heard from again. Some say he never died; but later, Bedevere found a fresh grave that a hermit had dug for a corpse borne by three ladies dressed in black garb.

When Lancelot sensed that Arthur was dead and heard that Guinevere had entered a convent as a nun, he became a priest. Both died soon afterwards. Guinevere's grave was hollowed next to Arthur's, even as the remaining knights, led by King Constantine, set off to fight the holy wars. The Round Table, excepting for a place in history, was no more.

Commentary:

Malory, a knight-turned-thief, wrote *Morte d'Arthur* around 1469. *Tales of King Arthur* is the abridged version that renders Malory's Middle English prose into a more readable form and deletes some of the numerous combats and conquests.

The story revolves around those who would achieve knighthood and fame—at any cost. Malory depicts a group of honorable knights, dedicated to the chivalric code, who fall prey to corruption, savagery, incest, lust, intrigues, and, in the end, near annihilation. Though there is much good in most of the knights, even Arthur ultimately pays the price of incest by having to kill his own son—then losing his own life. Indeed, Lancelot, the "noblest" of knights, is responsible for the deaths of those he most loves. In the end, it is the abandonment of virtue and honor in favor of a more desperate warfare that rescinds the Age of Chivalry.

THE FAERIE QUEENE

by
Edmund Spenser
(c. 1552 - 1559)

Type of work: Epic poetic allegory

Setting: Mythical Fairy Land; medieval times

Principal characters:

Queen Gloriana, the glorious Fairy Queen (symbolic of queen Elizabeth)

Prince Arthur, hero of heroes (embodying all virtues in one)

Una, a beautiful maiden (symbol of truth)

The six commissioned knights:

Red Cross (epitome of holiness),
Guyon (hero of temperance),
Palmer (patron of prudence),
Britomart (defender of chastity),
Artegall (champion of justice), and
Calidore (sovereign of courtesy)

Commentary:

In a whirlwind of action and a complication of plot that rivals the most intense modern thriller, Edmund Spenser's *The Faerie Queene* is an allegorical *tour de force.* Holiness, justice, and chastity are presented as glorious virtues in the symbolic form of mighty knights, whose duty it is to battle vice. Wizards, witches, dragons, and giants serve as extended metaphors in this moral conflict, portraying the hosts of evil wrestling against the good within us.

Alongside these extensive allegories, Spenser also addresses the political atmosphere and historical conflicts that dominated Elizabethan England. As the Faerie Queene herself, Gloriana represents the supreme virtue and authority of Queen Elizabeth's lineage and position; crucial issues of the time, such as the conflict in Ireland, are addressed through such devices as Irena's restoration to her throne. Thus, Spenser's moral and historical fable serves not only to entertain the modern reader, but also to provide valuable insight into the composition of daily Elizabethan life.

While Spenser's pragmatic message may at first seem naively moralistic and heavy-handed to our modern tastes, it is not necessary to read the piece as though it were a sermon dictated from a pulpit; it can just as easily be seen as an archetypal Jungian myth. The incredible scope of *The Faerie Queene* easily accommodates any reader's interpretation, and, in fact, this expansiveness has recently spurred a renewed scholarly interest in Spenser's writings.

A near contemporary of Spenser, John Milton (*Paradise Lost*), proclaimed the author of *The Faerie Queene* as "our sage and serious poet." Spenser's genius lay in his ability to lift the English language into an exalted realm of respectability and decorative beauty that had previously been dominated by the Romance languages. Such a breakthrough required innovative vocabulary, rhyme, and poetic structure. Thus, Spenser invented his own stanza—now known as the nine-line "Spenserian" stanza.

Finally, as a "poet's poet," Spenser framed *The Faerie Queene* to attest to his inner yearning for growth, change, and knowledge: "O how I burne with implacable fire," he wrote, "yet nought can quench mine inly flaming syde, / Nor sea of licour cold, nor lake of mire, / Nothing but death can do me to respire." The work, then, serves as profound testament to the bottomless well of poetic possibility and discovery.

Story Overview:

In the highest and holiest of all courts in Fairy Land, knights and warriors of great virtue received their commissions from Gloriana, the Fairy Queen. Upon accepting these commissions, the bold knights set out upon great adventures, inaugurating the ultimate victory and perfection of virtue over vice.

The first of six knights, Red Cross Knight, the embodiment of holiness, found that his assigned task was to chaperon the maiden Una, or truth, on her journey home, and to rescue the kingdom of her family from the seething dominion of a hideous dragon. Embracing his mission, Red Cross left the court of Gloriana, leading the fair Una and her attendants into a savage and threatening wilderness.

Laboring through this dense forest, the party took shelter from a raging storm in the cave of the evil half-woman, half-dragon, Error. A grotesque battle ensued wherein Red Cross displayed such valor and strength that "from her body full of filthie sin / He raft her hatefull head without remorse."

With Error vanquished, the party then advanced to the hermitage of the deceitful wizard Archimago. Through trickery and spells of illusion which presented the chaste Una as a flirtatious harlot, Archimago managed to convince Red Cross to abandon her. Now alone in his sojourn, Red Cross came upon the revolting witch Duessa, who, disguised as a beautiful damsel, successfully seduced the knight of holiness. Afterwards, Duessa and her minions, the Saracen brothers, captured the weakened Red Cross and imprisoned him in the House of Pride, where he was at the mercy of Orgolio, a "hideous Geant horrible and hye, / That with his talnesse seemd to threat the skye [whose] stature did exceed / The hight of three the tallest sonnes of mortall seed."

Una, meanwhile, had found safety under the watchful eye of a lion companion, accompanied by a small group of satyrs and the honorable knight Satyrane. With the aid of the noble Prince Arthur, she set forth with this ragtag crew to rescue Red Cross—an endeavor that culminated in a triumphant and ferocious battle. During the combat, the monumental Orgolio was slain and the evil Duessa was revealed in her true and disgusting form: "Her teeth out of her rotten gummes were feld, / And her sowre breath

43

abhominably smeld . . . more ugly shape yet never living creature saw."

Weary from his encounter with Duessa and her insidious minions, Red Cross recuperated at the House of Hope, where his faith in Una's purity was restored. As a result, the valorous warrior soon advanced to do battle with the flaming dragon that held Una's ancestral lands in terror. The dragon was finally defeated after a three-day battle, succumbing to the renewed physical and spiritual superiority of the heroic Red Cross. Not only did he free Una's family from their confines, he also reinstated health and peace in the Kingdom of Truth. Fulfilling his commission, Red Cross was wed to Una with the blessings of all.

A second knight, Guyon, representing the virtue of temperance, was commissioned by Gloriana to find and destroy the Bower of Bliss, where the enticing enchantress Acrasia transformed her victims into gluttonous beasts. In his quest, Guyon repeatedly called upon the "golden mean" of humility and godliness, powers which enabled him to vanquish Braggadoccio, or boastfulness, Pryocholes, anger, and Cymochles, the lure of sensual pleasure. Ultimately, it was the virtue of his companion, Palmer, the epitome of prudence, which helped Guyon to resist the enticements of Mammon in the Cave of Riches, which lay at the gates of hell. There, in a swoon after a clash with temptation, Guyon was rescued by Prince Arthur, and the two proceeded to the Castle of Temperance, where Arthur remained to battle the evil passions of the giant Melager.

Guyon and the faithful Palmer, meanwhile, set sail for the isle where the Bower of Bliss spread its leaves. There, the two repulsed the seductive and sensual wiles of the sorceress Acrasia. Thus the triumphant Guyon fulfilled his commission: he had withstood the threat to his temperance, and "blisse he turn'd into balefulnesse . . . And of the fairest late, now made the fowlest place."

In yet another commission conceived by the Fairy Queen, the warrior maiden Britomart—who represented chastity—sought the conquest of lust by virtue, so as to preserve the purity of all fair maidens. In this enterprise, Britomart ranged in pursuit of Foster, who had attempted to compromise the chaste damsel Florimel. As soon as the warrior maiden freed the maiden from Foster's vile advances, Prince Arthur and Guyon remained with Florimel to serve as her courtly protectors.

In the meantime, Britomart marched on to the Castle Joyous, where Malecasta, advocate of amorous and sexual indulgence, kept his den of iniquity. There, "much disgusted," Britomart seethingly condemned Malecasta's excess, and then left in search of her dear Artegall.

In addition to chastity, Gloriana espoused friendship as a most necessary and lofty virtue in the struggle against evil. With the help of Britomart's beloved Artegall, the agents of true friendship—personified both in the brotherly alliance between the youthful knights Campbell and Telamond and in the love relationship between Scudamore and Amoret—overwhelmed vice and false friendship in a three-day tournament, ultimately proving that true friendship could vanquish deceit and disloyalty. Afterwards, in the midst of celebration and feasting, Britomart and Artegall came forward to take their wedding vows. Artegall then set off on a mission to dispense justice, his ultimate goal being to fulfill his commission to restore Queen Irena to her kingdom, Ireland, which had previously been subdued by the mighty ogre Grantorto.

In attempting to fulfill his commission, Artegall encountered many threats to the virtue of justice. First, in supreme combat, he avenged the beheading of an innocent damsel by the evil Saglier. As punishment for his abhorrent actions, Artegall sentenced Saglier to carry the head of his victim on his chest for a year so that all might see the dishonor of his tarnished soul. Artegall then faced the Queen of Amazons, Radigund, in a gripping battle. But on the verge of victory, the knight became briefly mesmerized by Radigund's striking beauty, which resulted in his defeat and imprisonment.

Meanwhile, however, having received a vision of justice at the Temple of Isis, Britomart sensed Artegall's predicament and set out to meet Radigund in combat. The brave woman, after beheading Radigund with a blow "so rudely on the helmet smit, / That it empierced to the very brain," rescued her husband. Thus was Artegall enabled at last to advance to the kingdom of Irena.

In Irena's realm, Artegall challenged the beast Grantorto, and after receiving a severe wound, summoned his remaining wit and might to best the giant with a hefty, lethal stroke. But once restored to power, Irena's court was besieged by still another threat: a triad of strifes, Envy, Detraction, and the Blatant Beast of slander. And so it became the commission of Sir Caldore, a man of great courtesy, to capture the Blatant Beast and preserve the reputation of Irena through chivalric virtue. While Caldore's gallantry eventually succeeded in saving Irena, the victory was short lived: the Blatant Beast of slander who had been imprisoned by Caldore, soon escaped and spread its cancerous venom throughout wayward lands for generations thereafter.

Hence the battle between virtue and vice raged on, with no apparent end in sight—for such was the condition and curse of humanity. At last, however, the Fairy Queen's commissions culminated in a trial against Mutability, a Titaness who had gained control over the earth and who sought to rule heaven as well. Nature, as judge, cast her deciding verdict against Mutability, and so validated the desire for virtue and, ultimately, perfection.

However, while staunchly affirming the rights and powers of goodness and virtue, this verdict did not eradicate the influence of corruption in human affairs. The verdict thus served to assign humanity—well outside the scope of Fairy Land—the responsibility of carrying on the great virtuous quest to achieve victory over vice.

IVANHOE

by
Sir Walter Scott
(1771-1832)

Type of work: Historical Romance
Setting: Late 12th-century England
Principal characters:
  Sir Brian De Bois-Gilbert, a Norman aristocrat and knight
  Sir Cedric, a Saxon aristocrat
  Sir Ivanhoe, Cedric's son and a brave Saxon knight
  Lady Rowena, Cedric's charge, a Saxon beauty of exalted lineage
  Isaac of York, a wealthy Jewish merchant
  Rebecca, Isaac's enchanting daughter
  Richard I, King of England

Story Overview:

Two Normans, Sir Brian De Bois-Gilbert, a Knight Templar, and Prior Aymer de Jorvaulx, a monk, had been searching in vain for Rotherwood, the manor of the Saxon noble, Sir Cedric. It was with great relief, then, that they happened upon a cloaked and hooded pilgrim who guided them to their destination.

Observing the approach of visitors, Sir Cedric announced to his warder that whether the strangers be "Norman or Saxon the hospitality of Rotherwood must not be impeached . . ."

That night at dinner, Cedric and his beguiling young ward Rowena were thus joined by the two Norman travelers and the anonymous pilgrim who had guided them to Rotherwood, as well as by one other remarkable guest: Isaac of York, a wealthy Jewish merchant. Despite his wealth, Isaac was marked by his Hebrew lineage as an outcast—fated to be "detested" by commoners and "persecuted by the greedy and rapacious nobility"; only one of Cedric's guests, the kind pilgrim—whose facial features remained obscured by a swarthy cloak—engaged the Jew in conversation.

Sir Brian, meanwhile, regaled the others in attendance with accolades for the great "renown in arms" of Cedric's son, the Knight of Ivanhoe. Actually, however, Cedric had banished his son to the crusades because of Ivanhoe's devotion to Rowena, whom Cedric wished to ally in marriage with the illustrious Saxon noble Athelstane.

Thus when Sir Brian expressed a desire to joust with Sir Ivanhoe, Cedric bristled at Rowena's response: "My voice shall be heard, if no other in this hall is raised, in behalf of the absent Ivanhoe. I would pledge name and fame that Ivanhoe gives this proud Knight the meeting he desires."

Rowena's words elated the cloaked pilgrim; for, in reality, he was none other than Ivanhoe himself in disguise. To his further delight, Rowena later invited him to converse secretly in her chamber. " . . . You this night mentioned a name," faltered the lady. "—I mean . . . the name of Ivanhoe in the halls where by nature and kindred it should have sounded most acceptably . . . I only dare ask you where, and in what condition . . . you left him of whom you spoke?"

"He hath, I believe, surmounted the persecution of his enemies in Palestine," Ivanhoe lied, "and is on the eve of returning to England . . ."

"Would to God," Rowena exclaimed, "he were here safely arrived, and able to bear arms in the approaching tourney . . ." She then retired to her bed, and Ivanhoe paid a visit to Isaac's guest chamber—with the warning that he had overheard Sir Brian earlier discuss a plan "to abduct him and steal his money." "Holy God of Abraham!" Isaac despaired. Ivanhoe, however, reassured him. "I will guide you by the secret paths of the forest, known as well to me as to any forester than ranges in it, and I will not leave you till you are under safe conduct of some chief or baron going to the tournament . . ."

As promised, Ivanhoe safely conducted the fugitive through the forest. When Isaac later appeared with his daughter Rebecca in the spectators' gallery at the tournament, Prince John—who was acting as regent while his brother and "mortal enemy" King Richard fought in the Crusades—was immediately smitten with the enchanting girl. "Yonder Jewess must be the very model of that perfection whose charms drove frantic the wisest king that ever lived!" he marvelled. Indeed, the Prince even considered naming Rebecca as the tournament's Queen of Beauty and Love.

Ivanhoe, however, under the anonymous title of a "Disinherited Knight," fought superbly in the tournament's first matches, defeating six other knights, including Sir Brian; and as a reward, he was given the honor of naming the tournament Queen. Of course the Lady Rowena was selected. On the second day of the tournament, according to custom, "the Prince marshalled Rowena to the seat of honour opposite his own." And as the day's events unfolded, it appeared that the Disinherited Knight would again defeat all his challengers. Suddenly, however, the horseman was set upon by three knights at once—led by the Norman Sir Brian: *The masterly horsemanship of the Disinherited Knight, and the activity of the noble animal which he mounted, enabled him for a few minutes to keep at sword's point his three antagonists, turning and wheeling with the agility of a hawk . . . and rushing now against the one, now against the other . . .* Before long, however, "it was evident that he must at last be overpowered."

Then, just at the crucial moment, "the course of the day [was changed]." A knight dubbed the Black Sluggard, who "hitherto had evinced little interest in the event of the fight," suddenly rushed into battle; and with the assistance of this enigmatic ally, the Disinherited Knight again proved victorious. He "waved his fatal sword over the head of his adversary," Sir Brian, who had fallen from his wounded horse.

Proclaiming the Disinherited Knight the tournament champion, Prince John instructed him to receive the "chaplet of honour" from Rowena. Then, over the knight's protests, as he knelt before his lady his "helmet was removed." And though "his countenance was as pale as death, and marked in one or two places with streaks of blood," Rowena recognized Ivanhoe. With a "faint shriek," she placed the chaplet on his head. Ivanhoe then kissed his lady's hand—and fainted.

When "Cedric the Saxon saw his son drop down senseless in the lists of Ashby, his first impulse was to order him into the custody and care of his own attendants." His pride, however, prevented him. And he was further vexed when Rowena subsequently refused to "share a throne with Athelstane"; nevertheless, the three set off together for Rotherwood.

En route, they were shocked to find Isaac and Rebecca shrieking by the roadside in distress. They, having set out for Rotherwood along with their wounded friend Ivanhoe—who lay huddled and concealed in the litter—had been stopped by the news "that there was a strong band of outlaws lying in wait in the woods before them"; meanwhile, their frightened servants had fled with all the horses.

Isaac now begged the Saxons to accompany them on their journey. Athelstane at first refused; touched by Rebecca's pleas, however, Rowena persuaded Cedric to help. The travelers thus journeyed together until twilight, "when they were assailed in front, flank, and rear" by three Normans: Sir Brian, Maurice de Bracy, and Reginald Front de Boeuf.

The Normans immediately led their Saxon prisoners to Front de Boeuf's castle. Here, the Saxons were confined together, Ivanhoe, the enshrouded and sickly "Jew-man," was tended to by a Saxon "hag" named Ulrica, and the others were led to separate chambers.

In his chamber, Isaac learned that Front de Boeuf sought a ransom of "a thousand silver pounds" for his release. If Isaac refused to pay, de Boeuf would torture him to death. Although unaware of her father's plight, Rebecca, in her chamber, was horrified to hear Sir Brian demand her hand in marriage. To silence him, she threatened "to jump from her turret-chamber."

Not long thereafter the Norman castle was attacked by Saxons—including not only the renowned Robin Hood, along with his outlaw band, but King Richard himself, still riding under the dark trappings of the Black Sluggard Knight. During the ensuing battle, the captives managed to make their way outside. There they saw that a "fire was spreading rapidly through all parts of the castle." And as the blaze roiled upward, "Ulrica, who had first kindled it, appeared on a turret, in the guise of one of the ancient furies, yelling forth a war song," until at last she was engulfed by the hungry flames.

Robin Hood then directed de Bracy and the erstwhile captives to "the trysting-tree near Hartwalk Walk." Here, everyone was apprised of the events that had transpired during the battle: Athelstane and de Boeuf had both met their deaths, and Rebecca had been abducted by the proud Sir Brian. "Oh," Isaac lamented, "Better the tomb of his fathers than the dishonourable couch of the licentious and savage Templar."

When Isaac visited the Grand Master of the Templars to arrange a ransom for his daughter's return, however, the Grand Master was outraged. "Spurn this Jew from the gate," he commanded his men. "Shoot him dead if he oppose or turn again." He then sent a messenger to find Sir Brian, who was stunned to hear, "Rebecca . . . is a sorceress and must suffer as such."

"She shall not, by heaven," Sir Brian exclaimed. But Rebecca's fate was now out of his hands. The Jewish maiden was "brought before the tribunal of the Grand Master" on charges of sorcery.

After various witnesses had related incidents purporting to demonstrate her bewitching of Sir Brian, at last Rebecca spoke. "To invoke your pity," she began, "would . . . be as useless as I should hold it mean." She then continued: " . . . I maintain my innocence, and I declare the falsehood of this accusation. I challenge the privilege of trial by combat . . . "

Thus, on the day scheduled for her execution, Rebecca was led to a "black chair arranged near a stake surrounded by faggots, where she awaited a champion to fight for her life." None appeared. At last the Grand Master announced, "Let her prepare for death."

Suddenly "a knight, urging his horse to speed, appeared on the plain." Ivanhoe had come to defend Rebecca. The combat began; and the Saxon's opponent, Sir Brian, soon lay unhorsed on the ground, unable to arise. "Slay him not," the Grand Master commanded. Sir Brian, however, had already died—not by "the lance of his enemy," but by "the violence of his own contending passions."

Then a "clattering of horses' feet" could be heard. King Richard—who was in the process of wresting control of his throne from the treacherous Prince John—had come with Robin Hood to arrest the Norman Knights.

Shortly afterward, the victorious King invited Sir Cedric to be "a guest at court for seven days." The Saxon now reconsidered his long quarrel with his son—and relented. With the blessing of Athelstane, who had miraculously come back to life at his own funeral, Ivanhoe and Rowena were soon wed, an event celebrated by both Normans and Saxons.

Following the marriage, Rebecca and her father left England for a safe and prosperous life in Spain. At Rotherwood, meanwhile, Rowena and Ivanhoe "lived long and happily [together], for they were attached to each other by the bonds of earthly affection, and they loved each other the more from the recollection of the obstacles which had impeded their union."

Commentary:

Sir Walter Scott noted that he had set *Ivanhoe* in the reign of Richard I because the period lent his narrative a "striking contrast betwixt the Saxons, by whom the soil was cultivated, and the Normans, who still reigned in it as conquerors . . . " In reality, hostilities between Saxons and their Norman conquerors had largely abated by the late 12th century—a fact that has long irritated critics of *Ivanhoe*. Despite this historical inaccuracy, Scott's novel has remained immensely popular largely because of his skillful dramatization of the daily life in Plantagenet England.

THE AENEID

by
Virgil
(70 B.C. - 19 B.C.)

Type of work: Epic poem

Setting: Carthage, Sicily, and Italy; ca. 1250 B.C., after the Trojan War and the destruction of Troy

Principal characters:

Aeneas, son of the Trojan prince **Anchises** and the love goddess **Venus,** and the leader of the Trojan exiles after the fall of Troy

Juno, the sister and wife of the supreme god **Jupiter,** and Aeneas' principal divine nemesis

Dido, the queen and founder of Carthage and, for a year, Aeneas' lover

Latinus, the king of Latium and the father of **Lavinia,** who is fated to marry Aeneas

Turnus, an Italian king who wages war against the Trojans

Deiphobe, the Prophetess of Cumae who guides Aeneas through the underworld

Commentary:

Written in the twilight years of Augustus Caesar's reign, the *Aeneid* recounts in epic form Aeneas' wanderings from the ruins of Troy to his settlement in Italy. The story was left unfinished at Virgil's death. Despite its lack of closure, however, it has remained a central work in our literary canon for over two thousand years. And with Robert Fitzgerald's superb English translation, the *Aeneid* continues to exert a vital influence on literature today.

The seeds of Virgil's plot are borrowed from Book XX of *The Iliad.* There, just as the Greek champion Achilles is about to kill Aeneas in combat, the sea god Poseidon (or Neptune, as he was called by the Romans) intercedes and spirits Aeneas out of harm's way, for, as Poseidon knows, Aeneas and his descendants are fated to be "lords over the Trojans born hereafter."

Story Overview:

The goddess Juno loved Carthage above all cities. She knew, however, that Fate had decreed that Rome, which had not yet been founded, would rise up and destroy Carthage in the Punic Wars. Moreover, she knew that the great Trojan warrior-leader Aeneas, whose Italian descendants were destined to build Rome, had just set sail with his fleet from Sicily.

Embittered by Fate, Juno conspired with the wind god Aeolus to send a storm that would make Aeneas' "long ships founder!" But before Aeolus could complete his task, the sea god Neptune intervened and calmed the waters. "Gale-worn," Aeneas laid anchor off the coast of Libya. Although several of his ships had been separated by the storm, Aeneas ordered the remaining Trojans ashore to make a feast of venison and wine.

The next day, Aeneas and his friend Achates set off to explore "the strange new places" along the coast. Midway through a forest, they encountered Aeneas' own mother Venus, disguised as a Libyan huntress. Venus related to them a brief history of Carthage and its founding queen, Dido. Then, before leaving them, she pointed out the road to Carthage and cloaked them "in grey mist" so that no one would "see or accost them" along the way.

Thus enshrouded, Aeneas and Achates entered Carthage and toured the city. Among its marvels, they were particularly struck by Dido's majestic temple, which was decorated with panels depicting "the Trojan battles in the old war, now known throughout the world." Their wonder, however, soon faded when Dido herself appeared, followed by the captains of the missing Trojan ships.

Dido welcomed the shipwrecked Trojans, also expressing her disappointment that Aeneas was not also present. And even as she said this, the mist around Aeneas and Achates vanished. "Before your eyes I stand," he addressed the queen, "the same one you look for." Pleased, Dido arranged a banquet that night to honor the Trojans.

Aeneas, meanwhile, sent word back to his ships that his son Ascanius should attend the banquet. Venus, seizing on Ascanius' imminent arrival as an opportunity to protect Aeneas, plotted with Cupid: disguised as Ascanius, Cupid would attend the banquet and cast a spell on Dido so she would fall in love with Aeneas. The trick worked, and that evening after feasting, an impassioned Dido asked Aeneas to tell his story of the "ruin" of Troy and his years of "wandering all the lands and all the seas."

Reluctantly, Aeneas agreed. When he had finished his tale of the Trojan Horse and the ruin it had brought him—the murder of his wife Creusa on their final night in Troy, the leveling of his country to ashes, and, in Sicily, the death of his father Anchises—Dido "ached [with] longing" for Aeneas and felt as if an "inward fire [was] eating her away." Aeneas, for his part, was equally beguiled by Dido's beauty and charms. Looking on, Juno and Venus decided that a union between the unrequited lovers would be mutually advantageous. Thus Juno caused a thunderstorm, which drove the pair into a secluded cave—there, to consummate their love.

Jupiter, incensed that Aeneas was now living with Dido in Carthage, dispatched his messenger Mercury with a warning: "If future histories and glories do not affect you," he told Aeneas, "Think of the expectations of your heir . . . to whom the Italian realm, the land of Rome, are due." Sobered by Jupiter's reprimand, Aeneas made secret preparations to make "the fleet ready for the sea."

Dido, having uncovered Aeneas' deceit, built a funeral pyre and threatened to take her own life if he left her. Jupiter, meanwhile, dispatched Mercury with a second warning, and, with this reproach fresh in his ears, Aeneas set sail late that night. At dawn, when Dido awakened and learned that Aeneas was gone, she cursed him and his descendants, climbed her pyre, and killed herself. And at sea, Aeneas looked "far astern" at Carthage, where, flaring on the horizon, he could see the blaze of Dido's pyre.

Back in Sicily, Aeneas sponsored Olympic games to observe the anniversary of his father's death. That night, Anchises appeared to Aeneas in a dream and informed him that he should sail for Italy. Once there, Anchises continued, Aeneas should seek out the Prophetess at Cumae, who would escort him to the underworld, where Anchises would reveal to Aeneas his fate.

Following his father's instructions, Aeneas sailed to Cumae and met with this esteemed prophetess, Deiphobe. There was a tree, she told Aeneas, sacred to Juno, whose "deep shade" concealed "the golden bough." This bough, which he would need to leave as an offering in the underworld, would be broken off "willingly" if he was "called by fate."

That evening, Aeneas returned to the Sibyl with the golden bough, and, together, they descended into the underworld. She first led him to the river Acheron, where they presented the golden bough to Charon, the ferryman who transported dead souls across the river. Crossing to the other shore, they continued their journey and, as night drew near, arrived finally at Elysium, where Anchises awaited them.

"Have you come at last?" Anchises wept with joy. "Your sad ghost impelled me," answered Aeneas, at which he tried three times to embrace his father—but each time Anchises "slipped through his hands, weightless as wind and fugitive as dream." The father and son made their way to a secluded grove, where Anchises pointed to a mass of souls gathered by the river Lethe. "Souls," intoned Anchises, "for whom a second body is in store."

As together they traversed among these disembodied souls, Anchises identified some of the "famous children" Aeneas' line would produce: Romulus, the fabled founder of Rome, and Julius and Augustus Caesar, who would "bring once again an Age of Gold." When the pair had "viewed it all," Anchises spoke briefly of the glory and wars that awaited Aeneas, and how he "might avoid or bear each toil to come." Then, after bidding his father farewell, Aeneas and Deiphobe made their way back "to the upper world."

Transformed and revitalized by the revelations of his fate, Aeneas returned to his ships at Cumae and sailed for Latium, the land where, as his father had foretold, he and his descendants would fulfill their destinies.

Shortly after they made landfall, Aeneas and the Trojans were greeted by Latinus, the king of Latium. Immediately, Latinus recognized that Aeneas was the foreign prince the oracles had decreed would conquer Latium and marry his daughter Lavinia. "Children of that stock," he knew, "will see all earth turned Latin at their feet, governed by them, as far as on his rounds the sun looks down on Ocean, East or West." Thus, to propitiate the Fates, Latinus offered his daughter Lavinia in marriage to Aeneas.

Meanwhile, Juno, rancorous because Aeneas now stood at the threshold of his destiny, unleashed the Fury Allecto to stir up enmity between the Latins and the Trojans. Juno accomplished her end by inspiring the Italian prince Turnus, Lavinia's principal suitor, to raise an army against Aeneas.

Rumors of impending war quickly spread throughout Latium, and Turnus soon commanded a large army anxious to expel the Trojans. While Aeneas enlisted the aid of the city-states Pallanteum and Etruria, Juno convinced Turnus to "raise the flag of war" over Laurenteum, Latium's capital city. "Now," Juno said, "is the time to sound the call for cavalry and war-cars, now!"

Apprised of the war, Jupiter called a council of the gods on Mount Olympus and made it clear to both Juno and Venus that he would not tolerate further interference. "The effort each man makes," Jupiter proclaimed, "will bring luck or trouble"; the Latins and Trojans would settle their dispute according to "the Fates."

In the meantime, Aeneas returned to the Trojan camps with new allies. In one of the battles that followed, Pallas, the son of the Pallenteum king Evander, was killed by Turnus and stripped of his armor. Aeneas, lamenting the loss, swore revenge and sought Turnus out on the battlefield.

As the war dragged on, Turnus fell into disfavor among the Italians, and members of his council suggested that he fight Aeneas himself. "Come, sir," one prince taunted him, "if any fighting blood is in you, any native legacy from Mars, go face the man who calls you out to combat!" After the Italian cavalry suffered another major defeat, Turnus reluctantly agreed to confront Aeneas: Lavinia, he declared, would marry the victor.

With their respective armies watching from either side, Aeneas and Turnus met in the field. A battle, however, soon erupted between the armies, and as the conflagration spread, Aeneas was struck by an arrow. While he retired behind battle lines to dress his wound, Turnus slaughtered a large number of Trojans in one of the bloodiest battles of the war.

Aeneas, now recovered, saw—and took—the opportunity to seize the undefended capital Laurenteum. When Turnus learned that Aeneas occupied the city, he again challenged him, and with the same terms as before: that the victor would marry Lavinia.

As the two champions met on the battlefield one last time, Jupiter reminded the gods that only Fate should determine the outcome of their combat. After dodging a stone, Aeneas threw his spear and hit Turnus, who fell to the ground. Seeing he was now defeated, Turnus asked Aeneas to "return me, or my body . . . to my own kin."

For a moment, Aeneas pitied his toppled foe and considered sparing his life. However, when he caught sight of the "swordbelt" at Turnus' side, the same weapon that had been stripped from his friend Pallas' body, the sight of this "trophy" brought on rage. "This wound," he cried at Turnus, "will come from Pallas: Pallas makes this offering, and from your criminal blood exacts his due." With that, Aeneas "sank his blade in fury in Turnus's chest. Then all the body slackened in death's chill, and with a groan for that indignity, his spirit fled into the gloom below."

THE ILIAD

by
Homer
(c. 9th century B.C.)

Type of work: Epic Greek poem
Setting: Troy; c. 1250-1240 B.C.
Principal characters:

The Achaeans (Greeks)
Menelaos, King of the Greek city-state Argos, whose wife Helen has been abducted by Paris, a prince of Troy
Agamemnon, Menelaos' brother and also a King of Argos
Achilles, mightiest and most feared of the Achaean warriors
Patroclus, brave Achaean soldier and close friend of Achilles
The Trojans
Paris, a Trojan prince, and abductor of the beautiful Helen
Hector, Paris' brother, a powerful Trojan warrior
Priam, King of Troy and father of Paris and Hector
Krypeis and Briseis, two women
Various gods and goddesses, each alternately favoring one side or the other

Commentary:

Since the age of Classical Greece, Homer's *The Iliad* and *The Odyssey* have been revered by the West almost as sacred texts. Throughout the ages, his epics have inspired a multitude of other great works in painting, sculpture, music, dance, and other literature.

Homer himself remains a baffling figure. According to legend, he was blind and lived on the island of Chios. All that can be said with certainty about the West's most celebrated poet is that he crafted his works in the Ionian dialect of ancient Greece.

It is not difficult to see why *The Iliad* and *The Odyssey* are considered two of the greatest prototypes of world literature. They possess what the critic Harold Bloom has called an "uncanny sublimity." That is, they have about them an imaginative and spiritual grandeur that competes not only "for the consciousness of Western nations," as Bloom says, but also as that consciousness—in its most powerful and instinctual form.

Prologue:

The Iliad focuses on events late in the Trojan War, a ten-year conflict between the Greeks and the Trojans which started when Prince Paris of Troy abducted Queen Helen, an Achaean woman famous for her beauty. King Menelaos, Helen's enraged husband, amassed Achaean troops and laid siege to Troy. The story line begins during the war's tenth year of conflict.

In response to the snatching of Queen Helen, the Achaeans have just kidnapped two comely maidens, Briseis and Kryseis, from towns near Troy; Kryseis was taken by King Agamemnon and Briseis was taken by the warrior Achilles.

As the fighting proceeds, the mythological gods also become important characters in the story, and influence the outcome of events at every turn.

Story Overview:

Hundreds of Achaean warriors lay dying in "transfixing pain" from a plague brought on by the archer god Apollo in response to a plea from Kryseis' grieving father. Soon an Achaean diviner came to prophesy that the plague would not abate unless the woman was returned. When he heard this news, King Agamemnon flew into a frenzy. "You visionary of hell," he thundered at the diviner, "never have I had fair play in your forecasts." Still, Agamemnon finally agreed to return Kryseis, but only under the condition that he be given Achilles' prize, the charming Briseis. Now it was Achilles' turn to be outraged. "You thick-skinned, shameless greedy fool!" the proud warrior confronted his king. Then he swore to fight in the Achaean cause no more, and even beseeched Zeus, the supreme god, to intervene instead on behalf of the Trojans.

True to his word, when fighting broke out again Achilles remained in camp. The Trojan who first came out to battle was Prince Paris, who, as Helen's abductor, was responsible for starting the war. He sported "a cowl of leopard skin . . . a longsword at his hip [and] two spears capped in pointed bronze." When Menelaos caught sight of him, he vowed, "I'll cut him to bits, adulterous dog!" Before he could do so, however, Paris changed his mind and retreated behind Trojan lines. His brother, the famed warrior Hector, regarded him contemptuously. "Paris, the great lover, a gallant sight!" he sneered. Thus humiliated, the cowering Paris announced that he would engage Menelaos in a personal duel for Helen and that the outcome would decide the war.

Menelaos agreed to his rival's challenge. Paris came out aggressively, but Menelaos quickly gained the advantage, pouncing on the prince in such a way that he lay "choked by the chin strap" of his own helmet. At that moment, however, the goddess Aphrodite intervened. She "hid [Paris] in mist / and put him down in his own fragrant chamber."

"Beyond question, Menelaos is victorious," Agamemnon proclaimed. But the Trojans renewed the conflict, with mortal foes "going for one another like wolves . . . / whirling upon each other, man to man," until countless combatants, "prone in the dust, were strewn beside each other." The brave Achaean warrior Diomedes was struck by an arrow in the shoulder; but, although "spirits of blood . . . stained his knitted shirt," he did not collapse. "Courage, Diomedes. Press the fight," the goddess Athena urged him, and Diomedes strode furiously back into battle. After slaughtering many of his foes, he was assailed by the warrior Pandaros. "Guided by Athena," Diomedes managed to strike Pandaros' "nose beside the eye / and shatter his white teeth: his tongue / the brazen spearhead severed, tip from root, / then plowing on came out beneath his chin."

Zeus had long since forbidden the gods and goddesses to aspire to sway men's fate. Nevertheless, many of them did choose to intervene at one time or another. When the balance of power tipped in favor of the Achaeans, Hector returned from the battlefield to the city to entreat his mother, Queen Hekabe, to make a sacrificial offering to "Athena, Hope of Soldiers." Then he kissed his child and bade an emotional farewell to his wife Andromache. "Unquiet soul," he said to her,

> do not be too distressed
> by thoughts of me. You know no man dispatches me
> into the undergloom against my fate;
> no mortal, either, can escape his fate
> coward or brave man, once he comes to be.

Andromache tearfully drew away from her husband's embrace; she was certain that he would not "be delivered from Achaean fury." But Hector, a soldier before a husband, met Paris by the gateway of Troy and rejoined the battle.

Meanwhile, Achilles, who was still angry with his king, pleaded to Zeus to give success to the enemy. As a result, Zeus sent thunder and "burning flashes of lightning against the Achaean army." All of the Achaeans despaired to see this fearful omen at the hand of Zeus. "Board ship for our own fatherland!" ordered Agamemnon, with tears trickling from his eyes. "Retreat! / We cannot hope any longer to take Troy." The king's advisors were shocked by this order of withdrawal and suggested a final maneuver before giving up: that Agamemnon make peace with Achilles and make use of his services. Agamemnon consented to the gambit and dispatched an embassy to speak with Achilles. The great warrior, however, shunned the embassy and ignored their request, announcing that he still planned to "sail homeward" the following day.

That night "Agamemnon lay beyond sweet sleep, and cast about in tumult of the mind," still looking for some way to avoid defeat. He thus decided to confer with a wise old man named Nestor "and see / what plan if any could be formed with him . . ." Sure enough, the old man devised a ruse to help his king: Patroclus, Achilles' good friend, would go to battle wearing the great warrior's armor in an effort to demoralize the Trojans. Patroclus, weary of war and anxious to break his enemy's spirit, readily agreed to Nestor's scheme.

The next day, when "Achilles," the great champion, appeared on the field of battle, the Trojans were stunned and terrified. But Apollo descended to allay Trojan fears and to address the imposter: "Back, Patroclus, lordly man! Destiny will not let this fortress town / of Trojans fall to you!" Obedient to the god, Patroclus "retired, a long way off," but not beyond the range of Hector, whose spear struck Patroclus "low in the shank" and killed him. The Trojans then removed Patroclus' battle gear and began desecrating his body.

When news of Patroclus' death reached Achilles, he "tore his hair with both hands [and] gave a dreadful cry":

> I must reject this life, my heart tells me,
> reject the world of men,

> if Hector does not feel my battering spear
> tear the life out of him, making him pay
> in his own blood for the slaughter of Patroclus!

The "lame god" Hephaistos, a designer of superior armor, undertook to outfit Achilles for the task at hand, creating for the warrior a magnificently crafted set of shield and armor. Girding the armor and taking up his shield, Achilles himself appeared on the field and "all the Achaeans gave a roar of joy." By now they had managed to reclaim Patroclus' body and fierce warfare had continued unabated. Agamemnon made amends with Achilles by returning Briseis to him, and before charging into battle, the two men sacrificed a boar to Zeus. With the aid of the gods, Achilles would not taste defeat.

After killing many brave Trojans, Achilles reached the gateway of the city, where Hector awaited him. When King Priam saw his son about to engage the mighty Achilles in battle, he begged Hector to withdraw: "Cut off as you are, alone, dear son, / don't try to hold your ground against this man, / or soon you'll meet the shock of doom . . ."

Achilles advanced "like the implacable god of war." At first Hector fled from him, and three times did the three men circle the walls of Troy. Finally, Hector turned and faced his enemy: "Now my soul would have me stand and fight, / whether I kill you or am killed." Achilles, the superior combatant, aimed his spear and "drove his point straight through the tender neck" of Hector, who was dressed in the armor Achilles had given Patroclus. "I beg you by your soul and by your parents," Hector whispered to Achilles before he died, "do not let the dogs feed on me."

The Achaeans gathered around the slain prince, "and no one came who did not stab the body." Priam wept at the defilement of his son's corpse. "Why could he not have died where I might hold him?" he lamented. Unmoved by the father's grief, Achilles persisted in heaping vengeance upon his fallen foe:

> Behind both feet he pierced
> the tendons, heel to ankle. Rawhide cords
> he drew through both and lashed them to his chariot,
> letting the man's head trail. Stepping aboard,
> bearing the great trophy of the arms,
> he shook the reins, and whipped the team ahead
> into a willing run. A dustcloud rose
> above the furrowing body; the dark tresses
> flowed behind, and the head so princely once
> lay back in dust . . .

Returning to the Achaean camp, Achilles left "Hector's body / to lie full-length in dust . . ." Thus it lay for eleven nights. As the twelfth day dawned, Zeus lost patience with Achilles' mad vengeance and sent his messengers to "beg [Achilles'] mercy" in accepting "ransom for the body." Afterward, Priam visited the Greek champion, who finally took pity on the anguished old man. His rage exhausted, Achilles ordered Hector's body bathed and rubbed with oil before it was returned to Troy:

> Then in a grave dug deep they placed it
> and heaped it with great stones . . .
> / So they performed
> the funeral rites of Hector, tamer of horses.

THE ODYSSEY

by
Homer
(c. 8th century B.C.)

Type of work: Epic poem

Setting: Greek islands; c. 1240-30 B.C., 10 years after the fall of Troy

Principal characters:

Odysseus, King of Ithaca and hero of the Trojan War

Penelope, Queen of Ithaca and wife of Odysseus

Athena, goddess of war

Zeus, supreme god of Olympus

Hermes, messenger of Zeus

Calypso, a beautiful sea nymph

Polyphemus, a Cyclops and the son of Poseidon

Circe, a beautiful goddess and enchantress

Story Overview:

Ten years after the Trojan War had ended, Odysseus, one of the great Greek heroes, languished on Ogygia, island of the sea nymph Calypso. Calypso, who was in love with Odysseus, had for seven years held him captive, refusing all appeals for release.

Pitying the plight of Odysseus, the goddess Athena called an Olympian council in the hopes of persuading her father Zeus to allow Odysseus to return home to Penelope, his wife, in Ithaca. Zeus agreed, and dispatched his messenger Hermes to Ogygia, ordering Calypso to release Odysseus. Reluctantly, Calypso relented and outfitted Odysseus with provisions and a small boat. And finally the homesick Odysseus again set sail for Ithaca. Poseidon, however, was enraged that the Olympian council had met in his absence only to rule in favor of Odysseus' release, so he sent a storm that shipwrecked Odysseus on the Phaeacian coast.

Meanwhile in Ithaca, Penelope was besieged by a group of marauding suitors. Led by Antinous, the suitors had encamped in the palace, and as they ate and drank their way through Odysseus' stores of food and wine, they informed Penelope that they would not leave until she selected a new husband from among them.

Having been washed ashore naked and unconscious, Odysseus awakened to find the beguiling Princess Nausica and her maids drying the palace laundry. By this stroke of good fortune, Odysseus was not only clothed but made welcome by Queen Arete and King Alcinous, who promised to give the stranger safe passage home.

The next night at a palace banquet, the Phaeacian court poet Demodocus unwittingly sang of heroic feats achieved during the Trojan War. Deeply moved, Odysseus wept into his cloak. Seeing this, Alcinous asked his guest why the song had made him so distraught, and, for the first time, Odysseus revealed to his hosts his true identity. At Alcinous' request, then, Odysseus agreed to tell the story of his ten years of wandering.

After the Trojan War, Odysseus began his story, he and his fellow Ithacans—like all the other Greek heroes of the War—had set sail for home. They first laid anchor at Ismarus, which he and his men then sacked and plundered. With their ships loaded with Ismarian wine, they then sailed on. Before reaching their next port of call, however, they were blown off course to the land of the Lotus-eaters. There, some of his crew ate the lotus and fell under its lethargic spell, wanting nothing more than "to stay forever, browsing on that native bloom forgetful of their homeland." Forcing the crew members back to their ships, Odysseus again set sail.

They next laid anchor in the land of the Cyclops, a race of one-eyed giants who lived in isolated mountain caves. Odysseus, taking his twelve best men, decided to explore the regions inland. During the expedition, they came upon the cave of the Cyclops Polyphemus, which, they discovered, contained a large cache of cheese.

Against the wishes of his crew, Odysseus decided to await Polyphemus' return and to trade his Ismarian wine for the Cyclops' cheese. When Polyphemus finally appeared with his flock of sheep, however, it was only to seal off the cave entrance with a huge stone, whereupon he snatched up two Greek crewmen "in his hands like squirming puppies to beat their brains out, spattering the floor. Then he dismembered them and made his meal, gaping and crunching like a mountain lion—everything: innards, flesh, and marrow bones."

Odysseus, known for his cunning, soon devised an escape plan. He offered Polyphemus several casks of wine—gifts, he reminded Polyphemus—that came from *Nobody*. "Nobody," Odysseus repeated. "Mother, father, and friends, everyone calls me Nobody." After the Cyclops had passed out, drunk, Odysseus sharpened a large pole, laid its point in the fire, and assisted his men in driving the smoldering stake into the Cyclops' eye. "Nobody, Nobody's tricked me," Polyphemus cried out. "Nobody's ruined me!"

Blinded, Polyphemus swore he'd avenge himself—but after he had pastured his sheep. Then, unsealing the cave, he let his sheep pass beneath his hands one by one, so as to ensure that none of his Greek meals were escaping. Again outwitting Polyphemus, Odysseus and his crew tied themselves to the bellies of the animals and delivered themselves, undetected, out of the cave.

After returning to their ships, Odysseus called out to Polyphemus as he shepherded his sheep, taunting him and acknowledging that it was he who had blinded the giant. "Cyclops," he shouted, "if ever mortal man inquire how you were put to shame and blinded tell him Odysseus, raider of cities, took your eye: Laertes' son, whose home's on Ithaca!" In frustration, Polyphemus called on his father Poseidon to curse Odysseus: "Let him lose all companions, and return under strange sail to bitter days at home." And Poseidon heard his son's pitiful request, and thereafter Odysseus and his crew were to be plagued by one catastrophe after another, including contrary winds, the slaughter of many of his crewmen, and the wreckage of a number of his ships.

On one occasion, having sailed to Aeaea, the land of the goddess and enchantress Circe, several of the crew were given a drug by their hostess that transformed them into swine. Odysseus, after much pleading, managed to persuade Circe to release his men from the spell—while himself falling prey to her charm and beauty and deciding to remain as her lover.

A year later, prompted by the complaints of his crew, Odysseus once more made ready to sail for Ithaca. These plans were interrupted when Circe informed Odysseus that he first had to make a trip into the underworld for a consultation with the blind prophet Teresias. Thus Odysseus, following Circe's instructions, steered his ship to the edge of the world, where Hades lay in perpetual darkness, and after offering up suitable sacrifices, Teresias appeared. The prophet, reading Odysseus' future, alerted him of those suitors who, even at that time, were pursuing his dear Penelope, predicted his ultimate victory over them, and prophesied that Odysseus would die a peaceful death in old age.

When Odysseus and his crew sailed back to Aeaea, Circe warned them of the many perils presented by the return voyage, the most serious of which concerned her father, the sun god Hyperion. In passing his island, she said, Odysseus was under no circumstances to allow his crew to eat the sacred cattle of the sun. Forewarned, Odysseus departed Aeaea for good.

As Circe had predicted, they passed the Sirens, whose captivating songs had been the undoing of so many sailors; then they sailed on through the narrow straits inhabited by the monsters Scylla and Charybdis; and, finally, having lost all but one ship, they reached the island of the sun god Hyperion, where the exhausted party laid anchor.

Weak from hunger, Odysseus' crew killed and ate several of Hyperion's cattle. Although they managed to leave the island intact, Hyperion soon discovered the slaughter of his cattle. Enraged, he sent a storm that claimed every soul except Odysseus, who was washed ashore on Ogygia. There, he spent the next seven years as Calypso's captive.

At this point, Odysseus ended his story; for his efforts Alcinous and Arete rewarded him with bounteous treasure from the palace coffers. And that night, just as they had promised, the generous king and queen put him on a Phaeacian ship bound for Ithaca.

On board, Odysseus fell into a deep sleep, only to wake the next morning on a beach with his treasure beside him. Momentarily, Odysseus believed that the Phaeacians had tricked him and left him marooned on yet another foreign shore. Athena, however, appeared and convinced Odysseus that he was in fact on the island of Ithaca. She then revealed to the intrepid voyager her plan to take revenge on Penelope's obstinate suitors.

Thus it was that Odysseus, disguised in beggar's clothes, went to the farmhouse of Eumaeus, one of his old family retainers, where he was offered food and a bed.

Three days later, Odysseus, still disguised as an old beggar, paid a visit to his palace. The suitors, in the midst of a feast, mocked and derided him. Biding his time, Odysseus covertly set aside the weapons he would soon be needing and secured the rest; lastly, he instructed the women servants to lock themselves in their rooms.

Later that night, Penelope, thinking once more of ways to discourage her rapacious suitors, devised what she considered an impossible feat of strength: she would consent to marry whoever among them could string Odysseus' bow and shoot an arrow through twelve axes, she announced. Then she returned to her room. Each suitor attempted and failed even to string the bow. Finally, Odysseus asked if he could try. To the roars of laughter, Odysseus picked up the bow, applied its string, and sent an arrow whistling through the air. The arrow's flight was checked only after piercing the twelve axes.

Throwing off his disguise, Odysseus sent his next arrow into Antinous' throat, initiating a slaughter that did not cease until every suitor lay slain.

Upstairs in her room, Penelope was informed that Odysseus and the old beggar were one and the same, and that he had killed every last one of the greedy suitors. Finally, the pair were reunited:

> Now from his breast into his eyes the ache
> of longing mounted, and he wept at last,
> his dear wife, clear and faithful, in his arms,
> longed for
> as the sunwarmed earth is longed for by a
>   swimmer
> spent in rough water where his ship went down
> under Poseidon's blows, gale winds and tons of
>   sea.
> Few men can keep alive through a big surf
> to crawl, clotted with brine, on kindly beaches
> in joy, in joy, knowing the abyss behind:
> and so she too rejoiced, her gaze upon her
>   husband,
> her white arms round him pressed as though
>   forever.

As Teresias had foretold, the couple lived happily into old age.

Commentary:

"Where shall a man find sweetness to surpass his own home and his parents?" Odysseus asks in Book IX. This is the question that inaugurates the tale of Odysseus' wanderings and, in a larger sense, the quest that forms the narrative structure of *The Odyssey*. Odysseus' answer is a pained one, made all the more so because the way back to his island home is vexed by the sea god Poseidon: "In far lands," Odysseus answers, the wanderer "shall not [find the sweetness of home], though he find a house of gold." In this respect, writes the critic Harold Bloom, Odysseus the wanderer is confronted with two choices: "heroic endurance or death."

This powerful theme begins with the *Odyssey* and recurs in some of the great masterpieces of Western literature. Virgil's *The Aeneid*, for instance, borrows this theme of nostalgia—of an exile's longing for a *nostos*, or home. Similarly, in our own times, Joyce's *Ulysses* (the Latin name for Odysseus) takes up Homer's theme with the character of Leopold Bloom, the archetypal wandering Jew.

THE SHORT STORIES OF H.P. LOVECRAFT

(taken from *The Haunter of the Dark and Other Tales of Horror*, Victor Gollancz LTD, London, England, 1971)

Commentary:

In 19th-century England many writers penned wonderful tales of horror. America, however, with the notable exceptions of Edgar Allan Poe and Nathaniel Hawthorne, produced few such authors. All this changed in the 1920s. With the advent of pulp science fiction/horror magazines, America acquired a new interest in fantasy. Among the many writers of this genre, H.P. Lovecraft, who died in 1937 at the age of 47, "became a master of the macabre who had no contemporary peer in America."

Lovecraft clearly understood the power of the imagination to produce horrific visions. In contrast to contemporary writers like Stephen King, Lovecraft subtly but ominously evokes the imaginative places that make us dread the dark.

The Outsider

The castle was infinitely old and infinitely horrible, full of dark passages and having high ceilings where the eye could only find cobwebs and shadows. The damp stones were always over-shadowed by giant trees, and the rooms were so dark that candlelight barely helped. Although during my many years there I must have been cared for by someone, I cannot recall any person other than myself. I never heard a human voice and I never thought to speak aloud. *My aspect was a matter equally unthought of, for there were no mirrors in the castle.* I imagined myself akin to the figures I saw drawn and painted in books.

Finally there came a time when my longing for light grew so frantic that I could not rest. Even though the castle had one ancient tower that rose above the trees, it no longer ascended to the upper part. Soon, however, *I resolved to scale that tower, fall though I might; since it were better to glimpse the sky and perish, than to live without ever beholding day.*

I climbed the pitch-black stairs as far as possible, then raised myself perilously on whatever small footholds I could find until I reached a large dark chamber. Finding a door, I forced it open and saw the light of the moon shining through an opening.

I ran to the opening and peered out, expecting to see the tops of trees in the moonlight. What I saw instead astonished me: the monuments and stones of a cemetery. How could I be at ground level?

As I walked through the opening, I was driven by some vague memory to move along a road toward another castle. Unlike the castle I had been raised in, this castle was not in ruins. In fact, the moat was filled and the windows were lit. Guided by the light, I approached the castle and heard sounds of revelry.

I could see joyous people when I peered in a window and I wanted to join them so I stepped over the low sill. The people began to scream. In their panic, a few swooned and were dragged away by fleeing companions.

I trembled at the thought of what might be lurking near me unseen. As I moved across the room, I made my first sound, a ghastly moan, as it came into view: *I cannot even hint what it was like, for it was a compound of all that is unclean, uncanny, unwelcome, abnormal, and detestable.* As I raised my hand to ward it off, it came closer: *In one cataclysmic second of cosmic nightmarishness and hellish accident my fingers touched the rotting outstretched paw of the monster beneath the golden arch.* And in that second all the horrific memories returned. I finally recognized the abomination that stood leering at me.

Crashing out of the doorway, I ran back to the cemetery, but I could not force myself down into the dark. Instead, I remain here in hiding, even to this day. *I know always that I am an outsider; a stranger in this country among those who are still men.* I have known this since my reaching hand touched a cold and unyielding surface of polished glass.

The Color Out of Space

As a surveyor, I had been sent to help with a new reservoir under construction in a rural area of New England. The region was virtually uninhabited. And the few who did live there had a positive aversion to the place. In fact, as I worked in the five acres of grey ash that the locals called "the blasted heath," I found the place quite unsettling.

Once, however, I happened upon the cabin of old Ammi Pierce. Not only was Ammi unusually excited about the reservoir, but he also knew the story of the heath. Naturally, I listened with interest.

Apparently a meteorite had fallen one day near Nahum Gardener's trim white house. Scientists came from the university to chip samples from the meteorite, but when they dropped the pieces of glowing coals into a bucket, the pieces flared and then shrunk before their eyes—as did the meteorite itself, until, finally, there was nothing left of the mass of metal.

Although the region's fruit seemed to flourish that Fall, it in fact was bitter in taste, wholly inedible. When the grains suffered a similar fate, Nahum claimed that the meteorite had poisoned the soil. Before long, the animals became sick and died, and then Nahum's family also became sluggish and dispirited.

Nahum's son Thaddeus now swore that the trees swayed when there was no wind. Nahum's house and barn, as well as the ground they sat on, took on a glowing luminescence. Then, exactly one year after the meteorite's fall, Nahum was forced to confine his lunatic wife to an attic room. Soon afterward, as all the trees and bushes began to crumble to a grey powder, Thaddeus started to see colors dancing in the water well. He later died and turned to dust. Little Zenas, the middle son, just stared into space, while the youngest, Merwin, had taken to screaming. Finally, one day he went to the well, and never returned.

As winter approached, Nahum's wife was transformed into a colorful pile of rags disintegrating in a corner of the attic. Nearby there was the sound of *a sort of heavy dragging, and a most detestably sticky noise as of some fiendish and unclean species of suction.*

Finally Nahum called Ammi to come to the sickly, glowing house. In the kitchen he found Nahum, slowly turning to ash. "The color . . . it burns," Nahum whispered. "It lived in the well . . . it beats down your mind . . . it comes from some place whar things ain't as they is here . . . "

Ammi returned later with the medical examiner and policemen. After draining the shallow well, they found the skeletal remains of many animals and of Nahum's three sons. Finally, as the sun began to set, the well started to glow intensely until its bright colors *poured* out and filled the night sky. Then, from the top of a ridge, the flabbergasted men watched as the hideously glowing farm crackled and shot into the air before dissolving into grey ash. Still, colors danced in the well.

The residue left behind was never analyzed, however, because scientists rarely listen to rural hearsay. Ammi told me, though, that there were probably two other capsules in the meteor: one that escaped back into space and one that stayed behind in the well. Although I'll be glad when the reservoir is finished, I know I will never drink there.

The Thing On the Doorstep

Edward Derby and I had been friends for years. Because I was a painter and Edward a poet, we shared an interest in the dark side of life. Like many of his friends, I was concerned when Edward married the much younger Asenath Waite—daughter of a reputed family of witches.

On the rare occasions when I saw Edward after his marriage, he often expressed a hunch that Asenath had captured him in her shadowy, hypnotic spell. Before long, many people commented on the changes that had come over Edward: although he had never before driven, he now went for long rides in the car; he seemed to be getting younger, even as his wife rapidly aged; he alternately dabbled in the occult; and he had eerily begun to resemble Asenath, both in appearance and deportment.

Finally, I received word from a rural town marshall that he had found Edward, crazed and stumbling out of the woods. When I went to see him, Edward raved, "I'll kill that entity before I let her, him, it, take me again." After a while, I was able to calm him. Then, as I drove him home, he stunned me by saying that his wife wanted to become male, because

a *male* witch could do so much more. In fact, Asenath gradually had been taking over his body, while she had ordered his mind to reside in *her* body, which she kept locked in a room. Worst of all, she had begun to increase the time that she spent in Edward's body.

Edward actually believed that neither he nor Asenath existed any longer. Her father, he speculated, had now inhabited her body so that he could live eternally. "Tell me," Edward said quite lucidly, "what devilish exchange was perpetrated in the house of horror where that blasphemous monster had his trusting weak-willed half-human child at his mercy?"

Suddenly Edward fell silent. Then, he explained that he was again himself and that all of his recent studying of the occult had made him ramble on. Clearly, however, I knew that Edward was *not* himself.

One night, a few months later, Edward paid me a visit. Before long, he began to sob, saying, *"My brain, my brain . . . it's tugging from beyond—that she-devil—even now—I might have known—nothing can stop that force; not distance nor magic, nor death . . . "*

From that point on, Edward's health rapidly failed. After he was institutionalized, I visited him at the sanitarium twice weekly and listened to him rave. Then, in late January, the sanitarium called to inform me that Edward had recovered. I rushed over to see him, but I immediately realized that the person sitting before me, while rational, was not the Edward I had known.

Later, when my phone rang that night, I answered only to hear strange noises coming from the receiver. Then, after my doorbell rang a few hours later, I went to the door. Crouched on my porch was a slight figure, wearing Edward's clothes and emanating the rankest odor I had ever smelled.

The figure lunged forward with a piece of paper. It was a message in Edward's handwriting, explaining that Edward had killed Asenath to prevent her from inhabiting his body. Even after burying her in the basement, however, he could still feel her struggling to enter his body. In fact, earlier that day he had suddenly found himself inhabiting her dead body. After managing to free himself from the grave, he had written the note. I was the only one who knew the truth and could kill it; it wasn't Edward Derby anymore, but rather something—a demon, maybe—that might have plans to inhabit my body. The only recourse was to cremate it.

As I came to the end of this pitiful message, the horrid creature on my doorstep disintegrated into dust.

When the police investigation was launched, Asenath's crushed skull was found protruding from Edward's clothing. So you see, dear reader, I really didn't kill Edward Derby at the sanatarium. I put holes into some terrible *thing*. But please stop delaying the cremation for post mortems. *I [will not] change souls with that bullet-ridden lich in the madhouse!*

ON THE BEACH

by Nevil Shute, William Morrow & Company, New York, N.Y., 1957

Type of work: Apocalyptic novel

Setting: Australia; the late 1950s in the aftermath of nuclear war

Principal Characters:

> *Commander Dwight Towers*, heroic captain of the U.S.S. *Scorpion*
>
> *Moira Davidson*, Towers' heavy-drinking female companion
>
> *Lieutenant Peter Holmes*, Australian liaison to the *Scorpion*
>
> *Mary Holmes*, Peter Holmes's wife
>
> *John Osborne*, a civilian radiation scientist assigned to the *Scorpion*

Commentary:

Written during the 1950s at the height of the Cold War, Nevil Shute's *On the Beach* depicts the aftermath of a nuclear holocaust. As survivors in Australia await imminent death from fallout, some meet their fates with dignity and others with dread. *On the Beach* thus delves compassionately but forcefully into the human psyche, and, while many of Shute's characters ultimately fail to attain a state of grace, their anger and sorrow are nevertheless profound. Perhaps, then, Shute's purpose in portraying his characters so vividly is to paint nuclear war as a possibility so repellent as to be unthinkable.

Story Overview:

Presumably all life in the northern hemisphere had been destroyed a few years earlier by nuclear detonations and radioactive fallout. Survivors in Australia now awaited the inevitable arrival of the billowing mists of fallout that would eventually kill them.

Peter Holmes, a lieutenant in the Australian Navy, had been reassigned as a liaison officer on the *U.S.S. Scorpion,* a former American submarine that had come under Australian command after America's annihilation. Holmes' new commanding officer, Commander Dwight Towers, was a soft-spoken man who, like most displaced Americans in Australia, kept to himself. Thus, in a gesture of goodwill, Holmes invited the Commander to stay the weekend at his oceanside home south of Melbourne. At first, Dwight was disinclined to undertake even the most casual of friendships, as he was about to embark on a long and dangerous research mission up north. Finally, however, he decided to accept the invitation.

When they arrived at Holmes' house, Peter introduced Dwight to his wife Mary and to Moira Davidson, a boisterous, single young woman who drank to excess in order to escape from the war's painful effects. Dwight nevertheless soon developed a very close relationship with Moira. In truth, grief-stricken over the loss of his family in Connecticut, Dwight's pain was every bit as intense as Moira's: ... *His wife and family were very real to him, more real by far than the half-life in a far corner of the world that had been forced upon him since the war. The devastation of the Northern Hemisphere was not real to him, as it was* not real to her. He had seen nothing of the destruction of the war, as she had not; in thinking of his wife and of his home it was impossible for him to visualize them in any other circumstances than those in which he had left them. He had little imagination, and that formed a solid core for his contentment in Australia. In Dwight's eyes, then, his wife and children were still alive. "I suppose you think I'm nuts," he once remarked to Moira. "But that's the way I see it, and I can't seem to think about it any other way." Moira, of course, understood.

As it happened, Moira's cousin John Osborne had also been assigned to the *Scorpion* as a civilian radiation specialist. The Australian government intended to send the submarine to the Northern Hemisphere to measure radiation levels and to investigate the source of some recently received radio signals: transmitted from the Seattle area, the infrequent signals indicated that someone might have survived the nuclear devastation. Although John felt flattered that the Navy had recruited him for such important work, he wanted to stay in Australia for a reason that once might have seemed petty: to work on the Ferrari he had purchased from an elderly widow. For John, the race car—which ran on a methanol derivative rather than ever-scarcer petrol—diverted his thoughts from the radiation which was gradually moving southward. Moreover, a lively amateur racing club had sprung up in Melbourne, and the prospect of speeding around curves with other equally reckless drivers invigorated him. Even dying in a fiery collision was preferable to succumbing to painful radiation poisoning.

Finally, however, John, Dwight and Peter were ordered to board the submarine for its northern mission; both Mary and Moira were left with the fear that they would never again see the men they loved. In fact, before Peter left he also became quite worried, and advised his wife what to do in the event of his death if she and their baby became caught in radiation's grasp: she was to give the baby a lethal injection and then take one of the lethal red pills. "I think you're crazy," Mary shot back at him in disgust. "If you say one more word, I'll murder you!" Now it was John's turn to lash out in anger. Staring fiercely at his wife, he murmured, "This is a time when you've just got to show some guts and face up to things!" Later, Mary told him, sobbing, "Oh, Peter, I'm sorry I've been such a fool." Still, she could not really accept the fact that they were all going to die by summer's end: she would simply tend to her garden and try to savor life until her husband's return.

In contrast, Moira had come to grips with the inevitable, but longed to have more time with Dwight before their lives ended. Now, however, she sensed that she would not see him again. Keeping her feelings to herself, however, Moira, in saying goodbye, tried to ease Dwight's mind about the submarine's dangerous mission.

Moira, feeling forsaken, stayed with Mary

for a while and then went to her parent's farm, where she thought the chores would provide a distraction. Since beginning her relationship with Dwight, Moira had taken control of her life: she had curtailed her drinking and had even enrolled in a secretarial class at the local university.

Meanwhile, the farther north the submarine went the more restless became its crew. Even after staying submerged for two weeks, the men did not dare to step onto the bridge when they surfaced because of the high radiation levels.

When the submarine finally approached the American coast near Seattle, the crew hoisted the periscope to survey what remained of the small suburb of Edmonds, fifteen miles north of the city. Suddenly a sailor, an Edmonds' native named Lieutenant Swain, disappeared through a rear escape hatch and began swimming towards his home town. Stunned, the crew watched Swain emerge from the water, climb the rocks, and disappear amid a cluster of houses. Dwight, in fact, knew that he likely would react similarly if the sub had been sent to Mystic, Connecticut, where he had last seen his own family.

Later, as the submarine entered the region of Puget Sound near where the radio transmissions had originated, John Osborne was fitted into a radiation suit equipped with two hours of air and sent ashore to inspect the radio station. He found no survivors; someone had apparently left a transmitter on, and an open window pane—slapped by occasional gusts of wind—had activated the switch panel.

After this disappointing discovery, the crew set course to test radiation levels further north. Near the Alaskan shoreline they found the levels to be consistently lethal, disproving a popular theory that the fallout gradually was being filtered out of the atmosphere as it blew toward the polar ice caps. Now there was no hope for survival, either on land or at sea.

The submarine headed southward on its long journey back to Australia. After Dwight and Moira were reunited, however, their relationship quickly began to deteriorate. As Dwight continued to grieve for his dead family, Moira slowly came to realize that she would never marry and have children. For her, the end had already come.

Peter and Mary, on the other hand, coped with their impending fate by retreating into themselves—focusing only on their home, their garden, their baby, and the deep love they felt for one another. They planted seeds in the sterile earth, even though they knew they would never germinate.

Australians, in single-minded reverence, savored each day; before long the ever-advancing death-tide would overtake them. John Osborne, for one, persisted in fixing up his Ferrari—the glimmering sports car that would carry him to death in the upcoming "Grand Prix."

Now radio broadcasts reported that the southward seepage of radiation had quickened; the end of life on earth, once calculated for September, would actually come sometime around the end of August. And as predicted, one by one the cities of the Southern Hemisphere—Rio, Cape Town, Sydney—blacked out, as their remaining inhabitants perished. Now there was only Melbourne.

The lone Australian station still sending out newscasts saw a certain bitter irony in the continent's plight: the pesky rabbits that had long plagued Australia's countryside—and escaped all attempts at eradication—would outlive human beings by at least a year.

As radiation sickness beset Melbourne's remaining inhabitants, the red suicide pills began to appear, free of charge, in all the local pharmacies. In fact, when Moira's parents became gravely ill, the older couple ended their lives with the pills.

As the days passed, Dwight, who had finally come to terms with his wife and children's deaths and had taken many pleasant outings with Moira, decided to release the *Scorpion* from its moorings and sink it out beyond the end of the bay. Under skies that were already turning an unnatural color of gray, he bid Moira a tearful goodbye. And as the *Scorpion* made its way out of port, Dwight emerged from the below deck and walked out onto the bridge. Moira, standing on the gangway, looked on as if in a trance. So, this was the end. *[She] watched as the lower end of the gangway was released, as the lines were singled up . . . watched the water swirl beneath her stern as the propellers ran slow ahead and the stern swung out. . . . Only Dwight with one other was left on the bridge. [He] lifted his hand in salutation to her, and she lifted hers to him, her eyes blurred with tears, and the low hull of the vessel swung away around Point Gellibrand and vanished in the murk.*

Moira drove her car carelessly around the tip of the Point and parked in a spot overlooking a cliff, where she continued watching the submarine as it glided out of the bay and finally plunged out of view. *[She] looked at her little wrist watch; it showed one minute past ten. Her childhood religion came back to her in those last minutes; one ought to do something about that, she thought. A little alcoholically, she murmured the Lord's Prayer.* Then, closing her eyes, she took the pill in her palm, put it to her mouth, and swallowed for the last time.

John Osborne later triumphed in his Grand Prix race, but to his disappointment did not suffer the heroic death he had planned. He retired to his shop to do a final tuneup on his Ferrari. Afterwards, he donned his racing suit and goggles, and then he, too, popped a red pill into his mouth.

Waiting for death together at home, Mary and Peter Holmes had made peace with reality. When they finally became too weak to go on, they enjoyed one last cup of tea. Then Peter prepared the syringe, gave the baby her shot, and extracted two pills. "I've had a lovely time since we got married," Mary said gently, touching his arm. "I've had a grand time, too," he replied, kissing her. "Let's end on that."

STRANGER IN A STRANGE LAND

by Robert Heinlein, Putnam, New York, N.Y., 1961

Type of work: Science fiction

Setting: United States; post-20th century

Principal characters:

Valentine Michael Smith, a human earthling
    raised by Martians

Gillian "Jill" Boardman, a nurse who helps
    teach Michael

Jubal Harshaw, a learned doctor, lawyer,
    and writer who befriends Michael

Story Overview

Earth's second mission to Mars produced a surprising discovery: a human child born during the first Mars mission had survived his parents' death and the Martians had nurtured him to adulthood.

When the young man, Valentine Michael Smith, was brought back to Earth—or "Terra," as the planet was officially known—the Terran government was understandably anxious to study him, and he was promptly sequestered in a hospital. Not for long, however. Fearing that this stranger in a strange land would be an easy prey to bureaucratic exploitation, Jill Boardman, a nurse in the hospital, surreptitiously removed Michael to the home of her friend Jubal Harshaw, a respected author-journalist-doctor-lawyer, and a veteran cynic. Under the tutelage of Jill and Harshaw, the "Man from Mars" began learning about Terran society. In the process, Michael also instructed them and their assistants about Martian ways.

The central goal and fixture of Martian culture was known as "grokking." "To grok" meant to achieve complete understanding of an object or individual—in rational, emotional, as well as existential terms; to empathize so thoroughly that the observer actually became part of what he observed. Martians placed an especially high value on "Growing Closer" to their companions, and grokking was the doorway to this intimacy. One could never grok properly with his associates, however, without first calling on the "Old Ones"—the "ghosts" of Martians who had voluntarily "discorporated"; who had allowed their bodies to die while their spirits lived on without material substance.

"Sharing water"—the act of offering water to someone—was one of the chief symbolic signs of Growing Closer. In fact, if one shared water with you, he became your "water brother," a loving companion. Everyone in Harshaw's household, including Jill and Harshaw himself, quickly became a water brother to their transplanted visitor.

Along with a disarming otherworldly naivete', Michael also possessed totally *unearthly* powers. Not only did he show extraordinary intelligence, but he could read with the speed of an electronic scanner and remember even minute details with photographic precision. Then there were his "magic tricks": he could make people and objects disappear—"twisting them into neverness"—read minds, levitate, and induce telekinesis and teleportation. When his body needed rest, he could put himself into a cataleptic trance, at the same time allowing his "spirit" or "essence" to roam about and do as it wished.

In the meantime, after Michael's removal from the hospital, Jill had immediately been charged with kidnapping. Realizing that their protege could not be hidden forever, she and Harshaw attempted to contact J. Edward Douglas, Secretary General of the Federation—the planetary government of Terra—to open negotiations which they hoped would save Michael's life and grant him his freedom—and, incidentally, ensure their own immunity from prosecution.

At first they were refused contact with Douglas; instead, a State Security patrol was sent to storm Harshaw's estate. But Michael, grokking threats of "wrongness" to his new water brothers, twisted the entire patrol—guns, ships, soldiers and all—into neverness. Afterward, Harshaw was quickly granted access to Douglas. After ascertaining that Michael Smith was well and that he was not being held against his will, the Secretary agreed to meet with a hastily organized Martian Diplomatic Delegation.

As the Terran delegation's spokesman, Harshaw negotiated masterfully. In return for recognizing Michael's status as Mars' earthly ambassador and heir to a vast fortune (since he, the first human to be born on Mars, was legally entitled to a portion of the planet's resources), Douglas was appointed the young man's business manager. Regarding Michael's alleged ownership of Mars, Harshaw rejected the notion that anyone could be said to "own" a planet, particularly an inhabited one; rather, Michael would serve as an ambassador representing Martian interests. This settlement caused grumbling among those members of the Federation council who had sought to gain rich trading concessions on Mars, but at the moment, with the Secretary General's public recognition of Michael's ambassadorial status, their voices were powerless.

At this point, Michael grew curious about Terran religion, which he perceived as a special human means of Growing Closer. (What humans distinguished separately as religion, philosophy, science, and medicine to a Martian, through "grokking," were fused as one.) After reading much about human religions, he was especially interested in conversing with Earth's "Old Ones" as he had with the Old Ones on Mars.

Of course, each of Terra's various religious sects was eager to claim the Man from Mars as a convert. The most prominent of these was the Church of the New Revelation, whose adherents, known as the "Fosterites," made no bones about their calling to be the "salespeople for God." Since Michael concurred with the Fosterites' prime doctrine—that humans were created to "be Happy"—he went to meet with their leader, Supreme Bishop Digby. But upon seeing the man, Michael immediately grokked "wrongness" and twisted the Bishop into neverness.

For a long time Michael told no one of what he had done, fearing that Harshaw and the others would be angry with him. For their part, the Fosterites simply announced that Supreme Bishop Digby had been translated to heaven, a miracle which further strengthened the prestige of the sect.

Another part of Michael's education was learning about sex, which was both unknown and unnecessary for reproduction on Mars. Until he had come to earth, he had never seen a woman—Martians were not sexually distinct beings—and was totally ignorant of sex as practiced by humans. Now he saw sex, like religion, as a wonderful way to Grow Closer and obtain happiness.

After thinking the matter over, Michael came to the conclusion that intercourse between freely consenting adults ought to be encouraged, without regard to marriage. Jealousy and rivalry, he concluded, had caused humans to institute marriage as a form of "property rights" to prevent love from being cultivated between two unmarried individuals. To Michael, sex—at least sex that was liberated from the cultural baggage imposed on it—was the source of all that was good about humanity.

Reflecting on his "education" and the generally unhappy state of the human race, Michael finally founded his own "religion," which, in truth, was a facade to attract recruits who could be trained in what Michael called "the discipline." The discipline's purpose was to hone in on a select but slowly-widening group of humans, teaching them the advanced, innate skills of Martians. Its highest level was called the "Inner Nest," and those non-territorial humans found worthy of gaining this status engaged in what outsiders denigrated as spouse-swapping. The Inner Nest, of course, referred to it as "Water Sharing," a symbolic expression of closeness, brotherhood, togetherness, and unity of mind, heart, and purpose.

Michael's soon-thriving "church" directly challenged the Fosterites, who vigorously fought the "decadent" movement—even while secretly engaging in similar sexual practices themselves. As their power and membership began to erode, the hypocritical Fosterites, using their political connections, were able to focus public outrage on the teachings of the Man from Mars. Local governments soon began cracking down on Michael's organization, burning down its main temple and, finally, putting its leader in jail.

Of course, with his superhuman powers, Michael readily escaped from prison and rendezvoused with his followers at a hotel. Wondering if he had failed his disciples, Michael discussed their predicament with Harshaw. He had tried to teach love; what could be wrong with that? "Thou art God and I am God and all that groks is God and I am all that I have ever been or seen or felt or experienced," he told Harshaw. "It's not a message of cheer and hope . . . " he continued. "It's a defiance—and an unafraid, unabashed assumption of personal responsibility. But I rarely put it over . . . No matter what I said, they insisted on thinking of God as something outside themselves. Something that yearns to take every indolent moron to His breast and comfort him. The notion that the effort has to be *their own* . . . is one that they can't or won't entertain."

The seed had been planted, Harshaw countered: " . . . In a matter of some generations the stupid ones will die out and those with your discipline will inherit the earth. Don't get faint-hearted because only a handful have turned into angels overnight." With this, the Man from Mars grokked in pleasure; truly he had accomplished something of great worth.

Meanwhile, a menacing crowd, whipped into a frenzy by the local Fosterites, had gathered outside the hotel to "do in" the Martian "antichrist." Michael stepped outside to speak to them, but the mob was in no mood for listening. Some of its elements threw bricks; others fired guns. Finally, the swarm closed in with fists and clubs. Valentine Michael Smith's final words before he discorporated were unmistakable: "Thou art God."

After burning what was left of Michael's earthly body, the mob at last dispersed. Michael's followers serenely exited the hotel and returned to Harshaw's estate, from there to continue spreading the discipline. They would succeed. It was just a matter of time.

Commentary:

Written in 1961, *Stranger in a Strange Land* was especially popular with younger readers, who enjoyed it for precisely the reason their elders abhorred it: Heinlein's irreverent treatment of traditional religious and sexual values. Similarly provocative was Heinlein's interpretation of marriage as a legal fiction allowing one person to establish "property rights" over another.

The Church of the New Revelation represents a composite of many Protestant religions, while the Fosterites' proselyting tactics savagely caricature the methods used by some contemporary radio and television evangelists. In spite of Heinlein's cavalier treatment of Christianity in general, Valentine Michael Smith is a strongly Messiah-like figure. In the book's final pages, Michael, like the New Testament's Jesus, perceives that his work on Earth is complete and goes willingly to his death at the hands of a mob. And, as Jesus' disciples did, Michael's followers continue to teach and apply his discipline, looking forward to the time when, not "the stupid ones," but *they* shall inherit the earth.

Stranger in a Strange Land can disappoint today's reader, for Heinlein displays none of the technical gadgetry modern science-fiction enthusiasts have come to expect. Instead, he creates and directs his theme on the social and cultural aspects of a futuristic society similar to today's. Although Heinlein's Terrans have avoided global thermonuclear war by kindling a form of world government, in the end, petty power-seekers continue to plague the human race. All in all, Heinlein is more interested in defining and examining the constants of the human condition than in exploring what to him were the trifles of technological wizardry.

WELCOME TO THE MONKEY HOUSE

(a collection of short stories by Kurt Vonnegut, Bantam Doubleday Dell Publishing, New York, N.Y., 1950)

Commentary:

Kurt Vonnegut established himself in the 1960s as an enormously popular yet enigmatic tragi-comic writer. Indeed, his novels all are notably *avant garde*, filled with irreverent descriptions and an unorthodox, off-center, underground view of life. Vonnegut's characters are particularly interesting: while they seem to have the world at their feet, fatal flaws always prevent them from gaining true happiness.

These characters in *Welcome to the Monkey House* explore a highly unusual scientific reality, one that may—or may not—determine the future world. Nevertheless, although Vonnegut maintains a guarded optimism about the future of mankind, he is skeptical that technology can make our lives any more safe or "real" than they already are.

Harrison Bergeron

In the year 2081, all American citizens finally became equal. No one was more attractive than anyone else, no one was smarter, and no one could exhibit any form of inequity without risking immediate punitive action by agents of the United States Handicapper General's office.

George Bergeron was a case in point. Clearly he would have been distinguished by his above-average intelligence, had it not been for the device implanted in his ear that spat a loud noise into his head every 20 seconds to disrupt intelligent thoughts. In contrast, George's wife Hazel wore no such device; she was naturally stupid.

Their son Harrison, taking after his father, was not precisely like everyone else. As 14 years old and seven feet tall, Harrison had been jailed for repeatedly bypassing the handicaps prescribed for him by law.

One day while watching some ballerinas on TV, George realized that *they weren't really very good—anyway, no better than anybody else. They were burdened with sashweights and bags of birdshot, and their faces were masked, so that no one, seeing a free and graceful gesture or a pretty face, would feel like something the cat drug in.* As these thoughts passed through George's mind, a news bulletin suddenly flashed on the screen: Harrison Bergeron, said to be extremely dangerous, had just escaped from jail.

As George listened in amazement, crashes were heard backstage at the TV studio and then Harrison appeared onscreen, laden with the Handicapper General's gadgets: "a tremendous pair of earphones . . . a red rubber ball for a nose," and black caps covering his teeth in order to offset his naturally good looks. Harrison, though, systematically stripping the artificial handicaps from his body, loudly proclaimed himself "The Emperor." Then he turned to one of the ballerinas and invited her to join him as his "Empress." After she, too, had removed her mask and untied the weights from her arms and legs, Harrison directed the musicians to likewise cast off their handicaps and play for them, while he and the woman danced across the stage.

Suddenly Diana Moon Glampers, Handicapper General of the United States, burst into the studio and fired a shotgun at the pair. Then as she turned the weapon in the direction of the musicians, she ordered them to again don their handicaps or face imprisonment.

At that point the Bergeron's television set burned out. George turned to say something to his wife, but the noise in his head drowned out his thoughts. And Hazel? She knew she had been crying, but could not remember why.

Welcome to the Monkey House

Billy the Poet was on a rampage. An infamous nothinghead, Billy refused to take his government-mandated birth-control supplements, even though he faced a $10,000 fine and ten years in prison. The World Government had legislated use of the pills when Earth's human population approached 17 billion. *The pills were ethical because they didn't interfere with a person's ability to reproduce, which would have been unnatural and immoral. All the pills did was take every bit of pleasure out of sex.* The government further tried to manage population growth by encouraging citizens to submit to suicide at "Ethical Suicide" parlors, where, upon request, they could be given a lethal injection.

As it happened, Billy the Poet "specialized" in deflowering the virgins who served as hostesses at the suicide parlors, and the Hyannis Ethical Suicide parlor was rumored to be Billy's next target. The local sheriff, in fact, arrived to warn hostesses Nancy McLuhan and Mary Kraft that if Billy were to show up, he should be kicked in the groin: nothingheads—unlike those who were numb from taking their ethical birth control pills—were especially vulnerable from the waist down.

Shortly after the sheriff had left, a light suddenly went on in one of the suicide booths that Nancy attended; an elderly man had entered, requesting that his life be taken. Before she could assist him, however, she was handed an envelope with a poem inside: "We were walking through the park, A-goosing statues in the dark," it read, "If Sherman's horse can take it, so can you." Obviously, this was the work of Billy the Poet.

Enraged, Nancy nevertheless stormed into the booth to help the old man, who, she learned, did not want to die right away; instead he began to reminisce about the good old days, those times before J. Edgar Nation had formulated his ethical birth control pills. One day, the old man muttered, Mr. Nation had apparently gone to the zoo, where he saw monkeys playing with their private parts. Shocked, he vowed to develop a pill to prevent monkeys from engaging in what he considered a disgusting habit—without realizing that later the pills would be used on humans as well.

While the old man droned on, Nancy was called away to answer a phone call—from Billy the Poet. After staying on the line so that the sheriff could trace the call, she returned to the booth. What a shock she received when she discovered that the "old man" was really Billy, wearing a mask and packing a revolver. He quickly forced Nancy out the window, down a hidden manhole, and into the sewers of Hyannis. Finally, after a subterranean journey that seemed to last for hours, the pair emerged into the Kennedy Compound, a museum featuring the Kennedy family yachts. Billy then waited for several more hours, until the effect of Nancy's ethical birth control pills could wear off. Finally, he and his "gang" of psychopath women dragged Nancy, fighting and screaming all the way, into Joseph Kennedy's former yacht, where they dressed her in lingerie. Afterward, Billy raped her.

When it was all over, Billy appeared terribly depressed. "Believe me," he told Nancy, "if there'd been any other way—"

"I suppose all the other women just loved it—couldn't get enough of it," she snapped back.

"Nope," Billy spat. "They've all been like you."

"What?" Nancy howled. "What about the women in your gang? You did the same thing to them?"

"Yes," Billy replied forlornly. "They are grateful. You will be too, in time." Then he explained his philosophy: "The world can afford sex, it just can't afford reproduction. The laws today were written by people that forgave themselves and their friends for such activity but were terrified by the natural sexuality of men and women . . . But this world is much poorer in the happiness that can be felt between two people now than in those days. That is why I did to you what I did tonight."

Billy placed a bottle of pills on the counter. "I am leaving you these," he said. "If you take one a month, you will never have children. And still you'll be a nothinghead." Then he left.

Nancy picked up the bottle. Its label read: WELCOME TO THE MONKEY HOUSE.

Report on the Barnhouse Effect

Professor Arthur Barnhouse is missing—and the world is looking for him. At the time the Professor went into hiding, I estimate he was probably fifty-five times more powerful as the atomic bomb dropped on Nagasaki. Who is he? He is the man who has disarmed the world. The phenomenon he discovered he named *Dynamopsychism*, or *force of the mind*; the press labeled it the "Barnhouse effect."

In a nutshell, Professor Barnhouse found a way to make luck a measurable and controllable force, something gamblers have sought to do for centuries. While shooting craps in the Army, he threw sevens ten times in a row. After bankrupting his roommates, he borrowed some dice and practiced again—with the same results. In both instances, he noticed that the thoughts that immediately preceded the dice roll were identical.

As time went by, the Professor's powers grew stronger. He learned to align his brain cells to create physical force. When discharged in 1945, he could remove bricks from a chimney more than three miles away.

I was a graduate student at Wyandotte the first time I met the Professor. Though he was looked upon by the faculty as a harmless eccentric, he and I became friends. I was fascinated by him; what he saw in me, nobody knows.

One day he came to me to ask my help in determining his sanity. "What you must do is simple," he said, speaking softly. "Watch the inkwell on my desk. If you see nothing happen to it, say so, and I'll go quietly—relieved I might add—to the nearest sanatarium." Dutifully I watched as *a high-pitched humming seemed to come from the inkwell; then it began to vibrate alarmingly, and finally to bound about the top of the desk, making two noisy circuits. It stopped, hummed again, glowed red, then popped in splinters with a blue-green flash.*

The Professor went on to tell me how he had cracked boulders, knocked down great oaks, and demolished abandoned farm buildings, using only the power of his mind. He confided that he had written a letter to the Secretary of State, asking his advice on how to best apply his remarkable gift in the interests of peace. For months thereafter he suffered the daily ordeal of having to demonstrate his unique power to the military. Although at first he had agreed to reveal the secret to developing these remarkable mental abilities, after constant pressure from the military brass he changed his mind.

The generals, meanwhile, captivated by the far-reaching possibilities of the Professor's gift, had initiated Operation Brainstorm, designed to prove the extent to which his powers could be used to destroy enemy weapons. Retired Navy ships, some 120 of them, were sent to a remote location in the Pacific, while ten V-2 rockets were readied for simultaneous launch and fifty radio-controlled bombers were prepared for a mock attack on the Aleutian Islands. Finally, at 11:00 A.M. on a given date, the Professor was told to *concentrate* on all of the material at once, and to destroy as much of it as possible.

The operation was a resounding success; everything was utterly decimated. But even as we sat, shocked at the totality of the destruction, the Professor escaped, leaving behind a signed message:

Gentlemen, as the first superweapon with a conscience, I am removing myself from your national defense stockpile.

Since that day, the Professor has systematically annihilated the lion's share of the world's armaments. He has become a willing participant in a rather amusing "war of the tattletales," a war in which each nation's spy network devotes itself to exposing the existence and location of the weapons of other nations.

Of course, the Professor cannot live forever. Until recently I believed that war would be imminent upon his death. However, not long ago I received an encoded note from the Professor. After deciphering the message, I have decided that I will soon be vanishing from society. In short, Professor Barnhouse may die, but the Barnhouse effect will survive him.

CHILDHOOD'S END

by Arthur C. Clarke, Harcourt, Brace & World, Inc., New York, N.Y., 1953

Type of work: Prophetic science fiction

Setting: Earth, in the late 20th through the 21st Centuries

Principal characters:
> *Overlord Karellen,* Earth's alien master/supervisor
> *Richard Stormgren,* Secretary-General of the U.N., Karellen's human liaison
> *Alexander Wainwright,* leader of Earth's "Freedom League," an organization fighting against Overlord rule
> *Rashaverak,* enigmatic Overlord researcher in the area of human psychology
> *Jan Rodricks,* a restless graduate student

Story Overview:

When the Overlords came to Earth in their enormous, gleaming ships, stationing themselves above every major Terran city, humanity was at once alarmed and relieved. For while the conquest of their planet eliminated international conflict, the very soul of humanity—in part defined by that struggle—was also now diminished.

Supervisor Karellen, the apparently beneficent Overlord who administered Terran affairs through the agency of envoy Richard Stormgren, Secretary-General of the U.N., was strangely evasive about his plans for the human race. Regardless, the Overlords had ushered in a Golden Age among the Terrans: with their technologically advanced rule had come true peace, plenty and freedom for the first time in history. Individuals at last were empowered to pursue any field they chose, albeit with limitations on the exploration of space and certain forms of scientific and artistic experimentation. And with pressure for supporting the arms race tidily removed, the world's wealth nearly doubled.

Apart from the question of their ultimate plans for mankind, one other major mystery remained concerning the conquerors: their physical appearance. For whatever reason, the Overlords refused to show themselves in the presence of humans. Even Stormgren, the one earthling authorized to deal directly with Karellen, communicated with the Supervisor only through an opaque grille. Alexander Wainwright, the vocal and devoutly religious leader of the planet's Freedom League, had used this argument to stir up a measure of protest against the Overlord rule—despite the futility of resistance. "We've lost freedom to control our own lives," Wainwright warned.

Finally the Overlords issued an announcement: "In fifty years—two generations from now—we will come down from our ships and humanity will at last see us as we are."

" . . . In fifty years," scowled Wainwright, "the damage will have been done. Those who remembered our independence will be dead; humanity will have forgotten its heritage."

"Karellen is working for a united world," Stormgren countered, "and I'll do nothing to help his enemies. What his ultimate plans may be, I don't know, but I believe that they are good."

Stormgren's faith may have been justified.

Fifty years later, humanity's new Golden Age was in full swing: the Overlords' laws of "Benevolence" were in force, religious faith had become a relic of the past, and the "mad tempo that had so characterized the 20th Century" was now a distant memory. "Humanity had lost its ancient gods. Now it was old enough to have no need for new ones." And now, at last, Karellen fulfilled his promise. In the presence of worldwide media, the Overlord stepped from his ship. A great collective gasp arose from the onlookers—for before them stood the Devil himself—horned, black-scaled, barb-tailed, and standing over two meters tall. "The most terrible of all legends had come to life out of the unknown past."

But after the Terrans' first collective shudders of shock the Overlords' planetary administration continued without a hitch. Meanwhile, bathed in the golden after-glow of "a past that could never return," human civilization drifted on. "And no one worried except a few philosophers."

By this time, freed by technology from the need to congregate in cities, humans had begun to imigrate to the far reaches of the globe. It was at one of these remote sites, a house owned by jungle caretaker Rupert Boyce on the southern tip of Africa, that a group of party-goers gathered some years later to commemorate Boyce's latest wedding. Among the celebrants were George Greggson, a noted theater designer, and his attractive and vibrant fiancee Jean Morrel, a researcher into the occult. The couple were surprised to find an actual Overlord also in attendance—a scholarly young devil named Rashaverak who had come to inspect Boyce's extensive library on paranormal psychology. Also present was the bride's brother Jan Rodricks, a graduate student in astronomy.

As the finally party wound down, Boyce prevailed upon his remaining guests, including Jan, George Greggson, and Jean Morrel, to join him in a seance. Rashaverak, however, elected merely to observe. As the seance unfolded, the Ouija board revealed several baffling messages, including: "BELIEVE IN MAN NATURE IS WITH YOU."

Finally Jan was invited to ask the board a question. Stealing a single glance at the impassive bulk of Rashaverak, the young scientist called out: "Which star is the Overlord's sun?" At once the plate began to move, spelling out the galactic coordinates: NGS 549672.

At this point the seance was interrupted; Jean Morrel, who had stood transfixed throughout the proceedings, suddenly toppled over into a faint.

But Jan Rodricks did not forget that configuration. After correlating the figures from the board with the direction in which the Overlord ships had been seen to exit the Solar System, he contacted a well-known oceanographer, a Dr. Sullivan. At that moment, Sullivan was busy readying a large ocean diorama—specifically, a display of a sperm whale fighting a giant squid—for the Overlords to take back to their planet for exhibition. Now Jan presented the doctor with a startling proposition: he himself would stow away, Jonah-style, aboard the whale and visit the Overlords' home.

Several years passed. George and Jean Greggson were now living with their two young children in a colony on a remote South Pacific island. At first the colonizers of New Athens had feared that their isolated community of artists and intellectuals and would invite the wrath of Karellen. However, the Overlords appeared to take little notice of the colony.

But the Greggsons were uneasy. Their oldest child Jefferey had begun to experience vividly haunting dreams of exotic, far-off worlds. At last even the skeptical George began to suspect his son's sleeping mind might be connecting with the aura of some remote universe.

Then one night Jean awoke to the faint, incessant hissing sound. Moments later, she stood transfixed in the nursery doorway: there before her, suspended in the air, was her infant daughter Jennifer's favorite rattle, beating rhythmically above Jennifer, who lay unmoving, her eyes closed placidly over a smile of bliss.

Just a few days later, Karellen delivered his final oration to humanity. George and Jean listened in silence; they had already learned the worst—and the best—from Rashaverak: The Overlords, it was at last revealed, had come to earth, ultimately, not as masters, but as midwives. From time immemorial their race had lived in the service of a vast, disembodied directive network of power which they called the Overmind. Of its origins and purposes they knew little; only that it pervaded the universe and yet remained somehow unfinished—seeking endlessly to expand the depth of its wholeness and awareness by merging with ripening sources of consciousness and creativity. And just such a source—teetering at the evolutionary crosspoint between self-annihilation and exaltation—was Karellen's collective mass of humanity. Now mankind was at last about to be liberated from its earthly prison of animal individuality; now at last the human race would rise into cosmic consciousness—*except*, of course, for those over the age of ten. With the onset of adolescence, Terrans were unredeemable, hopelessly sealed off from breakthrough under the armor of individuality. Only the children of earth would inherit the heavens.

The Greggson children had been the first chosen. Jean, during that long-ago African seance, had connected with the Overmind. And she could only have done so, Rashaverak surmised, through the medium of a child—her then-unconceived son-to-be, Jefferey. And now the chain reaction was accelerating. Very soon, children the world over would be conveyed to the remote interior of Australia, there to join together in an endless chain, dancing in wordless rhythm for months and years, while their minds expanded and blended, until they were ready to rise to their waiting destiny.

"My work here is nearly ended," Karellen concluded in his oration—but he did not speak with the ringing tones of triumph. For in fact the Overlords had come to Earth with a dual mission: First, and obviously, to incubate humanity within the safe, nurturing climate that would ensure a productive breakthrough for the Overmind. But

they had also come just as they had come before to other worlds on the verge of breakthrough—to search for their *own* salvation. And in this search they had once again failed.

Intellectually, the Overlords were far superior to the Terrans. *"Yet,"* confessed Karellen, *"there is something in your minds that has always eluded us . . . Our minds have reached the end of their development. So, in their present form, have yours. Yet you can make the jump to the next stage, and therein lies the difference between us."*

So the Overlords, with all their superb analytical and technological powers, would return again to their homeworld as barren midwives—still lacking the essential spirit or circuitry that might have made them into priests, poets, artists and prophets that, one day, might have lifted them into the Overmind.

Decades passed away. But due to the time displacement of faster-than-light travel, the stowaway Jan Rodricks—now returning to Earth after his 80-odd-year odyssey among the Overlords—had aged only six months. He found himself back home on a doomed and deserted planet. Of his race, only the one-time children remained—silently awaiting their liberation. Now, very soon, "like a growing plant that consumes the seed which originated and nourished it," the children would swell, merge, and vanish into the Overmind, absorbing the earth itself in their cosmic journey.

"When our ships entered your skies a century and a half ago," Karellen reminded the desolate Jan, " . . . you feared and recognized us . . . . . . We became identified with your race's death . . . even while it was ten thousand years in the future!"

It was time for the Overlords to leave. Jan, however, chose to stay behind; the last of a noble race, he awaited the ultimate exaltation—and annihilation—of his kind. And it was not long in coming. The Earth trembled slightly, then shimmered as its children, in a violent, outward-spinning wind, finally burst the bonds of their own flesh, devouring the fragile chrysalis that had nurtured them.

In his last radio transmissions to the Overlords, Jan described the tumultuous escape of the Earth's atmosphere and his own ghostly weightlessness as the planetary mass whirled into a pinwheel of disintegration. The transmissions ended in a blur of static.

And looking down "from the lonely height of the stratosphere, Karellen silently saluted the men and women he had known on the vanished planet. "Remember this," he had told them in his last message. "We will always envy you."

Commentary:

In *Childhood's End,* Arthur C. Clarke celebrates humankind's spirituality, the force that drives us to transcend, to create, to connect, to prophesy in a realm beyond words. And, in fact, from his seat in the 1950s when this book was written, Clarke himself proved to be a remarkable prophet.

Perhaps this prescience stands as testimony enough to the validity of the mysterious Ouija board message: "Believe in man. Nature is with you." And the world—*our* world—may end not in a holocaust after all, but in a triumphant metamorphosis.

THE DAY OF THE TRIFFIDS

by John Wyndham (John B. Harris), Michael Joseph LTD, London, England, 1951

Type of work: Science fiction narrative

Setting: London, England; mid-1950s

Principal characters:
   William Masen, a biologist (the narrator)
   Josella Playton, a writer
   Coker, a professional speaker and intellectual

Story Overview:

"Wednesday, May 8th was the day I was scheduled to have the bandages removed from my eyes," said William Masen as he began his story ...

But when I awoke in my hospital bed to hear the distant clock strike eight, I knew that something was very wrong: by this time I should have already been washed, dressed and fed. I rang the service bell to summon a nurse. When there was no response I felt my way to the door and shouted into the hall—only to hear hundreds of babbling voices sound an unintelligible response.

I tried to collect my thoughts. I had spent the evening before listening to the nurses' raving accounts of a spectacular meteor shower. What a pity it was that I had to miss it, they kept telling me. But nothing in what they said seemed to tie in with the chaos I now sensed around me.

Finally I reached up to remove the bandages from my eyes. Squinting against the sunlight, I saw a few people wandering aimlessly on the street below. I made my way out into the hall—and almost stumbled into a doctor who was reeling blindly toward me. I helped him, ranting and shuddering in pain, to his fifth-floor office, where he grabbed for the telephone. When he found the line dead, he turned before I could stop him and flung himself from the window.

Back in the corridors, I dodged between blinded, babbling fugitives and a litter of dead bodies. In the downstairs lobby, a sightless mob groped unsuccessfully for the main doors. I immediately fled.

Let me start at the beginning. I had landed in the hospital in the first place due to a triffid sting. You see, I was a biologist involved in triffid research. Years earlier, when laboratories in Communist-ruled Russia attempted to smuggle some triffid seeds out of the country, the jet carrying the seeds had been destroyed as it flew high in the stratosphere. The seeds, dispersed by air currents all across the globe, spawned a deadly menace. At maturity, the triffids stood some seven feet tall. They grew roots, so I guess you could call them plants; but they were like no plants anyone had ever seen before—at will they could pull themselves from the ground and lurch about on three leg-like appendages. Even more alarming, the whorl topping every triffid stem "could lash out as a slender stinging weapon ten feet long, capable of discharging enough poison to kill a man," whereupon it would feed upon its victim's flesh.

Scientists immediately launched into the all but impossible task of corralling the triffids, which by now had popped up everywhere. Since they could not be easily destroyed, the captured plants were commonly "docked"—a safety precaution involving removal of the whorl stinger—or else herded behind enclosures of safety netting. However, because of the valuable oil they produced, triffids by the thousands were soon under cultivation in scores of privately owned nurseries.

On one occasion while I was examining some rather unusual triffid specimens, a stinger had reached out and struck my mask. Poison splashed right through the mesh and blinded me; in fact, only quick medical attention had saved my life.

Ironically, I seemed to be the only human creature in the city who could still see. I wandered through the streets, watching as people felt their way down the sidewalks, occasionally colliding with one another. From time to time they broke into store fronts, searching for food.

Then, suddenly I heard a scream. I turned to see a woman, her hands tied behind her back, being beaten in an alley. Since her assailant was completely blind, I easily rescued her—and was delighted to discover that she, too, could see! Like me, this young woman had missed the fateful meteor shower.

Her name was Josella Playton; she was a writer. Together we commandeered an auto and set out toward her family home. When we arrived, however, we found only decaying corpses strewn upon the floor—and several triffids silently roaming the house. With a chill I recalled the words of one of my co-workers: "I tell you," he had said some days before his death, "a triffid's in a damn sight better position to survive than a blind man."

Josella and I drove on to Clerkenwell and supplied ourselves with "the best triffid-guns and masks in the world." The next morning we hooked up with a small group of people at the university who, for various reasons, had also missed the meteor shower. Working as a unit, we broke into warehouses and scavenged supplies, loaded up a lorry, and headed out of the city. When night came, we gathered in a small lecture theater and discussed our long-term plans. Eventually it was decided that we must abandon the blinded masses and work for our own survival.

Early the next morning I woke to shouted warnings. "Fire! Fire!" Hurrying down a smoke-filled staircase, I tripped and hit my head on the landing. When I again awoke, I found myself a captive. As it turned out, another group, led by a sighted intellectual named Coker, had hatched a plan different from ours. Coker's squads were collecting sighted prisoners to serve as the "eyes" for a company of blind people, scrounging up food and other necessities for them "until help arrived." When—and from whom—the help would come, however, Coker could not say.

My assigned scavenge district was

Hampstead, a London suburb; Josella, who had also been captured, was assigned Westminster. Chained between two rough-looking blind "attendant-guards," my 53-member team went to work. At first, my sightless captors could do virtually nothing without me. Soon, however, we began working as a team, rounding up the often infirm, sightless nomads.

On day five of my servitude, we came upon another work party, whose sighted guide straightway shot and killed one of my guards. Fearing for my life, when the other guard refused to release me, I instantly beat him to the ground, rifled through his pockets for the key, unchained myself, and ran.

Returning to base, I discovered that roving triffids and bands of human marauders had decimated our group. And many of the survivors were desperately ill with plague-like symptoms. Over the next several hours, most of them died or deserted the base. I knew the end for all of us was not far distant.

By the next morning, only the dead and the dying—and I—remained. Hoping to find Josella, I headed towards Westminster. When I arrived, however, I spotted only an occasional triffid and a random blind scavenger weakly stumbling about. No Josella; even the university had been abandoned.

It was then that I again ran into Coker. Desolated, he admitted that he had been wrong—it's just that he couldn't believe that some kind of help wouldn't come.

Coker and I finally scouted out another band of sighted survivors at Tynsham, led by a Miss Durrant. She reported that my original group, having rejected her ultra-religious, "brotherly" philosophies, had all gone on to Beaminster some weeks earlier.

Trudging to Beaminster, Coker and I merged with a trio of sighted men, a remnant of one of his squads of "hopefuls," and together we searched the countryside. Isolated bands of survivors huddled together for protection, but still there was no sign of the person who was uppermost in my own heart—Josella. Coker's plan was to return to Tynsham. But suddenly I remembered that Josella had said something about going to Sussex Downs. So, while the rest of our group proceeded toward Tynsham, I, in a crush of loneliness, headed for Sussex to find Josella.

Miraculously, she was there. My arms went around her in a relief that was too vast for words. After we stopped hugging and kissing long enough to speak, we shared our hair-raising stories. When Coker's group was overwhelmed by a combination of triffids and plague, Josella had made a terrified beeline for Sussex, the home of her friends Dennis and Mary Brent, who were now with her—and expecting a baby any time.

Several weeks later, I returned to Tynsham to see Coker, only to find that both his and Durrant's group had been obliterated; apparently, the typhoid-like plague had taken its horrible toll.

By the time I returned to Sussex, Mary's baby had been born. A few months later, Josella bore our own son, David. We spent the next several years at Sussex, frequently making runs into the nearby towns and cities to forage for the essentials that couldn't be grown on the land. Our only danger now came from the ever-present triffids pushing at our fenced perimeter. Over the years we came up with some ingenious schemes to kill or trap them, but none became a viable solution: the plants seemed uncannily capable of learning from their mistakes.

Then, in our fourth year at Sussex, a man by the name of Ivan, a friend of Coker's, appeared, piloting a helicopter. Ivan reported that Coker, who had survived the plague, had abandoned Tynsham when the epidemic struck. After eventually locating my original university group, which had established itself on the Isle of Wight, Coker sent Ivan to find us and bring us to join them on the island. We decided to go in the fall, after spending one last summer at Sussex.

But as it turned out, we were never to see Coker again. Droves of soldiers, who had spotted the smoke given off by the burning logs we had used to signal the helicopter, arrived in their half-tracks the following day. Their intentions were both simple and terrible: seventeen blind superintendents were to join us at Sussex. The soldiers spoke proudly of being "the first country to get on its feet." Indeed, they offered me an administrative post if I would aid their efforts.

I pretended to warm to this sinister plan; that night we even threw a party for our guests. But then at the height of the celebration, I slipped out and filled all but one of the vehicles' fuel tanks with honey. Finally, as the soldiers slept, we made our break in the one honeyless half-track. As we smashed through the fences of our enclosed compound, the triffids suddenly became our rescuers. Through the breach they filed, heading for the soldiers—who sat wide-eyed in their stalled vehicles.

"And there my personal story joins up with the rest," William Masen ended his narrative. "You will find it in Elspeth Cary's excellent history of the colony."

Commentary:

Written in 1951 at the dawn of the Cold War era, John Wyndham's *The Day of the Triffids* painted a dark portrait of humanity's future, a future filled with bizarre adversaries and horrific diseases. The blinding meteor shower and resultant mysterious plague, Wyndham implies, might actually have been the result of malfunctioning military missiles or satellites armed with deadly bacteria colonies. And the triffids themselves were probably developed by the Soviets for use as secret weapons.

Some of Wyndham's doomsday pessimism can be attributed to the general aura of McCarthy-era paranoia that hovered the early fifties. However, his assertion that a militant five percent of the world's population keeps the other 95% living in fear is as true today as it was then. And despite the powerful developed countries' claims that their "defensive" weapons are safely stored and in competent hands, we can never really know for sure.

SOMETHING WICKED THIS WAY COMES

by Ray Bradbury, Bantam Books, New York, N.Y., 1990

Type of work: Phantasmagorical coming-of-age novel

Setting: Green Town, Illinois; 1930s

Principal characters:

Jim Nightshade, a quiet and intense 13-year-old

Will Halloway, Jim's neighbor and best friend

Charles Halloway, Will's father, a janitor

Miss Foley, a kind spinster and Jim's and Will's teacher

J.C. Cooger, a carnival owner

G.M. Dark, Cooger's business partner

Story Overview:

When a salesman appeared in Green Town, Illinois one late October day and meandered up on the Nightshade's lawn to chat with Jim Nightshade and Will Halloway, storm clouds were gathering overhead. Jim and Will, both 13, were inseparable, although their personalities were quite different. Jim was quiet and somber, while Will seemed more spirited. The salesman handed the boys a bizarre-looking lightning rod and warned them that their house would soon be struck by lightning unless they attached the rod to its roof. Then he disappeared.

After affixing the finely etched rod to the peak of Jim's house, the boys headed for the local library to see Will's father, who worked there as a janitor. Will loved his father, although his stiff sluggishness, morose countenance and middle-aged anxiety were conspicuous—as they had been for some time now, following Mrs. Halloway's death. Despite his father's dismal manner, it was he who had first inspired Will's interest in books. But today the boys had too much energy to sit and read, and so, after greeting Mr. Halloway, they raced into town.

As they raced along the sidewalk, they came upon a crumpled piece of paper: *COMING, OCTOBER TWENTY-FOURTH! . . . Cooger and Dark's . . . A thousand and one wonders! . . .* Why, the carnival would arrive that very night! But instead of feeling excited by the news, the boys were strangely unnerved, and each quietly went to his own home.

At midnight, Jim heard a faraway sound. *A calliope began to play oh so softly, grieving to itself, a million miles away.* The carnival! Jim bolted out of bed and ran to the window; he could see that Will was also gazing out his window. Then the carnival train came into view, *dream-filled cars that followed the firefly-sparked churn, chant, drowsy autumn hearthfire roar.* Brimming with excitement, the boys quickly dressed and dashed outside.

As they ran toward the train, the boys saw shadowy figures climbing out—strangely quiet, like actors in some *silent theater haunted by black-and-white ghosts . . .* Somehow it all seemed unnatural. "I don't like it," Will whispered. "Yeah," Jim replied, and they ran back home.

The next morning everything was back to normal—or so it seemed. Will and Jim gulped down their breakfasts and rushed back to the site, where festive, lemon-colored side-show tents glistened in the bright sun. Scores of people milled about, and among them was Miss Foley, the boys' jovial schoolteacher. Spying them in the crowd, she strode toward them, gushing in childlike glee, "I love carnivals." Then, surveying the crowd, she said, "I'll buy hot dogs and you eat while I look for my fool nephew." Her nephew, Robert, she explained, had come for an extended visit. " . . . I think I'll spy through that Mirror Maze and—"

Will sharply cut her off, mid-sentence. "No," he cried. "People get lost in there." But Miss Foley would not be dissuaded; she *took a step, and vanished* in the maze of mirrors. "Oh God! Help!" they heard her shriek. Will and Jim took off after her and led her back into the sunlight. Shaking, the teacher explained that she had seen the image of a young girl in a mirror who looked just as she had many years ago. The girl spoke to her, and said, "*I'm* real. You're *not!*"

Just as the boys were about to head for home, they spotted a sign near the merry-go-round: *OUT OF ORDER! KEEP OFF!* Jim, unable to suppress his curiosity, climbed up among the painted animals and mounted *a plum dusk stallion.* Suddenly a man's voice brayed out, "Ho, boy, *git!*" Then a red-haired man reached up and plucked Jim off the horse and took hold of Will, who had rushed over to rescue his friend. A second man with yellow eyes then approached the boys. "Curious?" he asked. "The name is Dark," he went on, "and my friend with the red hair there is Mr. Cooger. Of Cooger and Dark's." The boys had found the owners of the carnival. Mr. Dark, whose arm was covered with tattoos—multi-colored eels, worms, and scrolls—also worked as the circus' "Illustrated Man." Dark asked their names. When both lied, he realized they were trying to fool him and spouted, "Show's over . . . Everyone out."

The boys pretended to leave the circus grounds, but when the carnival owners turned away, they scrambled up a nearby tree. There they watched as Dark activated the control box on the merry-go-round—sending it spinning backward, not forward. Then Mr. Cooger *leaped on the back-whirling universe of animals [and] flung himself into a seat.* Mr. Cooger's face began *melting like pink wax.* With each rotation of the carousel, the man grew younger—until he emerged from his seat as a boy, who quickly jumped off the merry-go-round and ran toward town. Scrambling down from the tree, Jim and Will followed after him.

They lost sight of the man-boy—until they turned onto Miss Foley's street and happened to look in her window. There, gazing out at them, stood little Cooger. With some hesitation, they walked up to the front door and rang the bell. "Miss Foley," Will ventured. "You *okay?*" She assured the boys that she was fine; then she invited them in to meet her nephew. Robert's face, however, was not that of an innocent child but of a demon, as *the eyes of Mr. Cooger* peered menacingly back at them. Jim and Will were desperate to warn Miss Foley, but they couldn't find the words to explain that her nephew was not who she thought he was.

That night, after everyone had gone to bed, Will and Jim sneaked out of their houses to make sure Miss Foley was all right. Hiding behind some bushes, they looked on as "Robert" opened the front door and raced off toward the carnival. Will and Jim sped after him. But to their horror, just as they reached the midway, the man-boy climbed onto the now forward-spinning merry-go-round and was transformed once more—this time into a seemingly 130-year-old man with long, spidery-white hair. Terrified, the boys fled the scene and called the police. By the time the officers arrived, Dark had strapped the withered old Cooger into an electric chair, who no longer assumed the role of Mr. Cooger, but that of "Mr. Electro." There was Dark, supplying the ancient figure with jolts of electricity. The officers were delighted with the illusion, and laughed off the boys' fears.

The police took the frightened youngsters home; however, the horrors were not over. Later that night, both boys awoke to find the carnival's enormous balloon hovering over the Nightshades' roof. At the very same moment the temperature abruptly dropped. "My God!" Jim exclaimed. "Now they know where we live!"

The next morning the boys warily made their way outside. They came upon a little girl weeping near a vacant lot. Staring into the child's eyes, Jim and Will were shocked to realize that she was Miss Foley! They rushed to her house, only to find it empty. "That carnival," Will said gravely. "They . . . change you so no one ever knows you again . . . "

When the boys went back to help the little girl, she had disappeared. Terribly frightened, they hid themselves in a space under the sidewalk that was covered with an iron grate. Above them they could hear the carnival parade passing by. And just as they had feared, several carnival freaks approached the iron grate and tried to reach the boys. To their relief, Mr. Halloway—who was on his way to the library—saw what was happening and came to their rescue. The boys were trying to explain the danger they were in, when Dark materialized out of nowhere and demanded to know the boys' whereabouts. Mr. Halloway sent him on his way, then bent down and whispered, "Oh, Jim, Will, something is going on." He ordered the boys to stay hidden for the rest of the day. Then he went on to the library to find a book that would offer solutions for such a situation.

For Mr. Halloway, that day was *the longest day of all the days he could remember in his life.* Although he didn't understand precisely why the boys were at risk, he was now convinced the carnival was a source of evil. While browsing through the shelves of books, he was struck while reading one of Shakespeare's couplets: *"By the prickling of my thumbs, / Something wicked this way comes,"* it read. The words sent a shiver up Mr. Halloway's spine. With the lines still echoing in his mind, he began to research the carnival's early history.

Later that evening, Mr. Halloway told Will and Jim what he had found: Cooger's and Dark's carnival had been on the road for nearly a century, always operating during the month of October. The carnival *was* evil, and those in it survived by *living off the poison of the sins we do to each other, and the ferment of our most terrible regrets.*

Mr. Halloway's ominous explanation was interrupted when the diabolical Dark, accompanied by his sinister and powerful associate, the Dust Witch, suddenly appeared and used their magical powers to transport Will and Jim back to the carnival. Seizing his pistol, Mr. Halloway hurried to the *dead tents*, raised the gun, and shot the Dust Witch through the heart, freeing Will from her power. Then turning, Mr. Halloway and his son saw Jim, as if in a trance, stumbling toward the spinning merry-go-round. Will ran after his friend, but couldn't reach him before he climbed aboard the carousel. His father, however, managed to find the power switch and shut off the mechanism.

Jim slumped and fell to the earth as if he were dead. Mr. Halloway tried to think of a way to break the carnival's spell of evil and misery. Then an idea struck him: "Shout, Will," he cried. "Sing, but most of all laugh, you got that, laugh!" Then, following his own advice, Will's father began to whoop, sing and giggle. Immediately, the carnival's sideshow tents began *blowing away like the petals of a great black rose.* And as the evil faded into the blackness of night, carried off by the winds of joy, Jim revived and joined in their joyous dancing.

All that remained of the horrible circus was the carousel. Before starting for home, Mr. Halloway took a hammer and smashed its control box. Then Jim, Will, and his dad started running *away from the wilderness,* toward home.

Commentary:

Best known for his science fiction, Ray Bradbury departs from this genre in *Something Wicked This Way Comes.* As a coming-of-age novel, it charts the passage of two boys from childhood to young adulthood. Will's father Mr. Halloway also profoundly "comes of age," as he teaches his son about both the reality and the sadness of death. Will cannot understand his father's preoccupation with death, until he himself must look death in the face.

Mr. Halloway also teaches the boys about the once-alien concept of a concrete evil. As the boys begin to accept this new and unpleasant reality, Mr. Halloway himself learns how to avoid being overcome by his fears. "Jump around! Whoop and holler!" he commands his son, as Jim lies close to death. Halloway's strategies, of course, prove successful: the evil carnival is vanquished, and Halloway rediscovers the exuberance and adventure of his youth.

HYPERBOREA

by Clark Ashton Smith, Ballantine Books, New York, N.Y., 1971

Commentary:

Clark Ashton Smith (1893 - 1961) frequently contributed to such early science fiction and horror pulps as *Weird Tales*. His stories rival those of J.R.R. Tolkien in their depth and character development, and rank among the best of early 20th-century fiction, notwithstanding their focus on horror and the supernatural.

This related collection of short stories describes the land and inhabitants of Hyperborea, the mythical country "beyond the North" that was celebrated by ancient Greek poets and historians. The stories often are intended to provide an important "lesson" for the reader—not unlike the morals of *Aesop's Fables*. Smith's protagonists accept challenges to carry out certain tasks. While some characters are driven by noble purposes, some by greed or arrogance, and others by force, their fates commonly depend on the merits of their intentions. Such resolutions are consistent with the stories' rather biblical tone.

The Seven Geases

The intrepid Lord Ralibar Vooz, high magistrate of Commoriom, had led an expedition of twenty-odd soldiers to hunt the elusive and menacing Voormis amid the towering peaks of Mount Voormithadreth. The Voormis, according to legend, were the half-caste offspring of human women and horrible monsters who lived deep within the mountain. Among these monsters was the god Tsathoggua, who supposedly come to Earth from the planet Saturn.

On the second day of their journey Lord Vooz and his party reached the highest peak of Voormithadreth. After gazing down and detecting a peculiar wisp of smoke wafting up from among the crags, Vooz left his companions to investigate. He then climbed ridge after ridge, dodging rockfalls and balancing on steep precipices, until he finally came upon an old man chanting incantations by a fire.

The old wizard, Ezdagor, cursed Vooz for his intrusion. Claiming that Vooz had prevented his spell from being effective, Ezdagor dispensed upon the stunned stranger a *geas*—both a curse and a heroic challenge that would lead its champion onto many deadly paths, but would ultimately set him on the road to glory and honor. Vooz thus could not avoid carrying out Ezdagor's command to follow a large raven-like bird named Raphtontis into the depths of Vormithadreth and offer himself as a sacrifice to the god Tsathoggua.

After barely surviving a battle with the Voormis in their outer caverns, Vooz found the god—in the form of a crouching mass—deep within the mountain: " . . . The mass stirred a little at his approach, and put forth with infinite slothfulness a huge and toad-shaped head." Its eyes seemed to open slightly, "visible as two slits of oozing phosphor in the black, browless face," as if the god had been disturbed from sleep. Because Tsathoggua had recently feasted upon a blood sacrifice, he had no interest in another.

Instead, he sent Vooz to report to the spider-god Atlach-Nacha, who resided in the depths of Vormithadreth. Aided by directions from the sorcerer Haen-Dor, Vooz followed Raphtontis into the very heart of the mountain. After traversing the strange genetic-regulating laboratory of the serpent-people, they passed through the Cavern of the Archetypes, immortal beings who controlled the original templates from which all earthly creatures were created. And finally, after many ordeals, Vooz arrived at the loathsome gulf of Abhoth, the father and mother of all cosmic uncleanness: *Here, it seemed, was the ultimate source of all miscreation and abomination . . . for the gray mass quobbed and quivered, and swelled perpetually; and from it, in manifold fission, were spawned the anatomies that crept away on every side of the grotto . . . like bodiless legs or arms that flailed in the slime, or heads that rolled . . .*

The wrathful Abhoth, angered that this trifling mortal should dare to appear before him, imposed upon Lord Vooz one final geas: after finishing his service to Atlach-Nacha, he must find some way to escape Voormithadreth and return to the Outer World—passing back through all the realms in which he had previously sojourned.

After a day's rest, Vooz resumed his journey, with the ugly progeny of Abhoth in pursuit. At last he reached the web of the spider-god Atlach-Nacha and was quickly forced onto its precarious filaments by his stalkers. Unfortunately, the web had been weakened by the crossing of an earlier creature, and thus gave way beneath Lord Vooz, plunging him into a bottomless chasm.

The god Tsathoggua at last had secured a most noble sacrifice.

The Weird of Avoosl Wuthoqquan

Fat Avoosl Wuthoqquan was Hyperborea's most avaricious—and prosperous—moneylender. Throughout the kingdom of Commoriom Avoosl supplied money to needy citizens at very high interest.

One day, while heading home for dinner, Avoosl chanced upon a beggar who petitioned him for a minor pittance in exchange for a prophesy, known as a *weird*. Avoosl, a selfish man, refused; whereupon the beggar intoned these words: " . . . *Harken to your weird: the godless and exceeding love which you bear to all material things . . . shall lead you on a strange quest and bring you to a doom whereof the stars and the sun will alike be ignorant. The hidden opulence of earth shall allure you and ensnare you; and the earth itself shall devour you at the last.*"

Indeed, months later, Avoosl Wuthoqquan sat conducting his usual business when a stranger entered his chambers and asked to borrow money, offering as security a pair of unusually large and perfect emeralds. Such fine gems, thought the moneylender, looking at his nondescript visitor, must certainly be stolen; and when the bargaining had ended, Avoosl had negotiated to give the stranger only two hundred djals for the stones.

After the stranger departed, Avoosl took the emeralds to the room where he kept his treasures, which included many carefully arranged diamonds, rubies, and sapphires. After adding the emeralds to this impressive collection, the moneylender stood back to ogle his hoard.

Suddenly, however, the two emeralds jerked themselves brusquely into motion and rolled off the table to the doorway. Then, to Avoosl's astonishment, they rolled out of his palatial house and down the street.

Needless to say, Avoosl was determined not to lose his precious new gems. Once he recovered his wits, he sprinted after them, but they were now a good distance ahead.

The jewels led him on and on, out of the city and into the surrounding farmlands. So intent on the chase that he ignored his growing fatigue, Avoosl was finally beginning to gain on the shimmering stones when they suddenly turned from the road and plunged into the woods. Frantically, the moneylender followed. Soon, he spotted an immense subterranean cavern in which the whirling jewels had disappeared. The moneylender, panting heavily now, entered deep into the cavern as the emeralds continued to roll just out of his reach. All at once, Avoosl noticed a glowing light in front of him and stepped onto a narrow ledge overlooking an expansive inner chamber—filled with a stockpile of jewels that reached to the roof. It seemed as if all the wealth in the world had been poured into one exquisite pit!

Letting out "a single cry of ecstasy, [Avoosl] leapt forward from the ledge, sinking almost to his knees in the shifting and tinkling and billowing gems." What his own treasure would look like with *this* roomful added to it!

Suddenly, however, Avoosl observed that his enormous body was gradually sinking into the jewels—as if he were being swallowed by quicksand. Panic-stricken, he struggled to regain the ledge from which he had vaulted.

Avoosl's shrieks were met by an evil cackling voice. Then a very large, pale, beastly entity appeared on the ledge and gaped down with contempt at the fat, greedy man below. "I came in search of my emeralds!" whimpered Avoosl, still slowly sinking amid his abundance. There was no reply. "Help me!" gasped the moneylender. Finally the entity responded: " . . . *The jewels you seek were stolen from this cavern, to which they always return upon hearing my call. I had let the original thief go, partly because he was but mere skin and bones. Now I realize my good fortune in doing so, for a fat, plump money-lender has taken his place.*"

Wielding a powerful tentacle, the entity then gently lifted Avoosl Wuthoqquan from the pile of jewels and devoured him.

Ubbo-Sathla

Paul Tregardis, a student of the occult and a frequent browser at London antique shops, stumbled upon a strange crystal during his scanning of a local curio. The milky stone was nearly the size of his fist, and its secondary colors seemed alternately to shift from light to dark. After haggling with the dealer, Tregardis purchased the crystal. Now as he again studied it, a strange familiarity burned in him—as if he and the crystal had had a previous encounter. But how? According to the dealer, the stone had recently been unearthed in Greenland—and Tregardis certainly had never traveled to that cold northern island.

When he returned home, Tregardis took out an old Hyperborean manuscript, the Book of Eibon, that made reference to crystals. Leafing through, he finally found a brief passage telling of a cloudy crystal owned by one Zon Mezzamalech, a wizard from the Mhu Thulan region of Hyperborea. The wizard had used his crystal to see into the past and to pursue Ubbo-Sathla, the being said to be the ultimate source of all life on Earth. Ultimately, the wizard had disappeared, and the crystal had vanished with him.

Once again Tregardis stared into the crystal orb, and now he began to sense an odd detachment with the object. It was as though he suddenly was imbued with two separate existences—one being that still lived in his London apartment and one that resided somewhere else. Sinking deeper and deeper into the auras of the crystal, Paul Tregardis suddenly became the lost wizard Zon Mezzamalech. As he stood in this other world and stared into the same crystal, he was now on a quest for knowledge of Ubbo-Sathla and the origins of life. The clouds of the crystal revealed that Ubbo-Sathla guarded two stone tablets, inscribed with the wisdom of the ancient gods who had died before the world was made.

At this point, Tregardis became alarmed. He felt he was being swallowed up by Zon Mezzamalech's overpowering persona. Although he turned away from the spellbinding orb, he could not help but again yield to its powers. From then on, each day he gazed dreamily into the crystal, grappling to unlock its secrets—and each day "his own person and the world about him became more tenuous and confused than before."

Finally came the day when Tregardis could no longer turn away from the crystal: at last his being had been absorbed by Zon Mezzamalech. Ever after, he would be one with the great wizards in an eerie succession of events that ran backwards toward the beginning of Time, retracing all of history, experiencing the savagery of the barbaric tribes who had invaded pre-Hyperborean civilizations, and even returning to the days of the giant saurian predators and their prey. As time returned from whence it came, Tregardis, now Zon Mezzamalech, allowed the backward-running stream of Time to carry him into oblivion, where he degenerated into a diffused and muddled being who blindly pursued the archetypes of earthly life.

When he finally reached the inscribed tablets guarded by the formless mass of Ubbo-Sathla, Tregardis himself was no more than a primeval ooze, without memory of why he had sought the tablets or of how to absorb their knowledge and wisdom. Paul Tregardis, like Zon Mezzamalech in the Book of Eibon before him, had mysteriously vanished into parts unknown, bearing the crystal with him.

FLOWERS FOR ALGERNON

by Daniel Keyes, Bantam Books, New York, N.Y., 1967

Type of work: Reflective science fiction

Setting: A big city; contemporary times

Principal characters:

Charlie Gordon, a retarded man with an I.Q. of 70

Miss Alice Kinnian, Charlie's adult-school teacher

Dr. Strauss and *Professor Nemur,* researchers in brain function

Algernon, a brain-enhanced white mouse

Commentary:

Like the best of science fiction, Daniel Keyes' *Flowers for Algernon* asks, "How different might a person act if just one thing was changed about him?" In this story, Charlie finds out.

Charlie is a not-quite-happy retarded adult who agrees to participate in an experiment in brain enhancement. For a time the treatments are effective, and as his intellect expands he begins to see a more truthful view of the world around him—but also a more painful view. In spite of the pain, Charlie likes being smart, and when he begins to lose all he has gained, he is shattered.

The story's vitality stems from the fact that, through reading Charlie's diary, we identify with and care about him. Indeed, in a sense, our superior viewpoint makes Charlie's eventual deterioration more painful to us than it is to him. This amplified sensitivity for those less fortunate in our society is undoubtedly what Keyes wanted to evoke in us.

Story Overview:

progris riport 1-March 3—*Dr Strauss says I should rite down what I think and remembir and evrey thing that happins to me from now on. I told dr Strauss and perfesser Nemur I cant rite good, but he says it dont matter.* Miss Kinnian at the beekman college center for retarted adults says they might make me smarter. I hope so, but I cant rite what i remember cause I dont remember anything.

progris riport 2-March 4—They told me I dont have to rite progris riport evrey time. Burt gav me a test today. *I think I faled it and I think mabye now they won't use me.*

Martch 6—Burt showd me a paper with a bunch of lines on it. One side said start and the other side said finish. I couldnt get what he wanted me to do. Finally he took me in a labertory and showed me a white mouse. He put him in a box with lots of sides like the lines on my paper. Burt said it was *amazed.* He showed me how Algernon, the mouse ran through the amazed. Burt said Algernon was a very smart mouse because he had the operation that I wanted to have. Burt had me try to do my amazed faster than the mouse, but Algernon beat me every time. Boy is that a smart mouse. *After the operation Im goona try to*

be smart. Prof Nemur says Ill be doing something for science and Ill be famus. *I dont care so much about being famus. I just want to be smart like othr pepul so I can have lots of friends who like me.*

March 11—*The operashun dint hert. Dr. Strauss did it while I was sleeping.* The skinny nerse took off the bandages today so I could write. She told me how to spell March. She said it was not rite what they done to me, they was tampiring with things they had no rite to. If god wanted me smart he would have made me that way.

March 13—I got a new nurse today. She showed me how to spell her name. Miss Kinnian came to see me and I told her I dont feel smart yet. She told me it would be a lot of werk and I would have to learn slowly to be smart. I told her after I got smart I was going to find my mom and dad. Maybe they wouldnt send me away no more if they see how smart I am. Miss Kinnian patted my hand and said I have faith in you Charlie.

March 15—I got out of the hospital but I get tested every day on the amazes. I hope I get smart soon. My head herts from trying to remember.

Mar 17—*Mabye the experimint dint werk. Mabye I wont get smart and Ill have to go live in the Warren home. I hate the tests and I hate the amazeds and I hate Alegernon. I never new before that I was dummer than a mouse.*

Mar 21—I went back to work at the bakery. I didnt tell anyone what the surgery was for because I wasnt supposed to. Joe Carp said maybe they opened me up to put some brains in. Frank said I opened a door the hard way. *That made me laff.* Sometimes when somebody does something wrong, they say, dont pull a Charlie Gordon. I dont know what they mean.

Mar 28—Prof Nemur and Dr Strauss put a thing in my room like a TV that whispers to me all night. I dont sleep well with that talking. I heard it say remember, remember, remember. And I did remember how I met Miss Kinnian at the school the first time.

Mar 29—I beet Algernon today. Burt told me that Algernon had the same operation so he was three times smarter than an average mouse. They sent Miss Kinnian to help teach me. She looks younger. I have started to read harder books like Robinson Crusoe. She showed me how to use a dictionary and think about how words sounded.

April 3—Im remembering lots more. I remember when my Mom brought a new baby sister home from the hospital. One day Mom found me holding the baby and started screaming and yelling and everything. I wouldn't have hurt the baby.

April 8—What a dope I am! I learned about punctuation. I want to go back and fix all my writing, but Miss Kinnian said they wanted it just like I wrote it to see my progress. I feel sick inside because I can see that Frank and Joe have been laughing at me. *Now I know what they mean when they say, "to pull a Charlie Gordon." I am ashamed.*

April 21—I remembered Frank and Joe and Gimpy trying to teach me how to make rolls at the bakery, but I couldn't do it on my own. "It's no use," they said, "It doesn't stick." Well, I'm reading lots of books now and its sticking. I would like to go to college and learn more.

May 1—I invited Miss Kinnian to the movie to celebrate the raise I got after I showed Mr. Donner a way to double the productivity of the bakery. I had never realized how attractive Alice Kinnian is. I didn't quite dare put my arm around her. After, we talked about movies and reality and logic. She said, "You're coming along so fast."

May 17—I am now studying at the University library. I am learning several languages and can read a page at a glimpse. I am having troubles in establishing a relationship with Alice. Whenever I try to as much as touch her I get dizzy and very ill. I remember that as a child, whenever I became aroused, mom would beat me with a belt and tell me to never, never go near a girl.

May 20—Today Mr. Donner fired me from the bakery. He said that the other employees had all signed a protest against me working there. *It had been all right as long as they could laugh at me and appear clever at my expense, but now they were feeling inferior to a moron. I began to see that by my astonishing growth I had made them shrink and emphasized their inadequacies. I had betrayed them and they hated me for it.*

June 6—I remember many things from my childhood now, all painful. Dr. Strauss is trying to help me deal with it through therapy. He says that my emotions have not grown as fast as my intelligence. I had a quarrel with Alice. She says I have changed since I became smarter, that I have no patience for anyone. *I am just as far from Alice with an I.Q. of 185 as I was when I had an I.Q. of 70. And this time we both know it.*

June 13—We went to Chicago so that Professor Nemur and Dr. Strauss could present a paper on Algernon and me. There I got into an argument with them because I realized they hadn't read some recent papers in Indian and Japanese that invalidated their theory. I also objected to being treated as an object, either in the past as a retarded child or now as an experimental subject.

July 9—I have been living on my own without contacting the others. I have a woman friend . . . I am finishing my concerto and the technical papers for publication. One thing bothers me, though: Algernon is getting very erratic in his behavior . . .

July 12—The foundation agreed to my demands for separate research facilities. Nemur and Strauss act like I am trying to steal some of their credit. *I've learned that intelligence alone doesn't mean a damned thing. . . . Intelligence and education that hasn't been tempered by human affection isn't worth a damn. 4:30 a.m.—I think I see the flaw in the experiment. I've got to get back to the lab and test it on the computer.*

August 26—I have discovered that artificially-induced intelligence deteriorates in direct proportion to its increase. I have sent the pertinent equations and proofs to Professor Nemur. Algernon can no longer do the mazes. Soon I will be like him.

Sept 27—Nemur says that others have confirmed my results. I went to visit my mother and Norma while I still could. I found my mother largely senile, but was surprised by Norma. She was delighted to see me. As we were talking mom suddenly came at me with the butcher knife in her hand. "Get away from her! I told you what I would do if you ever looked at your sister that way!" Norma took the knife from her. I realized that I could finally forgive her for trying to protect Norma. I wept on the way to my car.

October 3—Forgetting things. Going downhill fast. Have thought of suicide to end it all before I lose it all, but keep putting it off. *I'm trying to hold onto some of the things I've learned. Please, God, don't take it all away.*

October 10—Alice was in my apartment when I returned. She said that she wanted to spend what time she could with me, now that I am on her level. I kissed her and waited for the panic, but none came. I have finally experienced what sex can be with love involved!

October 21—Alice is gone. I have lost all languages and can't read the papers I wrote. About all I do is watch TV and sleep. Worse, I have spells of irritation when I hate everyone. Before she left Alice told me that I was worse off than I was before because I had lost Charlie's smile. I don't have anything to smile about.

November 21—*I did a dumb thing today I forgot I wasnt in Miss Kinnians class at the center any more like I use to be. She lookt at me funny when I came in and started to cry and run out. If you ever reed this Miss Kinnian dont be sorry for me. Im glad I got a second chance to be smart because I lernd alot of things that I never even new were in this werld and Im grateful I saw it all even for a littel bit. Im gone to keep trying to get smart so I can have that feeling agen.*

P.S. please if you get a chanse put some flowrs on Algernons grave in the bak yard.

THE DREAMING JEWELS

by Theodore Sturgeon, Dell Publishing Co., Inc., New York, N.Y., 1950

Type of work: Science fiction classic

Setting: Middle America of the 1950s

Principal characters:

Horty Bluett, an abused child who joins a carnival

Armand Bluett, his stepfather

Havana and *Bunny*, two midgets who befriend Horty

Zena, another midget friend who captivates Horty

Kay Hallowell, Horty's friend

Pierre "the Maneater" Monetre, a doctor/scientist who runs the carnival

Commentary:

Although frustratingly cryptic at times, Theodore Sturgeon's *The Dreaming Jewels* remains a classic because of its imaginative characters and plot. The winding narrative focuses specifically on people labeled as "freaks," how they view others and how other people view them. Thus, while Sturgeon fails to elucidate fully the genesis and extent of his characters' macabre powers, his insights into human nature are compelling.

Story Overview:

"What in Heaven's name made you do a filthy thing like that?" Judge Armand Bluett thundered at his eight-year-old adopted son Horty. "And do you plan to take up bug-eating for a profession?" Horty replied, "They weren't bugs, they were ants." Horty's enraged stepfather then sent him to his room.

Alone, Horty pulled his jack-in-the-box Junky off the closet shelf. Faded and worn, Junky's only redeeming features were his eyes: *They seemed to have been cut or molded . . . from some leaded glass which gave them a strange, complex glitter . . . Time and again Horty had been certain that those eyes had a radiance of their own, though he could never quite be sure.*

Junky had been given to Horty as an infant in the foundling home, and he gave the boy his only sense of security. As Horty began talking to his old confidant, Armand suddenly stormed into the room, struck Horty hard across the face and swept Junky to the floor, stomping the old jack-in-the-box into a heap of plastic and metal. When Horty struggled to prevent Armand from destroying Junky, his stepfather grabbed Horty, threw him into the closet, and slammed the door. Horty screamed as the door crushed his hand. "No use in your yelling," the man railed. "Now I suppose I'll have to get a doctor."

As Armand tramped downstairs, Horty crept out of the closet. Looking down at his mangled, bloody hand, he saw that the door had severed three of his fingers.

With his hand wrapped in a dirty napkin and Junky's pieces in a bag, Horty left the house and went to see his friend Kay Hallowell. He was running away, he told Kay, but someday he would return. Then he proceeded out onto the street, where he leaped into the bed of a passing truck.

The truck's driver was a strange alligator-skinned man named Solum, and to Horty's surprise, all his passengers were midgets. Among them was a small cigar-smoking man named Havana and two women: Bunny, a tiny giggling woman, and Zena, an enchantingly "beautiful little work of art." Gazing at the lovely Zena, Horty immediately decided to join the traveling carnival.

The next day, Zena introduced Horty to the carnival's owner Pierre Monetre. Monetre had once been a brilliant young surgeon who was barred from his medical practice when one of his patients died under mysterious circumstances. Rehired by a laboratory, Monetre had since become a devotee of the occult, particularly fascinated by the possibilities of cell regeneration.

Happening upon a jewel one day in the woods, he had made a remarkable discovery: the crystal was alive and had the capacity, when paired with a similar crystal, to duplicate human beings and other life forms. Monetre also discovered that he could communicate with the glistening crystal in thought frequencies.

As Zena soon discovered, Horty possessed a similar ability. When he spoke to Junky, the toy's eyes responded, glowing radiantly; the power behind the eyes even regenerated Horty's three severed fingers. After witnessing this miracle, Zena insisted that Horty hide the regeneration from Monetre by wearing gloves. Horty gladly complied with her request. Dear Zena had accepted him as he was—*and his starved ego soaked it up.*

One night as he slept near Zena, he heard an angry voice inside himself, saying, "Come here, come here. Come! Come!" Shaken, he got out of bed and saw Zena coming toward him. When Horty told her what had happened, she commanded, "You get back into bed." Then she walked outside into the darkness.

Often at night, Zena also heard a voice: the same voice Monetre "the Maneater" used when he practiced his dark mind control to summon her to his side, where, over wine, he'd speak to her about the crystals and their dreams: " . . . *Their dreams live in our world—in our kind of reality. Their dreams are not thoughts and shadows, pictures and sounds like ours. They dream in flesh and sap, wood and bone and blood. And sometimes their dreams aren't finished, and so I have a cat with two legs, and a hairless squirrel . . . They're not finished . . . they all lack formic acid and niacin . . . But— they're alive.*"

The Maneater's oppressive mind control had devastated Zena; indeed, his carnival had *exacted a bitter payment for giving her a place to belong . . . "You're different",* the gawking crowds seemed to say. *"Freak!"* In fact, only Horty could comfort her. "I love you, Horty," she'd tell him. "I love you."

As the years passed, Horty felt a sense of belonging that he never had felt before. He made wonderful friends at the carnival and Monetre usually left him alone. One day, however,

Monetre insisted on examining Horty's gloved hand. Consequently, Zena announced that it would be better if Horty left the carnival. She urged him to find Kay and to think about "getting even" with the monstrous Armand.

Horty, passing himself off as a touring guitar player, made his way to a bar Armand had been known to frequent, and there found his enemy, in the act of propositioning Kay, now a lovely young woman. But the past dozen years had not been kind to her. Her parents had died, and, to pay for her brother's medical school, Kay had left college to begin work at a law firm. And though she was not easily unnerved, she had always detested the way Judge Armand Bluett leered at her while she worked. Stung by Kay's rebuffs, he had hinted that he could arrange for her boss to fire her or that he could tie up the money from her father's estate. Intimidated by these threats, Kay had agreed to meet him for a drink.

Now seeing the two seated together, Horty's heart leapt. When Armand excused himself to go to the rest room, Horty quickly walked past and slipped three hundred dollars into Kay's hand, suggesting she use it to get out of town. Upon Armand's return, Kay resisted his offer to meet at his out-of-the-way apartment, but instead made a date to meet him the following evening.

"Kay" met Armand the next night; instantly he noticed that she now possessed a new radiance and confidence. Wholly unaware that it was not Kay in front of him, but rather Horty in disguise, Armand promptly hustled his date to his hideaway. However, to his dismay, "Kay" was not feeling the least bit amorous, but only wanted to know if he had ever hurt anyone. "Why, of course not," he replied. "You must remember—my business is justice." But "Kay" abruptly challenged this answer: Was it not true that he had brutally inflicted both physical and psychological pain on someone years before? Then, to Armand's horror, Kay calmly extracted a meat cleaver and chopped off three fingers of her left hand. As Armand vomited, his "date" walked out the door.

Still shaken two days later, Armand visited Monetre in hopes that the carnival owner—now a respected expert in both "strange people" and the regeneration of tissue—could tell him something about Horty, who he had begun to link to the apartment incident. Armand piqued Monetre's curiosity almost immediately when he mentioned that Horty had owned a jack-in-the-box with two jeweled eyes. Suddenly it all became clear: Horty had hidden his regenerated fingers beneath the gloves—fingers that had been restored by the two jeweled eyes. "Zena!" Monetre the Maneater now roared. "Come here!"

Furious, Monetre stalked to Zena's trailer and beat her into submission; the story of Horty's fingers came spilling out. Then he turned his wrath on Havana, breaking his neck, and on Bunny, hypnotizing her so that she might recall where to find the jeweled eyes.

Zena, meanwhile, grabbed some money and fled to Horty's apartment. As they spoke, Bunny arrived. Still hypnotized, she revealed that Kay, instead of leaving town, had come to the carnival in search of Horty, and that Monetre and Armand, thinking she was Horty in disguise, had kidnapped her. Hearing this, Horty jumped up. "Horty, wait, wait!" Zena screamed, grabbing the jeweled eyes from the table. "Junky's eyes, the jewels—they're you Horty!" But Horty had already darted past her and out the door.

Zena told Bunny about the jewels. "They're alive," she confided, staring at Junky's eyes. "They think and they speak. They mate. They're alive." Then she added, "These two are Horty." The jewels in the eyes had once belonged to the occultist Monetre, she continued. Thinking them "lifeless," he had thrown the jewels away. A craftsman later found them and used them for the eyes of the jack-in-the-box—which in time was donated to the foundling home where Horty lived.

Over the years, the jewels had worked their magic on their new owner, little by little transforming the boy until he wasn't human. And now if the sinister Monetre gained possession of the jewels, he would be able to exercise control over Horty.

When Horty returned home, Zena finally told him about his connection to the jewels. "Why didn't you tell me all this years ago?" he sighed. "All I tried to do was to have you accept, without question, that you were a human being," she finally offered, "a part of humanity, and grow up according to that idea." Still, Horty had one more question: As a boy, why did I eat ants? Zena answered bluntly: "Your formic acid was out of adjustment."

Equipped with this new awareness of himself, Horty located Kay. Then, concentrating with all his might, Horty used the gift of his supernatural mental powers to annihilate the old Armand. When he turned his powers on to Monetre the Maneater, however, the task of elimination proved more difficult. The wily occultist managed to slink behind Horty and inject him with a sedative. Then, with Horty sinking into oblivion, the Maneater, in a meandering speech, informed him that he had killed Zena—who, he said, like Horty, was also unhuman. What's more, she had been trying to destroy Monetre with a reverse form of mind control.

Finally, when the Maneater turned his back to snatch up the prized jewels, Horty, sensing his "strength seeping back into his exhausted frame," suddenly leaped up to confront his enemy. In his fear, the Maneater managed to crush one of the jewels in his hand before Horty could seize him by the head and twist the Maneater's head several times around. *There was a sound like a pound of dry spaghetti being broken in two, and the Maneater slumped.*

Horty's glorious victory, however, was mixed with bitter grief. Zena still lay, lifeless, upon her bed. Immediately Horty rifled through Monetre's supplies for some life-giving formic acid. And as soon as he removed the cap, he heard a voice say, "That smells so good, could I have some?" There was Zena, sitting up in bed. *She was big, now; a regular human girl, the way she always wanted to be.* Overjoyed, Horty *took her in his arms and sobbed.* At that moment, he knew she would become his wife.

**Personal Notes**:

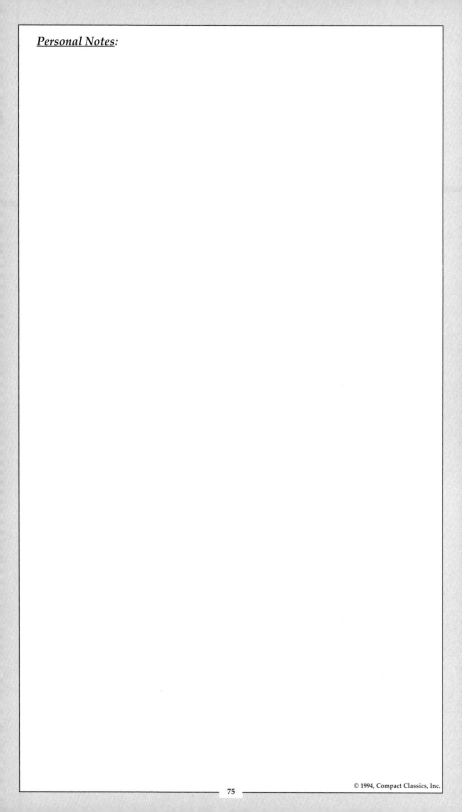

COMPACT
Classics®

LIBRARY #2: Realityscapes
confronting the waking world

Prepare for a wake-up call from dreams to daylight—and to sleet and drizzle and pea-soup midnight fogs. There are many surprises waiting for you in the Realityscapes library; and the biggest surprise of all may be the recognition that waking life is even more ambiguous and more dangerousthan the exotic world of dreams. The outside world assails us at countless levels and from all directions. And again and again we are left with the question: "What shall I do?" In fact, what would you do if you were Huckleberry Finn, drifting down the Mississippi with a runaway slave and trying to pick your way through the rights and wrongs of lawbreaking and deception in order to help a friend? How would you, as the partially crippled young Philip in Of Human Bondage, respond to the exclusionary pity of your associates? Or if, like one of Pam Houston's heroines, you found that cowboys were your weakness, could you also find the courage to face a trophy girl friend?

READER'S CHOICE TREASURY

compiled by the readers and editors of *Together* magazine, Doubleday & Company, Inc., Garden City, New York, 1964

The short stories included in this anthology first appeared in the popular "Reader's Choice" section of *Together*, a Methodist-sponsored family magazine, when its editors invited older readers to send in stories they remembered from their youth.

The Red Wagon
by Leon Ware

Janice Long loved her job working at the Sunset Valley School for children with special needs. She marveled at "their appreciation for all that was done for them [as well as] the almost complete lack on their part of any feeling of being ill-used by fate." Not all aspects of Janice's work, however, were as delightful as her interactions with the children. On the school's governing board were "some of the city's staunchest citizens," stalwarts who often disagreed with her on policy decisions. Fortunately, Janice had one ally on the board, a "housewife who usually backed [her in the] tussles with the board—most of which were about money and the 'sensible' use of it."

At today's meeting, though, Janice was certain that "there wouldn't be any squabble." A local philanthropist had given the school a check to buy a brand new station wagon for field trips. When the children heard about the check, they had "shouted and clapped and laughed in their delight"; and when Janice asked them to select a color for the station wagon, they had called out in unison: "Red!" One of the boys then wondered, "Please, Miss Long—will it have our name on it?"

"In gold," answered Janice.

But when Janice came before the board to obtain their blessing, "the OK was snagged on the objections of Mason Arnold," an auto-agency owner. It was "rather ridiculous under the circumstances," Arnold said, to insist on a red car—especially when they could save money by buying "a brand-new, last-year's model" from his dealership—a car that happened to be green. When Janice protested, Arnold shot back, "What difference does the color make?" Buying a red car, the teacher insisted, was "a matter of keeping faith with the children."

Finally, the housewife stepped into the discussion. "The color is a little thing—to us, perhaps," she explained. "But . . . I was never more sure of Miss Long's excellence in this position than I am right now: You have to keep faith with the children, Mr. Arnold." Moved by her words, the board decided that Janice should go immediately to pick up the red station wagon, bring it back to school, and beep the horn to summon the children as she drove into the parking lot.

When Janice returned, according to plan, and honked the horn, the children "came hurrying out of the school, almost before the . . . echo had subsided." As they gathered around the bright new car, "towheaded Whitney explored the lettering on the front door with his fingers. "Our name's here" he cried.

Then Miss Long invited a little girl named Peg to step forward. Grasping Peg's "soft, tiny fingers, Miss Long ran them along the slightly raised lettering and read the words aloud: "Sunset Valley School for the Blind."

The tiny girl's dark, blank eyes opened wide with delight. "And is it red, Miss Long?" she asked. Before Janice could answer, however, Whitney, his sensitive fingers still moving over the sleek front fender, answered for her: "Of course it's red, Peggy. Isn't that what we ordered?"

"Oh please," Janice whispered, catching her breath and biting her lip, *"let everyone keep faith with them always."*

The Last Leaf
by O'Henry

Among the many artists who scoured the streets for lodging in Greenwich Village's low-rent eighteenth-century attics were a pair of adventurous young women who went by the names Sue and Johnsy. At last they set up a studio together on the top floor of a squatty three-story brick building.

"That was in May. In November a cold, unseen stranger . . . called Pneumonia . . . stalked about the colony, touching one here and there with his icy fingers." And Johnsy, a native Californian unaccustomed to the harsh New York weather, was "touched" to the very bone. Gravely ill, "she lay scarcely moving, on her painted iron bedstead, looking through the small Dutch window-panes at the blank side of the next brick house."

"Sudie"—who had grown up in the cold climes of Maine—became distraught when the doctor informed her that Johnsy had only "one chance in—let us say, ten" of surviving through the winter. He was most concerned because Johnsy seemed to have lost her will to live. "If you will get her to ask one question about the new winter styles in cloak sleeves," he continued more optimistically, "I will promise you a one-in-five chance for her . . . "

As soon as the doctor left, Sue burst into tears. After composing herself, she swaggered into Johnsy's room and sat down next to the bed. Johnsy lay silent, her face turned towards the window, and Sue decided that her friend must be asleep. But soon she became aware of an intermittent murmur. "Twelve," said Johnsy faintly; then, a few minutes later, "eleven." With her eyes wide open, staring out the window, Johnsy was counting backwards.

"What is it, dear?" Sue inquired, unable to see what had caught Johnsy's attention outside the window: indeed, "there was only a bare, dreary yard to be seen, and the blank side of the brick house twenty feet away. An old, old ivy vine, gnarled and decayed at the roots, climbed half way up the brick wall."

Johnsy had counted down to five before she finally answered. "Leaves," she whispered. "On the ivy vine. When the last one falls I must go, too . . . "

"Don't be a goosey," Sue chided. "Why, the doctor told me this morning that your chances for getting well real soon—let's see . . . he said the chances were ten to one!" Johnsy, however, seemed not to hear. "I want to see the last one fall before it gets dark," she said dreamily. "I want to turn loose my hold on everything and go sailing down, down, just like one of those poor, tired leaves."

"Try to sleep," soothed Sue softly. "Don't try to move 'til I come back." Then she dashed downstairs to the studio of the girls' self-appointed protector, a fierce-tongued old emigre named Behrman who earned a sparse living as a fill-in model while drowning his own endless plans to paint "a masterpiece" in bottle after bottle of gin.

"Is dere people in de world mit der foolishness to die because leafs dey drop off from a confounded vine?" Behrman grumbled as he clambered upstairs behind Sue. But once in the apartment both Sue and Behrman fell silent. Together they stared despondently at the ivy vine outside the window, where a "cold rain was falling, mingled with snow."

Johnsy slept through the night. When she awoke the next morning, she asked Sue to draw back the green shade. "pull it up; I want to see," she whispered. Sue obeyed. *But, lo! after the beating rain and fierce gusts of wind . . . there yet stood out against the brick wall one ivy leaf. . . . Its serrated edges tinted with the yellow of dissolution and decay, it hung bravely from a branch some twenty feet from the ground.*

"It is the last one . . . " said Johnsy. "It will fall today, and I shall die at the same time."

But as the day passed into another stormy night, "the lone ivy leaf still [clung] to its stem against the wall." And when dawn again awakened the young women, the leaf was still there. Johnsy gazed at it for a long time. "I've been a bad girl, Sudie," she said finally. "Something has made that last leaf stay there to show me how wicked I was. It is a sin to want to die."

The following afternoon Sue came to Johnsy's bed, put an arm around her friend, and imparted the news she had just received from the doctor: "Mr. Behrman died of pneumonia to-day in the hospital." He had been found unconscious in his studio a day or so earlier. "His shoes and clothing were wet through and icy cold." Near his side lay "a lantern still lighted . . . a ladder . . . some scattered brushes, and a palette with green and yellow colors mixed on it."

" . . . Look out the window, dear," said Sue, "at the last ivy leaf on the wall. Didn't you wonder why it never fluttered or moved when the wind blew? Ah darling, it's Behrman's masterpiece—he painted it there the night that the last leaf fell."

Three Days to See!
by Helen Keller

[Blind and deaf, Helen Keller (1880 - 1968) lived out her life in a world devoid of both sight and sound but filled with the riches of inner vision. As a middle-aged woman in 1933, Miss Keller asked a friend what she had observed on her hour-long walk in the woods. "Nothing in particular," the friend replied. Keller was astonished. "How was it possible," she asked herself, "to walk for an hour through the woods and see nothing worthy of note? I who cannot see find hundreds of things to interest me through mere touch . . . "

Here, in her own words, are some of the magnificent woman's heartfelt reflections on the gifts of the senses and their supreme, often unawakened powers to connect us with each other and the universe.]

. . . I have imagined, selecting carefully, what I should most like to see if I were given the use of my eyes, say, for just a three-day period.

. . . On the first day, I should want to see the people whose kindness and companionship have made my life worth living. I do not know what it is to see into the heart of a friend through that "window of the soul," the eye . . . . . . I should call to me all my dear friends and look long into their faces, imprinting upon my mind the outward evidences of the beauty that is within them. I should let my eyes rest, too, on the face of a baby . . .

In the afternoon I should take a long walk in the woods and intoxicate my eyes on the beauties of the world of nature. And I should pray for the glory of a colorful sunset . . .

The next day I should arise with the dawn and see the thrilling miracle by which night is transformed into day . . . This day I should devote to a hasty glimpse of the world, past and present. I should want to see the pageant of man's progress and so I should go to the museums . . .

The evening of my second day I should spend at the theater or at the movies. How I should like to see the fascinating figure of Hamlet, or the gutsy Falstaff amid colorful Elizabethan trappings! . . .

The following morning I should again greet the dawn, anxious to discover new delights, new revelations of beauty. Today, this third day, I shall spend in the workaday world, amid the haunts of men going about the business of life . . . I stroll down [a busy street]. I throw my eyes out of focus, so that I see no particular object but only a seething kaleidoscope of color . . . [I] make a tour of the city—to the slums, to factories, to parks where children play . . . Always my eyes are open wide to all the sights of both happiness and misery . . .

At midnight permanent night would close in on me again. Naturally in those three short days I should not have seen all I wanted to see. Only when darkness had again descended upon me should I realize how much I had left unseen . . . .

THE SHORT STORIES OF H.H. MUNRO

by
Hector H. Munro
(1870 - 1916)

The short stories of Saki, the pseudonym of Hector H. Munro, comprise a series of independent vignettes, organized into sections, most of which center on a single character. To introduce Saki's works, two sets of vignettes have been summarized: "Reginald" and "The Chronicles of Clovis."

I: Reginald

Reginald

Against her better judgment, the young woman persuaded her cousin Reginald to go to the McKillops' garden party. It was not so much that she was afraid he would *say* anything; it was just that Reginald could be—well, so charmingly annoying. "There will be," he predicted, "the exhaustingly up-to-date young women who will ask me if I have seen *San Toy;* and a less progressive grade who will yearn to hear about the Diamond Jubilee—the historic event, not the horse . . . " She gave him two hours to dress before lunch; Reginald spent most of it debating about what tie to wear with which waistcoat.

Arriving at the McKillops, she parked Reginald near a dish of seductive looking desserts and drifted off to a safe distance. She heard with painful clarity the eldest Mawkby girl ask him if he had seen *San Toy.* A mere ten minutes later, Reginald wittily eviscerated old Colonel Mendoza. The Colonel was about to repeat for the umpteenth time how he had introduced golf into India—"When I was at Poona in '76—" when Reginald cooed, "My dear Colonel, fancy admitting such a thing. Such a give-away for one's age! I wouldn't admit being on this planet in '76." The Colonel turned the color of a ripe fig as Reginald calmly glided away.

Mrs. McKillop caught her. Apparently Reginald was doing the room—telling everyone about an irreverent and bawdy burlesque show he had seen. "Your cousin is discussing *Zaza* with the Archdeacon's wife," she winced. "At least *he* is discussing, *she* is ordering her carriage." But when she arrived at Reginald's side, the conversation had changed to weather and the war in South Africa. Reclining in a chair and pretending not to notice that the others were leaving, Reginald suddenly blurted out giddily, "What did the Caspian Sea?"

All at once, the room showed symptoms of a stampede. She grabbed her cousin and asked for their own carriage, vowing never to take him to a garden party again. "Never . . . you behaved abominably . . . `What did the Caspian see?'" Reginald, regretting a missed opportunity, replied, "After all, I believe an apricot tie would have gone better with the lilac waistcoat."

Reginald at the Theatre

Reginald and the Duchess regarded each other with mutual dislike and scientific interest. She thought him ethically below standard; he thought her inexperienced. Ethical conduct, said the Duchess, had certain well-defined limits. "So, for the matter of that, has the Russian Empire," Reginald answered dryly. "The trouble is that the limits are not always in the same place." The Duchess disapproved of the idea of evolution. Staring straight at the woman, Reginald replied that the process was far from complete in most of the people he knew.

Among numerous other things, the Duchess disliked Reginald's irreverence towards the Church of England, but she let that pass to skewer him instead on patriotism, Empire, Imperial responsibility, love of country, and Anglo Saxon brotherhood. "When the theatre season is over," Reginald rejoined, "and we have the time, you must explain to me the exact blood-brotherhood and all that sort of thing that exists between a French Canadian and a mild Hindoo and Yorkshireman, for instance." To her retort that, after all, England *was* "spreading the benefits of civilization all over the world" and organizing relief efforts for every case of misery and want, Reginald observed that each time one animal *feeds,* another is being *fed upon.* The Duchess gave up: "Oh, you're simply exasperating. You've lost all sense of moral proportion."

II: The Chronicles of Clovis

The Stampeding of Lady Bastable

Mrs. Sangrail virtually bribed Lady Bastable into watching Clovis while she went away to the MacGregor's by offering to cancel her outstanding bridge account in return for the favor. Clovis arrived at the breakfast table just as the deal was struck. "Just think," Mrs. Sangrail said coyly, "Lady Bastable has very kindly asked you to stay on here while I go to the MacGregor's." Clovis made suitable remarks in a very unsuitable fashion. He had hoped, after all, to teach the MacGregor boys how to play poker-patience, since they could afford to learn. Well, it was one thing to make a deal behind his back, but quite another to make him honor it.

Clovis soon found a way to foul his mother's arrangement. After breakfast, Lady Bastable retired, as usual, to her morning-room to read the paper, where she always expected to find news of the great social upheaval—the horrible "jacquerie" that she predicted would soon roll across the country to kill everyone of quality. ("It will come sooner than we think," the Lady often knowingly remarked.)

Shortly after her withdrawal, Clovis frantically burst into the kitchen, howling, "Poor Lady Bastable! In the morning-room! Oh, quick!" Moments later, a full coterie of servants, with Clovis several steps ahead, dashed into the room. "The jacquerie!" Clovis shrieked before fleeing out the French window. "They're on us!" Lady Bastable, confronted with a roomful of storming domestics—including the gardener, sickle still in hand—without hesitation followed Clovis through the window.

Alas, lost dignity is not quickly—nor inexpensively—restored. Half-way through lunch, Mrs. Sangrail was presented with an envelope on a silver plate. It contained a check for Lady Bastable's bridge account. And "the MacGregor boys learned how to play poker-patience; after all, they could afford to."

The Background

Clovis complained to his journalist friend of an art critic who talked of certain pictures as "growing on one," as though they were "a sort of fungus." At this, the journalist told him the story of Henri Deplis.

A Luxemburger and commercial traveller, Deplis had come into a small inheritance, most of which he frittered away. Once while on business in Italy, he contracted with Andreas Pincini, a renowned tattoo artist, to cover his back with a representation of the *Fall of Icarus,* in return for 600 francs. It was acclaimed by all who saw it as Pincini's greatest masterpiece, but before Deplis could settle his account, the artist died and Deplis discovered that he had but 405 francs to pay Pincini's widow. The widow, indignant, canceled the sale of Pincini's masterpiece and donated it to the city of Bergamo.

Deplis thereupon discovered that he could not publicly display his back, on which Pincini's masterpiece was etched, without permission from this city's governors, which permission was never granted. Nor was Deplis allowed to leave Italy, since the Italians had a strict law forbidding the removal of artwork from the country. After the initial excitement had died down, a German art expert came forward to testify that the *Fall of Icarus* was not a genuine Pincini, but had been executed by one of his students. Italian experts refuted this claim, and eventually all of Europe was drawn into the controversy. Deplis' testimony on the subject was felt to be invalid, since he had been under the influence of pain-deadening narcotics while the design was pricked into his skin.

Despondent, Deplis fell into the throes of anarchy. One day, during an angry debate held at the Italian Anarchists Congress, an opponent poured corrosive over Deplis' back, destroying the *Icarus*—and doing no small damage to the masterpiece's background, the blighted Deplis. When Deplis was well enough to leave the hospital, he was dropped off at the French border as an undesirable alien.

Today, the journalist concluded, Deplis can be seen on the streets of Paris. "He nurses the illusion that he is one of the lost arms of the Venus de Milo, and hopes that the French Government may be persuaded to buy him."

A Matter of Sentiment

It was the eve of the great horse race, the Derby, but no member of Lady Susan's house party had yet placed a bet. No clear favorite had emerged, no horse held a commanding position, as the sporting prophets had made no cogent predictions. Colonel Drake, a professor of military history, was the only guest with a definite choice, but he was completely useless because his choice altered every three hours. Unfortunately, Lady Susan objected entirely to racing. In fact, she disapproved of almost everything, it was said, and were it not for her great kindness and her equally great wealth, she would have been unbearable. Still, the house party found it maddening to drop such an enthralling discussion when Lady Susan approached and to suppress mention of it while in her presence.

Suddenly there was a breakthrough. Mr. Motkin, Lady Susan's butler, had a second cousin who worked in a stable at the track. Escaping the house on a ruse, he returned with a tip on the horse *Better Not*—and the next morning a packet of telegrams left the house with instructions for the bookmakers.

The afternoon telegram, however, brought bad news. Clovis reported to all assembled, including Lady Susan, that Sadowa had won the race. Lady Susan's countenance brightened at once: she had put money on Sadowa. "Why on this horse?" Mrs. Packletide asked, breaking the amazed silence. Smiling, Lady Susan explained, the Franco-German war had always interested her. "And when I saw there was a horse running in the Derby called after one of the battles in the Franco-German war, I said I *must* put some money it." Everyone groaned, but no one more deeply than the professor of military history, for Sadowa had most certainly been fought, *not* in the Franco-German War, but near the end of the Austro-Prussian conflict.

Commentary:

Hector Munro's stories, set in an upper-class English milieu during the late-nineteenth and early twentieth centuries, are invariably amusing and cleverly ironic concoctions. Even when the social context is unfamiliar to contemporary readers, Munro's wit connects and enlightens the scene, as when the hapless Mr. Deplis becomes captive to the work of art on his back, or when finicky Lady Susan, the most unlikely bettor, wagers on a horse and wins brilliantly—because of her own historical error.

Yet, beyond the wry humor, Munro savages the manners and attitudes of the Victorian upper crust. He uses Clovis and Reginald as critics, ridiculing the insularity, arrogance and snobbishness that typified the world Munro knew best. Reginald, acting the lampooning clever rogue at a stuffy party, sends out scores of pointed barbs designed to burst the Imperial English bubble. Munro, who would later die defending Britain in World War I, did indeed have some feeling for "the French Canadian and the mild Hindoo," and opposed all avowals of Anglo-Saxon superiority.

Even the unfortunate Henri Deplis is a vehicle for foresighted political commentary. That "all of Europe" became involved in the squabble over the authenticity of Deplis' tattoo pointed up for Munro's contemporaries the fragility of the European balance of power.

And finally, Munro's deftly drawn portraits of a people who take themselves too seriously, provide timeless targets of humor. Artfully intertwined with the author's political convictions, these portraits make Munro's tales so vivid, so lucid, that perhaps only Voltaire and Moliere could be said to write superior satire.

MAMA MAKES UP HER MIND

(and Other Dangers of Southern Living)
by Bailey White, Random House, New York, N.Y., 1993

One of the South's most gifted story-tellers, Bailey White mingles tall tales with poignant reminiscences in *Mama Makes Up Her Mind and Other Dangers of Southern Living*. White's spirited collection of vignettes features the antics of a decidedly cantankerous old woman: the irrepressible and willful Mama.

✧ ♦ ✧

Take, for instance, the time Mama's husband ran off with an archaeological expedition. *The leader of the expedition, a famous physical anthropologist, was a kind gentleman, and he took pity on my mother, who was to be left at home for a year and a half with a farm to run and three unruly children, and he gave her, as a parting gift, his telescope . . . The year and a half went by, and my mother studied every distant object she could find, from celestial bodies in the night sky to the pond a mile away from our house . . . My father came back, sunburned and irritable. He had presents for us: for my brother, a Persian dagger with a jeweled handle; for my mother, a lamp made out of the bladders of two camels . . . My brother developed amazing skills with the dagger and terrorized the neighborhood with feats of knife throwing, and my mother, on a creative whim, turned the camel-bladder lamp upside down and hung it by an electrical cord over the dining room table. . . . Soon my father went off on another adventure, but this time he never came back. The camel bladder chandelier could not seem to adjust to the climate of south Georgia: in the summer it would droop and swag and stretch in the damp heat until it almost touched the tabletop, and in the winter it would shrink and suck itself into a tight snarl up near the ceiling.*

✧ ♦ ✧

As the years slowly passed, Mama aged and she couldn't get around much anymore. It was then that she rediscovered the telescope. "Bring me my spyglass!" she'd bellow and as soon as someone obeyed, she'd perch by the window and gaze through the lens. Ultimately, however, one of Professor Meade's family members reclaimed the telescope, but, surprisingly, *Mama didn't seem to miss it. As a premium in the thirty-dollar pledge category for the local public radio station she got a pair of tiny plastic binoculars. Looking through those binoculars was the equivalent of taking three steps closer to your subject . . . Now, with the binoculars, she . . . could recognize family members when they came to call a moment before they opened the screen door, stepped inside, and said to her, "Put those damned binoculars down, Lila!"*

One summer we made a family trek to a wild island off the coast of north Florida . . . Every morning a boat from the local marine lab would pull up and anchor just off shore. People would wade around in the marsh grass with nets and spades and bottles. By the end of the first week the screen was bulged out from the pressure of Mama's binoculars. She didn't seem to understand that they did not give her the same dignity of distance she had achieved with the telescope. "They can see you, Mama," we hissed. But she just pressed the binoculars harder against the screen.

Then one evening a man came up to the house. We recognized him from the morning marine lab group . . . "Where is that old woman with the little tiny binoculars?" he asked. Someone went and got her from in the house . . . "Would you like to see what we're doing down there?" he said, and very carefully he helped her over the sand to the marsh . . . The last we saw of Mama that summer, she was heading for the open ocean. We stood on the dock and waved good-bye. But she didn't see us. She was leaning forward in the bow of the boat with her little plastic binoculars pressed to her eyes, peering out to sea.

✧ ♦ ✧

Apparently, Mama came by her willfulness naturally, as one "tough-looking Scandinavian woman" learned the hard way when she purchased Mama's ancestral home. *No one told her until the last papers had been signed that the house was haunted. The ghosts are not the ordinary kind—no doors creaking in the night or dogs watching the progress of nothing steadily mounting the circular staircase. These were eating ghosts. On nights near the solstices, people in the house would be awakened by the sounds of slurping, smacking, crunching, and the clink of cutlery. In the morning, something would be missing from the kitchen—a box of shortbread, a ham bone, a jar of artichoke pickles. And in my great-grandmother's garden there would be wide, winding, silvery trails in the dew, something like the tracks of giant slugs.*

✧ ♦ ✧

Unfortunately for Mama's dinner guests, eating ghosts were the least of the perils visitors might encounter: Mama' cuisine was more frightening still. *My mother eats things she finds dead on the road. Her standards are high. She claims she won't eat anything that's not a fresh kill. But I don't trust her. I require documentation. I won't eat it unless she can tell me the model and tag number of the car that struck it.*

Mama is an adventurous and excellent cook, and we have feasted not only on doves, turkeys, and quail, but robins, squirrels, and, only once, a possum. I draw the line at snakes. "But it was still wiggling when I got there," she argues. "Let's try it just this once." . . . And she won't even slow down for armadillos, although they are the most common dead animal on the road these days. "They look too stupid to eat," she says.

If guests survived dinner and were invited to spend the night, an even greater danger awaited them: the guest room bed. *An old aunt of mine temporarily took leave of her senses in 1890-something and went out and bought it. Her sanity returned soon afterward, but by then it was too late. Forty-five strong men had delivered the bed and had set it up in the guest room. . . . And it is not only a bed: by means of a series of hair triggers and precisely balanced weights and counterweights it can be made to swing up and fold itself into its headboard to reveal on the underside, now nearly vertical, an enormous beveled mirror . . . However, as you might imagine, in neither position is the thing satisfactory as a piece of furniture. In the mirror position the top leans out slightly, as if it were yearning to unfold itself and become a bed again, so that your image appears as a monster with a huge watermelon-sized head and dwindles down to a pair of tiny, remote feet almost hidden in the shadows. And as a bed it seems always to be on the verge of becoming a mirror, with the weights and counterweights groaning and the two iron legs at the foot lifting themselves ever so slightly off the floor . . . But the worst part is the tendency the bed has in the dead of night when all is quiet in the house, to transmogrify itself into a mirror . . . The poor guest wakes out of a strange dream to find the covers bunched on his chest, all his blood settling at his head, and his bare, drained, ice-cold feet pointing to the ceiling. It's hard to recover from this position in the dark of night in a strange house, and usually the guest falls into a trancelike swoon that lasts until morning, when Mama discovers his predicament, snatches the foot of the bed down again, briskly clicks the latch into position, and says, "We should have warned you about the bed."*

❖ ◆ ❖

Mama's sister Belle was every bit as fearless and headstrong as Mama was. *I remember as a little child watching my Aunt Belle's wide rump disappear into the cattails and marsh grass at the edge of a pond as she crawled on her hands and knees to meet a giant alligator face to face. She was taming him, she said. We children would wait . . . with our eyes and mouths wide open, hoping that the alligator wouldn't eat her up, but not wanting to miss it if he did.*

Finally Aunt Belle would get as close to him as she wanted, and they would stare at each other for some minutes. Then my aunt would jump up, wave her arms in the air, and shout, "Whoo!" With a tremendous leap and flop, the alligator would throw himself into the water . . . and my aunt would come up the bank drenched and exultant. "I have to show him who's boss," she would tell us.

Whenever Mama and her sister got together wacky adventures were sure to ensue. What happened during a vacation in North Carolina is a case in point. *Last summer it had been fossil hunting in Virginia. This year*

we were ferrying our way through North Carolina. Aunt Belle had a taste for the peculiar and the exotic. WORLD'S SMALLEST HORSES. SEE A LIVE PERFORMING BEAR. GHOST OF BLACKBEARD HAUNTS OUTER BANKS . . . [And during one of these wild adventures] Aunt Belle learned about the Devil's Hoofprints. People had been trying to fill the holes since 1813, when they first appeared, but they always came back, each one six inches deep and the size of a dinner plate . . . "Chickens will not eat out of those hoofprints," she mused. "Imagine that!"

[So, after procuring a live chicken], my aunt sprinkled a handful of chicken feed in each depression and then instructed," Now put that chicken down." She stood back to observe, and I set the old hen on the ground and stepped aside. The hen squatted there for a minute, then she puffed herself up with a little growl, gave us each a beady-eyed glare, and stalked off into the woods. Pretty soon she was out of sight. We stood there for a moment. Then my aunt said optimistically, "Well, she didn't eat out of them."

❖ ◆ ❖

Like her sister, Mama had her share of encounters with the supernatural. Her experiences must have been real: old woman though she was, she didn't tell lies and she didn't see visions. *That's why we didn't doubt her for a minute when she told us she had seen a flying saucer go over the house early one spring morning.*

She was lying in her bed on the screen porch when she saw it coming down. She unlatched the door and went out into the yard for a better look. It was round, flat, silent, and surrounded by yellow flames. It hovered over the garden for minute. Then, without a sound, it was gone. Our dog, who is not the excitable type, barked wildly and ran around and around.

. . . Since that day, Mama has read everything she can get her hands on dealing with UFOs and extraterrestrial life. I, not being as thorough a scholar as she, just skim the best parts: the pointy-headed creatures that creep and creep through your house at night and stare at you with their almond eyes as you sleep, and the dreaded "men in black" who cleverly insinuate themselves into your company . . .

Aliens, however, don't daunt Mama. And reptiles faze even less. *Once when I returned from a vacation in New England, she told me that "a big white oak snake" had taken up residence in my bedroom. "I started to put him out," she conceded, "but he gave me that look." So she'd left him there as a permanent guest!* Now *I don't have an unnatural fear of snakes, as some people do, but I'm not sure I like the idea of a having one living in the same room with me. "What if he crawls up the bedpost in the dark of night and creeps between the sheets with me?" I ask Mama.*

"These hot summer nights," she says reassuringly, "you'll just be grateful for the coolness of him."

CHICKEN SOUP FOR THE SOUL

101 Stories to open the Heart and Rekindle the Spirit
written and compiled by Jack Canfield and Mark Victor Hansen, Health Communications, Inc.,
Deerfield Beach, Florida, 1993

Like the fare that soothes your stomach when we're sick, Jack Canfield and Mark Hansen's chicken soup comforts and lifts the soul. After many years of "assisting individuals and organizations to live in alignment with their highest purpose and aspirations," Canfield and Hansen compiled the energizing stories, poems and vignettes for their bestselling *Chicken Soup for the Soul* from various talented authors and anonymous sources.

⋄ ♦ ⋄

ON LOVE

Harnessing the power of love is one of life's great assignments.

The Gift

In one seat [of the bus] a wispy old man sat holding a bunch of fresh flowers. Across the aisle was a young girl whose eyes came back again and again to the man's flowers. The time came for the old man to get off. Impulsively he thrust the flowers into the girl's lap. "I can see you love the flowers," he explained, "and I think my wife would like for you to have them. I'll tell her I gave them to you." The girl accepted the flowers, then watched the old man get off the bus and walk through the gate of a small cemetery.

- Bennet Cerf

The Smile

Smile at each other, smile at your wife, smile at your husband, smile at your children, smile at each other—it doesn't matter who it is—and that will help you to grow up in greater love for each other.

- Mother Teresa

After fighting in the Spanish Civil War, the author of *The Little Prince*, Saint-Exupery, wrote "The Smile." The story's main character Exupery, awaited execution by the enemy and asked one of his jailers to light his cigarette. Exupery continues: *As [the jailer] came close and lit the match, his eyes inadvertently locked with mine. At that moment, I smiled . . . In that instant, it was as though a spark jumped across the gap between our two hearts, our two human souls. I know he didn't want to, but my smile leaped through the bars and generated a smile on his lips, too. He lit my cigarette but stayed near, looking at me directly in the eyes and continuing to smile.*

I kept smiling at him, now aware of him as a person and not just a jailer . . . "Do you have kids?" he asked.

"Yes, here, here." I took out my wallet and nervously fumbled for the pictures . . . My eyes filled with tears . . . Tears came to his eyes, too.

Suddenly, without another word, he unlocked my cell and silently led me out. Out of the jail, quietly and by back routes, out of the town. There, at the edge of town, he released me.

My life was saved by a smile.

- Hanoch McCarty

Everybody can be great . . . because anybody can serve. You don't have to have a college degree to serve. You don't have to make your subject and verb agree to serve.

You only need a heart full of grace. A soul generated by love.

- Martin Luther King, Jr.

⋄ ♦ ⋄

ON PARENTING

When we attend to the needs of children, especially our own, we encounter love-reserves we didn't know we had.

What you are is as important as what you do;
Who you are speaks so loudly I can't hear what you're saying.

- Ralph Waldo Emerson

. . . *My friend and proud father Bobby Lewis was taking his two little boys to play miniature golf. He walked up to the fellow at the ticket counter and said, "How much is it to get in?"*

The young man replied, "$3.00 for you and $3.00 for any kid who is older than six. We let them in free if they are six or younger. How old are they?"

Bobby replied, "The lawyer's three and the doctor is seven, so I guess I owe you $6.00."

The man at the ticket counter said, " . . . You could have told me that the older one was six; I wouldn't have known the difference." Bobby replied, "Yes, that may be true, but the kids would have known the difference."

- Patricia Fripp

On Parenting

Your children are not your children.
They are the sons and daughters of Life's longing for itself . . .
You may give them your love but not your thoughts,
For they have their own thoughts . . .
You are the bows from which your children as living arrows are sent forth.
The archer sees the mark upon the path of the infinite, and He bends you with His might that His arrows might go swift and far.
Let your bending in the archer's hand be for gladness;
For even as He loves the arrow that flies, so He loves also the bow that is stable.

- Kahlil Gibran

Perhaps the greatest social service that can be rendered by anybody to the country and to mankind is to bring up a family.

- George Bernard Shaw

⋄ ♦ ⋄

ON LEARNING

Whether we are aware of the process or not, we are always learning.

Dear Teachr,

Today, Mommy cryed. Mommy asked me Jody do you rely kno why you are going to school. i said i dont kno why? She said it is caus we are going to be bilding me a fewchr. i said what is a fewchr wats one look like? Mommy said i dont know Jody, no one can realy see all your fewchr jest you. Don't wory caus youl see youl see. tats when she cryed and sed oh Jody i love you so.

Mommy says every one need to work realy hard for us kids to make our fewcherz the nicest ones the world can ofer.

Teacher can we start today to bild me a fewcher? Can you try espeshly hard to make it a nice pretty one jest for Mommy and me? I love you teacher.

Love,
Jody XXOOXX

- Frank Trujillo

You Are A Marvel

Each second we live is a new and unique moment of the universe, a moment that will never be again . . . And what do we teach our children? We teach them that two and two make four, and that Paris is the capital of France.

When will we also teach them what they are?

We should say to each of them: Do you know what you are? You are a marvel . . . In all the years that have passed, there has never been another child like you. Your legs, your arms, your clever fingers, the way you move.

You may become a Shakespeare, a Michelangelo, a Beethoven. You have the capacity for anything. Yes, you are a marvel. And when you grow up, can you then harm another who is, like you, a marvel?

You must work—we must all work—to make the world worthy of its children.

- Pablo Casals

We Learn By Doing

Not many years ago I began to play the cello. Most people would say that what I am doing is "learning to play" the cello. But these words carry into our minds the strange idea that there exists two very different processes: (1) learning to play the cello; and (2) playing the cello. They imply that I will do the first until I have completed it, at which point I will stop the first process and begin the second. In short, I will go on "learning to play" until I have "learned to play" and then I will begin to play. Of course, this is nonsense. There are not two processes, but one. We learn to do something by doing it. There is no other way.

- John Holt

❖ ♦ ❖

LIVE YOUR DREAM

If we didn't dream, we would have no dreams to make come true.

Encouragement

When Nathaniel Hawthorne's wife heard that Nathaniel had been fired from his job in a customhouse, she was not at all despondent:

"Now," she said triumphantly, "you can write your book!"

"Yes," replied the man, with sagging confidence, "and what shall we live on while I am writing it?"

To his amazement, she opened a drawer and pulled out a substantial amount of money.

"Where on earth did you get that?" he exclaimed.

"I have always known you were a man of genius," she told him. "I knew that someday you would write a masterpiece. So every week, out of the money you gave me for housekeeping, I saved a little bit. So here is enough to last us for one whole year."

From her trust and confidence came one of the greatest novels of American literature, The Scarlet Letter.

- Nido Qubein

Ask, Ask, Ask

. . . Markita Andrews has generated more than eighty thousand dollars selling Girl Scout cookies since she was seven years old . . . [She] has discovered the secret of selling: Ask, Ask, Ask! Many people fail before they even begin because they fail to ask for what they want. The fear of rejection leads many of us to reject ourselves and our dreams long before anyone else ever has the chance . . .

It takes courage to ask for what you want . . .

- Jack Canfield and Mark V. Hansen

People who say it cannot be done should not interrupt those who are doing it.

- Anonymous

❖ ♦ ❖

OVERCOMING OBSTACLES

None of the world's great feats just happened. Understanding the vast effort that individuals make inspires hope and courage.

Don't Be Afraid To Fail

You've failed many times, although you may not remember.

You fell down the first time you tried to walk . . .

R.H. Macy failed seven times before his store in New York caught on.

English novelist John Creasey got 753 rejection slips before he published 564 books.

Babe Ruth struck out 1,330 times, but he also hit 714 home runs.

Don't worry about failure.

Worry about the chances you miss when you don't even try.

- A message from United Technologies Corporation, Hartford, Connecticut, published in the Wall Street Journal

Obstacles

We who lived in the concentration camps can remember the men who walked through the huts comforting others, giving away their last piece of bread. They may have been few in number, but they offer sufficient proof that everything can be taken from a man but one thing: The last of his freedoms—to choose one's attitude in any given set of circumstances, to choose one's own way.

- Viktor E. Frankl, Man's Search for Meaning

❖ ♦ ❖

ECLECTIC WISDOM

The last ingredients in the recipe for *Chicken Soup for the Soul* pertain to commitment, perspective and miracles.

If I Had My Life to Live Over

Interviews with the elderly and the terminally ill do not report that people have regret for the things they have done but rather people talked about the things they regret not having done.

I'd dare to make more mistakes next time.
I'd relax. I would limber up.
I would be sillier than I have been this trip . . .
I would eat more ice cream and less beans.
I would perhaps have more actual troubles but I'd have fewer imaginary ones . . . Oh, I've had my moments and if I had it to do over again, I'd have more of them. In fact, I'd try to have nothing else. Just moments. One after another, instead of living so many years ahead of each day . . .

If I had my life to live over, I would start barefoot earlier in the spring and stay that way later in the fall.
I would go to more dances.
I would ride more merry-go-rounds.
I would pick more daisies.

- Nadine Stair (age 85)

LISTENING FOR THE CRACK OF DAWN

A Master Storyteller Recalls the Appalachia of the 50's and 60's
by Donald Davis, August House Publishers, Inc., Little Rock, Arkansas, 1990

Commentary:

Listening for the Crack of Dawn is a series of lively vignettes invoking the author's growing-up years in the down-home Appalachia of the mid 1900s. Vintage storyteller Donald Davis celebrates life as he remembers it through the innocent eyes of early childhood, the exuberance of boyhood, and the turbulent adventures of adolescence.

Although oral-based narratives like these inevitably risk loss when committed to paper, remarkably, Davis' tales come through with all the wry warmth of their home-grown flavor intact. Here are a few of his tangiest concoctions.

Aunt Laura and the Crack of Dawn

Very shortly after I was born, Aunt Laura came to live with us. She was, in reality, my great-aunt, Daddy's Aunt Laura Henry. She had lived, unmarried, with her sister-in-law, my Grandmother Henry, until Grandmother died the same year I was born. After Grandmother's death, Aunt Laura became what Daddy called a "floater." She would live in the spare front bedroom at our house for weeks at a time. After her first such visit [continued for over a month], Mother came out of her room one Sunday afternoon and looked harshly at my Daddy. "It's time," she said, "to take her for a ride." . . . We loaded Aunt Laura and her small cardboard suitcase into our old blue Dodge. After a long and scenic ride around Nantahala County, we ended up for a visit at Aunt Hester's house. We returned home alone.

And so the Aunts took their turns "hosting" their Great Aunt Laura. *My brother and I . . . loved it when she was with us. She was the first adult in my life who kept loving me no matter what I did. In fact, she liked it more the worse I was. She played with us all the time.*

Aunt Laura was renowned for thinking things through with a pure and poignant enthusiasm. One night in the middle of World War Two, when our Uncle William was off fighting someplace called "Oversees," she took Joe-brother and me outside to study the stars. When we asked why we needed to know the constellations, she answered, "Well, boys, sometimes people grow up and have to go places they don't want to go . . . Boys, if you ever . . . get homesick, just remember this: everybody lives under the same sky! Just wait until it gets dark, then go outside and look up. If you know them, those stars will take you right home."

Aunt Laura never got married. It was my observation that she simply had very little use for men as a group . . . But she did have one great love in her life: She was absolutely and totally in love with Dental Scotch Snuff, and if getting married meant that she had to give up dipping snuff . . . well no man on the face of God's earth was worth that.

Aunt Laura was always the first one up in the morning at our house. One day I asked her how she managed to get up so early. "Why law, son . . . I guess I just get up at the crack of dawn!" I was probably four or five years old at the time and had never heard anyone say that. "Can you hear the crack of dawn?" I asked. *She threw her old head back and laughed . . . "Why sure, son," she answered. "I hear the crack of dawn and it wakes me up. And I'll tell you what: once I've heard it, nobody else can . . . and everybody else in the whole countryside just has to get up the best way they can."* I must have looked pretty disappointed at hearing that, because Aunt Laura glanced down at me and said, "Don't you worry about that. When I'm dead and gone and don't need to get up anymore, I'll leave that to you . . . and you'll be the one who can hear the crack of dawn."

One mid-winter morning before sunup Dad roused Joe-brother and me from a sound sleep and took us out to the barn. We waited in silence while he milked the cow; then, without warning, he told us, "Aunt Laura died."

As we walked back toward the house, my mind was sinking under a load of questions. . . . *We had just passed my favorite black walnut tree, a split-trunked tree you could climb up in the summer and bounce on the long lower limbs of, when very suddenly, the heavy load of ice from last night's storm became too heavy . . . From right behind us with a deafening* **crack,** *the entire walnut tree split from top to bottom.*

When Daddy and I jumped around at the sound, we could just see the edge of the sun peeking over the hill below the Burgins' house . . . It was the crack of dawn! And I had heard it! And that hearing answered all my questions at once.

The first thing I knew was that Aunt Laura was really dead. I had heard the crack of dawn..she had left it to me the way she promised . . . But the most important thing was, and is to this day, that now when I hear the crack of dawn, I shall never, not even for one single day, be really very far away from my dear Aunt Laura.

Experience

Mrs. Amelia Harrison taught English, although she felt just as strongly about teaching us manners, and every third day she would stand contentedly at the door holding a brown paper bag and singing a little song about "please leave your chewing gum and razors at the door."

Long dubbed "Bad Boy" by friend and foe alike, Billy Barker had what the teachers called a "personality problem." He was also "orally dependent," and was constantly in trouble for chewing in school. At first it was tobacco, but after he was suspended from school and subsequently marched back to the building by his mother—who didn't want to be stuck with his personality problem either—Bad Boy switched to Juicy Fruit gum. In fact, by the time class was out, he usually had a whole pack of Juicy Fruit wadded up in his mouth.

Finally came the day of confrontation. It was during a vocabulary drill, and we couldn't find the word "hubris" in the dictionary. So *Mrs. Amelia . . . began to describe and define 'hubris' as "fatal pride. The kind of pride which makes you truly believe that you are not like everyone else . . . the kind of pride which makes you feel that none of the normal laws of life apply to you . . . the kind of pride which brings you to a great fall in the end . . . "* As she droned on, Bad Boy—lost in some dreamworld of his own—very slowly began to chew a full five-stick wad of Juicy Fruit. *Suddenly we realized that Mrs. Amelia, still talking, was looking straight at Bad Boy, unblinking, eyes open widely and set in a focussed stare as she talked. "Hubris is like," she went on, searching for an example, "it's like . . . it's like . . . well, it's like thinking"—she was on her feet now, and moving toward Bad Boy's desk—"you can chew gum out in the open in Mrs. Amelia Harrison's room and somehow get away with it."*

Face to face with Bad Boy, she held out her hand, and with unmistakable authority commanded him to spit it out. And then, just as Bad Boy spit out that gum into Mrs. Amelia's open palm, she reached up and plopped it right on top of his head and smashed it onto his hair with the dictionary she'd been holding in the other hand. *"Those who live by hubris," she kept talking as she walked back to her desk, "always get stuck in the end."*

"Mrs. Amelia had experience."

Daff-knee Garlic . . .

"I was born without kneecaps, so my knees will bend one way just as far and just as fast as they bend the other way. Why, I can run BACK-WARDS as fast as I can run forwards." At least that's how Clarence "Daff-knee" Garlic explained it to us. *"It is a great advantage," he would say, "to be able to look at what you're running from while you do it."*

Daff-knee Garlic was the owner, operator, and sole proprietor of the premier educational institution for teenagers in all of Nantahala County, the Sulpher Springs Big-Screen Drive In Theatre. He hired local boys to run the drive-in operation so he could "take charge" in the projection booth—and watch the movies, right along with the customers. One summer, three of my friends and I popped dozens of boxes of popcorn, manned the ticket booths and concession stands, col-

lared "slip-ins," cleaned up the grounds, and, of course, participated in "getting the light"—the really educational part of the job: *. . . Next to every car which had its parking lights turned on—for curb side service from the concession stand—there were cars in which the show was much better than anything going on on the movie screen. Who could possibly help it if . . . we happened to pass by and even casually notice the strange happenings in [these] cars . . . We would have worked all night free just . . . to "get the lights."*

Mowing the grass was another one of our professional duties—a job done with the aid of two Yazoo High Wheel Mowers. *There was no safety guard of any kind around the whirring rotary blade, which often slung rocks at tremendous velocity in totally random directions. There were actually several holes in the big-screen itself which had come from Yazoo-thrown rocks.*

In addition to his trick knees, Daff-knee had trick toes that pointed almost straight upwards, and he left his toenails uncut to protect the skin on his toes. "Those awful toenails . . . They're enough to make a dog sick," my mother once observed.

Once when Daff-knee was out helping us mow, he decided we needed a lesson in efficiency. So he grabbed the big lawnmower—and ran it straight into a wasps' nest. *Daff-knee grabbed the . . . mower and began to run backwards, letting go to slap at a new sting with every step. Running backwards as he was, he didn't see a speaker pole and ran straight into it. He stopped dead cold, but the big mower kept coming and rolled over his right foot . . . We looked up just in time to see [his] big toe, all in one piece, flying through the air over Budweiser Boulevard, across the fence and out of the drive-in theatre field.*

"There goes my toe," Daff-knee hollered, and took off to retrieve it, with the four of us right on his heels. But Rufus Stanley's big German shepherd/boxer cross-breed, Towser, was faster. Beelining for the falling toe, he opened his jaws, caught it in mid-air, and swallowed it in a single gulp.

In total shock, Daff-knee sat down and cried. We drove him to Dr. York's, who gave him a tetanus shot and stitched him together again. Then on the way home, we passed Rufus Stanley's house. And *there in the yard stood old Towser, gagging for all he was worth. We watched as, with a great retch, Towser vomited the intact toe onto the ground . . . "Whooo, look, Daff-knee," I shouted. "Mama always said that your toenails are enough to make a dog sick . . . Daff-knee didn't think it was funny. He also did not want the toe anymore. Later with the help of a long stick, the four of us boys reclaimed it from Towser's lot. We respectfully buried it and erected a small wooden cross over the grave-site. We were certain that the cross caused much confusion to those moviegoers who chose to park there afterwards.*

LAKE WOBEGON DAYS

by Garrison Keillor, Viking Press, New York, N.Y., 1985

Type of work: Semi-autobiographical parody chronicle

Setting: Lake Wobegon, Minnesota; 1940s-1980s

Prologue:

In the Preface to this nostalgic "family album," Garrison Keillor describes the impetus for *Lake Wobegon Days*. He, his wife, and their son had taken a train from their home in St. Paul to visit friends in San Francisco. Although their Pullman compartment was rather expensive, Keillor enjoyed feeling that he was "a successful American author who provided good things for his family." While they were in Idaho, however, the train derailed and they had to take a bus to Portland, where they finally caught another train to San Francisco.

Unfortunately, Keillor had left two of his prized manuscripts in the men's room of the Portland depot. The loss of his story "Lake Wobegon Memoir" particularly disturbed him. He would later observe that the "story shone so brilliantly in dim memory that every new attempt looked pale and impoverished before I got to the first sentence."

But as time passed, Keillor found that he was able to work his conception of Lake Wobegon into a radio show that he broadcast from Minneapolis—*A Prairie Home Companion*. While the show proved immensely successful, he could not help wishing that his lost story of Lake Wobegon would miraculously reappear. Frustrated, he finally sat down to write *Lake Wobegon Days*, the novel which he deemed "not nearly so fine" as the long-lost story he could no longer recall.

Story Overview:

Gary Keillor grew up in the town of Lake Wobegon, Minnesota. Although the body of water was no more than a "brackish puddle surrounded by mud flats that stank of fish," when the lake was named in 1855, the word "Wobegon" was euphemistically said to be derived from the Ojibwa word "Wa-be-gan-tan-han," sometimes translated as "patience." Indeed, patience was one of the many virtues the residents of Lake Wobegon extolled. There was also cleanliness, temperance, and contrition, depending on whether one was a Lutheran, a Catholic, or a member of the Sanctified Brethren.

Lutheranism was the town's most prominent creed, owing to the fact that most of the residents were of Norwegian stock and took great pride in their heritage. Among the earliest inhabitants of Lake Wobegon was Magnus Oleson, who, shortly following his arrival in America, had become a Confederate deserter in the Civil War. After stealing a horse and making his way to Minnesota, he had settled down near the lake, married three times, and fathered many children. As a result, "the name of Magnus Oleson was in the family tree of every Norwegian in town."

Oleson's male descendants had, for generations, made a ritual of frequently taking a bottle of whiskey to the cemetery to lay upon the "family grave." There they would talk "to the dead about home, the home in Norway, heavenly Norway." His female descendants still actively participated in the Daughters of the Pioneers—"membership limited to Norwegian families"—and devoutly followed Lutheran teachings.

The town's Catholics, of course, were equally devout, but seemed, at least to young Gary Keillor, "flashier" than the Lutherans. For one thing, they attended Our Lady of Perpetual Responsibility Church, where they seemed to enjoy an easygoing relationship with their priest, Father Emil. While not as liberal as Sister Arvonne or Father Todd, who wore "pant suits" and "T-shirts" respectively, Father Emil did preside over the flamboyant Blessing of the Animals, a sacrament "they did right out in the open, a feast for the eyes." Moreover, unlike most of the town's residents, Father Emil often traveled outside of Minnesota and the Dakotas. In August, for instance, he made his "annual bus tour of Civil War battlefields."

During Father Emil's absences, the Church always brought in a replacement. One year the "sub" was jovial Father Frank. At his farewell cocktail party, Father Frank sported "a sportshirt and yellow shorts," drank gin with the parishioners, and gave all the women "a good smack on the lips." Father Frank had even gone so far on this occasion as to create a new Psalm for his fellow golfers. "He maketh the ball to lie on the fairway and leadeth it around the water hazard," the priest had joked between sips of gin. "Yea. Though we walk through the rough, we will fear no bogey, for He prepareth the green before us in the presence of sand traps, and our putt runneth over to the cup and dwelleth there."

Such stories about the Catholics fascinated young Gary. He held a genuine "sneaking admiration" for them; their rituals seemed magnificent—so unlike the no-frills religion that he and his parents practiced.

As Sanctified Brethren, the Keillors met in "Uncle Al's and Aunt Flo's bare living room with plain folding chairs arranged facing in toward the middle. No clergymen . . . No organ or piano, for that would make one person too prominent. No upholstery, it would lead to complacency . . ."

Complacency, however, was exactly what young Gary longed for. For one thing, if he'd had any say in the matter, his family would have had "A/C." But air conditioning, at least from his father's point of view, was only "for the weak and indolent," the kind of luxury that had "brought down the Roman Empire" and that would ultimately cause Mom to start stepping out "in a skin-tight dress, holding a cigarette and a glass of gin, walking an ocelot on a leash."

Gary's father also held the belief that, like A/C, Christmas presents were shamefully extravagant: "It had all begun with Roosevelt who plunged the country into debt and now thrift was out the window and it was 'Live for today and forget about tomorrow' with people spending money they didn't have for junk they could do without and Christmas was a symptom of it."

As a cross current to his father's annual conviction that he would be sent to the poorhouse because of the Yule, however, there was Gary's mother's obsession with "incendiary" Christmas trees. "[The] danger of Christmas-tree fire some night killing us all in our beds seemed to point toward a live-for-today philosophy, not that we should necessarily go whole-hog and buy everything in the Monkey Ward catalog, but certainly we could run up a few bills, knowing that any morning could find us lying in smoldering ruins, our blackened little bodies like burnt bacon that firemen would remove in small plastic bags."

If Christmastime brought mixed emotions to Gary, the months following were fraught with impending calamities. Danger seemed omnipresent in the frozen Minnesota landscape. First, there were the icicles, "the fifty- and hundred-pounders" that his mother always warned him about. "One of those falls down," she'd say soberly, "it could go right through your head." Then there were the frozen pump handles and the hapless kids who put their tongues on them in the dead of winter to worry about; there were also the wild dogs in the woods that could "tear your flesh off in about two minutes" on the way to school; and, finally, there were the traps for bears, "covered with snow."

Of course, not everything in wintertime Lake Wobegon was fodder for January nightmares. There was, for instance, the Sons of Knute Ice-Melt Contest that began every year on Groundhog Day. Mr. Berge's old Ford—the town's Lutherans all drove Fords, while the Catholics drove Chevys—was towed out onto the ice of the lake, where it was left "forty yards off shore with a long chain around the rear axle." People then speculated as to "the day and the hour she would go down, at a dollar per guess." Because the winner received a boat, the contest always had a good turnout. Memorial Day—which boasted two "great bands" of Catholic and Lutheran marchers—and Flag Day—which included a "Living Flag" of Wobegon's citizens sporting red, white, and blue caps—also drew big crowds.

In addition to their town's festivities, the people of Lake Wobegon were genially proud of their newspaper. The *Herald-Star* had "some fifteen hundred subscribers," most of whom "didn't live there anymore (and wouldn't if you paid them)," but who nevertheless would "shell out $30 a year to read about it." The paper's owner, Harold Star, had long ago determined that the report of the high school game should be "five hundred words long and mention every boy who played in it," while a wedding deserved "a major literary effort." With this philosophy in mind, Harold, on one occasion, was forced to decide whether or not to print the "neatly typed manifesto" which a former resident of the town

had written anonymously to his parents. The document included some troubling accusations:

You have fed me wretched food, vegetables boiled to extinction, fistfuls of sugar, slabs of fat, mucousy casseroles, **lutefisk,** *a repulsive gelatinous fishlike dish that tasted of soap and gave off an odor that would gag a goat . . . Religious intolerance was part of our faith . . . We believed that Catholics were illiterate peasants, foreign born, who worshiped idols . . . We believed they poisoned the pets of Protestants . . . You brought me up to respect fastidiousness as an incarnate virtue . . . When Grandpa died, we tended his grave zealously . . . "He was a good man," someone said once in the cemetery. "Ja," you said. "I've been thinking of applying a little Turf-Builder. And maybe a fungicide." . . . You taught me not to be "unusual" for fear of what the neighbors would say . . . We knew they'd talk because we always talked about them. We thought they were nuts, but still we shouldn't offend them.*

Painful memories notwithstanding, people who had grown up in Lake Wobegon, including Gary, came home every now and again. It was comforting to know that the Statue of the Unknown Norwegian, Ralph's Good-Enough Grocery, and the Chatterbox Cafe were still there on Main Street, that the "Norwegian bachelor farmers" were still "combining in their antique McCormacks," and that old Elizabeth, the town's switchboard operator, still dispensed local gossip over the phone lines.

Of course, old Clarence Bunsen was still in town as well. "Anything that ever happened to me is happening to other people," Clarence had once said to Gary when he came home for a visit. "If that is true and our lives are being lived over and over by others, I don't know if I should laugh or cry," Gary had answered back. And at that moment a vivid image entered his mind of a man walking back to his house in the midst of a blizzard. *And as the man nears home, he knows that he will soon be "where people love him and will be happy to see his face."*

Commentary:

Garrison Keillor has been in the public eye since 1980, when his radio program, *A Prairie Home Companion*, became nationally syndicated. As popular as his show has proven to be, it has been Keillor's prose that has won him critical acclaim. Often compared to such masters as Mark Twain and James Thurber, Keillor has established himself as a distinctly American humorist who has never forgotten the writer's old adage, "Write what you know."

Keillor, as chronicler of Lake Wobegon, displays a sharp, endearing and intimate command of small-town Americana. Modeled on his own hometown of Anoka, Minnesota, Lake Wobegon emerges in his writing as both a grandiose "Philipoppolis" and a town so small that it is lost in the mysterious aerial "Minnesota jog" between time zones and doesn't even appear on a map. Lake Wobegon's appeal is ubiquitous, and, as *The New Yorker* once pointed out, Keillor's compilation of its universal idiosyncrasies "could well become a classic of our time."

THE KITCHEN GOD'S WIFE

by
Amy Tan, Ivy Books, New York, N.Y., 1991

Type of work: Intergenerational novel

Setting: 20th century China and California

Principal characters:

Pearl Louie Brandt, a forty-year-old Chinese American woman, married with two children

"Winnie" (Weili) Louie, Pearl's Chinese mother

Wen Fu, Weili's harsh first husband

"Helen" (Hulan) Kwang, Weili's friend and partner

Story Overview:

"Pearl-ah, have to go, no choice," Winnie informed her daughter by telephone. Pearl did not particularly want to attend the engagement party for her Aunt Helen's son or the Buddhist funeral for her Auntie Du, but, as usual, she dutifully agreed to go.

The first person to greet her at the engagement party was her cousin Mary. Pearl was very hurt and unhappy that Mary had told her mother, Helen, about a very private piece of news: Pearl's newly diagnosed multiple sclerosis. Helen and Winnie were very close friends, so it was only a matter of time, thought Pearl, until her own mother knew.

Pearl had meant to tell her mother herself—eventually. But, remembering the cancer that had killed her father, Jimmy Louie, years before, she could predict what Winnie's response would be: She "would search in her mind for the causes, as if she could undo the disaster by finding the reason why it had occurred. . . . According to my mother *nothing* is an accident. She's like a Chinese version of Freud . . ."

Now as Pearl gazed at her mother during the banquet, she felt sad. "I feel as lonely as I imagine her to be," she reflected. Then, suddenly she felt a hand on her shoulder and looked up to see her Aunt Helen. In a voice that could not be refused, the older woman invited her into the kitchen. "I have a brain tumor," Helen candidly announced once they were alone. "Everyone wants to keep this news from me, okay. They want to be nice before I die . . . [So, Pearl-ah], it makes my heart and shoulders heavy that your mother does not know [about your illness]. . . . You must tell your mother, Pearl."

"Auntie Helen, you know I can't tell my mother that," Pearl protested. "You know how she is." Auntie Helen's response came as a startling revelation: "Maybe [your mother] has secrets too."

The next day was Auntie Du's funeral. Afterwards, Winnie presented her daughter with a family heirloom: Auntie Du's famous good-luck icon, the Chinese Kitchen God. Elaborately stationed on what resembled a miniature stage and surrounded by gold-leafed Chinese characters signifying luck was the picture of a man with "two long whiskers, shaped like smooth, tapered black whips." According to Winnie, the Kitchen God was not "like Buddha," but one of the lesser gods.

Originally, Winnie explained, the Kitchen God had been a rich farmer named Zhang. One day Zhang brought a concubine to live in his household. Eventually the new favorite forced Zhang's wife to leave. Then when the concubine and Zhang had spent all of the family fortune, the woman left too, and Zhang, now too poor to buy bread, eventually fainted from hunger. When he came to, he found himself in the kitchen of his good wife. He was so ashamed that he jumped into the fireplace—and the wife watched "her husband's ashes fly up to heaven in three puffs of smoke."

And so farmer Zhang became the Kitchen God, "watching over everyone's behavior . . . And once a year, seven days before the new year, Kitchen God flew back up the fireplace to report whose fate deserved to be changed, better for worse, or worse for better."

Not long after giving her daughter the Kitchen God, Winnie's own life suddenly changed. Helen received a letter from China with astonishing news: Winnie's first husband, a harsh man named Wen Fu, had died on Christmas Day. "Can you imagine?" Winnie fumed. "Even to the end he found a way to make me miserable . . . How can I sing 'Silent Night,' 'Joy to the World,' when I want to shout and say, So glad he is dead!"

But this was only the beginning of Winnie's distress. Helen now insisted that she reveal the story of her own early life in China with Wen Fu. Winnie demurred; those secrets were shameful and sordid. But Helen's firmness prevailed. Reluctantly, Winnie called her daughter and asked Pearl to come the next day.

"It is the same pain I have had for many years," the older woman, seated next to Pearl, began. "It comes from keeping everything inside, waiting until it is too late. I think my mother gave me this fault . . . She left me before she could tell me why she was leaving . . ."

Winnie's mother had been raised between two worlds. She was born in Shanghai to a wealthy, educated family and attended a missionary school that encouraged her independence and enthusiasm for foreign customs. But later, she had followed tradition by entering into an arranged marriage with Jiang, a rich merchant with four other wives. When Weili—Winnie's Chinese name—was born, the young mother doted on the child. One day when Winnie was six-years-old, however, her mother argued with Jiang, and then ran away. Winnie never saw her again. Jiang sent Winnie to live on a distant island with her paternal uncle and his family so that her face and mannerisms would not remind him of his wife. Although the family treated her well, Winnie never really felt as if she "belonged."

After Winnie grew up and married Wen Fu, her husband showed her the meaning of cruelty in every way. He had married her only because of her family's great wealth, and she knew little happiness as a bride. "A woman always [has] to feel pain, suffer and cry, before she [can] feel love," her mother-in-law told her often. And this message was daily reinforced by Wen Fu, who forced the innocent girl to use language like "a salt water whore's" and to humble herself on her hands and knees to beg him for sex. " . . . He would complain," Winnie remembered, "telling me I was not a good wife, that I had not passion, not like other women he knew . . ."

It was in 1937, during the early days of her marriage, that Winnie first met Helen, "the wife of Wen Fu's military boss. Although Helen was an unschooled chatterbox with "the manners of a village servant," Winnie could not help but respond to her warmth and wit. Throughout the horrible years of war, the two women remained friends as they moved from one Chinese city to another to escape Japanese attacks.

Meanwhile, Wen Fu was impressing all the other men in the air force with his bravado. Even his boss mistook his swagger for courage. Secretly, Wen Fu disparaged his boss—and despised Helen.

As the war raged on, Winnie's relationship with her husband grew steadily worse. After her first baby, a girl, was born dead, Wen Fu's only comment was, "At least it was not a boy." Winnie gave the baby the name of *Mouchou*, or "Sorrowfree," because she had never known sorrow.

After injuring himself in a jeep accident, Wen Fu's behavior grew even more monstrous. He humiliated and beat his wife mercilessly, and when another girlchild, *Yiku*, was born to them, he beat her as well. Eventually, baby Yiku died as a result of Wen Fu's cruelties. "Good for you," said Winnie as she cradled the little corpse in her arms. "You've escaped. Good for you."

When she again became pregnant, Winnie decided to name her next child *Danru*, or "Nonchalance," in the hope that the baby would never become attached to anything. But when her son was born, little Danru adored his mother as much as she loved him.

Wen Fu did not beat his son as he had Yiku, but he continued to terrorize and humiliate Winnie, and invited a favorite mistress to live in their house. After his mistress left and the war ended, he moved his family back to Shanghai, where they lived in the mansion that belonged to Winnie's father. Jiang had been enfeebled by a stroke and was so weak that he gladly allowed his son-in-law to take over his finances. As Wen Fu busied himself spending the old man's fortune, Winnie and Danru took the opportunity to escape. They moved into a shelter, where Winnie struck up a romance with an old acquaintance, Jimmy Louie, a Chinese-American who worked as a translator for the U.S. government. Before long, she and Danru moved in with Jimmy, who provided them with the first real taste of family happiness. But, tragically, little Danru died during an epidemic, and soon afterwards Wen Fu had his wife imprisoned for stealing his son and "letting him die" and for deserting her Chinese husband to run off with an American . . . "

In great anguish, Jimmy returned to the United States. Thanks to his financial support and to Helen's tireless efforts, Winnie was eventually released from prison. After tricking Wen Fu into divorcing her, she prepared to join Jimmy in America. But when Wen Fu learned that he had been outwitted, he accosted Winnie and put a gun to her head. "Beg me, beg me to let you be my wife," he shouted. Then he raped her. Soon after, Winnie left China forever.

Still, there was one important fact left for Winnie to divulge. "And nine months later," she told Pearl, "maybe a little less, I had a baby. I had you." Stunned at the obvious implications of this confession, Pearl broke into sobs.

Her mother took her hand. "Of course every baby is born with **yin** and **yang**," she comforted. "This **yin** comes from the woman. The **yang** comes from the man. When you were born I tried to see whose **yang** you had. I tried to see your daddy . . . You looked like Mouchou. You looked like Yiku. You looked like Danru, Danru especially. All of them together. All the children I could not keep but could never forget."

Suddenly Pearl felt her shock begin to retreat—melting behind the dawn of a new awareness: Barriers were down; a bridge had been crossed. She and her mother were at last united as women. It was not hard at that moment for Pearl to reveal her own secret, the multiple sclerosis. "It's nobody's fault," she finished. "There's nothing you can do about it."

"How can you think this way?" Winnie protested. "What do you call this disease again? Write it down. Tomorrow I am going to Auntie Du's herb doctor. And after that, I will think of a way."

Minutes later, Pearl faced one last surprise. "I don't really have a brain tumor," confessed Helen. "I made it up! . . . Well, you had a secret, your mother had a secret. I said I was going to die so that you both tell each other your secrets . . . And now you are closer, mother and daughter, I already see this."

"I am laughing, confused," thought Pearl, "caught [between Helen and Winnie] in endless circles of lies. Or perhaps they are not lies but their own form of loyalty, beyond anything . . . that I will ever understand."

Commentary:

Like her first novel, *The Joy Luck Club*, Amy Tan's *The Kitchen God's Wife* has won universal acclaim. Through the intergenerational struggles of her characters, Tan evokes a marvelously mythic, complex and exotic world, a world that nevertheless remains startlingly contemporary and accessible.

And the fact that Tan's characters rarely forget to laugh, however desperate their circumstances, greatly increases this accessibility. The novel's humor, just as in the Greek epics, becomes a gallant response to fate. If Winnie has been victimized, she is not the victim of Wen Fu—whom she challenges—but rather of fate, of dynamic forces larger than life itself.

Even the Kitchen God himself is not exempt from Winnie's mockery. At the end of the novel Winnie buys her daughter "a lady statue" to replace the Kitchen God. "You should tell her everything," Winnie, smiling, urges Pearl. "She will wash away everything sad with her tears . . . See her name: Lady Sorrowfree, happiness winning over bitterness, no regrets in this world."

A RIVER RUNS THROUGH IT

by
Norman Maclean,
(1902-1990)

Type of work: Reflective nature novella

Setting: Western Montana; 1937

Principal characters:
> *Norman,* the eldest of two sons and narrator of the story
> *Paul,* Norman's younger brother, a master fly fisherman
> *Father,* Norman and Paul's minister father
> *Jessie,* Norman's wife
> *Neal,* Jessie's good-for-nothing brother
> *Old Rawhide,* a local prostitute

Story Overview:

In our family, there was no clear line between religion and fly fishing. We lived at the junction of great trout rivers in western Montana, and our father was a Presbyterian minister and a fly fisherman who tied his own flies and taught others. He told us about Christ's disciples being fishermen, and we were left to assume, as my brother and I did, that all first-class fishermen on the Sea of Galilee were fly fishermen and that John, the favorite, was a dry-fly fisherman.

Norman and Paul's most memorable time was spent with their father, zealously stalking the Big Blackfoot River for trout. A meticulous fisherman, he demanded the same conscientiousness from his sons. Using a metronome to practice the four-count rhythm, the boys were taught the proper casting angles, always staying between ten and two o'clock. They learned to fish; and they also learned to be tough, probing and proving each others' characters in the process. Paul, always ready to buck the establishment, showed his particular brand of mettle early: one day as a little boy he refused to finish a bowl of oatmeal at the breakfast table—and outlasted his father during the sit-in which ensued: *As the minister raged, the child bowed his head over the food and folded his hands . . . The hotter my father got, the colder the porridge, until finally my father burned out.*

Norman, on the other hand, was more of a conformist, with dreams of becoming a forest manager. During World War I most young men out of high school were off fighting, so at the tender age of fifteen Norman was introduced into the rugged, grown-up world of logging, where his love of the outdoors—and his interest in rivers—was strengthened.

The brothers' differences came to a final climax one summer when Norman and Paul were in their thirties. Norman was now married to Jessie, the daughter of a fellow Scotsman, and working in the forest service. The newlyweds lived with Jessie's mother. Paul, meanwhile, wrote and reported for the Helena newspaper. He loved to tell stories, even if they weren't quite true. Unfortunately, he also liked to gamble—and this was to be his undoing.

Both brothers loved to fish. And Norman was very good at it—but not as good as Paul.

One day while Norman worked the river, he saw that Paul had stopped to watch him. He remembered the moment: *Paul knew how I felt about fishing and was careful not to seem superior by offering advice, but . . . he couldn't leave now without saying something. Finally he said, "The fish are out farther." Probably fearing he had put a strain on family relations, he quickly added, "Just a little farther."*

It was soon after this that Norman came to talk with Paul about his brother-in-law Neal, a California emigre who was returning to Montana for a vacation. Norman wasn't particularly fond of Neal, but, at the request of his wife and mother-in-law, he asked Paul to accompany them on a fly-fishing excursion. Paul straightway voiced his disdain for Neal: " . . . *He's a bait fisherman. All those Montana boys on the West Coast sit around the bars at night and lie about their frontier childhood when they were hunters, trappers, and fly fishermen. But when they come back home they don't even kiss their mothers on the front porch before they're in the back garden with a red Hills Bros. coffee can digging for angleworms."*

Paul finally agreed to the trip, but asked a favor in return: he wanted to go out on the river alone with Norman before Neal arrived. The next day as Norman watched Paul work with the rod, he was awed by his brother's flawless casting. The type of fly had little to do with fishing success, Paul always said; it was technique—the suspending of the fly over the water before letting it touch, for instance—that caught fish.

When the brothers had reeled in their limits, Paul invited Norman home to eat and chat. Afterwards, Norman went to bed, while Paul left to attend to some business. Several hours later, Norman was awakened by the telephone: the police had just fished Paul out of a drunken brawl—one of the many gambling fights that had begun to muddle his life. When Norman arrived at the jail to claim his brother, he found Paul, along with his beautiful Cheyenne Indian girlfriend, sprawled on the jailroom floor. On the way home, not a word was spoken between the brothers.

The next day Neal arrived. At his wife's suggestion, Norman took him to the local bar to loosen him up a little. There, Neal captured the attention of Old Rawhide, a well-known local prostitute who easily had "weathered enough to deserve her name." As he left with Old Rawhide on his arm, he barely acknowledged Norman's reminder of the next day's fishing trip.

When morning broke, Paul was eager to get on the river. Anxious to find a good fishing hole, he set a blistering pace, leaving Norman saddled with Neal: *One reason Paul caught more fish than anyone else was that he had his flies in the water more than anyone else. "Brother," he would say, "there are no flying fish in Montana. Out here, you can't catch fish with your flies in the air." His outfit was set up ready to go the moment he stepped out of the car; he walked fast; he seldom wasted time changing flies . . .*

Norman could tell that Neal was too hung-over to fish, and after several attempts to rouse his companion, he headed off downstream, leaving Neal asleep in the grass; after all, "I wasn't going to catch many fish unless I quit fooling around."

A while later Norman met up with Paul, and tried to discuss the events of the night before. What was it Paul needed? Was he short on money? But Paul quickly changed the subject. He also pointed out that Norman was sure to get into trouble for leaving Neal alone—and sure enough, when they returned, they found Neal writhing in agony, badly sunburned.

Since Neal's arrival had disrupted his life at home, Norman proposed that he and Paul go to a vacation cabin for a couple of days. They had scarcely reached the cabin, however, when they saw another car drive up. It was Neal—incoherently drunk, but delivered to his rendezvous by the slightly less comatose Old Rawhide, who sportingly announced that she and "Buster" had come to fish. The brothers were furious, but, with true Scottish discipline, they put things into perspective. Sure the pair could fish; Paul and Norman would just let Neal and his gal follow them for as long as they could—meaning at most a few hundred yards—and soon they would be left behind.

With the unwanted guests safely out of the way, the fishing commenced in earnest. Once again, Paul showed his superior skills by catching a string of beautiful, large German browns. Then the brothers started back, looking forward to the cold beer they had cached in the river.

To their disgust, they found that Neal and Old Rawhide had already drunk the beer. Then they spotted the couple, lying bottoms up and totally naked, their bodies red as beets, asleep on a sand bar in the middle of the river. Norman knew he was in trouble again; the sleepers were already blistering with sunburn.

Back at the house Norman received the brunt of his wife's displeasure. "You bastard," Jessie wailed. Norman's frustrated thoughts turned to "the bait-fishing bastard who had violated everything that our father had taught us about fishing . . ."

"Woman," he finally told Jessie, "can't I love you without liking him?" "I am trying to help someone," replied Jessie. "someone in my family." Her husband shrugged. "I should understand that," he said soberly.

Setting aside the sunburn incident, Paul and Norman again escaped to the comfort of the river. But this trip would be different; this time their expedition would include their father, long since retired from both ministering and fishing.

After some gentle reminiscing on the banks, the brothers decided to separate while the father stayed near calmer waters. Heading upstream, fishing opposite sides of the river, Norman could not help but see how content Paul was again in his role as tutor. This time, however, it seemed that Norman had come upon just the right fly—the Bunyan Bug No. 2 Yellow Stone Fly—to simulate a particular insect in the area. He was having great success, while his brother, relying only on his casting skill, was struggling. Suddenly there were several large splashes in the water. Ruling out either fish or beaver as the cause, Norman saw that Paul was throwing rocks in front of him to spoil his fishing: *It didn't happen often in this life, only when his fishing partner was catching fish and he couldn't. It was a sight, however rare, that he could not bear to watch.*

Norman offered to wade across and give Paul one of the lucky flies, but Paul would have none of it; to admit that the fly made a difference would have been the height of humiliation. Smiling, Norman was pleased to see a tinge of jealousy in his brother. Satisfied with his catch, he turned back to join his father and rest for a while.

As father and son sat chatting, their attention shifted upstream, where they saw Paul, clearly struggling with a large fish on his line. Paul went underwater, floated downstream a ways, and, after a magnificent battle, finally landed his prize. *This was the last fish we were to ever see Paul catch . . . We sat on the bank and the river went by. As always, it was making sounds to itself, and now it made sounds to us. It would be hard to find three men sitting side by side who knew better what a river was saying.*

Months later Norman came to his father's house with a police sergeant to break the news of Paul's death. His brother's beaten body had been discovered in an alley. Pressing Norman for details and learning that nearly all the bones in Paul's right hand had been broken, the grief-stricken father seemed to take some consolation, as many Scotsmen would, in the fact that his son had died fighting for his life.

"All I really know," Norman finally said to his father, "is that he was a fine fisherman . . . Yes, he was beautiful. He should have been—you taught him."

Norman's father later added his own haunting and bittersweet commentary: "It is those we live with and love and should know who elude us."

Commentary:

Norman Maclean grew up and lived his life among the Montana rivers he wrote about here. Although this book was written as a novella, it is obviously semi-autobiographical. Maclean writes: "It was my children Jean and John who started me off [writing]. They wanted me to put down some of the stories I had told them when they were young." And so, near the end of his life, the fisherman decided to show his children "what kind of people their parents are—or hope they are." He returned to cast and probe the river for its secrets with language instead of a fishing rod: *Eventually, all things merge into one, and a river runs through it. The river was cut by the world's great flood and runs over rocks from the basement of time. On some of the rocks are timeless raindrops. Under the rocks are the words, and some of the words are theirs.*

I am haunted by waters.

MEMORY OF KIN

Stories About Family by Black Writers
edited by Mary Helen Washington, Doubleday, New York, N.Y., 1991

Commentary:

As Mary Ellen Washington compiled her collection of 19 stories and 12 poems, she gradually began to see "family as a living mystery, constantly changing, constantly providing us clues about who we are, and demanding that we recognize the new and challenging shapes it often takes." In fact, Washington's anthology challenges the notion that there is a single form of the "ideal" family.

Memory of Kin's writers explore various sides of the family. For instance, in "Just Like a Tree" (1968), a quilted, staccato tale of pilgrimage, Ernest J. Gaines' ten distinct narrators define "family" as *those who care* rather than those who are related by blood.

Likewise, in "Roselily" (1972) teacher and writer Alice Walker re-evaluates the function of marriage by revealing a bride's full range of giddy and troubled thoughts as she stands at the altar.

Finally, in "Adventures of the Dread Sisters" (1989), poet, playwright and political journalist Alexis de Veaux demonstrates that a "functional family" need not fit the traditional father, mother, 2.5 children, one-dog prototype.

Thus, Washington submits, "Like the 24 storytellers in this collection, we too become artists, re-creating our family in an imaginative act, retrieving what is lost by reconstructing our own 'memory of kin.'"

Just Like a Tree
by Ernest J. Gaines

Young Chuckkie tried to stay warm next to his mother Leola in the wagon. She, her husband Emile, her mother Gran'mon, and Chuckkie were on their way to say good-bye to "Aunt Fe," who was heading North to escape the unhealthy climate of the South. Chuckkie looked on in amusement as his father battled to get the family mule, Mr. Bascom, to pull the wagon.

As they lurched to a stop in front of Aunt Fe's house, Chuckkie jumped off the wagon to guide Mr. Bascom through the gate. As the wagon rolled through, however, it scraped the fence, tearing half of it down. At the sound of the ruckus, the whole housefull of family and friends who had come to see Aunt Fe off came bustling out.

Later, Chuckkie's mother found Aunt Fe sitting by the fireplace, trying to look happy. "Aunt Fe," Leola ruminated. " . . . The name's been 'mongst us just like us own family name. Just like the name o' God." She then recalled all the times she had washed clothes for Aunt Fe. Gloomily, Leola approached Louise and exclaimed, "Louise, moving her from here's like moving a tree you been used to in your front yard all your life." She even offered to take Aunt Fe home to live with her and her family, but Louise replied that it wouldn't be right: they weren't Aunt Fe's kin.

Louise's husband James, meanwhile,

decided that he needed to show these country folks a good time. He pulled out his whiskey bottle and began dumping it in the eggnog pot, though Louise held back his hand. Dumbfounded, he glanced around at all the poor, backward masses who were going to drink eggnog straight. "I mean, there's about ninety-nine of them. Old ones, young ones, little ones, big ones, yellow ones, black ones, brown ones—you name them . . . they're here. And what for? Brother, I'll tell you what for. Just because me and [Louise] are taking this old chick out of these sticks."

"I want me some eggnog," young Ben O repeated over and over. "Well, you ain't getting none," Gran'mon replied, picking up a potato chip and throwing it toward Ben O but hitting Chuckkie instead. Chuckkie then turned and hit Ben O, setting off a wrestling match. Leola rushed from the kitchen, snatched the two tussling boys from off the floor, shook them gently, and ordered them to kiss and make up. Chuckkie kissed Ben O on the jaw, but Ben O refused to kiss Chuckkie—until his mama whipped him with his daddy's belt. Then he kissed Chuckkie, "feeling like he wanted to spit."

In the meantime, Aunt Clo had been thinking of how heartless it was to take Aunt Fe away from the place where she had lived for so many years. "Be just like wrapping a chain round a tree and jecking," Aunt Clo believed. "Then you hear the roots crying, and then you keep on jecking, and then it give, and then you jeck some mo', and then it falls. And not till then . . . you see the big hole in the ground and piece of the taproot still way down in it—a piece you won't never get out no matter if you dig till doomsday."

Elsewhere in the room, Uncle Chris listened in delight as Lionel told the wildest lies. Everybody laughed; maybe it would take their minds off Aunt Fe's leaving. Why just the other day, when Pa had gone by to tell Uncle Chris about Aunt Fe's decision, Chris had broken down and cried, right there by the front gate.

Several miles away from the bustling house, Anne-Marie's car slithered through the mud toward Aunt Fe's. Despite the storm, she had to pay her respects to her former nanny. After her mother had died, Aunt Fe had cooked for her father—and had nursed her back to health several times.

Finally, Anne-Marie pulled into the drive. As she approached the house she heard laughter wafting out onto the porch; but the moment she stepped inside, the revelry stopped. Now everyone gawked silently as Anne-Marie handed a package to Aunt Fe. "Just think of it—a white lady coming through all of this for one old darky," one of the men mumbled. But Aunt Fe wasn't fazed in the least. Opening the package, she removed the 79-cent scarf, kissed it, and thanked Anne-Marie profusely—whereupon Anne-Marie knelt down and buried her face in Aunt Fe's lap, weeping. A few minutes later, she got up and walked out of the house.

Then Emmanuel suddenly appeared—and again the house turned deathly silent. Emmanuel was responsible for Aunt Fe's leaving. But Aunt Etienne spoke up to defend him; it wasn't his fault: "It started when one man envied another man for having a penny mo' 'an he had, and then the man married a woman to help him work the field so he could get much's the other man . . . And soon the other man had bought him a slave to work the ox so he could get ahead of the other man." The squabble had been going on for a million years, she continued; Emmanuel was just doing what the slaves had done in earlier times—except that instead of raising his arms he was bowing his head.

Emmanuel now stood before Aunt Fe. His voice barely above a whisper, he asked if she knew he loved her. She nodded. Then he turned and reminded everyone there of what Aunt Fe had told him when he was enraged over his great-grandpa's lynching: "I was so angry I felt like killing. But it was you who told me get killing out of my mind," he said, eyeing Aunt Fe. "It was you who told me I would only bring harm to myself and sadness to the others if I killed."

As the crowd began filing out of the house, tears streaming down their cheeks, Chuckkie's grandmother, Aunt Lou, sidled over to Aunt Fe, still sullenly seated by the fireplace. "Well, Fe?" Aunt Lou said, waiting quietly for Aunt Fe's response.

Finally, Aunt Fe, in her majestic yet quiet voice, said, "I ain't leaving here tomorrow, Lou." Aunt Lou, taking Aunt Fe by the hand, sang her a termination song; then she helped her into her nightgown. Leading her into the bedroom, Lou watched Aunt Fe kneel by her bed, praying for a long time, before she took one long last breath. "Sleep on, Fe," Lou said. "When you get up there, tell 'em all I ain't far behind."

Roselily
by Alice Walker

Dearly Beloved, we are gathered here . . .
Roselily's mind drifted into nothingness when the marriage ceremony began. As the preacher's voice droned on, she escaped into a fantasy of playing dress-up in her mother's white robe and veil—and of not already having three children. The man beside her glared at the congregation, whom he considered backward, while the bride thought "of ropes, chains, handcuffs, his . . . place of worship . . . where she will be required to sit apart with covered head." But after this ritual her groom would take her away from Mississippi to the South Side of Chicago, where she and her children would have a chance at respectability.

If there's anybody here that knows a reason why these two should not be joined together . . .
In her mind Roselily heard the preacher, but her thoughts had shifted to her fourth child—now living with his well-to-do father in New England. Then she reflected on her dead

mother, "and the long sleep of grandparents mingling in the dirt." Seeing her father and sisters in the yard, she wondered about her new life; her fiance had promised her a home, a place where she could sit down to an occasional rest. She regretted that she hadn't "asked him to explain more . . . But she was impatient. Impatient to be done with sewing. With doing everything for three children, alone."

Did she love this man standing next to her? There were, of course, *things* she loved about him—his pride, his sobriety. And she imagined she would "[love] the effort he will make to redo her into what he truly wants." But what did *she* want? Only "to live for once," something she'd never, ever done.

Let him speak now or forever hold his peace . . .
"The rest she does not hear . . . " Suddenly Roselily felt "a kiss, passionate, rousing, within the general pandemonium." And as the townspeople lined up to congratulate them, her new husband stood apart. He knew he was different; he was not a Christian. But he will take his bride to Chicago. "Her husband's hand is like the clasp of an iron gate. People congratulate."

Adventures of the Dread Sisters
by Alexis de Veaux

We crossing The Brooklyn Bridge. Traffic is slow going.
The Dread Sisters were on their way to Manhattan, trying to be on time for the "Rally Against Government Trucks Hauling Nuclear Waste Through Harlem." They were going to protest, even though for over a week they had been told that there was nothing to worry about. The girl reflected about this: *I might be only 15 but even I know ain't nothing safe. Not on no city street. Anything could happen. So I don't believe nothing the government says.*

Nigeria didn't like being late. Toni, another of the sisters, had refused to come along. She was in high school and boy crazy—and besides, she never could wake up before noon on a Saturday. Now the girl's mind again turned to their mission: *Nigeria and me, we call ourselves The Dread Sisters. We're not real sisters . . . But she raised me. So we are definite family.*

Dreadlocks trailed down the backs of both Dread Sisters, like African women shown in text books. Nigeria, in fact—like a carved African sculpture with a red leather Nefertiti-shaped crown—looked as if she stepped right out of one of the photos. She was a painter, who used to work on Atlantic City's boardwalk, drawing charcoal portraits. She still had the crisp 20-dollar bill she got for her painting of an old black lady dressed in black. The picture captured the woman's essence. That was in 1967, the year Langston Hughes died.

Now the wind was picking up; the girls shivered. They would never make it on time. Suddenly Nigeria jumped out of the car. "If you can't get to the rally when it starts," she bellowed, "start the rally wherever you are." And the Dread Sisters each took a lane, passing out anti-nuclear waste transport flyers to stranded motorists on Brooklyn Bridge.

THE SHORT STORIES OF JOHN CHEEVER

(taken from *The Short Stories of John Cheever*, Alfred A. Knopf, New York, N.Y., 1978, and *Yale Review*, 1937)

A writer for most of his seventy years, John Cheever (1912-1982) was insatiably fascinated by the dynamics of human relationships and the unique responses of ordinary individuals to the shifting entanglements of life. The following three stories, originally published in magazines as part of a series, illustrate in part the breadth of his interest and style.

The Brothers

When Tom was seventeen and his brother Kenneth was twenty, their parents had finally ended their bitter and hate-filled marriage. Now, four years later, the brothers still turned primarily to each other for love and support, and did most of their socializing together. Among their joint acquaintances was a vivacious matron named Amy, who, in a gesture of maternal warmth, extended a standing invitation for the brothers to visit her and her adolescent daughter Jane at their New England farm.

Late one Saturday afternoon the brothers arrived at the farmhouse. Amy greeted them happily and made small talk while they waited for Jane to return from riding her mare. Just in time for dinner, Jane finally came in—and immediately began to flirt with Kenneth. But the older boy seemed to be totally indifferent to her, preferring to converse with Tom instead. Tom noticed that Jane was stung by the rejection, and wondered what, if anything, he should do.

That night after dinner, the young people went for a drive. When they returned, Tom dropped Jane and Kenneth at the door while he parked the car in the barn; and when he entered the house and found the pair chatting on the couch, he silently crept upstairs to bed. Kenneth ignored Jane's gentle urging to stay and get better acquainted, and followed his brother up the staircase.

When Kenneth came into the bedroom, he chattered happily on and on about the brothers' upcoming trip to Canada. Sensing the excitement in his brother's voice as he spoke of the skiing and fishing they would do, Tom said nothing, although he began to feel concerned. "It was the first time it had occurred to [him] that their devotion to each other might be stronger than their love of any girl, or even than their love of the world."

The next morning, Tom awoke early and rowed a dinghy far up the Merrimack River, hoping to force Kenneth to pay some attention to Jane; instead, he found Kenneth waiting for him at the landing when he returned. Later that afternoon, Kenneth pried himself into a conversation with Tom about cars and barely acknowledged Jane's presence. She was seething with jealousy, but tried one last time to procure the older brother's attention. "Want to go for a walk with me, Kenneth?" she asked. Kenneth merely turned to Tom and asked if the younger boy wanted to join them. When Tom said no, Kenneth also declined. Jane, fed up, disappeared into the barn; she did not return until after nightfall, when the brothers had started back to the city.

Tom now knew he had to go away—not only for Kenneth's sake but for his own. On the night after their return from the farm, he caught a bus to New York City, claiming that he had to find work. Eventually, Kenneth realized why Tom had left, and decided to return to Amy's farm the next weekend. But now Jane showed no interest in him whatsoever. Kenneth wandered pensively into the cornfields. He and his brother, he mused, "had tried to give their lives some meaning and order, and for love of the same world that had driven them together, they had to separate. He walked through the fields clutching involuntarily at the air, as if something were slipping from his grasp, and searching and looking around him like a stranger at the new, strange, vivid world."

The Bella Lingua

Wilson Streeter, an American expatriate living in Rome, was struggling to learn Italian. His "sense of being an outsider would change, he thought, when he knew the language." His teacher was Kate Dresser, another American expatriate. The death of her husband, an officer with the foreign service, had left her with an adolescent son, Charlie, to support. By teaching Italian, doing translations, and dubbing English dialogue into old Italian movies, she was able to eke out a living without help from their relatives in Krasbie, Iowa.

Wilson met with Kate on Tuesdays, Fridays and Sundays, and began to move quickly through the nuances of Italian. After he finished studying the classic *Pinocchio*, he started on *I Promessi Sposi*, and planned to finish up the course with Dante's *Divine Comedy*.

One day Wilson's teacher asked him to come by on Thursday to do her an unspecified favor. Not until he arrived did Kate explain: "My father's brother—my Uncle George—is coming, to try and take Charlie home. I don't know what to do. I don't know what I can do. But I would appreciate it if there was a man here."

Wilson had known that there was tension between Charlie and his mother; now he understood why. Kate had easily embraced her adopted culture, while Charlie had done everything he could to preserve his identity as an American. He dressed in jeans and a leather jacket, and refused to learn Italian. Uncle George's arrival was sure to change the balance of power between them and give Charlie the upper hand; Kate wanted moral support from another expatriate. Good enough; he would help her out.

Uncle George's trip to Rome via Naples had done nothing to give him a positive impression of Italy. To celebrate his first vacation in forty-three years, he had signed up for one of those ill-conceived bus tours favored by blue-haired old women wearing costume jewelry. Lamentably, few of the natives had shown him the courtesy of speaking English. Then in some small nameless town, thieves had overpowered him and stolen his wallet. Not surprisingly, when Uncle George's bus finally pulled into Rome, he found it to be a rather ugly city, filled with "trolley cars and cut-rate furniture stores and torn-up streets and the sort of apartment houses that nobody ever really wants to live in."

When Wilson arrived at Kate's *sala* at seven, Uncle George had not yet appeared. As usual, Charlie showed up in his customary "American uniform"—tight jeans with upturned cuffs, pink shirt and loafers—and went on incessantly about baseball.

When at last Uncle George appeared at the door, he looked at Wilson and asked hopefully, "Speaka da English?" Wilson answered dryly, "I'm an American"—whereupon Uncle George launched into a diatribe on Italian culture: "All I see is statues of men without any clothes on . . ." Soon turning to his niece, he cut straight to the point: "The boat sails on Saturday, Katie, and I want you and the boy to come home with me." A heated discussion followed, which did nothing but reconfirm that while Charlie wanted to go with him, Kate insisted on staying in Italy. She countermanded each of Uncle George's arguments, replying, "No nice friends, no kitchen, no garden, no shower bath or anything else will keep me from wanting to see the world and the different people who live in it." Softly, she added, "You'll miss Italy, Charlie." The embrace between mother and son was one of goodbye.

At Wilson's next Italian lesson, he noticed that Kate's *sala* seemed bigger somehow; he rightly concluded that Charlie and his gear were gone. At the end of the lesson, Kate made no mention of her son nor of Uncle George; she simply complimented Wilson on his progress and reminded him to buy a copy of *Divine Comedy* for the next week.

The World of Apples

Asa Bascomb, aging American poet laureate, wandered through his villa in Monte Carbone, Italy, swatting flies and ruminating over the fact that he had not yet received the Nobel Prize. The flies notwithstanding, Asa preferred Italy to the States. On Fifth Avenue in New York, strangers were continually stopping him for autographs; in Italy he could lead a quieter, more peaceful existence and write without interruption.

But Asa was perturbed by something else now: his dreams had become blatantly obscene. Earlier in the spring, he had accidentally stumbled upon a couple making romantic overtures in the woods above his home. When he returned to work, the sight of the couple dominated his thoughts—and his mental images of their ecstasy were obstructing his creative energies.

As time passed, he found himself producing work that was increasingly banal and mediocre, such as the ballad of "The Fart That Saved Athens"—which he crumpled up and burned in the stove. The next morning he could come up with nothing better than a lurid tale which he called "The Confessions of a Public School Headmaster." To top things off, that same

afternoon fourteen students from the University of Rome appeared at his villa and, in a chorus of adulation, began chanting "The Orchards of Heaven," the opening sonnet from his latest book, *The World of Apples*. Asa was embarrassed by the praise, especially when he thought of his morning's work on the salacious adventures of the schoolmaster.

Inexplicably, the hapless laureate now seemed fixated in the course of a pornographer. In ten days, he wrote the most ribald stories: "The Confessions of a Lady's Maid," "The Baseball Player's Honeymoon," "A Night in the Park," and some sixty dirty limericks, all of which he burned. A trip to Rome even failed to clear his head. He returned to his villa only seeking to take comfort in the works of Petronius and Juvenal, so full of sexual merriment. But then, those poets were classicists; their works did not inspire the guilt that writing his own poems did.

Ultimately, Asa grew desperate, and climbed to the church at the top of Monte Giordano to offer such prayers as he knew: "God bless Walt Whitman. God bless Hart Crane," he prayed, hoping this would invoke his muses. "God bless Dylan Thomas. God bless William Faulkner, Scott Fitzgerald, and especially Ernest Hemingway." When daylight faded, he spent the night at a nearby inn.

The next morning, Asa walked down from Monte Giordano past a mountain pool. There he discreetly watched as an old man undressed, bathed in the cold mountain water, and innocently played in the small waterfall that fed the pool. After his bath, the old man dressed and left, and Asa, too felt cleansed somehow. He remembered a similar incident involving his own father that had occurred when he was child. Now in a rite of emulation he stepped, naked, into the torrent of water, and bellowed the way his father had. And "when he stepped away from the water he seemed at last to be himself."

Asa returned triumphant to Monte Carbone. "In the morning he began a long poem on the inalienable dignity of light and air that, while it would not get him the Nobel Prize, would grace the last months of his life."

Commentary:

John Cheever is considered a virtuoso of characterization. The people in his stories are a unique blend of individual glory and idiosyncrasy: an old writer purges himself of his vices through a self-styled rite of self-baptism; a woman decides to move on with her life and away from her American roots, even at the price of losing her son; two grown brothers cling to one another at the expense of their individuality—until they must part to grow any further.

Many of Cheever's characters feel a compelling need for rebirth. The innate desire human beings have for some sort of cleansing or baptism is universal; Cheever uses a variety of devices to symbolize his characters' personal awakenings—and perhaps, vicariously, our own.

LONG DAY'S JOURNEY INTO NIGHT

by
Eugene O'Neill
(1888-1953)

Type of work: Tragic autobiographical drama
Setting: New England; August, 1912
Principal characters:
  James Tyrone, a handsome 65-year-old actor
    of Irish descent
  Mary Tyrone, his wife
  Jamie Tyrone, their 33-year-old son
  Edmund Tyrone, their younger, more fragile
    son of 23

Play Overview:

After breakfast, Tyrone placed his arm around his wife and led her into the living room of their summer home. "You're a fine armful now, Mary, with those twenty pounds you've gained." Still quite attractive, Mary did not mind her husband's teasing. "You were snoring so hard," she quipped affectionately, referring to the night before, "I couldn't tell which was the foghorn."

Then their two sons came into the room, and the conversation—as it so often did in the Tyrone home—turned ugly. Tyrone himself started things out by chiding Jamie, the older son, for his spendthrift ways. "Let's forget it," said the younger brother Edmund, nervously sensing Jamie's rising defense. Gaunt and sallow, Edmund was easily exhausted by these family arguments. "Yes, forget! Forget everything and face nothing!" their father retorted angrily.

Later, after Mary and Edmund had left the room, Jamie seized the opportunity to ask his father about Edmund's condition. Was it consumption? It might be, Tyrone answered; the doctor would soon let them know. Hearing this, Jamie snapped, "It might never have happened if you'd sent him to a real doctor when he first got sick." And indeed, in a typical bid to save money, Tyrone had sent Edmund to see Dr. Hardy, a local practitioner who only charged a dollar per visit.

Adding to Jamie's foul mood that morning was the fact that he had begun to suspect the source of his mother's recent edginess. Ever since giving birth to Edmund, she had been a morphine addict, trapped in an endless cycle of withdrawal and relapse. Surely it was some "cheap quack like Hardy" who had been responsible for hooking her on pain killers in the first place.

As Tyrone and Jamie stepped out onto the front porch together, Mary sank into a chair and waited for Edmund, her special pet, to reappear. When he came downstairs, she complained about how lonely she felt; furthermore, she said, it disturbed her that her family seemed to suspect another drug relapse. "I've been so worried ever since you've been sick," she told her frail son. Consoling his mother, Edmund promised her that he would soon recover, and encouraged her to take a nap.

The morning wore on. Toward noon, Jamie and Edmund sat drinking, waiting for lunch to be served. "Why did you leave her alone so long?" Jamie railed at his brother. It was true; Mary had spent much of the morning alone upstairs.

Edmund hadn't checked on her because he didn't want to confirm her fears that the family was "spying on her."

Suddenly the brothers heard their mother's footsteps on the stairway. Mary shuffled into the living room "as if she were . . . withdrawn from her words and actions." And she certainly was not pleased to see Edmund drinking. "Don't you know it's the worst thing?" she scolded. Then, when Tyrone entered the room, she erupted: "You're to blame! . . . How could you let him?" A moment later she excused herself—but by then it was clear that she was totally out of control.

After lunch, Mary's tirade took up where it had left off. Why had Tyrone insisted on sending Edmund to Dr. Hardy? "Because he's cheap," she sneered. "When you're in agony and half insane, he sits and holds your hand and delivers sermons on willpower!"

Edmund himself, meanwhile, had gone upstairs to dress for his doctor's appointment while his father spoke with the doctor over the phone. "He's got consumption," Tyrone confided to Jamie as he hung up.

In impotent fury, Jamie stormed upstairs. A moment later, Mary drifted back into the room, looking even more detached than before. Embracing his wife, Tyrone implored her: "Dear Mary! For the love of God, for my sake, and the boys' sake and your own, won't you stop now?" But Mary was now dallying dreamily in the past: how happy she had been as a young girl in the convent school, she remembered; and how miserable she had felt when Eugene, her second child, died—a death she still half-consciously blamed on Jamie, whose measles had infected the infant.

And now as Edmund—her beloved Edmund—appeared to ask for carfare, Mary only stared vacantly out the window. Finally, Edmund steeled himself to approach his father. To his amazement, the tight-fisted Tyrone handed him much more money than he had requested. "Did Doc Hardy tell you I'm going to die?" Edmund snorted sarcastically.

"I won't have it!" Mary rose up with a frenzied howl. "Saying you're going to die!" Not in the mood for another outburst, Tyrone got up and left the room. And when her boys finally drove away for Edmund's appointment, Mary watched them go. "Mother of God," she wondered, "why do I feel so lonely?"

Afternoon settled around the Tyrone house in heavy gray folds. "How thick the fog is," Mary remarked to her servant Cathleen. "I wish it was always that way." For some time now, Mary had been secretly plying the girl with her husband's liquor in exchange for weekly trips to the pharmacy to buy morphine. The medicine controlled the pain of her rheumatism, as she now pointedly reminded Cathleen. "So maimed and crippled!" she moaned, looking down at her hands. Her eyes shining "with unnatural brilliance," Mary then began to regale the maid—who was quite tipsy herself by now—with tales from the past. In the convent school, Mary had wanted to become a concert pianist; instead, she had married Tyrone, a "great matinee idol" at the time. "Women used to wait at the stage door just to see him come out," she reminded herself, half tearful and half exultant. Then she sighed, "You were much happier before you knew he existed." And as these words seared through the walls of her cocoon, the woman started to pray: "Hail Mary . . ." she quavered—but she could not continue. "Do you expect the Virgin Mary to be fooled by a lying dope fiend reciting!" she taunted.

After Edmund returned from Dr. Hardy's office, Mary, fueled by the sight of her ailing son, lashed out at her husband. Night after night, she accused, he had left her alone in "ugly hotel rooms" to go out drinking. "Can't you forget it—?" Tyrone begged. "No, dear," she told him. "But I always forgive"; and, again caught up in her idyllic vision of the past, she strayed onto the subject of her wedding gown.

"I've got to go to a sanitarium," Edmund finally blurted out. "No, I won't have it!" Mary shot back, stunned briefly into reality. At last, in a burst of pent-up rage, Edmund screamed at his "dope fiend" of a mother. Though he immediately apologized, Mary refused to be comforted, and Edmund ran from the house. After gazing for a long while out the window, Mary turned to Tyrone and said, "I hope sometime, without meaning it, I take an overdose."

It was close to midnight when Edmund returned home. Mary was upstairs; Jamie was still out. "I'm glad you've come, lad," said Tyrone drunkenly. "I've been damned lonely." By now every bit as intoxicated as his father, Edmund stumbled over a hatstand and cursed Tyrone for being too cheap to turn on the lights—triggering yet another argument: Edmund was a "good-for-nothing"—like his brother, ranted their father. Tyrone's stinginess was to blame for Mary's addiction, Edmund countered. "You lie again!" Tyrone retaliated. " . . . if you hadn't been born—" Then he stopped mid-sentence. The fleeting mention of this thought had stricken and sobered them both.

For a while son and father passed the time talking and playing cards. However, when Edmund learned that his father intended to send him to a state-run sanitarium, another dispute ensued. This time Tyrone surrendered, overcome with worry and remorse. His voice softened. "You can go anywhere you like," he said. "All I care about is to have you get well . . . "

"What ho! What ho!" Jamie's voice, thick with alcohol, came from just outside the door. Tyrone, fearing yet another quarrel with Jamie, retreated to the porch. Tottering into the living room, Jamie poured himself a drink.

The brothers spent the rest of the evening on the verge of tears, alternately arguing and declaring their love for each other. "I love your guts," Jamie sobbed. "I'd do anything for you." Soon, however, he started in again on Edmund: " . . . Just because you've read a lot of highbrow junk, don't think you can fool me! You're an over-grown kid! Mama's baby and Papa's pet! The family White Hope! You've been getting a swelled head lately!" Entirely incoherent by now,

Jamie finally grunted, "Think of me as dead"— and fell into a fitful doze.

"Thank God he's asleep," Tyrone said, coming back into the room. He poured himself a drink, and scoffingly remarked on what a miserable "drunken hulk" Jamie was. At this, Jamie's eyes opened wide and he let out a string of swear words. The threesome began to argue once again, but, drowsy with drink, they could barely stay awake.

Suddenly the chandelier lights in the adjacent room came on and a tortured version of a Chopin waltz could be heard on the piano. Then, just as abruptly, the sound stopped and Mary appeared in the doorway, dressed in her wedding gown and looking curiously innocent. "The Mad Scene. Enter, Ophelia!" Jamie laughed. The joke, however, was none too funny to Jamie's father. "I'll kick you out into the gutter tomorrow," he threatened, whereupon Jamie began to cry inconsolably.

"Let me see," Mary went on, seemingly oblivious to the anger and anguish that permeated the room. "What did I come here to find?" and again began to mumble something about the Blessed Virgin.

"Mama!" Edmund cried, taking hold of his mother's shoulders, "I've got consumption." Breaking free of his grip, Mary whimpered, "You mustn't try to hold me. It isn't right when I'm hoping to be a nun." Slowly, she meandered back into her reverie, her eyes fading into her own, private dream. "Yes, I remember," she said finally. "I fell in love with James Tyrone and was so happy for a time."

Commentary:

Long Day's Journey Into Night is one of Eugene O'Neill's most popular and powerful plays. O'Neill's unremitting—and at times unforgiving—attention to the four central characters creates an often devastating impact. The deeply troubled members of the Tyrone family can neither tolerate one another nor leave one another alone; self-revelation is their forte, but, tragically, it is revelation without redemption. In contemporary jargon, the Tyrones present all the trappings of a genuinely "dysfunctional" family.

On the stage, characters are graphically defined by contrasts of light and darkness. In one revealing scene, Tyrone begins to grope around the room turning off lights, dimming the stage little by little. Though this is, on one level, an obvious demonstration of his incorrigible miserliness, the audience is also presented with a more symbolic significance: Tyrone suffers an incurable craving for darkness.

As bleak as the play's vision seems, it is no more bleak than the playwright's own early life. Using the first names of his actual family members (with the exception of his mother), O'Neill has evoked the whole tragedy of intimate disconnection with scenes from his own tormented youth as the son of a hard-drinking, tyrannical, once-famous-actor father and a morphine-addict mother. In view of the deep personal agony that went into this drama, it is not surprising that O'Neill decided to name the Tyrones' dead child "Eugene."

THE ACCIDENTAL TOURIST

by Anne Tyler, Alfred A. Knopf, New York, N.Y., 1985

Type of work: Realistic character novel

Setting: Contemporary Baltimore and Paris

Principal characters:
  Macon Leary, a middle-aged author of travel guides
  Sarah Leary, his wife
  Muriel Pritchett, an eccentric young dog trainer

Story Overview:

Macon Leary was startled to learn that his wife wanted a divorce. Sarah calmly informed him that she intended to find a place of her own when they returned home after their vacation, which, like so many other events of the past year, they had been unable to enjoy. Ever since their twelve-year-old son Ethan had been murdered during a hold-up at the Burger Bonanza, the once-exuberant Sarah had become withdrawn and the ever-guarded Macon had turned into an insomniac. Although they both knew that losing a child put "a terrible strain" on a couple—even people like the Learys who had been together for almost twenty years—they were now too depressed to envision a means of saving their marriage.

After Sarah moved out, Macon "marveled at how an empty space could be so full of a person" who was absent; he was not, however, entirely opposed to living alone. Unlike his wife, Macon had countless strategies for getting things done efficiently, such as wearing "tomorrow's underwear" to bed "so he wouldn't have to launder any pajamas."

In addition to being spared Sarah's "lack of method," Macon could now become totally immersed in his work. The author of *The Accidental Tourist* travel guides—designed for business travelers who liked to "pretend that they had never left home"—Macon loved "the virtuous delights of organizing a disorganized country" on paper, "classifying all that remained in neat, terse paragraphs [and] dithering over questions of punctuation."

Unfortunately, Macon hated to travel. So it was only with the greatest effort that he could force himself to prepare for a trip to England shortly after Sarah had left him. As always, he followed the advice he gave in his guide books: *One suit is plenty . . . The suit should be a medium gray. Gray not only hides the dirt; it's handy for sudden funerals . . . Bring only what fits in a carry-on bag. . . . Add several packets of detergent so you won't fall into the hands of foreign laundries.*

Nevertheless, Macon was now confronting a particular problem that had not found its way into *The Accidental Tourist:* how to find someone to care for a temperamental pet. Edward, the Welsh corgi that his son had adored, had become cranky since Ethan's death. Sometimes he even nipped at people—and who wants to dog-sit a nippy, cranky dog? Finally, in desperation, Macon hit upon a solution: the Meow-Bow Animal Hospital.

The receptionist at Meow-Bow, a thin young woman with "aggressively frizzy black hair," surprised Macon by asking, "Can't you leave him at home with your wife?" When Macon explained rather coolly that he was divorced, the woman ignored the snub. "I'm a divorcee myself," she responded. She then went on to introduce herself as Muriel Pritchett.

Upon Macon's return from England, Muriel told him that she and Edward had "just got on like a house afire." In fact, she continued, "He just fell in love with me." Muriel, it so happened, prided herself on being a dog trainer who specialized in dogs that bite, and she was eager—overly eager from Macon's point of view—to train Edward. She was not "some amateur," she assured Macon; she had success with "biters, barkers, deaf dogs, timid dogs," even attack dogs.

"You think it over and call me," she prodded him before he managed to get out the door with Edward in tow. "Or just call for no reason! Call and talk." Macon, of course, who abhorred superfluous conversation of any kind, had no intention of phoning a stranger, least of all one who sported "blackish lipstick" and "preposterously high-heeled sandals." A few days later, however, Muriel called *him*. "I was just wondering how Edward was doing," she said. "I still think he ought to be trained." Macon tried to brush her off, but Muriel jabbered right on. "You and me could have a drink or something," she suggested, or, if he preferred, she would cook Macon dinner. "I think for now I'll try to manage on my own," he said as he hung up.

As it happened, Macon soon found that he could *not* manage. One day, carrying Edward down to the basement—where lately he had begun to feed the dog—he tripped and broke his leg. As a result, he was reluctantly moved back to the house where he had lived as a child so that his younger sister Rose could care for him. Rose already cooked and cleaned for her other two brothers, Porter and Charles, with whom she still shared the house. Perhaps because they had been raised by their grandparents, the Leary children had grown up to be rather stodgy and peculiar. Rose, for example, alphabetized canned goods on the kitchen shelves and painstakingly planned menus. She had certainly never expressed much interest in romance. Consequently, Macon was stunned and embarrassed about the way she fussed over his publisher Julian on the day he dropped by to check up on Macon. He was also shocked by Edward's behavior that day: the dog barked ferociously at Julian; when Macon intervened, the dog snarled and then bit his hand. And so, a few days later, Macon called Muriel.

Naturally, Muriel was delighted that Macon needed her help. "Five or six times a week I'll come out for however long it takes," she told him. And true to her word, she arrived the next day. To Macon's surprise, simply by hissing, clucking her tongue, and gently prodding Edward, Muriel induced the dog to obey. Throughout their session, Muriel yammered on enthusiastically about her family—and even about her hair, which she herself referred to as a "fright wig."

Macon had never met anyone like Muriel. Although he tried to deny it, he became increasingly drawn to her each time they met. Predictably, his family considered the woman to be utterly outlandish. "Imagine a flamenco dancer with galloping consumption," Rose said to Charles and Porter one day. "That's Edward's trainer." Still, Macon marvelled at Muriel's honesty and exuberance. She—unlike Sarah—was an optimist, a survivor who had worked hard to rear her young son and to make something of her life after her husband had walked out on them.

But Muriel's son, Alexander, left Macon feeling uneasy. He was a "small, white, sickly boy with a shaved-looking skull," and despite the fact that he bore no resemblance to Ethan, he nonetheless evoked memories of Macon's own son. In fact, when Muriel invited Macon to her house for dinner, he thought, *"I just can't."*

"I lost my son," Macon eventually blurted out. "I can't go to dinner with people! I can't talk to their little boys!" Silently, Muriel took Macon in her arms and hugged him; a while later, they made love for the first time. That night Macon felt a sense of well-being that he had not experienced since Ethan's death.

Not long afterwards, Macon moved in with Muriel and Alexander. He discovered that despite her endless banter about make-up, cellulite, and thrift stores, Muriel had the uncanny ability to "pierce his mind like a blade." He also began to bond to Alexander: he worried about the boy and wanted to please him; he found himself helping him with homework, buying him pizzas, and taking him shopping for new clothes. Muriel, however, still shell-shocked from her husband's abandonment, began to fear that Macon too would leave. "Oh for pity's sake," he'd say in response.

Still, on the day his sister married Julian Edge, Macon found himself reconsidering his relationship with Muriel. Moreover, talking again with Sarah, who was Rose's matron-of-honor, seemed "so natural," so pleasantly intimate. He had always been a traditionalist, he remembered. He was still a Leary, uncomfortable with flamboyance and change.

To add to his alarm, Macon now realized that Muriel reminded him of his mother Alicia, a "war widow" who had left her young children in the care of her Leary in-laws so that she could enjoy the company of various men. Observing his mother at the wedding standing beside Muriel, Macon had a disturbing thought: "Maybe in his middle age he was starting to choose his mother's style of person, as if concluding that Alicia—silly, vain, annoying woman—might have the right answers after all."

Soon after the wedding, Macon left Muriel—the woman with whom he had planned a trip to Paris and had even discussed marriage—to return to Sarah.

For a while both Sarah and Macon were delighted by the familiarity of their old routines: they bought furniture and flowers and ate at their favorite restaurant. They became increasingly aware, however, that Ethan's death had created a void in their companionship that they were still unable to fill. Before long, Macon called Muriel.

Their strained conversation didn't last long.

Then, embarking on another reluctant European business trip, Macon was astonished to see Muriel suddenly materialize on the plane that was transporting him to Paris. "I called your travel agent," she told the blustering traveler. "You don't own this plane!"

Try as he might, Macon could not avoid Muriel once they landed in Paris. She had booked a room at his hotel and she persisted in inviting him to dinner until he acquiesced. The first night they went to the Burger King on the Champs-Elysees; the next they went to an elegant restaurant. However, when Muriel later asked him to spend the night with her, he declined. Alone in his room, he slept fitfully. Then, when he awoke the next morning, he hurt his back and had to stay in bed all day because of the fierce pain.

Sarah immediately flew to Paris to be with her husband. In addition to bringing him medicine and vowing that she intended to fulfill his business obligations while he was laid up, she announced that they could enjoy a "second honeymoon, sort of." Sarah also told him, rather nonchalantly, that she had run into Muriel. Despite her insistence that she had been unfazed, Sarah could not help asking Macon, "Was the fact that she had a child what attracted you to that woman?" A few moments later, Sarah said evenly, "You could have stopped her if you'd really wanted . . . You could have taken steps."

That night Macon lay awake, thinking. It was true: he had not taken steps very often in his life and it was time to "learn to do things differently." He was packing his bags when Sarah woke up the next morning. "You're going back to that woman," she said. "You'll be one of those mismatched couples no one invites to parties. No one will know what to make of you."

"I'm sorry, Sarah," he sighed, putting his arm around her. "I didn't want to decide this."

Macon walked out of the room, down the stairs, and out of the hotel. Two blocks away, he found a taxi. On his way to the airport, the driver passed the hotel and Macon saw Muriel standing there. *"Arretez!"* he commanded the driver. As the taxi lurched to a halt, he saw a "sudden flash of sunlight" before Muriel opened the door and got in.

Commentary:

Anne Tyler, born in 1941, is a prolific Pulitzer-Prize-winning writer. Acclaimed most frequently for her compassionate depictions of offbeat characters, Tyler has also earned accolades for her imaginative renderings of Baltimore, the city where she has spent much of her adult life.

Baltimore has nourished other notable writers, such as Poe and Mencken; Dickens, however, is the author with whom Tyler shares the greatest affinity. As the writer Joseph Mathewson has noted, Tyler's "writing has a lot of Dickens's humanity . . . as well as a certain lack of fear, which came more easily to his own century than it does, alas, to ours." Truly, fearlessness—as it is so movingly embodied in the character of Muriel—emerges in **The Accidental Tourist** as a necessary prerequisite to happiness and survival.

RABBIT, RUN

by John Updike, Ballantine Books, New York, N.Y., 1960

Type of work: Psychological novel

Setting: Mt. Judge, Pennsylvania; ca. 1960

Principal characters:

Harry "Rabbit" Angstrom, a 26-year-old former high-school basketball star, who now demonstrates kitchen gadgets for the Magipeel Peeler Co.

Janice Angstrom, Rabbit's pregnant wife and mother of their son, Nelson

Marty Tothero, Rabbit's former high-school basketball coach

Ruth Leonard, a prostitute

The Reverend Jack Eccles, a young Episcopal minister who seeks to "heal" Rabbit, but soon finds himself as confused as his protege'

Story Overview:

It was late March, the month when "love makes the air light" and "things start anew." Harry "Rabbit" Angstrom was walking home along the back alleys of Mt. Judge, a suburb of Brewer, when he happened on a group of kids playing basketball. Although he was still dressed in the cocoa-colored suit he'd worn to work that day as a demonstrator for the Magipeel Peeler Company, Rabbit couldn't resist the impulse to show these kids how a "natural" played the game. Indeed, during his junior and senior years of high school Rabbit had broken the county's *B-league* scoring records. "Hey," he called out, taking off his coat, "O.K. if I play?"

Reluctantly, the youngsters chose up sides. As he raced with the kids up and down the asphalt court, Rabbit sank "shots one-handed, two-handed, underhanded, and out of the pivot, jump, and set." Finally, after a while, the kids grew sullen. "O.K.," Rabbit finally said, "the old man's going." Picking up his coat in one hand, "like a letter," he began to run.

When he reached home, he found his seven-months-pregnant wife, Janice, in front of the T.V. set watching the *Mouseketeers*. As often happened in the afternoons, Janice had been drinking Old-fashioneds. "Jesus," her husband told her, "you're a mess." Rabbit, who didn't drink, couldn't help baring his disapproval, even if it meant initiating a quarrel—which, as usual, it did.

When their argument had subsided, Rabbit agreed to retrieve their car, parked at his mother-in-law's house, and to pick up their son Nelson from a friend's house on the way back. Just as he was about to leave, Janice called out to him from the kitchen to ask if he minded buying her a pack of cigarettes while he was out. Squinting down at his faint yellow shadow on the door, Rabbit suddenly felt certain he was about to be caught in some sort of "trap."

It was already dark by the time Rabbit sprinted up to the curb in front of the Springer home. Rather than confront Janice's parents, he ducked into the car and drove off. Still caged by the same stifling sense of claustrophobia, he was suddenly struck by the thought that he never again wanted to see downtown Brewer—"that

flowerpot city" where he worked. An overpowering impulse hammered against his ribs, and Rabbit aimed the car southwest. He would "drive all night, through the dawn through the morning," he decided. Then he would "park on a beach, take off [his] shoes and fall asleep by the Gulf of Mexico."

But after several hours it seemed that the farther he drove into West Virginia away from Pennsylvania, the more the landscape resembled "the country around Mt. Judge." Indeed, if anything, the net of the trap felt "thicker now." Instinctively, Rabbit swung the car around and headed north again, following the radio's "warm-weather reports" back to Brewer.

At dawn, as he approached the outskirts of town, Rabbit stopped at the apartment of his old basketball coach, Marty Tothero; perhaps Tothero could give him a place to sleep—and maybe some advice on how to redeem his crumbling marriage.

Tothero was delighted to see "wonderful Harry Angstrom" again and gladly put him up. But when Rabbit awoke later that afternoon, he discovered that his coach was less interested in advising him on his marital problems than in taking him out to dinner. "Have I got a girl for you!" Tothero smiled. The girl turned out to be Ruth Leonard, a prostitute and Rabbit's prearranged date. "Well," Ruth greeted him when they arrived at the restaurant, "you're a big bunny."

That night Rabbit slept at Ruth's apartment; the next morning he decided to move in with her. "In all the green world," he thought, "nothing feels as good as a woman's good nature." He had, however, two concerns: first, since the car had been a gift from Janice's father, he wanted to leave it for his wife at their apartment; and second, he needed to get his clothes.

Everything went smoothly at first; Rabbit was able to drop off the car and pack his clothes at the apartment without bumping into Janice. As he was leaving, however, he was spotted by Jack Eccles, the young Episcopal minister whom Janice's parents had called in to mediate their daughter's marital problems. Eccles flagged Rabbit down and asked him bluntly if he intended to return to Janice. No, Rabbit replied, he didn't. Then, almost in the attitude of confession, he described his relationship with his wife. It was as if he had been "glued" to their marriage, he said, until it had suddenly occurred to him "how easy it was just to get out . . ." Eccles, realizing it would be unwise to pressure Rabbit further, invited him to play golf the next Tuesday. For some reason, Rabbit accepted.

Tuesday arrived. While the twosome made their way around the golf course, Rabbit explained to Eccles that he felt he was on some sort of "quest." There was "something" out there, he said, gesturing vaguely toward the landscape, "that wants me to find it."

"All vagrants think they're on a quest," the minister replied. Then, since Eccles knew that Rabbit's flight from Brewer had cost him his job with Magipeel, he notified him that Mrs. Smith, a wealthy widow, was looking for a gardener at her estate. Rabbit applied, and easily got the job.

For a time, Rabbit's life seemed idyllic. He delighted in the "simplicity" of planting a garden, a labor he likened to getting "rid of something by giving it to itself." And surprisingly, as his friendship with Reverend Eccles deepened, Rabbit discovered that the man of God had lost his faith; the center of his existence had been shattered. Although Rabbit had never experienced anything remotely comparable to faith, Eccles was now—like him—a man hungering for new meaning and companionship.

Rabbit's ties to Ruth also grew more rooted. As she blithely pointed out to him one day: "You've got Eccles to play golf with every week and to keep your wife from doing anything to you. You've got your flowers, and you've got Mrs. Smith in love with you. You've got me." Later, Rabbit conceded to her that leaving Janice had taught him an "interesting" lesson: "If you have the guts to be yourself, other people'll pay your price."

But after a few months Rabbit's life once more began to sour. First it seemed to him that Ruth, lately, had been "trying to make him feel guilty about something." And then, early one June morning, there was a call for him. "Harry," Eccles told him in muted tones, as though his buried voice were reaching up for Rabbit from beneath the ground, "your wife has started to have the baby."

It was still dark as Rabbit dressed; repeatedly he assured Ruth that it was his duty to go to the hospital. Ruth did not respond. "Hey," he said finally. "If you don't say anything I'm not coming back." Still, Ruth remained silent.

That morning, when little Rebecca June Angstrom was born, Rabbit decided to give his marriage a second chance. And for a brief period after Janice and the baby came home from the hospital, he felt "lucky, blessed, forgiven"—in a state of grace; he even attended services at Eccles' church "to give thanks" for his daughter. "God, Rebecca, thank you," he said as he kneeled, adrift on "the senseless eddies of gladness."

But once again Rabbit's bliss was short-lived. Later that same Sunday night as they lay in bed, he and Janice argued: he wanted to have sex; she, reminding him that she was not yet fully recovered from childbirth, refused. Angry, Rabbit bolted out the door and headed for Ruth's apartment—leaving Janice to drink her misery away.

The next afternoon Janice's mother called. Sensing that something was wrong, she announced over her daughter's protests that she was on her way to the apartment. Janice, by then drunk almost to oblivion, blundered through the house for awhile in a desperate effort to tidy things up. Then she drew a bath for the baby. As she knelt by the tub and placed the child in the water, however, suddenly little Rebecca slipped from her hands and sank "like a grey stone." By the time Janice was able to wrest her daughter from the water, she knew that "the worst thing that has ever happened to any woman in the world [had] happened to her": she had drowned her own daughter.

When Rabbit returned home that evening after a futile search for Ruth, he walked into the nightmare of his daughter's death. Now he began to think that if he and Janice could endure *this* tragedy, their marriage might survive. At Rebecca's funeral, though, it struck him that everyone somehow blamed *him* for what had happened. "Don't look at *me*," he finally said. "I didn't kill her." Then to clarify his own confusion, he pointed at Janice and blurted, "*She's* the one." A sea of faces, "blank with shock," turned toward Janice—and Rabbit whirled around and began to run.

He ended up once again at Ruth's. This time he found her home—with the news that she was pregnant. Rabbit tried to convince her to have the baby. "Will you marry me?" she demanded. When Rabbit replied that he'd "love to," she challenged him to divorce Janice. "If you can't work it out," she said, "I'm dead to you; I'm dead to you and this baby of yours is dead too."

"That's fair," Rabbit, blinded by hope, answered.

Rabbit suddenly felt hungry now; he decided to step out to buy some groceries. "I'll be right back," he told Ruth. But once he got outside, an air of apprehension overtook him. Instead of heading to the market, he turned and began walking in the opposite direction. Then, as he groped with the old indefinable, elusive urge to be free, his junket picked up speed; "his heels hitting heavily on the pavement at first but with an effortless gathering out of a kind of sweet panic growing lighter and quicker and quieter, he runs. Ah: runs. Runs."

Commentary:

Rabbit, Run (1960), the first in a tetralogy of novels which follows with *Rabbit Redux* (1970), the Pulitzer-Prize-winning *Rabbit Is Rich* (1981), and *Rabbit At Rest* (1990), elicited widely divergent critical views. Alfred Kazin, for instance, praised the book for its rich language and its insightful portrayal of a society characterized by "an increasing disbelief in marriage as the foundation of everything." Norman Mailer, in contrast, found Updike's prose deeply flawed, too often filled with "self-indulgent, tortured sentences," and the narrative "routine" and lacking in real moral vision.

Kazin and Mailer did agree, however, on one point: Rabbit's anxious evasions and escapes gradually erode his moral center of gravity, and leave him unable to act decisively. While Eccles agonizes over his own lost moral center, Rabbit, who never had a moral center in the first place, continues to run from his future, hoping to return to the shining past of his carefree, basketball-star high-school self—a past where he was in charge, where he knew how to act and what to do. As a result, his growing need for escape—both from the "trap" of social conventions and institutions (his marriage) and from the price of personal freedom (the assumption of responsibility for his own acts and decisions)—becomes an end in itself. "Running," as the book's title implies, becomes Rabbit's one "moral imperative," the symbolic flight of an escape artist *par excellence*.

THE CANTERBURY TALES

by
Geoffery Chaucer
(c. 1343 - 1400)

Type of work: A series of tales told in verse

Setting: 14th-century England

Principal characters:
Thirty pilgrims on their way to Canterbury, among them:
the Wife of Bath, an earthy, middle-aged woman;
the Friar, "a wanton and merry" priest;
the Franklin, a generous older gentleman; and
the Pardoner, a greedy merchant of supposed "holy relics"

Story Overview:

"When in April the sweet showers fall . . . people long to go . . . from every shire's end of England, down to Canterbury." Thirty pilgrims en route gathered at an inn to rest for the night. Their host, a gracious, merry man, gave them all a great welcome, and as they ate their supper and drank strong wine, he made a proposal: "Each one of you shall help to make things slip by telling two stories on the outward trip to Canterbury . . . and on the homeward way to journey's end another two, tales from the days of old; and then the man whose story is best told, he shall be given a supper paid by all." Readily agreeing to this modest wager, the pilgrims drew straws to determine who would be the first storyteller.

The chivalrous Knight went first, relating the tale of Palamon and Acrite, two Theban cousins who were captured by the armies of the Athenian general Theseus. Imprisoned in a dungeon atop a tower, the cousins stared down longingly at Emily, who graced the garden below. Even though Emily was Theseus' sister-in-law, Palamon and Acrite both instantly fell in love with the beautiful maiden. Although Acrite was ultimately banished and Palamon escaped, both remained enchanted by the woman.

To determine who would win his sister-in-law's hand, Theseus arranged a joust. Palamon then prayed to Venus, the goddess of love, while Acrite prayed to Mars, the god of war. Acrite won. Just as he rode up to accept his prize, however, his horse threw him—and it was with his dying breath that Acrite yielded Emily to Palamon.

After the Knight's noble tale, the Miller followed with a ribald story about an old carpenter and his philandering wife. Everyone laughed at this bawdy anecdote, except the Reeve. Once a carpenter himself, he took offense. So, in retaliation, he launched into a tale about an unscrupulous miller whose wife and daughter were dishonored by two common scholars, a punishment that "comes of the cheating that false miller's do."

When the host heard yet another vulgar tale after the Reeve's, he decided that it was high time to turn the storytelling over to the poet Chaucer. Settling on a didactic tale, Chaucer spoke of a man named Melibee, who, returning from his fields one day, discovered that three of his enemies had killed his daughter and beaten his wife. Melibee vowed revenge. Before he could act, however, his level-headed wife Prudence advised her husband to curb his anger. Ultimately reason won out; Melibee forgave his enemies.

After Chaucer had finished, the Merchant began his tale with some information about himself. As a man who sold "relics," he had become adept at duping his customers. "When the yokels have sat down," he boasted, "I preach and tell a hundred lying mockeries more. The curse of avarice and cupidity is all my sermon. I preach against the very vice I make my living out of—avarice."

Following this confession, the Pardoner began his tale of three revelers who tried to kill Death. One morning after a night of drinking and gambling, the three watched as a coffin was led down the street. One of the revelers asked the tavern-knave to find out who had died. "He was a friend of yours in days of old," the knave reported, "and suddenly, last night, the man was slain, upon his bench, face up, dead drunk again." Then the knave spoke of the murderer: "They call him Death, who kills us all round here, and in a breath he speared him through the heart . . . And then Death went his way without a word. He killed a thousand in the present plague." The three men, much disturbed by this account, raised their hands and vowed that they would "kill this traitor Death."

The men had not traveled far when they came upon an old beggar. After their rough treatment of him, the old man pleaded that death might come. Surely, this old beggar knew where Death cloaked himself, the three reasoned. "If it be your design to find out Death," the man answered them, "turn up this crooked way towards that grove. I left him there today under a tree and there you will find him waiting." The three gentlemen hurried to the tree, where they found a pile of gold coins—and "no longer was it Death those fellows sought."

Soon the youngest went into town to buy food and wine. One of his older companions devised a plan so that the youngest would not share in the fortune: when the youth returned the other two would wrestle him, seemingly in jest. "I'll up and put my dagger through his back," he said, "then you draw your dagger too and do the same. Then all this money will be ours . . . divided equally, of course, dear friend."

Meanwhile, the returning youth entertained similar thoughts. "To think that I might have all that treasure to myself alone," he mused. Hence he settled on poisoning the wine he carried. Entering an apothecary, he said, "Sell me some poison if you will, I have a lot of rats I want to kill." Then, returning with the spiked wine, he entreated his comrades to drink. But without warning "they fell on him and slew him, two to one." Their evil deed done, they sat down, drank the wine and perished.

The Wife of Bath followed this morbid story of duplicity with one about a knight who had raped a virgin. As punishment for this misdeed, he was sent abroad to discover the secret of what women want most. En route, an old crone tricked him into marrying her. And, indeed, after living with the hag for several weeks, the knight finally discovered what women want most: to be loved for themselves. Having heard his marvelous revelation, the ugly old woman was transformed into a beautiful maiden:

> He took her in his arms and gave her kisses
> A thousand times on end; he bathed in blisses.
> And she obeyed him also in full measure
> In everything that tended to his pleasure.

After this happy tale, the Friar told the story of a sly Summoner, a man whose job it was to deliver legal summons for a strict archdeacon, who used information obtained from his spies to extort the guilty and innocent alike.

Once, on his way to blackmail some money from a poor sickly widow, the summoner met a yeoman. As fate would have it, the yeoman was also a summoner in his town; therefore they both thus "swore to be brothers to their dying day." Now the first summoner openly acknowledged having done his dastardly deeds. Upon hearing this confession, the yeoman then made his own confession: he himself was, in fact, an agent of the devil; now he had sufficient evidence to drag the summoner down to Hell. Of course this did not stop the summoner from honoring his vow of fraternity. "You take your share—whatever people give," he said.

The summoner and yeoman proceeded to the widow's cottage, where the summoner made his demands on the poor old woman. She protested that she was too sick to make the journey to a court. And so the summoner struck his deal: if she paid him 12 pence, he assured her, she would be forgiven. "Show kindness to a miserable wretch!" the woman protested. The summoner, however, replied, "If I excuse you, may the devil fetch me off. I'll carry off your frying pan for debt." The old woman shot back, "As for you and your frying pan, the hairiest, blackest devil out of Hell carry you off and take the pan as well." And at these words, the demon yeoman "made a swoop and dragged him, body and soul, to join the troupe in Hell."

None too pleased with the previous account, the Summoner returned the Friar's evocative tale with one of his own—which, in sum, suggested that all friars are doomed to Hell's most repulsive corner.

Soon, the Franklin took his turn, sharing a chivalric story about a knight, his wife, and the man who loved her: "In Brittany, there was a knight enthralled to love who served his lady with his best. He freely gave his promise as a knight that he would never darken her delight . . . ." One day the knight was called off to England, "to seek high deeds of arms of reputation and honour." Though the knight vowed he would be gone for only two years, his poor lady grieved over her husband's absence.

In an effort to cheer her up, the lady's friends one night took her to a dance. There, a handsome squire approached her; it so happened that this "lusty squire" had been in love with her for a very long time, and, seizing the opportunity, he confessed his devotion. The lady, of course, spurned his advances. However, she did relent a bit: Looking out over the nearby rocky cliffs, she said, "I might perhaps vouchsafe to be your love on the day the coast of Brittany are stone by stone cleared of these hateful rocks. I'll love you more than any man on earth."

Time went by and the lady's knight-husband returned home, and she received him warmly. The young squire, however, was terribly discouraged; his beloved's conditions were most difficult to meet. Then one day he made acquaintance with a sorcerer who, if the squire promised to pay him a thousand pounds of gold, would remove the rocks. The deal was made, and the rocks vanished—whereupon the squire went to retrieve his lady. Distressed that the clever squire had somehow met her demands, she confessed to her husband the promise she had made. The knight, being a man of honor, told her that she must keep her word. The squire, however, could not bear to see how unhappy it would make her to leave her husband, and so he released her from her oath. And, when the sorcerer heard this woeful tale, he, too, released the squire from his debt.

Commentary:

Although of middle-class origins, Chaucer was highly esteemed for his intelligence, loyalty and hard work. Widely regarded as an excellent scholar, he served in many diplomatic posts, including an ambassadorship to Italy.

The Canterbury Tales—left unfinished at the time of Chaucer's death and later arranged by scholars—are often rowdy, filled with images of naked buttocks hanging out of windows or of the sounds of thunderous flatulence. Nevertheless his tales also reflect strong Christian morals. Indeed, this diversity of themes—which, over the centuries, has shed some doubt as to Chaucer's sole authorship of his narratives—has served to heighten the fame and impact of his distinctive anecdotes.

In his final retraction of his writings, Chaucer "taketh the maker of this book his leave," humbly saying: *Now pray I to all those who hear this little treatise or read it, that if there be anything in it that pleases them, that they thank our Lord Jesus Christ for it . . . And if there be anything that displeases them, I pray them also that they attribute it to my want of skill, and not to my purpose, which would gladly have said better if I had had skill . . .*

THE LAST DAYS OF POMPEII

by
Edward Bulwer-Lytton
(1803-1873)

Type of work: Historical fiction

Setting: The luxurious city of Pompeii, Italy, at the height of the Roman empire, 79 A.D.

Principal characters:

Glaucus, a young and wealthy Athenian living in Pompeii

Ione, a beautiful young Neapolitan

Apaecides, Ione's secretly religious brother

Arbaces, an evil, shadowy and magical Egyptian who is guardian of Ione and Apaecides

Nydia, a blind and faithful flower girl

Story Overview:

Glaucus, an Athenian of means, and Ione, a Neapolitan beauty new to Pompeii, were deeply in love. Enjoying the leisure that privilege brings, the young couple spent many hours delighting in poetry, song, and intimate conversation. They also took great pleasure in roaming the splendid city arm in arm engaging in marketplace debate with the Pompeiians.

One bright sunny day, Glaucus awoke feeling awed by his good fortune. He dressed quickly and crossed the city towards Ione's dwelling place. On this particular morning, the melodious voice of Nydia, a blind flower girl, called out to Glaucus to buy some flowers. "Ah, Nydia—how you have grown!" answered Glaucus. "Your flowers might come from Flora herself. I renew again my vow to the Graces, that I will wear no other garlands while thy hands can weave me such as these." The young girl trembled beneath her tunic at the sound of his voice. But Glaucus, dazed by his charming Ione, could not see that Nydia was in love with him.

That same day, still another person's ardor received a blow when Arbaces, a sinister Egyptian priest, paid the nymph-like Ione a visit. He had been legal guardian of both Ione and her brother from the time they were orphaned, but he harbored more than a paternal interest in his lovely charge. And seeing Ione so enraptured by Glaucus only served to fuel Arbaces' determination to exercise his influence; somehow he would eliminate the Greek and take Ione for his wife. "She is beautiful, yes, but that is not all . . . " Arbaces thought to himself. "She has a soul worthy to match with mine. She has a genius beyond that of woman—keen—dazzling—bold." The next day Arbaces sent Ione an invitation to dine at his home, situated on the outskirts of Pompeii. Since he was her custodian, she could not refuse.

As the time for Arbaces' dinner arrived, Nydia, who had learned of the invitation and knew the workings of the Egyptian's heart, hastened to alert Glaucus and Apaecides, Ione's brother. The trio stormed into a small shrine behind Arbaces' home, and found a desperate Ione struggling to free herself from the Egyptian's grasp. He had pledged his love and

entreated the terrified Ione to accept it, but she could not love him—she loved only Glaucus.

Now Arbaces whirled around to give full fury to Glaucus. Inasmuch as neither was armed, both fought like uncaged animals, trying to tear out each other's neck. In the heat of combat, Arbaces, clutching a column of the shrine and gazing at the image perched atop, called out for deliverance: "O ancient goddess! Protect thy chosen—proclaim thy vengeance against this thing who with sacrilegious violence profanes thy resting-place and assails thy servant."

Overwhelmed by the Egyptian's incantation, Glaucus slipped and fell to the marble floor, whereupon Arbaces snatched up a knife and sprang forward to slay him. At that awful instant, the floor suddenly shook and convulsed beneath them: a mightier spirit than the Egyptian's goddess had intervened! The earth shuddered once more, and the column supporting Arbaces' esteemed deity came crashing down, gravely wounding him.

Even so, the lovers did not remain free of Arbaces' rancor for long. Julia, a spoiled young woman of noble birth, had for some time coveted the handsome Glaucus. She realized the futility of her desire, however, and implored the recovering Arbaces for a love potion that would turn Glaucus' heart to her. Sensing an opportunity to be rid of his Greek rival, the Egyptian told Julia to visit a powerful witch living at the base of Vesuvius—an ash-born mountain that lay to the south of the city. But before Julia could seek the cave beneath the volcano, the mighty Arbaces made the journey himself, and commanded the much-frightened witch to substitute lethal poison for the elixir. "Let the lover breathe his vows to the Shades," he chortled to himself.

Even as the witch trembled with fear, she spoke thusly: "If instead of that which shall arrest the heart, I give that which shall sear and blast the brain—which shall make him who quaffs it unfit for the uses and career of life—an abject, raving, benighted thing—smiting sense to drivelling—will not thy vengeance be equally sated?" Smiling, Arbaces replied, "Oh, witch! how much brighter is woman's wit, even in vengeance, than ours! How much more exquisite than death is such a doom!"

Julia came to the witch on the following evening. However, the potion she eagerly took away did not last long in her possession. Having suffered terribly for Glaucus' unrequited love, the blind, sweet Nydia substituted water for Julia's potion and pilfered the real "charm" to use in her own cause.

When Nydia gave Glaucus the tainted drink, he took but a sip before a cold pang shot to his heart, followed by a wild dizziness. He let out a shrill, involuntary laugh, then broke into delirious song. Nydia, little understanding what had happened, cried, "Glaucus, oh dear Glaucus, do speak to me!" But her love had already

---

107

passed through the doors and into the streets, raving.

At the same time, Arbaces had by chance met up with Apaecides in a secluded grove by the river. Sensing the young man's wrath toward him, Arbaces spoke in a convincing yet false show of repentance": "Thou art enraged that I would have offered violence to thy sister . . . " and begged the young man's forgiveness. But Apaecides answered, "Egyptian, were even I to consent, my sister loathes the very air thou breathest; nay, I forgive thee not!"

Having spoken his mind, Apaecides turned to leave. In a flash, Arbaces unveiled a knife and plunged it twice into the youth's breast. But despite the secluded location, a man, crouched low in the bushes, had witnessed the callous deed.

A moment later, Glaucus wandered onto the scene. Seeing his opportunity, Arbaces placed the knife in Glaucus' hand and began to shout, "Ho, citizens, oh! help me! A murder, a murder before your very face!" As a result, Glaucus was arrested for the slaying of his betrothed's brother.

By and by, the witness to the crime, a greedy priest named Calenus, approached Arbaces and demanded that the Egyptian pay him to remain silent. Instead of paying him money, Arbaces imprisoned Calenus in a dungeon and left him there to starve. Nydia and Ione were also imprisoned, for Arbaces could not risk leaving the women to testify on Glaucus' behalf. But Nydia, ever resourceful, tricked a domestic into freeing her. She also overheard Calenus relating his woeful tale to another prisoner.

A farcical trial had meanwhile ended with Glaucus' conviction. The condemned man waited serenely in his call to be taken to confront the lion in the Coliseum, and listened to the wild roar of the multitude. Truly these Pompeiians were keen to see Athenian blood spilt! Then a voice rang out: "Glaucus . . . thy time has come. The lion awaits thee."

A murmur rippled through the crowd as Glaucus strode into the arena. Then the lion was released—but the animal, who had been starved for the occasion, only sniffed the air and emitted a mournful groan before creeping back into his den. "How is this?" cried the keeper. "Take the goad, prick him forth, and then close the door of the den."

Then there came an urgent cry: "Remove the Athenian!—Quick! or his blood be on your head!" Haggard from his imprisonment in Arbaces' dungeon, the priest Calenus stood boldly before them. "Arbaces of Egypt is the murderer of Apaecides; these eyes saw him deal the blow. Release the Athenian—he is innocent!"

"It is for this, then, that the lion has spared him," the keeper shouted. "A miracle! a miracle!" Whereupon the people also took up the cry: "A miracle; a miracle! Remove the Athenian—Arbaces to the lion!" The crowd rushed forward to seize the Egyptian, but he brazenly lifted his hand toward the sky: "Behold how the gods protect the guiltless! The fires of the avenging Orcus burst forth against the false witness of my accusers!"

The eyes of the multitude followed the gesture of the Egyptian, and saw a huge cloud shoot from the summit of Vesuvius. There followed a dead silence—and then an anguished roar rang out from the lion's den. At that very moment, the earth delivered a tremendous shake, causing the walls of the amphitheater to quiver. The volcano had erupted. Amidst prayers and shrieks, the throng emptied into the streets.

Glaucus rushed off in search of Ione, but Nydia blindly called Glaucus' name again and again until he answered her cries. Then she revealed Ione's whereabouts. After rescuing his beloved from the Egyptian's house, Glaucus propelled Ione and Nydia through Pompeii's panic-filled streets toward the sea. Masses of Pompeii's citizens bustled about; some were trampled by the mob, while others lay sobbing on the steps of their homes, coughing on the ashes that were spewing from the volcano.

As Vesuvius angrily vomited thick rising columns of smoke and hurled steam and cinders down on the city, day seemed to turn to night. Calenus, still clutching an armload of looted treasures, lay dead amid the bedlam and falling ash. Elsewhere in the doomed city, the lifeless body of Arbaces rested beneath a toppled column, his malevolent magic having finally abandoned him.

Not until the next day did the early-morning sun spread a faint light on the survivors of Pompeii. These fugitives had been carried away from Vesuvius' grasp by a blessed vessel, which now drifted placidly in the harbor. Among them was Nydia, who rose gently, bent over Glaucus and sadly kissed his brow. " . . . She felt for his hand—it was locked in the embrace of Ione; she sighed deeply, and her face darkened . . . 'May the gods bless you, Athenian!' she murmured: 'may you be happy with your beloved one!—may you sometimes remember Nydia! Alas! she is of no further use on earth!'" Then, with hardly a splash, she slipped into the glassy water.

When Glaucus and Ione awoke, they embraced each other joyfully, then searched in vain for the faithful Nydia until they guessed her fate. Then they drew near one another, "forgot their deliverance, and wept as for a departed sister."

Commentary:

No other work could inspire a reader to make a long trek to the dead city of Pompeii as readily as *The Last Days of Pompeii*. Bulwer-Lytton uses the mysterious, sad ruins of a once beautiful city to frame a story about living, breathing, feeling Pompeiians; in a skillful blend of fact and fiction, the reader relives the tragic fate of these people.

The book also forces the reader to think of the casualness through which we lead our daily lives, as well as the shortness of life and the power of nature. It also prompts reflection upon the universal power of the human heart—a heart that beats with the same emotions from generation to generation, and century after century.

THE NAZARENE

by Sholem Asch
(1880-1957)

Type of work: Religious/historical fiction

Setting: 20th-century Poland and Biblical Judea

Principal characters:
  Jochanan, a young Hebrew scholar
  Pan Viadomsky, an aged, classical scholar
  Miriam of Migdal, Mary Magdalene
  Yeshua, Jesus Christ

Commentary:

Though a fervent practitioner of Judaism, all his life Sholem Asch dreamt of writing the story of Jesus, whom he called "the outstanding personality of all time and all history." For thirty years Asch prepared by studying all available information and making frequent visits to the Holy Land.

First published during the Holocaust, the book infuriated many in the Jewish community, who believed that the novel would encourage anti-Semitism. Paradoxically, Asch apparently hoped that *The Nazarene* would actually promote greater understanding between Christians and Jews.

The Nazarene exercises the concept of soul transmigration to bring to life its characters. It paints a vivid portrait of the ancient city of Jerusalem as a fertile cosmopolitan, shackled by Roman rule. Most importantly, it tells the tale of one of history's most enduring figures offered from three separate viewpoints: a Roman official, a troubled disciple, and a young citizen of Jerusalem.

Story Overview:

Pan Viadomsky's reputation was unsettling to Jochanan. Not only had Pan kept company with forgers, but he was also an outspoken anti-Semite. Nonetheless, the young scholar decided to make available his "knowledge of the Hebrew language" to the distinguished Classical academician.

Despite Pan's repugnant disposition and lewd pomposity, he was in possession of a document that Jochanan longed to see and to translate: an ancient Hebrew text from the time of Christ.

Pan, however, did not show Jochanan the prized document for quite some time. Instead, during their first meetings the old scholar simply talked to the young man, making anti-Semitic remarks while teaching him about "the greatness that had been Rome." One cold night, Pan demanded of Jochanan, "Jew, do you not recognize me? . . . I am Cornelius . . . the lieutenant and representative of Pontius Pilate in Jerusalem." Jochanan attributed Pan's words to his "sick imagination"; nevertheless, they left him with an "eerie sensation."

As the days passed, Pan continued to insist that he indeed was "Cornelius, commander of the Antonia Fortress" in Judea, and that he had never before revealed his true identity to any other "contemporary." Moreover, he expected Jochanan to inscribe, "word by word, and letter by letter," the things he, as Cornelius, had witnessed in ancient Judea. To placate the old man, Jochanan took down his words.

In Rome, began the old man, Cornelius had held the "titular rank . . . of Cilarch." As such, he was sent to Jerusalem, where he was responsible for "keeping a restraining hand" on the Jews. While in Jerusalem, Pilate commanded Cornelius to mount the imperial eagle and shields, emblems of Roman authority, in the sacred temple. Infuriated, the Jews attacked the fortress.

Cornelius' soldiers delighted in this chance "to teach the insolent Jews a lesson": the Romans slaughtered them en masse. In desperation, a Jewish High Priest requested an audience with Pontius Pilate. Following the meeting Pilate announced that the Roman insignia would be removed from the temple.

Although Cornelius had "nothing but hatred" for Jewish men, he found the women alluring, especially Miriam of Migdal. He had first met Miriam at a banquet given by the same High Priest who had later bribed Pilate. Observing Miriam from his couch, Cornelius was overcome by her beauty and grace.

In her garden above the city, Miriam often meditated on "the problems of eternity, of the ultimate end of man, and of the purpose of life." It surprised no one, then, when Miriam left to follow this "new visionary," Yeshua.

In a synagogue one Sabbath morning, Yeshua was invited to read from the Torah. To the astonishment of the congregation, Yeshua did not stand, but sat in the Seat of Judgment, as would a king. "I am the bread of life," he began. "He that comes to me shall not hunger . . . . . . I am the good shepherd; the good shepherd lays his life down for his sheep . . . "

Some who witnessed this blasphemous oration were terrified, and thought Yeshua a demon. Yet, he became known throughout Jerusalem as a champion of the poor. Local Jewish authorities were reluctant to punish him, as was the incensed Roman governor Pontius Pilate.

Cornelius first beheld this "wonder-worker" of Galilee while on business in Judea. Afterwards, he could not rid himself of the image of the bearded, slender Yeshua. For weeks Cornelius listened in secret to Yeshua's teachings—to the neglect of his official duties. Yeshua, who associated with the poor and spiritually deprived, however, was different from the many other Jewish holy men, and Cornelius soon found himself "yielding to the man's magic."

Cornelius reminded himself that the charismatic Yeshua was an enemy, who could incite his followers to rebel against Rome. Thus resolved to free himself of Yeshua's influence, he went to warn both Herod and the High Priest of the danger posed by "the prophet of Nazareth."

Cornelius named Judah Ish-Kiriot, as Yeshua's disciple. The High Priest, however, was not interested in this information nor in this petty follower of Israel's newest prophet.

Meanwhile, Judah had been keeping a secret record of Yeshua's teachings which he left "in the tomb cave of Sepphoris, in Galilee." And almost two thousand years later, these writings had mysteriously passed into the hands of Pan Viadomsky.

Jochanan was stunned when Pan finally disclosed that this was the manuscript he wanted translated. As Pan presented him with the "bundle of ancient papyri," the young man's heart pounded with delight. Jochanan could not refuse the opportunity to translate Judah's words.

"It is written," Judah's text began, "Thou shall inquire and seek out and ask diligently." Judah then told about how Yeshua had "called together a great multitude of people on a hill" and fed them with only a few fishes and loaves of bread, and how he and the other disciples had left their wives and children, houses and fields, to follow this Nazarene miracle-worker. Miriam of Migdal had joined them, as well.

"I am a man of unclean lips and evil heart," Judah himself had once lamented. Unlike Miriam, however, Judah, who struck upon a new "messiah" every week but eventually became disappointed in each, remained deeply troubled by Yeshua. Even after Judah had visited Yeshua's mother and had observed "that her eyes were like the Song of Songs," and even after he had seen that Yeshua could calm the Canaanite woman whose grandchild had been sacrificed, he was still racked by doubt.

Unfortunately, just as Yeshua and his disciples approached Jerusalem, Judah's gospel writings broke off. It was as if a "brutal hand" had torn away the final page of the manuscript. Thus, having translated the last of Judah's words, Jochanan brooded endlessly on the life of Yeshua. And, in time, he too became convinced he had a "personal memory" of that ancient era. Pan, recalling his former life as Cornelius, startled Jochanan one night by asking, "Were you not one of the pupils of Nicodemon?"

Now Jochanan surrendered to Pan's invitation, and immersed his entire mind, soul and heart into the past, renewing the narrative, himself now speaking as a student of Nicodemon. Quite vividly, he remembered how he, along with Judah Ish-Kiriot, had been Nicodemon's student, who one day had burst into the professor's home, shouting, "It has begun! The redemption has begun!" Yeshua, who had disappeared into the wilderness for some days, had now emerged radiating the terror of God—even as the prophet Elijah had foretold the King-Messiah would do.

A great crowd had gathered at the city gate, hailing Yeshua king of kings. As the palm-carrying procession steered Yeshua toward the Temple to be crowned, a Roman legion appeared—the escort of the Pilate, the Procurator. This, the faithful Jews reasoned, would be the moment of truth; at last the Messiah would crush Rome's insolent might, inaugurating the Redemption.

But Yeshua only moved out of the way, allowing the Romans to pass. "How astounded, how bitterly disappointed they were," Jochanan lamented. "Not a single miracle did he perform! The heavens were not split, no heavenly hosts descended; everything was as it had been yesterday!"

Now Judah was desperate. His Messiah had betrayed him; he had foretold that Israel's temples would one day be utterly defiled, that great wars would follow, that when the sun no longer shone,

only then would the Son of Man return in glory. Judah wept bitterly, and begged Nicodemon to explain why he must wait for the ultimate deliverance of the Jews. Rabbi Nicodemon answered that Yeshua had come into the world to save, not the Jews, but the gentiles, the stray sheep of the world. Judah rushed out, unable to hold back his biting malice.

Later, still in his former life, Jochanan had been horrified to see the prophet Yeshua's "pallid face, marked with streamlets of blood," and to hear the prophet's "single cry to God" in the Garden of Gethsemane.

The following day, Yeshua was taken captive by the Romans. Cornelius, who headed the detachment, admitted that Judah had divulged his master's whereabouts for money.

Despite Nicodemon's compelling defense, the Jewish high priests ruled that Yeshua's fate lay in Pilate's hands.

Now, according to custom, Pilate was given authority to release one of his prisoners. But rather than free Yeshua, whom he found innocent of insurrection, he left the decision up to the people—who chose to discharge Abba, the leader of the armed rebels. Looking at Yeshua for the last time, Pilate issued a command to his guards: "Go! Deliver this man to the soldiers. Lash him and crucify him! Crown him the King of the Jews!"

Pilate's instructions were carried out. Later, the body of Judah Ish-Kiriot was found outside Jerusalem, hanged by his own hand. And after Yeshua had "died in sanctity and purity" on the cross, Jochanan had been one of the men who had lifted him off and placed him on the back of Nicodemon so that the nails could be withdrawn from his feet.

Hearing Jochanan's account, Pan now intoned, "He laid upon me the curse of [eternal] being." Indeed, as Cornelius, he had orchestrated Yeshua's arrest and, afterwards, had taunted the prophet, "If you are the King of the Jews, come to your own help."

"The last look with which he pierced me," Pan told Jochanan through his tears, "pursues me and is forever with me. . . . When he asked me for water as he hung on the cross I took a sponge dipped in vinegar and lifted it to his lips . . . He moved his lips and I heard these words issued from them: 'From this day on let vinegar be your drink!' I asked him in a jeering voice, though my heart already wept, 'And when will my drink turn to water?' He answered: 'When a tear of mine will fall into it.' [Now] my drink is vinegar . . . and I long for the clear water of the brook."

Pan Viadomsky, not wanting to die with questions still lingering in his mind, now begged Jochanan to tell him what had happened after the crucifixion. His young friend reported that it was rumored throughout Jerusalem that Yeshua had risen from the dead and ascended into heaven. Then Jochanan asked the dying scholar what had become of Cornelius. "I am here today," Pan exhaled.

Now Pan Viadomsky wept openly, unashamed. "Glory to God in heaven . . . God! Have mercy on my sinful soul," he murmured as he surrendered to death, a "blissful expression" etched on his face.

TWO FROM GALILEE

by Marjorie Holmes, Bantam Books, Old Tappan, New Jersey, 1972

Type of work: Biblical novella

Setting: Palestine, shortly before the birth of Jesus Christ

Principal characters:
> *Mary*, a Galilean maiden
> *Joseph*, a young carpenter
> *Hannah and Joachim*, Mary's mother and father
> *Elizabeth*, Hannah's sister, mother of John the Baptist

Commentary:

Two From Galilee dramatizes both the love of God for man and the love of Joseph and Mary—a young betrothed couple living in the land of Palestine—for each other. The New Testament accounts serve as an outline for the story of the pair who were called upon to raise Jesus Christ to adulthood.

When Joseph of Nazareth learned that his betrothed had conceived a child before the consummation of their union, under Jewish law he could have broken his marriage contract—and, in fact, he was encouraged to do so. But Joseph chose to share Mary's life as well as her persecution. His love for Mary—like the love of God for mankind, which according to Christian doctrine inspired the miraculous birth at Bethlehem—would redeem her and reclaim her—"even in her shame."

Story Overview:

Hannah adored her first child Mary, and she was determined that her precious daughter—this chosen girl who carried the blood of the great King David in her veins—should marry into wealth and station. Hannah brought Mary up in truth and love, and as Mary matured into a beautiful and gracious young woman, several young men in the village vied for her attentions. She, however, was interested in only one: Joseph, the handsome young son of a local carpenter, but she did not dare to hope that he would choose her.

Then one day Mary summoned the courage to approach Joseph. "Why haven't you ever been betrothed?" she asked shyly. "Can't you guess?" he smiled. "I'm waiting for you, little Mary." After that, they kept their love a secret between them, a special secret almost too precious to put into words.

Mary's mother, however, knew her daughter too well to be entirely oblivious to this liaison, and she resisted the idea that Joseph, who was six years older than Mary, should think of her daughter as a marriage prospect. "Mary, their Mary, was meant for a finer fate than toiling and bearing children for a poor young carpenter."

Fortunately for Mary, her father Joachim doted on her. She never asked for much, and she was always obedient, so on the day when she came of age and asked that she be betrothed to Joseph, though he knew that Hannah would be furious, he could not find it in his heart to deny her.

Even before their engagement was announced, Joseph began to build the home he and Mary would live in. At night, he worked on the gifts he would present to his bride at the wedding: a sewing box, a pair of doeskin slippers, and a table. And now he found that, even as he worked, "a great silence had come upon him"—a euphoric silence akin to music. "The music within him was too mighty for words, even those of David or Solomon. He could make music only with his hands."

In due time, the couple's betrothal was announced. Some weeks later, Mary went to her family's stable to bring the donkey some water. Bending to her task, she heard a voice call her name. Then a shaft of light descended and within the light she beheld an angelic presence. "Behold," pronounced the angel solemnly, "you will conceive in your womb and bear a son and you shall call his name Jesus . . . He will be great and will be called the Son of the Most High . . . and the Lord God will give to him the throne of his father David, and he will reign over the house of Jacob forever, and of his kingdom there will be no end."

"The Messiah!" Mary gasped. "But I am unworthy . . . How can I be the mother of this long awaited child?" The angel gently replied, "God knows the secrets of his handmaiden's heart. He does not expect perfection. This child that he will send you will be human as well as holy. The Lord God wills it so, in order that man, who is human, can find his way back to God."

"I will strive to be worthy," Mary whispered, her hands still gripping the donkey's fur. Then, suddenly, a dreadful thought occurred to her: What would Joseph and her family think when they learned she was going to bear a child? Fearful of their responses, she delayed telling anyone about the miracle that had transpired until her pregnancy began to show.

Just as she had feared, her father was the only person who embraced the wondrous disclosure that she was the vessel chosen to bear the holy Messiah. Hannah simply presumed the worst: that her daughter had either lost her mind, or, worse still, her virtue. And as for Joseph, his response was one of deep distress and bewilderment; he simply could not comprehend—nor believe—Mary's halting, though sincere, explanation.

Mary herself was now deeply grieved; but then she remembered the angel's second pronouncement: that her mother's sister Elizabeth was also to bear a child of prophecy, a child whose mission was to prepare the way for her own godly son. Thus, to allay her own doubts as well as those of her mother, the troubled young woman traveled to Ain

Karem, where her Aunt Elizabeth lived. When Elizabeth saw Mary, she knew at once why she had come. "Blessed are you among women," she greeted her niece, "and blessed is the fruit of your womb." Then, weeping, Elizabeth knelt and kissed the girl's dusty feet.

"Then you know?" Mary asked. "You already know how it is with me, my aunt?" Elizabeth, overjoyed, answered: "I know. I knew it on the instant that my own child leapt. How is it that I have deserved to be thus visited by the mother of my Lord?"

Mary stood at the door, shaken and dazed. Her aunt had borne witness; Elizabeth believed her. It must be true, then.

Mary spent the next several months with her Aunt Elizabeth and Uncle Zacharias, healing and strengthening her soul. *Now in new ways she heard the voice of God. It roused her at dawn when his seven silver trumpets at the Temple heralded the day's first sacrifice. And every few hours the hills were pierced again by these wild and holy signals for songs and psalms.*

Joseph, tormented both by his own doubts and by the malicious rumors that had begun to spread through the village, awaited Mary's return to Nazareth. Even his usually sympathetic mother suggested that he should break the marriage contract and put Mary aside, as Jewish law prescribed. But though Joseph could not bring himself to accept Mary's wild claim, neither could he bring himself to give her up to disgrace.

To clear his mind, Joseph retired to the solitude of their still unfinished house. After hours of prayer and meditation, sleep began to overcome him. Then, as he rested, sudden-ly *a chill breeze blew through the open door, though a great moon seemed to have risen. A moon whose light was so intense that he must shield his eyes. He half-roused, blinking, his blood racing. For it seemed to him that he was not alone.* "Who is it," he demanded. "Where are you and what do you want?"

Joseph was startled by the sound of his own voice. Then another, heavenly voice spoke to him: "It's all right, Joseph. Fear not. Be calm . . . I am sent to tell you that you must not fear to take Mary for your wife, for that which is conceived in her is indeed of the Holy Spirit, as she has said. She will bear a son, and you shall call his name Jesus, for he will save his people from their sins."

Joseph rubbed his eyes and whispered under his breath, "Don't mock me. Whoever you are, whether from God or the devil, in God's name don't torment me further!"

"But it is true, Joseph," the voice answered, "even as she has told you. Remember the prophecy: `Behold, a virgin shall conceive and bear a son, and his name shall be called Emmanuel.' That prophecy is to be fulfilled, Joseph, son of David. So delay no longer in taking her as your wife. But know her not until she has borne this holy one."

The next morning Joseph prepared to travel to Jerusalem to bring Mary back for their marriage. However, on that very day his father died. It seemed impossible that one heart could hold within it such conflicting emotions as Joseph's now did. Jewish law bound him to stay in Nazareth through the time of mourning, "but he made his plans for the journey even as he grieved for Jacob."

On the last day of Joseph's period of bereavement, Mary returned to Nazareth. Because Joseph had touched his father's dead body, he was prohibited by law from embracing her until the sun had set. Mary had long since conquered her impatience; all that mattered now was that she knew Joseph believed her and wanted her for his wife.

But Hannah, the unhappy mother, was shocked when she learned that Joseph still planned to make Mary his bride. "He's always loved you beyond all reason," she said, almost accusingly. "But Joseph believes! . . . " Mary interceded. "He is not taking me out of kindness to spare me, or even because of his love for me. But only because at last he too believes."

That very night Joseph came to claim Mary as his wife—and they entered together into their new home. Life was not easy for the newlyweds; many of the villagers sought to twist their great and sacred honor into something shameful. Still, the couple found joy in their abiding love, and awe at the holy calling which they shared.

As the time for the birth of Mary's child drew near, word of a decree from the Roman ruler Augustus Caesar reached Nazareth: Rome planned to levy new taxes on the Jews, and had ordered that a census be taken of all the males in Israel. Each man was required to return to his place of birth to be registered and taxed. In Joseph's case, this meant a trip to Bethlehem. Mary chose to make the journey with him, knowing that the child who was to become the Jewish Messiah must be born in that tiny, insignificant city.

As they neared Bethlehem, Mary began to experience the pains of labor. Joseph frantically searched for a private room, but all the inns were full; even the stables were crowded with travelers. Finally an innkeeper took pity on the couple and gave them shelter in some caves he used for storage.

At the caves, Joseph did his best to make things comfortable for Mary. He knew that he had to find a midwife, but he also knew he could not leave his beloved alone. In the end, Joseph was forced to deliver the child himself.

Though it was forbidden for men to witness childbirth, Joseph felt strangely justified in breaking with this tradition, as if it somehow emphasized the reality of a new beginning. He lifted the child up for Mary to see: *And they looked upon him together and marveled at him, his wholeness, infinitely small and red and perfectly formed. And when he squirmed in Joseph's arms and uttered his first cry, the thrill of all mankind ran through both of them, for this was life, human life, and they knew that a miracle had been achieved.*

THE TALISMAN

by
Sir Walter Scott
(1771 - 1832)

Type of work: Historical novel

Setting: Syria; 1191-1192

Principal characters:
Sir Kenneth, a Scottish Crusader
Theodorick of Engaddi, a holy man and mediator
Richard the Lionhearted, King of England
Lady Edith Plantagenet, Richard's cousin
Saladin, the Moslem leader
El Hakim, a physician sent by Saladin to cure Richard
Conrade, Marquis of Montserrat, Captain of the Crusades
The Grand Master of the Knights Templar, another Crusader

Story Overview:

Sir Kenneth, brave knight of the Couchant Leopard, had traveled to Syria to fight in the crusades, and there the Christian leaders had entrusted him to take a message to a local holy man named Engaddi, who served as a mediator between the Christians and the Moslems.

One day as he rode through the desert searching for clues to Engaddi's whereabouts, Sir Kenneth spied the form of a sworn Saracen enemy approaching on horseback. He did not hesitate to accept the infidel's challenge to battle, but after a brief skirmish both men realized that they were evenly matched. "Let there be peace betwixt us," the Saracen generously proposed, to which Kenneth agreed. Thus a friendship was forged between the former enemies, and, learning of Kenneth's mission, the Saracen offered to lead him to Engaddi.

After a long ride, Kenneth and the Saracen arrived at the cavern where Theodorick of Engaddi lived. The holy man received both men graciously, giving them food and drink and beds on which to rest.

But Kenneth hadn't slept long when he was roused again by Engaddi. "Speak not," said the holy one, "but tread lightly and follow me." And to Kenneth's surprise, Engaddi led him through a small iron door in the side of the cavern, up a staircase, and into a magnificent Gothic chapel. There Kenneth knelt before a shrine that contained a large shard of wood reported to be from the actual cross of Christ. While gazing at the sacred relic Kenneth discerned an angelic blend of voices in song, and turned to see a glorious procession of nuns, "beautiful boys," and "noble Christian maidens" entering the chapel.

As the choir filed past, one of the maidens dropped a cluster of roses by the side of the kneeling knight. Although she was veiled, Kenneth immediately recognized the "ruby ring on [her] snow white finger": this was none other than Lady Edith Plantagenet, whom he had long loved—even though as a member of the lesser Scottish nobility Kenneth could never hope to marry her, for Lady Edith was the cousin of Richard the Lionhearted, King of England.

The enraptured knight remained for some time in the chapel, praying and murmuring endearments to his lady; at length, however, he forced himself to leave so that he might relay the crucial message to Engaddi: King Richard, the leader of their crusade, lay gravely ill, and the remaining Christian authorities now sought lasting peace with the Moslems. However, jealous of the English monarch and his sovereign power, they had not informed King Richard of Kenneth's errand.

Engaddi relayed the message to the Moslems, where it seemed to find favor. In fact, as a gesture of good will, the Moslem leader, the honorable Saladin, sent a highly skilled physician, El Hakim, under the escort of Sir Kenneth, to tend to the ailing English monarch. The physician was confident of his powers. Should his remedies fail to cure the king, he promised, he would forfeit his own life. Then, employing a mysterious talisman, an amulet with magical power, Hakim prepared the medicine. Miraculously, soon after the king had quaffed it, his fever began to dwindle. The king offered Hakim payment from the royal coffers, but he would not accept it. Richard thus remained indebted to the humble physician.

King Richard's feelings toward Kenneth, however, were another matter. Knowing all too well that some of his commanders longed to usurp his power in the Holy Land, he was displeased that the knight had naively assisted in arranging a truce without his consent.

Meanwhile, the power struggle within the Christian camp was erupting into open rebellion. Already the Archduke of Austria, refusing to submit to "the grandson of a Norman bastard," had torn down the banner of England and displayed his own in its stead. But the king remained unaware of even more serious threats: Conrade, the Marquis of Montserrat, who intended to conquer parts of Syria for himself, was acting in concert with the Grand Master of the Knights Templar to plot Richard's death.

Thus, as the maddened Richard, still weak from fever, leaped from his bed to go tear down Austria's "paltry rag," suddenly one of his own warriors drew his sword and lunged toward the king. Had it not been for Kenneth, who fended off the blow with his shield, the monarch would surely have perished.

"Valiant Scot," declared Richard, "I owe thee a boon, and I will pay it richly." Then, in accordance with the code of chivalry, the king asked Kenneth to stand guard over the banner of England. This was a high and holy honor indeed. With his beloved hound at his side, Kenneth stood stalwart at his post. But suddenly the dog barked a warning, as a lone dwarf approached—tendering a well-remembered ruby ring along with an urgent petition to visit the lady who had sent it. Sir Kenneth was faced with a grave dilemma: should he hurry to the service of Lady Edith, who owned both his heart and his knightly pledge to protection, or should he stay and guard the banner, the post in which he had pledged his life to maintain? At last the knight spoke: "Let us hasten to obey the commands thou hast brought," he told the dwarf.

Following the dwarf to one of the royal pavilions, the knight was greeted, not by Lady Edith, but by his sovereign's smiling wife, Queen Berengaria, who had summoned him "for an idle frolic." Aghast at the news of this folly, Lady Edith instructed her beloved to keep the ruby ring and to return immediately to his post. But he arrived too late, finding his faithful dog wounded and the English banner gone. Then, suddenly Hakim appeared before him in the moonlight. Kenneth's life was in grave danger, reported the Moslem, and he urged the knight to flee "from the vengeance of Richard to the shadow of Saladin's victorious banner." To his horror, Kenneth also learned that Saladin was planning to create an alliance with Richard by taking Edith as his wife. But even in his profound distress, Kenneth would never consider deserting to the Moslem camp.

As Kenneth had expected, his dismayed sovereign summarily condemned him to a traitor's death for the loss of the English banner. "I have deserted my charge," assented the gallant knight. "When the headsman and block are prepared, the head and trunk are ready to part company." But at the last moment, Hakim reappeared, reminding Richard that he owed him a debt—in fact, "a life"—and asked that Kenneth be spared. "Take this Scot . . . to thy keeping," the king at last responded, and Kenneth was left to Hakim.

Meanwhile, word of Saladin's plan to wed Lady Edith had reached Conrade and the Grand Master. Realizing that the marriage would only increase Richard's power, the king's rivals decided that he must be immediately done away with. Thus, a Turkish dancer was soon brought into the camp—ostensibly to perform. As the dancer spun towards the King, he suddenly drew a poison-tipped dagger and lunged toward Richard—landing instead in the embrace of a vigilant Nubian slave, who quickly struck down the Turk. In this brief struggle, however, the Nubian's arm was pierced by the dancer's deadly dagger—whereupon, to the awe of all onlookers, the chivalrous King himself descended to apply his lips to the wound. With the amulet's power still coursing through Richard's veins, the venom was extracted, and, miraculously, monarch and slave both survived.

Shortly thereafter, the devoted Nubian offered his royal master another service: If all the Christian leaders were made to pass in front of him, averred the slave, then his talismanic powers would enable him to discern which man had stolen the King's banner.

And so the fateful procession was convened. And as the wary leaders paraded before the stern Nubian, not one guessed that in truth it was the blue Scottish eyes of Sir Kenneth which appraised them behind the veiled turban.

At last Conrade approached—and Kenneth's faithful hound, remembering its old injury, let out a furious yelp. "I impeach thee of treason," roared Richard, stepping before the crusader. But Conrade protested vigorously: "I never touched the banner. Thus, at length, the King decreed that the question of Conrade's guilt would be decided in combat with another Christian knight, and that the great Saladin would be invited to judge the contest.

At the appointed hour, Saladin rode up to the pavilion. When Richard went out to meet him, the two men dismounted to "embrace each other as brethren and equals." Then King Richard led his guest to a courtyard where a splendid banquet awaited them. There, Saladin removed his veiled turban. "A miracle—a miracle!" Richard exclaimed: to his utter astonishment, he found himself staring into the eyes of Hakim, his faithful friend and physician. But Richard too had a surprise in store. He now called forth his Nubian slave—to reveal that he had known his true identity all along. Now to the brave Scot the King granted the honor of dueling with Conrade.

This time Kenneth did not disappoint Richard. Locked in mortal combat, Kenneth easily speared his enemy. "I am guilty," confessed the wounded Conrade, "but there are worse traitors in the camp than I." Hearing this, the Grand Master rushed forward to seal the lips of his fellow conspirator with a fatal sword stroke. But Saladin, who had learned of the Grand Master's treachery, raced after him—and summarily lopped off the traitorous Christian's head.

King Richard applauded the Moslem leader's "great act of justice" and proclaimed that he would "lay down [his] gauntlet on behalf of Christendom." Their strife ended, the two leaders assured each other of their abiding good will.

There now remained but one final noble gesture. After leaving the king's camp, Saladin sent Kenneth a wedding gift—his "celebrated talisman." Richard then betrayed a secret: out of fear that Kenneth would be barred from the Crusades, Richard had for years kept hidden his true royal heritage; in truth, Kenneth was "Earl of Huntington, Prince Royal of Scotland"—and as such, he was a fitting groom for Lady Edith.

Unfortunately, the mystical talisman that Saladin had so generously bestowed on the English crown never proved as effective in Europe as it had in Syria.

Commentary:

Educated as a lawyer in 18th-century Edinburgh, young Walter Scott was soon diverted from his work at the bar by his lifelong intrigue with the literature, history, and trappings of the age of chivalry. His special interest was the Crusades—the centuries-long series of medieval Christian Holy Wars *founded [both] on the spirit of chivalry, and on the restless and intolerant zeal . . . blended by the Churchman with the military establishment.*

In *The Talisman,* as in the Waverley novels and many of his other works, these chivalric themes are artfully intertwined with Scott's staunch pride in his own Scottish heritage and history and with the gothic aura of the early romantic period in which he was actually writing, to produce an unforgettable arabesque of adventure.

In 1820, Sir Walter Scott was made a baronet in recognition of his rousing and prolific contributions to British literature.

THE SHORT STORIES OF O. HENRY

(taken from *Collected Stories of O. Henry,* Crown Publishers, New York, N.Y., 1979

Commentary:

O. Henry—the pseudonym of William Sidney Porter—was born in Greensboro, North Carolina in 1862. Trained as a pharmacist in his uncle's drug store, at age 20 Porter left home and went to Texas, where, for several years, he supported himself by working a string of itinerant jobs. In 1887, he moved to Austin where he met and married Athol Estes Roach. It was here that Porter found a job with the First National Bank of Texas, a job which eventually led to his being charged with having embezzled $5000.

Porter, rather than stand trial, fled the country and ended up in Honduras, where, apparently, he hoped to establish himself and then send for his family. In the interim, however, his wife contracted tuberculosis, and so, in 1897, he returned to the States and was arrested. His wife died, and shortly thereafter Porter began a five-year sentence in the Ohio State Penitentiary. It was while in prison, one story goes, that he adopted his pseudonym, after the prison's warden, Orrin Henry.

Porter served three years and was released in 1901. In 1903, he moved from Pittsburgh to New York, and it was here—in the "rush and throb of real life"—that he enjoyed his most productive years as a writer. In the tradition of Bret Harte—whose gold camp stories had mythologized the California frontier of the 1850s—Porter's stories of turn-of-the-century New York sought to ennoble the struggle of immigrants to survive, perhaps enrich themselves on the economic margins of urban society. It is in this context, and employing Harte's device of the so-called "trick ending," that these stories come to us.

The Furnished Room

The unending stream of residents in the "red brick district of the lower west side" was as ephemeral as time itself. There, among the decaying red mansions of an earlier era, the newly-arrived immigrants and transients of the city could find, for a modest weekly rate, a furnished room in which to live. Thus, as a result of having been host to a thousand dwellers, each of the district's houses had accumulated its own ghosts, its own "tales to tell."

One night a young man set his bag down on the steps of one of these houses—the twelfth he had been to that evening—and, "wiping the dust from his hatband and forehead," rang the bell. "Come in," said the housekeeper when asked if she had a room. "I have the third floor, back, vacant since a week back."

He followed her upstairs and down a long lichen-colored carpeted hallway and pushed open a door. "It's a nice room," she said. "It ain't often vacant." Then she pointed out its amenities, which included a large closet and cooking gas, and recalled that its most

recent occupants—a vaudeville team—had been happy there that summer. "Do you have many theatrical people rooming here?" the young man wanted to know. In particular, he was interested in a "Miss Eloise Vashner"—a stage singer who was "medium height and slender, with reddish, gold hair and a dark mole near her left eyebrow." The housekeeper replied that she didn't know the woman, adding with a shake of the head, "Them stage people have names they change as often as their rooms."

The young man, who in fact loved Miss Vashner, remained convinced that she was living somewhere in New York. Ever "since her disappearance from home" five months earlier, he had searched the city—from the most elegant theaters to the meanest dance halls—and always the answer to his "ceaseless interrogation" had been the "inevitable 'no.'" Now, he was beginning to worry he might never find her in a city that seemed increasingly like a "monstrous quicksand, shifting its particles constantly."

He paid an advance on his room and settled into a chair, listening "while the room, confused in speech as though it were an apartment in Babel, tried to discourse to him of its diverse tenantry." Every mark, it seemed, from the "splattered stain" on the wall to the "chipped and bruised" furniture, was a sign, a signature left by the long procession of tenants who'd preceded him. The young man sat there, "inert," reading these "characters of a cryptograph," when he suddenly detected the "sweet odor of mignonette," the same "odor she had made her own."

"She has been in this room," he breathed, springing to his feet. Suppressing his excitement, he rushed down the hall and knocked on the housekeeper's door, again asking her to recite the names of all those who had occupied the room in the weeks before he had. None, however, fit Miss Vashner's description, and, dejected, he returned to his room. It seemed "dead" now, and the "perfume of mignonette" had disappeared. Staring at the yellow, singing gaslight, he walked over to the bed and began to tear its sheets into strips, which he then stuffed "into every crevice around windows and door." Then, he "turned out the light, turned the gas full on again and laid himself gratefully upon the bed."

The housekeeper sat in her room with a friend. "I rented out the third floor, back, this evening," she said. "And did ye tell him, then?" the friend asked, referring to the girl who had killed herself "wid the gas" there the week before. The housekeeper replied that she hadn't. "Rooms," she said, were "furnished for to rent," and people were likely to "rayjict the rentin' of a room if they be tould a suicide has been after dyin' in the bed of it." Then, in a casual reference to the suicide, the housekeeper observed that the girl would have been considered "handsome"—if it were not "for that mole she a-growin by her left eyebrow."

Brickdust Row

Alexander Blinker was annoyed. His trip to the "North Woods" would have to be postponed a day so that he could meet with his lawyer and sign some documents pertaining to his "lands, tenements, [and] hereditaments."

"Oh, property!" shouted an exasperated Blinker. "Let's have it all at one dose tomorrow," he said to his attorney, Mr. Oldham, "signatures and property and snappy rubber bands and that smelly sealing-wax and all." Oldham glanced at his client and sighed, "I'll try to remember to drop in at eleven tomorrow."

At the unfolding of a hot afternoon, Blinker decided that rather than dine at the Club that night he would go to Coney Island. He caught a cab to a North River pier, stood in line to buy a ticket like everyone else, and then, after being "trampled upon and shoved forward," at last "found himself on the upper deck of the boat staring brazenly at a girl who sat alone upon a camp stool." He hadn't meant to stare; it was just that "the girl was so wonderfully good looking" that he had forgotten his manners.

She, however, was also staring back at him, and as a gust of wind blew up, he grabbed his straw hat and sat down next to her. "How dare you raise your hat to me," she said with a mocking smile. "I didn't," he replied, and then corrected himself. "I didn't know how to keep from it after I saw you."

They talked pleasantly for a while, and in the course of their chat he learned that "she was twenty, and her name was Florence." She trimmed hats, she told him, in a millinery shop, and shared a "furnished room with her best chum Ella."

Soon the boat landed at Coney Island, and before they knew it they were swept ashore on "a great human wave of mad pleasure-seekers." Blinker was disgusted by the "vulgarity" of it all, by the "shrieking" masses of sticky children and insolent youths who, in his view, brutally contradicted "all the tenets of a repression and taste" he'd so carefully cultivated in his life. When he glanced at Florence, however, his impression suddenly changed. She returned his look of repugnance with a "quick smile and upturned, happy eyes, as bright and clear as the water in trout pools." He saw in her eyes, for the first time in his life, the "right" to be happy—a look that humbled him. Now, with Florence on his arm, they joined the "hundred thousand true idealists" and took "everything in, one by one."

At 8:00 that evening they caught the "returning boat and sat, filled with pleasant fatigue, against the rail of the bow, listening to the Italians' fiddle and harp." The morning's anxieties about signatures and property had melted away, and in their place was "Florence," this extraordinary girl whose "name was as pretty as she was."

The boat had just "turned its nose towards its slip" at the pier when it was struck on the side by a steamer, up near the stern. As the boat began to take on water and passengers to panic, Blinker turned to Florence and called out how much he loved her. She smiled and said, "That's what they all say." Blinker could only assure her he was serious and that, because he was rich, he could "make things all right" for her.

"That's what they all say," the girl repeated, as if the words were a refrain in some "little, reckless song." And Blinker, at this second censure, found himself quite disturbed—not only because she didn't believe him but also because she grouped him with an anonymous "they." She was not a "wallflower," she insisted, and she met these men she referred to either "on the boat, sometimes in the park, sometimes on the street." Blinker was even more exasperated that she found "it necessary to pick up every Tom, Dick, and Harry" she met in public. "Why don't you entertain your company in the house where you live?" he asked incredulously.

Florence gazed at him calmly. "If you could see the place where I live," she explained, "you wouldn't ask that. I live in Brickdust Row. They call it that because there's red dust from the bricks crumbling over everything . . . There's no place to receive company. You can't have anybody come to your room. What else is there to do?" she asked him. "A girl has got to meet the men, hasn't she?"

The boat, though severely damaged, managed to dock safely, and Blinker walked Florence to within a block of her home. She thanked him for the pleasant evening, and he, after muttering something in reply, "plunged northward till he found a cab."

The next morning at 11:00, Blinker met with his lawyer. After signing his name at least thirty times, he barked at Oldham that now he wanted to "get to the woods."

Oldham, however, had one piece of business to conclude, having to do with "some buildings, fifteen in number," which, he reminded Blinker, had "new five-year leases to be signed." Blinker's father, Oldham continued, had "contemplated a change in the lease provisions, but never made it. He intended that the parlors of these houses should not be sub-let, but that the tenants should be allowed to use them for reception rooms." Oldham was about to describe the location of the house when "Blinker interrupted him with a loud, discordant laugh."

"Brickdust Row for an even hundred," Blinker guessed. "Do what you want with it," he told Oldham, rising to put on his hat. "Remodel it, burn it, raze it to the ground. But, man, it's too late, I tell you. It's too late."

JAZZ

by Toni Morrison, Alfred A. Knopf, Inc., New York, N.Y., 1992

Type of work: Contemporary lyrical novel

Setting: New York City and rural Virginia; mid 1800s to 1926

Principal characters:
>*Violet Trace*, a thin and attractive fifty-year-old woman
>*Joe Trace*, Violet's handsome husband
>*Dorcas Manfred*, Joe's eighteen-year-old girlfriend
>*Alice Manfred*, Dorcas's aunt
>*Felice*, Dorcas' best friend

Story Overview:

There were actually *two* Violets—or so Violet often thought to herself. There was the Violet whom neighbors had begun to call "Violent" after she'd brandished the knife at Dorcas's funeral. Long before the funeral however, *that* Violet, after suffering a series of miscarriages, had tried to steal another woman's baby. Mostly, though, *that* Violet seethed quietly. At night she would tiptoe into the living room to stare at the photograph of Dorcas. It sometimes confused and worried her to think that she might somehow be falling in love with the dead girl, even though she used "brand-new cuss-words" to curse her husband Joe because he loved Dorcas, too.

The *other* Violet slept with a doll, despite the fact that she was fifty years old. Of course, she had once been strong, "a snappy, determined girl and a hardworking young woman, with the snatch-gossip tongue of a beautician"—the trade that she had taught herself. This second Violet, though less dangerous than the first, was also extremely tenacious. Not only had she obtained a spacious uptown apartment near Lenox Avenue "by sitting out the landlord, haunting his doorway," but *this* Violet had also won the love of Joe Trace.

Joe Trace was, in fact, the only thing Violet had ever won. She had met him when she was seventeen years old, back in the days when she was baling hay in Virginia. She remembered how they "rode all day" in haying time—she and her sisters, and her grandmother True Belle—then "assembled at dawn, ate what was handed out and shared the meadows and the stars with local people who saw no point in going all the way home for five hours sleep."

Despite the hardships, Violet's Grandma True Belle never complained. She had spent her entire life toiling on behalf of other people, first as a slave, then as a laborer, and finally as a surrogate mother to the children of her daughter Rose Dear, who had thrown herself down a well. After Rose Dear's suicide, True Belle had raised her grandchildren, including little Violet, whose mother's death haunted the girl so terribly that it often seemed that "the well sucked [Violet's] sleep."

So it was not surprising that when Joe Trace fell out of a tree one night and landed with a thump on the ground near her sleeping place, Violet "claimed him." The moment she saw him in the moonlight, she determined never to let go of him.

What Violet did not know about Joe Trace was that he, too, was haunted by the ghost of his own lost mother. Raised from infancy by a kind-hearted foster family, Joe had grown up without any knowledge of the birth parents who abandoned him. In fact, he had chosen his own last name to commemorate his unknown origins: his father and mother had "disappeared without a trace."

But Joe had finally learned who his mother was when he casually asked one of his companions about the fiercely deranged woman who haunted the woods—"Wild," as she was known among the locals. What would it take "to kill Wild if they happened on her?" Joe wondered coolly. But his companion had lashed out at him, saying, "Now, learn this: she ain't prey . . . You know that woman is *somebody's* mother and *somebody* ought to take care." As soon as Joe heard these words he had realized that Wild was his birth-mother, and from that moment "Wild was always on his mind." The rest of his life was devoted "to hunting her," to killing the dazed mother who lived in the woods, constantly shaming her son: *Whispering into hibiscus stalks and listening to breathing, he suddenly saw himself pawing around in the dirt for a not just crazy woman who happened to be his mother . . . who orphaned her baby rather than nurse him or coddle him or stay in the house with him. A woman who frightened children, made men sharpen knives, for whom brides left food out (might as well—otherwise she stole it). Leaving traces of her sloven unhousebroken self all over the country.*

Joe became obsessed with Wild. Even after he met Violet, married her, and moved to New York, he could not get his mother out of his mind. Even after he had peddled Cleopatra beauty products in the city for years, he could still not help wishing "he had never been born."

For a while, after Joe turned fifty, it had seemed to him that Dorcas Manfred was a reason to live. At eighteen, "Dorcas should have been prettier than she was"; but even though she "had all the ingredients . . . the hair, the color, the shape," there was something about her that "didn't fit." Dorcas seemed as if she wanted men "to do something scary all the time." Joe, however, failed to see that aspect of her; instead, he saw a frightened young girl, a child whom he thought he could take care of. And there was another side to Dorcas that Joe responded to as well: the girl "knew better than people his own age what that inside nothing was like"; Dorcas filled the nothing in him, "just as he filled it for her." So Joe spoiled Dorcas with gifts: phonograph records, silk stockings, Schrafts chocolates, and scented water, a liquid "in a blue bottle that smelled like a whore." And Dorcas promptly became Joe's "personal sweet—like candy."

Like Joe, Dorcas had been adopted. Her aunt Alice Manfred had taken Dorcas in after her parents died, and Alice had always been worried about the little girl who "went to two funerals in five days and never said a word." Her father had been "stomped to death" during a race-riot and her mother had subsequently been "burnt alive." When Dorcas finally broke down and told Joe Trace about her mother's tragic death, she cried in his arms. At such times, Joe would tell Dorcas things he never would have thought of telling his wife: things such as how he longed to find his mother in the woods, how he wanted to see her "give him a sign, her hand thrust through the leaves, [which] would be enough to say that she knew him to be the one, the son she had . . . and ran away from, but not too far."

Given his attachment to Dorcas, it stunned everyone—especially Joe himself—when he ended her life. After telling him one day that she'd grown tired of him, that he made her "sick"; that if he ever "brought her another bottle of cologne" she would "drink it and die," Dorcas walked out of the room, got on a streetcar, and took up with another man—younger, "tireless and a little cruel." Her new boyfriend never gave "her a present or even thought about it," but she was happier with him than she had been any time before.

Joe was staggered. He could not believe that Dorcas would leave him—abandon him—as his mother once had. Hearing one evening that Dorcas was attending a party, Joe went there, hoping to find her sitting there sad and all alone. Instead, there she was, smiling and dancing in the arms of her new beau. Overcome by pain, Joe raised his gun, took aim, and squeezed the trigger. Because no one in the crowded room was certain just who had killed the girl, Joe was never arrested.

But Violet knew. For a few days she waited, wondering when her husband would come home again. Then, finally, on the day of the funeral, she recalled the knife she used to clean the parrot's beak and claws. Snatching up the knife, Violet rushed out of her apartment and down the street to the church, pushed through the mourners at the funeral, and slashed "the girl's haughty secret face," just as they were preparing to close the casket.

Horrified, the boys and men in the gathering joined to tackle the kicking and growling Violet and throw her out onto the street. The frenzied woman then turned and ran home. As soon as she reached her apartment, she opened the doors to all her caged birds "and set them out the windows to freeze or fly, including the parrot that said, 'I love you.'"

Following Dorcas' death, time seemed to almost stand still for Violet. Joe finally returned home, but in their apartment "a poisoned silence floated through the rooms" as, for each, the memory of the deceased girl persisted. Grief-stricken over what he had done, Joe became sluggish, while Violet grew more and more obsessed with discovering everything she could about her dead rival. Persistently, Violet called on Dorcas's Aunt Alice. And gradually softening to the strange, sad woman who had carved up the face of her niece, Alice finally forgave and befriended her. Eventually Alice even gave Violet a picture of Dorcas.

At night, Joe and Violet frequently tiptoed into the living room to stare at the photograph, which Violet had gently placed on the mantle. "Dorcas? Dorcas," they would take turns saying.

One day Dorcas's friend Felice unexpectedly showed up on their doorstep. The girl had been at the party on the night when Dorcas was murdered. In fact, she had phoned for an ambulance—an ambulance that hadn't arrived until the next morning, Felice explained, "because it was colored people calling it." If the ambulance had arrived that night, Dorcas, who was slowly bleeding to death, would probably have lived.

After Felice's visit, the Traces' lives took a turn for the better. Joe found a new job at a nearby speakeasy called "Paydirt," while Violet cooked for him and tended to the new bird she had bought. Now, they would often crawl into bed after dinner, and Joe would take Violet's hand and "put it on his cheek, his stomach." And Violet would rest her hand there contentedly, as though on "the sunlit rim of a well."

Commentary:

Toni Morrison, born in 1931, is the first woman and the first Afro-American writer to have won both the Pulitzer and Nobel Prizes. Since the publication of her first novel *The Bluest Eye* in 1970, Morrison has captivated readers with her lyrical prose and unforgettable characters, characters who often have been violently uprooted from their families and who spend their lives searching for lost mothers, for the nurturing and security they have never known.

In *Jazz,* as in her earlier works, Morrison powerfully evokes a well-honed sense of Afro-American history for her readers. For her, history achieves its greatest impact when viewed through the filter of individual experience—through "the interior life of . . . a small group of people" who give voice to the collective sufferings of a race. Within this historical context, her characters live, struggle, and ultimately achieve grace.

Time, in Morrison's novels, is cyclical; it is mythical, sacred, a sort of time that defies contemporary notions of progress and linear development. Indeed, Morrison's characters find the strength to survive only insofar as they can integrate their own experiences with those of the past.

Morrison's *Jazz* shifts back and forth between rural, Antebellum Virginia and New York City, shortly after the Armistice. Furthermore, she allows the events of the novel to unfold from the point of view of various characters—including an enigmatic narrator, a strangely insistent anonymous "I" who leads us into the novel's harmonic idioms and compelling rhythms so reminiscent of musical jazz. It is through this anonymous narrator that we gain profound respect for Joe, Violet, and Dorcas. Whatever their transgressions, the narrator reminds us that there is always a hidden reason that must be explored, a context, a complex "state of mind" that must be understood.

SEIZE THE DAY

by Saul Bellow, Viking Press, New York, N.Y., 1956

Type of work: Psychological novel

Setting: New York City; 1950's

Principal characters:
> *Wilhelm Adler*, an emotionally ravaged young man
> *Dr. Adler*, Wilhelm's perfectionist father
> *Margaret*, Wilhelm's ex-wife
> *Olive*, his girlfriend

Commentary:

Saul Bellow's *Seize the Day* chronicles one day in the life of "Tommy" Wilhelm Adler—a day which captures the whole agony of a man's descent into emotional and financial ruin. Though he is already well into middle age when we meet him, Wilhelm is still not free to accept responsibility for his life; forever frozen into his early role as the family failure, he behaves as a helpless, forsaken child, flailing and howling as he slides down into hell.

"I expect help!" wails Wilhelm. But his cries are left unanswered; help is not forthcoming; no kind, wise parent appears to rescue the doomed spiritual orphan. Release and "help" are at last attained only through his own symbolic "death."

As the book's introduction conveys, Wilhelm's "search to affirm his own humanity not only moves the reader through deep pity, but arouses an identification with that search as expressive of what everyone who would come to terms with himself must undergo." At the same time, Bellow raises some probing questions for each of us: Just how much and what kinds of financial, emotional, or spiritual support do parents and children owe to one another? And to what extent does a man's monetary worth determine his inner value?

Story Overview:

Emotional brutality had marked the forty-odd-year relationship between Wilhelm Adler and his father, "Doctor" Adler, the respected diagnostician. Fastidious in both dress and manners, Doctor Adler had a face marked by "a wholesome reddish and almost translucent color, like a ripe apricot. The wrinkles beside his ears were carved deep because the skin conformed so tightly to his bones. With all his might, he was a healthy and fine small old man." The doctor had little tolerance for his son's slothful ways, and, even long years after Wilhelm had reached adulthood, he treated him as if he were a spoiled, messy child. The fact that Doctor Adler insisted upon calling Wilhelm by his childhood nickname, "Wilky," typified the doctor's domination over his son. In fact, whenever he found himself trapped in his father's presence, "Wilky" actually reverted to markedly childlike behavior, stammering and fidgeting uncontrollably.

It was characteristic of Dr. Adler to judge a man on the size of his bank account. As a matter of pride, he often lied to friends about Wilhelm's earnings, pretending that his son—who had recently been laid off from his latest job with a toy manufacturer—was a successful businessman.

Wilhelm's pleas to his father for financial relief, however, were met only with formulated homilies from the doctor's well-rehearsed litany: "There's a poor man with a bone condition which is gradually breaking him up . . . I've learned to keep my sympathy for the real ailments."

That Wilhelm was also "gradually breaking up," not from any physical disease but from a progressive state of financial and spiritual decay, was a reality which Doctor Adler refused to apprehend. To him, only money and medicine—the two palpably useful commodities that he knew and respected—were real. Doctor Adler's only recommendation was that his son undertake hydrotherapy or muscle massage.

And now, as Wilhelm confronted his father with a last desperate plea for money, the doctor's disgust erupted into an irrevocable dismissal: "Go away from me now, it's torture for me to look at you, you slob! . . . You want to make yourself into my cross. But I am not going to pick up a cross. I'll see you dead, Wilky, by Christ, before I let you do that to me."

Wilhelm's estranged wife Margaret also had dismissed him from her conscience. She refused to give him the divorce he asked for, yet still insisted that he "agree to support her and the two children"—despite the fact that he was nearly bankrupt. In addition, she held him solely responsible for everything that had gone wrong with his life: for his unemployment, his sexual impotence, and their family breakup. When he begged for mercy, her reply was immediate and brutal: "How did you imagine it was going to be, big shot? Everything made smooth for you?"

Margaret had even denied Wilhelm the companionship of the family dog. "Four years ago when we broke up I gave her everything—goods, furniture, savings," he remembered bitterly. "I tried to show good will, but I didn't get anywhere. Why when I wanted Scissors . . . she absolutely refused. Not that she cared a damn about the animal . . ."

Margaret's unyielding, unsympathetic spite had spilled over to contaminate Wilhelm's new attachments, too. After his separation, he had fallen madly in love with a girl named Olive who promised to marry him "once he was divorced"—but Margaret would not let him go." Now his romance with Olive had begun to crumble. "When she would get up late on Sunday morning she would wake him almost in tears at being late for Mass. He would try to help her hitch her garters and smooth out her slip and dress and even put on her hat with shaky hands. . . . She got out a block from church to avoid gossip . . . "

Perhaps Wilhelm's pain had really begun as a teen, with the death of his mother. He was, after all, his mother's son; it was from her that he had inherited "sensitive feelings, a soft heart, a brooding nature, a tendency to be confused under pressure."

The doctor's mistreatment of both his wife and son had also made them equal partners in sorrow; they shared the iron bonds of the mutually oppressed. "You were set free when Ma died," Wilhelm once accused his father. "You wanted to forget her . . . "

Though other authority figures in his life had generally ignored him, Wilhelm could recall that his mother had cared enough at least to attempt once to dissuade him from what she considered a "foolish" course of action. On the day he had announced his decision to become an actor, Doctor Adler, ashamed of his son, had literally turned his back on Wilhelm. "Mama was the one who tried to stop me," Wilhelm remembered, pondering the incident, "and we carried on and yelled and pleaded . . . Poor Mother! How I disappointed her."

Declining his mother's appeal that he "go into medicine" with his father, Wilhelm had moved to Hollywood anyway and taken on the name "Tommy Wilhelm"—dropping the searing "Adler." And he had actually been hired a few times, though only as an "extra." (Dr. Adler had often tried to explain his son's new name: "I uphold tradition. He's for the new.")

But "Tommy" had left Hollywood when his "agent" finally shared with him the fact that he was wasting his time trying to be an actor; and since then, his forays into various business ventures had all somehow led into shadowy dead ends. Finally, desperate to earn his father's approval and to meet the support payments demanded by his wife, Wilhelm had invested his last seven hundred dollars in lard futures. His investment partner, Dr. Tamkin, a self-proclaimed psychologist with the mesmerizing gift of persuasion, had promised him huge returns. "I am at my most efficient," Tamkin had boasted with customary exuberance, "When I don't need the fee. When I only love . . . The spiritual compensation is what I look for. Bringing people into . . . the real universe. That's the present moment. The past is no good to us. The future is full of anxiety. Only the present is real—the here and now. Seize the day."

But Wilhelm's association with Dr. Tamkin had proved only one in a long line of disastrous attempts to find nurturance—to be loved and watched over by a sympathetic parent. Once again he had placed his trust—not to mention his money and his fragile psyche—in the wrong hands. Tamkin had

claimed that the "whole secret to this type of speculation is in the alertness. You have to act fast—buy it and sell it: sell it and buy it again. . . . Get to the window and have them wire Chicago at just the right second." Yet when the time came to sell, Tamkin had dawdled—and the golden moment was lost. And then, predictably, the wizard had disappeared, leaving his raving, almost lunatic disciple to search for him in the streets.

"What a creature Tamkin was when he took off his hat!" Wilhelm now marveled in despair. "The indirect light showed the many complexities of his bald skull, his gull's nose, his rather handsome eyebrows, his vain mustache, his deceiver's brown eyes."

In the end, even God the Father had seemed to fail Wilhelm. His petitions to heaven all went unheard or ignored. "Oh, God," he prayed. "Let me out of my trouble. Let me out of my thoughts. For all the time I have wasted I am very sorry. Let me out of this clutch and into a different life. For I am all balled up . . . " But God did not release Wilhelm from his weighty burden of selfhood. No, "the spirit, the peculiar burden of his existence lay upon him like an accretion, a load, a hump. In any moment of quiet when sheer fatigue prevented him from struggling, he was apt to feel this mysterious weight, this growth or collection of nameless things which it was the business of his life to carry about."

Now, jobless and destitute, abandoned by every being whose love he had craved and solicited, Tommy Wilhelm Adler realized that his only hope for relief lay in death. Wandering randomly into the funeral service of a stranger, he gazed enviously down at the figure in the coffin. "The dead man . . . had two large waves of gray hair at the front. But he was not old. His face was long and he had a bony nose, slightly, delicately twisted. His brows were raised as though he had sunk into the final thought. Now at last he was [at] the end of all distractions . . . And by his meditative look Wilhelm was so struck that he could not go away."

Then the funeral music started up—and Wilhelm's moment of epiphany swelled into being. "The flowers and lights fused ecstatically in [his] blind, wet eyes; the heavy sea-like music came to his ears. It poured into him where he had hidden himself in the center of a crowd by the great and happy oblivion of tears. He heard it and sank deeper than sorrow, through torn sobs and cries toward the consummation of his heart's ultimate need." Jolted out of his lonely, vulnerable trajectory into another, more peaceful orbit, he had experienced a catharsis, an annihilation of his faltering former self and an acceptance of himself as a lone, free creature. In a single climactic moment of rebirth, Wilhelm Adler had at last come to terms with his own humanity; at once he found himself resurrected, strengthened, serene, intact, whole.

THE ADVENTURES OF TOM SAWYER

by
Mark Twain
(1835 - 1910)

Type of work: Juvenile adventure novel

Setting: The small town of St. Petersburg in antebellum Missouri

Principal characters:
Tom Sawyer, a ten-year-old boy
Aunt Polly, Tom's guardian
Huckleberry Finn, Tom's best friend
Injun Joe, a half-breed scoundrel
Muff Potter, the town drunk
Becky Thatcher, a girl who captures Tom's interest
The Widow Douglas, an elderly townswoman

Story Overview:

For Tom Sawyer, St. Petersburg was more than a friendly frontier town located on the banks of the Mississippi. It was a place of adventure. A resourceful and scrappy lad, Tom lived with his Aunt Polly, and spent his free time fishing, playing, and trying to avoid school and chores.

One beautiful Saturday afternoon when most boys were at play, Aunt Polly stuck Tom with the task of white-washing her fence. But Tom heard another boy, Ben Rogers, coming down the lane and had an idea. He began to paint with great zeal.

"Say, I'm going in a-swimming I am," Ben crowed. "Don't you wish you could? But of course you'd druther work—wouldn't you?" Tom answered nonchalantly, "What do you call work?"

"Why, ain't *that* work?" Ben asked, referring to the white-washing. "Well, maybe it is, and maybe it ain't," Tom countered. "All I know is, it suits Tom Sawyer." Ben guffawed; surely Tom couldn't "*like*" the task. "Like it?" Tom asked. "Well, I don't see why I oughtn't to like it. Does a boy get a chance to whitewash a fence every day?"

This line of reasoning "put the thing in a whole new light. Ben stopped nibbling his apple . . . 'Say, Tom,' he offered, 'let *me* whitewash a little . . . '" Before long, other children came by and wanted a turn at white-washing. Not only was the fence soon finished, but Tom also had collected many treasures in exchange for the privilege of whitewashing, including Ben's apple, a kite, and a dead rat (and some string to swing it on).

A boy as inventive as Tom had no trouble figuring out how he could attract the attention of sweet Becky Thatcher later that summer. Tom would woo Becky by winning a Bible in a Sunday School contest—and he'd be sure to win by trading marbles and toys for the tickets that the Sunday School superintendent awarded the children each time they memorized a scripture. The superintendent was amazed when Tom, who had recited very little scripture, proudly presented 28 tickets. To Tom's surprise, when he stepped up to claim the Bible, he was asked to give the names of Jesus' first two apostles. The eyes of the whole congregation were fixed upon

him, and although the question was repeated, the boy remained silent. Finally, Tom breathed deeply and almost shouted, "David and Goliath!"

In fact, in all of St. Petersburg there was only one other boy half as high-spirited as Tom: Tom's friend, Huckleberry Finn. The envy of all the boys in town, Huck had no family except for a drunken father, and so could do whatever he pleased. Thus, one night he and Tom stole off to the graveyard to perform a wart-curing spell. When they arrived, they happened upon a frightening scene: Muff Potter, young Doc Robinson, and a local criminal named Injun Joe were digging at a fresh gravesite. The men hoisted up a coffin and opened it.

When the drunken Potter demanded more money from the doctor for helping him secure a cadaver, a fight ensued. Snatching up a knife from the ground, Injun Joe went for Robinson, who had already felled poor Potter with a board. When the doctor spun around, Injun Joe thrust the knife into his chest.

After killing Doc Robinson, Injun Joe placed the knife in Potter's limp hand. Then when the man came to, Injun Joe convinced the bewildered fellow that it had been he who had killed the doctor. "Why, you two was scuffling," he related, "[you] snatched the knife and jammed it into him . . . " Potter sputtered, "It was all on account of the whiskey . . . I never used a weapon in my life . . . " The two men then fled the graveyard.

Terribly shaken, Tom and Huck finally reached safety—and swore that they would never breathe a word of what they had seen. Nobody crossed Injun Joe without paying with his life.

As it happened, the next day the whole town was abuzz about the murder. After one of the townsmen recognized the knife left at the scene as Muff Potter's and Injun Joe had given his statement to the Sheriff, Muff was put in jail to await trial.

Tom, Huck, and a friend named Joe Harper, meanwhile, had decided they wanted to leave town and become pirates. Late one night the three boys set sail on a makeshift raft for Jackson Island. As they spent the next day swimming, fishing, and exploring, it struck them that they had discovered the perfect life—no school, no washing, and no one to tell them what to do.

That afternoon, however, the boys heard the sounds of a cannon and saw a ferryboat approaching. "Somebody's drownded," Tom cried. "It's us!" That night after Joe and Huck fell asleep, Tom quietly left camp and returned to his house. Peering inside, he saw his Aunt Polly, his sister Mary, his brother Sid, and Mrs. Harper, all mourning the boys' death. This gave Tom an idea. He paddled back over to the island and announced to Huck and Joe that they would attend their own funeral!

Disguised, the three boys sat through the first part of the service in the church gallery.

Then they rustled down the stairs and walked down the church aisle. Needless to say, Aunt Polly and Mrs. Harper were ecstatic to see the boys alive.

Doc Robinson's murder, meanwhile, was on everyone's mind—and, finally, the date for Muff Potter's trial arrived. What, with the stack of evidence against him, Muff had to have done the deed. When Injun Joe took the stand and convincingly lied about how Muff had murdered the good doctor, Tom and Huck stood by "expecting every moment that the clear sky would deliver God's lightnings upon his head." God's judgment, however, did not come. Tom couldn't stand by and see Ol' Muff hanged. So, on the third day of the trial, he came forward to tell what he had seen that night. In the middle of his testimony, a loud crash rang out and Injun Joe sprang from his seat and disappeared out the window.

Now that he had established Muff's innocence, Tom went back to pirating—and to courting Becky. Once she accidentally tore a page in the schoolmaster's book and the schoolmaster began questioning all the children about it. Knowing that Becky would be unable to lie, Tom suddenly leaped up and confessed. He received a whipping—but won Becky's admiration.

Having succeeded with Becky, Tom now set out in earnest with Huck to find hidden treasure. They had just started prying up the floor in an old house when they heard voices. After they crept upstairs, they peered down through the floorboards, and saw Injun Joe and another bandit. Tom almost fainted on the spot.

The men dug until one of their knives hit wood. They then removed a box that was filled with gold coins. After discussing where they might re-bury the gold, the scoundrels grabbed the box and left the house—while the two boys scurried home.

Determined to discover where the treasure was re-hidden, Huck kept an eye on the tavern where Injun Joe was staying. When he noticed Injun Joe and his accomplice leave the tavern toting a large bundle one night, he trailed the criminals, who headed straight for the home of the kind Widow Douglas. "Her husband was rough on me . . . " Huck heard Joe say. "He had me *horsewhipped*! . . . do you understand? He took advantage of me and died. But I'll take it out on *her*." Huck was horrified. Quickly, he enlisted the help of a nearby farmer, and Widow Douglas was rescued from harm. Soon the whole town was chattering about how Huck had saved the widow's life.

That same evening Tom, Becky, and some of their friends went on a picnic to McDougal's Cave. After exploring the many splendid caverns, most of the children returned to town. Tom and Becky, however, got lost in the cave. When Aunt Polly and Becky Thatcher's mother discovered that the children were missing, they became hysterical.

Poor Tom and Becky wandered from one narrow chamber to another. Becky soon began to cry. Finally settling down to sleep, they hoped someone would find them. When they awoke some hours later, Becky shared with Tom a piece of cake she had brought. Then their candles burned out.

Finding a kite-string in his pocket, Tom tied one end to a protruding rock and set out in search of an exit. Just as he reached the end of the string, a candle and a hand suddenly appeared twenty yards ahead of him; then Injun Joe came into view. Tom stood paralyzed by fear—but Injun Joe in his haste had apparently failed to see Tom. Badly shaken, he returned to Becky, and eventually they discovered a small opening—a whole five miles away from the cave's main opening—and managed to crawl out and hitch a ride back into town.

Tom and Becky spent nearly a week recovering from the ordeal. When Huck finally was able to visit his friend, Tom told Huck about seeing Injun Joe in the cave and about his suspicion that the gold was hidden there. Judge Thatcher, however, already had had the cave's entrance barricaded with a triple-locked iron door to prevent other children from being lost there. When Tom heard this news, he turned white. "Injun Joe's in the cave!" he cried. A posse was organized to ride to the cave, and when the door was unlocked, Injun Joe lay just behind it, dead.

The morning after Injun Joe's funeral, Huck and Tom made their way back inside the cave. Tom led Huck to a large rock marked with a cross. They hoisted up the rock and found a natural chasm—where the treasure-box lay. Filling two sacks with coins, the boys stashed the rest of the gold in the Widow Douglas' woodshed. But by the time they reached her house, a crowd had gathered to hear the Widow's news. Putting her arms around the mangy Huck, she told him he could come and live with her; why, he'd saved her life, and forever after she'd clothe, educate, and take excellent care of him. "Huck don't need it," Tom broke in. "Huck's rich!" Then he ran outside to fetch the money. The coins amounted to over twelve thousand dollars! Judge Thatcher put the money into safe-keeping and promised the boys an allowance of a dollar a day.

Huck moved in with the grateful Widow Douglas; he went to school, used a knife and a fork, and washed regularly. But he never would have consented to such "civilized" things if Tom, true adventurer that he was, had not promised to assemble a "respectable" band of robbers—with Huck as one of its chief marauders.

Commentary:

Samuel L. Clemens was born in Hannibal, Missouri in 1835 and spent his boyhood on the banks of the Mississippi. He began writing under the pen name "Mark Twain" when he was about twenty-six. He is best known for his characters Tom Sawyer and Huckleberry Finn. Tom, the adventurous, all-American boy, is in reality a rather complex character. On the one hand he does everything possible to avoid school and church; at the same time he is highly principled, always trying to do the right thing—according to his rather romantic ideals. The importance of this novel—and its equally beloved companion volume, *Huckleberry Finn*—is in the rich, colorful portrait Twain paints of an unforgettable American era.

THE ADVENTURES OF HUCKLEBERRY FINN

by
Mark Twain
(1835 - 1910)

Type of work: Juvenile adventure novel and satire

Setting: Missouri's mid-19th-century backwoods and the banks of the Mississippi River

Principal characters:
Huckleberry Finn, a lively country boy
Tom Sawyer, Huck's friend
Pap Finn, Huck's reprobate, drunkard father
Jim, a runaway Negro slave
The Widow Douglas, Huck's guardian

Commentary:

According to Ernest Hemingway, modern American literature begins with *Huckleberry Finn,* Twain's sequel to *Tom Sawyer.* Mellowed by the introduction of real pathos; deepened by a new attention to Huck's developing consciousness—and conscience; and broadened by its undercover exploration of social and political ambiguities, the book is obviously a richer and more sophisticated work. But what distinguishes it as proudly and quintessentially *American* is its unabashed use of the first-person Missouri vernacular narrative voice.

Naturally, Twain's characteristic humor peppers *Huck's* pages. Indeed, Twain prefaces the story with a warning that "Persons attempting to find a motive in this narrative will be prosecuted; persons attempting to find a moral will be banished; persons attempting to find a plot in it will be shot." Nevertheless, the novel explores significant—and very American—issues, including the legitimacy of hierarchal social relationships.

Story Overview:

This story starts out sometime in the mid-1800s in the placid little Mississippi township of Hannibal, Missouri. Some months earlier, Tom Sawyer and his friend Huck had discovered an honest-to-God chest of gold. The two lucky, lively boys had split the twelve-thousand-dollar treasure, and trustworthy Judge Thatcher was safeguarding their money in trust. Meanwhile, the Widow Douglas and her sister Miss Watson took the rough-hewn boy under her wing—and into their home—to try to "civilize" him. Although he managed to put up with school, and even learned some religion, Huck didn't take too well to Miss Watson's determined efforts to squelch his swearing and smoking.

Then one day Huck saw some footprints in the snow, and realized that his no-good, drunken father was back in town, no doubt with an eye to Huck's money. Huck, in response, immediately rushed over to Judge Thatcher's to sign away his rights to the treasure. He left feeling unburdened and satisfied; now he owned nothing at all to fret over.

Late one night not long afterward, Huck found his Pap, pale and ragged, crouched in the corner of his room. "You've put on considerable many frills since I been away," Pap spat in contempt. "You drop that school, you hear? I'll learn people to bring up a boy to put on airs over his own father." Then Pap asked outright about the money. Huck gave him the dollar he had, and the old man left; but the next day—declaring himself Huck's legal guardian—Pap showed up on Judge Thatcher doorstep, demanding more money. Naturally, the judge refused to turn over a single red cent.

Well, Pap got to feeling more and more desperate, until finally one pleasant spring day, the elder Finn kidnapped his son and took him to stay in a remote log hut on the Illinois side of the Mississippi. Huck reveled in the fishing and hunting, but he didn't like being kept under lock and key when Pap went into town, nor was he fond of the beatings he received when Pap staggered home drunk. One night after Pap almost killed him, Huck decided it was time to escape.

The next night, while Pap was in town, Huck sawed a piece out of one of the logs in the cabin wall, crawled out the hole, and carefully replaced the chunk. Then he smashed in the cabin door with an ax, dribbled pig's blood on the ground, and stuck a few of his own hairs on a bloody ax for effect: He sure hoped Pap would think that he had been killed.

For three days the boy happily camped out on Jackson Island. Then, out on a ramble one night, he saw something that caused his heart to jump "up amongst [his] lungs": a campfire. To his relief, though, he soon saw that the blaze was tended to by Jim, Miss Watson's Negro slave. Jim, meanwhile, stared wildly at what he presumed was Huck's ghost. "Doan' hurt me—don't!" he wailed. "I alwauz liked dead people, en done all I could for 'em . . . "

When Huck finally calmed Jim down enough to explain that his death had been fabricated, Jim confided that he'd run off from home after hearing that Miss Watson was planning to sell him downriver. And so the fugitives made camp together.

Then one night after a heavy storm had swollen the river, Jim and Huck found a frame house floating by on the current. Inside they found a dead man lying amongst a scattered deck of cards and empty whiskey bottles. Jim warned Huck not to look at the man's face—it was too "gashly." Together they searched the rooms for useful goods and sent the house on its way.

As time passed, Huck found himself itching for news from town. Finally one day he dressed up in a girl's calico dress and bonnet and stepped daintily into Hannibal to gather some gossip. Lisping out questions in a high-pitched voice, he learned that some townsfolk thought poor dead Huck had been killed by his Pap, who had up and disappeared himself just a few days earlier; others thought Jim must have done the deed, since he and Huck had vanished on the same night. In fact, some men were talking about going to Jackson Island later that night to see if they could roust Jim. Double-fast, Huck hurried back to Jim's side. "There ain't a minute to lose," he warned. "They're after us!"

Within minutes, the fugitives had loaded up Jim's raft and started down the Mississippi. Their plan was to board a steamship north, where Jim could earn money to buy the freedom of his wife and children. But Huck couldn't help feeling guilty; after all, Jim was a runaway: he was Miss Watson's property. Huck finally decided that he would turn Jim in the next chance he got. But when a boatload of men appeared looking for runaways, Huck told them that he was sharing the raft with his sick father—who was lying inside the tent with a bad case of smallpox. That sent the men paddling away in a hurry. Huck felt a few pangs about helping a "nigger" on the lam, but he knew his conscience would kill him if he betrayed a good friend like Jim.

So, the travelers continued downstream, encountering one adventure after another. Then one night after drifting into a bank of thick fog, they heard the unmistakable sound of a steamboat bearing down on them and leaped into the water to avoid being mashed. When Huck finally pulled himself up on shore and called out for Jim, there was no answer.

Soon afterward, Huck was taken in by a rich family named Grangerford. The Grangerfords were good, generous people, and they treated Huck to all the comforts he could want. But they were somehow caught up in a bitter feud with another family named Shepardson—for reasons no one could remember.

One day the Grangerford slave who attended Huck asked him to come into the woods to see "some snakes." Rather than snakes, however, Huck found his old friend Jim there, hidden in the underbrush. But tragically, that very night, while Huck was gone, a battle was touched off between the feuding families in which the entire Grangerford clan was killed. "I wished I hadn't ever come ashore that night to see such things," Huck later grieved. "I ain't ever going to get shut of them."

So once more the raft-mates set off down the Mississippi. A few days later, they took two fellows on board with them who professed to be from royal families: one said he was a duke, while the other claimed to be a king. Although Huck knew that they were lying, he decided to play along.

The two hucksters stopped periodically at towns along the river to carry out get-rich schemes. At one village the King learned that a rich man named Peter Wilks had just died, leaving three thousand dollars to his three daughters, and that Wilks' deaf-and-dumb brother would be arriving soon for the funeral. He gathered as much information as he could about the brother and then coached the Duke to impersonate him. Sure enough, the poor daughters entrusted the "uncle" with their entire inheritance.

Disgusted by these shenanigans, Huck sneaked into the scoundrels' room that night to reclaim the money, which he then stashed safely in the dead man's coffin for the daughters to retrieve.

The next day the real brother showed up, and the Duke and the King were hauled away to jail. But just as Huck and Jim were untying their raft to move on, the two escape artists came running down the bank to rejoin them. It was all Huck could do to keep from crying.

The next day the foursome stopped off at another town. After running some errands, Huck returned to the raft to find Jim gone. The Duke had sold the runaway, complained the King— "and never divided with me, and the money's gone."

Immediately Huck set off to the rescue. But to his surprise, at the plantation where Jim had been imprisoned he was greeted by a woman who gave him a loving squeeze and called him Tom—Tom Sawyer! She was Tom's own Aunt Sally—and obviously she had taken Huck for her nephew, who was due to arrive for a visit. So, in order to help out Jim, Huck gladly assumed Tom's identity.

When Tom eventually showed up, the boys shared a grand reunion. They decided that Huck would pretend to be Tom's cousin, Sid, whenever they were around Aunt Sally. Then Huck told Tom about Jim's situation and revealed his plan to steal the key, unlock the door to the hut where the slave was being kept, and then head down the river. Tom, however, had been reading pirate books; he favored digging a tunnel into the hut. That plan sounded infinitely more complicated and dangerous, so naturally they immediately settled on it.

When the tunnel was finally completed, Tom wrote an anonymous letter to Mr. Phelps, the plantation owner: *There is a desperate gang of cutthroats going to steal your runaway nigger tonight.* Then the boys made their way through the tunnel into Jim's hut. Fleeing into the darkness, the three were chased by Phelps and a posse of gun-toting farmers.

Alive and free for the moment, they reached the raft. But Tom had caught a real live bullet in the leg, and the group was soon recaptured. Back at the Phelps' farm, there were cries to hang the double runaway, and Jim was again securely locked up. Suddenly Tom sat upright in bed. "They hain't no right to shut Jim up! . . . He's free as any cretur that walks this earth. Old Miss Watson died two months ago, and she . . . set him free in her will."

"Then what on earth did *you* want to set him free for?" cried Aunt Polly. "I wanted the adventure of it!" Tom replied.

Jim was immediately released. Phelps then fed him and gave him a suit of clothes, while Tom gave him forty dollars for being such a respectable prisoner. Although Tom was now ready to return home, Huck was reluctant to join him for fear of his Pap. Hearing this, Jim made a sad confession: "He ain't a-comin' back no mo', Huck. Doan' you 'member de house dat was float'n down de river, en dey wuz a man in dah, kivered up, dat wuz him."

And so Huck headed back on the double toward the Widow Douglas' house—before Aunt Sally made good on her threat to adopt him.

COWBOYS ARE MY WEAKNESS

by Pam Houston, W. W. Norton & Company, New York, N.Y., 1992

Commentary:

With the modern West as a backdrop, Pam Houston examines the trials and imbalances of modern relationships. Her male characters display all the steadfast stoicism and "don't-fence-me-in" autonomy of the classic 19th-century cowboy, but very little of his mystery, chivalry, or underlying sense of purpose. With his fail-safe aura of silent strength and "wildness," the cowboy invariably attracts women; but without purpose or commitment, he is unable to give back strength or comfort to the attachments that ensue.

Each of the following three stories is narrated by a woman entangled with a pick-up-truck cowboy. As each is brought face to face with her predicament by a moment of subtle crisis, each responds to the grim epiphany in a different way. Through it all, the cowboys drift and dare in aimless, arrogant detachment, ultimately functionless in the inconsonant sunshine of the modern West.

How to Talk to a Hunter

Although she was in love with the hunter, she felt as if she should have known early on that there would be trouble. After all, in the months she had lived with him she had never once asked herself why he listened so religiously to top-forty country music or why he balked at replaying his phone messages when she was around. And now, as he talked about spending the summer in Alaska or the spring in Hawaii, it was impossible for her to tell whether or not she was included in his plans.

One day, while the hunter was outside splitting wood, the phone rang. It was "Janie Coyote" the voice said into the answering machine. She was getting off work and just wanted to hear the sound of his "beautiful voice" before she left.

The week before Christmas, while she sat with the hunter in front of the TV screen watching *It's a Wonderful Life*, she finally mentioned the word "monogamy." He said that he would be perfectly happy spending every night with her—but there were still "just a few questions he [didn't] have the answers for."

When the heavy snows arrived, Janie Coyote came down from Montana. The hunter called his woman to say that he couldn't see her because a friend had unexpectedly come into town. He even went so far as to give eight separate facts about this so-called "friend," careful never to identify the friend as "she."

When she and the hunter met again, it was at her house. The hunter hugged her, but she did not hug him back. He told her that if she would just be a little patient, things might work out. She forced herself not to cry. She knew she shouldn't let things go on, but in spite of all the deceit, she also knew that they *would* go on.

Selway

Jack and his girlfriend had driven several hours to ride the rapids of the Selway River, only to learn that it was far above the recommended water level for boating. Nevertheless, they decided to enter the river, almost capsizing their boat before they finally found a place to put ashore for the night.

The next morning, they met three men on a training run in a self-bailing boat, who suggested that Jack and his girlfriend run the rapids with them. "It'll be safer for us both," they said. Jack still preferred to go it alone, but then one of the men told him about an accident that had happened earlier that day: a boat had flipped over and a girl had been drowned in the current. Even as he spoke, the helicopter bearing the girl's body passed overhead and disappeared behind the cliffs. Jack reluctantly decided they would run the river together.

The next morning, as they floated towards the rapids, Jack's girlfriend thought back to what an old Southern hunter's widow had once told her about men: that "the wild ones were the only ones worth having" and that a woman had to do whatever it took to keep them wild. She knew that Jack's wildness was the reason she loved him—even if that same wildness might very well get them both killed. If he ever gave up his undomesticated ways to live the "safe life" for her sake, she thought ruefully, he would wind up losing her.

The party made it through the first day without any problems, after which Jack and his girlfriend separated from the group and camped for the night. Both were exhausted, but when the morning broke Jack insisted that they go on. It wasn't long before they came upon a string of rapids for which they weren't prepared. All at once the boat turned sideways and rolled, trapping Jack's girlfriend in the current. Shivering in the river's bone-drenching cold, she somehow made it to shore. Jack followed her, but their boat continued drifting downstream.

Jack found the boat stuck in a sandbank near the other side of the river. He decided that, if he was reading the current right, he could launch himself from upstream, ride the current, and come ashore at the spot where the boat had lodged. "And if you read the current wrong?" she asked. "Then it's over Selway Falls," Jack grinned.

He set out swimming confidently. But as she watched from shore, the powerful flow soon carried him far past his mark. She started to pray then, and though it might have been coincidence, at that moment she saw his svelte body accelerate towards the shore. It took all of fifteen minutes, but he made it.

Later, in the truck on the way home, Jack remarked nonchalantly that he had never been in any real danger. "I let him get away with it," his girlfriend mused, "because I knew that's what he had to tell himself to get past almost losing me." They stopped along the dirt road, built a fire and rolled out their sleeping bags. The night was so still that she "could imagine a peace without boredom."

Cowboys Are My Weakness

Homer's girlfriend held a picture in her mind of a small ranch house on the edge of the forest: a woman in blue cutoffs stood at the door to kiss her bearded husband goodbye before watching him drive off to work in his pickup truck. "I always had this thing about cowboys," she told Homer. "Maybe because I grew up in New Jersey." Now she hoped she had found a real cowboy of her own.

She and Homer both lived in Fort Collins, Colorado, only a mile apart. But for the past six years, Homer had divided his time between Colorado and the Montana ranch where he worked as a wildlife specialist studying the mating patterns of white-tail deer. Lately, she had been going with him. She knew that if she didn't go, he would just take up with someone else—and even though she wasn't all that crazy about spending her days following rutting does, she *still* hoped that Homer was her dream cowboy.

Later she found out that Homer had a long history of stirring up trouble around the ranch. He had slept with several of the ranch hands' girlfriends and wives, and there was a rumor circulating that he had been the reason for the ranch owner's recent divorce.

Nonetheless, she stayed. When she went along with Homer to watch the deer, he made her sit still, only permitting her to change positions once every two hours. Even worse, she wasn't allowed to say a word all the way home. When they did get home, she hungered to talk with him, endlessly, about the things they had seen that day. Invariably, Homer elected to sit in front of the TV with his dinner.

Dave, the ranch owner, was the kind of man she knew she *should* have fallen in love with. He didn't seem like the typical ranch owner. He was more gentle and refined, "a poet, a vegetarian. He listened to Andreas Vollenweider and drank hot beverages with names like Suma and Morning Rain."

It was around Thanksgiving when the relationship began unraveling. Homer's contract required him to stay in Montana until the Sunday before the holiday, and he had promised her they would leave the ranch early enough to spend the long weekend at home. But when she asked him about it, he got upset. "You don't know anything about it," he protested. "Thanksgiving is the premium time. Thanksgiving is the height of the rut."

Her illusion about Homer all but crumbled the day she told him she might be pregnant. Homer had always said that they would get married and have a family. In fact, every time the subject had come up she had imagined her dream cowboy and wondered how *he* would react to such news—maybe he'd sing the music from *Father Knows Best* or do a swan dive in the deep snow. But Homer's response had nothing of the magic she had envisioned. He simply said, "Well, in that case we better get back to Colorado before they change the abortion laws."

That was the moment she sensed that if a relationship like the one in her picture was in any way possible, it wouldn't happen with Homer. Homer was no cowboy, "just a capitalist with a Texas accent who owned a horse."

On the very next morning, a real cowboy entered her life. Monte, one of the ranch hands, caught her attention and asked her to the stockgrower's ball. She was hesitant at first, but finally agreed to go.

As the night of the ball wore on, she realized how exhilarating it was to be with Monte. She had forgotten how much she loved dancing, and here she was, having fun for the first time in a long while. "It had taken me ten years, and an incredible sequence of accidents," she reflected, "but that night I thought I'd finally gotten where I'd set out to go."

After the ball, they were driving back to the ranch, discussing, of all things, horses, when she asked Monte's opinions on other things she had enjoyed doing before she met Homer—things like music and sailing. But Monte, true to the cowboy tradition, was too polite to tell her what he thought for sure.

When they pulled into the driveway between their two cabins, Monte eyed her sideways and said, "I'd love to give you a great big kiss, but I've got a mouthful of chew." Smiling, she exited the truck and went inside. She could hear Homer snoring before she got past the kitchen.

After that, she made plans to go back to Colorado, partly because of the way Homer and Monte began to eye each other and partly because she couldn't bring herself to spend another Thanksgiving watching does in heat.

The morning she was to leave, Homer approached her: after thinking it over, he had decided that she was the woman he wanted to spend the rest of his life with. She tried, and tried again, but just couldn't take him seriously.

Monte intercepted her on the way out the door. He asked her to write, and promised to take her dancing again the next time she was in the area. They smiled at each other, and he rode off toward the west. She gazed after him to see whether he was the cowboy in her picture, but he was already too far off on the horizon for her to tell.

Why, she suddenly wondered, had she always imagined her cowboy-husband *leaving* her; why hadn't she seen him *coming home* to her instead? Then she understood: *she* had changed. *She* had evolved into someone totally different than the woman she was in her dream. It was not her dream anymore.

COLD SASSY TREE

by Olive Ann Burns, Dell Publishers, New York, N.Y., 1984

Type of work: Coming-of-age novel

Setting: Cold Sassy Tree, Georgia; early 20th century

Principal characters:
    Will Tweedy, the story's perceptive adolescent narrator
    Will's Grandpa Ruck Blakeslee
    Love Simpson, a milliner from Baltimore who marries Grandpa following the death of his wife

Story Overview:

According to the tale young Will Tweedy spun for his friends, his flat-chested Aunt Loma, a new mother, didn't have enough milk to feed a jaybird and eventually had to resort to nursing a pig to increase her flow. When Loma heard the story, she decided to help her nephew channel his creativity in a different, more appropriate direction. "I've decided you ought to be a writer," she told Will, presenting him with a "special" notebook. Will then faithfully recorded subsequent events as they happened.

The town of Cold Sassy had got its name from the ancestors of Will's grandmother when they migrated from North Carolina to Georgia. While they were building their houses, the family camped on a ridge under some big sassafras trees. Later, visitors referred to the settlement as "thet cold sassafras grove" or "them cold sassy trees." Although in 1906 many townspeople figured they had "out-growed" the tawdry name and wanted to change it, Ruck Blakeslee, Will's grandpa, would not hear of it. Inasmuch as he owned the town grocery store—and thus was an influential man—the official name remained Cold Sassy, Georgia.

Ruck Blakeslee was known for doing the unexpected, but on the day he announced to his two daughters, "I'm aimin' to marry Miss Love Simpson," they were appalled: not only was Miss Love young enough to be their sister, she was also a free-thinking suffragette who was undoubtedly only after their father's money. And worst of all was the fact that their father was planning to remarry only three weeks after their beloved mother had died. "She's dead as she'll ever be ain't she?" he responded to their protests. "Well ain't she?"

Unlike his mother and his Aunt Loma, Ruck's 14-year-old notebook-scribbling grandson could see the advantages to the marriage. After all, Grandpa had explained he could either "hire . . . a colored woman or get married . . . And tell you the truth, hit's jest cheaper to have a wife." In the few weeks since Granny's death, both Grandpa and his house already had begun to look a mess. Now Love would be there to take care of both—and Will was sure she would never try to take Granny's place.

Grandpa had truly *loved* Granny. Although she was a no-nonsense Southern woman, she had always struck Will as gentle and refined. *She didn't fuss at Grandpa about not having the house wired for electricity, [nor his refusal] to hook into the new water main and sewer system.* Instead, she and Grandpa kept on "going to Egypt," which was what everybody in town called going out to the privy. Although some folks gossiped that the hardships of her primitive life with Grandpa had finally brought on the stroke that killed her, Will knew better. Like her garden, where she had cultivated over 60 varieties of roses, Granny had enjoyed a full life. As she lay in bed dying, Grandpa had presented her with one of the scarlet buds from the garden. "I remember you had a red rose like this'n in yore hair the day I decided to marry you," he whispered. And he remembered how Granny had once told him, "Mr. Blakeslee, I wouldn't even mind dyin' if'n I could be buried in a bed of roses." After she died, Grandpa had worked tirelessly making blankets of roses to fill the "deep yawning hole" at her gravesite.

So, at any rate, Grandpa and Miss Love eloped. And afterwards no one but Will went to call on them. When he arrived to help Miss Love get settled in her new house, he found Grandpa hard at work and Miss Love playing the piano and singing "Ta-ra-ra-boom-de-ay," followed by "I'm Only a Bird in a Gilded Cage." At the sight of Grandpa's new wife, Will felt as if he were on fire: Miss Love wore a dress cut so low that if she had "bent down in that dress, her bosoms would of looked like two puppies trying to climb over a fence."

Miss Love was full of plans for the house; already it looked different from when Granny had lived there. To Will's surprise, when Grandpa came in from work he said very cheerfully, "Miss Love, do you think you could trim my hair some?" Miss Love was delighted. "With a close haircut, a thin mustache and no beard, you'll look—distinguished!" she said. And when she was finished Grandpa looked years younger. "I do recollect seeing thet feller somewheres before," he mused, gawking at himself in the mirror. "Ain't he a buster though!"

"How come you married my grandpa?" Will asked Miss Love after Grandpa returned to the store. "Partly I married your grandfather so I would have a family," she answered, adding that everyone in her own family had died. Then she went on to explain that she and Grandpa had "a marriage in name only"; they didn't love each other, but Grandpa needed someone to be his housekeeper, and he'd agreed to deed the house and furniture to Miss Love after his death.

Their conversation was interrupted when a stranger barged in on them, a man in a cowboy hat with a fancy saddle draped over his arm. Miss Love *stood there like she'd gone numb, her hands on her mouth.* Then to Will's complete amazement, the man strolled over to Love and *kissed her right on the mouth . . . like he was starved and she was something to eat.* And Miss Love—why she was *kissing him back, no doubt about it.* To Will's horror, the man proposed to Love on the spot. The saddle was an engagement gift he'd brought all the way from Texas, he explained. Tremulously, Miss Love replied, "You write me I'm not good enough for you, and now two years later—"

"I've come back for just one reason," the man broke in. *"I love you."* And just about that time, Grandpa walked back in through the door. When he heard about the proposal, he seemed neither angry nor jealous. Instead, he offered the man a drink and *was the friendliest host you ever saw.*

"So do you want to marry him or don't you?" Grandpa finally asked Love when the stranger had left. Miss Love sobbed and shook her head: "If I weren't married to you, I still wouldn't marry him." And no more questions were asked.

Grandpa's affection for his bride grew stronger with each passing day. He was a new man, far more adventuresome and warm than he'd ever been. Not only did he buy Love a race-horse to go with her new saddle, he also was planning to take her on a buying trip to New York. Although he normally sent Will's Papa to do the buying for the store, this time Grandpa wanted to enjoy the trip with Miss Love.

The news depressed Mama. For once, *she'd* hoped to accompany Papa on the trip north—and now she had yet another reason to dislike her father's new wife. To cheer her up, Papa bought a big shiny red Cadillac car that made everyone in Cold Sassy *proud for Mama.* Thrilled, Mama exclaimed, "Oh, won't she be jealous"—and Will knew that the "she" referred to Miss Love.

As it turned out, though, Will himself enjoyed the car more than anyone. Quickly learning how to drive, he savored climbing behind the wheel to run errands for his father. One day, he happened to see his pretty schoolmate Lightfoot McClendon walking along the road, and he pulled over to pick her up. After driving for a while, they stopped to take a leisurely walk on the grounds of a cemetery. "I shore wisht I could get one a-them angels for Pa," Lightfoot said pointing to a beautiful headstone. Then she began to cry, mumbling to Will about her father's tragic death. Without thinking, Will took the girl in his arms and kissed her. The memory of that kiss stayed with him for a long time.

After Grandpa and Love returned from New York—with presents galore and a new car for themselves—Will developed a new, more compassionate appreciation for his grandfather. One night when the three of them went out for a drive in the Blakeslee's new Pearce, they had an accident and were forced to spend the night in a stranger's house. Time passed, and Will couldn't get to sleep. Finally, around midnight, he heard his grandfather get out of bed and go to his wife. "Don't, Mr. Blakeslee," Miss Love began to cry. "How dare you try to . . . to use me like I'm a . . . Why, I trusted you!"

"I love you, dang it!" Will, wide-eyed, heard Grandpa grouse. "Love, I've been waiting for this minute ever since the day I laid eyes on you!" Although he'd hated himself, he'd "hankered after" Love "like a schoolboy," and, while he'd loved his wife and prayed for her recovery, Grandpa also knew "thet if'n she died" he wanted to marry Love. "You poor, dear man. I'm so very sorry," Miss Love murmured. Then she made a confession of her own: when her old

cowboy fiance learned that many years earlier she had been raped by her father, he had broken their engagement; hurt and rejection followed. Tenderly, Grandpa told her, "Hit don't make no difference, Miss Love."

Soon Will had his own problems to confront. Learning that Lightfoot was going to marry a boy who worked in Grandpa's store, Will found himself praying that *something would happen to his rival that would prevent their marriage.* But to Will's horror, *the one something happened to was Grandpa.* One night robbers broke into the store and hit Grandpa, knocking him out. When he regained consciousness it wasn't the pain that bothered him so much as it was his sense of humiliation. "You're alive," Love sighed tenderly. "That's all I care about." Then, she confessed, "You dear, dear man. I love you."

But that wasn't the end of it: Grandpa was injured more severely than anyone suspected; soon he developed a bad chill and a cough that turned into pneumonia. Miss Love, heartbroken, nursed him, as the rest of the family gathered at his side. Closing his clouded eyes, Grandpa spoke to Granny—presumably, the last words that would ever leave his lips. Then—as Will duly recorded in his notebook—suddenly his fever broke, and Miss Love delightedly told him that she was expecting their baby. Afterwards, holding hands, Grandpa and Miss Love fell asleep. Hours later, when Love awoke, Grandpa was dead.

As he had requested, Grandpa was buried in a plain pine box next to Granny. A band played parade music, and there was a "funeral party" after the burial. Miss Love took this opportunity to speak to Grandpa's family and friends about her love for Grandpa. And now that she was expecting his baby, Cold Sassy seemed like home to her—a place where she should raise their child.

A month after Grandpa died, the town's name was changed. He had always said the only way it would happen was "over his dead body." And, Will wrote, he had been right.

Commentary:

When journalist Olive Ann Burns (1924-1990) learned that she was chronically ill, she began her work on *Cold Sassy Tree.* Burns' semi-autobiographical novel grew out of vignettes from her own family's history in Georgia, just as Will Tweedy's story grows out of his journal notations.

At first reluctant to write in the notebook his Aunt Loma gives him, Will quickly discovers that his journal can memorialize all the changes that are taking place around him. He is, of course, preserving recollections of bewildering and exhilarating transformations in both his own adolescent life and the world around him. The arrival of Love Simpson in Cold Sassy, with her low-cut bodices and her newfangled enthusiasms seems both to symbolize and to catalyze the reformative rhythms of Cold Sassy. Eventually, the town turns against its own name—both endearingly and embarrassingly quirky in a new age dedicated to rounding off rough edges. And an era ends, along with an old man's life, as a new child is born.

WHERE THE RED FERN GROWS

The Story of Two Dogs and a Boy
by Wilson Rawls, Garden City: Doubleday, New York, N.Y., 1961

Type of work: Coming-of-age novel

Setting: The Ozark mountains; early 20th century

Principal characters:
> *Billy Colman,* the story's narrator, a ten-year-old boy
> *Old Dan and Little Ann,* Billy's hounds

Commentary:

Author Wilson Rawls' early-twentieth-century rural childhood was similar to that of his narrator, Billy Colman. Rawls' parents were so poor that they could not even buy a writing tablet and pencil for their son. Nevertheless, their strength and courage inspired him. "Son," he recalls his father saying, "a man can do anything he sets out to do, if he doesn't give up."

Rawls apparently took these words to heart, teaching himself how to write the fiction for which he would later become famous. *Where the Red Fern Grows* first appeared as a serial in the *Saturday Evening Post;* after overwhelming acclaim by young audiences it was published in book form by Doubleday, receiving numerous awards.

Story Overview:

Billy Colman, a young half-Cherokee farm boy, wanted only one thing out of life: a pair of coonhounds. Unfortunately, despite his fervent prayers, his parents were poor and simply could not afford such expensive animals. And although it saddened them, they could do nothing to cure the ten-year-old's "dog-wanting disease."

Billy, however, was determined to fulfill his dream. An inventive and diligent boy, he decided to earn money by selling minnows and providing berries for his grandfather's general store. In fact, Billy worked so hard that in just two years he had saved up the fifty dollars he needed to buy his hounds. He then enlisted his grandfather's help in writing a letter to a kennel that sold the extraordinary dogs. A short while later, the kennel sent a notice saying that two puppies would be shipped to the Tahlequah depot within a couple of weeks.

At last, Billy received word that his puppies had arrived. Although Grandpa offered to take him to Tahlequah sometime later in the week, Billy decided that two-odd years had been a long enough wait; he would head for Tahlequah by himself. That night, as soon as his mother, father, and three sisters had bedded down, Billy crept into the kitchen, filled a sack with food, and left.

After a long, dusty journey, he arrived in Tahlequah. The normally intrepid boy was awed by the busy town and its bustling people, who laughed at his tattered clothes and bare feet. It was not easy for Billy to muster up enough courage to enter the depot. To his great relief, however, the stationmaster turned out to be quite friendly. "They sure are fine looking pups," he told Billy when he learned why the boy had come. Then he handed over the pups—and

Billy's "heart started acting like a drunk grasshopper." Rubbing his face against the animals' wriggling bodies, he suddenly burst into tears. Putting the puppies in a sack, he thanked the stationmaster and began the long trek home.

Although his parents weren't angry with him for "stealing off," when Billy arrived home he felt awful about the terrible worry he had caused Mama. Still, he couldn't remain sad for long, now that he had his precious puppies.

Not surprisingly, the little hounds soon endeared themselves to Papa, Mama, and Billy's sisters. "Do you believe God heard your prayer . . . and helped you?" Mama asked. With a smile, Billy assured her that he believed exactly that. "I'll always be thankful," he added. Indeed, every day the boy became more and more pleased with his two extraordinary hounds. He named them Old Dan and Little Ann, and they became his loyal companions—as well as first-rate hunters.

Grandpa, who had "caught coon upon coon" during his own childhood, helped Billy to construct and set traps. After snaring his first raccoon, Billy used its hide as a lure to teach his pups how to trail the critters. The dogs complemented each other perfectly: Ann was more intelligent than Dan, while the male was more aggressive in pursuing the scent. As they grew, the dogs turned out to be smaller than most of their breed, but their reputation as excellent coonhounds had begun to "spread all over" the Colmans' region of the Ozarks.

Unfortunately, the hounds' reputation had sparked the jealousy of the wild Pritchard brothers who lived nearby. The older brother, Rubin, had once "cut a boy with a knife" during a brawl; his brother Rainie was generally "disliked by young and old." Although Billy always tried to avoid the pair, the Pritchards confronted him one day outside Grandpa's store. Rubin, swaggering, was willing to wager two dollars that Billy's hounds couldn't tree the legendary "ghost coon"—a huge, elusive creature who somehow always found a way to outwit its hunters. Initially Billy was reluctant to make a bet with the Pritchards; but egged on by their taunts of "yellow," at last he agreed.

After nightfall, Billy took his hounds to meet the Pritchards in a thick canebrake near the river. As soon as the hounds picked up the scent of a raccoon, they dashed off on its trail, jumping in and out of the river and scrambling back and forth through the undergrowth. Suddenly, "all hell broke loose" and Billy glimpsed the biggest coon he'd ever seen. Then, as the hounds closed in, the raccoon "cried." Billy had heard a similar sound scores of times before, but *this* raccoon's howl unnerved him, and he told the Pritchards that he didn't want to kill the ghost coon.

"Are you crazy?" Rubin shrieked as he took off after the critter himself. Unable to catch it, he turned to vent his anger on Billy. But just as he was about to lay into the boy, Dan and

Ann took up a skirmish with the Pritchard's hound. Rubin let go of Billy, grabbed an ax, and chased after the dogs. But as he raced toward them, he stumbled, dropped to the ground, and lay there, very still. Rubin had fallen on his own ax.

As the young man gasped out his last breaths, Billy drew the ax from the gaping wound. Horrified, he called out to Rainie; but Rubin's brother had vanished into the brush. In shock, Billy led his dogs home. Hearing the awful news, Mama broke down sobbing. Papa, sadness etched on his face, stood up and walked out into the darkness to fetch Rubin's body.

During the next several days, Billy moped around in a daze. At last he roused himself and set off to pay his last respects to Rubin. On the freshly dug grave, he laid a bouquet of flowers.

Days later, Billy was still reliving "the horrible tragedy," when Grandpa opened a newspaper and pointed to a notice: *"CHAMPIONSHIP COON HUNT TO BE HELD."* Clearly elated, Grandpa said, "I've got it all fixed, Billy. We can enter Old Dan and Little Ann in this championship hunt." To Billy's surprise and delight, Papa also decided to accompany them on the long trip to the huntsite in the woods near Bluebird Creek.

On the day before the competition, Billy felt like his head had "swelled up as big as a number four washtub." Not only was he certain that his dogs would win, but he was doubly thrilled to hear Grandpa and Papa praise the hounds' skill and loyalty. In fact, everybody at the Bluebird Creek camp was cordial and extremely complimentary toward Dan and Ann. And even though Billy certainly had *not* expected either of his dogs to shine in the preliminary contest for "best-looking hound," Ann won a modest silver cup that brought tears to her master's eyes.

But on the next day, the coon hunt itself nearly ended in disaster. After some initial success—as well as several frightening ordeals—the three Colmans found themselves stumbling through a blinding, "wind-driven sleet" across treacherous icy terrain. "We'll freeze to death," Papa feared. Then suddenly Papa and Billy realized that Grandpa had disappeared. Frantically, Billy sent Ann off on Grandpa's trail. At last the dog's howl led them to the place where the weakened hunter had twisted his ankle and "fallen face down in the icy sleet." Papa and Billy revived Grandpa and together they struggled back to the warmth of the camp. And tears of panic turned to tears of joy when Billy discovered that the slew of raccoons they had managed to bring in before Grandpa's accident had won the gold cup for his dogs—and three hundred dollars for him.

When he got home, Billy put the prize money in Mama's hand. "Thank God," she wept, "my prayers have been answered." For a while, anyway, the Colmans' money worries were behind them, and the doctor had said Grandpa's injury was not as serious as it had first appeared.

Not long after the coon hunt, Billy once again took the hounds out on the trail. As he struggled to keep up with the swift-moving animals, he became alarmed by the "deep baying of Old Dan" somewhere ahead of him. He ran forward to investigate—only to find himself face to face with a mountain lion, "the devil cat of the Ozarks," poised in a tree above his baying hound. At that moment, the frightened cat let out a blood-curdling scream and sprang from the tree. Dan, ever fearless, met the lion in midair. And as Ann loyally darted into the fray, Billy himself "went berserk," hacking at the beast with the cutting blade of his ax.

After what seemed an eternity, the huge cat lay motionless on the ground. Even then, Dan would not unfasten his jaws from the animal's flesh. When Billy finally managed to pry him loose, he found that deep gashes covered the hound's body. Carefully he lifted Old Dan in his arms and headed home, Ann at his heels. Mama doctored the dogs: Ann's wounds were not severe, but Dan's were fatal. Before he died, his loving gaze fixed on his master's face, the heroic warrior gave a last "feeble thump of his tail" and then "his friendly gray eyes closed forever."

The boy buried his coonhound on a hillside, "at the foot of a beautiful red oak tree." After that, Little Ann refused food, and her eyes turned "dull and cloudy." Finally one day she dragged herself to the hillside, lay down on her companion's grave, and closed her own eyes in death.

Heartsick, Billy buried Ann by the side of Old Dan. Later, he asked Mama if "God made a heaven for all good dogs." "I'm sure He did," she replied quietly. Papa then explained that God had taken both dogs away because "he doesn't like to see families split up."

As it turned out, Billy's parents had thought not too long ago of moving into town so that their children could receive better schooling; at that time they had decided against it in order to avoid separating Billy from his dogs. Now, however, they knew that the move was meant to be; it was the "will of God."

That spring the Colmans packed all their belongings in their wagon. Just as they were ready to leave, Billy decided to make a final visit to the two graves on the hillside. As he drew near, "I saw something was different. It looked like a wild bush had grown up and practically covered the two little mounds . . . I took out my knife, intending to cut it down." But then he stopped cold and gaped wide-eyed at an extraordinary sight: "There between the graves, a beautiful red fern had sprung up . . . and its long red leaves had reached out and in rainbow arches curved over the graves of my dogs."

In Billy's part of the country, the red fern was a legendary symbol. Once, after a young Indian boy and girl had frozen to death in a snowstorm, the fern had appeared on their graves. From then on it was said "that only an angel could plant the seeds of a red fern, and that [the ferns] never died; where one grew, that spot was sacred."

Billy Colman never returned to his childhood home, the place where his boyhood innocence was replaced with deeper understanding. But throughout his life he knew that an important part of himself lay buried beneath the place where the red fern grows.

THE EDUCATION OF LITTLE TREE

by Forrest Carter, The University of New Mexico Press, Albuquerque, New Mexico, 1991

Type of work: Autobiographical pseudo-fiction
Setting: Tennessee hill country; 1930s

Story Overview:

The boy's Ma lived for only a year after his Pa had died. Once her funeral was over, the five-year-old went to live with Granpa and Granma in a mountain hollow deep in Tennessee. As soon as they reached their cabin, the boy found his bedroom and lay down. Granma, "her full skirts around her, the plaited hair streaked with silver," sat down beside him, stroked his hair, and began to sing: *They now have sensed him coming/ The forest and the wood-wind/ Father mountain makes him welcome with his song/ They have no fear of Little Tree/ They know his heart is kindness/ And they sing "Little Tree is not alone."*

As Granma sang, the boy knew that *he* was Little Tree. And suddenly he could "hear the wind talking" and the water "singing." He knew he was loved; he did not cry.

No, Cherokees did not cry. That was what Granma and Granpa said. Even though Granpa was only half Cherokee, he, like Granma, his full-blooded Cherokee wife, "thought Indian."

Granpa, for example, "held his palm up to show peace," demonstrating that he held no weapon. He often explained that "the white man meant the same thing by shaking hands, except that his words was so crooked, he had to try to shake a weapon out of the sleeve of the feller who claimed he was a friend."

Despite the fact that Granpa's own Pa had been a Scot, the explorer "did not lust for land or profit, but loved the freedom of the mountains"—where Granpa had met Red Wing, his Cherokee bride. At the wedding, they had held their "marriage stick"; now the marriage stick was well mellowed, the notches they carved in it to mark each new sorrow and happiness, each new quarrel mended, in their lives.

Even after all these years Granpa and Granma occasionally quibbled, but they had a special "understanding" that Granma said grew "deeper as the years went by, and she reckined it would get beyond anything mortal folks could think about or explain." She knew their spirits would be together, always.

To express these deep feelings, Granma and Granpa had their own word: *kin.* Sometimes at night Little Tree would hear Granpa say to Granma, "I kin ye." A long time ago, according to Granpa, the word *kinfolks* "meant any folks that you understand . . . it meant 'loved folks.' But people got selfish and brought it down to mean just blood relatives."

Generally speaking, words bothered Granpa. "If there was less words," he reasoned, "there wouldn't be as much trouble in the world."

Unlike Granpa, Granma loved words. In fact, she insisted that Little Tree learn five words a week from the dictionary and then practice the words in sentences. One day while he was working on the *A*'s, Little Tree came across the word *abhor*, which he decided to try out on Granpa. "I

abhor briers, yeller jackets and such," the boy said, smiling importantly. "What in hell," Granpa wondered, "has whores got to do with yeller jackets and briers?"

Books, in general, also bred some dissension between Granpa and Granma. On the one hand, Granpa loved to sit in front of the fireplace at night and listen to Granma read. On the other, he firmly believed that too many books begat confusion, and he "was put out about the number of books" that he had to carry home from the library for Granma.

But if Granpa didn't have much respect for books and their fictional characters (particularly Shakespeare's Mrs. Macbeth, who, Granpa argued, should have minded her own business and stopped meddling in Mr. Macbeth's affairs), George Washington captured his unyielding admiration. In him rested the hope that there "could be a good man in politics." Since Granpa saw politicians in general as "powerful monsters who had no regard for how folks had to live and get by," Granma carefully selected what she read to him about Washington so that Granpa still would have "someone to look to and admire." One night, though, Granma slipped up: she forgot to omit a reference in the passage she was reading to Washington's whiskey tax. The very thought of such a tax "hit Granpa deep." After all, he himself made whiskey for a living, and he had always contended that no one had the right to interfere with the trade that had been in "the Scotch side of his family for several hundred years."

Granpa thought Little Tree should learn whiskey-making too—even if later on he "might want to switch trades." As they worked, side by side, Little Tree and Granpa listened to the birds and to the animals. Granpa knew all about bird signs. Whippoorwills brought "night peace and good dreams"; mourning doves "mourned and remembered the dead." And when his hounds were out fox hunting, Granpa knew which hound's bay was "a damn lie" to make him think it had picked up a trail-scent and which hound communicated "the real thing."

Fox hunting, though, was just a sport; Granpa never let the hounds kill a fox. In fact, Granpa and Granma never killed anything unnecessarily. "It is The Way," they explained. "Take only what ye need." All life was sacred because it had sprung from Mon-o-lah, the "Earth Mother." And indeed, after a short time with his grandparents, Little Tree could actually feel Mon-o-lah beneath his moccasins as he walked across the warm, spongy ground.

There was much more for Little Tree to learn about his Cherokee heritage. "If ye don't know the past, then ye will not have a future," his grandparents told him. Then they recounted the story of how one autumn, long ago, thousands of Cherokees were brought together "in bunches like cattle," by soldiers who planned to send them "far toward the setting sun, where the government had . . . land that the white man did not want." Although the soldiers had brought wagons, the Cherokees "would not ride . . . They walked." Not one among them was willing to "let the wagons steal his soul."

Soon the exhausted people "began to die . . . by the hundreds—by the thousands . . . The soldiers said they could only bury their dead every three days." So the Cherokees carried them. The white men called the march to Oklahoma the Trail of Tears, because it sounded romantic. But there were no tears—"for the Cherokee would not let [the white man] see his soul"—and there was nothing romantic about the husband carrying his dead wife, or "the death-stiffened baby in his mother's arms . . ."

Fortunately, Granma revealed, it was possible for a person to have many lives. She also told Little Tree that "everyone has two minds": one took care of "the necessaries for body-living . . . to get shelter and eating" and to "have young'uns and such"; the other was the "spirit mind," which could get "bigger and stronger" until there was "no body death at all."

To help ensure that their spirit minds were as strong as possible, Granma made certain that everyone went to the Baptist church each Sunday. Granpa, however, didn't care much for "churching," nor for preachers: " . . . If God was as narrer-headed as them idjits that done the arguin' about piddlin' such, then Heaven wouldn't be a fit place to live anyhow." In fact, the only thing Granpa liked about going to church was that there he could visit with his friend Willow John, a Cherokee who rarely spoke but always brought a game to share with Granma, Granpa and Little Tree after the service.

One day, two visitors whom Little Tree had never seen before arrived at the cabin. They brought a paper that said Little Tree could no longer stay with Granpa and Granma; besides being uneducated, whiskey-making Indians, they were too old to care for Little Tree. There was nothing Granpa and Granma could do: Little Tree would have to go to an orphanage. But before he left, Granma asked him, "Do ye recollect the Dog Star, Little Tree? Wherever ye are—no matter where—in the dusk of evening, ye look at the Dog Star. Me and Granpa will be looking too." Then Granpa, head down, led Little Tree to the bus.

Being the only Indian in the orphanage, Little Tree was treated poorly, but he didn't mind: he was left alone more often than the other children, and so he could sit by himself in the evening and gaze up at the Dog Star.

Then one Christmas Eve, after Little Tree had watched the Dog Star "rising bright" in the cold, clear sky, he spotted Granpa on the grounds of the orphanage. The next day Granpa took Little Tree home. Granpa later explained that Willow John had convinced the Reverend to sign some "give-up papers" for Little Tree. "Thankee Willow John," Little Tree told his old friend the following Sunday. The old warrior simply laid his hand on the boy's shoulder.

The next time Little Tree's family visited Willow John, he had "begun his passing song, telling the spirits he was coming." Little Tree, Granpa, and Granma watched "the spirit slip-

ping away," little by little; and then Willow John was gone.

After they had buried Willow John's body beneath a huge gnarled fir, Little Tree knew that his time with Granpa and Granma might also be drawing to a close. Still, the three of them "lived it full" for two more years, pointing out to each other "the reddest of the leaves in the fall" and "the bluest violet in the spring."

Then one day as they wound their way up the trail to stare at the mountains, Granpa tripped and fell. He never stood upright again, and not long afterwards a friend named Pine Billy came to the cabin to play the fiddle music Granpa loved. As Pine Billy played, tears streamed "down his face onto the fiddle" and the bedclothes. "Quit crying, Pine Billy," Granpa said. "Ye're messing up the music." Moments later, Granpa's "spirit mind" took over, and he died.

And on another day, just before spring came in that year, Little Tree was walking back to the cabin, when he noticed Granma sitting silently in her rocker on the back porch. She didn't look up to greet Little Tree, and he knew that she, too, was gone. Affixed to her best dress, the one Granpa especially loved, was a note:

Little Tree, I must go. Like you feel the trees, feel for us when you are listening. We will wait for you . . .

Granma

Little Tree and Pine Billy buried Granma beside Granpa. Then the boy took their old marriage stick and laid it down so that it touched the head of each grave. Before covering it up, he studied the notches they had carved for him "right down near the end of the stick. . . . Deep and happy notches."

When spring came, Little Tree, now ten years old, set off for Oklahoma, where Granma had always told him they had "kin."

Commentary:

After publication of his extraordinary semi-autobiographical novel in 1977, Forrest Carter (1927?-1979) explained, "I just write down what I've experienced by living with my granpa and what I studied in small-town libraries." For Carter, who spent much of his life as an itinerant laborer, libraries were "the most wonderful places in the world." Even after he became a popular writer and had one of his books made into a movie ("The Outlaw Josey Wales" starring Clint Eastwood) he still believed that "the greatest honor would be for a man to have a library named after him."

After reading *Little Tree,* notes Rennard Strickland in the book's introduction, "one never again sees the world in quite the same way." The vision of Granma and Granpa shimmers with life; their world is wholly animate: every star, fish, and rock has a language of its own. The "past" and "future" of this world belong to the Cherokee, but the present—its "life springing from Mon-o-lah," the Earth Mother—accommodates Shakespearean prose, Scotch whiskey, Baptist prayer meetings and George Washington as graciously as it does Granpa, Granma, and Little Tree.

HATCHET

by Gary Paulsen, Puffin Books, New York, N.Y., 1987

Type of Story: Young adult survival adventure

Setting: The contemporary Canadian wilderness

Principal character:
    Brian Robeson, a city-boy who must fight for his life in the timberlands of Canada, a small hatchet and common sense his only tools

Story Overview:

When thirteen-year-old Brian Robeson's mother insisted that he strap a survival hatchet onto his belt, he scoffed. After all, he was only going to visit his father; the Alaskan oil fields, though rugged, were hardly wilderness. What's more, Brian was angry with his mother. Unbeknownst to her he had found out about the secret extramarital affair she was enmeshed in—and Brian planned to tell his father everything immediately upon landing in Alaska.

As the small, two-engine plane roared out over the Canadian back-country, Brian was still so upset about his mother's Secret that he didn't pay much attention to the scenery. Suddenly, though, the plane lurched to one side and Brian was jolted from his thoughts. Searching the pilot's face for reassurance, he found only terror: *The pilot's mouth went rigid, he swore and jerked a short series of slams into the seat, holding his shoulder now . . . "Chest! Oh God, my chest is coming apart!" . . . The pilot was having a heart attack!*

Panic-stricken, Brian grabbed the controls. As the pilot's body went limp, the boy, half screaming and half praying, begged him to "just be asleep."

Brian brought the plane under control— but it had been pulled off course. How could he correct the error? Although he was momentarily able to contact someone on the radio, the connection quickly faded out. Brian began to cry hysterically. Now all he could hear was "the sound of his own sobs in the microphone, his own screams mocking him, coming back into his ears."

Gradually, though, Brian forced down his panic and began to think more clearly. He made up his mind that he wouldn't try to land the plane until he found a lake; crash-landing into dense forest would mean certain death.

To his relief, he soon spotted an L-shaped lake on the right: *He pushed the right rudder pedal gently and the nose moved over . . . Trees suddenly took on detail . . . There was a great wrenching as the wings caught the pines at the side of the clearing and broke back . . . He was momentarily blinded and slammed forward in the seat, smashing his head on the wheel. Then . . . the plane rolled to the right and blew through the trees, out over the water and down, down into the lake.*

Someone was screaming, screaming as the plane drove down into the water. He saw nothing but sensed blue, cold blue-green, and he raked at the seat belt catch, tore his nails loose on one hand . . .

clawed up into the blue . . . he sucked water, took a great pull of water . . . and his head broke into light and he vomited and swam . . . until his hands caught at last in grass and brush and he felt his chest on land . . . everything stopped and he was gone from it all, spiraling out into the world, spiraling out into nothing.

Brian awoke just before dawn. He was alive—but how could he survive in this harsh timberland?

Now as the sun rose over the mountain, *swarming hordes of mosquitoes . . . flocked to his body, made a living coat on his exposed skin, clogged his nostrils when he inhaled, poured into his mouth when he opened it to take a breath . . . In moments his eyes were swollen shut and his face puffy and round to match his battered forehead.* Frustrated and miserable, Brian started crying.

He soon became aware, however, of an even more painful sensation—hunger. His stomach screamed for food. But there was no way to get food. Even his survival hatchet was useless; he was too weak and unskilled to use it.

Then, in the midst of his despair, Brian noticed noisy flocks of birds circling in the distance. Intrigued by their reckless, teeming eagerness, he made his way toward them. As he approached the bushes where they were clustered and "saw they were eating berries," he rushed forward, "scattering the birds, grabbing the branches, stripping them to fill his mouth . . . "

With renewed strength, Brian at last set out to scout the area. Near the lake he discovered a cave-like indentation in the cliffs. Gratefully he pulled himself inside; through the night he stayed there—between violent bouts of nausea and diarrhea from gorging on the berries.

The next morning, a weaker but wiser Brian realized that his survival—and, ultimately, his rescue—would require both temperance and patience. Nevertheless, it was by accident that he learned his next lesson. One night soon afterwards, as he threw his hatchet at a porcupine who had invaded his shelter, he noticed the sparks that flew up as the hatchet struck the rock. After hours of persistent and frenzied experiments using a piece of obsidian, Brian was able to start a fire.

Now, tending the blaze and gathering food required Brian's constant energy and attention. At night he would often wake up to add wood to the coals. Sometimes he dreamed of home; but the days of feasting on cheeseburgers and milk shakes were far away.

As the weeks passed, Brian began to think of himself as a part of the forest; he depended on his hatchet as if it were his right arm. His hair matted with grime and his face stained with smoke, he felt wild, strong, governed by his primal instincts.

Spotting a large blue kingfisher by the lake one afternoon, Brian noted how it dove into the water and then "emerged a split second later" with a small fish fastened on its beak. Weary of eating berries and bird eggs, the boy fashioned a bow and arrow—which he used as a spearing kit like the kingfisher's beak so that he, too, could dine on fresh lake-trout. Later he constructed a retaining fence to trap the fish in a shallow pond. Then, fortified by his new diet of fish, he built a log wall to protect his cave, carved a sharp-pointed spear, and refined his bow and arrow in order to kill birds.

As time passed the boy became attuned to the subtle sounds of the forest and the area's sudden shifts in weather. One day while he was hunting, however, Brian stopped cold in his tracks: between him and the lake stood a large wolf, staring at him with large yellow eyes.

That first encounter was terrifying; but in time Brian became accustomed to the predator's visits. *He knew the wolf now, as the wolf knew him, and he nodded to it, nodded and smiled . . . He was not the same now . . . In measured time forty seven days had passed since the crash. Forty seven days, he thought, since he had died and been born as the new Brian.*

Having long since given up hope of rescue, Brian began to think of the approaching winter. He was proud of his new survival skills and confident that he could weather nature's cruelest tricks—until one night a terrible storm ravaged his campsite, destroying his wall, scattering his food supply, and shattering several of his tools. Later, while drinking at the lake, he was inexplicably trampled by a cow moose.

With bruised ribs—and a bruised ego—the boy sat down. Then he noticed it: " . . . Something curved and yellow was sticking six or eight inches out of the water." At first he could not place it, but then, under his breath, the words tumbled out: "It's the tail of the plane." It had been upended during the storm.

Determined to retrieve a survival pack from the craft, Brian built a makeshift raft and floated out to the wreckage. Straddling the plane's belly from the water, he hacked through its aluminum hull with his hatchet. Then, in a careless moment, he dropped the hatchet. Despondently he realized that "without the hatchet he had nothing—no fire, no tools, no weapons—he was nothing. The hatchet was, had been him." Fortunately, however, after a few difficult forays to the murky lake bottom, Brian retrieved the irreplaceable tool.

Then, chopping his way through the plane's exterior shell and wriggling through the opening, Brian was met with a horrific sight. *In the light coming through the side window . . . he saw the pilot's head. only it wasn't the pilot's head any longer. The fish . . . They had been at the pilot all this time, almost two months nibbling and chewing and all that remained was the not quite cleaned skull . . .* Fighting back his horror, Brian grabbed the survival kit and made his way up to the surface.

Back at the camp he inspected his newly-won treasures: a sleeping bag, a foam pad, an aluminum cook set, matches, two small butane lighters, and a sheath knife with a compass in the handle. At the bottom of the kit, he also found an emergency transmitter—which appeared to be broken—and a .22 rifle with ammunition. *It was a strange feeling, holding the rifle. . . . The rifle changed him the minute he picked it up, and he wasn't sure he liked the change very much.*

Now ravenously hungry, Brian ripped open a package of freeze-dried food. *And at that precise instant, with his mind full of home and the smell from the food filling him, the plane appeared . . . There was a tiny drone . . . then suddenly, roaring over his head low and in back of the ridge, a bushplane with floats . . . passed directly over him . . . then turned and glided back, touching the water gently . . . and settling with a spray . . . in front of Brian's shelter.* Before the boy could fully fathom what he was seeing, the pilot cut the engine and got out of the cockpit, stepping onto the float so as not to get his feet wet. *"I heard your emergency transmitter . . . "* He trailed off . . . *"Damn. You're him aren't you? You're that kid. They quit looking, a month, no, almost two months ago. You're him, aren't you? . . . "* Brian looked down at himself—dirty and ragged, burned and lean and tough—and he coughed to clear his throat. "My name is Brian Robeson," he said. *"Would you like something to eat?"*

Brian returned to civilization. Now, however, he was more thoughtful and introspective than before, with a new interest in nature and a firm resolve not to take everyday conveniences for granted. And although he often found himself longing for the solitude of his wild lake home, to his surprise he was no longer angry with his mother.

. . . After the initial surprise and happiness from his parents at his being alive . . . things rapidly went back to normal. His father returned to the northern oil fields, where Brian eventually visited him, and his mother stayed in the city . . . Brian tried several times to tell his father, came really close once to doing it, but in the end never said a word about the man or what he knew, the Secret.

Commentary:

Brian Robeson, as he suffers through his ordeal, learns more than just how to survive in the out-of-doors: he also learns some things about nature—and, most importantly, about himself.

And who is Brian Robeson, beneath civilization's indulgent and often forged veneer? When challenged, he is a person who can and does make the most of his talents, bringing his latent intelligence and judgment to the fore and depending only on his own personal hand tool for survival. And eventually he goes home to forge his own spiritual path as well, leaving his mother to grapple with her Secret and his father to retreat from involvement, while he, Brian, seeks his own way. Brian has grown up to become—as we must all inevitably become in order to claim our adulthood—a survivor in life's harsh and humbling wilderness.

ANPAO

An American Odyssey
by Jamake Highwater, Harper Collins Publishers, New York, N.Y., 1977

Type of work: Young adult Native American oral history

Principal characters:
Anpao, the illegitimate offspring of the Sun and an Earth Woman
Oapna, Anpao's contrary brother
Ko-ko-mik-e-sis, Anpao's true love
The Moon, the Sun's vengeful and jealous wife

Commentary:

Written in the spiritual language of legend and chant, Jamake Highwater's *ANPAO* succeeds on at least two levels: first, it preserves a small but significant part of American Indian oral tradition and mysticism; and second, it introduces Native American culture to the world at large. In so doing, it reads like a delightful New World fable, one in which inanimate objects (including not only the forces of nature but even dwellings, musical instruments and diseases) are routinely personified and given souls of their own.

Highwater's mythic novel also self-consciously recalls one of the oldest, most venerated texts of Western literature: Homer's *The Odyssey.* As *The Boston Globe* reported, ANPAO is "an Indian 'Ulysses,' whose odyssey will help illuminate the Indian concept of nature and man's place in the cosmos. Clearly in this he has succeeded."

The author himself beautifully captures the spirit of his 1978 Newbery Award-winning book when he writes: *Some of these tales are very old, so old that no one quite knows where they originated. Others are quite recent, coming out of the experience of the Indians since the white man invaded their country . . . But old or new, the stories have no known authors. They exist as the river of memory of a people, surging with their images and their rich meanings from one place to another, from one generation to the next—the tellers and the told so intermingled in time and space that no one can separate them.*

Story Overview:

Anpao's heart beat like a triumphant war drum when the beautiful Ko-ko-mik-e-sis agreed to be his wife. But the sadness in her eyes soon muted his joy. "Wait!" she said, "The Sun has asked for me. He says that I must not marry, that I belong to him . . . You alone can find the Sun because you are brave and adventurous. You must tell him that you want me for your wife. Then you must ask him to take the scar from your face. That will be his sign to me. I will know he is pleased and will not punish me. But if he refuses, or if you fail to find his lodge, then you must never return to my village and I will never marry."

Faced either with the prospect of great triumph or great despair, both for himself and his beloved Ko-ko-mik-e-sis, Anpao set off with his twin brother Oapna on the arduous journey in search of the Sun's lodge. Along the way, many questions haunted Anpao: How had he been marked by the red scar that stained his cheek? Why could he not remember his parents? And why did his puzzling twin brother always say the opposite of what he meant?

The brothers journeyed "over great prairies, through precipitous canyons in which the water leapt along wooded ridges, and among grass-rich valleys," their food sack becoming lighter each day. One night, as the Moon rose high in the sky, Anpao exclaimed, "Look, Oapna! The Moon is very beautiful tonight." Oapna agreed: "No, it is very ugly!" Positively enthralled by the luminous globe that rose in a great arc across the black sky, Oapna could not contain himself. "It is the ugliest thing I have ever seen!" he shouted.

The vain Moon, who was not pleased by the ardor of Oapna's contrary sentiments, immediately caused a great ring of light to form around the twins. When it vanished, Anpao found himself standing alone. His brother had been spirited away, and beside the Moon he could see a bright new star in the sky. Determined to shoot down the beautiful star for Ko-ko-mik-e-sis, he drew an arrow onto his bow and let it fly. The bright star plunged to earth, but when Anpao arrived at the spot where it had fallen, he found, to his horror, the battered and bloody body of Oapna, swinging limply in the branches of a tree. Mad with grief, Anpao staggered into the woods. Crumpling into a lonely heap on the ground, he slept until morning.

When Anpao awakened, he found a swan-girl standing before him. She led him to an island, where he met Swan Woman, who, wise and powerful, presented him with a magical stone pipe and revealed the mystery of his parentage.

Long ago, Swan Woman began, the Sun had fallen in love with an Earth Woman, and had taken her to his lodge in the World-Above-the-World. For a time the woman was very happy, and bore a son. This son was Anpao. However, in time the woman became homesick and attempted to escape the World-Above-the-World through a hole she had dug out of the sky. She lowered herself and Anpao downward with a rope she had secretly plaited. But, alas, the rope was too short, and as the woman dangled above the Earth, not knowing what to do, the Sun discovered her. Furious, he struck his traitorous wife with a fiery hoop of willow, killing her. The rope gave, and mother and son, along with the magical hoop, fell to the ground, Anpao landing on his mother with such force that her belly split open. Her blood splashed on Anpao's cheek—and left the scar.

The orphaned Anpao had been found and cared for by Grandmother Spider, who warned him never to toss his hoop into the air, for its magic was very strong. Nevertheless, one day Anpao disobeyed Grandmother Spider—and, sure enough, the hoop plunged down and struck him on the head. The blow was so powerful that it split him in half and he became two children—Anpao and Oapna, twin brothers who were opposite halves of each other.

Now Anpao, stunned by the revelation of his origins, fell into a deep sleep. When he awakened, he found himself held fast by roots and

Oapna curled up next to him. Oapna, however, had been transformed "into some unimaginable thing . . . golden and fibrous and hard—like a gigantic cocoon." An astonished Anpao "could see Oapna's translucent body slowly pulsating" inside the gourd-like structure. "This newly born body feebly rubbed its limbs together as if to dry itself and undulated blindly like a great worm. Then after it had rested it began to slide toward Anpao," gradually fusing the twin brothers into one.

Whole again, Anpao set off again on his quest to win Ko-ko-mik-e-sis for his bride. But on the next day, Anpao fell into a ravine and broke his leg. He had almost given up hope, when a grotesque and smelly dwarf appeared and offered to mend his leg on one condition: that Anpao become his slave. Fearing death, Anpao agreed, and for the duration of the winter he hunted game for the vile little man.

Then one day in spring, while he was out hunting bear, Anpao came upon three "cloud men" who called themselves "Thunders." Since they were old enemies of Anpao's loathsome captor, they asked Anpao if he would lure the ravenous dwarf from his lair with the promise of bear meat. Anpao agreed. When the old dwarf came out and found himself confronting the Thunders, he began shooting his poisoned quills. When the air exploded with blue sparks as the Thunders hurled lightning bolts in return, the old dwarf "fell slowly to the ground, where his body smoldered until at last it vanished entirely."

After a winter of harsh servitude, a grateful Anpao wandered into a friendly village. There, two adventurous brothers offered to join him in his search for the Sun. Soon their travels led them into a vast desert, where they suffered much from hunger and thirst. To make matters worse, when they finally found some eggs to eat, Anpao discerned them to be sacred. Despite his warnings, one of the brothers devoured the sacred eggs, and shortly thereafter he was turned into a great water serpent. "Do not be afraid," the serpent hissed. " . . . I am still your friend. And do not weep, for I have finally found the place where I truly belong."

Anpao and the lone grieving brother returned to the village, where Anpao danced the story of Snake Boy, unaware that the vengeful Moon was still plotting his death. Thus, when Anpao took ill, Snake Boy's sister Amana—who had fallen in love with Anpao—suspected enchantment. After guiding Anpao to a Wise Man who saved his life, Amana expressed her desire to marry Anpao. "Forgive me," he answered, picturing Ko-Ko-mik-e-sis in his mind. "When I hear singing, it is not the song you sing . . . I have become my journey, and my journey has become me. Without it I am nothing." Then, with heavy heart, Anpao left Amana's camp and continued his search.

After passing through many other trials, Anpao at last reached the edge of the desert, "where the light of the Sun was so strong that only the humblest of creatures and plants could survive among the crags and drifts of sand." There he came upon a young man named Morning Star, who invited him to his home. As he entered the lodge, Anpao could not help but tremble with fear. "There was only one person sitting inside—the Sun's wife and Morning Star's Mother. It was the Moon!" Anpao felt certain now that the Moon would destroy him. But to his surprise, she offered him food instead; and as they conversed, Anpao slowly perceived that his purifying journey had so altered his appearance that his nemesis no longer recognized the mature young man seated before her. Calling himself "Scarface," Anpao consented to stay on as Morning Star's companion.

One day, against the Moon's warning not to hunt near the lake, Morning Star crept away to see the "magic dogs" (horses) his father kept hidden there. Anpao followed after to protect his friend. When they arrived and nothing more menacing than six tiny yellow birds fluttered over their heads, Morning Star laughed. But his frivolity quickly ceased when he realized that the birds "were only decoys riding on the beaks of giant beings with the barbed wings of bats." While Morning Star panicked and ran in circles, Anpao bravely fought the birds with his axe, slaying the lot of them.

In gratitude, the Sun removed the scar from Anpao's face: "He was transformed at once. The Sun, the Moon, and Morning Star stared at him in amazement, for he looked exactly like his celestial brother and great father . . . So Anpao became the first person in whom the power of the Sun, the Moon, and the Earth of his mother were united."

Accepting the blessings of his celestial companions along with their rich gifts of weapons and horses, Anpao rode furiously to reach his treasured Ko-ko-mik-e-sis. As he drew closer to her village, however, he grieved: "The world was changed. Where deer had leaped across the grass, there was now gray land with scattered herds of animals . . . The great river which once ran abundantly with clear water was soggy with sludge and rust." Men with pale faces were polluting the land and killing the people.

When he arrived at Ko-Ko-mik-e-sis' village, he was relieved to see that the plague had not yet touched it. But when he warned her people of the approaching destruction and begged them to follow him to safety, they mocked him. Only Ko-ko-mik-e-sis believed his words. Together they departed the village, and before long "the spirits of the Raven and the Sun took Anpao's hand. The spirits of the Moon and those of Morning Star and the Kit Fox took the hand of Ko-ko-mik-e-sis. Together they chanted by the water and sang 'Come with us to safety in the village below . . . '" When the song ended, "the spirits led Anpao and Ko-ko-mik-e-sis slowly down into the beautiful water. For a moment, she gasped with fear as the water touched her face, but she smiled and gazed at Anpao as they descended. Then they were gone."

Years later, hearing the singing, laughing voices of men, women and children issuing from beneath the water, the old Holy Man Wasicong whispered to his people: "It is Ko-ko-mik-e-sis and Anpao and all their children! . . . Do you hear . . . ? . . . We shall live again. We shall live again."

ISLAND OF THE BLUE DOLPHINS

by Scott O'Dell, Houghton Mifflin Co., Boston, Mass., 1960

Type of work: Adolescent adventure novel

Setting: An island off the California coast; mid-1800s

Principal characters:
Karana, a native American girl
Ramo, her little brother
Rontu, a dog
Tutok, an Aleut girl

Story Overview:

The Russian captain and his Aleut crew had anchored their ship on the shores of the Island of the Blue Dolphins, where they arranged with the Ghalasat natives to spearhunt otter in the tribal waters. In return for this privilege, the Russians agreed to turn over half their catch to the villagers. When their hatches were loaded, however, the hunters tried to leave without making full payment. The chief of the village objected, touching off a battle in which most of the men of the village were killed, including the chief himself.

Throughout the long winter the villagers mourned their dead. In the spring, the new chief paddled away in his canoe to find a safer home for his people. Two years later, he sent a white man's ship to carry his people to a new island.

Black clouds were gathering behind the vessel as it dropped anchor in the waves off the island, and the villagers rushed to clamber aboard before the storm broke. Among them was a young girl named Karana, the daughter of the slaughtered chief. But in the midst of the confusion as the ship moved off through the rough waters, Karana suddenly jumped overboard: she had just seen her little brother Ramo standing forlorn on the shore, still clutching the forgotten fishing spear that he had gone back at the last minute to retrieve. *I kept thinking over and over as I swam how I would punish Ramo when I reached the shore, yet when I felt the sand under my feet and saw him standing at the edge of the waves . . . I forgot all those things I planned to do. Instead I fell to my knees and put my arms around him.*

Karana and Ramo spent the day gathering food. As night fell, Ramo suddenly remembered the village's canoes that lay hidden on the beach—their one means of escape from the island. Karana expected to help her brother retrieve the boats, but when she woke up the next morning, Ramo was already gone. Reluctantly, she decided not to follow him; he would have to learn to do things himself and become a man.

Karana waited a long time, but Ramo did not return. At last she set off to search for him. Nearing a cave, she discovered his mutilated body, savaged by the pack of wild dogs that roamed the island. *All night I sat there with the body of my brother and did not sleep. I vowed that someday I would go back and kill the wild dogs . . . I thought about how I would do it, but mostly I thought of Ramo, my brother.*

Karana soon found that she could not bear living alone among the empty huts of the village. One day she burned them and moved to a tall rock by a spring. There she waited for the return of the ship which had taken her people.

Karana knew she needed weapons to protect herself from the dogs. Since the laws of her village prohibited women from making weapons, she searched the island to find some, but to no avail. In desperation, she decided to break the tribal taboos and fashion her own. *Would the four winds blow in from the four directions of the world and smother me . . . ? Or as others said, would the sea rise over the island in a terrible flood? Would the weapons break in my hands at the moment my life was in danger, which is what my father had said?*

After many failed attempts, Karana finally formed a crude spear, a bow, and a handful of arrows. She spent her days scavenging for food, and her nights watching the stars over the island. Every day she watched the harbor, but the white men's ship never came.

At last Karana decided that she must leave the island. The dangers of the sea terrified her, but it was better to face them than to stay alone on the Island of the Blue Dolphins, "where everything reminded [her] of those who were dead and those who had gone away."

Swallowing her fear, the girl pushed off in her canoe towards the island that lay to the east. But halfway through the first night of her journey, the canoe began to leak. Finally submitting to her fears, she paddled back, fighting sleep and the pain of her blistered hands, guided only by the blue dolphins which surrounded the canoe. Reaching home, Karana knew she should never again try to cross the sea alone.

Resigning herself to remain on the Island of the Blue Dolphins, Karana built herself a hut. To keep the dogs out, she shaped the ribs of a whale into a fence. Then, in order to make a good fishing spear, she set out to hunt down a sea elephant and pull out one of its teeth. But once again nature was treacherous. As Karana tracked down one of the mammoth sea elephants, she fell and injured her leg. For several days she could not walk at all. Then the water supply in her hut ran out. Forced to drag herself to the spring, she stayed in a nearby cave until her leg healed. All the while, the dogs waited for her outside the cave's entrance.

Karana finally pulled out the spear-point teeth she needed from the carcass of a dead sea elephant. Now, she concluded, with a proper weapon and her leg strong and whole again, it was time to take her revenge on the pack of dogs. Creeping close to the mouth of their cave, she quietly set a fire. When the smoke-stunned animals emerged, she killed three of them outright with her spear. Their wounded leader, a big gray Aleut dog with yellow eyes, escaped; but Karana easily caught up with him. However, she did not kill the dog; instead, she took him to her hut and nursed him back to health. She named him Rontu, or "Fox Eyes," and he became her close companion.

Karana constructed a new canoe from the damaged hull of the old boat, then spent the winter making a special spear to catch a "devilfish," or octopus—a catch that would provide many meals. One day, out in her canoe, she spotted the giant devilfish that she had been stalking for months. With her new spear she managed to hook the creature, and, after a long struggle in which both she and Rontu were injured, she finally landed it.

As the months turned into years, Karana and Rontu explored every corner of their island. They visited Black Cave, where Karana's ancestors had created images of people with gleaming abalone-shell eyes. Together they spent a night there, while Karana pondered the images and played her flute.

One summer, another party of otter hunters—this time an Aleut band—disembarked on the island. Remembering the bitter encounter that had killed her father and driven her people from the island, Karana hid in another cave-house by the spring. And there, while she waited for the hunters to take their leave, she made herself a beautiful skirt out of cormorant feathers—which were "black, but underneath were green and gold [and] shimmered as though they were on fire."

Karana also met up with an Aleut girl, Tutok, who had wandered away from the ship to explore the island. Even though the Aleut were an enemy to Karana's tribe, the two girls became friends and spent many days exchanging gifts and teaching each other to speak their separate languages. *I had not heard words spoken for so long that they sounded strange to me, yet they were good to hear, even though it was an enemy who spoke them.*

After the Aleut hunters had left the island, Karana missed Tutok sorely. Eventually, she found some solace in the companionship of a young crippled sea otter; she also tamed many birds and kept them at her hut. *With the young birds and the old ones, the white gull, and Rontu, who was always trotting at my heels, the yard seemed a happy place . . .*

Karana loved her animal friends so strongly that she resolved not to ever kill animals again. "Animals and birds," she thought, "are like people, too, though they do not talk the same or do the same things. Without them the earth would be an unhappy place."

Then one summer day when Karana let old Rontu out of the fence, he did not return. She found him just before he took his last breath and buried him in a crevice in a rock, covering his body with colored pebbles from the cove. Later that summer, by placing a drug in the water where the wild pack drank, she captured another yellow-eyed dog and named him Rontu-Aru, or "Son of Rontu." They had many happy times together; but Karana now

thought more and more about human friends she had known. She wondered if her sister Ulape was married, and if so, how many children she had. Sometimes she imagined she heard "their voices in the wind," or "in the waves that lapped softly against the canoe" when she was at sea. Indeed, "[strong] was the wish to be where people lived, to hear their voices and their laughter."

The next summer a powerful tidal wave hit the island. Karana survived by hunching in the crevice of a cliff. She also weathered an earthquake, during which the ground "rose and fell like a great animal breathing."

Not long afterwards, as she sat building a canoe, Karana saw a ship on the horizon. It was neither like the white man's ship which had taken her people away nor like an Aleut ship. When the crewmen came ashore and she saw that they were not Aleut, she resolved to leave the island with them. But before she could reach them, the ship had again sailed away.

Two years later, the same ship returned. This time, Karana readied herself, drawing the mark of an unmarried girl across her nose. As she advanced toward the men, one, a priest, spoke to her. *Though his words meant nothing to me, they now seemed sweet. They were the sound of a human voice. There is no sound like this in all the world.*

The men made a dress for Karana out of two pairs of trousers, and although her cormorant skirt and otter cape were far more beautiful, she put them in her basket to wear when they reached their destination. Sailing away from her beloved island, her thoughts turned to her animal friends; they had given her many happy memories. And beside the ship's bough, as if to say goodbye, blue dolphins leaped through the water, escorting the ship toward the land to the east.

Commentary:

Island of the Blue Dolphins is a speculative re-creation of the adventure of a Native American woman who actually lived alone on the island of San Nicolas, about 75 miles southwest of Los Angeles, from 1835 to 1853. Little is known of "The Lost Woman of San Nicolas" except that she did jump into the sea from a ship, made her way back to shore, and was found on the island 18 years later, dressed in a cormorant feather skirt, with a dog at her side.

Written in a simple, straightforward narrative style, Scott O'Dell's novel powerfully develops Karana's strong character. Her loneliness, for instance, echoes throughout the book. Despite the fact that Karana is skilled, intelligent, and strong enough to survive alone on the island, she never quite overcomes her ache for human companionship.

Karana comes to appreciate and love her animal friends, and at the same time achieves a sense of the greatness of human worth. When she meets Tutok, she does not kill her, as she might have earlier. Instead, two enemies become friends, forming a bond that remains in Karana's heart years later.

RISING SUN

by Michael Crichton, Alfred A. Knopf Inc., New York, N.Y., 1992

Type of work: Modern detective fiction

Setting: Present-day Los Angeles, California

Principal characters:

Lieutenant Peter Smith, Special Services Division police detective and liaison with the Los Angeles' Japanese community

John Conner, a Special Services detective on indefinite leave

Eddie Sakamura, a wealthy Japanese playboy

U.S. Senator John Morton, a powerful player in Japanese trade

Mr. Ishigura, a respected Japanese businessman

Story Overview:

Lieutenant Peter Smith received a call informing him that there had been a murder at the grand opening of Nakamoto Towers and that the Japanese hosts were demanding a Special Services liaison officer at the crime scene. On his way, Smith picked up Captain John Conner, who spoke fluent Japanese and was one of the most knowledgeable men in the division.

Upon their arrival, a Mr. Ishigura stepped forward. After introductions, he said, "The only reason there's a problem here tonight is that your colleague is unreasonable." Apparently an imprudent agent named Graham had threatened to interrogate everyone at the reception regarding the murder—including highly influential U.S. senators and a number of celebrities. At best, Graham was "a pain in the ass," and it was generally known he had no liking for the Japanese.

As they approached the crime scene on the 46th floor, Smith and Conner noticed that a Japanese was standing behind the yellow tape taking photographs. The man was part of the corporation's security staff, Mr. Ishigura explained.

They learned that the strangled woman, Cheryl Lynn Austin, 23, was a known party girl, having been seen with some of the city's highest rollers. Next the detectives met with the building's security guard. They wanted to view the security video tapes for the 46th floor.

The guard told them he had come on duty after the murder took place, and that the guard he was to relieve was nowhere in sight. Instead, he found a Japanese man in his office. It soon became evident that this man had removed one of the security tapes.

The following morning Smith and Conner found the other security guard sitting in a bar, who told them that he had left his shift early the night before after his supervisor had replaced him. His supervisor? "Japanese . . . New guy . . . Never seen him before." When the agents stood to leave, the guard said, "I'll write down my phone number for you," and scribbled something on a napkin. When they got in the car, Conner handed his partner the napkin, which bore a message in block letters: "THEY STOLE THE TAPES."

The next day, acting on a hunch, Smith and Conner visited the TV station that had covered the Nakamoto opening. They viewed the tapes of the celebration and saw Cheryl Lynn "laughing with Eddie Sakamura . . . But from time to time, her eyes flicked away [as] if she was waiting . . . for someone to arrive . . . " When Sakamura "became aware that he did not have her full attention," he pulled her roughly to him. Then someone stepped in front of the camera and they were lost in the crowd.

Smith and Conner drove to a Beverly Hills club that Eddie Sakamura often frequented, but were told that he was attending a party at a house in the hills. As the detectives approached the house, a large man appeared at the front door. After showing their badges and asking to speak with Eddie, they stepped inside and immediately spotted both Eddie and Senator John Morton, a powerful framer of Japanese trade.

A guard confronted the pair; unless they had a search warrant, he told them, they would have to leave. "Mr. Sakamura is a friend of mine," Conner insisted. Now the guard moved toward him threateningly, but Conner quickly pinned the man to the floor.

At the disturbance, Eddie Sakamura ambled over and agreed to answer questions about Cheryl's murder. He coolly denied that he'd been with Cheryl that night or that he had taken the tapes, though the guard had said the man who took the tapes had a burn mark on his hand, exactly like the one on Eddie's.

After leaving the club, the detectives headed to the morgue. There the medical examiner described the peculiarities of the woman's wounds, and concluded, "I don't think there's any question: we're looking at a case of sexual asphyxia." Just then, Conner received a telephone call: Mr. Ishigura of Nakamoto Corporation had delivered a box of video tapes to police headquarters. At last, it seemed, Mr. Ishigura was cooperating in the investigation.

When the detectives examined the tapes showing the murder scene, Conner found a spot where Eddie Sakamura's face appeared reflected in a mirror. They gathered up the tapes and left.

Smith dropped Conner off at his home and was headed to his own apartment when the car phone rang. It was agent Graham; he was outside Eddie Sakamura's home with a warrant for Sakamura's arrest, and wanted Smith's help with the bust. For once, Graham was doing things by the book.

When Smith joined him, the two detectives went to the door and kicked it open. Behind two shrieking party girls, both men suddenly spied a "dark figure running down the stairs." By the time they had dashed back outside, Eddie's Ferrari was already speeding away, a police backup unit in hot pursuit. "I got to the concrete embankment about thirty seconds after the Ferrari hit it flat out at a hundred and sixty kilometers an hour," Smith later reported. Upon impact the gas tank exploded and flames shot into the sky, leaving the car nothing more than a smoldering hulk of metal.

The following morning, dispatch sent Smith two intriguing messages. Eddie had called at 1:42 a.m. with urgent news about the missing tape, followed by a call from the assistant chief of police—which left him very nervous, because Jim Olson never called before ten in the morning unless there was a problem.

"Looks like we got ourselves a rattlesnake by the tail," Olsen told Smith when he returned the call. " . . . Last night was a prime screwup . . . nobody got the names of the girls . . . They're cutting Sakamura's body out of the wreck this morning to ship what's left to the morgue." The chief, assuming that the videotapes proved that Sakamura had killed the girl, was closing the investigation.

Smith hurried to the lab to make copies of the tapes—before anything happened to them. Along with a technician there, Theresa Asakuma, Smith scrutinized the tapes and found that some of them depicted the murder quite plainly, though the murderer's face was still obscured. Theresa volunteered to study them for more clues. Smith and Conner then went to see Senator Morton—who had seemed strangely interested in knowing whether or not the investigation was formally wrapped up.

When the detectives returned to the lab, Theresa informed them that the tapes had been doctored. "The shadows don't match," she reflected. "They're in the wrong place . . . " Then Smith and Connor remembered the man they had found taking pictures at the murder scene. "Do you remember how he moved?" Conner asked excitedly. Yes, there had been something odd about him. "He never turned around," Smith answered. "He backed up all the way . . . He was repeating the walk of the girl and the killer in reverse, so . . . he would have a good record of where the shadows in the room were."

Conner left, but Theresa and Smith continued to examine the altered tapes. "There," she suddenly exclaimed. "They forgot to erase that one." And peering at the monitor, Smith could make out the indistinct image of a third man—not the man who had been involved with, and murdered, Cheryl, but another. And, after many more hours of video enhancement, they could clearly make out the face of this other man: Eddie Sakamura.

The tapes had definitely been tampered with. Using clever imaging techniques, there they could see, superimposed on the tape, a reflected image of what appeared to be Eddie Sakamura. Theresa kept working to generate more detail. Then suddenly they saw the face of the real murderer. They were stunned into silence, as they recognized the smiling countenance of Senator John Morton. After snapping a Polaroid photo of the screen, Smith left to find Conner.

The detectives tracked down Morton, and found him preparing to appear in a commercial about how America was losing its economic competitiveness to foreigners. "I have nothing to say to you gentlemen," Morton grunted. But when Conner told him that he had a videotape that revealed the real identity of Cheryl Austin's killer, Morton began pacing the room. He sidled

toward the window and looked down on the soundstage, where he saw a familiar figure. It was Eddie Sakamura—alive. Just at that moment the phone rang. It was Theresa Asakuma; she had uncovered another flaw on one of the last tapes.

During the few minutes Smith was on the phone, the senator disappeared upstairs. Conner raced after him, but caught up with him too late: Morton had already put a gun in his mouth and pulled the trigger.

The detectives reported the suicide and stayed on the scene until police officials arrived. Then they had something else to worry about. "That damn Eddie," Conner said. " . . . Didn't you notice how he acted around Ishigura? He was too confident . . . He should have been frightened and he wasn't." Racing to Eddie's home, they found his body floating face down in the swimming pool.

The next morning both detectives met with Theresa, who said she had something to show them on the tapes. In one sequence, the men saw Cheryl's body lying motionless on the conference table; but although the tape was rolling, nothing was happening. Then Theresa began to describe the next scene as they watched it. "It was a static scene. And then I saw, clearly, the girl's leg twitch . . . Now the girl's arm . . . The fingers closed and opened." At that point in time, Cheryl was still alive.

"Now watch the clock," Theresa said, pointing at a spot on the tape. It said 8:36. The tape ran for two more minutes, but the clock, frozen at 8:36, never moved. Smith then produced a tape he had found—one presumably left by Eddie Sakamura—in his apartment the night before. There, "in crisp black and white . . . they saw Morton leave the girl behind on the table." Then the figure of another man appeared, cautiously entering the room. "It was Ishigura," Smith said aloud; it was he who had actually done the killing in hopes of fingering the senator. Ishigura was seeing to it that Morton would pay for his threats to back down on several important trade agreements. There was Ishigura, cool as can be: "very deliberately, he walked to the edge of the table, placed his hands on the girl's neck and strangled her."

Rushing to Nakamoto Towers, Smith and Conner found Ishigura in a meeting. All at once a young Japanese aide passed into the conference room, approached a distinguished-looking gray-haired man, and whispered something to him. The older gentleman stood and slowly left the room; one by one, the others followed. After some time Smith and Conner entered the room. "Mr. Ishigura," Conner said, "would you please stand?" The man didn't move. "Show them the tape," Conner said. Peter played the tape, which showed Ishigura strangling the girl. "When you are through with your charade, you will find me outside," Ishigura said indignantly. Then he stood, left the room, and walked out onto the terrace.

By the time the tape had ended, the terrace was empty. From the railing, the detectives saw that Ishigura had landed in freshly-poured concrete. In the distance, sirens wailed, echoing through the streets.

THE HUNT FOR RED OCTOBER

by Tom Clancy, Naval Institute Press, Annapolis, Maryland, 1984

Type of work: Military suspense fiction

Setting: The United States, the Soviet Union, and aboard the Soviet submarine *Red October*; 1980s

Principal characters:

Marko Ramius, Captain First Rank of the *Red October*

Jack Ryan, agent of the Central Intelligence Agency

James Greer, Ryan's superior

"Judge" Moore, Director of the Central Intelligence Agency

Ronald Jones, U.S. Navy sonar technician

Story Overview:

When *Red October,* the most powerful nuclear submarine ever produced by the Soviet Union, plunged deep into the sea on December 3, only Captain Marko Ramius knew that this would be her final voyage. Rather than keep his scheduled rendezvous with a group of attack subs and battleships of the Soviet fleet, Ramius intended to defect to the Americans, making the *Red October* his personal weapon of vengeance against the motherland.

Before setting out, the captain mailed a letter announcing his defection; the news would reach the high levels of Soviet government only after he had made his move. Of course it would only be a matter of time before the Soviet fleet would be dispatched to sink or expropriate his vessel and to execute him as an enemy of the state. But Ramius had great confidence in his own abilities and felt sure that he could escape detection.

Even as Ramius' scheme was being played out in the Atlantic, Jack Ryan, a mid-level analyst for the Central Intelligence Agency, sensed something unusual afoot. Called back to Washington from his post in London, where he had been given a set of classified documents obtained by the British Secret Service, Ryan began to unravel the mystery of *Red October.*

Arriving in the Washington office of his boss, James Greer, Ryan and his superior examined photos of the submarine and speculated about the reasons for the two large doors in its fore and aft sections. Having obtained proper clearance, Ryan took the photos to a friend, Skip Tyler of the Naval Academy. Tyler advised Ryan that the doors probably indicated a tunnel drive, a propulsion system the U.S. Navy had once tried and then abandoned as unworkable. Tyler noted that the jet-like action of a tunnel drive greatly reduced noise and that if *Red October* boasted such a system, the sub would be able to travel virtually undetected.

As Ryan gathered intelligence, the USS *Dallas,* an American sub in the North Atlantic, was routinely monitoring Soviet submarines. Ronald Jones, a top-notch sonar technician, sat at his station in his usual trance-like pose. All at once there came over his earphones a short rumbling noise, but computer analysis attributed the "funny signal" to mere magma displacement. Jones felt uneasy with that analysis and asked his superior officer to inform the Captain.

"You against the machine again?" the captain complained good-naturedly. Jones was still struck by the easy informality of his commanding officer, even after three years on nuclear subs.

"Skipper," Jones replied, "the computer works pretty well most of the time, but sometimes it's a real *kludge* . . . For one thing, the frequency is all wrong." Jones couldn't really say what the signal meant: "I don't know, Captain. It isn't screw sounds, and it isn't any naturally produced sound that I've heard. Beyond that . . . "

"Well, keep at it," the captain advised. "No sense letting all this expensive gear go to waste."

Back in Washington, CIA Director "Judge" Moore summoned Greer and Ryan to his office. Moore, whose nickname "Judge" derived from his years as a federal magistrate, had received a communique from "CARDINAL," a well-placed CIA mole working in the Soviet hierarchy. The message revealed the reason for a recent surge in Soviet naval activity: one of the USSR's most state-of-the-art nuclear subs was missing. All available Soviet ships had been put on alert to retrieve her at any cost, lest she sink—or, worse, fall into American imperialist hands.

The Soviets knew the Americans would immediately detect their massive naval force, steaming for U.S. shores. It seemed to give the impression of an all-out invasion aimed directly at the United States—if it were not for the obvious flaws of such a transparent strategy and the lack of accompanying air power.

Because he had done his homework on Ramius, Jack Ryan was able to guess the true motive for the massive enemy fleet action: the Soviet captain intended to defect—and now the Soviet Union knew it too. Ramius, Ryan had learned, was disillusioned with the Soviet government and sought revenge for two reasons: first, for his wife's death at the hands of an incompetent Red Army physician; second, for years of oppression by the Communist Party that he had come to view as abusive and ridiculous. Ramius wanted Party *apparatchiks* to pay for their abuses with the loss of *Red October.*

Ryan felt that the facts supported his hypothesis—unless CARDINAL's story was misinformation aimed at duping or misdirecting the CIA. Even though such a possibility was real, Judge Moore instructed Ryan to brief the President and Joint Chiefs of Staff about his theory and to investigate the accuracy of CARDINAL's story through independent sources.

Aboard the *Red October*, Ramius was maintaining radio silence—supposedly to avoid being detected by the Americans; the ruse worked, as most of his crew became convinced of the secrecy of their mission. In fact, he had first secretly killed the *Zampolit*, or political officer, who posed a threat to the defection, and convinced the enlisted men that the officer had died in an unfortunate accident. Next he had consulted with his fellow officers, who intended to defect with him. Little did Ramius and the *Red October* officers realize that sonarman Jones had succeeded in tracking their vessel and that the Americans were now entirely aware of their intention to defect.

Ramius and his officers plotted their strategy: when *Red October* neared American shores, the officers would create a fake radiation leak in order to distract the crew. By creating this feeling of imminent danger, they would then prepare the crew to evacuate the sub, voluntarily putting themselves into American hands.

For Jack Ryan, meanwhile, events were moving very quickly—perhaps too quickly. He was sent to the *HMS Invincible*, a British ship in the North Atlantic, with orders to have the battleship assist in defusing a possible Soviet threat. The *Invincible* was to make contact with *Red October* and ascertain Ramius' intention to defect. If a defection was verified, the British ship was to evacuate the crew from the sub, and transfer them first to the United States and then back to the Soviet Union. The *Pigeon*, another British ship in the *Invincible's* battle group, was to protect the *Red October* until two American attack subs could escort her safely into American waters. Once the *October's* crew had been removed, Ryan himself, assisted by several others, was to board her and guide her into a hiding place in an American missile submarine bay, shielded from Soviet satellites. The Soviet crewmen would be tricked into believing *Red October* had been destroyed when the Americans detonated an old submarine in the vicinity.

Tensions ran high and many cat-and-mouse confrontations with Soviet aircraft over the Atlantic ensued as both superpowers raced to reach the *Red October*. The American *Dallas* reached her first and convinced Ramius to surface near the *Invincible*. Morse Code messages were quickly transmitted to the Russian captain via his periscope, and his intent to defect was verified. However, when Ramius realized that, despite the silent tunnel drive, he had been discovered by the Americans, he was nothing short of incredulous: "How can this be? They knew where to find us—Exactly! How? What can the Americans have? How long has the . . . USS *Dallas* been trailing us?"

By means of a prearranged signal—a single solar ping—Ramius agreed to rendezvous with the American force at 33N 75W, where the evacuation plan would be set in motion. Ryan was elated that his theory had been vindicated and *Red October* secured.

His delight was short-lived, for a deadly confrontation lay ahead. As the American subs and *Red October* sped northward, an Alfa-class Soviet sub, the *V.I. Konovalov*, under command of the brilliant Captain Tupolev, a former student of Ramius', waited to intercept them.

Although *Red October* was flanked by three American subs, Tupolev recognized her unique sonar signature: undoubtedly, it was that of a Soviet sub, the very submarine he had been sent to hunt and destroy. Quickly, he moved to attack. "Range seven thousand, six hundred meters. Elevation angle zero," the sonar operator reported. Tupolev donned a headset allowing direct communication with the fire control officer, who was entering data into the on-board computer. It was a simple problem of target geometry. "We have a solution for torpedoes one and two . . . Prepare to fire . . . Flooding tubes," Tupolev ordered. Impatient, the officer reached past the petty officer and flipped the switches himself. "Outer torpedo tube doors are open . . . Recheck firing solution!" Tupolev barked. "Solution confirmed, Comrade Captain," came the reply, bringing Tupolev's command: "Fire one and two!" Two *Mark C* torpedoes were released in the direction of *Red October* at a slow but certain forty-one knots.

Who would win this battle of wits—former student Tupolev, or Ramius, his teacher? Ramius adroitly ordered the *October* to turn *into* the torpedoes, in order to display a minimum profile—but the move was made too late. One torpedo struck the *October* midship, tearing a huge hole in her side. The only thing that saved her were her huge nickel-cadmium battery arrays, which had been designed for just such a blow.

The tense chase continued, with the three American subs alternately lunging toward the *Konovalov* and then withdrawing—until Ramius took a bold step. He rammed the Soviet ship, sending it to the bottom of the sea.

A few days later, *Red October* was brought into the American missile submarine dock to be scrutinized. Ramius and his officers were whisked away by the CIA—first to be debriefed, then to enjoy free lives in the United States. Ryan, bleary-eyed from lack of sleep, was routed home on a flight to London. However, his superiors had no intention of letting him rest long; this bright young analyst would be a key member of many future intelligence efforts.

Commentary:

The Hunt for Red October presents a fascinating look into the sophisticated war machines of the Cold War era. The CIA and its intelligence operations are shown in a favorable light, while Soviet characters are depicted as serving their country capably and honorably, albeit with thinly veiled disgust for the Party and its trappings.

Perhaps the most significant objective of the book is to educate the reader as to the vast scope of international military activity that goes on from day to day and the mutual respect between soldiers and sailors of all nations.

KING SOLOMON'S MINES

by
Sir Henry Rider Haggard
(1856 - 1925)

Type of work: Adventure novel

Setting: 19th-century South Africa

Principal characters:

Alan Quatermain, a British explorer

Sir Henry Curtis, a British aristocrat in search of his lost brother

Captain John Good, Sir Henry's devoted friend and fellow explorer

Umbopa, a native guide of uncertain origins

Gagool, an aged Kukuana shamanness

Foulata, a beautiful Kukuana girl

Story Overview:

Having endured a disappointing elephant hunt, the intrepid colonial explorer Alan Quatermain was returning home to Natal by ship. During the passage, chatting over whiskey and pipes, he made the acquaintance of two distinguished English gentlemen: Sir Henry Curtis, an enormous man with thick yellow hair and beard, and Captain John Good, a stout, dark naval officer who sported a monocle in his right eye. The two were journeying together to Africa in search of Sir Henry's estranged younger brother George. The brothers had quarreled after their father had died without a will, leaving his estate to pass through rights of progenitorship to the firstborn son, Sir Henry. Embittered, George had changed his surname to "Neville" and vanished into the African outback "in the wild hope of making a fortune." Sir Henry had since come to realize that "blood is thicker than water." Now he hoped to find George and make amends.

As it happened, Quatermain had heard of this "Neville" chap; he had set out on a safari in search of the "countless diamonds" of King Solomon's legendary mines. In fact, Quatermain himself had some connection to the mines. Ten years earlier a Portuguese treasure hunter dying of a "bilious fever" had bequeathed him a fragment of linen—proportedly a map showing the way to the remote and fabled treasure.

Upon receiving this information, Sir Henry immediately arranged an expedition to search for the mines. If Quatermain would join him, he promised he would pay any amount requested. Quatermain acquiesced; the money would help provide for his son, a medical student in London.

But even Quatermain, who regarded himself as a cautious and conservative man, underestimated the hardships that would befall them in Africa's remote bush country. The party left Durban in high spirits; not until one of their Zulu bearers was trampled by a rampaging wild bull elephant did the explorers take a more sober appraisal of the dangers that might await them. "Man must die," intoned their native guide, Umbopa, enigmatically. "Like a storm-driven bird at night we fly out of Nowhere; for a moment our wings are seen in the light of the fire, and, lo! we are gone again into the Nowhere."

The expedition soon entered a region that seemed to fit Umbopa's cryptic designation of Nowhere: a boundless wilderness of desert. But despite the native's somber admonition to turn back, the explorers pressed forward. There in the vast, waterless sands, heat "danced over the surface of the desert as it dances over a cooking stove"—but still the thirst-maddened men trudged on. At last, at the moment of total despair, one of the bearers happened upon an oasis, and the rejuvenated party pressed forward on their blazing 520-mile trek to the walled mountain range that allegedly sheltered Solomon's mines.

According to Quatermain's map remnant, the mountain peaks concealed a "great road" which would lead them on a three-day journey to the King's Palace. The company scaled the narrow, volcanic cliffs and finally gained the summit. And there beneath them, "cut out of solid rock [and] fifty feet wide," winding in splendor across a plain bordered by green forests and undulating rivers, stretched King Solomon's Road.

Descending to the road, the men stopped to rest near a small brook. Good had just scrubbed himself and was in the process of shaving, when suddenly a throng of towering natives appeared, clad in short cloaks of leopard skins covered with black plumes. " . . . No strangers may live in the land of the Kukuanas," announced a fierce old warrior in broken English. Good responded to this ominous decree by removing his false teeth. The sight of his detachable jaw, his toothless, half-shaven face, his bare white legs, and his strange eye-piece, probably saved their lives. The awed warriors promptly escorted these "white lords from the stars" to meet their king, Twala the Terrible.

Twala was an enormous, dreadfully cruel, repulsive man with "one gleaming black eye." To underscore his power, the King ordered that one of his own servants be slain in full view of the explorers.

After the visitors were housed in a Kukuana hut, Umbopa slipped out of his clothes, and, to their surprise, displayed the royal image of a great snake that had been tattooed around his waist. His true name was Ignosi, he revealed; and he was *"rightful king of the Kukuanas!"* Many years earlier, his father had been murdered by Twala, and Ignosi's mother had fled the land with her young son. Now his one wish, as legitimate heir to the throne, was to avenge his father's death, "overthrow this tyrant and murderer," reclaim his royal birthright, and lead his people in peace.

Hearing these words, Infadoos, their aging Kukuana escort-guard, suddenly knelt before Ignosi, took his hand, and, presenting himself as Ignosi's uncle, vowed to help his nephew and his white friends overthrow Twala. Their attack would be launched, they decided, from the town of Loo, where the "great annual witch hunt" was to be held on the following day.

The witch hunt proved to be a gruesome affair, led by a wizened old witch-doctoress named Gagool. Yielding to her fearful, monkey-like countenance and thin, piercing hate-filled voice, attendants moved through the crowd, dooming victim after victim to death with a ghoulish shriek: "I smell him, the evil-doer!" Then, with corpses of Loo's citizens littering the ground, Gagool closed the hideous spectacle by choosing an extraordinarily beautiful young woman named Foulata to be sacrificed to the gods.

Once again, however, Good's quick-wittedness came through. Remembering that his almanac for that day had predicted the occurrence of a solar eclipse, he now commanded that the sun's light be dimmed; and sure enough, all witnessed at "the edge of the great orb . . . a faint rim of shadow." The distraction was working—until Twala's son, infuriated that a white man would possess such wondrous power, tried to spear Good. But somehow the Englishman managed to turn the spear on the false prince; and in the ensuing panic the expedition party fled into the hills. They were accompanied by Foulata along with a large number of Kukuana chiefs who had long opposed Twala's atrocities and now wanted to help Ignosi reclaim his throne. Together they mustered a force of some twenty thousand Kukuana warriors.

At dawn, Twala's army struck; but although they were severely outnumbered, Ignosi's gallant band overcame the odds. Twala, his warriors either scattered or dead, found himself deserted by all but Gagool. His final wish to "die fighting" was quickly fulfilled as Sir Henry beheaded the tyrant with a single, mighty blow from a Kukuana battle-ax.

Once enthroned as king of Kukuanaland, Ignosi commanded the crone Gagool to lead his white benefactors, along with the girl Foulata, into the "deep cave in the mountain" where Solomon's treasure was hidden. She had no choice but to obey.

A three-day march led them to a labyrinth of caves dotting the secluded slopes of a snow-capped mountain: they had found King Solomon's mines! Through the entrance portal the group passed into a huge, vaulted cathedral-like cavern, half-a-mile round and pillared by exquisite stalactites. However, the next cavern proved to be a chamber of horrors: there, seated on benches beneath a huge figure of Death himself, was a roomful of petrified human corpses—the past kings of Kukuanaland. And on a table in front of these silent stonewatchers lay Twala's decapitated body.

"My lords are not afraid?" jeered Gagool in contempt as she advanced into the shadows of a narrow passageway. At this point she triggered a hidden lever, lifting a massive stone door. Inside lay one last chamber brimming with untold stores of gold and ivory, and countless heaps of huge diamonds, glimmering in the lamplight.

But while the men stood gaping, awestruck by the marvelous hoard before them, Gagool "crept like a snake" toward the doorway and pulled the lever that would entomb her adversaries alive. When she saw Foulata moving to block her escape, Gagool stabbed her ferociously. Then, grappling to disentangle herself from the grip of the dying girl, the old sorceress lunged again for the opening. But she was too late: all thirty tons of the massive door came crashing down upon her.

For a while, all was silent within the chamber. After the gentle Foulata had breathed her last, tenderly enfolded in Good's loving embrace, the three Europeans desperately scanned the sealed room. They found no exit, however, and eventually the flames of their lamps dimmed and died. For hour upon hour they sat in darkness, "buried in the bowels" of a lost mountain, quietly awaiting death. " . . . Around us lay treasures enough to pay off a moderate national debt," Quatermain mused, "yet we would have bartered them gladly for the faintest chance of escape . . . "

Then suddenly Quatermain noticed how "perfectly fresh" the air in the chamber was. There must be a vent somewhere to the outside. Quatermain's hunch soon paid off. In the blackness, a loose stone was discovered in the floor, beneath which they found a staircase descending into a lair-like earthen enclosure. Some hearty digging followed, and at last they were free!

Before leaving their underground prison, however, Quatermain had filled his pockets with enough diamonds to ensure many lifetimes of wealth. This was indeed a provident act, for when the men returned later to search for the opening to the treasure chamber, they could find no trace of it.

Having bid farewell to honorable King Ignosi, Quatermain, Sir Henry and Good started out on the grueling return trip home. Again they passed through the scorched desert, and, chancing on an oasis that had previously eluded them, they encountered a rude yet cozy hut situated under a fig tree. Limping out to greet them came a lame "white man clothed in skins and an enormous black beard." "Great Powers!" cried Sir Henry. "It is my brother George!" Disabled by a leg injury on his quest for Solomon's diamonds, George Curtis had been living by the spring for nearly two years.

Sir Henry at last could smile. Pressed upon to accept a third part of the diamonds which Quatermain had carried from the treasure vault, Sir Henry declared "that his share should be handed to his brother" as a token of his love and joy. Another third portion was generously bestowed by Quatermain on Good.

And so the four adventurers set off for Durban, where Quatermain bid a reluctant good-bye to his friends. His farewell was a vow to take up a pen once he was safely home and set down an account of their most remarkable adventures.

Commentary:

King Solomon's Mines, an obvious prototype for the exploits of modern movie heroes like Indiana Jones, is a fine example of what was once termed a "boy's adventure tale"—a genre which emphasized plot over character and moved from one action-packed scene to another.

But H. Rider Haggard's novel is an adventure story with remarkable moral depth. Haggard refrains from stereotyping either his characters or the landscapes they traverse, taking great care in characterizing the Kukuanas, who, despite their warlike appearance, emerge as expert craftsmen, gifted storytellers, and fundamentally peace-loving citizens who must endure the cruelties of a tyrant.

Furthermore, underlying the grandiose adventure and break-neck action of the storyline is a deeper theme of loyalty and familial devotion: from the outset, Sir Henry's search for King Solomon's mines is not motivated by greed but rather his concern for his brother. Likewise, Good accompanies Sir Henry as an act of fellowship; Quatermain joins them in order to provide for his son; and Ignosi guides them to Kukuanaland with the aim of fulfilling his own birthright and restoring order in his homeland. Camaraderie, then, and not bravado, inspires these characters to tackle and surmount the odds of their journey. And the diamonds carried from the Kukuana burial vaults are not trophies of greed but tools of good. Long may Haggard's characters adorn the worlds of literary and cinematic adventure.

THE HOUSE OF THE SEVEN GABLES

by Nathaniel Hawthorne
(1804-1864)

Type of work: Gothic mystery

Setting: New England; the mid-1800s

Principal characters:

Hepzibah Pyncheon, a sour-faced but tender-hearted old maid

Clifford Pyncheon, Hepzibah's brother

Phoebe Pyncheon, her delightful young cousin

Jaffery Pyncheon, another of Hepzibah's cousins, heir to the Pyncheon fortune

Mr. Holgrave, Hepzibah's tenant, a daguerreotypist (i.e., a primitive photographer)

Commentary:

Nathaniel Hawthorne describes this novel as a "romance." Not to be outdone by other writers of his day, however, who placed great import on framing their work around definite moral lessons, Hawthorne also provided a moral for his story: "That the wrong-doing of one generation lives into the successive ones, and, divesting itself of every temporary advantage, becomes a pure and uncontrollable mischief."

Hawthorne's work is often preoccupied with the themes of witches' curses, family influences, and the decay of ancient lineages—and *The House of Seven Gables* is vintage Hawthorne, capturing each of these elements somewhere within the novel's two-century time span.

Story Overview:

The House of the Seven Gables, which stood halfway down Pyncheon Street, bore "traces not merely of outward storm and sunshine," but also of "the long lapse of mortal life, and accompanying vicissitudes that [had] passed within."

But the house was not the first habitation erected on that spot of ground. The carpenter Matthew Maule had originally built a hut for his family on the site, near a pleasant natural spring. As the town grew, however, the land had come to the attention of Colonel Pyncheon, "a prominent and powerful personage, who asserted plausible claims to [its] proprietorship . . . on the strength of a grant from the legislature." Matthew Maule, however, though an obscure man, stubbornly defended what he considered his property.

The dispute was settled only by the death of Matthew Maule. In fact, Maule was executed for witchcraft—and Colonel Pyncheon's had been among the loudest of those voices who had joined in the cry to expedite his sentence.

But who on this earth can be assured of ultimate victory? At the moment of his execution, Maule had pointed his finger toward Pyncheon and proclaimed a curse upon him and his entire posterity. Pyncheon, his energy of purpose undeterred, had torn down Maule's shack and erected in its stead the House of the Seven Gables—though the townspeople had expressed amazement that he would choose the site of an unquiet grave to build a house where "future bridegrooms were to lead their brides, and where children of the Pyncheon blood were to be born." And perhaps they were correct in their forebodings, for on the day of the great public opening of his new structure, Colonel Pyncheon was found within, sitting dead at his desk beneath his own imposing portrait. The clutter of letters, parchments and blank sheets of paper before him bore mute testimony to the coroner's verdict of "sudden death."

Upon the death of the Colonel, his only son acquired a rich estate, including claim to a vast tract of Eastern lands in the state of Maine. But, unfortunately, Colonel Pyncheon had died without leaving a clue as to where the deeds to those lands might be found. And over the generations, the Pyncheon family wealth slowly deteriorated.

For the better part of two centuries the Pyncheons, though a family filled with eccentrics, lived much like any other New England family. In recent years, however, a particularly onerous calamity had befallen their descendants: one member of the clan, Clifford Pyncheon, was adjudged to have murdered his uncle in a fit of rage. When this shamed and ruined family member was finally released from prison as a broken old man, he took up residence with his sister, Hepzibah—who had been willed a life estate in the House of the Seven Gables. These two, along with the current heir, Judge Jaffery Pyncheon, and the youngest of the family, Phoebe, were all that remained of the Pyncheon lineage. The Maule family, it was supposed, had by now become extinct.

Hepzibah, an old maid, tall, with a "long and shrunken waist" and a perpetual scowl upon her face, was mistress of a now dark and chilly house, its once beautifully sculpted grounds withered and overgrown with weeds. She was thankful, therefore, when her young relative, Phoebe, came to live with her.

A slender young girl full of sunshine and song, Phoebe brought a smile and a cheery glow with her, quite a contrast to Clifford's "wasted, gray, and melancholy figure." This unfortunate man still loved beautiful things, however, and was especially drawn to Phoebe. For her part, Phoebe also dearly loved her uncle and delighted in cheering him with flowers from her garden.

Still, living with the two reclusive old people was a lonesome task. "The only youthful mind with which Phoebe had an opportunity of frequent intercourse was that of the daguerreotypist" who boarded at Seven Gables, Mr. Holgrave. It is doubtful either would have taken a liking to the other, so different were they, except they both loved working in the gardens and were regularly drawn together there in conversation. During one of these chats, Mr. Holgrave spoke up. "Now, this old Pyncheon House!" he began. "Is it a wholesome place to live in, with its black shingles, and green moss that shows how damp they are? . . . its grime and sordidness, which are the crystallization on its walls of the human breath that has been drawn and exhaled here in discontent and anguish? The house ought to be purified with fire,—purified till only its ashes remain!" Holgrave regretted that he was forced to board there in order to pursue his studies: "I dwell in it for a while, that I may know the better how to hate it," he declared. In fact, Holgrave continued, he had written down a Pyncheon legend which he meant to have published in a magazine:

Matthew Maule, a grandson of the original Maule, had apparently inherited from his ancestor some traits of witchcraft. These powers were enlisted by Gervayse Pyncheon, a descendent of the Colonel, to help him locate the missing document that would secure the family's Pyncheon properties: Under a hypnotic spell cast by Matthew, Gervayse's daughter Alice reported that, as part of the Pyncheon curse, the document was destined to remain hidden until it was too late to slake a claim.

After securing this knowledge, however, Maule chose not to release Alice from his control. For the rest of her life, whenever he raised his hand, she would do as he bade. He thus induced her to laugh during solemn occasions and to commit all sorts of other undignified acts over the years. Finally, when he forced her go out on a cold night to wait upon his wife, Alice caught pneumonia and died. Maule followed the funeral procession, "the darkest and woefullest man that ever walked behind a corpse! He meant to humble Alice, not to kill her; but he had taken a woman's delicate soul in to his rude grip, to play with—and she was dead!"

Rolling up his manuscript as he finished relating this story, Holgrave found that Phoebe's eyelids were drooping. "A veil was beginning to be muffled about her . . . It was evident, that, with but one wave of his hand . . . he could establish an influence over this good, pure, and simple child, as dangerous . . . as that which the carpenter of his legend had acquired and exercised over the ill-fated Alice."

Not long thereafter, Phoebe withdrew to the country for a few days to visit her family. Mr. Holgrave remarked that he would not be surprised if the shattered Clifford now crumbled away and the impoverished old maid Hepzibah lost what "little flexibility" she had; both seemed to exist—indeed, breathe and live—because of Phoebe. He now expressed the portent that some new, unforeseen trouble was hovering over Phoebe's relatives, and that the dilapidated house had become a sort of theater stage on which the last of the Pyncheons would meet their doom.

Holgrave's forebodings were finally fulfilled the day Judge Jaffery Pyncheon came to visit and presumptuously announced his certainty that Clifford knew the secret of the Pyncheon land grant, lost now for centuries. But when Hepzibah hurried to summon her brother to the Judge's imperious presence, Clifford was not in his room. Panic-stricken, she returned to the parlor to inform Jaffery of his disappearance—only to find Clifford himself at the parlor's threshold. "His face was preternaturally pale," and his finger pointed towards the Judge, who slumped dead and silent in his seat before him. The brother and sister fled the house in fear, leaving Judge Jaffery alone in the home of his forefathers.

On the following day, when Phoebe returned to the House of the Seven Gables, she was met by Mr. Holgrave, looking extraordinarily pale. "His smile, however, was full of genuine warmth, and had in it a joy, by far the most vivid expression that Phoebe had ever witnessed, shining out of the New England reserve with which Holgrave habitually masked whatever lay in his

heart." The Judge was dead, he announced, and both Clifford and Hepzibah had mysteriously vanished. Phoebe could not understand the calmness of Holgrave's demeanor. "He appeared . . . to feel the whole awfulness of the Judge's death, yet had received the fact . . . without any mixture of surprise, but as an event preordained, happening inevitably, and so fitting itself into past occurrences that it could almost have been prophesied." Phoebe longed to throw open the doors and call for the police, but Holgrave convinced her that with Hepzibah and Clifford gone, suspicion would naturally fall upon them. And this, he asserted, would be a grave injustice, "because if the matter can be fairly considered . . . it must be evident that Judge Pyncheon could not have come unfairly to his end . . . This mode of death has been an idiosyncrasy with his family for generations past . . . usually attacking individuals about the Judge's time of life, and generally in the tension of some mental crisis . . . Old Maule's prophecy was probably founded on a knowledge of this physical predisposition in the Pyncheon race"—a hereditary condition that brought early death to its bearers.

Phoebe still could not fathom what "mental crisis" could have led to such an end—until Holgrave continued with his narrative. The man sitting dead in the parlor, he contended, had thirty years earlier made a desperate search for a will which would cut off his inheritance. In fact, concluded Holgrave, the elder Jaffery Pyncheon had recently drawn up a new will bequeathing his estate to Clifford. Under the shock of discovering his nephew rifling through his papers, however, the uncle had suffered a fatal seizure—to become another victim of the Pyncheon curse. Jaffery had then destroyed the will—and framed Clifford as his uncle's murderer.

When Hepzibah and Clifford returned to the House of the Seven Gables, the truth of Holgrave's account was at last made known to the world. Clifford, released from the decades of anguish heaped upon him by Jaffery, finally remembered the secret sought after by long generations of Pyncheons: As a child, he had discovered an opening concealed behind the portrait of the original Colonel Pyncheon—a compartment containing the long-lost land grant. The document was now worthless—but no matter; the last of the three Pyncheons would inherit Jaffery's wealth.

Holgrave and Phoebe, drawn together through companionship and crisis, now found themselves in love. However, there was one more secret still to be revealed. "My dearest Phoebe," said Holgrave, "how will it please you to assume the name of Maule? As for the secret, it is the only inheritance that has come down to me from my ancestors. You should have known sooner (only that I was afraid of frightening you away) that, in this long drama of wrong and retribution, I represent the old wizard, and am probably as much a wizard as ever he was. The son of the executed Matthew Maule, while building this house, took the opportunity to construct that recess, and hide away the . . . deed, on which depended the immense land-claim of the Pyncheons. Thus they bartered their Eastern territory for Maule's garden-ground."

LORD JIM

by
Joseph Conrad
(1857 - 1924)

Type of work: English morality and adventure novel

Setting: Malaysia and the Far East

Principal characters:

Lord Jim, an intelligent young man who brands himself a coward

Captain Marlow, a seaman who takes an interest in Jim

Dain Waris, a young Patusan warrior, and Jim's friend

Doramin, father of Dain Waris

Cornelius, a skulking Patusan trader

Jewel, Cornelius' daughter, and later, Jim's wife

Rajah Tunku Allang, an evil Patusan chieftain

Brown, a treacherous buccaneer

Commentary:

Joseph Conrad's **Lord Jim** ranks among the best novels ever written. Through the enigmatic Jim, Conrad explores the many faces of human character—courage versus cowardice, honor versus dishonor, as well as the fall and redemption of self esteem and the plight of society's lost souls.

Conrad's writing evolved from his own experience as a seaman. He forsook his native Poland after the Russian oppression of the 1800s—a self-condemned act of cowardice with which he came to terms when he wrote **Lord Jim.**

Story Overview:

The boy, an outcast known simply as Jim, was raised in obscurity on the English coast and trained to go to sea, where he would experience a series of crises which would bring him face to face with his own human frailties.

During Jim's first voyage, all hands were summoned to recover passengers from two vessels that had collided during a storm. Caught up in the confusion of the moment, Jim hesitated to risk his life—and so another boy carried out the heroic rescue. Although Jim later felt guilty, he made light of the incident and claimed he was brave enough to confront any peril.

While aboard another ship some time later, Jim was injured and set aground at an eastern port to convalesce. Thirsting for action, when he recuperated he immediately signed onto the *Patna,* an archaic iron-sided ship whose captain disdained the 800 Mecca-bound Muslim pilgrims who were his passengers. Jim, considering himself superior, remained aloof from the *Patna's* gross skipper and his liquor-soaked crew.

In the middle of the Red Sea one night the ship struck some floating wreckage and sustained damage to the hull. Sent to check the bulkhead, Jim saw that it was half-full of water and assumed it would soon burst apart and drown everyone. Before long, a storm hit and the panicked skipper gave orders to abandon ship. At first Jim was bent on standing by his post. But at the last minute, certain that any moment the ship's hull would rupture, he flung himself over the side of the ship into the lifeboat: "His confounded imagination had evoked for him all the horrors of panic, the trampling rush, the pitiful screams, boats swamped." Then came the awful realization that, with that single act of cowardice, he had descended into an "everlasting deep hole" of fear and self-loathing.

Jim later learned that the *Patna* and its passengers had not sunk, but had been towed safely to port by a French vessel. When the skipper and crew learned that there was to be an official inquiry conducted on the incident, they either disappeared or descended into panicked dementia, leaving Jim, alone, to face the inspectors. Although Jim also had a chance to escape, he wanted to salvage what was left of his tattered honor.

Jim insisted on a hearing, infuriating the conducting officer, Brierly. With a flawless record to protect, Brierly was not about to have a young man's lack of mettle ruin it and asked a Captain Marlow to give Jim two hundred rupees to run away. But Jim refused to defect: "I may have jumped but I won't run away. I'm not good enough."

Drawn to the wholesome-looking lad, Marlow saw in Jim a reflection of his own soul and defended the young man before the tribunal. In the end, however, Jim's seaman's certificate was revoked and news of his humiliation followed him to every harbor.

In time, with his friend Marlow's aid, Jim took on employment as a water clerk, brokering cargo for ships. But still ashamed of his actions and feeling "no better than a vagabond," he fled to yet another port. "Dash it all!" the youth exclaimed to Marlow as they again perused Jim's misadventure with the *Patna.* "I tell you [the bulkhead] bulged. A flake of rust as big as the palm of my hand fell off the plate all of itself."

While guilt over the incident often haunted him, Jim eventually came to believe that he had done his penance. One day he cried, "Jove! I feel as if nothing could ever touch me." But Captain Marlow knew from experience that Jim would not be completely free of guilt until he could redeem himself. Meanwhile, he would have to "face it out and wait for another chance."

Months later, Marlow introduced Jim to a wealthy merchant named Stein, who operated a trading post near the Malaysian port of Patusan. Right away Stein was impressed with Jim. In fact, he hired the intelligent young man to replace Cornelius, an inefficient Patusan trader who had been overseeing Stein's trading post. When Stein gave Jim his silver ring so that he could convince the local Malay chief, Doramin, that he was a trusted ally, Jim again felt powerful, as if he might overcome the specter of his own cowardice and self-hatred.

While traveling up the river to Patusan territory, however, Jim was captured by Rajah Tunku Allang, a ruthless chief who routinely tortured and killed the Patusan people. Jim managed to escape by vaulting over the wall of Allang's stockade and running away before the surprised guards could overtake him. When he reached the next village, he collapsed, but managed to gasp Doramin's name in the hope that the locals would help him. The villagers took him to Doramin's house, where Jim produced the silver ring "and was received . . . into the heart of the community" as a trusted comrade. Jim befriended Doramin's son, Dain Waris, and the two young men worked together to overthrow Rajah Tunku Allang.

Finally Jim made his way to the trading post, where he found Cornelius indeed to be despicable—a man who exhibited "an inexpressible . . . stealthiness, of dark and secret slinking." Cornelius greatly resented Jim for coming to displace him; even more, he feared Jim would take his daughter, Jewel, away from him. Jim stayed at the trading post for the next six weeks, during which time he and Jewel did fall in love. Infuriated by the young sailor's presence, one night Cornelius tried to kill him in his sleep, but Jewel arrived just in time to forewarn her lover.

The couple decided to marry and to remain in the Patusan empire—but far away from Cornelius. Although they were very happy, Jewel could not help but fear that Jim in time would become homesick and leave her.

In Patusan, meanwhile, Doramin's people suffered many abuses at the hand of Tunku Allang and his attaché, Sherif Ali. Jim, like a modern-day Moses, resolved to deliver their victims from bondage. First he commanded Doramin's warriors to drag two seven-pound cannons to the hill overlooking Serif Ali's fort and to open fire. The bombardment quickly reduced the fort's walls to rubble. After leading an assault on the ruined encampment, Jim and Dain Waris routed Ali's men and took Tunku Allang prisoner.

When Jim returned from the battle, the villagers greeted him as a hero, appointing him as the great *Lord Jim*. They even attributed divine powers to him, insisting that "Jim had carried the guns up the hill on his back, two at a time." And so the legend of Lord Jim expanded throughout the land.

But peace would not last long. Soon a notoriously cruel Australian buccaneer named Gentleman Brown was led to Patusan by Cornelius. Brown and his fellow cutthroat seamen were in search of provisions to plunder. Although Jim was absent at the time, the Malay people drove Brown and his marauders onto a hillock near Sherif Ali's ruined fortress. Brown nevertheless plotted to enslave the Malay and to kill Lord Jim.

When Jim returned, Doramin and Dain Waris urged him to attack the wily pirate. But Jim decided first to appeal to Brown's sense of honor; surely he could persuade Brown to give up his weapons and leave Patusan in peace. Jim thus arranged a meeting.

Without knowing Jim's history, Brown nevertheless detected the young man's guilty past, hinting that he and Jim were alike—both hiding from society and its harsh indictments. Thrown off guard by Brown's words, Jim failed to convince his adversary to give up his weapons. "You shall have a clear road or else a clear fight," Jim warned. Brown, however, refused to strike a deal. Doramin again prodded Jim to lead a raid against Brown and his men, but Jim persuaded the chief to allow Brown and his men to leave, pledging to give up his own life in the event any Malay was harmed.

After Jim had sealed the agreement with Brown, his men, led by Cornelius, began their retreat downriver. Cornelius, however, still lusting after revenge, coaxed Brown's pirates to open fire on the Malays' riverside camp. Amid the heavy volley of bullets, the chief's son, Dain Waris, along with many of his men, fell. Afterwards, Brown's men escaped, but Cornelius was caught and stabbed to death.

Following the attack, Dain Waris' body was brought to Doramin. On the young man's finger was Jim's silver ring, worn as a symbol of love and trust. Now Lord Jim had broken that trust. As the ring was removed from his son's lifeless hand, Doramin let out a "fierce cry, deep from the chest, a cry of pain and fury."

Meanwhile, Jim's servant tried to convince him either to fight or flee for his life. Jim refused, announcing that at dusk he would surrender himself up to Doramin as promised. "Nothing can touch me," he declared. Jewel, however, was hysterical that her beloved Jim would forfeit his own life to pay for a scoundrel's crime. She clung to him so fiercely that Jim had to summon a servant to break her grasp. "You are false," she shrieked as he marched off toward Doramin's village. "Forgive me," he called to her, refusing to look back. But Jewel replied, "Never! Never!"

Jim boldly made his way to Doramin's house, while villagers whispered their disbelief that he would honor his word. As he drew near, Jim saw the shrouded body of Dain Waris. Approaching it, he lifted a corner of the sheet and gazed at his dead friend's sallow face. "He hath taken it upon his own head," said one onlooker. Jim then turned to face the chieftain. Surrounded by torches, he sat, a scowl on his face, with two flintlock pistols resting on his knees. "I am come in sorrow," Jim murmured. "I am come ready and unarmed." Doramin said nothing, but "from his throat came gurgling, choking, inhuman sounds [and] his little eyes stared with an expression of mad pain, of rage, with a ferocious glitter."

Two servant men then helped Doramin to his feet, whereupon the ring rolled from his lap, coming to rest at Jim's feet. Jim stood in the light of the torches, his head bowed. Doramin "clung heavily with his left arm round the neck of [the] bowed youth, and lifting deliberately his right, shot his son's friend through the chest." Then, according to legend, "the white man sent right and left at all those faces a proud and unflinching glance. Then with his hand over his lips he fell forward" at the grieving father's feet.

In death Lord Jim had finally overcome fear. Ironically, even in the minds of Doramin and his people, he was a hero.

THE DEERSLAYER

by
James Fenimore Cooper
(1789 - 1851)

Type of work: Realistic North-American colonial
adventure novel

Setting: Lake Glimmerglass, New York; 1740

Principal characters:

Natty Bumppo, a skilled young woodsman
known as Hawk-eye to the Mingo
Indians and as Deerslayer to the
Delaware

Henry March (Hurry Harry), a large, reckless
woodsman

Tom Hutter, a settler living on a
Glimmerglass-Lake houseboat

Judith Hutter, Tom's beautiful daughter

Hetty Hutter, Judith's half-wit sister

Chingachgook, Mohican chief and friend of
Deerslayer

Hist (Wah-ta-wah), Chingachgook's love

Rivenoak, a Mingo chieftain

Commentary:

The Deerslayer (1841) is the first of
Cooper's classic *Leatherstocking Tales* about early
American frontiersman Natty Bumppo, stories
that address many conflicting themes that have
been revisited in the twentieth century: reverence
for nature, contrasted with the contention that
civilization must destroy nature; the paradox of
considering Native American "savages" somehow
both inferior and superior to Christian colonists;
and the sad truth that people of integrity often
find themselves isolated from the community in
which they live. Cooper also implies that the
Christian settlers were hypocritical, preaching
one thing and doing another insofar as their treatment of Native Americans was concerned.

Deerslayer's code of conduct is based on
respect for every living thing, a belief that proves
a source of conflict for many who seek to seize
upon "the American dream." When he engages in
a shooting contest with a Mohican chief and kills
several waterfowl, he later expresses regret:
"We've done an unthoughtful thing in taking life
with an object no better than vanity."

Cooper lived both in Europe and America.
After writing some 32 novels, he died in 1851
near Lake Glimmerglass in Cooperstown, New
York.

Story Overview:

Natty Bumppo, known as the Deerslayer,
and Henry "Hurry" March were traveling
through the woods to Tom Hutter's home at Lake
Glimmerglass. Deerslayer planned to rendezvous
in the area with Chingachgook, a Mohican chieftain, and Hurry had come to see Hutter's eldest
daughter, Judith, whom he adored. If she were
already married, Hurry vowed, he would kill her
husband. When Deerslayer threatened to inform
the other settlers if Hurry went "a murdering,"
the enormous woodsman grabbed Deerslayer
and shook him until his bones rattled. But
Deerslayer remained calm. "You may shake until
you bring down the mountain," he said, " . . . but
nothing but the truth will you shake from me."

When the two men reached Hutter's fortified cabin, they could not find Hutter or his
houseboat. Remembering that Hutter occasionally moved it from one side of the lake to the other,
they took a canoe and went in search of him.

They were in Mingo territory, and it was
natural to speak of Indians as they paddled.
Hurry regarded Indians as "half-human"; to him,
taking their scalps for money was totally justifi-
able. Deerslayer strongly disagreed. Even though
it was a customary practice for "savages" to take
scalps, it was wrong for Christians, who understood that "God made all . . . alike."

Finally the men came upon Hutter's houseboat and Hurry introduced Deerslayer to Hutter
and his two daughters. Judith was just as beautiful and refined as Hurry had boasted, while her
younger sister Hetty was sweet, but dull and
slow-witted. There was little time for talk, however; the Mingos were on the warpath, and Tom
was anxious to maneuver the boat away from
shore. Even as he sank his pole into the lake, six
Indians bolted from the trees and attempted to
jump aboard. Five warriors landed in the water,
and as the sixth struggled to gain his balance on
deck Judith pushed him in after them. Shots rang
out from other Indians on the bank, and
Deerslayer urgently pulled Judith inside the boat
as her father guided their craft safely out of
range.

Deerslayer had come to the area on a mission of mercy: to help his friend Chingachgook
rescue his lover, Hist, from the Mingos. But now
Hutter and Hurry wanted Deerslayer to help
them raid the Mingo camp for scalps. On moral
grounds alone Deerslayer strongly opposed the
idea, but finally did agree to stay behind on the
boat and defend Hutter's two daughters. Hutter
and Hurry paddled off toward the Mingo camp.
But as Deerslayer made his way back to the
houseboat, he heard the screams of his friends
coming from the forest, and knew the white men
had already been captured.

As Deerslayer's canoe approached the
shoreline, he was confronted by a Mingo. The
two discharged their weapons simultaneously.
The Mingo's bullet missed; Deerslayer's did not.
The maimed Indian, before crumpling to the
ground, rushed forward in a frenzy of rage and
threw his tomahawk, which Deerslayer caught in
mid-flight. Before returning to the boat, the
woodsman tended to the needs of his dying
enemy. Then, after informing the girls of their
father's and Hurry's predicament, he paddled to a
nearby rendezvous with Chingachgook to plan
the rescue of all three prisoners. He found that
Chingachgook had already scouted the Mingo
camp, and had caught a glimpse of Hutter and
Hist, his love. But as the two friends talked,
they saw Hetty resolutely rowing by in one of the
canoes toward the enemy camp, on a rescue mission of her own. Deerslayer did not go after her,
and later assured Judith that her sister was safe;
Indians did not harm those they considered slow-

witted.

At the Mingo camp, Hetty argued with Chief Rivenoak, trying to convince him to release her father. "Love your enemies," she preached, quoting from the Bible. "Do good to them that hate you." Rivenoak replied, "Why does [the white man] forget himself all [the Bible] says?" Confused, the simple girl broke down in tears.

The white prisoners were soon freed in exchange for some ivory chess pieces which Judith and Deerslayer had found in Tom Hutter's weathered old sea chest—whereupon Hurry tried improvidently to shoot his erstwhile captors. Although he was thwarted in his attempt by Deerslayer, the Mingos then threw a bundle of blood-dipped sticks on the white men's boat to show that they were still on the warpath. And by the time Hurry, Tom, and Chingachgook returned to the Mingo camp to rescue Hist, the Indians had moved.

When they finally located the new camp-site, the men crept forward and found Hist in one of the tepees. But before they could free her, a Mingo squaw detected their presence and ran to alert the rest of the camp. Deerslayer, acting as a decoy, distracted the Mingos so that the others could escape, but was captured in the process.

The jubilant Mingos hauled the woodsman to the center of their camp, where Chief Rivenoak, calling Deerslayer by his Mingo name, tried to persuade him to abandon his friends and join up with the tribe. "Hawkeye should have been born a [Mingo]," he declared. Deerslayer, who had been raised by the Delawares, admitted that, though "white in blood," he was "a little red-skin in feelin's and habits . . . [Hutter] is not a man to gain my love," he added, but still he could not betray his companions.

After Chingachgook and Hist had arrived at the houseboat, Hutter and Hurry decided to backtrack to Hutter's lakeside cabin. There, how-ever, they found the Mingos awaiting them. As the two entered the cabin, the Indians struck, and within seconds, Hutter lay dying on the ground. Hurry managed to escape out the back door.

Judith and Hetty returned to the cabin, just in time to hear Hutter direct them with his last gasp to "look in the chest—'tis all there." And indeed, following a fitting ceremony and after depositing their father's body into the lake, the young women opened his old sea chest. Inside they found documents showing that Hutter was not, in fact, their father. He had married their mother when they were babies, after their own father had abandoned them. And what's more, Hutter had apparently once been a pirate—which explained why he had insisted on living on a boat.

Meanwhile, the Mingos sent Deerslayer back to the cabin with a proposal: all the men, including himself, could depart in peace if Hist and the Hutter girls would agree to surrender themselves in their stead and live among the Mingos. Deerslayer promised to deliver this ulti-matum and to return to his captors if the bargain was rejected.

Judith, who had come to care for Deerslayer, was stung that he would even consid-er these conditions. "And do you bring such a message to me?" she retorted. "Am I a girl to be an Indian's slave?" Humbled by her words, Deerslayer prepared to return to the Mingos and face certain torture.

He left his mournful friends, and returned as pledged to the Mingos, who marvelled at his sense of honor. "My people are happy in having captured a man and not a skulking fox," Rivenoak told him. Then he offered Deerslayer his life if he would marry the widow of the Indian he had killed earlier. When Deerslayer declined the offer, the widow's brother, furiously insulted, launched a tomahawk at his chest. With cat-like quickness, the woodsman caught the weapon in flight and flung it back, striking the Indian between the eyes. Then, in the resulting pandemonium, Deerslayer fled.

The Indians lost no time in recapturing their quarry. This time they bound him and began to use his body for target practice, bringing their bullets closer and closer with each shot. But Deerslayer, wounded and bleeding, did not flinch. Then, completely unexpectedly, Hetty again appeared in camp, pleading once more for the Indians to exercise Christian mercy. "You are tormenting your friend in tormenting this young man," she said. But Rivenoak ignored her. "Let the paleface show how little he cares for [Mingo] bullets." They shot at him again, but Deerslayer only mocked them, saying, "We've squaws among the Delaware that could outdo your great-est endeavors." At these words, the Indians became more inflamed.

Then Judith also appeared, disguised as an old woman, and attempted to barter for Deerslayer's life. Her efforts failed, however, when the confused Hetty exposed her sister's true identity. By now thoroughly enraged by the events, Rivenoak lit a circle of fire around his bound enemy. But at just the last moment, Chingachgook and Hist raced into camp, leapt the flames, and cut Deerslayer loose. As he sprang free, a Mingo lunged at Chingachgook with his knife. Hist deflected the blade, and Chingachgook then launched his own knife at the warrior, killing him. Deerslayer seized a rifle, and he and his friends, greatly outnumbered, pre-pared to fight for their lives.

All at once, at the height of the fighting, a British army platoon broke through the clearing, with Hurry March at the lead. The soldiers opened fire on the Mingos, sending them scurry-ing into the brush. But Hetty was fatally wound-ed in the skirmish. "I wish you would try to be more like Deerslayer," she told Hurry with her dying breath. Then, raising her eyes to the sky, she gasped, "I see Mother and bright beings beyond her in the lake." Like Tom, she was buried in Lake Glimmerglass.

Weeks later, Judith bluntly asked Deerslayer to marry her. Turning to her, he gen-tly explained that he desired freedom more than he desired the lovely Judith.

Fifteen years later, Deerslayer again visited Lake Glimmerglass, with Chingachgook and Chingachgook's son, Uncas. There, by the side of the water, they found Hutter's cabin and boat, both ravaged by time—melancholy monuments to the people who had lived and died there.

UNCLE TOM'S CABIN

by
Harriet Beecher Stowe
(1811-1896)

Type of work: Abolitionist novel

Setting: Antebellum Kentucky, Louisiana, Mississippi, and Ohio

Principal characters:

Tom, a saintly old man, a slave affectionately called "Uncle Tom"

Eliza, a young part-negro slave woman

George Harris, Eliza's husband, also a slave

Augustine St. Clare, a rich white slaveholder

Eva St. Clare, Augustine's benevolent young daughter

Simon Legree, a cruel planter and slave dealer

George Shelby, the son of a slave-owner

Commentary:

The northern based movement to abolish slavery was in full swing, and Connecticut-born Harriet Beecher Stowe was an ardent sympathizer in her forties when she sat down ten years before the outbreak of the American Civil War to breathe life into her idealized long-suffering plantation slave Uncle Tom and the colorful galaxy of characters who surround him. Soon afterwards she found herself spotlighted as one of the foremost novelists of her age. *"So this is the little lady who started this big war!"* said Abraham Lincoln when he met her in 1863.

Ironically, Stowe's meek and patient martyr has often met with scathing ridicule among social crusaders. The character of George Harris—proudly flaunting the law and his master, and finally shooting his family's way out of slavery—is much closer to the contemporary "hero" ideal. But it should be remembered that for Stowe, the Uncle Tom whose name so acutely embarrasses black activists today represented something much more than either a model *or* a stereotype of black manhood. Tom was her Christian paradigm: the idealized, moral victim, suffering through all the indignities and brutalities conferred by a deranged world on its noblest children—and emerging with his soul intact.

Seen in this light, Tom's gentle, optimistic endurance becomes the ultimate show of human strength. Not incidentally, it also becomes the one instrument capable of moving Tom's white masters to turn against their own worldly interests and start working for the dismantlement of the very evil that empowers them. In the end it is not the courage of George or Eliza or the tears of little Eva, but the unquenchable "forgiveness" of Uncle Tom which hastens the end of slavery.

Story Overview:

A well-mannered Kentucky gentleman, Mr. Shelby, was trying to convince his creditor, a coarse slave-trader named Haley, that the requital of an old negro slave named Tom was sufficient reimbursement to settle Shelby's debt: *I mean, really, Tom is a good, sensible, pious fellow. He got religion at a camp meeting, four years ago . . .*

and I always find him true and square in everything.

Though he realized that Shelby was on the verge of losing his plantation, Haley was bent on squeezing the honeycomb dry. Just then a captivating four- or five-year-old little black boy entered the room. "Tell you what," said Haley, "fling in that chap, and I'll settle the business—I will."

"O, missis," cried the child's young mother Eliza to Mrs. Shelby after overhearing this conversation, "*do* you suppose mas'r would sell my Harry?" Stunned, Mrs. Shelby replied, "No, you foolish girl! You know your master . . . never means to sell any of our servants, as long as they behave well."

Eliza tried to take comfort from this, but later in the day she had another wrenching jolt. Her husband George Harris, who belonged to an owner of a nearby plantation, had discovered that his master was resentful of the admiration George had won among his fellow slaves for his hard work and intelligence. Now, George reported, "he says he'll bring me down and humble me, and he puts me to just the hardest, meanest and dirtiest work on purpose!" So George had resolved to flee to Canada and earn money to buy freedom for Eliza and little Harry. Eliza wept and embraced her husband, then watched as he fled into the darkness.

Still later that night, Eliza's distress turned to horror when she discovered that the Shelbys, looking to save their plantation, had indeed sold Harry. There was no time now for useless protests. The young mother hurried to her room to pack some belongings. Then she took her son up in her arms and made her way to the cabin of Uncle Tom.

As soon as Tom and his wife Chloe opened the door, Eliza blurted out her news: Shelby had sold both Tom and her own little Harry, and she was running away with the little boy. Chloe tried to convince Tom to flee with Eliza, but he refused. "It's better for me to go [to the new plantation]," he explained, "than to break up the place [entirely]." Then, staring at his own brood of children, his pride and joy, Tom began to sob.

The next morning Haley set off on horseback in pursuit of Eliza and Harry. But when he caught up with them on the banks of the Ohio River, Eliza, "nerved with strength that God gives only the desperate," seized her child and raced to the water's edge: *. . . With one wild cry and flying leap, she vaulted sheer over the turbid current by the shore, on to the raft of ice beyond. It was a desperate leap—impossible to anything but madness and despair . . . With wild cries and desperate energy she leaped to another and still another cake; stumbling—leaping—slipping—springing upwards again . . . till dimly, as in a dream, she saw the Ohio side . . .*

Across the borders of a free state, Eliza was led to refuge in a Quaker shelter for runaways. And miraculously, George was eventually guided to the same house.

But soon after the family's tearful and joyous reunion, they learned that Haley, still bent on reclaiming his prize, had commissioned two unsavory slave hunters to scout the area for Harry. Under the cover of darkness, the runaways fled again. When the bounty seekers managed to track them down, George dispatched one of them with a bullet. And at last the fugitives made their way into Canada.

Back at the Shelby plantation, Haley was furious that Harry had escaped. Still, he came to take possession of Tom. The grizzled old slave bid his heartbreaking farewell to his own family and to Shelby's adoring son, young master George—who promised to someday buy Tom's freedom. Then, chained to Haley's wagon, he followed it down the road.

During the voyage down the Mississippi to the New Orleans slave markets, Tom's quiet demeanor impressed even the callous Haley. Unshackled, the old man was allowed to "come and go freely." In his walks on the boat's deck, Tom soon became acquainted with Little Eva St. Clare, a beautiful white child who often made secret visits to the slaves in their chains—sometimes with her hands full of food for them.

One day, as Little Eva stood on the dock with her father, Augustine St. Clare, she "suddenly lost her balance and fell sheer over the side of the boat into the water." In a moment, Tom "was after her," saving her life. The next day the grateful St. Clare purchased Tom from Haley.

After returning to New Orleans with the St. Clares, Tom became the family carriage driver. He soon learned that his wealthy new master loved his daughter above all else and that he also cared deeply for his slaves. In fact, St. Clare even allowed Little Eva to read to old Tom from the Bible.

Everyone on the estate loved good-natured Eva. Even a mischievous, ragamuffin little slave girl named Topsy succumbed to Eva's kind nature. "O, Topsy . . . " Eva told her one day. "I love you and I want you to be good!" Eva's heartfelt kindness made Topsy weep, and thereafter she tried hard to behave.

Thus it was that a great gloom spread over the entire estate the day news came that Little Eva was dying of a fatal fever. Flushed and tearful, the child told her father, "I feel sad for our poor people . . . I wish, Papa, they were all *free* . . . "

"O, Tom, my boy," wailed the distraught master as the old slave held his hand, "it's killing me!" Moments later, Eva's suffering ended: "a glorious smile came over her face and she was gone."

In the dismal days that followed, St. Clare made plans to follow his daughter's dying wishes and free his slaves. Before the formalities were completed, however, St. Clare himself died in an accident, leaving his widow with the task. Marie St. Clare, the stepmother of poor Little Eva, who had long berated her husband for his "wild, extravagant notions" about the dignity of slaves. At her direction Tom was sold to a particularly loathsome planter named Simon Legree. Upon his arrival at the new cotton plantation, Tom

despaired at the bleak sight of the slaves in Legree's charge: . . . *Human beings of whom nothing good was expected and desired; and who, treated in every way like brutes, had sunk as nearly to their level as it was possible for human beings to do.*

Two specially-trained, singularly brutal black overseers stood guard over the laboring slaves. One day a guard saw Tom trying to help a sick and feeble woman with her work; immediately he took a whip to the old man. Later, Legree demanded that Tom himself flog the woman. Horrified, Tom refused. " . . . Mas'r," he said, "if you mean to kill me, kill me; but as to my raising my hand again' anyone here, I never shall—I'll die first!"

Tom was beaten savagely on the spot, and then dragged to "an old forsaken room." Later, a slave woman named Cassy sneaked in to tend to his wounds. Cassy told him her own story, recalling the agony of having her daughter sold to another master—before she herself was forced into Legree's bed. When Tom urged her to trust in God, Cassy shook her head. There's no use calling on the Lord," she said. "He never hears."

Not long afterward, Cassy ran away with another slavewoman, and Tom was accused of complicity in the escape. "Well, Tom!" roared Legree, "do you know that I've made up my mind to KILL you?"

"O, Mas'r!" replied Tom, "don't bring this great sin on your soul!" Unmoved, Legree summoned his guards. "Take every drop of blood he has, until he confesses!" he commanded. Then he watched while Tom was beaten senseless. But when Legree had stalked off, the guards tended Tom's injuries. "We's been awful wicked to ye!" they cried. Tom's reply came tenderly: "I forgive ye with all my heart!"

Two days later, George Shelby—now a grown-up young gentleman—arrived at Legree's plantation. George had not forgotten his childhood promise to purchase Uncle Tom's freedom. But it was too late. "O, Mas'r George . . . " Tom sighed from his cot. "The Lord's bought me, and is going to take me home . . . " Moments later, he died.

When Legree strode into the room, grinning, George "knocked [him] flat upon his face." Then he took Tom's body up onto a shady knoll nearby and buried it, vowing, "I will do *what one man can do* to drive out this curse of slavery from my kind!"

After leaving the plantation, George ran across Cassy, in the company of another runaway, Madame de Thoux, on a riverboat going north. To his delight, he was able to help them: from his own family plantation records he soon ascertained that Cassy was Eliza's mother and that Madame de Thoux was George Harris' sister. With this knowledge, the women were eventually able to locate their families in Canada, where they celebrated a joyous reunion.

Meanwhile, George Shelby returned home to Kentucky. True to his word, he freed his slaves. As they circled around to thank him, he pointed to his old friend's cabin. *"Think of your freedom every time you see UNCLE TOM'S CABIN; and let it be a memorial to put you all in mind to follow in his steps, and be honest and faithful and Christian as he was."*

GREAT EXPECTATIONS

by
Charles Dickens
(1812 - 1870)

Type of work: Fictional study of moral values

Setting: 19th-century England

Principal characters:

Philip "Pip" Pirrip, a gentle and well-mannered orphan boy

Joe Gargery, Pip's brother-in-law, a kind-hearted blacksmith

Mrs. Joe, Joe's cantankerous wife and Pip's sister

Miss Havisham, a wealthy and reclusive woman who lives at the Satis House estate

Estella Havisham, Miss Havisham's conceited yet beautiful adopted daughter

Abel Magwitch, an escaped felon

Compeyson, another escaped convict

Mr. Jaggers, Abel Magwitch's aggressive and intimidating lawyer

Molly, Jaggers' housekeeper

John Wemmick, Jaggers' chief clerk

Biddy, Joe Gargery's childhood friend and maid

Orlick, a surly brute employed at Satis House

Herbert Pocket, Pip's close friend and later business partner

Story Overview:

Seven-year-old Philip Pirrip, or "Pip" as he was called, was "brought up by hand" in his sister's home after their parents and five brothers had died. Her blacksmith husband, Joe Gargery, was fond of the boy and protected him, when possible, from his wife's cruel abuse.

One Christmas Eve as Pip made his way to the churchyard to visit his family's graves, he was accosted by "a fearful man . . . with a great iron on his leg." The convict ordered Pip to bring him food and a file, or he would "have his heart and liver out." Terrorized, Pip returned with a pork pie and a file, and while the convict devoured the food and began to grind off his manacles, Pip made his escape.

Later that day, when a unit of soldiers stopped to have Joe repair a set of handcuffs, Pip learned that they had apprehended two convicts, one of whom had threatened Pip. The boy was relieved to hear that the man had confessed to stealing the pie and other "wittles" from Joe's house.

Not long afterwards, Pip was hired by the eccentric Miss Havisham of Satis House as a playmate for her adopted daughter Estella. Pip found Miss Havisham a puzzling woman: jilted by her fiance years ago, she had stopped all the clocks in the house, left the rooms untouched, and made revenge her chief aim in life. One of her weapons in this aim was Estella, who treated Pip with contempt because of his "coarseness." Pip, however, loved Estella from the beginning.

One day, Pip was attacked by a "pale young gentleman." After Pip soundly trounced the lad, Estella, who had been thrilled by the fight, allowed Pip to kiss her. From that time forward, Pip, in order to win Estella's favor, was determined to make himself into a real gentleman.

His hopes were dashed, however, when Miss Havisham abruptly returned him to Joe to learn blacksmithing. Back in his familiar surroundings, Pip, ashamed of his trade and of his brother-in-law Joe, felt that "all was coarse and common."

One day Pip returned to Satis House for a visit and discovered that Estella had gone off to school. Then on the way home, he found his sister, who had been assaulted and lay unconscious on the road. The only clue left at the scene was a filed leg cuff—which Pip recognized as the one worn by his convict.

Over the next week, "Mrs. Joe" partially recovered her hearing and sight, but not her temper. Biddy, an uncouth domestic who had been hired to care for her, soon fell in love with Pip—and now Pip grew even more disenchanted with his station in life.

Four years later, a lawyer, Mr. Jaggers, came to the Gargerys' door to buy Pip's services on behalf of an anonymous benefactor. Pip was to be removed from Satis House, given a "handsome property," and "brought up as a gentleman—in a word, as a young fellow of great expectations." Astounded, Pip imagined the offer had come from Miss Havisham, certain that she was grooming him to marry Estella.

Pip soon traveled to London to learn the fine art of foppery, with Jaggers as his new guardian. There, Pip met two of Jaggers' employees: Molly, the housekeeper, and John Wemmick, Jaggers' trusted clerk.

When Pip located his lodgings, he was startled to find that he had a roommate, Herbert Pocket—the very "pale young gentleman" he had boxed at Miss Havisham's. Nevertheless, Herbert and Pip soon became friends.

The novelty of Pip's situation, however, began to wear off. London was not a beautiful city, and though Pip had managed to distance himself from Joe and Biddy, he was still not the gentleman he had hoped to become.

Years passed, and Pip, now a "gentleman," received a visit from Joe. Mortified by the blacksmith's clumsy ways and his "bird nest of a hat," Pip could hardly bear Joe's presence. The next day, when Pip left for his home village, he decided not to stay at Joe's home, since true gentlemen boarded at the Blue Boar Inn.

During his visit, Pip went to Satis House and, to his dismay, was greeted by a gruff and hateful servant named Orlick. Estella, who had returned from her schooling, was now a ravishing young woman. Sensing Pip's renewed interest in her daughter, Miss Havisham encouraged him, and Pip, thinking she was now "intended" for him, tried to court her. Estella informed him, however, that he was the only man she would not marry. Pip was crestfallen.

When Pip returned to London, he learned that his sister had been murdered. In her death throes, she had somehow written the words "Joe,"

"Pardon," and "Pip." Also in an apparent effort to leave clues as to her murderer's identity, she had drawn a "T," though Pip could not help but suspect Orlick.

The day Pip turned 21, his anonymous benefactor decreed he was to receive the sum of 500 pounds a year, which Pip gladly accepted. Then two years later, a weather-beaten stranger appeared at Pip's door. "You're a game one," the man uttered with deliberate affection. "I'm glad you've grow'd up a game one!" Pip suddenly recognized the stranger: it was "his convict"; and Pip became even more horrified to learn that this man had been his long-time benefactor. Indeed, the felon, whose name was Abel Magwitch, had acquired the money he had sent to Pip by herding sheep in Australia. Now he had come back to England—despite penalty of death—to see Pip.

Disillusioned, Pip "shrank from him as from some terrible beast." When Magwitch lay down and slept, though, Pip pondered his situation. He had shunned Joe as being too coarse; the guilt welling up, he saw now "how fully wrecked he was and how the ship in which he had sailed had gone to pieces."

Meanwhile, Pip learned that the convict with whom Magwitch had been captured, a man named Compeyson, had played the part of a gentleman at their trial and thus had received a milder sentence. Magwitch had sworn revenge. The felon also revealed that it was this same Compeyson who had jilted Miss Havisham years ago.

Dejected, Pip returned to London to find a note from the clerk Wemmick, warning him not to go home: Compeyson was in London spying on Magwitch. Wemmick also suggested that Magwitch be relocated, and Herbert promptly moved him to a house near the waterfront.

Herbert and Pip now devised a scheme to spirit Magwitch out of the country. Purchasing a boat, the two began to row up and down the river for a period of weeks. When their rowing would no longer attract suspicion, Pip would transport Magwitch to a ship and they would sail away.

Jaggers invited Pip for dinner one day. Seeing the housekeeper Molly again, it finally occurred to Pip that she bore a striking resemblance to Estella. Later, Wemmick admitted that Jaggers had once defended Molly on a murder charge, and, in return, she had become his servant. Molly's child had always been thought murdered—but Pip knew otherwise.

Armed with this new information, Pip returned to Satis House. Regretting her earlier treatment of Pip, Miss Havisham offered to do something to prove to him that she was "not all of stone." Pip forgave her, after which Miss Havisham acknowledged that Jaggers had in fact, many years earlier, entrusted two-year-old Estella to her care.

Pip left, but sensing some danger, he immediately returned to the house, where he found Miss Havisham enveloped in flames, her yellowed wedding dress having brushed against the fire. Pip flung her to the ground and beat out the flames with his cloak, saving her life.

Back in London, Magwitch confessed to Herbert that Molly, before she was tried for murder, had been his wife. Just a year after their marriage, Estella had been born, and he had given the

child to Miss Havisham to save her from being sent to an orphanage.

Some days later, Pip received a mysterious note summoning him to a local limekiln. When he arrived, however, he found no one. Just as he turned to leave, he was overpowered and bound by Orlick. Orlick, who was one of Compeyson's spies, gruffly confessed to Mrs. Joe's murder; then he picked up a long-handled hammer with which to dash out Pip's brains. But just then a group of men, led by Herbert, heard Pip's shouts and came to his rescue. Orlick dropped his weapon and fled into the night. Herbert, it turned out, had found the note and, suspecting mischief, had followed Pip.

The next morning, Pip and Herbert embarked on their plan to smuggle Magwitch out of the country. Compeyson, however, intercepted them before they boarded the escape vessel. In the melee that followed, Magwitch fought with Compeyson and the two rivals plunged off the boat into the water. After a brief struggle, it was Magwitch who swam back to the boat.

The magistrate, who by now had arrived at the dock, shackled the severely injured man. In spite of Jagger's able defense, Magwitch was found guilty and sentenced to hang.

Pip visited kind-hearted Magwitch in his cell and told him about Estella. This news proved to be the only consolation Magwitch would take to his death.

Soon, Pip fell violently ill. Once more Joe stepped in and nursed his brother-in-law back to health. Pip, finally having learned from Joe and Magwitch the true meaning of love and humility, returned to his boyhood village, only to find that Miss Havisham had died of her burns. With the marriage of Joe and Biddy, it was now Pip who found himself no longer needed.

Herbert and Pip decided to sign on as mates aboard a ship bound for India. When Pip returned to England eleven years later, he found that the Gargerys had been blessed with both a daughter and a son—a son named Pip.

Pip once again stopped by Satis House to call on Estella, who had by then been married and widowed. Now, as the more mature couple reunited, Pip "saw no shadow of another parting from her."

Commentary:

Dickens, himself the product of a large family blighted by hunger and privation, knew firsthand the experiences of which he wrote. *Great Expectations* is at once a superbly constructed mystery and a profound examination of moral values.

Few writers of fiction have matched Dickens' genius for creating characters who are both believable and intriguingly complex. The reader at first views Pip, for instance, with humor and compassion, a view that soon turns to scorn as he systematically spurns those who love him to pursue high social status. Indeed, Pip must suffer before his own humanity can be restored—a humanity mastered through and reflected in Magwitch's love, Joe's loyalty, and Biddy's abiding trust. In fashioning his grand host of characters, Dickens seems to mock those who seek fame and fortune, arguing instead that it is the pure in heart who are most praiseworthy and virtuous.

ROLL OF THUNDER, HEAR MY CRY

by Mildred Taylor, Dial Books, New York, N.Y., 1976

Type of work: Young adult fiction

Setting: Mississippi; 1933

Principal characters:
Cassie Logan, a fourth-grade girl
Stacey Logan, her twelve-year-old brother
"Mama," Mary Logan, their mother
"Papa," David Logan, their father
"Big Ma," their grandmother Caroline
T.J. Avery, Stacey's bothersome friend

Story Overview:

Even though their mother was a teacher, the Logan children didn't like going to school. Their days were filled with rote lessons, drab textbooks, and whippings. Nevertheless, every morning from October to March—when they were not needed to pick or plant cotton—Cassie Logan, her big brother Stacey, and their two younger brothers set off on the hour-long trek to the dismal old schoolhouse.

The children "could have more easily endured the journey" however, if it had not been for the Jefferson Davis school bus that always zipped up behind them and doused them in mud. Stumbling to avoid the mud-shower, the children knew they were simply "comical objects" for the white driver and students on the bus, who yelled "Nigger! Nigger!" as they passed.

"Big Ma, it ain't fair," the children complained. Though Big Ma knew far better than her grandchildren how difficult it was to be scorned by "ignorant white folks," she "was not one for coddling." She simply replied, "You jus' keep on studying and get a good education and you'll be all right."

Big Ma untiringly maintained the land that her husband had bought for the family way back in 1918. Born a slave, Paul Edward Logan had worked long hours as a carpenter so that he could purchase 400 acres of good farmland from the Grangers, who had once owned the largest plantation in the area. But now Paul Edward was dead, and Harlan Granger, who still owned a ten-square-mile tract abutting the Logan's acreage, was out to reclaim the property that his family had sold. Big Ma, however, would never consider giving up her family's land. She made sure that the taxes and mortgage were paid, even if everyone had to do without. And from spring to fall, Papa worked in Louisiana laying railroad track to reduce the debt. "You ain't never had to live on nobody's place but your own," he'd once told Cassie, "and long as I live and the family survives, you'll never have to . . ."

In the meantime, Cassie had concerns of her own, not the least of which was the horrid school bus. Stacey, though, devised a plan to stop that bus from splashing them. One day he, Cassie, and their little brothers dug dirt from the road's center, forming a pothole; then they hid in the bushes and watched as the bus "careened drunkenly" in the drooping earth and "died." While the white students piled out into the mud

and "moved spiritlessly toward home" on foot, Cassie thought gleefully, "A well-maneuvered revenge!"

That night, however, Cassie's glee turned to terror when Joe Avery, the father of Stacey's talkative, pesky friend T.J., arrived at the Logan home. "They's ridin' t'night," he told Mama. "It don't take but a little of nothin' to set them devilish night men off."

Immediately the children were sent to bed. But Stacey and Cassie already knew all about the night riders. Just a few days earlier, T.J. had related how the night men had gone over to the Berrys' house and put "a match to 'em." Mr. Berry and his nephews had been "burnt near to death." Tonight, thought Cassie, they must be out to avenge the school bus. "Stacey," she whispered, "they're coming after us!"

It was a long time before Cassie finally succumbed to sleep. When she woke, it was "still nightly dark" outside and she could see "a caravan of headlights" moving toward the house. One of the cars pulled into the driveway and a man got out. He "stared at the house for several long moments" before he got back in and drove away, followed by the others. "Waves of terror swept over" Cassie as she lay trembling into the dawn.

It was not until a week later that Cassie found out from T.J. that the night riders had at first mistaken the Logans' house for Sam Tatum's. It seems Tatum had called a white merchant named Wallace a liar; in retaliation the night men had hunted Tatum out and tarred and feathered him.

Even though everyone knew that the Wallaces were among the night men who had "poured kerosene over Mr. Berry and his nephews and lit them afire," the black sharecroppers had no choice but to shop at their store: despite the high interest rates they charged and the drinking and gambling that went on at the store, the town's black citizens relied on credit with the Wallaces to buy their wares. Although Mama had gone from house to house in the black community, trying to convince them to do their buying in Vicksburg, even she knew her plan would be difficult to carry out. Who in Vicksburg would extend credit to the sharecroppers?

Then over the Christmas holidays Mr. Wade Jamison, Big Ma's white estate lawyer, offered to back the credit himself. "I'm a Southerner born and bred," he explained in his soft-spoken way, "but that does not mean that I approve of all that goes on here."

In the days following Mr. Jamison's offer, Mama took shopping orders from various black families, and then one morning Papa and his friend Mr. Morrison climbed into the wagon and set off to Vicksburg.

The shopping trip was a success. But shortly after Papa's return, he received a visit from Mr. Harlan Granger, who was piqued because Papa's brother Hammer had recently bought a silver Packard almost identical to his own. But what really disturbed him was the Logans' "traveling store." "Seems to me," Granger frowned, "you folks are just stirring up something." Then he threatened to foreclose on their mortgage if they missed a payment. "You plan on getting this land," Papa said, "you're planning on the wrong thing." Harlan Granger only grinned.

One day after Mama caught T.J. cheating on an exam, the boy stormed out of her class to report her to Kaleb Wallace, a member of the School Board. Wallace immediately appeared at Mama's classroom—accompanied by fellow board member Harlan Granger. Granger interrupted Mama's history lesson on slavery in the South. "I don't see all those things you're teaching them in here," he said, holding up a textbook. "All that's in that book isn't true," explained Mama evenly. "You so smart," Granger hissed, "I expect you'd best forget about teaching altogether . . . thataway you'll have plenty of time to write your own book." Mama had lost the job that helped pay the mortgage.

Papa insisted on taking Stacey along on his next shopping trip to Vicksburg. "I want [Stacey] strong . . . not a fool like T.J.," he said, although Mama worried because she had heard that Wallace might make trouble for them.

On the night that Papa, Stacey, and Mr. Morrison were due to return, the family waited nervously. "Something's happened to them! I can feel it!" Mama finally blurted out. And her fears were soon confirmed. When the wagon appeared, Papa lay cradled in Mr. Morrison's arms. Men in a truck had driven by and shot him, the bullet just grazing his head. Then, as he had fallen to the ground, the wagon had rolled over Papa's leg. Mr. Morrison had struck one of the Wallace boys as the truck sped away, and it was rumored that the boy's back was broken.

Mr. Morrison brought Papa into the house and laid him on the bed. He was barely conscious, and his broken left leg jutted awkwardly out. "But who'd shoot Papa?" Cassie cried in disbelief. "Can't nobody just shoot Papa!" But the concern for now was Mr. Morrison's safety; the Wallaces surely would retaliate.

Sure enough, just days later, while Mr. Morrison was out on an errand, Kaleb Wallace found him. "You big black nigger," Wallace railed. "I oughta cut your heart out. I'm gonna come get you for what you done!"

Before long, the bank—at Granger's and Wallace's urging—demanded that the Logans pay off their mortgage in full. "Said our credit's no good anymore," Papa told his family. Then he promised, "We ain't gonna lose the land . . . Trust me."

In fact, his brother's Packard provided unexpected help: Hammer sold it to pay off the loan. "What good's a car?" he smiled. "It can't grow cotton. You can't build a home on it."

Still, the Logans could not forget Wallace's threat. One night Cassie lay listening to Mr. Morrison's singing on the front porch: *Roll of thunder, hear my cry; Over the water, bye and bye. Ole man's comin' down the line; Whip in hand to*

beat me down. But I ain't gonna let him, Turn me round. Suddenly the girl heard a strange sound and opened the door to her room. There stood T.J. She stared "in horror at the deep blue-black swelling of his stomach and chest." T.J. explained that after he and some white friends had broken into a gun shop, one of the white boys had smashed the owner's head in with an axe, before turning on T.J., beating him and leaving him behind to take the blame.

Terrified, Cassie and her brothers helped T.J. to the Avery house. Then, as they turned towards home, they saw the headlights of the night riders. Within seconds the white men had broken into the house and wrenched the Averys out by their feet. Pulling T.J. aside, they began kicking at his mutilated stomach.

Just then, Mr. Jamison arrived. "Y'all let the sheriff and me take the boy," he called out. The mob ignored him. Ropes in hand, they began dragging T.J. outside. "Papa'll know what to do," Stacey frantically whispered to his sister as they turned and ran for home.

Hearing what had happened, Papa grabbed his shotgun and "disappeared into the night." And as "the thunder banged menacingly" outside her window, "Big Ma fell upon her knees and prayed a powerful prayer." Then everyone waited silently. Suddenly, Mama "sniffed the air." The cotton was on fire. Big Ma and Mama instantly began filling buckets and dipping burlap in water. "You set one foot from this house," Mama told her children as she dashed out the door, "and I'll skin you alive."

Early the next day, the youngsters learned what had happened. Seeing the flames, everyone in the community—both black and white—had rushed to the cotton fields to put out the fire. They all thought that lightning had caused the blaze. But the Logan children knew better: Papa "had started the fire [to] stop the hanging."

T.J. was arrested; the law would now determine his fate. The long night was finally over. Yet, before she slept, Cassie cried for T.J.—and she cried for the land.

Commentary:

Mildred Taylor, one of the country's foremost writers of children's literature, received the coveted Newbery Medal in 1977 for *Roll of Thunder, Hear My Cry*. Like most of Taylor's fiction, this novel reflects the author's fascination with the vivid oral narratives that she heard as a child during summer visits with her Mississippi relatives. She credits the South for the sense of family, community and history that reinforces her writing.

The impact of history is everywhere apparent in *Roll of Thunder;* it fills the Logans' lives and shapes their thinking. Mama, especially, sees an honest confrontation with history, no matter how painful, as essential. Even when her job is on the line, she will not teach the sanitized version of Southern slavery found in the white textbooks. This portrayal of a "docile, subservient people, happy with their fate" is contrary to her heritage. For Mary Logan, truth and freedom are synonymous.

THE GOOD EARTH

by
Pearl S. Buck
(1892-1973)

Type of work: Naturalistic novel

Setting: Pre-revolutionary China; twentieth century

Principal characters:

Wang Lung, a peasant who becomes wealthy
O-lan, his wife, once a slave
Lotus, a prostitute
Pear Blossom, Wang Lung's slave and concubine

Commentary:

With the appearance of Pearl S. Buck's *The Good Earth* on bookstore shelves in 1931, many American readers got their first real glimpse into Chinese life. Readers and critics alike were captivated. Heralded as "a work of genius," the novel became a national best-seller and Pulitzer Prize-winner. But while highly acclaimed in the west, *The Good Earth* was not well received in China. Among its detractors were Chinese academics, who believed that the novel oversimplified their country's multifaceted culture by focusing on the peasant class. Other detractors attacked its honest attention to sexuality, which they felt demeaned the sensibilities of the Chinese.

Still, Buck's simple yet explicit depiction of Chinese life gave her work a universal appeal that humanized and demystified a country which, to the Western world, had long been an enigma.

Story Overview:

On his wedding day, Wang Lung nervously made his way to the gates of the illustrious house of Hwang to meet his new bride. As the gateman led him into the opulent hall, the peasant heard "tinkles of laughter on every side" that increased his anxiety. He was, after all, a poor man, whose father had negotiated his marriage to an unpretentious slave woman there.

When O-lan, Wang Lung's bride-to-be, was presented to him, he could see that "there was not a beauty of any kind in her face." Nevertheless, he felt a "secret exultation" during the wedding feast and ceremony, for, at last, "he had his woman!"

After his marriage, as his new wife attended to his needs, Wang Lung discovered, for the first time, a "luxury of living." Not only did his bride's cooking, housekeeping, and work in the fields please him, but her "untouched" and "beautiful" body satisfied him as well. And before long, O-lan presented him with his first man-child. Informing his father that he was now a grandfather, Wang Lung listened as the old man cackled joyfully.

A short time later, the hard-working and fertile O-lan gave birth to yet another son. And to add to this luck, after much hard work and sacrifice, Wang Lung and O-lan were able to buy a new tract of land from the great House of Hwang. Wang Lung firmly believed that the earth was "one's flesh and blood," and now at last he felt himself "equal to [the] people in the foolish, great, wasteful house." O-lan, meanwhile, rejoiced that she was the wife of a man who could buy land from those who had enslaved her.

The family's happiness, however, was short-lived. Hearing of his nephew's new prosperity, Wang Lung's destitute uncle began to make demands. All too well acquainted with the ways of the libertine man, Wang Lung observed acerbically, "If [we] have a handful of silver it is because . . . we do not, as some do, sit idling over a gambling table or gossiping on doorsteps never swept, letting the fields grow to weeds and our children go half-fed!" Nevertheless, bound by family honor, Wang Lung assisted the uncle and his family as often as he could.

In time, a terrible drought took hold of the land, killing many crops, and there came a point where Wang Lung could no longer afford to give even "a small heap of beans" or "a precious handful of corn" to his uncle without starving his own family. The uncle went around the village, complaining bitterly: "My nephew, there, he has silver and he has food, but he will give none of it to us, not even to me, and to my children, who are his own bones and flesh." Incited by the uncle's words, the villagers descended on Wang Lung's home and pocketed the family's last few bits of food. For a moment Wang Lung felt great fear, but he immediately comforted himself: "I have the land still, and it is mine."

Meanwhile, two daughters and a third son had been born to Wang Lung and O-lan. The younger daughter had a vacant gaze and dull mind, but her father loved her; sadly and affectionately he referred to her as "the fool." Now, however, he could no longer bear to look at any of his emaciated children. At last, though he knew the journey would be difficult in their weakened state, he decided in desperation to take his family south.

As Wang Lung and O-lan led their children out of the village, they discovered a horde of other desperate families struggling towards the railroad to board the "fire wagons" that would take them south. With his last two pieces of silver, Wang Lung also bought tickets, then loaded his family on a train bound for the city of Kiangsu.

Kiangsu's well-fed residents often hurled "scornful and haughty" glances at their new neighbors from the north. After pulling together a rude hut from cheap floor mats to shelter his family, Wang Lung went to work pulling a ricksha through the city; his father, wife, and children, meanwhile, set out to beg on the streets. "Unless you give, good sir, good lady—we starve—we starve," they called out to passersby. But even as his kin coaxed coins from strangers, Wang Lung's hope and pride burned on. He never let the one most important thought drift from his mind: "We must get back to the land."

Before long, a class war erupted between

the city's poor and rich. As penniless mobs ransacked Kiangsu's palatial mansions, a handful of pilfered silver finally came into Wang Lung's grasp. The silver not only paid for return tickets to Wang Lung's home village, but it also bought a new ox for his family, and "seeds the likes of which he had never planted before."

To Wang Lung's further delight, O-lan had pillaged a "heap of jewels" from a rich man's house in Kiangsu. As she surrendered this treasure, she asked only that she be allowed to keep two small "wife pearls" to wear around her neck. Wang Lung promptly marched to the house of Hwang to exchange the rest of the fortune for more land. His property holdings were now vast, and he would no longer permit his wife to work in the fields. In her place, he contracted the services of Ching, his gentle and loyal neighbor.

As the years passed, Wang Lung hired more laborers to tend to his fertile lands. At last, he had achieved the status of a wealthy man, and, as such, he naturally encouraged his sons to become scholars—although he occasionally worried about how accustomed they had become to privilege. He was also troubled by his beloved daughter, "the fool." She could not speak, but could only display a sweet, empty smile that filled him with intense love and sadness.

Strangely, the richer Wang Lung became, the more overwhelmed he was by sadness, often mixed with anger. One day as he stared at O-lan, he was suddenly struck by how plain she looked: she was "a dull and common" old woman indeed. And, soon, Wang Lung found himself longing for a young and beautiful woman.

He met just such a woman only a few days later at the new tea shop in town. Although Lotus worked as a prostitute, she was "like a flower on a quince tree," an exquisitely beautiful and fragile creature who "kept him fevered and thirsty, even if she gave him his will of her." When she demanded silver and jewels, Wang Lung happily complied, going so far as to compel O-lan to turn over her treasured wife pearls in order to pacify his charming Lotus. At last he moved her into his own house, and even agreed to build an addition for her. There in her polished shrine, Lotus "lay indolent upon her bed . . . nibbling sweet meats and fruits, and wearing nothing but single garments of green summer silk . . ."

Wang Lung's life became increasingly difficult and complicated. Not surprisingly, O-lan never spoke to her rival; and Wang Lung's aged father often scolded loudly, "There is a harlot in the house!" If these troubles weren't enough, his conniving uncle's family also moved into Wang Lung's house to enjoy a life of leisure. And things became even more awkward when Wang Lung discovered his oldest son in Lotus' bedroom. Consequently, the distraught father hastened his son's marriage to the courtesan. Now, despite his great wealth, "Wang Lung found himself in such a coil as he never dreamed of"— and he longed to return to the land.

True to the prevailing run of luck, the long-frail O-lan died on the very day her son was wed. And only days later, as if "death could

not easily leave the house where it had come once," Wang Lung's frail father also died. Grief-stricken, Wang Lung selected "a good place in his fields under a date tree for the graves . . . And out of his heaviness there stood out but one clear thought and it was a pain to him . . . He wished that he had not taken the two pearls from O-lan that day . . . and he would never bear to see Lotus put them in her ears . . ." In fact, his ardor for his daughter-in-law had begun to cool long before O-lan's death.

Finally, in an attempt to free himself once and for all from the humiliating entanglements with his uncle, Wang Lung, after consulting with his second son, turned over his old residence to the avaricious old man and bought the "great house of Hwang" for himself and his family to live in. Shortly after they were settled into the lavish new dwelling, Wang Lung's first grandson was born, and a new aura of peace came into his life. But then he received another blow: the death of the trusted Ching, caretaker of his beloved land. Wang Lung wept openly; the earth that he had once esteemed and coveted with unbridled fierceness now left him unfulfilled and desolate.

Over the years, the great house of Hwang, which he had taken so proudly into his possession, began to dishearten him as well. His two eldest sons and their wives feuded constantly, and Lotus became jealous of a lovely young slave girl called Pear Blossom who had recently been added to the household. When Lotus one day accused Wang Lung once of lusting after the girl, he laughed; but then he noticed for the first time how "very pretty and pale" she was, and "something stirred in his old blood that had been quiet" for many years.

"Child!" he called to Pear Blossom one day as the girl went about her duties—and immediately she submitted to him. Afterward, as he lay fondling her gently, he delighted in her words: "I like old men—I like old men—they are so kind." His youngest third son felt betrayed, however; for he had fallen in love with Pear Blossom himself. Now unable to endure her adoration of his father, he withdrew from the house.

In grief and repentance, Wang Lung sighed to Pear Blossom, "I am too old for you, my heart, and well I know it." Now his "passion died out of him," and life itself seemed to retreat from his being. But faithful Pear Blossom always helped him to recover his spirits when he was downhearted. What was more, the servant-girl promised to look after her master's cherished "little fool" after he died, and to remain steadfastly by his side until that day.

As Wang Lung's passing drew near, he could see that his two greedy eldest sons had become preoccupied with thoughts of their inheritance—the good earth which years earlier he had left in favor of riches. "If you sell the land," he warned his sons, "it is the end." In an attempt to placate their dying father, they promised that the land would not be sold.

And Wang Lung, his tired eyes closed, did not see their expressions of conspiracy as "they looked at each other and smiled."

I KNOW WHY THE CAGED BIRD SINGS

by Maya Angelou, Bantam Books, New York, N.Y., 1971

Type of work: Autobiography

Setting: Arkansas and California; 1930s and '40s

Commentary:

I Know Why the Caged Bird Sings is an account of Maya Angelou's early life. Other, more complete autobiographies have received greater critical acclaim, but this one, her first, remains the most popular. Indeed, since she read her inauguration poem for President Clinton, *I Know Why the Caged Bird Sings* has reappeared on the national best-seller lists.

Despite her traumatic childhood, Angelou's intelligence and determination have helped her both to survive and to flourish. The grace, energy, and tenacity that emerge in all of her writings have won the admiration of countless readers.

In her mix of work, which also includes essays, poetry, and screenplays, Angelou reveals a deep attachment to her religious and cultural roots. Without this connection, she suggests, a "caged bird" may never learn to sing—or to escape the oppressive confines of its cage.

Story Overview:

Accompanied by her four-year-old twin brother Bailey, Marguerite Johnson boarded a train in California. The two "poor motherless darlings" quickly drew the attention of other passengers. In fact, Bailey and Marguerite did have parents, but for reasons they never understood, their mother and father had decided to send them to "Stamps, Arkansas, c/o Mrs. Annie Henderson," their tall, imposing paternal grandmother, who soon became known to the children simply as "Momma." Momma was a woman of great personal integrity and abiding faith, and she commanded the respect of everyone in Stamps' black community.

Together with her crippled son Willie, Momma owned and operated the Wm. Johnson General Merchandise Store. At first, Bailey and Marguerite thought of the store as a "Fun House of Things," things to eat and enjoy. As the years went by, however, their grandmother expected them to work in the store, and they took almost as great a pride in their work as they did their play.

Some of their grandmother's other expectations, though, were harder for the children to fulfill. For instance, they realized early on that their "total salvation" depended on obeying Momma's Two Commandments: "Thou shall not be dirty" and "Thou shall not be impudent." In terms of cleanliness, the children cringed at the prospect of going out to the well to wash in the ice-cold water. But with Momma's admonition to "wash as far as possible—and then wash possible" echoing in their ears, they managed to comply.

The battle to curb impudence, however, was not so easily won. Once, when a frenzied Sister Monroe yelled "Preach it!" to Reverend Thomas during his Sunday sermon and then hit him so hard that his false teeth fell out onto the floor, Marguerite and Bailey began to laugh and holler uncontrollably. For this impudence, they received a whipping from Momma and Uncle Willie.

"Impudence" around white folk, however, took on a whole other meaning—one that could quickly lead to racial friction. As a young child, Marguerite once watched as Momma packed a black man in a barrel to prevent his lynching by the Klan. But the harsh reality of racism didn't personally touch the young girl until the day "a troop of powhitetrash kids" marched onto Momma's property. "Sister, go on inside," Momma ordered. Gazing out the window, Marguerite looked on, horrified, as the girls taunted and mimicked Momma. When one of the older children did a handstand so that Momma had to view the girl's uncovered crotch, Momma began to sing, "Bread of Heaven, bread of Heaven, feed me till I want no more." Then, just as strangely as the game had begun, the girls grew tired. "'Bye, Annie," they called out, and Momma answered, "'Bye Miz Helen, 'bye Miz Ruth, 'bye Miz Eloise." Marguerite marvelled at Momma's poise in the face of cruelty; here was a woman who, despite the fact that she knew white folk "couldn't be spoken to insolently" or spoken to at all "without risking one's life," nonetheless retained her dignity.

Marguerite came to recognize at an early age that Momma's world "was bordered on all sides with work, duty, religion, and 'her place.'" Yet, within that world, she was her own master. Even on the day she said good-bye to them, she didn't cry. Her son—their father, Bailey Sr.—had come to take them to St. Louis to live with their mother before he returned to California. At first Marguerite was reluctant to leave Stamps with this handsome stranger who persisted in calling her "Daddy's baby." She soon realized, however, that with or without her, Bailey Jr. was going to St. Louis, and she couldn't imagine living out her life without him.

On the appointed day, Marguerite cried in the back seat of the car. Not only was she leaving Momma, Uncle Willie, and her friends, but she was also being ignored by her father and Bailey, who joked and laughed in the front seat. But, she decided, that was natural: they were father and son, while she was only a girl—and a rather unsightly one at that.

Marguerite's unhappiness did not immediately subside when they reached St. Louis. The city, with its "crowded-together soot-covered buildings," was both "a new kind of hot and a new kind of ugly." But when Bailey Sr. introduced them to their mother Vivian Baxter Johnson, Marguerite was flabbergasted: "My mother's beauty literally assailed me . . . Her smile widened her mouth . . . seemingly through the walls of the street outside. I was struck dumb. I knew immediately why she had sent me away. She was too beautiful to have children."

Slowly, Marguerite, now eight years old, adjusted to life in St. Louis and became acquainted with her parents and other relatives, including her flashy and highly regarded

Grandmother Baxter, a woman so charismatic she even "had pull with the police." There were the three Baxter brothers—all of them possessing a cruel streak and "best known for their unrelenting meanness." In fact, Marguerite learned that her uncles had once tracked down a man who had made the mistake of cursing at their mother. When they had restrained the culprit, they encouraged their sister to attack him; and Vivian had obligingly "crashed the man's head with a billy enough to leave him just this side of death."

This incident aside, Vivian always behaved lovingly towards her children. Preparing a "special place" for them in her house and letting them visit her at Louie's, the tavern where she danced and sang the "heavy blues." But, because she was often away working, her children spent many evenings alone in the house with her live-in boyfriend, Mr. Freeman. And while Bailey and Marguerite read their books—everything they could find from Shakespeare to cheap paperbacks—Freeman kept to himself and "put his whole self into waiting for Vivian to come home."

When she returned, he was obviously delighted. But Vivian frequently interrupted their time together by bringing Marguerite—who suffered from nightmares—into their bed. Then one morning, when Vivian was out on an errand, Marguerite awoke to find Freeman curled up naked beside her. After she had complied with his feverish fondling, he held her in his arms, and the thought came to her that "he'd never let me go or let anything bad happen to me."

Weeks later, Freeman raped Marguerite again, threatening to kill her brother if she ever told anyone about them. It was only when Vivian changed Marguerite's sheets and found her bloodied underwear that she determined what had happened.

Vivian pressed charges against Freeman. Marguerite, frightened almost beyond words, had to testify in court, but the child molester still walked out free. Later that day, however, he was "kicked to death . . . behind the slaughterhouse"—undoubtedly by Marguerite's uncles.

The girl was now convinced that she had lost "her place in heaven"; her feeble testimony had resulted in Freeman's death. What's more, Marguerite decided that her words somehow had the power to "poison people"—and she stopped speaking to everyone but Bailey. At first her muteness struck her family as a natural reaction to the rape; but as the weeks passed, her silence was mistaken for impudence and she received multiple beatings, "given by any relative who felt himself offended." Before long Marguerite and Bailey were on a train back to Stamps.

Everyone in Momma's community believed that the girl's muteness was simply a sign of her "tender-hearted" disposition—an "affliction" which was like "being a little sick or in delicate health." But it was Mrs. Bertha Flowers, "the aristocrat of Black Stamps," who took a special interest in the shy, sensitive girl. She lent Marguerite many fine books and encouraged her to take pride in her intelligence.

Before long, Marguerite again began to speak; through Mrs. Flowers, the girl felt "liked and respected . . . just for being Marguerite Johnson."

Marguerite's discovery of her self-worth proved invaluable. Strengthened by her childhood ordeals, she managed to keep her self-respect in the face of many other brutal encounters with life.

Understandably, the girl disliked crossing over into "whitefolk's country." One day, however, Momma led the hesitant girl across the bridge. Marguerite suffered from two rotten-to-the-gums cavities and the excruciating pain would not go away. Promising her granddaughter that the white dentist would attend to her because he owed her a favor, Momma was not prepared for their reception. "Annie, you know I don't treat . . . colored people," the dentist frowned. But Momma reminded him, "When you came to borrow money from me, you didn't have to beg. . . . You stood to lose this building and I tried to help you out." Icily, the dentist replied, "Annie, I'd rather stick my hand in a dog's mouth than a nigger's."

"They don't really hate us," Uncle Willie explained afterward. "They don't know us. How can they hate us? They mostly scared." But later that evening Bailey arrived home in a state of shock, unable to "let go of the horror" of having seen the mutilated body of a black man who had just been lynched. It was then that Momma decided it was time to send her grandchildren back to California.

The Johnson children were forced to adapt once more, this time to life in San Francisco. Marguerite worked hard in high school, earning good grades, and Bailey, eager to face life on his own, found work on the Southern Pacific Railroad. As the months passed by, however, Marguerite felt certain her life was at a crossroads. She had made up her mind to become a street-car conductorette. Intrigued by the prospect of "sailing up and down the hills of San Francisco in a dark-blue uniform," she was determined to land the job even after being told that the city didn't accept applications from "colored people." In the end, Marguerite was hired.

She soon realized, though, that her life was far from complete. She had no boyfriend and felt insecure about her sexuality; her body seemed to her to be more manly than womanly. To overcome these feelings Marguerite resolved to seduce a popular boy whom she knew casually. But their awkward encounter proved disappointing to both of them. Then, a few weeks later, she discovered that she was pregnant. Although relieved that she was, in fact, a "real woman," a "massive pushing in of fear, guilt, and self-revulsion" now tormented her.

When she at last informed her family, she encountered "no overt or subtle condemnation." Finally, she began "enjoying the imminent blessed event." Her beautiful baby boy delighted Marguerite—but motherhood frightened her. Still concerned about her own awkwardness, Marguerite thought about what her mother had said: " . . . You don't have to think about doing the right thing. If you're for the right thing, then you do it without thinking."

MOSCOW TO THE END OF THE LINE

by Venedikt Erofeev, Northwestern University Press, Evanston IL, 1992

Type of work: Introspective tragedy

Setting: A train car traveling between the Russian cities Moscow and Petushki; the mid-1960s

Principal characters:

Venedikt Erofeev, a drunken but eloquent ex-cable fitter

Venedikt's unnamed sweetheart, a young woman who waits for him at the end of the train line

Various other people, all of whom Venedikt meets on the train car

Commentary:

Although Erofeev's book does not claim to be an autobiography, the author has endowed his fictive narrator with his own name and background, thus lending a grimly realistic tone to his commentary on life in the Soviet Union of the 1960s. While the plot unfolds within a time frame of only a few hours, the book manages to address—through the painful ponderings of Erofeev, a "typical" Russian worker—issues ranging from politics and poetry, wealth and poverty.

During the Communist era, when Soviet leaders forbade any criticism of their policies, *Moscow to the End of the Line* was circulated underground in hand-written copies. Open publication was finally permitted in 1987, and the work was subsequently translated and published in the United States in 1992.

With the exception of the first and last few chapters, Erofeev's dark thoughts unfold entirely within the confines of a train car journeying from Moscow to Petushki, the city at the end of the rail line. The author uses phrases that are at once vulgar and stunningly poetic to document the hopelessness that many Russians felt during this time. In the introduction he labels the work as a meditation, a nightmare, delirium tremens, and even "a hymn to thirteen kinds of Soviet vodka which the almighty government distills in order to keep the plebs complaisant . . . " Whichever of these labels is attributed to the narrative, it befits the first-person account of this "merry, brave, educated man falling into despair."

The call of various unnamed train stops often interrupts the flow of the narrative in mid-sentence, and neatly divides Erofeev's encounters—and those of his comrades—into a series of chapters. The energy of the language and the many intoxicating images effortlessly carry us, along with the narrator, to the end of the line.

Story Overview:

. . . *On the sixth day, I was so soused that the boundary between reason and heart had disappeared and they both recited in one voice: "Go, go to Petushki. In Petushki you'll find your salvation and your joy, go."*

And so Venedikt, weary of Moscow, begins his journey to Petushki where his sweetheart, his lover, his "most beloved of trollops" awaits him. He launches his morning journey with a glass of Zubrovka vodka, "since I know from experience that they've not come up with anything better by way of an eye-opener." Later, to brace himself against the pain and poverty of the workingman, he adds two beers and still more vodka. And on his way to the train station, he hugs a suitcase close to his heart—it carries vodka as well.

Once aboard the train car, Venedikt notes the empty, swollen eyes of his fellow Russians and makes specific observations about them in his ever-present notebook. Most of the passengers are intellectuals, caught up in spouting off all that is good about the State, yet inwardly they are as disgruntled about the economy, the politics, and the inequities between poor and rich as Venedikt is.

Venedikt's musings are cut short by a heated argument between two heavy-drinking intellectuals seated nearby. He duly notes the crux of their spat, while roundly condemning the pettiness of their reasoning. These academic vagabonds, he writes, imbibe only to feel superior; he, on the other hand, drinks out of a superior purpose: vodka, to Venedikt, is "the most intimate of intimacies."

As the train rolls into its next station, Venedikt turns away from his fellow passengers and remembers incidents in his youth, when many "insignificant" differences set him apart from his companions. Unlike the other boys, he never—ever—either used a bathroom or passed gas in the presence of anyone else—never in his life. Now, however, he could laugh at his past predicaments; they were but additional examples of an exceptional personage caught up in the midst of a coarse environment. Nevertheless, they did result in Venedikt often feeling isolated from his peers, almost as if he were a leper.

As these painful reminiscences cascade over Venedikt's heart, he now confesses his innermost fear of "being understood not just wrongly, but in exactly the opposite way to what I intend."

The train rumbles on. A fuzzy-headed Venedikt thinks back to his recent week-long drinking binges. He was working underground laying cables, and when he was not actually on the job, most of his time was spent on the bottle. When he became foreman on his job, he "simplified" the work by scheduling his men to play blackjack one day and drink away the next. Sometimes the men would guzzle Freshen-up Eau de Cologne and speak of Pushkin, the great early-nineteenth-century poet. "Oh, the sweetness of unaccountability," Venedikt sighs. "Oh that most blessed of times in the life of my people, the time from the opening until the closing of the liquor stores!"

Venedikt and his co-workers even created graphs that recorded the patterns of their drinking sprees and the amount of alcohol they consumed. One day, however, the graphs were accidentally discovered, and Venedikt realized that the days of their "exclusively spiritual life" were numbered. "They fired me," Venedikt says. "Me, the thoughtful prince, the analyst lovingly inspecting the souls of his people . . . "

Venedikt's musings on the real world meander on for quite some time, until they are courteously interrupted by a chorus of commiserating angels. "We understand, we understand everything," they cry. "They insulted you. You and your beautiful heart." The angels also make use of the occasion to chide Venedikt for his bad language. They remind him that his lover waits on the platform at Petushki, and preview what will follow their reunion: "Trapper's vodka and port wine, bliss and writhing, ecstasy and convulsions . . . " Venedikt exhorts the angels to pray for him—to let him see the city he has longed to see. The angels smile agreeably, nod, and fly away.

The train has finally reached the halfway point between Moscow and Petushki. Venedikt takes to pacing the train vestibule while he puffs on a cigarette, and comes to another, important insight: "Drink more, eat less. This is the best method of avoiding self-conceit and superficial atheism." Throughout his confused journey, as throughout his life, alcohol acts as the key, both opening his mind to the subtle call to duty in the Soviet state and dulling his mind to the frustration and futility so conspicuous all around him. Accordingly, in a spasm of generosity, he begins to share the secret recipes for his choice cocktails with his fellow passengers, promising them that these exotic concoctions will bring them into the presence of God. Among his favorites are "Tear of a Komsomol Girl," "Balsam of Canaan," and best of all, "Bitches' Brew," a beverage which requires a precise mixture of beer, "Sadko" shampoo, dandruff treatment, athlete's foot remedy, and bug killer. After combining these ingredients, one must steep the cocktail for a week in cigar tobacco, and chill before serving.

Venedikt Erofeev's ruminations turn to panicked exclamations when he discovers that someone has stolen the 100 grams of "Aunt Clara's Kiss" from the suitcase containing his private store of liquor. By the process of elimination, he whittles down the suspects to a grandfather and grandson sitting nearby, licking their lips. But instead of accusing them, Venedikt merely asks the pair to sit down and share another drink with him. Upon hearing this invitation, the two intellectuals whom Venedikt observed at the beginning of his journey—anxious to share a drink among comrades—anchor themselves to him like common leeches.

"Everyone drank, throwing their heads back like pianists." Then the little group begins to pontificate about the necessity of alcoholic beverages in Russia. "All thinking Russia . . . drinks and never wakes up," they argue. "Ring all bells of London—no one in Russia will raise his head, everyone's lying in vomit, and life is hard for everyone." Amid this revelry of swaying, bumping monotony and human grimness, Venedikt notes, there runs a thread of droll sarcasm; perhaps it is the giggling remnant of good humor that these giggling drunks share.

Before long, a burly, mustachioed woman approaches the rowdy gathering. In a voice that seems to emanate from her very innards, she intones, "I also want to drink to Turgenev." Everyone stops, and with a shrug of defeat, they invite her to join them. "Nice women like that," one of the intellectuals mumbles sadly, "nice women like that should be shipped to the Crimea and fed to the wolves."

Soon, darkness closes in. And through the darkness the occupants of the train car—from the ticket inspectors (paid off in grams of vodka per kilometer) to the scholars, to the mustachioed woman who has no teeth—roll along the tracks on their way to Petushki.

The closer Venedikt comes to his destination, the wilder his hallucinations grow. As he ambles from car to car, demanding to know his location and direction, he carries on conversations with the Devil, Christ, a black-clothed woman, and a man who speaks in nothing but riddles. Finally, total confusion overcomes him, and he exits the train—only to discover that he is once more back in Moscow. Or is it really Petushki? A dense fog has come up, and he can't be sure.

Staggering through the misty blackness, Venedikt confronts another man, who is also caught up in the torpor of his own mind. All at once, the stranger unsheathes a knife and stabs Venedikt in the chest. Vision and reality merge briefly, and Venedikt cries for help. A peasant woman hears his screams and approaches, but instead of offering relief, she strikes him with a hammer. "Oh, this pain," Venedikt's hoarse voice shrieks from the recesses of his mind. "Oh, this devilish cold. Oh, the impossibility of it. If every one of the Fridays ahead is like this one, some Thursday I'll hang myself."

Venedikt wishes in all earnestness that he could have twenty swallows of vodka; with only twenty swallows he could convince himself that he was in Petushki with his girl, and not back in the misery and sorrow of Moscow's streets. Now, four men are chasing him; now he sprints away, past the Kremlin, where, once more, angels appear, laughing—and God is silent. Then the men overtake Venedikt and begin torturing him.

Venedikt's parting words seal an indictment on his culture and its intellectually dispassionate, soul-spoiling, hard-liquor, Soviet-party, inequitable ways: "Since then I have not regained consciousness, and I never will."

THE SHORT STORIES OF GUY DE MAUPASSANT

(taken from *The Complete Short Stories of Guy de Maupassant*, Hanover House, New York, N.Y., 1955)

Guy de Maupassant became one of the predominant short story writers of the 19th century. Rivaled only by Anton Chekov in his mastery of the genre, de Maupassant wrote some three hundred short stories in the span of ten years. These accounts often examine what he saw as the hypocrisy of contemporary French society and the decadence of its citizenry.

A Lucky Burglar

One evening as three young men sprawled drunkenly in an art studio "discussing war and the uniforms of the empire," the host tippler suddenly leapt to his feet and pulled out the military uniforms of a Hussar, a grenadier, and a cuirassier. Arranging themselves in their battle gear, the friends executed an intricate drill. Then, after commanding his men to "drink like troopers," the host brought down weapons from the studio wall: a pistol, an enormous gun with a bayonet attached, and a battle ax. Appointing himself general, the host split open a dummy's head with his ax while his second in command lunged into its breast with his bayonet. After thoroughly maiming the dummy, all three reeled about the studio.

Opening a cupboard, the companions were startled to find an old man crouched inside—doubtlessly a burglar. Immediately, they slammed and locked the cupboard door. Consultations ensued. Should they starve the intruder, "blow him up with dynamite," or perhaps just smoke him out? Finally, starvation impressed them as most fitting. This decided, they merrily toasted the health of their victim.

Eventually, the general decreed that it was time to take a peek. Barking like lunatics, his fellow "madcap" cronies dashed to the cupboard, hauled their captive out, bound him hand and foot, and stood back to observe this "haggard-looking, white-haired old bandit, with shabby, ragged clothes."

"We will try this wretch," the general determined. Accordingly, the prisoner was officially condemned to die. Moreover, it seemed appropriate to execute him on the spot. "Say, you don't mean it, do you?" the old man groaned. But they demanded that the recreant kneel—"for fear that he had not been baptized"—and then poured a glass of rum on his head while ordering him to confess his sins.

Suddenly the prisoner began to scream. They quickly gagged him and put their guns to his head. But when they pulled the triggers, nothing happened—evidently, the weapons had not been loaded. Then one soldier intervened; in reality, he said, "they had no right to shoot a civilian," so the poor wretch was tied to a board and lugged to the police station. The chief of police, however, saw their effort as nothing more than a "great lark," and declined to keep the man in custody. The three captors dragged their prisoner back to the house.

"By jingo!" the old fellow cried when they ungagged him. "I have [had] enough of this." Moved by the old man's ordeal, the three still tipsy friends plied him with punch and exchanged toasts as if he were "a long-lost friend." Finally, when dawn broke, the captive stood up, saying, "I am obliged to leave you; I must get home." No matter how hard they begged, the man declined to stay. "Look out for the last step," the host cautioned as the old burglar walked out the door.

The Devil

As the aged peasant woman lay on her deathbed, the physician chided her son: "Honore, you cannot leave your mother in this state; she may die at any moment." But Honore, a thrifty farmer of Norman descent, thought otherwise: he needed to collect his wheat; it was, after all, the season for reaping. His 92-year-old mother—though almost too sick to speak—was also "still possessed by her Norman avariciousness"; she agreed that her son should "get in his wheat and leave her to die alone." The incensed doctor threatened that if Honore did not find someone to attend to his mother, that he would leave Honore himself to "die like a dog" should he become ill.

Troubled about the cost of hiring an attendant, Honore went to call on La Rapet, the old washerwoman who "watched the dead and dying of the neighborhood." La Rapet was herself avaricious in the extreme; nevertheless, she welcomed Honore cordially and even offered him the special price for her services—"twenty sous by day and forty by night"—that she reserved for clients of modest means. "No, I would rather you . . . fix a price until the end," Honore said. "I will take my chance one way or the other." La Rapet, though "tempted by the idea of the possible gain," feared that the miserly farmer might take advantage of her. Hence, she insisted on first seeing the patient.

After examining the dying woman, La Rapet grunted, "You will have to give me six francs, everything included." Immediately, Honore flew into a rage. Yet, remembering his crops, he agreed to her price. Then he left La Rapet to tend to his mother.

La Rapet went home that night and returned the next morning, bitterly disappointed to find the old woman still alive. How long *would* she live? After waiting impatiently for a few hours, La Rapet asked her patient, "Have you ever seen the devil?" The poor woman said weakly that, no, she had not. La Rapet went to work: "She took a sheet out of the cupboard and wrapped herself up in it; then she put the iron pot onto her head so that its three short, bent feet rose up like horns." Next she "took a broom in her right hand and a tin pail in her left," and threw the pail suddenly upward, so that it clattered noisily to the ground. La Rapet then climbed on a chair near the bed, shrieking and prodding the old woman with the broom. Although the dying woman "made a superhuman effort to get up and escape," she was too frail. After letting out a deep sigh, she finally expired. La Rapet closed the dead woman's eyes and said the prayers for the dead with dutiful solemnity—and with great contentment, for she had come out twenty sous ahead. This fact did not escape Honore either when he came home that evening and found his mother had died.

The Necklace

Mathilda Loisel lamented "the shabby walls, the worn chairs, and the faded stuffs" of her apartment. Life had disappointed her; she had been born "into a family of clerks" and then had "allowed herself to marry a petty clerk," although her looks and charm had once seemed to promise better things.

One night her husband thought he would surprise Mathilda with an invitation to a ball at the residence of the Minister of Public Instruction. To his amazement, Mathilda flung the invitation angrily onto the table. "What do you suppose I have to wear to such a thing as that?" she challenged him, bursting into tears. "How much would a suitable costume cost?" he asked. Calculating silently, she finally told him that four hundred francs would cover the expense. Against his better judgment, the frugal clerk agreed to give his wife the money.

Soon after buying the dress, Mathilda again became distraught. Now she was "vexed not to have a jewel, not one stone, nothing" to adorn herself with. Perhaps she could borrow jewelry from her modish and well-fixed friend, Madame Forestier, suggested her husband. Mathilda realized this was so.

To Mathilda's delight, Madame Forestier presented her with a stunning array, inviting her to choose whichever piece she liked. Mathilda had to try on much of the jewelry before selecting "a superb necklace of diamonds."

The ball turned out to be a dazzling event, and Mathilda was "a great success." Resplendent in her new dress and sparkling necklace, she felt "intoxicated with pleasure." Basking in "the triumph of her beauty," Mathilda did not even think of leaving until four in the morning, whereupon she dashed out of the ballroom—so the other women wouldn't notice that she did not have rich furs—and into the street where her husband was hailing a cab.

When she had closed the door to their apartment, Mathilda could not resist "a final view of herself in her glory." Removing her cloak, she gazed at herself in the mirror, only to shriek in dismay: the necklace was missing!

Immediately, her husband hastened to retrace their steps—without success. All he could do was contact the police and put a notice in the newspaper.

Her husband, beside himself with concern, instructed Mathilda to write a letter to Madame Forestier to the effect that the clasp of the necklace had broken, so they had taken it in for repairs. A week passed, and Mathilda's husband reached despair. "We must take measures to replace this jewel," he resolved.

Spotting a replica of the lost necklace in a shop window, the unhappy couple inquired after it. To their horror, the price was thirty-six thousand francs. What else could they do but resort to Mathilda's husband's inheritance and borrow the rest, about half the total amount.

When Mathilda returned the necklace to Madame Forestier, the Madame did not even bother to open its case; rather, she gently rebuked Mathilda for keeping the necklace for so long.

Subsequently, Mathilda's life changed radically. No longer able to afford a maid, she discovered the "horrible life of necessity": washing, scouring, doing the laundry, and going to the market. When she and her husband finally paid off their debt—some ten years later—Mathilda had become "the crude woman of a poor household." So when it happened that she spotted Madame Forestier out on a stroll, Mathilda was at first hesitant to approach her old friend. Still, so many years had passed; why not reveal the truth?

"Oh! my poor Mathilda! How you have changed," the gentlewoman exclaimed when Mathilda addressed her. "Yes," Mathilda continued, "I have had some hard days since I saw you, and some miserable ones—and all because of you!" Madame Forestier, of course, was taken aback. And on hearing Mathilda's story, her friend was thoroughly shocked—the diamonds had been "false," a trifling piece of costume jewelry: "Oh my poor Mathilda! They were not worth over five hundred francs!"

Commentary:

Born in Normandy, France, Guy de Maupassant (1850-1893) developed an early interest in literature. He was more fortunate than most aspiring writers, however, in that one of his mother's friends was the great French novelist Gustave Flaubert.

Indeed, in a story like "The Necklace," many elements are reminiscent of Flaubert. Clearly, the character of Mathilda owes something of her temperament to Flaubert's *Madame Bovary*.

De Maupassant, however, did not become a strict adherent of any epochal movement. Instead, he borrowed techniques from various schools to highlight the milieu of his complex and pathetic characters, who, like Mathilda, the dying woman, and the burglar, are often destroyed by greed, materialism, or the cruel whims of others.

THE SHORT STORIES OF RAYMOND CARVER

(taken from *Where I'm Calling From: New and Selected Stories*, Vintage Contemporaries, New York, N.Y., 1989)

"It's possible to write about commonplace things and objects using commonplace but precise language, and to endow those things . . . with immense, even startling power," Raymond Carver once said of his stories. The message of this statement may, in part, account for the broad appeal of Raymond Carver's truly startling tales.

What We Talk About When We Talk About Love

They sat at the table drinking gin, and as the afternoon light poured into the kitchen from the big window behind the sink, they "somehow got on the subject of love." Mel McGinnis, a cardiologist, was telling his friends, Nick and Laura, and his second wife, Terri, that, in his opinion, the only "real love" was "spiritual love." Terri, however, remembered more complex experiences with love; she related how her ex-boyfriend Ed had "loved her so much he tried to kill her." According to Mel, that kind of love belonged to "the kick-me-so-I'll-know-you-love-me school." In the kind of love he was talking about, Mel affirmed, "you don't try to kill people."

"If you call that love," he insisted, "you can have it." Mel reached up and got a second bottle of gin from the cupboard and poured another round of drinks. They raised their glasses in a toast: "To love." Then they "grinned at each other like children who had agreed on something forbidden." Then he launched into a gently bombastic discourse on what real love wasn't. First, he said, there was "carnal love"; then, "sentimental love." And there had been a time once, he confessed, when he'd loved his first wife "more than life itself." But now he hated her guts, he said flatly; and this change of heart had led him to conclude that "all this love we're talking about" would, in the end, "just be a memory" anyway. "Am I wrong?" he wanted to know, by now just a little drunk. "Mel, we love you," Laura said. "Love you too, Laura," Mel replied. "And you, Nick, love you too . . . You guys are our pals."

But Mel still hadn't said all that he wanted to say about love. The bottle made its way once more around the table, and he commenced a story; a story that would "make us feel ashamed," he said, "when we talk like we know what we're talking about when we talk about love."

He told of a case in which an older couple had suffered "the works" after a youthful drunk driver had plowed his dad's pickup into their camper. Following two weeks in intensive care, the injured twosome was transferred to a private room, where they lay covered in bandages from head to foot. Their only exposed parts were the little "eye-holes and nose-holes and mouth-holes."

Mel shook his head in disbelief, then resumed. Every day, he said, when he treated the husband for his wounds, he would press his ear against the husband's mouth-hole, and the husband would tell him how his "heart was breaking" because he couldn't turn his head to *see* his wife. "Can you imagine?" Mel asked.

By then everyone was more than a little drunk, and daylight was fading. Finally Mel suggested they polish off the gin and go out to dinner, but no one moved from the table. Nick thought he could hear his heart pounding—in fact, he could hear everyone's heart, beating in rhythm. Still, he didn't move. He was overcome by "the human noise [they] sat there making, not one of [them] moving not even when the room went dark."

Feathers

Jack and Bud were friends at work, and one day in the lunchroom—about eight months after Bud and his wife Olla had had their first baby—Bud invited Jack and his wife, Fran, out to their house for supper. It would be just the four of them, he announced. "You and your missus, and me and Olla. Nothing fancy. Come around seven."

When Jack got home that night and told Fran about the invitation, she "wasn't too thrilled." Fran felt that the two of them didn't really "need other people." In fact, it was this very attitude that explained why Jack and Fran were not planning on having children of their own.

As Jack and Fran pulled up the long, graveled driveway to Bud and Olla's house, they heard a strange wailing cry—"*May-awe, may-awe!*" Then they saw "something as big as a vulture" flap "heavily down from one of the trees" and land right in front of the car. Fran had never seen a live peacock before and she said so. Jack could only repeat "Goddamn" over and over again.

Later, after supper, the peacock again took up wailing, and Olla told Bud to let the bird in. Bud boasted that he had paid "a hundred bucks for that bird of paradise," and then grinned, saying, "I got me a woman with expensive taste."

Just then the baby awoke and began to cry, and Olla brought him to the table. Jack "drew a breath" and stared: to call the baby ugly, he thought, would be to do it credit. The child had "no neck to speak of," and it was so "pop-eyed" that it looked as if "it was plugged into something." Bud allowed that "he's no Clark Gable," then quickly added, "But give him time."

Fran had just begun to play patty-cake with the child when the peacock once again appeared. As the peacock "ran its long neck across the baby's legs" and "pushed its beak in under the baby's pajama top and shook its stiff head back and forth," it was all too obvious the two creatures were playing a game they had played before.

There was a moment during that evening when Jack realized he "felt good about almost everything." He could barely "wait to be alone with Fran," to tell her what he was feeling—how he'd closed his eyes at the table and wished to "never forget or otherwise let go of that evening."

Jack's wish came very tangibly true. When they got home that night, Fran turned to her husband and said, "Honey, fill me up with your seed!" For her, that evening had immediately changed everything. "Goddamn those people and their ugly baby," she would later say. "And that smelly bird."

For Jack, though, the change had come about more gradually. In fact, he was still adjusting to having his own family—not to mention the fact that he and Fran almost never talked anymore. Still, he remembered how that night at Bud's they had hugged each other goodnight and Olla had given Fran some peacock feathers to take home. He remembered how Fran had sat close to him in the car and had "kept her hand" on his leg all the way home.

A Small, Good Thing

It was Saturday afternoon, and Ann Weiss ordered a birthday cake for her son, Scotty. The baker, an older, sullen man, took down her phone number. Then, looking up at her just once, he said, "Monday morning."

But on Monday morning Scotty was hit by a car on his way to school. After the accident, he was able to walk home, but as he started telling his mother what had happened he suddenly "closed his eyes, and went limp."

Of course, the birthday party was canceled. Day passed into night at the hospital, and the boy had not regained consciousness. Still, Ann and Howard were reassured by Dr. Francis' diagnosis that Scotty was "in a very deep sleep—but no coma."

Late that evening, Howard decided to go home to wash up and change clothes. The phone was ringing as he entered the house. When he picked up the receiver, a voice on the other end said, "There's a cake here that wasn't picked up." Distraught and tired, Howard shouted, "I don't know anything about a cake," and hung up.

The next morning Scotty was taken to Radiology for a brain scan. Howard and Ann had sat up all night, hugging each other and praying; "they were together in it, this trouble." When Scotty was finally brought back to the room, Dr. Francis spoke for the first time about the possibility of a coma. Still, he insisted, there was "no good reason" why Scotty "shouldn't come around. Very soon."

Finally Howard persuaded Ann to go home for an hour or so to freshen up. She had just arrived when the phone rang. "Mrs. Weiss," said a male voice. "It has to do with Scotty, that problem. Have you forgotten about Scotty?" Then the speaker hung up, leaving Ann half-crazed with anxiety.

When Ann returned to the hospital, her husband broke the news: the doctors had decided to operate. But just then, Scotty opened his eyes. They tried talking to him, but after awhile "his eyes scrunched closed, and he howled until

he had no more air in his lungs." It was all over in less than a minute.

The doctors explained that the cause of death was "a hidden occlusion . . . ; it was a one-in-a-million circumstance." When Howard and Ann, grief-stricken, returned home, once again the phone began to ring. "Your Scotty," the man's voice said, "I got him ready for you . . . Did you forget him?"

By now thoroughly overwrought, Ann screamed and hung up; she would "like to shoot" the man and "watch him kick," she told her husband. Then it dawned on her that it was the baker's voice. "Drive me down to the shopping center," she said, turning to Howard.

Warily, the baker let the distraught couple in. Instantly Ann took out after the man, shouting that they were Scotty's parents and that Scotty was dead. At this, the man cleared a table and asked them to sit down. "Let me say how sorry I am," he began. He was "just a baker"; years ago, perhaps, he had been "a different kind of human being." The truth now, he explained, was that he didn't "know how to act anymore."

"Please," he begged, "let me ask you if you can find it in your hearts to forgive me?" Seeing the sincerity mirrored in the old man's eyes, Howard and Ann took off their coats as the baker set coffee and hot cinnamon rolls on the table. "I hope you'll eat," he urged them. "Eating is a small, good thing in a time like this."

For the first time since Scotty's accident, Howard and Ann were hungry. As they ate, the baker spoke of his own isolated existence; of what a dismal loneliness it was to be "childless all these years." Then he brought out a loaf of dark bread, and, breaking it open, asked them to smell it. "It's a heavy bread," he told them, "but rich." They ate as much as they could. And as they continued to talk into the night, "they did not think of leaving."

Commentary:

Raymond Carver (1938-88) writes in a friendly, familiar style that puts most readers instantly at home. At the same time, there is within his conventional working-class characters a profound sense of estrangement. Perhaps it is this paradox that gives the stories their edge and resonance.

In "A Small, Good Thing," for instance, the baker is so isolated by his work that he barely remembers what it once felt like to be a "human being." In "Feathers," Jack and Fran's marriage is so fragile that a simple dinner with casual acquaintances forever alters the course of their lives.

The things-really-are-as-bad-as-they-seem pathos and bleakness evident in Carver's sketches, however, are what make his hard-luck stories at once memorable, meditative and funny. We see in them a series of American grotesques—similar in nature to the urban paintings of Edward Hopper or the frontier tales of Bret Harte; a chain of events, of human beings at once disfigured by progress and cut off from their pasts.

THE SHORT STORIES OF PEARL S. BUCK

(taken from *Fourteen Stories*, The John Day Company, New York, N.Y., 1961)

Commentary:

Pearl S. Buck (1892-1973) was a prolific writer. And as in her most famous novel, *The Good Earth*—in which cultural differences between East and West are explored—"home" often emerges as an important theme in her short fiction.

In the stories profiled below, there is a sense in which the characters, to the extent that they are turned against their homes, become identical in their sufferings. In this respect, the accounts may be seen as versions of the same narrative—a narrative of expulsion and exile.

Enchantment

Boarding the commuter train, Roger Kentwell fought his way through the crowded cars looking for a place to situate himself for the hour-long ride home. In the third car, he spotted an empty seat and, though he "hesitated . . . to sit beside a strange woman," he made his way down the aisle and asked, "Is this seat taken?"

"No, it isn't," the woman replied. But it was only after he had seated himself that he "felt a shock of surprise" at seeing a woman so "absolutely beautiful." As he closed his eyes, he thought immediately of his wife Ruth, who would be waiting for him outside the station. Ruth was more than just a part of his life: she was "the earth in which were his roots." Now, however, it occurred to him that, until now, he had never really thought about how women looked.

"Will you help me?" the woman suddenly whispered to him. "What can I do for you?" he asked her, suddenly on guard. She smiled weakly and said, "Just let me walk beside you, wherever you get off. As soon as we leave the station I shall not need you."

Roger reluctantly agreed to help her, then settled back in his seat. "Ruth was not beautiful," he thought to himself, and yet it was also true that "beauty was the last essential to happiness between a man and a woman . . . a chance possession."

Soon the train pulled into the station and Roger found Ruth standing on the platform. Though he wasn't sure why, the sight of her made him feel uncomfortable: he hadn't wanted Ruth to see him walking beside this beautiful woman. "Well, dearest," he greeted her, ignoring the woman who had now fallen a step behind him. Roger could tell instantly that Ruth had noticed the woman, who thanked him and went her way.

In the car, Ruth remarked how "terribly pretty" the woman appeared. "I always notice really beautiful women," she told Roger, "because I'm so ugly." He protested that she was "the dearest woman in the world and the only one I have ever thought of." Yet, he knew that something had changed between them; it was as though "the beautiful woman . . . had

set a standard of beauty between them . . . "

At dinner, Ruth startled her husband. "It's ridiculous of me," she said, referring to their years of happiness together, "but I'd trade them all for this moment, just to hear you protest that I am really—quite beautiful." Then she excused herself from the table, saying she would join him shortly in the living room for coffee. "The fire," she added, "is laid ready just to touch with a match."

Upstairs, Ruth undressed in front of the mirror; a sense of "lonely wretchedness" crept over her. She had always known that Roger had fallen in love with her not "passionately, but slowly, half unwillingly. She had courted him with exquisite skill, never pursuing, always gently making herself indispensable to him." Then, in the years after their marriage, she "had done nothing but built around him the enchantment of her pleasantness." That night at dinner, however, she felt certain that her "enchantment" had been shattered—her husband had almost seen her as she was.

After removing her pale green dress, Ruth put on one of dull red velvet, and returned downstairs to Roger, who was sitting by the fireplace. For a moment, she thought she detected in him a sign that, in fact, her enchantment was broken. "You know?" she said of her mood, "I think it was that green dress! I don't think I'll ever wear it again."

Roger examined her, and as he did she could see an expression of relief pass across his face. "Silly," he said to her. "Come and pour my coffee!"

Parable of Plain People

If only the overlords could be "removed by some stroke of heaven," lamented Wang the Eldest, "he could have managed very well." Wang was the first to admit that his life was uncommonly blessed. He owned a small but productive farm, where, with the exception of luxuries like tea and cloth, he was able to raise everything his family needed.

Wang was also fortunate to have two sons, both of whom were good young men. The oldest had married the daughter of his best friend, and shortly after she had borne twin sons. Thus, to Wang's delight, the "affairs of his house were arranged and the generations were proceeding in order." His second son, though frail and sickly, proved no less a delight to him. In an effort to bring "silk-making in the house and take his second son from the fields," Wang had managed to betroth him to a silk weaver's daughter. And only a few months after their marriage, his new daughter-in-law—this "Fairy of Silk-weaving," as he called her—had brought so much money into the house that Wang's family became more prosperous than it had ever been. Surely, if not for his overlords, "he would have had no troubles" at all.

Even when his second son's first child

was still-born, Wang remained stoical, if not sanguine. There would be other children, he prophesied; and, less than a year later, a daughter was born. When famine struck, Wang assured his family that they would weather it "as they had weathered other famines, generation after generation." Again, they survived. In every way, Wang felt "he could have lived in peace and in plenty if it had not been for these overlords."

In all, there were three overlords in the village: the first, Li, "was a rich and powerful man" whom Wang feared most; the second was a magistrate, who routinely had men beaten and imprisoned when they failed to pay their taxes; and the third overlord was an outlaw, a marauding warlord who plundered from the rural peasants. "I have no troubles except for these men," Wang repeated. "Of what use is any good I have, when these men are my overlords?"

After giving his problem a great deal of thought, Wang lit upon a solution. He cut down his orchards, burned his house, torched his fields, and flooded his land. "Now," Wang told his family, "now we are free. We are beggars, but we have beggared ourselves at least."

The Silver Butterfly

"I tell you of my mother," the Chinese man began. And so, even though it was already dark, the American man shut his eyes and listened. He had come to Hong Kong "to hear the true stories of men and women" who had escaped mainland China, and now this storyteller began a story about his mother's life in a small village by the Yangtze River.

His mother, he said, had been a concubine, and before he was born she had lived on his father's estate. The first son born to them, this man's oldest brother, had died at the age of five. His mother, he surmised, had loved his brother best, because each time she "saw a little child about [his brother's age], a boy, she coaxed him to come to her and fed him sweets."

When the revolution dawned on China some years later, his "father was accused, as a landlord, by his tenants." It didn't matter that he was well-liked in the community; it was simply the custom that tenants demanded "the execution of their landlords." Consequently, his father was strung up by his thumbs in a tree and, as the family watched, flayed to death.

Afterwards, the man continued, the Party moved his family into a one room "co-operative" on a commune. He was married by then, and he and his wife would work each day digging in the riverbank to lay the pilings for a great bridge. His mother, however, whose "brain was muddied," was by then too old and confused to work. Since food in the commune was rationed according to one's work, his family was forced to survive on only two rations. When he finally broached this subject with his "commander," he was told that his mother would have to work.

Inasmuch as his family's house had been converted to a nursery for the commune, the Party assigned his mother to work there. One day, however, "a little boy of five years, or thereabouts, was brought to the nursery, crying." The moment his mother saw the boy, she was reminded of her son who had died, and so she began to love the child, which "was her great crime."

His mother's return to her old house had stimulated memories of her life as a concubine. One day, in this "dream of confusion," she remembered that years ago she had hidden three pieces of jewelry behind a brick in the wall in the shed. Of these pieces, the most valuable among them was "a butterfly of filigree silver set with small good pearls."

"The next day, it happened that the boy [whom she had taken for her son] cut his hand." Wanting to comfort him, the mother led the boy to the shed and showed him the silver butterfly. "See how pretty," she told him. "This is your butterfly. I will keep it for you, so that no one can take it from you, but it is yours. We will look at it every night. Here, take it in your hand."

Each night they would return and gaze in secret at the silver butterfly. But the boy told another child about the butterfly and that child, for "a bit of sugar," told the directress. Since luxuries were not allowed in the commune, the boy was severely beaten and the man's mother was "sentenced to be denounced at the next meeting of the commune."

"On the day of the meeting," the man said, "I hid myself in the crowd." His mother, her hands bound behind her back, was forced to make her way through the vicious mob. When she fell to the ground, the man said, he knew "it was time to kick her. Everybody was watching me and I was afraid. I stepped forward to do what I had to do. In that moment she looked up and saw me . . . When I saw that she knew me, I tried to look angry. She was bewildered for a moment, and then she smiled."

"Is that the end?" the American man asked.

"No," said the man, "but there is an end." After his mother was released from the hospital, she went to the little boy, who was still recovering from his own beating, and "coaxed him to come with her to the shed." Once there, she held him and whispered to him that she had now become "a burden" to her son—the son who had been made to strike her. "I cannot help him by living," she told the boy. "I see this . . . So come with me, my child, my little one. Let us go to a better place."

The boy responded by asking if he could see the silver butterfly, and she answered, "We will go to the river. There are butterflies there." At the river's edge, the woman picked the boy up in her arms and "walked into the water until it covered her head and the child's head and she did not step back." That, the man said, "was the end."

ULYSSES

by
James Joyce
(1882 - 1941)

Type of work: Experimental novel

Setting: Dublin Ireland; June, 1904

Principal characters:
    Leopold Bloom, a canvasser at the local newspaper
    Molly Bloom, his wife
    Stephen Dedalus, a recent college graduate
    A host of characters, including a number of journalists, an old mariner, a caretaker, priests, and several drunken soldiers

Commentary:

In nearly every imaginable way, James Joyce's novel is like no other—and that's *aside* from its presenting such anomalies as a fifty-page-long running sentence (filled with a wife's ruminations), its stream-of-consciousness flavor, and its innovative, twisting, 750-plus-page pseudo-plot. Massive, mythic—and, due to its earthiness, still frequently placed on the "adult" shelf at the library—*Ulysses,* first published in 1922, is probably the most ambitious and multi-dimensional jigsaw puzzle ever assembled out of the English language. But the novel is also something much more pivotal than a juicy literary crossword: it is the work that ushered the world's English-language readers and writers into the landscapes of 20th-Century modernism.

In a sense, modernist and post-modernist narrative *begins* with Joyce. Like T.S. Eliot's influential poem "The Waste Land," Joyce's *Ulysses* grows out of the early 20th century's drastic redefinition of civilization. While Europeans of the late 19th century had assumed that technological advancements would foster peace, prosperity, and unchecked progress, artists and intellectuals of the new century not only started questioning technology's contribution to humanity on moral and ethical grounds, but they also began to allocate "progress" to the realm of myth. Thus, writers like Joyce and Eliot focused on the dissolution of the old order.

In the tragic wake of World War I, writers discovered both a profound pessimism and a new emphasis on the individual. Freud, of course, had recently posited the existence of the *id*—a great psychic repository of unconscious impulses and urges that lay deep within the human soul. Thus, armed with this new knowledge, writers and artists like Joyce courted a far less sanguine view of the individual and his experiences than previous Romantic-era writers had entertained.

In *Ulysses,* for example, Joyce chooses to depict individual experience as far too fragmentary and multi-textured to be subjected to the constraints of traditional plot. Thus, no "story" of any real consequence emerges in the novel. In lieu of a traditional narrative, Joyce focuses on the psychology and perceptions of Leopold Bloom, the "middle-aged Irish Jew" who is Joyce's modern Ulysses. Like Homer's timeless Greek voyager wending his way home to Ithaca after the Trojan War, Bloom lives a life of exile, wandering from adventure to adventure, before he returns home to his wife.

In contrast to Homer's epic *The Odyssey,* in which heroes and gods are truly heroic and godly, Joyce's Ulysses—Bloom—is left trudging the wasteland streets and pubs of lower-middle class Dublin in search life's meaning—or, at very least, some sort of steppingstone on the pathway leading "home."

Bloom's errant wanderings are depicted in a single, "ordinary" Dublin day. And as the routine of this day unfolds, the reader is offered what critic A. Walton Litz calls "an encyclopedia of modern life." Litz goes on to say that no matter how we view *Ulysses,* the ways in which we can approach it are "almost endless. We can only conclude that the best reading of the work is the one that yields the greatest number of related perspectives."

Story Overview:

June 16, 1904 was an ordinary day in the city of Dublin, Ireland. As the early summer sun began to spread her majesty over that vast borough, Stephen Dedalus awoke. Dawn had come, as usual, much too soon. The life of the young Latin poetry instructor lacked any hint of happy anticipation. Still in mourning for his mother, who had died of pneumonia the year before—vainly pleading with her son to pray for her soul—Stephen brooded once again over his guilty memories and the appallingly aimless condition of his life. He had no faith, no true friends. What's more, he received no sympathy in his grief from his roommate and only close companion, the vulgar, bullying medical student Buck Mulligan. "O, it's only Dedalus whose mother is beastly dead," offered Mulligan.

After breakfasting, Stephen and Buck walked to the beach with a new houseguest, a Mr. Haines. Buck Mulligan sang as they went:

> *I'm the queerest young fellow that ever you heard.*
> *My mother's a jew, my father's a bird.*
> *With Joseph the joiner I cannot agree,*
> *So here's to disciples and Calvary.*

Later, Stephen made his way to the academy. "Tell me now, what is a pier," he asked a pupil. But he did not get the expected Latin translation. "A pier, sir. A thing out in the waves," explained the boy, helpfully. After spending the entire morning in such tedia, Stephen finally realized what it was that kept him in a sort of paralyzed, hopeless conspiracy with these boys: in them he saw his own awkward, fearful, impoverished childhood.

When, at last, class was dismissed, the principal of the academy, Mr. Deasy, approached Stephen with a manuscript in his hand. "It's about the foot and mouth disease," Deasy explained. He wanted Stephen to use his influence with the local newspaper to have the article published as a public service item. And since Stephen did not feel he was in any position to deny the request, he made his way to the newspaper offices.

On the other side of town, meanwhile, a middle-aged Jew named Leopold Bloom was just beginning his day with an appetizing breakfast of grilled mutton kidneys, which "gave to his palate a fine tang of faintly scented urine." Bloom worked as an ad salesman at the newspaper, and carried a dead weight within him: since the death of their infant son Rudy he had found himself unable to complete the act of sexual intercourse with his wife Molly. And yet, in the aftermath of Rudy's death, both had often sought comfort in the arms of others.

After breakfast, Bloom rode off in the carriage to the funeral of his friend Patrik "Paddy" Dignam. As the service commenced, however, he suddenly decided that he detested funerals. "My kneecap is hurting me," he thought as he knelt in prayer. In truth, the whole affair reminded him of little Rudy, and of his own father, who had died a suicide. At one point, gazing ahead at the coffin, he wondered, "Which end is his head?" And then, as his mind strayed further and further from the here and now, Bloom's brief respite from work was over.

Most of Bloom's dismal working day was spent trying to negotiate the terms of advertising space with a tea merchant named Keyes. The editor, Myles Crawford, was aghast when he reviewed the final agreement for approval. Keyes was a bloody cheat, he screamed. "He can kiss my royal Irish arse."

Later in the day, Stephen Dedalus arrived at the newspaper office to talk with the staff about the Deasy article. Crawford, still peeved by the Keyes incident, was not in favor of printing a piece dealing with the loathsome and ridiculous subject of foot and mouth disease. His readers wouldn't stand for it; they'd read anything *but* an article about a damned disease. "All balls!" howled the editor. "Give them something with a bite in it. Put us all into it, damn its soul. Father Son and Holy Ghost and Jakes M'Carthy."

At daylight faded, Stephen, still flushed from drink, met up with Mulligan and some other young scholars at a local tavern. In time their talk turned to a rousing analysis of Hamlet. *Hamlet* was a *Jew,* one of the young men spat out, scowling. Stephen quickly rebutted this with the proposal that the Prince of Denmark indeed represented the playwright Shakespeare himself. "He wrote the play in the months that followed his father's death," Stephen contended.

As for Leopold Bloom, after he left the office he made his way from the pubs to the seaside. There happened upon a flirtatious lass named Gerty, who leaned back against a rock, exposing her bare thighs and knickers: . . . *She was trembling in every limb from being so far back he had a full view . . . and she wasn't ashamed and he wasn't either to look in that immodest way like that because he couldn't resist the sight of the wondrous revealment half offered . . .* "O sweet little, you don't know how nice you looked," thought Bloom as the girl left. "I begin to like them at that age. Green apples. Grab at all that offer."

Bloom staggered back toward the taverns, the pictures in his mind coming one right after another: there was his dearly departed Rudy; why did his eleven-day-old man-child have to

die? Then came the lurid vision of his wife—in bed with one of his cordial acquaintances. Now his only recourse was to "drown his sorrows." He arrived at the pub just in time to catch the last of Stephen's discourse on *Hamlet.* The conversation then moved on to civic issues. Frequently Mulligan would turn to stare in the direction of a certain Jewish patron while he voiced his supercilious views: "For the enlightenment of those who are not so intimately acquainted with the minutiae of the municipal abattoir as the morbid-minded esthere and embryo philosopher who for all his overweening bumptiousness in things scientific can scarcely distinguish an acid from an alkali."

After a few more hours of drinking and enduring such bluster, Bloom made his way to Mabbot Street, a nearby lane of enticing ill-repute. Stumbling onward, he received sad, ethereal visitations from his dead father, then from an anonymous bearded woman, then from his wife, and, finally, from his lover. In this state, he came across Stephen again, who, in a similar state of despondency, was revisited on the spot by the ghost of his dead mother, begging her son once more to pray for her soul.

Strolling on together, Bloom and Stephen stopped to cavort with a group of prostitutes—until two soldiers happened upon the scene and took exception to Stephen's surly demeanor. In concert, they struck the young scholar and knocked him, bleeding, to the ground.

As the soldiers continued on down the lane, Bloom helped Stephen up, brushed him off, and handed him his hat. For refreshment, they then trudged on to a seaside cafe, and listened to a scruffy old sea veteran recount his grandiose tales. "I seen a crocodile bit the fluke of an anchor," he boasted. " . . . I seen icebergs plenty, growlers. I was in Stockholm and the Black Sea . . . " Bloom and Stephen listened on in rapturous envy; never had either of them braved such wonderful explorations.

Quite recovered from the beating he had taken, Stephen accompanied Bloom home, where they mulled over the intricacies of music, religion, and life. As the night wore on, Bloom implored his new young friend to stay—to leave his reckless circle and come live with him and his wife. And even though Stephen refused, both men now knew that, despite an age difference of sixteen years, their lives were irrevocably intertwined.

After commanding his wife to arise early and prepare his breakfast, Bloom now finally drifted off to sleep—leaving Molly Bloom lying there awake, thinking. Thinking of her most recent lover . . . of her girlhood . . . of the mysteries of the human body . . . of the possibility of Stephen Dedalus—a refined young writer—coming to live with them . . . and, at last, of her long-past courtship with Leopold Bloom—of "how he kissed me under the Moorish wall and I thought well as well him as another and then I asked him with my eyes to ask again yes and then he asked me would I yes to say yes . . . "

And so the woman's thoughts flowed on, pungent, earthy, and homey, while her far-wandering husband snored in the darkness at her side.

THE PRINCE OF TIDES

by Pat Conroy, Houghton Mifflin, Boston, Massachusetts, 1986

Type of work: Mythological realism

Setting: South Carolina and New York City; the 1940s to the 1980s

Principal characters:
Tom Wingo, an unemployed coach/ English teacher
Savannah Wingo, Tom's twin sister, a poet
Luke Wingo, Tom and Savannah's older brother
Lila Wingo, their beautiful mother
Henry Wingo, their father, a shrimper
Susan Lowenstein, Savannah's psychiatrist, and, later, Tom's confidante

Story Overview:

Although thirty-six-year-old Tom Wingo had a wife and three daughters whom he dearly loved, he was still tormented by the "wreckage" of the family that he had been born into. He had grown up near the town of Colleton, on a small island that his great-grandfather had actually won in a horseshoe game. The island's natural beauty had delighted Tom, his twin sister Savannah, and their older brother Luke; all three of them spoke of the place "religiously." Their home life, however, was nightmarish: Lila, their beautiful mother, was obsessed with her social standing and refused to acknowledge the pain her husband Henry inflicted on all of them when he berated and beat them. She ignored the cruelty, even as it happened, insisting instead on maintaining "family loyalty."

Inwardly unable to endure this "egregious" charade, the Wingo children bore wounds, deep and festering. As an adult, the oldest son Luke became a loner who ultimately "heard voices and began to see the faces of his family materialize on the branches of trees." Wandering the marshlands where he had been born, he was to suffer an early and violent death, a tragedy still contained by an aura of mystery.

Like her brother Luke, Savannah often hallucinated. As a young woman she had moved to New York and become a famous poet. Though she tried valiantly to repress her pain, Savannah nevertheless had more than once been crushed by the bone-deep urge to destroy herself. Horrified by his twin sister's anguish, Tom desperately tried to impart the appearance of normalcy by striving to become the "irreproachable figure [that his] parents always wanted."

But in the end, the past overwhelmed Tom, too; he suffered a nervous breakdown and lost his job teaching English and coaching high school football. He still longed to please his wife Sallie, a medical internist who was now the sole support of their family, but Tom's depression prevented him from satisfying Sallie emotionally or sexually. Adding to his despondency was the fact that he had not seen Savannah in three years. He had also become increasingly troubled by Luke's death and by the growing hatred he now felt for his mother.

Tom arrived in New York that day, a devastated man. Not only was Savannah in the hospital after yet another suicide attempt, but he

had also just discovered that his wife was having an affair. "Hold me tight, Tom," Savannah had often said to him while they were growing up, and he had always tried to defend his sister—first from the blows of their father and from the coldness of their mother, and later from her "own screams and wounds, [which] sustained the imperishable beauty of her art. [Yet] there were no dark poems in Savannah's work, only beautiful fruit surrounded by flowers that could put the taster forever to sleep on thorns dusted with cyanide . . . "

It became immediately clear to Tom that Savannah's poetry fascinated her psychiatrist, Susan Lowenstein. "Who is *The Prince of Tides*?" Dr. Lowenstein demanded the moment Tom walked into her elegant New York office. Completely unnerved, Tom retorted, "Why don't you ask Savannah?" He simply could not bring himself to tell this stranger that the phrase—the title of Savannah's most recent book—referred to their dead brother Luke. The doctor's reply to this was cool: "I will when she's able to speak to me." Until then, however, Susan wanted Tom to tell her about his sister's background.

Susan Lowenstein grated on Tom. She was "breathtakingly beautiful, one of those go-to-hell New York women with the incorruptible carriage of a lioness"—and, as the soft-spoken, smooth-mannered, Southern-Catholic gentleman who had fulfilled Lila Wingo's best visions for her son, Tom resented the doctor's brash, polished, Jewish intensity.

Although Tom had confronted Savannah before in states of catatonic retreat, he was still deeply saddened when Susan took him to her room. Protectively, he knelt by the bed where his mute sister lay "curled like an embryo" and gently crooned her a melody they had sung together as children.

Later, when Tom learned that Savannah had been "covering herself with her own excrement"—after narrowly escaping death from this latest wrist-slashing—his antagonism toward Susan Lowenstein eased. Their dinner-date that night initiated the first in a line of probing and intimate conversations. Finally Tom decided to stay in New York to meet with Susan regularly in hopes of coming to terms with his own torn feelings as the son of a family whom "fate had tested a thousand times, and left defenseless, humiliated, and dishonored."

At one of their dinners, Tom told Susan about the day when life had literally begun for him and Savannah: The tide was rising and a hurricane was gathering force off the South Carolina coast. The 85-year-old former slave who attended the twins' birth, had died protecting the infants from the storm. Every year afterward, the Wingo children had visited her grave.

Aside from the isolation of being "raised Catholic in the deep South" on a remote island, the Wingo children had also suffered terribly from the violence that permeated their lives. In addition to their father's sadistic and unpredictable beatings, they had been terrorized by a

171

stalker, an immense man with murderous eyes. After chasing the children out of the woods one day while their father was away in the Korean War, the giant had walked out to stare lasciviously at their mother, "I want you," he had shouted to Lila. And as he turned away, they heard the giant laughing. "I'll be back."

The following week the stalker reappeared, only this time he was brandishing a knife in his meathook-like hand. But Lila and her children pelted him with open jars full of black widow spiders from their basement—and once again he retreated into the darkness.

As the extraordinary history of the Wingo household slowly unfolded, Susan listened with deep interest. Tom found himself increasingly aware of the vibrant, compassionate and vulnerable woman that lay beneath the assertive, clinical poise. After hearing about Tom's anguish over his wife's affair, Susan confessed that her husband, Herbert, a famous violinist, was also involved with another woman. Now more than ever, Savannah's two protectors seemed of one heart.

Then Susan asked Tom if he would coach her adolescent son Bernard, who longed to play football. When Tom agreed, the developing relationship with Bernard soon incited Herbert Lowenstein's jealousy. Aware that both his son and his wife had become smitten with this enigmatic Southerner, Herbert accosted Tom in Central Park and announced that he was sending Bernard away to music camp.

Shortly after this confrontation, Tom was taken aback by an invitation from Herbert to a dinner party. Not surprisingly, the dinner had been engineered as an occasion for Herbert to embarrass his wife and insult his Southern rival. However, the plan backfired. When he heard Susan repeatedly belittled and himself publicly branded as anti-Semitic, Tom simply turned and left the party—and, to his delight, Susan followed. Soon afterward she moved in with Tom.

While Tom still cared deeply for his wife, in Susan's arms he found both comfort and excitement. With her, Tom could let out all the horrors and wonders of his early life. By now he had told her all about his father Henry Wingo—how on one occasion he had brought home a Bengal tiger to rent out at parties.

And then, at last, Tom disclosed details of the day when the stalker had arrived for a third time at the door of the Wingo house, accompanied by two depraved companions. Bursting into the living room, the three men had raped Lila, Savannah, and Tom, and threatened to kill them. It was Luke who had saved them—along with the Bengal tiger. Lured from its cage by Luke, the tiger came padding into the house to confront his mother's attacker, tearing him into a hundred bloody shreds. In the ensuing chaos Tom grabbed a marble statue and beat in the head of his own assailant, driving "fragments of his skull deep into his brain," while Savannah "cut her rapist in half" with a shotgun.

"This didn't happen," Lila had gasped afterwards. "This did not happen." Then, at their mother's direction, Tom and Luke had carried the three savaged bodies into the woods for bur-

ial, while Lila and Savannah cleaned the blood and viscera from the walls and floor. True to her word, Lila never mentioned the horrific events to anyone, not even to her husband. Henry Wingo came home from work later that night to a clean house and a fish dinner—and afterwards Savannah made her first attempt at suicide.

Lila's children were not surprised years later when she divorced their brutal and bewildered father to marry into a prominent local family. It was this marriage that set the events into motion which would lead to Luke's undoing: In her divorce settlement, Lila was awarded the family's small island, a property which her new husband convinced her to sell to a company that produced materials for nuclear weapons and power plants. Luke, with his passionate attachment to the island, had been outraged.

A former Vietnam War hero, he "initiated guerrilla actions," unintentionally causing the death of four men in the derailment of a train. Now a wanted man, Luke disappeared into the wild coastal marshes which he knew so well. While he had never meant to kill innocent people, Luke was considered to be extremely dangerous, "a murderer and a crackpot." Having slipped into madness, he was finally spotted and callously shot down while making "a sentimental visit to the island where he grew up." After Luke's funeral, Tom and Savannah took the body of their beloved brother out on a boat and dropped it overboard.

As Tom's story came to an end, Susan held him in her arms. Shortly afterwards, Tom realized that, while he might never be able to "measure the cost of loving a family so deeply and with such a cold fury," he now had finally found the strength to put his life in order. With great sadness and gratitude, he said goodbye to Susan and set off on the journey home.

Long after he and Sallie had reclaimed and forgiven each other, long after he and Savannah had turned to the task of reforging their lives, Tom still often found himself alone in his car late at night, whispering, "Lowenstein, Lowenstein, Lowenstein . . ."—affirming once more the healing relationship that had led him back home.

Commentary:

Like his narrator Tom Wingo, Pat Conroy grew up along the coast of South Carolina. *The Prince of Tides* undoubtedly draws heavily on many of the author's own experiences as the self-professed son of a domineering father and a class-conscious mother, whose rigidity helped precipitate their children's rebelliousness.

The fictional story of Tom, Luke, and Savannah Wingo, however, takes a decidedly idiosyncratic form. Not only do the adult children of Henry and Lila Wingo find themselves unable to conform to the distorted expectations of their parents, they remain in a denial so deep that it not only recolors but often obliterates memory. Alienated from both themselves and each other by the madness of dissociation, it is only through restored memory and disclosure, which Susan Lowenstein so powerfully invokes in the novel, that the Wingos can begin to heal and to share their "capacity for homage and wonder."

THINGS FALL APART

by Chinua Achebe, McDowell, Obolensky, New York, N.Y., 1959

Type of work: Ethnographic adolescent novel

Setting: Nigeria's Igbo villages; turn of the 20th century

Principal characters:

Okonkwo, a middle-aged Igbo farmer and warrior

Nwoye, Okonkwo's disappointing, "womanly" oldest son

Ikemefuna, a virile boy who comes to live with Okonkwo

Story Overview

Okonkwo lived with his three wives and their children in the Igbo village of Umuofia, feared by all its neighbors for its power "in war and in magic." Subsisting largely on yams, the villagers were obliged to appease the wrath of many gods each season in order to secure a plentiful harvest. And when they finally reaped their yams, they always held a great harvest feast.

Unlike the other villagers, however, Okonkwo did not find release or joy in this celebrating; he much preferred the daily rounds of tending his fields. In fact, his dedication had made him a prosperous man. Okonkwo also distinguished himself as a warrior. In his youth he had routed the notorious "Amalinze the Cat" in a wrestling match and, recently, he had taken his fifth head in combat with Umuofia's enemies.

Thus Okonkwo's fame, resting "on solid personal achievements," had spread through all the adjacent Igbo villages. This particularly gratified Okonkwo because it set him apart from his dead father, Unoka.

Unoka was said to have been cursed by a bad *chi*—the personal god-spirit who accompanied each man through life and swayed his fate. In life, the spiteful little god had caused his crops to fail; even more deplorable, Unoka had acquired a reputation as a man who disdained war. Unoka's *chi* also had plagued his death, causing him to suffer a fatal "swelling" that "was an abomination to the earth goddess." Due to the loathsome nature of this disease, Unoka's body had been carried away to be buried in the Evil Forest to prevent polluting Umuofia or its people. Unoka had been so ill-fated in every respect that Okonkwo's "one passion" was "to hate everything his father had loved."

Then an event occurred in Umuofia that was to profoundly change Okonkwo's life. To compensate for the murder of a woman from Umuofia by a villager in Mbaino, a virgin and a young boy from Mbaino were sent to Umuofia. The boy, Ikemefuna, was placed under Okonkwo's care and sent to live in the house of Okonkwo's first wife, who treated him as kindly as she treated her own sons.

In contrast to his wife's tenderness, Okonkwo dealt harshly with Ikemefuna, standing over him with a "big stick" when he would not eat his yams. Indeed, all of Okonkwo's children and wives "lived in perpetual fear of his fiery temper," an anger which he reserved most passionately for his eldest son, Nwoye—whose disposition reminded Okonkwo of his own bedeviled father. Preferring to stay home and hear the "womanly" stories of his mother rather than joining in the manly labors of his father, Nwoye was as gentle and peace-loving as his grandfather had been. The disappointing boy was even less virile and intrepid than his beautiful younger sister Ezinma, in whom Okonkwo found some consolation.

It was with relief, then, that Okonkwo watched as his new charge, Ikemefuna, ripened into a lively, popular, and highly industrious youth. As the seasons passed, Okonkwo grew very fond of the boy, and in many respects thought of him as an ideal son. Moreover, this exemplary new brother gradually "kindled a new fire" in the meek and sluggish Nwoye.

Then one day, three years after Ikemefuna's arrival, Okonkwo received a visit from one of Umuofia's respected patriarchs. The esteemed visitor told Okonkwo that the "Oracle of the Hills and the Cave" demanded Ikemefuna's sacrifice. The wizened patriarch cautioned, however, that Okonkwo must "not bear a hand in his death."

Two days later the village elders came for the young man. Told that he was being led back to Mbaino, Ikemefuna nevertheless felt a great foreboding as he trudged through the forest alongside the men of Umuofia. Frequently Ikemefuna's mind turned to his mother and sister in Mbaino: Would they recognize him? What if his mother was dead? To soothe his nerves, Ikemefuna recalled a song from his childhood, and sang to himself.

All at once, one of the men "growled at him": the boy had fallen behind. Glancing around, Ikemefuna realized with a chill of fear that Okonkwo had quietly joined the group. An instant later, he found himself struck down by a blow from an unseen machete. "My father, they have killed me!" he cried out. Afraid of being thought weak, Okonkwo immediately dashed forward and slashed at the fallen boy with his own machete.

When Okonkwo returned from the forest, Nwoye avoided him. Instinctively he knew that Ikemefuna had been killed. Deeply shaken, "something had given way inside" Okonkwo's eldest son. Nwoye would never again be the same.

But Ikemefuna's death had also deeply shaken his great lion of a father: "[Okonkwo] tried not to think about Ikemefuna, but the more he tried the more he thought about him. [In time], he was so weak that his legs could hardly carry him. He felt like a drunken giant walking with the limbs of a mosquito. Now and then a cold shudder descended on his head and spread down his body."

Subsequent events deepened Okonkwo's despair. First, the ancient patriarch who had brought word of Ikemefuna's sacrifice died. Umuofia's warriors, their bodies painted and adorned in "raffia skirts," danced in the great sage's honor. In a frenzy, they then dashed about brandishing machetes and firing guns. Among them, Okonkwo raised his gun for the final salute to the deceased and, by accident, his bullet struck and killed the dead man's son. Okonkwo knew that the only atonement for this deed was seven years banishment, for it "was a crime against the earth goddess to kill a clansman."

Early the next morning, Okonkwo set off with his three wives and their children to begin their new life in exile, withdrawing to the village where his mother had been born. Okonkwo straightaway set to work building huts for his family and planting yams so that he might prosper in the new village. But still he was troubled: Okonkwo's deepest desire had always been to "become one of the lords of the clan" in his home village of Umuofia. Now it occurred to him that his own *chi* might be as malevolent as his father's had been.

Seeing Okonkwo's distress, his maternal uncle offered solace: "A man belongs to his fatherland when things are good and life is sweet. But when there is sorrow and bitterness he finds refuge in his motherland. Your mother is there to protect you. She is buried there. And that is why we say that mother is supreme." Okonkwo took these words to heart, and soon he had adapted to his new home.

During his second year in his motherland, however, Okonkwo received troubling news: white Christian missionaries had settled in Umuofia, bringing with them their "great evil" and gradually winning many converts. One of these converts was his own son Nwoye, who, upon baptism, had renounced Okonkwo, declaring, "He is not my father."

Okonkwo fumed with hatred; he despised the white intruders and hoped the villagers would wage war on them. How he missed the "bold and warlike" men they once were!

Finally the seven years of exile elapsed, and, after providing a great feast for his maternal kinsmen, Okonkwo and his family set off for home, eager to rebuild their lives.

But upon his return Okonkwo found that his fatherland had undergone profound changes. White men had begun to govern the whole region with support of those who had converted to the new faith. Outraged, Okonkwo sought to convince the villagers to "drive away" or slaughter the foreigners, but to no avail. Then one day a Christian profaned the earth goddess by removing the mask from one of the village's ritual dancers; for this grave sacrilege the people of Umuofia burned down the new Christian churchhouse.

For a brief moment Okonkwo knew once more a feeling akin to happiness; the men of Umuofia had not lost their courage after all. But his joy evaporated when, a few days later, he and other villagers were arrested and sent to jail to pay for the burning. Starved and beaten, Okonkwo's old fury returned.

After his release from jail, Okonkwo made his way to the village marketplace, where a council was to be held. "All our gods are weeping," said one of the speakers. "We must root out this evil." Suddenly, five court messengers, Okonkwo's former friends who now worked for the new government, appeared in the crowd. "The white men," one of them announced loftily, "whose powers you know all too well, have ordered this meeting to stop."

Okonkwo immediately drew his machete and decapitated the nearest messenger. Then, cleaning his blade on the sand, he turned and disappeared into the crowd.

The local District Commissioner and his soldiers set out to re-arrest the Igbo warrior. But upon reaching his compound, they were disappointed: In a nearby bush, Okonkwo had hanged himself.

"It is an offense against the Earth," one of the villagers said, referring to Okonkwo's suicide. Thus, like his father before him, Okonkwo was doomed to be "buried like a dog" in the forest and to suffer forever afterward the scorn of his people.

Commentary:

"Things fall apart," reads William Butler Yeats' classic poem. "The center cannot hold."

Chinua Achebe, born in 1930, grew up in an Igbo tribal village. Like the characters in *Things Fall Apart*, Achebe and his family lived through the trauma of being trapped between radically distinct cultures. "I think that I'm much more a part of a transitional generation than any other," Achebe once stated. "And this is very exciting. Of course it carries its penalties, since you're in no-man's-land." And it is just this anguished journey through no-man's-land that underscores the whole narrative in *Things Fall Apart*.

In the opening pages we find Okonkwo, who has managed to carve himself a "place" in Umuofia, working feverishly to avoid spiritual exile from his "fatherland." His tender firstborn son Nwoye pursues the "womanish" interests that leave him stranded between Umuofia's separate male and female worlds, already an inhabitant of a literal no-man's-land where the torch of Okonkwo's own legacy—one hitherto sired by his outcast father—will obviously be extinguished.

Upon this scene Ikemefuna—a young exile from his own fatherland—seems to descend as a miraculous savior, redeeming and reconciling father and son. But when the hour of the young redeemer is come, and he is led away for sacrifice, Okonkwo makes a rash, unsanctioned leap towards the glory of final self-denial—and falls, cursed, into the abyss of the outcast.

The nourishing womb of the Motherland constitutes yet another no-man's-land; and when Okonkwo re-emerges into the world of manhood, Umuofia, his fatherland, has already been lost to the foreign fathers of white Christian civilization. Okonkwo's suicide completes the tragic cycle, as the evil *chi* that so viciously plagued his father completes its work on him.

THE SHORT STORIES OF VLADIMIR NABOKOV

(taken from Nabokov's Dozen: A Collection of Thirteen Stories, Doubleday and Company, Garden City, N.Y., 1958)

Vladimir Nabokov (1899 - 1977) once remarked, "While I keep everything on the very brink of parody, there must be, on the other hand, an abyss of seriousness." The interplay of solemnity and humor in his work underscores the double-edged nature of life, which contains elements of both comedy and pathos. In addition, Nabokov's vagueness about time and place hurls his readers into a fractured and unreal world.

"That in Aleppo Once . . ."

Although I can produce documentary proofs of matrimony," V.'s friend wrote him in a letter, "I am positive now that my wife never existed." They had married, the letter continued, not long before the "gentle Germans" thundered into France. The groom was a journalist, and his criticisms of the Nazi regime were sure to breed trouble, so the couple wanted to flee to New York, where the bride's uncle lived. But they could not get proper emigration papers, and so were forced to settle for a move to Nice. His wife greatly mourned the loss of their dog, which they were obliged to leave behind. "The honesty of her grief shocked me," he wrote, "as we had never had any dog."

The newlyweds traveled by train, stopping along the way at the city of Faugeres. Unfortunately, while he was in the station buying food, the train left without him. He sent frantic messages to all the stops between Faugeres and Nice, to no avail. After several months, he finally found his wife in Marseilles. They were enormously relieved to be together again, and promptly began the long, torturous process of applying for visas to America.

In the meantime, he tried to get his wife to tell him what had transpired during the time they were separated. She told him several tales; they all differed wildly. According to one story, she had taken up with a group of refugees and found shelter at a Russian church. Later, she claimed that she had met a traveling salesman who abducted her and took advantage of her. In still another version she told how she had run off with the salesman of her own accord.

On the day their visas were issued, he arrived at their apartment to discover that she had disappeared with all of her belongings. He made a few inquiries, all without success. He did run into an elderly acquaintance, who berated him for having done away with the dog back in Paris.

Despondent, he took a boat to America. On board, he encountered a doctor who claimed to have known his wife in Marseilles. The doctor said she had told him about her husband, who was planning to meet her shortly with their bags and visas. "It was at that moment," read the letter's final paragraph, "that I suddenly knew for certain that she had never existed at all." Her uncle's address in New York, he later ascertained, was no more than an alley between two buildings.

Still, sometimes he had the desire to look for her; at the same time, he feared to make the attempt. "It may end in Aleppo if I am not careful," he closed. The war was raging on, and Aleppo was a dangerous place to be.

Scenes From the Life of a Double Monster

Floyd was trying to resolve a question that he and his brother had been asked years ago. Could they recollect, a doctor had once asked, the very first time either of them realized the peculiarity of their condition and destiny? Floyd and Lloyd had been born conjoined twins, and were wed forever at their navels. They had shared the same umbilical cord in the womb. Their mother had died immediately after their birth—shocked beyond measure by their condition, Floyd conjectured—and were left to be raised by their Grandfather Ibrahim.

After thinking it over, Floyd remembered that by the age of three or four he had started wondering about his strange relationship with his brother. By the age of nine, he decided, "I knew quite clearly that Lloyd and I presented the rarest of freaks."

Soon Grandfather Ibrahim began exhibiting them for money. Floyd had never felt shame or revulsion at his condition. However, the first time he ever saw another child—a "normal" child, a child other than Lloyd, that is—he concluded that he must be a person with two shadows. He reflected on the strangeness of it all: he and the other child both cast shadows in the sun, but Floyd "possessed yet another shadow, a palpable reflection of my corporal self." And looking on at the awestruck boy, who stood gazing at the conjoined twins, Floyd merely wondered if he "had somehow managed to lose his [shadow], or had unhooked it and left it at home. Linked, Lloyd and Floyd were complete and normal; he was neither."

The twins, though unashamed, lived in fear of one person: their Uncle Novus. They knew that he was determined to steal them from their grandfather and sell them to a showman or a carnival. So, one day, thinking they had little time left to enjoy themselves, they decided to visit the Black Sea. They had lived near its shores their entire lives, but had never seen it. This was their only chance to "do what we were absolutely forbidden to do: go beyond a certain picket fence, open a certain gate."

But as they emerged from a stand of cypress trees onto the beach, they saw Uncle Novus waiting for them with his carriage. They tried to flee, but he easily snatched them up and pitched them into a large box. They would never again see their home.

Now, twenty years later, Floyd thought back on the moment of their abduction. Had some adventurous mariner stepped out on the shore just then, would he have experienced the thrilling trace of some ancient enchantment as he confronted a gentle, two-headed mythological monster framed by cypress and white stone?

"But, alas," Floyd reminisced, "there was nobody to greet us there save . . . our nervous kidnapper, a small doll-faced man wearing cheap spectacles . . ."

Conversation Piece, 1945

"I have a disreputable namesake," the writer began, "complete from nickname to surname, a man whom I have never seen in the flesh but whose vulgar personality I have been able to deduce from his chance intrusions into the castle of my life." The writer's double did indeed seem to be both real and disreputable. For example, in Nice once, a young woman called on the writer at his hotel, took one look at him, apologized, and left. The writer also learned that his double had once borrowed (and never returned) a copy of the "Protocols of the Wise Men of Zion," a fraudulent document whose only use was to incite anti-Semitic pogroms. And while lecturing in Zurich, the writer had been arrested in a restaurant for the other man's crime of violence: smashing three mirrors.

After emigrating to the United States, the writer thought he had escaped his evil twin. But one month he had received a phone call. A woman's voice on the other end invited him to attend a lecture about the war. The caller had assured him that he "would be very, very much interested in the discussion."

Yes, when he attended the lecture he found that he was interested—but also deeply disgusted. The lecturer, a Doctor Shoe, made apology after apology for German atrocities committed against the Jews, but then turned around and equated those atrocities to the Allied bombing of Leipzig, Munich, and Dresden. When the writer could stand no more, he retrieved his coat and galoshes, and stormed out. But not before he had announced to his hostess, "You are either murderers or fools, or both, and that man is a filthy German agent."

A week later, he received a letter:

Esteemed Sir,

You have been pursuing me all my life. Good friends of mine, after reading your books, have turned away from me thinking that I was the author of those depraved, decadent writings. In 1941, and again in 1943, I was arrested in France by the Germans for things I never had said or thought. Now in America, not content with having caused me all sorts of troubles in other countries, you have the arrogance to impersonate me and to appear in a drunken condition at the house of a highly respected person. This I will not tolerate. I could have you jailed and branded as an impostor, but I suppose you would not like that, and so I suggest that by way of indemnity . . .

The amount demanded was actually quite modest.

Time and Ebb

A ninety-year-old scientist had survived a disease that he and everyone else thought would kill him, and now he was resolved to write his memoirs. He discovered, however, that while his early memories were remarkably clear, his recent recall was frustrat-ingly confused. "I cannot," he scrawled, "remember the name of the eminent scientist who attacked my latest paper, [just] as I have also forgotten those other names which my equally eminent defenders called him." Stymied by this phenomenon, he decided to content himself with contrasting the world of his childhood with the world of his old age.

He was born a Jew in Paris, but his family had fled to the United States to avoid the tortures another nation had inflicted upon his race. He remembered thinking that the "skyscrapers" of New York were quaintly misnamed. To his childish eyes, they did not grate against the sky at all, but seemed to merge delicately and serenely into the sunset, their pulsating lights merging softly with the twilight.

As a child, he had also been fascinated by airplanes, though he doubted anyone born since the 1970s would remember them as fondly as he did. There was such a romance about them in those early days. "A boy would know planes from propeller spinner to rudder trim tab," he recalled, "and could distinguish the species by the pattern of exhaust flames in the darkness." One of his most cherished boyhood experiences was imitating the drone of an engine as he watched a plane approach, growing larger as it roared overhead. Then slowly it would shrink into the distance until "nothing but a lone star remained in the sky, like an asterisk leading to an undiscoverable footnote."

Commentary:

Tragicomedy is Nabokov's stage; timelessness is a major component in his fiction. Consider the newlyweds in "That in Aleppo Once . . . " At the beginning of the story, we chuckle at the thought of a man deducing that his wife never existed. As we read on, however, the story turns to tragedy when we comprehend that she is a woman who in fact physically exists, and lives in a web of lies and deceit.

A similar development occurs in "Scenes From the Life of a Double Monster." Initially it is amusing when Floyd says that the first child he ever saw was neither complete nor normal. But the mild humor is transformed into pathos when we learn that the conjoined twins have previously been abducted by their uncle, sold to strangers, and made to live out their lives under the gawking eyes of circus goers.

"Conversation Piece, 1945" also stretches the limits of credibility. A writer is haunted by an apparent double throughout his life; finally, he is contacted by this disreputable *doppelgager* —who has likewise been troubled by the antics of the writer.

"Time and Ebb" is a more tender and melancholy story. An aged scholar writing his memoirs, perhaps in an attempt to liberate himself from the painful thoughts of his own mortality, becomes lost in reverie about the early days of flying machines. In the end, he leaves his readers in a state of wistful reminiscence, in much the same way as he was left behind by his vanishing airplanes.

THE SHORT STORIES OF ISAAC BABEL

(taken from The Collected Stories of Isaac Babel, Criterion Books, Inc. New York, N.Y., 1955)

Isaac Babel (1894 - 1941) published his first story in 1916, the year before the onset of the Russian Revolution. Subsequently he participated in both the Revolution and the Civil War that followed. Stark, realistic, violent, and intensely personal, many of his tales are based on his experiences and observations during these periods, and on his service with Russian forces in Poland during the 1920s.

The following stories focus on characters caught up in personal predicaments: the devastation of personal identity amid one's high hopes and the harsh and very private realities of pre-holocaust conditions.

Gedali

Sabbath evenings made the young man melancholy. Since the Revolution, the Jewish quarter of Zhitomir was a shadow of its former vibrant self. He walked to the market, but beheld there only its death; gone were the days of fat and plenty. Later on, he found half-blind Gedali, who had continued to hold onto his shop even after all the other shopkeepers had fled or been killed. Gedali and his young, dispirited visitor sat on empty beer barrels and talked of the Sabbath—and of the Revolution.

Gedali blessed those high-spirited days in Poland, when the revolution had interrupted a pogrom that had cost him his sight. Though Gedali loved music, he had handed over his phonograph to the State when threatened with a firing squad. The young soldier who had come to collect had told him, "She cannot do without shooting, because she is the Revolution." Gedali, puzzled, had replied, "The Revolution is the good deed of good men. But good men do not kill . . . Then how is Gedali to tell which is Revolution and which is Counter-Revolution?"

Now the two men, one jaded with age, the other still touched with youthful hope, became quiet as they watched the first star pierce the sunset sky, marking the beginning of the Sabbath. "Jews should be going to the synagogue," Gedali stated solemnly—but the young man could only think that there was a scarcity of good people, of good Jews in Zhitomir. He asked of Gedali if Jewish biscuits and a glass of tea could be made available for the Sabbath. "Not to be had," Gedali answered over his shoulder as he limped away. The Sabbath was coming, and Gedali, founder of Zhitomir's revolutionary front, made his way to the synagogue to pray.

The Story of My Dovecot

Young Babel yearned to own a dovecot, a coop or home for pigeons. His father promised the wherewithal to build and populate it, but only if Babel passed the entrance exams to the preparatory class of the secondary school of Nikolayev. After much angst and many long nights of rote memorization, Babel at last did pass the exams, and in the autumn of 1905, as promised, his father gave him the money he sought.

Grandfather Shoyl helped build the dovecot with materials secured by Babel. Then, on the morning of October 10, 1905, the very day Emperor Nicholas bestowed on the Russian people a constitution, Babel set out toward the bird market to purchase his six doves—even though gunshots could be heard off in the distance. As he left the bird dealer's stall, a neighbor walked by and reported that "Grandfather Babel has been constitutioned to death." Grandson Babel commenced the walk back to his home, only to be accosted by Makarenko the Cripple and his wife, Kate. "What's that you've got in your sack?" Makarenko asked, snatching the bag from Babel's hands. Opening it to find Babel's long-coveted pigeons, the crippled man took one out and examined it for a moment, then dealt young Babel a crushing blow with the hand holding the bird, knocking him to the ground. "Their spawn must be wiped out," growled Makarenko's wife. "I can't a-bear their spawn, nor their stinking menfolk." Babel, stunned, felt the bird's blood and guts trickle down his temple. Weeping bitterly, he staggered to his feet and furtively made his way home down secluded alleys and backstreets. When he arrived, he found Grandfather Babel lying dead in the dusty yard.

Awakening

All the people among Babel's family acquaintances—merchants, fishermen, carpenters, clerks, and brokers alike—had insisted that their children study music. Naturally, Babel's parents wanted the same for him. After all, many master musicians had grown up in Odessa: Mischa Elman, Zimbalist, Gabrilowitsch, even Jascha Heifetz. The boy's father could endure poverty, perhaps, but fame he must have. Thus, thrice weekly, young Babel went to Zagursky's house for violin lessons. Much to his father's displeasure, however, no amount of practice could make Babel a master violinist. " . . . The sounds dripped from my fiddle like iron filings," he later recounted, "causing even me excruciating agony, but my father wouldn't give in."

What Babel really wanted was to be a writer. Even as he scraped his way through violin exercises, he devoured the pages of Turgenev or Dumas secreted under the pages on his music stand. During the day he told his friends improbable tales; at night he committed them to paper.

The bookish lad finally managed to escape from Zagursky's den of horrors. As a fugitive schoolboy loitering near Odessa's harbor, he met up with Mr. Trottyburn, a retired sailor who befathered the multitude of young truants spending their days in the port, far away from work, school—and violin lessons.

Trottyburn encouraged his young charge to write. "One must suppose there's a spark of the divine fire in you," he remarked after a brief scrutiny of a story Babel had composed. Yet Trottyburn was scandalized that Babel cared nothing for the natural world; the boy cold not name a single bird, tree, shrub, or flower. "A man who doesn't live in nature, as a stone does or an animal," the old man scolded kindly, "will never in all his life write two worthwhile lines." Babel pondered these words as he returned home. Where could he acquire a feeling for nature?

The aspiring writer's answer did not come that afternoon, for Mr. Zagursky finally arrived to check on the reason for Babel's three-month absence. Catching a glimpse of his former instructor coming up the walk, Babel hurriedly locked himself in the bathroom to escape his father's almost certain wrath. After everyone had gone to sleep, he emerged and stole outside. In the depths of night he headed towards the port, only to be corralled by his Aunt Babka and taken to his grandmother's house. "The moonlight congealed on bushes unknown to me, on trees that had no name. Aunt Bobka held me firmly by the hand so that I shouldn't run away. She was right to. I was thinking of running away." Still the thought ran through his head: How would he attain a feeling for nature?

How Things Were Done in Odessa

Babel asked Arye Lieb how it happened that Benya Krik had ascended the ranks to become "King" of Odessa's gangsters; why not Froim Grach, Kolka Pakovsky, or Chaim Drong? So Lieb recounted to his assemblage of boys the story of Benya Krik, bidding them to "forget for a while that you have glasses on your nose and autumn in your heart," to forget their studies and let their imaginations roam.

Krik was the son of a wagon driver, but he dreamed of being something bigger. He went to Froim Grach and confided that he wanted to be *somebody*—and to be somebody, he was willing to rob anybody. A council of gangsters was held and a decision rendered: unleash Krik on Tartakovsky the storeowner— also known as "Nine Holdups," because he had already been robbed nine times, and as "Kike-and-a-half . . . because no one Jew could hold all of the sheer nerve and all the money that Tartakovsky had." And so it was arranged.

The tenth robbery of Tartakovsky's store was progressing quite smoothly, until Savka, a member of Krik's gang, staggered drunkenly onto the scene and improvidently shot and killed the store's clerk, who had been meekly handing over the money and jewels.

Later, Tartakovsky offered one hundred rubles to the aunt of the dead clerk, Pesya, as a token compensation for the loss of her nephew. Krik became enraged when he heard of this perfidy. Immediately he raced over to the aunt's home, barged into the negotiation with Tartakovsky, and won for the bereaving Pesya a much better settlement: a five-thousand-ruble lump sum and fifty rubles each month. Krik, himself mourning the clerk's untimely death, arranged for the unfortunate young man to have the grandest funeral Odessa had ever seen. And after the funeral, Krik entreated the mourners to attend a similar ceremony for Savka, the group's reckless—and unfortunate— gunman, who had been interred in the Jewish cemetery next to the grave of the hapless clerk.

Following the funerals, everyone but Krik and his three associates had fled the graveyard as if they were running from a fire. "I wasn't there personally," Lieb concluded his account, "but the fact that the cantor, the choir, the Burial Society didn't ask any payment—that I did see with the eyes of Arye Lieb."

And Arye Lieb ended with this declaration: "Now you know everything . . . You know who was the first to utter the word 'King.' That was Moses [the Lisper]. And you know why he didn't give this name to Grach the One-Eyed or to Kolka the Crazy. You know everything. But what's the use, if you still have glasses on your nose and autumn in your hearts?"

Commentary:

Babel brings to vibrant life the experience of growing up as a Jew in his hometown of Odessa, mixing objectivity and tenderness with humor, cruelty, and elements of wild fantasy. These surrealist components are especially evident in "How Things Were done in Odessa." We enter the action through the eyes of young boys being told a story—itself a soft, sentimental scene. The tale of Benya Krik which unfolds, however, is at once cruel and fantastic. Early on, the story seems credible enough (and, sadly, in all our modern age, all too familiar). As the events progress, though, the picture of a gangster negotiating with one of his victims to secure a pension for the aunt of another victim begins to stretch the bounds of credibility. Yet, only after we finish the story do we wonder how we were able to suspend disbelief.

The more realistic "Awakening," on the other hand, involves a familiar dilemma: the struggle of a growing child to choose between parental expectation and the assertive demands of his own soul.

Though Babel's stories were ostensibly political, presented as portraits of life among the peasant and Jewish populations of pre-World-War-II Russia, apparently many Soviet officials were not at all pleased by the works: Isaac Babel disappeared forever during the Stalinist purges and pogroms of the late 1930s. It is unclear whether he was executed by Stalinists or if he died later in a Nazi concentration camp after Germany invaded Russia in 1941. Whichever is the case, Russian and Jewish literature were made the poorer by Babel's untimely death.

THE SHORT STORIES OF ERNEST HEMINGWAY

(taken from *The Snows of Kilimanjaro and Other Stories*, Macmillan Publishing, New York, N.Y., 1986)

Ernest Hemingway (1899 - 1961) served as a volunteer ambulance driver at the Italian front during World War I and in later years became a big-game hunter, a restless adventurer, and an American expatriate who lived in 1920s Paris. These experiences emerge in much of his fiction, particularly in the following stories, which are among his most popular.

The Snows of Kilimanjaro

Harry, living with his wife in the wilds of Africa, was dying from the gangrene that had spread down his right leg. Yet he felt no pain and no horror at what he knew was coming. His only regret was that he had so much more to write—all the tales he had saved for the time he could do them justice. Now he was determined not to fail; he would pick up a pen and write those stories.

"I wish we'd never come here," sighed Harry's wife. If only they had remained in Paris, where this sort of thing was unheard of. "What have we done," she murmured, "to have this happen to us?"

Harry, a pragmatist in such matters, only could respond that he'd either forgotten to put iodine on the deep abrasion he had received or had acted too late. Then he turned on her; she was to blame. It never would have happened, he mumbled, if she hadn't left her people, the old Westbury, Saratoga, Palm Beach people, for him. That's why it had happened.

"That's not fair," she said. "I love you. Don't you love me?"

"No," he answered.

Searching his mind for times when all was right with the world, Harry saw himself standing with his pack at a railway station in Karagatch, saw the woodcutter's house with the big porcelain stove at Gauertal, and remembered the time the deserter had come there with bloody feet in the snow to escape the gendarmes who were tracking him. "He had never written a line of that, nor of that cold, bright Christmas day . . . [when] . . . Barker had flown across the lines to bomb the Austrian officers' leave train, machine-gunning them as they scattered and ran."

Now, in the stark light of the real Africa, here was Harry's wife, crying because of his words. He told her he was sick, that he was crazy and that he did love her as he'd never loved another. Then he turned, contradicted himself, and called her a bitch, crying, "I'm full of rot and poetry!"

Harry awoke later that evening and found her gone, out shooting game. He thought back to how he'd become involved with her, of how the relationship was over for him the moment it had begun. He'd told himself he was going to write about rich people, that he was not really one of them, merely a spy in their country. But now he would never do it; he'd grown soft sharing in his wife's opulent life. And now his abilities had dulled and his desire to work had ebbed to a halt—until he did no work at all.

She returned later with some meat. As they talked and drank together, he realized how cruel he'd been earlier. And then it occurred to him, with jolting clarity and remorse, that he was really dying. "It came with a rush; not as a rush of water nor of wind; but of a sudden evil-smelling emptiness and the odd thing of it was that the hyena slipped along the edge of it."

He thought of how he had quarreled with his wife, how he'd argued with all of the women he'd loved. One time before traveling to Constantinople, he and the woman who was then his wife had argued. Afterwards, he'd slept with whores, trying to lessen the hurt; when that didn't work, he sent his wife a letter telling about his activities and how he couldn't kill the hurt. He'd witnessed the horrors of battle, but lived to return to Paris to find the lovers' quarrel over and forgotten—until the day his letter had arrived, ending the relationship. " . . . He had always thought he would write it finally. There was so much to write . . . but now he never would."

But maybe he could write something, he contemplated, before he died. But he had no strength, and his current wife had never learned to take dictation.

So he was just left to ponder all those things he *should* have written: the log house and the Black Forest after the war, the passionate and gay French quarters, and the ranch. His mind turned to the half-wit boy who'd shot a man, and who, afterwards, had allowed himself to be taken to the sheriff under the mistaken certainty that he would be rewarded for having kept the man out of the hay. He thought of his war buddy, Williamson, hit by a stick bomb, caught in the barbed wire, begging for someone to kill him.

Now, as Harry's head drowned in such thoughts, he felt a very real weight upon his chest. "It crouched now, heavier, so he could not breathe. And then, while [the servants] lifted the cot, suddenly it was all right and the weight went from his chest."

Morning had dawned, and Harry could hear the droning of old Compton's plane. Compton, a veteran pilot, had earlier loaded him into the craft. Then—just the two of them—they had lifted off, soaring high into the sky, through a storm, and then "all he could see, as wide as all the world, great, high, and unbelievably white in the sun, was the square top of Kilimanjaro."

The woman awoke to the whimpering of a hyena. As she lay in the darkness, she could not hear her husband breathing.

A Clean, Well-Lighted Place

"It was late and everyone had left the cafe except an old man who sat in the shadow the leaves of the tree made against the electric light." Two waiters watched him. One, the more seasoned of the two, remarked to his companion that the old man had tried to hang himself the week before; his niece had found him and cut him down. "Why?" asked the younger one. "Fear for his soul," the older waiter replied.

Mention of the elderly gentleman's attempt on his own life brought a new turn to the conversation. The younger waiter immediately wanted to know if he was a man of wealth. Yes, he had plenty of money. And so the question lingered: Why had he tried to kill himself?

"I wish he would go home," grumbled the young waiter. "I never get to bed before three o'clock. I have a wife waiting in bed for me." At this, his companion revealed that the old man had also once had a wife, and maybe he would be better off if he still had her. Now all he had was his niece to look after him.

Some minutes later, when the old man ordered another drink, the young waiter refused to bring it. Resigned to his fate, the old man sighed, paid his tab, and left. "The waiter watched him go down the street, a very old man walking unsteadily but with dignity."

As the two waiters closed up for the night, the unhurried one asked why the younger hadn't let the old man stay and drink. His answer was harsh: he was in a hurry to get home to his wife. Upon hearing this, the older one responded that he hated to close up so soon; there were those who needed a clean, well-lighted place—those who did not want to go home to bed. He would stay behind and close up later. "Good night," said the younger waiter, disappearing out the door.

Later that night, making his way home after closing down the cafe, the older waiter stopped by a bar and tried to speak with the barman. The barman, however, wasn't at all interested in conversation, and the waiter left after one drink, deciding that "he disliked bars and bodegas. A clean, well-lighted cafe is a very different thing."

Now he would go home and maybe sleep before daylight. He was sure it was only insomnia, and many people must have it.

Fathers and Sons

One lazy Sunday morning Nicholas Adams steered his car down the empty streets of a small town, "under the heavy trees . . . that are part of your heart if it is your town and you have walked under them, but that are only too heavy, that shut out the sun and dampen the houses for a stranger." He drove straight through into the countryside, through fields forgotten until springtime. In his mind, Nick hunted those fields, sizing up each clearing for signs of quail.

His father had taught him to hunt, his keen-sighted father, who, Nick judged, "saw as a big-horn ram or an eagle sees, literally." He had loved his father very much, but, for Nick, it was not good to call up such a remembrance too often—for his father had killed himself. Someday, Nick resolved, he would write about that—but not yet; he wasn't ready yet for such a painful burden. Perhaps he would write about other things first, like his first love, an Indian girl named Trudy.

Suddenly Nick's thoughts were interrupted by his own son, who, sitting beside him on the seat, asked what it had been like when he was little. Nick hesitated, then told the boy about hunting with Trudy and her brother, and with his father. Yes, the boy's grandfather had been a good shot; in fact, Nick had always gathered that his dad was disappointed with his son's shooting skills. "I don't feel good never to have even visited the tomb of my grandfather," the boy said finally.

"We'll have to go," Nick said. "I can see we'll have to go."

Commentary:

Ernest Hemingway is renown for his ability to conjure up powerful characters and storylines using a minimum of narrative. In "A Clean, Well-Lighted Place," for instance, the characters reveal themselves almost entirely through dialogue. The old man is the most defined of the three main characters, yet he says very little. Rather, his character unfolds from the waiters' discourse.

Hemingway's settings are likewise characterized by an economical use of language, a skill perhaps developed during the author's early days as a journalist and war correspondent. Though widely regarded as a man of action, most of Hemingway's shorter works employ very little action, relying on dialogue and description rather than dramatic events to propel the story along. "Fathers and Sons," for instance, consists almost entirely of conversation; "action" occurs only within the protagonist's private thoughts.

THE SHORT STORIES OF JAMES JOYCE

(taken from *Dubliners*, Random House, New York, N.Y., 1969)

The characters who appear in the fifteen short stories that comprise Dubliners, though widely diverse in age, occupation and ethical constitution, are bound by a common setting—the city of Dublin—and by the quirks of Irish culture, a subject of which Joyce never tired.

Counterparts

"Mr Alleyne wants you upstairs."

Farrington muttered an oath and stood up from his desk. Heavily, for he was a large man, he climbed the stairway and entered his boss' office. There was Alleyne, his head "so pink and hairless that it seemed like a large egg" as he bent over his papers.

"Farrington! What is the meaning of this? Why have I always to complain of you?" Mr Alleyne began his reprimand. As Alleyne carried on, Farrington "stared fixedly at the polished skull which directed the affairs of Crosbie & Alleyne, gauging its fragility"; yet he managed to stifle the rage that rose in his own throat. Suddenly he felt the need for a drink. At length, the red-faced executive officer finished his not uncommon tirade and growled, "Are you going to stand there all day? . . . Go downstairs and do your work."

Farrington returned to his desk, but he was so angry that he could only "stare stupidly at the last words he had written." Exiting the premises with a practiced deceit, Farrington sought O'Neill's shop, where he could soothe his dry throat with a beer. He downed it in one swallow, then "retreated out of the snug as furtively as he had entered it."

Upon Farrington's return to the office, the chief clerk informed him that Mr Alleyne had been asking for him again. He knew that he had no time to complete the transcription his boss was expecting, and hoped Mr Alleyne would not notice that "the last two letters were missing." Now he found his anger returning. "He felt strong enough to clear out the office single-handed. His body ached to do something, to rush out and revel in violence."

All at once Mr Alleyne was standing in front of him, shouting in a fury: "Do you think me an utter fool?" Caught off guard, Farrington took a moment to respond—and when he did, his answer surprised him as much as it did his co-workers. "I don't think, sir," he stammered, "that that's a fair question to put to me."

Mr Alleyne turned scarlet; he twitched and shook his fist. "You impertinent ruffian! . . . " he screamed. "You'll apologize to me for your impertinence or you'll quit . . . !"

When the work day was over, Farrington "felt savage and thirsty and revengeful, annoyed with himself and with everyone else." He had apologized to Mr Alleyne, but he knew that his boss would now harass him relentlessly—and things were bad enough already. Once again he craved a drink. And as he walked through the crowded streets of Dublin, he began to compose a witty narrative about his momentary triumph over Mr. Alleyne, as he

would relate it to the boys in the bar.

Flynn, O'Halloran and Leonard, his drinking chums, thought Farrington's telling of the incident at work highly amusing and found his final rejoinder superb. Each bought Farrington a round of beers, and Farrington himself bought two.

A little later Leonard introduced his friends to another young man named Weathers, a performer of sorts who volunteered to take them to a pub where some "nice girls" of his profession could be met. In mock politeness, O'Halloran offered to excuse Farrington from the adventure—"because he was a married man"—but Farrington declined to be excluded.

At the pub, Weathers greeted two young women who were seated with a man. Farrington exchanged a few glances with one of the women, but when she left the room she brushed past him without looking back. Suddenly Farrington's anger flared again—anger at his lack of money, and anger at Weathers, whom he now saw as a sponge.

Now Weathers sat at their table, displaying his biceps and boasting. Farrington's friends called upon him to upstage the braggart in an arm-wrestling contest. But Weathers bested the hulking Farrington, not once but twice. When another man dared to voice approval of Weathers' technique, Farrington rose up to challenge the meddler. But O'Halloran tactfully called for a final round of drinks.

After a night of arm-wrestling and noise-making, Farrington, discontent, found himself alone, waiting for his tram to appear. Arriving home at last, he let himself in at the kitchen door and bellowed for his wife. A little boy, one of his five children, greeted him and lit the lamp. Farrington roared at the tyke, "What's for my dinner?"

An expression of agony came over the boy's face. "I'm going . . . to cook it, pa," he answered.

But his father had reached his breaking point. "You let the fire out!" he brayed, seizing a walking stick from behind the door. The child sank to his knees, awaiting the blows. "By God, I'll teach you to do that again. Take that, you little whelp!"

With blood streaming from his thighs, the boy begged, "Don't beat me, pa! And I'll . . . and I'll say a *Hail Mary* for you . . . I'll say a *Hail Mary* for you, pa, if you don't beat me . . . I'll say a *Hail Mary* . . . "

The Dead

When Miss Julia and Miss Kate staged their annual dance, it was guaranteed to be the success it had always been. But on this occasion the elderly sisters were feeling a certain agitation due to the unexpected tardiness of their favorite nephew, Gabriel Conroy. It was, after all, well past ten o'clock, and the dance was already in progress. The doting aunts were also fretting over the possibility that Freddy Malins might arrive even more drunk than usual.

At last Gabriel and his wife Gretta appeared on the snowy doorstep and were met by the maid. While his aunts accompanied Gretta to the ladies' dressing-room, Gabriel followed the maid into the pantry that served as the men's cloakroom. Making conversation, he teased, "I suppose we'll be going to your wedding one of these fine days with your young man, eh?" The girl replied, "The men that is now is only all palaver and what they can get out of you." Gabriel blushed, and after pressing a coin into her hand, hurried up the staircase to wait for the waltz to finish. As he entered the drawing-room, Gretta, Aunt Julia and Aunt Kate emerged from the ladies' dressing room to join him—Aunt Kate seizing the opportunity to cross-examined her nephew and his wife.

Soon, Aunt Julia came to announce the arrival of Freddy, hinting that Gabriel must hasten to assess the newcomer's condition. "It's such a relief" said Aunt Kate to Gretta, "that Gabriel is here."

When the waltz ended, a young lady sat down to play the piano. Gabriel "liked music, but the piece she was playing had no melody for him." Retreating from the drawing-room, he returned only when he perceived the recital's conclusion.

For the next dance, Gabriel was paired with a Miss Ivors, a "frank-mannered" young woman who invited her partner to bring his wife on a tour of the Atlantic coast. When Gabriel replied that he was more inclined to take a cycling excursion of Belgium or France, Miss Ivors became indignant. "And haven't you your own land to visit," she sputtered, "that you know nothing of, your own people, and your own country?" Suddenly annoyed, Gabriel retorted, "O, to tell you the truth, I'm sick of my country, sick of it!" The dance ended and Gabriel escaped to a "remote corner of the room." Alone at last—that is, until his wife found him. "Gabriel, Aunt Kate wants to know won't you carve the goose as usual."

After assuming his position at the head of the table, Gabriel commenced carving while Aunt Julia and Aunt Kate circled the table, "getting in each other's way and giving each other unheeded orders." When all were served Gabriel announced, "Kindly forget my existence, ladies and gentlemen, for a few minutes," and with that he commenced eating his meal.

Near the end of the feast, "a few gentlemen patted the table . . . as a signal for silence," whereupon Gabriel rose from his seat to address the assemblage on the merits of Irish hospitality as personified by his aunts. (The fact that Miss Ivors had retired from the party prior to supper seemed to have boosted his confidence.) He finished his eloquent discourse by proposing a rousing toast to the hostesses, who were quite overcome with emotion. Indeed, his speech was a great success, as was the event which it capped.

Gabriel and Gretta left the house in the company of a certain conceited tenor who would share their cab until they got out at the hotel. His wife strolling before him, Gabriel walked along, remembering some of their intimate moments together, but the tenor's presence forced Gabriel to restrain his passion.

Despite the tenor's objection, when they arrived home Gabriel tipped the driver handsomely. When Gretta took his arm, the light pressure she applied filled him with a rush of desire. The aged porter saw them to their room, then departed.

Gretta immediately came to her husband's embrace, but the "serious and weary" expression she wore defied him. "You look tired," Gabriel said, at which she stretched upwards and kissed him, cooing, "You are a very generous person, Gabriel." The words filled his heart with joy. "Just when he was wishing for it she had come to him of her own accord." He stroked her hair—and yet again he sensed a resistance. "Gretta dear, what are you thinking about?"

Breaking free from his arms, she turned and collapsed in tears on the bed. Gently, Gabriel urged her to tell him what was troubling her. "I am thinking about a person long ago," she finally replied. He was a young man, a boy really, she sniffed, named Michael Furey, who had died at the tender age of seventeen. Then she added: "I think he died for me."

At this confession, a vague terror overcame Gabriel: "While he had been full of . . . tenderness and joy and desire, she had been comparing him in her mind with another . . . He saw himself as a ludicrous figure, acting as a pennyboy for his aunts . . . orating to vulgarians and idealizing his own clownish lusts." The disillusionment in his voice betrayed him when he next spoke: "I suppose you were in love with this Michael Furey, Gretta." But she broke down in a fit of grief; Gabriel, holding in his sorrow, walked to the window and peered out at the darkness.

Later, as Gabriel imagined Gretta's "first girlish beauty," without which Michael Furey had been unwilling to live, tears welled up in his eyes and his thoughts "approached that region where dwell the vast hosts of the dead."

All across Ireland the snow was falling—even settling upon Michael Furey's cold grave. The soul of Gabriel Conroy "swooned slowly as he heard the snow falling faintly through the universe and faintly falling, like the descent of their last end, upon all the living and the dead."

Commentary:

In the preceding two stories, even the apparently dissimilar protagonists, Farrington and Gabriel, share a comparable sense of impotence: Farrington is forced to submit to a man he detests while Gabriel—caught up in Gretta's memories of a dead youth—feels powerless to seduce his own wife. However, the two men react to their common frustrations in totally opposite ways. The scorned office worker explodes in a flurry of rage and brutality; the *bon vivant*, on the other hand, manages to move beyond anger to a deeper understanding, a higher spiritual plane.

EAST OF EDEN

by
John Steinbeck
(1902 - 1968)

Type of work: Allegorical novel—a study of good and evil

Setting: California's Salinas Valley; early 1900s

Principal characters:

Adam Trask, a wealthy idealist
Cathy "Kate" Ames Trask, his wife
Aron and Caleb Trask, their twin sons
Lee, the Trask's Chinese houseboy
Samuel Hamilton, Adam's friend, a Salinas rancher

Story Overview:

"There are monsters born in the world to human parents." And Cathy Ames, "born with the tendencies, or lack of them, which drove her all of her life," was just such a creature. As though nature concealed a trap, Cathy was beautiful and innocent in appearance; a pretty child who grew to become a pretty woman. But "even as a child she had some quality that made people look at her, then look away."

On a farm in Connecticut in the wind-up years of the 19th century, lived two bachelor brothers, Adam and Charles Trask. The sons of a Civil War veteran who'd left them a fortune, the Trask brothers had never gotten along; they simply didn't agree on anything. Recently, Adam had been trying to convince his brother that they should move to California, the land of opportunity. But Charles wasn't interested.

One night as the brothers debated this issue, they heard a scratching at the door. Investigating, they found a woman on the stoop, beaten and left to die. Adam immediately brought her inside.

Despite his brother's opposition, Adam was determined to keep the woman at the house and nurse her back to health. She healed slowly, but "Adam couldn't remember ever having been so happy. It did not matter that he did not know her name. She said to call her Cathy and that was enough for him."

But just as Adam fell utterly in love with Cathy, Charles grew to utterly mistrust her. Even on the day when the couple married, Charles made no attempt to hide his displeasure; Cathy would destroy Adam, he warned. And that very night, while Adam slept, Cathy slipped out of the room and went to Charles' bed. The next day, Adam took his new bride and headed for California.

They moved into a ranchhouse situated in the Salinas Valley. When Cathy discovered that she was with child, Adam immediately hired a Chinese servant, Lee, to help her through her pregnancy. He also contacted a neighbor, Samuel Hamilton, about digging some new wells on his property.

Over the course of that first summer, Adam and Samuel became friends. Like Charles, however, Samuel too distrusted Cathy. He couldn't put his finger on anything in particular; all he could say was "something's wrong."

Eventually, Cathy gave birth to twin boys. She rested for a week, then announced that she was leaving. When Adam tried to stop her, she picked up his Colt revolver, shot him through the shoulder, then walked out of the house.

Adam withdrew in despair. A year went by, and he remained immobilized. Finally, Lee, who'd been single-handedly raising the still-unnamed twins himself while trying to take care of Adam, appealed to Samuel Hamilton for help. Samuel tried talking to Adam first; when talk failed to jolt his friend out of his detached, greywater world, he raised one of his heavy fists and struck Adam in the face.

It worked, and the two men went to the long-overdue task of naming the twins: the dark-haired boy—curiously resembling his uncle Charles—Adam called "Caleb"; the other, fair-haired child was given the name "Aron."

Time passed, and Adam and Samuel grew older. One day when the twin boys were eleven, Samuel came to visit. Over dinner, the two men, together with Lee, discussed the Biblical story of Genesis. Lee remarked how, for many years, the question of Cain's redemption had puzzled him. In the King James Bible, for instance, Jehovah *promises* Cain that he will conquer sin; in another translation, God *commands* Cain to conquer sin; while in the original Hebrew version, according to Lee, Jehovah says that Cain *MAY* conquer sin—an idea expressed by the word "Timshel." Adam favored the latter concept. Cain's fate was *not* set in stone; it offered possibilities of human freedom and choice.

After dinner, Samuel told Adam a secret he'd kept hidden for many years: Cathy was in Salinas; she owned the most vicious and depraved whorehouse in the county. He'd never told Adam for fear of hurting him, but now felt he could no longer hold his silence.

A few weeks later, Samuel died. After attending the funeral in Salinas, Adam, curious, sought out his estranged wife. "She was still pretty . . . " was his first thought on seeing her, "but her outlines were not sharp anywhere. . . . The work of the years had been subtle." He saw this woman, who now went by the name "Kate," as she truly was: twisted and filled with anger. Before he left town, Kate told him how much she hated him; Adam answered that it didn't matter anymore. Truly, "Samuel's funeral and the talk with Kate should have made Adam sad and bitter, but they did not. Out of the grey throbbing, an ecstasy arose. He felt young and free."

The twins sprouted quickly. Now virtually grown men, they very much reminded Adam of himself and his brother in their youth. Caleb—or "Cal" as he preferred to be called—was cynical, worldly and cruel—much like Charles; Aron, like his father, was an idealist, loved by everyone. He refused to hear the occasional rumors about his mother; instead, he scrupulously trusted his father's sentimental stories about her death.

When the Trask family moved into Salinas so that the youths could attend a better school, the same pattern continued. Cal soon took to wandering the streets late at night. Since the restless youth made no trouble, however, the police let him alone.

From fragments of talk overheard in pool halls, Cal slowly came to a knowledge of his mother. Finally one night he located Kate's house and saw what went on there. He reacted strangely to this unveiled truth: instead of hurting for himself, he became concerned for his father. Toward Adam, he grew more and more protective; he wanted to make up somehow for his father's suffering. The old rebellious hatred and jealousy he had previously held toward his brother seemed to have retreated from his soul.

As his father's new self-appointed guardian, Cal took it upon himself to learn all he could about Kate. He shadowed her for weeks until she finally confronted him. When Cal introduced himself, distant memories turned to clear recollections; the shadows of years past faded from her eyes. Finally she escorted her son into her grey, windowless "inner sanctum." As they spoke, Cal began seeing the sinister, sinful side of his mother, and vowed never to become like her. She was not part of him.

The nation was plunging headlong towards world war. Adam had recently lost a great deal of money in a disastrous business venture, while Aron yearned to complete college but lacked the funds. As the war fever heightened, Cal came up with a plan to help his father—and maybe Aron, too: he borrowed $5000 from Lee and enlisted Samuel Hamilton's son Will to be his partner. They would grow beans on the old King City ranch—a crop that would skyrocket in price when the fighting broke out. Aron, meanwhile, left for college, still financially strapped, with visions of becoming a minister.

Adam Trask was appointed to the Salinas draft board, a job he performed well and honestly, but also sadly. "He could not get over the feeling that the young men he passed to the army were under sentence of death." What's more, he feared that someday he would be forced to induct his own boys.

Aron returned home for Thanksgiving, disillusioned with the monotony of college life and ready to quit. Cal, on the other hand, was exuberant; his moneymaking scheme had flourished and he planned to present his father with a gift over dinner.

At last, dinnertime arrived. After picking at the pudding, Cal handed his father a red-ribboned package. Inside was fifteen thousand dollars in cash.

Adam Trask's face folded into a frown. From whom had his son stolen this money? When Cal answered that he'd *earned* it by selling beans to the Army, Adam shook his head: "I send boys out . . . and sons will die . . . not one will come back untorn . . . Son, do you think I could take a profit on that?"

Later that evening, Cal took his reluctant brother Aron to visit their mother. Early the next morning, Kate was found in her inner sanctum, dead from a drug overdose. When her will was read, it was found that she had left her entire estate to her son, Aron Trask.

Cal sat in his room, thinking about what he'd done, of how his brother had sobbed like a child leaving Kate's place, and then disappeared into the night. Hoping beyond hope that some sort of sacrifice might bring his brother back, Cal burned, one at a time, each of the crisp, new bills that he'd tried to give his father.

A few days later, Adam Trask, now suffering from forgetfulness, deteriorating eyesight, and deepening depression, received a letter from Aron: "Dear Father," it began. "I'm in the Army. I told them I was eighteen."

On May 28, 1918, American troops carried out their first major offensive of the war. And within the day a telegram had arrived at the Trask home: Aron had been killed in action. When he heard the news, Adam immediately fell to the floor, the victim of a massive stroke.

At the hospital, after Adam had been stabilized, Cal shuffled up to his father's bedside and confessed everything he had done that pivotal Thanksgiving night. By taking Aron to see Kate, he was indirectly responsible for his brother's death. He was sorry, he explained. But Adam only stared into the blackness.

Adam's ever-faithful servant Lee begged on Cal's behalf, imploring Adam to forgive his only remaining son. Adam, trembling with exertion, arose and whispered a single word: "Timshel!"

Then he slept.

Commentary:

Steinbeck's *East of Eden* can be interpreted as an elaboration of the Book of Genesis: a good and pure man seeks to create a paradise in California but is thwarted by the deeds of his helpmeet; their two sons bear names and traits much like those of Cain and Abel—Aron, the favorite, can do no wrong while, in contrast, Cal's every deed is a vain attempt to win favor from his father. And in the end, like Cain, he figuratively slays his brother after his own "offering" to Adam is rejected.

Though intimations appear throughout the book to the effect that a pattern of good balanced against evil repeats itself in every generation, the real question seems to be what *is* good and what *is* evil. Steinbeck's work also carries the message that no human being is all good or bad.

The notion of "Timshel" is vital to Steinbeck's purposes. Wrapped up in the word's meaning is the possibility of redemption, not through delivering up an offering, a hollow gift of grace, but through personal, proper choice and action. Adam denies evil, and thereby fails to cope with it. Cathy, by contrast, is "born" evil; she has no choice. Her rage fills the void left by her inability to love. And Aron symbolizes innocence betrayed—an individual locked out of the chance to become either good or evil. Cal, as the only member of his family to have developed to the point where he really is human, at first refuses to recognize his evil, then eschews it and tries to "protect" the innocence of others, and finally betrays it altogether, taking upon himself the consequences of his own actions.

OF HUMAN BONDAGE

by
W. Somerset Maugham
(1874 - 1965)

Type of work: Semi-autobiographical account of a young man's painful progress towards maturity

Setting: England, Germany and France; late 19th, early 20th centuries

Principal characters:
Philip Carey, an awkwardly handicapped but intelligent and responsive young student
Hayward, Philip's intellectual friend
Sally, Philip's long-awaited bride

Commentary:

W. Somerset Maugham refers to *Of Human Bondage,* published in 1915, as an "autobiographical novel." In a sense, perhaps, writing this book helped Maugham to exorcise the unhappy recollections of his own early life.

The plot is almost void of explicit action; instead it transports the reader on a journey through one young man's developing selfhood as he struggles to find a center of meaning in the callow world around him. The intensely personal drama follows Philip Carey through his many new beginnings, aborted careers and relationships, and finally to his epiphanic proclamation: " . . . If one has lived thoroughly, then life has a meaning and a pattern as rich, though as unsymmetrical, as those formed by the colors [of] an oriental rug."

Story Overview:

Torn from the home of his dying mother as a young boy, Philip Carey was sent to live with his uncle, the vicar in a small English village. It was with mixed feelings, however, that the childless clergyman and his wife took on the guardianship of their sensitive, club-footed nephew.

Soon after Philip's arrival at the vicarage, they decided to enroll him in a religious boys' school where the students were encouraged to aspire to Holy Orders. Though at times bitterly frustrated by his impairment, nine-year-old Philip relied on his astute mind to survive and excel among this classmate.

Over the next several years, a wave of religious fervor spread through the school. Always eager for new experiences, Philip joined the circle of the devout, and every night before the lights went out he read earnestly from the Bible.

One night he came across a passage that particularly excited him: *If ye have faith, and doubt not . . . ye shall say unto this mountain, be thou removed, and be thou cast into the sea; it shall be done. And all this, whatsoever ye shall ask in prayer, believing ye shall receive.* When he heard the same words repeated in a sermon on the following Sunday, the young boy received them as an epiphany. Fervently he fell to his knees and asked God to make his club foot whole; for the rest of his holiday break he continued in this attitude of prayer.

When at last school reconvened and Philip saw that his abnormality was still not repaired, he consulted his uncle. "Supposing you asked God to do something, and really believed it was going to happen, like moving mountains, and you had faith and it didn't happen, what would it mean?" he asked. The uncle replied curtly: "It would just mean that you hadn't got faith." Although he did not see how his faith could possibly have been any stronger, Philip did not demur. Perhaps this passage, like many other Biblical verses his elders had explained to him, somehow meant something quite different from what it actually said.

But as the next few years passed, Philip found he could no longer fully embrace the passion of his former faith; daily religious exercise slipped into mere formality, his classes became cumbersome, and the prospect of ordination oppressed him. After much argument, Philip's aunt and uncle allowed him to continue his studies in Germany under the guidance of a local professor. There, Philip experienced for the first time in his eighteen years a sense of beauty and freedom.

After three months at school in Heidelberg, Philip was assigned a new roommate, a scholarly 26-year-old Englishman named Hayward. Though new acquaintances generally tended to disgust him, Philip rapidly took a liking to his fellow student and soon found himself thirsting for their daily walks and discussions.

When Hayward left Heidelberg to tour Italy, Philip was at a loss. Back home in England, however, he struck up a close friendship with the daughter of a former rector, a Miss Wilkinson. In the meantime, his guardians took him aside to discuss his future. Philip flatly refused to attend Oxford University, where his uncle had hoped he could study on a scholarship for his degree. But his aunt continued to aver, however, that there were only three professions worthy of a gentlemen: Army, Church, and Law. With his club foot and his unwillingness to accept ordination, the first two options were ruled out; this left only Law.

Immediately, Philip's uncle contacted the family solicitor. Though this gentleman said that though he had no room for Philip as an apprentice in his own law firm, he knew of a position elsewhere. Philip, sensing that a move to London would be a great opportunity, accepted the position and made plans to leave within the month.

Meanwhile, over time Philip had grown ever fonder of Miss Wilkinson. One Sunday evening while he was calling on her family, the object of his interest complained of a headache and coyly retired to her room. Not surprisingly, Philip offered to stay and attend her, if necessary, while the others left for an engagement. When the house had emptied, he crept up to the door of Miss Wilkinson's room. After what seemed like hours, he finally turned the handle—and there she stood, wearing just her petticoat. In that instant, a sensation of horror washed over him. Was this love? But despite his revulsion, he also felt a tinge of conceit. After all, even with his deformity, another human being had finally

185

demonstrated an attraction to him.

Not long after the tepid consummation of his attachment to Miss Wilkinson, Philip set off for London. Unfortunately, the novelty of his new work quickly evaporated. Some nights he would just sit outside a window, watching the people and wondering if he would ever experience any sense of true belonging or joy.

Spring came, and Philip looked forward to Hayward's London homecoming. His hopes were dashed, however, by a letter from his friend that extolled the delights of springtime in Italy; Hayward had decided to stay on and enjoy them. "There are only two things in the world that make life worth living, love and art . . . " the letter continued. "My feeling is that one should look upon life as an adventure [and] expose oneself to danger. Why do you not go to Paris and study art? I always thought you had talent."

When the end of the year came, Philip decided to act on Hayward's advice. But his uncle would have no part of this plan: " . . . Going to Paris to be an artist," he sputtered. "What a Bohemian idea." Why, no Christian gentleman, his uncle added, would participate in such an act. "Well," Philip replied disgustedly, "I know I'm not a Christian and I'm beginning to doubt I'm a gentleman."

Since his uncle had refused to provide for him in Paris and it was still three long months before Philip, now twenty, would receive his small inheritance, he ended up scrounging for bed and board at Anitrano's Art school in Paris, where he learned there was very little work to be found in painting unless one did portraits for rich Americans.

With the advent of summer, many Parisian artists retired to the countryside. Philip, finally sustained by his inheritance, joined in the sabbatical. He had but one life to live, he reminded himself earnestly, and it was important to do things right.

But after two years of the artist's life, Philip received some frank advice from his art teacher to the effect that he should get out while he could. Feeling sufficiently liberated, if not successful, he returned to the vicarage, where his aunt had recently died.

It was during this interlude at the vicarage that Philip first read Darwin's *The Origin of Species*. In the "struggle for life" depicted so graphically between its covers, the young man found an intensity and grandeur that he had never before encountered. Raptly turning the pages, he was swept by a flood of new religious elation. On one side of his life lay society's barren and repressive formalities; on the other, like a sun, shone the laws of natural selection. At last he had found the true measure of Good and Evil.

Now twenty-five and resplendently armored in his new Darwinian vision, Philip once again set out to conquer life in London. The exam he had passed earlier to certify for his accountancy easily qualified him to enter medical school; and romance soon crept back into his life in the emaciated form of a consumptive young waitress named Mildred.

But the star of Darwinian optimism soon burned itself out. Every morning Philip awoke with tortured thoughts of Mildred—who snubbed and belittled him at every turn. Desperately the lover persevered—only to find himself recoiling in disgust when Mildred at last relented to his advances. In some perverse way, spurning the love he had finally won from the woman who had once enthralled him brought a new dimension of freedom to Philip's life.

Philip returned to his medical studies with a new—and well-grounded—vigor. Having failed twice, this time he worked harder than ever. When he took the exam for the third time, he passed it with honors and stepped into his new career as an out-patient clerk at the hospital.

Then, when he was in his late twenties, life suddenly passed once again out of Philip's control. It was 1914, and world war had reared its hideous head. Soon nearly all of Philip's old friends and classmates were dead or fighting in the trenches; no one knew where the future of Europe lay.

To distract himself, Philip carelessly played the stocks—and disastrously lost. He could no longer afford medical school, and he was soon put out on the street. Though he had always been poor, until now the possibility of starving had never entered his mind. Poverty of this order was for Philip—as it was for every respectable middle-class Englishman—a disgraceful and dehumanizing disease. The crippled orphan from the vicarage who had fought to form a niche for himself in the world now once again found himself on the outside looking in.

Through the next months, Mr. Altheny, a kindhearted acquaintance from Philip's hospital, often invited the young man to dine with him and his family. And finally, with Mr. Altheny's assistance, Philip landed a job as a clerk in a department store.

As the war raged on, Philip avoided the places he had frequented in happier times. His great consolation was a ripening friendship with Mr. Altheny's daughter Sally. That same year, his uncle passed away, leaving him enough of an inheritance to finish medical school—and to ask Sally to marry him.

Finally, at the age of thirty, Philip Carey was able to find peace in a world that had both enslaved and rejected him. He now saw the underlying sameness of all the elusive dreams and passions that had once repressed him. From his first childhood ardor for a Biblical God, through his worshipful pursuit of Hayward's intellect, of art and Bohemianism, of Darwinian struggles, and of an unobtainable woman, he had been chasing the same chimera: " . . . All his life he had followed the ideals that other people, by their words or their writings, had instilled in him, and never the desires of his own heart. Always his course had been swayed by what he thought he should do and never by what he wanted with his whole soul to do."

Now, "with a gesture of impatience," Philip put all of this aside. Henceforth, he would follow his own soul. As he pressed his hand in Sally's and walked out onto the street, he saw that the cabs and omnibuses and people were hastening in every direction—and that "the sun was shining."

CATCH-22

by Joseph Heller, Simon & Schuster, New York, N.Y., 1961

Type of work: Satirical black humor

Setting: Pianosa, an island off the coast of Italy; the last months of World War II

Principal characters:
    Captain John Yossarian, an unwilling American Air Force bombardier
    Orr, Yossarian's tentmate
    Doc Daneeka, the squadron's flight surgeon
    Captain R.O. Shipman, the chaplain
    Colonels Cathcart and Korn, two vain and scheming group commanders

Story Overview:

During the closing months of World War II, Colonel Cathcart resolved to get his picture in the *Saturday Evening Post* and be promoted to the rank of general. In a characteristic act of false valor, he volunteered his 256th Squadron for a bombing mission to destroy the bridge at Ferrara, boasting that the squadron could execute the mission within 24 hours. They missed their target, however, for seven days in a row.

In a bid for redemption—and possible early discharge—Lieutenant John Yossarian offered to take his unit of six bombers over the bridge a second time. Their first run over the target had been a dismal failure when Yossarian's navigator had become disoriented and was unable even to *find* the Ferrara bridge. But this time out, he vowed, he would prove himself.

That Sunday, as the American planes approached the target again, every German anti-aircraft cannon in the area was aimed directly at them. Yossarian concentrated on his sights while releasing his bombs. When he finally looked up, he noticed the plane above him was engulfed in flames. He watched in horror as it crashed unceremoniously into the sea, its pilot killed on this "the seventh day, while God was resting."

The loss of the plane and its crew disturbed Colonel Cathcart: "It's just that it looks so lousy on the report," he told Yossarian. "How am I going to cover up something like this in the report?" Yossarian suggested that the colonel award him—as squadron leader—a medal. The colonel agreed, and Yossarian received the Distinguished Flying Cross—and a promotion to the rank of captain.

Yossarian believed that virtually everyone around him was crazy, especially Colonel Cathcart, who had successively raised the number of flying missions from 25 to 30, and then to 35. Moreover, Yossarian found it incredible that even "strangers he didn't know shot at him with cannons every time he flew up into the air to drop bombs on them." Others, of course, thought it was Yossarian who was crazy. His symptoms, as recorded by the squadron's physician, included "a homicidal impulse to machine-gun strangers, retrospective falsification, and an unfounded suspicion that people hated him and were conspiring to kill him."

The 256th Squadron was next assigned to fly a mission over Bologna, and Yossarian did all in his power to ensure that nobody even got near the target. Yossarian knew that his fellow bombardiers shared his feelings. Luckily, rainy weather delayed them at first. When the skies cleared, Yossarian added laundry soap to the sweet potatoes in the mess hall, inducing an epidemic of diarrhea. Another whole day was lost to allow the rain-soaked runway to harden enough for the planes to take off. Then later that night he stole into the compound and redrew the bomb line so that it extended above their target city. When Cathcart saw the map in the morning, he was overjoyed to see that Bologna had already been miraculously bombed and this week's reports would be spared the smirches of Yossarian's blunderings.

Eventually, however, the commanding officers realized that the city had not yet been bombed and ordered their fighters to shell it. As Yossarian approached the target, however, he tore out the cords of his intercom, thus breaking communication with the pilot and forcing his plane to turn back. The other men flew on to complete the mission successfully.

The next day Colonel Cathcart received orders to bomb the city again, and this time Yossarian was assigned to fly lead. As his plane flew in over the target and the enemy's anti-aircraft gun let loose with a furious barrage, Yossarian lost his nerve. He dropped his bombs prematurely, and left the formation. From a safe distance, he watched his own and another squadron of planes get blasted out of the sky. Among them was the plane belonging to Orr—Yossarian's stocky, buck-toothed tentmate—which was forced to crash land. In fact, almost every time Orr went up he had to ditch his craft or make a crash landing.

Several days later, Orr invited Yossarian to go up with him in his plane so that he could teach him how to ditch and crash-land—in case it ever came in handy. Yossarian refused, thinking Orr, like all the rest, was crazy.

Later, during a mission over Avignon, Yossarian realized that his buddy Snowden, the plane's radio gunner, had been shot. "I'm cold, I'm cold," Snowden whimpered, ashen-faced, as he reached toward a stain near his armpit. Yossarian "ripped open the snaps of Snowden's flak suit and heard himself scream wildly as Snowden's insides slithered down to the floor in a soggy pile and just kept dripping out."

After that, Yossarian vowed never again to put on a uniform; he'd "lost his nerve . . . because Snowden lost his guts." This time when the heroic bombardier lined up to receive his medal, he stood in formation stark naked; he had made up his mind to spend the rest of the war in the hospital, easily confusing the doctors with symptoms from a blessed liver condition that fell just short of being jaundice.

Yossarian had always felt comfortable and safe in the hospital. For one thing, he could distract himself by opening and censoring the enlisted men's letters, closing each with an amazingly different and inventive signature. For another, he knew that there, if he started screaming, someone would come running to help. Besides, fewer people died there. "They couldn't dominate Death inside the hospital, but they certainly made her behave."

It was in the hospital that Yossarian was visited by company chaplain R.O. Shipman, a quiet, introverted Anabaptist who doubted his own usefulness. During one visit, Yossarian's comrades asked the chaplain to speak to Colonel Cathcart to convince him not to raise their bombing quota again. Summoning his nerve, the chaplain suggested that Cathcart bring in troops stationed in Africa to replace his men. The colonel brushed off Shipman's advice, but Shipman persisted. In particular, he mentioned Yossarian: "He's in a very bad way, sir. I'm afraid he won't be able to suffer much longer without doing something desperate." Cathcart was unconvinced.

After the chaplain had departed, however, Cathcart began to second-guess himself: "Maybe sixty missions were too many for the men to fly. . . . But he then remembered that forcing his men to fly more missions than everyone else was the most tangible achievement he had going for him."

Yossarian, meanwhile, tried a different tack: he would feign insanity and force the doctors to send him home. "You're wasting my time," Doc Daneeka told him flatly. "Sure, I can ground you by filling out a slip saying you're unfit to fly. But there's a catch"—Catch-22. The contradictory essence of Catch-22, the doctor explained, was that he could send home anyone whom he thought was crazy; if, however, Yossarian asked to be sent home, then the doctor could not consider him crazy, because feeling threatened by a dangerous situation was a purely rational response. Besides, Daneeka added, if he started grounding men or sending them home, Headquarters might up and reassign him to the Pacific: " . . . All they've got in the Pacific is jungles and monsoons. I'd rot there." Yossarian pleaded: "I'm asking you to save my life." But the doctor only smiled sullenly: "It's not my business to save lives."

After completing a total of 71 missions, Yossarian made a last-ditch effort to stay alive: he refused to fly again. Even as fat-cat officers and supply clerks were profiting from the war by selling government goods on the black market, the absurdities of Catch-22—which by now had cost the life of his friend Orr—were sending countless men to their graves. When word of Yossarian's defiance spread, other fliers' attitudes deteriorated, too. Before long, the commanding officers realized they had a problem on their hands: "The men with seventy missions were starting to grumble because they had to fly eighty . . . Morale was deteriorating and it was all Yossarian's fault."

While they pondered what to do, Yossarian took an unauthorized leave to Rome. He knew that going A.W.O.L. could lead to a court-martial, but the pressure he felt was even less bearable than the thought of losing his freedom. Walking through the dark, rain-swept streets of the city, he witnessed horrible scenes of poverty and brutality. A youngster without shoes or a coat plodded along in the freezing drizzle. Further on, a man

cudgeled a small boy, while an uncaring crowd looked on. "The night was filled with horrors, and he thought he knew how Christ must have felt as he walked through the world, like a psychiatrist through a ward full of nuts, like a victim through a prison full of thieves." When the bombardier returned to his bed, two military policemen arrested him for having left without a pass.

By now the officers had decided what to do with their resident nonconformist. Colonel Korn greeted Yossarian with a smile and told him they were sending him home—with a promotion and another medal. But only on one condition: he had to play along with the big boys and give a good report. The alternative, they told him, was a court-martial. They still did not acknowledge that they were assigning the men too many missions. But the other fly-boys would be easier to discipline after Yossarian was gone, especially if he consented to endorse their authority.

Yossarian reluctantly agreed to the deal, but guilt soon overwhelmed him; he would be betraying his men. When he asked Shipman for advice, the chaplain replied only that "You must do whatever you think is right . . . " It was then that Yossarian knew he could not double-cross his men; but he also knew he could not fly another bombing mission.

Within minutes after Yossarian had made the decision to desert, Chaplain Shipman rushed in with news that Orr, whom they all had thought dead, was still alive and had made it to Sweden. Yossarian was elated; Sweden was neutral territory, and American soldiers could stay there under comfortable conditions for the duration of the war. Now he understood why Orr had gotten shot down on practically every mission he had flown: he had been practicing crash-landings in the ocean so that he could escape to Sweden. "It's a miracle of human perseverance, I tell you," the chaplain added. "And that's just what I'm going to do from now on! I'm going to persevere . . . "

Following Shipman's lead, Yossarian laced up his boots and headed north. He had survived war's insanity.

Commentary:

Joseph Heller's imaginative, irreverent use of comedy in Catch-22 forces the reader to re-examine what at first may seem insanely funny. Combat scenes often begin on a humorous course, only to be replaced by overwhelmingly horrible scenes. A similar form of "black comedy" is apparent in the different motives of the commanding officers, resulting in a heightened perception of the frightening effects of misused power.

Yossarian's moral progression is an important theme in the novel. After deserting and being brought back to the squadron, he confronts three choices: save his own life and thereby leave his buddies to deal with the irrational Colonel Cathcart; go to prison for crimes he did not commit; or desert, knowing he has already served his country beyond the so-called "line of duty." By choosing to run away instead of submitting to Korn's "odious deal," Yossarian is not escaping from his problems: he is finally accepting the responsibility to act on his moral beliefs.

TESS OF THE D'URBERVILLES

by
Thomas Hardy
(1840-1928)

Type of work: Impressionist novel

Setting: 19th-century England

Principal characters:

Tess Durbeyfield, a beautiful farm girl
Alec d'Urberville, her wealthy suitor
Angel Clare, her lover and, later, husband

Story Overview:

"Don't you really know, Durbeyfield, that you are the lineal representative of the ancient and knightly family of the d'Urbervilles, who derive their descent from Sir Pagan d'Urberville . . . ?" the parson asked.

"Never heard it before, sir," said John Durbeyfield, a penniless chicken-trader.

"Well, it's true."

Once Durbeyfield had digested this news, it was not long before the entire village had heard about the distinguished heritage of "Sir John."

John and his wife soon began a busy round of pub-hopping to celebrate their new-found nobility and formulate plans for reclaiming the wealth of the d'Urbervilles, leaving their oldest daughter, Tess, with the chores of caring for her six brothers and sisters, making deliveries for her father—and dragging her parents from the pub each night.

Then, after an accident killed the family horse, Mrs. Durbeyfield dispatched Tess to see Mrs. d'Urberville, one of their newly claimed relatives, who lived close by. It was suggested that after telling Mrs. d'Urberville of their kinship, Tess might appeal for money to purchase a new horse.

At the d'Urberville estate Tess was greeted by Alec d'Urberville, the woman's handsome yet manipulative son. Alec explained to his attractive visitor that his invalid mother was unable to appear. He also revealed that his family were not in fact d'Urbervilles at all, but from a line of Stokes who had simply appropriated an unused title as their own. Though the young man made her vaguely uncomfortable, Tess chatted politely for a while, then took her leave—unaware that she had left her host enamored and intrigued.

Thus the thing began. . . . She was doomed to be seen and marked and coveted that day by the wrong man, and not by a certain other man, the right and desired one in all respects.

Days later, Tess received a letter, ostensibly from Mrs. d'Urberville—but actually written by Alec—inviting her to come and manage the d'Urberville's fowl farm. At her parents' urging, she agreed to go.

For weeks Tess labored at the d'Urberville farm, all the while hounded by the infatuated Alec. At every opportunity, he tried to force himself upon her. She held off his advances—until one night when she accepted his offer for a ride home. On the way, Tess fell asleep; she was still deep in slumber when Alec veered off the main path. When she awakened, they were lost in a dark fog deep in the forest. Out of fright and exhaustion, Tess finally succumbed to Alec's passion.

Soon afterwards, Tess learned that she was pregnant. Ashamed, she returned home and recounted what had happened. Her mother, only mildly shocked, was disappointed when Tess told her she was not going to marry Alec. Tess spent most of that winter indoors to hide her swelling belly. Then, after the child was born, she returned to work in the fields.

Just a few months after its birth, Tess's baby died. She tried to give it a Christian burial, in spite of the fact that it hadn't been baptized.

The sorrows of the past two years had taken their toll. Longing to start a new life away from her heartless parents, Tess took a job as a milkmaid in Talbothay, a village to the south. Once she had left home, she became more and more hopeful that she could put the past behind her.

She settled comfortably into her new position, boarding with a dairyman, his family, and three other milkmaids, Marian, Izzy and Retty. Though the male hands good-naturedly teased Tess, she ignored them all.

Then one day, Angel Clare, a fellow farmworker, came to call on Tess. She recognized instantly that Angel was intelligent, educated—and something of a dreamer. He was also unimpressed by religious dogma and saw nothing special in Tess's d'Urberville heritage. He told her that he was apprenticing at the dairy in order to someday establish a farm of his own. Hearing of his high aspirations, "Tess seemed to regard Angel Clare as an intelligence rather than as a man."

The three other dairymaid boarders were fascinated with Angel, and talked about him constantly. Tess, for her part, tried to persuade Angel that any of the three would make a worthier companion than herself. Angel, however, was captivated by Tess; and despite her protests and lack of formal education, he found her "an exceedingly novel, fresh, and interesting specimen of womankind."

One day when Tess and Angel were alone, he took her by the arms and pulled her close to him. She was at once pleased and distraught; the experience with Alec was still too near the surface, and she was afraid to tell Angel of her past. Angel sensed her discomfort. After apologizing, he reprimanded himself for allowing his feelings to overcome his judgment, and left.

But Angel soon returned to ask Tess to marry him. At first she hesitated. Though she loved him, she felt she could never be worthy of him. Nevertheless, after much persuasion, Tess agreed to marry Angel on New Year's Eve.

But as the marriage date drew nearer, she fell into despair. How could she reveal her secret and still keep Angel's love? A few weeks before the wedding, Tess resolved to tell Angel about her past. Since she could not bring herself to confront him in person, she wrote him a letter and slid it under the door of his room. She was puzzled the next day when Angel, cheery as usual, said nothing about the letter.

Finally the day of the wedding arrived. Still guilt-ridden and baffled by Angel's reaction to her confession, Tess went to his room. There she found the letter, unopened—still jammed under the carpet near the door, just as she had left it. Panicking, Tess tried again to confess her secret to Angel, but he put her off; they could trade confessions after the wedding, he said. So the simple ceremony took place as planned, and the newlyweds left for their honeymoon at the old d'Urberville family manor.

During dinner that night, Angel announced that it was time to set the record straight: He had earlier had an encounter with a prostitute in London. Relieved beyond measure that his confession was so similar to hers, Tess related the events that had marred her own past. But to her utter dismay, Angel—the Angel whom she had always known as so generous and charitable—would not forgive her. "Forgiveness does not apply to the case!" said her new husband. "You were one person; now you are another." Beneath his layers of kindness and generosity, Angel was, in fact, a moralizing hypocrite. He could not love someone who had proven to be so different from the pure and innocent young girl he had imagined.

To avoid a scandal, Angel refused to accept a divorce. At last, he gave Tess some money and sent her away with the hope that they might reconcile at a future time.

Angel's family, waiting eagerly to meet his bride, was naturally disappointed when he returned home alone. He explained that his plan was to open a farm in Brazil and gave them the impression that his wife would stay with her family until she could join him there.

Meanwhile, at her home a few miles away, Tess, feigning that she was happily married and would soon join her husband in South America, turned over half the money Angel had given her to her family and left in search of employment. A letter from Marian, one of the Talbothay milkmaids, informed her of a job on the Flintcomb Ash farm—a place as bleak and formidable as its name. The labor there turned out to be brutal; but worse, at Flintcomb Ash, Tess discovered that after rejecting her, Angel had asked Marian's friend Izzy to accompany him to Brazil. This revelation shattered any hope for a reconciliation.

On her way into town one day, Tess passed by a large crowd gathered to hear a preacher. The preacher's voice was a familiar one: it was Alec d'Urberville! Alec had apparently repented of his predations and become a barnyard preacher. Tess hurried away, but not before Alec had sighted her.

Not long afterwards, Alec showed up at Flintcomb Ash. Converted to Christianity, the preacher had come to an understanding of his moral obligation; now his wish was to wed the woman he had dishonored. Tess begged him to leave; she was already married. But Alec insisted that she forget about her estranged husband and marry him instead. Following months of Alec's vows and visits, Tess wrote a last impassioned letter to Angel, imploring him to come back or send for her before something regrettable happened.

In the meantime, Tess learned that her parents had taken ill, and once again she returned home. Life there became progressively hopeless. First, her father died; then the lease expired and the family was turned out of their house. Resolved in his pursuit of Tess, Alec proposed that the family stay at his estate. She initially rejected his offer, but facing the prospect of being homeless, she relented. Once she was installed at the d'Urberville estate, Alec convinced Tess to marry him.

Meanwhile, Angel had made his way home, sick and weak from the hardships he had suffered in Brazil. Deeply moved by the pleas in Tess's letter, he was now determined to find her and make amends. When he found her, however, Tess greeted him with sobs. "It is too late," she told him. Alec "has won me back to him."

When the confused and painful exchange was over, Alec angrily inquired about Angel's visit. Tess turned and rebuked him bitterly: "You have torn my life all to pieces. My sin will kill him and not me. O God I can bear this no longer." Alec's only response was to mock her, cursing Angel to her face. At this, Tess seized a knife, thrust it into his chest, and ran from the house.

" . . . I have killed him!" Tess confessed when she reached Angel's side. "I have done it—I don't know how. Still I owed it to 'ee and to myself, Angel." Embracing desperately, they took a vow never to part again.

Fleeing into the woods, the couple came to an abandoned house, where they remained for five days. At last, in quiet and seclusion, they found the bliss that had so long eluded them. On the sixth day they moved northward to Stonehenge. But feeling that her fate was closing around her, Tess made Angel take a vow: For her sake, should anything happen, he should marry her younger sister Liza Lu. Angel promised to abide by her wish.

The next morning, Tess was arrested.

She was sentenced to hang for the murder of Alec d'Urberville. From atop a hill, Angel and Liza Lu watched as a black flag was raised, signaling that Tess's worldly trials were over.

Commentary:

Like many of Hardy's works, this novel was publicly rejected due to its dark and sensual themes. Hardy eventually turned to poetry, forsaking novels entirely.

The plot of *Tess* is built around an indiscretion. At first it appears the author condemns Tess for her act and sides with Angel Clare, whose very name connotes virtue. However, as the story progresses the reader is led to feel that Tess is the one who has been ill-treated by the "monstrously cruel," self-righteous Angel. This growing sympathy for Tess, along with the portrayal of Alec as a scheming, sadistic predator, leaves Tess somewhat justified in her killing the man who has destroyed her life. Indeed, afterward, she is granted a brief measure of happiness with Angel. But the author never quite condones her crime, and in the end justice prevails as Tess is punished for what she has done.

Personal Notes:

<u>*Personal Notes:*</u>

COMPACT

Classics®

LIBRARY #3: People, Places and Times
the drama of history

All the world's a stage, and its people merely players. . . wrote William Shakespeare in "As You Like It." And the bard had a point. History seems to display much of both Shakespeare's literary and casting skills, and his flair for the dramatic.

People, Places and Times offers you living, breathing, colorful casts of characters, changes of scenery, and dramatizations that make history real, vital, and relevant. This collection of book summaries starts out with the spotlight focused on current dramas—with all their heroes, villains, and chanting choruses. A Kaffir Boy from apartheid South Africa tells the story of his struggle, along with a defecting Soviet MiG pilot and a British traveler who follows the footsteps of Marco Polo.

Then the scene shifts—to highlight crucial and colorful regional subplots. And for the final act, we go back in time to recorded history's earliest cradles, until we have experienced at least a sizeable fragment of what has gone before.

Finally led full-circle back to the world we know today, we find ourselves better able to frame more coherent visions for the next act in the ever-unfolding drama of history.

The actors are waiting in the wings; the props are in place. So, part the curtains, and let the play begin!

The Stages of Mankind—colorful theatres of history

Changing Backdrops—in search of the "best of times"

Immortal Voices—words from history that live on

WHAT IS HISTORY?

by E.H. Carr, Random House, New York, N.Y., 1961

Author/historian Edward Hallett Carr was born in London in 1892 and educated at Trinity College, Cambridge. His collection of essays titled **What Is History?** was published in 1961. Now considered a classic, it is a work invaluable to anyone willing to gaze beyond what previous generations regarded as "inherently historical."

French philosopher Voltaire once defined history as "a pack of tricks played upon the dead by the living." Carr is slightly more kind, suggesting instead that history, in fact, is "the perspective of historians," a perspective which is in a constant state of transformation. "When we attempt to answer the question, What is history?" he writes, "our answer, consciously or unconsciously, reflects our own position in time, and . . . the society in which we live." The just-give-me-the-facts stance—of 19th-century historians, for example, often saved them from thinking for themselves. Though this no-nonsense viewpoint at least encourages the historian to get the facts straight before plunging into the realms of interpretation, it also eventually runs straight up against the next big question: "*Which* facts?" In effect, "Not all facts about the past are historical facts, or are treated as such by the historian." So, asks Carr, What facts *will* we select to enshrine as valid "historical" facts? In *fact,* is there *any* way to discern the existence of *one* authentic, solid, irrefutable, "backbone" of historical fact?

No, replies Carr; there is not. By the second half of the twentieth century, the factual backbone of 19th-century history had come under close scrutiny—and relegated to the status of a mirage. "History" was found to be, in effect, *the creation of the persons writing it;* and our notions of truth as shaped by the careful arrangement of selected "facts." Historians must inevitably sift among an infinity of facts to choose those he will pass along. He must interpret and judge from the very beginning. All history, then, is "subjective."

"This element of interpretation enters into every facet of history," notes Carr. "Our picture has been pre-selected and predetermined for us, not so much by accident as by people who were consciously or unconsciously imbued with a particular view and thought the facts which supported that view worth preserving."

"What had gone wrong [in the 19th century]," Carr continues, "was the belief . . . that facts speak for themselves and that we cannot have too many facts . . . " As historian Benedetto Croce cogently observes, these "fact-fetish" historians fail to grasp the point that "All history is 'contemporary history' . . . Essentially [we look at] the past through the eyes of the present and in the light of its problems . . . " Or in other words of another con-temporary historian, Michael Oakeshott, "History is the historian's experience. It is 'made' by nobody save the historian . . . "

Carr finally puts all these arguments into one compact capsule: "The facts of history never come to us 'pure' . . . : they are always refracted through the mind of the recorder."

And the message here to the reader is equally to the point: "Study the historian before you begin to study the facts. [Remember that] by and large, the historian will get the kind of facts he wants." Of course "the duty of the historian to respect his/her facts is not exhausted by the obligation to see that [the] facts are accurate. He must seek to bring into the picture all known or knowable facts relevant, in one sense or another, to the theme on which he is engaged and to the interpretation proposed."

If this rule is not taken into account, Carr insists, the historian will likely fall into one of two historical heresies: The "scissors-and-paste history," where history is "a child's box of letters with which we can spell any word we please," or the heresy of propaganda, where the historian warps facts to suit a ruling party. "Either you write scissors-and-paste history without meaning or significance; or you write propaganda or historical fiction, and merely use facts of the past to embroider a kind of writing which has nothing to do with history." Hence, what the historian must do, Carr avers, is as follows: *The historian starts with a provisional selection of facts and a provisional interpretation in the light of which that selection has been made—by others as well as by himself. As he works, both the interpretation and the selection and ordering of facts undergo subtle and perhaps partly unconscious changes through the reciprocal action of one or the other. And this reciprocal action also involves reciprocity between present and past, since the historian is part of the present and the facts belong to the past. The historian and the facts of history are necessary to one another. The historian without his facts is rootless and futile; the facts without their historian are dead and meaningless.* So how does Carr finally answer the question *What is history?* In essence he replies that there is *no* final answer. He sees "good" or "true" history as a dynamic, evolving relationship; as "a continuous process of interaction between the historian and his facts, an unending dialogue between the present and the past."

Now Carr addresses the roles of society and the individual: *As soon as we are born the world gets to work on us and transforms us . . . into social units. Every human being at every stage of history or pre-history is born into a society and from his earliest years is molded by that society . . . Both language and environment help to determine the character of his thought; his earliest ideas come to him from others, [as] the individual apart from society would be both speechless and mindless. The lasting fascination of the Robinson Crusoe myth is due to its attempt to imagine an individual independent of society. The attempt breaks down. Robinson is not an abstract individual, but an Englishman . . . ; he carries his Bible with him and prays to his tribal God. The myth quickly bestows upon him his Man Friday; and the building of a new society begins.*

"We shall arrive at no real understanding either of the past or of the present if we attempt to operate with the concept of an abstract individual standing outside society," Carr insists. "Civilized man, like primitive man, is molded by society just as effectively as society is molded by him. You can no more have the egg without the hen than you can have the hen without the egg." In a few words, no one can stand completely outside his or her own society.

The effects of *individual* experience are equally as biasing as those of social experience. The common-sense view of history spoken of earlier treats history as "written by individuals about individuals. This view was certainly taken and encouraged by nineteenth-century liberal historians, and is not in substance incorrect. But it now seems oversimplified and inadequate, and we need to probe deeper . . . The men whose actions the historian studies were not isolated individuals acting in a vacuum: they acted in the context, and under the impulse of a past society."

[The individual historian is merely] another dim [human] figure trudging along in another part of the procession. And as the procession winds along, swerving now to the right and now to the left, and sometimes doubling back on itself, the relative positions of different parts of the procession are constantly changing, so that it may make perfectly good sense to say, for example, that we are nearer today to the Middle Ages than were our great-grandfathers a century ago or that the age of Caesar is nearer to us than the age of Dante. New vistas, new angles of vision, constantly appear as the procession—and the historian with it—moves along.

In essence, the historian, as a *product* of history, is an integral *part* of the history he is recording. Taking these views even further, Carr writes: "Great history is written precisely when the historian's vision of the past is illuminated by insights into the problems of the present"; there exists an interactive, ongoing dynamic relationship between the historian's *present* and the *past*. Carr's purpose here is to validate two important truths: "First . . . you cannot fully understand or appreciate the work of the historian unless you have first grasped the standpoint from which he/she approached it; second, that standpoint is itself rooted in a social and historical background."

To demonstrate how easily history can be twisted to the individual historian's unique pen and the rapidity by which historians can change their personal points of view—and through their writings change not only one society or social order, but a succession of dif-

ferent orders—Carr cites the example of the great and copious German historian Meinecke, who covered a lengthy series of "revolutionary and catastrophic changes in the fortunes of his country":

Here we have in effect three different Meineckes, each the spokesman of a different historical epoch, and each speaking through one of his three major works. The Meinecke of **Weltburgerthum and Nationalstaat,** *published in 1907, confidently sees the realization of German national ideals in the Bismarckian Reich and—like many nineteenth century thinkers . . . —identifies nationalism with the highest form of universals . . . The Meinecke of* **Die Idee der Straatsrason,** *published in 1925, speaks with the divided and bewildered mind of the Weimar Republic: The world of politics has become an arena of unresolved [moral] conflict external to politics . . . Finally, the Meinecke of* **Die Entstehung des Historismus,** *published in 1936, when he had been swept from his academic honors by the Nazi flood, utters a cry of despair, rejecting a historicism which appears to recognize that whatever is, is right, and tossing uneasily between the historical relative and a superrational absolute. Last of all, when Meinecke in his old age had seen his country succumb to a military defeat more crushing than that of 1918, he relapsed helplessly in* **Die Deutsche Katastrophe** *of 1946 into the belief in a history at the mercy of blind, inexorable change . . . What interests the historian is the way in which Meinecke reflects back three—or even four—successive, and sharply contrasted, periods of present time into the historical past.*

The point is that "it is not merely that [history] is in flux. The historian himself is in flux. [So], if the philosopher is right in telling us that we cannot step into the same river twice, it is perhaps equally true, and for the same reason, that two books cannot be written by the same historian." It follows that "the historian who is most conscious of his own situation is also more capable of transcending it . . . more capable of appreciating the essential nature of the differences between his own society and outlook and those of other periods and other countries . . ."

Hence Carr suggests to any student of history to first study the historian, "study his historical and social environment." *The historian, being an individual, is also a product of history and of society; and it is in this twofold light that the student of history must learn to regard him.*

And so, Carr's question *What is history?* must be answered—not once, but every time a reader's eyes flow over the words and accounts of society's historians, present past or future. "History cannot be written unless the historian can achieve some kind of contact with the mind of those about whom he/she is writing." Once that connection has been established, one can truly begin to understand past societies and individuals. For "the function of the historian," Carr concludes, "is neither to love the past nor to emancipate himself from the past, but to master and understand it as the key to the understanding of the present."

ROOTS

by Alex Haley, Dell Publishing, New York, N.Y., 1974

"Alex Haley's taking us back through time to the village of his ancestors is an act of faith and courage," says James Baldwin of Haley's extended family record, "but this book is also an act of love, and it is this which makes it haunting. . . . It suggests with great power how each of us . . . can't help but be the vehicle of the history which produced us."

The 200-year saga of *Roots* certainly compels us to listen to the chronicles of modern-day African-American families, to grieve for the brutal mistreatment of the slaves, whose lives we relive through Haley's feeling narrative, and to rejoice in the hard-won triumph of Kunta Kinte's descendants. Ultimately, *Roots* confers upon all non-Native Americans, as the children and grandchildren of immigrants from throughout the world, a renewed appreciation of our own progenitors and a strengthened sense of both our own individual roots and identities and the common links of humanity that unite us.

In a Mandinka village upriver from the coast of Gambia, West Africa, a manchild was born to Omoro and Binta Kinte. The parents named the boy Kunta Kinte to designate him as a member of the Kinte family who would become a proud and honorable hunter, provider, and tribesman.

Filled with love for his firstborn, Omoro carried Kunta into the brush, lifted him toward the stars, and uttered the traditional words of blessing and oblation: *Behold—the only thing greater than yourself.*

Raised to take his place as a village leader, Kunta grew quickly. At fifteen he had finished the "manhood training" required of Mandinka boys and emerged from his initiation rites as an accomplished hunter, tireless, dignified, courageous, and well versed in his tribal lore.

Kunta thus began to assume the responsibilities of a young bachelor in the village. After a morning prayer to Allah in the mosque, he would inspect various huts to ensure their cleanliness. He also farmed his own rice patch, which contributed to his family's supply.

Fruitful at all of his tasks, Kunta felt most virile when he took his turn as a village sentry, watching to warn the people if *toubob*, or white men, appeared. Tragically, however, one day as he went to the forest to search for wood to build a drum, Kunta himself was captured by the *toubob*. Beaten senseless, stripped naked, and chained, he was carried away to the beach. Then, with his head shaven, he was loaded along with hundreds of other captives onto what seemed a huge canoe, with a vault where people were crowded in the darkness onto small shelves. As the ship lurched into deeper waters, Kunta knew he would never again see his home.

During the four long months that followed, the captives were taunted and beaten, fed wretched food, and left for days to swelter in the hold. Enduring many sicknesses as well as the ever-present stench of death, Kunta only vowed more deeply to always remember who he was—the son of the Kintes, a circumcised Moslem, and "mighty Mandinka man."

When the boat finally touched land, Kunta was appalled to see more throngs of *toubob*. Even worse, were those laboring among them who possessed the skin of Africans yet dressed and talked like the *toubob*.

Kunta was poked, spat upon, and whipped. Finally he was sold to work in the plantation fields, where his only thought was of escape. One day, he finally ran away. *His muscles, so long unused, screamed with pain, but the cold, rushing air felt good upon his skin, and he had to stop himself from whooping out loud with pleasure of feeling so wildly free.*

Kunta was soon recaptured. But the exhilaration of this short burst of freedom impelled him to flee the fields again and again and again. After his fourth flight, two white men finally cut off half his foot. Half delirious from shock and blood loss, Kunta promised himself that "he would take revenge—and he would escape again. Or he would die."

Kunta was then relocated to a new plantation, where a fierce and gentle slave woman named Bell nursed him slowly back to health. Although he would never condone the heathen ways of the pork-eating slaves around him, Kunta now knew that, like them, he would have to learn some of the *toubob's* words in order to survive. One word "in particular was extremely puzzling to him . . . What, he wondered, was a 'nigger'."

As Kunta began to learn the new language, he came to value his associations with the other slaves. He also found himself drawn closer to middle-aged Bell, though he retained the conviction that "no matter what, he must never become anything like these black people." Eventually they "jumped the broom" together in a slave-sanctioned gesture of marriage. And when their daughter was born, Kunta, with "Africa pumping in his veins," hobbled out under the stars and, baring the "infant's small black face to the heavens . . . spoke aloud to her in Mandinka: *Behold, the only thing greater than yourself!*" He named her Kizzy, which in Mandinka meant "you stay put"—referring to his wish that she should never be sold away.

But Kizzy did not stay put. Her downfall was ordained when her parents broke the great decree in slave-holding society: they allowed her to learn to read. Thus, at sixteen, when Kizzy was caught trying to forge a traveling pass for the young runaway slave with whom she had fallen in love, she was promptly sold. On her first night at the new plantation, she was visited by her new "massa," and was soon heavy with child.

Even though her baby was not the deep beautiful black of her father and mother, Kizzy adored little George. Proud of her ancestry and determined to never let the memories of her father slip away, she taught her son everything African that she could remember. "Dat river is de

Kamby Bolongo," she would tell him, just as her father had told her. "An' dat ol' guitar, dat dere's a *ko* in African . . . You always 'member dat you grandaddy's name be *Kintey!*" And George did remember. "I gwine tell my chilluns 'bout gran'-pappy," he promised his mother.

Years later, as an adult, George was put in charge of raising and matching his "Massa Lea's" gamecocks; ever after he was referred to as "Chicken George." And soon the gifted George himself became his master's prize possession. He ultimately married a slave named Matilda, with whom he had eight children. And after each new birth, the family would gather around to hear their father relate the story of his noble grandaddy: *He were a African dat say he name "Kunta Kinte." He call a guitar a ko, an' a river "Kamby Bolongo," an' lot mo' things wid African names. He say he was choppin' a tree to make his li'l brother a drum when it was fo' mens come up an' grabbed 'im from behin'. Den a ship brung 'im 'crost de big water to a place call 'Naplis. An' he had runned off fo' times when he try to kill dem dat cotched 'im an' dey cut half his foot off!*

The recitation of these African stories took on even greater meaning as George's master fell upon hard times and spoke of selling off his slaves. But before any selling could take place, George was lost in a wager over a cockfight and was sent to England to train roosters for a British master. The remaining family—except for Kizzy, who by then was too old to "fetch a decent slavin' price"—was sold to a nearby plantation owner.

Tom, the fourth son of Chicken George and Matilda, was now the head of the family. He learned the blacksmith trade, a skill which allowed him to travel to various plantations where he was paid for his labor. Tom saved every penny that the master allowed him to keep.

It was on one of his "smithin' rounds" that Tom met a half-Indian slave girl named Irene, with whom he promptly fell in love. When they were married, Tom's kind master, Murray, bought Irene and moved her into her husband's cabin.

Meanwhile, after nearly three years in England, Chicken George returned home with the freedom papers that his master had promised him. When he arrived, he found his wife and family gone and his mamma, Kizzy, dead. Locating his family's new plantation, though he longed to stay there with them, he found that it was unlawful for a free black man to live in slave quarters. George thus headed north to find work so that he could buy his family's freedom.

Back on the plantation, Irene, who often overheard conversations in the master's house, became enthralled by accounts of someone "up nawth called massa Lincoln," who wanted to set the slaves free. Later, on the day they learned that Lincoln had been elected President, Tom enlisted as a blacksmith for the Southern cavalry. War had begun.

The Southerners were jubilant; there was steady talk of "kickin' those Yankees clear back to England . . . !" Such talk nearly crushed the slaves' hopes; freedom was a long way off.

Then, on New Years Day, 1863, Matilda dashed from the Master's house to the cabin, shrieking, " . . . It jes come over de railroad tele- graph wire Pres'dent Lincoln done signed 'Mancipation Proclamation' dat set us free!" A wild celebration broke out. Tom's nephew raced to the chicken coop, shouting, "Ol' hens quit layin', you's free!—and so's ME!"

However, the family's jubilation was short lived. Without provisions, they soon realized that they could go nowhere until Chicken George returned. Within a week, they were back sweat- ing in the fields.

But finally, one happy afternoon, Chicken George swept in rambling on about a settlement in western Tennessee that needed families to build the town. And before long the family was on their way to Tennessee, "where de land so black an' rich, you plant a pig's tail an' a hog'll grow."

The land truly was rich, and, at last, they were together. Tom, who took on the last name "Murray," after his former master, quickly estab- lished himself as the town's blacksmith. And now unimpeded, he prospered. Tom and Irene's daughter, Cynthia, married a hard-working and highly respected young black man named Will Palmer, and soon the couple were blessed with a young child named Bertha. Once again the fami- ly—who had by now built both a church and a general store—assembled to hear the stories of "dat ol' African Kintey . . . "

Well-versed in her heritage, Bertha grew into a bright young woman who went to college to become a teacher. She fell in love with a young man named Simon Alexander Haley, and after their marriage, she gave birth to a baby boy—a boy whom his parents named Alex.

Young Alex Haley, always hungry for sto- ries about "the old days," spent more time with Grandma Cynthia and Grandpa Will than with anyone else. He listened intently to each tale about "ol' African Kintey."

As an adult, Haley became an accom- plished writer. For thirty years he traced his family's past; finally he traveled to Juffure, his ancestral village in Gambia, where he studied the language and spoke with a *griot*, or storyteller. In stunned silence, Haley listened to the old man as he recited the history of a Moslem holy man, Kairaba Kunta Kinte, who, by a second wife, Yaisa, over two centuries earlier, had begotten a son named Omoro. Omoro, at "thirty rains," took to wife a Mandinka maiden named Binta Kebba, and they begat four sons, Kunta, Lamin, Suwadu, and Madi. Then one day their oldest son, Kunta, "went away from his village to chop wood . . . and he was never seen again . . . "

This old village griot, Haley wrote, "had no way in the world to know that he had just echoed what I had heard all through my boy- hood years on my grandma's front porch in Henning, Tennessee . . . "

Tracing the steps of his abducted forefa- ther, reliving the long voyage from West Africa to Maryland, the author Alex Haley had unearthed his roots. Even after the passing of seven generations, he was able to introduce to the world the wrenching and wonderful story of his forbearers—the family of Kunta Kinte.

THE HIDING PLACE

by Corrie ten Boom, with John and Elizabeth Sherrill, Chosen Books, Washington Depot, Connecticut, 1971

The Dutch survivor of a German extermination camp, Corrie ten Boom (1892 - 1983) inspired countless admirers around the world with her faith- and compassion-promoting "speaking ministry." Her story radiates a faith in God's love and forgiveness that will never die.

❖ ♦ ❖

In January 1937, the ten Boom family celebrated the 100th anniversary of their watch-making business. That happy day, with the threat of war still distant, 45-year-old Corrie, her brother Willem, her father, her sisters Betsie and Nollie, as well as virtually everyone else in the city of Haarlem joined in the festivities at the *Beje*—as the ten Boom house was called. After the party, Corrie went upstairs to think: *I didn't know it then . . . that there was any future to prepare for in a life as humdrum and predictable as mine. I only knew as I lay in my bed at the top of the house that certain moments from long ago stood out in focus against the blur of years.*

Corrie recollected how as a young girl her father had often read aloud to them, and how once she had been particularly baffled by the words of a psalm: *Thy word is a lamp unto my feet, and a light unto my path . . . Thou art my hiding place and my shield.* The words made Corrie wonder, "What kind of hiding place? What was there to hide from?"

Although life had been exciting and happy in the Beje, Corrie learned over the years to accept the fact that she—like Betsie—would never wed. She had been devastated in her youth when Karel, the man she had loved, married another woman. "God loves Karel, even more than you do," her father had tried to comfort her, "and if you ask Him, He will give you His love for this man, a love nothing can prevent, nothing can destroy. Whenever we cannot love in the old, human way, Corrie, God can give us the perfect way."

Corrie later learned that her father's words had given her "the secret that would open far darker rooms than this—places where there was not, on a human level, anything to love at all."

A few years after the ten Boom's anniversary party, these "darker rooms" became reality when the Germans invaded Holland. The ten Booms had long used the ample rooms of the Beje to house many of Haarlem's Jews. As Willem, a minister, became active in the Dutch underground, he helped his father and sisters aid their Jewish friends. The ten Booms were able to meet the many needs of their boarders, including the ration cards that Corrie obtained illegally. The underground even surveyed the Beje to find a "hiding place" for Jews in case of a raid and then built an elaborate secret chamber leading to Corrie's bedroom.

When the dreaded raid finally came, Corrie was in bed with the flu. "So you're the ring leader!" a Gestapo agent said, bursting into her room—where, moments earlier, Corrie had groggily looked on as the Jewish boarders scrambled to safety. "Tell me now, where are you hiding the Jews?" Admitting nothing, Corrie was led downstairs where another Gestapo agent beat her and demanded, "Where is your secret room?"

"Lord Jesus," Corrie cried. The Gestapo agent flew into a rage. "If you say that name again I'll kill you! . . . If you won't talk, that skinny one will"; then he began clubbing Betsie.

Before the day had ended, all the ten Booms were arrested. The next day they were transported to a Gestapo "court" in the Hague, where Corrie and her sisters were separated from their father. "God be with you!" Corrie called to him as she and her sisters were led away by a matron. "And with you, my daughters," he replied.

In the women's prison at Scheveningen, Corrie and her two sisters were assigned to separate cells. As the months wore on she learned that Willem, Nollie, and several of the others had been released. But not long after receiving this happy news, a letter from Nollie arrived: "I have news that is very hard to write you. Father survived his arrest by only ten days. He is now with the Lord . . . "

That same month in 1944 Corrie finally received a hearing. Led to a hut where she met her interrogator, Corrie was surprised when the man treated her kindly and allowed her to speak about the Bible. The following day, after again calling her to his hut, the man confessed, "I could not sleep last night, thinking about the book where you have read such different ideas. What else does it say in there?" Corrie replied, "It says . . . that a Light has come into this world, so that we need no longer walk in the dark. Is there darkness in your life, Lieutenant?" After a long pause, he sighed. "There is great darkness," he told her. "I cannot bear the work I do . . . I wear a uniform, I have a certain authority over those under me. But I am in prison, dear lady from Haarlem, a prison stronger than this one."

A few weeks later, the lieutenant arranged for Corrie to see her family under the pretext of a reading of her father's will. She learned that Willem's son Kik had been arrested and deported into Germany. Still, she was relieved to learn that some of their Jewish boarders were safe, and she was grateful to receive a small Bible from Nollie.

This Bible proved to be a source of comfort during the terrible months ahead. Not long after her reunion with her family, Scheveningen was evacuated. In the crowd of women herded into a train car, Corrie was reunited with Betsie—a blessing for which Corrie was immensely grateful. "The four months in Scheveningen had been our first separation in fifty-two years," she later wrote. "It seemed to me that I could bear whatever happened with Betsie beside me."

When the train stopped, the ten Boom sisters found that they were still in Holland, at Vught, "a concentration camp for political prisoners." Malnourished and exhausted, the women were questioned, fingerprinted, and finally "marched along a path between twisted rolls of barbed wire and through a wide gate into a compound of low tin-roofed barracks." Locked in their new quarters, Corrie asked her sister, "How long will it take?" Betsie answered, "Perhaps many years. But what better way could there be to spend our lives? . . . Corrie, if people can be taught to hate, they can be taught to love! We must find the way, you and I, no matter how long it takes . . . "

Betsie's capacity for love constantly amazed her sister. Although Corrie frequently raged silently at her German captors, Betsie forgave and sought to understand everyone, even the Dutch informant who had facilitated the raid on the Beje. "I . . . pray for him whenever his name comes into my mind," Betsie explained one night. "How dreadfully he must be suffering!"

As the months in Vught slowly passed, Corrie learned that "the usual prison term for ration-card offenders—as she and Betsie had been designated by the Germans—was six months," and she began to count the days until their release. They were not discharged on that date, however; instead they were sent on an overcrowded freight train to Ravensbruck—a "women's extermination camp" in Germany.

Ravensbruck, for the few who were not sent to the crematorium, would be far worse than Vught. Not only were the women herded naked into the shower room past jeering S.S. men, but they also had to submit to the "recurrent humiliation of medical inspection," backbreaking labor, and the nightly crowding onto reeking, flea-infested straw-covered platforms.

Although she had been searched upon arrival at the camp, Corrie had managed to retain her Bible. The Gospel proved to be the only solace for the ten Boom sisters and their fellow prisoners, who held covert nightly religious services in the barracks. As Betsie's faith multiplied, however, her health deteriorated amid daily beatings and inadequate food. Only after she had contracted a blistering fever did the guards permit her to receive medical treatment and to be reassigned to the "knitting brigade," which worked inside the barracks. Nonetheless, the winter chill, which was extreme even indoors, further weakened Betsie, and she was eventually moved to the hospital.

Mercifully, a hospital worker arranged for Corrie to spend one final moment with her beloved sister, who, appearing as "a carving in old yellow ivory," lay naked on a cot. Corrie prayed, in gratitude: *For there lay Betsie, her eyes closed as if in sleep, her face full and young. The care lines, the grief lines, the deep hollows of hunger and disease were simply gone. In front of me was the Betsie of Haarlem, happy and at peace.*

Three days after Betsie's death, Corrie was unexpectedly called into the admission barracks and given a slip of paper that read

CERTIFICATE OF DISCHARGE. Stunned, Corrie was presented with new clothing and a railway pass, before being taken into a room for a physical examination. But then came another turn: "Edema," the doctor snapped as he studied her feet. "Hospital!" As a guard led Corrie away, he explained, "They only release you if you're in good condition."

The hospital turned out to be "the most savage place yet." She recalled: *Around me were survivors of a prison train which had been bombed on its way here. The women were horribly mutilated and in terrible pain, but at each moan two of the nurses jeered and mimicked the sounds.* Corrie tended to the wounded—finding bedpans and presenting one particularly sensitive woman with her prized Bible—until the day came when the doctor finally approved Corrie's discharge and she boarded the first of many trains on her long journey home. "It was New Year's Day, 1945," and Corrie now recalled with wonder a few of the optimistic words Betsie had murmured the day she died: "By the first of the year, we will be out of prison!" She recalled more of her sister's final remarks: "We must tell people, Corrie. We must tell them what we learned."

Reunited with those who remained of her family, Corrie began to organize meetings; she would see that Betsie's dream of "a home here in Holland where those who had been hurt could learn to live again unafraid" was realized. Following one of these meetings, a wealthy woman offered her estate, Bloemendaal, to serve as just such a home. Later, after Holland was liberated, Corrie donated the Beje to widely-hated former Dutch informants for the Gestapo, while Bloemendaal opened its doors to the Gestapo's victims.

In the years following the war, Corrie ten Boom traveled the world, raising contributions for Bloemendaal and speaking about Betsie's life and faith. Of all the countries that Corrie visited, Germany was the country she perceived to be most in need.

Speaking in Munich once, Corrie recognized the face of one of the S.S. men "who had stood guard at the shower room door in the processing center at Ravensbruck." With no hint of embarrassment, he approached her and said, "How grateful I am for your message, *Fraulein!* To think that, as you say, He has washed my sins away!"

Face to face with one of her captors, Corrie's blood ran cold. "I have become a Christian," he went on. "I know that God has forgiven me for the cruel things I did there, but I would like to hear it from your lips as well. Fraulein," he said, extending his hand, "will you forgive me?"

Corrie, momentarily stunned by the gesture, wrestled with her feelings until a calm came over her. She took his outstretched hand—and in that instant, she said, *a current seemed to pass from me to him, while into my heart sprang a love for this stranger that almost overwhelmed me . . . "I forgive you, brother!" I cried. "With all my heart!"*

ALL THE PRESIDENT'S MEN

by Carl Bernstein and Bob Woodward, Simon and Shuster, New York, N.Y., 1974

All the President's Men is a compelling record of an American president's fall from power. Moreover, it is a fascinating account of two reporters' dogged pursuit of a story which takes them and the country on an unlikely, behind-the-scenes tour of Washington politics and power. As the characters and their illegal activities are paraded before the American public, they come to represent a sort of contemporary Vanity Fair—Washington Style.

Of all Woodward's and Bernstein's carefully groomed sources, it is the enigmatic "Deep Throat" who most adds a human dimension to the scandal. Described simply as a frail, chain-smoking figure whose fatigue registers in his blood-shot eyes, Deep Throat is the book's moral center of gravity, the wise teacher who despairs for the country. It is he who knows, first hand, that the United States is being governed by a band of "not brilliant guys" who will "stop at nothing" to serve their own ends.

❖ ◆ ❖

On the calm Saturday afternoon of June 17, 1972, the city editor of the *Washington Post* was startled to learn that five men, wearing "business suits" and "surgical gloves," had been arrested for burglarizing the Democratic National Committee headquarters in Washington's posh Watergate Complex. Policemen had seized more than $2,000 from the prowlers, along with "a walkie-talkie, 40 rolls of unexposed film, two 35-millimeter cameras, lock picks, pen-size tear-gas guns, and bugging devices . . ."

Post reporter Bob Woodward "snapped awake" the moment the city editor called him to cover the burglary. When he arrived at the newsroom, Woodward learned that he was not the only reporter assigned to the break-in: Carl Bernstein was already on the phone tracking down information on the case. A 28-year-old college drop-out who had the reputation for being able to overpower other reporters, Bernstein had a nose for pushing himself into a good story and getting his byline on it. Neither Bernstein's tactics nor his "counterculture" appearance impressed Woodward, a Yale graduate and a registered Republican.

Woodward had no time to waste worrying about his competitive colleague, and he left for the courthouse to attend the preliminary hearing of the burglary suspects. All of the suspects claimed to be "anti-communists," and three of them were Cuban-American. But the one who most intrigued Woodward was James W. McCord, Jr., who told the judge that he was a security officer for the CIA. "Holy shit," Woodward murmured, and rushed back to the *Post* to write his story. As yet, however, he could not give an "explanation as to why the five suspects would want to bug the Democratic National Committee offices, or whether or not they were working for any other individuals or organizations."

In addition to Woodward's story about the burglary, a piece by Bernstein also appeared in the Sunday *Post*, reporting that four of the suspects "had been involved in anti-Castro activities and were also said to have CIA connections." That same morning the Associated Press reported that McCord had served as the security coordinator of the Committee for the Re-election of the President (CRP).

"What the hell do you think it means?" Woodward asked Bernstein. Bernstein shrugged; he knew nothing about McCord or his involvement in the break-in, but this new facet of the case suggested that it was time they pooled their resources. By the end of the day, the reporters had a profile of McCord, an ex-FBI agent and former CIA officer. He had apparently worked full-time for the CRP, despite a public denial issued that day by former Attorney General John Mitchell.

After assimilating this information, Woodward began typing the day's story. Bernstein studied the crude draft and went back to his desk to rewrite it. Within a short time they had established an efficient work pattern: "Woodward, the faster writer, would do a first draft" and Bernstein would later rework it. Often they worked through the night, all the while maintaining individual master phone-number lists, which they used to unearth leads and document their facts. "The working relationship between Bernstein and Woodward" soon developed into a formidable alliance.

Woodward developed a profound respect for the aggressiveness and tenacity that had once made him resent Bernstein. Similarly, Bernstein came to value Woodward's talent for eliciting information from his sources. Indeed, as the months went by, these sources revealed the identities and activities of various high-level CRP executives. Woodward learned that Maurice Stans, "Nixon's chief fund-raiser and CRP finance chairman," had received a check for $25,000 that was later deposited in the bank account of one of the Watergate burglars, suggesting White House involvement in the conspiracy.

Meanwhile, Bernstein pursued his own contacts. A bookkeeper at CRP disclosed that the committee's Finance Counsel, G. Gordon Liddy, had been involved in the conspiracy as well as "Mitchell's principal assistants . . . the top echelon." Another source, Hugh Sloan, former Treasurer of the CRP and the committee's "sacrificial lamb," provided Bernstein with the most damning information of all. Sloan maintained that John Mitchell, while still the Attorney General of the United States, "had authorized the expenditure of campaign funds for apparently illegal activities against the political opposition."

When Mitchell learned that the *Post* planned to run a story linking him to the break-in, he was furious. When Bernstein phoned Mitchell for a reaction, he ranted, "All that crap, you're putting in the paper? It's all been denied." Mitchell then proceeded to threaten the *Post's* publisher Katherine Graham, making it clear that when "the election was over *they* could do almost anything they damned well pleased."

Shocked by Mitchell's outburst, Bernstein called the *Post's* Executive Editor Benjamin Bradlee, who was equally stunned. Bradlee instructed Bernstein to quote Mitchell verbatim, and, in spite of desperate pleas from the CRP's Deputy Press

Director, the *Post* printed the story.

Mitchell's involvement in the conspiracy was soon confirmed by one of Woodward's favorite sources. "Deep Throat"—as the *Post* staff had dubbed the anonymous voice—held a "position in the Executive Branch" of government, and clearly deplored the "switchblade mentality" that permeated Nixon's administration. As Woodward secretly met with Deep Throat in a garage early one morning, he was shocked by the picture of the White House and the CRP that Deep Throat painted. "You can safely bet," Deep Throat told the reporter, "that fifty people worked for the White House and CRP to play games and spy and sabotage and gather intelligence. Some of it is beyond belief." Then Woodward asked if the White House had "been willing to subvert . . . the whole electoral process." Deep Throat just nodded.

During their meeting, Deep Throat warned Woodward that the government wanted "to single out the *Post*. They want to go to court to get your sources." And, sure enough, after the *Post* ran stories denouncing Republican smear tactics and implicating in the conspiracy attorney Donald H. Segretti and Dwight Chapin, Deputy Assistant to the President, the CRP and the White House retaliated. The CRP's Campaign Director issued a statement at a press conference on October 18 charging that the *Post* had used "innuendo," "hypocrisy," and "huge scare headlines" to attack the President and promote Democratic rival George McGovern. Then, on October 25, White House Press Secretary Ron Zeigler accused the newspaper of "shabby journalism" and of a "well conceived and coordinated" effort "to discredit [the] Administration and individuals in it."

"This is the hardest hardball that's ever been played in this town," Bradlee told Woodward and Bernstein. Despite Bradlee's and Graham's steadfast support, the two journalists were occasionally unnerved by the magnitude of the situation in which they had involved themselves. In fact, when they began to connect White House Chief of Staff H.R. Haldeman to the conspiracy, there were times when they actually feared for their lives. Deep Throat, for example, had warned Woodward to "Be careful!" By all accounts, Haldeman was a man who would stop at nothing and who took pride in calling himself "the President's son-of-a-bitch."

Bernstein also felt unsettled by Haldeman, though for very different reasons. At times he wondered if he and Woodward were being set up by unscrupulous sources. "What if Haldeman had never asked for authority over the money," he worried, "or had never exercised his authority."

At this point the reporters made a serious mistake: They had misrepresented a statement that Sloan—always an amiable and reliable source—had made and had then "compounded their mistakes" by over-zealously prejudicing a source at the FBI. As Deep Throat would later point out, their hasty deductions had made everyone feel "sorry" for Haldeman, initiating for the reporters "the worst possible setback."

It wasn't until after Election Day on November 11 that Bernstein found a long-awaited opportunity to meet with Segretti, who confirmed that Chapin received "his orders from Haldeman . . . Everyone is out to crucify me," Segretti added, tearfully, " . . . the White House, the press." Shortly afterward, Bernstein met with a CRP secretary who informed him that John Erlichman, Nixon's Assistant for Domestic Affairs, had met with the conspirators, including Hunt and Liddy, in the Executive Office Building.

In January of the following year, Liddy and McCord were found guilty of various counts of conspiracy. Judge John Sirica, however, noted that he was not satisfied that "all the pertinent facts" had become available and hoped that the upcoming Senate investigation might very well "get to the bottom" of Watergate.

Before the trial began, Woodward and Bernstein collected more incriminating evidence that reached into the highest echelons of the White House. Deep Throat confirmed that, like Mitchell, Charles Colson, Special Counsel to the President, "had direct knowledge" of Watergate. Moreover, the investigators learned "that Hunt and Liddy were being routed information from national-security wiretaps." Infuriated by the Washington *Post* stories, the CRP issued subpoenas for the reporters and their notes.

Although the subpoenas were thrown out of court, the *Post* received another, far more serious threat: *"Everyone's life is in danger,"* Deep Throat told Woodward just before the Senate hearings on Watergate began. Apparently the CIA had bugged both the *Post* building and the reporters' homes, and Nixon, by now a "secretive, distrustful" man, was suffering "fits of . . . depression."

Presumably, the President's indignance and depression did not diminish, for there was even more "rampaging" to come. As the Senate hearings progressed, Presidential Counsel John Dean was fired and Haldeman and Erlichman resigned; the White House was in a state of utter confusion. "It's every man for himself," one source told Woodward, "get a lawyer and blame everyone else."

By the spring of 1974, the House Judiciary Committee had begun investigating the possibility of Nixon's impeachment. The president reportedly possessed taped conversations from the Oval Office—conversations which could prove damaging not only because of their content but also because they had apparently been "tampered with." That spring, many of Nixon's men, including Magruder, Segretti, and Dean, pleaded guilty to various obstruction and conspiracy charges; others—Haldeman, Erlichman, Colson, and Mitchell—were indicted. By now, the entire country spoke of little else but the conspiracy Woodward and Bernstein had uncovered.

President Nixon, under threat of impeachment, resigned his office as President of the United States on August 9, 1974. Although his successor Gerald Ford officially pardoned the deposed President the following year, Nixon's documented participation in illegal efforts to ensure re-election and the subsequent cover-up attempt proved not only to shatter his political career but to tarnish the office of President. As a result of having violated the public's trust and tampering with one of the chief features of democracy—free and open elections—Nixon's involvement in Watergate also placed an element of doubt in the minds of Americans about all successors to the office, a doubt that persists to this day.

OUT OF AFRICA

by Isak Dinesen, Random House, New York, N.Y., 1938

Type of work: Autobiographical recollections

Setting: A coffee plantation in the Ngong Hills, near Nairobi, in the former colony of British East Africa (present-day Kenya)

Prologue:

In 1914, Karen Blixen (1885 - 1962) sailed to British East Africa to marry her Swedish cousin Baron Bror Blixen. When the couple divorced seven years later, Karen remained as manager of the coffee plantation that she and the Baron had jointly owned outside Nairobi. When the coffee market collapsed in 1931, however, she finally had to leave her beloved Ngong Hills. Returning to her native Denmark that year, she compiled her recorded excerpts and published them under the pseudonym Isak Dinesen.

The resulting work, *Out of Africa* is neither novel nor autobiography, but rather a collection of personal essays which vividly reveal the author's great admiration for Africa's people, wildlife and landscape. These individual observations and reminiscences can, in most instances, stand on their own, apart from the larger work. But taken together the writings form an elaborate and intricate mural, with each phrase contributing an indispensable pictorial element. Through Dinesen's eyes, we see the interaction between two very different cultures—the cosmos of the African natives and the world of the European colonists. We discover a land of varied geographical features: lush forests, burning deserts, soaring mountains, and expansive valleys. And we learn of a woman's immense love for a place and its inhabitants, the affinity of an immigrant who has found her spiritual home.

Overview:

Baroness Karen Blixen first met Kamante, the son of one of her squatters, while he was herding his family's goats on the grass plains. Observing the gaunt boy whose legs were covered with sores, Madame Blixen reflected, " . . . He looked extraordinarily small, so that it struck you as a strange thing that so much suffering could be condensed into a single point." After trying unsuccessfully to cure the boy with home remedies, the baroness carried him to a nearby church hospital.

Three months later, Kamante returned to his goats, healed—and converted to Christianity. "I am like you" he beamed, apprising Madame Blixen of his new religion. From then on he remained at her home as a houseboy. It was "as if he took it for granted that now he belonged there."

Kamante shared a unique relationship with the European woman; without her, as he explained, "he should have been dead a long

time ago." He demonstrated his appreciation with a "benevolent, helpful, or perhaps the right word is, forbearing, attitude" towards the baroness. In a particularly touching example of concern for his mistress, he pointed out that the book upon which she was working was not really a book, but rather merely a loose bundle of papers. As evidence, he brought in a copy of *The Odyssey,* announcing, "This is a good book. It hangs together from the one end to the other. Even if you hold it up and shake it strongly, it does not come to pieces . . . But what you write . . . is some here and some there. When the people forget to close the door it blows about . . . It will not be a good book."

Madame Blixen responded to this critique, assuring the boy that "in Europe the people would be able to fix it together." But a few days later she overheard Kamante explaining to the other houseboys that, in Europe, the book Madame Blixen was writing could be "made to stick together, and . . . even made as hard as the Odyssey . . . He himself, however, did not believe it could be made blue."

Kamante was an unusual character, defying many of the traits Karen Blixen attributed to the natives. "Natives have usually very little feelings for animals," noted Madame Blixen, "but Kamante differed from type here, as in other things." It was Kamante who took charge of Lulu, a young bushbuck antelope who, as a fawn, had become a member of the household. Bottle-fed by Kamante, Lulu grew to be a "slim delicately rounded doe, from her nose to her toes unbelievably beautiful . . . On the strength of this great beauty and gracefulness, [she] obtained for herself a commanding position in the house, and was treated with respect by all."

Nevertheless, Lulu was still a wild creature at heart, and one evening she disappeared. A week-long search ended in vain. When Madame Blixen expressed her fear to Kamante that Lulu had fallen prey to the leopards by the river, Kamante reassured her: "Lulu is not dead. But she is married." A few days later the two watched as Lulu returned to the house to eat the maize Kamante had left out for her. Delighted, the baroness wrote:

It also seemed to me that the free union between my house and the antelope was a rare, honorable thing. Lulu came in from the wild world to show that we were on good terms with it, and she made my house one with the African landscape, so that nobody could tell where the one stopped and the other began.

Equally important to Karen Blixen were those visitors who brought news from the outside world, news "good or bad, which is bread to the hungry minds in lonely places." Guests at the plantation varied from the Prince of Wales to Kinanjui, Chief of the Kikuyu tribe. Sometimes the farm was the site for tribal dances, known as

Ngomas; at other times it served as a sanctuary for fellow Europeans who found themselves down on their luck in Africa.

Probably Karen's favorite guest was Denys Finch-Hatton, a British immigrant to Africa; when not leading a safari, he was frequently to be found at the farm. There the two expatriates would sit "into the small hours of the morning, talking of all the things we could think of, and mastering them and laughing at them."

"When I had no more money, and could not make things pay, I had to sell the farm," explains the author, recounting her last year in Africa. The news saddened everyone: the squatters who worked the farm, the servants in the house and the large circle of travelers to whom the farm was a second home. And for Karen Blixen herself, who awakened each morning and thought, "here I am, where I ought to be," a state of denial set in:

It was a curious thing that I myself did not, during this time, ever believe that I would have to give up the farm or to leave Africa. I was told that I must do so by the people round me, all of them reasonable men . . . and all the facts of my daily life pointed to it. All the same nothing was farther from my thoughts, and I kept on believing that I should come to lay my bones in Africa.

It had been arranged that she would remain on the farm only until the last crop of coffee was harvested. Still reluctant to accept her destiny, the baroness nevertheless prepared to leave, like "a blind person who is being led, and who places one foot in front of the other, cautiously but unwillingly." Because the new owners intended to sell the land rather than farm it, she began making frequent trips to Nairobi to find new land where the squatters could live. She then proceeded to sell her furniture and many of her possessions. Later, she would reflect:

When in the end, the day came on which I was going away, I learned the strange learning that things can happen which we ourselves cannot possibly imagine, either beforehand, or at the time when they are taking place, or afterwards when we look back on them. Circumstances can have a motive force by which they bring about events without aid of human imagination or apprehension.

Madame Blixen had carefully instructed her houseboys to close the doors of her empty house once she was out of sight. They did not obey, but left the doors wide open to show they wished her to come back again. Undoubtedly a door would always remain open in Karen Blixen's heart, a doorway of hope through which she might someday return to her beloved Africa.

Commentary:

The theme of *Out of Africa,* like the continent itself, is an imposing and unwieldy mosaic for any writer to conjoin, but perhaps even more so for one who has lived within the African experience and thus passed beyond simplistic preconceptions and superficial observations. Dinesen superbly presents an Africa of contradictions and extremes. It is a community articulated by natives and immigrants; it is a land inhabited by creatures as common as fireflies and as majestic as lions. For Dinesen, however, each is an essential part of the African landscape; singly and combined, they *are* Africa.

Like Africa itself, Karen Blixen, the woman behind Dinesen's narrative voice, is made up of contradictions and extremes. For instance, Dinesen is an astute observer of Africa's people and cultures. Yet, paradoxically, she frequently and strangely seems unaware of the destructive impact of her own colonial enterprises. She can assail, for example, a colonial policy that strips the native population of its land, and, at the same time, fail to see her own complicity in the very policy she attacks. Dinesen, in fact, owned six thousand acres of land in a country that prohibited its own native-born "noble savages" from owning even one acre.

Dinesen's whole attitude toward the "noble savage" is yet another of the author's incongruities. At times she seems oblivious to the suffering of the native people; at other times she seems to suffer along with them, accurately recognizing, for instance, both the relationship and the difference between the *discovery* of the "noble savage" and the subsequent *destruction* of the cultures and cultural wisdom of Africa's native inhabitants by imperialistic Europeans: " . . . It is more than their land that you take away from the people . . . It is their past as well, their roots and their identity."

Another area wrought by contradictions and extremes is seen in passages where Dinesen discusses animals, both wild and domestic. She frequently praises the beauty and majesty of the native wild animals, but also finds sport in hunting these same beasts. One moment she extols the virtue of the lion or giraffe, and the next she is taking a bead on the splendid creature down the scope of a rifle. Dinesen's fondness of hunting and her respect of the African wilds are not necessarily irreconcilable; but they do form an intriguing manifestation of the contradictions she embodies.

Perhaps these contradictions escaped her shrewd eye—or possibly her own complicity merely made the paradox an uncomfortable subject for her to confront. Perhaps the ability to live among contradictions, to adapt between one extreme and another, was requisite in a land that was itself in tremendous flux; a land at once being divided asunder and pushed forward by the clash of cultures, yet held together by the tenacious grasp of its inhabitants—wild animals, native dwellers, and immigrants alike. Regardless of Dinesen's intent, the incongruities she presents in her work ultimately serve to challenge the reader to examine his or her own preconceived notions.

KAFFIR BOY

by Mark Mathabane, Macmillan Publishing Company, New York, N.Y., 1986

Kaffir Boy is the autobiography of Mark Mathabane, a black boy who grew up during the days of apartheid in South Africa—where the word "kaffir" has the same connotation as the term "nigger" in the United States. He was born in the crowded ghetto of Alexandra, where his parents gave him the name of Johannes. Somehow, through a combination of talent, great discipline, and a series of happy accidents, he found his way past the sealed ghetto to become one of the few black South African tennis stars of the early 1970s.

◇ ♦ ◇

The Road to Alexandra

Many of Johannes' first gripping childhood memories are of police raids on the shack where he lived with his parents and a growing number of brothers and sisters. Typically, the boy would be sleeping naked on a piece of cardboard, covered with newspaper, when the black "Peri-Urban" policemen came pounding at the door. All blacks had to have a legal pass to live in Alexandra or they could be carried off to jail.

The worst finally happened when Johannes was seven years old: His father Jackson was laid off from work as a laborer, and a few weeks later was arrested at a bus stop for "being unemployed." Almost a year later, when the starving family had given him up for dead, Jackson Mathabane returned from jail—gaunt, his proud faith in his manhood irreparably shattered. And as the father retreated sullenly into drink, gambling, and hopeless fantasies of revived tribal glory, Johannes' mother became the champion of her son's dream to get ahead.

Other early memories were of coping with hunger. For a time Johannes and his family scavenged for scraps in a garbage dump. On one occasion, he accompanied a gang of boys to an address where they had been promised food for easy work, only to learn it was a house of prostitution. Sometimes he suffered dreadful hallucinations brought on by semi-starvation.

Life in the South African ghettos held many lessons to be learned. For instance, when Johannes taunted some laborers, performing what he considered the demeaning work of emptying the ghetto latrines, the men promptly forced him to jump in a bucket of excrement. The boy never made fun of *anyone* again. And at the age of six he grasped another critical reality, when he was introduced through movies to the white world. It didn't take long for Johannes to realize that in South Africa whites had everything and blacks had nothing.

Passport to Knowledge

One day when he was about seven, Johannes' mother woke him early and took him to stand in a long line to be registered for the Bovet Community School—a local outlet for white-ordained "Bantu" (black) education. Students at the black community schools had to provide their own books, uniforms, and fees; they were discouraged from any associations with European (white) culture or literature, and were taught exclusively in African tribal languages. Nevertheless, it was recognized that education "embodied the hope for a meaningful future for black people," and it was hoped that some students would stay in school at least long enough to learn to write their names. Johannes' mother knew that without an education, her son would probably wind up on a dead-end road as a *tsotsi*—one of the many murderous ghetto gang members.

Johannes resisted the school's harsh discipline and inflexible code of behavior, but loved learning and became the top pupil in his class. Even the heart of his father was touched; smiling, Jackson gave Johannes 60 cents to pay for his next year's expenses.

The boy continued to do well in school—although he was often caned for lacking books, not wearing the established uniform, or for failing to pay his fees. Between these canings and a growing sense of isolation at home, the young boy stopped eating and sleeping. At one point he even considered suicide. But his mother, then jobless and six months pregnant, reminded him that his sisters and brother looked up to him. "Stay in school," she said. "As soon as I find a [new] job, I'll buy you books and uniforms."

Johannes' father opened a beer-selling business, and things briefly improved for the family. Johannes even brought in a little extra money by reading and writing letters for migrant workers. Then, when he was ten years old, his life hit a turning point: his Granny took him to meet the Smiths, the white family who employed her as a maid. Impressed with the boy, the Smiths began paying him to do odd jobs; they also provided him with used books and hand-me-down clothes. These were precious items to Johannes, but the Smith's adolescent son, Clyde, still stung the "kaffir boy" with his taunts.

Clyde's insults, however, only made Johannes more aware that learning to express himself effectively in English would be a key tool in lifting himself above the chronic violence of the ghetto.

Meanwhile, Johannes had found a new love: the Smiths had given him a used tennis racket, and he began pounding a tennis ball against the walls of the Alexandra Stadium. He liked the thought of playing tennis because he knew that his success would depend largely on his own efforts—under the direction of a "mulatto" coach named Scaramouch, who soon became Johannes' full-time coach, as well as a surrogate father.

Passport to Freedom

As Johannes' life revolved more and more closely around school, reading, and tennis, he resisted both his mother's efforts to win him to Christianity and his father's insistence that he spend three months in "mountain school" and be initiated into tribal manhood. Even as this family tug-of-war intensified, Johannes' relationship with his father steadily worsened. The boy greatly feared that all this turmoil would hurt his school work; yet when primary exam results came out, he had scored so high that he was awarded a government scholarship for all three years of secondary school. His mother sobbed with joy—and even his father's harsh rebukes were softened.

Although classes in the black secondary school were taught in English rather than the familiar tribal Isongas, Johannes' grades remained high—and his interest in tennis jumped to a new level. Toting along a notebook, he visited bookstores to copy pointers from tennis books. Then, to help focus all his energies on schoolwork and tennis, he took up yoga and committed to sexual abstinence.

In 1972 and 1973 Johannes began to compete in tennis tournaments. He also began to work at a white tennis ranch called Barretts, where, in an impulsive rebellion against the oppressive Afrikaner government, he gave his name as the English-sounding "Mark."

For years black South Africans living under apartheid had idolized American black heroes like Martin Luther King, Jr. and Muhammad Ali. Now all black South Africans, including Mark, looked forward to the visit of Arthur Ashe, the distinguished black American tennis star. Ashe was cheered wildly as he won matches against local white professionals, and Mark wondered if he could ever hope to become like him. As he returned to the dreary reality of life in the ghetto, that hope seemed more impossible every day.

Then in 1974 Mark won his first tournament championship; his trophy was prominently displayed in the bar at Barretts. The following year he became the first player from Alexandra chosen to represent the southern Transvaal black junior tennis squad in the national tournament. But more and more he felt like a stranger in his own country. His wide and voracious interests—which included reading and classical music as well as the desire to match up against the best tennis players in the world—all convinced him that he belonged in another world.

In June of 1976, black riots scarred the country, triggered by a new legal requirement to conduct secondary Bantu school classes in Afrikaans rather than English. Police opened fire on students in Soweto, cutting them down mercilessly. The rebellion soon spread to Alexandra, where Mark angrily joined in the looting. Finally, though, he came to ask himself whether he was willing to kill to obtain black freedom. He found the very question demoralizing.

Meanwhile, Andre Zietsman, one of South Africa's rising white tennis stars, befriended Mark and taught him the finer points of the game. While they played together illegally on white courts, Andre, who had been to America, told an incredulous Mark how blacks in the United States were able to use the same libraries, gymnasiums and taxies as whites. As he listened, Mark felt a great longing to see this "promised land" for himself. Whenever he met an American player, he asked for addresses to universities so that he could write for information about tennis scholarships.

Then the death of imprisoned black activist Steven Biko spawned a new wave of interracial violence. In response, the Afrikaner government cracked down hard, and army vehicles became a common sight in Alexandra. Although some blacks considered him a pacifist traitor, Mark sought his familiar refuge in books and tennis.

During all this unrest, the Black Tennis Foundation tried to force the total integration of tennis by boycotting the prestigious South African Breweries Open tournament. Mark, contending that the boycott only enabled whites to turn their backs on the black cause, played anyway; as a result the Foundation banned him for life from its ranks. But soon afterwards, he had the good fortune to meet Stan Smith and Bob Lutz, the number-one doubles team in the world. Eventually Smith became a close friend, and encouraged Mark's efforts to go to the United States. He also sponsored Mark as a player in two white tournaments.

As the first black to be admitted to a white junior tennis squad, Mark was soon invited into the homes of his team members, where he was able to debunk some of their misconceptions about blacks and to revise some of his own biases against whites. But there were still setbacks and discouragements: for example, when a prestigious white club called The Wanderers agreed to admit Mark to membership, they added that, because of apartheid laws, he would have to shower with the servants. Angered, Mark became more intent than ever on getting out of the country.

Then one night the inevitable occurred: Mark was arrested and jailed for "intruding" in a white neighborhood without a pass. Since the only route to get a pass was a job outside the ghetto, Andre Zietsman helped him land a position with a bank at the kingly sum of 290 rands a month—three times the combined earnings of his parents.

Meanwhile, Gaffney College in South Carolina offered Mark an all-expense-paid tennis scholarship. But he still had to wait—for the South African government did not favor blacks leaving the country. *"Why do you want to study in America?* he was asked. *You leave the country and start telling Americans lies about how bad things are . . . "* But at last Mark had in hand all the necessary papers—and a plane ticket.

When it was his time to get on the bus to the airport, Mark's family bid him a tearful good-bye. He turned for a last look at them, standing in a row in front of their shack, and was so overcome with emotion that he wanted to turn back. Instead, he followed his destiny.

Epilogue:

Though tennis was the vehicle that helped lift Mark Mathabane out of the Alexandra ghetto, he ultimately dedicated himself to a notable career in journalism and public speaking. "Using the pen to fight against injustice and racism" remains his goal and mission.

MIG PILOT

The Final Escape of Lieutenant Belenko
by John Barron, McGraw-Hill Book Company, New York, N.Y., 1980

Lieutenant Viktor Ivanovich Belenko, deputy commander of the Soviet Air Force's 3rd Squadron, awoke on a September morning in 1976, and peered out the window of his apartment at the blinding sunrise. Today, he told himself, would be the day. Yes, today would definitely be the day . . .

After a distasteful breakfast at the officers' mess, Belenko met with his regimental commander. "Today we fly," the commander barked. "Our mission is a vital mission, for we will fire our rockets."

Belenko knew that he must maintain an air of normalcy. He donned his tattered cotton flight suit and inspected his automatic pistol. That he even carried a gun stemmed from a tragic incident: several months earlier a pilot had successfully ejected from his plane in a wilderness area—only to be found weeks later dead of starvation. Now all Soviet MiG pilots carried a pistol, and the furnishings of their MiG-25s included basic survival gear.

Today Belenko's squadron would practice intercept maneuvers, then return to base. But the day's plans held much more for Belenko: If he was successful, today would mark his first step away from a barren existence; today he would begin fulfilling his dream.

At 12:50 P.M. the pilot lined up with the rest of his squadron, released his brakes, and surged down the runway. Then, climbing to 19,000 feet, he suddenly jammed the stick forward and plunged into a power dive. At 100 feet he leveled off, hoping to evade the ever-probing Soviet radar. For him to attempt to take a MiG-25 so low was potentially suicidal; even at 1,000 feet the cumbersome planes were difficult to control.

Flying so low, Belenko twice had to swerve to avoid hitting fishing vessels. Soon he would have to bring the jet back up to the thin air at 20,000 feet so as not to deplete his fuel supply. But for now he had to fly low to avoid long-range Soviet radar, as well as the missile-bearing ships which patrolled offshore.

At 1:11 P.M., when it finally rose from the sea to 20,000 feet, Belenko's MiG appeared as an unidentified blip on Japanese radar. Eleven minutes later he breached Japanese airspace. Immediately several F-4 Phantom jets scrambled to intercept him. They would have to find him on their own; the band on his radio was so narrow he could only communicate with other MiGs.

Thirty minutes after takeoff, the fighter pilot throttled back and began gliding downward. Scarcely sustaining airspeed in order to facilitate interception by the Japanese Phantoms, he hoped that by descending he would also break free of the clouds.

Three times during his descent the MiG pilot sliced through the clouds into thin layers of blue sky—only to be engulfed anew in a blanket of dirty gray clouds. Now, worry crept in: Where were the Phantoms that would guide him to a safe landing?

An airstrip at the city of Chitose, which lay toward the middle of Hokkaido behind a range of mountains on the island's southwestern peninsula, was Belenko's target. But by the time he finally spotted land, he had no more than 18 minutes of fuel left. Hopefully this would carry him to Chitose. He could always eject from the craft, but the preservation of the MiG-25 was his utmost concern. He decided to stay low for visibility, even though it would further compromise his fuel.

At 1:42 a red warning light flashed and a panel lit up with the message "You Have Six Minutes Of Fuel Left." Then, suddenly a calm, firm female voice advised him from a hidden recording device: "Caution, Oh-six-eight! Your fuel supply has dropped to an emergency level. You are in an emergency situation." Continuing his flight into the unknown, Belenko replied aloud: *Woman wherever you are, tell me something I don't know. Tell me where is that aerodrome.*

Thus progressed Viktor Belenko's escape from the Soviet Union. But why Belenko, of all people? He had never been in trouble, never associated with dissidents.

The answers began in Belenko's childhood. Having been raised by an aunt in Donbas after his parents' divorce when he was two years old, he had lived out his boyhood in a mud and straw hut. Confined to the hut every winter for lack of suitable footwear, the boy's first shoes were actually a pair of slippers sewn from the sleeves of an old jacket.

In school Viktor became a voracious reader, devouring everything he could put his hands on. Authors were his true parents, his role models and his best teachers. One of these mentors in print, the French aviator and author Antoine de Saint-Exupery, instilled in the life-hungry boy a desire to fly. Later, after suffering a beating by four older boys, Viktor also devoted himself to boxing and physical fitness.

But above all, throughout his life, Viktor had asked himself questions: *Why is our country always unprepared for the harvest? . . . How can we have a cholera epidemic when we are told we have the best medicine in the world? . . . You mean they have a Communist party in the U.S.? They allow it? . . . If people in America are starving and out of work, who is driving all those cars I see [on the news and in movies]? . . .*

Upon graduation from school, Viktor had joined a military auxiliary, where he was selected as one of forty men for pre-flight training. In time he became a pilot, one of the most coveted jobs in the Soviet Union.

But even in flight school questions about America kept vexing the young man's mind. America was filled with decadence and internal strife, he was told. America was the "Main Enemy"; Americans were the "Dark Force." The *My Lai* massacre in Vietnam was portrayed as the ultimate example of American inhumanity and degeneracy; Lt. William Calley had ordered the slaughtering of hundreds of innocent men, women and children. *But why are the Dark Forces putting him in jail?* Belenko reflected. *If they are pure and true Dark Forces the officer did just what they wanted. Why not give him a medal?*

Then one day, while scanning an intelligence report on the U.S. Navy's F-14, Belenko had learned that its radar could detect aircraft 180 miles away, lock onto multiple targets moving at four times the speed of sound 100 miles away, and fire six missiles simultaneously. He could not believe the report: *Our radar, when it works, has a range of fifty miles. Our missiles, when they work, have a range of eighteen miles. How will we fight the F-14? It will kill us before we ever see it! If our system is so much better than the Americans, why is their technology so much better than ours?*

Belenko's skepticism had gradually grown into a deep-seated rejection of the Soviet system. And now, faced with the loss of his only son, who had been taken by Belenko's estranged wife to a city thousands of miles away, the pilot had no ties to bind him to his country.

Now barely maintaining airspeed, Belenko watched the altimeter drop. Then at 250 feet the world lit up and he could see an airstrip—a commercial airfield at Hakodate. The runway was only two-thirds long enough to land a MiG. But with no fuel left for any other choice, he jerked the controls into the tightest turn possible, pulled up to avoid an oncoming Boeing 727, dove at the runway, and touched down at 220 knots. Deploying his drag chute and slamming down again and again on his brakes, he grimaced as the craft screeched toward the end of the runway and skidded into a field, finally stopping just short of hitting a huge antenna.

Viktor was quickly ushered into the airport and closeted with officials. But the pilot would say little: his only stated wishes were that his aircraft be put under guard and concealed, and that he be granted political asylum in the United States. These requests, when translated, brought an outburst of cheers and applause. Within minutes the news flashed around the globe: Belenko had delivered the Soviets' most super-secret aircraft into the hands of the Free World.

Not long afterwards a KGB officer, functioning as a Soviet embassy official, was sent to interview Belenko: "All your relatives, your wife, your father . . . your mother, your aunt . . . have joined in sending a collective letter to you," the agent said. Belenko knew it was a lie: *How could they get them together so quickly from all over Russia?* "I flew to Japan voluntarily and on purpose," he told the agent matter-of-factly. "I on my own initiative have requested political asylum in the United States. Excuse me. Our conversation is over."

Aboard a 747 on his way to Tokyo, Belenko was admitted to the flight deck: *How could only three men manage such an enormous plane?* he wondered. *The rest of the crew must be hidden somewhere*

On his arrival in America, the Soviet pilot's doubts persisted. Meeting with CIA officers, Belenko mused on their appearance: *They are too trim, too healthy, dressed too expensively . . . too friendly. . . . They are trying to fool me.* Later, on visiting a supermarket for the first time, he laughed at the expensive shopping carts and the seemingly endless isles of food: *If this were a real store, a woman in less than an hour could buy enough food in this one place to feed a whole family for two*

weeks. But where are the people, the crowds, the lines? . . . This is not a real store . . . It's a showplace of the Dark Forces. And upon entering a modest apartment for the first time, it finally struck him as too much: *Who ever heard of a worker's apartment with two bathrooms and carpet all over the floors and machines that wash the dishes . . . ?*

The CIA were disposed to grant Belenko almost anything he asked. After all, the enormity of what he had supplied them, in the MiG-25, defied calculations in both monetary and defense terms. But they were surprised by the still-suspicious pilot's first request: he wanted to work on a farm—absolutely the worst place to live in his homeland. Now, however, he witnessed firsthand the modern equipment and growing and harvesting techniques, the high standard of medical care, the lavish availability of high-tech TVs, radios and calculators—not to mention the fact that they were available to American farm workers and their families.

And, above all, Belenko saw the autonomy of the people. He was astonished: *Why, a common laborer on this farm is better off than a Soviet fighter pilot . . . They are free people . . . Look at the harvest!*

What! You mean they pay a doctor twice as much as a fighter pilot? You mean you pick your own doctor, and if he makes you wait too long or you don't like the way he treats you, you go to another doctor? . . . They lied. All these years, they lied, and they knew they were lying.

A color television set in the Soviet Union cost a worker approximately five months' wages . . . You can buy a car in this country as easily as a loaf of bread! . . . How can they afford to let everybody just get up and go anywhere he pleases whenever he wants? What keeps order in this country?

At the close of his interrogation by CIA agents, Belenko was informed that his great service to the United States was to be repaid via "a generous income for the rest of his life." Not a materialist by nature, Belenko did not rejoice at financial security; he still saw much that he needed to accomplish—with English language proficiency at the top of the list. Accordingly, now cloaked under a new identity, Belenko did two things: he bought a car and enrolled in an intensive English program.

When, after making rapid progress, he hit a patch of resistance in his language studies, Belenko's teachers suggested that he "tramp around the country, practicing English." And this he did. From Appalachia to the Rockies, from Kansas City to San Francisco, Belenko traveled compulsively, still astounded by American "superabundance." Speeding across "the breadth of Texas in fewer than twenty-four hours," Belenko struggled with the impulse to drive straight to the Soviet Embassy. "Great stakes rode with him"; what a boost for Party morale his rejection of American society would mean: all Soviets would be inspired by this "New Communist Man who had seen and judged."

At last, however, the "fever broke." Exhausted, Belenko pulled over to the side of the road. His heart already told him just what a CIA friend would soon be reassuring him: "Viktor . . . the United States is more your homeland than the Soviet Union ever could be."

TOUCHING THE VOID

by Joe Simpson, Harper & Row, New York, N.Y., 1988

After ten days of hard climbing in the Andes, Joe Simpson found himself in a pitch-black icy chasm with no food or water, his leg severely fractured. His climbing partner—his only hope—had, in desperation, cut his safety rope and left him for dead.

Touching the Void is Joe's riveting account of their adventure—their heroic struggle to reach the mountaintop, the terrifying series of incidents that left Joe disabled in an icy abyss, and the superhuman tenacity that brought him home alive.

DAY 1-6: At base camp 15,000 feet high in the Peruvian Andes, Joe Simpson and Simon Yates prepared to scale the unclimbed west face of Siula Grande, rising another 6,000 feet above them. They spent two days selecting their route and waiting for a break in the weather—well aware that the towering cumulus clouds moving in to rain on them in the afternoons were bringing fresh snow—and the risk of avalanche—at higher elevations. At one point they started up the fractured, contorted glacier spilling over the mountain's south ridge; but waist-deep, powdery snow soon forced them back in exhaustion.

On day six, after gorging from their supply crates to fortify themselves for the rigorous struggle ahead, the climbers loaded their backpacks with equipment and set out again. That night they bivouacked in a snow hole, hoping for warmth.

DAY 7: At five the next morning, peering from their snow hole, the climbers were greeted by blue ice fields sparkling under clear, sunny skies—perfect climbing weather. Simon led out, hammering iron pitons into the ice with frost-brittle fingers; Joe, tethered by a 150-foot rope, followed, constantly off balance by the obtruding angle of the sheer wall. Alternating the lead, they continued up another 1,000 feet, then 2,000, wondering when the icefields would ever end.

As night fell, the pair climbed cautiously over the crumbly, honeycombed ice. Finally a tube-shaped wall reared up sharply out of the dark and the good ice gave way to mushy powder. With one last desperate move, the climbers propelled themselves onto the slopes above, where they dug in for the night.

DAY 8: Joe and Simon had bivouacked at 19,000 feet, roughly 2,000 feet from the summit—just a few hours' climb. Despite the thin air, they made good progress ascending up a 55-degree ramp of ice. Then, for the first time, they caught sight of the summit itself—nothing more than a huge overhanging cornice.

From that point on, they encountered every possible deterrent from bare rock to waist-deep snowfields. After four hours of wrenching work—and a sparse, hard-won 300 feet—they decided to bed down for the night. Two hours and one hundred feet later they gulped down their last freeze-dried meal, and settled into their sleeping bags.

DAY 9: Morning dawned with clear skies and no wind. It looked like the climbing would be easier—and before them rising another 100 feet was the summit. Simon took the lead, leaving Joe behind to take photos. Then Joe also clambered to the top, the euphoria reflecting in his face.

Then, suddenly, another storm moved in and the climbers watched the ridge below them disappear into the clouds. Within minutes, they were totally enveloped in a white-out. It was 2:30 P.M.

Together the men weighed their options: Should they stay put or move down? Then for a brief moment the sky brightened and Joe caught a glimpse of the ridge. Encouraged, Simon set out towards it, but within a minute the clouds swirled back in and he was lost from Joe's sight. The rope slowly running through Joe's gloves was the only sign that his partner was still there. Then suddenly the rope whipped through his hands, a deep explosion echoed through the clouds, and Joe was pulled chest first into the snow. He called out to Simon; no answer. He waited. A full fifteen minutes passed before he heard Simon's relieved, exultant cry: "I've found the ridge!"

"One minute I was climbing, the next I was falling," Simon explained when Joe finally reached him. He had broken away a 40-foot cornice and fallen with it; only the rope had saved him from a 4500-foot drop.

DAY 10: As they felt their way along the mountain, often sinking in snow up to their chests, a feeling of helplessness descended on the pair; their fingers were showing signs of deep frostbite. Finally they realized that the ridge they were traversing was one vast horizontal cornice.

At last, Joe spied another way off the ridge. Crouching down on his knees, he lowered himself over the edge and kicked the steel-plate crampons attached to his boots into the ice wall below. Without the slightest warning, there was a sharp crack—and he was falling. He hit the slope below with both knees locked—and with a second, bone-splintering crack below his left knee, his body exploded in pain. The impact catapulted him over backwards and down the east face.

"I've broken my leg, that's it. I'm dead," were Joe's first thoughts. The impact had driven his lower leg bones all the way up through the knee joint. His rope slackened, a sign that Simon was coming his way.

Hour after hour, Simon lowered Joe patiently down the mountain face, slackening the rope until it ran out, then digging himself out of his snow seat, and climbing down to where Joe was waiting—to begin the procedure all over again. Nightfall brought a relentless storm, making communication impossible. Each time Joe was lowered, his crampons would snag, wrenching his mangled leg up toward his body. " . . . There would be a flare of agony as the knee kinked back, and parts within the joint seemed to shear past each other with a sickening gristly crunch." By the end of the fourth descent, Joe was in so much agony that his leg shook uncontrollably.

Visibility worsened, as did the angle of the slope. At one point Joe screamed for Simon to go slow, but his words were lashed away by the savage wind. Then all at once Joe felt himself hurled outward into space. Clawing at the near-vertical cliff-face, he had triggered an avalanche of loose snow, and now he was dangling in mid-air, suspended over a deep crevasse.

The constant, ever-increasing pull on his line soon told Simon that Joe was in trouble. Then the rope began to cut into his own waist, draining strength from his body; within seconds he would be pulled out of his snow seat. If that happened, both of them would be killed. He weighed the options—then, with trance-like calm, he reached down and cut the rope.

Moments earlier, Joe's lamp had gone out; above him all he could see were stars. Then all at once the stars went out, too, and he was falling. "I fell silently, endlessly into nothingness, as if dreaming of falling," Joe recalled. And then a blinding thud against his back shattered the stillness of the dream. He bounced, and fell again, deeper into a crevasse. When next he struck something solid, he lay there, stunned. "I couldn't breath. I retched . . . Nothing . . . I shut my eyes, and gave in to gray fading shadows . . . "

Joe was overwhelmed by panic and pain as breath and consciousness returned to him. Groping through the dense blackness with his fingers, he discovered that he had landed on some type of ledge or snow bridge. He anchored himself with a piton to the ice. Then Joe decided that if he was going to die, he would at least die trying. Pulling his hammer up from below, he beat a piton into the ice to anchor himself. Then he drew in the rope—and stared in disbelief at its end: it had been cut. Cut!

In shock, grief, and anger Joe began lowering himself even deeper into the void. When he came to the end of the rope, he resolved, he would simply slip off and die in the plunge. But as he descended, ever so slowly, a surprising shaft of sunlight caught his eye, and a glimmer of hope welled up in him. With renewed strength he began hacking steps in the ice wall; somehow he must reach the light. Planting his axe, he gingerly pulled himself up the jagged steps towards salvation, hopping with his good leg. An ascent that would have taken the average hiker no more than ten minutes took Joe more than half a day of agony. But finally, near total collapse, he poked his head like a gopher out of the abyss to behold the most awesome, gratitude-inspiring sight of his life: he was free again.

DAY 11: Joe was now 200 feet above the glacier and six miles from base camp—a half-day's stroll for a healthy climber, but for him at least a three-day ordeal. In torturous anguish, he began hopping, dropping and sliding downward. From time to time his crampons would catch, wrenching his broken leg up behind him. Finally, in anguish, he reached down, unhooked the spikes with his axe, and rid himself of them entirely.

All the while Joe kept hearing a voice in his mind that prevented him from drifting off into a death sleep: *"Go on, keep going . . . faster. You've wasted too much time. Go on . . . "* Darkness fell, and a heavy wind came up. Once again he fell face down in the snow; and for a long while he lay there, defeated. But then the voice intensified: *" . . . Don't sleep, don't sleep, not here. Keep going. Find a slope and dig a snow hole . . . don't sleep."*

DAY 12: Joe awoke half-frozen and screaming; then he realized he was no longer in the crevasse. Everything now hinged on his ability to maintain his bearings and find a route that would take him off the glacier. Halfway through the day he found himself in what looked like familiar surroundings. Trying to stand, he peered towards the horizon, fighting the sharp, prickling pains which he recognized as the onset of snow-blindness. Then he caught sight of the rockfields, the pass where they had set up base camp.

When Joe finally reached the rocks, his stamina was spent. Nevertheless, he struggled onward, fighting drowsiness, pain, and the urge to quit. Using his foam mat and the straps from his crampons, he fashioned a splint around his knee, and again stood. His head reeled in torment as he took a weak step, then another. Each time he collapsed, he lay exhausted in a timeless semi-stupor.

DAY 13: *"Must reach camp today,"* Joe thought. *"Surely Simon had to be there, he'd have been there two days now."* Again and again he clawed his way up to take a hop, and again and again he fell. *"I thought how far I had to go and how far I had come. Part of me wanted to give up and sleep . . . The voice countered this."* At one o'clock, he finally stumbled into the narrow, lake-dotted pass that opened onto their base camp, Bomb Alley—home territory at last.

By three o'clock Joe had come to the end of the rock fields. Every now and then he would spot a boot print, and his confidence soared. Then it was four o'clock—close to dark; now he had to hurry. An hour later he inched his way along the divide that led to the campsite. Then, using his axe as if on ice, he hacked into the mud wall and hauled himself up. It was almost dark. "SIIMMMOONNN!" he groaned. Only eerie echoes returned.

Hours of darkness sifted by; all sense of time and place were lost. Staggering dazedly onward, Joe found himself in a dry river bed. Somewhere on the edge of the bed were the tents. "SIIMMMmoonn . . . Please be there, you must be there." A crisp snow beat against his face—and the night remained black and silent.

Then, as if out of nowhere, lights appeared. *Something floated and glowed ahead of me. A semicircle of red and green . . . a space ship . . . then muffled sounds. A spray of yellow light suddenly cut out from the colors in a wide cone . . . voices, not my voices . . . the tents!! They're still there. Then, [Simon's voice.] "Joe! Is that you? JOE! Joe! God! Oh my God! . . . look at you. Lift him, lift him . . . God Joe, how? How?"*

KON-TIKI: Across the Pacific By Raft

by Thor Heyerdahl (trans. by F. H. Lyon), Rand McNally & Co., Chicago, Illinois, 1950

Once while Thor Heyerdahl and his wife were visiting a little island in the Marquesas group called Fatu Hiva, they listened intently as old Tei Tetua—the sole survivor of his tribe—discussed the ancient Polynesian god and chief, offspring of the sun, Tiki. "It was Tiki who brought my ancestors to these islands where we live now," Tei Tetua explained. "Before that we lived in a big country beyond the sea." As Tei Tetua spoke, the sea continued to come crashing in on the eastern shore—always from the east. As the old man's words haunted his brain late into the night, Heyerdahl pondered: "It was as though time no longer existed, and Tiki and his seafarers were just landing . . . on the beach below." Then a thought struck him, and he said to his wife, "Have you noticed that the huge stone figures of Tiki in the jungle are remarkably like the monoliths left by extinct civilizations in South America?"

Heyerdahl returned to his native Norway with a plan to research the ancient origins of the South Sea islands' native cultures. Although oral tradition held that the earliest Polynesians had been immigrants from Asia (the first groups disembarking around 500 AD and the second in 1100 AD), Heyerdahl could not reconcile the technologically advanced civilizations of the orient with the less sophisticated cultures of the Pacific. He supposed that the first Polynesians had come from the opposite direction, from the Americas. Not only did the stone heads and the waves breaking on the eastern shore of Fatu Hiva lead him to this conclusion, but while in Peru he had read the Inca legends of the sun-king: Kon-Tiki had been the Incan leader of the legendary white, bearded men who, after being defeated in battle, had escaped to the Pacific coast, and then disappeared to the west. In fact, the first European explorers had been surprised to find entire Polynesian families—said to be direct descendants of Tiki—who looked almost white.

Heyerdahl examined the possible connection between ancient Peru and Polynesia in a manuscript, which he later submitted to various experts. All flatly rejected his theory. One professor of anthropology insisted that no South American culture had the technology in 500 AD to cross the 4000 miles of Pacific Ocean to reach the first of the Polynesian Islands. When Heyerdahl protested—citing evidence that, far from being a primitive people, these early sailors were expert astronomers and were equipped with well-constructed balsa-wood rafts—the professor smiled, "Well, you can try a trip from Peru to the Pacific islands on a balsa-wood raft." And so the Norwegian resolved to do just that.

Heyerdahl calculated that the minimum time for a raft to make the trip would be ninety-seven days—four months at the outside. He then turned his attention to finding a crew. Herman Watzinger, a Norwegian engineer,

was the first to link up with Heyerdahl. After determining that they would need four additional crew members, Heyerdahl and Watzinger enlisted the services of Erik Hesselberg—an experienced seaman—who could use a sextant to plot their course, and two Norwegian war heroes, Knut Haugland and Torstein Raaby, who could work a radio to receive reports on weather conditions.

Still lacking a sixth crew member, Heyerdahl and Watzinger tended to other aspects of the expedition: first they obtained financing from private lenders and free food rations from the American War Department; then they attended to legal matters with the government of Peru; and finally they traveled to South America to a jungle area near the city of Quevedo—a region frequented by headhunters and bandits—in order to obtain the large balsa logs.

After floating the logs down the Rio Palenque to the coast, Heyerdahl and Watzinger began to assemble their raft in the Peruvian naval docks, where they came across their the sixth crew member, Bengt Danielsson, a Swede who had studied Amazonian Indians. Before long, the other crew members also arrived to help build the raft. Supporting a bamboo hut and a large square sail, the raft was made up of nine huge balsa logs lashed together with long ropes—which experts insisted would fall apart within a few weeks—and long centerboards to keep the forty-foot craft gliding forward, as well as a long steering oar. It was an exact replica of rafts described by the earliest Spanish explorers.

On April 28, 1947, the day after the raft had been christened *Kon-Tiki* in honor of the legendary voyager, a tug boat pulled the raft out to sea. Without an engine, the first few days would prove to be the most difficult and dangerous. Still trying to learn how to steer their raft, the crew worried that cross-currents would smash them back into the rocky coast rather than keeping them afloat on the Humboldt Current that could carry them across 4,000 miles of open water to their destination.

The genius of the raft's design, however, soon presented itself. Unlike a large ship—designed to plow through surging waves—the relatively tiny raft could ride up and down on the surf. If several large waves came in succession, though, whoever was steering had to hold on tight and wait for the water to drain, to avoid being swept overboard.

That first night, the waves were so big that two men had to struggle with the steering oar to keep the raft from capsizing. For the next three days they battled the sea, taking turns at the helm. By the fourth day the sea had calmed, and the exhausted crew was relieved to find that their craft's ropes showed no sign of wear. Although the logs seemed to be absorbing water, the voyagers later learned that the balsa sap in the freshly cut logs kept water from saturating—and sinking—their raft.

Well out on the open seas the crew became acquainted with their new sea neighbors. Flying fish regularly came thudding onto the deck, which the crew gathered up for breakfast. On one occasion they found on their raft a "snakefish" *(Gempylus)*, previously thought to be extinct.

For their own safety, the crew used hooks, harpoons, and ropes to discourage sharks from approaching the raft. Harpoons often shattered on the shark's rough skin; several heavy fish hooks hidden in a dolphin fish and lashed onto a strong line proved to be more effective. But later a more exciting method of clearing the area of sharks was discovered: holding a piece of fish over the edge of the raft, a daring "fisherman" would lure the shark to jump up out of the water. In that instant the sailor would seize the shark by the tail and haul it on board.

Sharks were not the only potential menace. The crew had been warned against the giant octopuses found in an area of the Humboldt Current. While they never saw one of the enormous creatures, they were surprised several times when smaller specimens came flying on board, using a sort of jet propulsion to leap high into the sky in order to avoid their pursuers.

On board the *Kon-Tiki*, each man performed daily duties: Bengt worked as steward; Herman took readings with meteorological and hydrographical equipment; Knut and Torstein operated the radio equipment; Erik patched the sail and spliced ropes; and Heyerdahl tended to the logbook, collected fish and plankton specimens, and filmed the expedition. In addition, everyone took turns cooking and steering.

For both solitude and amusement during the long journey, a few of the men would tie a safety line to a rubber dinghy, climb in, and row off alone for a few hours. At first the sight of the tiny, crude *Kon-Tiki* bobbing in the waves made them laugh. But later, as Heyerdahl recalled, "when we saw the silhouette of our craft grow smaller and smaller in the distance . . . a sensation of loneliness sometimes crept over us."

Because the current made it impossible for the raft to turn around, the crew knew anything or anyone that fell behind the raft's path would be irredeemably lost. Understandably, then, the crew was momentarily horrified when Herman fell overboard. Quickly, Knut tied a safety line around his waist and swam out to where Herman floundered, and they were drawn safely back to the raft.

Although two storms ended up damaging the steering oar and loosening the ropes and centerboards, they were nonetheless confident that the *Kon-Tiki* was still sound enough to reach their destination.

Heralding land days in advance, boobies and other short-range fowl first appeared, followed by increasing numbers of birds. Then,

just after six o'clock on July 30, Herman woke Heyerdahl. "Come out and have a look at your island!" Now, for the first time in over three months, they saw land. The current, however, had already pulled them too far past the island for the *Kon-Tiki* to land. Although they spotted two more islands the next day, the voyagers decided to head for Angatau. Three days later, when they reached Angatau, the crew deemed the south side the most suitable for a landing—if they could find a break in the treacherous reef that surrounded it. All day they maneuvered in and out of the reef, elated by the prospect of soon setting foot on solid earth after ninety-seven days at sea.

As they circled the island, there appeared two natives, rowing through a passage in the reef to greet them. Astonished to find that the *Kon-Tiki* lacked a motor, the natives helped the crew as they tried to breach the shallow reef. Despite the efforts of natives from four additional sea-going canoes, the unrelenting current swept the raft farther and farther from shore.

Unable to reach Angatau, the crew maneuvered the *Kon-Tiki* through the dangerous reef of Raroia. Though they hoped to sail north of the Raroia shoal, the wind changed and they quickly decided to head for the southern side of the reef. There they became caught in a northern current, however, and realized that within a few hours the Kon-Tiki would strike the reef.

During their final hours on the *Kon-Tiki*, the crew scrambled to save what remained of their provisions. Finally the moment came when the raft, with its confident crew, crashed through the breakers and onto the reef. Wave after wave passed over the vessel, battering the hut, before the crew could salvage the raft's provisions and leap onto the reef, away from the murderous breakers.

The six men waded to one of the palm-shaded islets and set up camp. "When I reached the sunny sand beach, I slipped off my shoes and thrust my bare toes down into the warm, bone-dry sand," Heyerdahl recalled. " . . . The voyage was over. We were all alive."

A few days later, natives arrived from a neighboring island. They listened spellbound to the story as it was translated by their chief of the *Kon-Tiki*, named after their ancestor, and then helped to pull the wrecked craft over the shoal and into the lagoon. Returning to the natives' village, the crew happily waited for the ship that would transport them and the battered *Kon-Tiki* to the world beyond.

Although *Kon-Tiki's* voyage had not proven that the Polynesians initially had emigrated from South America, the journey demonstrated conclusively that a balsa-wood raft could sail the 4,000 miles from Peru to Polynesia—a feat perhaps accomplished many millennia earlier in which a similar craft carried a people who would plant coconut palms, create a paradise for themselves, and foster a new civilization.

THESE GOOD MEN

by Michael Norman, Crown Publishers, New York, N.Y., 1989

On Friday, April 19, 1967 the soldiers of Golf Company, Second Battalion, 9th Marine Division moved out on a routine rescue mission. As they moved cautiously into North Vietnam, Michael Norman's ten-man Charlie squad paused at Bridge 28, which spanned the Quang Tri River. There they found not only the bodies of those troops they had hoped to save, but also the enemy. For the next three days Norman's company engaged in an intense fire-fight. When the battle was over, only half of the company's 110 men survived to walk away.

Five years later Norman began to feel overwhelmed by rage. As he later recalled: *I was sure that I had walked off the battlefield a more knowing man. Those who survive such a long and lethal assault emerge with at least a small piece of truth, some little lesson, a sliver of light. Maybe, across the years, chasing bylines and a bigger house, I had simply lost it.* Longing to understand the full impact of his experiences in Vietnam, Norman finally decided in the Spring of 1984 to organize a reunion of war buddies. . . . *In search of the ineffable, I set out to find the men I once held close, intimates side by side under a flame-white sun and at night belly to back in a fighting hole . . . Those men had been a mirror of me; likely they, too, carried home some small verity. Perhaps my comrades had been more provident and not let a thing so dearly won slip so easily away.*

Norman first flew to Mesquite, Texas to see Craig Belknap, whom he could still remember seeing that day on the bridge, crouched behind the bullet-riddled body of Tommy Gonzales. Although Norman vividly recalled Craig, drenched in blood, being lugged down the road on a stretcher, now, almost 20 years later, he was unprepared for the shock. Craig's right foot and leg, which had been hit by mortar fire, were stunted and twisted so that he limped badly. All that remained of his right hand were two semi-rigid fingers and a fused thumb. Embracing his old friend, Norman wept.

Craig later explained to Norman that he had come home from Vietnam a hero, he also "had come home a drunk." His girlfriend Jean, Craig went on, left him soon afterward, and although he had married another woman with whom he had children, he remained an alcoholic who suffered extreme physical and emotional pain: "I wanted to understand it," Craig shook his head. "I wasn't getting any answers."

Finally, after years of anguish, Craig had gone into treatment and had emerged a recovered alcoholic. He subsequently began counseling addicts and alcoholics, and, although he and his wife divorced, Craig found comfort in a resumed relationship with his old girlfriend Jean.

Next, Norman contacted Michael Tom Williamson, a tall, thin Oklahoman who had been nicknamed "Squeaky" because an operation he had undergone as an adolescent had left his voice with a distinct whine. Squeaky had been among the first in Norman's rescue squad to set foot on Bridge 28. Although he had escaped the ambush unscathed, Squeaky remained psychologically tormented by the death of his close buddy Gonzales. Months after the incident, Squeaky, as an eager new lieutenant, had led his men into another ambush and had stepped on a mine. Suffering eye injuries and brain damage from exploding metal fragments, he was sent home.

After "recovering," Squeaky enrolled in college. It was a miracle that he attended his classes at all, not only because he had been partially blinded, but also because he had remained in mental anguish all those years. In any case, one class short of graduation, Squeaky dropped out of college and out of life—as, earlier, he had dropped out of a marriage.

With his second wife Georgia, Squeaky launched a cross-country junket, bedding down in a tent and surviving on government disability checks. Because he suffered continual vision loss, he finally contacted a surgeon who performed cornea transplants—and who located and removed a remaining "floating" metal fragment from his eye. When he submitted his insurance claim, however, the government refused to pay for the surgery unless Squeaky could identify the person who had caused the injury. Though he was able to laugh at his misfortune, the terrible absurdity did not escape Squeaky's notice.

Soon Norman found himself on a flight to Newark, New Jersey to see Frank Ciappio, his old platoon commander. Nicknamed "Demo Dan"—"because he liked to blow things up"—Frank was a real soldier's soldier, surviving many battles in Vietnam. In fact, because he served as a father figure for many of his men, Frank had signed up for an extra tour of duty.

One day, however, in the middle of a firefight, Frank found one of his buddies lying face down in the mud, dead, and something just snapped inside of him. He suddenly became afraid. Gone was his concern for his men; his only thought now was to get out of the war alive. As it happened, Frank contracted malaria and was soon shipped home—but "he never forgot his kids or recovered from the feeling that he had abandoned them."

Frank later married and became a stock broker. But the war—and his kids—continued to haunt him; he drank heavily and frequently turned violent. Marine psychologists told him that he suffered from "Post Traumatic Stress Disorder," but identifying his "disorder" did little to cure him. All treatments failed. Embittered by his experiences, Frank now claimed that he would send his son to Canada before he let him fight in a war like Vietnam's.

After spending several days with Frank, Norman traveled to Savannah, Georgia to look up Bob Hagan and Charles Whitfield. Second Lieutenant Hagan had once bragged that he was going to win the Congressional Medal of Honor. When the fighting on Bridge 28 broke out, however, Bob froze, paralyzed with fear. Now, as Norman talked to Hagan's parents, he learned that Bob had been awarded the Silver Star for heroism in a later battle, had re-enlisted, and then been reported missing in action. "The more I heard, the more I wanted to know," Norman writes. "Hagan was a conundrum; the man who had wanted to cut and run; the man who had tried to shoulder the standard." What was the difference between a coward and a hero? Norman couldn't say. Bob was probably just a man at war with himself.

Charles Whitfield, however, was still living in Savannah. In a campaign after the "bridge battle," "Whit" had received a sniper bullet in the back of the head—a bullet, incidentally, that had been intended for Norman. Over a period of months as he recuperated in a hospital, Whit had managed to overcome his bitterness about the war and his injuries, and had found peace by acknowledging the abilities he retained. As his wife now told Norman, "I think the war was where Charles derived a lot of his strength, his values, and character."

Norman next located Mike Caron and Dave Buckner. He was pleased to find Mike doing well and working as a manager-in-training for a tire company in West Haven, Connecticut. "Quite simply . . . the bravest man I'd ever met," at Bridge 28 Mike had repeatedly risked his own life to drag the dead and wounded from the field of fire. In spite of what he had gone through in Vietnam, the experience had left his psyche fairly intact.

In contrast to Mike, whose wife comforted and supported him, Dave Buckner's wife had recently left him and filed for divorce. Now living in London, Dave had remained in the Marines, even though he had once threatened to "do in" a superior officer: Dave had refused to take a hill as ordered, and instead had simply raised his rifle and squinted down its sights at the officer—who backed down. The humiliated officer had subsequently kept Dave from being promoted to Lieutenant Colonel—though he had deserved the promotion many times over. Eventually, Norman learned, Dave won his promotion. Norman grinned widely when he heard this news, because, as Dave so often expressed, "I love the Marines. When they triumph, I just love it."

Dave's enthusiasm for the military was not at all shared by Doc DeWeese, who had been the company's senior medical corpsman. A former divinity student who hated war and death, Doc had always been a gentle, compassionate soul. In fact, the day after Bridge 28, Doc had cared for Norman when he suddenly went into convulsions. After Norman had been stabilized, Doc refused to allow his evacuation after hearing that psychiatrists behind the lines were treating battle fatigue with electro-shock therapy. Instead, Doc gave Norman tranquilizers and stayed by his side for two weeks until he recovered.

After so many years, Doc had seemed excited when Norman talked with him over the phone. When they met at the airport, though, Doc seemed rather cold and distant. As they drove into Seattle, Doc finally admitted that Norman's visit had upset him. "It's like somebody coming back from the dead," he explained.

In Doc's case, it wasn't just damaging memories that bothered him: the war had literally destroyed his faith in God and he had been unable to return to divinity school. "Every man I zipped in one of those horrible green body bags," he confessed, "a little bit of me died."

After beginning work as a guidance counselor, Doc had finally realized that he was gay, a revelation that troubled him. Nevertheless, the prospect of the reunion seemed agreeable, and he promised to come.

Indeed, when the reunion finally took place in the spacious backyard of the Norman home in Montclair, New York, Doc was there to honor their comrades who had died on Bridge 28. Beth, Norman's wife, had set empty chairs at the flag-adorned tables to mark their ultimate sacrifice.

The weekend passed by too quickly; men wept openly when they bid their goodbyes. It was then that Norman knew why he had gone to so much trouble to arrange the reunion: *I know now why men who have been to war yearn to unite. Not to tell stories or look at old pictures. Not to laugh or weep on one another's knee. Comrades gather because they long to be with men who once acted their best, men who suffered and sacrificed, who were stripped raw, down to their humanity . . . I know them in a way I know no other men. I have never given anyone such trust.*

◇ ♦ ◇

Psychologists studying Vietnam War veterans and the phenomena of post-war stress often contend that the veterans' anger is related to politics. Perhaps to some extent this is true, but what the veterans primarily suffer from is their terrible memories—memories that just won't let them live in peace. In fact, Norman maintains that the Vietnam War experience is unique in that it *exposed more dramatically . . . the lunatic motives that lead to organized butchery and the awful waste that results from it. In our era, it was easy to see that the sacrifice had been for nothing and that perhaps nothing was worth that sacrifice.*

In the end, however, Norman was able to find within his Vietnam experience a deep and abiding consolation. When his second son was born, Norman and his wife Beth asked Craig Belknap to be the infant's godfather, an rite that reunited them, not merely as comrades in arms, but as best friends. There was Craig, holding the baby. For Norman, it was a pivotal scene: *On that Saturday in September, far from the field of battle . . . I knew that the men of Golf Company had done more than just survive the fighting or come through the long aftermath. . . . We had truly come out ahead . . .*

DANZIGER'S TRAVELS

Beyond Forbidden Frontiers
by Nick Danziger, Random House, Inc., New York, N.Y., 1987

Nick Danziger, a 24-year-old British artist, set out with a backpack and a dream to retrace the Silk Road, the ancient trade route described by Marco Polo that stretches from east China to the gates of Europe. Traveling by foot and local transport, with only $1500 in his pocket, Danziger journeyed from London to Peking in the space of eighteen months. En route, he lived with the local people, pitted his wits against government bureaucracies, and broke formidable cultural barriers at every new way station.

As he planned his itinerary, Nick applied for travel permits from Middle Eastern and Asian countries. After months of waiting, however, only Pakistan had responded. He finally decided to forgo visas and make the journey by hook or by crook. In the end, he felt that the experience would be worth the risk of jail--or perhaps even worse--for it would "promote greater understanding of the people along its route . . ."

London to Istanbul

Nick traveled by rail from Victoria Station in London to Istanbul, the same city where Marco Polo had begun his journey in the late thirteenth century. Then, hitch-hiking south along the Aegean and Mediterranean coasts, he stopped intermittently to pick tomatoes and converse with the locals. After meandering inland through southern Turkey, he ended up in Cappadocia. The surreal landscape of this Turkish backland is filled with rock cones, capped pinnacles and craggy ravines, forming endless warrens in which thousands of early Christians once took refuge from Arab raiders. Even today entire cities are built right into the soft rock; the homes and furniture, including tables, chairs, beds, windows and disc-shaped doors are all carved from stone.

Into Syria

With no visa to cross the Turkish border south into Syria, Nick tried to slip past a secondary border post. At the ramshackle hut, two frontier guards apprehended him—and then invited him to join them in tea and backgammon. With a one-week visa in hand, he hopped a battered bus east to Aleppo, where he found his way into a dark, smoky night club. Out of the smoke and pulsating music emerged a sultry belly dancer, swishing between the tables as patrons stuffed folded bills into her gold-braided bikini. Later Nick discovered the exotic siren was a Canadian national who taught dance at UCLA. It was, after all, a small world.

Back to Turkey

Crossing back into the eastern part of Turkey, Nick discovered a culture entirely different from that of the west; both the landscape and the people were hard and angry. Bitter Kurds, hailing from enclaves in many Middle-Eastern countries but denied a homeland of their own, made up most of the population. There, camped along the border of Iran, he found tens of thousands of Kurdish refugees, displaced by the recent Iran-Iraq war. As he continued southward, he doubted that the Iranian border guards, with their hatred of "the Great Satan in the West," would let him pass into their country. But he decided to try anyway, using some forged documents he had obtained. And as luck would have it, the Iranian guard, nursing a machine gun, stamped Nick's passport and put him on the first truck that happened by. Dropped off on the edge of a dusty little town and unable to speak a word of Farsi, he eventually wandered into a bus station and called out, "Tehran," which fortunately sounded the same in both Farsi and English.

Revolutionary Iran

Nick found Tehran to be a city of dualities: Buildings were covered with slogans proclaiming the virtues of the "People's" Revolution, radios blurted out extremist chants, and television channels aired a continuous barrage of military propaganda. However, subtle signs of defiance appeared everywhere: a word whispered against Khomeini, forbidden water sipped during Ramadan, rock music played low late at night.

Near Shiraz, Nick made a dangerous junket to the ancient city of Persepolis, founded by Darius the Great about 500 B.C. Marveling at the immense bas-relief sculptures portraying representatives of vassal peoples to the Persian court, Nick lamented, "It's one of the world's cultural tragedies that such a work of art should now be so inaccessible."

In the northeastern Iranian province of Khorassan Nick lobbied the Afghan mujahideen—the Islamic guerrilla at war with Soviet invaders—to smuggle him into their country. At first the soldiers refused; but a few days later a stranger cornered him and surreptitiously whispered, "You will leave here for a place near the border tomorrow afternoon!"

Clandestine Afghanistan Crossing

As it turned out, Danziger didn't leave Iran the next day, but he was taken to a safe house by two Afghani brothers who swapped his British clothing for the garb of the mujahideen—turban, baggy pants and a *shalwar camise*, the long-tailed Afghan shirt worn outside the trousers. After several failed and frightening attempts, he finally was spirited across the border into Afghanistan. "We traveled at night, skirting Soviet patrols and trying to make the next village before sunrise."

When he reached the fabled city of Herat, which over its twenty-five hundred years of existence had witnessed the passage of Alexander, Ghengis Khan, and Tamerlane, Danziger was shocked to find it a bombed-out ruin under Soviet seige; the Soviet MiG attacks were unrelenting; a number of times he barely escaped death.

Eventually a respected mujahideen commander Ismail Khan befriended Danziger and allowed him to accompany his band of freedom fighters, who were heading towards Pakistan to secure arms from supporters. The group traveled on horseback, alternately evading and attacking Soviet forces. Nick came to love these proud and courageous freedom fighters; to show his solidarity with their struggle, he wore the guerrilla "uniform" they had given him throughout the rest of his journey.

At the Pakistani frontier, the mujahideen learned that the Soviets were preparing to seal off the border; Nick would be trapped inside war-torn Afghanistan. Miraculously, the night before the Soviet assault began, a smuggler offered to sneak the entire company across the border in a battered army truck. It was a harrowing trip as they crept past Soviet patrols and inched around land mines in narrow desert canyons. Three times the truck broke down, and three times Nick concluded that "it was all over." But just before dawn they saw a glow on the horizon and recognized the frontier town of Chaman. They were in Pakistan.

Across Pakistan

Nick's objective now was to traverse Pakistan and cross into China through the Himalayan Khunjerab Pass—before this still-prominent trade route was closed by winter snows. Afghan freedom fighters were welcome in Pakistan, so Khan's group of mujahideen hired a bus to take them to the mountain city of Quetta, along the way passing some three million tent-dwelling refugees from the recent civil war. In Quetta, Nick bought a first-class ticket to the northern city of Peshawar, near the western border of China, and for the first time in months enjoyed a bed and a shower. Because winter was fast approaching, however, he hurried on by transit wagon from the Pakistani capital of Islamabad to Gilgit.

The Roof of the World

At 15,000 feet above sea level, the Himalayan highland where China, Russia, Pakistan and Afghanistan meet is one of the most remote areas on earth. After venturing through several high mountain villages, Nick bribed a Pakistani official with a bottle of Scotch to stamp his passport and allow him to cross over into China on a truck convoy.

Xinjiang Province, China

In the city of Tashkorgan, near the border of then-Soviet Nadzhikistan, Nick was struck by the beauty of the Tadzhik people—tall and lean with a beautifully exotic combination of Eastern and Western facial features. "The people gazed at our convoy of trucks as though they were spaceships."

After winding through steep mountain passes, the convoy reached the Uighur town of Kashgar, a major center of commerce during the Middle Ages. The faces of the Uighurs, a Muslim people, were tanned, wrinkled and hardened by the extremes of temperature in the high mountains. The men were proud and dignified, and wore long black corduroy coats fastened at the waist with scarves.

On the next day, Sunday, the town held a great bazaar. As Nick roamed through the marketplace, the awe-struck Uighurs all wanted to touch his beard and feel his skin. "Never in all my travels have I enjoyed so much my first day in a new country." Two weeks later, a Chinese official granted him special permission to traverse inland China over the great Takla Makan Desert, an honor that had not been accorded a foreigner since the Communist revolution.

The Great Takla Makan Desert

After beginning the trek, Nick quickly learned that other officials were not pleased to see him wandering so far inside China. They insisted that he be accompanied by a guide. When he managed to slip away for a few days and take a camel caravan to some nearby villages, he was arrested and almost jailed. Finally he resigned himself to completing the long, cold and tedious trip through the heart of China by bus—a vehicle which broke down many times, once for as long as 27 hours.

At his wits' end, Nick left the bus at the town of Dunhuang and, after walking along the main highway for three days, hitched a ride to Lhasa—the forbidden city. The gun-toting drivers of the vehicle must have been bandits; military men would have turned him in. It was a long but spectacular journey, winding past yak herds and glaciers scattered over the plateaus of Tibet.

Forbidden City

In Lhasa, the holy center of Tibetan Buddhism, Nick saw a group of people who were making a ritual walk around a carved deity. In order to earn merit in the next life, occasionally they would stop and bow before the object.

The women of Lhasa were considered so disarmingly attractive that a former Dalai Lama had once ordered them to blacken their faces with soot so he would not be distracted by their beauty. Nick found that he wholeheartedly concurred with the Dalai Lama's assessment.

Leaving Lhasa, Nick spent several more weeks in Tibet. Again he was arrested, but this time there was no room for compromise: he was ordered to leave the country by plane the next day. But that night the dauntless traveler, determined to avoid deportation, slipped passed a drowsy sentry, made his way to the road, hitched a ride with a convoy of Muslims, and headed northeast for the Mekong River in central China.

Into the Heart of China

Nick entered into the densely populated Sichuan Province. "In an hour of traveling," he observed, "I passed more people than I'd seen in the whole of Tibet." He was low on money, but it was now late spring and warm enough for him to sleep outdoors. Ranging freely, he took a boat down the Yangtze River to Wuhan, and then an east-bound train to Peking. He writes that it's "worth traveling by train to Peking just to see the station. I felt positively ant-like."

Home

His money now exhausted and his goal of traversing the famed Silk Route achieved, Nick could not even afford a flight back to England—nor, in light of the incredible journey behind him, did he desire such a facile method of travel. Instead he chose to work his way home on a cargo ship—completing a travel adventure that may have been unparalleled since the days of Marco Polo.

THE MEDIEVAL UNDERWORLD

by Andrew McCall, Dorset Press, New York, N.Y., 1979

In *The Medieval Underworld,* Andrew McCall provides a compelling but disturbing analysis of lawbreakers during the Middle Ages. Contextualizing medieval criminality in terms both of history and religion, McCall explains how society regarded and punished witches, prostitutes, thieves, swindlers, beggars, heretics, and homosexuals. Moreover, McCall makes it clear that legal compliance and social conformity were essential survival mechanisms during this period of intolerance, violence, and social strife.

✧ ♦ ✧

In treating the history of the Middle Ages, the points of interest McCall chooses to focus on are fascinatingly unique.

The Middle Ages

The Middle Ages are often thought of as a dark interlude in the progress of Western civilization. Coined by an Italian of the fifteenth century, the term "Middle Ages" designates the eleven centuries of ignorance and fear that elapsed between the fall of Rome in about A.D. 395 and the emergence of the Renaissance in 14th-century Italy.

In essence, the Middle Ages began with the barbarian conquest of the Roman Empire. The ensuing society was developed from an uneasy synthesis of Christianity and paganism. Thus, as Western Europe was steadily raided by Magyars, Saracens, Moors, and Vikings, the early Middle Ages were wrought with violence. Ordinary citizens, powerless to defend themselves, consequently turned to territorial warlords for protection. Although these relationships initially were voluntary, they eventually spawned Western European feudalism. In fact, by the end of the eleventh century, not only had Christianity become the established religion but feudalism had also determined the established social order. However, over the next few centuries as trade routes gradually extended into far-off regions, more towns emerged, money circulated, the demand for labor increased, and many serfs liberated themselves from their lords. Clustering in towns, the freed serfs began to change the order. As McCall points out, *The Middle Ages had in fact been, for all the talk of an Immutable Order, an age of evolution and flux; an age during which ideas and institutions, secular and ecclesiastical, had been developed, adapted and amended . . . an age during which the whole fabric of Western European civilization had, in short, been in a state of continual metamorphosis.*

Crime and Punishment

Medieval society had two conflicting sets of laws: the law of each autonomous region and the law of God (or, Canon law). Secular law combined elements of Roman and Germanic legal systems: Germanic law demanded that the accused prove his innocence, while Roman law put the burden of proof on the accuser (a defendant was presumed "innocent until proven guilty"). In contrast to secular law, religious law maintained that authority from God was transmitted through God's representatives on earth. Moreover, according to the

Church, every "crime" was a "sin" requiring penance, and it was the Church's duty to extract confessions so that the guilty might repent. Besides various means of torture, barbarous rituals were instituted to "draw out" these confessions.

Among these rituals, trial by ordeal was one of the most commonplace. The accused was scalded with boiling water, and judged guilty or innocent depending on whether or not welts formed once the bandages were removed. In another popular ritual, trial by battle, the accused was deemed innocent only if he was victorious on the field. Although the Church later tended to rely more heavily on sworn testimony to determine guilt and to put more trust in human evidence, the rack, the pulley, the iron boot, and various forms of water torture and other instruments to inflict pain still continued to be used.

If medieval society was not known for its amiable judicial standards, it nevertheless demanded *active* and *observable* justice; thus, in order to preserve social order, punishment became an important public event. Not only were stocks and gallows usually set up outside churches, but executions were also carried out in town squares, where corpses of the executed remained for days. Criminals who escaped death often had their flesh branded with hot irons or their limbs crudely amputated. According to McCall: *Conformity at every level . . . and in all matters became essential for the salvation of the soul: to achieve the purpose of his earthly life the Christian was obliged not only to submit to the decisions of the Church courts and of royal justice but also to abide by the customary law of the region in which he lived or was staying.*

Richman, Poorman, Beggarman, Thief

Although medieval armies and mercenaries were bellicose, the poor were responsible for much of the period's violence and crime. During the thirteenth and fourteenth centuries, for instance, when people were devastated both by unemployment and by the plague, crime became a way of life. Thus as new and larger towns sprang up along travel routes and rivers, beggars and thieves flocked there to prey on the numerous urban dwellers. Certainly, it was much easier to "make a living" scavenging along city streets than in rural yards.

Of all medieval towns, those in France entertained the most organized groups of beggars and thieves: the *Malingreux,* for example, collected charity by making themselves appear as if they were suffering from horrible lesions, while the *Pietres* patronized street corners feigning disability. Similarly, in London men gathered on curbs to collect alms by perpetrating a more novel hoax: they pretended to have had their tongues torn out by an iron hook, displaying the appendage—which actually was a piece of tongue-shaped leather—to sympathetic passersby. "It was seldom difficult," McCall writes, "either for locals who turned to crime, or for fugitives from other areas, to become absorbed into the shifting underworld of thieves, beggars, fences, pickpockets and receivers of stolen goods which no medieval town of any size was without."

Prostitutes

The Church denounced prostitution as an invention of the Devil. However, St. Augustine inferred more than once that if prostitution were suppressed "erratic lusts would overthrow society." Consequently, the enterprise became an "admissible evil" in medieval society—a least-of-two-evils type accord.

In fact, as new towns were established, prostitution flourished and eventually took on a more organized demeanor. Official brothel zones proliferated just outside city walls, often contributing sizeable revenues to both church and state. Kings and town councils taxed the brothels, while Popes and bishops leased the "official" property. Indeed, in 1347, Queen Joamma of Naples built a splendid brothel quarter for the prostitutes of Avignon. Other luxurious establishments soon followed at Toulouse, Angers, Strasbourg and elsewhere. However, "prostitution in general remained, throughout the Middle Ages, closely linked with poverty, misery, crime and disease."

Homosexuals

It is difficult to determine how widespread homosexuality may have been in the Middle Ages because there were not many records of cases brought before the authorities. As Christianity took hold of medieval Europe, however, it is clear that the Old Testament story of Sodom became a parable against homosexuality, inasmuch as the crime of the Sodomites was widely presumed to have been homosexual relations. Because St. Augustine had declared that "those sins which are against nature, like those of the men of Sodom, are in all times and places to be detested and punished," people in the Middle Ages viewed death by burning as an appropriate penalty for homosexuality. Interestingly, although female homosexuality was denounced, it was not criminalized as was male homosexuality, probably because of the superstitious reverence for semen that many medievals held.

Heretics

In 311, Emperor Constantine found that an alliance with the Church would boost his power. He realized that it was essential for the Church to command obedience and to retain Christian uniformity of belief by stamping out heresies. Therefore, in 1230, the Inquisition was enacted by Pope Gregory XI. Though it was intended to stop heresies from spreading, it eventually caused them to multiply. Consequently, in the twelfth century many groups such as the Arius and the Montanists emerged to preach against the corruption of the Church.

In the eyes of the Church, some of the worst heretics belonged to the Beguines, a female cult who possessed vernacular translations of the Scriptures. Because the Church strongly opposed public use of the texts, maintaining that proper training was required to make correct scriptural interpretation, the ability to read and write and understand Latin was usually confined to the clergy. Many Christians indeed suspected that there were things in the texts that the Church did not want them to learn. Actually, however, there were doctrines that the Church taught that did *not* appear in the Scriptures. There was no mention of Purgatory, for instance, of indulgences, or of the Pope's all-encompassing influence in the church. "It was chiefly as a result of the Catholic Church's inability to fulfill the role which the Bible-reading dissenters thought it should play," notes McCall, "rather than because of the spread of Eastern gnosticism or the agitation of fanatical revolutionaries, that the medieval Papacy's battle to preserve uniformity of religious belief in a total Christian society was finally lost."

Sorcerers and Witches

As far as the medieval Church was concerned, anyone who practiced magic for any purpose was trying to control the universe, and thus was engaging the Devil. Inasmuch as subjects such as alchemy or astrology were considered evil, anyone who possessed such books was accused of sorcery. Furthermore, the accumulation of knowledge, especially in the natural sciences, was considered a dangerous practice.

Such ideas derived from the earlier Roman and barbarian cultures, which affirmed that certain people possessed the power to work magic. In the Middle Ages these people were labeled "witches." Most "true" witches were women, since females were thought to be more susceptible than males to the persuasions of demons. McCall writes: *Most accusations of sorcery and witchcraft seem to have been made as a result either of personal quarrels or actual attempts to work magic . . . like curing illness or turning metal into gold, which would not today be considered in any way reprehensible.*

Jews

Persecution of Jews inevitably resulted from their cultural practices or religious beliefs. Jews of the classical period became regarded as outcasts; their rights and property were seized. Later during the Middle Ages, anti-Semitism became more virulent, and the Jews had to take their place among those of the medieval underworld.

Thus while the seeds of anti-Semitism were planted shortly after the crucifixion of Jesus, Christians—in their bigotry—normally did not associate the fact that both Jesus and his apostles were Jews. Nor did they fathom that it was Romans who carried out the crucifixion.

Inasmuch as medieval Jews had been sentenced by Christians as social subordinates, it was easy to connect any stroke of bad fortune to the "monstrous Jews." Whenever a disaster occurred, it was a Hebrew affliction. Jews were even accused of poisoning wells to spread the Black Death. Although Christians considered Jews to be sub-human, they believed that in the Last Days the Jews would be spared eternal punishment by their conversion to Christianity. In other words, those Jews who accepted Jesus as their Messiah would avoid Hell. Those who refused to embrace their Lord, however—prostitutes, homosexuals, heretics, thieves, sorcerers, and other social misfits—would be perpetually hurled backwards by a black howling wind, immersed in a river of boiling blood, or forced to run through the burning desert of Hell.

CANNON FODDER

by A. Stuart Dolden, Blandford Press, Poole, England, 1980

Few who fought in World War I are still alive. For most of us, the "war to end all wars" seems a rather quaint and pale precursor to both the high-tech threat and the savage chaos that distinguish our current conflicts around the globe.

But all wars create their own versions of hell. During the years of World War I, the Twentieth Century was still in its infancy, and aircraft were still daringly experimental. Thus, across Europe, infantry foot soldiers advanced slowly, digging trenches every few feet while contending with massive artillery fire and poison gas. Generals used their young fighters to gain ground, apparently unmoved by the loss of life. Because the generals regularly "fed" their front-line soldiers to the enemy cannons, their infantrymen soon became known as "cannon fodder."

One of these young infantrymen, an English Private named A. Stuart Dolden, kept a journal to record his four years as a soldier. Dolden's journal—pages filled with the horror, the day-to-day misery, the occasional boredom, and the inevitable bright and dark humor that colored life for him and his war-stressed comrades—was later published as a book, *Cannon Fodder*.

1914-15

In November, 1914, after completing his schooling as a solicitor (attorney), Dolden enlisted in the London Scottish infantry regiment. After several months' training, he was assigned to a battalion commissioned to dig trenches near the front lines. In July the battalion arrived in the small village of Varennes, France, where they set in with pick and shovel under the summer heat. Their first battles were not with the German enemy, but with the ravenous lice that sucked their blood. Then, in August they headed, first by train and then by foot, toward the front lines.

Near Vermelles, Dolden and his Company-D colleagues moved into behind-the-lines trenches. Their new homes consisted of dugouts—four- or five-foot deep holes tunnelled off to the side of the main trench. Some of the trenches, like "Park Lane," were named nostalgically; others took on more foreboding monikers, like "Rotten Row" and "Death Valley."

Dolden was assigned a box of "bombs" (grenades) which had to be kept at the ready, even as he slept. For four days straight, under nearly constant artillery fire, he dug trenches and dugouts and carried water up the communications trenches towards the front. Finally he was sent to the rear—and allowed to remove his boots. He also had his first hot bath in four months—a great luxury, even though the bathwater was only one inch deep.

One night while he was on guard duty in the rest area, Dolden heard the footfalls of a drunken non-commissioned officer coming up the path—followed by a sudden groan as the officer stumbled into the *midden* where the farm manure was stacked. The officer emerged in an indescribably unsavory but intact condition—only to discover later that he'd lost his false teeth in the manure pile. Just as well he didn't find them, Dolden guessed.

A grenade of 1914 was an unpredictable adventure. Soldiers were instructed to light the detonator, hold the bomb for three or four seconds, then throw it as far as possible. It never worked right, especially when things got wet—as they usually did.

On one assignment to storm a German position, Dolden's company followed a shallow trench up toward the front lines, then, as ordered, they lit and tossed their grenades. As usual, however, it was raining and the devices didn't explode. All at once bullets began hailing down on them from all sides—they were caught in the crossfire between the Germans and their own troops. A bullet splattered through the head of their lead grenadier, and they were forced to crawl in file over his limp body in the struggle back to their regiment—picked off one at a time along the way. One of the soldiers who died that night was Dolden's best friend Johnny Walker. Now Dolden knew first hand—and bone deep—the meaning of the term "cannon fodder."

Soon the regiment was moved to a new area so close to the front that while they spaded the rocky earth they could hear their German counterparts at work just yards away. During the day Dolden's unit cowered in their trenches under continual artillery fire. *No matter which way we turned, we seemed to run into bursting shells. The only thing to do was to crouch down at the bottom of the trench and with palpitating hearts wait and hope for the best.*

One day, after digging a trench far in advance of their lines, Dolden's unit mounted a surprise attack on the enemy. As they rushed forward, German machine-gun fire cut into their ranks. Dolden felt a bullet strike his right thigh. Unable to move in either direction, he huddled in the open along with a few others as the shells rained down around them. The Sergeant-Major handed him a German trenching tool, and Dolden, lying flat, burrowed until he could cover his head and shoulders with earth. Then he turned to hand back the tool to its owner; but the Sergeant-Major did not respond: He had already taken a hit. *I was lying there with dead all round me . . . Behind me I could hear the groans of the wounded. Every now and then one of them would call out, "Mother, Mother."*

Out of a brigade of 5,000 men, only six hundred survived that day's combat. Of the twenty soldiers in Dolden's platoon, he was one of three who returned alive to his unit.

1916

His thigh healed quickly, and Dolden soon found himself assigned to serve as cook for a new company. He "had not the faintest idea about cooking," he noted in his journal, and followed with the observation that "ignorance seemed to be the only qualification for a job in the army."

The camp came under bombardment almost every day as they prepared for the Battle of the Somme. Dolden's quartermaster often bragged that he brought his cooks closer to the action than any other company—and he wasn't lying. But after a few months, since two-thirds of the company had been killed and "we didn't need so many cooks" anymore, Dolden was reassigned to combat duty. For seven successive nights he and two other privates were ordered to crawl out in advance of the front lines, and whatever situation they encountered, to hold their position until dawn. After that week-long nightmare of endurance, Dolden was gratefully reinstated as a full-time cook.

Back in the world of gourmet cookery, the chef began to wonder about all the engorged bluebottle flies that swarmed through the camp. Then, climbing a ridge one day, he almost stepped on a corpse. French and German bodies lay strewn everywhere, feeding the bloated flies.

In addition to the constant shelling, the flies, the rain, and the corpses, Dolden's regiment had to contend with one other formidable challenge: mud. As Dolden wrote: *We had already experienced . . . all the incidences of warfare on other sectors of the line . . . but after our trip to the Somme I realized what a truly demoralizing effect mere mud could have.*

Finally, in November, Dolden was granted leave to go home. After ten days of hot baths and meals with real silverware, however, he returned to the battle lines—to sleep at night on boards floating on the trench waters.

1917

The shelling persisted unabated through New Year's. By then the weather had grown absolutely frigid, and as natural food became scarce, rats became the soldiers' most prolific enemy. Dolden suspected that they were feeding on the dead. Once a rat fell on Dolden's face while he was sleeping, its filthy feet slipping into his mouth before he could reach up and kill it.

When Dolden's unit was transferred to Arras in the spring, conditions were no better: the soldiers had to battle the mud again, while their bodies were attacked by vermin of every sort. As they stumbled toward their destination, covered from head to foot in the muck, one horse harnessed to Dolden's cookstove wagon became so swamped in mud that they had to shoot the delirious animal and then drive over it to continue down the road.

But at last, by late June, Dolden could see that the Allies were making progress. Their unit took possession of more and more abandoned German trenches. Some of these huge excavations were 30 feet deep, and capable of housing fifty men.

Summer passed and the weather again turned colder. The troops slipped on the icy floor boards of the trenches and battled the chill in their bunkers covered only by a ground cloth. Christmas Day of 1917 brought only short rations and more cold; but a few days later Dolden and four companions were able to visit an old French lady in the countryside, who cooked ten-egg omelettes for each of them,

served with potatoes, chicken, chocolate, cigars and champagne. At that moment, Dolden could believe that perhaps it wasn't such a bad war after all!

1918

Upon returning to his unit in France after taking another brief leave, Dolden's unit was sent to stay at a reserve area. One day a shaggy, smelly goat ambled by and started helping himself to their food. When the men tried to drive it away, the outraged goat launched a counterattack, sending them scurrying onto tables for refuge. *The animal stayed just as long as it wished, and then just before dark ambled gently out of the yard, and we were able to come down from our perches.*

Back at the front, the Germans dug in and began a furious barrage of artillery and bombing. They shelled so far into the rear of the Scottish regiment that the front-line fighters were often safer than the men in the reserve areas.

This was also the point during which gassing became a real hazard. All Company A cooks had to visit the hospital for poisoning; one Company B cook was blinded by gas. Once, after a particularly explosive German shelling, Dolden and a companion named Robertson discovered a whitish substance covering the bottom of the trench. They argued awhile about whether it could be gas—the enemy had never before been known to lace their shells with chemicals—and finally an expert was called in. He took one whiff and bolted—with Dolden and Robertson not far behind. The gas made them gravely ill. After a painful recuperation, he accompanied his regiment, cooking faithfully away, as they assumed various front-line positions.

Whenever the troops were about to march to the front, and whenever they came trudging back, Dolden boosted their British spirits with—what else?—hot, steaming tea. Ironically, in fact, after four years of fighting the Germans, it was tea that nearly took him permanently out of action. One day as he struggled to pry open a tea canister that had stood near the fire, he was scalded by a blast of steam that might have left his face scarred for life had it not been for the quick action of a comrade who rubbed the Company's entire one-day butter ration over his burns.

Finally, Dolden's regiment found themselves chasing the Germans back home through France and Belgium. During this "orderly retirement," as the Kaiser's army euphemistically called it, the retreating enemy routinely scorched the earth—burning field, killing farm animals, and then poisoning the carcasses in order to deprive the advancing Allies of provisions.

Finally, on November 11, 1918, Dolden received word that a cease-fire was in effect. When the Armistice followed a month later, he went home. After four years of marching over half of Europe—and watching so many others march straight into needless death—Dolden vowed never again to walk any further than he had to. It was a vow he kept religiously throughout the rest of his life.

WOMEN OF THE WEST

by Cathy Luchetti, in collaboration with Carol Olwell, Antelope Island Press, St. George, Utah, 1982

In the West women experienced an autonomy never before dreamed of, and with this freedom came the necessity to solve their problems in any way they could. Making do became an art shared by both sexes, and "women's work" soon came to mean whatever had to be done . . .

Concerned that "history seldom tells the stories of the eight hundred thousand women who also came West," Cathy Luchetti offers "not an academic history" of those American women who ventured west between 1830 and 1910, but a "document of human experience." She makes use of letters, diaries, journals, and photographs to reconstruct the life stories of eleven female pioneers of the western frontier.

Luchetti's informative introduction offers an overview of both the hardships and the opportunities that confronted the women of the West. Those who migrated on the wagon trains, for example, encountered not only "limited water supplies and scant privacy [but] unsanitary trail conditions [that] contributed to disease and death," and women died at a rate twenty-two percent higher than their male counterparts. Those who managed to maintain their health were expected to serve as nurses to the less fortunate. As a result, women developed a mastery of "herbs, bone-setting, and delivering children" which made their "value to the pioneer community inestimable."

In "Minority Women," the book's second section, Luchetti challenges the stereotype of the "slave-like" position of early Native American women. "While some tribes did hold women in very low esteem," she writes, "other tribes were matrilineal, tracing their ancestry through the mother and bestowing great importance upon women." In fact, while "white women were . . . unable to vote, to own their own property or to sign a contract unassisted . . . Indian women went into marriage fully endowed with their own property, which remained their own and could not be touched by male relatives."

In this section Luchetti also relates the moving stories of the thousands of Black and Chinese women and girls who occupied the West. Many were sold as slaves and then consigned to a life of prostitution on the West Coast.

The eleven personal histories that round out the remaining chapters of *Women of the West* reflect the author's concern with diversity; the women profiled emerge from varying religious, racial, and economic backgrounds. Three of the most illuminating are featured here.

✧ ◆ ✧

Miriam Davis Colt (1817-   )

The twelfth child of seventeen coming into the home of a poor New York City tanner, Miriam Davis began working as a housekeeper at the age of fifteen, using her modest earnings to supplement the family's income and to pay for her own education. After eight years of work and study, Miriam earned her teaching certificate and took a position in Parishville, New York, where she met and married fellow teacher William H. Colt. The two were working and living in Montreal when Colt and his affluent parents decided to join an experimental vegetarian settlement in Kansas. The family immediately purchased 720 acres of land—sight unseen—from the U.S. government and set out for the rugged frontier.

Despite the privations and perils of the journey west, Miriam faithfully recorded in her personal journal the family's itinerary and the way the West of 1856 appeared through her urban eyes: *May 1st—Take a walk out to the levee—view the city, and see that it takes but a few buildings in this western world to make a city.*

But as the Colts drew near to their new home, Miriam's sense of wonder gave way to a sense of uneasiness. On May 12 she mused: *The ladies tell us they are sorry to see us come to this place; which shows us that all is not right. [We] are too weary to question . . .* But the very next day, she asks her journal: *Can any one imagine our disappointment this morning, on learning . . . that no mills have been built; that the directors, after receiving our money to build mills, have not . . . ?* Miriam found herself even more devastated to learn that many families, feeling duped by the directors, had accepted their financial losses and abandoned the project long before the Colts' arrival.

Living in cloth tents, surviving on milk and cornbread, and occasionally waking to find rattlesnakes in their beds, the Colts and other remaining members of the colony began to see some yield from their labors, when, in mid-June, Miriam's journal reports: *. . . Pumpkins, squashes, melons, cucumbers, beans, peas, potatoes, and tomatoes are thriving finely.* Miriam, tired of burning the hems of her dresses while cooking over open fires, soon dismissed her Victorian mores and adopted a new mode of dress—shorter "Bloomer dresses," in which she "can bound over the prairie like an antelope."

But the colony's revival was short-lived: malaria struck several members and the water supply was nearly dried up by the first of July. The sickness, threats from local Indians, and the loss of the family oxen convinced Miriam and William to leave Kansas. And when the couple and their two children departed on September 2 after only four short months on the prairie, they were nearly penniless. William's parents and sister—all of whom chose to stay behind with the colony—died shortly thereafter.

Miriam and William's infant son died a few weeks into their journey, and William himself perished in the ensuing weeks, leaving Miriam and her daughter, Mema, stranded in Missouri until local citizens came to the rescue and arranged for their return to New York. In an effort to earn money to support herself and her daughter, Miriam Davis Colt again picked up her pen and wrote about her year on the prairie. The memoir, *Went to Kansas*, was published in 1862.

Sarah Winnemucca (c. 1844-1891)

The granddaughter of a Piute chief, Sarah Winnemucca roamed the northern Nevada deserts. Having spent part of her youth with a trader's family, she became fluent in English and served as a translator between her tribe and the U.S. Army. During her life Sarah traveled and lectured on behalf of her people; one result of this dedication is her book *Life Among the Piutes* (Luchetti's source for Winnemucca's biographical profile).

Sarah Winnemucca writes of her own beginnings: *I was born somewhere near 1844, but am not sure of the precise time. I was a very small child when the first white people came into our country. They came like a lion, yes, like a roaring lion, and have continued so ever since.* Before long rumors began to spread through the Nevada territories that white men were killing and eating Indians. Then came that memorable morning: sensing that whites were approaching Sarah's tribal village, the alarmed Piute women buried Sarah and the other young girls in order to protect them from the fearsome Caucasians: *... Our mothers buried me and my cousin, planted sage brush over our faces to keep the sun from burning them, and there we were left all day ... Can any one imagine my feelings buried alive, thinking every minute that I was to be unburied and eaten up ... ?*

The following spring, Sarah suffered more heartache when whites fired on her father, grandfather, and uncles as they fished in the Humboldt River: *The widow of my uncle who was killed, and my mother and father all had long hair. [After the massacre, we] cut off their hair, and also cut long gashes in their arms and legs ... for this is the way we mourn our dead.*

Increasingly aware that her people were called "savages" by the whites, Sarah interpreted the difference between whites and Indians. Piute children are "taught to love everybody," she explained, and "don't need to be taught to love [their] fathers and mothers. Among her people, all were equal: "a tenth cousin is as near ... as [a] ... first cousin." Moreover, Sarah continued, Piute women were honored and respected by their husbands, who, following the birth of a baby, assume all of the wife's household work for the twenty-five days afterward. And, "if [the father] does not do his part in the care of the child, he is considered an outcast."

Throughout her life Sarah attempted to bridge the gap between her people and the white settlers, most notably when she worked for the U.S. Army as an interpreter during the Bannock war. Though she helped save many lives on both sides, the outcome of the war was not favorable to her tribe, whose members, half-starved, were forced to walk in the dead of winter to a prison camp in the Washington Territory. Though half her family perished during the trek, Sarah continued to work for some

time as an interpreter. Finally disgusted with the white government's broken promises, she retired from public life around 1884 and founded an Indian school near Lovelock, Nevada, which closed shortly before her death in 1891.

Elinore Pruitt Stewart (1876-1933)

Born in Fort Smith, Arkansas, Elinore Pruitt was one of nine children in a family so poor that she did not own a pair of shoes until she was six years old. When her parents died of a fever, Elinore, just fourteen, took a job with the railroad and assumed responsibility for her brothers and sisters. Elinore compensated for her lack of a formal education by reading newspapers and asking questions. At the age of twenty-two, she married and began writing articles for the Kansas City Star, but her career as a journalist was cut short by the death of her husband just four years into their marriage. With a young daughter to support, Elinore moved to Denver to work in the home of the genteel Mrs. Coney (to whom all of Elinore's published letters are addressed).

Finally, at age thirty-three, Elinore answered an advertisement for a housekeeper that had been placed by a Wyoming sheep rancher, Clyde Stewart. And, as fate would have it, they married after Elinore had spent only six weeks in his employ. Still, she never allowed the union to interfere with her desire to homestead her own parcel of land.

Shortly after her arrival in Wyoming, Elinore proudly wrote to Mrs. Coney: *Well, I filed on my land and am now a bloated landowner. I waited a long time to even see land in the reserve ...* But not content with merely owning a plot of ground—which was, in itself, quite an accomplishment for a woman in her time—Elinore learned how to work it, and to "do many things which girls more fortunately situated don't even know have to be done": *Among the things I learned to do was ... run a mowing machine. ... I got sunburned, and my hands were hard, rough, and stained with machine oil, and I used to wonder how any Prince Charming could overlook all that in any girl he came to. For all I had ever read of Prince Charming had to do with his "reverently kissing her lily-white hand," or doing some other fool thing with a hand as white as a snowflake. ... Well, when my Prince showed up ... he was delighted as well as surprised. I was glad because I really like to mow.*

Indeed, Elinore came to believe that involvement in homesteading could raise women from subjugation and lift the poor out of poverty. In one of her later letters, she urged women to *get out and file for land. ... Any woman who can stand her own company ... and is willing to put in as much time at careful labor as she does at the washtub, will certainly succeed; will have independence, plenty to eat all the time, and a home of her own in the end.*

Elinore Pruitt eventually lost her life as a result of her labor of love: in 1926, she was seriously injured when a covey of quail scattered in front of her horses, causing her to fall beneath the hay mower she was driving. Having never fully recovered from those injuries, she died in 1933.

BLACK COWBOYS

by Paul W. Stewart with Wallace Yvonne Ponce, Philips Publishing, Inc, Broomfield, Colorado, 1986

"Look at that drugstore cowboy," Paul Stewart said to his cousin, pointing to a black man in a cowboy hat. "Who's he trying to fool? Everybody knows there are no Black cowboys." Stewart's cousin assured him, however, that the man was in fact a real cowboy, and since that day in Denver in 1960, Stewart has been on a quest.

What Stewart learned in the intervening years is that after the Civil War more than 8,000 black cowboys—and girls—lived in the Old West; many worked as cattle ranchers, rodeo stars, farmers, and sheriffs. The result of Stewart's long quest is *Black Cowboys*, a history he compiled from taped interviews with these pioneering men and women and their descendants. A blend of true-life stories and photographs, the book makes for fascinating reading.

❖ ◆ ❖

When the Civil War ended in 1865, Americans resumed their westward expansion. Not surprisingly, the Indian tribes resisted this encroachment on their lands, and to combat this "threat" Congress organized four black regiments—the 9th and 10th Cavalries and the 24th and 25th Infantries. Given a monthly salary of thirteen dollars as well as food, clothing and shelter, young blacks eagerly signed up for five-year tours of duty. The Indians called the black troops "Buffalo Soldiers," and held in great esteem their fighting ability, valor, discipline, and loyalty to their superior officers.

For the most part, the contributions of these units have gone unrecognized. For example, the black 10th Cavalry in Cuba rescued Theodore Roosevelt and his "Rough Riders" at the battle of San Juan Hill, but only Roosevelt and the Rough Riders are acknowledged in the history books. "Though their contributions have been downplayed," writes Stewart, "the Buffalo Soldiers truly were the super heroes of the often violent, savage and barbarous West."

Many of these Buffalo Soldiers went on to distinguished careers after their military service. Willie Kennard, for example, applied for the job of marshal in the wild mining town of Yankee Hill, Colorado in 1874. The mayor promptly sent Kennard to arrest a man, holed up in the saloon, who had just killed the father of a girl he'd raped. Kennard shot the man's guns off his belt before he could grab them, and brought him in for trial. Kennard later served as town sheriff.

Stewart points out that not all the blacks in the Old West were men. Mary Fields, for instance, who stood six feet tall and weighed upwards of 200 pounds, was born a slave in 1832. After her escape from slavery, she held a number of jobs in Montana. When her restaurant business folded, Fields got a job as a mail coach driver, regularly "combatting extremely inclement weather, fending off wild wolves, and earning a reputation for delivering the mail."

In her later years, Fields managed a laundry. Once, spotting a man who owed her money, she seize him by the coat, threw him to the ground, and put her foot on his chest. "If you don't pay me the $2.00 you owe me for that laundry," she growled, "you won't get up." The man paid her.

The unsavory Ned Huddleston (alias "Isom Dart") and Benjamin J. Hodges were the black versions of Butch Cassidy and the Sundance Kid. Huddleston, also known as "The Black Fox," was an outlaw with a compassionate streak but a lot of bad luck. Born a slave in 1849, he moved down near the Mexican border after emancipation and made a living stealing horses. Later he gave up outlawing for mining, but an unscrupulous partner spent all his money and drove him off the claim.

Huddleston was later jailed when a cook for whom he worked mysteriously disappeared. When the cook returned and the hapless cowboy was released, he turned to breaking wild horses for a living and took an Indian wife named Tickup. Later, he joined a group of horse thieves, moved to Oklahoma, and spent his remaining days ranching—though many claimed he supplemented his own stock with that of his neighbors. In 1900, as Huddleston sat in front of his cabin, a hired killer gunned him down.

Benjamin Hodges—a forger, cattle thief, trail driver and confidence man—lived in Dodge City, Kansas. A rancher once dickered over the price of some cattle Hodges was selling. After the rancher struck what he thought was a good bargain and swaggered into the saloon to boast of it, someone suggested that he check the brands on the cattle: Sure enough, many of the steers he had bought were his own. The embarrassed rancher refused to pressed charges. Although Hodges did go to trial many times, he was never convicted, and lived to a ripe old age, regaling children with his tales of the old West.

A more respectable, law-abiding cowboy was John Ware, who referred to himself as "the first 'Smoked Irishman' to raise cattle in the Southwest." The six-foot-three, 200-pound Ware became known for his great strength while working on the Quorn ranch in 1888. *The Quorn boys were proud of their top rider's strength so they arranged a lifting contest between John and a hefty newcomer . . . The first lift with hay hooks on a weigh scale was a draw, so the beam was set up a couple of hundred pounds. John lifted mightily and the hay hooks straightened out in his hands. The contest was over.*

On another occasion, a couple of strangers came to the Quorn ranch to dispute the ownership of a horse. Ware convinced them to leave by taking out his .45-caliber Colt revolver and asking, "Shall I kill'em now, boss, or will I wait 'til they take the horse?"

Some black cowboys distinguished themselves for their innovative horsemanship and rodeo riding. Around 1900, rodeo rider Bill

Pickett originated an event called bull-dogging (steer-wrestling). Using no hands, Pickett would bite into the animal's tender nose and thus bring it to the ground. Eventually Pickett earned a fortune performing in Wild West Shows. He was later enshrined in the National Rodeo Hall of Fame.

Jessie Stahl, another remarkable entertainer, sometimes rode his broncs backwards. He was also famous for a practice called "Hoolihanding," in which he chased a steer on horseback, leaped onto its neck, grabbed its horns, and drove them into the ground with such force that the steer couldn't pull them out. (The stunt was later outlawed by the Humane Society.)

James Arthur Walker, an all-around cowboy of considerable talents, was born in Texas in 1868. His sister remembered that as a young man he would often perform the trick of spurring his horse to a gallop, jumping off, hitting the ground, and jumping back on—a feat perfected by Walker years before this "Hollywood Hop" was made famous by the cowboy stars of the silver screen.

Some black cowboys achieved great financial success as ranchers and businessmen. Two prominent examples from Colorado were Andrew Jackson Steele and his sons and Harvey Groves. Steele, who owned three farms, several rental houses, and a number of coal mines, began with only a livery stable and a saloon. He fathered four sons, all of whom went on to attend universities and to hold jobs of considerable responsibility.

In 1890, rodeo cowboy Harvey Groves achieved a measure of fame denied most black cowboys in the West. President Theodore Roosevelt presented Harvey with angora chaps and gold spurs for taking first prize in a broncoriding contest in Colorado Springs. Groves later became a successful businessman and was often mentioned in the *Colorado Statesman,* one of the first black newspapers.

The Groves family lived in Manitou, Colorado at a time when the Ku Klux Klan had a strong following. In 1916, when drinking fountains in Manitou began displaying "For Whites Only" signs, one of the Groves brothers took a shotgun and an ax and destroyed all the drinking fountains in town, while the town sheriff looked on. *He told the sheriff, "Don't bother me and I won't bother you." He was later fined $40 for . . . destroying public property, but that ended the segregated drinking fountains.*

During his life of 83 years, Matthew "Bones" Hooks engaged in three fruitful careers and made the transition between the era of the Old West and that of modern-day America. He also had a reputation of returning good for evil.

Born in 1868, young Hooks worked at several different ranches. In Texas, one owner had "Bones" castrated to prevent him from impregnating any of his seven daughters. After working on the range for almost thirty years, in 1909 Hooks became a porter for the Santa Fe railroad. *His love of horses and talent for riding never left*

him . . . While he was on duty as a porter, he overheard a conversation about a horse that had a reputation of being impossible to ride . . . "Bones" . . . rode the horse to a standstill . . .

In 1930, Hooks left the railroad and became a social and equal rights activist. He started the "Dogie Club," an orphanage for boys, as well as the first boy scout troop in Amarillo, Texas. Hooks died in 1951, deeply mourned by the community he'd serve so well.

Other blacks in the West found success as blacksmiths. Dennis Brown, born in 1878, was a blacksmith apprenticed at the age of twelve. Those who knew him said "he had the uncanny ability to just look at something and tell its measurements." By the time he mastered his craft, he "could fashion most anything out of iron." People from hundreds of miles away would take their horses to him to shoe.

Racism prevented many great black rodeo cowboys from achieving the fame and fortune they deserved. Marvel Rogers, one of the finest riders of all time, was banned from competing in white rodeos and had to make "hat rides"—passing a hat around to the spectators. He wowed onlookers by riding with a lit cigar in his mouth and emitting puffs of smoke at every leap of the horse or bull. This legendary rider, however, suffered much abuse from white riders. "Frequently his boots were used as comfort stations," Stewart notes, "and they'd set fire to the bales of straw where he slept."

Mose Reeder, a rodeo cowboy born in 1885, often rode under the name "Gaucho the Corral Dog." Reeder, says Stewart, best summed up the hardships of the black cowboy on the rodeo circuit: *Your lot as a Black cowboy meant that you drew the roughest horse. If that didn't eliminate you, the next horse you got would be one that wouldn't buck. A non-bucking horse meant no points and that would definitely rule out any hopes of winning. Or, they'd classify you as a professional which would automatically eliminate you or they'd tell you that all the applications for an event were already filled.*

Despite persecution, black cowboys continued to make inroads. Willie (Smokey) Lornes, for example, staged the first Black rodeo in Denver in 1947 to give black cowboys the opportunity to compete for prize money. Marvel Rogers later founded the American Black Cowboy Association and worked as the arena manager for the first Black rodeo in New York City. In 1982, three years after Marvel's death, Charles Sampson became the first Black World Champion bull-rider.

After having long neglected the history of black cowboys, writers and historians have finally begun to acknowledge their substantial contributions to the development of the Old West. Stewart writes: *Some were hardworking, law-abiding citizens, others were noted because of their lawlessness . . . The dangers of the trail were not the only worries of the Black cowboy. Racial prejudice was practiced openly, sometimes at the hands of a trail boss who could inflict indignities of the worst kind . . . It is important that these men . . . not be forgotten—for they too played a prominent role during*

BRAVE ARE MY PEOPLE

Indian Heroes Not Forgotten
by Frank Waters, Clear Light Publishers, Santa Fe, New Mexico, 1993

A preeminent chronicler of Native American history and culture, Frank Waters has been nominated for the Nobel Prize in Literature five times. His book **Brave Are My People** recounts the tragic lives of fifteen noted Native American heroes who lived on the North American continent between 1600 and 1900.

According to Waters, when Columbus arrived the Indian population of North America was about five million. By 1910, however, the population had been reduced to fewer than 200,000.

Although the Native American population has subsequently increased to nearly two million, indigenous Americans still contend with *prejudice, injustice, [and] the lowest poverty level in the country.* But Native Americans, Waters points out, are an extraordinarily resilient people: *They have endured through the centuries because of their loving respect for the earth and their sense of unity with all that exists . . .*

❖ ◆ ❖

POWHATAN

In the late 1500s, the Algonquians—led by Wahunsonacock, who was later named Powhatan by his tribe, after the name of his village—were united in a two-hundred-village confederacy that stretched across the whole Eastern seaboard. Not long after the English settled Jamestown in 1608, Captain John Smith led a group of colonists upriver to meet with Powhatan. The chief offered to trade corn for weapons, but Smith refused. Eventually Powhatan did provide the starving colonists with corn, but he expressed his concerns to Smith: *Captain Smith, I know the difference between peace and war better than anyone else in my country . . . But that you are said to come to destroy my country so much affrights all my people as they dare not visit you . . . What will it avail you to take that by force which you may quietly obtain with love, or to destroy them that provide you with food?*

Nearly half of the 900 Jamestown colonists died that winter, and more would have perished if the Powhatans had not taught them to make wigwams and to plant indigenous crops. In spite of the many deaths, however, new bands of colonists were sent to America with strict orders to "make a profit for the [British] stockholders by any means." *Instead of clearing new forest land [the colonists] drove the Powhatans off their own fields, burned their villages, and worked those captured as slaves.* In retaliation, the Powhatans killed a number of colonists and captured John Smith, whose life was spared by Chief Powhatan's daughter, Pocahontas.

When the British settlers decided to grow tobacco, they took possession of additional lands, which the Powhatans defended. In retribution, the colonists took Pocahontas as a hostage.

For months Powhatan received no word of his beloved daughter. Eventually he learned that she had converted to Christianity and had married a planter named John Rolfe. Soon after her marriage, Pocahontas sailed to England, where she was received at court. Three years later, she died of smallpox, and within a year of her death, her aged father Powhatan, a disillusioned old peacemaker, also died.

THAYENDANEGEA (JOSEPH BRANT)

Because of his abilities, the trustworthy young Mohawk Thayendanegea was chosen as a Pine Tree Leader. Clearly, like the stalwart and upright pine tree, Thayendanegea was destined to not only assist the hereditary chieftains in carrying out their decrees, but, in his own right, he would become a leader of his people. Since the whites called his Mohawk father "Brant," he became known as Joseph Brant.

In the early 1760s, Brant's sister married the Englishman William Johnson, who encouraged the Indians to join the British in fighting the French. Thirteen-year-old Joseph was among those who eagerly joined the conflict, and in return for his services Johnson helped to educate him.

Eventually Brant sailed to England and served as secretary to Colonel Guy Johnson, a post which allowed him to address some of England's most influential government ministers. In one speech before Parliament in 1775, Brant proclaimed: *Indeed, it is very hard, when we have let the king's subjects have so much land for so little, they should want to cheat us in this manner of the small spots we have left for our women and children to live on. We are tired out in making complaints and getting no redress.* Bolstered by these words, the British government promised to restore Mohawk lands if the tribe would support the crown against the American revolutionaries.

Brant returned to America, but his alliance with the British divided the Iroquois League because some tribes chose to ally themselves with the colonists. The Mohawks and British lost the war, of course, but Brant was never captured to stand trial. Still loyal to the British, he escaped to Canada, where he spent the rest of his life translating the Bible into Mohawk.

Interestingly enough, when the Iroquois Confederation of Five Nations was replaced by a new confederation—a realm comprised of thirteen colonies—the new American nation followed Mohawk tradition by adopting the eagle and the pine tree as prominent national symbols.

RED JACKET

The Seneca Sagoyewatha became known as Red Jacket because of his distinguished service to the British during the Revolutionary War. Later, however, he allied himself with the Americans in the War of 1812. But throughout all of these conflicts he always remained a strong opponent of Anglo encroachment. In a speech to the British Parliament, for instance, Red Jacket, a renowned orator, said the following: . . . *Your forefathers crossed the great water and landed on this island . . . They found friends and not enemies. They told us they had fled from their own country for fear of wicked men and had come here to enjoy their religion . . . We took pity on them . . . We gave them corn and meat; they gave us poison in return . . .*

After growing increasingly dependent on alcohol, Red Jacket was deposed as chief in 1827 and died three years later.

MANGUS COLORADAS

As a boy, Mangus Coloradas was called Don-ha, "He-Who-Just-Sits-There," because he always sat up late listening to the discussions of his Apache elders. This habit continued into adulthood, when he is said to have remarked: "Action is useless unless it is the fruit of thought. The heart, the mind, the time must work together."

Toughened by their environment, the Apaches (originally a Canadian people who had migrated southward into Southwestern regions United States) disdained farming and herding. Instead, they supported themselves by raiding Mexican settlements across the border—raids often led by the towering Don-ha. It was during one of these raids that Don-ha chose a Mexican girl to be his third wife. The story goes that the brothers of his first two wives became enraged at this, and he was obliged to kill them. When he appeared before his new wife with his arms covered in blood, Don-ha received his adult name: Mangus Coloradas, or the quasi-Spanish version of "Red Sleeves."

When the Mexicans put a bounty on Apache scalps, American trappers set an ambush as a means of collecting as many as they could. Their plan was to invite Chief Juan Jose and a large group of Indians to a feast. As the women and children came forward to accept a gift of free corn, however, the Americans fired a cannon upon them, killing many Apaches. The suspicious Mangus Coloradas, who had kept himself apart from the crowd, escaped and returned to his people with news of the massacre.

After suffering other similar atrocities, the Apaches finally turned the full brunt of their rage against the Americans. In 1861, the *Arizonian* newspaper reported: *We are hemmed in on all sides by unrelenting Apache. Within six months, nine-tenths of the whole male population have been killed off, and every ranch, farm and mine in the country has been abandoned in consequence.*

By the time the territory of Arizona was created in 1863, Mangus was seventy years old and knew he had little time left. He agonized over which of his sub-chiefs [Victorio, Cochise, Cadette, or the young renegade Geronimo] to appoint to take his place.

As his final act of bravery, Mangus Coloradas marched into a U.S. Army camp carrying a flag of truce. He wanted to discuss the problems of his people with the commanding officers, but they refused to listen. Instead, they tried to provoke him to violence so that they would have an excuse to kill him. At first Mangus, standing erect, ignored their provocations, but when the soldiers began prodding his flesh with red-hot bayonets, he flinched, whereupon the soldiers shot him for "attempting escape."

SEQUOYAH

The half-breed Sequoyah had obtained some schooling. Therefore he became fascinated by the "talking leaves" that the white men used to communicate with others far away; that black marks on paper could convey meaning seemed almost magical.

After joining other Cherokee to help Andrew Jackson fight the Creek Indians, Sequoyah, crippled in the fighting, returned home frustrated by the American government's insatiable hunger for Indian land. He reasoned that if the Cherokee had a written language of their own, they would be better equipped to defend themselves. For four years he labored to develop a Cherokee script, attempting to model it after the ancient Chinese system which used a different character for each word—an overwhelmingly enormous task.

Unfortunately, the tribe became impatient with Sequoyah's delay and burned down his cabin—and with it his painstaking work.

Meanwhile, the American government had forced the Cherokee to accept territory in Arkansas in exchange for their land in their Tennessee and the Carolinas. So it was in Arkansas that Sequoyah resumed his work. In three years he devised a new, more efficient written language that employed eighty-six phonetic characters, one for each sound in the Cherokee tongue. Although he repeatedly demonstrated it to the chiefs, they remained unimpressed.

Sequoyah's fellow Cherokees, however, avidly adopted the script after discovering that it took a Cherokee child only about a month to become proficient in the new writing, whereas mastering the English script took all of four years. As the popularity of the written language spread, Sequoyah purchased a printing press and began publishing a newspaper in Cherokee. Sequoyah became famous and, for a time, his people prospered.

Meanwhile, the U.S. government continued to coerce the Cherokee into accepting more bad land trades. Then, when gold was discovered in Cherokee territory and white settlers tried to uproot them again, the Cherokee fought back in the American courts. However, despite having won a Supreme Court decision protecting their property, thirteen thousand Cherokees were forcibly removed to Indian Territory in an exodus that became known as the "Trail of Tears." During the trek, forty-six hundred Cherokee died.

Sequoyah subsequently disappeared into the Southwester regions of the U.S. and began a search for the remains of the Cherokee language in the languages of other tribes. Later, when the Indian Territory applied to become a state, Indians voted almost unanimously to name the state "Sequoyah." The U.S. government, however, insisted that it be called "Oklahoma."

THE INCAS

The Royal Commentaries of the Inca
by Inca Garcilaso de la Vega (1539 - 1616) translated by Maria Jolas, The Orion Press, New York, N.Y., 1961

El Inca Garcilaso de la Vega was born seven years after the Spanish conquest. As the son of a Spanish conquistador and his native concubine, a Peruvian princess directly descended from the twelfth Inca, de la Vega grew up hearing the oral histories of the Incas that later provided the foundations for his *Royal Commentaries*.

De la Vega's European heritage, of course, also shaped his points of view. The teachings of the Catholic church, for example, formed his distaste for Incan gods and icons, which he referred to as "demons." Despite his orthodox Christian convictions, however, his history of the Incas and their subsequent defeat by the Spanish is generally free of the cultural biases so common among the early European chronicles. Indeed, Garcilaso's privileged understanding of both the Spaniards and the pre-Columbian Peruvians makes his *Commentaries* arguably the most illuminating of all the early histories that delineate the New-World conquest.

Written in 1604, the first of the *Commentaries'* two volumes depicts some four-and-a-half centuries of life under the Incas before the Spaniards' arrival; the second, written in 1616, details events of the Conquest and its aftermath.

❖ ♦ ❖

"Once we were kings, now we are vassals!" the young future historian often heard his grown-up Peruvian relatives exclaim. In response, the curious young boy finally asked his uncle to tell him the history of their ancestors, the Quechua peoples of the Andes who were led by the Great Incas.

" . . . At one time, all the land . . . was nothing but mountains and desolate cliffs," began the storyteller. "The people lived like wild beasts, with neither order nor religion . . . Seeing the condition they were in, our father, Inti, the Sun was ashamed for them, and he decided to send one of his sons and one of his daughters from heaven to earth, in order that they might teach men to adore him and acknowledge him as their god . . . "

Thus, to his son Manco Capac and his daughter Coya Mama, the Sun gave a rod made of gold. "At the spot where, with one single thrust, it disappears entirely," the father advised them, "there you must establish your court." Then the Sun-father set his children down on the shores of Lake Titicaca and pointed them north. They began their journey along the Andean plateau-lands, trying the rod as they went; but not until they reached the Cuzco Valley did the rod disappear into the ground when they pushed it.

Finding the radiant Lord "and his sister-bride" in their valley, the Quechua inhabitants joyfully "assembled around the two Incas [their word for 'divine leaders'], ready to follow them wherever they might lead."

Manco Capac and Coya Mama spent the rest of their lives establishing "natural and reasonable laws" in their mountain kingdom.

Among the most important rules were those governing royal succession: so that the Sun's blood would "not be mixed with human blood," the great Incas would emulate Manco Capac, marrying only their own sisters, passing their thrones in turn to their eldest sons. The ten legitimate Incas who followed Manco Capac obeyed these royal laws of succession, and, in accordance with the Sun's wishes, continued to expand their territories and to build magnificent temples in honor of their gods.

Sometime near the beginning of the European fifteenth century, however, the eleventh Inca, Huaina Capac, modified the divine rule of succession. Abrogating his throne required him to install his legitimate son, Huascar, as sovereign over all the Inca dominions. Instead, however, he proposed to install his illegitimate son, Huascar's half-brother Atahualpa, as ruler over the Andean kingdom of Quito, while leaving coastal Peru and other conquests to Huascar.

Huascar agreed peaceably to this division; but shortly thereafter, the Inca received unsettling news: "strange people, of a type that was quite unknown" had been spotted sailing along the coast. Unaware, of course, that the ship belonged to the great Spanish explorer Balboa, who "had just discovered the Southern Sea," the Inca regarded the sighting as an omen—the first of many "bad omens," including floods, earthquakes, and comets, that began appear in his kingdom. Subsequently, he predicted that the "strange people" would eventually conquer his dominions. "I order you to obey and serve them," the Inca said before he died.

A few years after the death of Huaina Capac, the new Peruvian Inca, Huascar, began to worry about his half-brother's growing power. He sent a message to Atahualpa, demanding that he refrain from further territorial expansion and that he acknowledge Quito as a "vassal state" of Peru. Enraged, Atahualpa sent "more than thirty thousand warriors" to capture Huascar in his capital of Cuzco. Then, after imprisoning Huascar and torturing and slaughtering thousands of his friends, relatives, and loyal subjects, Atahualpa boldly proclaimed himself sole Inca.

Encamped on the isthmus of modern-day Panama, meanwhile, two Spaniards "of very noble lineage," Diego de Almagro and Francisco Pizarro, had formed an alliance with the purpose of conquering Peru. Pizarro, who had first laid eyes on the Inca kingdom from Balboa's ship, now immediately commandeered another ship and left for the southern coast. He was soon followed by Almagro.

The expedition was plagued by hardships. Whenever the Spaniards attempted to go ashore, they encountered hostile Indians. Almagro was blinded in one eye by Quechua arrows, and many of his crew members were killed. And although they were elated to see natives "decorated with emeralds and turquoises, [and] gold nails driven into their faces," once again they were driven away by arrows. Utterly exhausted, Almagro and Pizarro finally sighted the beautiful city of Tumbez, "with its fortress, its temples, palaces, and countless houses." Still, only one brave man, Pedro de Candia, dared go ashore. Convinced that the bearded Candia "was the son of the Sun and that he had come from heaven, [the Quechuas] brought him to the temple, which was entirely paneled with gold, in order that he might see how deeply they revered their god, who was also his father."

When Candia returned to the ship and told his story, the Spaniards, fortified by the realization that Peru "promised to be richer than anything . . . encountered thus far in the Indies," promptly disembarked for the march inland.

As the conquistadors, led by Pizarro and the noble Hernando de Soto astride their magnificent steeds, approached the capital city of Cajamarca, they were greeted by Atahualpa's soldiers. Bowing down at the feet of their awe-inspiring visitors, the Indians led them to the Inca's sumptuous palace, and Pizarro and de Soto bowed themselves down in turn before the ruler's "solid gold throne." Then, as a sign of love and peace, Atahualpa rose to embrace the Spanish commanders and to offer them food and drink—including "all sorts of fresh and dried fruits, various breads, [and] resin wine." The Spaniards were "dumfounded to see such . . . courtesy among people who, until then, they had imagined to be rustics and barbarians." They retained enough presence of mind, however, to advise Atahualpa that "of all the princes in this world," the Pope and King Carlos V of Spain were the most powerful, and that it was their will that the Peruvians give up their idols and worship "the only real God."

Unable fully to comprehend the miserable translation of the Spaniards' inept native interpreter Felipe, Atahualpa nonetheless answered: "I am delighted, divine lords, that you and your companions should have succeeded in reaching such remote regions as these, and that, thus, you should have confirmed the exactness of the events forecast by our ancestors . . . I should like to consider this moment as the happiest we have ever experienced . . . "

The following morning the Spanish visitors "divided their cavalry . . . into three groups of twenty men, [who] went and hid behind a wall," while Pizarro "went to await King Atahualpa at one end of the main square." As soon as the king arrived—on a litter surrounded by thousands of his subjects—Pizarro sent a Dominican priest, Vincente de Valverde, to speak to him.

With "cross in hand," Friar Vincente told the great ruler that if he wished to avoid war, he would have to become a Christian and yield up his kingdom to Spain. Atahualpa replied eloquently: "My vassals and I accept death and whatever else you may choose to do with us . . . in order that the last wishes of my father, Huaina Capac, may be fulfilled"; Atahualpa added, however, that he was surprised to be asked to pay tribute to King Carlos, rather than to God or to Jesus Christ . . . But if you say that I owe nothing to any one of these three, it seems to me that I owe even less to Carlos, who was never lord of this land, and has never even seen it."

At this point, impatient with the long exchange, the Spaniards suddenly "sprang from their hiding places and attacked the Indians," seizing their jewelry and defacing a gem-encrusted gold icon. Since Atahualpa had forbidden the Peruvians to wound the Spaniards—even if his own person came under attack—the ambush ended in a massacre. "More than five thousand Indians were killed, [even though] there were on hand more than thirty thousand armed Indian fighters, and the Spaniards numbered one hundred and sixty!" Then they seized and shackled Atahualpa—and jailed him within his own temple.

Atahualpa assured his captors that his envoys would ransom him with gifts of unprecedented wealth. Indeed, soon after his imprisonment, immense quantities of "gold and silver began to flow into Cajamarca." But even with this, the Spaniards soon started "to grumble, saying that the Inca was poking fun at them, and that his envoys, instead of collecting gold and silver, were simply levying troops to come and free him."

Two Spanish parties, meanwhile, had left Cajamarca to explore other regions of Peru. While Pizarro traveled to the fabled temple of Pachacamc and marvelled at its "unbelievable riches," de Soto and his men visited Sausa, where they met with the imprisoned Inca Huascar. "When your commander-general hears what injustice has been done to me," Huascar told de Soto, "he will surely return my kingdoms to me, and I shall give him much more gold than my brother could ever have promised him." Impressed, de Soto's Spaniards left with Huascar's promise for Cuzco.

Meanwhile, Atahualpa had concluded "that poor Huascar's death would assure him life and liberty"—since the conquistadors would then have all the riches they could possibly desire—and thus had surreptitiously sent orders to guards in Sausa to execute the deposed Inca. After his half-brother's death, however, Atahualpa was not set free; instead he was "tried for the death of Huascar" and for conspiring "to massacre the Spaniards"—a false charge leveled by the unscrupulous interpreter Felipe. Despite the objections of many Spaniards, Atahualpa was sentenced to be burned alive—a common fate for "pagans" of that era. In order to avoid this grisly prospect, Atahualpa agreed to be baptized—after which he was "garroted on a stake driven into the ground." Although Pizarro had agreed "to have him put to death in order to be freed of the responsibilities that Atahualpa's captivity entailed," the Spaniard "went into mourning for him, and ordered solemn funeral rites in his honor."

Thereafter, "even until this very day," as de la Vega concludes the sweeping narrative that his Quechua uncle began for him when he was a child, "the Spaniards [have] remained supreme masters of [the] Peruvian kingdoms, there being no one left to oppose them or even contradict them, because all the Indians, whether they belonged to Quito or to Cuzco, had remained, after their kings were gone, like sheep without a shepherd."

THE FATAL SHORE

The Epic of Australia's Founding
by Robert Hughes, Alfred A. Knopf, Inc., New York, N.Y. 1986

Robert Hughes' magnificent history examines the painful colonization of Australia. Between 1788 and 1868, he relates, 160,000 British castoffs of the "criminal class"—men, women and children— were shipped to the newly discovered continent. Although Australia had never before been inhabited by Europeans—and thus seemed strange and hostile to its new arrivals—they gradually established settlements that grew in size and number, until the vast land was transformed into a flourishing nation.

To vividly depict the lives of Australia's early settlers, Hughes studied hundreds of documents, including numerous letters and diaries. Consequently, as he has written, **The Fatal Shore** "is largely about what [the convicts] tell us of their suffering and survival, their aspirations and resistance, their fear of exile and their reconciliation to the once-unimagined land they and their children would claim as their own."

The Harbor and the Exiles

England's 18th-century rulers had so mismanaged the nation's economy that the vast majority of people were impoverished, unable to eat unless they stole food. In hopes both of discouraging theft and of ensuring a cheap labor force in the nation's horrid factories and industrial plants, the government passed extremely harsh laws: theft of property of less than 40 shillings was punishable by seven years in prison, while theft of property worth more than 40 shillings was punishable by hanging. Despite these severe punishments, however, thievery continued, and by the 1770s England's prisons were vastly overcrowded. Even though many convicts had previously been sent to America, the Revolution had put an end to that practice. Thus, England—which now had begun "warehousing" prisoners on retired, disease-ridden ships—sought a new solution.

A Horse Foaled by an Acorn

When crime first took its dramatic rise, the Georgian citizenry deduced that England's population largely consisted of criminals who should be eliminated. Public hangings thus became commonplace. Often viewed as social events, hangings were attended by hundreds, even thousands, of people, who frequently referred to the tripod-shaped gallows as the "three-legged mare" and to the condemned as one who was to be "foaled by an acorn."

As time passed, however, the public increasingly viewed the condemned as heroic rather than criminal, and fewer convicts were sentenced to death—which put the government right back in the position of having to deal with increasingly overcrowded prisons. The government soon hit upon the idea to ship convicts to the vast Southern Continent discovered by Captain James Cook in 1770.

The Geographical Unconscious

Before Cook's discovery, "the lands south of the equator were thought, even by educated Europeans, to be inhabited by grotesque humans and strange mythical creatures." This notion, however, was somewhat dispelled by Cook, who wrote that the Aborigines "are far happier than we Europeans; being wholly unacquainted not only with the superfluous but the necessary conveniences so much sought after in Europe . . ." Concluding that such a primitive and timid people would pose no threat, the British subsequently encountered larger groups of Aborigines on the southern, New South Wales coast; and as a result of this contact, the native population was reduced from 300,000 to 30,000 within one hundred years.

Having deemed Australia the appropriate place to deposit the dregs of England, the British loaded 736 prisoners (including 155 women) on to a fleet of eleven vessels on January 26, 1788. Most of these inmates had been imprisoned for petty crimes: "Thomas Hawell went down for seven years for stealing one live hen . . . Elizabeth Powley, twenty-two . . . raided a kitchen and took a few shillings worth of bacon, flour and raisins . . . Elizabeth Beckford, seventy, got seven years [for having] stolen twelve pounds of cheese."

However minor their infractions, all of the prisoners—most of whom were seasick and in shock throughout the journey—had to endure abominable conditions. Not only were they deprived of light and fresh air on the ships' lower decks, but they were also chained together, assaulted by vermin and the stench of excrement, vomit, and rotten food. What's more, they had no idea that "they were going on the longest voyage ever attempted by so large a group of people. If they had been told they were off to the moon, the sense of loss and fear could hardly have been worse . . ." Finally, on the evening of January 19, 1789, land was sighted, and the surviving 696 feeble passengers disembarked at Botany Bay.

The Starvation Years

As the fleet's captain, Arthur Phillip, and his officers surveyed the landscape—"a flat heath of paperbark scrub and gray-green eucalyptus, stretching featurelessly away under the grinding white light of the Australian summer"—they realized they were ill-prepared to work the land—and most of the provisions left on the ships had spoiled.

However, by February 7th, after huts and tents had been erected for the convicts, Phillip sensed that hunger was not their only problem. On that day, as "the judge-advocate read the Royal instructions giving Phillip, as Governor, the power to administer oaths, appoint officers, convene criminal and civil court and emancipate prisoners," the captain surmised that no one else in the First Fleet shared his dream of a colony of free immigrant settlers. Indeed, it soon became evident that the marines and officers hated both the convicts and Aborigines, and despised the impartial way justice was meted out by the governor. Moreover, relations between the Aborigines and the convicts were hostile.

Then in 1790, the colony became desperate for food. Rations were cut to survival level. Soon work-weary convicts began to turn against each other, and what little morale they had was destroyed. To make matters worse, the guards "grew peevish; they could not make up their minds on simple matters; they hallucinated . . . They often beat the convicts senseless, sometimes killing them . . . Shortages bred stony, grasping men who robbed one another like jackals snarling over a carcass . . ."

Bolters and Bushrangers

The convicts quickly realized that "in Australia it was easy to escape. The hard thing was to survive." While some were able to hijack or stowaway on ships, most were caught, only to be shot or hanged. Some escaped convicts became "bushrangers." With their "long ratty hair, thick beards, roughly sewn garments and moccasins of kangaroo hide, a pistol stuck in a rope belt, a stolen musket [and] a polecat's stench," they roamed the bush for over 80 years killing countless kangaroos and Aborigines, or terrorizing newly-arrived settlers. Despite their brutalities and outlaw deeds, the bushrangers—similar to America's Old West outlaws—became Australian folk-heroes.

The Government Stroke

After the turn of the century, convicts were assigned to work for settlers who emigrated with the promise of free land and cheap labor. For example, Gregory Blaxland, "the first capitalist-farmer to emigrate," received from the government some "4,000 acres of land in perpetuity . . . and forty convicts to work them with."

Critics of "assigned service" considered the practice slavery. Convicts, however, could be paid for a portion of their labor, and they could also sue their masters—who were forbidden to inflict corporeal punishment—for ill-treatment. Moreover, convicts were freed after serving a fixed term of labor, and their children were always born free. While not as brutal as slavery in America, Australia's system of enforced labor soon created a stagnant economy.

Gentlemen of New South Wales

Most of Australia's first settlers suffered either from a rather violent obsession with land acquisition or from a pronounced boredom with their former lives. After relocating, their new rural lives tended to exacerbate their British class-consciousness. Thus, for instance, they believed that Australia's men "could be roughly sorted into three kinds of people. There were opportunists struggling to be gentlemen; convicts and outcasts waiting to be opportunists; and the failures, who could never become anything." Indeed because most colonials had come to New South Wales to make their fortunes quickly and then return to England, few identified with the more prominent residents of the land they called Australia—a term from *austral,* meaning "southern," which was initially synonymous with condescension or abuse. In fact, decades passed before Australians took pride in their sovereign nation and unique culture.

Metastasis

In the early 1820s, back in England, an unsuccessful attempt at prison reform was made: a famine, coupled with a deteriorating economy quickly impoverished rural workers, who turned increasingly to crime. Even as the crime rate surged out of control, liberal opposition to the "transportation" (deportation) system was strident. " . . . The English authorities knew—and in fact had come to accept—that their ways of dealing with crime had failed . . . The crime rate in England had not dropped; thus one had to conclude that transporta-

tion did not deter." Nevertheless, now addicted to transportation, England had increased the yearly shipment of convicts to almost 3,000 by 1824, but by then Australia's voluntary settlers had begun to outnumber convicts and emancipists. In 1825, responding to the settlers' demands for harsher treatment of prisoners, newly appointed governor Ralph Darling approved the use of "cat-o'-nine tails, whose whistle and crack [became] as much a part of the aural background to Australian life as the kookaburra's laugh."

The Aristocracy Be We

By 1850 the liberals' clamor against transporting convicts had grown louder. The end of the system did not come about because of moral outcries, however, but rather because of two miners, John Lister and Edward Hargraves, who had discovered gold west of Australia's Blue Mountains. Two months after their discovery in February of 1851, a thousand diggers were tunneling on the banks of Summerhill Creek and the road over the Blue Mountains was choked with columns of men. By mid-1852, 50,000 miners were unearthing hundreds of tons of gold, most of which was shipped back to England. The following year, as over 30,000 more emigrants flooded the Southern Continent, England slowed the shipping of convicts to eastern Australia and Tasmania to a trickle.

The End of The System

Early in 1868, "the last convict ship to Australia landed . . . at Fremantle [Western Australia], eighty years to the month . . . since Arthur Phillip brought the First Fleet to . . . Sydney Cove." Twenty years later, when colonial Australia celebrated its centennial, few convicts were still alive, and the government actually tried to suppress the memory of their "stain." For decades, no Australian history book even mentioned the transportation of convicts; records of trials and convictions were burnt so as not to inflict "social pain" on innocent descendants.

In 1901 the six Australian colonies were federated to form an independent Commonwealth—and at this point, ironically, measures were introduced to prevent immigration by non-whites. In 1974, Australia, under Gough Whitlam, abolished the "white Australia" policy in favor of one which was nondiscriminatory.

Although for eighty years England had dumped its refuse on the "fatal shores" of what it deemed a worthless land, Australia struggled to develop a distinctive culture, and, until quite recently, chose to ignore its so-called tarnished origins. Nowadays the thriving nation credits these rejected "criminals" as the cornerstone of its strong, vibrant culture.

Perhaps the history of Australia's "fatal shore" was best captured in 1918 by poet Mary Gilmore, who wrote of the debt Australia owed its unwilling founders:

I was the convict
Sent to hell,
To make in the desert
The living well:

I split the rock;
I felled the tree—
The nation was
Because of me.

INDIA

by Stanley Wolpert, University of California Press, Berkeley and Los Angeles, California, 1991

All of us who wear cotton cloth, use the decimal system, enjoy the taste of chicken, play chess or roll dice, and seek peace of mind or tranquility through meditation are indebted to India. Surprisingly few Americans have much more than a superficial understanding of her deep-rooted civilization, or the causes of her complex modern problems and recurring conflicts.

Stanley Wolpert's compelling book **India** not only sheds greater understanding on the societal and religious differences between East and West, but allows readers to vicariously experience that nation's centuries'-long contributions to world culture and the frustrations endured by her people. India is unique for its sheer endurance. The nation has survived "every invasion, every natural disaster, every mortal disease and epidemic, transmitting an unmistakable imprint on three-quarters of a billion modern bearers."

Wolpert further states: *India is the world's most ancient civilization, yet one of its youngest nations. Much of the paradox found there is a product of her antiquity and youth. Everything is there, usually in magnified form. No extreme of lavish wealth or wretched poverty, no joy or misery, no beauty or horror is too wonderful, or too dreadful, for India. Nothing is 'obviously true' of India as a whole.*

One example of the India paradox is that Indians are among the world's most sensual and yet most austere people. Indeed, sex is worshiped as religious ritual in the same land that invented monasticism. Alongside the cars of the upper classes and buses of the middle-class, roll "bullock carts" loaded with market produce, and people riding bicycles or walking to their daily destinations.

In a similar way, India is a land that is at once startlingly beautiful and menacing: *Heat is to India what fog is to England and smog is to California. She sizzles from March to early November. Crop yields are considerably lower than other nations, but may be attributed to the enervating heat.* Birds and lizards make their nests in the beams of urban dwellings, and snakes, even poisonous ones, are considered good luck. Still, "children are taught early never to reach under a tablecloth or into any dark closet that might have insufficient light to reveal the coiled body of a sleeping cobra."

Even India's famous mountains are marked by paradox. The Himalaya range, which includes both the tallest and the youngest mountains in the world, provides runoff waters to the fertile lower plains and acts as a barrier against outside invasion; yet it also acts as a wall, segregating the national sections from each other and contributing to divisiveness within India—a condition which has left her actually more vulnerable to conquest by outsiders.

India's history, though shrouded in myth, has its roots in historic reality; the epic tales must be sifted for whatever genuine gems that remain. Apparently, more than 4,000 years ago an Aryan people living along the river Indus enjoyed a highly sophisticated, urban, commercial civilization, which was destroyed by severe earthquakes and floods. An oral history was preserved by scattered groups of priests, or *Brahmans*. Later, around 2000 B.C., their writings were recorded in books called the *Vedas*, early scriptures comprising hymns, prayers, and rituals of war and religious sacrifice.

About 1000 B.C., India discovered iron, ushering in an era of rapid change during which territorial kingdoms evolved. The *Mahabharata* and *Ramayana* epics were recorded during the next 300 years. These literary works, rich in legend, lore, character and custom, tell much of what is known of the period. During this time, when many Indians became tired of war and sought ways of achieving peace, *Karma*, the doctrine of reincarnation and teachings of the relationship between the illusory material world and the profound reality of the spiritual world, came into existence. Roughly 500 B.C., Buddha's teachings of peace, as opposed to the Brahmans' warlike offerings, gained popularity.

At the end of the 6th century B.C. there were a dozen religiously affiliated princely states in India engaging in miniwars that continue even today. A common strategy of the competing princes was to release a white stallion—followed by cavalry—let him run free for a year, and then claim all the lands that the animal had traversed. Of course, the current landowner would try to kill or capture the stallion to protect his land from being taken and prove his own sovereignty, and thus "ancient India's miniwars began."

Alexander the Great crossed into India in 326 B.C. His dreams of world unity inspired Chandragupta Maurya to unite the Ganges and Indus valleys for the first time. Maurya's philosophy of government included such ideas as "spying on the loyalty of wives and closest ministers, also generals and lesser bureaucrats." Maurya's grandson, Ashoka, who reigned from 269 to 232 B.C., emulated his grandfather's policies for nine years. Then a particularly bloody war, costing hundreds of thousands of lives, forced him to change strategies. "He decided to follow the paths of war no more, advocating love and nonviolence as the worthiest ideals for empires." These ideals are still remembered today, and many would seek to return to the "golden age" of the Mauryan Empire.

Persians, Scythians and Chinese now poured over the border, each influencing politics. Chandra Gupta II, a Hindu imperial ruler who lived about A.D. 375, resumed India's era of glory. He also inspired Kalidasa, "the Shakespeare of India," to write "Shakuntala," a drama about human weakness which has since provided historians with great insights into the daily life of that period.

In A.D. 711, adherents of Islam slashed their way through southern India for the first time; they would "continue their assault on Indian soil for the next thousand years," and during the last 500 years their monarchs—including

Mahmud of Ghazni, who annually raided Hindu temples—ruled much of India.

Those jihads *("holy wars") left a bitter legacy of communal hatred in the hearts and minds of India's populace, undermining all attempts to reunify the nation under Muslim rule.* The final Islamic wave came about 1526 with Akbar the Great's fifty-year reign over the Empire, his Mughal court initiating a "general policy of religious tolerance of Hindus," and wood royal Hindu families with "beauty, luxury, sensuality, pageantry, and the trappings of power." Soon after, Muslim monarchs returned to Islamic orthodoxy with a vengeance, beheading gurus for refusing to convert to Islam. The Sikhs, another important Indian religion, turned more militant as a result of their persecution.

As the Mughal empire diminished, the forces of the West began to encroach on India. Vasco da Gama began to trade in spices, which allowed Portugal to prevail upon India for almost 100 years. British rule then came to India under the auspices of that country's East India Company—an alliance that would forever change the face of the nation. *Many new ideas, techniques and institutions came to India as a consequence of Western Rule. Private ownership of land, as well as technological inventions, including post and telegraph systems, made enduring changes, whose legacies continue to help modernize Indian life.*

Change brought problems as well as profit. The East India Company, increasingly corrupt, ran roughshod over the Indian people, multiplying abuse that climaxed in the Indian War of 1857. "But [the country] was too divided by unbridgeable gulfs of belief, by doctrines that taught them to hate or mistrust one another." So much brutality would be remembered from the War that Indians would always have difficulty in thinking of themselves as Indians rather than as Brahmans or Afghans or Mughals. Indeed, "even after scar tissue appeared," and "long after the bleeding actually stopped," *young Indians began to awaken to the realization that before they could free India from the shackles of British rule they would have to unite themselves.*

Mohandas Gandhi was probably the greatest leader in Indian history. He returned to his homeland in 1906 after a 13-year stint in South Africa, where racial discrimination changed his life forever. Gandhi was also inspired by Christian concepts of love and self-effacing poverty, the Vedic belief in "the Real" as "the True," and the Buddhist and Hindu ideal of non-violence, which he defined as "Love." In India, Gandhi argued that he could "move the world" by combining these forces in non-violent measure. Subsequently, "he adopted the dress (dhoti) and preached that modernity was 'Satanic,' crushing human souls and destroying all the good and beautiful things of nature."

After World War I, the British imposed martial law upon India. Gandhi, denouncing such "heinous" laws, organized protest marches across the country. When Reginald Dyer, a British brigadier ordered his troops to open fire on Indians without warning, Gandhi, in an effort to throw off the British yoke, "called upon Indians everywhere to boycott any and every-thing British until it ground to a halt." Gandhi sought the support of Muslims as well as Hindus and instructed his disciples "to welcome suffering, to court prison, even death, if need be." But when an angry mob burned two dozen Indian police, Gandhi confessed that he had made a "Himalayan blunder" in assuming his followers were ready to carry out a peaceful mass protest. He retired to an isolated village for almost ten years.

Still, Gandhi did not forget his dream of independence for India. In 1930 he led a band of disciples in gathering their own salt at the seashore near Dandi. This act was illegal, since the government had decreed that salt could only be purchased from British stores. Millions if Indians followed Gandhi's example, and soon the jails were full. At the same time, the leader of the Muslim faction, Jinnah, was demanding a separate Moslem state—an independent state that would be called Pakistan.

In 1942, with Japanese troops at India's gates, Britain partially acquiesced by proposing "Dominion Status" for India. In 1947, however, when the British balked at these terms, a year of civil war commenced. *Gandhi walked from village to village trying to restore peace, but when he moved the madness returned, the mayhem and bloodlust continued.* He died January 30, 1948, never seeing the peaceful India he had so often envisioned.

India's first general election, held late in 1948, took four months to complete, owing to the monumental task of preparing lists of 173 million Indians qualified to vote, 80 percent of whom were illiterate. The Nationalist candidate Jawaharlal Nehru, who had taken over the reins of government at Gandhi's death, was elected. Nehru, himself incorruptible, realized that great power also brought a degree of impotence. Although he was able to articulate the problems of the people, he presented few palpable solutions to India's social and economic troubles.

Nehru's daughter, Indira Gandhi was elected as India's Prime Minister in 1966. Indira made many needed changes, but her fatal weakness was "her passion for power and her unbridled ambition for herself and her sons." She postponed elections so often that militant Sikhs eventually murdered her.

Indira's son, Rajiv, was elected President in December 1984. In his inaugural address he declared: *We talk of the high principles and lofty ideals needed to build a strong and prosperous India . . . But we obey no discipline . . . follow no principle of public morality, display no sense of social awareness . . . Corruption is not only tolerated but even regarded as the hallmark of our leadership.*

In closing, Wolpert remarks: *All of the above is but to say that India's present and future continue to reflect her past. So India keeps changing, but Indian faith in cyclical change makes every return to past norms or traditional values and beliefs seem somehow natural, more proper than what might be viewed as "backsliding" in the West. Indira Gandhi once noted, "India has not ever been an easy country to understand. Perhaps it is too deep, contradictory and diverse, and few people in the contemporary world have the time or inclination to look beyond the obvious.*

CHINA: A MACRO HISTORY

by Ray Huang, M.E. Sharp, Inc., Armonk, New York, N.Y., 1988

In *China, A Macro History*, Ray Huang traces Chinese history from 1600 B.C. to the beginning of the 20th century.

Characterizing China's history as the struggle between the traditional ruling dynasties and the great social and geographical forces that eventually defeated them, Huang writes: *Chinese history differs from the history of other peoples and other parts of the world because of an important factor: its vast multitudes . . . Presiding over the land mass of the East Asian continent, the center of gravity of this enormous entity seems always to have been wrapped in some form of mysticism. In the imperial period as well as in the very recent past, practical problems had to be translated into abstract notions in order to be disseminated . . . Sometimes form counted more than substance. For the bureaucracy operating under such a system, truth resided with authority; both had to move from the top downward.*

❖ ◆ ❖

The Shang Dynasty

Although an ancient *Xia* dynasty was purported to have existed around 2000 B.C., the first dynasty for which there is archaeological evidence is the *Shang* dynasty, founded around 1600 B.C. The Shang, primarily a pastoral people, moved their capital more than six times in their 500-year history. They differed from later Chinese civilizations in that they allowed women relatively more freedom, consumed more alcoholic beverages, and practiced human sacrifice without remorse. More importantly, however, they possessed a sophisticated writing system that even modern Chinese readers can understand.

The Start of the First Empire: The Zhou and Han Dynasties

Around 1000 B.C., the warrior King Wu conquered the Shang, inaugurated the *Zhou* period, and inaugurated an age of "culture, peace and virtue."

However, the Duke of Zhou, King Wu's younger brother, soon devised a schematic infrastructure for the new empire, indiscriminately dividing land along preconceived, geometric lines and taking no thought of the people's needs. *If today such a system were to be imposed on the United States, the uneven shore lines of Michigan would be ignored; in organizing the state we would endow it with boundaries as straight and neat as those of Wyoming . . .* The vast country then consisted of series of small farms laid out on a grid, an agricultural society ruled by a highly ritualistic central government.

In 771 B.C., invasions from "barbarian" tribes caused the Zhou to move their capital to the eastern part of the country. Hence, historians designate the Zhou period before 771 as the time of the Western Zhou and the period from 771 B.C. until 221 B.C. as the Eastern Zhou. The power of the Zhou kings declined during this period and ended between 403 and 221 B.C., when land was divided according to a feudal system.

During this period two schools of thought

formed. Mencius, a philosopher often referred to as the "Second Sage" (Confucius being the first great Sage), spoke of "charity" and "universal compassion." *Legalism*, on the other hand, was used to justify even the most tyrannical acts of China's first sovereign emperor, Qin Shi-huang-di, who sent huge armies to subjugate weaker states.

Having conquered all rivals by 221 B.C., the king of Qin and first emperor of China, Shi-huang-di, immediately moved to consolidate and centralize his new dominions, organizing China along the lines of his native Qin state. Although he standardized the writing system and the units of measurement, Qin Shi-huang-di also had "seditious" books burned and Confucianist scholars who opposed his views buried alive. No philosophy but Legalism, which sanctioned his atrocities, could be read or discussed.

Qin Shi-huang-di's dynasty died along with him in 206 B.C. Divided into factions, the government then dissolved. Four years passed before a former police officer named Liu Bang founded the *Han* dynasty. Laying claim to the first emperor's dominion, the Han ruled China's sixty million inhabitants.

Emperors who succeeded Liu Bang worked in stages to centralize the government. The fifth emperor, Han Wu-di (141 - 87 B.C.), for example, encouraged a Confucianist code of conduct for the empire's civil servants and proclaimed "the promotion of Confucianism to the disparagement of all other schools." *The teachings of Mencius, which held that the state had a stake in the livelihood of the populace, were similarly endorsed without reservation.*

In practice, however, the Confucianist code of honor proved unrealistic when it came to guiding everyday government operations. The heavy taxes imposed on China's millions of farmers, for instance, were impossible to collect, and the government collapsed under its own weight and corruption. As the Han period ended, Zhang Rang, a palace eunuch who wielded political power, reflected the general cynicism of the time when he said to his opponents: "You said that we inside the palace are corrupt. Please tell me, Sir, from the ministers on down, who is loyal and who honest?"

The Second Empire: The Sui, the Tang, and the Song Dynasties

In A.D. 220, China experienced a period of disunity, which lasted until the year 581. The North split into 16 "transient & overlapping" kingdoms, while the South passed through four short dynasties. A warlord named Yang Jian united the North in 581, then conquered the last of the four Southern dynasties in 589, reunifying China and ushering in the Second Empire, under the Sui, Tang, and Song dynasties.

The short-lived *Sui* dynasty was first to offer its people literacy examinations, a practice the later *Tang* dynasty (618 - 906) also adopted. Whereas the recommendation system of the Han had led to the domination of government offices by clans, the examination system created a highly educated bureaucratic class.

Under Tang rule, the empire experienced "the most splendid and satisfying period in the history of China's imperial era." Government efficiency prevailed, and many glorious battles were fought and won.

Then, in 906, the ruling empress Wu Zetian effected a small but real revolution. Empress Wu rejuvenated the bureaucracy in her time, but the Tang fell into decline after her death. Indeed, Huang notes: *. . . The ideal state did not endure because, gradually, the central leadership became indolent and irresponsible . . . The bureaucracy not only expanded its membership but also multiplied its pay scale. Emperors and ministers degenerated in character [and] there were no common efforts that profitably tied the governing and the governed together . . .*

After the collapse of the Tang, the empire again dissolved into separate states. Thus the Song dynasty, lasting until 1279, never ruled over the whole empire, yet was marked by prosperity, cultural advancement, and artistic excellence. Decentralization also proved beneficial: *. . . With the government's center of gravity shifting down to the provincial level, the governance was more responsive to the local situation.*

The Third Empire: The Yuan, the Ming, and the Qing Dynasties

In 1279, the Mongols under Khublai Khan conquered China, inaugurating the Third Empire. The Mongols' mobile culture helped make them superior horsemen and irrepressible warriors but did not prepare them to rule: *The Chinese used to say that the Mongols, after conquering the world on horseback, intended also to rule it on horseback.* The Mongol dynasty, the *Yuan,* lasted until 1368, when the *Ming,* an "introverted and noncompetitive state," came into power.

The founder of the Ming, Zhu Yuanzhang, installed the most centralized government China had yet seen. Moreover, he outlawed sea voyages and forbade participation in warfare outside the empire's boundaries. As the Ming government began its slow decline, its system of taxation failed. And as supply lines broke down and armies were left to scavenge for food, an army of peasant rebels rose up to seize the capital city of Beijing. Emperor Zhu Youjian hung himself before the rebels could overtake him, leaving behind a message that read: "Bandits, I invite you to quarter my body, but I forbid you to do harm to my subjects, any one of them!"

Unable to crush the peasant revolt, the Ming commander invited the Manchus into Beijing to kill the rebels. The Manchus, alien conquerors though they were, quickly adapted themselves to Chinese culture, and initiated the *Qing* dynasty. While at first the Qing did much to reinvigorate the Ming institutions, they made few fundamental changes.

Now as the Renaissance transformed European life, the Celestial Empire remained static, isolated from the world, content to live under the "self-restraint and mutual deference" of the Confucian code: *The calm and orderliness that emanated from this system commanded admiration abroad. It was only in the early nineteenth century when the commercial interests of the West became established in force along the China coast that the Confucian style of statecraft, projecting an ideal perfection, more a fiction than a reality . . . quite suddenly appeared to be a cheap form of government that was neither solid nor flexible.*

Post-Dynasty Governments

In the 19th century, the empire suffered crushing defeats at the hands of English and French military expeditions. During the Opium Wars, the Chinese fought to stop Westerners from peddling the drug, but as the Chinese rose up to expel the Westerners, the wars that followed proved to expose the weaknesses of the nation's static system. Western domination of the Chinese was total. To compound matters, the empire also had entered into combat against Taiping rebels—Christian Chinese peasants who actually had lived in China for years—a fight which resulted in 20 million deaths before the rout of the rebels in 1864.

The Chinese soon instituted the massive "Self-Strengthening Movement," a program aimed at modernization. But the movement's purpose was singular: *China wished to take advantage of Western technology to boost its military strength . . . nothing else. It was guns and steamships that the reformers wanted . . .* These attempts to graft Western factories and machines onto the changeless, passive Imperial bureaucracy ultimately failed. But, Huang contends, *. . . We can now see that failures though they seemed to be, they were necessary steps toward an immense revolution . . .*

With Japan's increasing influence on the region's economy and trade, China's ability to control its own destiny waned. In 1898, for a period of 103 days, the emperor Guangxu issued a series of edicts calling for complete reorganization of government services along Western lines; China must be transformed into a modern nation, Guangxu implored. *But the move toward Westernization was proclaimed in a characteristically un-Western manner. The "Hundred Days' Reform," in line with traditional make-believe, invoked an age-old doctrine that truth always emanated from the top downward. A pronouncement from the throne was a deed accomplished, according to the practice.* Guangxu's brave attempt at reform failed, and the powerful Empress Dowager Cixi put him under house arrest. Then in 1900, Cixi, resenting increased foreign presence in China, declared war on all related foreign powers. The delegation of Westerners in Beijing was besieged, but eventually Western troops put down the Chinese forces in what was called the "Boxer Rebellion."

Following the deaths of Guangxu and Cixi and the failure of the Boxer Rebellion, the revolutionaries in China, led by Sun Yat-sen, managed to take over the government in October of 1911, forcing Guangxu's widow to abdicate. After 2,132 years, China's imperial age had ended; the giant hand of revolutionary Communism would rule the giant empire from that time forward.

Summary Note:

Although he does foresee an increase in pro-democracy militancy and expresses his hope that China is on the path leading to eventual liberation from Communist rule, Huang admits that it remains to be seen what the giant empire's future will be.

AFRICAN CIVILIZATION REVISITED

From Antiquity to Modern Times
by Basil Davidson, Africa World Press, Trenton, New Jersey, 1991

Basil Davidson's *African Civilization Revisited* provides a history of Africa from the vantage point of outsiders who came in contact with its early cultures. Drawing on more than a hundred sources, Davidson's book offers Westerners—who often define "civilization" as only a culture bearing armies and navies, with suit-and-tie-wearing inhabitants, and with a wealth of written chronicles—a uniquely pristine, though often tragic, view of African history.

❖ ◆ ❖

Anthropology, Davidson argues, seems to indicate that the evolution of humanity's ancestors from apes occurred in Africa. All non-human ancestors disappeared 12,000 years ago; humans were producing food across the vast plain of what is now the Sahara Desert 9,000 years ago. By the first millennium B.C.—well before any European contact was made—groups of African *homo sapiens* had developed an iron-based culture and had begun trading with other clans on the African continent.

Though African natives were at one time a single people, or possibly several peoples, according to Davidson, the advent of the iron-pointed spear paved the way for the eventual fracturing of ancestral stocks into a great number of "tribes." Ghana was the earliest of the West African kingdoms, awakening around A.D. 500. East Africa, a more isolated and developed nation, sprang up in the area of Katanga about 300 years later.

Around the eleventh century, during a time when large stone buildings were being built in South Africa—and large, sophisticated cities had sprung up in many parts of the continent—the white man arrived, interrupting the advance of African civilization: *European invasion arrived in the mid-stream of a time of major internal adjustment. It struck Africa at a moment of confusion that was itself the product of new pressures and needs. Thereafter nothing could ever be the same.*

ANTIQUITY

The oldest written records pertaining to Africa come from Egypt and are dated about 2300 B.C. The documents' author, Harkhuf, made four journeys south into Africa, bringing back ivory, ebony, incense, grain, panthers and even dancing pygmies: "My lord sent me," Harkhuf writes, "together with my father . . . in order to explore a road to this country [of the south]. I did it in only seven months and I brought all [kinds of] gifts from it . . . I was very greatly praised for it."

About 450 B.C., the Greek historian Herodotus traveled to a region now called Aswan and to the capital city of Meroe in northern Africa. Detailing his journey, Herodotus recalls watching the curious way in which the Carthaginians conducted trade with the people of western Libya: first the Carthaginians laid their wares on the seashore and returned to their boats; next the natives came to lay a quantity of gold on the beach, then retreated; finally the Carthaginians returned to look at the gold, and if they were not satisfied with the amount, retreated to the boat until more gold was added. "There is perfect honesty on both sides," writes Herodotus. "The Carthaginians never touch the gold until it equals in value what they have offered for sale, and the natives never touch the goods until the gold has been taken away."

EARLY EAST AFRICA

Many centuries separated Herodotus' visit to East Africa and that of the next reliable recordkeeper. The most successful East African city-state, situated on an island on the southern coast of Tanzania, was Kilwa, a municipality set up sometime in the blur of early antiquity. "Kilwa is one of the most beautiful and well-constructed towns in the world," recounts Ibn Battatua, an Arab adventurer. Kilwani legends tell of the island being settled by ancient sailors from Persia, but the inhabitants were clearly black Muslim, largely Swahili. The city of Kilwa controlled gold exports from southern Africa between the 13th and 16th centuries, before being conquered by marauding pagan Zanj bands and left in ruins.

The Portuguese, who for centuries had sought the source of Africa's legendary silver and spice deposits, also came to explore African coastal regions. Eventually their exploits spelled ruin for the East African traders, but it is through these Portuguese plunderings that we have any record of these early African civilizations. Vasco da Gama wrote about his landing on the East African coast: *They forthwith began to play on four or five flutes, some producing high notes and other low ones, thus making a pretty harmony for Negroes who are not expected to be musicians.* The Portuguese sailors, firing their cannons, then went about the business of subjugating the population and extracting the riches they come for.

Da Gama also recorded his landing on Mozambique Island, where he saw Muslims dressed in clothes of "fine linen or cotton stuff, with variously colored stripes, and of rich and elaborate workmanship" as well as Indian ships laden with great quantities of native treasure for transport back to India.

Chinese records also document trade with East Africa, dating to at least A.D. 863. Here were a group of people, Chinese historians wrote, who eat only meat and drink the blood from cattle mixed with milk. The Chinese expressed disgust to find that Arabs often raided the continent for slaves.

EARLY WEST AFRICA

African culture produced exquisite artistic creations. Anthropologists have found bronze and terra-cotta figurines in West Africa that have been dated to the Nok culture, which thrived there between 900 B.C. and A.D. 200. After the Nok reign, in-migration of Africans from the east resulted in a government that strictly controlled the indigenous artistic population. In A.D. 455 an Arabian merchant, Al Bekri, wrote his observations: *The king of Ghana can put two hundred thousand warriors in the field, more than forty thousand being armed with bow and arrow . . .* Following the proscribed regal and formal ceremonies, the king met with his people "to listen to their complaints and set them to rights," ruling fairly in all matters brought before him and delivering verdicts according to sound judgment.

In about A.D. 1240, the ruler of Mandingo prevailed in a great battle against a rival king; the result marked the beginning of the empire known as Mali, located in West Africa. Those who eventually migrated into Mali and settled there were of the Muslim faith. In 1324, the esteemed emperor of Mali, Kankan Musa, made a pilgrimage to Mecca. On his way, a historian writes, he passed through Cairo. As Musa made his way through the throng that had gathered to witness the meeting between Egypt's proud Sultan and the high emperor of Mali, it is recorded that Masa generously distributed so much gold to the people as he went that the price of gold in Egypt foundered for more than a decade.

CENTRAL AFRICA

The Portuguese Alcanova reported the sophisticated methods of the African's gold mining and refining: *. . . They dig out the earth and make a kind of tunnel, through which they go under the ground a long stone's throw, and keep on taking out from the veins the ground mixed with the gold, and when collected, they put it in a pot, and cook it much in fire; and after cooking they take it out, and put it to cool, and when cold, the earth remains and the gold is all fine gold . . .*

Portuguese records describing the inland empire of Monomotapa (Zimbabwe and western Mozambique) show that this area was the source of much of the gold exported from Africa in the early centuries of Western incursion.

By the late 17th century, the Portuguese had "fatally intervened in the affairs of Monomotapa," writes a Portuguese sailor, but they were too weak to impose a system of law and order, and so the door to chaos was opened.

WEST AFRICA MEETS EUROPE

A new phase of history began when West African gold, spices, jewels and ivory were taken for trade directly to Europe rather than traded through the middlemen of the Sahara: *[The trading] was brusque and bloody to begin with, an affair of squalid raids and running fights, but soon calmed to a more or less regular trading partnership.*

Seeing how wealthy they could become, the Portuguese claimed a monopoly on access to West Africa. In doing so, however, they insulted King Don Fernando of Spain, who authorized a navy to sail to Africa and humble the pride of the Portuguese. A band of Spanish fishermen, however, hearing of Don Fernando's plan, sent ships to Guinea in advance of the Spanish monarch's ships. There they offered to trade with the native king and hosted the people to a banquet on their fine vessels. After all had eaten, the fishermen offered to show their guests the holds of the ship, and when the entire assembly was below deck, the Spaniards closed and fastened the hatches and sailed away. In addition to the king himself, they had captured a total of 140 "African nobles of superb physique."

The king protested the captivity of his people, and when they reached Spain, he alone was freed. Alonso de Palencia records the ruler's response to his and his people's incarceration: *That savage [the king] maintained a certain regal authority during his captivity . . . dignity in his countenance, gravity in speech, prudence in conduct, and courage in adversity. On reaching his country, he exercised such cunning in order to avenge himself on his treacherous oppressors that, in spite of the distrust with which they traveled, he succeeded in securing some and keeping them as hostages for as many others of his relations.*

As England, France and others entered into trade with Africa, Portugal immersed itself in the slave trade to support its colonies in America. One tribal emperor in the Congo protested this practice to the Portuguese king: *. . . The merchants are taking every day our natives, sons of the land and the sons of our noblemen and vassals and our relatives . . . and so great, Sir, is the corruption and licentiousness that our country is being completely depopulated.* The Congo emperor recognized that his own people's desire for the Portuguese goods was so great that some would trade others of the tribe to obtain riches, so he begged the Portuguese monarch to end all such trade. His pleas went unanswered.

Richard Eden of England, in depicting the West African communities he visited, characterized himself as thoroughly "dumbfounded" to find advanced civilizations made up of highly skilled craftsmen—not at all the primitive, backward societies he had read about. In 1554, after describing the ingenious methods by which these people created their beautiful artifacts, fishhooks, daggers, and cloth, he wrote: *They are very wary people in their bargaining, and will not lose one sparke of golde of any value. They use weights and measures, and are very circumspect in occupying the same. They that shall have to do with them, must use them gently; for they will not trafique or bring in any wares, if they be evil used.*

Despite their wariness, however, the African civilizations were increasingly exploited by the Western world. All during the 18th century and most of the 19th, the various proud, independent African cultures suffered the expanding impacts of colonialism, bigotry, racism and slave trade. The riches of the continent were heavily exploited, while the interior went largely unexplored. As Davidson concludes: *The "technology gap" between Europe and Africa widened so far in the eighteenth century that Europe's conquest of Africa in the nineteenth was to seem, for most Europeans, right and even necessary. . . . By 1900 there was hardly any part of Africa which had yet to feel the impact of Europe's drive for material possession.*

LEGENDS, LIES AND CHERISHED MYTHS OF AMERICAN HISTORY

by Richard Shenkman, William Morrow and Company, New York, N.Y., 1988

We usually admit that Americans are somewhat ignorant of history, but we don't realize how ignorant . . . Not only have they forgotten what they should remember, but they have remembered what they should have forgotten . . . With time facts fade. But myths seem to go on and on.

Thus Richard Shenkman introduces us to our false memories of American history. Analyzing myths in seventeen categories from Art to War, each section—indeed, each page—shoots down dozens of myths.

Presidents

America's greatest Presidents have long been considered heroes, protagonists beyond reproach. Shenkman unmasks such illusions:

• George Washington was a veritable saint—and no one seems to remember anything that disagrees with that image. He admits to despising his mother—but we remember him only as a devoted son; he was a clever businessman who accumulated a fortune speculating in frontier lands—but we think of him as a simple and trustworthy farmer; his own records show that he was something of a dandy and wore all the latest fashions—but no one speaks of him as being vain. On the other hand, critics have suggested that he fathered several children by his slaves, a claim that is completely at odds with the historical record. In fact, Shenkman suggests, "Washington treated his slaves with respect and compassion and never once is known to have made any advances toward them." And, as near as we can tell, Washington was sterile, unable to have children.

• Likewise, the charge that Thomas Jefferson carried on for years with a beautiful slave name Sally Hemmings isn't easily proved or disproved. One of the most prominent Jefferson authorities discounts the rumor, arguing that Jefferson wouldn't have been willing to seduce a person who didn't have the right to say no. Jefferson's opinions about the press are also varied. Sometimes he asserted that the press was more important than the government itself; but on other occasions he would refuse to even recognize the rights of the press as included among the Constitution's basic freedoms.

• Fortunately, many of the myths told about Abraham Lincoln are true. He did carry important papers in his hat; he did grow a beard at the suggestion of a child; and he had worked as a rail splitter. However, there are also an abundance of fables. He winced when referred to as "Abe," and few called him by that name. The Gettysburg Address was not written on the train on his way to give the speech. In fact, he gave far fewer speeches than is generally believed, and seldom made extemporaneous comments—primarily out of a fear of appearing foolish. Although he did enjoy hearing and telling an occasional joke, he was quite serious and fiercely ambitious. Truly, he deplored slavery, but was not an abolitionist, until necessity forced it on him.

• So entrenched are the myths about the "American Camelot," that John Kennedy is still considered one of the two or three most admired U.S. Presidents. Among the many legendary tales are the ones about his war record and his literary skills. Kennedy, for instance, always maintained that his PT-109 was split in two during an attack on a destroyer; in truth, it was rammed during a lull in the fighting when he and his crew were caught napping. Kennedy rescued one man, not the three he claimed to have saved. Both his undergraduate thesis and his book Profiles in Courage, which won the Pulitzer Prize, were largely drafted by others.

The Family

The fundamental myth of the American family is that it is a fixed and stable institution. Not so, says Shenkman. For example, in colonial times most of the child-rearing was handled by the fathers and not the mothers. Children were treated as little adults, given heavy responsibilities, and provided with very few playthings.

Similarly, despite the myth, colonial Americans did not generally live together in extended families. In fact, elderly adults were often ousted from their homes by their children and sent off to fend for themselves. (It was during the Victorian era that epithets such as "old goat" and "geezer" came into use.)

Americans believe that the family today is suffering from new, unprecedented failures. History, however, does not bear this out. For example, divorce is not a recent scourge. In the 1880s America saw more divorces than any other civilized nation. Though the divorce rate is higher today than in previous decades, this may not be a symptom of a problem getting worse, but a sign of a problem getting better. That is, more people are willing to bring unhappy marriages to an end. We also perpetuate the fear that divorce creates a glut of one-parent homes, but America has always had one-parent homes, although from a different cause: the early death of a parent. As a matter of record, in the nineteenth century we had the same proportion of single parent homes as we have today. *Americans idealize the families of the past and fear the worst for present families. The facts show, however, that divorce is not unique to our times, single-parent homes are not solely the creation of modernity, and since colonial times American families have changed repeatedly.*

War

We tend to think of the American Revolution as being distinct from revolutions today, somehow more genteel and less bloody. In reality, America's fight for freedom had much in common with today's revolutions. No matter how unsullied it may appear in our myths, "real revolution is bloody and fearful." One measure of this violence is the way we treated those who stayed loyal to the English king. Loyalists commonly lost all their property, were tarred and feathered, and sometimes killed. Eighty thousand fled to Canada, to live out their lives in poverty. In truth, almost as many Americans fought *for* England as fought against it.

The minutemen, far from being middle-class patriots, were often farmers and tradesmen—poor, landless, out of work, and out of hope. What's more, they were not very good shots. We are infused with the image of the British Redcoats marching in line while the wily colonists bombarded them from behind rocks and trees. In reality, such guerrilla warfare was rare. For the most part the war was fought in classic European style, as Americans feared that the use of guerrilla warfare might diminish their society.

There is a myth that the dying Benedict Arnold put on his American uniform. In truth, he languished the last three days of his life in a delirious lethargy. Similarly, Davy Crockett did not die fighting to the end at the Alamo; rather, he and several others were captured and executed by Santa Ana's forces.

No two historians can fully agree about the causes and other details concerning the Civil War. For one, Shenkman asserts that the institution of slavery was no worse here than in other countries. Andersonville prison may have been a vile place to be held captive, but the Confederates didn't plan the deaths of twelve thousand Union prisoners: they just couldn't provide any better care; the prisoners were eating as well as their guards.

We often think the sinking of the *Lusitania* precipitated American intervention in World War I, but the fact remains that the United States didn't intervene until two years later. And the Germans, embroiled in the conflict, didn't invent submarine warfare: they just perfected it, as almost a century and a half earlier George Washington had commissioned a primitive one-man submarine to blow up a British warship during the Revolutionary War.

As for the infamous Nazi death camps of World War II and the well-publicized Allied accounts of the horrific sights discovered in them at war's end, these horrors, in fact, were not unexpected. Indeed, Shenkman insists, long before the publicizing of these death camps, the "evidence that Jews were being slaughtered by the millions had been abundant and overwhelming for years." Perhaps the Western world's journalists couldn't quite believe the early accounts themselves; hence the terse reports that were published in the newspapers were often buried on inside pages.

The myth remains that America was forced to drop the atomic bomb on Japan in order to spare millions of lives. The reality is, however, that the Japanese emperor was at the time on the verge of surrender. In like manner, claims that the American military misled the government into thinking that they could win an easy victory in Vietnam are wrong, says Shenkman. In actuality, the military warned that victory in Vietnam would require up to a million soldiers and seven years' time. Even the legendary French patriot Charles de Gaulle warned Kennedy against involvement. That warning and those that followed, however, went unheeded.

Holidays

Nothing is sacred, writes Shenkman—not even holidays. Americans, for instance, celebrate their Independence on the wrong day. Records clearly show that a break from England was declared in Philadelphia by the Continental Congress on July 2, 1776, and an announcement to that effect published in the papers that very night. True, the Declaration of Independence was adopted on July 4, but most didn't even sign it until a later date. Congress itself celebrated independence on July 8th.

"Until the Civil War, Christmas was but scantly observed," Shenkman notes. In 1659 the Massachusetts Bay Colony actually passed a law prohibiting any forms of Christmas observance, imposing heavy penalties on those who did not comply. Only after the Civil War, when retailers discovered the commercial possibilities of Christmas sales, did the holiday find favor. By 1870, December was a merchant's biggest month.

Folklore

Sometimes what we think of as mythical, is actually real—or at least has solid, historical roots. Casey Jones, John Henry, and Mrs. O'Leary were actual people, though most historians cannot substantiate the myth that O'Leary's cow triggered the great Chicago fire.

- Johnny "Appleseed" Chapman was a real person who tramped the Ohio Valley planting trees—but he wasn't poor and he wasn't a hermit. He was, in fact, a successful nurseryman.

- Sam Wilson, in his day, became America's own "Uncle Sam." Wilson supplied meat to the troops during the War of 1812 and it was stamped "US," for the United States. However, an imaginative dock worker once claimed that the initials stood for Uncle Sam—Sam Wilson's nickname—and, ever since, government property has been "Uncle Sam's."

"Just as there are real people falsely believed to be mythical," writes Shenkman, "so there are mythical figures falsely believed to be real." Mother Goose is one of these. The myth is that Mother Goose was Elizabeth Foster Goose from Boston. True, there really was an Elizabeth Goose, but she had nothing to do with the nursery rhymes, which were written by a Frenchman, Charles Perrault (who, incidentally, also invented the tales of Cinderella and Sleeping Beauty). The wrong connection with Elizabeth Goose resulted from a claim by a descendent many years later.

Everyone knows that Paul Bunyon was merely the product of American folklore. In reality, he was the creation of an advertising man to sell the products of the Red River Lumber Company. Thus he is as authentic a folklore hero as Mr. Clean or the Jolly Green Giant.

◇ ◆ ◇

Shenkman concludes that "many of the best-known stories from history are false." But, he adds, *Americans are not to blame for knowing so much that is not worth knowing. Even historians have been taken in. As E. M. Forster wrote, "Nonsense of this type is more difficult to combat than a solid lie. It hides in rubbish heaps and moves when no one is looking."*

THE CANADIANS

by Andrew H. Malcom, Time Books, New York, N.Y., 1985

In 1535, a French sailor named Jacques Cartier sailed up the St. Lawrence River hoping to find a passageway to the Pacific. As the river narrowed, Cartier put ashore at a Huron village and asked where he was. *"Kanata,"* the Hurons replied, referring to the name of their village. When Cartier returned to France, he announced that he had discovered a vast "new land" called "Canada."

"It was," writes Andrew Malcom, "a suitably symbolic beginning for Canada, misnamed, misunderstood, and mistaken for somewhere else." In his book *The Canadians,* Malcom takes his readers on an astonishing tour of Canada's unique history, vast landscape, diverse peoples, and burgeoning economy.

As Malcom reminds his readers, neither the French nor the British were the first settlers of Canada. "The first pioneers," he says, "came several thousand years before Cartier." Drawn by migrating animal herds, the Eskimos and other tribes wandered from Asia across the Bering Strait into Alaska. Once there, Malcom contends, they moved "down the coast and inland [to Canada], where they developed the languages and skills and patience and cooperative social structure so suitable for their survival in their harsh environment." Malcom illustrates their unique adaptation to the land by pointing out that while the Eskimos "had 100 words for different kinds of 'snow,' [they had] no words for 'war'; they were too busy fighting the Canadian climate to face off against each other."

Despite the fact that Cartier "discovered" Canada in 1535, Malcom notes that it took the French "another seventy-five years" before they were able to establish a permanent settlement near Quebec City: the Canadian winters were simply too harsh to endure. The British also had their difficulties colonizing the Canadian wilderness. "In 1610," for instance, the explorer "Henry Hudson pushed west through the ice until a mutinous crew, fearful of continuing farther into the depths of Canada's harsh elements, set him adrift to perish in the vast bay that later carried his name."

Malcom speculates that Canada's harsh geography and climate goes a long way in explaining its "mosaic" history and character. In a sense, he says, the isolation imposed by natural elements have created "archipelagos" of language, culture, and tradition. Thus, for instance, in the absence of a strong national identity, Canadians did not attain independence from Great Britain until 1867. Then, notes Malcom, it had to be forced on them "by a British government anxious to create some kind of political entity to forestall expansion from the south by the well-armed and newly re-United States."

One of the most remarkable characteristics about Canada is the disparity between its land mass and its population. Although its population barely exceeds 25 million, Canada is second only to Russia as being the largest country in the world. It is, writes Malcom, a sort of "distorted parallelogram of almost 4 million miles of land and water stretching far beyond the average citizen's scale of belief. East to west, it spans 4,545 miles and one-quarter of the world's time zones. Scattered across this area like a few specks of pepper on a huge freezer-room floor are the people, huddling together along the porous border with the United States."

While the majority of Canadians live in cities close to the U.S. border, much of Canada's northern tundra remains inhospitable, inaccessible, and unexplored. As Malcom remarks, "The North is but one of the many distinct geographical regions that have made Canada what it is today—and kept it from being more." Indeed, the tundra is so harsh that few animals or plants can survive. Nonetheless, the Inuits, as the "Eskimos" prefer to be called, have managed to endure in the frozen north for centuries. Perhaps, Malcom suggests, it has something to do with their rather unique perspective, a perspective that can best be summed up by their word ionumut, which means "It can't be helped."

Although most Canadians, however, never confront the harsh realities of the Inuits, many have learned to accept a degree of isolation and self-sufficiency that would be unthinkable to most Americans. As a result, perhaps, Canadians tend to identify themselves *regionally* rather than *nationally,* and, though they love their country, they generally disdain the displays of "patriotism and loud bragging" that might be seen in the United States. Also in stark contrast to its neighbor to the south, Canada does not think of itself so much as a "melting pot" for its myriad immigrants than as "a mosaic of separate pieces with each chunk becoming part of the whole physically but retaining its own separate color and identity."

Thus, while Quebec's separatist impulses may not be applauded, it is tolerated. Toronto, in fact, acquiesces to the demands of its many ethnic groups by sending out tax statements in "English, French, Chinese, Italian, Greek and Portuguese." Similarly, Newfoundland, which did not join Canada until 1949, enjoys a unique set of traditions and a "distinctive Irish flavored English" that refuses to give way to any form of "Canadian" identity. As one journalist recently told a foreigner, "Oh, I'm not Canadian either. I'm from Newfoundland."

Of all Canadians, perhaps none is more endangered than the Inuits. Although they have adapted to their unforgiving terrain for millennia, they are losing their traditional means of subsistence and face potentially disastrous consequences. Television, in the minds of many, is to blame. Now living in houses and buying their food in stores, many of the young Inuits must not only be retrained in "survival skills" to avoid death in the Arctic, but they must also learn to develop a perspective on the images of urban life they see daily on the T.V.'s: *"They come in for* the simple struggle of a nomadic life on the tundra," one worried high school teacher told me in a cafeteria serving hot dogs, hamburgers, and a strange delicacy called carrots to children reared on seal and caribou, "and they are exposed without any preparation to jiggling bosoms, talking horses, and colossal spaceship struggles for galactic dominance. If you're brought up with it, you can weed out the garbage. But if everything is a fantasy, how do you discern what is real and what values to embrace? It's a terribly disorienting for these kids."

Consequently, some Canadian schools have begun using television to help educate Inuit children. Teachers, for instance, use *Three's Company* to analyze and question mainstream culture as well as generate discussion about traditional Inuit values. Of course, educators find they must also adjust to Inuit customs: classes, for instance, must be scheduled around Inuit "hunting patterns," and recess is often cancelled when polar bears encroach on the schoolyard.

In contrast to their Arctic countrymen, urban Canadians enjoy the same comforts and high standard of living as their American counterparts. Not only do they take pleasure in the "delightful and delicious ethnic diversity" of large cities like Toronto and Quebec, they also have a strong tradition in the arts. Indeed, some of North America's finest musicians, dancers, actors, writers and journalists are Canadian. Interestingly, however, while native Canadians such as Peter Jennings, Hume Cronyn, Colleen Dewhurst, Margaret Atwood, and John Kenneth Galbraith are widely praised in the United States, Canadians often seem close-mouthed or even perturbed by the accomplishments of their countrymen. As Malcom contends: *It has often been true, especially to and for Canadians, that though famous in their own country, they did not really ever attain true fame until they had become widely known in the United States, where their fans or followers ignored their Canadianness. Then, by some perverse twist of the psyche, Canadians back home finally accepted them as worthy of note. In fact, their international fame might even be a signal back home for some to start tearing down the new star through some kind of "Venus envy."*

Such attitudes, however, seem to be changing. As Canada matures and Canadians become more appreciative of their richly diverse culture, they are rediscovering distinctively Canadian voices and images. Canadian arts are flourishing, while the "relics of the bad old days when being Canadian meant always having to say you were sorry" are rapidly vanishing.

Not surprisingly, then, Canada has strived to differentiate itself from the United States. According to Malcom, an essential aspect of "Canadian identity" is that they are not "Americans." Although Canadians enjoy a similar level of affluence and, at the same time, substantially lower crime rates and infant mortality, they nonetheless tend to feel "overwhelmed" by their southern neighbors. Despite its national sovereignty, Canada cannot help but be influenced by the economy, politics, defense strategies, and environmental policies of the United States: *The American influence is so widespread that American bashing is a frequent and often politically profitable phenomenon in Canada, requiring a certain sophistication that has not always been present among American politicians. They need to know when the tweaking of Uncle Sam's nose or the kicking of another anatomical part requires a response and when, being aired solely for domestic Canadian consumption, it had best be met by a dignified and possibly more powerful silence lest it seem to prove the point of American interference to no American advantage whatsoever.*

Given the "misunderstandings, frictions, and misinterpretations," Canada and the United States have enjoyed remarkably peaceful relations. The United States did invade Canada twice—once during the American Revolution and again during the War of 1812—but for the most part, the twin giants have shared an "unusual closeness" predicated on respect and convenience. As Malcom notes: *Each country has provided an accommodating and familiar safety valve for the discontented of the other. Thus, many draftees fled to Canada during the Vietnam War, while many Canadians emigrated to the United States during the 1930s when the economy did not begin to improve in Canada as it had in the south.*

Now, Malcom asserts, the movement from north to south tends to take the form of "bilateral trade," which exceeds $120 billion a year. Moreover, just as Americans have recognized for years that in North America the "natural market forces are north-south," Canadians themselves have recently begun to benefit from this realization.

According to Malcom, Canada's emergence has stimulated internal debate around "two broad areas: the use of imagination and research and development (R&D), and changing the country's ties with the United States." In terms of the first issue, Malcom writes that R&D has proved "a vital spark for future jobs and investments" and has helped to "spawn a kind of high-technology Silicon Valley North." As for its ties with the United States, Malcom observes that there is much dissent among Canadians. On the one hand, he notes, there is a reticence to identify too closely with the United States; as one Canadian professor expresses it, it's "[no] longer true that what is good for the United States is automatically good for Canada." On the other hand, there is a recognition that trade "is the fastest-growing element of the world's economy and that no two lands anywhere trade more than Canada and the United States [do]."

In Malcom's view, the two countries "would do well to face a hard fact: With the import of trade rising in most domestic economies, magnifying the already intimate relationship of Canada and the United States, scarcely anything is domestic anymore. Virtually everything has an impact somehow on the other country, whether it is a winter frost in Florida that hikes the price of Canadian salads or a government drilling policy that boosts the costs of Canadian natural gas piped into midwestern American homes."

FAMOUS LAST WORDS

by Barnaby Conrad, Doubleday & Company, Inc., Garden City, New York, 1961

One of the world's literary necrophilics, or "last-words" hobbyists, Barnaby Conrad offers his collection as a window into the lives and souls of their speakers. He remarks that, after reading thousands of deathbed utterances, one is struck and comforted by how comparatively pleasant dying is reported to be. Especially when compared with other ordeals. Such as living, for example."

This volume contains "bylines" that date from 600 B.C. to modern times. Many of the individuals are well known; some entirely unfamiliar. Yet their comments live on, evoking our compassion, our laughter, and our understanding. (For this summary, the book's "passing remarks" have been sorted into various categories.)

HEROIC LAST WORDS

Conrad notes, the dying often treat their deaths or the plights of their loved ones heroically in their final words.

Abigail Adams (1744-1818)
While lying upon her deathbed, President John Adams' wife told her husband: *Do not grieve . . . my dearest friend, I am ready to go, and—John, it will not be long.*

Robert O'Hara Burke (1820-1861)
One of the first white men to explore the Australian continent, Burke died of starvation on his journey, after writing these words: *I hope we shall be done justice to. We have fulfilled our task, but . . . we have not been followed up as we expected, and the depot party abandoned their post. King has behaved nobly. He stayed with me to the last, and placed the pistol in my hand, leaving me lying on the surface as I wished.*

John Calvin (1509-1564)
Thou bruisest me, O Lord, but it is enough for me that it is Thy hand.

Saint Joan of Arc (1412-1431)
Burned at the stake for heresy, she said in her dying breath: *Ah, Rouen! I have great fear that you are going to suffer by my death . . . ! Jesus, Jesus!*

AFFECTIONATE LAST WORDS

Tender souls, in spite of their suffering, prove their mettle to the very end.

Andrew Jackson (1767-1845)
The seventh President of the United States died surrounded by his family: *Oh, do not cry. Be good children, and we shall all meet in Heaven.*

Arria, wife of Caecine Paetus (c. A.D. 42)
Commanded by the emperor to kill himself, the Roman hesitated. But Arria plunged the knife into her own breast and said, *Paetus, it doesn't hurt!*

Augustus Caesar (63 B.C.-A.D. 14)
Live mindful of our wedlock, Livia, and farewell.

James, "The Just" (A.D. 62)
As the brother of Jesus was being stoned to death, he was said to cry out: *O Lord God, Father, I beseech Thee to forgive them, for they know not what they do.*

DUTIFUL LAST WORDS

At death's door, there are some who leave with their sense of duty and decorum intact.

Dominique Bouhours (1628-1702)
Bouhours was a grammarian to the end: *I am about to—or I am going to—die: either expression is used.*

John Jay (1745-1829)
The American statesman died after a long life of public service. *I would have my funeral decent, but not ostentatious. No scarfs—no rings. Instead thereof, I give two hundred dollars to any one poor deserving widow or orphan of this town, whom my children may select.*

Anna Pavlova (1885-1931)
The prima ballerina, most famous for the dance from *The Death of the Swan*, saw her own dying in terms of her art: *Get my "Swan" costume ready!*

Commodore Isaac Hull (1773-1843)
Hearing that he would soon die, Hull summoned the undertaker, his lawyer, and his biographer. He calmly put his affairs in order and then said, *I strike my flag.*

HUMOROUS LAST WORDS

Dying is serious business, yet some leave this life chuckling—or leave a smile on the faces of those left behind.

Anne Boleyn (1507-1536)
On the occasion of her execution, she said, *The executioner is, I believe, very expert; and my neck is very slender.*

Baron Henry Richard Vassal Fox Holland (1773-1840)
The English Whig statesman said about George Selwyn, who enjoyed executions and corpses: *If Mr. Selwyn calls again, show him up; if I am alive I shall be delighted to see him, and if I am dead, he would like to see me.*

Joel Chandler Harris (1848-1908)
Asked if his condition had improved any, the creator of the Uncle Remus stories replied, *I am about the extent of a tenth of a gnat's eyebrow better.*

Agemore de Gasparin (1810-1871)
Gasparin's wife wished to follow her frail husband up the steps: *No, you know I like to have you go before me.*

Ethan Allen (1739-1789)
When told by the parson that the angels were waiting, the former soldier shot back, *Waiting, are they? Waiting are they? Well, Goddamn 'em, let 'em wait!*

Comtesse de Vercelles
In his *Confessions*, Rousseau described the

Comtesse's aristocratic passing: "In the agonies of death she broke wind loudly. *Good!* she said, turning around, *a woman who can fart is not dead!*

Henry Ward Beecher (1813-1887)
An energetic orator and preacher of exceptional vitality, Beecher, at seventy-four, was a game patient. When the doctor asked him how high he could raise his arm, he replied: *Well, high enough to hit you, doctor.*

A.E. Housman (1859-1936)
After receiving sedation, Housman listened to his doctor tell a risque story and then said: *Yes, that's a good one, and tomorrow I shall be telling it on the Golden Floor.*

POIGNANT LAST WORDS
To the afflicted, death either comes as welcome relief or a time to reflect on lost opportunities.

John Keats (1795-1821)
After a long struggle with consumption, Keats consoled his devoted friend: *. . . Lift me up, for I am dying. I shall die easy. Don't be frightened! Thank God it has come.*

Queen Elizabeth I (1533-1603)
The queen silenced the Archbishop of Canterbury as he was enumerating her achievements: *. . . All my possessions for a moment of time.*

Sir William Schwench Gilbert (1836-1911)
At the age of seventy-five, Sir Arthur Sullivan's famed collaborator went for a swim in a lake with two young women. When one became frightened, Sir William swam to her saying: *Put your hands on my shoulders and don't struggle.* Gilbert died immediately of a heart attack from the exertion, but the girl was saved.

Paul Gauguin (1848-1903)
The French impressionist, dying in the South Seas, appealed to a missionary: *Dear Monsieur Vernier: Would it be troubling you too much to ask you to come to see me? My eyesight seems to be going and I cannot walk. I am very ill. P.G.* Minutes later he was found dead.

Benjamin Franklin (1706-1790)
"Poor Richard" delivered his last aphorism when his daughter urged him to roll over so that he could breathe more easily. He responded: *A dying man can do nothing easy.*

CHILLING LAST WORDS
Death delivers a deadline for regrets. Some, of course, do not give in to the promptings.

Carl Panzram (died 1930)
When asked for his last words for being executed, this murderer of twenty-three people replied, *I wish the whole human race had one neck and I had my hands around it.*

Michael Bestuzhev-Ryumin (died 1826)
A convicted Russian revolutionary, the first rope broke at his hanging, after which he said, *Nothing succeeds with me. Even here I meet with disappointment.*

PROFOUND LAST WORDS
As in life, many world greats died pondering on the imponderables.

John Luther Jones (1864-1900)
On his gravestone, famous Casey Jones' last words appear: *To the memory of the locomotive engineer, who . . . as "Casey Jones" became part of folklore and the American language. "For I'm going to run her till she leaves the rail—or make it on time with the southbound mail."*

Charles Hodge (1797-1878)
The Presbyterian clergyman said to one of his children: *Why should you grieve, daughter? To be absent from the body is to be with the Lord, to be with the Lord is to see the Lord, to see the Lord is to be like Him.*

Dr. Joseph Green (died 1873)
Looking up at his doctor, the surgeon said, *Congestion.* Taking his own pulse, he then remarked, *Stopped,* and died.

Anaxarchus (died c. 350 B.C.)
The Greek philosopher was bludgeoned to death, repeating the thought, *Pound pound the pouch containing Anaxarchus; yet pound not Anaxarchus.*

Leonardo da Vinci (1452-1519)
The gifted da Vinci died in the king's arms, saying: *I have offended God and mankind because my work did not reach the quality it should have.*

UNSPOKEN LAST WORDS
If actions do speak louder than words, at death's door they become all the louder.

Wolfgang Amadeus Mozart (1756-1791)
Mozart's last act was an attempt to vocally reproduce the sounds of the drum in his great work in progress, *Requiem.*

INSPIRING LAST WORDS
The dying often speak sagaciously or enigmatically.

Marquis de Pierre Simon Laplace (1749-1827)
The French astronomer and mathematicians' final comment was: *What we know is not much; what we do not know is immense.*

❖ ♦ ❖

Barnaby Conrad states that the best known of all last words are from Thoreau. " . . . Asked whether he had made his peace with his God, [Thoreau] answered calmly that he was not really aware that they had ever quarreled.

And a final word from the author expresses his sorrow for the great last words that have never been remembered: "What pains me is to think of . . . all the touching or inspiring or illuminating last moments of the unfamous that have gone unrecorded."

100 EVENTS THAT SHAPED WORLD HISTORY

by Bill Yenne, Bellwood Books, San Francisco, California, 1993

When he set out to compile a list of 100 events that have significantly altered world history, Bill Yenne knew some would object to his choices. However, his purpose was not to argue the merits of each event but "to make history accessible—and fun." The result is a collection of readable, single-page "event summaries" that are both entertaining and informative.

The great events in Yenne's list involve fields as diverse as law, religion, science, politics, communications and ideas. Included are discussions of personalities such as Moses, Christ, Buddha, Gutenberg, Genghis Khan, Newton, and Einstein as well as glimpses into world-altering "events" such as the Dark Ages, the plagues, the Renaissance, the Reformation, the discovery and development of the Americas, major world conflicts, and space travel. You are cordially invited to sample and savor them all in the complete work.

What follows is a scant version of Yenne's books. His self-imposed one-page limit and his chronological scheme force certain historical developments to show up in fragments. In the interest of space and continuity, some of his summaries have been recombined into a single review.

The Dawn of History

There was no particular moment when *prehistory* became *history*. Rather, it was a gradual process. There is evidence that humans lived on all continents at least 30,000 years ago. History began independently for each scattered group as they learned to communicate, then to tell stories; eventually the stories became legends, a kind of oral history. Although we have lost most of those early legends, a few remnants have been handed down to our day. "The dawn of history [began when] legends were first passed from one generation to the next."

Humans probably began banding together about 20,000 B.C., forming largely nomadic tribes. Then about 8000 B.C., people in the Middle East learned to cultivate fields and gardens and to herd sheep and cattle. It was there in ancient Mesopotamia that the first permanent cities were built. As these vestigial social units developed recognized sets of rules and traditions to govern themselves, the "Fertile Crescent" of land that arcs through present-day Iraq, Syria, and southern Turkey between the Tigris and Euphrates rivers became the cradle of Western civilization.

The Written Word

Although humans were drawing pictures on rocks as early as 35,000 B.C., it was not until about 3500 B.C. that the idea of developing a system of widely understood symbols, or letters, to represent speech and ideas was born. The first such phonetic alphabet was the cuneiform alphabet fostered by the ancient Sumerians. This system actually preceded Egyptian hieroglyphics, which used stylized pictures as symbols. The cuneiform alphabet was the forerunner of the Hebrew and Arabic alphabets, as well as those of the Romans and Greeks. The Roman alphabet forms the basis of most European alphabets of today, while the most profound influence on the Russian and Slavic alphabets was early Greek writing. Somewhat later, the Chinese picto-form alphabet was developed and became the cornerstone of other Asian alphabets.

The Might of Rome

"The *Roman Empire* was perhaps the most significant political entity in the history of the Western world . . . " The city of Rome was supposedly named after Romulus, the mythical survivor of twins, nursed by a wolf after a jealous relative threw them in the Tiber River. Around 750 B.C. Romulus or his counterparts founded Rome and began a policy of empire-building and annexing neighbors that lasted for a thousand years.

During the first 500 years, Rome consolidated its control over Italy; then it began looking west. The major power in the western Mediterranean was the city of Carthage on the north coast of Africa, founded in 814 B.C. by the Phoenicians. As Rome continued to expand its dominion, the two city-states collided, resulting in the three Punic Wars. The first (264-241 B.C.), won by Rome, was primarily a naval battle. During the second war (219-201 B.C.), however, the Carthaginian general Hannibal defeated Rome's allies in Spain, then crossed the Alps to win victories in northern Italy. In his hasty assault, however, Hannibal was outflanked by the Roman general Scipio, who promptly turned to strike at Carthage itself. Hannibal returned to defend the city, but lost to Scipio on the Plain of Zama in 202 B.C.

The third war was comparatively anticlimactic. Rome remained a republic until 44 B.C. By that time the city-state had come to see itself as "having a 'manifest destiny' to subjugate and rule as much of the known world as possible." Leading a military campaign that captured what is now France, most of Britain and parts of Germany, General Julius Caesar returned to Rome with his army, deposed the chief consul, Pompey, and proclaimed himself absolute "dictator for life." Fourteen years later, after Julius Caesar's brutal assassination, his nephew Octavian accepted the title of "Emperor"—and became the illustrious Augustus Caesar.

Rome's rise to prominence and Julius Caesar's dreams of expanding the realm in the Mediterranean converged at a historical turning point. By the time of Caesar's death, he had transformed Rome, the first European superpower, into an empire.

The Code of Hammurabi and the Magna Carta

As the city-states of Mesopotamia and the great kingdoms of Egypt evolved, their citizens intermingled and old tribal customs gave way to social chaos. The need for some new, unifying order became crucial. Finally, during the reign of King Hammurabi of Babylon (1792-1750 B.C.), the first true legal code was written. The Code of Hammurabi was engraved on a slab of stone for all to read, and consisted of 282 laws denouncing specific crimes against man and state and imposing penalties for each. The Code also stipulated Babylon's governmental structure and its religion, since the king was also the chief priest. Thus, the Code of Hammurabi represented the first time a subject people were allowed to hold a monarch accountable for his actions and demand that he rule by formal, accepted, published edicts rather than by his changing whims—a major milestone in the development of democratic civilization.

Much later, in 13th-century England, King John, described as "greedy, distrustful and incompetent" by all who knew him, held ultimate control over his subjects. John soon alienated the Pope, the commoners, and even his own nobles and land-owners. Finally, in 1215, these latter two groups united and sent John an ultimatum demanding that he agree to relinquish some control of the government to the tax-payers. Reluctantly, John thus signed this *Magna Carta* (Great Charter).

The Magna Carta recognized the rights of all "free" taxpaying citizens. Quickly it became the basis for the modern English legal system—and, eventually, legal systems world wide—affording individuals rights to trial by jury and to a fair tax structure. Even more importantly, the Magna Carta established that kings were not above the law, but must ultimately answer to the people.

The Magna Carta was further refined in 1679 when the English Parliament forced Charles II to accept the policy of *habeas corpus* ("you must have a *body of evidence*") as specific law. Thereafter, English courts had to possess reasonable evidence of wrongdoing before charging or jailing a person, and monarchs could no longer imprison anyone without demonstrable cause, a principle now embodied in most democratic governments.

The Decades of Discovery

Although Isaac Newton and others made a number of breakthroughs in basic science in the late 1600s, the major advances in *applied* science took place in the 19th century. In 1824, Joseph Niepce discovered that an image printed by the sun on a coating of silver chloride could be permanently fixed with other chemicals. The pictures produced by this technique he called heliotypes ("sun"-types). Niepce's partner Louis-Jacques-Mande Daguerre perfected the process in 1839 and called his pseudo-photographs daguerreotypes.

Then in 1879 inventor George Eastman found a way to mass produce photographic plates in quantity. Ten years later he was able to market strips of celluloid, or "rolls of film," inaugurating today's photographic wonders. Later, Friese-Greene of England and American Thomas Edison cultivated the concept of developing multiple images on a strip of film and then projecting a light through them. If the images were rolled past the light fast enough, the illusion of motion was reproduced on the screen. As early as 1895, the first "motion pictures" were shown in Paris.

In 1876, following the invention and implementation of Samuel Morse's Morse Code and Claude Chappe's high-speed telegraph system, Alexander Graham Bell demonstrated a device which electrically converted the human voice so that, like telegraph pulses, it could be transmitted over metal wires, then converted back to sound at the listener's end. Bell's patent application beat an independent competing application by only two hours—thus securing him credit as the inventor of the telephone system.

Later, in 1895, Guglielmo Marconi, employing Heinrich Hertz's discovery of radio waves eight years earlier, made possible the sending of wireless messages—which spawned the twentieth-century's telecommunications boom.

The Fall of Soviet Communism

By 1990, with the dramatic fall of the Berlin Wall and the disbandment of the Polish Communist Party under Lech Walesa's *Solidarity* government, "a wind of change was blowing through Eastern Europe."

Several revolts attempted by Soviet satellites had, years earlier, already been violently crushed, and Stalin, Khrushchev and Brezhnev in turn had come and gone, each having ruled with an iron fist. The Afghan uprising of 1979, however, had added a terrible burden to the USSR's already mounting economic problems. Then, in 1985, the new reform-minded Soviet president Mikhail Gorbachev promised the people a new system of government favoring *glasnost* (openness) and perestroika (restructuring). He also advocated greater autonomy for Eastern Europe, adding steam to the forces that were already splintering the Soviet Union. Gorbachev still hoped to hold the Union together; "however, Communism had already begun to crumble, and only the iron bands of totalitarianism held the pieces in place." Now as these bonds were loosened, the fifteen satellite republics spun out of Soviet control.

Thus ended a seventy-year experiment in expansionist centralized totalitarianism; and thus also ended an imposed world order. In the international and regional confusion that has manifested itself since the breakup of the Soviet Union, it remains to be seen what direction the world will take next from this latest historical turning point.

THE MARCH OF FOLLY

From Troy to Vietnam
by Barbara W. Tuchman, Ballantine Books, New York, N.Y., 1984

In *The March of Folly*, Barbara Tuchman treats a disturbing pattern in human history: folly in government. She defines *folly* as "the pursuit by governments of policies contrary to their own interests, despite the availability of feasible alternatives." Moreover, a policy must be deemed folly in its own time—because "nothing is more unfair than to judge men of the past by the ideas of the present."

To further expand her definition, Tuchman poses the question: Why does governmental folly so often prevail over common sense? She subsequently supports this premise through many historical examples of indecision, indiscretion, and recklessness.

The foolhardiness of Israel's King Rehoboam, for instance, divided the nation in two. When his people demanded that he ease the burden of forced labor, Rehoboam instead listened to his counselors' advice to heap additional abuses upon the people. Israel immediately seceded from the House of David, leaving Rehoboam to rule over Judah to the north. In response, the King declared war on his former subjects in hopes of reuniting the tribes of Israel. However, reduced and divided, they were conquered by the Assyrians and driven from their land.

The conquest of Mexico was also based on folly. Because the Aztec ruler Montezuma believed that the Spaniards were supernatural beings who had accompanied the god Quetzalxoatl to Mexico, Montezuma inadvertently invited the Spaniards to seize control of his kingdom. Although many Aztecs warned Montezuma that the Spaniards were not gods but altogether human, he ignored his people's counsel—and the invaders moved in to crush the native cultures. Perceived as a coward and a traitor, Montezuma was subsequently assassinated by his subjects. Still, his error in judgment has remained one of the costliest in history.

Another prime example of folly was Japan's World War II bombing of Pearl Harbor. Despite many warnings and the knowledge that a war with United States would probably occasion their defeat, the Japanese decided to attack the U.S. Pacific Fleet. Blinded by dreams of creating a Japanese empire, Emperor Hirohito apparently became incensed by the United States' refusal to make raw materials available to his country. Japanese leaders reasoned that in order to ensure unrestricted transport of such materials, it would be necessary to remove the threat of U.S. naval action in the Pacific. Clearly, Hirohito never stopped to think that an attack on American territory would instead push the United States into full-blown combat.

"The ultimate outcome of a policy is not what determines its qualification as folly," Tuchman emphasizes. "It qualifies as folly when it is a perverse persistence in a policy demonstrably unworkable or counter-productive." To demonstrate that poor decision-making has existed throughout history as a persistent attribute of government, she spotlights four major world events.

The Trojans Take the Wooden Horse Within Their Walls

The legend of the Wooden Horse may or may not be historically accurate; nevertheless it is one of the most famous stories of the Western world. Because of its significance to Western civilization and its reflection on human judgment, the sacking of Troy is a uniquely important example of folly.

Why would the Trojan commanders decide to bring a suspicious-looking wooden horse into their city while they were at war? Indeed, Trojan King Priam mocked those of his courtiers who advised him to destroy the horse, and instead brought it inside the city gates. Then, while the Trojans slept, Greek troops who had hidden themselves inside the structure crept out and laid siege to the city.

Tuchman attempts to put Troy's lesson into perspective: *Although the gods are its motivators, what [the tale of Troy] tells us about humanity is basic . . . It has endured deep in our minds and memories for twenty-eight centuries because it speaks to us of ourselves, not least when least rational.*

The Renaissance Popes Provoke the Protestant Secession

The Popes of the Renaissance era enjoyed great authority throughout most of Europe. Although the six Popes who reigned between 1470 and 1530 were extremely corrupt and perverse, they were nevertheless responsible for some remarkable undertakings, such as uncovering classical treasures, paving roads, assembling the Vatican library, and rebuilding St. Peter's Cathedral. And indeed the Popes were by no means the only decadent Renaissance rogues. Still, if the Popes had not made such a public display of scandal and corruption, the cry for reform would have been far more subdued.

As it was, Popes Alexander VI and Innocent VIII kept mistresses and sired many illegitimate children. These indiscretions did not bother their followers, however, nearly as much as the Popes' continual military rampages, lootings, tortures, executions, and their obsession with luxurious garments and jewels, the combined effect of which nearly drained the whole of the papal revenues.

Later, by the time Leo X was made Pope, the Church was focusing its attention on making money. "God has given us the Papacy, let us enjoy it," Leo cackled. Leo's favorite way to acquire money was by selling indulgences: partial remissions of God's temporal punishments. Although indulgences were not invented by Leo, he popularized the belief that by purchasing indulgences individuals could both atone for future sins and reduce the time their souls spent in Purgatory.

When Leo later authorized the sale of indulgences in Germany, he scoffed at the objections he received. Finally, after Leo had excommunicated many of his German detractors, Martin Luther led the "protestants" to an eventual break from Catholicism.

The Renaissance Popes thus displayed a persistent folly in that *they were deaf to disaffection, blind to the alternative ideas it gave rise to, blandly impervious to challenge, unconcerned by the dismay at their misconduct and the rising wrath at their misgovernment, fixed in refusal to change, almost stupidly stubborn in maintaining a corrupt existing system. They could not change it because they were part of it, grew out of it, depended on it.*

The British Lose America

Why did King George III insist on trying to force the American colonists into submission even though he was cautioned that the harm would outweigh any conceivable gain? Britain sought to maintain its sovereign status in America, and as such, believed it had the right to tax the colonists. The colonies, however, rejected the idea of taxation without representation; since they were denied any seats in Parliament, Britain had no right to tax them.

Taxation, then, was forced on the colonists. However, when the 1765 British Stamp Act was levied, requiring that colonists affix revenue stamps to all official documents, they rebelled. Although King George was fully aware that America yearned for greater independence and less interference, he was not about to bend.

While most colonists had never contemplated rebellion or separation, a decade of provocation from Britain caused them to rethink their position. George responded by immediately calling for a declaration of rebellion to "force those deluded people into submission," disregarding recurrent advice to send a peace commission to America, withdraw troops, recognize independence, and try to maintain rapport. Despite the fact that both Parliament and the British public protested sending a militia to quell the uprising, the King persisted, sensing the loss of America would bring him shame and ruin. As Tuchman points out: *If the British actors before and after 1775 had been other than they were, there might have been statesmanship instead of folly, with a train of altered consequences reaching to the present. The hypothetical has charm, but the actuality of government makes history.*

America Betrays Herself in Vietnam

One of America's own lessons in folly took place in Vietnam shortly after World War II. When President Franklin D. Roosevelt decided to help the French reestablish their colonial rule in Vietnam, he miscalculated the depth of commitment to self-rule of that country's citizens, believing that the Vietnamese would not be ready for self-rule until they were tutored by a democratic nation.

As French involvement increased, various resistance groups arose in Indochina, and the Indochinese Communist Party eventually took control of the scattered independence movement. Now under a consolidated power, the Communists declared that they would take up arms to win their autonomy. Roosevelt was disturbed that an anti-interference party had been formed, but was thoroughly infuriated that it was a Communist-based party. Washington thus intensified its efforts to help France retain power in Vietnam.

Later, during the late 1940s, Roosevelt's successor Harry Truman came up with the theory that any Communist movement in Indochina actually reflected a Soviet conspiracy to take over the world. In an attempt to squelch this plot, he gave France $10 million in military aid and urged the French to continue to maintain forces in Vietnam. Backed by Truman's guarantees that he was acting in their best interests, Americans soon became convinced that French victory was "essential to the security of the free world." The United States armed forces, meanwhile, took a passive stance. Even as the Soviets moved in to crush Hungary and assumed political jurisdiction of nearby Cuba, America minimized the danger: a band of Communists in faraway Vietnam did not pose a threat to American security.

Why didn't the American government learn from the French army and Foreign Legion's defeat at the hands of small companies of Asian guerrilla soldiers? Why did the government ignore French general Charles de Gaulle's advice that negotiation was the only path to victory, and that a war in Vietnam could not be won? According to President John Kennedy—who inherited the Vietnam impasse in 1961—the French and American struggles in Vietnam differed in that the French "were fighting for a colony, for an ignoble cause, [whereas] we're fighting for freedom, to free them from the Communists, from China, for their independence."

By 1963, America was fully involved in an undeclared war in Vietnam, and by the time Richard Nixon took office, public support for the war had dwindled. Indeed, the war's purpose was unclear to most Americans. In spite of urgings from Nixon's top advisors to find alternative solutions to end the war, Nixon—even as his predecessors had done—challenged conventional wisdom. Why did some of America's best minds underestimate the determination of Vietnam to resist foreign intervention? Ultimately, who or what was to blame? "Not ignorance," answers Tuchman, "but refusal to credit the evidence and . . . refusal to grant stature and fixed purpose to a 'fourth-rate' Asiatic country were the determining factors, much as in the case of the British attitude toward the American colonies. The irony of history is inexorable."

Clearly, in the case of Vietnam, possible losses and possible gains were not properly calculated. "Human casualties are bearable when they are believed to have served a purpose," Tuchman writes. "[However], they are bitter when, as in this case, 45,000 killed and 300,000 wounded were sacrificed for nothing." The misfortune for America, she believes, was the absence of a leader who had the courage to end the Vietnam War.

❖ ♦ ❖

Still, even today, the march of folly persists. It is, however, perhaps only in hindsight that we can realize how truly foolish governments can be. *The March of Folly* thus reveals far more than a few accounts of senseless choices; Tuchman's book leaves us wondering why we do not learn from history—and if we ever will.

SEEDS OF CHANGE

by Henry Hobhouse, Harper and Row, New York, N.Y., 1986

Men have always liked to believe in their own influence and direction in the course of time. These claims, however, sometimes conceal the truth. This book is about an unexpected source of change, which has hitherto been obscured because man has been looking too closely at his fellow men . . .

Scholars have long recognized the impact of crop failures and the rise of new crops on world history, but they have not always appreciated the full scope of that impact. Now, after meticulously studying eighty separate plants, Henry Hobhouse has identified five which have clearly changed the course of world events: quinine, sugar cane, tea, cotton and the potato.

QUININE

Malaria, a disease common to many parts of the world, is caused by a parasite transmitted by the *anopheles* mosquito. After the mosquito bites a victim, the parasite travels to the liver and damages the blood's red corpuscles. Fever, weakness and death often follow.

In ancient times, the concentration of people in cities near mosquito habitats led to the infection of whole civilizations. Malaria was also a major player in dictating the outcomes of wars: before World War I, more soldiers died of malaria than died in combat.

There is a story told that in 1638 the wife of the Spanish viceroy in Lima, Peru lay critically ill with malaria. A desperate physician finally tried a native cure containing the bark—or "kina" in the local Quechua language—of the cinchona tree. The wife was miraculously healed, and she and the physician later carried the cure back to Spain, where it was soon hailed as the wonder drug of the age. Elements of this story may be fictional, but cinchona bark did become a major new trading commodity during the mid sixteen hundreds. Because harvesting the bark usually killed the tree, however, over time the high demand for the new product—by now known in English as *quinine*—threatened to eliminate its source.

The British were particularly concerned about this scarcity because of debilitating malarial outbreaks in their Indian colonies. In the 1860s, British adventurer Clement Markham managed to bring a few cinchona plants from war-torn South America to England. Samples were also transported to India, where a Scottish gardener named McIvor found a way to harvest an annual crop from the trees without destroying them. The Dutch also began cultivating cinchona plantations.

The search for a chemical substitute for quinine began in 1834, with research efforts concentrated in England and Germany. By 1940 an artificial quinine had been developed from coal tar; it soon became one of the underpinnings of German industry.

Without quinine, India would still be an underpopulated country. What's more, the industrial development of much of the world in the 19th and 20th centuries has been based on cheap Oriental labor—a force that would have been vastly weakened without quinine. And finally, without artificial quinine for the Allied troops in Asia, Japan probably would have prevailed in World War II.

The triumphant success of quinine, clearly one of the pivotal plants of world history, leads one to ponder what other potential wonder drugs are being destroyed right now with the rapid destruction of the Amazon rain forest.

SUGAR CANE

Sugar cane is a grass native to Polynesia, but apparently roots of the plant washed up and flourished on other tropical shores. It was first refined for its sugar content in India about 700 B.C. Over the next 2000 years the demand for the substance—which many considered to hold magical properties—grew steadily, particularly in cold countries where grapes, with their natural sweetness, were not available. The value of sugar also expanded with the growth of bitter hot drinks—coffee, tea, chocolate—that required a sweetener to make them palatable. But Hobhouse argues that the dominant factor in the growing demand for refined sugar is its addictive power.

Extra energy is produced in a sudden flood when refined sugar is ingested, and demands on the digestive system are lessened. This means that enzymes needed to break down more complex, natural foods are not produced, so the stomach has more difficulty digesting them. As a consequence, fewer nutrients are absorbed and ever greater quantities of sugar are required to boost energy. Since the "sugar addict's" blood-level rises and falls rapidly with the intake of sugar, frequent reinforcement is necessary, spawning a craving "which is chemical, not psychological," claims Hobhouse. After illegal drugs, tobacco and alcohol, sugar "is the most damaging addictive substance . . ."

But even worse than the impact of refined sugar on the individual human body has been its impact on society. Soon after Columbus' voyages, sugar cane became the crop of choice in the Caribbean, which by 1800 boasted 80% of the world's sugar production—and 80% of the world's slave trade. As a labor-intensive crop during both planting and harvesting, sugar cane required many workers to supply enough of the commodity to meet demands. Whole tribes of Native Americans in the area resisted slavery—and died for their defiance. Africans were brought in, and soon the black slave trade became big business. "It was . . . the first time in history that one race had been uniquely selected for a servile role." An estimated 10 million African slaves were imported to the New World in the 1700s alone; five to ten million more died en route. And, for the most part, slaves didn't live long in sugar production; about ten percent of the labor force had to be replaced every year.

By the early 1800s there was growing opposition to the slave trade among civilized societies. About the same time, the cultivation of sugar beets in temperate countries aided in the decline of sugar cane production. Yet the tragic effects on the black race had already taken their inestimable toll. "It will take many generations to build the . . . sense of community [in the old slave-colony countries] that the humblest African peasant takes for granted," Hobhouse contends.

TEA

In 1700, fifty tons of tea were being imported annually to England; by 1800 the amount had increased to 15,000 tons a year. In the decade between 1830 and 1840 alone, tea exports from China averaged over 100,000 tons, worth about $3 billion in today's dollars. Smuggled, non-taxed tea imports may actually have doubled these numbers.

Tea is a product with more bulk than weight. The shippers hauling it needed to put their valuable cargo in the middle of the holds to keep it from water leakage and spray; the light weight of the tea, however, required that something heavier be used for ballast—preferably another marketable commodity. Fine Chinese porcelain, or "China," which was nearly as precious as the tea, soon became the product of choice.

At first, the tea and china were paid for mostly with gold, silver and copper. But as European wars created inflationary conditions, the costs of tea traders rose more rapidly than their revenues. In a bid to balance the books, opium was soon seen as a viable, though illegal, trade substitute. Since the profitability of the trade was great, both Chinese and European sovereigns looked the other way.

Thus, "for a pot of tea . . . Chinese culture was nearly destroyed." It remains to be seen whether the present Chinese government can restore the lost vitality of a brilliant civilization. (It is interesting to note that Japan separated itself from the opium trade and progressed at a time when China and India declined in influence.)

COTTON

Cotton cloth appears to have originated in what is now Pakistan; it appeared in Europe about 900 A.D. but remained a rare though coveted fabric. Then, at the beginning of the 19th century, the American South, putting Eli Whitney's newly invented cotton gin to use, captured the bulk of the market for its vast network of plantations, and cotton became king.

Most cotton weaving was done in the north of England, where the high value of the cloth inspired the invention of machines to speed up the work. The resulting Industrial Revolution, for all its benefits, soon obliterated the old cottage weaving industry and left the new class of British mill and factory workers in an even worse condition than many black American slaves.

But American slaves also suffered from the Industrial Revolution and the expanding cotton market. Before the cotton boom, land owners had worked beside their slaves under reasonably good conditions, but with the founding of huge plantations, owners left the control of their slaves to often brutal overseers.

After the importing of slaves was banned in 1834, American slave-owners turned to slave breeding to resupply their workforce. Meanwhile, several serious efforts to free the slaves foundered on the problem of how or whether to compensate the owners for their very valuable "property." It finally took a devastating war, and a million casualties, to free four million Negro slaves.

THE POTATO

The white potato originated in the highlands of the Andes mountains and was probably brought to Britain by Sir Francis Drake about 1586. For most Europeans, potatoes soon became just another garden crop.

But not in Ireland; there the potato was seen as a heaven-sent answer to the challenges of the land. Unlike grain crops, potatoes flourished in Ireland's mineral-poor soil. Furthermore, growing a potato crop took only ten to fifteen weeks a year. And the Irish people prospered.

Between 1760 and 1840, Ireland's population grew from 1.5 million to 9 million, a six-fold increase. But this phenomenal expansion only set the stage for disaster. In 1845-46, the great Irish potato blight struck, and for several years after potato crops were utterly ruined. About one million people died of starvation and malnutrition, and there followed great waves of emigration; by the commencement of World War I, a total of five and a half million Irish citizens had fled the island.

The British occupiers of Ireland reacted to this tragedy with massive indifference. "It is not unreasonable to share the Irish peasant's loathing of the English reaction . . . " Hobhouse writes. "They wanted food, they got words; they wanted work, they got eviction. Ireland needed investment; the island was told to look after its own poor . . . Soon, in some areas, there were not enough living to bury the dead."

When Irish immigrants flooded to America (in some cities making up 30% of the population), they brought their anti-English sentiments with them, eventually swaying much of American policy and profoundly altering much of recent history. Had the United States and England stood united, arm in arm against aggression in other parts of the world, Hobhouse contends, two catastrophic world wars that shaped the 20th century might have been avoided.

❖ ◆ ❖

In *Seeds of Change* Hobhouse has woven strands of data collected from agriculture, economics, history and other disciplines into a fascinating real-life, worldwide detective saga. But in the end, this book is not only about the influence of a small assortment of crop plants on the fortunes and failures of civilization; it is about the impact of our human choice on human destiny.

Even if readers take the stance that history is ruled by economics, and that nations and individuals must inevitably act to promote their own gain, it is easy to see that both 19th-century slave-breeders in the American South and self-serving Chinese sovereigns who "looked the other way" during the heyday of the opium trade were taking a disastrously short-sighted view.

As we approach a new millennium, faced with unprecedented potential for both the enhancement and the annihilation of human life, *Seeds of Change* and books like it can help in the urgent search for answers to the age-old human question, "What shall we do?"

DISEASE AND HISTORY

by Frederick Cartwright in collaboration with Michael D. Bidiss, Dorset Press, New York, N.Y., 1972

In *Disease and History*, Frederick Cartwright and Michael Bidiss succeed in making the connection between disease and historical change, arguing that disease may have altered the course of history by influencing significant world events. Theirs is a unique perspective, and within it they raise some interesting questions: Was plague more destructive to the Roman Empire than invading armies? Was the Black Death responsible for ending feudalism? Did syphilis turn Ivan the Terrible into a savage tyrant? Did typhus destroy Napoleon's empire? Was smallpox partially to blame for helping the Spaniards defeat the Aztecs? "The ills that have plagued man," Cartwright and Bidiss write, "are as much a part of their civilization as are their prevention and cure."

Disease in the Ancient World

One of the most significant events in history was the fall of the Roman Empire, and, insist the authors, one of the major contributors to its downfall was plague. The Rome of A.D. 300 had developed a system of public health and sanitation that remained unequaled until the middle of the nineteenth century. Aqueducts brought pure water into the city, public lavatories were plentiful, daily personal hygiene was an everyday part of life, government regulations saw to the freshness of perishable foodstuffs, and cremation instead of burial was almost exclusively practiced. However, though Romans were clean, they did not know the cause of disease, and therefore had no way of protecting themselves from it.

At its height, "all roads led to Rome." Stretching from the Sahara to Scotland and from the Caspian Sea to Portugal, the Empire's numerous sea routes and roads also ended up serving as the highways for disease, the authors insist. For example, in the first century B.C., a severe variety of malaria first appeared in Rome and remained for 500 years, killing hundreds of thousands. In A.D. 125, the plague of Orosius sent so many people to their graves that whole villages and towns had to be abandoned. The plague of Justinian soon followed, daily killing some 10,000 people; so many died that ships were often loaded with bodies and abandoned at sea. "When we consider the frightful sequence of pestilence that smote the empire . . . " the authors note, "we need hardly search for a more potent cause of disaster."

While the plagues of the first three centuries almost certainly contributed to the Empire's decline, they also helped Christianity establish itself as a world force. Christianity could not have succeeded at that time had Rome not been ravaged by disease. The new religion, with its belief in a life after death and its claim to healing powers, offered hope to the victims of plague, rapidly swelling Christianity's ranks.

The Black Death

The Black Death was a world-wide pandemic, reaching southward into Africa, northward to Scandinavia and Russia, and eastward to China. The tendency today is to assume that an outbreak of such a nature and on such an expansive scale "just cannot have happened." Italian humanist-poet Petrarch, who lived in France while the Death ravaged Europe, prophetically wrote that future generations would "not believe, could not imagine the towns and fields littered with the dead."

The Black Death was a pneumonic type of bubonic plague which could be spread by fleas from rats as well as by breath and saliva. It probably first broke out on the Crimean shore of the Black Sea, then spread east into Russia, India and China. It finally reached Italy through trade and quickly spread throughout Europe, reaching Moscow in 1352. Historians estimate that some 24 million people were exterminated.

The Black Death affected world history in at least two ways. First, it forced peasant laborers in England to become mobile, bringing an end to the already weak feudal system. Second, ships from the ravaged Scandinavian countries carried the plague to Viking settlements in Greenland. There, the inhabitants transported the disease to the coast of Canada, where the plague likely had a deadly impact and completely changed the early history of North America. "The Black Death was not just another incident in the long list of epidemics which have smitten the world. It was probably the greatest European catastrophe in history."

The Mystery of Syphilis

A puzzling question in medical history is how and why syphilis suddenly appeared in Europe at the end of the fifteenth century. One theory holds that it derived from the African *yaws*, a skin disease indistinguishable from syphilis. Yaws, the theory continues, after it was brought to Spain and Portugal through slave trade, underwent a transformation from the non-venereal variety to the syphilis we know today.

When the disease first emerged in Europe, however, it was much more virulent than it is now. Indeed, syphilis devastated Europe, and millions suffered, both directly and indirectly. For instance, one of the most intriguing, well-documented, and far-reaching cases is that of Ivan the Terrible. When at age 17 he first became the Russian czar in 1547, he established a judicious legal code, reformed the all-powerful Church, banished oppressive nobles, and instituted freedom of speech. Unfortunately for Ivan—and for Russia—he soon began to suffer from cerebral syphilis, and the savage tyranny began. Brain damage led to fits of insanity during which he routinely had people flogged, tortured, burned, boiled, roasted over slow fires, and pushed under lake ice. In one such episode, he even slaughtered his own son. Thousands of Russians died under Ivan's demented direction, and Cartwright and Bidiss argue that, as the disease dragged Ivan slowly down to paralysis and eventual death, millions of Russians were affected. In the end, the authors say, "it is possible that Russian history was radically changed by Ivan's failure to pursue the comparatively liberal and almost benevolent policy of his opening years."

General Napoleon and General Typhus

Napoleon's armies made up the greatest fighting force since Rome, and they helped him conquer all of Europe except Britain. Napoleon's power, however, was finally brought to ruin in 1812 with the destruction of his Grand Army. And, Cartwright and Bidiss suggest, Napoleon's primary adversary was not Wellington, but rather typhus.

Typhus, which is transmitted via body lice, became Napoleon's most formidable foe not long after he opted to invade Russia. Everything went as planned for the 600,000 invading troops until they reached Poland. There, in close, unsanitary quarters, many were quickly infected by the typhus bacteria. Forced into retreat by the combination of cold, hunger, Russian insurgents, and typhus, when it was all over, less than 40,000 men were left standing. One can only imagine what would have become of Europe and the rest of the world if Napoleon had fulfilled his dreams. Instead, "his Grand Army was destroyed by his own impatience and by the ill-luck of encountering typhus fever, and his empire never recovered from the destruction of that army."

The Impact of Infectious Diseases

Diseases which have developed and become tamed in civilized communities are generally lethal when introduced to distant peoples by explorers, missionaries, and traders. One such disease is smallpox, which had vexed Europe, Asia and Africa since the tenth century. Primarily a childhood disease in Europe, when smallpox was introduced to a new community, it was found to affect individuals of all ages.

In the early 16th century, after Spain had already established colonies in the West Indies, Hernando Cortez and his crew disembarked on the coast of the Yucatan peninsula, bringing with them smallpox, mumps and measles. Within six months, almost every village of New Spain was suffering the effects of one or more of the maladies. By the time Cortez defeated the Aztecs in 1519, nearly half of Mexico's indigenous population had been infected. "There is no doubt," the authors write, "that imported disease played as great a part as the Spanish conquerors in the destruction of the Aztec race, if not a greater one."

Queen Victoria and the Fall of the Russian Monarchy

In a sense, Cartwright and Bidiss argue, Queen Victoria was indirectly responsible for destroying the House of Romonov and bringing Lenin and the Bolsheviks to power in Russia. Victoria carried the gene for hemophilia, a disease that manifests itself in males and is induced by the lack of a clotting-agent protein in the liquid part of the blood. A hemophiliac may bleed to death if inflicted with even the most minor of injuries.

Victoria's daughter, Alice, and her granddaughter, Alix, both inherited the gene for hemophilia. Alix married Nicholas II, who became Czar of Russia, and they had one son and heir to the throne, Alexis, a victim of hemophilia. In the beginning of his reign, Nicholas was determined to uphold his autonomy, but after the near revolution of 1905, the Russians formed a parliamentary government called the Duma and presented Czar Nicholas, Alexis' father, with a compromise: they agreed to retain the Czardom only if Nicholas abdicated the throne in favor of his son, who would become a constitutional monarch under the tutelage of the Duma. Balking at the prospect of being parted with his ill son, Nicholas refused to agree to these terms.

At this time, anarchy and disillusionment spread among the Russians. Frequent famine led to a bread riot, which quickly escalated into a revolution led by the Bolshevik party, who rose up and began executing the imperial family. As Cartwright and Bidiss point out, one can only speculate what course Russian history might have taken had Nicholas agreed to the Duma's terms. The authors examine the myriad possibilities: "A young, helpless boy might have inspired sympathy, might have formed a rallying point and allowed the shaken Russian people to regain equilibrium. Russia might conceivably have rallied around her young [Czar]; then the history of the world would have been very different."

Man-made Problems of the Present and Future

"A great part of our civilized life depends upon the addition of amenities (technological advances), [and] very few of these amenities are entirely innocuous," note the authors. To prove their point, they cite the drug thalidomide, a common sedative administered to pregnant women during the early 1960s, which was later found to cause birth defects. In this case, the cure, while temporarily serving humanity's purposes, proved worse than the symptom.

For thousands of years man had no knowledge of the cause of disease, and therefore no means to cure disease. He accepted that out of one thousand children, 250 would die within the first year of life; it was common knowledge that an adult could not live beyond the age of forty. By the middle of the nineteenth century, however, man had gained a better knowledge of bacteria and thus could experiment in preventing and curing some diseases.

With rising life spans, populations shot upward. Between 1300 and 1750, Europe's population went from 80 to 150 million; in the following century, another 115 million were added. Since then, world population has increased at an astronomical rate. The authors thus end with an ominous warning: "Medicine, social, therapeutic, and preventive, has given the human race opportunities for a longer and more healthy life. It has enabled the world population to expand. In doing so, it has brought problems which may be insoluble. Advancing technology has given us comforts and amenities undreamed of two centuries ago. In doing so, it has brought problems which also may be insoluble . . . The solution will lie in the hands of one or all of man's age-old enemies, Famine, Pestilence, and War."

THE RISE AND FALL OF THE GREAT POWERS

by Paul Kennedy, Random House, Inc. New York, N.Y., 1987

"Why is it that throughout history some nations gain power while others lose it?" To answer this question, historian Paul Kennedy examines nearly half a millennium of history from 1500 to the early 1980s, tracing what he calls a recurrent "pattern" according to which "victory went to the economically strong side, while states that were militarily top-heavy usually crashed to eventual defeat."

Kennedy contends that *the triumph of any one Great Power . . . or the collapse of another, has usually been the consequence of lengthy fighting by its armed forces; but it has also been the consequence of the more or less efficient utilization of the state's productive economic resources in wartime, and further in the background, in the way in which that state's economy had been rising or falling, relative to the other leading nations in the decades preceding the actual conflict. For that reason, how a Great Power's position steadily alters in peacetime is as important to this study as how it fights in wartime.*

The Rise and Fall In the East

"The widely held image of extensive eastern empires possessing fabulous wealth and vast armies was a reasonably accurate one . . . and (their populations) seemed far more favorably *endowed* than the peoples of the states of western Europe." Among all of the great pre-modern civilizations, according to Kennedy, "none appeared more advanced . . . felt more superior, than that of China." Its population in the 1500s ranged from 100 million to 130 million in contrast to Europe's 50 to 55 million. Moreover, China boasted a highly refined culture, a "unified hierarchic administration," large cities, huge libraries, sophisticated technologies and agricultural methods. But China remained isolated, preoccupied with preserving and recapturing the past; creating a future based on foreign trade hardly entered their minds.

In contrast, the Ottoman Empire, which ruled over large parts of the Middle East as well as territories in Europe beginning in the 10th century, was intent upon conquering new lands. The Muslims posed a substantial threat to the Christians, who hoped to gain access to regions in India and Africa that ultimately became Islamic. Nevertheless, the Ottoman Empire began to suffer from "strategic overextension, with a large army stationed in central Europe, an expensive navy operating in the Mediterranean, troops engaged in North Africa, the Aegean, Cyprus, and the Red Sea, and reinforcements needed to hold a rising Russian power." The Ottoman Empire consequently began "to falter, to turn inward," as the Chinese had done, and finally "to lose the chance of world domination."

The Mogul Empire likewise deteriorated from within. Although enormously wealthy and strategically astute, the Moguls, starting with the Mongol Genghis Khan in 1526, became notoriously decadent: *The brilliant courts were centers of conspicuous consumption which the Sun King at Versailles might have thought excessive. Thousands of servants and hangers-on, extravagant clothes and jewels and harems and menageries, vast arrays of bodyguards, could be paid for only by the creation of a systematic plunder machine. Tax collectors, required to provide fixed sums for their masters, preyed mercilessly upon peasant and merchant alike; whatever the state of the harvest or trade, the money had to come in.*

As Mogul reign extended throughout India, the Empire, during the late 17th and the 18th centuries, declined in power in the face of opposition from Hindus and of European commercial expansion. Even while the Mogul Empire foundered, both Japan and Russia demonstrated signs of "political consolidation" and economic growth. In Japan, "nationwide peace was good for trade . . . and the increasing use of cash payments made merchants and bankers more important." They were not, however, permitted "social and political prominence" and thus had no access to the "new technological and industrial developments that were occurring elsewhere." Like China, Japan "deliberately chose . . . to cut itself off from the world."

In its early beginnings, Russia was similar to Japan. Both countries remained aloof from the West, although Western realms consistently challenged both countries' military expansionism. Unlike Japan, however, Russia was "economically underdeveloped" and encompassed a vast region inhabited by a number of different tribes. Compounding Russia's problems were "severe social defects: the military absolutism of the czars, the monopoly of education in the hands of the Orthodox Church . . . and the institution of serfdom, which made agriculture feudal and static." These problems, though, did not keep Russia from acquiring new lands and "imposing upon its new territories the same military force and autocratic rule which was used to command the obedience of the Muscovites."

The Rise and Fall In the West

Kennedy asks: "Why was it among the scattered and relatively unsophisticated peoples inhabiting the western parts of the Eurasian landmass, that there occurred an unstoppable process of economic development and technological innovation which would steadily make it the commercial and military leader in world affairs?" Sixteenth-century Europe's *weaknesses* were actually more apparent than its strengths. For instance, geopolitically speaking, the continent of Europe was quite "vulnerable." However, unencumbered by a "centralized authority and unilateral thinking"—hindrances that checked the economic growth and political diversity of other powers during this time period—"Europe's greatest *advantage* was that it had fewer *disadvantages* than the other civilizations." Playing on its economic, technological and military strengths, Europe eventually assumed world leadership.

Consistent with the prevailing patterns of struggle for world dominance, Europe's authority did not go uncontested. With the advent of Martin Luther's "revolt against papal indulgences," Europe became a "continent with large numbers . . . drawn into a *transnational* struggle over religious doctrine . . . and as a consequence, it became virtually impossible to separate the power-political from the religious strands of the European rivalries which racked the continent during this period." The major threat to peace in the region was the "Habsburg bid for mastery." The Habsburgs, a prominent European royal family/dynasty originating in Switzerland during the 10th century, had gained the imperial title and subsequent power through a series of advantageous "dynastic marriages," inheritances, and papal endowments. However, overextended by military conquests, the wealth of the Habsburg dynasty gradually dissolved—as did their power.

As Habsburg influence crumbled, various European states, step-by-step, evolved into "Great Powers" with distinctive national identities. The period between 1660 and 1815 was thus wrought with tremendous power struggles, which, Kennedy writes, resulted in "the maturing of a genuinely *multipolar* system of European states," where decisions were made "on the basis of 'national interests,' rather than for transnational, religious causes." During this period, "Spain, the Netherlands, and Sweden, fell into second rank" and five new, more potent nations emerged: France, Britain, Russia, Austria and Prussia.

Despite Napoleon's attempts to bring foreign European nations under French rule, the other Great Powers prevailed. Because the spiraling costs of war led Britain to create an advanced system of banking and credit, the country achieved an economic advantage that helped to frustrate Napoleon's campaign. Moreover, Britain, like Russia, at this time began to expand its sovereignty to other continents.

In the period from 1815 to 1915, a "strategic equilibrium" emerged, supported by all of the leading powers. Governments, particularly in the United States and Russia, now focused on domestic stability and expansion of their borders. During this period of relative stability the British Empire took its place as a global force. England owned a "virtual monopoly [on] steam-driven industrial production, [and] the spread of industrialization to other regions soon began to tilt the international power balances away from the *older* leading nations and toward those countries with both the resources and organization to exploit the newer means of production and technology." In fact, the Crimean War, the American Civil War and the Franco-Prussian War brought defeat to those nations which "failed to modernize their military systems."

Soon the pace of technological change and uneven economic growth created a complex and unstable international environment. After the 1880s, the Great Powers competed for strong military alliances and for additional Third World territories to increase economic and strategic capabilities. During this period, "indices of economic power were tending more and more to fundamental shifts in global balances . . . Despite their best efforts, traditional great powers [except for Germany] were falling out of the race," while the newly formed Soviet Union and the United States were moving to the forefront.

The period between 1900 and 1950 marked the beginning of a bipolarization of power that proved unusually stressful for the *middle* powers. Germany, for example, gained victory over the eastern front during World War I, only to be defeated within a few short months. To the west, Germany's "allies were similarly collapsing in the Italian, Balkan and Near Eastern theaters of the war," primarily as a result of American military and economic aid. "Austria-Hungary was gone, Russia was in revolution, Germany defeated; yet, even in victory, France, Italy and Britain itself had suffered heavy losses. The only exceptions were Japan, which further augmented its position in the Pacific, and the United States, which by 1918 was indisputably the strongest power in the world."

With the Soviet Union isolated under the Bolshevik regime and America withdrawing from foreign engagements after World War I, the international system was more "out of joint with economic realities than at any time" during the previous four centuries. Between the great world wars, *Britain and France, although weakened, were still at the center of the diplomatic stage, but by the 1930's, their position was being challenged by the militarized, revisionists states of Japan, Italy and Germany . . . The United States remained by far the most powerful manufacturing nation in the world, and Stalin's Russia was quickly transforming itself into an industrial superpower.* The shadow cast by these two giants produced a dilemma for "the status-quo middle powers" during World War II; "in fighting off German and Japanese challenges, they would most likely weaken themselves as well." Indeed, the apprehensions of the middle powers soon were confirmed: "France was eclipsed, and Britain irretrievably weakened. . . . The bipolar world had arrived . . . and military balance had once again caught up with the global distribution of economic resources."

Following World War II, the Cold War became a fact of life in the bipolar world. Nuclear weapons now guaranteed a completely transformed "strategic" and "diplomatic landscape." From the 1960s to the 1980s, the United States and the Soviet Union remained the dominant powers, their rivalry resulting in an "ever-escalating arms race which no other powers felt capable of matching . . . "

And today, "global productive balances have been altering faster than ever before; the Third World's share of total manufacturing output, depressed to an all-time low . . . after 1945, has steadily expanded"; Europe has become the world's largest trading unit; China is impressively "leaping forward"; and Japan's postwar economic rate has overtaken Russia in total GNP. Meanwhile, since the 1960s, both "superpowers" have shown "sluggish" growth rates, with "their shares of global production and wealth" steadily shrinking. Once again, a "multi-polar" world—including China, Japan, the EEC (European Economic Community), the Soviet Union and the United States—has emerged. Writing in 1987, before the unforeseen breakup of the Soviet Union and its "satellites," Kennedy nevertheless forecasts that those nations which vie to become one of the Great Powers must "grapple with the age-old task of relating national means to national ends. The history of the rise and fall of the Great Powers has in no way come to a full stop."

THE HISTORY OF THE DECLINE AND FALL OF THE ROMAN EMPIRE

by Edward Gibbon
(1734 - 1794)

Since publication of British historian Edward Gibbon's monumental six-volume *Decline and Fall of the Roman Empire* between 1776 and 1788, scholars have debated why Rome fell. Indeed, Gibbon asserts, for more than twelve centuries—from Rome's "golden age" (a two-century period beginning around A.D. 180) to its final political and physical disintegration in 1461—the city hastened its own ruin.

The massive work itself deserves all the adulation accorded it over the centuries. Manifesting a dramatic, polished style and an unparalleled depth of accuracy, it has been designated the most authoritative study of Rome ever written, though modern historians point to Gibbon's penchant toward taking the Roman perspective as a bias detrimental to his writing.

The lively and extremely complex history begins with a description of the Roman Empire at the height of its glory (A.D. 96-180). After the death of Marcus Aurelius, the Empire, under Commodus, began its long, leisurely decline—the causes of which Gibbon briefly explains. Actually, Gibbon was more interested in documenting and recounting historical events than in diagnosing Rome's ills. Thus the work is filled with a menagerie of fascinating anecdotes and milestones, with Rome's great and gradual fall taking a relative back seat.

It is beyond doubt that the Roman Empire was extremely powerful. Military strategists have for centuries studied its war machines, its generals' tactics, its awe-inspiring technological advances. Ironically, says Gibbon, the Romans destroyed themselves—their intricate government, their majestic cities—all while operating under a rich and vast society made up of highly knowledgeable citizens.

Myriad historians have puzzled over the fall of the Great Roman Empire. Some claim that a shortage of manpower played a part in its collapse. Others insist that its populace became debilitated by blood poisoning from the lead used to fashion pipes and pottery, or cite evidence that Rome fell victim to repeated bouts of plague. And still others argue that the intermixing of races—"strong" Aryan blood mixing with that of "weak" barbarian races—played a hand in its decline in power and in its ultimate destruction. Sexual permissiveness has also been widely touted as the cause, especially by Christian and Jewish clergy, who held in contempt the habitual orgies said to have been common among the ancient Roman aristocracy.

But Gibbon offers documentation suggesting more simple, plausible grounds for Rome's fall, reasons dealing both with politics and simple economics—and in fact focuses most of his attention on the Empire's *physical* decline.

Strangled by economic despotism from within, invasion from without, a subsequent intrusion of foreign beliefs, and a crumbling superstructure, Gibbon says, the prevailing successive Roman governments failed to uphold even the most basic social policies by which they had operated for almost one thousand years: *"keep the peace, keep the roads open, and do business with everyone."*

At the close of his history, Gibbon writes: "After a diligent inquiry, I can discern four principle causes of the ruin of Rome . . . I. The injuries of time and nature. II. The hostile attacks of the barbarians and Christians. III. The use and abuse of [building] materials. And IV. The domestic quarrels of the Romans." Throughout the lengthy narrative—filled with inquiries into emperors' actions both patriotic and tyrannical, accounts of barbarian onslaught, and Rome's gallant efforts to survive amid overwhelming odds—these causes are contested.

I. Physical Decay And Destruction

Certain that Rome's material decay gradually led to its societal, spiritual and intellectual decay, Gibbon wrote: *The art of man is able to construct monuments far more permanent than the narrow span of his own existence. Yet these monuments, like himself, are perishable and frail; and in the boundless annals of time his life and his labors must equally be measured as a fleeting moment. . . . The silent lapse of time is often accelerated by hurricanes and earthquakes, by fires and inundations . . . and the lofty turrets of Rome have tottered from their foundations.*

During Nero's despotic four-year reign (A.D. 64-68), when a fire struck Rome, *innumerable buildings, crowded in close and crooked streets, supplied perpetual fuel for the flames . . .*

[Then] in the full meridian of empire the metropolis arose with fresh beauty from her ashes; yet . . . memory . . . deplored [the] irreparable losses, the arts of Greece, the trophies of victory, the monuments of primitive or fabulous antiquity.

II. Christianity Triumphs; Rome Declines

In clarification of the assertion that "attacks of . . . Christians" was a principle cause of Rome's decline, Gibbon defended himself: He saw in Christianity an alien influence that ultimately served to dilute the already severely truncated spiritual fabric of Roman society. When the tenets upon which the Roman civilization was built were altered, Gibbon asserts, Roman society began to weaken and wobble. Just as a human being straying from his values—either through omission or commission—morally weakens, a state disregarding the ethics upon which it has rested for centuries becomes impotent. And what is lost cannot easily be regained.

In effect, Christianity's victory sent Rome's true "golden age" into decline; as Romans embraced the lofty new doctrines of the Christians, Rome's might faded, becoming nothing more than a distant mythology.

However harmful Christian presence was to Rome, the complex series of events leading to its downfall were only exacerbated by the Roman government's campaign **against** the Christians, which continued from the reign of Nero to that of early-fourth-century emperor Constantine the Great. While sincerely averring that the emperors were not as harsh in their treatment of Christians as some would claim, Gibbon of course denounces the atrocities perpetrated on Rome's perceived enemies: various "barbarian" tribes, Jews, and Christians: *Humanity is shocked at the recital of the horrid cruelties which [Romans] committed in the cities of Egypt, of Cyprus, and Cyrene . . . [However, the Jews were seen as] a race of fanatics whose . . . superstition seemed to render them the implacable enemies not only of the Roman government, but of human kind.*

Gibbon offers evidence supporting his claim that accounts of martyrdom were greatly exaggerated—both in terms of numbers and cruelty—and that, in many cases, Christians brought martyrdom upon themselves by goading the Romans to violence: *The personal guilt which every Christian had contracted, in . . . preferring his private sentiment to the national religion, was aggravated [to] a very high degree [by] the religious assemblies of the Christians, who had separated themselves from public worship . . . [Their] pious disobedience . . . made their conduct, or perhaps their designs, appear in a much more serious and criminal light.*

Five factors attributed to Christianity's rapid growth, as it came to gain total victory over the world: *I. The inflexible, and, if we may use the expression, the intolerant zeal of the Christians . . . II. The doctrine of a future life . . . III. The miraculous powers ascribed to the primitive church . . . IV. The pure and austere morals . . . V. The union and discipline of the Christian republic, which gradually formed an independent and increasing state in the heart of the Roman empire.* Thus, the Roman myths and creeds failed to hold its adherents, further rending the fabric of Roman society.

"The Edict of Milan"

In A.D. 313, Gibbon notes, the Emperor Constantine finally became weary of the persecution of Christians and made a radical turnaround. Hoping no doubt to put the devout passions and loyalties of this resilient sect at the services of the Empire, he "adopted Christianity as the official religion of the Roman Empire." Under his Edict of Milan, "Christians were ceded rights to inherit and dispose of property as they wished" and were empowered, under auspices of the Emperor, to elect their own church government. *Unfortunately, the universal toleration of Christianity had no sooner been decreed than the Church and Empire were split by the factions rising out of the Donatist and Arian heresies (i.e. dogmas of two rival schismatic Christian sects). The former were confined to Africa but the latter inflamed the entire domain which remained in bitter debate until Constantine intervened by convening the Council of Nice, in which he pronounced himself in favor of the Nicene Creed. This was the orthodox dogma of Christianity.*

This "insidious germ" of Christianity served not only to stretch the military forces of the Empire and to fuel heated contests between increasing numbers of religious and social factions, but resulted in bishops of the Church coming to have increasingly greater influence on matters of state, a condition which proved to mire the Empire in assorted entanglements for the next 700-odd years.

The Final Straw—Internal Strife Eventually

Brings About A Mistreatment of History's Relics

"I have reserved for the last the most potent and forcible cause of destruction," Gibbons writes, "the domestic hostilities of the Romans themselves." In A.D. 476 Odoacer, a German (barbarian) chieftain, serving under various Roman commanders, rebelled and deposed the last western Roman emperor, Romulus Augustulus. After acknowledging Zeno as overlord of the eastern empire, Odoacer ruled Italy for 27 years. With Odoacer's assassination by Theodoric the Great in 493, Rome entered into a series of alliances with other barbaric kingdoms. However, territorial expansion brought conflict with the Frankish king Clovis, and his death left the Empire leaderless—and ripe for Byzantine annexation.

In this confused and turbulent scene of personal and public bewilderment, the Romans themselves, fearful of further invasion, began disemboweling the city of its greatest treasures in order to supply building materials to construct their fortresses: *. . . The statues of the gods and heroes, and the costly ornaments of sculpture . . . became the first prey of conquest or fanaticism, of the avarice of the barbarians or the Christians.*

As the centuries wore on, Rome's continued rule by Byzantine and French emperors—who held vastly different beliefs and values than their subjects and were willing to violate the most sacred of Roman laws—triggered frequent periods of internal strife, sedition, and civil war in the city. *At such a time . . . when every quarrel was decided by a sword and none could trust their lives or properties to the impotence of law . . . the cities were filled with [hostility, and] to this mischievous purpose the remains of antiquity [such as temples and arches] were most readily adapted.*

With neither sovereign nor senate to protect it from Arab raids and the increase of papal authority, Rome—both its past might and its future promise—had nearly fallen. *Even the churches were encompassed with arms and bulwarks, and the military engines on the roof of St. Peter's were the terror of the Vatican and the scandal of the Christian world . . . "The houses,"* says a cardinal poet of the times, *"were crushed by the weight and velocity of enormous stones; the walls were perforated by the strokes of the battering-ram; the towers were involved in fire and smoke; and the assailants were stimulated by rapine and revenge."*

As the end of the great Empire's power was sealed, no emperor had the power to salvage it. As an ecclesiastical state in schism with its own, long history, Rome's influence was a relic of history: *"Behold,"* says the laureate, *"the relics of Rome, the image of her pristine greatness! Neither time nor barbarian can boast the merit of this stupendous destruction; it was perpetrated by her own citizens . . . Your ancestors have done with the battering-ram what the Punic hero could not accomplish with the sword."*

Rome's might had finally been laid to waste; it no longer commanded the respect of its neighbors. And on further reflection, many people would have to agree with Gibbon's concluding thoughts: " . . . Instead of inquiring why the Roman Empire was destroyed, we should rather be surprised that it had subsisted so long."

THE VANISHED LIBRARY

by Luciano Canfora (translated by Martin Ryle), University of California Press, Berkeley and Los Angeles, 1989

One of the great flowerings of Western civilization sprang to life at the end of the 4th century B.C. with the establishment of the Mediterranean port city of Alexandria. Bearing the name of its illustrious founder, Alexander the Great, and laid out—as many ancient visitors described it—"like an emperor's cloak" sweeping down to the Egyptian seashore, the capital of the Ptolemaic dynasty soon became the cultural center of the Hellenistic world.

At the heart of the city's glory stood the Library and Museum of Alexandria. Within the walls of this great complex, labeled by one Greek poet as "The Cage of the Muses" (hence the edifice's title of "museum"), the Ptolemies and their royal librarians managed to systematically collect, study, translate, and classify all the books of the ancient world. The debt we owe to the Library and its creators and curators is immeasurable. Similarly, the magnitude of the loss we have suffered through its mysterious destruction sometime between the first six centuries A.D. is incalculable.

In *The Vanished Library*, Luciano Canfora combines the intellectual rigor of a historian with the narrative gifts of a novelist to resurrect the ancient splendors of the Library and Museum. Dividing his fascinating work into two parts—the first a narrative history of the Library and the second an annotated bibliography of his sources—Canfora also lays out a carefully reasoned and provocative scenario to explain the mystery of the fire that destroyed the Library—a conflagration that has haunted Western culture for centuries.

Canfora begins his chronicle with an overview of the historical forerunners of the Library and Museum of Alexandria. There are two, in particular, to which he draws our attention: the Ramesseum in Thebes, which was the mausoleum of the Egyptian pharaoh Rameses II; and the Peripatos in Athens, which housed the *Lyceum*—the school founded by Aristotle.

Comparing ancient eyewitness accounts of the Library and the mausoleum of Rameses II, Canfora suggests that the Ramesseum served as the architectural model for the Museum complex. Indeed, Canfora argues that the "two buildings . . . were identical." Both contained a "covered walk" which "gave access to numerous rooms or chambers," including a "sacred library" in the Ramesseum. Both opened onto a huge, circular, "sumptuous room with the *triclinia* or couches." Finally, both buildings were "organized" around the *Soma*, or body, of a dead ruler. "The *Soma* of Alexander [the Great]," says Canfora, "was to be found [within] the Museum . . . precincts, just as the *Soma* of Rameses was to be found [within] the hall in the Mausoleum."

But if the Museum owed its architectural legacy to an Egyptian pharaoh, the spiritual breath that created and sustained it was Greek. Specifically, it was the breath of Aristotle, caught and molded into solid reality by the driving hand of Alexander the Great.

As Canfora reminds us, Alexander was born in the mid-4th century B.C. into the royal house of Macedonia—at that time still a semi-barbaric, untamed cultural outpost in the minds of the heartland Greeks to the South. His father, King Philip II, anxious to implant the refinements of high Hellenic culture within his borders, dared to invite Aristotle himself—appealing to the illustrious thinker's own origins as a native Macedonian son—to come back home and serve as the young Alexander's personal tutor.

Aristotle accepted; and, not surprisingly, by the time the Macedonian prince turned his hand to the conquest of the Middle East, the Hellenic vision, as embodied by Aristotle, had been burned into his blood. At the core of Alexander's great campaigns blazed the ideal of a great, new, unified world order, enlightened throughout by the culture and language of Greece. "Pray for a new heart among mankind," he told his generals; and the key to achieving that "new heart" lay in the establishment of new Hellenic cities and cultural centers throughout the lands of their conquest.

At Alexander's death in 323 B.C., the three generals who divided his empire among them retained this ardent—and shrewdly practical—vision. In fact, Ptolemy, now designated as the new ruler of Egypt, eagerly commissioned another disciple of Aristotle—Demetrius, the ex-governor of Athens—to educate his own son at Alexandria. And this son was to become Ptolemy II, the greatest ruler of the Ptolemaic dynasty, and the founder of the Library and Museum.

Following Alexander's vision and Aristotle's personal example at the Preipatos in Athens, Demetrius and Ptolemy quickly expanded the scope of the Library collection, beginning with a series of "books on kingship and the exercise of power." Canfora writes: . . . *They had calculated that they must amass some five hundred thousand scrolls altogether [in order] to collect at Alexandria "the books of all the peoples of the world." [Wherefore] Ptolemy composed a letter "to all the sovereigns and governors on earth" imploring them "not to hesitate to send him" works by authors of every kind: "poets and prose-writers, rhetoricians and sophists, doctors and soothsayers, historians, and all the others too." He gave orders that any books on board ships calling at Alexandria were to be copied: the originals were to be kept, and the copies given to their owners.*

In this way, Canfora observes, Ptolemy I and his successors quickly and purposefully built up a "Universal Library" of several hundred thousand scrolls. Endlessly acquisitive and curious, the Ptolemies and their royal librarians continued throughout several centuries to enlarge the Library's collection. In one project, for instance, the Library not only acquired all "the books of Jewish law," but also conducted a symposium in which "the Sages of Jerusalem" were invited to Alexandria to translate the

Pentateuch into Greek. All the while, the Museum's librarians made copies of the books and transcribed the rapidly deteriorating scrolls into book form.

As the Museum's collection grew, its curators undertook the operation of cataloguing and classifying all its holdings according to genres. The result—the famous *Catalogues* of Callimachus—gives us a tantalizing glimpse of the Library's extensive collection: *Callimachus devoted six sections to poetry and five to prose: his categories included epics, tragedies, comedies, historical works, works of medicine, rhetoric and law, and miscellaneous works.*

Of these works, many had been produced at the Library itself. The Greek geographer and historian Strabo, for example, wrote the Egyptian portions of his classic work *Geography* while he was a resident scholar at the Library. Apollonius of Rhodes compiled the classic epic *Jason and the Argonauts* while serving as the royal Librarian. In the field of literary scholarship, the Library and its staff amended and organized the *Iliad* and the *Odyssey* in the forms that we currently read them. The day's most distinguished scholars lectured in its great hall. In short, presided over by the ghost of Aristotle, the Library of Alexandria played a key role in conserving and shaping Western culture as we know it today.

It is easy to see, then, why the building's destruction, and the mystery surrounding it, have plagued the imagination of historians for some two millennia. The most widely accepted historical accounts attribute the catastrophe to Julius Caesar—who, ironically, frequently attended lectures there. According to Roman annals, during the Alexandrian war (48 to 47 B.C.) Caesar torched the Ptolemaic fleet which lay anchored in the city's harbor. Ancient sources go on to report that the fire spread to the shipyards and then to the warehouses "in which 'grain and books' were stored." The crucial question that then remains, of course, is whether these "forty thousand scrolls of excellent quality" were part of the Great Library. Canfora thinks not. Returning to his earlier discussion of the architectural resemblances between the Library and the Ramesseum, he notes that our uncertainty about the Library's location derives from the way we have come, over time, to define the word *library*. The Latin-based *-arium* ending which gives us our English "libr-*ary*," *does* in fact denote either a "room" or "receptacle" (solarium, planetarium, etc.). However, the etymological derivation of the word in the original Greek— and, for that matter, in Canfora's own Italian— *bibliotheke* translates instead to mean a "case," an "envelope," or a "shelf" rather than a room or building in which books are placed. Canfora maintains, then, that the Alexandrian *Library*, like the "sacred library" of the Ramesseum, must have been a shelf or a series of shelves which ran part way round the circular walls of the *inside* of the Museum: *Since the treasures of the Museum cannot possibly have been outside the palace walls, let alone stored in the port alongside the grain depots, we need hardly stress that the scrolls which went up in flames were quite unconnected with the royal Library.*

Canfora has another explanation for the forty thousand books that burned in the port warehouses. He recalls that Seneca often attacked "the fashionable taste that led so many rich people [in Rome] to fill their houses with thousands of books, collected [not for study but] for the sake of mere ostentation." So, he argues, the books that were destroyed might much more plausibly have been volumes waiting in storage for export to the personal libraries of wealthy Romans. Moreover, Canfora observes that the resident Library scholar/historian Strabo, writing just twenty years after the port fire, makes no mention of the loss of any books from the Library.

Canfora proposes another theory to account for the Library's ultimate ruin—a demolition of the royal palace and its attached Museum that took place some 600 years later. Using a history of the Islamic conquest of Alexandria in A.D. 641, he suggests that the Library's collection was burned on the orders of the Arab Caliph Omar. Shortly after Omar's general, Emir Amrou Ibn el-Ass, had conquered Alexandria, he apparently wrote to Omar asking him what he should do about the city's extraordinary library. After a delay of several weeks, Amrou received his answer from Omar: *"As for the books you mention, here is my reply. If their content is in accordance with the book of Allah, we may do without them, for in that case the book of Allah more than suffices. If, on the other hand, they contain matter not in accordance with the book of Allah, there can be no need to preserve them. Proceed, then, and destroy them."*

Canfora writes that Amrou, though greatly saddened by the Caliph's orders, then "set about his task of destruction": *The books were distributed to the public baths of Alexandria, where they were used to feed the stoves which kept the baths so comfortably warm.* [Islamic historian] *Ibn al-Kifti writes that "the number of baths was well known, but I have forgotten it . . . They say," continues Ibn al-Kifti, "that it took six months to burn all that mass of material."*

The only volumes spared, notes the Emir in his chronicle, were the works of Aristotle— whom the Arabs already knew and revered as an astronomer and logician from the days when his works were first made known to them by the Greek rulers of the Middle East after the conquests of Alexander the Great.

In the epilogue to his extraordinary history, Canfora attempts to contextualize the significance of the Library of Alexandria, noting that it was "the starting point and the prototype" of all libraries to come. Because of the vast historicity of the Museum's collection and its irreplaceable nature, Canfora considers the wanton destruction of the majestic edifice at Alexandria especially lamentable: *The great concentrations of books, usually found in the centres of power, were the main victims of [the] ruinous attacks, sackings and fires . . . In consequence, what has come down to us is derived not from the great centres but from "marginal locations," such as convents, and from scattered private copies.*

THE HISTORIES

(And *The History of the Persian Wars*)
by
Herodotus of Halicarnassus
(c. 484 - 425 B.C.)

This is the setting-forth of the research of Herodotus of Halicarnassus so that neither will the things done by men be forgotten with the passage of time nor will the great deeds and wonders which have transpired, some among the Greeks, and others among the barbarians, be without fame . . .

Thus begins Herodotus' massive nine-volume work, titled, appropriately, **The Histories**, considered to be the first true historical treatise. Though Sumerian and Egyptian scribes had earlier set down in print various events, they usually wrote their accounts to flatter their contemporary political authorities.

Herodotus was the first to organize divers events around a common narrative theme. In fact, his **Histories** stands as the first great work of prose extant in Western literature; all previous works had been written in verse for oral performance. Moreover, it is on the strength of Herodotus' work that the word has come to possess "history" its present meaning.

The **Histories** largely focuses on the conflict between East and West, Asia and Europe—or the Greeks and the "barbarians"—which culminated in the Persian Wars of 490 and 480 B.C. The first half of the **Histories**, Books I through V, deals mostly with the rise of the Persian Empire. The remainder details the conflict between the Persians and the Greek city-states.

Herodotus' purposes, however, were not strictly historical. His writing primarily was intended to be entertaining, for Herodotus was a great storyteller. He admits: "Digressions are part of the plan," and thus his history contains a large number of fascinating stories, including many of dubious authenticity.

The Story of Croesus

Typical of Herodotus' quasi-historical narratives is the story of Croesus of Lydia. Non-Greeks, the Lydians were most noted for their invention of coinage. Lydia's ruler, Croesus, belonged to a family called the Mermnadae. According to Herodotus, their dominion began when Gyges, Croesus' great-great grandfather, usurped the throne of King Candaules.

Now Candaules, or so the story goes, was exceedingly fond of his wife; to him, she was the most beautiful of women and he continually praised her comeliness to his bodyguard Gyges. To prove her beauty to Gyges, Candaules persuaded the reluctant servant to hide in the royal bedroom and observe her as she disrobed. Gyges did spy on the queen, but she spotted him doing so and suspected that her husband was responsible. The next day she summoned Gyges and presented him with an ultimatum: "Gyges, there are two courses open to you, and you may take your choice between them. Kill Candaules and seize the throne, with me as your wife; or die yourself on the spot, so that never again may your blind obedience to the king tempt you to see what you have no right to see." Not surpris-

ingly, Gyges opted for the first alternative.

Although many Lydians objected to the prospect of Gyges as king, they eventually were persuaded to accept him, so long as his authority was confirmed by a pronouncement of the oracle at Delphi. The priestess of Apollo indeed confirmed that Gyges would rule, but announced that Candaules' descendants would be avenged in the fifth generation.

Many years later, Gyges' descendant Croesus extended the Lydian Empire throughout the territory of the Greek city-states. As fifth in the line of Gyges, however, Croesus was destined to be deposed.

As it happened, among the many famous visitors to Croesus' city of Sardis was the Athenian constitutional reformer Solon. Croesus, quite smug about his own prosperity, asked the well-traveled Solon to name the man, among the many he had met, whom he regarded as the most happy. "An Athenian called Tellus," was Solon's reply.

Taken aback, Croesus asked the Athenian to defend his choice. Solon explained that Tellus had lived to see sons and grandsons born, and had died a glorious death in battle. The Athenians subsequently had provided a public funeral for this honorable, happy man.

Now Croesus demanded to know Solon's second choice, and this time he named Cleobis and Biton, two brothers who had pulled their mother in an oxcart to the festival of the goddess Hera, as the happiest. They died in answer to a maternal prayer that they be granted "the greatest blessing that can fall to mortal man." No man, regardless of his prosperity, added Solon, can be called "happy" until he has *died* happily. Croesus considered this explanation foolish, and sent Solon away.

Some years later, King Cyrus, founder of the Persian Empire, marched on toward Sardis, took the city, and captured Croesus. As predicted by the Oracle, Croesus and his great empire had fallen.

On the orders of Cyrus, Croesus and fourteen young Lydian boys were chained to a great pyre to be burned alive. Realizing that he was about to die, Croesus reflected upon his conversation with Solon long ago and thrice uttered the name of the Athenian: "Solon . . . Solon . . . Solon . . . " Cyrus, overhearing the invocation, sent an interpreter to find out what was meant by it. Upon hearing Croesus' explanation, Cyrus wanted to spare his life, but it was too late: the fire had been lit. As a last resort, Croesus called on Apollo to save him, whereupon that god sent a storm which doused the flames.

Such a tale, at least from a modern perspective, may seem out of place in a historical account. As stated earlier, however, Herodotus' purposes were different than those of a modern historian: "My business is to record what people say, but I am by no means bound to believe it—

and that may be taken to apply to this book as a whole."

Preserving the Ancient Tales

While entertaining, Herodotus' quasi-fictional accounts have also proven to be enlightening. There are at least two instances, for example, when he reports views which he did not find credible but which seem perfectly reasonable to the modern reader. The first deals with why the waters of the Nile rise at the summer solstice. Presenting three commonly held views, Herodotus denounces the third, although it is the one we know to be correct today: " . . . The water of the Nile comes from melting snow . . . " Since hotter climates were found to be farther south, and the source of the Nile is to the south, this explanation seemed highly implausible. He had no way of knowing, however, that many snow-capped mountains lie in the vicinity of the equator.

The second example of Herodotus' commitment to accurate recording is even more interesting. Herodotus relates that a Phoenician crew, commissioned by Pharaoh Neco, circumnavigated the African continent. While Herodotus does not question the fact that the voyage occurred, he doubts the report that "as they sailed on a westerly course round the southern end of Libya (by which he means Africa), they had the sun on their right—to the northward of them." We know that this is just what one would expect, traveling west in the Southern Hemisphere. But, of course, Herodotus was ignorant of the fact that the earth is roughly spherical. A more "scientific" historian would, no doubt, have neglected to mention such an unlikely detail.

The Culture of Ancient Egypt

One of the most important of Herodotus' digressions is the whole of Book II, which encompasses a detailed description of the cultural idiosyncrasies of ancient Egypt. Egyptian customs included both circumcision—which seemed frightening and distasteful to the Greeks—and mummification. He notes that, from a Greek point of view, the Egyptians often reversed the usual roles of men and women: Egyptian women went to the marketplace to shop, for instance, while the men remained at home, weaving.

Especially engrossing is Herodotus' comparison of Egyptian religious practices with those of the Greeks. He observed substantial underlying similarities between Greek and Egyptian religious practices and beliefs, and did not fail to draw an obvious conclusion: Greek gods were, in many cases, borrowed from the Egyptians. He then goes on to equate Egyptian deities with their Greek counterparts. Thus, the god Amun "is the Egyptian name for Zeus"; Osiris is simply an Egyptian Dionysus.

In some cases, Herodotus' assumptions are probably incorrect. He nevertheless was the first author to suggest that cultures borrow ritual practices and religious beliefs from each other.

The Persian Wars

From the latter part of Book V through Book IX, the historian focuses much more closely on his major theme: the famed Persian Wars.

When Aristogoras of Miletus persuaded the Ionian city-states to revolt against the Persian Empire in 499 B.C., he enlisted the help of the Athenians, who sent twenty warships. The combined Greek forces launched an attack on Sardis—by then a provincial capital of the Persian Empire—plundering the temples and burning much of the city. Soon afterward, around 494 B.C., the Greeks and Ionians first were defeated at sea by the Persian fleet, and then the Persians struck back, invading Greek and Ionian lands. By 493 B.C. the revolt had been completely suppressed.

Meanwhile, a formidable advocate of Athenian naval supremacy named Themistocles initiated two major confrontations between Greeks and Persians. He began by calling upon Persian Emperor Darius to send military aid. Still stung by the role the Athenians had played in Sardis' earlier defeat—Darius dispatched a fleet of ships carrying both infantry and cavalry to challenge Athens. The fleet landed on the east coast of Attica at the Bay of Marathon, leaving the Athenians, aided only by their allies the Plataeans, to confront a Persian force four times as large as their own. But against all expectations, the Athenians achieved a stunning victory: by what could only be attributed to "the graces of the gods," the Athenians and their allies suffered 192 casualties while the "barbarians" and their allies lost 6400.

The final Persian response was delayed by the death of Darius in 486 B.C. Six years later, however, his successor Xerxes—accompanied by a fleet of unprecedented size—personally led a mighty army to battle the Greeks. Although the Persian army initially met with little resistance, they were eventually confronted by a heroic force of three hundred Spartans at the narrow mountain pass of Thermopylae. A Greek named Ephialtes then covertly informed Xerxes of a second mountain pass by which, if followed, would allow the Persians also to attack from the rear. Xerxes and his legion subsequently were able to surround and annihilate the Spartan forces, then press southward to occupy Attica and burn to the ground the evacuated city of Athens.

By use of a clever ploy, the Greeks convinced the Persians to believe that they had "trapped" the entire Athenian fleet in the Bay of Eleusis. In the ensuing naval battle, however, the mighty Athenians showed their true strength and utterly defeated the Persian fleet.

His ships either sunken or badly crippled, Xerxes had no way to supply his massive land forces. Returning to Persia with some remaining ships, Xerxes left the core of his army on the Greek mainland under the command of Mardonius. During the next summer of 479 B.C., though, Mardonius was defeated at the Battle of Plataea and the remnant of the Persian fleet was overwhelmed and sunk at Mycale off the coast of Asia Minor.

Thus ends Herodotus' stirring narrative of the Persian Wars. While not always factual in every detail, his account largely is reliable, and every bit as exciting as the imaginative tales that illumine today's movie screens.

by, respectively, Thucydides (c.460-c.400 B.C.) and Xenophon (c.431-c.354 B.C.)

Played out against the backdrop of the classical Greek "Golden Age," the intermittent conflict between the city states of Athens and Sparta and their allies lasted from Hellenic 431 B.C. to 404 B.C. For a collective first- and second-hand narrative of the first twenty years of the conflict we have the remarkable *History of the Peloponnesian War* by the Athenian general Thucydides, who spent two decades in exile after a defeat in the battle for the city of Amphipolis.

Thucydides' work is a rare trove among ancient historical records. Aside from its great literary charm, the general's compilation sets a unique standard for accuracy. As the author himself explains: *And with reference to the narrative of events, far from permitting myself to derive it from the first source that came to hand, I did not even trust my own impressions, but it rests partly on what I saw myself, partly on what others saw for me, the accuracy of the report being always tried by the most severe and detailed tests possible.*

Only in the still-famous speeches he cites does Thucydides favor literary elegance over stringent accuracy: *... It was in all cases difficult to carry them word for word in one's memory, so my habit was to make the speakers say what was in my opinion demanded of them by the various occasions, of course adhering as close as possible to the general sense of what was really said.* Thus, for instance, Pericles' oration at the funeral of a fellow statesman was probably slightly embellished to help clarify the ideals of Athenian democracy: *"Our constitution does not copy the laws of neighbouring states; we are rather a pattern to others than imitators ourselves. Its administration favors the many instead of the few; this is why it is called a democracy. If we look to the laws, they afford equal justice to all in their private differences . . . The freedom we enjoy in our government extends to our ordinary life. . . . We throw open our city to the world, and never by alien acts exclude foreigners from any opportunity of learning or observing . . . . . . We cultivate refinement without extravagance and knowledge without effeminacy. . . . In short . . . I doubt if the world can produce a man [who is] graced by so happy a versatility as the Athenian . . . "*

Even with its self-congratulatory overtones, this 2500-year-old speech remains one of the most eloquent and widely celebrated defenses of an open society.

The Early Years

For years the great city of Sparta—located on the island of Peloponnesus (now known as Sicily)—had objected to Athens' expansionist gestures. As friction mounted between the governing Athens and the power-seeking peninsular city-state, relations between the two formerly neighboring—though discordant—cultures turned sour.

The first phase of the war—often known as the Archidamian War in honor of King Archidamus, who commanded Sparta's ground forces—lasted just over a decade, and ended in a virtual stalemate. Though the Athenians and their allies enjoyed an overwhelming naval superiority, the Spartans possessed enough of an advantage on the land to keep their rivals (literally) at bay.

During this period, nearly every spring the Spartans and their allies occupied the promontory of Attica, including the countryside surrounding Athens. Adhering to the policy of their great leader Pericles, the Athenians refused to fight and instead retreated behind the walls of their city. Unfortunately, this tactic brought tragedy: after their first retreat, Athens was beset by a plague, which killed a quarter to a third of the population, including Pericles. Overall, however, the occupation of Attica by Sparta and its allies had little political effect, since the Athenians were able to farm most of their own crops within the radius of the city defenses, and import their grain by sea.

With ample food supplies, the Athenians were thus able to conduct brief sorties into enemy territories to block ships from transporting goods. One of these sorties, in 425 B.C., led to the turning-point of the Archidamian War. On his way to Corcyra, the Athenian commander Demosthenes landed at Pylos on the west coast of the Peloponnesian peninsula. Finding a suitable and easily fortified harbor, Demosthenes took the radical step of securing it for permanent occupation, forcing the Spartan troops in Attica to sail back to Laconia in order to protect their homeland from Western invaders. The enormous Spartan fleet, however, was intercepted and destroyed by the vastly superior Athenian navy, led by Eurymedon and Sophocles. After a 72-day battle, a Spartan detachment of 300 infantrymen—trapped by the Athenians in Pylos—finally surrendered.

The defeat at Pylos was a severe blow to Sparta. Overly eager to recoup those who had been taken captive—many of them the sons of Sparta's most prominent families—the Spartans again left themselves vulnerable to attack by Athenian forces in Pylos, who found they could launch raids into Spartan territory virtually unimpeded.

Even after four long years of bitter attack, however, Sparta had some hopes for victory. The advantages of the city's enemies were partially offset by the campaign of the Spartan commander Brasidas, "liberator of Hellas," in Chalcidice, a peninsula where the Athenians held several major colonies. Brasidas set out in 424 B.C., and within two years, through conquest and coercion, had conquered several economically crucial Athenian allies. His campaign was almost as damaging to the Athenians as the capture of Pylos was to the Spartans. In 422 B.C., however, both Brasidas and his Athenian counterpart Cleon were killed in battle near Amphipolis.

After the demise of these two outspoken supporters of prolonged warfare, a peace settlement was arranged by the Athenian general Nicias and the Spartan king Pleistonax in 412 B.C. And for the next three years there was no more bloodshed.

The Sicilian Campaign

In 415 B.C., Sicilian leaders enticed the Athenians to undertake a campaign in their island, which was at war with neighboring Selinus. Although few Athenians were sufficiently knowledgeable of Sicily to warrant such an undertaking, they anticipated an easy and profitable victory. Encouraged by the popular and ambitious general Alcibiades, the Athenians dispatched a massive armada of 4000 troops and 300 horsemen, led by Alcibiades, Nicias and Lamachus.

After these three generals had arrived in southern Italy, a messenger arrived from Athens to demand that Alcibiades return: he was to be tried in Athens in connection with what was known as "The Affair of the Hermae," an incident involving a band of drunken young men who had blasphemously defaced many Athenian statues of Hermes. The trusted Alcibiades was allowed to return aboard his own ship. Instead of heading homeward for Athens, however, he turned sail to Sparta, where he sold his military expertise to his appreciative erstwhile enemies. On Alcibiades' advice, the Spartans soon sent a sizeable force to Syracuse, drawing Nicias and Lamachus to focus their attention on the capture of that city. This proved to be an absurd and highly futile project, inasmuch as Syracuse was almost as large and prosperous as Athens. Lamachus was killed early in the campaign, and Nicias confirmed his reputation as a fumbling and indecisive leader. In short order, the Syracusans, guided by the savvy Gylippus, blocked the Athenian troops by sea and by land.

The stubbornly determined Athenians sent Nicias reinforcements of another 73 ships and 5000 infantrymen, under the able command of General Demosthenes. Upon seeing what his forces would go up against, Demosthenes confided to his intimates that he favored abandoning the invasion; however, he never dared confront Nicias with this appraisal, and before long the entire Athenian fleet was blockaded in the harbor. In one of the greatest debacles of the war, after waging two unsuccessful sea battles against the Syracusans, the Athenians burned most of their own ships and attempted to escape overland. The retreat was suicidal: *. . . The dead lay unburied, and each man as he recognized a friend among them shuddered in grief and horror; while the living whom they were leaving behind, wounded or sick, were to the living far . . . more to be pitied than those who perished . . . They had come to enslave others, and were departing in fear of being enslaved themselves . . .*

Following this disastrous rout, most of the surviving Athenian forces surrendered. Nicias and Demosthenes were put to death and the captive Athenian soldiers were either sold as slaves or "deposited in the quarries." Thucydides writes: *This was the greatest Hellenic achievement of any in this war . . . [The Athenians] were beaten at all points and altogether . . . their fleet, their army—everything was destroyed, and few of the many returned home.*

The Final Decline of Athens

Towards the end of the Peloponnesian War, Athens gradually declined in influence. Sparta's allies, which now included the mighty city of Syracuse, built a fleet to rival that of Athens, and, one by one, the city lost almost all the client states which had comprised its empire. Some of the city's wealthiest citizens suspended operations of the Ekklesia, the governing body in Athens, and tried to make peace with Sparta on any terms. Due to military opposition, their attempt failed.

The account of Thucydides ends in 411 B.C. For a history of the last years of the war, we are indebted to the soldier-essayist Xenophon—unfortunately, neither as accurate nor as elegant as Thucydides. In his work *Hellenica*, Xenophon tells how Sparta and its allies entered into an alliance with the Persian Empire. Alcibiades was allowed to return to Athens and was elected supreme commander of the Athenian fleet, but the Athenians subsequently blamed him for their defeat near Ephesus, whereupon they elected ten new generals, including Pericles, the son and namesake of the celebrated early statesman.

Soon afterward, the Athenians enjoyed their last significant victory of the war with the Battle of Arginusae. A fleet of 150 Athenian ships met and defeated Lysander's 120-vessel force, sinking 70 of the Spartan ships, along with the 14,000 men they carried—including Lysander himself. A sudden storm, however, prevented the Athenians from rescuing the sailors from 25 of their own sinking vessels. And when Athens' citizens heard this, they angrily sought to depose the eight generals who had been present at Arginusae, eventually bringing six of them to trial. This was an unconstitutional act, but the members of the presiding committee, the *prytany*, eventually gave in to the public outcry and sentenced the generals to death in a near unanimous vote. The single dissenter was the philosopher Socrates, who "would do nothing at all that was contrary to the law."

As the war dragged disastrously on, the Athenian fleet was virtually destroyed after its commanding general Conon ordered it ashore on the European side of the Mediterranean in search of provisions. Under Spartan attack, Conon managed to escape to Cyprus along with eight ships. The *Paralus*, the official state warship of Athens, was subsequently sent to Piraeus, a Greek seaport, with an account of the defeat: *As the news of the disaster was told, one man passed it to another, and a sound of wailing arose . . . That night no one slept. They mourned for the lost, but still more for their own fate. They thought that they themselves would now be dealt with as they had dealt with others . . .*

Besieged by both land and sea, the starving Athenians were compelled to concede defeat in April of 404 B.C. There followed the Reign of the Thirty Tyrants—under Spartan dominion—during which Athens' most brutal oligarchs exercised their power to despoil their political enemies. After many executions and confiscations of estates, the Thirty were defeated by Athenian exiles returning from Thebes at the Battle of Munychia in 403 B.C. Soon thereafter, the Spartan King Pausanias proclaimed a general amnesty and dismantled the Spartan garrison which had controlled Athens. The Athenian democracy thus was restored, but never again would Athens attain the status of an imperial power.

A HISTORY OF GOD

by Karen Armstrong, Alfred A. Knopf, New York, N.Y., 1993

In *A History of God*, Oxford graduate and former nun Karen Armstrong argues that "social god-making" has largely determined "the nature of religious experience." Focusing on the social implications of religion, Armstrong presents a compelling historical analysis of Jewish, Christian, and Islamic monotheism.

Interestingly, Armstrong herself is not a monotheist but a self-professed agnostic, who contends that once she left the convent she felt her own "belief in God slip quietly away."

Armstrong argues that humanism—which she defines as "a religion without a God"—"has its own disciples of mind and heart and gives people the means of finding faith in the ultimate meaning of human life that were once provided by the more traditional religions." Humanism, in Armstrong's view, like all systems of belief throughout the centuries, "is highly pragmatic, [for] it is far more important for a particular idea of God to *work* than for it to be logically or scientifically sound."

❖ ♦ ❖

It was in the Middle East, Armstrong begins, that "the idea of our God gradually emerged about 14,000 years ago." The ancient Middle Easterners "personalized the unseen forces and made them gods, associated with the wind, sea and stars." Access to the sacred world allowed human beings to resemble gods: *If men and women imitated the actions of the gods they would share to some degree their greater power and effectiveness . . . The sacred world of the gods . . . was the prototype of human existence . . .*

In the mythology of the ancient people of Canaan (Phoenicia), the gods were born from chaos. Later, "other gods emerged from them in a process known as emanation, which would become very important in the history of our own God." In fact, the Canaan "High God *El*" seems to have developed into the prophet Abraham's god *Yahweh*, "a very mild deity" who bore a much stronger resemblance to El than to the "cruel and violent" Yahweh who later appeared to Moses in Exodus.

In contrast to Moses' all-powerful and dynamic Yahweh, the Greeks revered a "divine world [that] was static and changeless." As conceived by Plato, "divine forms . . . could be discovered within the self"; for Aristotle, God was "Unmoved Mover . . . pure being, and, as such eternal, immobile and spiritual . . . Pure thought . . . the highest object of knowledge." This remote Aristotelian "Unmoved Mover" was quite unlike the different Yahwehs of Abraham and Moses, or the Yahweh who later appeared to the Judean Isaiah. Neither "tribal deity" nor "war god," Isaiah's new Yahweh belonged to everyone, Jew, gentile or pagan: "his glory . . . filled the whole earth."

Although his message was often grim, the new Yahweh inspired many prophets, from Amos to the Second Isaiah, through whom the new God stressed "compassion" and "love" while denouncing "pagan gods." Once the Israelites worshiped Yahweh exclusively, Armstrong asserts, "the religion of Judaism was born."

Forced into exile after the Romans seized the Holy Land, the Jews began to form new sects including the Essenes and the Qumran, "who sought forgiveness of sins by baptismal ceremonies," and the Jewish Pharisees, whose Rabbis encouraged their people to "atone for sins with acts of loving-kindness to their neighbor." In their preachings, the Rabbis often spoke metaphorically: *One of their favorite synonyms for God was the Shekinah, which derived from the Hebrew shakan, to dwell with or to pitch one's tent. Now that the Temple [in Jerusalem] was gone, the image of God who had accompanied the Israelites on their wanderings in the wilderness suggested the accessibility of God. . . . Like the divine "glory" or the Holy Spirit, the Shekinah was not conceived as a separate divine being but as the presence of God on earth.* The image of the Shekinah helped the exiles to think of themselves "as a united community with 'one body and soul.'" Thus, even in exile, the Jews felt "enveloped by a benevolent God [who] stressed that Jews had a duty to keep well and happy."

Much later in human history, Christianity emerged, Armstrong suggests, from the teachings of the Pharisees, who preached that "charity and loving-kindness were the most important of the *mitzvah* (commandments)." Jesus may have been a Pharisee, Armstrong writes, for he clearly adopted the words of the great Pharisee Rabbi Hillel the Elder who had said, "Do not do unto others as you would not have done unto you." Ultimately, Jesus' disciples and the Jews parted company. Although Jesus referred to himself as "the Son of Man," his disciples believed "that Jesus had somehow presented an image of God"; as "passionate monotheists," the Jews could not accept the notion of a divine Messiah.

Christians had disagreements not only with the Jews, but also among themselves. Paul, for instance, did not believe in "the idea of Christ existing as a second divine being beside [Yahweh] from all eternity," while Peter, in contrast, insisted that after Jesus' crucifixion, "God had raised him to life and had exalted him to an especially high status 'by God's right hand.'"

In addition to their theological disagreements, many of the early Christian converts "felt lost, adrift and radically displaced." Among Christian sects, for instance, the Gnostics "did not experience the world as . . . the work of a benevolent deity." Indeed, contends Armstrong, God would not become a congenial God until the third century, when "some truly cultivated pagans began to be converted to Christianity" and the philosopher Clement reformulated God to be a peaceable being, "utterly impassable and serene." Later, Plotinus, the Roman Platonist, influenced Christian thinking by suggesting that the faithful withdraw into themselves to discover this serene God.

Whereas Eastern Christians embraced Platonists' tranquil deity, the Western Christians were increasingly convinced "that martyrdom was the only sure path to God." When the emperor Constantine converted to Christianity in 312, it became the state religion of the Roman empire and "began to attract new converts who made their way into the Church for the sake of material advancement."

According to Armstrong, the Church soon became bitterly divided over official doctrine: "Either Christ . . . belonged to the divine realm (which was now the domain of God alone), or he belonged to the fragile created order." After lengthy arguments in Nicaea, three Turkish theologians finally posited that "Father, Son and Spirit" were simply the outward manifestation (*hypostases*) of God, and not God himself, whose "divine nature *(ousia)* is unnameable and unspeakable." Thus the Trinity, which Western Christians would find "simply baffling" and Eastern Christians would consider "an inspiring religious experience," became part of Church doctrine.

The idea of the Trinity seemed "puzzling and even blasphemous" to Muslims, who, Armstrong says, denounced the concept as "self-indulgent guesswork about things that nobody can possibly know or prove." The Koran counseled Muslims "to see *through* the fragmentary world to the full power of original being, to the transcendent reality that infuses all things."

The Islamic prophet Muhammad ibn Abdullah, who introduced the Koran to Islam, was, writes Armstrong, "a man of exceptional genius": *When he died in 632, he had managed to bring nearly all the tribes of Arabia into a new united community, or ummah . . . Like many of the Arabs, Muhammad had come to believe that al-Lah . . . whose name simply meant "the God," was identical to the God worshiped by the Jews and the Christians.*

A merchant of the Meccan tribe of Quraysh, Muhammad lamented that his people had become capitalists and seemed "lost." In 610, Muhammad was visited by two angels but only later determined that he "had received a revelation from the God of Moses and the prophets, and had become the divine envoy to the Arabs."

"The Koran was revealed to Muhammad . . . over a period of twenty-three years," Armstrong notes, and when "each new segment was revealed, Muhammad, who could neither read nor write, recited it aloud and the Muslims learned it by heart and those few who were literate wrote it down."

The Koran encouraged the Quraysh "to become aware of God's benevolence," but also cautioned the Muslims that "if they failed to reproduce God's benevolence in their society, they would be out of touch with the true nature of things. [They therefore] had a moral duty to create a just, equitable society, where the poor and vulnerable are treated decently." Moreover, "Muslims were not to abdicate their reason, but to look at the world attentively and with curiosity."

While "it took the ancient Israelites some 7000 years to break with their old religious alliances and accept monotheism," Armstrong asserts, " . . . Muhammad managed to help the Arabs achieve this difficult transition in a mere 23 years." As Muslims, they embraced "no other deity but al-Lah the Creator of heaven and earth, who can save man and send him the spiritual and physical sustenance that he needs." And from

these monotheistic beliefs, Muslims became highly tolerant of other, non-Islamic theologies, reasoning that "because there was only one God, all rightly guided religions must be derived from him alone."

Following Muhammad's death, "egalitarianism would continue to characterize the Islamic ideal." New sects began to emerge, including the Shiahs—who believed "that only members of Muhammad's family had true knowledge of God"—and the Sufis—who sought God transcendentally. After the twelfth century, "the Iranian philosopher Yahya Suhrawardi linked Islamic Falsafah [the interpretation of the Koran from the perspective of Greek rationalism] indissolubly with mysticism and made the God experienced by the Sufis normative in many parts of the Islamic empire."

The Jews, meanwhile, had developed Kabbalah, in which "as in Sufism, the doctrine of the creation is not really concerned with the physical origins of the universe, but with the mystery of God." While mysticism preoccupied both Jews and Muslims, the Christians "began to see God in still more rationalistic terms." After battling Muslims in the Crusades to wrest control of the Holy Land and mounting brutal pogroms against Sephardic Jews in Spain, the Christians conquered the New World.

Having subjugated all enemies while acquiring considerable wealth, Christians were at leisure to question their own precepts, and thus the Reformation was born. Protestantism developed as an alternative to Roman Catholicism under the leadership of Martin Luther, who viewed "life as a battle against Satan," and later under John Calvin, who inspired people "to believe that they could achieve whatever they wanted."

When Protestantism took root in America, "the old proofs of God were no longer satisfactory . . . and philosophers, full of enthusiasm for the empirical method, felt compelled to create the objective reality of God in the same way they proved other demonstrable phenomena." (A similar preoccupation with "finding truth through reason" also occurred among 18th-century Jews under the elegant philosophical arguments of Moses Mendelssohn.)

But "Rationalism," Armstrong asserts, would in time foster atheism in many Christians. Indeed, "by the end of the nineteenth century, a significant number of people were beginning to feel that if God was not yet dead, it was the duty of rational, emancipated human beings to kill him." Likewise the Zionist Jews of this century propose that man "no longer needs God; he himself is the creator." So, even as Muslims continued to rely on God as "a force for transformation at a deep level," Westerners were increasingly secularizing their world.

As a response to atheism, says Armstrong, fundamentalists of all religions "are swift to condemn the enemies of God" and yet increasingly defy "a crucial monotheistic theme . . . the ideal of compassion"—an omission that causes Armstrong to conclude that "if we are to create a vibrant new faith for the twentieth century, we should, perhaps, ponder the history of God for some lessons and warnings."

WHEN EGYPT RULED THE EAST

by George Steindorff and Keith C. Seele, The University of Chicago Press, Chicago, Illinois, 1957

The history of Egypt as an autonomous, sovereign state begins around 2800 B.C. and ends with the Persian conquest in 525 B.C. Because of the sheer span of its history, then, it is difficult to give an adequate account of the ascent and ultimate decline of Egypt—nor a sufficient feeling for the great influence its culture has had on the world—in a single volume. Steindorff and Seele solve this problem in their masterpiece *When Egypt Ruled the East* by focusing on the period of the New Kingdom (1546 to 1085 B.C.), while treating the Old Kingdom, the First Intermediate Period and the Middle Kingdom more as preface, and the Decline (1085 to 322 B.C.), as epilogue. Their strategy has merit, since Egypt's most famous and colorful characters date from this period. Moreover, because the period is so rich, the authors can treat several aspects of Egyptian culture—such as religion, art, and hieroglyphic writing—topically. On the other hand, the reader should be aware that some very colorful aspects of Egyptian culture belong to earlier periods. In particular, the Great Pyramids of Giza were built for Khufu, Khafre and Menkaure, pharaohs of the Fourth Dynasty of the Old Kingdom (before 2500 B.C.); these remarkable edifices were already "ancient" when the New Kingdom began.

Steindorff and Seele begin their history with the Hyksos invasion and the subsequent war of liberation. The Hyksos, foreign invaders who ruled northern Egypt from about 1725 to 1600 B.C., set up their capital at Avaris in the Nile Delta. Nobody knows exactly who the Hyksos were. Since they had numerous fortified settlements in Palestine, however, scholars believe they must have been either Semites or Hurrians. The fact that they were skilled in the use of horses and chariots suggests they were a military aristocracy like the Hurrians. In any case, during the first century of Hyksos rule, a new line of Egyptian kings, skilled in the new arts of warfare, arose in Thebes. At first these Theban kings were vassals of the Hyksos, but by about 1600 B.C. the Theban ruler Sekenrere rebelled against his Hyksos overlords. From his mummified remains we know that Sekenrere met a violent end, having sustained blows to his left jaw and forehead, as well as a blow to the head so severe that it fractured his skull, exposing the brain.

Sekenrere's sons, Kamose and Ahmose, carried on a war of liberation against the Hyksos in the city of Avaris and their Nubian allies in the far south. Kamose, who died young, laid siege to Avaris, but failed to capture it. The younger son Ahmose succeeded in capturing the city and, once having driven the Hyksos out of the land, in pursuing them to Sharuhen, their stronghold in southern Palestine. After a three-year siege, Sharuhen fell as well, so that the victory over the Hyksos in Egypt was complete. Having defeated the Hyksos in the north, Ahmose attacked their Nubian allies, restoring Egyptian rule in the south as well.

Following a long and relatively peaceful reign, in 1546 B.C. Ahmose was succeeded by his son Amenhotep I, the first pharaoh of the Eighteenth Dynasty. Unlike the Egypt of the Old or Middle Kingdom, the Egypt of the New Kingdom was an imperial power with a standing, professional army equipped with chariots, archers and bronze weapons.

Amenhotep was succeeded by his son Thutmose I, who is generally regarded as the founder of the Egyptian Empire and the first pharaoh to fully exploit Egypt's newly acquired military prowess. Not content to exact tribute from just a few allies in southern Palestine, Thutmose led his armies all the way across Palestine and Syria to the shores of the Euphrates, which the Egyptians described as "that inverted water which flows southward when flowing northward." Although the "conquests" of Thutmose proved ephemeral and Egyptian rule was not established in Syria and Palestine until near the end of the long reign of Thutmose III in 1450 B.C., Thutmose I's Syrian campaign may be regarded as Egypt's emergence as an international power.

Thutmose I and his chief consort, the "Great Royal Wife" or crown princess, had two sons—Wadjmose and Amenmose—and two daughters—Hatshepsut and Nefrubity. Of these children, only the Princess Hatshepsut survived her father.

Tradition had for centuries dictated that only men could serve as pharaoh, and also that a pharaoh be succeeded by the *husband* of his eldest daughter; with this in mind, Thutmose married his daughter Hatshepsut to her younger half-brother Thutmose II, who took power upon his father's death in 1508 B.C. Yet when the frail Thutmose II died after a reign of only four years, his son, Thutmose III, was deposed by Hatshepsut, his mother-in-law, the Great Royal Wife herself.

For Hatshepsut, to rule Egypt as a mere regent or "power behind the throne" was not enough. Thus she openly assumed the title of pharaoh and claimed to reign by divine right as the daughter of Amun. In fact, between 1504 and 1482 the Egyptians lived in peace and prosperity under the rule of Hatshepsut and her chancellor, Senenmut. During her administration she rebuilt or restored the temples which had been destroyed or neglected by the Hyksos. She also erected two giant obelisks (one of which still stands in the temple of Amun at Thebes) and saw to the construction of one of the great monuments of Egyptian architecture—her temple at Deir el Bahri.

Hatshepsut designated her daughter, the Princess Nefrure, to succeed her, but her plans were thwarted when Thutmose III returned to Egypt in 1482 B.C. to have Hatshepsut killed and her allies banished. Afterwards, Thutmose III did his best to obliterate the memory of "Pharaoh" Hatshepsut and her consort. And, except for a few inscriptions he apparently overlooked, Hatshepsut's name was removed from most of the numerous monuments of her reign.

Having at last achieved undisputed rule, Thutmose III undertook a series of military campaigns in Syria to the northeast and in Nubia to the south. Over a period of nineteen years, Thutmose III brought the principalities of Palestine and Syria under firm Egyptian control. He replaced recalcitrant dynasties when necessary, installed princes sympathetic to Egypt, and educated the eldest sons of subject princes in Thebes to prepare them to replace their fathers if and when necessary.

Following the reign of Thutmose III, there was almost a century of peace in the Ancient Near East. The three great powers of Egypt, Mitanni and Babylon engaged in amiable diplomatic relations. This stability lasted until Egypt lost most of its Asiatic empire during the reigns of Amenhoteps III and IV, fanatics of religious reform who initiated a period of cultural and military neglect in Egypt that lasted from 1412 to 1366 B.C. Apparently disturbed by the growing wealth and political power of the priesthood of *Amun* (the personification of wind or breath, represented either as a ram or goose)—which constituted a long-term threat to the economic well-being and political stability of the Egyptian state—Amenhotep IV launched an attempt to systematize the complicated Egyptian pantheon, instituting a form of monotheism in its place, while decreeing that the worship of *Aton* would be the new and only state religion. (Akhnaton's new theology embodied a radical departure from Egyptian tradition. Aton was depicted not as a person or animal, but as a sun disk from which emanated hands [the rays of the sun] grasping the *ankh* [a cross with a loop at the top], the hieroglyphic sign for "life.")

In accordance with this proclamation, Amenhotep and his wife Nofretete had all polytheistic references stricken from the histories and chiselled from the temples. Thereafter, all persons bearing names compounded by "-amun" (meaning "Amun is satisfied") were ordered to change their names. Amenhotep himself gladly complied, and from that time forward adopted the name *Akhnaton,* meaning "He who is beneficial to Aton." Subsequently the government seat was transferred from Thebes to Akhetaton.

Akhnaton, his mind centered on religious reform, "not only made no attempt to reassure or lend material aid to the faltering representatives of Egyptian power in western Asia but rather, through his fanatical devotion to his religious innovations, brought Egypt to the brink of ruin." For this reason, no doubt, Akhnaton's religious reforms (which met with little resistance during his lifetime) were promptly overturned by the nobility shortly after his death. Still, his brief reformation was accompanied by a renaissance in the arts whereby a naturalism took hold in painting (doing away with traditional lateral representations of the face in which the observable eye appears in a frontal perspective), in bas relief, and especially in portraiture. The famous "caryatid statue" of Akhnaton with its long, floppy ears, thick lips and skinny, unmuscled arms carries naturalism to the extreme of caricature. And one of the best-known of Egyptian artifacts, the celebrated bust of Queen Nofretete, accurately portrays her long, thin neck.

Meanwhile, Egypt's Syrian empire crumbled. In the north, its dependencies fell to the Hittites and their allies; and southward "in Palestine the situation was no better." (It is worth noting in passing that this is the earliest Egyptian reference to the people who later came to be known as Hebrews. There is no corroborating Egyptian evidence to support the Old Testament claim of Hebrew captivity in Egypt proper. The Hebrews first appear as wandering mercenaries settling down in Syria-Palestine.)

Akhnaton and Nofretete had as yet failed to beget a male heir. With Nofretete having fallen into disgrace, Akhnaton tried to produce an heir through two of his daughters. Finally, approaching death, he gave the hand of a daughter to Tutankhaton (known to us as Tutankhamen), then a nine-year-old nephewprince. This fair boy-king would succeed the dying Egyptian pharaoh.

Tutankhaton's reign, however, was shortlived. Following his own untimely death in 1357 B.C.—and his well-publicized entombment—the aged regent Eye ruled as pharaoh. With Eye's subsequent death, one of Akhnaton's desperate daughters—who had been married to both her father and to Tutankhaton—wrote to the Hittite Emperor Supiluliumas I, requesting that he send one of his sons to be her husband and pharaoh of Egypt. But a group of assassins who did not like this arrangement murdered the son before the marriage could take place. Harmhab, a former commander-in-chief of the army of Tutankhaton, then marched with his army to Thebes, where he was hailed as new pharaoh by the priesthood of Amun. This mighty Harmhab, who ruled from 1353 to 1319, then set out to reclaim the lands lost under Akhnaton's rule.

Before the childless Harmhab's death, he named a favored general, Pramessu, to succeed him. Pramessu became known as Rameses I— the first in a long line of Ramesids, under which Egypt regained most of its previous lands. By 1284 B.C., the stability of the region was restored through a treaty with the Hittites. However, at the same time, all the great achievements of Egyptian culture belonged to the past. No subsequent achievement of Egyptian art bears favorable comparison with the best works produced under the reign of the Eighteenth Dynasty; no later literary work bears favorable comparison with the classical literature of the First Intermediate Period.

Indeed, after the death of Rameses III (1198 to 1167)—who had successfully repelled Hittite aggression—the history of Egypt is one of gradual political, economic, and cultural decline. Between 663 and 525 B.C. Egypt enjoyed a brief renaissance, induced by a vigorous foreign trade and by a nostalgic longing for the glories of the past. Following the conquest of Alexander the Great in 332 B.C., Egypt also enjoyed a cultural revival of sorts, since Alexandria became the greatest cultural center in the Eastern Mediterranean during the Hellenistic period. But the great scientific and literary achievements of Alexandria were triumphs of Greek rather than Egyptian culture. The great pharaohs ruled no more.

THE FACE OF THE ANCIENT ORIENT

A Panorama of Near Eastern Civilization in Pre-Classical Times
by Sabatino Moscati, Rizzoli, New York, N.Y., 1991

Three millennia before classical Greece and Rome flourished, Ancient Near Eastern civilization reached its apogee. Indeed, many of the fundamental aspects of civilized life began in the Ancient Near Eastern regions of Mesopotamia, Egypt, Syria-Palestine, and Anatolia. While the Greeks developed certain "modern-day" societal inventions such as philosophy, secularized drama, and abstract science and mathematics, the Greeks inherited many of their myths, writing, international trade, and urbanization from the Ancient Near East; hence much of Western culture derives from these archaic civilizations.

While specific Near Eastern cultures—including the Sumerians, the Egyptians, the Babylonians and the Hittites—have been treated individually by numerous authors, there are few like Sabatino Moscati, who attempt to survey the Ancient Near East as a whole. Indeed Moscati discusses the Ancient Near East from about 3500 B.C.—when the Sumerians arrived in the Tigris-Euphrates Valley—to 330 B.C.—when Alexander the Great put an end to the autonomy of the region by defeating the Persians.

Thus, to organize the diverse subject matter in *The Face of the Ancient Orient*, Moscati divides the civilizations of the Ancient Near East into three classes: the "components," the "catalysts," and the Persians.

(1) The *components* include the major civilizations that made autonomous contributions to their neighboring cultures—primarily the Egyptians and Sumerians, since the cultures of the Babylonians and Assyrians were largely patterned on the Sumerian model. Actually, the Egyptians too were profoundly indebted to the Sumerians for their writing and crafts. The earliest known Egyptian relief, for example, depicts a Sumerian Gilgamesh motif of a bearded king wrestling with lions. Thus Sumer was undeniably a seminal—if not *the* seminal—ancient civilization.

(2) The *catalysts* are ancient civilizations that were of minor political importance, but that were responsible for the spread of component-culture society. These civilizations include the Hurrians, the Hittites, the Hebrews, and the Mycenaean Greeks, all of whom possessed large merchant and explorer/military classes of citizens who were instrumental in dispersing the Mesopotamian cultural traits to neighboring states. Thus, subsequent Western civilizations frequently owed their conceptions of politics, weaponry, clothing, military strategy, languages, arts and religious pantheons and customs to the Ancient Sumerians, who initially inculcated their traits into the catalyst civilizations.

(3) The *Persians* ultimately conquered the entire region and created a civilization that synthesized the divergent cultures of the Ancient Near East.

❖ ◆ ❖

Living in prosperous city-states bordered by fertile, well irrigated farms, the Sumerians and their anonymous predecessors developed all the basic tools and skills required by an urban society, including: wheeled vehicles (such as chariots) and the potter's wheel; the architectural dome, vaults and arches; the cylinder seal, used to reproduce both written documents and artistic designs; the sexagesimal system of numeration (which we still use when we divide the circle into 360 degrees); and, most importantly, cuneiform script, from which all other writing systems derive.

With the development of cuneiform writing, the Ancient Near Easterners founded the institution of the *edubba*, or scribal school, and created the first legal codes, as well as most of the literary forms known in ancient times: epic poetry, proverbs, lamentations and love poems. In fact the only literary forms developed in the ancient world which were *not* invented by the Sumerians were Greek-inspired mathematical proofs, philosophical discourses, and sustained historical narratives. The Hebrew narratives of the Old Testament, Moscati surmises, were probably elaborations of previously existing forms; Biblical passages concerning the great flood, Cain and Abel, the tower of Babel, and the Job-motif, he says, were borrowed directly from Sumerian mythology.

Sumeria, Moscati believes, was the birthplace of civilization: . . . *Its literary works, its laws, and its artistic creations provide the basis for all the succeeding civilizations of Western Asia, in which we shall find them copied, adapted, and worked over, often being marred rather than improved in the process.* Thus, with the possible exception of Egyptian religion, Moscati argues that later religions of the Ancient Near East, including Judaism and Christianity, derive most of their form and content from Sumerian beliefs.

Sumerian mythology revolved around a pantheon headed by four creating goddesses and three astral deities. Just like the Biblical Yaweh's, the names of the four creating goddesses—led by the great *Ninhursag*—possessed magical powers: to effect change, a Sumerian needed only to conceive of the change and then pronounce the deity's name. While the names of all the male deities were similarly imbued, *An, Enlil* and *Enki* formed the "Mesopotamian Trinity." From these early beliefs, Moscati contends, the various gods (creators, patron beings, judges, war and love gods, the original "dying-and-rising savior god," and so forth) of the successive and scattered cultures of the Near East were born—albeit with new names reflecting the individual dogmas of the society.

Not only religious beliefs but also religious rituals and customs of the Babylonians, Hurrians, Hittites and Hebrews were based on Sumerian mythology, often with only minor modifications. For instance, the Babylonian creation epic *Enuma elish* was recited annually at the New Year's Festival and acted out by King Marduk. With only minor adjustments in style of dress and manner of speech, Marduk took the role of Babylon's patron-god the son of Enki, who was actually the *Sumerian* god of water and wisdom.

Similarly, in the Prologue to the *Code of*

Hammurabi, a Babylonian adaptation of earlier Sumerian legal codes, it is stated that Hammurabi received the laws from the Babylonian sun-god Shamash.

The Babylonians

Adapting the cuneiform script to their own Semitic language known as Akkadian, the Babylonians deliberately preserved the literature of the Sumerians. And, in at least one instance, they improved upon it. The elegantly crafted Babylonian *Epic of Gilgamesh* tells of mythical King of Uruk who befriended the wild man Enkidu, with whom, after Enkidu's death, he shared a series of adventures in a futile quest for eternal life. *Gilgamesh* has long been considered the supreme literary achievement of the Ancient Near East.

Over the centuries, the Babylonians also surpassed the Sumerians in their understanding and use of mathematics—in which they introduced the quadratic equation—and in the study of astronomy. The Babylonians, however, relied more heavily on divination (foretelling future events through signs) than the Sumerians; the two methods that the Babylonians favored entailed of the examination of animal livers and the practice of astrology. Although divination and other superstitious beliefs clearly impeded scientific and medical advancement in Babylonian society, it nevertheless managed to arouse an increase in astronomical scholarship.

The Egyptians

Egypt's great "component" civilization developed in conjunction with Sumer and its successors. Mesopotamia also influenced Egypt during certain crucial stages in its evolution. The Egyptian pyramid, for instance, derived much of its form from the Sumerian and Babylonian primary architectural monuments, the *ziggurats*. Pyramids and ziggurats, however, had different functions: ziggurats served as elevated platforms for the worship of the gods, while the pyramids encased a royal tomb. Actually, though, the differing functions were determined more by political ideology than by religious belief, inasmuch as in Egypt the reigning Pharaoh was regarded quite literally as a god.

The institution of divine kingship accounts for another difference between Egyptian and Mesopotamian society: the absence of written laws. In Egypt the person of the Pharaoh was the immediate source of all legal validity. As a god, the decrees of the Pharaoh had the status of law without any further justification.

Indeed, Moscati attributes what he calls the "optimism" of the Egyptians to their institution of divine kingship coupled with their belief in a glorious afterlife: ... *In Mesopotamia the king ... belongs to the human plane ... In Egypt, on the other hand, the king is a god descended among men. Hence the difference in the attitude to life: in Mesopotamia the constant anxiety, the fear lest the supreme will should remain uncomprehended and the harmony between the two spheres should be marred; in Egypt, a happy serenity, due to resignation to the predestined order which descends from on high without any break in transmission.*

Not surprisingly, then, Egyptian civilization became as rich as that of Mesopotamia. In fact, in the arts, Egypt may well have surpassed both Sumerian and Babylonian proficiency. Outside of the arts, however, Egypt's influence on other cultures was not nearly so profound as Sumer's. In religion, for example, the Egyptians were never as systematic as the Sumerians. Egyptian cosmologies never enjoyed universal acceptance. Hence it is impossible to provide any consistent summary of Egyptian belief. And while some aspects of Egyptian religion—such as the cult of Isis and Osiris, which were similar to the Sumerian cult of Dumuzi and Inanna—were adopted by other cultures, Egyptian mythology proved far less influential than its tidier, more systematic Sumerian counterpart.

Another reason why Egypt's culture was not widely adopted elsewhere was that it maintained a "defensive posture." From about 2800 B.C. until the Persian conquest of Egypt in 525 B.C., the Egyptians, under the rule of a single monarch, were both able and inclined to remain aloof, a stance which Mesopotamian peoples certainly never aspired to.

The "Catalyst" Civilizations and the Persians

Around 1500 B.C. the mountain-dwelling Hurrians—the forerunners of Iraq's Khurds—established a state known as Mitanni in northern Mesopotamia, which enjoyed favorable relations with the Egyptian Empire until it was overthrown by the Hittites in 1365 B.C. The Hittites rapidly appropriated and adopted the culture of their vassal state and, as a result, much of Hittite mythology is ultimately of Sumerian or Babylonian origin.

Two other "catalyst" groups that contributed to the Ancient Near East were the Biblical Canaanites, or Phoenicians, and the Persians, who, for a few centuries, united all of the Near East under a single imperial rule.

It is, perhaps, least misleading generally to refer to the Semitic peoples of Syria-Palestine—as opposed to, for example, the region's Hurrians or Hittites—as Canaanites, reserving the term Phoenician for those Canaanites who lived in seafaring coastal towns like Ugarit and Tyre. Given this usage we can confidently say that a phonetic alphabet was first employed by Canaanites—who were not necessarily Phoenician—sometime in the second millennium B.C. Subsequently, the use of such an alphabet was introduced to Western peoples, such as the Greeks, by Phoenicians, who were the most important maritime traders in the Eastern Mediterranean until well into the Hellenistic Age (c. 323 to 27 B.C.). And as a race of seafaring merchants, the Phoenicians facilitated not only a dispersal of basic goods but the spread of ideas among the diverse cultures of the eastern Mediterranean.

Finally, for almost two centuries from 525 to 332 B.C., the Persians united the entire region under sovereign Achaemenian kings. Intellectually and culturally, the Persians themselves had little to contribute. Pragmatically, however, their impact was enormous: they pursued a deliberate policy of religious toleration; they standardized the coinage that had been introduced into the region by the Lydians; and they built an extensive network of roads, including the famous royal road from Sardis to Susa, which facilitated an unprecedented level of trade between all the regions of the Ancient Near East.

JOHN F. KENNEDY

"Inaugural Address"

The thirty-fifth President of the United States, John F. Kennedy was 44 when inaugurated on January 20, 1961. His first address to the country was a clarion call for a new day of government. Delivered outside of the Capitol Building in Washington, D.C., the sermon exuded youth, idealism, and a sense of history. His Lincolnesque use of language was especially poignant, given both presidents were assassinated before their term of office was complete.

By the time he was elected, President Kennedy had earned the Purple Heart for heroic service in the Navy, had authored two prize-winning books, and had been elected to the House of Representatives and to the Senate. In *Profiles in Courage*, published in 1956, Kennedy wrote: *For without belittling the courage with which men have died, we should not forget those acts of courage with which men . . . have lived . . . A man does what he must in spite of personal consequences, in spite of obstacles and dangers and pressures—and that is the basis of all human morality.*

Bringing freshness and zeal to the office, this young chief executive also brought with him to the White House two young children—the youngest to live in the White House in over sixty years—and a gracious, intelligent wife, Jackie, who, with her husband, helped to popularize the presidency. Ultimately, they wrote themselves into the history books and hearts of America as legends in their time—and for all times.

❖ ◆ ❖

We observe today not a victory of a party but a celebration of freedom, symbolizing an end as well as a beginning, signifying renewal as well as change. For I have sworn before you and Almighty God the same solemn oath as our forbears prescribed nearly a century and three-quarters ago.

The world is very different now. For man holds in his mortal hands the power to abolish all forms of human poverty and all forms of human life. And yet the same revolutionary belief for which our forbears fought is still at issue around the globe—the belief that the rights of man come not from the generosity of the state but from the hand of God.

We dare not forget today that we are the heirs of that first revolution. Let the word go forth from this time and place, to friend and foe alike, that the torch has been passed to a new generation of Americans, born in this century, tempered by war, disciplined by a hard and bitter peace, proud of our ancient heritage—and unwilling to witness or permit the slow undoing of those human rights to which this nation has always been committed, and to which we are committed today at home and around the world.

Let every nation know, whether it wishes us well or ill, that we shall pay any price, bear any burden, meet any hardship, support any friend, oppose any foe to assure the survival and success of liberty.

This much we pledge—and more.

To those old allies whose cultural and spiritual origins we share, we pledge the loyalty of faithful friends. United, there is little we cannot do in a host of cooperative ventures. Divided, there is little we can do—for we dare not meet a powerful challenge at odds and split asunder.

To those new states whom we welcome to the ranks of the free, we pledge our word that one form of colonial control shall not have passed away merely to be replaced by a far more iron tyranny. We shall not always expect to find them supporting our view. But we shall always hope to find them strongly supporting their own freedom—and to remember that, in the past, those who foolishly sought power by riding the back of the tiger ended up inside.

To those peoples in the huts and villages of half the globe struggling to break the bonds of mass misery, we pledge our best efforts to help them help themselves, for whatever period is required—not because the Communists may be doing it, not because we seek their votes, but because it is right. If a free society cannot help the many who are poor, it cannot save the few who are rich.

To our sister republics south of our border, we offer a special pledge—to convert our good words into good deeds—in a new alliance for progress—to assist free men and free governments in casting off the chains of poverty. But this peaceful revolution of hope cannot become the prey of hostile powers. Let all our neighbors know that we shall join with them to oppose aggression or subversion anywhere in the Americas. And let every other power know that this hemisphere intends to remain the master of its own house.

To that world assembly of sovereign states, the United Nations, our last best hope in an age where the instruments of war have far out-paced the instruments of peace, we renew our pledge of support—to prevent it from becoming merely a forum for invective—to strengthen its shield of the new and the weak—and to enlarge the area in which its writ may run.

Finally, to those nations who would make themselves our adversary, we offer not a pledge but a request: that both sides begin anew the quest for peace, before the dark powers of destruction unleashed by science engulf all humanity in planned or accidental self-destruc-

tion.

We dare not tempt them with weakness. For only when our arms are sufficient beyond doubt can we be certain beyond doubt that they will never be employed.

But neither can two great and powerful groups of nations take comfort from our present course—both sides overburdened by the cost of modern weapons, both rightly alarmed by the steady spread of the deadly atom, yet both racing to alter that uncertain balance of terror that stays the hand of mankind's final war.

So let us begin anew, remembering on both sides that civility is not a sign of weakness, and sincerity is always subject to proof. Let us never negotiate out of fear. But let us never fear to negotiate.

Let both sides explore what problems unite us instead of belaboring those problems which divide us. Let both sides, for the first time, formulate serious and precise proposals for the inspection and control of arms, and bring the absolute power to destroy other nations under the absolute control of all nations.

Let both sides seek to invoke the wonders of science instead of its terrors. Together let us explore the stars, conquer the deserts, eradicate disease, tap the ocean depths and encourage the arts and commerce.

Let both sides unite to heed in all corners of the earth the command of Isaiah, to "undo the heavy burdens and to let the oppressed go free."

And if a beach-head of cooperation may push back the jungle of suspicion, let both sides join in a new endeavor; not a new balance of power, but a new world of law, where the strong are just and the weak secure and the peace preserved.

All this will not be finished in the first one hundred days. Nor will it be finished in the first one thousand days, nor in the life of this Administration, nor even perhaps in our lifetime on this planet. But let us begin.

In your hands, my fellow citizens, more than mine, will rest the final success or failure of our course. Since this country was founded, each generation of Americans has been summoned to give testimony to its national loyalty. The graves of young Americans who answered the call to service surround the globe.

Now the trumpet summons us again-not as a call to bear arms, though arms we need; not as a call to battle, though embattled we are; but a call to bear the burden of a long twilight struggle, year in and year out, "rejoicing in hope, patient in tribulation",a struggle against the common enemies of man: tyranny, poverty, disease and war itself.

Can we forge against these enemies a grand and global alliance, North and South, East and West, that can assure a more fruitful life for all mankind? Will you join in that historic effort?

In the long history of the world, only a few generations have been granted the role of defending freedom in its hour of maximum danger. I do not shrink from this responsibility; I welcome it. I do not believe that any of us would exchange places with any other people or any other generation. The energy, the faith, the devotion which we bring to this endeavor will light our country and all who serve it, and the glow from that fire can truly light the world.

And so, my fellow Americans, ask not what your country can do for you, ask what you can do for your country.

My fellow citizens of the world, ask not what America will do for you, but what together we can do for the freedom of man.

Finally, whether you are citizens of America or citizens of the world, ask of us here the same high standards of strength and sacrifice which we ask of you. With a good conscience our only sure reward, with history the final judge of our deeds, let us go forth to lead the land we love, asking His blessings and His help, but knowing that here on earth God's work must truly be our own.

ABRAHAM LINCOLN

"The Gettysburg Address" and "The Second Inaugural Address"

In a few paragraphs, President Abraham Lincoln dedicated the cemetery on the battlefield of Gettysburg, Pennsylvania in ceremonies honoring the 43,000 casualties of the three-day battle that marked the turning point of the long Civil War. The speech would long be remembered and revered, for his words not only dedicated a cemetery but unified a country that had for two years be torn by war.

Interestingly, however, the President had not been expected to speak at the cemetery's dedication on November 19, 1863—in part because he was not considered to be a particularly eloquent speaker and in part because Edward Everett had been invited to commemorate Gettysburg's dead. Everett, a Harvard professor, was widely regarded as the North's most gifted orator. After Lincoln had finished reading his three-minute "Gettysburg Address" to the crowd, Everett immediately congratulated the President and delivered his own speech. Everett clearly did not expect to have his own words diminished by Lincoln's.

Actually, the immediate impact of the President's address was minimal. Perhaps because Lincoln's high-pitched and Kentucky-accented voice was not ideally suited to oratory, few in the crowd were impressed by Lincoln's beautifully crafted words. The British *Times*, in fact, summarily dismissed his speech by stating, "The ceremony was rendered ludicrous by some of the sallies of that poor President Lincoln." Newspapers in the United States also found the speech "silly" or "embarrassing." And Lincoln himself, after the speech, commented, "That speech won't scour. It is a flat failure and the people are disappointed." On the farms where Lincoln grew up, when wet soil stuck to the mold board of a plow they said it didn't "scour."

However, as the days passed and Lincoln's sermon appeared in print, people began to marvel at the personal depth of compassion and presidential debt of gratitude that his words conveyed.

Indeed few speeches can rival "The Gettysburg Address." As scholar Gilbert Highet points out, Lincoln was a "literary artist, [and] 'The Gettysburg Address' [is] a work of art." Not only was Lincoln profoundly influenced by classic literature, the Bible, and Shakespeare, but he also fully understood and deftly manipulated rhetorical devices. Lincoln's powerful diction and profound allusions, Highet contends, have produced a literary masterpiece that "belongs to the same world as the great elegies and the adagios of Beethoven."

The great President's poetic words, spoken in only three minute's time, are engraven in stone at the Lincoln Memorial—and upon the hearts of freedom-loving people everywhere.

"The Gettysburg Address"

Fourscore and seven years ago our fathers brought forth on this continent, a new nation, conceived in liberty and dedicated to the proposition that all men are created equal.

Now we are engaged in a great civil war, testing whether that nation—or any nation so conceived and so dedicated—can long endure.

We are met on a great battlefield of that war. We have come to dedicate a portion of that field as a final resting place for those who here gave their lives that that nation might live.

It is altogether fitting and proper that we should do this.

But, in a larger sense, we can not dedicate, we can not consecrate, we can not hallow, this ground. The brave men, living and dead, who struggled here, have consecrated it, far above our poor power to add or detract.

The world will very little note nor long remember what we say here, but it can never forget what they did here.

It is for us, the living, rather, to be dedicated here to the unfinished work which they who fought here have thus far so nobly advanced. It is rather for us to be here dedicated to the great task remaining before us, that from these honored dead we take increased devotion to that cause for which they gave the last full measure of devotion, that we here highly resolve that these dead shall not have died in vain; that this nation under God, shall have a new birth of freedom, and that government of the people, by the people, for the people, shall not perish from the earth.

Born into poverty, Abraham Lincoln faced defeat throughout his life. He had lost eight elections, had failed twice in business, and had suffered a nervous breakdown. After serving in the Illinois state legislature and in Congress, he was not reelected and was subsequently rejected for the job of Illinois' land officer. Nevertheless, Lincoln doggedly pursued his political career. While he failed to be elected—twice—and lost his attempt at the Vice-Presidential nomination, Lincoln eventually was elected President of the United States of America.

Now taking the oath of the Presidential office for a second time on March 4, 1865, President Lincoln displayed his greatest strengths. He expressed his insights and convictions clearly, and in the process revitalized and healed a nation that had suffered four long years of internal strife. Though only subdued hand clapping and occasional cheers punctuated the address, reporters noted that tears coursed down the faces of those in the audience.

However physically drained the President must have been from presiding over a nation "torn from within," Lincoln continued to see those widows and soldiers who flowed from all parts of the country to visit him at the White House. Referred to as "Father Abraham" by millions of his countrymen, the President implored the nation to mend their differences and work together to rebuild the what had been so tragically shattered.

"The Second Inaugural Address"

Fellow countrymen: At this second appearing to take the oath of the presidential office there is less occasion for an extended address than there was at the first. Then a statement, somewhat in detail, of a course to be pursued, seemed fitting and proper. Now, at the expiration of four years, during which public declarations have been constantly called forth on every point and phase of the great contest which still absorbs the attention and engrosses the energies of the nation, little that is new could be presented. The progress of our arms, upon which all else chiefly depends, is as well known to the public as to myself; and it is, I trust, reasonably satisfactory and encouraging to all. With high hope for the future, no prediction in regard to it is ventured.

On the occasion corresponding to this four years ago all thoughts were anxiously directed to an impending civil-war. All dreaded it—all sought to avert it. While the inaugural address was being delivered from this place, devoted altogether to saving the Union without war, insurgent agents were in the city seeking to destroy it without war—seeking to dissolve the Union and divide effects by negotiation. Both parties deprecated war, but one of them would make war rather than let the nation survive, and the other would accept war rather than let it perish, and the war came.

One-eighth of the whole population were colored slaves, not distributed generally over the Union, but localized in the Southern part of it. These slaves constituted a peculiar and powerful interest. All knew that this interest was somehow, the cause of the war. To strengthen, perpetuate, and extend this interest was the object for which the insurgents would rend the Union,even by war, while the government claimed no right to do more than to restrict the territorial enlargement of it. Neither party expected for the war the magnitude or the duration which it has already attained. Neither anticipated that the cause of the conflict might cease with or even before the conflict itself should cease. Each looked for an easier triumph, and a result less fundamental and astounding.

Both read the same Bible, and pray to the same God, and each invokes His aid against the other. It may seem strange that any men should dare to ask a just God's assistance in wringing their bread from the sweat of other men's faces, but let us judge not, that we be not judged. The prayers of both could not be answered. That of neither has been answered fully. The Almighty has His own purposes. "Woe unto the world because of offenses; for it must needs be that offenses come, but woe to that man by whom the offense cometh." If we shall suppose that American Slavery is one of those offenses which, in the providence of God, must needs come, but which, having continued through His appointed time, He now wills to remove, and that He gives to both North and South this terrible war as the woe due to those by whom the offense came, shall we discern therein any departure from those divine attributes which the believers in a Living God always ascribe to Him? Fondly do we hope, fervently do we pray, that this mighty scourge of war may speedily pass away. Yet, if God wills that it continue until all the wealth piled by the bond-man's two hundred and fifty years of unrequited toil shall be sunk, and until every drop of blood drawn with the lash, shall be paid by another drawn with the sword, as was said three thousand years ago, so still it must be said "the judgements of the Lord, are true and righteous altogether."

With malice toward none, with charity for all, with firmness in the right as God gives us to see the right, let us strive on to finish the work we are in, to bind up the nation's wounds, to care for him who shall have borne the battle and for his widow and his orphan, to do all which may achieve and cherish a just, and a lasting peace among ourselves and with all nations.

GEORGE WASHINGTON

"The Temple Speech" and "The Farewell Address"

As the first Commander-in-Chief and first President of the United States, George Washington profoundly influenced his contemporaries and future Americans with his persistence, discipline, and sense of duty.

Born in Virginia, Washington received no formal education as a child, but read widely. He later was trained as a surveyor and subsequently explored his interest in land development. When the French encroached on Virginia territory, Washington began both his political and military careers, participating in local government positions and serving as leader of the state militia. After serving as an exemplary general of colonial forces during the Revolutionary War, he retired to his beloved Mount Vernon plantation—until the country would call on him again to lead the fledgling government.

On March 15, 1783, various officers sought grievance for back pay. As the angry and resentful commanders gathered in a hall called the Temple in New York, Washington unexpectedly arrived to speak to them. The tide of insurrection gradually turned as the President and Commander-in-Chief reminded his friends of their collective vision and purpose. His address left them in tears and once more willing to put their faith in Congress.

"The Temple Speech"

Gentlemen: By an anonymous summons, an attempt has been made to convene you together; how inconsistent with the rules of propriety, how unmilitary, and how subversive of all order and discipline, let the good sense of the army decide.

. . . If my conduct heretofore has not evinced to you that I have been a faithful friend to the army, my declaration of it at this time would be equally unavailing and improper. But as I was among the first who embarked in the cause of our common country. As I have never left your side one moment, but when called from you on public duty. As I have been the constant companion and witness of your distresses, and not among the last to feel and acknowledge your merits. As I have ever considered my own military reputation as inseparably connected with that of the army. As my heart has ever expanded with joy, when I have heard its praises, and my indignation has arisen, when the mouth of detraction has been opened against it, it can scarcely be supposed, at this late stage of the war, that I am indifferent to its interests.

But how are they to be promoted? The way is plain, says the anonymous addresser. If war continues, remove into the unsettled country . . . and leave an ungrateful country to defend itself. But who are they to defend? Our wives, our children, our farms, and other property which we leave behind us . . . If peace takes place, never sheathe your swords, says he, until you have obtained full and ample justice; this dreadful alter-native, of either deserting our country in the extremist hour of her distress or turning our arms against it (which is the apparent object, unless Congress can be compelled into instant compliance), has something so shocking in it that humanity revolts at the idea. My God! What can this writer have in view, by recommending such measure? Can he be a friend to the army? Can he be a friend to this country? Rather, is he not an insidious foe? Some emissary, perhaps, from New York, plotting the ruin of both, by sowing the seed of discord and separation between the civil and military powers of the continent? And what a compliment does he pay to our understandings when he recommends measures in either alternative, impracticable in their nature? . . .

For myself (and I take no merit in giving the assurance, being induced to it from principles of gratitude, veracity, and justice), a grateful sense of the confidence you have ever placed in me, a recollection of the cheerful assistance and prompt obedience I have experienced from you, under every vicissitude of fortune, and the sincere affection I feel for an army I have so long had the honor to command will oblige me to declare, in this public and solemn manner, that, in the gratification of every wish, so far as may be done consistently with the great duty I owe my country and those powers we are bound to respect, you may freely command my services to the utmost of my abilities.

While I give you these assurances, and pledge myself in the most unequivocal manner to exert whatever ability I am possessed of in your favor, let me entreat you, gentlemen, on your part, not to take any measures which, viewed in the calm light of reason, will lessen the dignity and sully the glory you have hitherto maintained; let me request you to rely on the plighted faith of your country, and place a full confidence in the purity of the intentions of Congress . . . And let me conjure you, in the name of our common country, as you value your own sacred honor, as you respect the rights of humanity, and as you regard the military and national character of America, to express your utmost horror and detestation of the man who wishes, under any specious pretenses, to overturn the liberties of our country, and who wickedly attempts to open the floodgates of civil discord and deluge our rising empire in blood.

By thus determining and thus acting, you will pursue the plain and direct road to the attainment of your wishes. You will defeat the insidious designs of our enemies, who are compelled to resort from open force to secret artifice. You will give one more distinguished proof of unexampled patriotism and patient virtue, rising superior to the pressure of the most complicated sufferings. And you will, by the dignity of your conduct, afford occasion for posterity to say, when speaking of the glorious example you have exhibited to mankind, "Had this day been wanting, the world had never seen the last stage of perfection to which human nature is capable of attaining."

[Washington then looked at his sullen audience and drew a letter from his pocket, to which he wished to refer. Squinting at the writing in the letter, the mighty General could not go on. He then drew from his waistcoat pocket an item very few in that audience had seen him use—a pair of glasses.]

Gentlemen, you will permit me to put on my spectacles, for I have not only grown gray but almost blind in the service of my country.

❖ ♦ ❖

After Washington had declined to serve a third term as President, in his last words to the young country, September 17, 1796, he issued warnings and beseeched the citizenry to seek harmony in the nation.

"The Farewell Address"

Friends, and fellow citizens: The period for a new election of a citizen, to administer the executive government of the United States, being not far distant, and the time actually arrived when your thoughts must be employed in designating the person who is to be clothed with that important trust, it appears to me proper, especially as it may conduce to a more distinct expression of the public voice, that I should now apprise you of the resolution I have formed, to decline being considered among the number of those out of whom a choice is to be made . . .

In looking forward to the moment which is intended to terminate the career of my public life, my feelings do not permit me to suspend the deep acknowledgment of that debt of gratitude which I owe to my beloved country, for the many honors it has conferred upon me; still more for the steadfast confidence with which it has supported me . . .

Here, perhaps, I ought to stop. But a solicitude for your welfare, which cannot end by with my life, and the apprehension of danger, natural to that solicitude, urge me on an occasion like the present to offer to your solemn contemplation, and to recommend to your frequent review, some sentiments which are the result of much reflection, of no inconsiderable observation, and which appear to me all important to the permanency of your felicity as a people . . .

Citizens by birth or choice, of a common country, that country has a right to concentrate your affections. The name of American . . . must always exalt the just pride of patriotism . . . With slight shades of difference, you have the same religion, manners, habits, and political principles. You have in a common cause fought and triumphed together. The independence and liberty you possess are the work of joint councils and joint efforts, of common dangers, sufferings, and successes.

. . . While, then, every part of our country thus feels an immediate and particular interest in union, all the parts combined cannot fail to find in the united mass of means and efforts greater strength, greater resource, proportionally greater security from external danger, a less frequent interruption of their peace by foreign nations, and . . . an exemption from those broils and wars between themselves . . .

Of all the dispositions and habits which lead to political prosperity, religion and morality are indispensable supports. In vain would that man claim the tribute of patriotism which should labor to subvert these great pillars of human happiness, these firmest props of the duties of men and citizens . . . And let us with caution indulge the supposition that morality can be maintained without religion. Whatever may be conceded to the influence of refined education on minds of peculiar structure, reason and experience both forbid us to expect that national morality can prevail in exclusion of religious principle.

. . . Promote, then . . . institutions for the general diffusion of knowledge. In proportion as the structure of a government gives force to public opinion, it is essential that public opinion should be enlightened . . .

Observe good faith and justice towards all nations. Cultivate peace and harmony with all. Religion and morality enjoin this conduct; and can it be that good policy does not equally enjoin it? It will be worthy of a free, enlightened, and, at no distant period, a great nation to give to mankind the magnanimous and too novel example of a people always guided by an exalted justice and benevolence . . . Can it be, that Providence has not connected the permanent felicity of a nation with its virtue? The experiment, at least, is recommended by every sentiment which ennobles human nature. Alas! is it rendered impossible by its vices? . . .

In offering to you, my countrymen, these counsels of an old and affectionate friend, I dare not hope they will make the strong and lasting impression I could wish, that they will control the usual current of the passions, or prevent our nation from running the course which has hitherto marked the destiny of nations . . . Though in reviewing the incidents of my administration, I am unconscious of intentional error. I am nevertheless too sensible of my defects not to think it probable that I may have committed many errors. . . . I fervently beseech the Almighty to avert or mitigate the evils to which they may tend. I shall also carry with me the hope that my country will never cease to view them with indulgence, and that after forty-five years of my life dedicated to its service, with an upright zeal, the faults of incompetent abilities will be consigned to oblivion, as myself must soon be to the mansions of rest.

Relying on its kindness in this as in other things, and actuated by that fervent love towards it which is so natural to a man who views in it the native soil of himself and his progenitors for several generations, I anticipate with pleasing expectation that retreat, in which I promise myself to realize, without alloy, the sweet enjoyment of partaking, in the midst of my fellow citizens, the benign influence of good laws under a free government, the ever favorite object of my heart, and the happy reward, as I trust, of our mutual cares, labors, and dangers.

MARTIN LUTHER KING, JR.

"I Have A Dream"

Dr. Martin Luther King, Jr., trained as a Christian minister, spoke out on behalf of the poor and the black in America. An intelligent and well-educated orator, Dr. King participated in and led non-violent protests against segregation and inequity.

The powerful and eloquent speech "I Have A Dream" was delivered August 8, 1963, at the Lincoln Memorial in Washington, D.C. Inspired by the enormity of the task before him, the Reverend had worked, writing out his speech in longhand, until four o'clock the previous morning. King then delivered his petitions to nearly a quarter of a million protesters who had assembled to urge Congress to pass President Kennedy's civil rights bill insuring jobs and equal rights. Although large marches previously had been held throughout the South, this was, as Philip Randolph, dean of the black American leaders, later described, a "convocation of national scope and gargantuan size."

Indeed, King was keenly aware of the volatile nature of the issue and of the gathering itself. His stirring call-to-action defined the moral basis of the civil rights movement—and became the highlight of the rally. King's eloquence paved the way for The Civil Rights Act of 1964, and earned him the 1964 Nobel Peace Prize.

❖ ♦ ❖

Five score years ago, a great American, in whose symbolic shadow we stand, signed the Emancipation Proclamation. This momentous decree came as a great beacon light of hope to millions of Negro slaves who had been seared in the flames of withering injustice. It came as a joyous daybreak to end the long night of captivity.

But one hundred years later, we must face the tragic fact that the Negro is still not free. One hundred years later, the life of the Negro is still sadly crippled by the manacles of segregation and the chains of discrimination. One hundred years later, the Negro lives on a lonely island of poverty in the midst of a vast ocean of material prosperity. One hundred years later, the Negro is still languished in the corners of American society and finds himself in exile in his own land. So we have come here today to dramatize an appalling condition.

In a sense we have come to our nation's Capital to cash a check. When the architects of our republic wrote the magnificent words of the Constitution and the Declaration of Independence, they were signing a promissory note to which every American was to fall heir. This note was a promise that all men would be guaranteed the unalienable rights of life, liberty, and the pursuit of happiness.

It is obvious today that America has defaulted on this promissory note insofar as her citizens of color are concerned. Instead of honoring this sacred obligation, America has given the Negro people a bad check; a check which has come back marked "insufficient funds." But we refuse to believe that the bank of justice is bankrupt. We refuse to believe that there are insufficient funds in the great vaults of opportunity of this nation. So we have come to cash this check—a check that will give us upon demand the riches of freedom and the security of justice.

We have also come to this hallowed spot to remind America of the fierce urgency of now. This is no time to engage in the luxury of cooling off or to take the tranquilizing drugs of gradualism.

Now is the time to make real the promises of Democracy.

Now is the time to rise from the dark and desolate valley of segregation to the sunlit path of racial justice.

Now is the time to open the doors of opportunity to all of God's children.

Now is the time to lift our nation from the quicksands of racial injustice to the solid rock of brotherhood.

It would be fatal for the nation to overlook the urgency of the moment and to underestimate the determination of the Negro. This sweltering summer of the Negro's legitimate discontent will not pass until there is an invigorating autumn of freedom and equality. Nineteen sixty-three is not an end, but a beginning. And those who hope that the Negro needed to blow off steam and will now be content will have a rude awakening if the nation returns to business as usual. There will be neither rest nor tranquility in America until the Negro is granted his citizenship rights. The whirlwinds of revolt will continue to shake the foundations of our nation until the bright day of justice emerges.

But there is something that I must say to my people who stand on the warm threshold which leads into the palace of justice. In the process of gaining our rightful place we must not be guilty of wrongful deeds. Let us not seek to satisfy our thirst for freedom by drinking from the cup of bitterness and hatred. We must forever conduct our struggle on the high plane of dignity and discipline. We must not allow our creative protest to degenerate into physical violence. Again and again we must rise to the majestic heights of meeting physical force with soul force. The marvelous new militancy which has engulfed the Negro community must not lead us to a distrust of all white people, for many of our white brothers, as evidenced by their presence here today, have come to realize that their destiny is tied up with our destiny and their freedom is inextricably bound to our freedom. We cannot walk alone.

And as we walk, we must make the pledge that we shall always march ahead. We cannot turn back. There are those who are asking the devotees of civil rights, "When will you be satisfied?" We can never be satisfied as long as the Negro is the victim of the unspeakable horrors of police brutality. We can never be satisfied as long as our bodies, heavy with fatigue of travel, cannot gain lodging in the motels of the highways and the hotels of the cities. We cannot be satisfied as long as the Negro's basic mobility is from a smaller ghetto to a larger one. We can never be satisfied as long as a Negro in Mississippi cannot vote and a Negro in New York believes he has nothing for which to vote. No, no, we are not satisfied, and we will not be satisfied until justice rolls down like waters and righteousness like a mighty stream.

I am not unmindful that some of you have come here out of great trials and tribulation. Some of you have come fresh from narrow jail cells. Some of you have come from areas where your quest for freedom left you battered by the storms of persecution and staggered by the winds of police brutality. You have been the veterans of creative suffering. Continue to work with the faith that unearned suffering is redemptive.

Go back to Mississippi, go back to Alabama, go back to South Carolina, go back to Georgia, go back to Louisiana, go back to the slums and ghettos of the northern cities, knowing that somehow this situation can and will be changed. Let us not wallow in the valley of despair.

I say to you, my friends, that in spite of the difficulties and frustrations of the moment I still have a dream. It is a dream deeply rooted in the American dream. I have a dream that one day this nation will rise up and live out the true meaning of its creed: "We hold these truths to be self-evident, that all men are created equal."

I have a dream that one day on the red hills of Georgia the sons of former slaves and the sons of former slaveowners will be able to sit down together at the table of brotherhood.

I have a dream that one day even the state of Mississippi, a desert state sweltering with the heat of injustice and oppression, will be transformed into an oasis of freedom and justice.

I have a dream that my four little children will one day live in a nation where they will not be judged by the color of their skin but by the content of their character.

I have a dream today.

I have a dream that one day in the state of Alabama, whose governor's lips are presently dripping with the words of interposition and nullification, will be transformed into a situation where little black boys and black girls will be able to join hands with little white boys and white girls and walk together as sisters and brothers.

I have a dream today.

I have a dream that one day every valley shall be exalted, every hill and mountain shall be made low, the rough places shall be made plains, and the crooked places will be made straight, and the glory of the Lord shall be revealed, and all flesh shall see it together.

This is our hope. This is the faith with which I return to the South. With this faith we will be able to hear out of the mountain of despair a stone of hope. With this faith we will be able to transform the jangling discords of our nation into a beautiful symphony of brotherhood. With this faith we will be able to work together, to pray together, to struggle together, to go to jail together, to stand up for freedom together, knowing that we will be free one day.

This will be the day when all of God's children will be able to sing with new meaning

My country 'tis of thee,
Sweet land of liberty,
Of thee I sing:
Land where my fathers died,
Land of the pilgrim's pride,
From every mountainside
Let freedom ring.

And if America is to be a great nation this must become true. So let freedom ring from the prodigious hilltops of New Hampshire.

Let freedom ring from the mighty mountains of New York. Let freedom ring from the heightening Alleghenies of Pennsylvania!

Let freedom ring from the snowcapped Rockies of Colorado!

Let freedom ring from the curvaceous slopes of California!

But not only that; let freedom ring from Stone Mountain of Georgia!

Let freedom ring from Lookout Mountain of Tennessee!

Let freedom ring from every hill and molehill of Mississippi, from every mountainside, let freedom ring.

When we let freedom ring, when we let it ring from every village and every hamlet, from every state and every city, we will be able to speed up that day when all of God's children, black men and white men, Jews and Gentiles, Protestants and Catholics, will be able to join hands and to sing in the words of the old Negro spiritual, "Free at last! free at last! thank God almighty, we are free at last!"

CHIEF JOSEPH

"Let Me Be A Free Man"

Leader of the Nez Perce, Young Chief Joseph worked to fulfill his promise to his "Old Chief" father by becoming a statesman and government advocate for the American Indians. Although his dying father asked that the tribal homeland never be sold, he of course could not foresee that the land in fertile Oregon would be taken from his descendants. "My father was the first to see through the schemes of the white men," Chief Joseph noted, "and he warned his tribe to be careful about trading with them. He had suspicion of men who seemed so anxious to make money. I was a boy then, but I remember my father's caution. He had sharper eyes then the rest of our people."

"Thunder Traveling Over the Mountains," as Young Chief Joseph was known to his people, deplored the violent fighting with the U.S. troops that broke out when the Nez Perce were required to surrender their land and move onto a reservation. Rather, the Chief resolved to lead his people to safety in Canada—a rambling march of 1,000 miles through the mountains of the Northwestern United States. Skillfully guiding his tribe, the Chief managed to avoid the troops, except once during a battle he won in Montana. Finally captured thirty miles from their destination, the Nez Perce were relocated onto reservations. His robes displaying bullet holes, Chief Joseph surrendered in 1877, with these words:

Tell General Howard I know his heart. What he told me before, I have it in my heart. I am tired of fighting. Our chiefs are killed, Looking-Glass is dead, Ta-Hool-Hool-Shute is dead . . . It is cold, and we have no blankets; the little children are freezing to death. My people, some of them, have run away to the hills, and have no blankets, no food. No one knows where they are—perhaps freezing to death. I want to have time to look for my children, and see how many of them I can find. Maybe I shall find them among the dead. Hear me, my chiefs! I am tired; my heart is sick and sad. From where the sun now stands I will fight no more forever.

❖ ♦ ❖

With the aid of an interpreter and from an enforced new "homeland" in Oklahoma, the Indian leader defended his people to the American public. In an attempt to sway public opinion and facilitate justice, Chief Joseph published the following essay in the April, 1879, issue of the *North American Review*. His eloquent plea for human rights is, as T.J. Stiles describes, "as powerful as anything written by the founding fathers."

My friends, I have been asked to show you my heart. I am glad to have a chance to do so. I want the white people to understand my people. Some of you think an Indian is like a wild animal. This is a great mistake . . . I will tell you in my way how the Indian sees things. The white man has more words to tell you how they look to him, but it does not require many words to speak the truth. What I have to say will come from my heart, and I will speak with a straight tongue. Ah-cum-kin-i-ma-me-hut (the Great Spirit) is looking at me, and will hear me.

My name is In-mut-too-yah-lat (Thunder Traveling Over the Mountains). I am chief of the Wal-lam-wat-kin band of Chute-pa-lu, or Nez Perces (nose pierced Indians). I was born in eastern Oregon, thirty-eight winters ago. My father was chief before me. When a young man, he was called Joseph by Mr. Spaulding, a missionary. He died a few years ago. There was no stain on his hands of the blood of a white man. He left a good name on the earth . . .

Our fathers gave us many laws, which they had learned from their fathers. These laws were good. They told us to treat all men as they treated us; that we should never be the first to break a bargain; that it was a disgrace to tell a lie; that we should speak only the truth; that it was a shame for one man to take from another his wife, or his property without paying for it. We were taught to believe that the Great Spirit sees and hears everything, and that he never forgets; that hereafter he will give every man a spirit-home according to his deserts: if he has been a good man, he will have a good home; if he has been a bad man, he will have a bad home. This I believe, and all my people believe the same.

We did not know there were other people besides the Indian until about one hundred winters ago, when some men with white faces came to our country . . . These men were Frenchmen, and they called our people "Nez Perces," because they wore rings in their noses for ornaments. Although very few of our people wear them now, we are still called by the same name . . . Our people were divided in opinion about these men. Some thought they taught more bad than good. An Indian respects a brave man, but he despises a coward. He loves a straight tongue. The French trappers told us some truths and some lies.

. . . All the Nez Perces made friends with Lewis and Clarke, and agreed to let them pass through their country, and never to make war on white men. This promise the Nez Perces have never broken. No white man can accuse them of bad faith, and speak with a straight tongue . . . But we soon found that the white men were growing rich very fast, and were greedy to possess everything the Indian had . . .

. . . There came a white officer (Governor Stevens), who invited all the Nez Perces to a treaty council. After the council was opened he made known his heart. He said there were a great many white people in the country, and many more would come . . . If they were to live in peace it was necessary, he said, that the Indians should have a country set apart for them, and that in that country they must stay. My father, who represented his band, refused to have anything to do with the council, because he wished to be a free man. He claimed that no man owned any part of the earth, and a man could not sell what he did not own.

My father left the council . . .

Eight years later (1863) was the next treaty council. A chief called Lawyer, because he was a great talker, took the lead in this council and sold nearly all the Nez Perces' country. My father . . . said to me: "When you go into council with the white man, always remember your country . . . The white man will cheat you out of your home. I have taken no pay from the United States. I have never sold our land." In this treaty Lawyer acted without authority from our band. He had no right to sell the a Wallowa (winding water) country . That has always belonged to my father's own people, and the other bands had never disputed our right to it . . .

. . . The United States claimed they had bought all the Nez Perces country outside of the Lapway Reservation, from Lawyer and other chiefs, but we continued to live on this land in peace until eight years ago, when white men began to come inside the bounds my father had set. We warned them against this great wrong, but they would not leave our land, and some bad blood was raised. The white men represented that we were going upon the war-path. They reported many things that were false . . .

. . . Our young men were quick-tempered, and I have had great trouble in keeping them from doing rash things . . . I know that my young men did a great wrong, but I ask, who was first to blame? They had been insulted a thousand times; their fathers and brothers had been killed; their mothers and wives had been disgraced; they had been driven to madness by whisky sold to them by white men; they had been told by General Howard that all their horses and cattle which they had been unable to drive out of Wallowa were to fall into the hands of white men; and, added to all this, they were homeless and desperate.

I would have given my own life if I could have undone the killing of white men by my people. I blame the young men and I blame the white men . . .

We retreated as rapidly as we could toward the buffalo country. After six days General Howard came close to us, and we went out and attacked him, and captured nearly all his horses and mules . . . We then marched on to the Yellowstone Basin.

On the way we captured one white man and two white women. We released them at the end of three days. They were treated kindly. The women were not insulted. Can the white soldiers tell me of one time when Indian women were taken prisoners, and held three days and then released without being insulted? . . .

I thought of my wife and children, who were now surrounded by soldiers, and I resolved to go to them or die. With a prayer in my mouth to the Great Spirit Chief who rules above, I dashed unarmed through the line of soldiers . . .

. . . We could have escaped from Bear Paw Mountain if we had left our wounded, old women, and children behind. We were unwilling to do this. We had never heard of a wounded Indian recovering while in the hands of white men . . .

. . . I could not bear to see my wounded men and women suffer any longer; we had lost enough already. General Miles had promised that we might return to our own country with what stock we had left. I thought we could start again. I believed General Miles, or I never would have surrendered . . .

. . . They all say they are my friends, and that I shall have justice, but while their mouths all talk right, I do not understand why nothing is done for my people. I have heard talk and talk but nothing is done. Good words do not last long unless they amount to something . . .

. . . When I think of our condition my heart is heavy. I see men of my race treated as outlaws and driven from country to country, or shot down like animals . . .

Let me be a free man—free to travel, free to stop, free to work, free to trade where I choose, free to choose my own teachers, free to follow the religion of my fathers, free to think and talk and act for myself—and I will obey every law, or submit to the penalty.

Whenever the white man treats the Indians as they treat each other, then we will have no more wars. We shall all be alike—brothers of one father and one mother, with one sky above us and one country around us, and one government for all. Then the Great Spirit Chief who rules above will smile upon this land and send rain to wash out the bloody spots made by my brothers' hands from the face of the earth. For this time the Indian race are waiting and praying. I hope that no more groans of wounded men and women will ever go to the ear of the Great Spirit Chief above, and that all people may be one people.

In-mut-too-yah-lat-lat has spoken for his people.

YOUNG JOSEPH

SUSAN B. ANTHONY

"Citizen's Right to Vote"

At the age of fifty-two, and shortly before her trial in June of 1873, Susan B. Anthony delivered a speech to defend women's right to vote in accordance with the Constitution. She had previously been arrested for voting in the 1872 Presidential Election, an event which attracted national attention. In defending her action, Anthony wielded the phrase: "it was we, the people; not we, the white male citizens; nor yet we, the male citizens; but we, the whole people . . . who formed the Union . . . to secure . . . the blessings of liberty."

Well-educated for a woman of her time, Anthony taught school between the ages of 15 and 30 while she and her family worked in support of the American Anti-Slavery Society. Always the crusader, she then organized and led America's first women's temperance league. Writing, lecturing and leading efforts for legislation, the women's rights leader traveled extensively in America and Europe. Together, she and Elizabeth Cady Stanton established the National Woman Suffrage Association.

Although her speeches often met with taunts and ridicule, Anthony's persuasive words and intelligent leadership inspired her followers. In fact, after her death in 1906, her followers picked up the work she had led until women won the right to vote with passage of the 19th amendment in 1920.

❖ ◆ ❖

"Friends and Fellow Citizens: I stand before you under indictment for the alleged crime of having voted at the last presidential election, without having a lawful right to vote. It shall be my work this evening to prove to you that in thus voting, I not only committed no crime, but instead simply exercised my citizen's rights, guaranteed to me and all United States citizens by the National Constitution, beyond the power of any State to deny.

Our democratic-republican government is based on the idea of the natural right of every individual member thereof to a voice and a vote in making and executing the laws. We assert the providence of government to be to secure the people in the enjoyment of their inalienable rights. We throw to the winds the old dogma that government can give rights. No one denies that before governments were organized each individual possessed the right to protect his own life, liberty and property . . . The Declaration of Independence, the United States Constitution, the constitutions of the several States and the organic laws of the Territories, all alike propose to protect the people in the exercise of their God-given rights. Not one of them pretends to bestow rights.

"All men are created equal, and endowed by their Creator with certain inalienable rights. Among these are life, liberty and the pursuit of happiness. To secure these, governments are instituted among men, deriving their just powers from the consent of the governed."

Here is no shadow of government authority over rights, or exclusion of any class from their full and equal enjoyment. Here is pronounced the right of all men, and "consequently," as the Quaker preacher said, "of all women," to a voice in the government. And here, in this first paragraph of the Declaration, is the assertion of the natural right of all to the ballot; for how can "the consent of the governed" be given, if the right to vote be denied? . . . The women, dissatisfied as they are with this form of government, that enforces taxation without representation—that compels them to obey laws to which they never have given their consent—that imprisons and hangs them without a trial by a jury of their peers—that robs them, in marriage, of the custody of their own persons, wages and children—are this half of the people who are left wholly at the mercy of the other half, in direct violation of the spirit and letter of the declarations of the framers of this government, every one of which was based on the immutable principle of equal rights to all. By these declarations, kings, popes, priests, aristocrats, all were alike dethroned and placed on a common level, politically, with the lowliest born subject or serf. By then, too, men, as such, were deprived of their divine right to rule and placed on a political level with women. By the practice of these declarations all class and caste distinctions would be abolished, and slave, serf, plebeian, wife, woman, all alike rise from their subject position to the broader platform of equality.

The preamble of the Federal Constitution says: We, the people of the United States, in order to form a more perfect union, establish justice, insure domestic tranquility, provide for the common defense, promote the general welfare, and secure the blessings of liberty to ourselves and our posterity, do ordain and establish this Constitution for the United States of America.

It was we, the people, not we, the white male citizens, nor yet we, the male citizens; but we, the whole people, who formed the Union. We formed it, not to give the blessings of liberty, but to secure them; not to the half of ourselves and the half of our posterity, but to the whole people—women as well as men. And it is downright mockery to talk to women of their enjoyment of the blessings of liberty while they are denied the use of the only means of securing them provided by this democratic-republican government—the ballot.

The early journals of Congress show that, when the committee reported to that body the original articles of confederation, the very first one which became the subject of discussion was that respecting equality of suffrage . . .

James Madison said:

"Under every view of the subject, it seems indispensable that the mass of the citizens should not be without a voice in making the laws which they are to obey, and in choosing the magistrates who are to administer them . . . Let it be remembered, finally, that it has ever been the pride and the boast of America that the rights for which she contended were the rights of human nature."

These assertions by the framers of the United States Constitution of the equal and natural right of all the people to a voice in the government, have been affirmed and reaffirmed by the leading statesmen of the nation throughout the entire history of our government.

. . . For any state to make sex a qualification that must ever result in the disfranchisement of one entire half of the people is . . . a violation of the supreme law of the land. By it the blessings of liberty are forever withheld from women and their female posterity. To them this government has no just powers derived from the consent of the governed. For them this government is not a democracy; it is not a republic. It is the most odious aristocracy ever established on the face of the globe. An oligarchy of wealth, where the rich govern the poor; an oligarchy of learning, where the educated govern the ignorant; or even an oligarchy of race, where the Saxon rules the African, might be endured; but this oligarchy of sex, which makes father, brothers, husband, sons, the oligarches over the mother and sisters, the wife and daughters, of every household-which ordains all men sovereigns, all women subjects, carries dissension, discord, and rebellion into every home of the nation.

. . . It is urged that the use of the masculine pronouns he, his and him in all the constitutions and laws, is proof that only men were meant to be included in their provisions. If you insist on this version of the letter of the law, we shall insist that you be consistence and accept the other horn of the dilemma, which would compel you to exempt women from taxation for the support of the government and from penalties for the violation of laws. There is no she or her or hers in the tax laws, and this is equally true of all the criminal laws.

Take for example the civil rights law which I am charged with having violated; not only are all the pronouns in it masculine, but everybody knows that it was intended expressly to hinder the rebel from voting. It reads, "If a person shall knowingly vote without his having a lawful right." . . . I insist if government officials may thus manipulate the pronouns to tax, fine, imprison and hang women, it is their duty to thus change them in order to protect us in our right to vote . . .

Webster, Worcester, and Bouvier all define a citizen to be a person in the United States, entitled to vote and hold office.

. . . I submit that in view of the explicit assertions of the equal right of the whole people . . . this omission of the adjective "female" should not be construed into a denial; but instead should be considered as of no effect . . . No barriers whatever stand today between women and the exercise of their right to vote save those of precedent and prejudice, which refuse to expunge the world "male" from the constitution.

The only question left to be settled now is: Are women persons? And I hardly believe any of our opponents will have the hardihood to say they are not. Being persons, then, women are citizens: and no state has a right to make any law, or to enforce any old law, that shall abridge their privileges or immunities. Hence, every discrimination against women in their constitutions and laws of the several states is today null and void . . .

Is the right to vote one of the privileges or immunities of citizens? I think the disfranchised ex-rebels and ex-State prisoners all will agree that it is not only one of them, but the one without which all the others are nothing. Seek first the kingdom of the ballot and all things else shall be added, is the political injunction . . .

. . . It is upon this just interpretation of the United States Constitution that our National Woman Suffrage Association, which celebrates the twenty-fifth anniversary of the woman's rights movement next May in New York City, has based all its arguments and action since the passage of these amendments. We no longer petition legislature or Congress to give us the right to vote but appeal to women everywhere to exercise their too long neglected "citizen's right." We appeal to the inspectors of election to receive the votes of all United States citizens, as it is their duty to do. We appeal to United States commissioners and marshals to arrest, as is their duty, the inspectors who reject the votes of United States citizens, and leave alone those who perform their duties and accept these votes. We ask the juries to return verdicts of "not guilty" in the cases of law-abiding United States citizens who cast their votes, and inspectors of election who receive and count them.

We ask the judges to render unprejudiced opinions of the law, and wherever there is room for doubt to give the benefit to the side of liberty and equal rights for women, remembering that, as Sumner says, "The true rule of interpretation under our National Constitution, especially since its amendments, is that anything for human rights is constitutional, everything against human rights unconstitutional." It is on this line that we propose to fight our battle for the ballot—peaceably but nevertheless persistently—until we achieve complete triumph and all United States citizens, men and women alike, are recognized as equals in the government.

FREDERICK DOUGLASS

"American Slavery"

Born a slave, Frederick Augustus Washington Bailey suffered greatly, and ultimately changed his surname to Douglass to avoid capture as a runaway slave. Douglass became a powerful orator, whose words moved his sympathizers and enraged his opponents. Because of his background as an ex-slave who tirelessly worked for abolition, he was regarded as an unusually credible speaker.

With the 1845 publication of his autobiography—seven years after escaping as a runaway—Douglass feared his identity would be revealed to his previous owners. He thus traveled to England to ensure his safety and to plead the cause of slaves. Shortly after his arrival in Britain, May 12, 1846, Douglass delivered this classic speech on American slavery.

Returning to America—his freedom now purchased—Douglass continued his work: he founded an anti-slavery newspaper, led attacks against segregated schools, supported the underground railroad for runaway slaves, recruited blacks for the Union Army, and worked in government.

❖ ◆ ❖

I feel exceedingly glad of the opportunity now afforded me of presenting the claims of my brethren in bonds in the United States, to so many in London and from various parts of Britain, who have assembled here on the present occasion. I have nothing to commend me to your consideration in the way of learning, nothing in the way of education to entitle me to your attention; and you are aware that slavery is a very bad school for rearing teachers of morality and religion. Twenty-one years of my life have been spent in slavery—personal slavery—surrounded by degrading influences, such as can exist nowhere beyond the pale of slavery; and it will not be strange, if under such circumstances, I should betray, in what I have to say to you, a deficiency of that refinement which is seldom or ever found, except among persons that have experienced superior advantages to those which I have enjoyed. But I will take it for granted that you know something about the degrading influences of slavery, and that you will not expect great things from me this evening, but simply such facts as I may be able to advance immediately in connection with my own experience of slavery.

Now, what is this system of slavery? This is the subject of my lecture this evening—what is the character of the institution? . . . I have found persons in this country who have identified the term slavery with that which I think it is not, and in some instances, I have feared, in so doing, have rather (unwittingly, I know,) detracted much from the horror with which the term slavery is contemplated . . . . . . I am here to say that I think the term slavery is sometimes abused by identifying it with that which it is not. Slavery in the United States is the granting of that power by which one man exercises and enforces a right of property in the body and soul of another. The condition of the slave is simply that of the brute beast. He is a piece of property—a marketable commodity, in the language of the law, to be bought or sold at the will and caprice of the master who claims him to be his property; he is spoken of, thought of, and treated as property . . .

. . . This is American slavery; no marriage—no education—the light of the gospel shut out from the dark mind of the bondman—and he forbidden by law to learn to read. If a mother shall teach her children to read, the law in Louisiana proclaims that she may be hanged by the neck . . . Three millions of people shut out from the light of knowledge! It is easy for you to conceive the evil that must result from such a state of things . . .

. . . The slaveholder resorts to all kinds of cruelty . . . starvation, the bloody whip, the chain, the gag, the thumb-screw, cat-hauling, the cat-o-nine-tails, the dungeon, the blood hound, are all in requisition to keep the slave in his condition as a slave in the United States . . . The bloodhound is regularly trained in the United States, and advertisements are to be found in the southern papers of the Union, from persons advertising themselves as blood-hound trainers, and offering to hunt down slaves at fifteen dollars a piece . . .

. . . And all this is necessary; it is necessary to resort to these cruelties, in order to make the slave a slave, and to keep him a slave . . . When I was treated exceedingly ill; when my back was being scourged daily; when I was whipped within an inch of my life—life was all I cared for . . . I was not thinking of my liberty; it was my life . . . But let him [the slave] know that the whip is burned; that the fetters have been turned to some useful and profitable employment; that the chain is no longer for his limb; that the blood-hound is no longer to be put upon his track; that his master's authority over him is no longer to be enforced by taking his life—and immediately he walks out from the house of bondage and asserts his freedom as a man . . .

. . . Some of the most awful scenes of cruelty are constantly taking place in the middle states of the Union . . . If you would see the cruelties of this system, hear the following narrative. Not long since the following scene occurred. A slave-woman and a slave-man had united themselves as a man and a wife in the absence of any law to protect them as a man and wife. They had lived together by the permission, not by right, of their master, and they had

reared a family. The master found it expedient, and for his interest, to sell them. He did not ask them their wishes in regard to the matter at all; they were not consulted. The man and woman were brought to the auctioneer's block, under the sound of the hammer. The cry was raised, "Here goes; who bids cash?" Think of it—a man and wife to be sold! The woman was placed on the auctioneer's block; her limbs, as is customary, were brutally exposed to the purchasers, who examined her with the full freedom with which they would examine a horse. There stood the husband, powerless, no right to his wife . . . She was sold. He was next brought to the auctioneer's block. His eyes followed his wife in the distance; and he looked beseechingly, imploringly, to the man that had bought his wife, to buy him also. But he was at length bid off to another person. He was about to be separated forever from her he loved. No word of his, no work of his, could save him from this separation. He asked permission of his new master to go and take the hand of his wife at parting. It was denied him. In the agony of his soul he rushed from the man who had just bought him, that he might take a farewell of his wife; but his way was obstructed, he was struck over the head with a loaded whip, and was held for a moment; but his agony was too great. When he was let go, he fell a corpse at the feet of his master. His heart was broken. Such scenes are the every-day fruits of American slavery . . .

. . . But you will ask me, can these things be possible in a land professing Christianity? Yes, they are so . . . While America is printing tracts and bibles; sending missionaries abroad to convert the heathen; expending her money in various ways for the promotion of the gospel in foreign lands—the slave not only lies forgotten, uncared for, but it is trampled under foot by the very churches of the land. What have we in America? Why, we have slavery made part of the religion of the land . . .

. . . Instead of preaching the gospel against this tyranny, rebuke, and wrong, ministers of religion have sought, by all and every means, to throw in the back-ground whatever in the Bible could be construed into opposition to slavery, and to bring forward that which they could torture into its support. This I conceive to be the darkest feature of slavery, and the most difficult to attack, because it is identified with religion, and exposes them who denounce it to the charge of infidelity . . .

. . . I love the religion that comes from above, in the "wisdom of God," which is first pure, then peaceable, gentle, and easy to be entreated, full of mercy and good fruits, without partiality and without hypocrisy . . . . I love that religion that makes it the duty of its disciples to visit the fatherless and the widow in their affliction. I love that religion that is based upon the glorious principle, of love to God and love to man; which makes its followers do unto others as they themselves would be done by . . . It is

because I love this religion that I hate the slave-holding, the woman-whipping, the mind-darkening, the soul-destroying religion that exists in the southern states of America. It is because I regard the one as good, and pure, and holy, that I cannot but regard the other as bad, corrupt, and wicked. Loving the one, I must hate the other; holding the one I must reject the other . . .

. . . I am here because you [Britain] have an influence on America that no other nation can have . . . There is nothing said here against slavery that will not be recorded in the United States. I am here, also, because the slaveholders do not want me to be here; they would rather that I were not here. I have adopted a maxim laid down by Napoleon, never to occupy ground which the enemy would like me to occupy. The slaveholders would much rather have me, if I will denounce slavery, denounce it in the northern states, where their friends and supporters are, who will stand by and mob me for denouncing it . . .

. . . I expose slavery in this country, because to expose it is to kill it. Slavery is one of those monsters of darkness to whom the light of truth is death. Expose slavery, and it dies. Light is to slavery what the heat of the sun is to the root of a tree; it must die under it . . . Slavery shrinks from the light; it hateth the light, neither cometh to the light, lest its deeds should be reproved. To tear off the mask from this abominable system, to expose it to the light of heaven, aye, to the heat of the sun, that it may burn and wither it out of existence, is my object in coming to this country. I want the slaveholder surrounded, as by a wall of anti-slavery fire, so that he may see the condemnation of himself and his system glaring down in letters of light. I want him to feel that he has no sympathy in England, Scotland, or Ireland; that he has none in Canada, none on Mexico, none among the poor wild Indians; that the voice of the civilized, aye, and the savage world is against him. I would have condemnation blaze down upon him in every direction, till, stunned and overwhelmed with the shame and confusion, he is compelled to let go the grasp he holds upon the persons of his victims, and restore them to their long-lost rights.

BORIS YELTSIN

"Eulogy" and "The Cost of Political Indifference"

Politically active during the breakup of the Soviet Union, Boris Nikolayevich Yeltsin will be remembered as the first popularly elected president of Russia. Thus in 1991, after the old Soviet Union had all but disappeared, Yeltsin suddenly was vitally important to the fate of all Russians.

Trained as a construction engineer, Yeltsin had joined the Communist party as a youth. Although a protege of Mikhail Gorbachev who came to oppose many items on the President's political agenda, Yeltsin did initially support—in concept, at least, the principles of *glastnost* (free and open discussion) and *perestroika* (economic and political reform). In fact, the up-and-coming statesman backed efforts to crush a coup attempt by Communist hard-liners.

Upon being elected, Yeltsin called a constituent assembly and drafted a new Russian constitution. When he later met with other world leaders, the President worked to end the Soviet-era deception in international relations.

The occasion of the following eulogy was the funeral of three young people who had been killed during a Communist uprising in August of 1991. The state used the emotion of the moment to rally public sentiment against old politics. The nationally televised funeral proceedings were conducted by religious leaders, a clear sign to the nation that the Communist regime had at last succumbed to the will of a free people.

"Eulogy"

Dear relatives and loved ones of Dmitri Komar, Vladimir Usov, and Ilya Drichevsky, dear fellow countrymen and Muscovites:

Today many millions of Muscovites, the whole of Russia, are parting with our heroes, with our defenders, and with our saviors. Of course, we are not parting with their names forever, because from now on their names are sacred names for Russia, for all the people of our long-suffering Russia.

When television and radio reported about the coup on Monday, the hearts of millions and millions of mothers and fathers trembled most of all, because they were scared for their children. Because it was young people, it was our children, who more than anyone else rushed to defend Russia's honor, its freedom, its independence, and its democracy, to defend its parliament.

Yes, from now on, this square, on which a battle raged for three days, on which tens of thousands of Muscovites kept vigil, will be called the Square of Free Russia.

The enemy is cruel and, of course, bloodthirsty, especially when he knows that if he loses no one will take him in. All the participants of the putsch are arrested. Criminal proceedings have been started against them, and I am sure that they will be made to answer for everything.

But even today, how cynical the words of arrested [former head of the KGB, Vladimir A.] Kryuchkov sound, the man who yesterday said that if he could do it over again he would have started a little faster and more energetically, and that the most important thing was to behead Russia.

This entire plot, and we must understand this very clearly, was aimed in the first place against Russia, its parliament, its government, its president. But all of Russia stood up to its defense: Moscow, Leningrad, the Urals, the Far East, the Kuzbass, practically all regions of the republic, although there were some regions which immediately put up banners and slogans expressing loyalty to the Extraordinary Committee. These officials already have been dismissed from their posts. And the prosecutor's office is considering their cases.

But we cannot resurrect those who died at the walls of our White House. We pay tribute to their courage, those who have become Heroes of the Soviet Union in death. I bow down to the mothers and fathers of Dmitri, Volodya, and Ilya, and I express to them my deep condolences, and to all their relatives and loved ones. Forgive me, your president, that I could not defend, could not save your sons.

In this day of Russia's national mourning, we, of course, need to strengthen our unity to energetically act further. We have cleared ourselves a path. Our deceased heroes have helped us to do so. This is a difficult day for us, a hard day. But it could have been even worse, because the enemies are already like cockroaches in a bottle, trying to eat each other. They are pointing fingers at each other, asking who played a more important role in the plot, revealing to each other the lists of people they wanted to kill first, second, third, fourth.

Only the first twelve victims in these lists were designated to be killed at 6 p.m. on August 19 during the storming of the House of Soviets. So it was not in vain the Muscovites were here, defending the honor of Russia.

It was a difficult loss, and the memory of it will be with us forever. For that reason, our heroes, sleep peacefully and let the earth be soft for you.

◇ ◆ ◇

In early October of 1993, President Yeltsin quashed another Communist coup—one that had joined forces with a Nazi faction. Subsequently, on October 6, 1993, Yeltsin delivered the following speech to the People of the Russian Federation.

"The Cost of Political Indifference"

Esteemed citizens of Russia, on October 3 and 4, Russia experienced a great tragedy. Gangs of murderers broke into state offices, they humiliated people who they took hostages. They captured city buses and trucks. The militants had a great amount of weapons, ammunition and military equipment. The lives of peaceful civilians were in mortal danger.

There was an armed mutiny, planned and prepared by the leaders of the former vice-president, the leaders of some parties and public organizations.

Among them were the National Salvation Front, including its arm "Labour Russia," some Communist parties and groups, the Nazi-style "Russian National Unity" and some others. Nazis and Communists merged in this damnable cause, the swastika joined the sickle and hammer.

Former people's deputies were among the organizers and active participants of the mutiny .... They used their deputy immunity as a shield from behind which to incite violence, stimulate mass unrest, organize mass-scale bloody rioting and unleash civil war.

The aim was to establish in Russia a bloody Communist-Nazi dictatorship. It is now clear that all this had been prepared for many months.

The bloodletting events of that night compelled [us] to bring regular army units into Moscow. The difficult decision was made to storm the Supreme Soviet building, which had turned into the stronghold of terrorism.

The actions of the militants were coordinated from the House of Soviets (parliament building). Illegal armed groups were formed inside it. Calls to storm the Mayor's office building, the Ostankino (television broadcasting centre) and the Kremlin came from the House of Soviets .... All preparations for the mutiny were carried out while sham negotiations were being conducted.

Why did we put up with the organizations in Russia which acted legally not only calling for violence but also preparing it. They were not duly rebuffed by either the prosecutors or by the law-enforcement agencies .... The Supreme Soviet and the Congress became their chief patrons. As a result every new sortie became more insolent and menacing.

The chief lesson for us is that democracy must be dependably protected. The State must use force wherever there is a threat of violence, a threat to the lives and safety of citizens. There can be no democracy without this.

All those who took part in the rioting with arms in their hands will be punished in accordance with law. All proponents of Nazi and Communist ideas who instigated the mutiny will be made answerable under the law. There can be no all-forgiveness to communistic nazism in Russia ever again.

I think that the constitutional court has to take much of the blame for what had come to pass. This agency has long since abandoned its most important principle-the court's independence from political time-serving.

The court appeared to overlook how endless amendments violated the Russian constitution, overlook the glaring contradictions in the constitution which were deliberately enhanced by the Congress.

I announce with full responsibility: most bodies of Soviet power are directly responsible for the extreme aggravation of the situation in Moscow. The system of Soviets showed full disregard for the security of the state and its citizens and thus put a full stop to its own political life.

Esteemed compatriots, having experienced the fearful days and nights, we can nonetheless be confident—no civil war has been unleashed in Russia. The mutineers in our capital remained strangers. The Muscovites despise and condemn them.

They failed to split the country, to split the Army and the State.

But the problems exposed by the mutiny are extremely serious. We need a normal democratic constitution as we need air to breathe. We need a united Russia. Playing at regional isolation is contrary to the interests and will of the majority of the country's population. We need full reform of the army and security agencies.

We need to consistently carry on economic transformations and support for all efforts the government makes in this direction.

But I would like to warn (people). If you think that the situation is completely back to normal, you are making a big mistake. Passions have not yet abated. Any careless, irresponsible word can enflame them again. I am appealing to the sense of civic responsibility of journalists.

Dear Russians, the most fearful things are now past. But in order to make peace and quiet inviolable in our country, we must pool efforts in strengthening our state, strengthening democracy. Elections to the Federal Assembly—and, I believe, new local bodies of representative power—will take place on December 12.

All politicians, parties and movements who have not smeared themselves with direct involvement in the mutiny are guaranteed equal opportunities.

In the past few days we came to understand the immense cost of political indifference. It is unable to save anyone or secure personal safety. Can one sleep quietly when one's house is being set on fire.

I am calling on you dear compatriots, to take an active part in the elections and vote for the worthiest, competent, clever and intelligent people. Those who are unable to betray.

Dear compatriots, the nightmare of the black days is over. Do not say that someone has won and someone lost. At this moment, these are inappropriate, blasphemous words. We have all been scorched by the deadly breath of fratricide.

People have died, our compatriots. They cannot be brought back. Grief and suffering have entered many families.

No matter how different outlooks may be, all of them are children of Russia, this is our common tragedy, our common grief, great grief.

Let us remember this insanity in order to never let it recur.

POPE JOHN PAUL II

"Jasna Gora" and "The Family Creates the Peace of the Human Family"

Despite Pope John Paul II's conservatism, he has taken his messages to a worldwide audience and has energized the papacy through his resolute yet very human character. The first non-Italian pope since 1523, John Paul was born Karol Wojtyla in Krakow, Poland.

Although an early devotee of both poetry and drama, John Paul eventually ended up working in a stone quarry and in a chemical factory while preparing for the priesthood. He received his doctorate at the Catholic University of Lublin and became an active participant in the Second Vatican Council before himself being elected pope in 1978.

Even before his shouldering the papal office, Pope John Paul II greatly influenced the restoration of democracy and religious freedom in his native Poland and throughout Eastern Europe.

John Paul delivered his speech "Jasna Gora" on his third visit to his homeland on June 18, 1983. At this time, the Polish workers' union *Solidarity* had just been banned by the Communist government. The Pope's impassioned and effective plea to the world to support these forgotten workers thus was etched into the history books and hearts of freedom-loving people everywhere. Those gathered at the monastery waved Solidarity banners at each mention of the word "workers" or "solidarity," or whenever he spoke of "truth," "oppression," or "human rights." As reported by *The Times*, when the Pontiff concluded his remarks, the cheers and applause that emanated from the massive, sequestered crowd was deafening, almost frightening.

"Jasna Gora"

Our Lady of Jasna Gora is the teacher of true love for all. And this is particularly important for you, dear young people. In you, in fact, is decided that form of love which all of your life will have, and through you, human life on Polish soil: the matrimonial, family, social and national form—but also the priestly, religious and missionary one. Every life is determined and evaluated by the interior form of love. Tell me what you love, and I will tell you who you are.

I watch! How beautiful it is that this word is found in the call of Jasna Gora. It possesses a profound evangelical ancestry: Christ says many times: "Watch" (Matt. 26:41). Perhaps also from the Gospel it passed into the tradition of scouting. In the call of Jasna Gora it is the essential element of the reply that we wish to give to the love by which we are surrounded in the sign of the Sacred Icon.

The response to this love must be precisely the fact that I watch!

What does it mean, "I watch"?

It means that I make an effort to be a person with a conscience. I do not stifle this conscience and I do not deform it; I call good and evil by name, and I do not blur them; I develop in myself what is good, and I seek to correct what is evil, by overcoming it myself. This is a fundamental problem which can never be minimized or put on a secondary level. No! It is everywhere and always a matter of the first importance. Its importance is all the greater in proportion to the increase of circumstances which seem to favour our tolerance of evil and the fact that we easily excuse ourselves from this, especially if adults do so.

My dear friends! It is up to you to put up a firm barrier against immorality, a barrier—I say—to those social vices which I will not here call by name but which you yourselves are perfectly aware of. You must demand this of yourselves, even if others do not demand it of you. Historical experiences tell us how much the immorality of certain periods cost the whole nation. Today when we are fighting for the future form of our social life, remember that this form depends on what people will be like. Therefore: watch!

Christ said to the apostles, during his prayer in Gethsemane: "Watch and pray that you may not enter into temptation" (Matt. 26:41).

"I watch" also means: I see another. I do not close in on myself, in a narrow search for my own interests, my own judgements. "I watch" means: love of neighbour; it means: fundamental interhuman solidarity.

Before the Mother of Jasna Gora I wish to give thanks for all the proofs of this solidarity which have been given by my compatriots, including Polish youth, in the difficult period of not many months ago. It would be difficult for me to enumerate here all the forms of this solicitude which surrounded those who were interned, imprisoned, dismissed from work, and also their families. You know this better than I. I received only sporadic news about it.

May this good thing, which appeared in so many places and so many ways, never cease on Polish soil. May there be a constant confirmation of that "I watch" of the call of Jasna Gora, which is a response to the presence of the Mother of Christ in the great family of the Poles.

"I watch" also means: I feel responsible for this great common inheritance whose name is Poland. This name defines us all. This name obliges us all. This name costs us all.

Perhaps at times we envy the French, the Germans or the Americans because their name is not tied to such a historical price and because they are so easily free: while our Polish freedom costs us so much.

My dear ones, I will not make a comparative analysis. I will only say that it is what costs that constitutes value. It is not, in fact, possible to be truly free without an honest and profound relationship with values. We do not want a Poland which costs us nothing. We watch, instead, beside all that makes up the authentic inheritance of the generations, seeking to enrich it. A nation, then , is first of all rich in its people. Rich in man. Rich in youth. Rich in every individual who watches in the name of truth: it is truth, in fact, that gives form to love.

My dear young friends! Before our common Mother and the Queen of our hearts, I desire finally to say to you that she knows your sufferings, your difficult youth, your sense of injustice and humiliation, the lack of prospects for the future that is so often felt, perhaps the temptations to flee to some other world.

Even if I am not among you every day, as was the case for many years in the past, nevertheless I carry in my heart a great solicitude. A great, enormous solicitude. A solicitude for you. Precisely because "on you depends tomorrow".

I pray for you every day.

It is good that we are here together at the hour of the call of Jasna Gora. In the midst of the trials of the present time, in the midst of the trial through which your generation is passing, this call of the millennium . . .

In it is contained a fundamental way out. Because the way out in whatever dimension—economic, social, political—must happen first in man. Man cannot remain with no way out.

Mother of Jasna Gora, you who have been given to us by Providence for the defense of the Polish nation, accept this evening this call of the Polish youth together with the Polish Pope, and help us to persevere in hope! Amen

❖ ♦ ❖

Pope John Paul's quest for democracy and individual freedom did not end with his own Polish countrymen but rather has expanded to fill the world community. On World Peace Day, January 1, 1994, he called on the families of the world to create within their homes a climate conducive to peace.

"The Family Creates the Peace of the Human Family"

The world longs for peace and has a desperate need of peace . . . which only feelings of solidarity and of love can usher in . . . In spite of everything, peace is possible, because it is part of the original divine plan . . .

The contribution which the family can offer to preserving and promoting peace is so important that I would like, on the occasion of the International Year of the Family, to devote this World Day of Peace message to a reflection on the close relationship between the family and peace . . . . The family, as the fundamental and essential educating community, is the privileged means for transmitting the religious and cultural values which help the person to acquire his or her own identity. Founded on love and open to the gift of life, the family contains in itself the very future of society; its most special task is to contribute effectively to a future of peace . . . through . . . the efforts of parents . . . committed to training their children to respect the dignity of every person and the values of peace.

In contrast with its original vocation of peace, the family is sadly, and not infrequently, seen to be the scene of tension and oppression, or the defenseless victim of the many forms of violence marking society today . . .

Frequent arguments between parents, the refusal to have children, and the abandonment and ill-treatment of minors are the sad symptoms that family peace is already seriously endangered; certainly it cannot be restored by the sad solution of separation of the spouses, much less by recourse to divorce, a true "plague" of present-day society.

Likewise, in many parts of the world, whole nations are caught in the spiral of bloody conflicts, of which families are often the first victims . . . War and violence not only constitute divisive forces which weaken and destroy family structures; they also exercise a pernicious influence on people's minds, suggesting and practically imposing models of behavior diametrically opposed to peace . . . . . . Even small children are playing a direct part in armed conflicts . . .

The very future of society is at stake. A community which rejects children, or marginalizes them, or reduces them to hopeless situations can never know peace . . .

An enduring peaceful order needs institutions which express and consolidate the values of peace. The institution which most immediately responds to the nature of the human being is the family . . .

It is the duty of the state to encourage and protect the authentic institution of the family, respecting its natural structure and its innate and inalienable rights.

The state also has an important role in creating the conditions in which families can provide for their primary needs in a way befitting human dignity. Poverty, indeed destitution—a perennial threat to social stability, to the development of people and to peace—in our day affects too many families.

In effect, no one can be at ease until an adequate solution has been found to the problem of poverty, which strikes families and individuals . . . Peace will always be at risk so long as individuals and families are forced to fight for their very survival.

I would now like to speak directly to families, in particular to Christian families.

Families, you have a mission of prime importance: that of contributing to the construction of peace . . . Knowing that peace is never secured once and for all, you must never grow weary of seeking it!

Finally, how can we forget the many people who for various reasons feel that they have no family? To them I would like to say that there is a family for them, too: The church is home and family for all.

May the family so live in peace that from it, peace may spread throughout the whole human family! This is the prayer which, through the intercession of Mary, mother of Christ and of the church, I offer to him "from whom every family in heaven and on earth is named" . . .

ANWAR EL-SADAT

"Address to Israel's Knesset"

Born in a village on the Nile River Delta, Anwar el-Sadat rose through the ranks of military and government leadership. After being trained in the military, Sadat worked to overthrow the government and rid Egypt of British influence. Twenty years before becoming Egypt's vice president in the 1960s, the young activist had served a prison sentence for his revolutionary activities. Sadat, however, ultimately became his country's president and served for eleven years until his assassination at the hands of Islamic extremists in 1981.

One of Sadat's primary goals was to end the longstanding Arab-Israeli conflict. Once an accord was reached, Sadat and Israel's prime minister Menachem Begin were awarded the 1978 Nobel Peace prize.

Although Sadat had refused to initiate diplomatic relations with Egypt's longtime foe, he finally, at the peril of his life, accepted an invitation to Jerusalem to plead his case for a peace treaty. In November 1977, Sadat spoke to the Israeli Knesset, charging his words with an emotional appeal for peace.

❖ ◆ ❖

I come to you today on solid ground to shape a new life and to establish peace. We all love this land, the land of God: we all, Moslems, Christians, and Jews, all worship God.

Under God, God's teachings and commandments are love, sincerity, security, and peace.

I do not blame all those who received my decision when I announced it to the entire world before the Egyptian People's Assembly. I do not blame all those who received my decision with surprise and even with amazement-some gripped even by violent surprise. Still others interpreted it as political, to camouflage my intentions of launching a new war.

I would go so far as to tell you that one of my aides at the presidential office contacted me at a late hour following my return home from the People's Assembly and sounded worried as he asked me, "Mr. President, what would be our reaction if Israel actually extended an invitation to you?"

I replied calmly. "I would accept it immediately. I have declared that I would go to Israel, for I want to put before the people of Israel all the facts."

I can see the faces of all those who were astounded by my decision and had doubts as to the sincerity of the intentions behind the declaration of my decision. No one could ever conceive that the president of the biggest Arab state, which bears the heaviest burden and the main responsibility pertaining to the cause of war and peace in the middle East, should declare his readiness to go to the land of the adversary while we were still in a state of war . . .

Here I would go back to the big question: How can we achieve a durable peace based on justice? In my opinion, and I declare it to the whole world, from this forum, the answer is neither difficult nor is it impossible despite long years of feuds, blood, faction, strife, hatreds, and deep-rooted animosity.

The answer is not difficult, nor is it impossible, if we sincerely and faithfully follow a straight line . . .

In all sincerity I tell you we welcome you among us with full security and safety. This in itself is a tremendous turning point, one of the landmarks of a decisive historical change. We used to reject you. We had our reasons and our fears, yes.

We refused to meet with you, anywhere, yes.

We were together in international conferences and organizations, and our representatives did not, and still do not exchange greetings with you. Yes. This has happened and is still happening.

It is also true that we used to set as a precondition for any negotiations with you a mediator who would meet separately with each party.

Yes. Through this procedure, the talks of the first and second disengagement agreements took place.

Our delegates met in the first Geneva conference without exchanging direct word. Yes, this has happened.

Yet today I tell you, and I declare it to the whole world, that we accept to live with you in permanent peace based on justice. We do not want to encircle you or be encircled ourselves by destructive missiles ready for launching, nor by the shells of grudges and hatreds . . .

I hail the Israeli voices that call for the recognition of the Palestinian people's right to achieve and safeguard peace.

Here I tell you, ladies and gentlemen, that it is no use to refrain from recognizing the Palestinian people and their right to statehood as their right of return. We, the Arabs, have faced this experience before, with you. And with the reality of the Israeli existence, the struggle which took us from war to war, from victims to more victims, until you and we have today reached the edge of a horrible abyss and a terrifying disaster unless, together, we seize this opportunity today of durable peace based on justice.

You have to face reality bravely, as I have done. There can never be a solution to a problem by evading it or turning a deaf ear to it. Peace cannot last if attempts are made to impose fantasy concepts on which the world has turned its back and announced its unanimous call for the respect of rights and facts.

There is no need to enter a vicious circle as to Palestinian rights. It is useless to create obstacles; otherwise, the march of peace will be impeded or peace will be blown up. As I have told you, there is no happiness based on the detriment of others.

Direct confrontation and straightforwardness are the shortcuts and the most successful way to reach a clear objective. Direct confrontation concerning the Palestinian problem and tackling it in one single language with a view to achieving a durable and just peace lie in the establishment of that peace. With all the guarantees you demand, there should be no fear of a newly born state that needs the assistance of all countries of the world.

When the bells of peace ring, there will be no hands to beat the drums of war. Even if they existed, they would be stilled . . .

Ladies and gentlemen, peace is not a mere endorsement of written lines. Rather , it is a rewriting of history. Peace is not a game of calling for peace to defend certain whims or hide certain admissions. Peace in its essence is a dire struggle against all and every ambition and whim.

Perhaps the example taken and experienced, taken from ancient and modern history, teaches that missiles, warships, and nuclear weapons cannot establish security. Instead, they destroy what peace and security build.

For the sake of our peoples and for the sake of the civilization made by man, we have to defend man everywhere against rule by the force of arms so that we may endow the full of humanity with all the power of the values and principles that further the sublime position of mankind.

Allow me to address my call from this rostrum to the people of Israel. I tell them, from the Egyptian people, who bless this sacred mission of peace, I convey to you the message of peace of the Egyptian people, who do not harbor fanaticism and whose sons—Moslems, Christians and Jews—live together in a state of cordiality, love and tolerance.

This is Egypt, whose people have entrusted me with their sacred message. A message of security, safety, and peace to every man, woman, and child in Israel. Let all endeavors be channeled toward building a huge stronghold for peace instead of building destructive rockets.

Introduce to the entire world the image of the new man in this area so that he might set an example to the man of our age, the man of peace everywhere. Ring the bells for your sons. Tell them that those wars were the last of wars and the end of sorrows. Tell them that we are entering upon a new beginning, a new life, a life of love, prosperity, freedom, and peace.

You, sorrowing mother, you, widowed wife, you, the son who lost a brother or a father, all the victims of wars, fill the air and space with recitals of peace, fill bosoms and hearts with the aspirations of peace. Make a reality that blossoms and lives. Make hope a code of conduct and endeavor.

The will of peoples is part of the will of God. Ladies and gentlemen, before I came to this place, with every beat of my heart and with every sentiment, I prayed to God Almighty. While performing the prayers at the Al Aksa mosque and while visiting the Holy Sepulcher I asked the Almighty to give me strength and to confirm my belief that this visit may achieve the objective I look forward to for a happy present and a happier future.

I have chosen to set aside all precedents and traditions known by warring countries. In spite of the fact that occupation of Arab territories is still there, the declaration of my readiness to proceed to Israel came as a great surprise that stirred many feelings and confounded many minds. Some of them even doubted its intent.

Despite all that, the decision was inspired by all the clarity and purity of belief and with all the true passions of my people's will and intentions, and I have chosen this road considered by many to be the most difficult road.

I have chosen to come to you with an open heart and an open mind. I have chosen to give this great impetus to all international efforts exerted for peace. I have chosen to present to you, in your own home, the realities, devoid of any scheme or whim. Not to maneuver, or win a round, but for us to win together the most dangerous of rounds embattled in modern history, the battle of permanent peace based on justice.

It is not my battle alone. Nor is it the battle of the leadership in Israel alone. It is the battle of all and every citizen in our territories, whose right it is to live in peace. It is the commitment of conscience and responsibility in the hearts of millions.

When I put forward this initiative, many asked what is it that I conceived as possible to achieve during this visit and what my expectations were. And as I answer the questions, I announce before you that I have not thought of carrying out this initiative from the precepts of what could be achieved during this visit. And I have come here to deliver a message. I have delivered the message, and may God be my witness.

I repeat with Zachariah: Love, right, and justice. From the holy Koran I quote the following verses: We believe in God and in what has been revealed to us and what was revealed to Abraham, Ishmael, Isaac, Jacob and the thirteen Jewish tribes. And in the books given to Moses and Jesus and the prophets from their Lord, who made no distinction between them. So we agree. Salam Aleikum—Peace be upon you.

MARGARET THATCHER

"Let Me Give You My Vision" and "The Falklands Factor"

Dubbed the "Iron Lady," Margaret Thatcher earned the distinction of being the first woman to hold the office of Prime Minister—and the first prime minister in Great Britain to serve three consecutive terms. Among her primary objectives included reversing Britain's economic decline and reducing the role of government in the lives of its people.

Before entering politics, Thatcher received degrees in chemistry from Oxford University. Later, as a research chemist, she studied to become a tax lawyer and, eventually, after joining the conservative party, she was elected to the House of Commons. Her goal in government was to reintroduce "Victorian values" and to encourage state thrift and self-reliance.

In her first speech as party leader on October 10, 1975 at Brighton, Thatcher was met with cheers and foot-stamping as she encouraged national pride and financial responsibility.

"Let Me Give You My Vision"

Whenever I visit Communist countries their politicians never hesitate to boast about their achievements. They know them all by heart; they reel off the facts and figures, claiming this is the rich harvest of the Communist system. Yet they are not prosperous as we in the West are prosperous, and they are not free as we in the West are free.

Our capitalist system produces a far higher standard of prosperity and happiness because it believes in incentive and opportunity, and because it is founded on human dignity and freedom. Even the Russians have to go to a capitalist country—America—to buy enough wheat to feed their people—and that after more than fifty years of a State-controlled economy. Yet they boast incessantly, while we, who have so much more to boast about, for ever criticize and decry. Is it not time we spoke up for our way of life? After all, no Western nation has to build a wall round itself to keep its people in.

So let us have no truck with those who say the free enterprise system has failed. What we face today is not a crisis of capitalism but of Socialism. No country can flourish if its economic and social life is dominated by nationalization and State control.

The cause of our shortcomings does not, therefore, lie in private enterprise. Our problem is not that we have too little Socialism. It is that we have too much . . .

Of course, a halt to further State control will not on its own restore our belief in ourselves, because something else is happening to this country. We are witnessing a deliberate attack on our values, a deliberate attack on our heritage and our great past, and there are those who gnaw away at our national self-respect, rewriting British history as centuries of unrelieved gloom, oppression and failure-as days of hopelessness, not days of hope. And others, under the shelter of our education system, are ruthlessly attacking the minds of the young . . . intimidation designed to undermine the fundamental beliefs and values of every student, tactics pursued by people who are the first to insist on their own civil rights while seeking to deny them to the rest of us.

We must not be bullied or brainwashed out of our beliefs. No wonder so many of our people, some of the best and the brightest, are depressed and talking of emigrating . . . They are giving up too soon. Many of the things we hold dear are threatened as never before, but none has yet been lost, so stay here, stay and help us defeat Socialism so that the Britain you have known may be the Britain your children will know.

These are the two great challenges of our time—the moral and political challenge, and the economic challenge. They have to be faced together and we have to master them both.

What are our chances of success? It depends on what kind of people we are. What kind of people are we? We are the people that in the past made Great Britain the workshop of the world . . .

We are a people who have received more Nobel Prizes than any other nation except America, and head for head we have done better than America, twice as well in fact.

We are the people who, among other things, invented the computer, the refrigerator, the electric motor, the stethoscope, rayon, the steam turbine, stainless steel, the tank, television, penicillin, radar, the jet engine, hovercraft . . . carbon fibers, et cetera—and the best half of Concorde.

We export more of what we produce than either West Germany, France, Japan or the United States, and well over ninety per cent of these exports come from private enterprise. It is a triumph for the private sector and all who work in it, and let us say so loud and clear.

With achievements like that who can doubt that Britain can have a great future, and what our friends abroad want to know is whether that future is going to happen.

Well, how can we Conservatives make it happen? Let me give you my vision: a man's right to work as he will, to spend what he earns, to own property, to have the State as servant and not as master—these are the British inheritance. They are the essence of a free country and on that freedom all our other freedoms depend.

But we want a free economy, not only because it guarantees our liberties, but also because it is the best way of creating wealth and prosperity for the whole country, and it is this prosperity alone which can give us the resources for better services for the community, better services for those in need.

By their attack on private enterprise, this Labour Government has made certain that there will be next to nothing available for improvements in our social services over the next few years. We must get private enterprise back on the road to recovery, not merely to give people more of their own money to spend as they choose, but to have more money to help the old and the sick and the handicapped. And the way to recovery is through profits, good profits today leading to high investment, leading to well-paid jobs, leading to a better standard of living tomorrow . . .

Some Socialists seem to believe that people should be numbers in a State computer. We believe they should be individuals. We are all unequal. No one, thank heavens, is quite like anyone else, however much the Socialists may pretend otherwise. We believe that everyone has the right to be unequal. But to us, every human being is equally important. Engineers, miners, manual workers, shop assistants, farmworkers, postmen, housewives—these are the essential foundations of our society, and without them there would be no nation. But there are others with special gifts who should also have their chance, because if the adventurers who strike out in new directions in science, technology, medicine, commerce and industry are hobbled, there can be no advance. The spirit of envy can destroy; it can never build. Everyone must be allowed to develop the abilities he knows he has within him, and she knows she has within her, in the way they choose.

Freedom to choose is something we take for granted until it is in danger of being taken away. Socialist Governments set out perpetually to restrict the area of choice, and Conservative Governments to increase it. We believe that you become a responsible citizen by making decisions for yourself, not by having them made for you. But they are made for you by Labour all right!

❖ ◆ ❖

Thatcher's strength and resolve during the Falkland Islands crisis greatly increased her popularity. The strong-willed stateswoman delivered the following speech at a rally of Conservative women in Cheltenham on July 3, 1982.

"The Falklands Factor"

Today we meet in the aftermath of the Falklands Battle. Our country has won a great victory and we are entitled to be proud. This nation had the resolution to do what it knew had to be done—to do what it knew was right.

We fought to show that aggression does not pay . . . We fought with the support of so many throughout the world . . . Yet we also fought alone—for we fought for our own people and for our own sovereign territory.

Now that it is all over, things cannot be the same again, for we have learnt something about ourselves—a lesson which we desperately needed to learn. When we started out, there were the waverers and the faint-hearts: the people who thought that Britain could no longer seize the initiative for herself; the people who thought we could no longer do the great things which we once did; and those who believed that our decline was irreversible . . . There were those who would not admit it . . . but—in their heart of hearts—they too had their secret fears that it was true: that Britain was no longer the nation that had built an Empire and ruled a quarter of the world.

Well, they were wrong. The lesson of the Falklands is that Britain has not changed and that this nation still has those sterling qualities which shine through our history. This generation can match their fathers and grandfathers in ability, in courage, and in resolution. We have not changed. When the demands of war and the dangers to our own people call us to arms—then we British are as we have always been—competent, courageous and resolute.

When called to arms—ah, that's the problem. It took . . . the demands of war for every stop to be pulled out and every man and woman to do their best.

British people had to be threatened by foreign soldiers and British territory invaded and then—why then—the response was incomparable. Yet why does it need a war to bring out our qualities and reassert our pride? Why do we have to be invaded before we throw aside our selfish aims and begin to work together as only we can work, and achieve as only we can achieve?

That really is the challenge we as a nation face today. We have to see that the spirit of the South Atlantic—the real spirit of Britain—is kindled not only by war but can now be fired by peace.

We have the first prerequisite. We know we can do it—we haven't lost the ability. That is the Falklands Factor. We have proved ourselves to ourselves. It is a lesson we must not now forget. Indeed, it is a lesson which we must apply to peace just as we have learnt it in war. The faltering and the self-doubt has given way to achievement and pride. We have the confidence and we must use it.

Just look at the Task Force as an object lesson. Every man had his own task to do and did it superbly. Officers and men, senior NCO and newest recruit—every one realized that his contribution was essential for the success of the whole. All were equally valuable—each was differently qualified. By working together, each was able to do more than his best. As a team they raised the average to the level of the best and by each doing his utmost together they achieved the impossible. That's an accurate picture of Britain at war—not yet of Britain at peace. But the spirit has stirred and the nation has begun to assert itself. Things are not going to be the same again.

NELSON MANDELA

"The Rivonia Trial," "Our March to Freedom," and "Glory and Hope"

From prisoner to president, Nelson Mandela sacrificed his personal life for the cause of his fellow South Africans. After he gave up a promising legal career, his public actions quickly carried him to the heights of civil rights leadership and made him a symbol of heroic black resistance to the government's apartheid regime.

As an integral member of the *African National Congress* (ANC) and the *Umkhonto we Sizwe* ("Spear of the Nation"), Mandela sought the liberation of blacks, who had endured untold hardship and violence. Indeed, Mandela and other political colleagues were hunted by police and ultimately jailed.

Charged under the Suppression of Communism Act, Mandela defended himself against the death penalty in the Rivonia Trial. Late into the night he wrote his statement—an explanation of the ANC, of Umkhonto, of himself and of his people—then collapsed from exhaustion. Six months after the trial opened, on April 20, 1964 Mandela delivered his four-hour defense. After hearing it, the judge sentenced Mandela and seven other defendants to hard labor and life imprisonment.

❖ ◆ ❖

"The Rivonia Trial"

. . . Our fight is against real, and not imaginary hardships, or, to use the language of the State Prosecutor, "so-called hardships." . . . We fight against two features which are the hallmarks of African life in South Africa . . . These features are poverty and lack of human dignity, and we do not need Communists, or so-called "agitators," to teach us about these things.

. . . The whites enjoy what may well be the highest standard of living in the world, whilst Africans live in poverty and misery. Forty per cent of the Africans live in hopelessly overcrowded and in some cases, drought-stricken reserves . . . Thirty percent are labourers, labor tenants, and squatters on white farms and work and live under conditions similar to those of the serfs of the Middle Ages. The other thirty per cent live in towns where they have developed economic and social habits which bring them closer, in many respects, to white standards. Yet forty-six per cent of all African families in Johannesburg do not earn enough to keep them going.

The complaint of Africans, however, is not only that they are poor and whites are rich, but that the laws which are made by the whites are designed to preserve this situation. There are two ways to break out of poverty. The first is by formal education, and the second is by the worker acquiring a greater skill at his work and thus higher wages. As far as Africans are concerned, both these avenues of advancement are deliberately curtailed by legislation.

. . . The present Government has always sought to hamper Africans in their search for education. There is compulsory education for all white children at virtually no cost to their parents . . . Similar facilities are not provided for African children . . . The present Prime Minister said during the debate on the Bantu Education Bill in 1953: "When I have control of Native education, I will reform it so that Natives will be taught from childhood to realize that equality with Europeans is not for them . . . People who believe in equality are not desirable teachers for Natives. When my Department controls Native education, it will know for what class of higher education a Native is fitted, and whether he will have a chance in life to use his knowledge."

. . . The other main obstacle to the economic advancement of the Africans is the industrial colour bar by which all the better jobs of industry are reserved for whites only. Moreover, Africans are not allowed to form trade unions, which have no recognition under the Industrial Conciliation Act. The Government often answers its critics by saying that Africans in South Africa are economically better off than the inhabitants of the other countries in Africa. Our complaint is not that we are poor by comparison with people in other countries, but that we are poor by comparison with white people in our own country, and that we are prevented by legislation from altering this imbalance.

. . . Hundreds and thousands of Africans are thrown into gaol each year under pass laws. Even worse than this is the fact that pass laws keep husband and wife apart and lead to the breakdown of family life.

Poverty and the breakdown of family life have secondary effects . . . This leads to a breakdown in moral standards, to an alarming rise in illegitimacy and to growing violence . . . Life in the townships is dangerous [and] violence is carried out of the townships into the white living areas. People are afraid to walk alone in the streets after dark. House-breakings and robberies are increasing despite the fact that the death sentence can now be imposed for such offenses. Death sentences cannot cure the festering sore . . .

. . . We want to be part of the general population, and not confined to living in our ghettos. African men want to have their wives and children to live with them where they work, and not be forced into an unnatural existence in men's hostels. Our women want to be left with their men folk, and not to be left permanently widowed in the Reserves. We want to be allowed out after 11 p.m. and not to be confined in our rooms like little children. We want to be allowed to travel in our own country, and seek work where we want to, and not where the Labor Bureau tells us to. We want a just share in the whole of South Africa; we want security and a stake in society.

This then is what the ANC is fighting. Our struggle is a truly national one. It is a struggle of the African people, inspired by our own suffering and our own experience. It is a struggle for the right to live.

During my lifetime I have dedicated my life to this struggle of the African people. I have fought against white domination, and I have fought against black domination. I have cherished the ideal of a democratic and free society in which all persons live together in harmony with equal opportunities. It is an ideal which I hope to live for, and to see realized. But my lord, if needs be, it is an ideal for which I am prepared to die.

❖ ◆ ❖

When released from prison twenty-seven years later, Nelson Mandela was seventy-one and white-haired. Smiling as he left the jail, he raised his hand in the clenched-fist salute of the ANC and made his first speech since his trial. A crowd of 50,000 and a television audience of millions heard Mandela once again pleading for human rights.

"Our March to Freedom"

Friends, Comrades and fellow South Africans, I greet you all in the name of peace, democracy and freedom for all. I stand here before you not as a prophet but as a humble servant of you, the people. Your tireless and heroic sacrifices have made it possible for me to be here today. I therefore place the remaining years of my life in your hands . . .

The apartheid destruction on our subcontinent is incalculable. The fabric of family life of millions of my people has been shattered. Millions are homeless and unemployed. Our economy lies in ruins and our people are embroiled in political strife . . .

. . . We have no option but to continue . . .

. . . Our march to freedom is irreversible. We must not allow fear to stand in our way. Universal suffrage on common voters' roll in a united, democratic and non-racial South Africa is the only way to peace and racial harmony.

. . . It is an ideal which I hope to live for and to achieve. But if needs be, it is an ideal for which I am prepared to die!

❖ ◆ ❖

Though Nelson Mandela, his family, and his compatriots suffered persecutions and bans for three decades, they unrelentingly struggled to draw attention to the plight of Africans. Finally, as President of South Africa, Mandela addressed the people of Pretoria on May 10, 1994. Displaying an uncommon graciousness toward his former captors and opponents, Mandela expressed his hopes for reconciliation and democracy in his inaugural speech.

"Glory and Hope"

Your majesties, your royal highnesses, distinguished guests, comrades and friends: Today, all of us do, by our presence here, and by our celebrations in other parts of our country and the world, confer glory and hope to newborn liberty.

Out of the experience of an extraordinary human disaster that lasted too long must be born a society of which all humanity will be proud.

Our daily deeds as ordinary South Africans must produce an actual South African reality that will reinforce humanity's belief in justice, strengthen its confidence in the nobility of the human soul and sustain all our hopes for a glori-

ous life for all.

. . . To my compatriots, I have no hesitation in saying that each one of us is as intimately attached to the soil of this beautiful country as are the famous jacaranda trees of Pretoria and the mimosa trees of the bushveld.

. . . That spiritual and physical oneness we all share with this common homeland explains the depth of the pain we all carried in our hearts as we saw our country tear itself apart in terrible conflict, and as we saw it spurned, outlawed and isolated by the peoples of the world, precisely because it has become the universal base of the pernicious ideology and practice of racism and racial oppression.

. . . We deeply appreciate the role that the masses of our people . . . have played to bring about this conclusion. Not least among them is my Second Deputy President, the Honorable F. W. de Klerk.

We would also like to pay tribute to our security forces . . . for the distinguished role they have played in securing our first democratic elections and the transition to democracy, from bloodthirsty forces which still refuse to see the light.

The time for the healing of the wounds has come.

The moment to bridge the chasms that divide us has come.

The time to build is upon us.

We have, at last, achieved our political emancipation. We pledge ourselves to liberate all our people from the continuing bondage of poverty, deprivation, suffering, gender and other discrimination.

. . . We dedicate this day to all the heroes and the heroines in this country and the rest of the world who sacrificed in many ways and surrendered their lives so that we could be free.

Their dreams have become reality. Freedom is their reward.

We are both humbled and elevated by the honor and privilege that you, the people of South Africa, have bestowed on us, as the first President of a united, democratic, non-racial and nonsexist South Africa, to lead our country out of the valley of darkness.

We understand it still that there is no easy road to freedom.

We know it well that none of us acting alone can achieve success.

We must therefore act together as a united people, for national reconciliation, for nation building, for the birth of a new world.

Let there be justice for all.

Let there be peace for all.

Let there be work, bread, and water and salt for all.

Let each know that for each the body, the mind and the soul have been freed to fulfill themselves.

Never, never and never again shall it be that this beautiful land will again experience the oppression of one by another and suffer the indignity of being the skunk of the world.

The sun shall never set on so glorious a human achievement!

Let freedom reign. God bless Africa!

WINSTON CHURCHILL

"The Locust Years," "Blood, Toil, Tears and Sweat," "Be Ye Men of Valour," and "This Was Their Finest Hour"

"It was the nation and the race dwelling all round the globe that had the lion's heart. I had the luck to be called upon to give the roar." Not only was Sir Winston Leonard Spencer Churchill one of the world's greatest statesmen, in his lifetime he was a noted speaker, painter, soldier, war reporter, historian and biographer. Writing history, Churchill also made history during his political career in Great Britain.

Having resigned from the position of First Lord of the Admiralty, the post he held for four years and would hold again in three years, Churchill participated in the House of Commons' debate on defense in London on November 12, 1936. Warning that Germany was stronger in the air than France and Britain, in this, one of his greatest speeches, Churchill urged a confrontation with the enemy.

"The Locust Years"

. . . The Government simply cannot make up their minds, or they cannot get the Prime Minister to make up his mind. So they go on in strange paradox, decided only to be undecided, resolved to be irresolute, adamant for drift, solid for fluidity, all-powerful to be impotent. So we go on preparing more months and years—precious, perhaps vital to the greatness of Britain—for the locust to eat. They will say to me, "A Minister of Supply is not necessary, for all is going well." I deny it. "The position is satisfactory." It is not true. "All is proceeding according to plan." We know what that means . . .

Owing to past neglect, in the face of the plainest warnings, we have now entered upon a period of danger . . . The era of procrastination, of half-measures, of soothing and baffling expedients, of delays, is coming to its close. In its place we are entering a period of consequences. We have entered a period in which for more than a year, or a year and a half, the considerable preparations which are now on foot in Britain will not, as the Minister clearly showed, yield results which can be effective in actual fighting strength; while during this very period Germany may well reach the culminating point of her gigantic military preparations, and be forced by financial and economic stringency to contemplate a sharp decline, or perhaps some other exit from her difficulties. It is this lamentable conjunction of events which seems to present the danger of Europe in its most disquieting form. We cannot avoid this period; we are in it now. Surely, if we can abridge it by even a few months, if we can shorten this period when the German Army will begin to be so much larger than the French Army, and before the British Air Force has come to play its complementary part, we may be the architects who build the peace of the world on sure foundations.

Two things, I confess have staggered me . . . The first has been the dangers that have so swiftly come upon us in a few years, and have been transforming our position and the whole outlook of the world. Secondly, I have been staggered by the failure of the House of Commons to react effectively against those dangers . . . I never would have believed that we should have been allowed to go on getting into this plight, month by month and year by year, and that even the Government's own confessions of error would have produced no concentration of Parliamentary opinion and force capable of lifting our efforts to the level of emergency. I say that unless the House resolves to find out the truth for itself it will have committed an act of abdication of duty without parallel in its long history.

❖ ♦ ❖

Three days after becoming Prime Minister of Great Britain, Churchill spoke to the House of Commons on May 13, 1940. Aired on BBC radio that evening, Churchill's words became famous throughout the world both for their memorable phrases and their refusal to acknowledge the prospect of defeat.

"Blood, Toil, Tears and Sweat"

It must be remembered that we are in the preliminary stage of one of the greatest battles in history, that we are in action at many points in Norway and in Holland, that we have to be prepared in the Mediterranean, that the air battle is continuous and that many preparations have to be made here at home. In this crisis I hope I may be pardoned if I do not address the House at any length today . . . I would say to the House, as I said to those who have joined the Government: "I have nothing to offer but blood, toil, tears and sweat."

We have before us an ordeal of the most grievous kind. We have before us many, many long months of struggle and of suffering. You ask, what is our policy? I will say: It is to wage war, by sea, land and air, with all our might and with all the strength that God can give us: to wage war against a monstrous tyranny, never surpassed in the dark, lamentable catalogue of human crime. That is our policy. You ask, What is our aim? I can answer in one word: Victory—victory at all costs, victory in spite of all terror, victory, however long and hard the road may be; for without victory, there is no survival. Let that be realized; no survival for the British Empire; no survival for all that the British Empire has stood for, no survival for the urge and impulse of the ages, that mankind will move forward towards its goal. But I take up my task with buoyancy and hope. I feel sure that our cause will not be suffered to fail among men. At this time I feel entitled to claim the aid of all, and I say, "Come, then, let us go forward together with our united strength."

❖ ♦ ❖

After the Germans invaded Holland and Belgium, and destroyed French defenses at Sedan, Churchill issued a call to arms. The Prime Minister wrote his speech in just three hours and then delivered it live over the radio on May 19, 1940.

"Be Ye Men of Valour"

Our task is not only to win the battle—but to win the War. After this battle in France abates its force, there will come the battle for our island—for all that Britain is, and all that Britain means . . . In that supreme emergency we shall not hesitate to take every step, even the most drastic, to call forth from our people the last ounce and the last inch of effort of which they are capable. The interests of property, the hours of labour, are nothing compared with the struggle for life and honour, for right and freedom, to which we have vowed ourselves.

I have received from the Chiefs of the French Republic, and in particular from its indomitable Prime Minister, M. Raynaud, the most sacred pledges that whatever happens they will fight to the end, be it bitter or be it glorious. Nay, if we fight to the end, it can only be glorious.

Having received His Majesty's commission, I have found an administration of men and women of every party and of almost every point of view. We have differed and quarreled in the past; but now one bond unites us all—to wage war until victory is won, and never to surrender ourselves to servitude and shame, whatever the cost and the agony may be. This is one of the most awe-striking periods in the long history of France and Britain. It is also beyond doubt the most sublime. Side by side, unaided except by their kith and kin in the great Dominions and by the wide Empires which rest beneath their shield—side by side, the British and French peoples have advanced to rescue not only Europe but mankind from the foulest and most soul-destroying tyranny which has ever darkened and stained the pages of history. Behind them . . . gather a group of shattered States and bludgeoned races: the Czechs, the Poles, the Norwegians, the Danes, the Dutch, the Belgians—upon all of whom the long night of barbarism will descend, unbroken even by a star of hope, unless we conquer, as conquer we must; as conquer we shall.

Today is Trinity Sunday. Centuries ago words were written to be a call and a spur to the faithful servants of Truth and Justice: "Arm yourselves, and be ye men of valour, and be in readiness for the conflict; for it is better for us to perish in battle than to look upon the outrage of our nation and our altar." As the Will of God is in Heaven, even so let it be.

❖ ♦ ❖

Broadcast to millions four hours after being delivered in the House of Commons, this address became the most famous of all the war's speeches. Noting that French resistance to Hitler had deteriorated, Churchill braced his country to continue the fight alone.

"This Was Their Finest Hour"

We do not know what will happen in France or whether the French resistance will be prolonged . . . The French Government will be throwing away great opportunities and casting adrift their future if they do not continue the war in accordance with their Treaty obligations, from which we have not felt able to release them. The House will have read the historic declaration in which . . . we have proclaimed our willingness at the darkest hour in French history to conclude a union of common citizenship in this struggle. However matters may go in France . . . we in this island and in the British Empire will never lose our sense of comradeship with the French people. If we are now called upon to endure what they have been suffering, we shall emulate their courage, and if final victory rewards our toils they shall share the gains, aye, and freedom shall be restored to all. We abate nothing of our just demands: not one jot or tittle do we recede. Czech, Poles, Norwegians, Dutch, Belgians have joined their causes to our own. All these shall be restored.

What General Weygand called the Battle of France is over. I expect that the Battle of Britain is about to begin. Upon this battle depends the survival of Christian civilization. Upon it depends our own British life, and the long continuity of our institutions and our Empire. The whole fury and might of the enemy must very soon be turned on us. Hitler knows that he will have to break us in this island or lose the war. If we can stand up to him, all Europe may be free and the life of the world may move forward into broad, sunlit uplands. But if we fail, then the whole world, including the United States, including all that we have known and cared for, will sink into the abyss of a new Dark Age made more sinister, and perhaps more protracted, by the lights of perverted science. Let us therefore brace ourselves to our duties and so bear ourselves that, if the British Empire and its Commonwealth last for a thousand years, men will still say, "This was their finest hour."

MAHATMA GANDHI

"Nonviolence Is . . . My Faith"

Slight of build, yet possessing impressive physical and moral strength, Mohandas K. Gandhi led the people of India in a fight for independence. His unique approach to social change required courage, nonviolence and truth. Noncompliance, self-suffering—including fasts and hunger strikes, positive programs—hand spinning and weaving industries, media campaigns, and public speaking were his nonviolent methods for social action.

Trained as a lawyer in London, Gandhi spent 21 years in South Africa working for *Indian rights*. Constantly shadowed by the police, he was arrested many times by the British, and these arrests provided the impetus for the reform Gandhi was seeking. Thus, in 1922, he was charged with sedition for articles published in *Young India*. On March 23, in Ahmadabad, upon the conclusion of his trial, Gandhi was allowed to give the following prepared statement to the packed Indian courtroom prior to his sentencing. In his preliminary remarks, he welcomed full punishment for his activities against the government. However, had he not acted as he did, he would have failed in carrying out his duty to his people. When the judge finally sentenced him to six years in prison, Gandhi thanked him for his courtesy.

Two years before, Gandhi had become leader of the Indian National Congress, which adopted his *satyagraha* (passive resistance) principles. His political path included further imprisonments, great personal suffering, and, ultimately, collaboration with the English when, in 1967, they acceded to Indian self-government.

❖ ◆ ❖

I want to avoid violence. Nonviolence is the first article of my faith. It is also the last article of my creed. But I had to make my choice. I had either to submit to a system which I considered had done an irreparable harm to my country, or incur the risk of the mad fury of my people bursting forth, when they understood the truth from my lips. I know that my people have sometimes gone mad. I am deeply sorry for it, and I am therefore here to submit not to a light penalty but to the highest penalty. I do not ask for mercy. I do not plead any extenuating act. I am here, therefore, to invite and cheerfully submit to the highest penalty that can be inflicted upon for what in law is a deliberate crime and what appears to me to be the highest duty of a citizen. The only course open to you, Mr. Judge, is . . . either to resign your post or inflict on me the severest penalty if you believe that the system and law you are assisting to administer are

good for the people. I do not expect that kind of conversion. But by the time I have finished with my statement, you will perhaps, have a glimpse of what is raging within my breast to run this maddest risk which a sane man can run.

I owe it perhaps to the Indian public and to the public in England . . . that I should explain why from a staunch loyalist and cooperator I have become an uncompromising disaffectionist and non-cooperator. To the court too I should say why I plead guilty to the charge of promoting disaffection toward the Government established by law in India.

My public life began in 1893 in South Africa . . . My first contact with British authority in that country was not of a happy character . . . I discovered that I had no rights as a man because I was an Indian.

But I was not baffled. I thought that this treatment of Indians was an excrescence upon a system that was intrinsically and mainly good. I gave the government my voluntary and hearty cooperation, criticizing it freely where I felt it was faulty but never wishing its destruction.

Consequently, when the existence of the empire was threatened in 1899 by the Boer challenge, I offered my services to it . . . Similarly in 1906, at the time of the Zulu revolt, I raised a stretcher-bearer party and served till the end of the "rebellion." On both these occasions I received medals and was even mentioned in dispatches . . . When the war broke out in 1914 between England and Germany, I raised a volunteer ambulance corps in London consisting of the then resident Indians in London, chiefly students. Its work was acknowledged by the authorities to be valuable. Lastly, in India, when a special appeal was made at the War Conference in Delhi in 1918 . . . I struggled at the cost of my health to raise a corps in Kheda . . . In all these efforts at service I was actuated by the belief that it was possible by such services to gain a status of full equality in the empire for my countrymen.

The first shock came in the shape of the Rowlatt Act, a law designed to rob the people of all real freedom. I felt called upon to lead an intensive agitation against it. Then followed the Punjab horrors beginning with the massacre at Jallianwala Bagh and culminating in crawling orders, public floggings, and other indescribable humiliations. I discovered too that the plighted word of the prime minister to the Mussulmans of India regarding the integrity of Turkey and the holy places of Islam was not likely to be fulfilled. But in spite of the forebodings and the grave warnings of friends . . . I fought for cooperation . . . hoping that the prime minister would redeem his promise to the Indian Mussulmans, that the Punjab wound would be healed, and that the reforms, inadequate and unsatisfactory though they were, marked a new era of hope in the life of India.

But all that hope was shattered . . . The Punjab crime was whitewashed, and most culprits went not only unpunished but remained in service and in some cases continued to draw pensions from the Indian revenue, and in some cases were even rewarded. I saw too that not only did the reforms not mark a change of heart, but they were only a method of further draining India of her wealth and of prolonging her servitude.

I came reluctantly to the conclusion that the British connection had made India more helpless than she ever was before, politically and economically. A disarmed India has no power of resistance against any aggressor if she wanted to engage in an armed conflict with him . . . She has become so poor that she has little power of resisting famines. Before the British advent, India spun and wove in her millions of cottages just the supplement she needed for adding to her meager agricultural resources. This cottage industry, so vital for India's existence, has been ruined by incredibly heartless and inhuman processes . . . Little do town dwellers know how the semi-starved masses of India are slowly sinking to lifelessness. Little do they know that their miserable comfort represents the brokerage they get for the work they do for the foreign exploiter, that the profits and the brokerage are sucked from the masses. Little do they realize that the government established by law in British India is carried on for this exploitation of the masses. No sophistry, no jugglery in figures can explain away the evidence that the skeletons in many villages present to the naked eye. I have no doubt whatsoever that both England and the town dwellers of India will have to answer, if there is a God above, for this crime against humanity which is perhaps unequaled in history. The law itself in this country has been used to serve the foreign exploiter . . . My experience of political cases in India leads me to the conclusion that in nine out of every ten the condemned men were totally innocent. Their crime consisted in the love of their country. In ninety-nine cases out of a hundred justice has been denied to Indians as against Europeans in the courts of India. This is not an exaggerated picture. It is the experience of almost every Indian who has had anything to do with such cases. In my opinion, the administration of the law is thus prostituted consciously or unconsciously for the benefit of the exploiter.

The greatest misfortune is that Englishmen and their Indian associates in the administration of the country do not know that they are engaged in the crime I have attempted to describe. I am satisfied that many Englishmen and Indian officials honestly believe that they are administering one of the best systems devised in the world and that India is making steady though slow progress. They do not know that a subtle but effective system of terrorism and an organized display of force, on the one hand, and the deprivation of all powers of retaliation or self-defense, on the other, have emasculated the people and induced in them the habit of simulation. This awful habit has added to the ignorance and the self-deception of the administrators . . . Affection cannot be manufactured or regulated by law. If one has an affection for a person or system, one should be free to give the fullest expression to his disaffection, so long as he does not contemplate, promote, or incite to violence. But the section under which Mr. Banker and I are charged is one under which mere promotion of disaffection is a crime. I have studied some of the cases tried under it, and I know that some of the most loved of India's patriots have been convicted under it. I consider it a privilege, therefore, to be charged under that section. I have endeavored to give in their briefest outline the reasons for my disaffection. I have no personal ill will against any single administrator, much less can I have any disaffection toward the King's person. But I hold it to be a virtue to be disaffected toward a government which in its totality has done more harm to India than any previous system. India is less manly under the British rule than she ever was before. Holding such a belief, I consider it to be a sin to have affection for the system. And it has been a precious privilege for me to be able to write what I have in the various articles, tendered in evidence against me.

In fact, I believe that I have rendered a service to India and England by showing in Non-Cooperation the way out of the unnatural state in which both are living. In my humble opinion, non-cooperation with evil is as much a duty as is cooperation with good. But in the past, non-cooperation has been deliberately expressed in violence to the evildoer. I am endeavouring to show to my countrymen that violent non-cooperation only multiplies evil and that as evil can only be sustained by violence, withdrawal of support of evil requires complete abstention from violence. Nonviolence implies voluntary submission to the penalty for non-cooperation with evil. I am here, therefore, to invite and submit cheerfully to the highest penalty that can be inflicted upon me for what in law is a deliberate crime and what appears to me to be the highest duty of a citizen. The only course open to you, the Judge and the Assessors, is either to resign your posts, and thus dissociate yourselves from evil if you feel that the law you are called upon to administer is an evil and that in reality I am innocent, or to inflict on me the severest penalty if you believe that the system and the law you are assisting to administer are good for the people of this country and that my activity is therefore injurious to the public weal.

<u>*Personal Notes:*</u>

COMPACT
Classics ®

LIBRARY #4: Issues and Insights
piecing together the fragments of a changing world

The Issues and Insights library turns over a "hot handful" of the core crises and controversies behind all this sound and fury. Here you will find provocative and informative discussions on gang violence, child abuse, crime, homelessness, abortion, AIDS, addiction, cultural chauvinism, capital punishment, suicide, and environmental pollution. These selections- -especially taken in conjunction with our summaries on ethics and human relations in Volumes I and II— can provide crucial "border" pieces to help you form a framework for the dynamic, social jigsaw; then you can flesh out a finished picture with segments of your personal values and experience. The result will be uniquely yours—a coherent vision of where the world is going, of where you want to see it go, and of how you can help shape the direction of accelerating social change.

AMUSING OURSELVES TO DEATH

Public Discourse in the Age of Show Business
by Neil Postman, Viking Penguin Inc., New York, N.Y., 1985

We congratulated ourselves in 1984 when Orwell's ominous prophecy of government intrusion, long associated with that year, did not prove true. But we had forgotten Aldous Huxley's equally chilling vision, described in *Brave New World*. Huxley proclaimed that no Big Brother is required to deprive people of their independence, for people would come to adore the technologies that undo their capacity to think. In his *Amusing Ourselves to Death,* Neil Postman concurs with Huxley's forecast and affirms that the age of television has brought it to pass. "What Orwell feared were those who would ban books," Postman explains: *What Huxley feared was that there would be no reason to ban a book, for there would be no one who wanted to read one . . . Orwell feared that what we hate will ruin us, Huxley feared that what we love will ruin us.*

The Medium is the Message
Postman bases his arguments on the premise that the *form* of public discourse helps dictate its *content*. The medium itself classifies, shapes and regulates what we see, and even "argues a case for what the world is like." In the case of smoke signals, for example, the medium at least partially dictated the message; clearly, if only for lack of firewood and blankets, these signals would not have been appropriate for carrying long-range philosophical discussions.

The invention of the printing press heralded the birth of a *print culture*. As the traditions of oral story-telling and epic poetry gradually disappeared, a new mode of thinking took their place: *In a culture dominated by print, public discourse tends to be characterized by a coherent, orderly arrangement of facts and ideas.* It was no accident that the dominance of print coincided with the Age of Reason. And now television has replaced print as our culture's principle mode of learning about itself. *Therefore, how television stages the world becomes the model for how the world is properly to be staged.*

Obviously word-centered and image-centered cultures produce very different modes of thinking. Whereas print media favor *logic* and *rationality*, television favors *image* and *entertainment: It is not merely that on the television screen entertainment is the metaphor for all discourse. It is that off the screen the same metaphor prevails . . . In courtrooms, classrooms, operating rooms, board rooms, churches and even airplanes, Americans no longer talk to each other, they entertain each other. They do not exchange ideas; they exchange images. They do not argue with propositions; they argue with good looks, celebrities and commercials. For the message of television . . . is not only that all the world is a stage but that the stage is located in Las Vegas, Nevada.* Indeed, downtown Las Vegas is the most apt symbol of our national culture and character. We are, then, a people on the verge of "amusing ourselves to death."

America Before the Age of Show Business
During the late 18th and throughout the 19th centuries, America was a nation of readers:

- In 1776, Thomas Paine's *Common Sense* sold between 300,000 to 500,000 copies. Proportionately, a book published today would have to sell 24,000,000 copies to be as successful.

- Alexis de Tocqueville and other visitors to America in the 1800s were impressed by Americans' immersion in printed matter and the high level of literacy.

- "When Charles Dickens visited America in 1842, his reception equaled the adulation we offer today to television stars, quarterbacks and Michael Jackson."

The Shape of Television Discourse
The cultural mind-set fostered by television is captured in the TV phrase "now . . . this," used to indicate that what you have just heard or seen has no relevance to what is about to follow—or perhaps to anything else. From moment to moment the audience is bombarded with skewed and dissimilar bits of information. Furthermore, the world as depicted on TV "has no order or meaning and is not to be taken seriously": *There is no murder so brutal, no earthquake so devastating, no political blunder so costly . . . that it cannot be erased from our minds by a newscaster saying, "Now . . . this." The newscaster means that you have thought long enough on the previous matter (approximately forty-five seconds) . . . and that you must now give your attention to another fragment of news or a commercial.*

Television is *not* neutral; it demands something of us. And our culture has contorted itself to fit the requirements of the medium:

- All messages must entertain.

- Make the viewer feel, not think.

- Image is more important than substantive argument.

- Quantity is more important than quality of information.

- Each communication must be able to stand on its own; programs must not require prerequisites.

- Complexity is not allowed. A perplexed or bored watcher will change the channel.

- The theatrical quality of the presentation is more important than an argument's content or logic.

Public Discourse in the Age of Show Business
Television has shaped our world so gradually that we are now blind to the distortions of the worldview it offers: *The most disturbing consequence of the dominance of television in our culture [is that] the world as given to us through television seems natural, not bizarre.* Nor are we fascinated or perplexed by its machinery: *We do not tell stories of its wonders. We do not confine our television sets to special rooms. We do not doubt the reality of what we see on television, and are largely unaware of the special angle of vision it affords.* And in spite of the enormous amount of time we devote to it, we no longer talk about television itself, but only about what is *on* television.

If you doubt that we have molded our national character to fit the agenda of television—

its advertisers, its neon heroes, its highest virtues and most salient vices—consider the following differences between today and the America of the 1800s:

Advertising:
- During the 1800s, advertisers attempted to sell their products by *making a claim*, if often a disputable one. Today, advertisers rarely make declarative statements about their product, preferring instead to pair it with an *image*, with a feeling.
- Business has discovered "that the quality and usefulness of their goods are subordinate to the artifice of their display."

Politics:
- Political candidates receive support based on appearances and TV sound-bites. *The emergence of the image-manager in the political arena and the concomitant decline of the speech writer attest to the fact that television demands a different kind of content from other media.*
- Today, William Howard Taft, our twenty-seventh president, would not be considered a viable political candidate. The voting television audience would not see beyond his three-hundred-pound image long enough to even consider his politics.
- Neither would Abraham Lincoln—who rarely, if ever, smiled, and was prone to introspection, self-reproach and long bouts of depression—have been well suited for image politics.
- The Lincoln-Douglas debates, each lasting several hours (one as long as seven), were largely a product of their time. It is not coincidence that the electorate was willing to sit through lengthy intellectual discussion, nor that they were able to navigate the maze of complex declarations and counterpoints; they were a people oriented toward and shaped by the written word.
- Contrast the Lincoln-Douglas debates with those held currently. Arguments are limited to five minutes, rebuttals to a minute or two. *In such circumstances, complexity, documentation and logic can play no role, and, indeed, on many occasions syntax itself [is] abandoned entirely. It is no matter. The [candidates are] less concerned with giving arguments than with "giving off" impressions, which is what television does best. Post-debate commentary largely avoids any evaluation of the candidate's ideas, since there [are] none to evaluate.* Instead, the analysis focuses on the candidates' *style*—"how they looked, fixed their gaze, smiled, and delivered one-liners."

Religion:
- The well-known preachers of the previous century were literary men, relying upon logical argument and exposition to convince their audience. Today, instead of soliciting astute or experienced advice, televangelists seek endorsements from those with real clout: sports or show business celebrities.
- Adopting the television mentality, many religious leaders today seem concerned more with the size of their audience than with the content of their message. A Chicago preacher delivers her message with the wit—and with the same

reception—as a comedienne. Another mingles his Gospel radio message with rock-and-roll music. Even Billy Graham can be seen on the air trading jokes about eternity with George Burns.

The Print Media:
- *America's newest and highly successful national newspaper, USA Today, is modeled precisely on the format of television. It is sold on the street in receptacles that look like television sets. Its stories are uncommonly short, its design leans heavily on pictures, charts and other graphics, some of them printed in various colors. As a consequence, it has become one of the largest dailies in the United States.*

While our culture's adjustment to the demands of television is not yet complete, it has certainly distorted our collective vision. Even those who attempt to remain independent of the show business mind-set pay the price: *If some of our institutions seem not to fit the template of the times, why, it is they, and not the template, that seem to us disordered and strange.*

The Phrase "Serious Television" is a Contradiction in Terms

The answer to these problems, Postman observes, is *not* better television. In fact, he feels that we would be better off if television got worse: *I raise no objection to television's junk. The best things on television are its junk . . . We do not measure a culture by its output of undisguised trivialities but by what it claims as significant. Therein is our problem, for television is at its most trivial and, therefore, most dangerous when its aspirations are high, when it presents itself as a carrier of important cultural conversations. The irony here is that this is what intellectuals and critics are constantly urging television to do.*

Breaking Television's Spell

A critical analysis of television, demonstrating how it recreates and degrades our conception of the world, *cannot be accomplished on television: In order to command an audience large enough to make a difference, one would have to make the programs vastly amusing, in television style. Thus, the act of criticism itself would . . . be co-opted by television. The parodists would become celebrities, would star in movies, and would end up making television commercials.*

Education, thus, is the only forum left with the chance to break television's heinous spell. To begin with, educators must not continue to look to television for the answers to educational challenges. Indeed, we must *rethink the questions.* Instead of "How can we use television to control education?" our question ought to be, "How can we use education to control television?"

Regarding television and other pervasive media, Postman feels we must each ask ourselves some hard questions: *What conceptions of intelligence, wisdom and learning does each form insist upon? What conceptions does each form neglect or mock? What is the kind of information that best facilitates thinking? What redefinitions of important cultural meanings do new sources, speeds, contexts and forms of information require?*

Asking the right questions is enough, believes Postman; it's not necessary that we agree on specific answers. For once, if it is dissected and de-mythologized through critical analysis, the spell of television will have been broken.

MANUFACTURING CONSENT

The Political Economy of the Mass Media
by Edward S. Herman and Noam Chomsky, Pantheon, New York, N.Y., 1988

This controversial view into the inner workings of the mass media has been both heralded and renounced. Edward Herman and Noam Chomsky propose a startling yet believable model of propaganda that shapes and constrains the mass media—disclaiming objectivity as an illusion and exposing the powerful, invisible arm of the establishment at work.

Manufacturing Consent is a study of governmental and corporate use of propaganda in the mass media "as a force in engineering democratic consent by management of public opinion." According to the co-authors, *the "societal purpose" of the media is to inculcate and defend the economic, social, and political agenda of privileged groups that dominate the domestic society and the state. The media serve this purpose in many ways: through selection of topics, distribution of concerns, framing of issues, filtering of information, emphasis and tone, and by keeping debate within the bounds of acceptable premises.*

Herman and Chomsky argue that newsworthy items must pass through five successive "filters" in order to get into print or the nightly newscast. As news passes through each successive filter, it is further refined and shaped. The "distilled" or "cleansed" information that remains often reflects the campaigns of any number of special interests, but may or may not reflect the unaltered truth. Therefore, through their purging mechanisms, these five filters set the context of media reporting, fix the premises of discourse, and define newsworthiness. They allow for objectivity only within these constraints. Taken together, they effectively "narrow the range of news that passes through the gates," and determine which stories will become "big news" and which ones will not.

The First Filter: Size and Ownership

Only the wealthy have access to ownership of the media, argue the authors. And, moreover, media operations are often connected to major manufacturing corporations. Thus, they function as integral participants in the market system, sharing in the unrelenting corporate focus on profitability. NBC, for example, is owned by General Electric and has a board of directors dominated by corporate and banking executives. The authors suggest that such close corporate ties not only make the media more sensitive to the interests of a wealthy minority but give this wealthy minority the power to push their own, special regulatory tools through Congress.

The Second Filter: Advertising

In order for a media source to survive in the modern arena, it must rely on advertising; funds generated through advertising are what keeps the enterprise solvent. Thus, any media outlet is put at a competitive disadvantage—and media are placed at the mercy of their advertisers' good graces.

Herman and Chomsky cite the example of *The London Daily Herald*, which was the largest daily newspaper in post-World War II England. At the time of its demise, *The Herald* had almost double the readership of *The Times*, the *Financial Times*, and *The Guardian* combined; nevertheless, the newspaper experienced a "progressive strangulation by lack of advertising support," due to its earnest desires to remain a media tool rather than a commercial tool.

Because newspapers cannot survive on revenues from circulation, advertising is the primary source of financial support for most dailies. But there is an inherent conflict of interest in such an arrangement: "With advertising, the free market does not yield a neutral system in which final *buyer* choice decides. The *advertiser's* choices influence media prosperity and survival."

The authors suggest that successful media corporations are primarily interested in attracting an audience with buying power, an audience that will in turn attract advertisers. Hence media content is tailored *not* to the interests or service of customers who might buy the paper, but to the *seduction* of customers who fit the advertisers' profile—who will buy what the ads want to sell.

The Third Filter: Sources

Because most media sources simply cannot afford to keep reporters on hold in every area of the world to await newsworthy events, they must rely on other sources to receive their news. Their primary sources usually consist of wire services and other credible, first-hand newspeople who concentrate their attention on major news hubs (i.e. The Pentagon, The White House, The State Department, major corporate headquarters, etc.). In fact, however, many of these "primary" sources themselves must rely on secondary, often self-serving sources in order to obtain raw news material. Government media sources flagrantly promote their own interests—as do major corporations—while wire services, which to the average citizen appear as disinterested sources, suffer from the same innate bias of information obtained through government and corporate sources. And an end to the cycle of "media-making" is nowhere in sight: "The magnitude of the public-information operations of large government and corporate bureaucracies that constitute the primary news sources is vast and ensures special access to the media."

Herman and Chomsky also discuss the so-called experts employed by the government, corporations, and the media itself to echo and add legitimacy to the wishes of the establishment. "The steady flow of ex-radicals from marginality to media attention shows that we are witnessing a durable method of providing experts who will say what the establishment wants said."

The Fourth Filter: Flak and the Enforcers

"Flak" is a term the authors use to refer to any negative response to a media statement or program: "It may take the form of letters, telegrams, phone calls, petitions, lawsuits, speeches and bills before congress, and other modes of complaint, threat, and punitive action." Flak may come from advertisers, consumers, the public, or the government, and, Herman and Chomsky contend, often encouraged by special-interest "plaintiff parties"—i.e. the NRA or the Sierra Club, for example—it is used as a prime method of control.

A newspaper that loses its advertisers as a result of its persistence in exposing an uncomfortable topic may quickly find itself in the throes of bankruptcy. Herman and Chomsky cite a classic historical example of governmental flak. During the McCarthy era of the fifties, newspapers that were in any way critical of Senator Joseph McCarthy's efforts to rid the United States of Communists and their influence, were branded "red" and frightened into submission. Herman and Chomsky contend that American papers today have not essentially changed. As arms of the establishment, the media only rarely attack "flak machines"; it doesn't matter whether the flak machine is a liberal or conservative organization, or whether it is anti- or pro- any particular cause. The machines are seen as too powerful, too widespread. "Although the flak machines steadily attack the mass media, the media treat them well. They receive respectful attention, and their propagandistic role and links to a larger corporate program are rarely mentioned or analyzed."

The Fifth Filter: Anti-Communism as a Control Mechanism

Maintaining the ideology of anti-Communism is a kind of "national religion" underlying all other mechanisms of control; its subsistence "helps mobilize the populace against an enemy, and because the concept is fuzzy, it can be used against anybody . . ."—regardless of political or ideological persuasion. [*Manufacturing Consent*, written in 1988, predates the fall of the Soviet Empire. Although a post-Cold War ideology has yet to take solid hold, the concept of an underlying "national religion" exerting control over the populace is a central theme of Herman and Chomsky's propaganda model.] Propaganda has proven its mind-bending strength, they say, in numerous historical examples from the U.S. and elsewhere: Nazi Germany, for instance, used propaganda to effective and deadly ends.

◇ ♦ ◇

The second part of *Manufacturing Consent* involves the application of the Herman/Chomsky propaganda model to various world happenings, contrasting hard facts with media accounts of the events. Variations in the quantity as well as the quality of news coverage of different events are strikingly noted.

Applications: Worthy and Unworthy Victims

In 1984, a Polish priest and outspoken supporter of the Solidarity trade union named Jerzy Popieluszko was kidnapped and murdered by the secret police. In this case the media ensured—through various techniques such as printing graphic pictures of the scene and editorializing on the event to reinforce its senselessness—that it was not only well remembered, but that it shocked and outraged readers. The media, in other words, in an effort to expose the evils of

Communism, *made* the Popieluszko case a high-profile news item—even as a hundred or so nuns, missionaries and other members of the clergy were being murdered in a strikingly similar manner throughout various Latin American countries. The media, however, gave the Latin American killings only a fraction of the coverage. One reason in the discrepancy could have been that Latin American news sources were lacking; more likely, Herman and Chomsky submit, the American media had no incentive to bring the facts of these priests' murders to public light, and their story faded quickly from the media spotlight. "A propaganda system will consistently portray people abused in enemy states as *worthy* victims," the authors write, "whereas those treated with equal or greater severity by its own government or clients will be *unworthy.*"

Inaccurate Portrayals of Third World Elections

Herman and Chomsky contend that American media support and legitimize U.S. Government exploits in Central America. For instance, successful attempts made by the Nicaraguan government in the 1980s to hold peaceful and democratic elections were snubbed by the media, while the oppressive terrorist regimes in El Salvador and Guatemala received warm praises from newscasters and the press. As the authors put it: "Given the earlier similar performance of the mass media in the cases of U.S.-sponsored elections in the Dominican Republic in 1966 and Vietnam in 1967, we offer the tentative generalization that the U.S. mass media will always find a Third World election sponsored by their own government a step toward democracy, and an election held in a country that their government is busily destabilizing a farce and a sham."

Herman and Chomsky point to signs of unfair and inconsistent media intervention in many inconspicuous places around the globe, the motives for which may not always be immediately evident. Such situations include the KGB-Bulgarian plot to kill the Pope—in which the enemies of NATO were incriminated after the assassin was forced to recant his story—and the Indochinese wars throughout Vietnam, Laos, and Cambodia—in which "deception, propagandistic journalism, and destruction" were rampant.

Herman and Chomsky are careful to point out that bias within the media is a by-product of a highly complex, market-based system, and *not* the reflection of a conscious, concerted effort of a few interested individuals nor of any one political party. In concluding their detailed report, they also distinguish the U.S. mass media from the media of propagandistic totalitarian regimes, in which all debate is discouraged. Indeed, independent, autonomous media are important to a free society. However, when the media become puppets of government special-interest groups and powerful corporations, then a change is in order: *In sum, the mass media of the United States are effective and powerful ideological institutions that carry out a system-supportive propaganda function by reliance on market forces, internalized assumptions, and self-censorship, and without significant overt coercion.*

THE CRY FOR MYTH

by Rollo May, Norton, New York, N.Y., 1990

In *The Cry for Myth,* Rollo May argues that psychoanalysis has usurped the role of myth in Western society. And as our traditional mythologies fade away, May contends, we experience a profound emptiness that is manifested in an increase in cults, drug addictions, and suicides.

The loss of "meaning and significance" which results from the vanishing of myth is not unique to our own culture. As May points out, when the myths of ancient Greece disintegrated in the third and second centuries B.C., the poet Lucretius saw "aching hearts in every home, racked incessantly by pangs the mind was powerless to assuage . . . " And like the ancient Greeks, May suggests, we, too, without a cohesive mythology to help us regulate our "anxiety and excessive guilt feelings," must now endure such pangs.

The absence of myth may be so devastating that some may feel driven to create private mythologies. May points to the autobiographical novel *I Never Promised You a Rose Garden* for a sketch of just such a person. The novel's narrator Deborah, who is battling schizophrenia, invents mythical characters to inhabit her imaginary kingdom of Yr, where she retreats when "terrified or unbearably lonely in the so-called real world." Deborah's therapist understands the pain that has driven her to escape inside the fanciful walls of Yr. While he is away on an extended leave, however, a less experienced therapist treats Deborah confrontationally in an attempt to destroy the delusions. Stripped of her "whole system of gods," Deborah rapidly deteriorates and regresses, finally setting fire to the hospital and behaving "like a human being whose humanity is destroyed." According to May, Deborah's mental breakdown illustrates the powerful influence of myth on the psyche's equilibrium as well as the extent to which a disappearance of myth can profoundly muddle both individuals and societies.

Cults, May notes, are equally illustrative of the chaos that erupts in a culture from which myths have fled. Young people, who feel particularly confused in a society that has "little sense of the present" and "no life-sustaining beliefs, secular or religious," are highly susceptible to the communal spirit and proscribed mythology that cults appear to offer. Tragically, in turning to cults in their desperate "longing for something to fill the vacuum of their lives," these youth suffer catastrophic effects: they often experience a deeper sense of emptiness—especially when they break from the spell of the cult's mythology—that may lead to drug abuse or even suicide.

How, then, can we recover the equilibrium that myth provides? First, according to May, we must realize that myth does not denote "falsehood." We tend to favor the rational over the mythical in Western civilization to the degree, as May points out, that the phrase "only a myth" is deprecatory.

However, throughout history, May posits, there have been two distinct and equally important forms of communication: "rationalistic language," which involves "specific and empirical" thought and discourse that have culminated in formal "logic," and "mythic language," communication which emphasizes "totality rather than specificity," and unites all of life's experiential feelings and spiritual sensations: "conscious and unconscious, historical and present, individual and social . . . the meaning and significance of human life." May insists that "mythic truth," which speaks to the "quintessence of human experience," *transcends* time, while "empirical truth" changes with every new judiciary breeze and with the publication of each new scientific journal.

Before their widespread debunking, myths provided us with a sense of ourselves, of our "roots" as well as a "sense of community" and belonging. Furthermore, myths once served as models for solving individual and cultural crises and to reinforce our moral values by answering questions concerning the mysteries of nature and the "great beyond." In other words, myths bound us together into a harmonious society, a community of allies. Alex Haley in writing his award-winning *Roots,* felt compelled to trace his ancestors in order to "find his own myth," his identity and his place in the world. Without this understanding, he acknowledged, he felt utterly empty.

Mythical stories, passed through family lines, gave parents a method of teaching values to their children and helped each generation develop a sense of heritage and purpose. May contends that in America, a land of immigrants isolated from their cultural roots, we have always had a special need for restorative myths. And it was this need, he argues, that led Americans to embrace the theories of Sigmund Freud. Freud, the father of psychoanalysis, isolated two conflicting types of myth: those of *Eros,* pertaining to love, and those of *Thanatos,* pertaining to death. In Freudian terminology, Eros represents "friendship, interdependence, and . . . unity with our fellow men and women" whereas Thanatos signifies "illness, fatigue . . . and non-being . . . the forces that tear us apart." Freud concluded that out of the conflict between Eros and Thanatos, "civilization is wrought." Interestingly, each needs the other to survive: Eros alone is "insipid, childish, indeed, as irrelevant as the little boy 'Cupid' . . . " and Thanatos, unmitigated by Eros, points to "an emptiness beyond even cruelty."

Related to the necessary balance between these two great forces of love and death, is what Freud called the "healing power of myth." For Freud, the "regressive" function of myths brings to the surface of consciousness the "repressed, unconscious, archaic urges, longings, dreads, and other psychic content" so they can be openly confronted, while the "progressive" function of myth penetrates to a "greater meaning which was not there before," allowing the patient to confront his problem at "a higher level of integration."

According to May, America's singular need for restorative myths likewise led early pioneers and gold-seekers on a "wonderfully mythical" western migration. To compensate for their "rootlessness," Americans looked to the vast frontier as an outlet; mythologies (in the form of legends such as Paul Bunyan, Pecos Bill, Johnny Appleseed, as well as religious and folk beliefs) sprang up and spread accordingly as "the rebirth of humanity, without the sin or evil or poverty or injustice or persecution which had characterized the Old World." Also from this "frontier" mentality grew the doctrine of "manifest destiny," which, as a policy, gave settlers a "divine right" to the New World and the justification to resist any outside interference.

Of all the American myths, May contends, none was more potent than the myth of the "Wild West." Not only was the Wild West said to possess "a sense of destiny [and] was reputed to have a healing power," but American folk heroes emerged from what Paul Tillich called the "holy void." Kit Carson, Calamity Jane, Annie Oakley, Butch Cassidy and the Sundance Kid were distinctly American personalities, and from them came an American archetype, embodying "loneliness and the myth of the west." The valiant cowboy—who "lived a life of relative isolation and bragged about it"—won the admiration of all "independent Americans." Believing that "every person must be ready to stand alone," Americans valued the cowboy's courage and freedom, and embraced the ideal of "rugged individualism," in which "each individual must learn to take care of himself or herself and thus be beholden to no one else." Unfortunately, May argues, the myth of individualism deprived Americans of any "solid community" to call their own. Citing Robert Bellah, Americans' ideals focused so "exclusively on individual self-improvement that the larger social context hardly comes into view." Ultimately, adds May, this self-oriented society spawned the "narcissistic personality . . . the modern myth of lonely individualism."

In their narcissism, Americans have lost the ability to criticize their own behavior and have acquired a "split personality," parodying the people in commercials who are "always smiling . . . running in the fields . . . dancing, and driving Cadillacs" and yet simultaneously experiencing "the reality of depression . . . fear of nuclear disaster, [and the insecurity of] sexual activity without lasting relationships." One consequence of this splitting of the American psyche is a country of citizens with "many acquaintances, but no close friends." Moreover, May contends that Americans are "sexually liberated" but lacking in "passion," "well educated" but devoid of intellectual curiosity, and well-paid but dismal and downcast. In essence, in pursuit of "The Myth

of the American Dream," Americans—so commonly duped into thinking that what "is promised in the TV ads [will] bring happiness"—find their factual lives to be "exasperatingly empty."

Indeed, the "American Dream" was, in May's view, "probably the most important in American history in the last century." Emerging from the supposedly factual saga of Horatio Alger—suggesting that "the man of wealth was therefore a good man, for his wealth showed that God approved of him"—and culminating with President Ronald Reagan's "all-American" news conference narratives of going from eating "oatmeal-meat" as a boy to becoming a millionaire, the dual-edged "American Dream" has persisted in the national psyche. Indeed, throughout Reagan's presidency "the stock market boomed to a height never dreamt of before," owing, May hints, largely to an increase in risky financial undertakings; America's "split personality" daily grew more dramatic, as investors tried to "win big on the stock market or lottery" and put "less effort forth in honest work."

But, for May, no loss was as devastatingly pivotal as that of those myths and rituals which once gave vital order and meaning to the lives of men and women, elevated their daily tasks "above boredom, mindlessness, and despair," and provided them with a sense of community and cooperation within society. When mythology prevailed in the daily lives of people they were better equipped, not only to deal with their daily lives, May argues, but to deal with tragedy and mortality as well.

In many Greek myths, human suffering and mortality were considered gifts—positive virtues. In the story of Alcmene and Amphytryon, for instance, Zeus becomes passionately attracted to a mortal woman, Alcmene, and dons the guise of her husband Amphitryon in order to make love to her. When he returns to Olympus, a very troubled Zeus speaks to Mercury about Alcmene, and of how, during their tryst, she had spoken of being young, growing old, and someday dying—all held in the arms of her beloved Amphitryon. In the end, Zeus learns something that all mortals know: "This stabs me, Mercury," Zeus says dismally. "We miss something . . . the poignancy of the transient—the sweet sadness of grasping for something we know we cannot hold." In May's view, Zeus' admission that mortality enriches life soothed the Greek mind: by believing the myth, they could at once accept the inevitability of death and, even in the face of this ultimate, dire fate, revere and savor life.

May concludes that, in marked contrast to the ancient Greeks, human beings in the twentieth century have lost touch with myth and the power it brings; however, the time for a global mythology has arrived. "After a sleep of many centuries" he writes, the mythic consciousness of the world has already awakened to create "a new and irrefutable sense in the myth of humankind."

GENERATION X

Tales for an Accelerated Culture
by Douglas Coupland, St. Martin's Press, New York, N.Y., 1991

Douglas Coupland's controversial fictional novel *Generation X* salutes Americans born in the late sixties and early seventies. From Coupland's point of view, this "twenty-something generation" remains almost pathologically ambivalent about the future. Lacking cultural and religious dictums, Coupland's all-grown-up-but-no-place-to-go generation complains of having little to look forward to except a "McJob": a low-paying, zero-prestige, no benefits-package job in the service industry. Needless to say, a McJob offers a future that Generation Xers prefer not think about.

Coupland's under-employed but over-educated misfits focus on the present, filling their lives with media-images and inventing catch-phrases to convey their angst:

- *Brazilification:* The widening gulf between the rich and the poor, accompanied by the disappearance of the middle classes.

- *Emotional Ketchup Burst:* A sudden and explosive eruption of long-bottled-up opinions and emotions; often shocks and confuses employers and friends who thought that everything was fine.

- *Fame-Induced Apathy:* The attitude that no activity is worth pursuing unless one can become very famous pursuing it; mimics laziness, but goes much deeper.

- *Option Paralysis:* The tendency, when given unlimited choices, to make none at all.

- *Poverty Jet Set:* A group of individuals given to chronic traveling at the expense of long-term job stability, permanent residence, and an exorbitant phone bill; tends to discuss frequent-flyer programs at parties.

- *Safety-Net-Ism:* The belief that there will always be a financial and emotional safety net (usually parents) to buffer life's hurts.

Generalizations aside, Coupland's unflinching view of his fellow Xers is ultimately compassionate. "Could the situation be that . . . we were promised heaven in our lifetimes," he wonders, "and what we ended up with can't help but suffer in comparison?"

Coupland's experiences, after all, have not been wholly different from his peers': *I was a terrible employee to have around during my brief foray into time-clockdom—chronically and cheerfully late, insubordinate and rude to anybody who copped an attitude. People gripe that it's some horrible curse against society not to work a creepy job that has no loyalty to you and is killing you . . . But . . . I'm happy to know there are dreamers out on the edge, characters out of key, in and out of love, drifting, slightly twisted, still willing to listen—childlike and full of wonder with their world—people I would consider my friends.*

Coupland thus establishes his affinity to *Generation X's* three main characters: Andy, Dag, and Claire.

The Sun is Your Enemy

Back in the late 1970s, fifteen-year-old Andy Palmer joined the Poverty Jet Set when he spent his life savings on airfare in order to witness a total solar eclipse in Manitoba, Canada. On the morning of the once-in-a-lifetime event, the "pencil thin and practically albino" took a bus from the TravelLodge to the edge of town, where, all alone, he made his way into a wheat field. There, "chest-high in cereal," as Andy later recalled, *I lay myself down on the ground . . . and held my breath, there experiencing a mood that I have never really been able to shake completely—a mood of darkness and inevitability and fascination—a mood that surely must have been held by most young people since the dawn of time as they have crooked their necks, stared at the heavens, and watched their sky go out.*

Now, one and a half decades later, Andy's ambivalence lingers as he sits on the porch of his rented Palm Springs bungalow. Soon he hears his friend Dag rifling through the kitchen cupboards. Coming outside to sit with Andy, Dag is still on a "vandal's high" after scraping a boulder across the hood of a Cutlass Supreme with a bumper sticker that read, *WE'RE SPENDING OUR CHILDREN'S INHERITANCE.* "I don't know, Andy," Dag says, "whether I feel more that I want to punish some aging old crock for frittering away my world, or whether I'm just upset that the world has gotten too big—way beyond our capacity to tell stories about it, and so all we're stuck with are these blips and chunks and snippets on bumpers. I feel insulted either way."

Later, Claire returns from her "date from hell." Grabbing a glass of mystery drink from the refrigerator, she joins her two friends on the porch just as dawn breaks. "What do you think of when you see the sun?" Dag asks, morosely. "Quick. Before you think about it too much and kill your response. Be honest. Be gruesome." Claire then responds by saying that she sees an image of a Russian farmer on a tractor, "but the sun's gone bad on him—like the fadedness of a black and white picture in an old *LIFE* magazine . . . killing his crops."

In response, Dag describes his vision of "an Australian surf bunny, eighteen years old, maybe, somewhere on Bondi Beach, and discovering her first keratosis lesion on her shin."

Finally, Andy explains, "I think of this place in Antarctica called Lake Vanda, where the rain hasn't fallen in more than two million years." There is a long silence, which Claire finally breaks: "Either our lives become stories, or there's just no way to get through them." They all agree. That is the very reason they have come to the desert—"to tell stories and to make our own lives worthwhile tales in the process."

Eat Your Parents

It was only a minor nuclear waste accident. A jar of "possibly radio-active trinitite beads"—that Dag had brought Claire as a gift—had shattered on the floor. Now Andy and Dag are busy picking up the "plutonium" beads from the hard wood floors of Claire's apartment. Because of his upcoming trip home for Christmas, Andy is in a "morbid" mood. "Trust me, you have *nada* to worry about," Dag reasons. "Look at me. I just made someone's apartment uninhabitable for the next four and a half billion years. Imagine the guilt I must feel."

Dag's comments do nothing to keep Andy' thoughts from home, and he now recalls his mother's inability to grasp the concept of recycling. Last Thanksgiving, in fact, she had used a non-biodegradable bag to dispose of left overs and so Andy had pointed out that she might want to use a degradable bag. "You're right! I forgot I had them," she replied—then proceeded to put the non-biodegradable bag *inside* the degradable bag, and throw the whole thing out.

"Have you ever wanted to set your parent's house on fire just to get them out of their rut?" Andy now asks. Wrinkling his brow, Dag ponders the question. "Andy," he replies, "I'm the last person to be saying this, but, hey—your parents are getting old. That's what happens to old people. They go cuckoo, they get boring and lose their edge." Andy should take a lesson from his brother Matthew, Dag suggests, who is continually arguing with his agent over who gets to eat the FAX bill—that is, who writes it off as a business expense. "I suggest you do the same thing with your parents. Eat them," Dag says, smiling. "Accept them as a part of getting you to here . . . Write them off as a business expense."

Define Normal

Very soon now Andy will go home for Christmas and his mind turns to an old family portrait. All nine family members had endured what seemed to be an "endless sitting" as the photographer yelled out "fromage!" Although the photo is dated, the family looked *perfect*. The portrait no longer hangs above the fireplace, but rather has been moved to the den, where it sometimes attracts a nostalgic family member who wants to marvel, "but we were all so innocent once."

"Wasn't that a great year Andy, remember?" his sister Diedre asks on the phone. Recently, Diedre has called more frequently and more frantically as her divorce becomes uglier. Diedre isn't going home for Christmas; in fact, with the exception of Andy and his young brother Tyler, none of the six Palmer kids will be there. Now that they have grown up, they have their own problems to worry about: the pressures of uncertain income, of cheating on spouses, of dabbling in cocaine, or of moving into and then out of *the nest*.

"Oh Mr. Leonard," Andy asks quietly, "how *did* we all end up so messy? We're all looking hard for that *fromage* you were holding—we really are—but we're just not seeing it anymore. Send us a clue, *please*."

Jan. 01, 2000

Andy was driving to Calexico, across a landscape of "overwhelming fertility," when his eyes fixed on an ominous and alarming sight. A giant mushroom cloud cloaked the horizon, "angry and thick, with an anvil-shaped head the size of a medieval kingdom and as black as a bedroom at night." He waited for sirens and turned on the radio to see if there were any emergency warnings, but everything seemed to be normal. Could it be that nobody yet was aware of the disaster at hand? Still, he continued down the road, "possessed with lurid curiosity" as to what would happen next.

Finally he reached the source of the cloud: local farmers were burning off stubble from their fields. Scores of motorists had climbed out of their cars to watch the carbonized fields ascend into the air. Amid the horde of rubber-neckers, a van stopped, "and out of it emerged . . . a dozen or so mentally retarded teenagers, male and female, gregarious and noisy, in high spirits and good moods with an assortment of flailing limbs and happy shouts of 'hello!' . . . " But soon the noisy teens turned silent, as a "cocaine white" egret flew in from the west to collect the offerings of the freshly burned fields.

The crowd was oohing and aahing as the bird swooped and dipped, until it appeared to be leaving. Then, suddenly, the egret circled back. "We quickly and excitedly realized that it was going to swoop right over us," Andy said. "We felt chosen . . . Suddenly the children were turning to look at *me*. I felt something sharp drag across my head, there was a *swoop swoop swoop* sound. The egret had grazed my head—its claw had ripped my scalp. I fell to my knees but did not remove my eyes from the bird's progress." Without warning, Andy felt himself in the grasp of a pair of "fat arms bearing fat dirty hands with cracked fingernails." It was one of the mentally retarded kids, a girl, who pulled him gently to his knees in order to examine his head. Then, with indescribable gentleness, she tapped Andy's head; indeed, it was "an optimistic healing staccato caress."

Within seconds Andy was surrounded by the teens and, as he recalled, enveloped in "their adoring, healing, uncritical embrace, each member wanting to show their affection . . . They began to hug me—too hard—as if I *were* a doll . . . I was being winded—crushed—pinched and trampled." Their bus driver came over to yank them away—"But how could I explain to him . . . that this discomfort, no this *pain* . . . was no problem at all, that in fact, this crush of love was unlike anything I had ever known . . . Well maybe he did understand, [because] he removed his hands from his wards . . . I can't remember whether I said thank you."

A NATION OF STRANGERS

by Ellis Cose, William Morrow and Company, Inc., New York, N.Y., 1992

In *A Nation of Strangers* Ellis Cose evaluates 200 years of American immigration history and the impact that each new wave of immigrants has had upon the social and political landscape in this country. Although the United States unquestionably has absorbed more immigrants than any other nation, its citizenry has also experienced periods of intense xenophobia.

Except for African slaves, early immigrants overwhelmingly were British Protestants who assumed that they would always predominate. But by the mid-nineteenth century, countless numbers of Irish Catholics and Germans had made the journey; and blacks, meanwhile, were granted citizenship. Then, by the late 1800s many Jews and Catholics from Eastern and Southern Europe began to arrive in the United States, followed by Asians. Subsequently, the number of new immigrants from western Europe declined.

The United States today is experiencing a resurgence of immigration. With increasing floods of immigrants arriving on its shores every year since the turn of the century, America must now evaluate its ability to absorb newcomers from widely divergent cultures. Providing insight into the history of U.S. immigration, Ellis Cose's *A Nation of Strangers* explores the complex problems that cultural diversity engenders.

Years of Confusion, Days of Rage

In the fifteen years before the Civil War, the United States experienced unprecedented expansion. Vast tracts of western lands once owned by Mexico were seized by the United States, and as soon as gold was discovered in California, many new immigrants arrived to settle the region. Homesteaders came from all around the world, but nothing rivaled the huge influx of eager Chinese immigrants. Although the Chinese provided desperately needed manpower, their sheer numbers incited a backlash. Many settlers complained that the Chinese immigrants drove white immigrants away, and as a result, California's governor John Bigler sought and won special measures to stop the Chinese from entering the country.

Anti-Chinese propaganda soon appeared in the press—then quickly spread to the courts. Popular newspapers ran articles proclaiming the inferiority of the Chinese and their danger to the community at large, while a California appellate court invalidated the conviction of a white man in the murder of a Chinese worker. At the time, Blacks, Mulattoes and Indians—and now Chinese—were barred from seeking redress through the legal system.

In the eastern United States, meanwhile, another form of nativism was taking hold. The "Know-Nothing" movement of the American Party promised stability by protecting the country from foreign influence. Membership was often secret; thus, when asked by the uninitiated about their activities, members would invariably respond that they knew nothing. Know-Nothings demanded that the period required for naturalization be extended from five to twenty-one years

and wanted laws ensuring that only native-born Protestants could hold political offices—since, they reasoned, all Catholics were under control of the pope. Indeed, at the height of their influence, the Know-Nothings and their allies dominated the legislatures of many Eastern states.

Politicians and journalists now were loudly publicizing supposed "scientific findings" showing that immigrants were more likely to become criminals or paupers than native-born Americans. However, no one suggested a ban on immigration—only that citizenship be restricted to white Protestant Europeans. Others felt that by allowing immigration but denying citizenship, the country would be capsized in that non-citizens would be less apt to uphold traditional American values. Still others argued that denying citizenship was the only way to keep some foreigners "in line."

In 1854 the American Party—and, indeed, the country in general—found itself violently divided over the issues of slavery and immigration. Many legislators believed that in order to preserve the delicate balance between slave and master, influence from any possibly detrimental outside sources should be outlawed. Thus, legislation was soon passed prohibiting the importation of Chinese Coolies and curtailing Chinese immigration in general.

Before the onset of the Civil War, President Lincoln supported immigration from Europe; indeed, the Union cared little about religious diversity or ethnicity. Then, as the war raged, Lincoln vehemently endorsed immigration, telling Congress that workers were needed to bolster the economy, especially in mining and agriculture: "While the demand for labor is thus increased here, tens of thousands of persons, destitute of remunerative occupation, are thronging our foreign consulates, and offering to immigrate to the United States if essential, but very cheap, assistance can be afforded them." Thus, an aggressive campaign was undertaken by politicians to increase European immigration; in fact, Britain was only too happy to send its mass of poor English and Irish workers to America.

At this time, because Irish Catholics were considered near the bottom of the socio-economic ladder, many native-born workers blamed them for keeping wages low and for taking too many jobs. Many Irish workers, in turn, resented blacks, and opposed efforts to enfranchise them while they supported efforts to crowd them out of low paying jobs.

Subsequently, the Emancipation Proclamation of 1863 generated additional resentment among the Irish, since it promised to increase their competition with blacks. Further angering New York's Irish immigrants was the new military draft that exempted blacks—who many saw as the cause of the war—as well as anyone who could pay three hundred dollars. All other married men up to the age of thirty-five and all other single men to age forty-five were eligible to be drafted.

Finally, in June of 1863, three thousand

angry New York longshoremen, striking for higher wages, looked on as strikebreakers—many of them black—were brought in under police escort to take their jobs. Soon after, the most violent riot in the city's history broke out. As draft officials conducted a lottery, a crowd which had gathered to watch turned violent and destroyed draft headquarters. For several days the predominantly Irish mobs roamed the city assaulting blacks at random. No one was ever tried for the thousands of deaths that resulted from the rampage.

The decades that followed brought little change, either in race relations or in immigration policy improvements.

A War Ends, An Era of Isolation Begins

Two months before the United States entered World War I, Congress, via the Anti-Anarchist Act, authorized deportation of any alien "found advocating or teaching the unlawful destruction of property, or advocating or teaching anarchy . . . " Years later, only a month before the war's end, Congress broadened the statute to include any foreigner who "believed" in anarchy. Then, in 1920 the statute was once more expanded to cover all aliens who wrote, commissioned, distributed, published, printed, circulated or possessed with the intent to circulate any materials advocating violent overthrow of the government. However, this burst of legislative activity proved to be ineffective at weeding out the "violent foreigners."

The Justice Department boasted plans to deport sixty-thousand radicals, but the policy was never enacted. Nevertheless, many arrests were made: FBI agents and local police raided meeting halls and private homes, seizing any evidence which might point to membership in illegal organizations. Hundreds of innocent people were tried as traitors or saboteurs, and both citizens and aliens were deported to their alleged countries of origin.

The Supreme Court and most if not all state appellate courts, meanwhile, had sanctioned the notion of "Eugenics," the belief that some races were simply inferior to white Europeans. "The intention [of the original naturalization statute]," Cose writes, "was to confer the privilege of citizenship upon that class of persons whom the fathers knew as white, and to deny it to all who could not be so classified."

In 1923, for instance, a case came before the Supreme Court in which Bhagat Sinh Thind, a high-cast Hindu, claimed to be an Aryan and therefore eligible for naturalization. Justice Sutherland, writing for the court, responded: "It may be true that the blond Scandinavian and the brown Hindu have a common ancestor in the dim reaches of antiquity, but the average man knows perfectly well that there are unmistakable and profound differences between them today . . . The children of English, French, German, Italian, Scandinavian, and other European parentage quickly merge into the mass of our population and lose the distinctive hallmarks of their European origin. [However], children born in this country of Hindu parents would retain indefinitely the clear evidence of their ancestry."

Because so many unemployed Americans resented immigrants taking their jobs, the depression era saw some of the most restrictive immigration laws in history. Even as Hitler's armies marched across Europe, hundreds of thousands of people fearing for their lives were unable to immigrate to the United States. In fact, during World War II, more than one hundred thousand persons of Japanese extraction—the vast majority of them longstanding U.S. citizens—were placed in internment camps in remote regions of the nation. Conversely, the Chinese, traditionally enemies of the Japanese, were recognized as allies, and moves were made to repeal exclusion orders which barred all but token numbers of Chinese immigrants.

The Centrality of Race, The Challenge of Diversity

The last fifty years have seen radical changes in the way most Americans view cultural diversity. As late as the 1940s, trials were still being held in America to determine a person's "whiteness."

Then in 1952, the McCarran-Walter Act finally eliminated all racial restrictions to naturalization. Soon afterward, the success of the civil-rights movement made exclusion based solely on race legally unacceptable. And with the shattering of the last vestiges of legal restrictions, "lower" Europeans—i.e. Italians, Russians, Rumanians and Poles—whose immigration once was thought to be detrimental to the stability of America, now were being rapidly assimilated into the mainstream.

Today, in contrast to past decades, almost three fourths of all immigrants coming to the United States are from Asia—an influx that will radically change the country. Even now, in the "politically correct" nineties, some citizens fear that the new immigrants, coming from such widely divergent cultures, may have a detrimental effect on the United States. History, however, suggests that such a fear is unwarranted. America is an increasingly mature and capable nation. In the past two hundred years it has made great strides towards tolerance and racial and ethnic diversity—even while much of the rest of the world has not.

Still, the United States certainly is not free of racial or ethnic bigotry. Despite widespread belief that affirmative action programs have led to rampant "reverse discrimination," a 1991 Urban Institute study found that when young white and black men seeking entry-level jobs in Chicago and Washington were matched for age, qualifications, experience, education, demeanor, and physique, whites were three times as likely as blacks to receive preferential treatment; this is roughly the same advantage that whites were found to have over Hispanics in a similar study.

Thus, racial and cultural intolerance in America is still a major problem—a problem that can not be solved through legislation alone, since it stems more from an *individual's* or *community's* unwillingness to accept differences. With so many of the country's immigrants now belonging to "minority" groups and so many Black and Hispanic citizens still excluded from the mainstream, it behooves Americans to try to make America's diversity a strength rather than a weakness.

MONSTER

An Autobiography of an L.A. Gang Member
by Kody Scott (with acknowledgement to others), The Atlantic Monthly Press, New York, New York, 1993

There is troop movement throughout the city, and in some areas the fighting is intense. The soldiers are engaged in a "civil war." A war without terms . . . this conflict has lasted nine years longer than Vietnam . . . Neither side receives funding from any government . . . they are maintained by proceeds from major narcotics deals . . . The death toll is in the thousands . . .

This is not a war correspondent's description of an intertribal uprising in a distant land; it is Kody Scott's account of life in South Central Los Angeles, "the concrete jungle—battlefield of the Crips and Bloods." As a former Crip gang member, Scott offers a thought-provoking glimpse into the mentality of the "bangers" who initiated him into adulthood. Although *Monster* offers few if any direct solutions to the growing problem of gang-related crimes and violence, Scott's book does examine the attractions that compel youth to join and remain in gangs. However nightmarish the lives of the black Eight Trays and the hispanic Rollin' Sixties in *Monster* may seem, these teenage guerrillas and their "sets" are an all-too real and rapidly expanding feature of modern life—as are the mayhem and brutal deaths they bring about. In their world, *bangin' ain't no part-time thang, it is full-time, it's a career. It's being down when ain't nobody else down with you. It's gettin' caught and not tellin'. Killin' and not carin', and dyin' without fear. It's love for your set and hate for the enemy.*

With these words, eleven-year-old Kody Scott—who had just pumped eight blasts from a sawed-off shotgun into a group of rival gangsters—was initiated into L.A.'s Eight Trays Crip set. Earlier that day, Kody had graduated from the sixth grade of his 54th-Street Elementary School. It would be his last graduation; Kody now had other activities to keep him busy, a new "moral obligation" to smoke pot and drink beer, to submit to beatings, to stand guard with a .38 revolver as older gangsters stole a car, and, finally, to end lives with rounds from a 12-gauge shotgun.

The Eight Trays, like other gang sets, had their own turf, explains Scott. Depending on which groups they perceived as rivals in their area, the Eight Trays could as easily declare war on other Crip gangs as on their traditional enemies, the largely hispanic Bloods. Sometimes the Eight Trays preferred to attack strangers instead of rival gangsters. As Scott recalls: *When I was thirteen, while robbing a man . . . I was hit in the face . . . I stomped him for twenty minutes before leaving him unconscious in an alley. [Later], police told bystanders that the person responsible for this was a "monster." The name stuck, and I took that as a moniker over my birth name.*

Through the late seventies Scott worked on living up to his new name. By "putting in

much work and dropping many bodies," he rose from "little homie" to "homie" (for "home-boy"), and now he longed to be an O.G.—an "Original Gangster." Becoming an O.G. meant first building a reputation within your particular set and then establishing yourself as "a promoter of Crip or Blood, depending, of course, on which side of the color bar you live."

By the fall of 1980, a war between the Eight Trays and its rival Blood gang the Rollin' Sixties was in full swing. This clash set a precedent for future gang relations: *[The two gangs] became . . . superpowers not unlike the former Soviet Union and the United States. . . . Our war, like most gang wars, was not fought for territory or any specific goal other than the destruction of individuals, of human beings. Points were scored when individuals with prestige were hit.*

It was in this climate that sixteen-year-old Scott finally found himself charged with murder. One day, after surviving two drive-by shooting attempts, he had decided to take revenge. Dressed in combat black, he picked up his sawed-off, double-barrel shotgun, jumped on his brother's bike, and made his way to Horace Mann Junior High, the gathering-place of the Sixties. Ditching the bike, he stole across the schoolgrounds, quickly fired two rounds of buckshot into the crowd, then beat a hasty retreat. Safely home, he turned on the TV and watched The Benny Hill Show.

On his way to a party the next night, Scott was arrested by two undercover cops. "You cannot keep going around killing people and leaving witnesses," one of them told him.

Two days later, Scott's mother came to see him: "Kody, what has happened to you?" she asked. "What is wrong?" Sobbing uncontrollably, the boy could only answer, "I don't know."

But there was, in fact, one thing Kody *did* know: he enjoyed being a Crip. . . . *The total lawlessness was alluring, and . . . the sense of importance, self-worth, and raw power was exciting, stimulating, and intoxicating beyond any other high on this planet.*

Scott's addiction to gang life was not unique. As he notes: *Per year, gangs in South Central recruit more people than the four branches of the U.S. Armed Forces do. Crack dealers employ more people in South Central than AT&T, IBM, and Xerox combined.* And as each new generation of "bangers" has brought a greater level of complexity to the organizations, gang recruitment has accelerated. In fact, Monster says: *. . . The notion of the "war on gangs" being successful is as realistic as the People's Republic of China telling Americans to stop being American. When gang members stop their wars and find that there is no longer a need for their sets to exist, banging will cease. But until then, all attempts by law enforcement to seriously curtail its forward motion will be in vain.*

Scott's "gangbanging" certainly didn't stop when the District Attorney declined to prosecute his case and he was released from jail. Motivated by news that the Sixties had raided an Army surplus store and made off with hundreds of automatic and semi-automatic weapons, he decided to hit a Western Surplus store himself on New Years Eve: *A weapon in South Central is a part of your attire, a dress code. "This gun goes with these pants and this shirt," or "I can put this weapon here with this outfit and still be chic."*

As Scott, unarmed, approached the store's entrance, three strangers suddenly appeared. "Ain't you Monster Kody?" one said. "Yeah," he answered, "I'm Monster Kody, Eight Tray Gangsters, what's up?" In response, the men opened fire. The first bullet entered Scott's stomach with such force that he was knocked up against the wall; the second hit him in the hand as he reached to deflect the third, which had been aimed at his heart. Turning to run, he was shot twice in the back; then, as the bullets slammed him into the ground, his attackers charged forward, firing into him at close range as he raised his legs to protect his torso.

After regaining consciousness in a hospital bed, Scott decided that he had come of age. At 16, he had already been banging for five years, and he actually thought of himself as well into his mid-twenties. "I recognized early that where I lived, we grew and died in dog years," he later wrote. "Actually, some dogs outlived us . . . "

Shortly after his release from the hospital, Scott was finally arraigned on charges of murder and attempted murder. He was subsequently held in L.A. County Jail's juvenile division, which he decries as "the most blatant exercise the state has ever devised for corrupting, institutionalizing and creating recidivism in youths . . . "

Nevertheless, Scott's conception of jail was not entirely negative: *Those in . . . foster homes . . . looked up to those in juvenile hall, those in juvenile hall looked up to those in . . . Youth Authority, and those [in Youth Authority] looked up to those in prison . . .* Now he was a "righteous . . . stone cold" criminal; he had finally achieved the status of O.G. In his own mind, at least, he was a star.

At his trial, the jury, judging a lack of hard evidence, found Kody Scott not guilty on all charges. Soon he was back on the street "needing to shoot somebody," tracking down the rivals who had testified against him. Unexpectedly, he received help from the police, who had apparently decided that providing information about gangs to their rivals would help thin their ranks, as the troublemakers annihilated one another. So, following police tips, Scott quickly met up with—and killed—the Blood who had betrayed him.

Scott was not apprehended for this shooting. In July of 1981, however, he found himself convicted and sentenced to four years in Juvenile Training School—ironically, all for a robbery he had not committed. It was in Juvenile that Scott learned how to intimidate other prisoners. But he also came into contact with members of the Consolidated Crip Organization or C.C.O., a group who taught a new order of peace among blacks, African pride, and self-esteem. Its "New Afrikans" spoke to each other in *Kiswahili*, a quasi-African vernacular. They were "upright, respectful, physically fit and mentally sharp. They were socially conscious . . . but weren't Muslims." The C.C.O. had ruled that "CRIPS" meant "Clandestine Revolutionary International Party Soldiers" and that its leaders were subversives working to destroy the African heritage of the gangbangers.

"Monsta, you've done too much damage to the Crip Nation," a C.C.O. leader told Scott one day. "We can't let you continue to kill our citizens. Either you hook up or you must be destroyed." Of course, Scott joined.

In prison, Scott, now a full-fledged C.C.O. ally, passed ample time in solitary for various infractions. In 1985, after striking a guard, he was put in maximum security, received an additional seven years, then transferred to Fulsome State Prison and, later, to Soledad. After seven "Americans" (white prisoners) there were stabbed and shot, he was sent to San Quentin, where the C.C.O. eventually was disbanded.

Having spent thirteen years of his young life behind bars, Scott was finally becoming disenchanted with the banger mentality. Tired of the gangs' insatiable appetite for destruction, he resolved to break away from the Crips—a long process, and "something, which in banging, is tantamount to treason." Then, before his parole, he attended electronics classes, worked as a clerk, and developed an interest in writing.

Once he was paroled in November of 1988, Kody Scott reestablished ties with his family and began work as a file clerk. Having fathered a child, he accepted his role as a father, working in the city on weekdays and commuting to his home outside L.A. on weekends. In time he broke all ties with his set.

In 1991, however, Scott was arrested for assault and grand theft after beating a crack dealer who had refused to stop selling in his neighborhood—a fact which the court chose to dismiss. But by then his attitude had changed: *I make no excuses . . . Because of my terrible record, I faced a sentence of seven years. I eventually pleaded guilty and received seven years.*

He will be paroled in the year 1995.

❖ ◆ ❖

At the time of his book's printing, Kody Scott—deemed a threat to "institutional security"—was in his third year of solitary confinement. He has expressed a "dedication" to finding the means to end gang warfare, concluding: *. . . Time is of the essence, and every thinking person with a stake in life—especially those involved in the fighting—should put forth an effort . . . to deal with this tragedy.*

CHILD ABUSE

An American Epidemic
by Elaine Landau, Simon and Schuster, Inc., Englewood Cliffs, N.J., 1990

Elaine Landau's *Child Abuse: An American Epidemic* explores abuse in contemporary American families. Landau describes how abuse occurs, manifests itself, and increases in troubled homes. Although our society has often failed young abuse victims, Landau explains what some are doing to reverse the frightening trend of domestic violence and neglect.

⋄ ♦ ⋄

Kevin, his "arms and legs visibly discolored with bruises . . . was not a stranger to pain." During numerous visits to the doctor his parents had insisted that his injuries resulted from falls. Although Kevin's grandmother had confronted his parents and reported the situation to local child-protection agencies, Kevin's father, a practicing attorney in upstate New York, persisted in harshly disciplining his son.

To the boy's delight, "on Kevin's third birthday, his grandmother took him out to celebrate." As he ate his dessert, however, "the waitress was horrified to see blood leaking from the toddler's mouth." This birthday would be Kevin's last. When his father came home that night, he brushed past his wife and headed for Kevin's bedroom. Seconds later, several "thumping" sounds were heard. "Kevin didn't live through the night. His father had kicked him to death."

In thousands of homes across America, similar, horrifying stories are repeated. Abusive parents often seek medical treatment for their children only in life-threatening situations, or when their abuse might be "found out." Those who take their children in for treatment frequently change doctors and hospitals to avoid "embarrassing" questions. Nevertheless, X-rays normally reveal the truth of how their children were injured.

It often seems that only news at the most sensational levels of child abuse reaches the public. "Stories of babies left to die in garbage cans, incinerators and subway stations" are those that, regrettably, are most quickly snapped up by the media. But we need to become aware of the quiet pervasiveness of abuse.

Sadly, there are many ways to neglect or inflict harm on a child, including:

- Failure to give adequate food, sanitation, or clothing
- Disregard or disdain of educational, medical or emotional needs
- Inadequate supervision (statistically, the deadliest of all forms of abuse)

PHYSICAL ABUSE

Child abuse occurs for a number of "reasons." One common notion perpetuating abuse—a premise first challenged in 1874 by Henry Bergh—is that parents "own" their children. Bergh, founder of the American Society for the Prevention of Cruelty to Animals (ASPCA), was searching for wounded and abused animals one day in New York when he heard screams from a nearby apartment. He entered to find "a ten-year-old girl . . . being repeatedly stabbed by her parents, who

thought she was a witch." At that time, there were no legal means of having the child removed from the home; it was assumed—and often still is—that children don't need protection from their parents. Tragically, this notion is often reinforced by the common belief reported by attorney and child advocate Donald Bross that "government shouldn't meddle in people's lives by telling them how to raise their children."

Other factors which contribute to child abuse include:

- **Substance abuse:** "The National Committee for the Prevention of Child Abuse estimates that at least 40 percent of all abuse cases involve a parent's use of alcohol or drugs."

- **Spousal abuse:** According to a recent issue of *People Weekly* magazine, "In 30-40 percent of child-abuse cases, the wife was also a victim of abuse." And *Newsweek* reports that "Children from abusive homes are six times more likely to become abusive parents than are those from 'normal' homes."

- **A general lack of parenting skills:** Parents are often poorly educated to deal with the everyday problems that arise in families.

Although experts postulate that poverty increases the likelihood of abuse, there is no evidence to support this position. In fact, the National Committee for the Prevention of Child Abuse reports numerous instances of abuse from well-to-do, well-educated families.

EMOTIONAL ABUSE

Physical scars and broken bones can heal, but emotional scars last a lifetime, and may go untreated for many years because they are unseen.

The 250,000 cases of emotional abuse reported each year clearly cut across racial, ethnic and economic lines. Like physical abuse, emotional abuse is often generational: abusers mirror their own parents' techniques for dealing with their children. Until they learn more effective ways to handle their own stress, the pattern will be passed down the line indefinitely from parent to child.

Emotional abuse may take the form of name-calling, labeling, ignoring of positive behavior, neglecting psychological needs, or exploiting of the child for the parent's own gratification. Exploitation, for instance, may take place in homes where sick or disabled parents place their children in "caretaker" roles that rob them of normal, rewarding childhood activities. Forced to accept such heavy responsibilities, children often become "pleasers," unable to give or receive unconditional love.

SEXUAL ABUSE

From the time Cheryl was eleven, she had been sexually assaulted by her 240-pound father. On those occasions when she attempted to resist, he threatened to harm her younger sisters.

Then one day in school, Cheryl and a classmate came upon a newspaper article about an abused wife who had hired someone to kill her husband. Three months later Cheryl's classmate shot and killed her father as he left for work. Both classmates were subsequently found guilty of manslaughter. "This is not a place I want to be in," Cheryl lamented as she served out her term in a correctional center, "but nothing could compare with what I went through. I just couldn't see another way out."

A sexually abusive family may appear, on first glance, "normal," or even extraordinary; behind closed doors, however, a destructive pattern prevails, a pattern often encompassing repeated instances of male domination, wife-beating, restrictions on a daughter's outside activities, and alcohol or drug abuse by incestuous fathers. Parental unemployment—and related decline in self-esteem—also seems to trigger abuse: studies done in a typical Chicago neighborhood showed that "sexual abuse rose and fell with the unemployment rate."

Why don't mothers come to the aid of their traumatized daughters? Many do, but others are too economically or emotionally dependent to confront their husbands. Tragically, they often "side" with their mates, leaving their children to deal with feelings that they are to blame for what is happening to them. Of course, sometimes mothers are also guilty of sexually abusing their children.

A parent's power usually prevents children from feeling "in control." Fearful of being abandoned or rejected, children readily obey, and in sexually abusive families obedience spawns ever increasing feelings of guilt, fear and shame. For girls, incestuous relationships often end during their teenage years. Still, during this time fathers may become more possessive, placing ever greater restrictions on their daughters' lives. Profoundly angry and depressed, daughters typically leave home or, ideally, seek help.

THE EFFECTS OF ABUSE

Young children who are the victims of abuse often evoke the sympathy of adults, while adolescents—whose anti-social behavior often provokes the opposite reaction—are frequently viewed as "deserving of what happened to them." Adolescents, however, are often as unable as children to extricate themselves from destructive relationships.

Regardless of a victim's age, the potential consequences of abuse are many and varied: Physical, emotional and mental impairment; paralyzing fear of separation from the parent; impaired personal development; feelings of guilt and shame; severing of family ties; bed-wetting problems or chronic insomnia; low self-esteem; hostility and other disruptive and anti-social behaviors; a sense of desperation or unresolved anger; involvement in gangs, drugs, prostitution and/or crime; a pathological uncertainty about self and the world; either a profound lack of empathy for others, or an excessive vulnerability to the pain others feel; extreme dependence on friends or an exaggerated "search for love"; hopelessness; and suicidal and/or homicidal impulses.

FINDING SOLUTIONS

In 1971, Faye Yager claimed that she "saw her ex-husband, Roger Jones, molest their 18-month-old daughter." Yager sued for full custody of their daughter. The jury, however, awarded custody to the father. In desperation, Yager fled with her daughter. Then a few months later she discovered that her daughter had contracted gonorrhea, and, convinced that this medical evidence would prove her case, she returned to court. Instead of gaining custody of her daughter, Yager was jailed for defying the court's first order: "Custody was awarded to her husband's parents and Roger Jones was granted continued access to his daughter."

Yager subsequently became the director of Mothers Against Raping Children, a national organization assisting mothers and children "on the run." Increasingly mothers, frustrated by the justice system, have gone "underground"—giving up homes, friends, jobs, and support payments to escape an abuser.

Many psychologists and child advocates, however, stress that hiding a child may only aggravate an already difficult situation. Although children forced to live as "fugitives" may develop psychological disorders and social alienation, many mothers firmly believe that protecting their children from further sexual abuse is their first priority.

Clearly, neglected and abused children live in desperation. They often suffer silently, too afraid or ashamed to seek help. In response to this national tragedy, legislation has been enacted to provide better protection:

- *The Child Abuse Prevention Act of 1974*, Promotes research and provides information on the prevention of child abuse.

- *The Adoption Assistance and Child Welfare Act of 1980*. Requires states to offer support services to families before removing a child from the home. If removal is necessary, a specific plan for the child, while in foster care, must be established and reviewed every six months.

- *Reporting laws*. By law, professionals working with children must report suspected child abuse and neglect.

- *The Child Protection Act of 1984*. Raised the age limit in child pornography cases from 16 to 18. The act also increased fines for offenders and specified that sexually explicit pictures of children constitute pornography.

- *The Child Support Enforcement Act Amendments of 1984*. Required states to withhold wages from parents who are delinquent in child-support payments.

Although hampered by inadequate funding, these laws have begun to effect changes in law-enforcement personnel, school staff and resources, child-welfare bureaus and mental-health agencies. When these agencies work together, children in need are more likely to receive treatment.

Landau stresses that government agencies are only a second-line defense: child-abuse prevention is *everyone's* responsibility. Children are not "property" but beings worthy of life, love, and the fulfillment of hopes and dreams. One person's involvement *can* make a difference; intervention by someone outside the child's family may be the only hope for an abused child. Every few seconds, Landau reminds us, "a child is being hurt. . . . That child's tears will not stop until our society is transformed into one in which all young people can grow up free of the fear . . . "

ADDICTION

by Gilda Berger, Franklin Watts, New York, N.Y., 1992

A 25-year-old man steals to get his daily fix of heroin; a business executive must have a cup of coffee as a jump-start for the day; a teenager cannot give up "crack," even though it killed his best friend; a teacher secretly gulps shots of whiskey between classes; a TV star must snort cocaine in order to perform; a young mother takes pills to sleep—and then pills to wake her up again. Each case is different, but each is a case of addiction, the subject of Gilda Berger's book.

The term *addiction* is derived from the Latin word *addicere*, which means "surrender . . . or give oneself up to something." Addiction also implies two additional characteristics: 1) a degree of physical *tolerance*, in which the body develops an increased need for a particular substance; and 2) *withdrawal*, or actual pain or discomfort if the substance is abandoned.

A substance may be categorized as either *illicit* (illegal) or *licit* (legal). "All told, there are about one hundred separate illicit substances subject to abuse." These substances are divided into five major groups: *narcotics, depressants, stimulants, hallucinogens* and *cannabis* (marijuana).

Licit substances are easier to come by and are generally accepted by most of society. Nevertheless, many of these substances, which include *inhalants, alcohol, nicotine,* and, to a much lesser extent, *caffeine*—and even *food,* when ingested to the extreme or used improperly—can be very damaging.

The author's exhaustive research clearly points to the seriousness of addiction in America today:

- 72.5 million Americans have used illicit drugs one or more times.
- 57 million Americans are hooked on cigarettes.
- 18 million are addicted to or abuse alcohol.
- 21 million have tried cocaine, and over one million are hooked on cocaine or heroin.
- 7 million smoke marijuana at least once a week.
- 10 million abuse tranquilizers and other psychotherapeutic drugs.
- 1 million regularly use hallucinogenic substances.
- 80 percent of AIDS cases are the result of intravenous drug abuse or of sexual contact with intravenous drug abusers.
- Over 5 million women of child-bearing age are current users of illicit drugs; and one of every ten babies born in the U.S. is exposed to potentially harmful drugs in the womb.
- A recent study among adolescents ages 12 to 17 showed a 39-percent increase in the prevalence of obesity and a 64-percent increase in "super-obesity."

Despite extensive research, Dr. Alan Lang of Florida State University insists that "there is no single characteristic or constellation of traits that is inevitably associated with addiction." Nevertheless, Berger is able to submit a report which suggests that "the reason most addicts give for starting substance abuse is social." At one time, the prevailing notion was that "only people on the fringes of society abused substances. Now most agree that . . . addiction permeates the total of society." Factors that contribute to this widespread addiction include: (1) easy availability of drugs; (2) limited access to educational and occupational opportunities; and (3) influence of family members or peers who use drugs.

ILLEGAL SUBSTANCES OF ABUSE

Narcotics: Most narcotics are derived from poppy seeds. As early as 6500 years ago Egyptian physicians used opium to kill pain, relieve anxiety, and give pleasure. In the nineteenth century, morphine was first extracted from opium, and became the "wonder drug" of choice for wounded Civil War soldiers. However, throughout history "little attention was paid to the addiction problem."

Heroin was first touted in 1898 as a safe alternative to morphine. Although use spread quickly, by the early 1900s society became aware that heroin was two to three times more addictive than morphine.

Depressants: Millions of people of all ages use—and abuse—depressants (barbiturates, quaaludes, tranquilizers) to attain a calm, relaxed feeling. Depressants affect the "thinking" part of the brain as well as the central nervous system. Tolerance is quickly reached, and gradually leads to dependence and often death, unless the user chooses to withdraw.

In the 1940s a campaign against prescribing barbiturates resulted in the fabrication of tranquilizers (Valium and Librium)—which were more readily accepted by the medical community, yet can be just as addictive.

Stimulants: Stimulants generate an increase in energy, alertness, and euphoria. Cocaine, a derivative of the coca plant and once considered a "wonder drug," is the most powerful of the natural stimulants. Crack, a purified form of cocaine, is an especially strong drug that can hook the user after only one use.

Drug counselors consider amphetamines, or speed, to be one of the most dangerous of all abused drugs. Like cocaine, speed is used to maintain alertness. Because it suppresses the appetite, however, it may result in serious undernourishment. Also prevalent among users of speed are sleep disorders and discordant behaviors from violence to severe depression or paranoia.

Hallucinogens: The group of mind-altering drugs known as hallucinogens "work on the brain and nervous system to bring about changes in thought, self-awareness, emotion and sensation." They distort the senses and trigger hallucinations. Some can literally cause the "violent side of a person to take over the whole person." Flashbacks may occur even when the drug is not being actively plied. Long-term effects range from depression to psychoses.

Cannabis: The last and most widespread of the illegal drugs is marijuana and hashish, made from the hemp plant *cannabis sativa*. Marijuana grows freely worldwide in both hot and temperate climates. In the U.S. during the '60s and '70s, it quickly became a "source of identity among people with a common point of view; namely that parents were stupid, government immoral, and the war in Vietnam—wrong."

The 400-plus chemicals in "pot" work together to produce a dream-like state. Although physical dependence is *not* likely, the use of cannabis in any form can lead to psychological and emotional addiction.

TREATMENT

Cal is a typical example of the user's approach to treatment. He entered a hospital confessing, "I'm hooked on smack . . . pot, and I drink until I am completely wasted." The hospital assigned Cal to a drug treatment team, who prescribed medications to ease withdrawal and enlisted him in group therapy. Feeling "cured" after the first week, Cal left the clinic against medical advice, only to return three months later, hooked again.

Addiction was once considered a "personal matter," but today it is not only an illness that requires professional intervention by a doctor but a *societal crisis* that deserves society's attention. Thus, drug interventionists handle addiction in a more direct, team-oriented manner. Programs, facilities and staffs band together to fight both the individual cases of addiction they run across *and* the spread of addiction in society by initiating and overseeing public service and community programs.

"Detoxification" is a "cold turkey" approach of ridding the body of poisons. Prescription drugs are used to help "ease anxiety and physical pain during withdrawal . . . " The success rate is low, however, and the average "detox" addict is back on drugs within eight days.

"Maintenance" programs employ a synthetic narcotic named Methadone to gradually wean users from drugs. Though Methadone is cheap, easily accessible, and allows the individual to function well between doses, the drug itself is addictive, and can induce unpleasant side effects.

Non-drug therapies are perhaps most effective in the long run, says Berger. Support groups such as Alcoholics Anonymous and Narcotics Anonymous emphasize drug abstinence and behavioral modification. Addicts are given an opportunity to share common experiences in therapeutic group sessions, and clients help each other "come out from behind their defenses." Such programs have a long-term success rate of fifty percent, and are currently considered the "best single solution."

Other non-drug programs help addicts ease back into society by providing much-needed financial, educational and employment assistance.

LEGAL SUBSTANCES OF ABUSE

Inhalants: Typically used by the younger generation, inhalants (including glue, nail polish remover, and spray paint) are relatively cheap, accessible, and "legal" substances which produce a short-term effect similar to alcohol. Even so-called "moderate" use can disrupt young lives, impede psychological development, lead to family problems, and promote delinquency. Long-term use damages liver, kidneys, bone marrow, brain cells, and may result in death.
Alcohol: Alcoholism and alcohol-related tragedy (traffic fatalities, liver disease, etc.) are the nation's number one cause of death. Alcohol, produced by fermenting the sugar in fruits and grains, has long been used for recreational and religious purposes and is still the legal "drug of choice" in the United

States for young and old alike. And because of its widespread use, Berger and most other experts deem it the most persistent problem in the country. Alcohol is also "the drug most commonly abused with illicit drugs."
Smoking: Nicotine, a colorless oil with a sharp taste, is the most active ingredient in tobacco. Taken alone, a tiny 70-milligram drop can kill a human being. It is extremely addictive, with "tolerance increasing with each cigarette." Smoking women endanger their unborn children, and second-hand smoke produces harmful effects on non-smokers. But with appropriate treatment, "ninety percent of those who do not smoke after a year will not resume . . . As a rule of thumb, anyone who has not smoked for two years is considered cured of nicotine dependency."
Caffeine: Coffee, Colas and Tea: How often do you say or hear, "I can't get through this morning's staff meeting without coffee!"

"Caffeine, widely used in society, is found in almost every popular beverage. An average person drinks about 34 gallons of soda and 28 gallons of coffee a year." The mild stimulant, which speeds up the central nervous system and makes the user feel more "alert and active," is also present in chocolate, cough and cold remedies, and over-the-counter drugs. Physical effects of caffeine are confusing: it opens blood vessels in the skin, while closing them in the brain (often leading to headache); small amounts raise body temperature, while higher amounts lower it. "Regular use seems to develop a tolerance in some users, but rarely does anyone die of an overdose . . . "

"Although far milder than any other drug," Berger adds, "caffeine is addictive," and can be used to the point where it exacerbates health problems and disrupts behavior.
Food Addiction: Food, too, is commonly abused as a substitute for love, pleasure, enjoyment, comfort and friendship. "Overeating differs from other forms of abuse in that there is no evidence of tolerance and physical withdrawal is nothing more than hunger pains, [although] psychological withdrawal varies from person to person. . . . Obviously, it is not possible to 'kick' the habit and never eat again."

Hypnosis has proven a successful treatment for weight loss as well as other eating disorders (i.e. *anorexia nervosa*—self-imposed starvation—and *bulimia*—a cycle of overeating and purging of food). Weight-loss victims—those caught up in the yo-yo syndrome (weight-loss, then gaining more back than lost), for example—are treated against subconscious difficulties and provided with inner strength to fight the addiction. Organizations such as Weight Watchers and Overeaters Anonymous use group therapy, nutritional education, and emotional support to help people adapt to a "new self-image."

❖ ♦ ❖

The fight against substance abuse is one that must be waged at all levels of government and society, for addiction, Berger warns, "has reached epidemic proportions in the United States today, cutting across almost all social, ethnic, and economic barriers . . . Addiction costs the nation over $300 billion a year"—not to mention the tragic cost in failed relationships, physical and emotional suffering, and lost lives.

TELL THEM WHO I AM

The Lives of Homeless Women
by Elliot Liebow, The Free Press Division of MacMillan, Inc., New York, N.Y., 1993

In his book *Tell Them Who I Am*, Elliot Liebow artfully explores a hidden niche of American society: that of homeless women. Through the words of these women and through Liebow's insights, readers are presented with a portrait of daily life among these "outcasts" that will forever change the way the homeless are viewed in America.

The genesis of the book is as momentous as its subject. When Liebow learned in 1984 that he had terminal cancer and a short life expectancy, he quit his job as an anthropologist with the National Institute of Mental Health and began working as a volunteer at soup kitchens and homeless shelters in and around Washington D.C. In a suburb of the city, he found the *Refuge*, a woman's shelter: "Almost immediately, I found myself enjoying the company of the women. I was awed by the enormous effort that most of them made to secure the most elementary necessities and decencies of life that the rest of us take for granted."

Soon he was visiting the shelter four or five nights a week. Perhaps because of his training, with the women's permission he started taking notes of their conversations. He didn't treat them as research subjects, but as friends—and that's what many of them became.

❖ ♦ ❖

"It is, perhaps, all too easy to fall into homelessness," Liebow notes, "but being there is not easy at all. Just surviving is a constant struggle; retaining your humanity in inhuman conditions is even harder . . . "

For many homeless women, the daily travail begins with getting enough rest. In the shelters they sleep in one big room, tossing and turning amid an endless cacophony: coughing, sneezing, wheezing, retching, snoring, mumbling, and people getting up to go to the bathroom. At 5:30 AM they are roused, then turned out onto the streets by 7:00. This happens every day of the week, every morning of the year.

Being turned out so early contributes to a problem that's most destructive to those on the streets: boredom. For most of the women this is high on their list of hardships. "I walk the streets," said Betty, a bright, distinguished-looking alcoholic in her mid-fifties. "Twelve hours and 15 minutes a day, every day, I walk the streets. Is that what I got sober for?" For Sara, another of Liebow's acquaintances, leaving the shelter is the worst part of the day, in that it brings home the fact that no one needs you, no one wants you, no one cares about you—and . . . you have nowhere to go.

With so much time to kill, the homeless either work at "filling time" or making it more bearable. They might frequent the library, but they are not allowed to sleep there. And they don't dare sleep on park benches for fear someone will steal their belongings.

A routine appointment with a doctor or case worker—or any human contact, for that matter—is relished and given a lot of attention for several days beforehand. "Thus," Liebow recalls in his book, "what often seemed to be procrastination or laziness or exasperating inefficiency to those looking in from the outside may well have been, from the women's point of view, an attempt to distribute structure and meaning over as many days as possible."

It is easy to think of homeless people as having no possessions, but one of the most talked about predicaments among Liebow's group was caring for one's "things." Most tote around with them a bundle filled with all their belongings: clothes, an emergency supply of food, essential medicines and toiletries, and the personal documents that identify them and qualify them for public assistance. More important, however, are the personal items, like family photos, Bibles or other inspirational material, tokens of some treasured time in their past. And it is these possessions in particular to which they so fiercely cling: "To lose one's stuff, or to have to jettison some of it, was to lose connections to one's past if not the past itself."

Protecting these treasures consumes a large part of a homeless person's energy and resources. As the reality of her situation gradually sinks in, she may go to great lengths to store possessions, using money that could better be used for subsistence to rent a storage garage. When she inevitably falls behind in her payments, often her most precious belongings are put up for auction.

After two failed marriages and four times as many failed jobs, Shirley, now on the streets, had fought to keep her valuables from being auctioned off. Finally, when she missed another deadline, Liebow drove her to the storage facility. As Shirley had suspected, her things had been put up for sale—but they were safe, because no one would pay even five dollars for what she was paying $42.50 a month to store!

Another serious problem that homeless women suffer is poor health. While health care is usually available for emergencies or critical disabilities, minor illnesses that normally would respond within a day or two to proper medication can linger on for weeks or months, sometimes becoming life-threatening. When a homeless woman does receive medical help, the doctor often says, "Spend the next few days in bed."

In addition to basic problems of survival, homeless women commonly endure hundreds of persistent annoyances: not having access to a toilet on Sunday mornings or holidays; sexual harassment on the streets; and finding a place to stay during cold or bad weather. The blend of these day-to-day irritants has the power to drain homeless women, leaving them with insufficient strength to go on. But most push on, seeking a job or some other method of bonding with the outside world.

"For most of [them], jobs are a principal source of both independence and connectedness to others," Liebow writes. "It should come as no surprise that, in the work force or out, work and jobs are important themes in the lives of homeless women." A job is not only a way out of the shelters but it provides pocket money, expands self esteem, and establishes a work history. Unfortunately, however, homeless women are often kept out of the work force by something as simple as the lack of a phone: prospective employers and agencies can't call them for a job interview. The lack of a phone also signals to employers that the applicant is homeless—definitely *not* a plus. Moreover, once a homeless woman has secured a job, maintaining her personal appearance becomes a struggle, if not a losing battle.

A homeless woman's employment problems do not end there. Better paying jobs frequently are not in reach of public transportation. She may also feel both socially unfit to compete for the better jobs and inadequate to perform their tasks well, even when equipped with the skills to succeed. All these factors combine to keep the women in low-paying jobs; thus, public assistance becomes both a more comfortable and more lucrative alternative.

There are essentially three ways for a woman to free herself from the constraints of the shelter: (1) she works two jobs, (2) she finds a job as a live-in housekeeper or baby sitter, or (3) she sticks with her low-paying job in hopes of qualifying for public housing assistance. Following one of these paths, some women do find their way out of homelessness. Others find their way out and then fall back into the poverty pit.

In terms of families, Liebow found that some homeless women do maintain regular contact with living children and/or parents. The contact, however, is usually strained at best. For instance, one 44-year-old shelter resident named Grace, the product of abusive parents, had all her assets taken away from her by her husband. Still, she tries to be a "mother-at-a-distance," calling her children regularly.

Similarly, relationships with parents are often troubled. The worst cases are the women who have been officially classified as retarded or learning disabled. While Liebow expresses sympathy toward those parents who are unable to personally deal with their handicapped children, he condemns those who keep all or most of the government Supplemental Security Income they receive and then turn their daughters out on the streets. Judy, a heavy-set, slightly retarded and mentally disturbed young woman, is a case in point. Her parents routinely begged her to come home, but heaped so many restrictions on her that she would always refuse.

In most cases homeless women came from families who lacked the resources to deal with each other, and, either consciously or subconsciously, forced the weakest one out. In spite of such painful experiences—and in spite of families often being as much a source of pain

as of comfort and support—the women Liebow met often seemed to derive some strength from their families, even if it was from remembering past good times rather than current realities.

Communication with husbands and ex-husbands is almost non-existent. In fact, recalls Liebow, the women didn't talk much about spouses, probably because the memories were too painful. Some homeless women initially came to the shelters to escape abuse; others were abandoned outright. Dulcie's case is not atypical: after 29 years of marriage, her husband went back East to be with his mother when his father died—and he never returned.

There are, of course, homeless couples and entire families who wander the streets during the day and hole up in vacant buildings or bed down in separate shelters at night, not knowing or expecting any other kind of life.

Support in the shelters varies according to facilities and staff. "Some shelters are terrible places," Liebow emphasizes, "[while] some are as nice as one can reasonably expect a shelter to be. [But] even under the best of circumstances, there is a coarseness, a rudeness, even a brutishness to life in the shelters and on the street." This harsh manner seems to rub off on those who run the shelters, and plays a significant role in the fear that staff and volunteers have of violence from the homeless. On the other hand, the homeless fear the powers of the staff to reduce their meager privileges. As a result, an ever-present circle of anxiety filters through the shelters.

Different shelters emit different moods, depending on whether the main staff consists of professionals or volunteers. Professional social workers seem to be continually trying to change the homeless and provide them with the skills to improve their situation, while volunteers tend to be content with trying to provide a safe refuge for the night—both important emphases. Liebow witnessed some incredible acts of compassion and love by various staff members. However, he found that the thing that bothered the homeless women most was the continual questioning they received from the professionals. As they saw it, the questions were just one more example of a "crazy" bureaucracy.

The homeless bear great difficulties, but they also receive a significant amount of support, says Liebow. That support, however, for the most part, does not come from outsiders, but from two other sources: from other homeless individuals and from their relationship with God. "They [turn] to God for hope and a sense of self-worth and to give their lives meaning; and they [turn] to themselves for the strength to keep going, day in and day out, even when, for the moment, their friends and God [fail] them."

Liebow concludes that homelessness in America is a national shame. "Shame on you, shame on me, shame on America," he writes. "Shame because it is the result of choices we have made; shame because it does not have to be."

THE ENIGMA OF SUICIDE

by George Howe Colt, Summit Books, New York, N.Y., 1991

George Howe Colt's lucid and compassionate analysis of suicide began as an article for *Harvard Magazine*. He explains that the purpose of his book is "to chip away at some of the cultural barriers our society erects between 'normal' . . . and 'suicidal' people—barriers that . . . we erect from the fear that the difference is so slight."

In *The Enigma of Suicide*, Colt explores various "ethical, philosophical, biological, [and] cultural" perspectives on suicide and presents revealing case studies of victims and survivors in the United States.

Adolescent Suicide

During the past three decades the rate of adolescent suicide has nearly tripled; the trend has bred a national crisis. Which young people are most at risk for suicide? Three times as many males as females commit suicide, Colt reports, "and the rate rises with age." According to statisticians, *One of every seven suicides in 1984 was a male between the ages of fifteen and twenty-four. Blacks of both sexes, young and old, commit suicide less frequently than whites, but the suicide rate of young black males has more than doubled in the last twenty-five years. Native Americans may have the highest adolescent suicide rate of any group.*

Although the majority of suicidal adolescents are *not* mentally ill, most have "had clearly discernable and long-standing difficulties." Researchers have isolated various factors more common to the lives of adolescent suicide victims than to those of other teenagers. Surprisingly, although depression often accompanies suicidal thoughts, the most common risk factors among teens include:

- "loss of a parent through divorce, death or desertion,"
- "constant parental quarreling," and
- "physical or emotional abuse."

Many suicidal adolescents reveal their intentions by "giving away prized possessions" or by speaking directly or indirectly of their own deaths. To help teens to recognize the warning signs of suicide both in themselves and in their friends, many schools now offer suicide prevention programs.

History of Suicide

Throughout history, suicide has provoked sharply divided opinions, depending both on the culture and the era in which it is viewed. In ancient Egypt, for example, religious zealots commonly hurled themselves into the Nile to achieve "blessed immortality." Similarly, in feudal Japan a samurai who committed *hari-kari* "would have been praised as a man of principle." For the most part, however, suicide victims were reviled, their bodies often horribly mutilated, their possessions awarded to the state, and their families ostracized. It wasn't until the early seventeenth century that Europeans began to soften their views, due in large part to writers such as Richard Burton, John Donne, and William Shakespeare, who "managed to humanize suicide, showing it as an object of sympathy."

The Range of Self Destructive Behavior

"No one ever lacks a good reason for suicide," the Italian writer Cesare Pavese once noted. According to suicidologist Edwin Shneidman, killing oneself "is an attempt to solve a problem." Commonly the problem involves some sort of *loss:* loss of a loved one, "loss of status, career or power," or the "loss of sanity—or fear of its loss." Conversely, those recovering from mental illness may commit suicide because they fear "getting well." Success can trigger people with unusually low self-esteem to take their lives "shortly *after* something wonderful has happened or some long-sought goal has been attained." Paradoxically, then, *gain* can be as strong a motivating factor in suicide as loss.

The method of taking one's life "depends on race, sex, occupation, availability, psychology, and, to some extent, fashion." In ancient Rome, for instance, "chic suicides fell on swords or opened the veins in a warm bath," while hanging was considered tasteless—a view that persisted at least into the eighteenth century. Responding to the hanging of a friend, a late-18th-century Englishman commented, "What a low-minded wretch to apply the halter. Had he shot himself like a gentleman I could have forgiven him."

In contemporary American society, statistics confirm that suicide methods are related to profession. Ninety percent of policemen who chose to end their lives did so with service revolvers; most doctors—"who commit suicide at three times the rate of the general population"—prefer drugs, while dentists prefer "anesthetic gas." In fact, researchers have found that some of the strangest suicides—occasioned "by swallowing poisonous spiders," "by driving nails or barbecue spits into . . . skulls," or "by injecting [into the bloodstream] paraffin, cooking oil, peanut butter, mercury, deodorant, or mayonnaise"—are job-related.

Prevention

Suicide prevention once seemed a mix of superstition and social hand-slapping. It was not until 1958 when psychologists Edwin Shneidman and Norman Farberow opened the Los Angeles Suicide Center (LASPC)—"a sort of international think tank devoted solely to suicide"—that the idea of suicide prevention became commonplace.

The LASPC introduced and developed the landmark idea "that some suicidal people are at a higher risk than others, and for each person the degree of risk or 'lethality' fluctuates over time." To better understand causative factors in suicide, the LASPC also devised the "psychological autopsy," a procedure that first received national attention after the death of Marilyn Monroe. The work of the LASPC, as well as later research by the National Center for Studies of Suicide Prevention, has demonstrated that *listening* to a potential candidate who is discussing—or threatening—suicide is of utmost importance. "Anyone who talks about suicide is serious," one psychiatrist stresses. "It is not up to us to make a judgment about whether he or she will do it or not."

Unfortunately, however, many therapists are poorly trained to treat suicidal individuals: "Psychiatrists, in fact, score no better than radiologists on tests determining their knowledge of risk factors; other mental health professionals score only slightly higher than college students and the clergy." While "50 to 80 percent of people with mental health problems come first to the clergy," apparently these ministers often feel ill-equipped to handle such problems.

Another distressing facet of suicide prevention concerns "suicide landmarks"—suicide sites which have proved to be powerful magnets for those contemplating taking their own life. The Japanese volcano Mihara-Yama, for instance, has become "the most powerful suicide magnet of all time"; before access to the volcano was closed in 1935, 940 people in a short two-year period had leapt to their deaths, and police had prevented another 1,208 people from doing the same. While "Niagara Falls, the Cathedral at Milan, St. Peter's, the Eiffel Tower, [and] the Empire State Building" have all attracted suicides, none has lured as many as the Golden Gate Bridge, where more than 800 people have jumped to their deaths.

Despite, however, therapeutic incompetence and a plethora of suicide landmarks, many suicidal people do find substantive help through some interventive psychotherapy. As psychiatrist Robert Litman says, "Many, many things together bring a person to suicide, and many, many things together can prevent a suicide." In addition to seeking out professional counseling, effective preventive measures include:

- talking to some trusted friend or family member about ones feelings;
- immersing oneself in some worthwhile, challenging, or self-satisfying endeavor; and
- engaging in some diversion.

The Right to Die

There has been a long controversy around the ethics of keeping terminally ill patients alive. One medical ethicist has openly wondered, "Where can we draw the line between prolonging a patient's life and prolonging his dying?" Because physicians "are trained to regard preservation of life as their highest goal," they may use technology to cause "unintentionally sadistic scenes" in the hospital rooms of their patients. In fact, before he switched off his own ventilator, one patient wrote: "Death is not the enemy, doctor. Inhumanity is."

Of course, some doctors do *allow* their patients to die; still others *practice* euthanasia. Famous heart surgeon Christaan Barnard, for instance, admits to having for years "practiced passive euthanasia"—by such means as leaving potent, life-taking drugs on the tables of terminally ill patients.

Certainly, opposition to euthanasia is enormous. Religious groups cite the sixth Commandment, "Thou shall not kill," while others simply object on the grounds that a cure might be "just around the corner." Other opponents of euthanasia are outraged by the idea that *anyone* has the right to assist in the death of another human being.

Survivors

By all accounts, those individuals who take their own lives sentence their friends and families to years of agony. "Suicide is the cruelest death of all for those who remain," one therapist relates. Although survivors typically spend years in agony, struggling to come to grips with the tragedy and trying to discover what brought about the suicides of their loved ones, they rarely are able to find any comprehensible motives. "Even if there *is* a reason," a therapist explains, "that's never answer enough."

In fact, some experts insist that "survivors never recover from suicide." And, tragically, survivors have been found to be at much higher risk to kill themselves than the general population: "25 percent of seriously suicidal people have a suicide in the family"—a statistic that perhaps points to both a genetic disposition to suicide as well as the terrible constant grief that a survivor suffers.

Although she did not take her own life, Merryl Maleska contemplated killing herself for months after her husband Carl's suicide. Merryl had worked tirelessly to help Carl free himself from depression while he finished his doctoral dissertation. Just as it seemed he was recovering, however, he checked into a YMCA and promptly hung himself. When Merryl learned of his death, she screamed, ran outside, and "threw herself repeatedly on to the space in the driveway where Carl's car had been": *The world suddenly seemed so unnatural and misshapen and wrong and dangerous that the only place that she could be comfortable was between the car and the gravel. If she had her way, she would have stayed there forever, screaming.*

Four years passed before Merryl found the strength to sort through Carl's personal possessions. Finding a picture of him, she spoke softly: "You cared so much about life, you wanted so much from it—why did it go awry for you? . . . Oh, how you hurt me. And how I loved you." Then Merryl whispered, "That was a different life, that was down another path . . . You suffered a lot, Carl . . . But I have to put you away."

CRIME IN AMERICA

by Milton Meltzer, Morrow Junior Books, New York, N.Y., 1990

In *Crime in America*, Milton Meltzer takes a sobering look at a vast spectrum of illegal activities ranging from random street violence to the "clean" white-collar crimes, and from "organized" criminal mobs to corruption in public office. He observes that not only are *all* Americans feeling the effects—direct and indirect—of our swelling crime rate, but that the public is increasingly frustrated and appalled by the labyrinthine ineffectiveness of our criminal justice system. What can be done? There *are* no easy answers. But, says Meltzer, Americans *can* become more aware of what crimes are being perpetrated upon them and more involved in seeing to it that, ultimately, crime does not pay.

No Easy Answers

In every society and century of recorded history, thieves, murderers, rapists, gangsters, and swindlers have plagued the homes, businesses, and streets of towns and cities. And today, crime touches the life of every American, in every walk of life:

- **Street crimes** include robberies, muggings, and burglaries.
- **Organized crime** is the province of professional gangs or "mobs," traditionally dealing in drugs, prostitution, gambling, extortion, and loan-sharking.
- **White-collar crime** includes such infractions as tax evasion, price fixing, embezzlement, and consumer fraud.
- **Corruption in public office** involves such activities as bribes, payoffs, and conflicts of interest at all levels of government.

It is important to realize that no crime is "just a crime": *All crimes are tied together, threads in the fabric of the society we live in . . . Crime has to do with the way we manage our society, run our lives and connect with one another. It has to do with human behavior . . . with personal conscience and social morality.*

Crime Rates: Are They Going Up?

What we know about crime rates comes from three official sources: the Federal Bureau of Investigation (FBI), the United States Justice Department, and the United States Census Bureau. According to official statistics, crime rates, especially in urban areas, have skyrocketed over the past two decades. Some criminologists assert that this is due more to the increased willingness of today's victims to report crimes than to an actual increase. Meltzer notes, however, that the experience of the average person on the street likely contradicts this claim.

Crime in the Streets

Experts indicate that robbery rates are an indicator of how "safe" a city is. New York reports more robberies per capita than any other major city in the U.S. In all major cities, drug-related robbery is a growing problem. Drug robberies are nearly impossible to prevent, as hard-core addicts will do almost anything, no matter how rash, to support their habit. Car theft is a favorite gambit because breaking into a car and lifting the stereo—or stealing the car outright—is the most convenient way to get fast money. One car owner left a **NO RADIO** sign in his window when he parked, and returned to find his car windows smashed and his sign flipped over with a message scrawled on the back, reading: **GET ONE!**

According to official data, only a tenth of all crimes are violent. But since violence, in its worst form, means murder, that one tenth is important. Regrettably, the United States suffers a higher homicide rate than any other industrial country, a fact which many attribute to the wide availability of handguns in the U.S. Also, it seems that violent resolution to disagreements is more acceptable in the United States than elsewhere.

Battered Women, Battered Children

Nearly one out of every three American families experience some degree of domestic violence. Battery within American homes inflicts more injuries on women than rape or muggings combined. If the abuse becomes too great, many women strike back—often with equally tragic consequences.

Rape is legally defined as engaging in sexual intercourse with another person without that person's consent. Although men and boys are often the target of other men, the primary victims of rape are still women and girls. The FBI estimates that one in ten women will be raped during her lifetime—and that 90 percent of rape victims either know or are acquainted with their attackers.

In the United States, more than 1.6 million children are abused by their parents each year. Sadly, this figure appears to be escalating. Because child abuse is often a "family" crime, its impact reaches not only the young victims themselves but into future generations. And children who are victims of violence at home later inflict their pain on the community. Nearly three-fourths of the people convicted of violent crimes grew up in violent homes.

The Hell of Addiction

In Jersey City, one of the leading black churches no longer holds Sunday evening services because too many churchgoers have been mugged by crack addicts on their way home. Crack, cheap and easy to obtain, has become a popular drug among addicts seeking relief from their poverty and pain. Middle- and upper-class citizens are also increasingly turning to drugs for "recreation," escape or consolation, but their problem is more easily hidden from public view.

By the end of 1988, Washington, D.C. had tallied up a record homicide rate, an increase directly attributable to increased drug use. Quarrels between buyers and sellers frequently leads to the exchange of gunfire—which kills not only drug users and dealers, but innocent bystanders. "As new drug gangs compete for control of the market," says Meltzer, "the level of violence climbs higher and higher."

The Mob Takes Over

Organized crime involves thousands of criminals, all operating by their own standards and rules. Most Americans are affected by the clandestine operations of organized crime, and cannot fathom the extent of their influence. The price we pay for building materials, appliances, and other products is often doubled after the mob takes its cut. Furthermore, if the mob paid taxes on their vast earnings, every American would see a significant tax cut.

Organized crime today now controls many production and service industries—most of them legal enterprises. Crime syndicates also enjoy great profits from their influence in trade unions. In the early '80s, the Teamsters Union, linked to the Mafia, collected such huge illegal profits that building costs skyrocketed nationwide.

Crime at the Top

White-collar crime seems remote to most Americans, yet it costs the country more than all other crimes combined.

- **Business fraud** costs the nation $100 billion per year, reports the National Association of Attorneys General.
- **Faulty goods and monopolistic practices** annually cost consumers $174 billion to $230 billion, estimates the Senate Judiciary Committee.
- **When corporations violate federal regulations,** taxpayers lose $10 to $20 billion a year, says the Department of Justice.

Statistics show that no social group is immune from the temptations of larceny. Few blue- and white-collar employees regard themselves as thieves, of course, but 50 percent of the nation's work force commit embezzlement by stealing from their employers. "This aspect of wrongdoing by 'business persons' includes everyone from corporate owners to . . . unskilled workers."

Everybody's Doing It

Examples of white-collar crime in federal, state and city government abound:

- More than 110 senior officials of the Reagan administration came under investigation for improper fiscal conduct.
- A group of New York City Health Department inspectors habitually held up their fingers as they walked into restaurants to signal how large a payoff they wanted from the owner. Two fingers meant $200; five fingers meant $500.
- Housing officials in New York were charged with accepting bribes from private contractors.

Justice: Imperfect but Improvable

Meltzer admits that "law is not a divine creation or a fixed body of rules that tells people where they belong in the order of society and what they can do or not do. It's an instrument that the people at the levers of power use to move toward some particular goal. The law changes constantly as human needs and desires change."

Over the centuries, American law has grown and developed organically as needs and priorities have changed. Because of deeply rooted complexities in our history, the United States now has 52 separate legal systems (besides the Supreme Court), 95 federal district courts, and 12 circuit courts of appeal. Though general laws, or *statutes,* are passed by the legislature, the actual workings of our criminal justice system are based upon common law, which is defined by rulings of judges in deciding individual cases. These *precedents,* or past

rulings, are what judges refer to in deciding current cases. Combined with the many, often inane, legal "technicalities" that can be brought before the courts, it is these precedents that often cause the American criminal justice system to break down, allowing proven criminals to walk away unpunished and unrepentant.

In many cases the reverse is also true, and disadvantaged, possibly innocent citizens are punished to the full extent of the law. These injustices are partly due to our court system. Trials in the American courts of law are governed by the *adversary* method, a system of rules and procedures in which neither judge nor jury is allowed to take sides. A fair trial requires that each side of an issue be thoroughly presented; this is where attorneys come in. Attorneys are found everywhere in American life; in fact, two out of every three lawyers on the planet live in the United States. It is recognized that attorneys for both sides *should* be equally skilled in presenting the evidence and organizing their case. However, in practice, this is a rare scenario: records indicate that those defendants or plaintiffs who can *pay* for the best attorneys are the most likely to win the case.

Juries and Judges

At the heart of the American legal system is trial by jury, in which a group of six or twelve citizens hears the case under the guidance of a judge. A trial by jury is supposed to be impartial, but impartiality under the adversary system is an unlikely accident. Attorneys attempt to select jurors who will be most beneficial to *their* side, and anyone with any prior knowledge or opinion of the case is ruled out by one side or the other. "If the jury's main function is to determine the facts . . . the adversary system works to prevent precisely that."

Furthermore, with the common manipulations of plea bargaining—a court-approved deal struck privately between the accused and the prosecutor, often dictating that a lesser sentence be passed down—the great majority of legitimate criminal cases never make it to trial.

What Can Be Done About It?

Unfortunately, Meltzer has no conclusive solutions to ending or reducing crime in America. He returns instead to the premise that "there are no easy answers." Noting the general, social causes of crime, however, he does urge parents, teachers, lawmakers, and businesses to become involved in the fight for legal and social reform.

Meltzer cites poverty, illiteracy, and humankind's aggressive instincts as the three primary causes of the growing crime rate in the United States. Education, he contends, is the only ingredient which will turn potential criminals into productive citizens. He also suggests that individuals with mental illnesses and/or learning disabilities are responsible for a significant number of crimes, and urges educators to more carefully attend to such persons' needs. "Better education for all classes of society is the major solution to the problem of crime in America."

Finally, says Meltzer, "We need to examine what we do to each other. When we see someone go wrong, someone doing harm, we need to think about such behavior and make a judgement. Is this the way we want to live?"

IN THE BELLY OF THE BEAST

by Jack Henry Abbott, Random House, New York, N.Y., 1981

In his introduction to *In the Belly of the Beast*, Norman Mailer writes: "I love Jack Abbott for surviving and for having learned to write as well as he does." Mailer was at work on *The Executioner's Song*, his book about Gary Gilmore—who had been executed for murder—when he first received a letter from inmate Abbott, whose "direct, unadorned, and detached" prose impressed him. Aware that Abbott could provide him with a view of prison helpful to his study of Gilmore, Mailer began corresponding with the convict. Abbott and Gilmore, in fact, had quite a bit in common: both had been "juvenile delinquents, both had been incarcerated for most of their adolescence in state supported institutions . . . and both men knew very little of liberty." Indeed Abbott has spent most of his life in prison: *First imprisoned at twelve, he was out once for nine months, then imprisoned again at the age of eighteen for cashing a [bogus] check [and] given a maximum of five years. As he tells us in this work . . . he then killed a fellow convict and was given an indeterminate sentence of nineteen years. He has been in jail ever since but for a six-week period when he was on the lam in America and Canada.*

During his many years in Maximum Security, Abbott read voraciously and later won Mailer's praise for the scope—if not always the content—of his learning. While Mailer admitted that he was "much more impressed by the literary measure of Abbott's writing in prison than by his overall analysis of foreign affairs and revolution," Mailer was instrumental in arranging for sections of Abbott's letters to be published in book form as *In the Belly of the Beast.* Supported by many others in the literary world, Mailer lobbied for Abbott's parole. Tragically, however, six weeks after winning parole in 1981, Abbott stabbed a stranger at a New York cafe and, convicted of murder, was sentenced to fifteen years to life.

❖ ◆ ❖

Born in 1944, Abbott spent his early years in a series of foster homes. At the age of nine he was taken out of elementary school and placed in a reform school for what he describes as the "juvenile crime [of] failure to adjust to foster homes." At age twelve, he was transferred to the Utah State Industrial School for Boys where, Abbott claims, he was beaten and put on a semi-starvation diet. Eventually he began to spend long stints in solitary confinement, developing a profound distrust that quickly turned to paranoia.

Free only "nine and a half months since the age of twelve and consequently highly suspicious by nature," says Abbott, "at age thirty-seven I am barely a precocious child. My passions are those of a boy." Not only

does he view himself as emotionally stunted, he also sees within himself something far more destructive: . . . *the other half—which concerns judgment, reason (moral, ethical, cultural.) It is the mantle of pride, integrity, honor. It is the high esteem [state-raised convicts] have for violence . . . It is what makes us . . . dangerous killers who act alone and without emotion . . . to avenge themselves, establish and defend themselves with acts of murder that usually evade prosecution by law: this is the state-raised convict's conception of manhood, in the highest sense.*

Practicing brutality did nothing to make Abbott's incarceration any easier. On the contrary, Abbott writes, "I cannot adjust to daily life in prison. I feel that if I ever did adjust to prison, I could by that alone never adjust to society." Claiming that he doesn't consider himself responsible for his initial incarceration, Abbott protests that he could "never accept guilt for things I never did": *If I were beaten to death tomorrow, my record would go before the coroner's jury—before anyone had the power to investigate—and my "past record of violence" would vindicate my murderers. In fact, the prison regime can commit any atrocity against me, and my "record" will acquit them.*

Despite the punishments that Abbott claims were inflicted on him by guards while spending "five and a half years in Maximum Security,"—during which he spoke to no one but his sister—Abbott used this time to "read all but a very few of the world's classics," and often experienced, through literature, a kind of transcendence: *Shorn of a gracious God, the mind surrenders to nothing, to Nothingness.*

According to him, in prison reading is deemed "dangerous": Prison officials are afraid that knowledge will empower convicts. In fact, Abbott claims that "the most dangerous prisoners . . . are 'readers and writers.'" Books of course offer freedom, and "a taste of freedom in prison," he contends, "is not unlike the taste of heroin—a taste that obsesses you: a 'taste' that addicts you—you'd *kill* for it in a literal sense."

Inhumane confinement, the antithesis of freedom, apparently had "a more adverse and profound spiritual effect" on Abbott than any of his childhood experiences. When he was first put into long-term confinement he was claustrophobic: His hands and feet shackled all night, he felt as if the oppressive darkness and loneliness of his cell were causing him to be "crushed to death." A few years in solitary, however, ultimately cured him of his claustrophobia.

Upon trying to escape from prison following his murder of another convict, Abbott was placed in a "blackout cell": *It was in total darkness, not a crack of light entered that cell anywhere—and I searched, in the days that followed, for such a crack along every inch of the door and the walls. The darkness was so absolute it was like being in ink.*

Abbott subsequently spent months in "strip-cells," where the cubicle is kept constantly lit and the "floor inclines from the walls inward to the center [where] there is a *hole* about two inches in diameter" that serves as a toilet. The prisoner can wear nothing but "a pair of undershorts" and he must beg the guards for water. *Any sane man may wonder: What grievous crime would a man have to commit to be thus treated: The answer: In prison anything at all. Any indiscretion. A contraband book. A murder. A purloined sandwich. This does not even square with the savage's conception of justice:* An eye for an eye.

Even worse than the strip cells, according to Abbott, is "the starvation diet." This punishment is now outlawed, but Abbott had to endure the diet for six months. Once a day for ten days he was given water. Although on the eleventh day he was supposed to receive three full meals, he was not always granted that privilege. After surmising that sixty days of starvation was tantamount to "the death penalty," Abbott soon discovered that "cockroaches are a good source of protein"; he thus began to "mash the day's catch together . . . in a piece of bread and swallow it like a big pill."

Alternately starved, beaten, "teargassed," and tranquilized with powerful drugs, none of these punishments seemed to weaken Abbott's resolve: *I have been made oversensitive—my very* flesh *has been made to suffer sensations and longings I never had before. I have been chopped to pieces by a life of deprivation of sensations; by beatings so frequent I am now a piece of meat and bone; by lies and by drugs that attack my nervous system. I have had my mind turned into steel by the endless smelter of* time *in confinement.*

Abbott contends that guards, or "pigs," are responsible for most of his suffering in prison: they treated him "so violently" that he couldn't recall "ever having anything but the deepest, aching, searing hatred for them": *The law does forbid the methodical use of torture and corporeal punishment. [However, there has never been] a single instance in which a prisoner's complaint of cruel and unusual punishment has ever at any time been affirmed as true either by the government in general or the prison regime in particular. [Nevertheless], in every instance on which a prisoner is lucky enough to air his complaint in a courtroom . . . he always has been vindicated. Always proven to have told the truth.*

While Abbott supports the rights of prisoners, he certainly does not romanticize his fellow inmates: *Walking into the new maximum security units is exactly like walking into a room lined with animal cages . . . All day there are arguments and threats hollered all over the place. It is not too different, really, than the "monkey houses"* at the zoo.

Prisoners, Abbott says, being constantly forced into proximity with other desperate convicts, either "are so afraid of violence that they will degrade themselves in every con-

ceivable way to maintain peace" or they "accept violence, committing it to survive *morally* as well as biologically." Morality, in prison, is the inability to be "broken"; it entails a "hard code of survival" in which "dignity and sanity" must remain intact. Indeed, Abbott likens prisons to "gladiator schools," where optimally the combatants learn how to die honorably. "All violence in prison is geared for murder," he states. "You can't have someone with ill feelings for you walking around. He could drop a knife in you any day . . . You learn to 'smile' him into position. To *disarm* him with friendliness." Then, as one who has himself murdered in prison, Abbot traces the gruesome details: *Here is how it is . . . The enemy is smiling and chattering away about something. You see his eyes: green-blue, liquid. He thinks you're his fool; he trusts you. You see the spot. It's a target between the second and third button on his shirt . . . you have sunk the knife to its hilt into the middle of his chest. Slowly he begins to struggle for his life. As he sinks, you have to kill him fast or get caught. He will say "Why?" or "No!" Nothing else. You can feel his life trembling through the knife in your hand. It almost overcomes you, the gentleness of the feeling at the center of a coarse act of murder. You've pumped the knife in several times without even being aware of it. You go to the floor with him to finish him. It is like cutting butter, no resistance at all. They always whisper one thing at the end: "Please." You get the odd impression he is not imploring you not to harm him, but to do it right. If he says your name, it softens your resolve. You go into a mechanical stupor of sorts. Things register in slow motion because all of your senses are drawn to a new height. You leave him in the blood, staring with dead eyes. You strip your cell and destroy your clothing flushing it down the toilet. You throw the knife away. You jump under the showers. Your clarity returns. There is no doubt you did the only thing you could.*

Murder is commonplace in prison—and is rarely investigated. Moreover, Abbott claims that guards and prison officials frequently encourage prisoners to liquidate inmates they consider trouble-makers.

In spite of having murdered in prison, Abbott claims that he is not "a callous punk"; in fact, he says, "you want to stop in the middle of it and hold him so tight you can force his life back into him and save him . . ."

Because Abbott has "seen what 'blind justice' has done in all its horrors," he denounces the United States—denounces not only its penal system, but the whole of American society. Citing institutional violence, racial hatred, and an aggressive foreign policy, Abbott argues that "a violent government, a violent class, *breeds* the violence that will someday violently bring them to their knees." Consequently, he embraces Marxism and holds on to a dream: *To walk with comrades in patched-up suits from every corner of Europe and America across a country we just conquered and to feel that it is at last ours.*

WITHOUT CONSCIENCE

The Disturbing World of Psychopaths Among Us
by Robert D. Hare, Pocket Books, New York, N.Y., 1993

Psychopaths abound. According to Robert D. Hare, an internationally acclaimed expert in psychopathy, *there are at least two million psychopaths in North America; the citizens of New York City have as many as 100,000 among them. And these are conservative estimates. Far from being an esoteric, isolated problem that affects only a few people, psychopathy touches virtually every one of us.*

Thus, most of us have had unpleasant encounters with these "social predators who charm, manipulate, and ruthlessly plow their way through life, leaving a broad trail of broken hearts, shattered expectations, and empty wallets." Because psychopaths initially may strike us as unusually bright and affable, they may easily win our trust. And by the time we realize that we have been victimized, it is too late.

Hare attempts to address three common questions about psychopaths: "Who are these people?" "What makes them the way they are?" and "How can we protect ourselves?"

Identifying Psychopaths

Many psychopaths are in prison; most are not. Psychopaths work in every profession, live in every community, and—on the surface, at least—resemble everyone else. What sets them apart, however, is their "stunning lack of conscience." Psychopaths suffer no qualms about the fates of their victims, and may even savor the pain they inflict.

Even though most of us will manage to avoid contact with the deadliest of psychopaths (Ted Bundy-type serial killers) we probably will be harassed, bullied, swindled or driven to despair by psychopathic friends or family members who view us as mere objects.

Parents of psychopaths may be horrified by their child's "unpredictable, unusually destructive, and often expensive behavior." They may blame themselves for the violent, destructive and perverse acts committed by their son or daughter and ask themselves, "Is my child crazy, or just plain bad?"

This questions cannot easily be answered, says Hare. Although psychopathy has been regarded since the early 19th century as a mental disorder, it was not widely studied until this century, when psychiatrist Harvey Cleckley first published his classic *The Mask of Sanity* in 1941. Cleckley's research into psychopathy profoundly influenced Hare's *Psychopathy Checklist*, a "scientifically sound means of measuring and diagnosing psychopathy" that defines these six common "emotional/ interpersonal" traits:

1. **Glib and superficial.** While psychopaths frequently are "very likeable and charming," they may also "seem too slick and smooth." They often speak authoritatively about subjects they know little or nothing about and display a "smooth lack of concern" about being deemed impostors.

2. **Egocentric and grandiose.** Psychopaths tend to "have a narcissistic and grossly inflated view of their self-worth and importance . . . and see themselves . . . as superior beings who are justified in living according to their own rules."

3. **Lack of remorse or guilt.** Even though psychopaths may claim to be aggrieved by the pain they cause, they frequently express surprise—or even anger—at their victims' suffering. After being reminded that he had stabbed a man during a robbery, one psychopathic prisoner snapped, "Get real! He spends a few months in the hospital and I got here."

4. **Lack of empathy and sensitivity.** Psychopaths often seem "like the emotionless androids depicted in science fiction, unable to imagine what real human beings experience."

5. **Deceitful and manipulative.** Psychopaths are often "proud of their ability to lie" and take delight in deceiving others.

6. **Shallow emotions.** "Psychopaths are prone to dramatic, shallow, and short-lived displays of feelings." Such outbursts tend to result from the welling-up of the most primitive responses to the environment. "I believe in emotions: hate, anger, lust, and greed," notorious night stalker Richard Rodriguez once remarked.

In addition to the six "emotional/interpersonal" symptoms of psychopathy, Hare determined that there are six characteristics of "Social Deviance" that chronically impair psychopaths' adaptations to their environments:

1. **Uninhibited Impulsivity.** Because psychopaths are unable to delay gratification, they do not "spend much time weighing the pros and cons of a course of action." One psychopath remarked, "If I always think about tomorrow, I won't be able to live today."

2. **Poor behavior controls.** Psychopaths react fiercely to perceived slights. They normally view these "aggressive displays . . . as rational responses to provocation."

3. **Need for excitement.** Since they prefer life "on the edge" and are unable to endure "routine or monotony," many psychopaths turn to daredevil pranks and criminal activities to find excitement.

4. **Lack of responsibility.** While they frequently voice "good intentions," psychopaths "do not honor formal or implied commitments to people, organizations, or principles."

5. **Early behavior problems.** As children, psychopaths tend to be unusually callous and destructive. Their symptoms include "persistent lying, cheating, theft, fire-setting, truancy, class disruption, substance abuse, vandalism, violence, bullying, running away, and precocious sexuality." In extreme cases, young psychopaths "torture animals and other children."

6. **Adult Antisocial Behavior.** Psychopaths resent and rebel against the dictates of society. For some this antisocial behavior may lead to frequent arrests; others prey only on their families, friends or business associates, who may hesitate to take legal action.

Causative Factors in Psychopathy

No one knows whether people are born as or develop into psychopaths. Although most researchers nowadays assume that psychopathy—like most other mental disorders—probably results from the complex interplay of "nature" and "nurture," few have had success attributing specific symptoms to either genetics or the environment. What is clear, however, is that psychopathy results from a *failure in the learning process.*

To be specific, psychopaths seem to lack the ability to learn from experience. While for most of us "early childhood punishments produce lifelong links between social taboos and feelings of anxiety," psychopaths apparently do not experience such anxiety, nor do threats of punishment deter them.

Moreover, psychopaths may perceive tacit approval from society for some of their exploits. "Clearly, evil is alluring," writes author Bruce Weber, "and not just to those who would dramatize it. From mild naughtiness to vicious criminality, the performance of bad deeds is something the rest of the population wants to know about." Thus, Hanibal Lector becomes a national phenomenon, young executives learn to flatter "their senior but brutalize their juniors," and groupies bombard serial killers with visits and love letters.

Psychopaths often exhibit linguistic distortions, which many researchers attribute to abnormalities in the cerebral hemisphere. While the left hemisphere of the brain normally governs "the use of language" and the right "processes information," psychopaths tend to process language bilaterally. Because both hemispheres of psychopaths' brains govern language, their "speech is poorly integrated and monitored." Thus, they often make illogical and contradictory statements. One psychopath, for example, was asked if "he had ever committed a violent offense," and he responded, "No, but I once had to kill someone." Another, a serial murderer, proudly declared, "I've got enough *antidotes* [sic] to fill five or six books—enough for a *trilogy.*"

In contrast to the linguistic idiosyncrasies of psychopaths, few other symptoms of psychopathy have been convincingly linked to physiological disturbances. "Failure to bond," deprivation, or abuse during early childhood may contribute to psychopathy, but it is a conjecture that has not yet been proven. Rather, Hare writes, *Psychopathy emerges from a complex—and poorly understood—interplay between biological factors and social forces.* Even a "good family life" will not deter psychopaths from their "lives of callous self-gratification." However, statistics do bear out that "psychopaths from unstable backgrounds [commit] many more offenses that [do] those from stable backgrounds."

Protection and Damage Control

The prognosis for psychopathy is extremely poor. Inasmuch as psychopaths "are perfectly happy with themselves" and thus have no desire to change, their disorder is exceedingly difficult to treat. For most of us, then, "the best strategy is to avoid becoming entangled in the first place." Hare offers some "awareness advice" about how we can protect ourselves:

- *Know what you are dealing with.* All of us are potential victims, and need to familiarize ourselves with the symptoms of psychopathy.

- *Don't wear blinkers.* Because psychopaths tend to conceal "their dark sides [and to] give vague, evasive, or inconsistent replies to queries about their personal lives," we should be suspicious of people who hide even the most trivial aspects of their lives.

- *Keep your guard up in high-risk situations.* Places like "singles' bars, social clubs, resorts, ship cruises, [and] foreign airports" particularly attract psychopaths—as well as an abundance of lonely "potential victims."

- *Know yourself.* We should become acutely aware of our weaknesses, because psychopaths will happily exploit our need for companionship, flattery, or adventure.

Given the prevalence of psychopaths, completely avoiding them is not feasible, so Hare offers these recommendations for "damage control":

- *Obtain professional advice.* Find a clinician who fully understands the symptoms of the disorder.

- *Don't blame yourself.* Psychopaths have a propensity for blaming us for the many things that go wrong in their lives, but we need to remember that they are responsible for their own behavior.

- *Be aware of who the true victim is.* Although psychopaths frequently "give the impression that it is they who are suffering and it is the victims who are to blame," we need to remember that their pain is much less than our own and results only from not being able to manipulate us.

- *Recognize that you are not alone.* Virtually everyone has been targeted at one time or another by a psychopath.

- *Be careful about power struggles.* Because psychopaths have an especially strong desire to dominate others, we must remember that aggressively matching our wills against theirs may result in "serious emotional or physical trauma."

- *Set firm ground rules.* Without acting defensive or overly standoffish, it is important to set limits in dealings with psychopaths.

- *Don't expect dramatic changes.* Since psychopathic traits rarely disappear, we have to realize that our feelings and actions are going to have little or no positive impact on psychopaths.

- *Cut your losses.* The more psychopaths are able to weaken us, the more we awaken their "insatiable appetite for power and control." Seeking out professional help, if necessary, we need to find the way to take charge of our own lives.

- *Use support groups.* While there are few groups available for the victims of psychopaths per se, there are many excellent ones for the victims of various crimes and other forms of abuse.

While these strategies may help us cope with individual psychopaths, their collective impact on society continues to increase. Hare urges researchers to initiate further studies, for psychopathy "is responsible for far more social distress and disruption than all other psychiatric disorders combined." Instead of the billions of dollars we spend to "rehabilitate" or "resocialize" psychopaths, Hare recommends funding studies "to search for effective early interventions."

HISTORY OF AIDS

Emergence and Origin of a Modern Pandemic
by Mirko D. Grmek, Princeton University Press, Princeton, N.J., 1990

I am not so naive, in the middle of an epidemic still in full advance, as to believe its history can be written with serenity and knowledge afforded only by distance from the events. But I am bold enough to think that, even at this early date, a look back by a physician trained in historical method might be of benefit.

So begins Mirko Grmek's *History of AIDS*, a comprehensive narrative account of a virus which, the author claims, is "the first of the post-modern plagues." Divided into four parts, Grmek's book examines the origins of the epidemic, analyzes the scientific community's efforts to isolate and identify the virus, surveys the history of AIDS, and, finally, seeks to uncover the biological and social issues surrounding this new pandemic.

A Calamity for Our Times

Between 1980 and 1981, physicians in Los Angeles, San Francisco, and New York began to see patients who presented a set of symptoms that included "lassitude, weight loss, and slow consumption of the body, but without specific signs." When physicians reported their findings, they discovered that their patients shared an array of other symptoms as well—specifically, all were infected by an unknown virus that attacked their immune systems. In addition, several patients later developed opportunistic infections like *Pneumocystis carinii* pneumonia, while others contracted a rare form of skin cancer called Kaposi's sarcoma. Finally, and perhaps most significantly, all the patients were young men, and all were gay.

By the end of 1981, Grmek reports, the Center for Disease Control in Atlanta had come to believe that the unknown virus was "spread by sexual contact." Researchers had found, in fact, that the majority of the Los Angeles patients shared a common sexual network. And at the center of this network they had discovered "a young man" they called "Patient Zero" because, as an airline steward, "he had sown the disease and death all along his route, at the rate of about 250 partners a year." Patient Zero, apart from emphasizing "the danger of contagion" by sexual contact, confirmed "a profound epidemiologic truth": that carriers of the virus, "who in another day may have taken the stagecoach, the long haul trains, and ships, now take to the skies: in a single day infectious diseases can now cross continents, or jump between them."

"This diabolical AIDS virus," Grmek explains, "first disrupts the organism's immune defenses, disorganizes its internal regulation. It then ricochets outward to disturb sexual relations and finally, dangerously, to poison social habits in a new way, more subtle and more insidious than medieval leprosy, Renaissance syphilis, or machine-age tuberculosis." Indeed, it presented a terrifying prospect, and its horror was only underscored when, in 1982, scientists learned that the virus had spread to new "target populations." Strangely, Grmek notes, scientists and the media mentioned only those risk groups who were already considered "marginal" or "stigmatized in advance either by their behavior, by their ethnic origin, or by some inborn defect." Thus, although scientists and journalists acknowledged that intravenous drug users, Haitians, and hemophiliacs were now at risk, they failed to mention two "innocent" groups in "this club of the damned: recipients of blood transfusions, and newborns infected in utero."

In the summer of 1982, the disease the media had been calling "the gay cancer" and "the gay pneumonia" was formally dubbed *AIDS* by the scientific community, an acronym for Acquired Immune Deficiency Syndrome. The malady was now not a "disease" per se but rather "a *syndrome*, that is, a constellation of symptoms" that included various opportunistic infections and malignancies.

Naming the epidemic meant that statistics could begin to be compiled. Grmek notes that the World Health Organization reported that AIDS cases "increased from 408 at the beginning of 1982, to 1,573 in December 1982, then to 5,077 in 1983, and 12,174 at the end of 1984. All such numbers," he hastens to add, "underestimated the real situation. Only after serologic [blood] findings fully emerged could the real measure of the catastrophe be taken."

The Oracles of Science

Among the research institutes vying to be the first to identify and isolate the virus were the National Cancer Institute (NCI) in Bethesda, Maryland and the Pasteur Institute in Paris. Both institutions enjoyed venerable reputations within the scientific community; there, however, their similarities ended.

The NCI, as a government research center, was generously endowed. Led by Robert Gallo, its research labs aggressively pursued a hypothesis that AIDS was caused by a retrovirus called HTVL, a pathogen linked with certain kinds of leukemia that could "lie dormant for a very long time, possibly even forty years after the initial infection." Unfortunately, writes Grmek, the "American teams had rushed down the wrong path [and] lost a year trying to justify their initial intuition."

By contrast, the Pasteur Institute, a private, less well-funded research institution headed by Luc Montaigner, took a different route. First, they isolated a new retrovirus they called LAV, which later became known as HIV. Then, after finding the virus in blood and tissue samples in ten pre-AIDS and AIDS patients of "widely differing ethnic, social, and biological settings," Montaigner's labs proposed that the HIV virus was the "causative agent."

Although initially greeted with skepticism, the French team's hypothesis gradually gained support in the scientific community. In the meantime, however, Gallo and the NCI teams had isolated another strain of HTVL and claimed, after initial testing, to have discovered the AIDS virus itself. When analyses revealed that Gallo's HTVL-III seemed to be a clone of Montaigner's HIV, a dispute erupted between the NCI and the Pasteur Institute as to who should receive discovery credit

329

and, on a more practical level, who should receive patent rights to an AIDS diagnostic kit.

In March 1987, the two sides reached a compromise on both issues. "The Americans," Grmek writes, "would add the name of Montaigner to that of Gallo to their patent for the diagnostic kit." Additionally, the scientists would co-author a "chronological history of AIDS research, promising not to 'make or publish any statement which would or could be construed as contradicting or compromising the integrity of said scientific history.'"

Once the AIDS virus had been discovered and diagnostic tests devised to detect its presence, the history of AIDS entered a new phase. While researchers worked on various drug therapies, scientists and the media did some public relations work. The public, for instance, was reassured that AIDS could not be "contracted from a handshake, a swimming pool, or a toilet seat." Instead, its path of transmission was confined to "sexual activity, the biology of maternity, the injection of drugs, or medical intervention." At the same time, the progression of AIDS was delineated from its "silent stages" of flu-like symptoms to its advanced clinical forms where "opportunistic infections, Kaposi's sarcoma, and non-Hodgkin's lymphoma predominate."

"From this time on," says Grmek, "AIDS was a true pandemic."

A Look Back

"Is AIDS a new disease?" Grmek asks. The answer, he says, depends on how one defines "disease" and how one defines "new." For Grmek, AIDS is not "a disease in the old sense of the word, inasmuch as the virus . . . affects the immune system and produces symptoms only through the expedient of opportunistic infection or malignancy." Nor is AIDS "a newborn in the absolute sense, a mutant whose ancestors were never pathogenic." Rather, AIDS is "new in its present epidemiological dimension."

For instance, Grmek asserts that past "biological and social conditions" precluded a retrovirus outbreak of such proportions. "A disastrous epidemic of this type," he argues, "could not have occurred before the mingling of peoples, the liberalization of sexual and social mores, and, above all, before progress in modern medicine had accomplished the control of the majority of serious infectious diseases and introduced intravenous injections and blood transfusions."

The Origin and Spread of the AIDS Agents

According to Grmek, pathogenic viruses "do not spring up *ex nihilo*. They come from ancestors that must have similar genetic characteristics and must replicate somewhere, be it in an animal population or human population in which they have struck a sort of biological equilibrium." Among the numerous hypotheses regarding the origin of the AIDS virus, Grmek cites three in particular.

The first is the so-called "simian hypothesis," which suggests that AIDS was transmitted by monkeys to man; the most plausible scenario for this to have occurred is found in the rise of animal medical experimentation since the 1950s.

French scientist Luc Montaigner proposes another scenario. "The virus," he says, "existed for quite a long time in certain isolated African tribes without causing the least damage: there was no AIDS because the tribe had genetically adapted to the virus, and tolerated it . . . " Only when, "for reasons that remain to be determined," the virus was transmitted beyond this limited environment into populations much more sensitive to the virus did AIDS ensue.

And yet a third theory synthesizing elements of the other two is offered by American researcher Robert Gallo. In his estimation, the virus "originated in Africa, where it infected many species of Old World primates, including human beings. It reached the Americas along with the slave trade.

Curiously, it may well have arrived in Japan in the same way. In the 16th century, Portuguese traders traveled to Japan and stayed specifically where the HTVL-I [virus] is now endemic. Along with them they brought both African slaves and monkeys, as contemporary Japanese works of art show, and either one or the other may have carried the virus."

No matter what the actual origin of the AIDS virus may be, what seems certain, insists Grmek, is that the modern pandemic originated at three sites: on the east and west coasts of the U.S. and in Africa. From these epicenters the virus then spread to Europe and beyond, primarily through sexual contact and contaminated blood supplies.

Modern medicine, for its part, has had its triumphs and failures during the AIDS epidemic. As Luc Montaigner puts it, "We've identified the enemy, we know how to avoid infection from blood products, we've got the prevention campaigns rolling. And we have a little hope, on the therapeutic side, thanks to a drug, AZT, which, while it doesn't cure, slows down the disease's progress and prolongs patients' lives . . . What we haven't managed is either a complete recovery from AIDS by means of medication, or its prevention by means of a vaccine."

While scientists pursue strategies to treat and eventually cure AIDS, Grmek maintains that the pandemic will only worsen: "Around the world in the next five years, a million people in their prime will become gravely ill. It will be the main cause of death for persons under the age of fifty." But, Grmek notes, whether a vaccine is found or not, gradually "a new equilibrium will be established between humans and the virus . . . Natural selection will see to it that the virus adapts to the human host." In the meantime, Grmek concludes, "We should not presume that humankind is done with this blood tribute once and for all. Heavy burdens still await us as the price of our action, disturbing the dynamic equilibria between humans, their physical surroundings, and the totality of living beings."

◇ ♦ ◇

Without a doubt, the pathogenic horrors of AIDS have forever rent the fabric of our society; as we approach a new millennium, the specter of the virus has come to dominate the way we view ourselves and our interactions with others. "With its links to sex, drugs, blood, and informatics," Grmek says in conclusion, "and with the sophistication of its evolution and of its strategy for spreading itself, AIDS expresses our era."

LAWFUL EXIT

The Limits of Freedon for Help in Dying
by Derek Humphry, Norris Lane Press, Junction City, Oregon, 1993

"Individual freedom requires that all persons be allowed to control their own destiny, especially at life's end . . . " However, in the United States existing laws do not allow the terminally ill to ask for death and to solicit the help of a willing physician. Therefore, argues Dr. Derek Humphry, the laws must be changed.

Most of us have heard the passionate legal and ethical arguments currently raging against euthanasia, or "assisted suicide." We have also heard the urgent clamor for the right to "death with dignity." In *Lawful Exit*, Humphry gives a calm and well-reasoned analysis of both sides of the issue and then comes down clearly in favor of legislation granting carefully monitored voluntary assistance to terminally ill patients who choose to end their lives. Whether one agrees with him or not, most readers will appreciate his clear exposition of a painful, complex, and often volatile subject.

Humphry insists that he is not trying to impose his choice on others, but only to keep "others" from imposing their choice on the rest of society. Certainly, he allows, no physician should be compelled to assist in a suicide; nevertheless, a physician must be allowed to do what he or she feels is morally right without fear of prosecution. Since existing laws do not provide this prerogative, the laws must be reformed.

Two factions have been instrumental in defeating proposed legislation dealing with voluntary euthanasia: religious groups, who oppose euthanasia on moral grounds, and physicians themselves, who are concerned with the responsibility involved. The religious right will probably never be swayed from its stand, admits Humphry; but many physicians are beginning to call for new guidelines and legislation. In fact, some doctors and nurses have personal knowledge of practitioners in their profession who have helped patients die gracefully. They may even have agreed clandestinely to provide the same service for each other should the occasion arise. But with no clear standards to draw from, there is always the risk of "whistle-blowers" calling attention to their actions and bringing legal retribution.

"Without a law in place, there are no criteria or guidelines," says Humphry. Physicians like Dr. Jack Kevorkian, who flout the current statutes and help the terminally ill end their lives, only stiffen resistance to what Humphry sees as a compassionate and democratic solution to the dilemmas created by medical and technological advances that have overwhelmed us.

It would be much more effective to work towards changing our outmoded codes than simply to ignore them. Unfortunately, however, if new legislation is not passed soon, more and more people will be taking the law into their own hands. Recent polls conducted in the states of Washington and California showed that 46% of all registered voters supported revising their current euthanasia laws. There is a growing trend towards acceptance of assisted suicide among both physicians and the public.

Humphry stresses that *voluntary* participation—on the part of both patient and physician—must be the key ingredient of any new euthanasia legislation. His proposed *Death with Dignity Act* states that only an adult who is terminally ill, appears likely to die within six months, and has the mental capacity to understand the consequences of assisted death and any viable alternatives, may request the assistance of a willing physician in dying. The Act will benefit not only the dying, but also those patients in the earlier stages of a terminal illness, who will know that they have a dignified way out if the pain becomes unbearable. This knowledge may give such patients the strength to carry on gracefully *without* assisted dying.

The proposed act still does *not* allow assisted death in many other cases. For example, help would be withheld in the early stages of a terminal illness, because radical medical breakthroughs are always possible—and because many "terminal" patients are still living high-quality, functional lives. Those who have already lapsed into unconsciousness or who are incompetent or too young to decide their own fate would also be ineligible for assistance. This may often be regrettable, but it is necessary, since the ethical and legal complexities of euthanasia without patient consent remain overwhelming.

Neither does the Death with Dignity Act allocate assistance to "terminally" depressed or mentally ill patients. Many intelligent and caring persons have made the case that the mentally ill can suffer just as much as those with terminal cancer. "I believe them," says Humphry, "[but] that is a minefield across which I do not choose to walk. The chance of misdiagnosis, the possibility of successful treatment or cure, or the risk of a hoax could cause this to blow up in the faces of those who practiced it." And Humphry does not favor granting the option of assisted dying to those who find their health deteriorating and their problems mounting. Some critics are concerned that as society does become more "accepting" of such choices, the "right to die" will instead become the "*duty* to die," with seniors feeling an obligation to "get out of the way" of the young. And, finally, the statute will not apply to those who are severely handicapped but not terminally or hopelessly ill. Many disabled and chronically deteriorating patients have chosen to fight their problems and live active, productive lives. Those who choose otherwise should have that choice respected as well, thinks Humphry; but, again, the medical profession is not yet ready to extend help to this circle.

Many critics are also troubled by what they refer to as the "slippery slope," arguing that passing the Death with Dignity Act today will open the door to more permissive laws in the future. Would passage of the Act empower governments to do away with the needy, the old, or whomever they may choose to judge as unproductive? Humphry thinks not, reasoning that societal limits would be drawn to keep euthanasia within the ethical bounds.

The term *euthanasia* embraces two possible levels of involvement: *assisted dying*, where a physician or other person helps provide the means for death but does not take part in the actual procedure, and *active euthanasia*, where the helper not only provides the means but takes part in the act itself. Some supporters have proposed separating the two concepts of "assisted suicide" and "voluntary euthanasia," and then trying to get "assisted suicide" accepted first. But Humphry believes that such a move would result in discrimination. In a case where there were two terminally ill patients, both in great pain, and one was strong enough to commit suicide while the other was not, only the stronger patient would receive legal assistance.

To illustrate the agonizing and hair-splitting distinctions involved in real-life cases, Humphry reveals his own most personal ordeal with euthanasia: "I helped my first wife, Jean, to die in 1975 when she was suffering from advanced bone cancer. Jean took her own life and I provided the drugs, sat beside her, and gave her moral support." Without the assistance of a physician, the procedure would have been very difficult, admits Humphry, if not impossible.

Other opponents have voiced concerns about the risk of misdiagnosis. Most physicians, however, do not share that fear. While mistakes are not inconceivable, "a patient with an advanced terminal disease, existing in a body undergoing serious deterioration, and with pain requiring huge amounts of analgesics, hardly requires a physician to tell him that death is imminent."

In 1985, a few years after Humphry had drafted his model statute, two California attorneys began outlining new guidelines for those physicians who want to help patients requesting assistance in dying. Their efforts to pass them into law failed, but Humphry feels that as people come to grasp the good such laws could do, public sentiment will change.

A national poll indicates that more than half of all physicians would assist patients in dying if they were given the legal right to do so. Says one doctor: "Physicians in America would not allow themselves to die in the terrible ways they put their patients through."

Humphry has now experienced three failed attempts to modify state euthanasia laws. He says that the most important lesson he has learned is that "a law which specifically, directly and constantly affects ordinary people must be written in easily understood language." In Washington, for instance, people were confused when the law also incorporated contingencies for the reversal of Living Wills. Still, more than 46% of Washington voters opted for the change. And in a second California attempt, Humphry's campaign spent most of its money gathering signatures, and did not educate the public about the fine distinctions addressed in the law. Opponents from the religious right hammered home the line that the law had "no real safeguards," which Humphry strongly contends simply wasn't true; but, unfortunately, it was written in "legalese," so lay voters remained skeptical, puzzled as to its true and full meaning.

Several other modifications have been suggested for the model law. Some cautious proponents want to lengthen the waiting period between the time when assisted death is requested and the time when assistance is granted; others want to eliminate altogether the current 24-hour waiting period. Humphry takes a middle-ground stance: some period of time—he finds 24 hours reasonable—is necessary to allow a patient to change his mind; but extending the interval only prolongs suffering, not to mention multiplying both medical and legal expenses.

Other critics charge that unscrupulous doctors will immediately start opening "suicide clinics" if the law is passed. Humphry counters that the proposed law largely eliminates such a prospect by controlling the fee that can be charged and requiring that physicians meet careful qualifying standards before they are authorized to participate in assisted deaths. He also points out that countries such as Holland, which allow euthanasia, have seen no improper facilities opened.

If one or two states pass Humphry's model law, will we see a rush of indigent patients flocking in from around the country for help, thereby bloating local social and medical expenses? Perhaps, Humphry replies, but that problem can largely be rectified by adding a simple residency requirement.

Humphry believes that two additional documents should accompany future attempts to pass a "Death with Dignity" act:

1. A set of plainly worded legal and ethical guidelines, both to assist medical professionals and to calm the fears of the public;

2. An explanatory booklet outlining the built-in protections that have been incorporated into both this law and pre-existing laws which will not be rescinded by the new statute. Even "if a thousand protections were built in," Humphry alleges, some voters would persist in being offended by the law. But, he proclaims, we must press forward: *This is the ultimate civil liberty, the freedom to select one's own manner of dying without interference from others, but with help if we choose. If we cannot die by our choice, then we are not free people.*

ABORTION: THE CLASH OF ABSOLUTES

by Laurence H. Tribe, W.W. Norton & Company, New York, 1990

In *Abortion: the Clash of Absolutes*, Laurence Tribe examines a debate that has long divided America. Seeking to define both sides of the issue (though he favors the "pro-choice" position), he asks: Does the U.S. Constitution protect the right to abortion? Is abortion a private or public matter? Is a fetus a living person? Will our decisions about abortion rights affect other rights that we consider to be fundamental?

Approaching Abortion Anew

The abortion debate in America, according to Tribe, is essentially a conflict between two basic values: the right of a fetus to live and the right of a woman to control her own body and destiny. Those opposed to abortion ask: If infanticide is wrong, is the destruction of a fetus any different? However, as the opposition argues, to be forced into parenthood is an infringement on liberty; and if it is wrong to force a woman to suffer a pregnancy that may in the process kill her, is it not just as wrong to force her to suffer a pregnancy that may shorten or ruin her life? Tribe searches for ways to approach the issue of abortion that will avoid pitting such absolute positions against one another.

Many who argue fiercely for the right of the "human" fetus to live, contends Tribe, have difficulty seeing the human plight of the woman who is carrying it. Conversely, those who argue for the right of the woman to control her own body often cannot envision the reality of the developing fetus within her. "If each of us reexamines the complex issues that make up the question of abortion," he hopes, "we may yet find more common ground than we currently imagine."

From Roe to Webster

On January 22, 1973, in the *Roe v. Wade* decision, the Supreme Court announced that the U.S. Constitution protects a woman's right to choose to end her pregnancy. "Jane Roe" was in this case actually Norma McCorvey, a Texas woman who wanted an abortion but could not obtain one because the procedure was illegal in her state of residence. McCorvey didn't have the resources to travel to a neighboring state in which the procedure was legal, and so decided to challenge Texas' ban on abortion.

The immediate effect of the Supreme Court's decision was to render the abortion legislation in forty-nine states invalid; and since the constitutionally protected right to choose abortion made direct political action to restrict abortion impossible, anti-abortion forces were left with only two options: either try to amend the Constitution, or seat pro-life Supreme Court judges by electing a pro-life President. Thus the election of abortion-foe Ronald Reagan resulted in the appointments of Justices O'Connor, Rehnquist, Scalia, and Kennedy, moves which were largely interpreted as a victory for the "right-to-life" movement.

The anti-abortion campaign won its first Supreme Court decision in 1989, when the ruling on *William Webster v. Reproductive Health Services* was handed down. The case presented an abortion clinic's challenge to a Missouri law requiring that tests of fetal viability be performed at the twentieth week of pregnancy on all women seeking an abortion. After years of striking down restrictive abortion laws, the Court upheld the Missouri law. Although *Webster* did not overrule *Roe*, it did clear the way for state legislators to attempt to further regulate abortion.

Two Centuries of Abortion in America

To consider whether *Roe* was or was not fairly decided, Tribe suggests that it is important to examine the history of abortion in the United States, for "while the clash over abortion is one of absolutes, absolutes themselves may be contingent; they arise out of particular social contexts, problems, and concerns that change as society changes."

In post-Revolutionary America, abortion in early pregnancy was neither prohibited nor uncommon. The procedure was permitted up until movement of the fetus was first discernable because only at that point in gestation could one be certain that a woman was in fact pregnant. In the late eighteenth and early nineteenth centuries, abortion was not unusual, nor was it considered a deep moral issue; unmarried sex was the real target of concern.

Not until the late nineteenth century were the first anti-abortion laws passed, their main purpose being to protect women from what was then a dangerous procedure. The Catholic Church, then absent from debate, held that a fetus was not human until it was infused with a soul, which, according to Church doctrine, ensued in male fetuses at forty days and in females at eighty days of gestation.

With abortion laws firmly in place in over forty states, the early twentieth century did not see the rise of any significant controversy. Though Tribe contends that data show one in three pregnancies was still terminated during this period, the abortion debate in the United States did not resurface until the 1950s, when hospitals established review boards to decide when abortions were necessary in order to save the mother's life.

Between 1950 and 1970, crucial changes occurred in the roles and lifestyles of American women: the number of married women working outside the home nearly doubled, and, in the 1970s alone, college enrollment increased 57% among white women and 112% among black women. The growing freedom of women to work and study as equals with men led to an increase in women's use of all types of birth control—including abortion.

Concurrently, the procedure itself became safer and more hygienic. Still, each year during the late 1960s, 1,200,000 women were undergoing illegal abortions in substandard conditions, and thousands of them died. Fueled by this tragic loss of life, reforms were enacted to allow abortion in cases of rape or incest or where the fetus had an incapacitating defect; however, many women were still dying from illegal abortions. Then in 1969 the National Association for the Repeal of Abortion Laws was formed and became the principal grass-roots organization of the pro-choice movement. On the other side, the Catholic Church at this time took a strong public position against the legalization of abortion.

Finding Abortion Rights in the Constitution

Roe v. Wade considered the question of what protections the Constitution extends either to a woman seeking an abortion or to the fetus. One argument often used against *Roe v. Wade* maintains that the decision protects a right to privacy which appears nowhere in the Constitution. However, pro-choice factions cite the Fourteenth Amendment, which reads: *No state shall . . . deprive any person of life, liberty, or property without due process of law.* It is this guarantee of liberty that protects us from government infringements on privacy, argued attorneys for *Roe v. Wade*. Opponents of the Supreme Court decision contend, however, that only *enumerated* rights, such as freedom of speech and religion, are constitutionally guaranteed—and the right to privacy is not enumerated. Pro-choice advocates reply, however, that the Supreme Court has never limited the application of the liberty clause to only those rights enumerated in the Bill of Rights—and that if the Court ever did so, government could control almost every aspect of our lives. Moreover, *Roe* supporters argue, the Supreme Court has protected the right of privacy as constitutional in previous cases, such as *Pierce v. Society of Sisters* in 1923, when the Court held that states could not force all students to attend public schools; to do so would "violate the students' right to privacy." Another decision, *Griswold v. Connecticut* in 1965, upheld the right to privacy by striking down a Connecticut law that made the use of contraceptives by married couples illegal.

The Other Side of the Debate: The Rights of the Fetus

The irreducible conflict between the pro-life position and the pro-choice position surrounds the question: When does a human life begin? The primary pro-life argument is that the fetus is a person from the moment of conception, and therefore is entitled to human rights; abortion thus deprives the fetus of life without due process of law. John Wilke of the National Right-to-Life Committee holds that the embryo must be considered a person from the moment of conception because the forty-six chromosomes that determine an individual's separate genetic identity are all present at that time. Pro-choice supporters, on the other hand, respond that the question of when human life begins is a religious one, and therefore cannot be legislated. Attempting to locate a gray area in the debate, Tribe points out that modern embryology reveals fertilization to occur not in a "moment" but as a *process,* lasting about 24 hours and ending with the intermingling of the chromosomes.

Many opponents of *Roe v. Wade* argue that the question of when life "as a person" begins should be decided by the democratic political process, not by nine judges or by a woman and her doctor. And on the other side, supporters of the Court's 1973 decision express concern that debate over the "personhood" of an embryo distracts Americans from the question of whether the state can force a woman to incubate that embryo. Tribe assesses the stalemate by stating that "too often, when activists on either side present their picture of the abortion issue, they leave room for only the fetus or the pregnant woman."

In Search of Compromise

As Tribe points out, there are potential legislative compromises that fall somewhere between the *Roe v. Wade* decision and the wholesale criminalization of abortion. One commonly offered compromise is a requirement which obligates the consent of the pregnant woman's husband before an abortion can be carried out. In the case of minors, consent laws require pregnant girls to secure permission from a parent before obtaining an abortion.

However, pro-choice advocates argue that consent requirements transfer the power to choose from the woman to her husband, or from the pregnant girl to her parent or guardian. Furthermore, "choice" proponents argue that if a parent can *stop* his pregnant daughter from obtaining an abortion, he could just as well force her to *get* one.

Another possible compromise to the question of abortion is enforcing a mandatory waiting period. Again, however, pro-choice supporters contend that a compulsory waiting period is tantamount to saying that women cannot be trusted to think for themselves or make a sound decision.

For Tribe, the best and most obvious solution is to reduce the number of unwanted pregnancies through sex education and the wide availability of effective birth control. However, many "pro-lifers" believe that the only moral way to prevent pregnancy is through abstinence.

Beyond the Clash of Absolutes

Tribe writes: *If the clash of absolutes is a clash between life (the life of a fetus) on the one hand, and liberty (that of a woman) on the other, solutions that split the difference—denying some fetuses life and some women liberty—hardly offer a solution.* It is problematic, he adds, that the pro-choice movement draws support disproportionately from scientists, intellectuals, and high-earning men and women, while the pro-life movement draws support disproportionately from those with less education and wealth. Such differences in the social position of opponents in the abortion debate create a sense of mutual distrust. Abortion foes are inclined to denounce "pro-choicers" as immoral, while pro-choice advocates decry the inconsistency of those in the pro-life movement who also oppose gun control and support the death penalty. For everyone, on both sides of the debate, Tribe offers one final prescription—that of mutual respect: *For both sides . . . a greater measure of humility seems in order. If we genuinely believe in the democratic principle of one person, one vote, then each of us will have to treat the votes, and hear the voices, of our "opponents" as being no less worthy or meaningful than our own.*

SEXUAL HARASSMENT ON THE JOB

by William Petrocelli and Barbara Kate Repa, Nolo Press, Berkeley, California, 1992

The American workplace has changed radically over the past few decades. More women than ever have entered the workforce, assuming jobs that once were exclusively considered "men's work." As a result of these changes, the problems of recognizing and dealing with sexual harassment in the workplace have become more important than ever. According to William Petrocelli and Barbara Kate Repa, employers and employees alike need to educate themselves on the current laws governing sexual discrimination and harassment. Female workers, in particular, need to learn what constitutes sexual harassment and what they can do about it.

In *Sexual Harassment on the Job*, Petrocelli and Repa address these issues in a style that is eminently readable, informative, and precise. By examining numerous case histories at both the state and federal levels, the authors manage to clarify just what constitutes harassment and to let readers know what can be done about it—in the interests of a richer and more productive working environment for everyone.

❖ ◆ ❖

Background, Causes and Effects

Sexual harassment is legally defined as any instance of "unwelcome sexual advance or conduct on the job that creates an intimidating, hostile or offensive working environment." Simply put, explain the authors, sexual harassment is "any offensive conduct related to an employee's gender that a reasonable woman or man should not have to endure." This definition obviously covers a wide range of illegal conduct, all the way from making belittling or sexist comments to actually demanding sexual favors—either overtly or covertly—in order for a worker to attain or keep a job. In most cases, the authors note, sexual harassment goes unreported because victims fear embarrassment, degradation, or retaliation—and sometimes because they simply do not know how to report or confront their harasser.

Petrocelli and Repa begin with an interesting observation: *Sexual harassment results from a misuse of power—not from sexual attraction.* In this sense, the authors claim that men most often harass women out of resentment: they see them as competitors for jobs and promotions. Even when the conscious intent is not to force women into lower-paying jobs, the authors argue that this is often the effect.

Petrocelli and Repa enumerate several effects of sexual harassment. Women, they say, may be fired for failing to accede to employers' demands; they may be denied raises and promotions, forcibly reassigned or even pushed into resigning; or they may suffer stress-related and other kinds of physical and mental injury. The ultimate impact of abuse is that women are forced to endure limited job options and stereotyped roles.

Obtaining legal protection from sexual harassment, however, has been a long, ongoing struggle. Ironically, the authors note, the Civil Rights Act of 1964 was amended to include sexual discrimination only in an attempt to get the whole law thrown out. Even after it became law, the Equal Employment Opportunities Commission (EEOC) did not enforce the statute for several years.

In 1980, under the direction of Eleanor Holmes Norton, the EEOC finally issued regulations acknowledging that "sexual harassment" was in fact tantamount to "sexual discrimination." The implications of these new regulations were clear: sexual harassment in the workplace was now deemed illegal. In late 1991, more teeth were put into the law when employees were allowed to sue for compensatory damages. Petrocelli and Repa note, however, that initiating a proper complaint often requires following a step-by-step, company-established complaint procedure, which usually includes: confronting the harasser; filing a complaint with an appropriate government agency; filing a lawsuit under the Civil Rights Act or state FEP law; and, finally, filing a common law tort suit.

Most harassment cases that come to court are tested by four fundamental legal questions:

1. **Was the conduct sexual in nature?** Legally, "sexual conduct" includes not only sexual advances but also outright hostility to women; pranks, threats and intimidation; or the use of lewd, sexual or pornographic pictures, language or jokes that create a "sexually-poisoned" workplace.

2. **Was the conduct unreasonable?** Demanding sexual favors in order to obtain a raise or promotion is clearly not reasonable behavior. Many other areas of "unreasonable" behavior, however, are not so clear. For example, for years the courts interpreted "reasonable" only from the man's point of view (putting an arm around an employee's waist is just a way to "engender a more cordial boss/employee relationship"). Fortunately, more recent decisions have recognized that a woman often sees sexual behavior from a different viewpoint (the arm around her waist may, to her, be conveying a totally different message), and that she has the right to set her own standards for what is reasonable to her.

3. **Was the conduct severe or pervasive in the workplace?** EEOC investigators look at:
   - *whether the conduct was verbal, physical, or both;*
   - *how frequently it occurred;*
   - *whether the conduct was hostile and patently offensive;*
   - *whether the alleged harasser was a direct supervisor;*
   - *whether others joined in perpetuating the harassment;*
   - *whether the harassment was directed at more than one individual.*

4. **Was the conduct unwelcome?** "The problem is timing," say the authors. "The woman must show that the conduct was unwelcome and offensive to her at the time it occurred. Sometimes that can be difficult." Recent court

decisions, however, have indicated that neither a woman's appearance, her previous activities, nor her prior consent to sexual activity forfeit her right to file a harassment claim.

First Steps to Stopping Harassment

There is no one "best" way to handle such harassment; however, before "deciding whether to take informal or formal action," a woman should carefully examine the behavior that is making her "uncomfortable, angry or frustrated" and gather her personal feelings. Talk to fair-minded friends, the authors advise. Then, if her gut feeling still tells her that she is being harassed, it is time to take action.

The first step they suggest is *confrontation:* the woman should tell her harasser specifically what behavior she finds objectionable. If the harasser persists, she can either tell him a second time or put her complaint in writing.

Some harassers will continue their behavior even after they have been warned. In these instances, the authors point out, a woman can chose one of three courses: quit her job, stay on and hope for improvement, or, preferably, take some action.

The authors suggest that an employee take action first by obtaining "official help either from your employer or a state or federal agency." She then should collect as much detailed evidence as possible about the harassment—including any evidence in the form of notes, drawings, photos or other material either given to her personally or posted on bulletin boards. She should also keep a detailed journal of what is said and done to her, how it makes her feel, and the names of any witnesses. Particularly she should include her own verbal and physical responses to the advances or lewd comments. She might then consider writing a letter to the harasser and her supervisor detailing the harassment, retaining a copy for possible further action. And finally, if after all these measures the harassment does not cease, she should seek legal counsel and take action—either through the court system or through company procedure. At the same time, she should consider joining a support group for victims of sexual harassment.

Workplace Policies and Procedures

"In the past," the authors write, "most employee manuals were little more than puff pieces . . . Now, however, employee manuals are used to define and obtain workplace rights . . . An employer can set out the conditions of employment . . . And an employee can legally enforce them." Unfortunately, however, many companies still act as if ignoring sexual harassment will make it go away. In these instances, Petrocelli and Repa suggest that employees band together to reinforce existing policies—or to initiate new ones.

For a company's "sexual harassment policy to be effective, it must be tailored to the needs and sensibilities of the employees." When harassment problems are present in a company, an employer may better determine employee needs by conducting an informal, clandestine survey:

1. Evaluate the level of sexual hostility in the company: Is there an observable motive behind much of the sex-based friction, jokes or pin-ups? (e.g. latent resentment of the harassed, a desire to be thought of as macho by peers, a hidden wish to impress or strike up a romance with an employee.)

2. Measure employee comfort level: Is there too little—or too much—gender mixing?

3. Casually peruse the office gossip quotient: How much of it contains sexual content?

4. Compare company promotion records: Do men and women receive equal recognition and advancement?

5. Evaluate the criteria for equity and advancement in the company: Are female employees pressured in any way to trade sex for promotions or equal treatment?

If the employer's informal "survey" signals problems in any of these areas, the employer needs to ensure that new policy is implemented to resolve these issues. Such a policy should begin with a short, clear statement that sexual harassment will not be tolerated in the office. Then it can articulate particular areas of concern. Specifically it should answer seven basic questions:

- **What behaviors are prohibited**—including verbal harassment, ogling, displaying offensive materials, and physical harassment?

- **What actions will be taken** for first-time and repeat offenses?

- **What are the guidelines for reporting** any offenses?

- **What are the provisions for prompt and confidential investigations**—or appointing an outside investigator to look into the complaint?

- **How will the results be made known**—to both the accused and the accuser?

- **What stands will be taken** against any forms of retaliation?

- **How will further training and monitoring be provided** within the company?

As Petrocelli and Repa also note, "The tone and tenor of the investigation of a harassment complaint often means the difference between achieving a prompt and satisfactory resolution of the problem or having it escalate into an expensive legal battle." A prompt and fair company investigation can contribute significantly to bringing problems to a quick and satisfactory conclusion.

Legal Remedies

When company rules are non-existent, not observed, or not enforced, a harassed employee can appeal to legal remedies in various arenas. For instance, most states are equipped with *Fair Employment Practice* (FEP) statutes. Similarly, *common law tortes* can be effective instruments for obtaining compensation—including money for personal injuries, punitive damages and attorney fees.

Generally, however, torte and FEP statutes are ineffective in efforts to reinstate jobs or promotions or to change company procedures. In these cases, the employee's attorney will often file a complaint to include any and all possible legal remedies.

EDUCATIONAL RENAISSANCE

by Marvin Cetron and Margaret Gayle, St. Martin's Press, New York, N.Y., 1991

In *Educational Renaissance*, Marvin Cetron and Margaret Gayle concede that in recent decades the American educational system has failed its students, in large part due to the fact that our school systems have been "designed more for organizational and political convenience than for learning." However, after examining hundreds of reform efforts underway throughout the United States, the authors claim that there is "substantial good news about our schools." Indeed, their purpose in writing the book "is to spread the good word . . . The lessons in this book, all of them drawn from today's experience, offer an encouraging preview of education as we will soon come to know it."

Rebuilding the System

Cetron and Gayle report that there are numerous positive trends in our school systems, among them systemic reforms that include the textbook selection process and school funding. The authors note, for instance, that recently Texas and California have begun to resist both liberal and conservative pressures to choose the "right" textbook and have rededicated themselves to their original purpose: to provide students with texts that best give them "the skills and information needed to function in society." Because Texas and California dominate the textbook market, the authors note that these states' reforms will "soon improve textbooks throughout the country."

School systems have also begun to redress funding inequities from district to district. For instance, some states have revised "property-based school funding" in order to equalize school budgets. Elsewhere, states and school districts have experimented with "parental-choice" plans and with "school-based management" programs. A parental-choice plan, which emphasizes a school's *quality* over its location, allows parents to enroll their children in schools outside their districts. In a school-based management program, state and federal bureaucrats have no influence on school curricula; instead, principals and teachers decide "what to teach, how to teach it, when to schedule classes, how to maintain discipline, and what criteria to use in weighing their students' performances."

Other reform initiatives aim directly at the quality of classroom instruction. These initiatives, however, despite challenges from the National Education Association, have centered on recruitment practices, teacher training, and merit-pay increases. For example, the authors report that there is an increase in the recruitment of teachers from business and industry, with the idea of getting "practicing chemists to teach chemistry, accountants to teach arithmetic, and so on." Similarly, schools are revising their teacher-training and competency standards. Connecticut, the authors note, now refuses to hire teachers with education degrees. Instead, "would-be teachers must now major in the subjects they hope to teach." Finally, the authors observe that merit-pay programs have had some success. In these schools, teachers are evaluated by their school principals and then rated according to their performances: "Those who receive the top rating qualify for a merit-pay raise . . . Those who receive the lowest rating could be fired." Whatever the approach, the authors believe that any reforms designed to improve classroom instruction "will serve our students well."

Because research data show that a child's personality is determined during preschool years and that by age ten a child likely to drop out is "already scoring lower on standardized achievement tests," the authors say that elementary school curricula will undergo a radical transformation in the 1990s. The trend, they note, is toward an elementary school that provides not only a standard curriculum but also offers comprehensive day care, preschool, and kindergarten programs. Already, pilot programs like "Schools of the 21st Century" are operational. Developed by Yale psychology professor Dr. Edward Ziglar, this system proposes to "keep our public schools open throughout the working day, and long enough before and after so that parents could drop their children off on the way to work and pick them up on the way home. During that period, a separate faculty would provide competent, reliable care for children aged three through twelve whose parents were unavailable." By implementing programs like Schools of the 21st Century, the authors believe that "our national dropout rate will fall, test scores will climb, and we will know that the difficult task of building a whole new educational infrastructure was well worth the cost and effort it required."

Yet another reform the authors predict "will sweep our schools in the 1990s" concerns vocational alternatives. Because "some 75 percent of new jobs will not require a college degree" but rather "specialized training of the kind in which vocational schools once excelled," our school system will be forced to meet this challenge. To fail to do so, they argue, will spell economic disaster. Among the features "critical to the success of vocational training in the 1990s," Cetron and Gayle emphasize three: *rigorous focus on the job market; accessibility for the student from 7:00 A.M. to 10:00 P.M. five days a week throughout the year;* and *equal importance placed on academic as well as vocational subjects.*

The last kind of systemic reform the authors foresee is that "American business will become ever more deeply involved in our schools." Having examined our school system, say Cetron and Gayle, "corporate executives are frankly scared." With undereducated workers, how are they supposed to "win back their markets from the Japanese, who may have the highest average literacy any society has yet achieved?" To combat this deficiency, Cetron and Gayle note that businesses across the country have already formed partnerships with "more than 40 percent of the nation's grammar and high schools." Regardless of whether these "educational partnerships" provide tutoring or funding, the authors remain convinced that "this trend will gain such momentum that no school system in need of help will have to go without it."

Classroom Reforms

One of the key issues educators are now debating is *what* children should learn. Surprisingly, note Cetron and Gayle, the United States is the only developed country in the world without a national core curriculum for its students. According to the authors, however, "this situation should improve dramatically" over the next decade because educators will concentrate on developing a standardized curriculum for our schools. Likely to be included in this core curriculum are "the most essential subjects: English, math, science, and computer literacy."

Indeed, if Cetron and Gayle are correct, computers might very well have to compensate for expected teacher shortages in the coming decade. In that worst-case scenario, "computerized instruction will be our only hope of making up the deficit." With the advent of interactive, multimedia educational software, the authors believe that computers can be "more than automated drillmasters, or substitutes for human teachers." Rather, as sources of both "information and feedback," computers can help students "develop analytical and creative abilities that are required for any productive role in the modern world, [which, after all] is the real promise of computerized education."

One of the most radical trends in classroom reform, however, will "rebuild schools almost from the ground up." Such reform will not only dispense with "today's watered-down course elements" and give students "a more hearty intellectual diet," but it will also replace "standard teaching methods with more difficult and effective techniques." In essence, say the authors, classrooms will likely follow some variation of the philosopher Mortimer J. Adler's Padeia model, which is organized around "three modes of learning": "the acquisition of organized knowledge" in the arts, humanities and sciences; "the development of intellectual skills" that improve analytical thinking; and "the enhancement of *understanding* of basic ideas and values." The authors feel that one of the benefits of this kind of reform will be that "academic performance should rise quickly, and dropout rates fall, in the years to come."

Profiles of Progress

Cetron and Gayle examine four school systems that, in their estimation, represent possibilities of progress in the next decades. These model school systems extend across the nation from Virginia to California; yet each one in its own way addresses current problems of *attendance, performance, resources,* and *funding.*

In Fairfax County, Virginia, for instance, the authors highlight a school system which, if one measures success by "dropout rates, SAT scores, and the number of children who go on to college," is clearly an educational triumph. The authors attribute a large part of the county's success to widespread public support: "If parents and their childless neighbors genuinely want good public schools, almost no force in the country can stop them." As a result, the Fairfax County school system enjoys quality teaching, a decentralized bureaucracy, a full-day kindergarten, and a model preschool program. Cetron and Gayle write, "If there is a single lesson to be drawn from Fairfax County's experience that other districts can use, this has to be it: If would-be reformers make sure that local residents know what they are doing, and what benefits any proposed reforms have to offer, then they will give school reform all the support it needs."

In Rochester, Minnesota, school administrators and educators grew tired of "reactive, short-term problem-solving and set the stage for lasting improvement. Their approach was to create a systematic process for long-range strategic planning"—a forward-thinking strategy that produced results. For instance, district residents, teachers, and Board of Education members collaborated on a five-year plan that established "learner goals" for its students as well as "long-range goals" for its administrators. At the end of the first five-year plan, writes the superintendent of schools, "we accomplished all of our original goals. Perhaps more important," the superintendent adds, "we still have a firm sense of where we are going in the years ahead."

In California, state educators committed themselves to a "reform strategy" that promises, in only six years, significantly improved students' SAT scores and decreased dropout rates. The strategy was guided by two simple premises: first, that the "ability to abstract, conceptualize, and solve problems" is essential if we wish "to prepare thinking citizens who understand democracy and its ways"; and second, that "all children can learn to think, understand democracy and the culture around them, and become prepared for the changing job market." According to the California Superintendent of Public Instruction, within a decade reform-minded educators "will transform our nation's schools into the world class systems that our children deserve."

Toward a More Literate Tomorrow

Cetron and Gayle are encouraged by the reform initiatives they have encountered across the country, from which, in their view, we can draw nine key lessons:

1. We must *raise educational standards* at all grade levels.

2. We must ensure that schools and teachers *meet* these new standards.

3. Educators and students alike must spend more time in school.

4. We must reward educators and students for *performance,* not "time served."

5. We must establish a comprehensive national program of preschools and day-care centers.

6. We must *increase school budgets* in order to pay teachers a living wage and give them the resources they need to do their jobs.

7. We must use computers both to compensate for teacher shortages as well as to take advantage of technology's unique benefits.

8. We must seek a *partnership* with business and industry.

9. We must ensure that everyone involved in educational reform has "bought into" the program.

If, the authors conclude, "the United States is to survive as an economic leader, parents—and everyone who reads this book—must accept responsibility for the performance of their local school system." Accepting this responsibility means volunteer work in the schools, lobbying legislators to increase school budgets, and collaborating with teachers and administrators to see that the money is spent wisely. "Above all, we must make certain that our children understand the importance of a good education and have the support required for the difficult job of learning."

REINVENTING GOVERNMENT

by David Osborne and Ted Gaebler, Penguin Books, New York, N.Y., 1993

Our governments are in deep trouble today. This book is for those who are disturbed by that reality. It is for those who care about government . . . or simply want their governments to be more effective.

Every day, say David Osborne and Ted Gaebler in this book, we witness the legendary inefficiency of our national, state and local governments. *Bureaucracy* was once a complimentary word. But times—and the world—have changed, and governments have failed to keep up with the changes. Today, citizens are simultaneously demanding more and better services—all at less cost. Proposition 13 in California and similar legislation around the country, for instance, have forced small communities to survive on half their usual tax income.

A few progressive governments have learned to survive—and even flourish in this climate—by taking some fundamental steps in a revolutionary direction. Those who have succeeded in reinventing government for the most part share ten basic operational concepts—philosophies which, the authors claim, make up the heart and soul of any attempt to reinvent government.

1. *Catalytic Government: Steering Rather Than Rowing*

Traditionally, governments have had two functions: taxing the populace and providing services in exchange. This worked for as long as tax incomes kept pace with economic growth. But today, with the advent of an ever tighter economy, there often isn't enough money to provide the services sought by a more demanding public.

In 1975, Mayor George Latimer of St. Paul began to search out creative ways to solve his city's problems, using less money rather than more. He established a Development Corporation that offered loans and loan guarantees, made deals with banks and investment companies, and expanded volunteer organizations. In doing so, Mayor Latimer discovered one of the keys to modern governmental success: to redefine government's role so that it acts primarily *not* to provide services itself, but to see that services *are* provided through the enlistment of volunteer and private enterprise.

This approach to governing has many advantages. It allows governments to steer, rather than row, the boat. Passing the rowing on to others frees governments to do that which they do best: shaping policy and seeing that it is carried out. Governmental entities simply should see that required services are delivered in the most efficient way; if the lines between the public and private sectors get blurred in the process, does it really matter?

2. *Community-Owned Government: Empowering the People*

When Lee Brown became Houston's chief of police, he overcame major hurdles by assigning the majority of his officers to neighborhood beats and giving them the charge to *solve problems* rather than react to them. These officers in turn worked with local individuals and groups to get to the direct causes of crime. " . . . Police can be most effective if they help communities to help themselves," Brown says.

In the post-depression years, government agencies were required to step in and deal with huge financial crises. As a result, people came to depend on their leaders rather than on themselves. Many neighborhoods and cities are now seeking ways to rejuvenate "old" ideas about self-help and neighbor-helping-neighbor, to a sense of true community.

"Government cannot force people to take control of their housing or schools or neighborhoods," but they can enable or encourage such efforts. A reinvented government will seek out all possible avenues—including offers of seed money, training, and technical assistance—to encourage and enable its citizens to take control.

3. *Competitive Government: Injecting Competition Into Service Delivery*

Phoenix, Arizona, reacting to a tax revolt, put its garbage collection out for bid. As expected, the city-owned system, pitted against private suppliers, consistently lost out. But employees in the city system, determined to keep their jobs, found ways to cut costs, and eventually won the bids. As they did, private competition became sharper, forcing the public system to become even more competitive. Clearly, competition rewards innovation, makes for greater efficiency and responsiveness, and boosts the morale and pride of public employees.

4. *Mission-Driven Government: Transforming Rule-Driven Organizations*

Rules are necessary. But today we have so *many* rules that they prevent good things from happening. HUD, for example, "one of the most centralized, bureaucratic, dysfunctional systems in American government," controls public housing using a big book of regulations. "Every rule was originally laid down with the best of intentions. But the cumulative effect is gridlock." Louisville, Kentucky, however, managed to bypass most of this stifling red tape—at the same time enhancing both the quality and promptness of construction—by founding a nonprofit subsidiary of its own.

Mission-driven governments have abandoned massive rule books in favor of simply-stated "shared visions" and "sets of values"—that focus on aims and purposes. These *mission statement* directives give service organizations more motivation and flexibility for meeting changing circumstances; thus they can respond more quickly, for example, to the ebb and flow of tax revenues.

Mission-driven governments are generous in giving rule waivers to those who can accomplish the objectives at hand. They organize around clear goals, creating accountability systems which measure performance against those goals.

5. *Results-Oriented Government: Funding Outcomes, Not Inputs*

Recently, the state of Illinois discovered

that by giving more funds to those nursing homes that provide for bedridden patients, they were unknowingly encouraging the homes to keep patients in bed rather than getting them back on their feet! When they began instead to reward recoveries and releases from the homes, measured quality of care improved and costs decreased.

Governments reward their staff members for "longevity," schools for "number of students attending," welfare programs for "number of recipients," and police departments for "amount of crime." These are all *inputs*, and as a result, public employees are not inspired to solve problems.

"Because they don't measure results, bureaucratic governments rarely achieve them. But when they are funded according to outcomes, they become obsessive about performance." When governments begin to measure results, the need to improve measurements generally drives performance upward. Budgets, pay levels, and managing efforts, then, should all be shaped by *results.*

6. *Customer-Driven Government: Meeting the Needs of the Customer, Not the Bureaucracy*

Do you feel like a valued customer at your children's school, at the motor vehicle office, or at city hall? "American governments," the authors note, "are customer-blind, while *McDonald's* and *Frito-Lay* are customer-driven. This may be the ultimate indictment of bureaucratic government." Government programs, driven by the turf wars of *politics* rather than by sound customer *policy,* proliferate today because most government agencies don't receive their funds directly from the people they serve. If motor vehicle registration offices were only paid on the number of registrations they processed, employee action and accountability would change in a hurry.

"Entrepreneurial governments" ignore the political rhetoric; they listen directly to their "customers"—the total citizenry—through surveys and focus groups. And then they *help* and *enable* these "customers" to solve problems. Some governments, like the California Department of Motor Vehicles, for example, are now installing self-service computer terminals to renew driver's licenses.

7. *Enterprising Government: Earning Rather Than Spending*

In 1990, a reporting service offered to pay a local government agency for the privilege of transcribing its hearings, knowing it could then sell the transcripts to interested attorneys. The agency, however, turned the offer down. Why? It couldn't find a way to process money coming in. "We have 15 million trained spenders in American government, but few people who are trained to make money."

However, some government agencies are now learning to be "earners." They raise money by charging fees for services, allowing managers to keep savings/earnings in their departments, and gauging the return on spending as if it were an investment. "An enterprising government exposes its subsidies to public light, relies on public pressure to do away with them—and then finds ways to make money from the services involved."

8. *Anticipatory Government: Prevention Rather Than Cure*

As government became more involved in delivering services, it shifted its focus from anticipating problems to fixing them. In other words, firemen became more adept at fighting fires than at preventing them. But "anticipatory governments," those able to respond to rapid change, work on two fronts, use an ounce of prevention to save a pound of cure, and build foresight into the planning process.

Governments are now beginning to look to the future by implementing long-term strategic planning and budgeting, and by creating "rainy day" funds. They would also do well to look at fuller utilization of more efficient regional and area government coalitions.

9. *Decentralized Government: From Hierarchy to Participation and Teamwork*

With the onset of the information explosion, highly centralized organizations have become both impractical and inadequate. Decentralized organizations are more efficient, more adaptable, more effective, more innovative, and have higher morale than their slow-witted centralized cousins. Compare the Vietnam War—where control was extremely centralized—with the Gulf War—where control was delegated: decentralized. Decentralization involves more in-the-know people in the decision-making process. This participation brings high rewards both to the individual involved and to the governmental unit.

10. *Market-Oriented Government: Leveraging Change Through the Market*

"Our governments must consciously use their immense leverage to structure the market," the authors contend, "so that . . . businesses and individuals have incentives to meet our health care, child care, job training and environmental needs." Consider, for example, recycling. Some states, instead of instituting expensive recycling programs for bottles and cans, simply charge a refundable deposit for them, with excellent results.

None of this reflects conservative urgings to "leave it to the market." Indeed, it amounts to just the opposite—a *proactive intervention* in the marketplace to create incentives for solving or preventing problems.

Intervention can take place in several ways: providing information to consumers, creating or augmenting demand, making deals with private sector suppliers, developing new markets, and sharing risks.

◊ ♦ ◊

Attentive public officials and private citizens are already taking the lead, increasingly demanding that we push our present, outdated governments to move forward using more productive methods of meeting the needs of its citizenry and redefining their role from "provider" to "enabler." It's only "the lack of a vision—a new paradigm—[that] holds us back," the authors insist. "We hope our road map will empower *you* to reinvent *your* governments."

EARTH IN THE BALANCE

by Vice President Al Gore, Houghton Mifflin Co., New York, N.Y., 1992

At a time of personal upheaval—after the near-death of his son in an accident—Senator Al Gore, now Vice President of the United States, became deeply concerned about the growing prospects of environmental disaster looming over our world today. "The search for truths about this ungodly crisis and the search for truths about myself have been the same search all along," writes Gore. " . . . This life change has caused me to be increasingly impatient with the status quo, with conventional wisdom, with the lazy assumption that we can always muddle through . . . " Clearly, Gore sees a planet already in crisis. He wants a lot done—and he wants it done immediately.

We are all aware of the current social trends which portend environmental breakdown; yet up to now our response has been somewhat equivocal. It would seem that the impending mass extinction of entire species has less bearing on our actions than the news of a little girl falling in a well. Some of the environmental problems of the past have been local or regional, but now we are facing global problems—or more correctly, as Gore asserts, we are *refusing* to face our urgent global predicament.

Our current environmental threats have been triggered by two human factors: population growth and technological growth. But the biggest danger of all, Gore insists, is our indifference and ignorance: *Most people do not yet accept the fact that this crisis is extremely grave.* Some argue that we need to continue studying the problem. According to Gore, however, further investigation will just postpone the implementation of real solutions.

He points out, for example, that while the exact impact of elevated levels of carbon dioxide (CO2) in the atmosphere is unknown, we do know that our rising levels of CO2 will inevitably raise global temperatures and incur the risk of catastrophic climactic changes. Even minimal climactic change—like the "little Ice Age" of millennia past and the dust bowls of the American Midwest in the 1930s—can cause great hardship for people; and we are now in the process of inviting much more significant alterations in temperature and precipitation. The "correlation between CO2 levels and temperature levels over time is well established. "Our procrastination in dealing with this problem of the "greenhouse effect" while we wait for the outcome of "definitive" studies, is unjustified: "The insistence on complete certainty about the full details of global warming—the most serious threat that we have ever faced—is actually an effort to avoid facing the awful, uncomfortable truth . . . "

AIR

Apart from the catastrophic potential of the greenhouse effect, our air, Gore claims, is being degraded in other pernicious ways. He cites several examples:

First, chemicals are devouring our ozone layer. As a result, we can expect the "ozone hole" above the Antarctic to grow, causing increased exposure to ultraviolet rays. Among other things, this will result in an increased incidence of skin cancer and in the eventual failure of certain less tolerant crops.

Second, the atmosphere has become so polluted that it no longer functions as a self-cleaning agent. Deadly methane gases are no longer being properly broken down, and the air we breathe has become a toxic cocktail.

WATER

Global warming, with the attendant rise in sea levels as ice packs and glaciers melt, will also have a major impact on our freshwater supplies. Gore warns that this factor, combined with pollution, may drastically diminish the availability of drinking and irrigation water in the not-too-distant future—perhaps bringing about the deaths of millions. And since one-third of humanity currently lives within sixty kilometers of a coastline, rising sea elevations may create significant socioeconomic upheavals and dislocations.

An additional threat to our water supply is posed by radical changes to the land, especially deforestation. When forests are destroyed and natural cycles of transpiration, evaporation and condensation are disrupted, rains may eventually be reduced to a trickle.

Still another threat to our freshwater is the increasingly widespread chemical contamination of streams and rivers. In the U.S. and Europe, some progress has been made in reducing the amounts of pollutants pumped into the water; but in the world as a whole, Gore notes, chemical pollution continues to grow.

LAND

Deforestation not only diminishes our freshwater supply but also presents a significant threat to land and air. Since forests absorb carbon dioxide, destroying them leaves more CO2 in the atmosphere—once again boosting global warming. Gore observes that tropical rain forests are currently disappearing at the rate of one and a half acres per second. At that rate they will have totally vanished midway through the next century. The only type of land we are presently creating, he sadly notes, is desert.

As if these stark prospects were not enough, deforestation also destroys the earth's reserve of wild plant species. From opium to quinine to penicillin, most of our wonder drugs throughout the ages have been discovered and developed from plants. Now as our jungles and forests roll back into oblivion, a whole trove of unrevealed curative powers will be forever lost.

Finally, Gore touches on the problem of waste disposal. Statistically speaking, "every person in the United States produces more than twice his or her own weight in waste every day." This gross accumulation of waste (e.g. garbage, sewage, automotive refuse, etc.) is hazardous to our health and our environment. Unfortunately, recycling efforts have not been totally effective, in large part because most manufacturers are not in the market for recycled materials. To remedy the problem, Gore says, regulations must be passed to make recycling both easier and obligatory.

WHAT CAN GOVERNMENT DO?

A crisis of government has befallen us. As mass media probes further into the private dealings of our elected leaders, politicians are now often more concerned with "image" and re-election strategies than with digging in to solve unsavory problems. *Politically expedient* gestures are favored over *real*—and potentially unpopular—solutions. For instance, most Americans favor an improved environment. Who wouldn't? But when we balk at the price tag attached to specific programs, our legislators waffle. Instead of sticking to their guns and educating voters about real alternatives and outcomes, they pander to our shortsightedness with face-saving compromises that promise "everything for nothing."

So what is the solution? "Men and women who care must be politically empowered to demand and help effect remedies to ecological problems wherever they live." Our industries and businesses, Gore alleges, cannot—and will not—solve the problems by themselves. They operate within a system that rewards industrial productivity and ignores the potentially harmful side-effects. Hence, appropriate economic incentives must be put in place that encourage business and industry to consider the ecological impact of their competitive strategies.

Our religious values teach us that we are stewards of our planet. Now, we, as individuals, and as a society, need to apply those values to the environmental challenges that surround us. Empowered by knowledge and by a renewed sense of stewardship, society can alter both its attitudes and its approach to these crucial problems. Enlightened individuals who are sickened by the abuse they see heaped upon the planet will serve as catalysts for change and will succeed in bringing about a global response.

Gore points to a historical precedent for such a response to global crisis: the post-World War II Marshall Plan, in which several nations united to rebuild shattered Europe. What we need now, Gore writes, is a "Global Marshall Plan" headed up by a UN-sponsored/maintained "Stewardship Council." With the United States as a leading partner, individual nations would host a yearly Environmental Summit, similar to the annual Economic Summit.

Gore suggests that the first tasks of such future global summits would be to establish goals in five strategic areas:

1- **Stabilizing World Populations:** The world population will double to nine billion in the next 45 years, with 94% of the growth occurring in developing countries. Population growth is already putting a severe strain on the ecology of these nations—and even the ecology of the world—as rain forests are turned into cash crops. In order to control their growth, developing nations must work on three fronts: (1) raising literacy levels, (2) decreasing infant mortality, and (3) making birth control an acceptable practice.

2- **Developing and Sharing Appropriate Technologies:** Gore argues that we must rigorously search out technologies that are friendly to the environment but that will not curtail economic progress. A Strategic Environment Initiative should be established that will offer businesses tax incentives for clean technologies as well as funding for research and development, while restricting or banning outdated technologies.

3- **A New Global "Eco-nomics":** We must redefine "prosperity" and "productivity" (including the archaic GNP) and make it economically expedient to use recycled/recyclable materials. For example, a "virgin materials" fee could be instituted to invite recycling. Similarly, tougher mileage and efficiency standards for vehicles could be enacted.

4- **A New Generation of Treaties and Agreements:** Gore favors fashioning international treaties aimed at protecting the environment. However, such enactments, he observes, will only be initiated if politicians are convinced that the public demands them.

5- **A New Global Environmental Consensus:** We need fundamental changes in both the ways we gather information about the environment and the ways we use that information to educate the world, Gore argues. Somehow people need to become convinced that the globe is their personal "backyard"— and certainly no thinking, responsive individual would sully his own property. He suggests that the Space Program, via public education, might become a partner in this effort to revise the way we see our planet.

Each day that we deplete our natural resources and produce more waste, we do serious damage to our planet's ability to sustain life. For Gore, "the key to reversing the current pattern of destruction and beginning the process of restoration and recovery is to dramatically change attitudes and to remove the constant pressures exerted by population growth, greed, short-term thinking, and misguided development." There is a strong correlation between the wise, ethical choices that we make and what we and the world become. As he reminds all citizens of the world: "The choice is ours, earth is in the balance."

SOUND AND FURY

by Patrick J. Michaels, Cato Institute, Washington, D.C., 1992

The Environmental Protection Agency's spokesman John Hoffman held a press conference in 1983 to announce that unprecedented climactic changes would occur within a few years. Asserting that hundreds of independent scientists supported the Agency's findings, Hoffman cautioned that the predicted changes would raise sea levels so high that many major cities would be flooded.

"What I witnessed," Patrick J. Michaels writes in his best-selling book, *Sound and Fury*, "was the first grand attempt at environmental science (and therefore policy) by press release, a process that has since become numbingly repetitive . . . I also sensed that the issue was sufficiently emotional that people who did not go along might be subject to rough treatment."

Michaels, head climatologist for the State of Virginia and a columnist for the *Washington Post*, contends that the media and politicians are fabricating environmental crises as a result of either misinformation or self-interest. When he published an article on global warming in 1986, Michaels claims, he was severely criticized by Senator Al Gore, who, in 1989, told *Time* magazine that Michaels was, in effect, "destroying the world."

Subsequently, Michaels expanded his argument against ultra-environmentalism in *Sound and Fury*. Comparing his own views with those of the Vice-President, Michaels writes: *Gore's book* [Earth in the Balance] *begins with some suppositions and generalizations and quickly moves to firm convictions and necessary world change; I, on the other hand, start off examining the scientific evidence, then move cautiously, not wanting to solve problems—squandering vast amounts of taxpayer funds in their wake—before we know they exist.*

Global Warming and the Greenhouse Effect

Citing global warming as a phenomenon which elicits unnecessary panic, Michaels argues that although few climatologists believe global warming will cause global disaster, press releases from environmentalist-controlled sources have convinced the public that ice caps will melt, oceans will flood cities, and drought will be widespread. Moreover, Michaels contends that the effects environmentalists link to global warming would be prohibitively expensive to eradicate. The cost to reduce greenhouse gases, for instance, has been estimated at five trillion dollars, an expenditure that would cut the GNP of the U.S. by 2% a year and cost at least 600,000 jobs. Arguing that such expenditures are not warranted, Michaels writes, "The climactic history of the planet is inconsistent with forecasts of gloom and doom."

The greenhouse effect responsible for global warming *is* real, in Michaels' view, but he argues that it is in fact creating a *superior* climate with warmer winters and longer growing seasons. While certain gases in our atmosphere, such as water vapor, carbon dioxide (CO_2), and methane keep the earth heated, he explains, other forces in nature—namely, day-time cloud cover—prevent heat from increasing to dangerously high levels. Hence, Michaels argues, greenhouse effects are far more complicated than environmentalists can imagine.

Even if we were to remove all the CO_2 from our atmosphere—a process that would endanger Earth's vegetation—the mean temperature would drop only 1.5 °C. In fact, throughout most of our planet's history, the earth has had *more* CO_2 in its atmosphere than at present; the earth, in other words, is presently CO_2 *depleted*. True, the atmospheric gases have grown to a level some 60% higher than before industrialization, but "therein lies one of the most intriguing mysteries of science: if greenhouse enhancement invariably leads to an increase in surface temperature, where's the warming?"

In an effort to debunk the correlation between CO_2 production and global warming, Michaels points out that in 1988, when James Hansen, a NASA scientist, testified before Congress that world temperatures had risen over the last hundred years, no one realized that temperatures had actually risen *before* the largest increases in CO_2 occurred. Moreover, while the levels of CO_2 and other greenhouse gases in the atmosphere continue to rise, the cost of reducing the concentration would be enormous.

Environmentalists' base their catastrophic forecasts on computer models which attempt to link the increase in CO_2 to changes in weather patterns. But because climatological forecasting is so complex, Michaels contends, models are not really accurate. Since the models are unable to accurately predict *current* conditions, he argues, how can these models reliably predict future climactic changes?

Furthermore, Michaels insists, half of the CO_2-doubling that was forecast by climatologists has already occurred, and yet world temperatures have increased far less than the models predict.

Measuring temperature variations is not an easy task, notes Michaels: relocations of weather stations, adjustments in instrumentation, and revised directional readings all contribute to both inaccurate readings and temperature fluctuations. In fact, when Tom Karl of the U.S. Department of Commerce developed a comprehensive weather record of the United States, he found that even variables such as nearby construction caused measurements to oscillate, making 97% of previous weather records invalid. Michaels asserts that when Karl recalculated temperatures to account for such variables, he discovered that there had been no warming effect. Finally, Karl's findings are supported by measurements from weather satellites between 1979 and 1990 which show no warming trends and thus contradict the records used by environmentalists.

"The temperature history of the planet supports neither the Popular Vision of climactic apocalypse," says Michaels, "nor the mid-1980's . . . forecasts of global warming, either in pattern or in magnitude. Yet both the Vision and those forecasts are driving the most comprehensive experiment in central planning of energy in the history of the human race."

Although Michaels recognizes that greenhouse gases are accumulating, he asserts that global warming is far less significant than environmentalists have predicted and that the warming which has occurred results from increasing cloudiness. Greenhouse gases probably cool the upper atmosphere, he posits, and this cooling transforms the particulate produced by industry into clouds. Increasing clouds lower daytime and summer temperatures and, since clouds help trap the heat given off by the earth, *elevate* temperatures in the winter at night. In support of his theory, Michaels points out that measurements from around the world show increased cloudiness; additionally, when dissolved CO_2 is extracted from polar ice cores and analyzed, no long-term trend is found. In other words, regardless of temperature fluctuations and other climactic variables, CO_2 levels rise and fall *at random*.

According to Michaels, four signs would be evident if clouds are responsible for mitigating greenhouse warming:

(1) On long, hot summer days, the cooling effect from clouds should be pronounced; (2) On shorter, winter days, the cooling effect from clouds should be attenuated; (3) On long winter nights the warming effect from clouds should be more pronounced; and (4) On shorter, summer night the warming effect from clouds should be attenuated.

According to Michaels, Karl's adjusted U.S. temperature data remarkably follow these exact four patterns. Likewise, Karl's data analysis of his recently-developed weather data base (that takes in the U.S., the former USSR, and China), when evaluated by time-of-day and season, suggests that, in accord with Michael's theory, clouds are offsetting the greenhouse effect and that warming at night is ten times greater than warming by day.

Doomsdayers and Their Strategies

According to Michaels, those who use environmental science for political ends tend to follow these strategies:

1. *Define the Problem As Apocalyptic.* First acid rain, then ozone holes, and now global warming have been successively defined as global crises that threaten lives and property on a massive scale.

2. *Present the Apocalyptic View As a Mainstream View: Dissenters Are Crackpots.* Sweeping statements such as "all scientists agree that the greenhouse effect is real" emerge, followed by other statements to the effect that scientists also anticipate a catastrophe.

3. *Play Up the Lurid Prognostications and Imagery of Doom Because Apocalypse Sells Newspapers and Television Time.* Because the media favor sensational news, their reports are neither objective nor unbiased; and these biased reports often incite the public to side with the environmentalists. What's more, the media, says Michaels, frequently suppress vital facts that unmask the real picture of environmental non-crisis. As *Newsweek's* Gregg Easterbrook states: *Lately Gore and the distinguished biologist Paul Erhlich have ventured into dangerous territory by suggesting that journalists quietly self-censor environmental evidence that is not alarming.*

4. *Build Massive Financial Support.* Contributions to the largest environmental groups in 1988 totalled $300 million; during the same period, the contributions to all the presidential election campaigns were about $90 million.

5. *Use That Lobbying Support to Pass Economically Profound Legislation Before the Necessary Science Has Been Completed.* This is a favorite tactic of legislators. For example, the members of Congress were once so busy preparing to pass the Clean Air Act at a cost of $40 billion that they couldn't hold a hearing to familiarize themselves with the results of a $600 million study that concluded that there was no catastrophe associated with acid rain after all.

6 *Invent a New One.* They start the cycle all over again to enhance their images as environmental protectors.

When policy-makers are confronted with evidence that fails to support their hypotheses, Michaels contends, they offer improbable reasons why their dire predictions did not prove true or they respond as one environmentalist did: "The data don't count!"

Michaels comes down especially hard on Vice-President Gore, who, the author charges, won a platform to express his views by basing much of Clinton's Presidential campaign on the environment, "commandeer[ing] global warming as an issue . . . "

Michaels argues that we now have three competing environmental apocalypses: acid rain, ozone depletion, and global warming. In reality these phenomena are interrelated, Michaels says: the same particulate which apparently cause acid rain also help to create the clouds that offset global warming; in turn, these same clouds offset the ultraviolet burning caused by ozone depletion. And the higher CO2 of global warming offsets vegetation damage from acid rain.

Recently, scientists have worked hard to eliminate errors from the climactic forecast models. In each case the corrections have reduced warming to one-half the former projection. And though Michaels admits that even the newest models don't accurately predict present temperatures, he considers them useful in showing that most of the warming that is taking place originates in winter, at night, and in extremely cold climates. Clearly these are not catastrophic scenarios.

Michaels suggests that, in making their apocalyptic cases, environmentalists imply—wrongly—that a consensus exists among scientists. In fact, a survey of the authors and reviewers of a 1990 pro-environmentalist report published by the U.N. found that 40% disagreed with the information; nearly all of a group of equally qualified scientists *not* involved in putting together the U.N. report agreed that no crisis is evident; and most professional climatologists, meteorologists and geophysical scientists argue on one point, according to Michaels, and that is: we lack evidence of any crisis. "Historians in the 21st century will note that, even by the mid-1980s," Michaels writes, "the best available data indicated that the then Popular Vision of climate catastrophe was a failure . . . On warm nights we will look out at green fields and wonder how we could have been so foolish." Unfortunately, Michaels concludes, the money will have already been spent.

HEALING THE PLANET

by Paul and Anne Ehrlich, Addison-Wesley Publishing, New York, N.Y., 1991

Environmentalists Paul and Anne Ehrlich feel that the enormous and still-expanding scale of human activity on our planet is setting the stage for a disaster of global proportions. "A billion or more people could starve in the first few decades of the next century . . . the health and happiness of virtually every human being could be compromised, and social breakdown and conflict could destroy civilization as we know it . . . " Nevertheless, the authors hold out the hope that Earth's inhabitants will change their pattern of overdevelopment in time: "There remains a chance that civilization can alter its headlong rush toward the brink, that Earth can be healed, and that our descendants could live lives of plenty, dignity, and peace."

In *Healing the Planet*, the Ehrlichs first describe the increasing threat of overpopulation, then undertake to investigate the destruction of the ozone and the pollution of land and water. Finally, they turn their attention to the need to develop an effective, functional global environmental policy.

Our Life-Support Systems

Our earth consists of a complex ecosystem in which all matter—animate and inanimate—is interrelated. For example, earth's ecosystem generates and maintains soil, which provides for the disposal of wastes and the cycling of nutrients. It controls the carbon cycle of natural fuels, the nitrogen cycle of our air, and supplies food. The ecosystem also contains a vast library of genetic material from which we can design new crops and create new medicines.

Unfortunately, overpopulation jeopardizes the health of the ecosystem by disrupting the conditions necessary for maintaining life. Plant and animal species are becoming extinct at a faster rate than at any time since the death of the dinosaurs. And, as the authors point out, what may be even more alarming is the fact that all of our attempts to provide substitutes for our vanishing natural ecosystems have failed, except on a very small scale.

Energy Traps and Global Warming

The environmental impact of overpopulation can be illustrated with a simple equation: *Environmental impact* (I) is determined by *Population* (P), *Affluence* (A), and *Technology* (T). In other words, I = PAT; the greater the population, the affluence and the technology of a society, the greater impact it has on the environment.

The authors suggest that energy consumption may be the best single index of these three factors, and point out that the average American expends about 11 kilowatts (KW) of energy each day, or the equivalent of a hundred 100 KW light bulbs. By contrast, a citizen of sub-Saharan Africa consumes only about .03 KW. As a result, "the average American does about 70 times as much damage to the global environment."

The environmental impact of energy consumption on a global scale is far reaching. In the year 1990, the world consumed about 13 billion kilowatts—or 13 "terawatts" (TW) of energy. If earth's population continues to grow at its present rate, energy consumption will double in 40 years. If the average per capita consumption of energy in affluent countries increases by half during this same time—which is not unlikely, considering the speed of technological advancement—consumption will quintuple to 65 terawatts! And even if we find ways to consume less energy, the Ehrlichs argue, the PAT is likely to double—sending out intensely devastating environmental shock waves around the planet.

How can we escape this energy trap? "The only chance we see for a planet on which everyone could lead a decent life," the Ehrlichs say, "depends on successful improvement of energy efficiency everywhere."

Part of the solution may lie in using renewable energy resources instead of fossil fuels, particularly coal. Because the development of hydro, geothermal, and wind-generated power all pose some technical problems, the Ehrlichs are clearly in support of solar power as the best choice for the future. *If* safety and waste disposal issues can be resolved, nuclear power may also prove useful as an energy supplement.

In any case, the continued use of fossil fuels contributes to global warming, which may have serious repercussions. Unchecked global warming will reduce agricultural production worldwide, damage natural ecosystems, raise sea levels, and threaten fresh water supplies. Hurricanes will be intensified and other natural disasters may follow. Many consider such dire predictions as mere hype, spouted in order to gain some sort of political or financial advantage. The Ehrlichs, however, insist that scientific evidence is on their side. What's more, they feel as if we simply cannot take chances with such a fragile—and obviously indispensable—ecosystem: "Do we want to keep it up and find out what will happen? What do we gain by playing 'environmental roulette'?"

So, how do we go about reducing our dependence on fossil fuels and halt the resultant global warming? The authors suggest that we can impose a "carbon tax" on electric power plants to encourage conversion to non-fossil fuel consumption. Such a tax might work like the dollar-per-gallon gasoline tax, except that power plants would be taxed several hundred dollars per ton of pollutants. They also favor making a concerted effort to end deforestation and to replant our forests. Although this step would be difficult and expensive, they argue that "the benefits of forest restoration and widespread tree planting would far outweigh the costs."

Finally, the Ehrlichs suggest that we research ways to control other greenhouse gases such as methane and CFC (chlorofluorocarbon), with each country taking a specific role in solving these problems. For example, affluent, energy-efficient countries like Japan might help China develop a solar energy economy; energy inefficient countries like Poland and the United States could pledge themselves to cleaning up their own messes.

Unfortunately, "the United States so far has not initiated any measures specifically designed to slow global warming"—citing the specter of cost as a determining factor in the debate. One cost estimate suggests that the price tag for doing so could reach a trillion dollars by the year 2010. Even so, "it would still be a small payment for insurance against economic losses that could run into tens of trillions of dollars over that period if the worst happened . . . "

Ozone: A Cautionary Tale

Only in the early 1970s did scientists begin to trace the effects of fluorocarbons on the ozone layer—the thin, ozone-concentrated region in earth's upper atmosphere (lying at between ten and twenty miles in altitude), that absorbs solar ultraviolet radiation not screened out by other atmospheric components. In brief, they discovered that the release of CFCs or "Freon" from refrigerators, air conditioners, and aerosol sprays destroyed large amounts of the ozone, the mantle that protects us from the Sun's. This discovery, however, elicited little interest. Later, when other groups of scientists discovered a "hole" in the ozone above Antarctica, concern in the scientific community turned to public alarm. Not only can a thinning of the ozone layer increase the risks of skin cancer, but it could also cause massive damage to ecosystems, climates, and agricultural production around the world. Happily, after twenty years of discussion, international agreements to ban CFCs entirely are now being signed and implemented.

The Ehrlichs point out, however, that there is an important lesson to be learned here: in the endless political debates, scientific studies, and other delays in coming to the solutions for environmental calamities, the damage—much of it irreparable—continues to mount.

Pollution: Dead Trees and Poisoned Water

Another serious threat to our environment is air pollution. The Ehrlichs estimate that it causes some 70,000 deaths and millions of injuries a year. Greater still is the hazard air pollution poses to natural and agricultural ecosystems. Air pollution produces acids, which are eventually deposited on plants in the form of "acid rain." And when combined with global warming, acid rain creates many serious problems. " . . . The fundamental long-term solution to problems of air pollution," write the authors, "[requires a significant] reduction in the scale of human activities," such as taking the bus instead of driving a car, dressing warmly in the winter rather than turning up the heat, and finding ways to cut back on electricity usage. According to the authors, the 1990 Clean Air Act, which requires that an annual air emissions test be performed on every vehicle, is a giant step forward in keeping our air at an acceptably healthy level.

As serious a threat as it is, air pollution is only part of an even more profound pollution problem. A "witches' brew" of toxic substances has found its way into our groundwater supplies, our rivers, our streams, and our oceans. If the fresh water reserves become contaminated, the effects on natural ecosystems could be catastrophic.

Fortunately, the effects of water pollution appear to be reversible, the Great Lakes being a case in point in which "a reversal [was] both technically and economically feasible." But the authors warn that one positive example does not take into account all the factors involved in cleaning up a polluted system; and "the consequences to both the region's ecosystem and human health are sufficiently subtle that action may be delayed while the problems are studied—and unnecessarily perpetuated."

Risks, Costs, Benefits and Policy

The Ehrlichs claim that we need to make decisions now to protect the future of our world. "There is no question as to whether or not we should affect our environment—the questions all center on the *scale and consequences* of our involvement."

One way of measuring the effects of our environmental impact is by running risk- and cost-benefit analyses. Even though some critics complain that these kinds of studies "can result in serious errors," they can also serve a useful, illustrative purpose. For instance, many of us choose to use private cars for convenience. If, however, we take into account that traffic congestion reduces convenience and increases direct risk (accidents) as well as indirect risk (air pollution), then perhaps we'll be less likely to use our cars so frequently.

As a hedge against environmental catastrophe, the Ehrlichs also suggest in effect that America take out a figurative "insurance policy" with a yearly premium of $100 billion—a figure, they say, that represents only about one-third the total amount it spends on military security—money that can be used to promptly research and resolve environmental impact issues. We also need to cultivate more conservative environmental risk philosophies—if only to increase humanity's margin for error: "The basic way to [put that philosophy into action]," they write, "is to reduce the scale of human activities . . . The dilemma facing human societies, rich and poor alike, is how to manage the unavoidable population and economic expansion ahead while reducing the scale of total impact on the environment."

None of us will be able to escape the large-scale environmental issues: we must either change our habits and come up with better, more efficient energy solutions, or we must pay the consequences. In addition to recycling or driving our cars less, many more of us need to become politically active and demand that all politicians respond to environmental concerns. "We have to take responsibility ourselves for a far-reaching transformation of our society. We wish you luck; all of us will need it."

THE HUNDREDTH MONKEY

by Ken Keyes, Jr., Vision Books, Coos Bay, Oregon, 1982

As its author says, "this book does not deal with petty matters," but with a grave problem that has threatened planet Earth for half a century: the possibility of our self-annihilation by means of nuclear war. It might be claimed that the danger of self-destruction is largely past, given the collapse of the Soviet Union and the perils of the "Cold War," and the fact that nuclear power is no longer seen as the best answer to our energy needs. But unfortunately, though the nature of the nuclear threat has changed, it has not disappeared. More nations than ever are now armed with atomic bombs, and there is renewed world-wide pressure to build nuclear power plants.

Ken Keyes is clearly committed to abolishing the use of all forms of nuclear energy. He has not copyrighted his book and makes it available at cost. What sets it apart from others like it is the importance Keyes places on the role of the individual citizen in dealing with a critical, planet-wide concern. He illustrates the power of "collective consciousness" by describing a phenomenon that has come to be known among scientists as "the hundredth monkey."

❖ ♦ ❖

Social scientists have been observing the Japanese macaque at several locations in the wild for over forty years. In 1952, the observers gave the macaques on one island sweet potatoes to eat—sweet potatoes that had been dropped in the sand. The monkeys relished the delicacies, but made it obvious that they *didn't* relish the sand stuck to them. Then one young female macaque found she could get rid of the sand by washing the potatoes in a nearby stream. Before long, she had taught her mother and friends the same trick.

Over the next six years, all the young monkeys on the island learned to wash their potatoes. Most of the older monkeys, however, continued to eat them dirty.

Then one day in the autumn of 1958, almost all the macaques on the island suddenly began to wash their food! Not only that, but it was soon found that in some inexplicable way, the monkeys' new habit had spontaneously vaulted both to other islands and to the Japanese mainland. In a very short time, virtually the whole of the macaque population in several locations began to wash food.

Scientists theorize that once some pivotal, "critical-mass" number of monkeys discovered the potato-washing solution, *all* became aware of it. Keyes sums up this "collective consciousness" phenomenon concisely: *when a certain critical number achieves an awareness, this new awareness may be communicated from mind to mind.* Perhaps it was the hundredth monkey whose discovery triggered the explosion of awareness; perhaps it was the seventy-fifth, or the hundredth and thirtieth. The crucial point is that as long as only a limited number of individuals share the awareness of a new and better way of doing something, that awareness *remains* limited; but at some point, the addition of one more "aware" individual results in the mass diffusion of awareness throughout the group.

This phenomenon has far-reaching implications when applied to human beings. To Keyes it means that *your* personal awareness may be a critical catalyst in saving the world from nuclear war. You may be, so to speak, the "hundredth monkey."

Frighteningly, says Keyes, every large or small nation will soon have a supply of nuclear bombs as a "deterrent" to aggression. And, as past world events have already demonstrated, "the passions of many military and political leaders and terrorists are such that sooner or later they will unleash every bit of destructiveness they can get their hands on." As Herbert Scoville, Jr., a former deputy director of the CIA commented in the late '70s: *"The unfortunate situation today is that we are moving . . . toward the probability or the likelihood that a nuclear conflict will actually break out—and that somebody will use one of these nuclear weapons in a conflict or even by accident."* And no one, as Scoville reminds us, could ever "win" in a nuclear war. The global consequences would be catastrophic. Hundreds of millions of people would probably be killed outright—leaving most of the survivors to die from radiation sickness.

Any dictator who becomes angry, fearful, discouraged or overconfident could conceivably set off the fatal chain of events. Likewise, a nuclear accident could be triggered by mechanical failure, human error, the crash of a ship or plane carrying nuclear weapons, or even the inadvertent bombing of a power plant during a "conventional" war. In the past, despite every technical precaution, both the United States and Russia have suffered major accidents at nuclear power plants.

But we *don't* have to resign ourselves to this scenario. "In case you are feeling there is nothing you can do about the increasing nuclear menace that hangs over our heads," Keyes reminds us, "remember the story of the Hundredth Monkey. Your own awareness and action can be the added energy needed to make the difference between life and death . . . " Nuclear war and nuclear accident *can* be prevented. An aroused public has the power to demand and achieve change. Mass action has caused policy changes in the past; we need to work together to solve this present—and future—threat.

Unfortunately, too many people are ignoring the warning signals. Imagine yourself as part of a family floating down a river in a raft or canoe. You carefully steer away from the hazards you see, but pay no attention to the rushing noise that indicates a steep waterfall downstream. Are citizens of planet Earth in just such a position? Are we ignoring the unmistakable signs of impending catastrophe?

Nuclear contaminants are already damaging the health of a significant number of people. The incidence of lung cancer among Navajo Indians working in uranium mines in the southwestern United States has increased 85 percent. Nuclear submarine workers in New Hampshire are contracting cancer at double the normal rate.

In 1954, a cast and crew of 220 people filmed a movie on the sandy dunes outside St. George, Utah. For three months they unknowingly breathed dust laced with radioactive particles from nuclear tests. Within twenty-five years, 91 of the 220 had contracted cancer, and half of that group had already died of the disease—including John Wayne, Susan Hayward, Agnes Moorehead and producer Dick Powell.

"All exposure," Keyes points out, "however small, has a cumulative effect on your body." Even when nuclear detonations occur many miles away from a populated area, the radiation may cause deaths from leukemia within five years, or from other cancers within twelve years. A single tiny particle of plutonium can cause cancer or alter genetic structure in humans. Furthermore, a nuclear explosion could quickly deplete the ozone in the atmosphere, threatening human life and blinding wildlife, destroying ecological balance, perhaps forever. The safest option is to avoid *any* further nuclear insanity.

Sadly, our atmosphere and our bodies already carry significant traces of deadly radioactive plutonium and strontium. In other words, says Keyes, "We've already trapped ourselves in a small degree of irreversible nuclear damage."

In addition to the individual and mass action required of us to raise worldwide collective consciousness, we must also surmount the "habits of the heart" that led to the creation of nuclear power in the first place. For Americans, this implies striving to understand the conditions and viewpoints of those in other nations rather than erecting barriers against them; it means ceasing to demand that *our* way or *our* will must always prevail. Scientists developing nuclear weapons were able to go from textbook theory to a working device in only four years, Keyes notes. What would happen if we applied the same energy now to resolving world tensions?

Keyes maintains that *emotional separateness* is a sickness more threatening to human well-being and survival than all other diseases combined. He defines three kinds of "separateness":

1. **Mental separateness**—where the mind is divided against itself, leaving the individual self-conscious, self-critical, and self-preoccupied.

2. **Bodily separateness**—where the mind is divided against the body, so that the act of thinking itself gradually undermines and crowds out the ability to feel, and striving for success replaces the capacity for joy.

3. **National separateness**—where other cultures or countries are approached with an "us-vs.-them" mentality. In many ways, we earthlings are still living like our primitive ancestors, struggling to survive and never fully abandoning a threat/counter-threat mentality. Americans today are no exception. As the world leader, we still stand divided against the four-plus billion other human beings who share the planet with us.

"Understanding, cooperation and love are the keys to human survival!" Keyes writes. Of course, it is an error to believe that loving someone means we must love everything about them.

Instead, by separating the person from the action and ceasing to judge others by their mistakes or faults, Keyes believes that we can train ourselves to achieve a "consciousness in which patience and understanding will compassionately harmonize the flow of our activities so that we all want to help each other work things out"—as individuals, as groups, and as countries.

Linked by our common ancestry and our shared destinies as denizens of the same small sphere in space, all human beings are more alike than different. And in some way each individual is affected by the increase or decrease in harmony anywhere on the planet. We are all interconnected. We have long realized that our health may be damaged if we live among those who have contracted certain diseases and that our happiness can be jeopardized by associating with those who are chronically unhappy; in the same way, the life of every person on earth is threatened by the proliferation of nuclear power, and especially nuclear weapons.

In the United States alone some 50,000 nuclear devices have been stockpiled in an unrivaled expression of national separateness. We must quit acting like spoiled children fighting over the marbles. "No matter what illusions may dominate our minds, nuclear devices are suicidal for our species."

How, then, as a world, can we become more united? First and foremost, we can acknowledge that happiness doesn't come from accumulating more marbles, but from the joy of playing together:

- *We can learn to disagree in appropriate ways.* "Winning" at the bargaining table is not as important as saving countless people—and the world as a whole—from nuclear destruction.

- *We can cultivate love*—and with love, the desire to live together and help one another. A student writing letters to a pen pal halfway around the world; sister cities understanding and helping one another; universities exchanging cultural/technological information—these help generate "heart-to-heart love."

- *We can increase our skill in living together cooperatively.* A proliferation of nuclear weapons only serves to multiply misunderstanding. " . . . We cannot afford to play such enthusiastic games with loaded nuclear pistols any more! The marbles just aren't worth it!"

Besides enriching our interpersonal skills and laboring to love others, Keyes suggests other ways to make our world a safer place to live: read and become more aware of the nuclear predicament we find ourselves in; meet with others who share the same concerns; pass along copies of *The Hundredth Monkey*; talk or write to public officials. It is up to us to replace nuclear myths with nuclear knowledge, and to see to it that verifiable facts are used to enlighten others regarding the dangers of nuclear war or accident.

"Be informed, hopeful and energetic," Keyes urges. "Be vigilant with your thoughts of peace and love. Sense your power to lift the mood of despair. Let your enthusiasm seep in and penetrate the collective consciousness!" You are essential. You may be the hundredth monkey.

SILENT SPRING

by
Rachel Carson (1907-1964), Houghton Mifflin Company, Boston, Massachusetts, 1962

Rachel Carson's *Silent Spring* was distinctly disquieting when it was first published in 1962, and it remains so today. In 1963, responding to the furor generated by Carson's book, President Kennedy appointed a Scientific Advisory Committee to investigate the inappropriate use of pesticides. The committee report urgently concurred with Carson's findings, and advised that stringent guidelines be immediately adopted to control toxins in the environment. Today, three decades later, however, many of the poisons Carson warned of are being used even more indiscriminately than they were at mid-century.

Carson's early career was devoted to marine biology. But her participation during the government studies of pesticides so alarmed her that she shifted her attention from the wonders of the sea to the horrors of chemical contamination.

During the evolution of *Silent Spring*, the author struggled both with her own poor health and with rejections from magazine editors, who were loathe to publish anything on a subject as unpleasant as the chemical contamination of the environment. Although Carson had not intended to expand her draft into a book-length manuscript, she finally decided that her work would only be accepted by a publisher who did not have to contend with pressure from advertisers. Reaction to the release of *Silent Spring* was immediate—and virulent. Chemical companies spent fortunes on campaigns to denounce the author as "an ignorant and hysterical woman who wanted to turn the earth over to insects." Ironically, these campaigns generated so much interest that the book quickly became an ecological classic.

Carson opens her book with a dedication to the Nobel-prize-winning physician Albert Schweitzer, who once offered this sobering prophecy: *Man has lost the capacity to foresee and to forestall. He will end by destroying the earth!* Then she goes on in the first chapter to create a fictional town in the heart of America that is suddenly plagued by mysterious maladies and unexplained deaths. Children were being stricken with fatal illnesses, and "the few birds seen . . . trembled violently and could not fly." Surely this was the first spring of its kind: "a spring without voices."

Worst of all, this catastrophe had been caused unwittingly by the people themselves. Once "all life had . . . lived in harmony with its surroundings," but the townspeople, oblivious to the intricate balances of nature, had poisoned their environment until even the prospects for future life were utterly destroyed.

To quote another of Schweitzer's observations: "Man can hardly even recognize the devils of his own creation." The "devils" in Carson's fable are pesticides. She warns that although the town and its denizens are, for now, imaginary, the uncontrolled use of insecticides and weed

killers is sure to result eventually in "a stark reality we all shall know." Our greatest concern, maintains Carson—paralleled only by the threat of nuclear warfare—should be "the contamination of man's total environment with such substances of incredible potential for harm [as those commonly found] in herbicides and pesticides." These toxins have been proven to accumulate in the tissues of plants and animals, destroying not only those we wish to exterminate but also those that are vital for our own survival; these chemicals "shatter or alter the very material of heredity upon which the shape of the future depends."

Unlike previous generations, we are "subjected to contact with dangerous chemicals from the moment of conception until death." In fact, Carson asserts, scientists find it virtually impossible to locate plants and animals free from chemical contamination. Furthermore, few people have been educated about these lethal ingredients. Because the use of substances like *DDT* has become widespread, we have come to see them as harmless. Actually, DDT has long been classified by scientists as a *chlorinated hydrocarbon*—a chemical that in "minute quantity can bring about vast changes in the body," particularly in the liver, kidneys, and the membranes protecting the intestines.

Other equally toxic chlorinated hydrocarbons used in pesticides include *chlordane, heptachlor, dieldrin, aldrin* and *endrin.* Endrin, considered the most toxic of the group, has not only fatally poisoned cattle grazing in sprayed orchards, but also purportedly killed a baby and a dog whose home received a tiny amount of the chemical during a routine extermination for cockroaches.

Even more deadly than insecticides containing chlorinated hydrocarbons are those utilizing *organic phosphates*. While chlorinated hydrocarbons change the carbon structure of molecules, organic phosphates destroy enzymes that perform necessary functions in the human body. Without these enzymes, "movements of the whole body become uncoordinated: tremors, muscular spasms, convulsions, and death quickly result." It is sobering to learn that organic phosphates have been used in the production of nerve gases intended for chemical warfare.

Two frequently-used phosphate pesticides, *malathion* and *parathion,* have long been known to interact with each other as catalysts, significantly boosting their joint toxicity. This interaction, according to Carson, presents a threat to society at large because any mixture of common vegetables—as in salads, for example—may easily combine the two potent insecticides.

In addition to leaving residues in meats, fruits, and vegetables, organic phosphates and chlorinated hydrocarbons seep into our water supplies. Because these pollutants seem to defy destruction, the scientists who monitor water purity often have no way to remove them. In fact, there is not even a routine test to *detect* them. Rain carrying the toxins can settle into pores and cracks in the ground, spilling into "a dark underground sea beneath the earth" and traveling great distances before it finally resurfaces as groundwater.

Indeed, this was just exactly what happened in a Colorado farming district during the 1940s, when insecticides from a chemical manufacturer several miles away diffused into local wells. As a result, crops in the district died and people and livestock became ill. Surprisingly, scientists found that most of the damage had not been done by the insecticides themselves, but rather by the toxin *2,4-D*, which had formed spontaneously in the wells when various chemicals had intermingled.

Equally devastating to the environment was the use of *DDD*, "a close relative of DDT," in Clear Lake, California. A favorite spot for anglers, the lake was home to a small but prolific gnat. In the 1950s, officials tried to exterminate the gnat population with DDD. The gnat menace was reduced, but within a few years, even after the lake waters had tested as nontoxic, local water fowl began to die. The birds had fed on fish from the lake, which, in turn it was discovered, had ingested toxified plankton organisms. In short, "the poison . . . had merely gone into the fabric of the life it supports."

Organic activity within the soil "consists of a web of interwoven lives, each in some way related to others." Similarly, the chemical contamination of the soil and the "green mantle" protecting it infects a vast array of life that both sustains the earth and takes food from it. Over a period of years, even minimal amounts of pesticides may build up and destroy this delicate balance. In 1960, a group of scientists ominously concluded that just "a few false moves on the part of man may result in destruction of soil productivity and the arthropods [i.e., "bugs"] may well take over."

Ironically, our *fear* that insects and spiders will "take over" may ensure that they *will do just that*—as we obligingly kill off their natural predators with toxins. In an attempt to eradicate Japanese beetles, many Midwestern American states sprayed fields with aldrin and dieldrin, killing in the process a great many birds and mammals and causing illness in humans—all without producing more than a temporary suppression of the region's beetle population. In contrast, the Eastern states effectively eradicated Japanese beetles by importing predatory insects from Asia that fed on beetle grubs—a much more effective and environmentally prudent solution. Nevertheless, it was deemed "too expensive" to be instituted elsewhere.

In reality, "insecticides are not selective poisons; they do not single out one species . . . " Instead, these chemicals frequently cause the slow and torturous death of various species, including humans. Carson notes, for instance, that organic phosphate poisoning in people, if survived, can cause paralysis and mental impairment, while chlorinated hydrocarbons can render the liver useless and leave the body defenseless against other poisons.

Tragically, as Carson points out, a sharp national rise in liver diseases such as hepatitis and cirrhosis coincided with the widespread use of insecticides during the '50s. The incidence of cancer in the United States also nearly quadrupled between 1900 and 1959, undoubtedly in part as a result of increased exposure to toxic chemicals in our air, water, and food. Before 1940, cancer in children was considered a "medical rarity," but now *"more American children die of cancer than from any other disease."*

As if our current pattern of illnesses were not reason enough to reconsider the uses of pesticides, Carson underscores that our entire "genetic heritage, our link with past and future" could be at stake. Toxic chemicals "have the ability to damage the chromosomes, interfere with normal cell division, or cause mutations." During the millennia through which humanity has evolved, she writes, "no threat has struck so directly and forcefully . . . as the mid-20th century threat of . . . man-made and man-disseminated chemicals."

Paradoxically, while pesticides threaten us, they are often a boon to insects. When chemicals prove more lethal to birds, bats and other insect predators than to the targeted insects themselves, the "bad bugs" are left to reproduce unhampered. In the Northwest, spider-mite colonies subjected to periodic spraying dispersed—but only to "scatter out in search of [new homes], where they [found] a far greater abundance of space and food than was available in the former colonies." And frighteningly, many of the world's more than half-million species of insects have now developed an unprecedented resistance to chemicals. Because "new insect generations arise in a matter of days or weeks," they quickly acquire a genetic adaptability or immunity to toxins that would take humans hundreds or even thousand of years to develop.

But even while she acknowledges these problems, Carson avoids arguing that chemical insecticides should never be used. Rather, she believes that toxic chemicals should be considered only after "their effect on soil, water, wildlife, and man himself" have been thoroughly examined.

Insects continue to be the main competitors for our food supply and the foremost carriers of human disease; but for Carson, nature's own solutions to this dilemma are both the safest and the most exciting. She recommends introducing natural enemies of insects to control troublesome species and using insect sterilization techniques, as was done in the American Southwest to reduce screw-worm populations. In addition, she advocates the implementation of natural venoms, attractants, and repellents. "Imaginative and creative approaches to the problem of sharing our earth with other creatures," believes Carson, will result in "a reasonable accommodation between the insect hordes and ourselves."

Meanwhile, the unnecessary—and often ineffective—use of pesticides has led many scientists, including Carson, to wonder urgently *"whether any civilization can wage relentless war on life without destroying itself, and without losing the right to be called civilized."*

DESERT SOLITAIRE

by Edward Abbey, Peregrine Smith, Inc., Salt Lake City, Utah, 1968

. . . Most of what I write about in this book is already gone or going fast. This is not a travel guide but an elegy. A memorial. Thus Edward Abbey, a part-time ranger, part-time teacher begins his description of the three seasons he spent working in Arches National Park in Southern Utah during the 1950s, when the Park was still undeveloped. Compiled years later from Abbey's journals, the book provides a stirring account of the natural world's beauty, its need for preservation, and its impact on one man's life.

Desert Solitaire, nevertheless, was not Abbey's own favorite among his books, nor was it initially accepted by the public. Through the years, however, and specifically as the environmental movement has gained prominence, the book has become a classic among environmentalists, who often view Abbey's work as the seminal and most eloquent account of their own theories of nature. Thus, in addition to Abbey's beautiful descriptions of the desert and of its inhabitants, he offers a thoughtful, intimate plea for the wilderness. His plea, of course, becomes ever more urgent as countries around the world develop agendas for their natural resources and for the destiny of humanity in relation to the earth.

Following the journalistic style of the book, this summary is written in the first person. Direct quotes from the book are set off in italics.

⬧ ◆ ⬧

. . . On my first morning at Arches National Park, I have already decided that this is the most beautiful place on earth. I know that people have many favorite places, of many kinds, but this place is special.

I arrived in Moab, Utah late last night and was directed to my new home, a metal trailer in the park where I would spend the next six months. When I awoke this morning, I lit the butane heater and then stepped out into the early light. Now, all around me I can see deserts and cliffs and canyons and plateaus. In the foreground are the arches themselves, massive windows cut into the rock by ice. *Standing there, gaping at this monstrous and inhuman spectacle of rock and cloud and sky and space, I feel a ridiculous greed and possessiveness come over me. I want to know it all, possess it all, embrace the entire scene intimately . . .*

I fight the tendency to see a stone god within the fifty-foot balanced rock ahead of me. I have come here not only to evade the clamor and filth of civilization, but to learn to see all the elements of nature, undefiled by the human beings.

Later this same day my supervisors leave me a shirt, a badge, and a pickup so that I can assist travelers and provide campers with firewood. As we tour the park, I realize that the impressive arches are only a small part of the naked rock all around. Back at the trailer, I eat supper and build a small fire. Then after a while I let the fire die out and go for a walk, a flashlight safely in my pocket.

Later, as I fire up the generator, it occurs to me that mechanical things such as the flashlight and the generator actually distance us from nature; in such conveniences we *[exchange] a great and unbounded world for a small, comparatively meager one.* I shut it off again and settle back to look at and listen to the night. *I am twenty miles or more from the nearest fellow human, but instead of loneliness I feel loveliness. Loveliness and a quiet exultation.*

Spring mornings dawn in stunning splendor. I fight the tendency to hear human messages in the cry of the mourning dove. One morning, watching the sunrise from the doorway of my trailer, I look down to find a rattlesnake just behind my heels. Swinging my feet out of the way, I gently remove the thrashing snake with a shovel. A week later, he—or one like him—is back, tempted by the mice living in my trailer. Later, I happen upon a gopher snake and bring him back to the trailer. I try my darndest to domesticate him. For a while he seems content, but in a few weeks he leaves—only to return a month later with a mate. While I watch, the two snakes writhe together in a strange, sinuous, and exciting dance; then they slither off. I don't see them again, but I sense that they are still nearby, eating mice and rattlesnakes. Am I ascribing human emotions to them? Not really. *I recognize that when and where they serve purposes of mine they do so for beautifully selfish reasons of their own. Which is exactly the way it should be.*

In May, the desert acquires a heavy coat of vegetation. It's certainly no jungle, but the ground suddenly yields up amazing arrays of shrubs and flowers. Their colors glow against the rocks' oranges and reds. A multitude of unusual rocks and minerals are found here, including uranium ore. Uranium once triggered a mining boom near Moab and the Arches, but most who prospered obtained their riches from other men's pockets rather than from the ground.

One day I spot three men in a jeep emerging from an off-limits site. Then I discover that they are surveyors, laying out a paved loop of asphalt in the park. After they leave, I pull up their stakes. I know it's futile; the Park Service has decided that people should enjoy parks from the comforts of their cars. Park officials are moving toward *more paving* and *less nature,* and, to me, that's the wrong direction.

Not long after this incident, I pick up a rock, pitch it at a rabbit, and kill it. I expect to feel remorse, but I don't; I'm relieved to know that my hands can provide me with food if they have to.

Still, there are times when solitaire becomes solitary . . . a prison term, and the inside of [my own] skull [grows] as confining and unbearable as the interior of a housetrailer on a hot day. Increasing my time in nature, I feel my isolation subside.

A tourist once said that this country would be an even more magnificent place *if* it had water. I answered him that if it did have water, it wouldn't be like this at all; it might look like an Ohio or a farm, but not like this.

When rain does fall here, it generally comes in cloudbursts and flash floods, not in quiet mists. After a rain, water-filled hollows in rocks host a joyful chorus of singing frogs. *Has joy any survival value in the operations of evolution? I suspect that it does; I suspect that the morose and fearful are doomed to quick extinction.*

In July's intense heat, the distant patches of snow on the mountains comfort me. *Mountains complement desert as desert complements city, as wilderness complements and completes civilization.*

When a friend and I raft down the Colorado River—which will soon be blocked by the Glen Canyon Dam—we float, losing track of hours, days. Once we reach the Glen Canyon area I explore the numerous winding canyons and finally make the six-mile ascent from the river to Rainbow Bridge. In fact, much of the marvelous natural span's beauty is in the effort required to reach it. Soon it will just be a short boat-ride away from civilization.

Away from civilization with its clocks, calendars, and human demands, there is an incredible sense of freedom. *Wilderness. The word itself is music . . . The sound of it draws all whose nerves and emotions have not yet been irreparably stunned, deadened, numbed by the caterwauling of commerce, the sweating scramble for profit and domination.*

By August, there is an oppressive stillness in the air. The desert heat makes the tourists weary. Even I am overwhelmed by a desire for mountains, running water and pine trees. In the evening after work, I head for the high hills to a different, greener world where humans are scarce. I camp on the shoulder of a mountain, then begin to climb through fields of wild flowers, rocky escarpments, and, finally, snowfields. When I reach the top I can see the entire vista of canyon country scattered below me. *I try for cosmic intuitions—and end up earthbound as always.*

Thunderstorms foreshadow September's resurgence of desert greenery. Nightly, coyotes serenade me: wails, barks, yelps and howls.

This morning my radio summons me to join the search for a hiker, lost in the vicinity of Grandview Point. Since the man has been missing for two days without water, we know that we are really looking for another casualty

of the desert. We find it, perched on a high bluff overlooking the junction of the Colorado and Green Rivers. Backtracking, we realize that the hiker must have become disoriented before dying of heat exhaustion. I almost envy him. *To die in the open, under the sky, far from the insolent interference of leech and priest, before this desert vastness opening like a window into eternity—that surely was an overwhelming stroke of rare good luck.* Still, we are grateful not to be in the body bag.

What is it about the desert that distinguishes it from other landscapes? Is it the color, the grandeur, the spaciousness? Is it the silence, the simple clarity? Or is it the veil of mystery, the sense of something unknown, unknowable? The desert seems to be waiting—but for what? There is something about the desert that the human mind cannot assimilate. The best artists and writers have failed to capture it . . . *Under the vulture-haunted sky, the desert waits—mesa, butte, canyon, reef, sink, escarpment, pinnacle, maze, dry lake, sand dune and barren mountain. Even after years of contact . . . this quality of strangeness in the desert remains undiminished.*

One can see, then, why 26-year-old Everett Reuss, the author of *On Desert Trails*, disappeared into the canyon country of Southern Utah, never to return. Although living in cities has its advantages and I do fine there, however, once I catch a whiff of juniper smoke, or a careless word or poem calls the desert to mind, I become as restless as a wolf in a cage.

I have been criticized for being anti-civilization. I am not. I just think that civilization should preserve the wilderness; civilization is simply not complete without wilderness. We need to be alone sometimes. For me, when the massive influx of people for the Labor Day holiday subsides, a sweet stillness falls over the park. I am with myself again.

Exploring a remote area called the "Maze" with a friend, we lower ourselves by rope into a windless labyrinth of winding gorges, untouched except perhaps by Indians hundreds of years ago. In the days we spend there, we are only able to explore a few of the countless ravines before the threat of the first snowstorm of winter forces us to turn back.

Now the tourists have gone home and today is my last day at Arches. Tomorrow I will leave to work for six months in the slums of a big city with a youth organization. *Balance, that's the secret. Moderate extremism. The best of both worlds.* After the many long months of solitude and quiet, now I find myself hungering for crowds and noise.

On my way to the train station, the sun breaks through the storm clouds and its rays cast a dazzling glow over the red rock country. I beg the driver to stop and take me back. "It'll all be here next spring," he grins. Will it? I hope so. *When I return will it be the same? Will I be the same? Will anything ever be quite the same again?*

COMPACT
Classics®

LIBRARY #5: They Made a Difference
lives that turned the world

Certain individuals—spouses, family members, close friends and associates—touch our lives, for better or for worse, in daily, direct and very personal ways. Yet ironically, many of the individuals who touch our lives most profoundly are people we never actually meet face to face. Think of the movie stars we worship, the sports heroes we try to imitate, the politicians we grumble about... These are the movers and the shakers of the world. And the waves they make reverberate on into the future. Lucille Ball, Charlie Chaplin, and Mark Twain are all dead, yet they still make us laugh. We still swivel to Elvis' early rock rhythms and move to the Gershwins' jazzy melodies; thirty years later, the glamor of Marilyn Monroe still dazzles; again and again we plunge into Spielberg's alternate worlds; we still marvel at the skill and determination of Muhammad Ali, the "Babe" and Billie Jean King; the legacy of warriors like George Patton and Margaret Thatcher is still outlined in borders on the map.

And then the occasional Helen Kellers, Albert Schweitzers, and Geronimos come along—to enlarge our human consciousness and to broaden the scope of our compassion and our ideals of justice.

There is a common thread that runs through the lives of all these diverse individuals: steadfast, even stubborn; creative, almost to a fault; confident, focused, and courageous, these are all people who have dared to stand out and to give their personal best in whatever vision of life they aspired to. And whatever their faults, these are those mortal champions who, over the past hundred years or so, have thrown themselves authentically, energetically, and wholeheartedly into life, and who, in the process, have shaped and colored the world we live in today. In other words, "they made a difference."

DON'T SHOOT, IT'S ONLY ME

by Bob Hope with Melville Shavelson, Putnam, New York, N.Y., 1990

Bob Hope is an American comedy legend. He has dispensed his dosages of on-the-road good will through four wars and countless other military engagements around the world. In giving tribute to his country, Hope's book *Don't Shoot, It's Only Me* reads like "a love song to my girl: America, warts and all."

❖ ◆ ❖

The terrible thing about growing older is that it lasts so long, Hope writes. *You start telling jokes to make a living and one morning you wake up and find you've written the history of half a century. Or your writers have. Accidentally.*

Bob Hope began entertaining the nation in 1938, first in films with *The Big Broadcast* and then on radio. To achieve his goal of becoming the most popular comedian on radio, he hired the best up-and-coming writers. He also honed an earthy, staccato, fast-paced delivery: *My method . . . was to deliver a series of one-liners, joke joke joke . . . I would zing a joke and then start on the next line and wait for the audience to catch up. Then I'd ad-lib, "laugh first, figure it out later." If someone laughed a little late, I'd ask, "Which one are you working on?"*

Hope began entertaining U.S. troops in 1941. During World War II everyone seemed to play a part—even President-to-be Ronald Reagan. Here's the story as Hope tells it:

An actor named Captain Ronald Reagan put in a short hitch at Armed Forces Radio Services Headquarters. Captain Reagan's only military experience up to that time had been saluting Colonel Jack Warner whenever Ronnie's option came up. On one careless occasion, someone decided to make Reagan Officer of the Day. One of my writers, now part of the unit, phoned him, disguising his voice.

"Captain Reagan? This is Lieutenant Colonel Whitney of the Fifty-Fourth on secret orders from General McNair. I have a company of one-hundred men en route to Camp Roberts and we're running late. Can you provide bivouac?"

There was a short pause while Ronnie quickly consulted his military dictionary.

"Yes sir!" he replied, and immediately hung up and called Abbey Rents to deliver a hundred army cots. There was no arrangement for sleeping at AFRS. All the sleeping was done at typewriters.

Almost immediately the telephone rang again.

"Lieutenant Colonel Whitney here. Very sorry, I miscounted, captain. Our unit on this maneuver actually consists of one hundred and fifty men. Does that present any logistical problem?"

"The impossible we do immediately," Reagan said, believing he had just coined a phrase. He hung up and frantically phoned Abbey Rents for fifty more cots.

Then came the final phone call.

"Captain Reagan? You know of course, the Fifty-fourth is a cavalry unit. Be sure you have enough hay."

Ronnie phoned the prop department at Warner Brothers. *They tell me there was straw blowing around in the wind at Sunset and Western for weeks after that.*

In another story, he tells of something that happened right after Reagan's re-election: *Ronnie topped all my jokes that year, making up one of his own. Testing the microphone for his weekly radio broadcast, he said, "My fellow Americans, I'm pleased to tell you today that I've signed legislation that will outlaw Russia forever. We begin bombing in five minutes."*

Somehow, the joke got put on the air. If it had been Orson Welles who had said it, it would have caused a national panic. But since it was Reagan, Hope writes, nobody took it seriously. "They just figured Nancy had forgotten to make out his cue cards."

Hope also shares stories about other American presidents—among whom were both his greatest victims and his greatest friends. During World War II, for example, Franklin D. Roosevelt—who "was either loved or hated," depending on whose side you were on—told a joke about himself that Hope enjoys retelling:

During the fighting on Guadalcanal in the Pacific, an American marine was disappointed because he hadn't had a chance to shoot at the enemy. He hadn't even seen one of them.

"Okay," his commanding officer said, "go up on top of the next hill and yell, 'to hell with Hirohito!' Believe me, that'll bring the Japs out of hiding fast."

So the marine went up on the hill and hollered, "To hell with Hirohito!"

A Jap came out of the jungle and shouted, "To hell with Roosevelt!"

"Just my luck," said the marine. "I can't shoot a fellow Republican."

Hope organized shows for the USO and went on tour, raising the spirits of American troops and their allies. During one show, he remembers, he was telling a joke, when *a tank burst through the crowd and [came] towards the stage. I didn't think the joke was that bad, but I'd never met a critic with a Sherman tank before, so I got ready to jump off the platform, when suddenly it stopped right in front of me. The turret popped open and a guy got out wearing a tanker's crash helmet. He dragged a folding chair up after him and sat down on it and crossed his legs.*

"Make me laugh," he said.

Hope has had them rolling in the aisles ever since.

Hope always made certain to surround himself with beautiful film stars, singers, and dancers when on tour. He recalls that one night it got so crowded at a party for service-men at the Hollywood Canteen *that if a sol-dier wanted to tune the radio, he had to squeeze past Lana Turner, Hedy Lamarr, Dinah Shore, and Betty Grable just to change the station. I must have heard 148 different programs.*

Everything was not always rosy for Hope and his band of "Hope Gypsies." A war was on, and enemy snipers and pilots rarely cared who was sleeping in a hotel or riding in a plane or bus. His entertainers often came under fire. As dangerous as touring was, however, sometimes it was just old-fash-ioned bad luck that caught up to Hope, as was the case in his first experience handling a plane, the *Catalina:*

I waited until everyone else in our group was asleep before begging our Navy pilot to let me do the driving. He was a little dubious about turning the controls over to a civilian, especially after I asked him which way was reverse, but he wanted an introduction to [my wife] Frances and he figured, how much harm could a stupid civil-ian do in a couple of minutes?

He put everything on automatic pilot and went back to talk to Frances. I have an idea the Catalina discovered who was flying it and the left engine fainted. The pilot came racing into the cockpit and ordered me out of the seat. He started checking the instruments and the motor kept complaining until finally he feathered the prop. We went into a dive, and he yelled, "Jettison everything we don't need!"

I raced into the back and tripped over Barney [one of the stage people], who was just getting out of his berth. I had kidded him so much about how the planes we were in were going to crash, he didn't believe me when I told him we were in serious trouble.

"How can it be serious?" he asked. "Your option was already picked up."

I dragged him up to the cockpit and showed him the feathered prop.

"That's supposed to be going around," I told him.

He swallowed hard and said, "Spare me the technical crap, how long have we got to live?"

The plane kept losing altitude and by that time everybody was awake and throwing every-thing overboard, including the scotch. Barney got indignant when we started eyeing him. [Then] he told me to throw my wallet overboard, since it was the heaviest thing on the plane.

When World War II ended, the Hope Gypsies hung up their fatigues and put away the box lunches—but by then their leader was already addicted to the thrills of "play-ing" for the armed forces. And when the "Korean Conflict" heated up, he was off and "playing" again. Entertaining during the Korean War, however, proved to be a differ-ent experience for Hope and his Gypsies. The war was unpopular back home as well as at the front. And the front itself fluctuated wildly; once, in a battle-torn area, they even arrived ahead of the Marines. The war kept Hope, Frances and company cracking jokes

and cheering the troops on for three years straight, both in sub-zero weather as well as in the sweltering heat of summer.

After the war's end, Hope went back to his TV and radio shows and film career; the Hope Gypsies were put into mothballs. Then in 1958, he decided to do one of his TV spe-cials from Moscow—a first of its kind. After much wrangling, his travel visa finally came through and, keeping his writers "chained to a typewriter on the way over," Hope set off. Using Russian talent to back himself, the show went off with few hitches—though the comedian had to convince Soviet officials that Americans made jokes about their lead-ers all the time before they would release the film for viewing.

In 1964, the Hope Gypsies were called out of retirement to play for thousands of advisers in a nasty little Southeastern Asian skirmish. The country was Vietnam:

There are some cynics who say I never met a war I didn't like. They're the ones who've never smelled it up close, in the hospital wards . . . Every time I walked out on stage, I was face-to-face with the kids who were doing the actual fighting. . . . They were very much alive and pre-ferred to stay that way. I was only interested in doing what I could . . . Toward the end in 'Nam, when the G.I.s at Lai Khe started booing the jokes, I knew it was finished.

Hope's tour, a goodwill phenomenon tethered by a long string of entertainment and jokes, had ended; Vietnam had been a long haul. All wars are terrible, but this one, Hope noted, proved to be even nastier than most: "less to laugh at." And the danger was greater than ever. There was even a plot hatched by the Viet Cong to assassinate the comedian. By the slimmest of margins, it didn't succeed.

Between 1974 and 1990, Hope worked on his occasional TV specials and made appearances on various other shows. In the late '80s and early '90s, he returned to the field, entertaining U.S. troops in Beirut and the Persian Gulf.

On October 2, 1989, Bob Hope did a vaudeville show. But not just any vaudeville. He was on stage with George Burns. Hope teased that between them they totalled 179 years old.

At the end of that special night, Hope, with the help of a ladies' hat from the audi-ence, played the feminine half of Burns and Allen. *It was a strange feeling, being half of Burns and Allen, even in fun,* Hope recounted. *The two of them had been the real vaudeville, and one of the true love stories of another generation. I wondered what George was thinking, but I couldn't see through the cigar smoke. But after we danced "Tea for Two" together, George said, "Say goodnight Gracie," and I said, "Goodnight Gracie," and he smiled and we walked offstage, arm in arm.*

The team of Burns and Hope had finally made the Big Time.

FOREVER LUCY

The Life of Lucille Ball
by Joe Morella and Edward Z. Epstein, L. Stuart, Secaucus, N.J., 1986

Lucille Ball, one of the world's best-loved comedians, was a "wild, tempestuous, exciting child with enormous energy, flair, and style," says her cousin. "She saw things in a way nobody else did. She was a reactor—she reacted to everything. Running away from home was reacting. It was always very dramatic when we were caught. And that was the point. What she really wanted was to play a scene."

Lucy was born August 6, 1911 in Celoron, New York. Four years later her father died and the family moved in with her grandfather, whose natural exuberance and love of life clearly influenced Lucy; her flair for acting rapidly emerged. One day she insisted on running next door to entertain some kids who had the measles. So, her mother looped a rope around the little girl's waist and hooked it to a pulley so "Miss Busybody" could run freely back and forth—still harnessed.

Throughout Lucy's school years her mother encouraged her to act, dance and sing. When she turned 15, she dropped out of high school to enroll in a drama academy in New York City. Shortly afterward, however, the academy notified Lucy's mother that she "was wasting her money."

Lucy decided to become a show girl. "I answered an Earl Carroll tryout," she recalled. "I rehearsed for two weeks, then a man told me I was through. I went home and cried. I got picked for a Shubert show. We rehearsed for two weeks and I was fired again. That time I really suffered."

Lucy often returned home to take any odd job she could find: soda jerking, clerking, anything at all to keep her going. She ate only when she could find a "one-doughnut man." This, she explained, "is a guy who sits at the counter and orders coffee and doughnuts. He drinks his coffee, eats one doughnut and puts down a nickel tip. I'd do a fast slide onto his stool, yell for a cup of coffee, pay for it with his nickel, and eat the other doughnut."

At 18, Lucy collapsed from malnutrition and fatigue while doing a modeling job. "It taught me that without your health, you ain't got nothin'," she explained. After recuperating, she signed a contract as a poster girl for a Goldwyn movie in California and appeared in ten films in 1933 and 1934. By then, however, she was a "last year's girl," so she moved to Columbia Pictures. She sent for her family, and they lived together in a rented house on Ogden Drive.

No sooner had they moved, however, than Columbia dropped Lucy's option. She hurried over to RKO and found a lower-paying job working "halfway between an extra and a bit." It was at RKO's talent school where she finally got her break while studying drama under Lela Rogers, Ginger's mother. "It was real acting experience," Lucy recalled. "We had a stage, scripts to get our teeth into, and an audience."

Lucy soon scored a hit in *Stage Door*. Busier than ever, she made seven films in 1938 and even more in 1939. One of her friends remembered, "Everything was an adventure, a great burst of joy and it was infectious."

During this joyful period, Desi entered Lucy's life. "I was in the room when Desi and Lucy first met, and it was like love at first sight," fellow dancer and actress Ann Miller recalled. "When he first was introduced to her, her eyes just lit up." Lucy's life changed noticeably when she began to date Desi. "We couldn't have learned more if we'd been in college," Lucy explained. "His department was facts, figures and sports, especially horse racing. Mine was women—I taught Desi a lot about women."

In 1940 the couple eloped. Justice of the Peace John P. O'Brien took them to the Byram River Beagle Club. "Maybe it doesn't sound very romantic," Lucy recalled, "but actually it was. The judge took us there because he said all young people who were going to spend a lifetime together should start off in as romantic a setting as possible."

"Marrying Desi was the boldest thing I ever did," Lucy confessed. "He frightened me." Desi lived dangerously, and danger did not appeal to Lucy.

Soon after her marriage, Lucy made some striking changes. While preparing for her first MGM movie, the chief hair stylist dyed her hair a bright red, which for ever after became her trademark. When people remarked that nobody ever had that shade of hair, she firmly said, "I do. When I chose this shade, things began to break for me. It gave me just the right finishing touch before the cameras." *Life* magazine regarded Lucy's first film at MGM as her "first real opportunity to become a big-time star."

During these years, according to friends, Lucy was "down to earth and refreshingly non-Hollywood." Desi, however, began to travel frequently, and the strain on their relationship increased. Then, as the country went to war, *Special Services assigned Desi to a hospital near Van Nuys. He was not far from their Northridge ranch but was still not living at home.* By now, Lucy's and Desi's marriage was in a shambles. Lucy was an old-fashioned young woman who believed in fidelity and "one man." Desi, on the other hand, liked to "fool around."

Their frequent separations and frenetic schedules soon made the couple long for tranquility. Even Desi grew tired of nightclub life and turned his thoughts to starting a family. Although Lucy became pregnant in 1940, it ended in miscarriage during a strenuous vaudeville tour with Desi.

In September 1944, Lucy filed for divorce. Although Lucy reconciled with Desi the day before, she felt obliged to act according to plan for fear the publicists would make her look foolish. The following morning, Lucy and Desi read the newspaper stories proclaiming them "divorced"; however their continued cohabitation automatically voided their divorce decree.

When Lucy again became pregnant, the duo conceived their famous television show. Working with a team of writers, they originated their characters: Desi would play a band leader named Ricky Ricardo and Lucy would play his zany wife. The first six scripts were sent to CBS and approved on the condition that the show be filmed live. "I Love Lucy" premiered on CBS-TV on October 15, 1951.

During the show's first season, 39-year-old Lucy gave birth to Little Lucie. Desi was overjoyed. Working hard both to care for their baby and to perfect their show, Lucy and Desi managed to keep their marriage intact.

Soon "I Love Lucy" was second in popularity only to "The Red Skelton Show." Not only did the series establish a new and energetic comedy team, but it also seemed to provide a glimpse into a real-life happy marriage. In fact, when Lucy became pregnant again, they decided to make Lucy's character "expectant"—a very wife-like thing to be in the 1950s. By this time the couple had pooled their talents to achieve stardom and financial security—and, outwardly, at least, they seemed the ideal couple.

Unfortunately, stardom also made them victims of McCarthyism. During the height of Senator Joe McCarthy's 1953 purges of Communist influence, Lucy found herself in the midst of a "witch hunt." Her grandfather had been a Socialist, and, to please him, Lucy had apparently registered as a Socialist in 1936. After newspapers reproduced her registration card without including the word "Canceled," Lucy testified, "I am not a Communist now. I have never been. I never wanted to be. Nothing in the world could ever change my mind."

Despite the McCarthy investigation, "I Love Lucy" remained popular until 1957. When the show ended that year, Lucy told a reporter, "We've loved our work and we've loved being pioneers, but the time has come to let somebody else 'enjoy' it. We're a little brain-weary, you know."

After the show went off the air, Lucy started Desilu workshops so other actors could benefit from her experience just as she had benefited from Lela Rogers' training. "It's the same old vicious circle," Lucy said. "You can't get a job unless you've acted, and you can't act unless you've had a job. We're just trying to give them exposure." Lucy's endeavor was hailed as the only practical workshop to come out of TV production.

The workshop kept Lucy's mind off her personal problems. Although she and Desi had quarreled constantly and had often separated, the public never knew. Following a bitter argument, Desi moved out for the last time and Lucy took the children to New York, where she was to appear in a Broadway musical comedy. The production, however, did not

enjoy a long run: Lucy became ill with a severe viral infection and lost the part to another actress.

Her health eventually improved and her spirits lifted. Then she met and married Gary Morton. "He's just a wonderful guy," Lucy explained. "I guess he was a candidate since he made me and my children happy."

For the next two years Lucy turned the management of Desilu Productions over to Desi. During this time, she introduced a new series, "Mission: Impossible," which became the biggest hit since "The Untouchables."

In 1967, Charles Bludhorn, president of Gulf and Western Industries, finally persuaded Lucy to sell Desilu, which gave Lucy the freedom to pursue acting. To her surprise, the first "not typically Lucy" story she had ever done— "Yours, Mine and Ours"—became a big hit. Subsequently, she formed Lucille Ball Productions and introduced a popular new show: "Here's Lucy." At first she sought to include her children in the series in an effort to protect them from the dangers of adolescence. Sadly, her plan wasn't successful: Desi Jr. soon began to abuse both alcohol and drugs.

Lucy, as always, was concerned about public opinion. Young Desi once explained, "The basic concern of my mother and stepfather has been protection of the family name. I never felt it was all that important." He eventually turned to them for help, however. According to Lucy, there was "a difference between being concerned and being nosy, but it took me a while to convince Lucie and Desi of that."

During the mid-70s, Lucie grew tired of being called "little Lucie," a feeling her mother didn't share. As time passed, she went all out to rid herself of the title. On one occasion she answered the telephone by saying, "This is young Lucie," for her mother's benefit. Irritated by it all, Mom snapped back, "And this is old Lucy!"

After completing a film version of "Mame," Lucy decided to cut back drastically on her schedule. Desi Jr. was still in and out of drug rehabilitation centers, and she wanted to spend as much time as possible with her family.

In 1983, Lucy was inducted into the Television Hall of Fame. Three years later, Desi died and Lucy underwent thyroid surgery— giving rise to reports that "she was resentful that she was having to slow down while others her age . . . still had the health to maintain full-time careers." In 1989, she did a show with Bob Hope. She looked wonderful at the time, but only a few weeks later she was rushed to the hospital after suffering a massive heart attack. Open-heart surgery at first seemed successful and she started to recover. Then her aorta suddenly ruptured. Lucille Ball, the queen of laughter, was dead.

Although Lucy is gone, the public has certainly not forgotten her. International syndication of the Lucy shows *reinforces in the public mind that Lucy will be forever young, forever funny, forever loved—Forever LUCY*.

IF I CAN DREAM: ELVIS' OWN STORY

by Larry Geller and Joel Spector, Simon and Shuster, New York, N.Y., 1989

In 1964, Larry Geller became Elvis Presley's personal barber. The first time he cut the young singer's hair, he was treated to a philosophical dissertation on life and its meaning. "I've always known that there had to be a purpose for my life," Elvis droned. "I've always felt an unseen hand . . . From millions and millions of lives . . . why was I picked out to be Elvis?"

Eight years earlier, at 21, Elvis seemed to materialize out of nowhere onto the entertainment scene, and in two short years he had become a "super-star," "larger than life," the King of Rock and Roll. According to Geller, *. . . Much of the appeal and the love people have for him transcends and probably has little to do with his talent . . . When asked about the reason for his success in [the] early days, he told one reporter, "Because God let me come along at this time."*

❖ ◆ ❖

Elvis Aron (later corrected to Aaron) Presley was born January 8, 1935, to Gladys Love Smith Presley and Vernon Elvis Presley, in East Tupelo, Mississippi . . . in the family's two-room shack. Gladys was a devoted mother, and made sure her son attended church and school by taking him herself.

As a member of the First Assembly of God Church, Elvis was introduced to music early. "Man," he once told Geller, "the first thing I could remember in life was sittin' on my mama's lap in church . . . all I wanted to do was run down the aisle and go sing with the choir. I knew it then; I had to sing." He made his first major step toward fulfilling that dream in July of 1953, when he made a recording at Sam Phillips' recording studio in Memphis, Tennessee. When asked who he sang like, Elvis is said to have answered, "I don't sound like nobody." This soon became evident; he had a sound all his own.

In July 1954, Elvis recorded "That's All Right," a song that became an overnight hit: *Following quickly came a series of firsts: first interviews, first press, first concerts. From the very start it was clear that Elvis had something—dark, potent, strange and irresistible. One Memphis paper headlined a piece on the new local star "He's Sex!" With a few exceptions, Elvis' early performances were as exciting as and possibly even more suggestive than what the nation finally saw in 1956.*

He went on to release a long line of hits, and his career skyrocketed. His personal appearances, including a landmark performance on the Ed Sullivan Show, were *enough to inspire girls to carve his name into their skin with penknives and demolish cars with their bare hands. [He] changed the way millions of kids viewed themselves and their world . . . Elvis was it.*

He achieved millionaire status almost immediately, and was soon being featured in movies. In 1957, he returned to Memphis and bought Graceland, a twenty-three-room mansion that had fallen into disrepair. The house sat on 13 acres of wooded land in Whitehaven, a Memphis suburb.

March of 1958 saw the rock idol inducted into the Army. After receiving basic training at Fort Hood, Texas, he rented a house off base where he and his parents could live. But shortly thereafter, his mother became ill and the family returned to Memphis. Two days later, she died. Elvis was devastated by the loss, and went into seclusion until the Army sent him to West Germany to complete his tour of duty. Returning to civilian life, at age 25 Elvis worried that "his moment of fame" had already passed him by. It was true that many things had changed. While in Germany he had met a girl, fourteen-year-old Priscilla Beaulieu, with whom he had fallen in love and whom he intended to marry.

During the sixties, Elvis committed to making several more movies, which kept him in Hollywood for several months of each year. However, he never did feel comfortable around "Hollywood types"; he was inherently a loner, "part of a crowd that only he belonged to." Still he craved companionship and found it in the "Memphis Mafia," his personal cadre of traveling friends and assistants. Geller, as his barber, joined this close-knit group and became Elvis' close friend, confidant, and spiritual advisor.

Elvis preferred to drive his motor-home back and forth between Memphis and the west coast. His loathing of Hollywood, however, usually caused him to delay leaving until the last possible moment, which led to non-stop junkets. It was during one such trip, that Geller first sensed that Elvis might have a problem with drugs. "Elvis [suddenly] extended his hand towards me," he relates. In it were Dexedrine tablets, a potent amphetamine. "Take these," he said, " . . . we'll be driving. We want to be alert."

The singer had also become a voracious reader of religious books. On another occasion, a road-weary Elvis confided to Geller, "All I want is to know the truth, to know and experience God . . . I believe, only nothing happens, and I want it to." Perhaps, Geller suggested, Elvis was trying to cram too much into his brain at once. "Before God," Geller told him, "you're no different from anybody else . . . You're not favored because you're Elvis Presley." Elvis then looked out the window of the bus at a cloud mass that had formed. "Do you see what I see?" he asked. In the shape of the cloud he had imagined the image of Soviet dictator Joseph Stalin. Perhaps God, Presley surmised, "[is] trying to show me what he thinks of me." And then he startled Geller by voicing his wish to die, to infuse God into his life in some way. *Then it happened! As they continued to watch the wind-driven cloud, the face of Stalin turned right into the face of Jesus.*

This incident had a lasting effect on Elvis. One minute he loved being "the King"; the next he yearned to become a monk so he could worship the *King of Kings*. "I want to be with God now," he moaned. Geller, for his part, was troubled by this state of Elvis' nature: *Elvis was an extremist . . . and spiritual studies were no exception. . . . Rather than using this experience to . . . correct and redirect his life, he embraced it as [an] excuse to abandon his life altogether.*

Elvis expressed his spiritual rebirth publicly in the album *How Great Thou Art*, a collection of gospel hymns that earned him a Grammy Award for "Best Sacred Performance." Two more Grammys would follow, one for *He Touched Me* ("Best Inspirational Performance," 1972) and another in 1974 for the song "How Great Thou Art."

Elvis' personality and star status meant *the outside world was a distant place he ventured into but never really lived in. . . . His life existed on the inside . . .* He never even went grocery shopping or on a vacation, but remained isolated in the past and in the company of his money. Money gave Elvis freedom, freedom to buy anything—which he did to excess. However, he was also very generous, giving away cars, condos, mobile homes—and not just to his friends: he lavished total strangers with extravagant gifts. If he heard of someone in need, he would help.

In April 1967, Geller was weighing the possibility of severing his ties with Elvis, when he received a call asking that he come to Graceland. "We're all going to Vegas," trumpeted Elvis' voice. Geller declined. The very next day, he was surprised by a newspaper headline: *ELVIS PRESLEY IS MARRIED*. He had finally wed his Priscilla. The teenage girl had moved to Memphis from Germany in 1962. In time, however, Elvis and Priscilla's marriage became one of appearance only: "Priscilla was like a little sister to me . . . She grew up, and the person that grew up and I are just apart. We're not in love with each other."

Finally Geller did retire from the Memphis Mafia, informing Elvis by letter that "their time together had been precious . . . but I feel that it is time to part . . . " For the next five years he had no contact with Elvis. During that time the star regained his title as King of Rock and Roll, principally by means of a "comeback special" on TV. By that time eight years had passed since he had performed for a live audience.

The following year, 1969, he made his Las Vegas debut, which put him back on the record charts as well: "Suspicious Minds" became a number-one hit; in 1970 a documentary on his Vegas show was released; the year after he was named to "America's Ten Outstanding Young Men" by the U.S. Jaycees. America's love affair with Elvis was on once again.

Then, in 1972, Priscilla left Elvis. Despite the distance that had grown between them it was a crushing blow. That same year, Geller went to Vegas to see Elvis perform, and their friendship took up right where it had left off five years before. But Geller was still uncomfortable with Elvis' lifestyle: the singer was touring constantly, eating all the wrong foods, and filling his head with drugs. News of the abduction of Patty Hearst had also made him paranoid someone would kidnap his daughter, Lisa Marie.

Further complicating his life was his association with agent/manager Colonel Parker, who had become a compulsive gambler. No casino would turn the Colonel away, and in one night alone Parker gambled away $1.4 million of Elvis' money. He also positioned himself "to take the maximum amount of Elvis' earnings as fast as possible." Among other things, he sold off the recording masters of all of Elvis' pre-1973 songs and took nearly half the $5.4 million sale price for himself. To satisfy his own vices, Parker put even greater pressure on Elvis to perform, and Elvis turned even more frequently to prescription drugs; he even experimented once or twice with cocaine and marijuana. Occasionally the singer would attempt to resolve his substance abuse by checking into a hospital. But he had been using drugs for so long, and his tolerance was so high, that his behavior usually seemed normal. Even on those occasions when he would forget his lyrics and he appeared on-stage overweight and under-prepared, the audience still loved him.

In 1976, Elvis found a new love, a woman named Ginger Alden. Their passion for each other, coupled with his love of entertaining, renewed his vitality, at least when he was on stage. Night after night he could pull off a magical performance, somehow, despite his weakening health.

Then one night as Elvis left the stage, he seemed to have lost his vision entirely. In this blinded state, he slipped and twisted his ankle. His staff became increasingly concerned.

On August 15, 1977, Geller returned to Memphis from Los Angeles and phoned his friend: "It's me, E. I just checked into my room." Elvis replied, "I'm in bed, trying to get rested . . . for the tour. Would you mind if I called it a night?" Then he asked, "Lawrence, did you bring that book on the Holy Shroud of Jesus?"

"Do angels have wings?" Geller asked in turn. Of course he had; Elvis had been wondering about the authenticity of the shroud of Turin for weeks, and had asked Geller to find him a book that probed the shroud's mysteries.

"Yeah, and don't forget," joked the King, "Angels fly because they take themselves so lightly." This was the last time Geller would ever hear him speak.

The next morning as he drove toward Graceland, Geller saw helicopters hovering overhead. *We were driving up to the gates when [Elvis'] Uncle Vester spotted me . . . He looked at me blankly . . . then said, "Didn't you hear what happened? . . . Elvis died."*

It didn't register . . . "Elvis what?"

"He just died, Larry. Elvis died."

MARILYN, NORMA JEANE

The Woman Who Will Not Die
by Gloria Steinem, H. Holt, New York, N.Y., 1986

Marilyn Monroe is still very much a part of everyday American life. Her famous smile and celebrated figure live on in posters and magazines; curiously, her persona seems to fit into the modern montage as well as any current actress or model. Other famous people have been remembered, but not like Marilyn Monroe.

"One simple reason for her life story's endurance is the premature end of it . . . " Gloria Steinem writes in this comprehensive biography. "When the past dies, there is mourning, but when the future dies our imaginations are compelled to carry it on." In fact, when she took her own life, many imagined that they might have helped her and ultimately saved her. Primarily, then, it is her vulnerability that has made her personal legend survive. As Steinem notes, "Her terrible openness made a connection with strangers."

Norma Jeane, The Girl

Norma Jeane Baker was born near Los Angeles, California on June 1, 1926, to Gladys Baker, a 24-year-old divorcee. Gladys had hoped to marry Norma Jeane's father, C. Stanley Gifford, a "Clark Gable-looking salesman," but on Christmas Eve, when she told him she was pregnant, he abandoned her. Gladys was devastated, and Marilyn, too, ultimately would be hurt: all her life she would yearn for a father. In fact, later in her life, when she tried to contact Gifford, he refused to have anything to do with his daughter.

Although Norma Jeane's mother loved her, she had to board her daughter with a neighbor family so that she could retain her job at a film lab. Eventually, however, Gladys was able to buy a small white bungalow where she and Norma Jeane could live together. Marilyn, a shy girl, recalled feeling a new sense of freedom and happiness when she moved in with her mother.

But the idyll was short-lived. In January of 1934, Gladys, weakened by the strain of working double shifts, withdrew into "her own interior world" and remained in an institution for most of her life.

Gladys' friend, Grace McKee, subsequently helped pay Norma Jeane's board as she moved to a succession of foster homes. When Grace remarried in 1935, however, she felt she had no option but to place Norma Jeane in an orphanage. "I saw this sign," Marilyn recalled, "and the emptiness that came over me, I'll never forget. The sign read: LOS ANGELES ORPHANS' HOME. I began to cry . . . When a little girl feels lost and lonely and that nobody wants her it's something she never can forget as long as she lives."

When Norma Jeane was 11, she left the orphanage, again to move from family to family, until Ana Lower (Aunt Ana), a loving, gentle woman, accepted her into her home. Unfortunately, Ana was too old to assume legal custody, and when Norma Jeane was 16, an arranged marriage seemed the best alternative.

Many biographers assert that Marilyn exaggerated the emotional neglect—and possible physical abuse—she may have experienced growing up. Notwithstanding, her pain *was* legitimate, and it did instill in her a remarkable empathy for people from all walks of life.

A Working Career

After marrying, Norma Jeane was singled out by a photographer who was taking action shots of people aiding the war effort. "I'm going to take your picture for the boys in the Army to keep their morale high," he beamed as he snapped picture after picture of the buoyant young woman at the factory where she worked. And upon seeing the photos, the largest modeling agency in California hired Norma Jeane full-time. "When she walked in," one of the agency's other models recalls, "it was like the room stopped, and everyone in the room knew she was going to get the job, and she did." Her career swiftly accelerated. Howard Hughes at RKO studios ordered a screen test, and his interest prompted Twentieth Century-Fox to quickly endorse her contract.

Norma Jeane promptly became "Marilyn Monroe"—and increasingly came to believe that her survival, her need "to prove she was alive, to be noticed, to belong, to be loved and to work, depended on her body." Although the budding actress initially resisted bleaching her hair, she finally relented in order to win a six-hour modeling assignment. She also lowered her "squeaky speaking voice" and mastered a new smile so that there would appear to be more space between her nose and mouth. By the time she had fully developed her "Marilyn" persona, she could turn it on and off like a light switch. "I just felt like being Marilyn for a moment," she would explain.

Although Marilyn appeared in roles as the standard "dumb blonde," she took her work as an actress seriously. Spending her weekly salaries on drama, dancing, and singing lessons, she once said, *I knew how third-rate I was . . . but, my God, how I wanted to learn! . . . I didn't want anything else. Not men, not money, not love, but the ability to act. With the arc lights on me and the camera pointed at me, I suddenly knew myself. How clumsy, empty, uncultured I was! A sullen orphan with a goose egg for a head. But I would change . . .*

Marilyn thus began studying with one of the foremost acting instructors of the time, Lee Strasberg, who later named her, along with Marlon Brando, as "one of the most talented actors" he had ever met.

But in spite of Marilyn's efforts to be taken seriously, Hollywood continued to offer her the same vapid roles—and she took them only because she wanted to work. Eventually, of course, she felt used and resentful. "Big breasts, big ass, big deal," she once said. "Can't I be anything else?"

Marilyn, though, shrewdly appraised Hollywood's attitude toward sex, and tried to use it to her advantage. "If [I] didn't go along, there were twenty-five girls who would," she explained. "You can't sleep your way into being a star . . . " she told a British journalist. "But it helps."

Despite owning a strong work ethic, Marilyn displayed some highly unprofessional habits. She was always late, a failing that prompted a reporter to blame her for several weeks of extra shooting on *The Misfits* set—a charge that led Marilyn to attempt suicide.

In addition to tardiness, Marilyn was known for her innate fear. Not only was she afraid to meet new people, she often, in "sheer primal terror," vomited before entering the sound stage.

Addicted to sleeping pills and tranquilizers, Marilyn once blamed her dependence on an inability to sleep—restlessness owing to earlier childhood trauma. In fact, studios of the '50s and '60s used drugs routinely to keep their most valuable performers working. Interestingly, Marilyn's addiction did not seem to interfere with her work; though too fond of pills and champagne, "she was still a beautiful and a good actress to the end."

In addition to acting, Marilyn's great passion was learning. Ashamed that she hadn't finished high school, she read voraciously and was particularly interested in poetry and politics. In her last interview, she pleaded with the reporter to end the story with something of substance: " . . . What the world really needs is a real feeling of kinship. Everybody: stars, laborers, Negroes, Jews, Arabs. We are all brothers. Please don't make me a joke. End the interview with what I believe." The reporter didn't listen.

Fathers and Lovers

Marilyn longed for someone to take the place of the father she had never known. Although Jim Dougherty was willing to fill this role, he was a merchant marine who was often away from home, leaving Marilyn to turn to her blossoming career and to other men for affirmation. After two years of marriage, she filed for divorce.

Freed from her marriage, Marilyn engaged in several affairs. However, finally—perhaps "to fulfill the pink-and-white American sex-goddess image that the public expected of her"—she chose baseball star and "handsome stoic" Joe DiMaggio to be her "true" first husband. But DiMaggio soon fell from the pedestal his wife had put him on, splintering the marriage: he resented her career and her immodest way of dressing, and did not share Marilyn's interest in education. In fact, on one special occasion she gave him a medal engraved with a quote from *The Little Prince*: "True love is visible not to the eyes, but to the heart, for eyes may be deceived." DiMaggio's mystified response was, "What the hell does that mean?"

Nine months after the marriage, the two separated. Following the split, DiMaggio became both paranoid and violent, once even raiding an apartment where he believed she and a lover were staying. Despite his anger and jealousy, ultimately it was DiMaggio who arranged her funeral, and who spent the night before the services in a vigil over her casket. As a fact of poignancy and irony, Marilyn "was buried with his flowers in her hands."

Upon divorcing DiMaggio, Marilyn promptly married Arthur Miller. She once said that talking with the famed playwright for the first time was "like a cool drink when you've got a fever." For his part, Miller was seriously in love; what's more, he was "touched by her profound connection to children and to nature, and even defended her sexual way of dressing . . . " However, problems developed as early as their honeymoon, when Marilyn discovered disparaging notes Miller had written about her, which set her to speculating that she was "only a grist for his writerly mill." After that, Miller took on the role, not of Marilyn's *father*, but as her caretaker; they never reconciled their differences and soon became, as Miller's maid Lena Pepitone remembers, "two people who were so polarized that Miller rarely emerged from his study or ate meals with his wife."

Marilyn again turned to the comforts of other men, including striking up a serious relationship with Yves Montand and probable relationships with Frank Sinatra and both Jack and Bobby Kennedy. Indeed, as she talked of remarrying and having a baby, "friends were stunned by both her lack of discretion and her lack of realism."

In 1962, following her rumored break-up with Bobby Kennedy, the increasingly erratic Marilyn was fired from the film *Something's Got to Give*. Shortly thereafter, on August 5th, Marilyn, "her image . . . so dependent on a sensuous youthfulness that it was bound to self-destruct," was found dead in her bedroom, the phone receiver in her hand. The official cause of death: acute barbiturate overdose.

The speculations as to the cause of Marilyn Monroe's death range from the well-reasoned to the bizarre. Having evaluated them all, Steinem concludes that, in all likelihood, Marilyn's death was by her own hand—though suicide may not have been her aim. Perhaps, writes Steinem, "she meant to die for the evening—but not to die forever."

Who Would Marilyn Be Now?

"We can imagine many futures for Norma Jeane . . . " Steinem muses. "If acting had become an expression of [her] real self, not an escape from it, one also can imagine the whole woman who was both Norma Jeane and Marilyn becoming a serious actress and wise comedienne . . . But Norma Jeane remained the frightened child of the past. And Marilyn remained the unthreatening half-person that sex goddesses are supposed to be. It is the lost possibilities of Marilyn Monroe that capture our imaginations. It was the lost Norma Jeane, looking out of Marilyn's eyes, who captured our hearts . . . If we learn from the life of Marilyn Monroe, she will live on in us."

THE AUTOBIOGRAPHY OF MARK TWAIN

edited and arranged by Charles Neider, Harper & Row Publishers, Inc., New York, N.Y., 1959

Samuel Langhorne Clemens—best known by the pen name Mark Twain—is one of the most original and gifted American writers. Since his death in 1910, his stories have been adapted countless times for stage and film productions, some fairly effectively; but the full beauty of Twain's works can be encountered only on the page.

A fan of Twain's works considering which of his books to read next could do no better than to pick up his autobiography. In setting down his life story, Twain withdrew from a traditional autobiographical format. Eschewing hard facts and definite chronological order in favor of a tangled series of journal entries, newspaper clippings, remembrances and banterings, he was, as usual, simply out to tell a good story.

Twain intended that his account be published posthumously. He wrote, as he said, "from the grave," offering an honest—sometimes *brutally* honest—audit of himself and others. As Charles Neider says in the book's introduction: *[Twain] had produced his share of work in the world; he had outlived most of the people he cared for; the world was in a bad way and he was not averse to leaving it. And so he reminisced, and by so doing he amused himself—reminisced on his own terms . . . not according to some theory of autobiographical composition.*

And so Twain begins his train of self-musings, appropriately enough, with his birth.

◇ ◆ ◇

I was born the 30th of November, 1835, in the almost invisible village of Florida, Monroe County, Missouri . . . The village contained a hundred people and I increased the population by 1 per cent. It is more than many of the best men in history could have done for a town.

The Clemens family consisted of Twain, his older siblings Orion and Pamela; and his parents, John Marshall and Jane Clemens. Another brother and sister, Benjamin and Margaret, would both die before he was seven. His brother Henry came along some two years later, and, according to Twain, "I think that the unbroken monotony of his goodness and truthfulness and obedience would have been a burden to [my mother] but for the relief and variety which I furnished in the other direction." In his book *Tom Sawyer*, Henry served as the inspiration for Sid.

When Twain was still very young, his family moved to Hannibal, Missouri. There he often spent a few months a year on the farm of his uncle John A. Quarles. A lot of the people, places, and events in Twain's most notable stories, he claimed, were plagiarized from his childhood. His Uncle John's farm, for example, was relocated to Arkansas in *Tom Sawyer, Detective,* and *Huck Finn.* Similarly, in the middle-aged slave "Uncle Dan'l," Twain said, he found a "faithful and affectionate good friend, ally and adviser," but also a model for "Jim." Thus, between the semi-fictional characters and the real-life people, Twain confessed that he sometimes got confused. *When I was younger I could remember anything, whether it had happened or not; but my faculties are decaying now and soon I shall be so I cannot remember any but the things that never happened.*

One of Twain's earliest memories was of an incident which occurred on his first day of school, when he was four and a half. He committed some small offense and, despite a warning that he had broken one of the rules, he proceeded to break it a second time. The penalty was a whipping, and Mrs. Horr, trusting in the boy's judgment, sent him out to find a suitable switch. The switch Twain presented to her was quite suitable for his purposes—but not for hers. *She said she would try and appoint a boy with a better judgment than mine in the matter of switches, and it saddens me yet to remember how many faces lighted up with the hope of getting that appointment. Jim Dunlap got it, and when he returned with the switch of choice I recognized that he was an expert.*

Twain's father died in 1847 and he was taken from school to serve as an apprentice printer for the Hannibal *Courier.* Two or three years later, his brother Orion returned from his job as a journeyman printer in St. Louis and purchased the other local newspaper, the *Journal.* Orion had never had much of a head for money, and it wasn't long before he had to move the whole works into the family's house. Finally, in 1853, Orion abandoned the paper altogether and ran off to Keokuk, Iowa to get married. Soon after that, Twain followed his brother's example and ran off himself to St. Louis. From there he went to see the big world—which, for Twain at the time, consisted of New York and Philadelphia. By the end of the following year he was back working for Orion amid the splendors of Keokuk.

Because Orion could never afford to pay his workers, however, Twain soon set off again. This time he found himself in New Orleans—where, for five hundred dollars borrowed money, he trained as a river pilot. "Within eighteen months," Twain reported, "I [had] become a competent pilot, and I served in that office until the Mississippi River traffic was brought to a standstill by the breaking out of the Civil War." In June of 1861 he served as a second lieutenant in the Confederate Army. His service was short-lived, however: *I resigned after two weeks' service in the field,* explaining that I was "incapacitated by fatigue" through persistent retreating.

A few years later, after signing on to work out west with the Virginia City

Enterprise, Twain was sent to Carson City to report on Nevada's legislative session. When several lines of his weekly column proved to be rather unkind to the legislators, they, in turn, became rather unkind towards him. And so, Twain writes, *I presently began to sign the letters, using the Mississippi leadsman's call, "Mark Twain" (two fathoms, or twelve feet) for this purpose . . .*

From Nevada he headed up to San Francisco to become the sole reporter for the *Morning Call;* later, the Sacramento *Union* sent him to do a story on the sugar interests in the Sandwich Islands (now Hawaii), where he was encouraged to "break into the lecture field"—and did so. After a slow start, he lectured his way throughout California and Nevada. Then he decided to tour Europe, sending letters about his travels to the *Daily Alta California* for twenty dollars each. His book based on this tour, *The Innocents Abroad,* was published in 1869.

Then, "In the beginning of February 1870," Twain writes, "I was married to Miss Olivia L. Langdon, and I took up my residence in Buffalo, New York." Once married, he gave up the lecture circuit for a few years. Unfortunately, during his absence the circuit became flooded with charlatans and money-grabbers. When he returned to it in 1884, he said, the audiences had to be taught all over again what to appreciate.

Their couple's first child, "Langdon Clemens, was born the 7th of November, 1870, and lived twenty-two months." This loss would have been greater had they not by then also had a daughter, Suzy, who was born a year and a half later. Suzy proved to be a blithe, happy yet contemplative girl with a direct conduit to her father's heart. Another daughter, Clara, was born two years after Suzy, and Jean some seven years after that.

In 1872 Twain wrote *Roughing It,* which, like *The Innocents Abroad,* was published through Elisha Bliss and the American Publishing Company. It was some ten years— and several books later—Twain dryly notes, that he was able to figure out just how badly he had been "swindled by those people." In his early years he knew nothing about royalties nor "above cost of manufacture profits" and such. "From my pen to their pockets" went the proceeds from some of Twain's most popular books—including *Tom Sawyer.* *[Now Bliss] has been dead a quarter of a century . . . My bitterness against him has faded away and disappeared. I feel only compassion for him, and if I could send him a fan I would.*

Despite the dishonesty of his publishers, Twain was far from impoverished; "my money and I undertook some great adventures." Once, for the cost of fifteen thousand dollar, he took out a patent on a minor invention. After watching his money fly away for a few years, he put the manufacturing and selling details into the hands of another, equally capable fellow. *At last, when I had lost forty-two thousand dollars on that patent I gave it away to a man whom I had long detested and whose family I desired to ruin. Then I looked around for other adventures*—the second of which cost him only ten thousand dollars; and his third, an attempt that kept him suitably occupied for sixteen months at a loss of some thirty-two thousand dollars, consisted of an investment in some sort of fantastic coal-burning steam engine thing. After all that, starting up an insurance company seemed like a good idea; and perhaps it was, since he lost just twenty-three thousand on the venture.

By then he was finally becoming more careful with his money. And it was then that a Mr. Alexander Graham Bell approached him with an offer to invest in some invention of his called the telephone, but Twain wasn't interested. Bell finally persuaded a dry-goods clerk in Hartford into investing his life's savings of five thousand dollars. *I was sorry for that man when I heard about it. I thought I might have saved him if I had had an opportunity to tell him about my experiences.*

In 1884 Twain set up his own publishing company—and put it in the incapable hands of his nephew-in-law Charles Webster. *Huckleberry Finn* soon appeared, and the author once again took to the lecture circuit.

As impossible as it sounds, my nephew-in-law, who specialized in printing only truly bad books, drove the publishing company into ruin by 1893. And at the age of fifty-eight, Twain found himself in debt to ninety-six creditors. To pay them off, his wife, his daughter Clara and he hit the lecture circuit again. By 1899, they were not only free from debt but eighteen thousand dollars in the black—the total sum of which was shortly gone after he trumpeted, "Put it in Federal Steel."

The last quarter of a century of my life has been pretty constantly and faithfully devoted to the study of the human race—that is to say, the study of myself, for in my individual person I am the entire human race compacted together. I have found that there is no ingredient of the race which I do not possess in either a small way or a large way . . . As a result, my private and concealed opinion of myself is not of a complimentary sort. It follows that my estimate of the human race is the duplicate of my estimate of myself.

In August of 1896, after a brief illness, Suzy Clemens died at the age of twenty-four. Then in 1902 his wife Olivia's health began to fail—mainly from nervous exhaustion. Jean was also ailing and bedridden at this time but, thanks to Clara, her mother was spared the details.

"Olivia, my beloved wife," Twain wrote, "died on June 5, 1904. She was my life, and she is gone; she was my riches, and I am a pauper." Jean died on Christmas Eve, 1909. "Possibly I know now what the soldier feels when a bullet crashes through his heart."

Twain himself died shortly afterwards, on April 21, 1910.

STEVEN SPIELBERG

The Man, His Movies, and Their Meaning
by Philip M. Taylor, Continuum Publishing, New York, N.Y., 1992

I think Hollywood will forgive me once I'm 55, I don't know what they'll forgive me for, but they'll forgive me when I'm 55.

Inspired filmmaker Steven Spielberg's success is unmatched in his field. His talent for creating films with universal appeal is certainly unique; however, it was a talent long unrecognized by the Academy of Motion Picture Arts and Sciences—who, as of this biography's 1992 publication date, had not awarded Spielberg even one Oscar. It seems Spielberg had been placed in a creative straightjacket: if he did films his audience loved, the critics hated it; when he broke out of his proven formula to please the critics, the audience hated it. This unfortunate phenomenon may be what he was referring to when he observes that we have probably seen the most *successful* films he will ever make, "but I don't think you have seen the best of what I can do as a filmmaker." In fact, Spielberg's colleagues often joked that a film could never hope for an Oscar if it suffered from the three S's: success, special effects, and Spielberg.

But Spielberg claims he is not bothered by the critics' view of his work. "I just make the kind of films that I would want to see," he shrugs.

So what is it about this man that makes the public love him, while the very industry in which he works ignores him? Critic Martin Amis astutely sums up the Spielberg phenomenon: *As an artist, Spielberg is a mirror, not a lamp. His line to the common heart is so direct that he unmans you with the frailty of your own defenses, and the transparency of your most intimate fears and hopes.*

❖ ◆ ❖

Spielberg admits that his best creations spring from a vivid collection of impressions engraved in his first memories. Almost all his films are geared to evoke the pure, primitive images and emotions of early youth—especially *his* youth. And his own preoccupation with childhood, adolescence, and nostalgia keeps us predictably spellbound.

Born in Cincinnati, Ohio, in 1947, Spielberg was raised in an era of great political agitation; surprisingly, however, he never really involved himself politically: he was too busy watching TV and the movies. "For children, it is the universe as it is," he reflects. "For adults, who think they know better, it is the universe as it should have been."

The character actors Spielberg uses in leading roles are very much like ourselves. Thus, by placing these people in extraordinary situations, he challenges his viewers with the critical question, "What would *you* do?" Again and again we are implicitly asked: "Would you board a giant alien spacecraft if one arrived?" "Would you hide a feeble alien in your room and ask the authorities for help if it were dying?"

This identification between audience and character has been a key element in Spielberg's success. Richard Dreyfuss has been chosen to star in a number of his films for that very reason. As Spielberg explains: " . . . Most of us are like Richard Dreyfuss. Few of us are like Bob Redford or Steve McQueen."

Spielberg speaks freely about his professional intentions and aspirations; however, he is not as willing to share the details of his private life. Yet, through his films we can glean a great deal. For example, there is the "yearning-for-home" theme that runs rampant throughout Spielberg movies. In *ET,* the plot centers around a lost alien's quest to return home; in the 1989 film *Always,* "home" is life itself; and in *Jaws,* Robert Shaw's character sings "Show Me the Way to Go Home." Spielberg explains: "I've lived in so many places since I was a child I felt I never really had a home, and that's a feeling many people can respond to."

The movie-maker describes a "semi-unhappy" childhood and parents who constantly bickered. He found a measure of escape by turning to television—though he admits to being frightened by much of what he saw. He specifically recalls a documentary on snakes that left him crying and trembling in fear—*a la* his future Indiana Jones hero.

As an adult, Spielberg was finally able to take out his revenge on TV through the movie *Poltergeist* (1982), a story about a family who is invaded by hostile supernatural entities via the television set.

Movies also left their early mark of inspirational trauma: "The first three movies I ever saw were all Walt Disney films, and they scared the bejeezus out of me . . . " remembers Spielberg. Ironically, however, he also credits Disney with influencing him more than any other filmmaker.

Spielberg's mother, Leah, played a leading role in his early life. She not only encouraged but catered to her young son's filmmaking obsession. Once she intentionally overcooked a gallon of cherries jubilee sauce in a pressure cooker until it exploded so her son could film the gooey mess all over the kitchen. "We never said no," she remembers. "We never had a chance to say no. Steven didn't understand that word."

"The weird skinny kid with acne," as Spielberg describes his boyhood self, was rarely accepted by his schoolmates. To make matters worse, just as he *would* begin to make friends in each new neighborhood, he found his family gearing up for another move. Thus, the perennial loner retreated for companionship into the recesses of his TV tube.

The introspective young TV addict began making movies when he was twelve. By age sixteen, he had mastered his father's 8mm movie camera and produced a two-and-a-half-hour science-fiction epic called *Firelight,* about a team of scientists investigating mysterious lights in the sky. His father, finally resigned to Steven's propensity towards film, rented the local cinema for one night, and the $500 epic made a profit of $100.

Soon after this initial success, the family moved to San Jose, California, where his parents, after years of turmoil, decided to divorce. In the film *Back to the Future,* Spielberg focuses on a boy's attempt to recreate his own life, sending his primary character back into the past to try to patch up—in advance—his parents' failing marriage.

Despite the trauma of his parents' split, the move to California proved happily fateful for Spielberg. To the detriment of his college studies, all of his efforts were now concentrated on getting his films before Universal Studio executives. And finally, with a hastily produced 22-minute dialogue-free flick called *Amblin,* his talent was recognized.

Before long, the 21-year-old Spielberg had quit college and signed a historic seven-year contract with Universal TV Production—a contract he soon came to resent. Still, driven to create films, Spielberg bit the bullet and worked out his professional apprenticeship by directing various episodes of shows such as "Night Gallery," "Marcus Welby, MD," "The Psychiatrists" and "Columbo."

It wasn't long before the college drop-out found himself exchanging script ideas with a diverse group of talented young filmmakers, including George Lucas, Francis Ford Coppola, Martin Scorsese, and Brian De Palma, who were able to share advice among themselves when there was none to be had elsewhere.

Spielberg and the American Present

In Spielberg's first cinema releases—*Duel* (1971), *The Sugarland Express* (1974), and *Jaws* (1975), he was able to experiment with techniques that would later become trademarks of his filmmaking style.

Then, because he "couldn't find anybody who would write it the way I wanted it," Spielberg took two years off and wrote *Close Encounters of The Third Kind* himself. He hired J. Allen Hyneck as a consultant for the film, an interesting choice since Hyneck was a former U.S. Government UFO expert who had resigned after seeing evidence that didn't concur with his skepticism. As he recalls: "I really found my faith when I heard that the government was opposed to the film. If NASA took the time to write me a 20-page letter, then I knew there must be something happening."

Close Encounters brought out one of Spielberg's greatest talents: directing children. The movie was first and foremost a celebration of innocence—as well as the first American film ever made suggesting that alien life might be amicable rather than hostile.

Spielberg and the American Past

The highly successful *Indiana Jones* trilogy was the product of a ten-year "gentlemen's agreement" with George Lucas—a joint pact to make a series of films patterned after the cliffhangers they had both enjoyed as kids.

In 1985, between the first and second *Indiana Jones* movies, Spielberg was prompted to depart from adventure to direct Alice Walker's *The Color Purple.* In this, his first major "people picture," he drew from his own memories to create a realistic portrayal of the pain involved in separation. The film was nominated for eleven Oscars, yet failed to win a single Academy Award.

Spielberg and the American Future

With the release of *E.T.,* his most personal film to date, Spielberg made a significant departure from Hollywood moviemaking. By portraying a race of ugly yet lovable aliens who, despite their superior technology, are just as afraid of us as we are of them, Spielberg made a statement against the Cold War which then still loomed over the world. *E.T.* was undoubtedly Spielberg's most inspired and memorable masterpiece—a long-awaited love story born out of his closest and innermost memories and fantasies. E.T. is a child lost from its parents, the universal human symbol of naked betrayal of innocence. "Towards the end of *E.T.,*" Taylor writes, "barely able to support my own grief and bewilderment, I turned and looked down the aisle at my fellow sufferers: executive, black dude, Japanese businessman, punk, hippie, mother, teenager, child. Each face was a mask of tears."

Nearly a decade after *E.T.'s* release, Spielberg began work on his ultimate autobiographical project: the story of Peter Pan. "I've always been Peter Pan," the filmmaker once admitted. "In a way it's typecasting for me." However, rather than focusing on lost childhood, *Hook,* starring Robin Williams, turned out to be a piece on lost fatherhood. "It's an allegory for all of us adults," explains Spielberg.

The Spielberg of the nineties is an even-tempered man who does not smoke, drink, or use drugs; he also works 20 hours a day. His only vice seems to be biting his nails. He does, however, occasionally suffer from bouts of depression, but he claims he does his best work when he is "in the pits emotionally." Although he elicits great love and joy from his children— the offspring of several different relationships—he is a man whose adulthood has "never quite proved as satisfying as his childhood."

Steven Spielberg will soon have lived for half a century. Yet he himself sometimes muses that he is simply becoming an older Peter Pan. And whatever he decides to do in the future, it is certain that if he is to be dragged from his childhood, it will have to be kicking and screaming.

Summary Note: In 1993, Spielberg may finally have achieved official Hollywood adulthood with Schindler's List, acclaimed by both critics and audiences, for which he at last received an Oscar as Best Director. In 1994, he was named the highest-paid entertainer in the world, earning 350 million dollars.

DISNEY'S WORLD: A BIOGRAPHY

by Leonard Mosley, Stein & Day, New York, N.Y., 1985

Walter Elias Disney was born on December 5, 1901 to Elias and Flora Disney, the last of their four sons. Walt's father had grown up in a rowdy, rambunctious family, but he had developed into a stern, religious man who tolerated no improper behavior. Elias' strict, tyrannical rule seemed to drive away all of his children at one point or another.

When Walt was five, his family moved to Marceline, Kansas. His father had worked in many trades, but now he wanted to settle permanently into farming. Walt always remembered the Marceline farm years fondly; he got along much better with the farm animals, however, than he did with his harsh father or the two domineering oldest brothers of the family. The ducks, cows and chickens that he tended on the farm became his first real friends. He called them by name, talked to them, and frequently sat down to sketch them.

Life in Marceline was also brightened for Walt by the visits of his Uncle Ed—a small, wizened-faced, elf-like man whom Walt took to calling "Uncle Elf." On every visit, zestful Uncle Elf would cavort with his nephew in the fields around the farm. In later years, Uncle Elf became the model for Jiminy Cricket, Pinocchio's loyal, spry and optimistic conscience.

Meanwhile, as Elias Disney's drought-stricken crops withered in the Kansas heat, his farming dreams slowly began to fade away. About this time, his two eldest sons, Herbert and Raymond, ran away from home, unable to tolerate his iron-fisted rule. Their embittered father disowned them, refusing even to acknowledge their existence. Not long afterwards, he became critically ill, and the Disneys finally had to sell their farm.

In Kansas City, their next home, Elias obtained a distribution route for a local newspaper. Though he had to hire and pay some "outside" paper boys, he also worked his two youngest sons, Roy and Walt, without compensation, claiming that he was investing their money. Roy vocally resented this, and finally stormed out of his father's door—just after Herbert had returned to try to make peace. When the family's finances dwindled, the Disneys were again forced to move, this time to Chicago, where Walt found summer work as a news carrier on the Union Pacific Railroad.

Walt spent the next school year in Chicago at McKinley High School—where he became enamored of Su Pitowski, the most beautiful and unattainable girl the shy young man had ever known. Her involvement in the school newspaper, *The Voice,* prompted him to volunteer his services as junior art editor and to originate a section in the paper for his cartoon, *The Tiny Voice.*

At the tail-end of World War I in 1917, sixteen-year-old Walt, too young and too skinny to enlist in the military, became a volunteer for a Red Cross unit. While traveling in Europe, he continued to correspond with Su and earned extra money around camp with his artwork.

Walt's homecoming was not all joy. First of all he discovered that Su Pitowski had already married another man. Then, for months on end there were quarrels with his father over what vocation Walt should now pursue. Elias insisted that his son go to work at a jelly factory; Walt wanted to be a professional illustrator. Walt chose to do it his way—and, true to family tradition, the last Disney son walked defiantly out the door.

Although one prominent cartoonist, Carey Orr, warned Walt off with the comment that he wasn't "cynical" enough for newspaper cartooning, his brother Roy finally secured him a two-month apprenticeship with the Pesmen-Rubin agency. There Walt met Ub Iwerks, another apprentice. When both Walt and Ub were let go at the end of the season, they went into business for themselves as "Iwerks and Disney." And soon they were earning twice their former wages.

But the ever adventurous Walt soon looked away from newspaper comics into the field of animation. He took a brief apprenticeship with a job at Kansas City Film Ad Company and thereafter formed his own company, Laugh-O-Gram Films. When Laugh-O-Gram went bankrupt, Walt was left with a handful of clothes, a camera, fifty dollars, and enough loose bills to buy a train ticket to Los Angeles. He headed for Hollywood to try his hand at acting while he tended brother Roy, who was recovering from tuberculosis.

Roy encouraged Walt to return to his cartoons, and finally persuaded him to send a copy of *Alice's Wonderland,* an old Laugh-O-Gram cartoon, to a distributor named Margaret Winkler. She liked it and immediately agreed to finance Walt's work. Taking on Ub Iwerks as a partner, he began producing more Alice comedies.

Within a couple years, however, Walt's new company was also foundering, inundated by mounting production costs. Meanwhile, Margaret Winkler had married and turned her business over to her husband, Charles Mintz, who was not nearly so appreciative of Walt's work.

Searching for a vehicle to recapture the slipping appeal of the Alice comedies, Walt worked with Iwerks to create "Oswald the Lucky Rabbit." The new character quickly became a hit, but now trouble arose in earnest between Walt and Charles Mintz. To keep the cartoonist in line, Mintz signed all of Walt's animators, except for Ub Iwerks and a few others, to contracts working for him. Then, as co-owner of the Oswald character, along with Universal Pictures, Mintz aspired to produce future Oswald cartoons without Walt. Walt replied by slamming an Oswald button down on Mintz's desk. "Here, you can have the little bastard, he's all yours!" he shouted. Within weeks, Walt had founded Walt Disney Studios and introduced a new character: Mickey Mouse.

At first, Walt's financial problems threatened to derail Mickey's career. The first two Mickey Mouse films met with polite applause at 1928 sneak previews, but no distributor offered to pick them up; and without Mintz, Walt found himself desperately short of capital.

Undeterred, Walt set to work on yet another Mickey Mouse cartoon—*Steamboat Willie*. Demonstrating the scenes for his animators, he would shrilly squeak out Mickey's captioned lines—for a silent cartoon. "If only we had sound," Ub said, "you'd bring the house down..."

In 1929 Walt announced that *Steamboat Willie* would be released with full sound. To achieve this, he agreed to work with sound expert Pat Powers, who demanded that Walt use his studio's equipment exclusively for the next year. By the end of that year, Powers saw what a sensation Mickey was and tried to steal the character by stealing the one man he figured Walt could not do without: Ub Iwerks.

Walt fought on. His staff of young animators rose to the occasion. In the end, he recovered all the rights to his Mickey Mouse films and distributed them through United Artists.

Understandably disillusioned with short cartoons, Walt now resolved to carry out a feature-length project based on the romantic fairy tale *Snow White*. Roy considered the idea ridiculous: no one would pay to see a full-length cartoon feature. But Walt went ahead with the project, and in 1938, thanks to his own obsessive vision and his animators' herculean efforts, *Snow White and the Seven Dwarfs* became a smash success.

The leaves on Walt's laurels for *Snow White* were still green when he came up with the idea for his next project: bringing *The Sorcerer's Apprentice,* a Dukas Symphony inspired by Goethe's classic fable, to film. Because the Dukas work was too lengthy for a short cartoon and too short for a feature, Walt engaged the services of Leopold Stokowski and the Philadelphia Symphony Orchestra to expand the score. Buoyed by the success of this daring experiment, he soon began piecing together another film, the frolicking semi-abstract musical adventure of *Fantasia*—working from an assortment of classical symphonies and ballets. But upon its release, Fantasia, undoubtedly a masterpiece, was a box office flop. It took years to recover its costs, and with the onset of World War II, Disney Studios found itself once more deep in the red.

Ironically, many of the Disney films that lost money in the late '30s and early '40s would later become his best-loved classics, including *Fantasia, Dumbo, Sleeping Beauty, Alice in Wonderland, Pinocchio* and *Bambi.* And of course the Disney characters "born" during this era— Mickey and Minnie Mouse, Donald Duck, Goofy, Pluto, the Three Little Pigs, and a dozen others— would become 20th-century legends.

The struggling Disney Studios, with its cadre of loyal employees, had previously been untouched by the union strife that struck every other major studio in Hollywood. However, in 1941 Disney became embroiled in a feud with Herbert Sorrell of the Screen Cartoonists Guild. In the heat of the power struggle, the Guild moved in and forced a strike. Instead of settling through a mediated vote, as proposed by Walt, the strikers called for a boycott, which forced the studio to concede to their wishes. Finally, Disney Studios became a unionized shop. After this defeat, Walt was a changed man, bitter and more demanding of his employees.

While on vacation in 1947, Walt flew to Alaska. His fascination with the antics of seals soon prompted another new adventure: *Seal Island*, the first non-animated Disney nature documentary. It was followed by a series of 30-minute nature films, the Disney "True-Life Adventures," which helped pay off the company's heavy debt and skyrocketed Disney Studios into the forefront of film-making—just in time for Walt to announce his *next* project: a recreational park in Anaheim, California.

Walt envisioned Disneyland as a theme park—a pioneer version of simulated reality that the whole family could enjoy. To come up with the needed capital, he created a new company, WED, and began searching for backers—only to find that the banks were not interested either. Amusement parks at that time were little more than carnivals—dirty, rickety and unsavory— and financiers had a hard time catching Walt's vision of "something different."

Finally Walt engaged ABC TV network to produce the weekly "Walt Disney Presents" series in return for funds to build his latest dream. At last, on land that had once been an orange grove, Disneyland became a reality. Since its opening in 1955, it has expanded through the decades—and made money every year.

After the release of his much-celebrated film *Mary Poppins* in 1964, Walt's enthusiasm for managing Disney Studios and WED began to wear thin. He had always smoked heavily, coughing and hacking his way through the halls of the studio over the years, and now his health was deteriorating.

But Walt Disney was congenitally unable to rest. Already he had begun work on a new secret project: Disney World. Disturbed by the horde of speculative businesses that had clustered around Disneyland, he had secretly bought up huge tracts of land near Orlando, Florida, amassing some 30,000 acres. Decades later, Disney World would arise there, just as Walt had envisioned it: a larger, more varied version of Disneyland, uncontaminated by commercial sleaze and housing a pristine "City of Tomorrow"—the EPCOT Center, a model community where the employees of Disney World could live and play.

But Walt didn't live to see the completion of his City of Tomorrow. In October 1966, a doctor informed him that cancerous nodules had been found in his lungs and immediate surgery was required. In November, he left the hospital with one less lung; but even as his health declined precipitously, Walt pushed ahead on EPCOT.

On December 15, 1966, Walt Disney, the tireless, true-life genius-magician loved throughout the world by children young and old, passed away. After a brief, informal funeral, his body was privately cremated—several hours before his adoring public and employees heard the news.

ME: STORIES OF MY LIFE

by Katharine Hepburn, Knopf (Random House), New York, N.Y., 1991

Katharine Hepburn was born on May 12, 1907 in Hartford, Connecticut to Thomas Norval Hepburn, a medical doctor and son of an Episcopalian minister, and Katharine Martha Houghton, a strong-willed social activist. Though the grandparents on her mother's side died when Kate was young, they instilled in her the value of education and self-sufficiency. "Knowledge! Education! Don't give in! Make your own trail," she remembers them saying.

The Hepburn household was lively—and *very free;* there were virtually no rules. The children were always climbing trees and swinging on a homemade trapeze, which draped all the way across the property. Hepburn's memories include exploring the nearby woods, organizing afternoon teas on tree stumps, riding on sleds behind Dad's car, and spending summers at their coastal home in Fenwick, Connecticut, where she learned to dive off a pier. Years later, when actress Jane Fonda was struggling to do a somersault dive during the filming of *On Golden Pond,* the seventy-year-old Hepburn teased, "If you can't do it, dear, I'll do it for you. It's one of my specialties."

They were also an upbeat household. Even upon the death of Kate's younger brother Tom, her parents refused to let themselves or their family wallow in remorse. "They moved on into life . . . They simply did not believe in moaning about anything . . . We were a happy family. We are a happy family."

Though she knew it was unavoidable, Kate was not too excited about going off to Bryn Mawr, the prestigious all-girl college which her mother had attended. She had spent most of her youth with her brothers, and the thought of living with wall-to-wall girls repulsed her. Her first year at Bryn Mawr was just as difficult as she had imagined. Her aloofness led a number of her schoolmates to label her as a conceited, "self-conscious beauty"—but during the second year she roomed with a girl she had come to know and trust, and college life improved.

Kate had always practiced "acting" as a child, putting on neighborhood shows and clowning around for the family; now, at school, she was given the opportunity to act in significant productions. During her senior year she met Edwin Knopf, who ran a reputable theater company in Baltimore. After graduation, she asked Knopf for work and was ecstatic when he hired her. "My God! I had a job!" she remembers exulting. "He gave me a job!"

Knopf's theater provided the neophyte actress with an ideal learning environment. She recalls the first time she had to be fitted for a costume. She arrived at the stage at 10:00 A.M., expecting to avoid the rush, only to find that she was *last* in line—and stuck with the *worst* costume.

"Then something very strange happened," she recalls. "One of the girls came up to me and said, 'I was the first here. I want you to take my costume. It's the prettiest.'" Kate protested—"oh no, I couldn't"—but the other girl insisted: "I'm not going to be an actor. And I think that you are going to be. I mean, I think you are going to be a big star. I want you to have it." Hepburn later looked back on that milestone: "Can you imagine anyone being so generous? Wasn't I lucky? Lucky."

Of course, the pieces of Hepburn's acting career didn't always fall into place so easily. Her first major stage performance was in a play called *The Big Pond.* During the first rehearsals she worked as an understudy for the lead actress, but she soon became convinced that she could do a far superior job as the lead herself. One day she was asked to stay and play a scene. "Pushed by a sort of frenetic boiling-over, I must have read it very well." Almost immediately the producers fired the lead and hired Hepburn. "This was happening just as I had imagined it would . . . I was arriving."

Then, early on during the play's first performance Hepburn feigned a French accent that brought the house down. "Well . . . that's that," she thought. "I'm a star." But her overconfidence caused her pitch and tempo to rise, the result being that no one could understand her for the rest of the night. She was swiftly replaced.

Her next big play, *These Days,* closed after only a week, and Hepburn again found herself on the streets, willing to accept any role she was offered. Then one night she got lucky again: a stranger approached and asked if she was in the theater. She would like to be, she said. And through this inauspicious exchange she received an invitation to work with the Theater Guild. The work was not steady, but she did appear in some lesser plays.

Hepburn's voice needed a lot of work. "I think that I was so excited by life and living and my future," she says of those first hectic years, "that I was simply wound up so tight I didn't—couldn't—relax." And this tautness was reflected in her vocal timber. With work and time, however, those same gravelly tones—which had once been considered her least valuable asset—became a Hepburn trademark.

In New York Hepburn also began spending more time with friends—men like Jack Clarke, who had first linked her up with Edwin Knopf, and Clarke's best friend, Ludlow Ogden Smith. Hepburn soon began pairing off with the debonair and sensitive Ludlow, or "Luddy," as she called him. It was with Luddy that she lost her "virtue." "I mean, I guessed that Luddy knew what he was doing—and I didn't object. So we did it," Hepburn recalls. "He was my beau from then on. Listen, let me tell you—yes, he was my beau but—and that's the biggest *but* you've ever heard: He was my friend!"

In time, Kate and Luddy were married. Hepburn had thought she could give up acting and settle down in Pennsylvania, but that lasted only two weeks. She was in love with herself as much as she was with Luddy, and she was compelled to pursue her acting career. And her husband supported her decision: "I don't know what I would have done without Luddy," Kate still professes affectionately.

Kate continued with her stage career. Then in 1930 she also decided to take on California and the movies. To get the part she coveted, starring alongside John Barrymore in George Cukor's *A Bill of Divorcement*, she knew she would have to beat out Lawrence Olivier's then-wife, Jill Esmond. On the trip by train to California, however, Hepburn caught several flecks of steel rail in her eye. When her agent, Leland Hayward, met her in Hollywood, her eyes were blood-red and sore. " . . . We got fifteen hundred dollars for *that* . . . ?" asked another agent when he caught a glimpse of her. "She's an original," replied Hayward. " . . . Get a load of those eyes," the other responded. "What's she been drinking?"

But Hepburn got the part. In fact, she made five movies in eighteen brief months after her arrival in Hollywood; and, just as important, she made her way into the industry's most prominent social circles, cultivating close friendships with some very influential men:

Motion-picture director George Cukor: "George really liked me—and I really liked him . . . [He] was my best friend in California. We made many pictures together—always happily . . . He loved to entertain and I loved to be his guest . . . It was as if George and I had been brought up together . . . The same liberal point of view—the same sense of right and wrong. I miss him."

Leland Hayward: After separating from Luddy, Kate spent much time with her agent. "We were like an old married couple . . . We just enjoyed—enjoyed—enjoyed . . . Leland wanted to marry me, but I really did not want to marry."

Billionaire-aviator-entrepreneur-movie producer Howard Hughes: Hughes began following one of Hepburn's plays on tour. In Chicago he stayed at the same hotel as the cast, and he and Kate had dinner together. They "had dinner the next night too—so . . . " The pair seemed to fall into a relationship out of loneliness. The newspapers said they were going to marry, "but when it came right down to 'What do we do now?'—I went East and he stayed West. . . . I always thought it was lucky that we never married—two people who are used to having their own way should stay separate."

Hughes suffered from hearing loss, a handicap that caused him much social discomfort and added heavily to an already deep sense of isolation. Later, after he had injured himself in a plane crash, his doctor gave him an open prescription for morphine—"and Howard found this blank road more comfortable than the endless life struggle. One cannot blame him, but it was very sad. He was a remarkable man."

L.B. Mayer, head of MGM: "He was not stupid, not crude. He was a very sensible fellow, and extremely honest. . . . I can say that he was the most honest person I ever dealt with in my life."

Mayer and Hepburn were sincere friends, and he came to rely on her judgment in important decisions. However, Hepburn recalls, " . . .

His life was his work. When the work ceased, he really sort of died . . . [He] would have loved to have been a most witty, charming and fascinating creature. I don't think he was particularly." But in his work "he was wild—He was a romantic. He *believed*."

And, of course, Katharine Hepburn knew **Spencer Tracy.** It was with Tracy that this strong and self-willed striver came to learn a new, self-less kind of love. "He was there—I was his. I wanted him to be happy—safe—comfortable. I liked to wait on him—listen to him—feed him—talk to him—work for him. I tried not to disturb him—irritate him—bother him—worry him, nag him. I struggled to change all the qualities which I felt he didn't like. Some of them which I thought were my best I thought he found irksome. I removed them, squelched them, as far as I was able . . . We lived a life which he liked. This gave me great pleasure."

The madcap Tracy, "Irish to the fingertips," was a master at making Hepburn laugh. They made nine pictures together and stayed with each other for twenty-seven years. During this time Hepburn finally divorced Luddy, but Spencer remained married to his wife until his death. She had given birth to a deaf child, and it did not sit right with Spencer to leave his family in such circumstances—though he did not actually *stay* with them, either. In retrospect, Hepburn thinks it would have been better to "straighten things out." Still, the time they spent together, at least for her, was "absolute bliss." And, she adds, "if he hadn't liked me [a lot too] he wouldn't have hung around."

Tracy died of a sudden coronary in 1967, shortly after he and Hepburn had completed filming *Guess Who's Coming to Dinner?* "I wonder if they found my little painting of flowers I put under his feet," the actress writes of the viewing and funeral. She continued living in the home they had shared for ten more years, making movies and trying to let go of "the thing called LOVE." By the time of her autobiography's publication in 1991, she had starred in forty-three films, among them *The Lion in Winter; Rooster Cogburn* (she was extremely fond of John Wayne, whom she likened to a cotton shirt—"It stays clean but it makes you sweat"); *On Golden Pond;* and *The Corn is Green.*

Today Katharine Hepburn spends much time at her childhood summer home in Fenwick, which she helped restore after a hurricane. There she can garden and relax. Although she is older now, she is as vital as ever. Having survived a serious automobile accident, she is grateful for the gift of life: "You suddenly realize what a tremendous opportunity it is just to be alive. The potential. If you can keep a-goin'—you actually can do it . . . It's when you stop that you're done." And if she is asked how she's doing, she'll probably reply, "Fine, if you don't ask for details. That's about it, isn't it?"

Her book's final chapter is filled with thank-you's, as Katharine Hepburn credits her friends, family, agents and others for helping to make her life memorable. "Memories—all there—Oh thank you . . . What would I have done without that backing? . . . Yes, lucky!"

THE GERSHWIN YEARS

by Edward Jablonski and Lawrence D. Stewart, Doubleday and Company, New York, N.Y., 1973

. . . True music . . . must repeat the thought and aspirations of the people and the time. My people are Americans. My time is today . . . They ask me what I am trying to do, and I can only say I am trying to express what is in me . . . There are thousands who have the same feelings and are mute. Those of us who can must speak for those who cannot—but we must be honest about it.

- George Gershwin, 1926

The children of Russian Jewish immigrants, George and Ira Gershwin were born within two years of each other—Ira in 1896 and George in 1898. They grew up in a family with a homelife that was both intense yet amazingly relaxed: Gershwin birthdays were never observed, the parents often couldn't remember that Ira's real name was Israel, they moved twenty-eight different times in the New York area, and worked in many different businesses. Their unusual background fostered in both boys a versatile sense of self-sufficiency.

At age six, for instance, George heard an automatic piano in a penny arcade playing Rubinstein's "Melody in F," and then began his life-long habit of keeping a scrapbook for music. "The peculiar jumps in the music held me rooted," he wrote. Thus was born his love for what would later become called "musical jazz."

In 1910, the family bought a piano so that Ira could take lessons. It was the younger George, however, who first pounded out, apparently by ear, a current popular song of the day, so it was decided that George, not Ira, should continue with the lessons.

George's teachers soon recognized his potential and began instructing him in musical theory. Influenced both by classical composers and by the ragtime music which defined the era, the fifteen-year-old boy took on work as a "piano pounder" for a Tin Pan Alley music producer.

Then in 1917, shortly before his twentieth birthday, George quit the piano-playing job so as to have more time for his own compositions. To support himself, he worked on producing piano rolls and as an accompanist. His first song was published that same year, and others soon followed.

During this early productive period George employed several different lyricists and wrote the score for several musicals. His first big success was a lively title song called "Swanee." Although the musical that showcased the tune soon folded, Al Jolson had heard the song and immediately adopted it as his trademark. Sales of Jolson's recorded "Swanee" shot into the millions; George Gershwin thus became a songwriter whose tunes enjoyed lasting fame.

While George pursued his path into the world of music, Ira had become fascinated with writing. As a teen he wrote bits for newspapers, but Ira, too, ultimately found his way into the music business. As a librettist writing the lyrics for different musicals, he first wrote under the name Arthur Francis, to dispel the idea that he was trying to ride on the coattails of his brother's success. While Ira eventually supplied lyrics for some of George's most famous songs, his collaborations with other songwriters were more successful.

Then in the early '20s, jazz stormed onto the musical scene. When bandleader Paul Whiteman thought of doing a concert based on the new music—to show the public that it was not a "tool of the devil" as some had suggested—he contacted George. Asked to prepare something for Whiteman's concert, George quickly began arranging a piece from scraps of music combining jazz with classical elements that had been floating around in his head. Finally, Ira suggested the title that has been famous ever since: *Rhapsody in Blue.*

Whiteman's concert failed to stir the audience—until Gershwin's piece began. As the last note played, the applause was spontaneous and tumultuous. While a few critics discredited the music, the public loved it.

The first complete all-Gershwin-scored musical, "Lady, Be Good," opened in 1924. Starring a pair of newcomers named Fred and Adele Astaire, it was an immediate hit. A year later, "Tell Me More" opened its long run in London. During this time George continued working on classical scores; the climactic triumph of this period was his beautiful and critically acclaimed *Concerto in F* for piano and orchestra. After its release, the critics lauded the "natural gift" of its creator and the "improvisatory . . . effortless quality" of the music. Granted, "he did not write by the book although he was thoroughly familiar with its contents."

In 1926, after attending London's premier of *Lady, Be Good,* George spent time in Paris. While there he received the inspiration for the opening theme of what later became *An American in Paris,* a symphonic, rhythmically exciting poem—and American through and through. Two years later he returned to France and completed the work. Due to its unique style, many referred to it as a "tone-poem"; others termed it "jazz ballet." Whatever it was, most listeners considered it fantastic.

Even after *An American in Paris,* some of George's friends begged him to give up serious music and stick to song-writing; others argued that if he gave up commercial composition he could be a great success as a classical composer. George resisted both bits of advice and insisted that he could do both "serious" and popular music—and do them both well.

One night George had trouble sleeping, so he picked up a new best-selling book: DuBose Heyward's *Porgy.* Struck by the book's powerful and dignified characterization of American blacks, he dashed off a letter to Heyward, suggesting a collaboration on a musical version of the story. But because of conflicting schedules, the two men would wait six years to formalize their agreement and to begin work.

During that six-year period, George and Ira together composed a number of well-received Broadway musicals, as well as one forgettable Hollywood musical. Included among their greatest works from these years were the sparkling musical comedies *Lady Be Good* (1924), *Tip-Toe* (1925), *Oh. Kay* (1926), *Funny Face* (1927), and *Girl Crazy* (1930). The duo then turned to political satire with the comedies *Strike Up the Band* (1930), *Of Thee I Sing,* (a 1931 spoof on presidential elections), and *Let Them Eat Cake* (1933). Each of these productions broke new ground in musical theater.

In *Of Thee I Sing,* for instance, rather than tacking verses and choruses onto the usual self-contained story, the Gershwins originated the idea of letting the songs themselves carry part of the story line—rather like an opera. The musical won a 1932 Pulitzer Prize for the story's authors, George Kaufman and Morrie Ryskind, and its lyricist, Ira Gershwin. (Oddly, the composer, George Gershwin, was overlooked.)

In 1933, the Gershwins and Heyward finally reached an agreement on *Porgy and Bess* and Heyward started to revise the script. But once again previous commitments slowed progress of the work. Heyward ended up doing the lyrics as well as the libretto, with Ira contributing ideas and suggestions.

For a while their commitments were such that they could only collaborate long distance. Then, when George returned to the project—becoming involved in all elements of the opera, including casting and stage design—two years passed before he could finish his score and orchestrations.

When *Porgy and Bess* finally opened in the fall of 1935, it was an initial success with audiences. The critics, however, didn't know what to make of something that was neither purely musical nor purely operatic. This lukewarm critical reception took its toll: the "folk opera," as George called it, failed at the box office—but only after 134 performances and a brief tour. Everyone involved lost money, but George was convinced that *Porgy* was some of his best work. Time has proved him correct, as the black folk opera is now considered the most popular piece ever written by an American.

Only a few months after the closing of *Porgy,* George and Ira signed up to work on three movies. The first, "Shall We Dance?" again featured Fred Astaire, now with Ginger Rogers; the second, "Damsel in Distress," was yet another Fred Astaire hit; and the final film was a Goldwyn review. Although George was generally displeased with the movie producers' use of his music, these films contained some of the Gershwins' best songs, including such favorites as "They Can't Take That Away From Me" and "Shall We Dance?"

Meanwhile, George fell in love—apparently for the first time in his life—with film goddess Paulette Goddard. The relationship was not to be, however. Tragically, he soon began to suffer disturbing personality changes, dizzy spells, and lack of coordination. Initial medical examinations failed to reveal a malady, but within a few months he was diagnosed as having a brain tumor. Surgery proved futile: George did not recover. On July 11, 1937, at only 38 years of age, one of America's most gifted, prolific, and innovative composers was gone.

After his brother's death, Ira worked with a variety of composers to produce several modest Broadway plays. He later achieved his greatest success in Hollywood, where he wrote lyrics for "The Barkleys of Broadway," starring Fred Astaire, "A Star is Born," with Judy Garland, and "The Country Girl," featuring Bing Crosby and Grace Kelly.

In stark contrast to the social dynamism of his brother, Ira was an avowed introvert. "I've always felt that if George [hadn't] pushed me into lyric writing," he divulged toward the end of his life, "I'd have been content to be a bookkeeper."

And true to his bookkeeper nature, Ira had kept photographs and personal accounts of his and George's early years, information which he gladly provided to biographers and musical historians.

The last refrain that the Gershwin brothers completed jointly was the chorus to "Our Love Is Here to Stay." After George's death, Ira completed the lyrics which summed up his feelings about his brother and himself:

The more I read the papers,
The less I comprehend
The world and all its capers,
And how it all will end.

Nothing seems to be lasting,
But that isn't our affair;
We've got something permanent
I mean, in the way we care.

A critic once purported that George and Ira Gershwin couldn't possibly write good music because they hadn't suffered enough. And aside from George's untimely death, the Gershwins' lives certainly always seemed to flow smoothly, but, in reality, the brothers had their share of flops to overcome, critics to silence, shattered professional dreams to rebuild. Their courage and determination were hallmarks of their success as clearly as was their talent.

Jablonski and Stewart's work points out the highs and the lows in the careers of the talented pair. It also provides us with peeks at score sheets, hand-written lyrics, and dozens of photographs. The biographers also detail how and why the Gershwin brothers' music has endured the test of time. Now, nearly sixty years after the Gershwins attained the pinnacles of their careers, musicians are still recording and performing their tunes, the many melodies and songs that still touch our heartstrings. After all, who can forget their penetrating musical comedies "Fascinating Rhythm," "I Got Rhythm," "All To Myself," "Lady, Be Good," "Clap Yo Hands," "Someone to Watch Over Me," "'S Wonderful," "Biding My Time," "Embraceable You," "But Not for Me," "Summertime," "I Got Plenty of Nuttin'," "It Ain't Necessarily So," "Shall We Dance," "They Can't Take That Away From Me," "Nice Work If you Can Get It," "Love Walked In," "Love Is Here to Stay," *An American in Paris,* or *Rhapsody in Blue?*

CHARLES CHAPLIN: MY AUTOBIOGRAPHY

by Charles Chaplin, Dutton Publishing, New York, N.Y., 1992

Charlie Chaplin was many things to many people. A comic genius, a lover, a dreamer, a fighter—and most assuredly, a legend. He rose from the humblest of beginnings in England to great fame across the world, and helped put a little town called Hollywood, California on the map. He made the world laugh and weep at the same time. Most of all, Chaplin, as the vulnerable and jauntily bedraggled Little Tramp, introduced *humanity* to the screen.

Chaplin penned his 480-page autobiography over a period of six years and endless rewrites. The final product is a neatly written and accurate tour de force. He neither glorifies any particular achievement nor minimizes his failures or the squalid settings of his youth. An inherently modest man, he portrays himself as a life-sized human being confronting life-sized challenges.

The Workhouse Years

Charles Spencer Chaplin was born to a pair of unrenowned vaudeville performers, Charles and Lily Chaplin, in 1889. About one year after the boy's birth, his father and mother separated, and Charlie spent his early years with his mother and older brother, Sydney, bunking in various back rooms of their Kensington Road home. The family led a meager existence, especially after Lily's damaged vocal cords curtailed her performances and her estranged husband refused to pay more for the family's upkeep. When Charlie was just over six years old, the family entered the Lambeth Workhouse.

With no means of support, Charlie and Sydney were sent to the Hanwell School for Orphans and Destitute Children. The school was not a happy place for the two homesick children, but Charlie did learn to read and write.

The Early Acting Years

A few years after she entered the workhouse Charlie's mother was declared insane, and the boys were sent to live briefly with their father and his new wife, both alcoholics. When Lily retrieved the boys after her recovery, the family eked out their meager existence with odd jobs. Sydney signed on as a ship's bugler, and, though he was often at sea, his wages helped the family survive. Then, during one of Sydney's absences, Lily suffered another mental breakdown. At eleven years old, Charlie was left to take care of himself.

At this point, Charlie's life finally changed for the better. He registered with Blackmore's Agency, a theatrical company, and was given the part of Billie, a page-boy in the play *Sherlock Holmes*. After two successful forty-week tours, he went without work for ten months. Sydney, meanwhile, had joined Karno's Comedy Company and pushed Mr. Karno to give Charlie a part. When the manager finally did offer the boy a tryout, Charlie's ad-libbing won him a one-year contract to play in a burlesque slapstick called "The Football Match."

After playing in England and France, Mr. Karno decided it was time to try America. The troupe was fairly well received in the United States, and Charlie at once fell in love with the welcoming towns of the Midwest.

Charlie accompanied the troupe on a second American tour, which received lavish reviews. But he did not stay with the company. During this second tour, Mack Sennett signed Charlie to star in movies.

As founder and owner of the Keystone Studios, home of the Keystone Cops, Sennett's early films always revolved around a chase. This didn't sit well with Charlie, and when directors tried to push him into the trademark slapstick style, he balked. There was a brief row; but when the box office receipts started rolling in from an earlier film—done more in Charlie's own style—Sennett allowed Charlie to call his own shots.

The Little Tramp is Born

One day, as the story goes, Sennett told Charlie that he needed some gags for a new movie. "Put on a comedy make-up," Sennett directed. "Anything will do." Looking through the studio's wardrobe, Charlie chose a too-tight jacket, baggy pants, a cane, a derby hat, and over-sized shoes, each item intended to contradict the others. Finally, because Sennett had mentioned that he looked too young, Charlie added a small paste-on mustache to lend an air of maturity.

Charlie began strutting about, swinging his cane in front of Sennett. The character evolved spontaneously, from the clothes and make-up. As gags and comedy scenes quickly flowed into a lively stream, Sennett giggled until he began to shake. "You know," he gasped finally, "this fellow is many-sided, a tramp, a gentleman, a poet, a dreamer, a lonely fellow, always hopeful of romance and adventure." And with that, "Charlot" the Little Tramp was born.

In the ensuing months, Charlie went on to write, direct, and star in many more Keystone Studio films.

The Middle Years (1915-1923)

Within a year, Charlie Chaplin had become a huge success. But the contract with Sennett expired at the end of 1914. Charlie had been making a film every two weeks and he knew he could not keep up such a furious pace. But in order to slow down, he needed a steady income. Sennett refused Charlie's request for a $1000-a-week contract, but Essanay Films came up with a better offer: $1250 a week in salary plus a $10,000 signing bonus, an immense amount of money for 1915. Charlie signed with Essanay.

Meanwhile, Charlie continued to produce a new film every two to three weeks, and began to burn out. He had few friends and socialized little, rarely fixing his gaze on anything but work. After finishing a film, he usually spent the next few days in bed, depressed and exhausted. Then, when another idea invaded his mind, he got up and went back to work.

Charlie's films were big box-office attractions. An adoring public eagerly awaited each one. The Little Tramp inspired merchandise, songs and poems. As the income from his films steadily climbed, Charlie negotiated a deal that gave him an additional $10,000 per picture.

By now, Sydney was working alongside Charlie and, because he understood legal jargon, took over the negotiations. When the Essanay contract expired, Sydney struck a bargain with The Mutual company, a major agreement which lasted for two years and produced twelve films.

Charlie never worked for one company for more than a couple of years. Always very aware of his triumphs, he was driven to achieve more and more. And, subsequently, he got more. As his fame grew, however, he didn't care for the attendant publicity. Whenever he traveled his destination was wired ahead by the studios, and all along the route people gathered and waited for him to speak. He had become America's reluctant darling.

After fulfilling the Mutual contract, Charlie entered the happiest time of his career. Twenty-seven years old and free, he was soon to be a millionaire; money flowed in from all his movies. Although he had few close friends, during this period he made several life-long associations—with a young actor named Douglas Fairbanks; with actress Edna Purviance, who stayed on the payroll at Chaplin Studios until her death; and with screen favorite Mary Pickford. Charlie also enjoyed cordial acquaintances with celebrities and dignitaries from across the globe: William Randolph Hearst, Gandhi, Sir Winston Churchill, Khrushchev, Einstein, and many, many others. He was never a lonely man; he simply preferred solitude to company.

In late 1917, Chaplin met Mildred Harris. After several months of dinners, dances and moonlit walks, he married her. At the time of the wedding, she thought she was pregnant—but this turned out to be untrue.

Meanwhile, Sydney negotiated a new contract with First National, for a whopping $1,200,000. When Sydney told his brother the sum of the deal, Charlie's laconic reply was, "Hum-um, I suppose that is wonderful." He would almost certainly have kept making movies even for far less money. He enjoyed the stimulation too much to let go.

First National lacked a studio to go along with its generous contract, so Charlie built a studio in California and started immediately on several films. Married life affected him, though, and he cut back to a couple of full-length movies a year.

Then, during the 1919 cutting of "The Kid," a wildly popular movie featuring Jackie Coogan's four-year-old son Jackie Jr., Charlie and Mildred separated.

After completing his First National contract in 1923, Chaplin began making movies for United Artists, the company he had created together with Fairbanks and Mary Pickford.

The Late Movies (1923-1957)

By now Charlie was making very few movies, averaging only one film every four years. He was busy with a second wife, whom he would not talk about—then a third wife, Paulette Goddard whom he starred with in "Modern Times" and "The Great Dictator"—and finally, a fourth, Oona O'Niel, the daughter of playwright Eugene O'Niel. In Oona, Chaplin finally found a woman who loved him not for money or fame, but for himself—and who did not aspire to a movie career of her own.

At this point, changing technology posed a problem for Chaplin. Talking pictures had been ushered in; silent films entered their twilight years. Although Charlie produced two more silent films, "City Lights" and "Modern Times," which proved to be roaring successes, it was obvious that he could not go on as he had.

Yet part of the Little Tramp's loveable, innocent appeal had always been tied to his muteness. Chaplin was faced with a dilemma. In his next film—a talkie called "The Great Dictator"—he found an ingenious way to let the Little Tramp stay on: Chaplin played two roles, appearing both as Hitler and as the dictator's look-alike, an amnesiac Jewish barber—who just happened to be a soft-spoken version of the Little Tramp.

With World War II looming on the horizon, Chaplin was invited by the government to speak on the question of American intervention on the Soviet front. Charlie, who considered himself to be a "citizen of the world," favored sending American and British troops to relieve "our Russian comrades" on the battle lines. Entering the war at all, however, let alone offering aid to Communist Russia, was unthinkable to many Americans, and Chaplin was harshly criticized. The media degraded him mercilessly, accusing him of being a Communist; eventually he was called before the Committee on Un-American Activities.

After that, Chaplin's stardom suffered and his films suffered several forms of censorship. Eventually, facing attempts by the IRS to discredit his name and cries to jail him, Charlie left for a vacation in Europe and was barred from returning to the U.S. Exiled from the land in which he had lived for over forty years, he moved to Switzerland and produced one final film, "The King in New York." He devoted his remaining years to his wife and daughters, and, later, to his grandchildren.

[In 1973, Chaplin returned to Hollywood to accept a special "Lifetime Achievement" Oscar at the Academy Awards presentations. A standing ovation and the tears that flowed down his own cheeks and those of the audience were testimony to the place that Charlie Chaplin had always retained in the hearts of Americans. In 1976 he was knighted by the British crown; a year later, in Switzerland, Sir Charles Spencer Chaplin passed away.]

ACCIDENTAL MILLIONAIRE

The Rise and Fall of Steven Jobs At Apple Computer
by Lee Butcher, Paragon House, New York, N.Y., 1988

Shortly after his birth in 1956, Steven Jobs, an orphan, was adopted by Paul and Clara Jobs of Mountain View, California. But the real story of Steven Jobs began in the eighth grade, when he formed a friendship with Stephen Wozniak, his future partner and co-founder of Apple Computers. It was an unlikely collaboration, however, because Jobs, in fact, had nothing to do with designing the first Apple computer. As Wozniak tells it: *Reporters would . . . ask "Well, did he develop the hardware?" I said "No." Then they would ask, "Well did he develop the software?" I had to answer "No . . . I created the whole computer."*

Jobs did take an electronics course in high school, but, far from being a computer prodigy, he dropped out of the program after a year. Instead, working nights and weekends at an electrical shop, he became an expert scrounger, reselling cheap finds at a profit.

Jobs, with his abrasive, aggressive style, made a negative first impression almost everywhere he went; but his persuasiveness was ultimately hard to resist.

After being caught up in the hippie movement of the late Sixties and early Seventies, Jobs enrolled at Reed College in Portland, Oregon. He quit, however, after only one semester, and, seeking enlightenment, turned to the study of Yoga and Zen Buddhism. It was during this period that he moved to a $25-per-month room, where, reportedly for a period of three weeks he lived on Roman Meal and milk from the college cafeteria.

Soon, Jobs fast-talked his way into a job at Atari Electronics, where he enjoyed his first business success. Atari had found that in Germany their games interfered with local TV reception, so they sent Jobs to resolve the problem. When he arrived at the German office, the local engineers were so stunned by his bizarre appearance and eccentric, often caustic behavior that they cabled Atari to make certain they had sent the right man. But somehow, to the amazement of everyone, Jobs solved the problem.

The next assignment for Atari's new wunderkind was in India, where he was dismayed by the abject poverty he saw. Rethinking his devotion to yoga, he went home convinced that "Thomas Edison had done more to improve the human condition than all the gurus that had ever lived."

Back at Atari headquarters—which at the time was in tremendous turmoil—Jobs was demoted to the level of consultant. Again, however, fortune prevailed. Atari offered him a bonus to design a game that used a ball to smash a brick wall, and Jobs asked his old friend Wozniak for help, offering to split with him the modest earnings.

Meanwhile, Wozniak had offered a new computer design to Hewlett-Packard, who, at the time, saw no future in personal computers. Jobs, however, saw the possibilities and convinced his friend that they could sell printed circuit boards to computer hobbyists. Within months they had signed a partnership agreement, and Apple

Computer was born on April Fools Day, 1976—"Apple" because it was sleek, simple, and possessed a wholesome, educational connotation.

Jobs first approached The Byte Shop, a store that sold computer kits, to market their circuit boards. Instead, The Byte Shop placed an order for fifty *completed* computers—promising to pay "between $489 and $589" per unit. Jobs and Wozniak were flabbergasted; the total return, $25,000 to $30,000, far exceeded their wildest expectations.

Next, a supplier agreed to sell them $20,000 in parts—enough to assemble 100 computers—on credit. With help from family members and friends, the pair put computers together in Jobs' parents' home and garage.

Even though these first "completed" computers were actually very incomplete—including no power supply, software, monitor, or keyboard—the Byte Shop accepted them. Wozniak then went on to create a cassette interface and BASIC software to enhance the computers, and finally to design a video interface. Jobs then convinced an Atari engineer to come up with a companion power supply—and, with a keyboard, at last they had a viable working unit.

Aside from securing a few personal loans, Jobs found no investors interested in Apple; amazingly, even as late as 1978, no one could fathom potential in an inexpensive "personal" computer. Bankruptcy threatened. Commodore, Hewlett-Packard, and Atari were all approached about buying the company, but each time negotiations fell through.

Finally Jobs decided Apple needed a better image. Using all his persuasive powers, he convinced the prestigious Regis McKenna Advertising Agency to represent them. *It was one of the most important associations the small company could have arranged.*

Over time, Jobs also interested "Mike" Markkula, a 33-year-old retired engineer and multi-millionaire, in Apple. Markkula gave the venture his *organizational skills, business experience, and a steadying influence over the mercurial Jobs . . .* On January 3, 1977, Markkula, Wozniak, and Jobs incorporated the Apple Computer Company.

Markkula, who "had no desire to run the business," soon convinced his new partners that the company needed to be professionally managed. He hired Michael Scott, an engineer he had worked with, as president of Apple.

With the addition of "professional guidance and a thin cushion of operating capital," Apple grew rapidly, moving from Jobs' garage to a building in Cupertino, California. Markkula created a business plan, Scott ran daily operations, and Wozniak pushed his team to ready the Apple II for the West Coast Computer Faire. Jobs, meanwhile, "who had no real responsibility," was content to "flit from desk to desk, ruffling feathers and . . . making himself feared and unpopular."

Jobs' semi-obscure vision now was to see the Apple II "stand out [aesthetically] as a swan against a background of ugly ducklings" and attract those in the hard-core business market. "Steve had a great deal to do with . . . the computer housing," Wozniak does admit. Indeed, it was Jobs who helped design a stylish plastic case and the Apple logo—a rainbow-colored apple with a bite taken out of one side.

But nothing went smoothly at Apple during those early days. "Steve had no ability to manage people," Wozniak says. "He ruled by intimidation, yelling and screaming . . . People were terrified of him." Jobs also gained "a reputation for being rude and overbearing with outside people with whom Apple did business."

By the time the Computer Faire rolled around, Apple had completed three computers. In the next few weeks, they received orders for 300—100 more than the total number of Apple I's already sold.

The company had finally achieved a strong sense of community. Its employees came early and stayed late, "partly because they wanted to and partly because Jobs expected it." But despite the company's cohesion, Apple soon acquired a reputation for not fulfilling commitments. Finances stayed tight. What's more, "Jobs' unwillingness to accept his own limitations did not prevent him from getting involved in things he didn't understand. People working on projects started to dread seeing him . . ."

Meanwhile, Scott, engaged in almost daily shouting matches with Jobs delighted in highlighting his adversary's sometimes peculiar behavior. With great glee he revealed that Jobs refreshed himself by sitting on the toilet tank, putting his feet in the bowl, and flushing.

In 1978, Apple introduced the first disk drive for a personal computer, beating out Commodore and Tandy. Sales immediately jumped. More investors came on board, while public relations pushed the rags-to-riches tale of two poor teenagers starting a computer company in a garage. Jobs and Wozniak quickly became cult heroes. Erroneously, Jobs got credit for much of the design for the Apple I and II, and accepted it as his due.

Jobs often talked about how much he cared for employees—but his actions seldom showed it. "You couldn't believe anything the guy said," Wozniak recalls, disgustedly. "He would say one thing and do another . . . Steve will use anybody to his own advantage."

Yet as one employee observes, Jobs "also had a sweet side, the hippie part of him who had gone to India soul-searching . . . " In fact, when another employee was hospitalized with cancer, Jobs visited him daily and "paid for . . . a private room and . . . all the medical expenses."

In 1979, Jeff Raskins, an Apple engineer, presented his idea for a new, more powerful computer to be targeted at business users—hooked up with something he called a "mouse." But, as Raskins relates, Jobs would not give the idea a chance: "He ran around saying, 'No! No! It'll never work.'"

Jobs fought Raskins's idea for two years. Then in 1982 he abruptly changed his mind and took over the Macintosh division of the company, driving Raskins out of the organization and splitting Apple into two bitter camps. "The Macintosh division had the best of everything: . . . biggest parties, highest salaries, and more stroking from Jobs," remembers Wozniak. " . . . You never heard the Apple II mentioned. We were generating most of the company's revenue and the Apple II was the best-selling computer in the world."

Then mighty IBM finally entered the personal computer market. "Apple looked at IBM with condescension and arrogance, much the way it looked at suppliers, retailers, and the personal computer infrastructure," and by 1983, IBM had managed to "steam-roller" its competition and grab a 30% market share.

In 1983 Apple hired John C. Sculley, formerly of PepsiCo, to replace Scott, who had resigned in 1981 as president of the company. Sculley struggled to turn Apple around, restructuring the firm and cutting much of its bloated bureaucracy.

But even as Sculley worked magic on one end of the company, Jobs' design constraints crippled the Mac. One disgruntled Mac owner complained: "It's like having a Maserati with a one-gallon gas tank." By November, 1984, only 200,000 Macintoshes had been sold. Apple had held back from ousting their folk-hero, but they finally brought Jobs to heel early in 1985—a move long overdue.

By this time, Jobs' nemesis, the Apple II, had set all-time highs in sales, generating a whopping two-thirds of Apple's 1984 profits. Sculley had promised that the Mac would be made expandable, capable of running IBM programs. But, since Jobs refused to make the enhancements, Sculley found himself in a dilemma: Even though Jobs, as the Macintosh division manager, technically worked under Sculley, the company president, "as chairman of the board, Jobs was Sculley's boss."

Finally Sculley chose to hire Jean-Louis Gassee, of Apple France, to replace Jobs as manager of Macintosh. In a last desperate maneuver, Jobs called for Sculley's resignation. At an ensuing emergency meeting of the executive committee, Sculley, however, made it clear that it was he who ran Apple—and Jobs was summarily moved to "a remote office . . . called Siberia."

Jobs still remained as Apple's board chairman, and with undimmed tenacity set out to start a new company. Presenting a list of employees he wanted to take with him—all key people at Apple, "it was clear . . . that Jobs intended to go into direct competition [with Apple]." Without delay, the board fired Jobs and sued for potential damages.

Jobs settled out of court, agreeing not to hire Apple employees for three years; not to produce products that competed with Apple's; and to submit any product developed by his new company, "NeXT," for approval by Apple prior to marketing. Then, in a typical act of defiance, he sold all but one of his shares in Apple.

Billionaire H. Ross Perot has since "invested twenty million dollars in NeXT, buying 16 percent of the company." In Perot, Jobs had "found a formidable ally, and, if he succeeds with NeXT, the stigma of his 'accidental' success at Apple may at last vanish."

DAVE'S WAY

A New Approach to Old-Fashioned Success
By R. David Thomas, G.P. Putnam's Sons, New York, N.Y., 1991

In 1940, at the age of eight, I dreamed that I would one day own the best restaurant in the world. All of the customers would love my food, and all of my employees would do everything they were supposed to do. But, most important, everyone would think I was a good boss, and every day when I walked into the restaurant, people would be glad to see me. The realization of that dream molded Dave Thomas into the man he is today—still a dreamer, a good boss who most of his employees know simply as "Dave," and the founder of one of America's most popular and successful fast-food restaurant chains.

Dave's earliest memories are of his adoptive mother dying: *It seemed like a strange dream to me. I didn't know people were supposed to die and I didn't know who would replace her. My grandmother, Minnie Sinclair, explained that my mother had gone to heaven where she would watch over me.*

After Dave's mother died, his father had a hard time settling into jobs. He and Dave were constantly on the move. Dave often speaks fondly of the summers he spent with his grandmother: *She could be tough if she wanted to, but you could see the warmth in her eyes. She was a special motivator. If you did the right thing, she could make you feel ten feet tall, and very, very special.*

One thing Dave especially admired about his grandmother was that she always seemed to have money: "She managed better than anyone I ever saw," he says, "She got so much out of so little, and she never acted poor." It was from her that he learned his most valuable lessons, lessons that made him the success he is: *Make a lot out of a little, but don't cut corners. Work hard and have fun. Be strict but caring, and pray.*

As two "hardy bachelors," Dave and his father constantly ate at restaurants, enabling Dave to become a restaurant connoisseur. Dave's favorite place was a hamburger stand close to their apartment, where he always ordered the thickest milk shake they made. Later it became the model for his Wendy's "Frosty" dessert: *I knew what customers expected and what kind of service and quality was acceptable. I overheard complaints and compliments and soaked them all in.*

Growing up, Dave worked many jobs. As a twelve-year-old he lied about his age to get a job at Walgreen's Drug Store. When the manager later became suspicious and confronted Dave, he wasn't fired: he simply refused to schedule Dave for any shifts. "You'll never keep a job!" his dad screamed when he heard of the incident. "I'll be supporting you for the rest of your life!" After that experience, Dave resolved never to lose a job again.

Realizing that "If somebody paid you, it was up to you to perform," Dave went to work at the Regas Restaurant, taking orders and filling out invoices. Six months later Dave and his father moved again, forcing him to ride the Trailways bus to work and back. Later, when summer came, Dave decided to rent a room in town so he could work twelve-hour days. He summed up his lessons at the Regas this way: *Make a clean, neat impression. Do everything you can to make customers happy. Set tough standards, but back up your employees when necessary. Build your peoples' confidence. Reward motivation and determination. TRY.*

Dave and his father moved once again, this time to Fort Wayne, Indiana, where the manager of the Hobby House hired Dave "because of his attitude." One day as Dave waited on tables, he noticed a man in a suit sweeping floors. He later learned that the man was the owner of the Hobby House, Phil Clauss. It was a revelation, and Dave determined then that one day he would be the kind of owner Phil Clauss was.

When his father moved yet again, Dave remained in Fort Wayne. He had a "family" at the restaurant, he told his dad. "Someday," he promised, "you'll be proud of me."

Fifteen years old and on his own, Dave attended high school and worked a full-time job. Finally, the pressure became too severe, and after the tenth grade, he quit school. Now he tells young people: *Get a job, don't be discouraged, try hard work and get an education. Find people you can learn from.*

Dave joined the Army at eighteen, and received some culinary training and experience as a mess-hall cook. When he was sent to Germany, "Sergeant Thomas" found that the mess halls were truly "a mess" and badly under-supplied. Trading surplus stock for necessary supplies, Dave gradually improved the quality of food.

The mess halls themselves were dingy, dismal places in which to eat. Again, through some shrewd trades, Dave obtained a truckload of 500 gallons of paint and ordered that the walls be given a good coat. Morale improved dramatically. This was one time, Dave chuckles, "I enjoyed being a big shot."

Before long, the manager of the Enlisted Men's Club hired Dave with the orders to turn around the failing operation. By focusing on more and better menu selections, he had the club running in the black within months.

After receiving his Army discharge in October 1953, Dave returned to Hobby House, where Phil was waiting for him, apron in hand. It was at this time that Dave met Lorraine, one of the spunkiest waitresses he'd ever known. After a year of courting, the couple were married.

Dave and Phil made a lot of adjustments to Hobby House's menu, which eventually hurt the business. However, the business partners worked well together—blending Phil's hustle and upbeat attitude with Dave's promotional and organizational talents. With their combined skills they built loyal core of customers.

On one occasion shortly after Colonel Sanders had come out with his new chicken franchises, Phil wanted to buy into one. In Dave's opinion it was a big mistake. Then one day, out of the blue, Colonel Sanders walked in the door at Hobby House, sat down, and ordered a meal. He and Dave started talking, and by the end of the conversation, Dave was sold.

The advent of Kentucky Fried Marketing was a turning point in the restaurant business for several reasons. Takeout food required proper packaging. In addition, people seemed to enjoy having a real person—the grandfatherly Colonel himself—back up their food. Sanders reinforced what Dave already knew: high standards and cleanliness make customers *feel good*—the real ingredient to business success.

In 1962, Dave and Lorraine moved to Columbus, Ohio to try to turn around four of Phil's poorly-managed stores. Dave's plan called for a complete overhaul, *firing all the managers (they just weren't cutting it), painting all the stores, daily reports so he could stay on top of things, slimming down the menus, focusing the business, and adding a large dose of promotion.* In just five short years, he made good on his plan. Not only had he acquired 40% ownership of the stores, but he had also purchased $10,000 in stock, which, in those five years had gown into a million-dollar investment.

Dave credits Lorraine with keeping his priorities in order: his family and personal life didn't suffer at all. As in most areas, he suggested a few simple rules for couples working together: *Guard your spouse's free time, share authority, think flexibility, keep an eye on the calendar and be careful of timing.*

In 1968 Dave sold his stock in the KFC franchise. About that same time the company offered him a 300-store regional managers job. Dave's ambition to own a burger place looked like it was still a distant dream.

Then came the turning point that put him on the right path: he lost his job at KFC over a disagreement involving stock purchases, conflicts of interest, and hurt feelings. At thirty-seven, Dave was out of work.

National Diversified, a restaurant enterprise in which Dave owned some stock, offered him a job with the Arthur Treacher's Fish and Chips chain. National's Len Imke, a friend and fellow manager, spent much time listening to Dave's plans and dreams. One day Len announced that he had a building for Dave to rent, a place where he could try out his ideas. Dave jumped at the opportunity.

The menu would be simple: three kinds of made-to-order burgers, chili, french fries, a Frosty, and assorted beverages. The name for the store came from the nickname of his fourth child, Melinda Lou, dubbed "Wendy" by the older children. At eight, little Wendy was the hit of the party when the first Wendy's opened on November 15, 1969. Within two years, three more outlets were opened, each fostering a down-home, family-type atmosphere.

Dave says the market trends that made Wendy's a success were obvious: *People wanted choices. They were tired of poor quality. People were on the move and adjusting to a more complicated way of life. People were ready for an upscale hamburger place.*

What exactly is it that makes Wendy's different? Dave believes that his way of doing business, which gives people what they want, is unique. For instance, he observes that most hungry customers don't want to stand in a lines: *Lines really say to the customer: self-service. Serve yourself, buddy, because we sure aren't going to serve you. This is a scramble system. You're either tapping a toe waiting or jumping for the next line that just opened up.* With this in mind, Dave came up with a more efficient, less frustrating system: a zig-zag line with just one, very outgoing, warm person taking orders: "They can make a little quick conversation, so we become a more personable place." If customers get too piled up, Wendy's sends another order-taker down the line: "As long as the line moves, people are happy." Dave employs the same time-and-money-saving techniques at Wendy's drive-through window.

Dave believes that customer feedback is crucial to Wendy's supplying better service. On any given day over 500 customer checklists are given out to gauge how customers are feeling and to assess overall employee satisfaction.

When Dave discusses advertising, he is the first to say: *Tell the truth. Have a sense of humor, don't expect it to be cheap and be believable.* Sometimes just the mention of a key word or the recreation of the right situation can capture the attention of a nation and give you the edge: Remember Clara Peller of "Where's the Beef?" fame?

Dave says his management philosophy is his most simple of all: *HARASSMENT.* By this, he means keeping at someone until they either do what you think they should be doing or until they prove that their way is better. But he cautions to uses restraint in this method of motivation: "Only harass people you care about."

Filled with humor and advice, **Dave's Way** is entertaining and valuable for anyone trying to find his way in an increasingly complex and competitive world. His down-to-earth suggestions for coping with everything from shyness to starting your own business epitomize Dave's dream—one he made come true: *There isn't anything in my life that I haven't been able to do. Well, maybe there is one thing. I would like to be able to sing like Perry Como or Nat King Cole . . . Maybe someday I'll wake up and decide to take singing lessons . . . imagine the commercials they could cast me in then!*

TRUMP: THE DEALS AND THE DOWNFALL

by Wayne Barrett, Harper Collins, New York, N.Y., 1992

In *Trump: The Deals and the Downfall,* veteran *Village Voice* reporter Wayne Barrett draws on fourteen file drawers of research relating to the business dealings and personal activities of Donald Trump. Although Trump refused Barrett's request for a personal interview, hundreds of other individuals acquainted with Trump assisted Barrett in telling the fascinating story of the business mogul's achievements and downfalls. Barrett writes, not dispassionately: *The story of Trump is a saga of unseemly liaisons, but Marla Maples was the least of them. Uncovering and recounting each of these often intricate episodes was what kept me going on this long and difficult journey. While I have, to a degree, used Donald as a window to a decadent age, he has not been a mere symbol to me. In these pages he is a man of cunning and will and achievement, who lives with his own peculiar, self-inflicted pain.*

UNRAVELING

Donald Trump once owned forty percent of Atlantic City's casino hotel rooms, and thousands depended on him for their livelihood. Many of his employees gathered in 1990 to celebrate his forty-fourth birthday, but amidst the crowd, Trump was alone, as he had always been alone. *Those who knew him best said he had virtually no real friends—because, in his own view, no one was actually worthy of his trust.*

Barrett suggests that because he trusted so few people he had made his own wife Ivana an officer in his gigantic corporation, then fired her when their marriage failed in 1989. Ivana, although hurt by his affair with model/actress Marla Maples, didn't want a divorce at first, but she did want $125 million in new post-nuptial agreement.

At the time, Donald's financial empire was reeling. Afraid that news of a separation and a public fight over a settlement would leave his bankers even more concerned, he offered Ivana $50 million—a sum which he simply did not have. Ivana rejected the offer. Soon after, reporters for *The Wall Street Journal, Forbes,* and the Philadelphia *Inquirer* began releasing stories of Trump's efforts to sell or refinance much of his empire and the Trump business debacle became as big a story as the Trump divorce.

The biggest blow to the Trump empire occurred when the Wall Street Journal reported that Trump had more than $500 million outstanding in unsecured, personally guaranteed loans. Regardless of the actual amount—which Barrett puts at closer to $800 million—the numbers were so large that the banks almost feared to force the issue.

But in the midst of all this, Donald told one reporter, "I take things very much as they come. I deal with the cards dealt me." He told another reporter who had asked about his future goals, "You keep winning and you win and you win . . . And then one day it doesn't mean as much as it used to."

In June of 1990, just weeks after his rather spiritless birthday party, Trump signed off on broad terms with the banks and accepted the fact that it would be a long time before he could make another major acquisition. Still, Trump claimed that he had a special magic, that he could always find an "upside."

ROOTS OF THE EMPIRE

Because of his family's wealth, Donald grew up isolated from other children. It was in military school where he first showed a desire to be an over-achiever, particularly in sports and leadership roles. After a short term at Fordham College, Donald abruptly transferred to Wharton, where he was content to just slide by.

Although Donald Trump has often described his life as a "rags to riches" story, in reality, he was supported by his father's multi-million-dollar real estate development business. Fred Trump founded his empire in the 1930s by winning the right to buy out of bankruptcy the prime assets of a failed mortgage servicing company. Fred went on to support politicians who could in turn help him secure public money for his real estate developments.

Donald was the only Trump son interested in some day taking over his father's business. When several failed business ventures and scandal took a toll on Fred, he retreated from public life, but remained a behind-the-scenes power in the business which he shared with Donald. But Donald had already learned from his father what has since become the Trump trademark: over-representing yourself, your experience, and your financing.

FIRST FORAY

In 1974, Donald saw an opportunity open up in the properties of the bankrupt Penn Central railroad. On the 60th Street rail yard, Trump planned to build 20,000 waterfront units and to purchase an additional forty-four acres of the 34th Street yard. Trump then demonstrated his political clout by setting up a meeting with the Mayor Abe Beame, who quickly announced his support for Trump's proposal.

Ned Eichler, then the new manager of Penn Central's non-rail real estate assets, immediately saw the beauty of Trump's plan. Over the next six months Eichler and Trump worked out a strategy for discontinuing use of the tracks, modifying zoning ordinances, and procuring housing subsidies and financing. Although other developers challenged the deal's legality in the courts, Trump won the right to use the rail yard. Later, other opponents argued that Trump had cut a deal with attorney David Berger, who earlier opposed Trump. In fact, *Their conclusion is supported by the pattern of Donald's business life before and since: The repeated wooing or retention of critical public or legal opponents would become a life-long hallmark of the Trump style.*

Although Trump won the battle, says Barrett, he lost the war when, in the late '70s, the City of New York found itself in a fiscal crisis and cancelled all funding for housing construction. Suddenly, Trump held a useless option on the yards, so he changed directions and instead focused on the least attractive of the four downtown hotels owned by Penn Central, the Commodore. While hard times froze *subsidized* housing expenditures, Trump realized, a tax-abated hotel renovation in midtown might be feasible.

Trump set up a meeting with Michael Bailkin, a mid-level bureaucrat, to discuss rebuilding the hotel, intimating that Hyatt would manage the place, Equitable Life would finance it, and the mayor would support it. All Trump needed was a property tax abatement to make the project viable—though he had neither the financier nor the manager lined up. Bailkin immediately came up with a plan for Trump to buy the property from Penn Central and donate it to the city in return for a 99-year lease. As a mere tenant and not an owner, Trump would owe no property tax, but would instead pay a negotiated rent to the city. As the plan unfolded, Trump proposed involving the state's Urban Development Corporation (UDC), and the project gained momentum. Trump later admitted that he could only obtain tax abatement if he had financing, and he could only secure financing if he had abatement.

Bailkin was assigned, in Barrett's words, to "camouflaging this tailor-made Trump giveaway" by representing the deal as a new city policy for economic development—with the Trump project as first in line for the new program. Long battles ensued before both the city and the UDC formally approved the Commodore abatement in the spring of 1976.

After obtaining final approvals from deputy mayor Stanley Friedman (who later became a Trump lawyer and subsequently spent time in prison for racketeering), Trump appeared to have risen to the top of his profession. He had found the pattern that he would stand by throughout his life—pursuing public projects for private profit.

A TOWERING TRIUMPH

Even before construction was complete on the renovated hotel, Trump was using his political connections to make the necessary contacts for acquiring the site of his next project: a downtown residential building at 56th and 5th Avenue, just off Central Park. Bonwitt Teller's department store, which occupied most of the block, agreed to sell their lease for $25 million. Equitable owned the ground and showed interest in striking a partnership with Trump—provided he could once again deliver on securing tax abatements and zoning changes. Trump delivered. He had Bonwitt Teller close down and then signed them on as tenants for the new building.

Although the structural design was well received by local architects, Trump's proposed building was plagued by controversy. Yet in spite of the strife that marked its fast-track construction—including charges that Trump was somehow being governed by crime syndicates—the edifice shot up. Even before work was completed on the Trump Tower in 1983, Trump had nearly secured the site for a nearby thirty-seven story residential co-op to be called the Trump Plaza.

A decade after he first moved into Manhattan to seek an option on the West Side yards, Donald had put together a string of successes with barely an entrepreneurial misstep. The dark side of his projects—from the brutality of his Hyatt condemnation actions to the shadiness of his construction compromises—was scarcely perceived and had no effect on the image he was inventing for himself . . . The banks and the development community judged him by the bottom-line results of his top-line projects. And on that scale, encouraged by an enthralled media, he was a colossal new force, a phenomenon whose day had come.

CAPTURING THE BOARDWALK

Trump had long been intrigued with the idea of owning a casino. While his New York properties were being developed, he worked hard to legalize gambling in New York. When it looked like a gambling ordinance would not be passed in New York, Trump worked out complicated lease options on several New Jersey properties in the middle of Atlantic City's Boardwalk and promptly did an about face and opposed legalized gambling in New York.

In order to secure a gaming license in New Jersey, Trump had to withstand an investigation. In spite of some uncertainties about the accuracy of his application, he was awarded a license in record time. True to his trademark, Trump claimed to have financial backing when in truth no mainstream source of funds was interested in casino operations. Finally he formed a partnership with Harrah's Casinos in which he would build and they would find funding and operation expertise. *Again . . . Trump had laid claim to a prime location with a minimal early investment, parleyed political advantages and a local downturned economy into a series of government concessions . . .*

Questions about underworld connections plagued the casino project when known mafioso bought into both the casino proper and the casino's parking garage. But with characteristic aplomb, Trump prevailed and the Trump Plaza Hotel and Casino was up and running.

At the end of 1985, Trump purchased the Atlantic City Hilton for $320 million and then bought out Harrah's half of the Trump Plaza for $250 million. *. . . The combination, one right after the other, was a reckless contrast to the measured development judgement Donald had demonstrated in the first ten years of his career.* Harrah's had decided that they couldn't afford two competing casinos and, according to Barrett, Trump should have learned from them. But "clearly determined to make the new casino the best that borrowed money could buy or build," Trump mortgaged all he had and renamed Harrah's Trump Plaza Hotel "Trump Castle."

Trump continued to buy everything in sight: an airline, a yacht, hotels and resorts, a giant estate in Florida. Then early in 1990, the walls of his financial empire started crumbling. *As suddenly as he had arrived, the Gatsbyesque posterboy was heading for mothballs, [to wait], ever the optimist, for another golden time when those with the balls to be rich would be idols again, embodying the appetites of an era.*

SAM WALTON: MADE IN AMERICA

My Story
by Sam Walton with John Huey, Doubleday Publishers, New York, N.Y., 1992

Branded the richest man in America, Sam Walton once said: "The next thing we knew all these reporters and photographers arrived, I guess to take pictures of me diving into a swimming pool full of money they imagined I had, or to watch me light big fat cigars with hundred-dollar bills while the hootchy-kootchy girls danced by the lake." The picture conjured up by this statement is so patently unlike the real Sam Walton that by the time you come upon it in the book, you just have to laugh. "We're not ashamed of having money," he added at the time, "but I just don't believe a big showy lifestyle is appropriate for anywhere. I'm not sure I ever figured out this celebrity business. I can't believe it was news that I get my hair cut at the barbershop. Where else would I get it cut?"

Walton grew up in Missouri during the Great Depression. He sold and delivered milk for the family, sold papers and magazine subscriptions, and raised and sold rabbits and pigeons. His mother was a special motivator. She told Sam that "he should always try to be the best he could at whatever he took on." So he always pursued everything he was interested in with a "passion to win." In high school, he was voted class officer several years, played every sport (never losing a football game), and earned his Eagle Scout award at age 13—"the youngest Eagle Scout in the history of the state of Missouri at that time."

Throughout college, Walton worked at least three jobs at once, carried a full class load, and was active in every organization he could join. He also learned a secret of leadership early in his campus years: *Speak to people coming down the sidewalk before they speak to you.* He called everyone by name whenever possible and soon they recognized him and considered him their friend.

When he realized that even with the same hectic pace he still couldn't afford to attend the Wharton School of Finance, he decided to look for a job. After accepting an offer to work for JC Penney as a management trainee, Walton would wander around the other two stores at the intersection on his lunch hour. Canvassing thus became his mode of informal job training.

In 1943, as an ROTC graduate, Walton was ready to ship out, but was sidelined by the Army because of a minor heart irregularity. Still in town, he stopped by a local bowling alley, where he met Helen, his future wife, out on a date with her boyfriend. Not in the least bit shy, Walton stepped up to her and blurted out the old line, "Haven't I met you somewhere before?" Helen could immediately recognize that Walton was someone who knew where he was headed. She told her parents she was "going to marry someone who

had that special energy and drive, that desire to be a success." Later she amended her qualifications: "I certainly found what I was looking for, but now I laugh sometimes and say maybe I overshot a little."

During their first two years of marriage, the new family moved 15 times—until Helen finally insisted that they settle down in a small town, one having no more than ten thousand residents. Sam willingly agreed, so they bought a Ben Franklin store in Newport, Arkansas. The operation, however, turned out to be a real loser; Walton knew little about running a store. Still, looking back, he says, "It was a real blessing for me to be so green and ignorant. I learned a lesson that has stuck all through the years: you can learn from everybody." That included John Dunhams' Sterling Store across the street. "Sam was always over there checking on John," Helen remembers. "Always. Looking at his prices, looking at his displays, looking at what was going on. He was always looking for a way to do a better job."

Walton ran his store by the book at first. Ben Franklin's supervisor sent all the merchandise and told him what to do. Then, however, Walton started doing things his own way. He wanted to buy direct from the manufacturer and run special promotions, but the manufacturers feared the wrath of Franklin's home office. So, Walton would "hitch a homemade trailer to the car, drive it into Tennessee and stuff it with whatever he could get good deals on. Then he'd haul it back, price it low, and just blow that stuff out the store. It drove the Ben Franklin folks crazy . . ."

As time went on, he tried lots of promotional things: a popcorn machine on the sidewalk; a soft ice cream machine in the store. "One of the biggest contributions to the later success of Wal-Mart may have been his constant fiddling and meddling with the status quo."

Before long, Walton opened a small department store next to the Ben Franklin and hired his brother Bud as manager. "That Newport store was really the beginning of where Wal-Mart is today," he said. "We did everything. We would wash windows, sweep floors, trim windows. We did all the stockroom work, checked the freight in. Everything it took to run a store. We had to keep expenses to a minimum. That is where it started. Our money was made by controlling expenses."

However, Walton's success commanded a price. Knowing Walton had nowhere else in town to move, his store's landlord decided not to renew the lease at any cost. He did offer to buy it at a fair price, with the idea of turning it over to his son. At that discouraging point, Walton had no other alternative: "It didn't seem fair. I blamed myself for getting suckered into such an awful lease and I was furious at the landlord. I didn't dwell on it. I've always thought of problems as challenges. I don't know if it changed me any. I did read the leases a lot more carefully after that. Helen and I started looking for a new town."

In the spring of 1950, Walton and his family went store hunting. They found a man willing to sell his store in Bentonville, Arkansas, about half the size of Newport. "It was just a sad looking country town," Helen said of the place, "but I knew right after we got here that it was going to work out."

By 1952 Walton had driven to Fayetteville and signed a lease on a site for a second outlet. Now called Walton's Five and Dime, the stores were set up as self-service, pay-at-the-front establishments, a new philosophy to the industry. In a bid to keep the store's name simple yet retain a part of himself, the name Wal-Mart was introduced. And by 1962, several Ben Walton franchises and three Wal-Marts were in operation.

Then the competition started moving in. Gibson's stores—taking a tip from Walton—began copying what Walton was doing, which propelled Walton to "roll out the stores" just as quickly as he could: "Had we been capitalized we would never have tried the small-town America stores. The big lesson that we learned was that there was much, much more out there than we ever dreamed of."

As the stores expanded, new ways of handling distribution, warehousing, management and accounting were needed. Walton continued to explore new ways of doing things with his management team. Saturday morning management meetings became a place to "share information, lighten everybody's load, and to rally the troops." The most important ingredient of Wal-Mart's success, according to Walton, "is that if you take care of the people in the stores, they will take care of the customers in the same manner. But you have to work at it because that little personal touch means a lot."

Walton hired good people wherever he could find them—most often from other stores. People liked him and were willing to risk coming into what at times may have seemed disastrous circumstances. He loved to buy huge quantities of an item, then advertise extensively. Such tactics set the company apart and were hard to compete with, especially price-wise. "The philosophy is that stores are full of items that can explode into big volume and profits if you are just smart enough to identify them and take the trouble to promote them." Walton often walked all over town to check out the competition, always with an eye to saving himself and his customers money on good merchandise.

Even with his busy schedule, however, he spent time with his family on long camping trips. His son Jim says, "Dad said you've got to stay flexible. We never went on a trip that wasn't changed at least once after the trip was underway. Dad thrived on change."

Despite Walton's success, problems did at times linger. Merchandise often didn't arrive at the stores on time, and there was a constant shortage of trained manpower. He opened 50 stores a year, hired managers with little retail experience, put them on the sales floor for six months and then "put them in line for the next store." Walton's belief in people gave them the confidence to try it "his way" in "their own store"—and they thrived. His motto that "desire and a willingness to work make up for a lack of experience" was not just a collection of idle words. He expected his executives to listen and then turn around and share good, workable ideas with associates. He realized that "folks who stand all day on their feet get exhausted and frustrated too and need someone to share it with who is in a position to find a solution."

In 1974, at 56, Walton was free of debt, his business was doing well, and he wanted to step back a little. After appointing Ron Mayer as CEO and chairman of Wal-Mart and Ferold Arend as president, Walton demoted himself to chairman of the Executive Committee.

Before long, however, things began to go downhill. "What they had was a semiretired founder who didn't want to go away, on top of an old-line bunch of store managers at war with an ambitious young guy with ideas of his own," conjectured Walton. Numbers were good during that period, but the company continued to line up on two different sides. When Walton finally called Mayer 30 months later and admitted that he wasn't going to retire after all, Mayer left, taking many of the senior managers with him.

The new team Walton succeeded in putting together "was even more talented, more suited for the job at hand than the previous one." As Walton became more comfortable in his limited hands-on role, he did learn to step back emotionally. As the company grew he continued to pursue the same principles that made it great in the first place: "Put the customer first, communicate, keep your ear to the ground, push responsibility and authority down, force ideas to bubble up, stay lean and fight bureaucracy, and always give something back."

Walton fought the effects of bone cancer during the final two years of his life. "He took his medicine," his son remembers, "but never dwelled on either the illness or its potential cures. He seized the day, flying his plane to visit his beloved associates, and worked on this book."

Just three weeks before his life ended at age 74 on April 5, 1992, he received a Presidential Citation from President Clinton, the Medal of Freedom. The down-to-earth atmosphere Walton stubbornly sought to marshal in his stores was not a put-on, but the real thing. Rising from Arkansas store clerk to the heights of a man having captured the

THE AUTOBIOGRAPHY OF ANDREW CARNEGIE

by Andrew Carnegie, Houghton Mifflin Company, Boston and New York, 1920

. . . I intend to tell my story, not as one posturing before the public, but as in the midst of my own people and friends . . . to whom I can speak with the utmost freedom, feeling that even trifling incidents may not be wholly destitute of interest for them.

And so begins the story of Andrew Carnegie, the Scottish immigrant who accumulated one of the great fortunes in America—then gave most of it away. Written in the warm, confidential voice one would expect of a friend, Carnegie's autobiography offers its readers a rich tapestry of advice, insight, anecdotes, and worldly experience.

Born in 1835, Carnegie grew up in the prominent Scottish town of Dumferline. The deep-seated history and poetic tradition of the hamlet touched him and "set fire to the latent spark within, making him something different and beyond what, less happily born, he would have become."

Carnegie descended from an intellectual and political family. His intensely patriotic forbearers despised the privileged classes, favoring instead American republicanism, specifically its "denunciations of monarchical and aristocratic government" and its belief in "a home for freemen in which every citizen's privilege was every man's right."

In 1848, when Carnegie was thirteen, his family fell on hard times and subsequently emigrated to America, settling with relatives in Pittsburgh. Andrew's father secured work for his son first as a bobbin boy in a cotton factory and later as a steam engine operator—work much too hard for a youth. "But . . . " Carnegie remembered, "my hopes were high, and I looked every day for some change to take place. What it was to be I knew not, but that it would come I felt certain if I kept on."

In 1850, Carnegie left the factory to work as a messenger boy for a telegraph office. "From the dark cellar running a steam-engine . . . I was lifted into paradise, yes, heaven, as it seemed to me, with newspapers, pens, pencils, and sunshine about me." In addition to becoming acquainted with "the few leading men of the city," soon he was supervising the delivery office, earning an unprecedented salary of thirteen dollars and fifty cents a month. His parents were elated. "No subsequent success," he wrote, " . . . ever thrilled me as this did."

At seventeen, Carnegie became a telegrapher, earning twenty-five dollars a month. He and his closest friends also joined a debate society, where he learned the art of public speaking. "Make yourself perfectly at home before your audience," he advised, "and simply talk to them, not at them. Do not try to be somebody else; be your own self and talk, never 'orate' . . . "

Young Carnegie quickly rose through the ranks of the firm. His family's situation improved, but in 1855 Carnegie's father died, "just as we were becoming able to give him a life of leisure and comfort . . . "

Around this time, Carnegie made his first investment—a hard-earned 500 dollars—and discovered the ease with which money could be generated: "It gave me the first penny of revenue from capital—something I had not worked for with the sweat of my brow." He also bought an eighth interest in a firm that manufactured the first sleeping cars for railroads. Then, in 1859, the 24-year-old Carnegie was named superintendent of the railroad's Pittsburgh Division at an annual salary of fifteen hundred dollars.

When the Civil War erupted, the young executive was called to Washington to help organize the railroad transport of soldiers and supplies. While there, he worked with both President Lincoln and General Ulysses Grant.

Near the close of the Civil War, Carnegie, back at work for the railroad, went into business forging new rails for the railroads and organizing the prosperous Pittsburgh Locomotive Works. He also helped form the Keystone Bridge Company, which thrived at a time when most other bridge builders were going under. Carnegie attributed his success to hard work and the quality production he demanded: *There has been no luck about it. We used only the best material and enough of it, making our own iron and later our own steel. We were our own severest inspectors, and would build a safe structure or none at all . . . This policy is the true secret of success . . . A high standard of excellence is easily maintained, and men are educated in the effort to reach excellence . . . The surest foundation of a manufacturing concern is quality.*

Carnegie and his partners implemented the first cost accounting system for the complicated manufacturing process. Also at this time he invested in the newly drilled Pennsylvania oil wells, and by 1865 his investments commanded so much attention that he retired from railroad service, determined to increase his fortune. "Thenceforth," he recalled, "I never worked for a salary. A man must necessarily occupy a narrow field who is at the beck and call of others."

In 1867 Carnegie moved to New York, where "the whole speculative field was laid out for me in its most seductive guise." He considered buying stocks to be a form of gambling, claiming that "speculation is a parasite feeding upon values, creating none." Hence, he resolved not "to own any stock that was bought and sold upon any stock exchange." Rather he decided that the proper policy was "to put all good eggs in one basket and then watch that basket."

I believe the true road to preeminent success in any line is to make yourself master in that line . . . My advice to young men would be not only to concentrate their whole time and attention on the one business in life in which they engage, but to put every dollar of their capital into it.

In 1871, Carnegie and his partners became the first American firm to utilize the "dross" (waste) from coal mines through an English process of washing and cooking. They were also first to hire a chemist to determine the quality of the ore from various mines. Utilizing recent scientific advances, they discovered that many manufacturers were discarding perfectly usable raw materials.

Carnegie founded a company in 1873 that manufactured steel rails using the new "Bessemer" process. For each of his ventures, he was able to choose the very best men to run the factories, handle the machinery, and manage the workers. It was this uncanny ability to perceive excellence in men—"the faculty of knowing and choosing others who did know better than myself"—for which he credited his success. Indeed, Carnegie wrote, "I did not understand steam machinery, but I tried to understand that much more complicated piece of mechanism—man."

In 1878 Carnegie embarked on a world tour, taking "several pads suitable for penciling" to make notes, which he later published as *Round the World,* his first book. While traveling, he read the works of Confucius, Buddha, "the sacred books of the Hindoos," and the teachings of Zoroaster: *The result of my journey was to bring a certain mental peace. Where there had been chaos there was now order. My mind was at rest. I had a philosophy at last. The words of Christ "The Kingdom of Heaven is within you," had a new meaning for me. Not in the past or in the future, but now and here is Heaven within us.*

Four years after his return, he published his second book, *An American Four-in-Hand,* from notes he made while on a coach trip through England and Scotland. Then in 1886 his mother and brother died within a few days of each other, and, he wrote, "I was left alone in the world." The next year, in his mid-forties, Carnegie married Louise Whitfield in New York. Soon a daughter was born to them. And in the decade that ensued Carnegie's business endeavors—and fortune—expanded threefold.

"The one really serious quarrel with our workmen in our whole history," Carnegie disclosed, arose in 1892 while he was away in Scotland. At the height of this Homestead Strike, which pitted disgruntled workmen against their bosses, Carnegie prepared to return to America. His partners, however, begged him to stay away, complaining that he "was always disposed to yield to the demands of the men, however unreasonable." In truth, he remembered, the bargaining philosophy which he pursued was quite rare: *"My idea is that the Company should be known as determined to let the men at any works stop work; that it will confer freely with them and wait patiently until they decide to return to work, never thinking of trying new men—never."*

Because of the ensuing Homestead riots and the massacre of ten picketers by security forces, much of the general public came to believe that Carnegie was unsympathetic to the working man. Ironically, the reverse was true; the industrial mogul had always enjoyed a friendly relationship with his laborers. In fact, once, upon learning that an employee named McLuckie had been forced to flee the country after the Homestead troubles, Carnegie immediately offered to send the destitute man money. McLuckie, upon receipt of the cash, remarked,

"Well, that was damned [good] of Andy, wasn't it?" The comment delighted "Andy." "I would rather risk that verdict of McLuckie's as a passport to Paradise," he quipped, "than all the theological dogmas invented by man." Another worker at the mill told the steel magnate that the Homestead predicament wouldn't have come up in the first place had Carnegie been there. When he confessed that he couldn't have offered a better settlement than his partners, the man replied, "Oh, Mr. Carnegie, it wasn't a question of dollars. The boys would have let you kick 'em, but they wouldn't let that other man stroke their hair."

In 1901 Carnegie elected to follow the advice he himself had given in his most recent book *The Gospel of Wealth;* that is, to cease his "struggle for more wealth." He sold The Carnegie Steel Company to John Pierpont Morgan and began "the infinitely more serious and difficult task of wise distribution." He eventually gave away more than 350 million pre-inflation dollars: four million dollars to a pension fund for his mill workers; a ten-million-dollar grant for the founding of the Carnegie Institution of Washington; and a five-million-dollar donation to create the Hero Fund (a pension for the families of heroes "who perish in the effort to serve or save their fellows"). He also founded libraries in his native Scotland and in America, established a pension fund for university professors, and donated millions of dollars to universities on both sides of the Atlantic.

Denouncing war as "the foulest blot upon our civilization," Carnegie devoted much of his last twenty years to the cause of world peace, providing funds for the building of a Temple of Peace in the Netherlands—"the most holy building in the world because it has the holiest end in view." He also wholeheartedly supported the idea of an International Court to arbitrate disputes between nations.

Carnegie conferred with many of the most famous men of his time: Mark Twain, Matthew Arnold, William Gladstone, Herbert Spencer, and President Benjamin Harrison, with whom Carnegie argued against going to war with Chili. When many speculated that Carnegie had been reserved in speaking with the President, Harrison replied, "I didn't see the slightest indication of reserve, I assure you." Carnegie also met the German Kaiser, whom he congratulated in 1912 for ruling for over 25 years without going to war. But Carnegie worried about the Kaiser's "military caste," saying, "Until militarism is subordinated, there can be no World Peace."

The great philanthropist ended his *Autobiography* on a sorrowful note: "As I read this today [1914], what a change! The world convulsed by war as never before! Men slaying each other like wild beasts! I dare not relinquish hope . . . "

Carnegie died in 1919, having given away the better part of his vast wealth. He spent his life and fortune striving to answer this single, most germane question: "What good am I doing in the world to deserve all my mercies?"

HENRY FORD

The Wayward Capitalist
by Carol Gelderman, The Dial Press, New York, N.Y., 1981

When Henry Ford left his Dearborn, Michigan farm at age sixteen and headed for Detroit, only one out of five Americans lived in cities; when he died in Dearborn at eighty-three, this proportion was exactly reversed. More than any other man, Ford helped bring about this revolution when he introduced industry to the assembly line and put the nation on wheels with his inexpensive Model T. Yet, as Carol Gelderman reveals in *Henry Ford: The Wayward Capitalist*, this pioneer of modern manufacturing despised cities, believing they were a cradle of social disorder.

Born in 1863, the grandson of an Irish immigrant and the son of a farmer, Henry took an early interest in mechanical things. But after he saw a self-propelled steam engine for the first time in 1876, he realized that he "knew only the periphery of the mechanical world which so fascinated him." So, three years later he moved to Detroit to work in a machine shop.

In Detroit, 25-year-old Henry married Clara Bryant, to whom he'd shown sketches of the "horseless carriage" which someday he would build. Clara put her whole heart into Henry's project. Recognizing her faith as an important factor in his success, he referred to her as "the great believer."

In 1893 Ford produced his first working engine from pieces of scrap: *The handwheel of an old lathe acted as flywheel. A piece of discarded pipe became a cylinder . . . A piece of fiber with a wire through its center served as a spark plug.* Then on June 4th, 1896, he completed his first vehicle, a "quadricycle," which had no brakes and no reverse gear.

In 1899 Ford lost the financial backing of three Detroit businessmen, who had grown impatient with his insistence on building the "perfect" vehicle. After either antagonizing or frustrating Detroit's wealthiest citizens over the next four years, Ford eventually joined forces with a coal merchant named Alexander Malcomson, who, along with other investors, contributed $100,000 to establish the Ford Motor Company in 1903. In the first year, the investors were paid dividends of $98,000 on their initial $100,000 investment.

"I think you are creating a social problem with your car," a young lawyer subsequently told Ford. "No, my friend, you're mistaken," Ford replied. "I'm not creating a social problem at all. I am going to democratize the automobile. When I'm through everybody will be able to afford one . . ."

True to his word, Ford introduced his Model T as the "motorcar for the great multitude." He then built an enormous assembly plant in Highland Park, near Detroit, where by 1913 he had put together the first moving assembly line, which eventually enabled the plant to turn out a new car every 24 seconds. As demand and production increased, he lowered the price of the Model T from $950 in 1909 to $490 in 1913. "The principle," Ford said, "is to decide on your design, freeze it, and, from then on, spend all your time, effort, and money on making the machinery to produce it, concentrating so completely on production that, as the volume goes up, it is certain to get cheaper per unit produced."

Not only did Ford keep lowering prices, but in 1914 he also doubled his employees' pay and shortened their work day from nine to eight hours. His generosity incited an uproar. Although most members of the press praised him and the "new economic era" he had inspired, Ford's fellow industrialists condemned him, protesting that the higher wages and shorter hours would "permanently undermine the peace and contentment of the lower classes [and would] breed revolution." But to Ford, the "mad socialist of Highland Park," the changes made sense: his workers now had more incentive to work diligently and efficiently. Indeed, Ford's profits soon skyrocketed.

While World War I raged, Ford, a staunch pacifist, nevertheless put his factory at the disposal of the U.S. government to produce cars, boats, tractors and ambulances. After the war, Ford went back to making Model T's again, and, at President Woodrow Wilson's behest, tried unsuccessfully to win a seat in the U.S. Senate.

The following year, 1919, Ford bought out his company's minority stockholders for $106 million and gained complete control of the Ford Motor Company: *Never had anyone risen so meteorically; in 1902 Ford had yet to design a car for the market, but seventeen years later he owned a complex of factories worth at least a billion dollars. Henceforth he could act with no restraint upon his massive power.*

That same year Ford sued the *Chicago Tribune* for libel. The newspaper had printed the editorial "Ford Is an Anarchist" attacking Ford's anti-preparedness stance during the early year of World War I. Subjected to a scathing interrogation by the *Tribune's* lawyer, Ford's ignorance, even in regards to common points of history, was exposed. After the trial, the major newspapers again released a bevy of statements belittling the auto maker. Unfortunately, Ford failed to realize that he had divided America: *It was no coincidence that the urban press damned Ford for his ignorance while provincial papers loved him for his simplicity.*

The mockery and abuse heaped upon him depleted Ford's natural optimism: *. . . His idealism gave way to cynicism, his faith in others' judgements was undermined, throwing him back on his own instinctive decisions.* Isolating himself from the public, Ford only sought the company of simple men who would not scorn him for his lack of education: *The cruel ridicule of his altruism, he perceived, came always from educated, highly literate city dwellers. Never did any farmer misunderstand Henry Ford . . . Ironically, the man who now looked on the city as the source of misanthropy had done more than anyone else to accelerate the rise of congested urban centers.*

Then, in 1921, while the country suffered from a recession, Ford had to lay off twenty thousand workers. Because of Ford's reluctance to deal with administrative duties, his secretary, Ernest G. Liebold, became the second most powerful man in the company. Charles Sorenson, Ford's production chief, also prospered by carrying out "unpleasant assignments," such as overseeing the firings of many employees in 1920 and '21. In addition to Liebold and Sorenson, Harry Bennett—a roughneck with ties to organized crime whom Ford had hired to protect his grandchildren from kidnapping—became increasingly powerful in the company.

The change in Ford's labor policy dismayed Henry's son Edsel, whom the elder Ford had made president of the company in 1918. As time went on, Ford, hiding behind his cadre of eager executives, began to visit the plant less often and became increasingly remote. Although he maintained all along that Edsel was in charge, Ford "refused to relinquish authority." In fact, Edsel "had to run to meet his father as if he were a junior executive." Clearly, Ford—the son of a tough farmer—considered his own son "too soft"; in addition, he resented Edsel's upper class friends.

Harry Bennett, meanwhile, took increasing control of the company: *He bragged that he was closer to Ford than Edsel was, and no one disagreed with him . . . When someone wanted something from the boss he went through Bennett, not Edsel . . . "Mr. Ford worshiped Edsel," Bennett admitted, "but he insisted that Edsel do everything his way."*

Edsel began urging his father to manufacture a sleeker, more modern automobile. Ford Motors, its outdated "Tin Lizzie" virtually unchanged from 1908 to 1927, had started losing ground on other, up-and-coming car manufacturers, and Ford dealers nationwide had asked for alterations in their product. But Ford's answer was short and sweet: "Well, gentlemen, so far as I can see the only trouble with the Ford car is that we can't make them fast enough." *What Henry failed to understand was that Americans wanted more than low price . . . They wanted style.*

Finally in 1927, Edsel, with Henry's support, designed a new car called the Model A, which proved wildly popular. To produce the new vehicle, however, the company had to re-tool all its factories, resulting in a tremendous backlog of orders. Eventually, Ford was able to increase production to a total of 6400 fully-assembled cars a day, a figure which accounted for one-third of all cars and trucks sold in 1929.

Indeed, Ford Motors became "America's first vertically integrated industrial empire." As the company acquired mines, ships, and a railroad, Ford controlled every step in the manufacturing process, from extracting the ore from the ground to seeing the finished car roll off the assembly plant. Even while he erected the company's mighty Rouge River, Michigan plant, Ford also collected artifacts of America's rural past, which were later placed in a museum of eighteenth- and nineteenth-century rural life. "All the relics have one thing in common," Ford proudly said of his collection, "they are all things used by run-of-the-mill people, not by the elite . . .

The everyday lives of ordinary folk have been overlooked by historians . . . "

Meanwhile, as the country wallowed in the midst of the Great Depression, Ford's mind, will and mouth got him into trouble. Blind to the severity of economic conditions, he optimistically pronounced that now that the people of Detroit had lost their jobs, they could "go back to their farms" where they belonged. A year later, in 1930, he offered this candid observation: "It was a mighty good thing for the nation that the condition which we misnamed prosperity could not last." And later that year he declared that the Depression was a "wholesome thing in general. If we could only realize it, these are the best times we ever had." Ford's off-the-cuff remarks struck his contemporaries as highly insensitive: *Never again would he be the untarnished hero of grass-roots America; his callous statements shocked and bewildered the millions who had always idolized him.*

His assembly-line workers were also quickly disillusioned. Goaded mercilessly by brutal foremen—consisting mostly of Harry Bennett's cronies—hundreds of workers, accused of loafing or of simply talking to other employees, were laid off. Although Edsel complained of Bennett's willingness to use violence and intimidation to break up union-forming activities, Ford continued to let Bennett handle such matters as he thought best.

Ford employees longed for the younger, considerate Henry Ford, the man who hadn't been afraid to address company matters. As Bennett accumulated more and more power, executives loyal to Edsel were summarily dismissed or transferred; Liebold's and Sorenson's teams of executives were also forced out.

Then, in 1943, debilitated by the stress of constant feuding, Edsel died. For all intents and purposes, Bennett—under Henry Ford's indifferent eye—now held the keys to the company.

Devastated by his son's death, Ford experienced periods of disorientation and memory loss, and became increasingly dependent on his wife Clara. Bennett quickly began purging the company of Edsel's supporters, replacing them with men who "knew nothing about production or business." Furthermore, many of Bennett's top people were ex-convicts, "ex-pugs and thugs," who terrorized company employees.

Finally, Clara, backed by Edsel's widow, convinced Henry to name Edsel's son, Henry II, president of Ford Motors. Seizing the reigns of the long-neglected firm, Henry II immediately fired Bennett and his henchmen. As the younger Ford reorganized the corporation from top to bottom, employee morale soared. "I guess young Henry knows what he's doing," his proud grandfather said months before his condition entirely deteriorated.

After Ford's death on April 7, 1947, one Detroit newspaper eulogized: *No other man ever so changed the face of the world in his lifetime as did Henry Ford . . . Not for the few but for the millions . . . he opened new vistas of space . . . [placed] in the reach of the greatest number of people a useful product which would lift the whole level of living . . . Ford established a new age—it might also be said a new civilization . . .*

HANG TIME

Days and Dreams with Jordan
by Bob Greene, Doubleday Publishers, New York, N.Y., 1992

Bob Greene published his insightful book about Michael Jordan prior to Jordan's retirement from basketball in 1993. Michael allowed Greene to travel with him during two world-championship seasons, and to share in his dreams.

Greene writes: *We had been talking about that word—that word "dream"—and how often people seemed to use it when referring to him.* Interestingly, Greene adds, Michael seldom dreams, and when he does it's rarely about sports. When he does dream about sports, however, it's about *baseball*—and being a pitcher.

Bob Greene met Michael Jordan quite by accident. At the time, Greene was a newspaper journalist who often wrote about child abuse. One case he reported involved a eight-year-old boy named Cornelius McGee, who had been systematically abused by his mother—abuse that had been so brutal and unthinkable that Cornelius' little brother Lattie had died at his mother's hands. Cornelius, Greene learned, had a passion for basketball, and when the Chicago Bulls' management heard about Cornelius they invited him to a game. Greene recalls that when he and Cornelius entered the arena, the boy was too overwhelmed; he just stared in awe. As Greene led him downstairs, "a door opened and a man came out. Cornelius looked up, and his eyes filled with . . . total disbelief." He tried to speak but no words would come out.

"Hi Cornelius," the man said. "I'm Michael Jordan." Michael knelt down, spoke quietly . . . then stood and said, "Are you going to cheer for us? . . . We're going to need it."

According to Greene, Michael often makes special efforts for children. Once, Greene reports, a little boy in a wheelchair was sitting outside the stadium after a game. As Jordan hurried to his car, he noticed the boy: *[He] had every excuse not to notice; the boy [couldn't even] motion to him. But he did notice. Something about Jordan—maybe it was the peripheral vision that serves him so well on the court, or . . . compassionate radar . . . he walked over to the boy and got down on the ground beside him and spoke . . . The boy's father had a camera, he tried to snap a picture. The camera didn't work. Jordan noticed . . . he stayed beside the boy until the father was able to make the shot.*

In the months that followed, Greene was frequently impressed by Jordan's heart-felt acts of generosity and affection. He seemed always to have time for people, especially those with handicaps. Greene learned many other interesting facts about Jordan as well. For instance:

- Jordan had once been cut from his high school team. "I went through the day numb," he recalls. "I had to wait until after school to go home . . . I hurried to my house and I closed the door of my room and I cried so hard. It was all I wanted—to play on the team." Writes Greene, *There can't be many professional athletes in any sport who were cut from their high school teams.*

- Jordan has set himself apart from most professional athletes by arriving early for every game, at a time when only the vendors, ushers and a few police officers are in the stadium. Then, all alone, Greene noted, he would embark on his routine—shot after shot. *Jordan would stand near the out-of-bounds line . . . his back toward the basket. The ball boy . . . would fire him the pass. Jordan . . . would wheel and jump . . . and shoot.* Then he would repeat the process, over and over.

- Jordan never appears undressed in the locker room. "It's not that I disapprove of women in the locker rooms," he says. "My feelings about it are the same for men as for women. Out of respect for myself, and for other people, I could not appear undressed in front of them." In fact, Michael normally likes to wear a suit and tie.

- Greene took immediate note of the impact Jordan has on the game as well as his team's success: *In the year before Jordan arrived in town, there had not been a single sellout. Some nights there had been scarcely three thousand souls rattling around the cavernous structure.* Now, however, the Bulls sell out nearly every game, and tickets are nearly impossible to buy for the Bulls' road games.

- If any of Michael's family attends a game, he has to know where they're sitting so he can look up and see them to know that they are safe. Otherwise, he can't concentrate on the game.

- Michael, undisputedly one of the world's greatest athletes, can't swim. When he's at a party where there is a pool, he stands far away from it. "I'll look to see where the deep end is," he grins, a little embarrassed, "Even when I'm . . . near the shallow end I won't stand very close . . ."

- Jordan once invited four impoverished boys who were standing outside the stadium in to see a game. Now, after *every* home game he makes it a practice to stop at a nearby street corner to talk with the boys. A garrulous multi-millionaire lingering in a rough neighborhood late at night to check up on how some boys are doing in school clearly isn't standard procedure.

- Michael Jordan is a hero and an inspiration to millions of basketball fans. Who are *his* heroes? "My heroes are and were my parents . . . I can't see having anyone else as my heroes . . . It wasn't that the rest of the world would . . . think they were heroic . . . But they were the adults that I saw constantly, and I admired what I saw."

- Jordan never pays attention during pre-game meetings: "I never follow along. I'm never paying attention . . . My whole life, I never did . . . I'm not listening." Why? "I know what to do." And watching him on the court, there's little doubt that he knows exactly what he's doing.

- Jordan doesn't feel pressure the way most people do. Leading his team to championships, *defending his NBA scoring title . . . knowing every fan expected him to play like Michael Jordan every night* might seem stressful to some, but Michael claims it's not for him: "The basketball court, during a game, is the most peaceful place I can imagine . . . I'm really by myself out there . . . the rules say that no one can talk to me or walk up to me when I'm playing . . . [it's] one of the few times in my life, I feel like I'm untouchable. I'm not untouchable anywhere else."

- On June 20, 1984, the NBA held its annual draft of college players. The Houston Rockets chose Akeem Olajuwon with the first pick. The second player selected was Sam Bowie, taken by the Portland Trail Blazers. *The team with the third pick . . . the Chicago Bulls . . . selected Michael Jordan of the University of North Carolina.* The third pick! How would the sports pages have changed if Portland or Houston had picked Michael instead?

- In terms of what his physical talent, his work ethic, and his mental preparation have contributed to his unparalleled success, Michael is typically self-deprecating. He says, "So much of it was timing, so much of it was just good luck . . . I'm serious," he adds. "Everyone tries to figure out why all of this has happened to me, and there are all these theories, and no one is willing to consider how much of it was just luck . . . I'm telling you luck has played more of a role than anyone understands."

Traveling with Michael, the journalist recalls: *All season long my companions at the press table had been telling me that when the playoffs started, it would feel as if something brand new was beginning.* "You'll feel it as soon as you walk into the building." And, confirms Greene, they were right. Now security was tighter: *no one without a ticket or a playoff credential slipped by . . . [The Bulls], for their part, were wearing black basketball shoes rather than their regular white ones*—a playoff tradition, Greene learned. *The most striking difference . . . was not the excitement of the games, but the fact that for the first time . . . the faces of the opponents were the same night after night.* The arena itself became frenzied, "almost claustrophobic." Because the opposing team was now a regular fixture, the fans' "hatred" for various players surfaced. Players like Isaiah Thomas, Dennis Rodman, and especially Bill Laimbeer had insults hurled at them constantly.

Laimbeer, as it turned out, could be quite disagreeable. At one of the 1991 playoff games against Detroit, Greene sat next to Consuelo Hill, who had sung the national anthem at one of the regular games against the Pistons and had

been invited back for the playoff game. As Greene spoke with her, she seemed rather disheartened. Then she said, "After the game in January, I went up to Bill Laimbeer to ask for his autograph, [telling him that she had sung the national anthem]. "He just looked at me and said, 'I don't care if you sang a whole concert.'"

Later, as the playoff game neared its end, it became obvious that the Bulls would win and Phil Jackson removed his starters. As they relaxed on the bench, Jordan gazed over in our direction "until he caught Consuelo Hill's eye . . . [and said], 'I just wanted to tell you that I thought you did a very good job on the anthem.'" The journalist observed: *Whatever would happen in the NBA Finals would happen. The real championships in life are not won on a basketball court.*

The Bulls went on to defeat Detroit and face Los Angeles in the finals—an best-of-seven-game event that brought the celebrities out of the woodwork. Jack Nicholson, Elizbeth Taylor, Arnold Schwarzenegger, even Princess Diana expressed interest in tickets—and a desire to meet Jordan.

In game five, with the Bulls up three games to one, the Lakers had made a strong run in the fourth quarter to take the lead. During a time out, Greene borrowed some binoculars: *I looked through the glasses at the Bulls' bench.* "Look at that . . . He's not going to let them lose." *Later I would learn that Jordan's father had said the same thing . . . he had looked at the bench during that time out, and he realized that there was no way his son was going to leave the Forum a loser tonight. Jordan . . . was as intensely focused as any person I could ever imagine seeing . . . [And when] the final buzzer sounded: Bulls 108, Lakers 101.*

Whenever Jordan had talked . . . about a championship, the words seemed uncharacteristically dry and cold; [there was] something missing . . . Now on a portable [TV] . . . there was Jordan . . . sitting in front of his cubicle, embracing the world championship trophy, weeping uncontrollably . . . Of course he had never been able to put into words what [this] would mean. There are only two reasons for us not being able to talk about something: When it means nothing to us. And when it means everything.

As the 1991-92 season arrived, Greene could see an undeniable media "backlash" against Jordan. Later that year, Jordan's gambling habits were exposed when a nightclub owner was found shot to death. In his briefcase were photocopies of three checks, totaling $108,000, all signed by Michael.

The season, however, went well for Chicago. The Bulls stormed through the playoffs to meet Portland in the finals. In just six games, the Bulls defeated the Blazers to repeat as world champions.

Greene writes of Jordan on that memorable night: *The last time I saw him . . . he was standing on top of the scorer's table . . . he had done his job, and he was free . . . He didn't dream about basketball. That's what he had told me all those months ago. But I do. I didn't used to, but now I do. The dreams are vivid and bright . . . and they will stay with me forever.*

BILLIE JEAN

by Billie Jean King, with Frank Deford, The Viking Press, New York, N.Y., 1982

I have always disliked the labels that were arbitrarily placed on me, whether in feminist, heroic, or less flattering terms. This book may serve to remove some of those misconceptions. At times I may be tough and at other times extremely sensitive. I'm an individual. In this candid autobiography, Billie Jean King reflects upon her personal life and upon her role as a trailblazer. After growing up in a working-class family, she broke into the world of country-club tennis and eventually became a popular champion to both sexes in a sport previously dominated by men. Though her career spanned two decades and included an amazing twenty "Grand Slam" titles (championships in tennis' "big four" tournaments: Wimbledon, and the U.S., Australian, and French Opens), this book deals more with her personal musings on the game, on her role in changing the game, on her rivalries, and on her personality.

King also offers her own version of her well-publicized lesbian affair with Marilyn Barnett. Once she feared that she would always be labeled by the affair, regardless of her other accomplishments. Now she uses the episode as a forum to attack all labels placed on her and on other people.

Growing Up Supplemental

As a child, Billie Jean King's first ambition was to be a missionary. However, she soon discovered that she was athletically inclined, but realized that there was no future for girls in team sports. Golf, to her, was too slow; she might drown in swimming. So she opted to play tennis, even though her working-class family did not have enough money to pay for a racket or a tennis dress.

Even now Billie Jean mourns that there are few underprivileged children who participate in tennis. She wants tennis to become a game that everyone plays. To this end, she visits and sponsors tennis clinics in low-income neighborhoods.

Feeling out of place with the country-club set didn't stop Billie Jean; in fact, she liked being different from everybody else. *I also like being successful. I somehow always knew that I would succeed. I had a great sense of destiny from the time I was very young. I remember one incident so vividly. When I was only about five or six years old, I was standing with my mother in the kitchen . . . I told her flat out that when I grew up I was going to be the best at something. She just smiled and kept peeling potatoes or doing whatever it was she was doing. She said, "Yes, dear; yes, of course, dear," as if I had simply said that I was going to* my room or . . . whatever. So, I always felt different that way.

Billie Jean suffered from bad knees, bad eyes, and breathing difficulties. But her will to succeed at tennis carried her over all these hurdles, and she was not surprised when she began to excel.

As much as she always loved the game, she was prepared to give it up when she married Larry King, and to "have babies—lots of them, as far as I was concerned." But Larry wanted her to continue. He also supported her when businessman Bob Mitchell offered to send her to Australia to train with world-renowned coach Mervyn Rose. Later, King was to recall: *I always wanted to be special, to be the best in one thing. I've always thought it would be easier for me just to be comfortable . . . but I really had no choice. I was driven.*

Always on the Cusp

That drive also led Billie Jean to accept the challenge to play a match against Bobby Riggs, a self-proclaimed male chauvinist. Their showdown in Houston's Astrodome created a media frenzy, drawing over 30,000 enthusiastic fans and a television audience of 40 million. In retrospect, King is convinced that the only reason she beat Riggs was that she despised what he stood for: not only the myth of male superiority, but also the dominance of men's tennis over women's tennis in terms of money and popularity. She admits that she was shaking until the crossover after the first game, when she glanced at Bobby and saw that he was scared, too. Suddenly all her doubts left her; all she feared was the unknown, and Bobby was now a familiar entity. After that, Billie Jean won the match quite handily. Only one thing bothered her: that everyone else at the match, including Bobby, seemed to have more fun than she did.

But even though King didn't enjoy herself much, she quickly perceived how saliently her victory had enhanced her reputation. Ironically, it gave her a certain credibility that even her victories at Wimbledon and Forest Hills had not. Even more importantly, she saw how much her victory over Riggs meant to others. Women still tell her that their husbands had to do the dishes for a week because she won that classic "battle of the sexes."

"This Would Make a Great Book"

Billie Jean is often disturbed by the inordinate amount of attention paid to female athletes' personal lives. She laments that, more often than not, they are stereotyped as lesbians. *I have often been asked whether I am a woman or an athlete. The ques-*

tion is absurd. Men are not asked that. I am an athlete, I am a woman.

This conflict made it all the more painful for King to go public with the fact that, while she was married, she had an affair with a woman. The woman was hairdresser Marilyn Barnett, who King had met in 1972; Billie Jean had never lived as a lesbian before that time. When Marilyn later threatened to sue Billie Jean for part of the fortune she had accumulated, King decided to hold a press conference rather than let Marilyn break the story. She knew that press attention would create a circus-type spectacle, for she was already a controversial celebrity, characterized as tough, loud, brash and insensitive.

What bothered her most about the publicity was that she would be judged on her perceived faults and failures rather than on her achievements and triumphs. The scandal completely ignored Billie Jean as a person and focused on labels. *It is important to keep me in perspective, and to remember the massive changes that I was experiencing at this time. My whole world was in flux.* She also feared that public disclosure of the affair would reflect unfavorably upon women's tennis in general.

Starting with Chris and Jimmy

Billie Jean complains that *players today have no sense of history. They don't feel a part of anything grand or dear or lasting.* As a matter of fact, most of them pretty much accept it that tennis began with Chris Evert on the women's side and Jimmy Connors on the men's.

Billie Jean believes that Connors is the one American player who is almost universally admired by female professional tennis players. She contends that although he can be vulgar and even foolish on the court, he gives so much of himself that women can't help but love him.

Evert's participation in the sport was also important, *not only for women's tennis, but for me personally because it gave the press a duel to play up.* Although King and Evert were portrayed as opposites by the press, Billie Jean does not feel they are so very different. Unfortunately, the arrival of the mild-mannered Evert on the tennis scene stereotyped King in an even more unfavorable light. When she finally decided to hire Pat Kingsley as her public relations agent, Pat turned down the account at first: she did not want to handle a "tough bitch."

Billie Jean does not identify with the image the media has created for her. In slugging it out with Evert on the tennis court, the press inevitably—and inaccurately, she claims—characterized the matches as contests pitting "monster" against "maiden." In fact, Billie Jean acknowledges nothing but great fondness and admiration for Evert.

Playing for the Love of It

Billie Jean admits that she is jealous of the money that team players make. However, she more deeply regrets the lack of recognition given to tennis players, when compared to that of other athletes. Entire towns unite to give their football and baseball teams parades or "days" in their honor. In contrast, when Billie Jean won Wimbledon three years in a row, few outside of the tennis community even knew about it.

But just as in other sports, the tennis community does spoil its stars. *It's really impossible for athletes to grow up. As long as you're playing, no one will let you. On the one hand, you're a child, still playing a game. And everybody around you acts like a kid, too. But on the other hand, you're a superhuman hero that everyone dreams of being. No wonder we have such a hard time understanding who we are. But either way, you see, the usual response is to spoil the athlete—child or god.*

She also explains that being a star can often be very annoying: *You can't ever win. Surely only a selfish bitch would refuse to donate one of her extra rackets to a worthwhile cause. Only, a hundred worthwhile causes a year asking for a racket apiece . . . plus autographed photos, clothes, shoes, balls . . . "Wouldja, couldja, canya Billie Jean? Just this one time . . . " The aggravation never stops.* The most important part of being a champion, she concludes, is playing the game.

In spite of the negative aspects of her fame, King believes that tennis has become *the* sport for today's woman, and that sports will become a vehicle for upward mobility among girls in the same way as it has always been for boys. *In fact, I would suggest that in tennis (and possibly other sports as well) women are every bit as tough as competitors as the men. If not more so . . . Making women's sports acceptable and making women's tennis into a legitimate big-league game was a crusade for me, and I threw my whole self into it in ways that exhausted me emotionally and physically.*

Billie Jean hasn't allowed the trials of that crusade to discourage her from carrying the banner a few more miles. Despite the trespasses into her personal life, she plans to continue her quest to vanquish labels. *So I'm not going to just wash away. I promise you that. I'm going to keep on trying. You know, I've never really cared what anybody did so long as they tried at it. I just plain like people who try. It doesn't matter what, so long as they get out there and work their bahoolas off.*

THE GREATEST: MY OWN STORY

by Muhammad Ali with Richard Durham, Random House, New York, N.Y., 1975

On September 30, 1975, heavyweight boxing champ Muhammad Ali retained his World Heavyweight Title after defeating the formidable "Smokin' Joe" Frazier. He recalls that victorious moment: *The screams are so loud they sound far away. Then the crowd, pushing, shoving, reporters shouting. They want something from me. Something more. Some words or comment. But I'm too tired. Besides, I already told them. And I already told you. Didn't you hear me? I said I was The Greatest.*

Ali's boxing career was characterized by a passion to win—a passion that gave him a tactical advantage over his rivals. In the ring he didn't seem to care about ego, money or titles as much as beating his ringmate. To him it was a mental game, a game he played with beauty and finesse, but with the zeal of a child. He fought for himself, for his home town, for his family and for the black race, battling not only his opponents, but the widespread prejudice of the time. He fought for Islam, for he is also a religious man as well as a political one. But most of all, he just loved to fight: broken jaws, torn muscles, split-open lips and cracked skulls were all a part of his mission, as he perceived it—a mission to bring power and recognition to black people everywhere.

❖ ◆ ❖

The Making of a Champion

In 1959 the boxer was still using the name he was born with, Cassius Clay. That year he won his first major title, the Chicago Golden Gloves Championship. Then in 1964, after deciding that his name would no longer reflect his heritage as the descendent of slaves, he began calling himself Muhammad Ali. In doing so, he wished to bring honor to the religion he had chosen: Islam. Three years later, citing both religious and political conviction, Ali refused induction into the Army and received a five-year jail sentence. Critics warned that his decision—not to mention a five-year layoff—would ruin his career. Instead, Ali's face has become the most widely recognized in the world.

Ali proved that his commitment to his religion was typical of his loyalty to his family and to his values. He is a complex man who was willing to forego his World Championship bout with Sonny Liston rather than renounce his ties with controversial Black Muslims. Despite his willingness to fight anyone, anytime, anywhere, he refused to fight the Viet Cong, saying he had nothing against them.

Ali may have displayed the most intense bravado the world has ever seen. His constant litany of self-praise and self-promotion outside the ring seemed decidedly un-American to some. He often made up poems that denigrated his opponents and proclaimed his own greatness.

Originally, the public scoffed at Ali's incessant claims to be "the greatest fighter that ever lived," but they soon fell in love with the man who could "float like a butterfly and sting like a bee!" Though the consummate showman, he came to command supreme respect from the most hard-nosed, celebrated fighters of his time.

"Invite Muhammad to fight, and your country will share in the world spotlight" was the advance campaign that attracted bids to host bouts from various national governments, including Zaire, Malaysia, the Philippines, Egypt, Saudi Arabia, Iran, Haiti, Ireland, Switzerland, Japan, Indonesia and Canada.

Two professional bouts especially stand out in the career of this champion. In 1973, Ali lost a devastatingly brutal 12-round split decision to Ken Norton in San Diego. In the other, he regained his World Heavyweight Title from George Foreman in a towering victory.

NORTON VS. ALI
Shorty Is Watching

Before the bell rings, [my manager] Bundini whispers in my ear, "Shorty is in the living room, watching. Shorty is sitting down, crossing His legs and watching you. Just remember that." Shorty is Bundini's name for God. And during the whole time I'm struggling to take Norton out before another blow crushes into my jaw, Bundini is screaming, "Shorty's watching!"

. . . The stadium explodes [when the decision is announced]. Wild shouts and screams come down from the bleachers. Some boo the decision, but the screams and cries of "NORTON!" "NORTON!" drown them out . . . Those voices out there are not just a "hometown reaction." It's the reaction of White America . . .

Why did I lose? I think back to the second round when Norton got in through my guard and crashed a left up against my jaw. I know exactly when the blow came. I felt a snap and a sudden gush of blood in my throat . . .

"If it's broke," Bundini is saying, "we've got to stop the fight." But he knows I won't stop. There are thirteen more rounds to go, and I can win.

After the loss, the former champion returned to Louisville to see if he would still be accepted. Until then, he had always returned home the conqueror: two Golden Gloves Championships, some AAU titles, an Olympic Gold Medal, the World

Heavyweight Title, and, after his exile from boxing, as The Undefeated. This time, he found the hometown fans loved him as much as ever.

FOREMAN VS. ALI

After the Norton defeat Ali was determined to regain the title. He hoped that George Foreman, then World Champion, would give him a shot and accept his challenge. A ten-million-dollar deal was signed for the Ali-Foreman match-up in Zaire on October 30, 1974.

Ali was ready to work his rope-a-dope move (a tactic in which he leans back against the ropes to rest, fends off blows with his arms and lets his foe punch himself out) and his "Ali Shuffle" (a quick, smooth shuffling of his feet followed by a thunderous hook). For Ali, the fight was more than just a chance to regain a title: it was the embodiment of his personal calling. . . . *George is The Champion, and the world listens to The Champion. There are things I want to say, things I want the world to hear. I want to be in a position to fight for my people. Whatever I have to do tonight, George will not leave Africa The Champion.*

The Half-Dream Room

CLANG! ROUND TWO . . . I move to the center, jab and dance and jab. But I know now that my danger is not in the corners or on the ropes, but in dancing six steps to George's three . . . It won't be George who'll be exhausted by round nine. It'll be me . . . I decide not to wait until I'm tired to play the ropes, but to take the corners while I'm fresh and still strong, to gamble on the ropes all the way . . .

A crowbar in George's right hand crashes through my guard into my head, knocks me into the room . . . the room I had planned to take George into, the half-dream room. My head vibrates like a tuning fork. Neon lights flash on and off.

CLANG! ROUND THREE . . . George's "murder" round. But if he expects me to be quiet on the day I'm supposed to die, he's mistaken . . . He throws his heaviest bomb, it curls around my head and we clinch so tight I feel his heart pounding. I bite his ear. "Is that the best you can do sucker? Is that all you got Chump? You ain't got no punch! You in big trouble, boy!"

When the round ends, my head is humming. But the round of my execution is over, and all I will do now is plot the time when my turn comes . . .

The Will to Win

The outcome of the Foreman fight ultimately turned on which man was to display the greater will to win. As the seventh round drew to a close, Ali still believed that he had the bigger heart:

The bell rings and I feel pain all over me. . . . How long can I stand up under this bar-

rage? I've got to go for the kill before he gets his second wind.

CLANG! ROUND EIGHT . . . George looks like King Kong when he comes at you . . . Only a man who knows what it is to be defeated can reach down to the bottom of his soul and come up with the extra ounce of power it takes to win when the match is even. I know George wants to keep The Champions Crown, but is he willing to pay the price? Would he lay out his life?

It's time to go all out. Toe to toe. George pours out a long left, and I cross my right over it. Now I've got to lay it all down on the line. If the price of winning is to be a broken jaw, a smashed nose, a cracked skull, a disfigured face, you pay it if you want to be King of the Heavyweights. If you want to wear the crown, you can play it careful only until you meet a man who will die before he lets you win. Then you have to lay it all on the line or back down and be damned forever.

The crowd eggs me on: "ALI! ALI! BOMAYE!" . . . I shoot a straight right to his jaw with all the snap and power that's in me. I strike him almost flush on the chin, and he stands still . . .

I'm ready to follow through with combinations, but I see he's slowly falling, a dazed look in his eyes. I know he's entering the room of the half-dream for the first time in his life. George is down, his eyes glazed. He's listening to the tuning forks humming in his head, bats blowing saxophones, alligators whistling, neon signs blinking.

The referee begins the count. George will later protest that he was the victim of a short count, and I can understand why. In the half-dream room time seems to stretch out slow, like rubber, and unless you've been there before, you'll never know how fast it goes by.

I watch every lift of the referee's arm. I remember thinking of Frazier. He would never lose the crown lying on the floor. No referee could count over his body as long as he had blood in it.

"Six . . . seven . . . eight . . . " George is turning over slowly.

"Nine . . . ten!" George is on his feet, but it's over. The referee raises my hand in victory.

And the stadium explodes! People break past the paratroopers and climb over the press tables, climb into the ring . . . and the whole world is screaming, ALI! ALI! ALI! ALI!.

A reporter claws his way through the crowd and yells at me, "How did you do it . . . What you think of George now?" I shake my head. I don't want to tell him what George has taught me. That too many victories weaken you. That the defeated can rise up stronger than the victor.

But I take nothing away from George. He can still beat any man in the world.

Except me.

JACKIE ROBINSON: A LIFE REMEMBERED

by Maury Allen, Franklin Watts Publishers, New York, N.Y., 1987

In 1947, Jackie Robinson—talented athlete, bona fide family man, and proud black-rights advocate—made history when he broke baseball's color barrier. In his time, he was also unquestionably the most exciting player in the major leagues.

In *Jackie Robinson: A Life Remembered*, Maury Allen compiles comments made by Robinson's teammates, opposing players, and family members to draw a revealing profile of this intensely competitive, courageous, and multifaceted man.

Robinson grew up in Pasadena, California, a predominantly white, middle-class community. After graduating from high school, the hyperactive young athlete attended Pasadena Junior College, then UCLA, starring at both institutions in football, baseball, basketball, and track. While at UCLA, he met his wife, Rachel Isum. She remembers how he immediately stood out in her mind, more for his character than for his athletic skills: "Jack was never ashamed of being black. In fact, he did something few blacks ever did. He always wore a white shirt. It showed off his dark skin."

After serving a stint in the Army, Jackie signed a contract with the Kansas City Monarchs of the Negro Leagues—in 1945, the only place a black athlete could go to play professional baseball. Fatefully, that same year, Branch Rickey, the operating head of the National League's Brooklyn Dodgers, told a few close associates that he'd decided to sign a black player for his team.

Rickey sent scouts out to look over the Negro Leagues and see what they had to offer. One of these Dodger scouts, Clyde Sukeforth, recalls that they were told to look for someone with more than just playing ability: "[Rickey] wanted a player who could turn the other cheek and fight back by exceptional play . . . keep his mouth shut, and [help] Brooklyn win . . . "

Rickey quickly became interested in Robinson. "There was something about the fellow that impressed me as his being somebody special," Sukeforth recalls. "Determination was written all over his face. This wasn't a young man who would be pushed around. It wasn't hard to tell he was a highly intelligent man."

Robinson played out the 1946 season with the Dodgers' top farm club, the Montreal Royals, leading the league in batting and winning the Royals their pennant. Though he was a fan favorite in Montreal, Jackie had to endure the segregation laws of the American South during spring training, staying in a different hotel from his teammates.

Then, in 1947, came a pivotal point in baseball history: Robinson moved up to the majors. A few of his fellow Dodgers, mostly Southerners, strongly opposed playing alongside a black man; one even went so far as to circulate an anti-Robinson petition. Other Dodger players, however, especially team captain Pee Wee Reese, went out of their way to make Robinson feel welcome.

In any case, Jackie's hitting and base-stealing abilities quickly convinced the whole team of his value. "Salaries weren't all that big in those days, and I wasn't going to make a big fuss over what color a player was if he was helping me win," remarked an appreciative teammate.

In those days, there were few blacks living in the middle-class Brooklyn neighborhoods of most Dodger fans; but stadium-goers flocked to Ebbets Field to see him play: *Into [our] narrow, traditional, segregated world . . . came the black face of Jackie Robinson. For many of us in 1947, it was the first black person we recognized by name . . .*

And the fans were not disappointed. Robinson was an electric player on the ball diamond, combining an intense will to win with tremendous natural ability. *He never stood still at third [base] . . . He bounced around . . . He made full runs toward home, just stopping at some perfect time so he could return without being caught.* "When he got caught in a rundown," remembers former catcher Joe Garagiola, "he'd have everybody in the park involved, including the vendors."

Still, the racial constraints of the time took their toll. "Those early days were awfully tough on Jackie," reflects one teammate. "I remember times on the train when nobody would sit with him or talk with him. Pee Wee always seemed to be the first to break the tension . . . " He received anonymous death threats; in Atlanta, the Ku Klux Klan picketed his hotel. "He was staying in those rat traps in the colored section while we were out in those fancy hotels, and that galled him . . . You could see him seething when the guys complained how slow the room service was or how the porters lost a bag . . . He would just take out that anger on the opposition."

Wherever he went, loudmouths, in an effort to distract him, shouted racial insults from the stands. It wasn't easy for Robinson to ignore these slurs. As another teammate recalls, he "was a combative person by nature and that restraint went against his personality. He had to hold a lot in, and it angered him terribly. Holding that much anger can really hurt a man, and I think all that name-calling in those years killed him. I really do think that."

In 1947 the Dodgers won the National League pennant, and faced the Yankees in the World Series—losing in seven games. Jackie didn't hit well in the series, but he did steal three bases. For his amazing rookie season, Robinson was awarded the National League Rookie-of-the-Year award.

More black players soon joined Robinson in the major-league ranks. The Dodgers signed Roy Campanella and Don Newcombe, and in the American League, Larry Doby signed with the Cleveland Indians midway through the 1947 season. But Jackie was the forerunner, and he remained the symbolic civil rights "man" of the late 1950s and early 1960s.

Roy Campanella was an entirely different person from Jackie. Everybody loved "Campy," while they either worshiped Robinson or else outright hated him. As Joe Black, another pioneer black player, explains, "He didn't buddy around with everybody. The biggest thing in his life was just playing ball and being with Rachel and the children." Another teammate remembered that "Jackie demanded respect as an athlete, and everything he did on the field seemed aimed in that direction. He felt responsible, as if the whole black race rested on his shoulders."

Campanella discusses their differing styles: "In the early days we couldn't stay in the same hotels with the rest of the club, and when we did we couldn't eat in the dining rooms. Jackie was always annoyed by that. I didn't care that much. But he fought that hard, and one day he just sat down in the dining room, and that was that. He was served and nobody made a fuss over it . . . He went after things his way, and I went after them my way."

When the Dodgers played their crosstown rivals the New York Giants, headed by former Dodgers manager Leo "the Lip" Durocher, Robinson and "the Lip" would often engage in vicious verbal battles, baiting each other to take the rivalry a step farther—perhaps into fisticuffs. The two teams had always hated each other, but Durocher and Robinson seemed to carry on an especially impassioned feud. One Dodger player looks fondly back at the spats: "The best times I ever had with Jackie were just listening to Jackie fight with Leo . . . Jackie had a real sharp tongue. It was fun playing with him."

But their enmity was never personal, Durocher maintains: "Sure we had our feuds, because he wanted to win and I wanted to win . . . I agitated him a little, and he agitated me back."

Still in 1951, after Bobby Thomson hit the famous home run to win the pennant for the Giants, Robinson approached Durocher after the game and congratulated him. "That was one of the hardest things any man ever had to do, and I really appreciated that," said Durocher later. "Jackie Robinson had class. He was some man."

As he had at UCLA and everywhere else he'd played, Robinson gradually assumed a leadership role on the team. In 1949, he won the National League MVP award. That same year the Dodgers went to the World Series again—and they would go on to five more Series during Robinson's playing career. They finally won the Series in 1955, when they beat the New York Yankees.

That time, Robinson, who'd entered the major leagues at the ripe-old age of 28, had begun to slow down, losing his fearsome quickness and speed. "Jack couldn't run the way he could earlier, but he was still some competitor," a young up-and-coming player reported. "[He] should have been the first black manager . . . When I think of Jackie now, I think of him as a great player and a great man, but also as somebody who was so competitive, so intense. Jackie

was like a great fighter getting ready for the heavyweight championship of the world before every game."

Robinson was a hero and a role model to young black Americans. He constantly sought out ways to use his fame as a tool to influence and inspire black youth. As a boy, future home-run king Hank Aaron was living in Mobile, Alabama, when Robinson paid a visit: "He was dressed in suit and tie and talked to us on the street in front of the drugstore. The kids just gathered around him and listened . . . He kept repeating, 'Stay in school, stay in school.' He stressed how important that was, and he said we all couldn't play in the big leagues, but we all could get a better education and make something of ourselves."

When he was traded to the Giants' organization in 1957, Robinson, 38, decided to retire from baseball. In ten seasons he had accumulated a batting average of .311 and broken Ty Cobb's base-stealing record. His final career hit had won game six of the 1956 World Series for the Dodgers and had proved to be his last performance in a baseball uniform. "Jack's knees were bothering him a great deal by then," remembers his wife Rachel. "He was also losing interest in baseball . . . He wanted to move on to other pursuits. He wanted to get involved in things that were now more important to him than baseball."

In 1959, Robinson took a job as personnel director for a restaurant and began writing a column for the *New York Post*. He spoke out on politics—especially on racial issues—and was involved in the civil-rights movements of the 60's. He also lobbied baseball to start hiring blacks in executive positions. By then there were many black players—in both leagues and on every major-league team—but still no black managers or black executives.

In his first year of eligibility, 1962, Robinson was inducted into the Baseball Hall of Fame. As the '60s moved into the '70s, however, his name and fame faded from the limelight. He worked and raised his family, while still making occasional personal appearances and speaking engagements. When his son, Jackie Robinson, Jr., died in a car accident in 1971, Robinson made a rare appearance on television to express his grief. Viewers were shocked; suffering from diabetes, their old hero now looked weathered and fragile. With his health steadily deteriorating, Robinson's final year was a difficult one.

Upon her husband's death in 1972, Rachel Robinson asked a young minister named Jesse Jackson to render the eulogy. Jackson lauded Robinson as a dynamic, chivalrous man and commended his dramatic pioneering role in securing for blacks the rights they deserved as Americans and as human beings. Then he ended his sermon with these words: *When Jackie took the field, something reminded us of our birthright to be free . . . He was the black knight. He was checking the king's bigotry and the queen's indifference. His body, his mind, his mission can not be held down by a grave.*

BABE: THE LEGEND COMES TO LIFE

by Robert W. Creamer, Simon and Schuster, New York, N.Y., 1974

Babe Ruth was the first American super-star, baseball's greatest and most beloved player, bigger in his time than any movie heartthrob or political hero. In *Babe: The Legend Comes to Life,* Robert W. Creamer, who as a boy watched the slugger play in Yankee Stadium, draws on interviews with Ruth's friends, teammates, rival ballplayers, and acquaintances to "produce a total biography, one that . . . would present all the facts and myths . . . the obvious and subtle things" that made Babe Ruth "a unique figure in the social history of the United States."

George Herman Ruth, born in Baltimore, Maryland to George and Katherine Ruth, always celebrated February 7th, 1894 as his birthday. His original birth certificate lists a later date, but as Ruth once observed with characteristic bluntness, "What the hell difference does it make?"

With both parents working outside the home, young Ruth habitually avoided school, "roamed the streets," and stole from his parents. *"Looking back on my boyhood," he wrote in his autobiography, "I honestly don't remember being aware of the difference between right and wrong." As a grown man . . . that carefree attitude toward moral and social codes remained . . . In the words of sportswriter John Drebinger, "He was the most uninhibited human being I have ever known. He just did things."*

Ruth's father eventually sent his recalcitrant son to St. Mary's Industrial School for Boys, where he would go on to spend the better part of his developmental years. The boys at St. Mary's attended classes, performed house chores, and, as part of their regular exercise regimen, played baseball. Ruth, playing as catcher, soon became the school's star player.

The prefect of discipline at St. Mary's was Brother Matthias, a giant of a man, six-and-a-half feet tall, whom Ruth later called "The greatest man I've ever known." Matthias started Ruth pitching, and it was as a pitcher that the young man attracted the attention of Jack Dunn, a baseball scout and owner of the minor league Baltimore Orioles, who signed him to a $600 contract for the 1914 season. "You'll make it, George," said Brother Matthias as Ruth walked away forever from Saint Mary's.

At spring training in North Carolina, Ruth impressed the professionals with both his pitching and his hitting. In a practice game—his first with other professional ballplayers—he pummeled a towering homer that, as an eyewitness reported, "will live in the memory of all who saw it." It was a taste of things to come.

The youthful and exuberant Ruth amused the older Oriole players, who began calling him "Dunn's Babe," in reference to his boyish behavior. It was with the Orioles that Ruth traveled outside Baltimore for the first time. Everything was new to him—eating in restaurants, traveling by train, staying in hotels, even the hotel elevators. Dunn kept boosting Ruth's salary, eventually to $1800 a season, and for the first time in his life, Ruth had spending money in his pocket.

The Orioles quickly rose to first place in their league. But attendance was low and Jack Dunn was losing money. One by one he sold off his players. Babe finally went to Joseph Lannin, owner of the major-league Boston Red Sox.

The Babe played little for the Red Sox in 1914; Sox skipper Bill Carrigan sent him down to the minors for most of the year. But life was not uneventful: it was during this time that Ruth met and married his first wife, Helen. *What a difference a year had made in his life . . . Months before he had [been] dirt poor, untraveled, totally unsophisticated. Now, at twenty-one, he was a successful professional athlete . . . He was rich . . . He was married . . .*

The next year Ruth became a starting pitcher for the Red Sox. He also hit four home runs, a remarkable feat for a pitcher—although, interestingly, at the time home runs were not routinely celebrated. *But there were signs . . . that the Ruthian home run was going to change things.* The ease with which Ruth hit his homers—and the length that he hit them—made them unforgettable to baseball fans.

Meanwhile, Lannin had raised Ruth's salary to $3500. Now Babe really took to the nightlife in the big cities where the team played. He was often seen driving down Broadway in New York in a "low-slung convertible, wearing a coonskin coat . . . " Carrigan later explained, "You have to remember, he had grown up in that Catholic reformatory. When they let him out it was like turning a wild animal out of a cage."

The Red Sox won the pennant and the World Series in 1915, and Ruth was an important part of the team's success. Boston won the series again in 1916 and 1918, seasons in which Babe was rated as the best left-handed pitcher in baseball. But even at this point the controversial ballplayer had a habit of not remembering the names of even those teammates he'd known for years.

Increasingly, it was Ruth's hitting, specifically, his home runs, that fans flocked to the parks to see. He hammered out 11 home runs in 1918, while still a pitcher, and the Red Sox, one of the weakest-hitting teams in baseball, began to play Ruth in the outfield or at first base when he wasn't on the mound.

During the 1919 season, the Red Sox moved Ruth permanently to the outfield. That year, he set his first home-run mark, smacking 29 "dingers" to break all previous major-league records—at the time seen as the ultimate accomplishment, even for him. But he would eventually more than double that mark.

After the 1919 season, the Red Sox, strapped for cash, sold Ruth to the New York Yankees. "I figure the Red Sox is ruined," one disgusted fan hissed. But Harry Frazee, the new Red Sox owner, claimed the trade would help the team: He was tired of Ruth's all-night partying and his tendency to get into fights with umpires, managers, and coaches. "While Ruth is undoubtedly the greatest hitter the game has ever seen," commented Frazee, "he is likewise one of the most selfish and inconsiderate men ever to put on a baseball uniform."

Ruth was also one of the most eccentric men who ever donned a baseball uniform. Once before a game, he offered an onion to a stranger as a cure for the man's cold; during a heat wave, he wore cabbage leaves under his ball cap to keep cool. But without Babe, Frazee's Red Sox suffered through almost a decade in last place, while the Yankees, flaunting the Home-Run King, were on the threshold of arguably the greatest dynasty in baseball history.

In his first two seasons as a Yankee, the swaggering Babe had the two best seasons in batting history. In the process, he launched—besides baseballs—a revolution. *The game changed more between 1917 and 1921 than it did in the next forty years.*

Up until Ruth's time, homers were rare, scores were low, and pitching dominated the game. A batter was expected to protect the plate and "punch out singles." But free-swinging Ruth, unafraid of striking out, broke the game wide open, slamming 54 homers in 1920 and putting 59 balls over the fences in 1921. "I swing big, with everything I've got," he expounded. "I hit big or I miss big. I like to live as big as I can."

Other players soon copied Babe's big swing, and home runs, along with scores, shot up throughout the majors. As fans flocked to the ballparks, the Yankees became the first club to draw more than a million in one season.

New Yorkers especially loved this larger-than-life character; the city's Italian immigrant population even christened him "Bambino." *And Ruth was made for New York.* Teammate Lee Allen remembered him as "a large man in a camel's hair coat and camel's hair cap, standing in front of a hotel, his broad nostrils sniffing at the promise of the night." On the road, Babe's room-mate, Ping Bodie, only saw him on the field, and ended up carrying Ruth's luggage on and off the train. "I don't room with him," Bodie once told a reporter, "I room with his suitcase."

Ruth's play was sub-par in 1922, brilliant in '23 and '24, and again turned sour—at least for his standards—in 1925. That season, after going to three straight World Series, the Yankees fell to seventh place. Babe's attitude was no help. His open contempt for Yankee manager Miller Huggins, whom he called "The Flea," infected other players, and Huggins lost control of the team.

At one point in the season, the over-weight Bambino had to be transported to the hospital with an intestinal abscess—dubbed by reporters as "the bellyache heard round the world." By then most writers prophesied that he would never return to his previous dominance. But the Babe had some of his greatest seasons ahead of him. *From the ashes of 1925, Babe Ruth rose like a rocket. In the next five years he put on the finest display of hitting that baseball has ever seen . . . 50 home runs a year [and] more than 400 yet to come . . .*

Ruth's team mirrored its slugger's success, winning three straight pennants. The '27 Yankees, considered by many to be the greatest baseball squad of all time, won 110 games. Ruth hit 60 homers that year, breaking his old record, and Lou Gehrig, his teammate, hit a whopping 47. Hitting three homers in the '28 series *was the apex of Ruth's career, the happiest moment of three years of great accomplishment and relative serenity. His life would never be as uncomplicated again . . .*

In 1929, Babe's wife Helen perished in a fire. Although they had been separated for three years, her death saddened him. But then Ruth met the love of his life: a widow named Claire Hodgson, whom he soon married. In 1931, Babe signed a two-year contract with the Yankees for an annual salary of $80,000. When someone mentioned that he was by far the highest-paid player in baseball, raking in even more earnings than President Herbert Hoover, the story has it that he replied, "Why not? I had a better year than he did."

In 1932, the "Sultan of Swat" began slow-ing down. *More and more he left the game in the late innings and let young Sammy Byrd or Myril Hoag finish up for him.* Still, the Yankees went on to another World Series—Babe's tenth.

It was in the third game of the 1932 series that Ruth hit the famous "Called-Shot" homer. Jeered by the opposing team and their fans, Babe, according to legend, pointed to the spot deep in the center-field bleachers where he would send the ball. He challenged the Cubs before 50,000 people—and went out and hit the home run.

In spite of his diminishing skills, Ruth con-tinued to play, partly because he had it in the back of his mind to manage the Yankees, or per-haps another club. But none of the major league owners would hire him. They saw him as a self-ish, undisciplined player who lacked the smarts to manage a team. "Could he have managed?" Creamer asks. *Of course . . . He was baseball smart, he was sure of himself, he was held in awe by his fel-low players and he was undeniably good copy. He may not have been a success . . . but he should have been given the chance.*

Babe finally retired. During his last years he played a fierce game of golf and traveled all over the world. In 1948, he returned to Yankee Stadium for the park's 25th anniversary. Thin, frail, and wasted from the cancer that would soon kill him, he donned his uniform and cap for the last time. One by one, his '23 Yankee teammates were introduced and walked out to applause from the stands. Then came Ruth's name: *He got to his feet . . . and took a bat to use as a cane . . . His name rang out over the public address system, the roar of the crowd began and, as W.C. Heinz wrote, "He walked out into the cauldron of sound he must have known better than any other man."*

Eight weeks later, on August 16, 1948, he died.

JIM THORPE: THE WORLD'S GREATEST ATHLETE

(published in 1975 under the title *Pathway to Glory*)
by Robert W. Wheeler, University of Oklahoma Press, Norman, Oklahoma, 1978

At the 1912 Olympic Games in Stockholm, the King of Sweden proclaimed Native American Jim Thorpe as "the greatest athlete in the world." One year later, Thorpe was forced to give up his Olympic gold medals in a scandal that changed the course of his life. With this warmly appreciative biography, Robert Wheeler convincingly pleads for Thorpe's exoneration, and for his reinstatement, 62 years later, as a "man of unbounded good nature combined with unlimited courage and determination . . ."

Born in 1888 on the Oklahoma prairie into the Sac and Fox tribes, the future athlete was named Wa-tho-huck, or "Bright Path" by his mother, Charlotte View, but he soon became known simply as Jim. He and his twin brother Charlie enjoyed an active childhood: *Our lives were lived in the open, winter and summer. We were never in the house when we could be out of it . . . I was always of a restless disposition and never was content unless I was trying my skill in some game against my fellow playmates . . .*

Jim's father, Hiram P. Thorpe, was in his own right a revered wrestler and track star. Not only did he teach his sons how to strengthen their bodies, he also counseled them to compete fairly. As one of Jim's childhood friends notes: *He made our Indian people known by his good sportsmanship . . .*

Jim's childhood, however, was marred by tragedy. First his brother Charlie died of pneumonia when the boys were eight; then several years later, while attending a military school for Indian youth, Jim learned that his father had been injured in a hunting accident and was near death. Immediately the boy set out for home on foot—covering a total of 270 miles in only two weeks. His father eventually recovered, but a few months later, Jim's mother died unexpectedly.

After a brief stint on a Texas ranch, Jim returned home to help his father with the farm and attended a nearby public school. In 1904, when he was sixteen, he was invited to attend the Carlisle Indian College on an athletic scholarship. Mr. Thorpe urged his son to accept. "Son, you are an Indian," he said. "I want you to show other races what an Indian can do."

At Carlisle Jim was coached by Glenn S. "Pop" Warner, the most innovative football genius of his time. Even as Jim's recruiter, Warner was amazed when he finally saw the full range of Jim's athletic prowess. One day while watching Jim practice the high jump, Warner exclaimed, "You've just broken the school record! That bar was set at five feet nine inches!"

Coach Warner was initially reticent to let Jim play varsity football because of his slender frame. But Jim pestered him until he agreed to play the fledgling in a few games during the 1907 season. By 1908, a seasoned Thorpe had made his presence spectacularly known—running for five touchdowns in one of the first games. In another game Jim was sidelined until the last few minutes. When Warner finally put him in, the young fullback immediately scored a touchdown in what one observer called "the single most dramatic play I have ever seen in sports": *Jim took the very first hand-off and blasted into the line with [a thunderous] crash . . . When he was able to continue into their backfield, I couldn't believe my eyes! He didn't use one block on his way to the goal line seventy yards away, while all the time he kept hollering, "Out of my way! Get out of my way!"*

Later in the season, the Carlisle "Indians" played against national champion Pennsylvania in what Thorpe later said was "the toughest game in my twenty-two years of college and professional football." After scoring Carlisle's only touchdown and kicking the extra point to preserve a 6-6 tie, Thorpe was named a third-team All-American. He was also a standout on the Carlisle track team, where he took first place in six out of seven events in one meet, generating the legend that he "single-handedly" defeated Lafayette College.

After the track season, Thorpe was leaving for a summer farm job when he ran into some friends at the train station. *A couple of Carlisle ballplayers . . . were going to North Carolina . . . to play baseball. I didn't enjoy farming, so I tagged along . . . The manager [at Rocky Mount] offered me fifteen dollars a week to play third base; I took it . . .*

Jim played for two seasons (1909-10) before the baseball league folded. Afterward, he drifted aimlessly around Oklahoma. Both his parents were now dead, and in his melancholy he jumped at the chance to return to the Carlisle football team for the 1911 season. He came back greater than ever, leading Carlisle to an 11-1 record. At season's end, Walter Camp named him a first-team All-American. Coach Warner was even more impressed: *[Jim] knew everything a football player could be taught and . . . could execute the play better than the coach ever dreamed of . . . He is the same way in all sports, always watching for a new motion which will benefit him. Then Thorpe has the marvelous concentrative power which he puts into every move he makes. It is a splendid sight to see him hurl a football thirty yards . . . with merely an abrupt snap of the wrist, direct to the hands of the receiver . . .*

Thorpe's long touchdown runs and accurate field-goal kicking soon brought him nationwide attention. Huge crowds began to come out to see him play and sportswriters praised him heartily as "the most versatile athlete ever."

Probably Thorpe's greatest moment came in 1912, when he traveled to Sweden to represent his country in the fifth Olympiad. To everyone's surprise, he won gold medals in both the decathlon and the pentathlon, taking first place in four of the five pentathlon events.

One American team official said: "It answers the allegation that most of our runners are of foreign parentage, for Thorpe is a real American, if there ever was one."

Thorpe's performance in the 110-meter hurdles for the decathlon—15.6 seconds—is truly amazing when compared with the 15.7-second time that won the individual event thirty-six years later. . . . *Improved diets, training procedures, hurdling techniques, and equipment had not been able to break track's longest-standing record.*

Following the Olympics, Thorpe played a final winning season at Carlisle and was again selected as a first team All-American. Pete Calac, one of Thorpe's teammates, recalled: *. . . He was the best. He was good at everything he attempted . . . [But he] never acted like he was better than any of us . . . He always tried to be just one of the guys.*

In 1913, reports came out that Thorpe had played minor league professional baseball three years earlier. The Amateur Athletic Union demanded an explanation. Hiding nothing, Thorpe wrote a letter to AAU president James E. Sullivan, readily admitting that he had been paid to play baseball, and adding: *I did not play for the money . . . but because I liked to play ball . . . I received offers amounting to thousands of dollars since my victories last summer, but I have turned them all down . . .*

The AAU, however, stripped Thorpe of his medals and divested him of his amateur status. The press was sympathetic. Sportswriter Damon Runyon mourned that "none of his marvelous records will stand. They will be wiped out completely . . . although it is rather doubtful if this . . . will remove them from the memory of the people who follow athletic events." And editorials across the country attacked the AAU: *AAU officials think nothing of taking money for their services as managers of athletic meets . . . still these men . . . are so "pure" that they cannot be approached.* Nonetheless, Thorpe only issued a single statement: "I must have time to consider my future plans."

Despite a bevy of lucrative offers from Vaudeville promoters who wanted to cash in on his fame, Thorpe finally signed to play professional baseball with the New York Giants in 1913. He earned much less than the promoters had offered him.

From the beginning, the Giants' domineering manager John McGraw clashed with the quiet Thorpe. Finally, in 1919, Thorpe was released by McGraw on the pretext that he couldn't hit a curve ball. In response, Thorpe said: "I hit .327 my last year in the National League; I must have hit a few curves." He went on to play nine more years in the minor leagues, then, in 1928, at the age of forty, he quit professional baseball.

Throughout the years Thorpe played for the Giants, he also played for football's semi-professional Canton Bulldogs, joining the team every fall at the end of baseball season. And in 1920, he had been named as president of the newly formed American Professional Football Association—the precursor of today's NFL—which he had helped to organize.

Thorpe's stamina continued to amaze his contemporaries. Walter Lingo, owner of the Oorang Indians, yet another team for which Thorpe played, revealed: *One of the secrets of his great lasting powers is the fact that he never quits training. Playing baseball in the summer, football in the fall, and [spending] the intervening months hunting, his body is in the pink of physical condition at all times . . . He is the real fighting type of man when occasion demands, but at all other times is both gentle and kind . . . His greatest virtue is his love of honesty and his hatred of untruthfulness or deception.*

After retiring from football in 1929, the 44-year-old Thorpe supported himself by working at odd jobs through the Great Depression, sometimes for only fifty cents an hour.

Then in 1938, a group of football greats published their picks for an "All-Time" All-American Team—and every one of them selected Jim Thorpe for his own team. As the only player so honored, Thorpe was hired to go on a cross-country lecture tour. In all his lectures, he pled the cause of his fellow Native Americans: *Indians, you know, are misnamed. We aren't Indians. We are Red Men and we settled this country long before the white people ever came to these shores . . . There were 30,000 Indian volunteers in the last war. They fought for this country. Many gave their lives for its people and its resources. In return, the Indians should be granted full citizenship with all the rights and privileges that go with it . . .*

The great Native American athlete believed that his fame could be used to help expose the "Red Man's" plight. He kept a copy of a newspaper article which, he felt, "placed the final, and most misunderstood, years of his life into proper perspective." *Pity the poor Indian?* it began. *Not Jim Thorpe! . . . One glance is enough to convince me that Thorpe is not a descendant of the Red Men who were rooked out of Manhattan Island . . .*

In 1950, two Associated Press polls voted Thorpe the greatest football player and greatest male athlete of the half-century. Thorpe, meanwhile, kept himself busy promoting a young pro-wrestler, advising Warner Brothers on the film *Jim Thorpe—All-American,* and "heading an all-Indian song and dance troupe," the Jim Thorpe Show.

In 1953, at the age of sixty-five, Thorpe died suddenly of a heart attack. Remembering the influence his own father had had on his life, Jim would have been especially proud of the eulogy offered by his daughter Grace: *[My father] had an enormous amount of personal integrity and never uttered a bad word about anyone . . . His posture was always erect and his manner mild. He exuded manliness and warmth.*

Jim Thorpe's life had thus left an unparalleled legacy not only in the world of sport, but in the hearts of his friends and family, where, for him, it counted even more.

HIGHER THAN HOPE

The Authorized Biography of Nelson Mandela
by Fatima Meer, Harper and Row, New York, N.Y., 1990

Fatima's Meer's biography *Higher than Hope* documents the remarkable life of South Africa's Nelson Mandela. Accused with Mandela in the 1956 treason trial, Meer was active in the organized resistance campaign of the African National Congress.

Although she was banned from her native South Africa in 1954, in 1976, and in 1981—when she and Winnie Mandela were imprisoned for five months awaiting trial—Meer subsequently returned. A professor of sociology in Durban, Meer wrote *Higher than Hope* at the Mandelas' urging. According to Winnie Mandela, "There was no better person to write such a narrative than Fatima Meer," who, through years of conversations and correspondence with Mandela, knows the man well.

❖ ♦ ❖

Nelson Mandela was born in 1918 in Qunu, South Africa. As his younger sister Nomabandla recalls: *Our father [Hendry Mphakanyoswa Gadla] was a chief but was subsequently deposed for insubordination. He rode a horse and he had enough cattle to marry four wives. Our mother, Nosenki Fanny, was of the Right-hand House and was his third wife . . .* A "devout Christian," Nelson's mother worried about the future of her son, "Buti," as he was then called, and after consulting with her husband, the boy was sent to the village of Mqekezweni, where he would get an education. Nelson lived with the village chief, his father's uncle, who adopted the ten-year-old after the death of his father.

Of the many chiefs who visited Mqekezweni, Chief Zwelibhangile Joyi was the oldest, "shriveled and bent and so black that he was blue." Nelson delighted in Tatu Joyi's knowledge of African history: *Tatu Joyi said that the white people divided brother from brother, and split the people of Ngangelizwe into pieces and destroyed them . . . A chief puts land beneath the feet of his people. Queen Victoria took away the land of the Thembu and put them into locations and put strange tribes between them, so that they would kill each other and remain forever weak against the white people.*

Nelson later researched Tatu Joyi's detailed accounts of the white man's arrival in South Africa when he studied at Fort Hare University. Indeed, Nelson confirmed that the whites had used gunfire and other forms of intimidation to suppress the African kings' *ubuntu* (humanity) and to establish their tyranny. . . . *Nelson, tutored at Tatu Joyi's feet, was fired to regain that ubuntu for all South Africans.*

Expelled from Fort Hare in 1941 for persisting in his "fanatical" studies, Nelson and his brother Justice moved to the sprawling city of Johannesburg. "They had come to South Africa's industrial heart," Meer writes, " . . . so they could begin to understand their own place and destiny in their motherland." But within days, Justice returned to live with Jongintaba, leaving Nelson, alone, to pursue an education.

Nelson became acquainted with Walter Sisulu, a young estate agent who would become Secretary General of the African National Congress (ANC). Walter gradually drew Nelson into the world of Johannesburg politics. While completing his B.A., attending law school, and marrying Walter's cousin Evelyn, Nelson became a leader in the ANC Youth League, an organization established to awaken popular political consciousness and fight oppression.

When ANC Youth League President Anton Lembede died in 1949, Nelson, as League Secretary, was catapulted into a more prominent role in the organization. Subsequently, the African National Congress adopted the Youth League's plan to protest against the Nationalist Government, and together they joined South Africa's oppressed Indian population to launch a national work-stoppage. However, the day ended tragically; 19 blacks and Indians were killed by police and thirty others were injured.

At Nelson's direction, the ANC called for a massive National Day of Protest in response to the killings. Rallies were held throughout the country; organized groups of Africans and Indians defied ordinances they deemed unjust. But when Walter Sisulu and others were jailed and Nelson was "jerked out of bed" in a first of many pre-dawn raids on ANC leaders, the demonstration was quashed.

Taking charge as president of the Youth League in 1951, Nelson thereafter replaced the exiled J.B. Marks as president of the Transvaal ANC. Now as he worked consistently to liberate his people, Nelson was often separated from his family.

The ANC's Defiance Campaign grew quickly and the South African government became desperate. *Realizing that the power of the Campaign and its international support lay in its non-violence, [the government] acted to slander [the campaign] with violence.* Although the government permitted the ANC to hold a mass prayer meeting in East London in October of 1952, within minutes the military moved in and "turned the peaceful gathering into a bloodbath." Committed to non-violence, and not knowing how to cope with such attacks, the ANC weakened. The government, meanwhile, outlawed any form of passive resistance and, by 1957, the campaign was all but lost.

Now forbidden to speak in public, Mandela was forced to change his tactics: he organized a "grassroots" effort relying on trade unions and covert operations. With more time on his hands, Mandela also studied for and passed his law exams, after which he opened an office at Chancellor House.

By now the Nationalists were at their strongest: . . . *Their tyranny appeared invincible. They passed laws . . . that deprived African, Indian and Coloured people of their homes and land;* the European-based African Education Movement went so far as to decree that there was "no place [for the] 'native'" in the South African literati. In response, Nelson Mandela called for the ANC to develop its own school system, announced a boycott of all public schools, and enlisted 1000 volunteer teachers for the ANC system. The government countered by declaring all "unregistered" schools illegal, before forcibly closing down the classes. Ultimately, Mandela conceded to government pressure, reasoning that some form of education was preferable to none at all.

Mandela's life was now so hectic that he was rarely at home. Consequently, he and Evelyn began divorce proceedings—and although he worried about the effect it would have on his children, he was able to console them. Just weeks later Mandela was arrested along with 155 other participants of the Congress of the People, an interracial alliance of South Africans who sought political freedom for all fellow countrymen. While much of the resistance movement became embroiled in the trial, the Ovamboland People's Congress—which would later become the South West African People's Organization (SWAPO), an ANC ally—was formed in Capetown in 1957. That year also marked the split within the ANC along racial lines, as black members accused certain white factions of emphasizing class conflict without regard to race.

Soon after Mandela was released from the Fort Prison on bail, he met Winnie Madikizela, and "wooed her in his own way within the confines of his banning order and in between his daily attendance at the Treason Trial." When his divorce from Evelyn was finalized in June of 1958, Nelson married Winnie.

Five years after the treason trial had begun, the court finally dismissed all charges and *Nelson was released from a stranglehold that had cost him his practice and seriously jeopardized his freedom to work for his people.* Although there were wild demonstrations of joy outside the courtroom, Nelson Mandela knew that his people were not winning the larger battle: *The Nationalists were . . . converting the traditional chiefs from patrons and guardians of the people into lackeys of the oppressor . . . African tenant farmers were expelled from white farms . . . pushed into already overcrowded reserves . . . forced to sell whatever livestock they possessed . . .*

Subsequently on March 26, 1960 in Sharpeville, South Africa, the police gunned down sixty-nine protestors and injured 180. As a result, 95 percent of the workforce went on strike; 30,000 marched on Caledon Square; a state of emergency was declared, both the ANC and PAC were banned, and thousands were temporarily detained by police. In response to the government's use of violence, Mandela and other ANC members set up Umkhonto we Sizwe, a clandestine organization that would force change through acts of sabotage against South African military installations.

In 1962, Mandela met with Ethiopia's Emperor Haile Selassie and the Commander-in-Chief of Algeria's Army of National Liberation in order to undergo military training in those countries. On his return to South Africa, he was arrested and subsequently sentenced to five years in prison for incitement to strike and for traveling without a passport. Thus Mandela was again brought to trial, along with Walter Sisulu and others of the High Command, charged with sabotage and attempting to overthrow the state. Winnie was permitted to attend what came to be known as the "Rivonia Trial"—"providing she did not dress or behave in a manner to cause 'incidents'." Mandela and all except two of his fellow ANC members were summarily found guilty of sabotage and sentenced to life imprisonment.

With Mandela out of the picture, *the ANC almost disappeared from the articulated consciousness of the country; a new generation of blacks grew into the Black Consciousness and confronted white tyranny with surly anger.* Winnie joined this movement, a choice that brought her frequent imprisonment and torture—as well as a citation as "Woman of the Year" from the British.

In 1976 the country experienced violence from which it has not yet recovered. That previous year the government had introduced Afrikaans (a derivative dialect of the early Dutch settlers) into the secondary schools as its state language—a tongue that African teachers could barely teach and pupils could barely understand. And in response to a simple Soweto student protest rally, police opened fire on children. *Overnight the children became defenders of their people against the government.* Clearly, the year 1976 paved the way for a sharpening of the military confrontation between apartheid and its opposition.

The South African government meted out a brutal revenge, swooping down on Black Consciousness groups and outlawing all such organizations. Winnie was not only again publicly scorned, but was banished from Soweto, where her circle of influence had been growing. *The one name that resounded above all others was that of Mandela. . . . Mandela came . . . to be celebrated internationally as the human symbol of freedom and human resistance against tyranny.*

The early and mid-1980s were marked by international pressure for South African reform. In January 1985, the Rivonia men were offered their release by the Nationalist State President P.W. Botha. Nelson's response was read at the Jabulani Stadium in Soweto on 10 February, 1985, where over 10,000 people had gathered. Mandela gave an unequivocal answer to Botha's offer: *Let him renounce violence. Let him say that he will dismantle apartheid. Let him unban the people's organization, the African National Congress . . . free all who have been imprisoned, banished or exiled . . . I cannot sell my birthright, nor am I prepared to sell the birthright of the people to be free.*

In December of 1988, the state announced that Mr. Mandela had been removed to a house at the Victor Verster prison, and that his family would be allowed to live with him there. But he declined to share his imprisonment with his family and refused any privileges denied his comrades in prison.

Then in July, 1989, *a government communique suddenly informed the world that Mr. Mandela had made a "courtesy call" on President Botha . . . and that the two* **leaders** *had talked for forty-five minutes . . . The government had openly referred to him as a "leader" . . . the most significant sign yet that the stronghold of Afrikaner domination was crumbling . . .*

◇ ♦ ◇

Summary Footnote:

In October, 1989, Walter Sisulu and others were freed unconditionally by new South African President F.W. deKlerk, who soon legalized the ANC. On February 11, 1990, Nelson Mandela was released from prison. He and deKlerk were awarded the Nobel Peace Prize later that year. Mandela is now serving as President of South Africa.

ALBERT SCHWEITZER, THE ENIGMA

by James Bentley, HarperCollins Publishers, New York, N.Y., 1992

In James Bentley's biography, Albert Schweitzer emerges as one of the twentieth century's most widely revered men. Schweitzer was also a man of enormous contradictions, "a man who cherished his family but spent months away from them, who despised racism but supervised a missionary hospital in which only whites held positions of power, who rejected Western civilization, but returned to it . . . " Moreover, although he worked tirelessly to promote peace and human dignity throughout the world, Schweitzer was given to periods of abject despair. On one occasion, he even revealed: *We believed once in the victory of truth . . . in our fellow men . . . in goodness, but we do not now. We trusted in the power of kindness and peaceableness; we do not now. We were capable of enthusiasm; but we are not so now.*

These bleak thoughts, however, ultimately gave way to optimism. After receiving the Nobel Peace Prize in 1953, Schweitzer told an audience, "It is my belief that one day we shall reach the point where we shall refrain from wars for moral reasons, because we feel that war is a crime against humanity."

Schweitzer was born on January 14, 1875, in the little town of Kaysersberg in Alsace, a German-speaking region of France. When Albert was one year old, the family moved to Gunsbach, where Albert's father served as a Protestant pastor. Young Albert soon became interested in religion himself and, when he was only eight, asked for his own Bible, which proved to greatly influence Schweitzer's humanistic vision. As he later recalled, "Out of the depths of my feelings of happiness there gradually arose inside me an understanding of Jesus's saying that we must not regard our lives as belonging to ourselves alone."

Albert clearly was not a typical child. Precociously, he had begun music instruction at the age of five, for example, and played the organ for Sunday Mass by the age of nine. Despite his accomplishments, however, his childhood was not particularly happy. Because his family was wealthier than others in the village, he was rejected and occasionally beaten up by his schoolmates.

Surprisingly, Albert was a poor scholar, but during this period he "found his voice." As he later recalled, "I emerged from the shell of reserve in which up till now I had hidden myself and became one who disrupted every amiable discussion."

Albert's passion for discussion, of course, proved quite advantageous when he entered the University of Strasbourg in 1893. Initially torn between his love for music and for theology, Albert ultimately decided to become a theologian. Years later he would tell a congregation: *People say that those who do theology are confronted with hard battles, because of the doubts which arise when they plunge themselves into the deep study and research of Christian doctrine and history. Such doubts and temptations have never assailed me . . . because I have been so certain of His spiritual presence.*

Indeed, Schweitzer proved to be gifted at working out intricate theological explanations which—influenced by the "inspired teachings of the brilliant theologians . . . at the University of Strasbourg"—focused his attention on psychological aspects of Jesus' life. Publishing articles which were later translated into many languages, Schweitzer's studies of Jesus soon made him famous throughout Europe.

After obtaining his degree in 1900, Schweitzer became a regular curate of the church of Saint-Nicolas in Strasbourg, where he was profoundly touched by a bust portraying a black man, sculpted at the hands of Frederic Auguste Barholdi. The sculpture's "melancholy expression" so moved Schweitzer that he began to reflect on the fate of contemporary black men and women. Consequently, he decided that when he reached the age of thirty, "he would devote himself to relieving the lot of the natives of Africa."

By 1910 Schweitzer had published his widely acclaimed *The Quest of the Historical Jesus* and had begun to establish himself as an internationally renowned scholar, but he decided it was now time to be "a simple human being, to do something small in the spirit of Jesus." Thus, he determined to fulfill his vow to provide "service to his fellow human beings" in Africa.

First, however, he moved to Paris to study tropical medicine. Schweitzer planned to become a "jungle doctor" and build his own hospital in Africa. As he explained to his congregation: *For me missionary work is essentially not a religious matter. First and foremost it is a human duty that our states and nations have never undertaken . . . This noble culture of ours speaks so piously of human dignity and the rights of man and then disregards the dignity and rights of countless millions, treading them underfoot simply because they live overseas or because their skins are of a different colour . . .*

When in February 1913 *Doctor* Schweitzer had completed his medical studies, he set about raising funds by giving recitals, and was soon able to afford a nurse and the equipment necessary for his first medical mission to Africa. *He also decided that his nurse [Helene Bresslau] ought to become his wife, or perhaps he felt obliged to marry her simply because few people, and particularly not her father, were pleased at the thought of an unmarried young woman leaving with her powerful male friend for the African jungle.* After marrying, Dr. and Mrs. Schweitzer, loaded down with books and supplies, took the train to Bordeaux and set out to sea on the steamer *Europe*. After a stormy journey, the couple reached the capital city of French Equatorial Africa. The afternoon of their arrival they went to work in a "filthy, leaking hut, till recently, used as a chicken coop."

While he slowly gained the trust of the Africans, Albert speedily charmed his fellow missionaries. Judging that his operating theatre in a former hen coop was inadequate, he designed and built a new hospital that "was oriented along the equator, so that the stifling sun never penetrated its wards." Mosquito netting and wooden shutters shielded the patients against insects.

By the end of their first nine months, the Schweitzers had treated nearly two thousand patients whose chief complaints were skin diseases, malaria, sleeping sickness, elephantiasis, heart problems, leprosy, osteomyelitis, tropical dysentery and hernias . . . " Schweitzer wrote: *From my own experience and that of other colonial doctors I can say that a single doctor . . . with the most modest equipment means very much for very many . . . who would otherwise have had to succumb to their fate in despair.*

In the summer of 1914 the World War created an "absurdly difficult" situation for the Schweitzers: *As Alsatians my wife and I were German nationals [and] since we were at war, my wife and I were regarded as enemy aliens—and treated as such.*

In September 1917, when the new French Colonial Government restricted even further the rights of German-speaking aliens, Schweitzer and his wife were sent to a prison in Bordeaux. Later they were moved to a small camp at Saint-Remy-de-Provence, a former mental hospital where, a few years earlier, Vincent van Gogh had died. By petitioning the camp director, Schweitzer was soon given permission to practice medicine in the camp.

Thus, though they grew more and more depressed, their internment became bearable. It was at this time that Helene conceived their only child, daughter Rhena. The pregnancy, however, did nothing to improve her already poor health. Finally, in July of 1918, the French government was persuaded to send them home to Strasbourg.

With Helene now suffering also from the terrible effects of tuberculosis, Schweitzer accepted an offer to return to his former positions as lecturer and preacher.

Salvation finally came from an unexpected source: Nathan Soderblom, archbishop of Uppsala, Sweden, who had read Albert's works, extended him an invitation to lecture. "His spirits were so low that he almost refused." But, exhausted and despondent, he went to Uppsala, and there he partially recovered his failing health. Soderblom also brought about the Schweitzers' financial relief by arranging for a lecture tour and the publication of Albert's life story, *On The Edge of The Primeval Forest.* Schweitzer "did not pull any punches" in the text: *We should perceive the task that needs to be done for the coloured people not as "good works" but as duty . . . not as benevolence . . . but atonement.*

In February 1924, Schweitzer wrote his *Memoirs of Childhood and Youth.* That same month, he left for Africa, leaving "the crippled Helene to care for their child." Permanently disabled as a consequence of her frequent illnesses and a skiing accident, his wife would have to experience the glory of Albert's mission vicariously, through his letters.

From this point on, he would only return to Europe for his extended fund-raising tours—and to accept numerous awards and honorary doctorates. Though he always remained a rather shy person and did not revel in publicity, he did what he had to do for the benefit of his hospital.

When he returned to West Africa in 1924, Dr. Schweitzer found his hospital in a shambles; the ravages of storms and looting had taken their toll. After designing and erecting a new hospital, which he called Lambarene, he added another forty structures which opened up space for several hundred patients. Doctors and nurses who wanted to join him in providing round-the-clock medical care poured in from all over Europe. In fact, Schweitzer's problem lay not in a lack of willing and able workers but in being able to pay their scant wages.

Often exhausted, Schweitzer considered his patients both a joy and a constant irritation: *[He] had endless problems persuading patients not to take their medicines all at once. Some of his recuperating patients would bathe, unwisely, in the filthy Ogowe River. Others inserted grubby fingers under their dressings to feel their wounds. Sometimes relatives crept inside his hospital and climbed into the patients' beds, forcing the sick to sleep on the floor.* In despair at such behaviors, he once exclaimed, "What an imbecile I am to have come to stay with these savages and devoted myself to them!" At hearing this, his black assistant Joseph replied, "Yes, doctor, on earth you are a fool, but not in heaven."

His work at the hospital had caused Schweitzer to completely neglect his marriage. The Second World War, however, proved to bring Albert and Helene back together. With the clouds of war looming over the world, the doctor traveled to Europe in 1939 to purchase a stockpile of food and drugs. While Helene subsequently accompanied him back to Africa, her poor health finally forced her to return to Europe. Helene visited her husband once more in 1957, but she died in Zurich only ten days later. Three months after her death, the 82-year-old Schweitzer brought Helene's ashes to Lambarene and buried them outside his study window.

Schweitzer would not abandon his work. Now aided by his daughter Rhena, he remained dedicated to humanity. Now, however, he was an old man. *Then on August 23, 1965, he startled his fellow workers by announcing arrangements for his death. The following Friday he walked through his orchard, saying good-bye to each individual tree.* A few days later, on September 4, 1965, Schweitzer died at the age of ninety.

Nearly a half century earlier he had delivered one of his most moving sermons: *If you study life deeply, looking perceptively into the vast and animated chaos that is creation, the profundity of it all will stun you. You will recognize yourself in everything. That tiny beetle which lies dead in your path was a living creature, struggling like you for existence, rejoicing like you in the warmth of the sun, like you knowing fear and pain. Now it is no more than decaying matter, as you too sooner or later will be.*

Later, one morning some days after Dr. Schweitzer's death, the natives sang for him, expressing their love and gratitude. One nurse remembered: "Once a native said to him, when you die we will have a tom-tom of a week to mourn you. The doctor replied, 'fortunately I won't hear it'."

THE STORY OF MY LIFE

by Helen Keller, Doubleday & Company, Garden City, New York, 1902

Have you ever been at sea in a dense fog, when it seemed as if a tangible white darkness shut you in, and the great ship, tense and anxious, groped her way toward the shore . . . and you waited with beating heart for something to happen? I was like that ship before my education began . . .

Helen Keller was born on June 27, 1880, in Tuscumbia, Alabama. For nineteen months, she lived a normal childhood, speaking her first words at six months and walking for the first time when she was one. *I am told that while I was still in long dresses I showed many signs of an eager, self-asserting disposition. Everything that I saw other people do I insisted upon imitating.*

All too soon, the happy signs of infancy ended. *One brief spring, one summer rich in fruit and roses, one autumn of gold and crimson sped by . . . Then, in the dreary month of February came the illness which closed my eyes and ears . . .* A high fever left Helen blind and deaf. Although her memories of her early life were vague, she later remembered "the agony and bewilderment with which I awoke after a tossing half sleep, and turned my eyes . . . away from the once-loved light, which came to me dim and yet more dim each day . . . Gradually I got used to the silence and darkness that surrounded me and forgot that it had ever been different . . ."

For five years Helen lived in darkness, her communication limited to "crude signs" or pantomimes. She realized that those around her didn't use signs to ask for bread or ice cream or water, but communicated by moving their mouths. *I stood between two persons who were conversing and touched their lips. I could not understand, and was vexed. I moved my lips and gesticulated frantically without result.*

As she grew older, Helen's frustration also grew. *My failures to make myself understood were invariably followed by outbursts of passion. I felt as if invisible hands were holding me, and I made frantic efforts to free myself.*

Helen's parents were willing to do anything to augment their daughter's limited life experience. When she was six they wrote to the Perkins Institution in Boston, an organization devoted to the education of the blind. In March of 1887, the Institution sent a woman named Anne Mansfield Sullivan to the Keller's home to teach Helen.

The day after she arrived, Miss Sullivan gave Helen a doll. Then, using an alphabet system in which different finger positions represented letters, she spelled "d-o-l-l" into the girl's hand. "I was at once interested in this finger play," Helen recalled, "and tried to imitate it." Although she learned to spell several words by using her hand, she did not realize that there was a connection between the "finger plays" and the actual objects they represented.

Then one day Miss Sullivan took Helen to the water pump, and while cool water splashed on the girl's outstretched palm, her teacher spelled "w-a-t-e-r" into her other hand. *[In that moment], somehow the mystery of language was revealed to me, a misty consciousness as of something forgotten—a thrill of returning thought . . . I knew then that "w-a-t-e-r" meant the wonderful cool something that was flowing over my hand . . . I left the well-house eager to learn. Everything had a name, and each name gave birth to a new thought . . .*

Once Helen learned the riddle behind language, her appetite was insatiable. *The more I handled things and learned their names and uses, the more joyous and confident grew my sense of kinship with the rest of the world.* Miss Sullivan encouraged her "to find beauty in the fragrant woods, in every blade of grass, and in the curves and dimples of my baby sister's hand . . ."

Miss Sullivan next employed a collection of words printed in raised letters to teach Helen how to read. The girl "quickly learned that each printed word stood for an object, an act, or a quality." The two of them made a game of learning about sentence structure by arranging a series of objects together with word cards to fill in the blank parts of the sentence. "Until then," Helen mused, "I had been like a foreigner speaking through an interpreter."

Throughout her life, Helen gave much of the credit for her amazing ability to process information and experience to Anne Sullivan: *It was my teacher's genius, her quick sympathy, her loving tact, which made the first years of my education so beautiful. It was because she seized the right moment to impart knowledge that made it so pleasant and acceptable to me . . . I feel that her being is inseparable from my own . . . All the best of me belongs to her—there is not a talent, or an aspiration or a joy in me that has not been awakened by her loving touch.*

On Christmas Day, 1887, Helen, who had previously understood little about the holiday, woke her family with her first signed "Merry Christmas!" In May of the following year, she took her first trip to Boston, to visit the Perkins Institution for the Blind. There she befriended many other blind children, with whom she conversed using Miss Sullivan's "manual alphabet." She walked on Bunker Hill and received her first history lesson. She even rode on an ocean-going steamboat, and touched Plymouth Rock: *As I recall that visit North I am filled with wonder . . . The treasures of a new, beautiful world were laid at my feet . . . I met many people who talked with me by spelling into my hand . . . the barren places between my mind and the minds of others blossomed like the rose.*

In 1890, Helen learned about Ragnhild Kaata, a deaf and blind girl in Norway who had learned to speak. No longer was Helen content to limit her conversations to hand-signing; she was "on fire with eagerness" to learn to speak. Another teacher, Miss Sarah Fuller, arrived to give Helen voice lessons. By feeling the position of Miss Fuller's mouth and tongue as she pronounced a word, Helen eventually managed to utter her first sentence: "It is warm." *It is an unspeakable boon to me to be able to speak in winged words that need no interpretation. As I talked, happy thoughts fluttered up out of my words that might perhaps have struggled in vain to escape my fingers.* Helen forced herself through the tremendous difficulties involved in learning to talk by constantly reminding herself, "My little sister will understand me now."

In Autumn of 1891, eleven-year-old Helen penned a little story which she titled "The Frost King." Although she didn't realize it, the story she wrote was mostly paraphrased from a story called "The Frost Fairies," which had been read to her in 1888. Her mind had retained the story's imagery, style and plot, and she later came to believe that they were her own. *I thought then that I was "making up a story," as children say, and I eagerly sat down to write it before the ideas should slip from me . . . Now, if words and images come to me without effort, it is a pretty sure sign that they are not the offspring of my own mind . . . It is certain that I cannot always distinguish my own thoughts from those I read, because what I read becomes the very substance and texture of my mind.* Eventually she even forgot that the story had been read to her. Nevertheless, some people persisted in spreading rumors that she had knowingly plagiarized the story. The accusations troubled Helen for many years: *Books lost their charm for me, and even now the thought of those dreadful days chills my heart . . . No child ever drank deeper of the cup of bitterness than I did. I had disgraced myself . . . I wept as I hope few children have wept [and] have never played with words again for the mere pleasure of the game. Indeed, I have ever since been tortured by the fear that what I write is not my own.*

In 1892, again encouraged by Miss Sullivan, Helen shook off the humiliation that had followed her first creative attempt and wrote a brief account of her life. The next year, now more confident, she traveled to Washington to attend the presidential inauguration of Grover Cleveland, and visited Niagara Falls. "I stood on the point which overhangs the American Falls," she wrote in her journal, "and felt the air vibrate and the earth tremble." The following summer she visited the World's Fair, accompanied by Dr. Alexander Graham Bell, the educator and inventor who had first advised Helen's parents to write the Perkins Institute. The exhibits at the fair—everything from industrial machines to Egyptian mummies—fascinated Helen, who was given free rein to touch anything she wished. *In the three weeks I spent at the Fair I took a long leap from the little child's interest in fairy tales and toys to the appreciation of the real and the earnest in the workaday world.*

In the Fall of 1894, after a year of attending "regular" school, Helen enrolled at Wright-Humason School for the Deaf in New York. There she studied "vocal culture" and "lip-reading," not to mention "arithmetic, physical geography, French and German." Two years later she began classes at the Cambridge School for Young Ladies and prepared to take the admittance exams at Radcliffe College, the women's college at Harvard. Attending the school was a lifelong dream: *When I was a little girl, I visited Wellesley and surprised my friends by the announcement, "Some day I shall go to college— but I shall go to Harvard!"*

With Anne Sullivan by her side interpreting the professors' words, Helen sat through lectures at the Cambridge School. She lived in a dormitory along with several seeing and hearing girls her own age, and for the first time enjoyed the full companionship of her peers.

Between 1897 and 1899, Helen took Radcliffe's admittance exams, passing the language and history subjects without difficulty. She also passed the mathematical examinations, despite complications with the braille notation. Some of the exam supervisors did not seem to appreciate the extra work it took to administer the tests to a handicapped girl. "But if they unintentionally placed obstacles in my way," Keller acknowledged, "I have the consolation of knowing that I overcame them all." She began classes at Radcliffe in 1900, determined to compete—and to succeed.

In 1902, while attending Radcliffe, Miss Keller completed *The Story of My Life*, a more complete account of her early years. It was published and became a best seller, as well as an inspiration to millions of readers worldwide.

The darkness that enshrouded Helen Keller's life at the age of two was lifted by her learning to speak and read. From the time she read her first story at age seven to the educational experiences of her adult years, Keller "devoured everything that [came] within the reach of my hungry finger tips." Reading became, of necessity, her primary past-time, her "utopia," and one of the few arenas in which she was not "disenfranchised." She went on to devote her life to improving conditions for the handicapped and fulfilling her desire that all children should enjoy the benefits of an education. She also received great joy from meeting with people and feeling the love of family and friends, among whom she counted writers Oliver Wendell Holmes and Samuel Clemens, poet John Greenleaf Whittier, and Alexander Graham Bell, some of the greatest minds of the age.

Sometimes, it is true, a sense of isolation enfolds me . . . as I sit alone . . . Beyond there is light, and music, and sweet companionship . . . So I try to make the light in others' eyes my sun, the music in others' ears my symphony, the smile on others' lips my happiness.

PATTON, THE MAN BEHIND THE LEGEND, 1885-1945

by Martin Blumenson, William Morrow and Company, New York, N.Y., 1985

A throwback to the Teutonic knight, the Saracen, the Crusader, George Patton was one of America's greatest soldiers, one of the world's great captains, writes Martin Blumenson in his biography of Patton. Blumenson, who once served in Patton's Third Army, reveals the man behind the uniform in an attempt to make the decorated general appear mortal.

George Smith Patton, Jr. was born on November 11, 1885 into a family of gentlemen and soldiers. Early in his life, young George decided to become a great military leader, following the tradition set by his ancestors, who *had displayed bravery, the highest manly quality . . . They became beacons for the future general. His kinsmen, he believed literally, watched from above, and . . . judged the actions of their descendants.*

George attended Virginia Military Institute as a teen and was later appointed to West Point. He resolved to be West Point's very best cadet, even though his dyslexia made schoolwork difficult. "I am either very lazy or very stupid or both for it is beastly hard for me to learn and as a natural result I hate to study," he wrote, expressing an "overpowering sense of [his] own worthlessness." Even though his military zeal impressed his instructors, George Patton had to repeat his first year at West Point.

Doubting his courage and wanting to test his mettle under fire, Patton soon began to perform feats of bravery that won the attention of his instructors and classmates. Patton succeeded, and the legend began, though the general would alter remark, "Naturally I am not over bold and am inclined to show emotion—a most unmilitary trait."

Perfecting "military traits" became extremely important to Patton: *All his life he honed his image, developing what he felt were the appropriate mannerisms—profanity . . . aristocratic bearing, the fierce scowl, ruthlessness. And in the process he killed much of his sensitivity and warmth and thereby turned a sweet-tempered and affectionate child into a seemingly hard-eyed and choleric adult.*

Joining the cavalry after his graduation from West Point in 1909, Patton drew both respect and scorn for publicly apologizing to an enlisted man, to whom he had said "damn you" instead of "damn it." And when his face was cut by a bucking horse, a bloodied Patton impressed his men by continuing to drill them, even as blood streamed down to his chest.

A year later, in 1910, Patton married Beatrice Ayer, a young woman from a wealthy family. Shortly thereafter, he and his wife relocated to Washington D.C., where he could be "close to those who mattered." However, it was not until 1915, when he was stationed on the Mexican border, that Patton found the chance to win the admiration of his superiors. After hostilities had broken out between Pancho Villa and American border forces, Patton, joining General John J. Pershing on an expedition into Mexico, led ten men in motorcars to the hideout of one of Pancho Villa's captains. This daring raid marked the first time that American troops had used motor vehicles in battle.

"I have at last succeeded in getting into a fight," Patton wrote to his family, which now included two daughters. Exhilarated by his own fearlessness, the officer boasted that when he first killed a man he "felt the same way he did when he hooked and landed his first swordfish, surprised by his luck."

Later, during World War I, Patton again joined Pershing, who led the American Expeditionary Force in France. Now promoted to Captain and longing for battle and personal glory, Patton quickly became an expert in the use of tanks in warfare and organized the First Light Tank Brigade. Awed by his vitality and singlemindedness, he was soon promoted to the rank of Lieutenant Colonel, and, as always, his men worshiped him.

Espousing a philosophy of "Attack . . . push forward, attack again," Patton once led his men to victory even after he had sustained a gunshot wound. Promoted to Colonel, he received the Distinguished Service Medal and the Distinguished Service Cross, and was lauded as the "Hero of the Tanks" in American newspapers.

The war's end came as a disappointment to the aggressive warrior, who would return to his peacetime rank of Captain in the Cavalry. "Peace looks possible," he wrote his wife, "but I rather hope not, for I would like to have a few more fights." Dismayed that Americans did not want to maintain a large peacetime Army, Patton was not altogether satisfied with his new life: *Although the glow of Patton's wartime achievements remained to cheer him, the interwar years for him were a time of frustration . . . Despite his external ebullience, he despaired. Was he growing too old to participate in another war adventure?*

When the United States entered World War II, Patton, who was first appointed to the rank of Colonel, then to Brigadier General, commanded an armored brigade. Conducting highly publicized war games in the Southwest to test deployment of large armored forces, he impressed George Marshall, Army Chief of Staff, and Patton was soon promoted to Major General and awarded his second star.

In 1942, leading a difficult amphibious landing in French Morocco, Patton quickly crushed Vichy French resistance and captured Casablanca. Now his hope was to confront Rommel's German troops in North Africa. But General Dwight Eisenhower, commander of the American forces, allowed the British to play the primary role in the operation against Rommel. Consequently, Patton lost respect for Eisenhower. The commander "lacked decision and a sense of reality," railed the younger Patton. What was worse, according to Patton, was that he'd gone "pro-British."

When a corps of Americans suffered a humiliating defeat at the hands of Rommel and the Germans, Patton assumed command of the corps. Its men fought so effectively in Africa under his leadership that Patton received a third star.

The rising general resumed command of his armored brigade—now called the U.S. Seventh Army—and successfully invaded Italy. Patton, of course, was elated: *In a tribute to his men, he wrote, "Soldiers of the Seventh Army: Born at sea, baptized in blood, and crowned in victory in the course of 38 days of incessant battle and unceasing labor, you have added a glorious chapter to the history of war . . . Your fame shall never die."*

But before long, Patton's jubilation turned to despair when he was reviled and publicly censured for two occasions on which he had slapped shell-shocked men. Convinced that the soldiers had simply succumbed to cowardice, Patton believed that the blows would reawaken their manhood and their sense of duty. *. . . Cowardice in the face of the enemy . . . was the ultimate dishonor. Saving an individual from that humiliation was, in Patton's view, justified and humane.*

After spending several months in disgrace, Patton was called back into service: *Eisenhower could ill afford to lose him. Yet because of his character flaws, Eisenhower would retain him as an army commander and permit him to go no higher.*

During the invasion of France, Patton was summoned to command the Third Army. Because most of his men were inexperienced in combat, however, they would not, much to Patton's chagrin, be allowed to invade the beaches; instead the Third Army would become active only after a beachhead had been established. Although disappointed, Patton prepared his soldiers to overrun the German positions.

The Third Army performed brilliantly at Normandy in 1944, and Patton once again became a national hero. However, Patton soon grew disillusioned with both Eisenhower—whom he deemed incompetent—and the British commanders. "Neither Ike or Brad has the stuff," Patton wrote in his diary. "Bradley and Hodges are such nothings." Indeed, Patton thought that if he had been placed in charge, the war would have ended much more quickly.

In 1944 and '45, Patton found himself fighting the Battle of the Bulge. The Germans had launched one last offensive, catching the allies off-guard and threatening to invade Antwerp. Patton, however, brilliantly crushed the German troops and reserved for himself a place in history. Yet he credited his troops for the victory: "To me it is a never-ending marvel what our soldiers can do . . . The people who actually did it were the younger officers and soldiers . . . Marching all night in the cold, over roads they had never seen, and nobody getting lost, and everybody getting to the place in time—it is a marvelous feat: I know of no equal to it in military history . . . I take off my hat to them."

After the Battle of the Bulge, Germany collapsed and the Allies advanced. Before the German surrender, Patton received his fourth star, becoming a full general: *Patton had . . . raised his Third Army to the level of the greatest fighting armies in history, comparable to Hannibal's, Cromwell's, Napoleon's, and Lee's.*

After the war's end in Europe, Patton, no longer in a command role, grew depressed, and asked to be transferred to the Pacific where the fighting continued. Instead, he was put in charge of a sector of Germany. It was then he realized that he was tired and old; he had lost his overriding confidence and zest. Sensing that he had finally fallen out of touch with the times, Patton mused: "Well the war is over . . . Now the horrors of peace, pacifism, and unions will have unlimited sway . . . It is hell to be old and passe and know it . . . Now all is left to do is to sit around and . . . await the undertaker and posthumous immortality."

Now in a fight against despondency, Patton left Europe to tour the United States. He had been away for so long that he actually felt alienated from his own country. Not long after his sixtieth birthday, Patton had a premonition of his imminent death. And shortly thereafter he broke his neck in an automobile accident. He lingered, incapacitated, for a week, and then, accepting his fate with fortitude, Patton died.

Hearing of his passing, the men he had commanded went into a state of mourning. One soldier still serving in Germany called him "one of the greatest men that ever lived," adding, "The men who served under him know him as a soldier's leader. I am proud to say that I have served under him in the Third Army . . . We are making every Heinie that passes stop and take off his hat. They can't understand our feelings for him. I don't know whether or not you can understand them either."

Patton's body was laid to rest in an American military cemetery in Luxembourg, alongside many of his fellow soldiers. After his death, Patton's popularity soared. *He died at just the right time, while his triumphs in the war remained fresh . . . Had he lived, he would no doubt have felt himself to be outside the mainstream of American life. He would have turned into an anachronism.*

In a letter written during the war, one Third Army veteran described Patton's dynamic aura: *General Patton walked out on the little terrace . . . and when the drum, ruffles, and bugles sounded the General's march, we stood transfixed upon his appearance. Not one square inch of flesh [was] not covered with goose pimples . . . that towering figure impeccably attired froze you in place and electrified the air . . . He said . . . "I can assure you that the Third United States Army will be the greatest army in American history . . . I shall drive you until hell won't have it . . . " He talked on to us for half an hour, literally hypnotizing us with his incomparable, if profane eloquence. When he had finished, you felt as if you had been given a supercharge from some divine source. Here was the man for whom you would go to hell and back.*

GERONIMO: HIS OWN STORY

The Autobiography of a Great Patriot Warrior
**(edited by S.M. Barrett, 1906; newly edited with an introduction and notes by
Fredrick W. Turner III) E.P. Dutton and Co., New York, N.Y., 1970**

" . . . What separates the enlightened man from the savage?" Herman Melville once asked. "Is civilization a thing distinct, or is it an advanced stage of barbarism?" Such questions are more than relevant to the bleak late-nineteenth-century Apache-Anglo conflict. The distinction between "savage" and "civilized" disappeared as white settlers often showed more ingenuity in killing than the Apaches.

In the clash that ensued, Native Americans not only lost their land, but—having also been spiritually displaced—lost their cultural heritage as well. Anglo-Americans also lost, among other things, the chance to understand from the Apache point of view to live in peace with their environment. Fortunately, Geronimo—the Chiricahua warrior whose feet were "planted in the roots of the soil of his Mother Earth, his hands open to receive the seasonal blessings of wind, sun, and rain, his heart reverent in the presence of wildness"—left his story as a testament to the lost legacy of his people.

Geronimo's story—supplemented by oral legends and excerpts from other memoirs and diaries—is tempered by his bitter burden as a prisoner of war. Consequently, his perspective, given in the great warrior's own voice, casts a new light on a history too often told only from the victor's point of view.

A boy-child was born in No-doyohn Canyon, Arizona in 1829 to a noble and proudly aggressive bloodline of Chiricahua Apaches. As an infant, Geronimo, whose tribal name was Goyahkla, was "warmed by the sun, rocked by the winds, and sheltered by the trees as other Indian babes." The boy's early childhood was relatively peaceful. His mother taught him to pray to the god Usen; his father educated him in the "pleasure of the chase, and the glories of the warpath." Thus, Goyahkla integrated the skills he would find necessary to lead his people: hunting, fierce resistance, and guerrilla warfare.

While still a boy, Goyahkla's father died, and he assumed the care of his mother. At the age of seventeen, he was admitted to the council of warriors and given the honor of going to war—something he had long desired. Before long, he had married and fathered three children of his own.

Then came the fateful summer of 1858, a period destined to earn him his now-famous warrior name *Geronimo*—a Spanish term connoting "Indian Resistance"—and to turn him into a vengeful, unapologetic fighter.

The entire Chiricahua tribe, which customarily ranged into Mexico each year to trade, returned to camp one evening to find that a large band of Mexicans had raided their camp and killed many of their women and children, among them, Geronimo's mother and his wife and children. The loss was devastating. He describes the numbness he felt when he encountered the scene: "I stood until all had passed, hardly knowing what I would do. I had no weapon, nor did I hardly wish to fight . . . I did not pray, nor did I resolve to do anything in particular, for I had no purpose left."

The survivors returned to Arizona, where Geronimo, according to Apache custom, burned his family's tepee and all other traces of his dead. Afterwards, he pledged ruthless vengeance on those who had murdered his family, and embarked on a campaign to persuade the other tribes to join in his raids. "I could not call back my loved ones," he remembered, " . . . but I could rejoice in this revenge."

The proud Chiricahua persisted with his forays into Mexico for the next fifteen years. Although he was wounded at least eight separate times—and lost another wife and child to counter-attacks—most of the raids were successful. Some, however, led to bitter censure for Geronimo's sometimes reckless nature, a temperament molded by his unyielding hatred. In fact, Geronimo chose not to tell his Anglo editor that he often resorted to tricks, lies, and kidnappings in his attempts to coerce his people to continue fighting when they otherwise were ready to surrender.

While carrying out the Mexican raids, the Apaches and the "Yankees" presented no threat to one another. Then, in October of 1860, when the half-breed son of a man named Ward ran away after a brutal beating by his father, Ward accused Cochise, the Chiricahua chieftain, of stealing him. Cochise appeared at the American soldiers' tent to pronounce his innocence, but the soldiers arrested him and his men. They were told they would be held prisoner until the boy was returned.

Cochise quickly escaped, but the incident ended formal relations with the whites and launched a bloody game of strike and retreat: if a man from either group was captured, it cost him his life.

In 1863, the chief of Geronimo's band, Mangus-Colorado (roughly translated "Red Sleeves"), negotiated a peace treaty with the whites. He was promised that if he brought his tribe to live near a specified white settlement, they would be protected and provided with ample supplies.

Mangus-Colorado moved part of his tribe, intending to send for the others after sincerity of the terms of the agreement had been tested. Notwithstanding his display of trust, the chief was immediately imprisoned and his guards were ordered to shoot him if he tried to escape. During his first night in prison, the guards brutally tortured and then murdered Mangus-Colorado, an act Geronimo later called "the greatest wrong ever done to the Indians."

In the spring of 1876, Geronimo was officially branded an American outlaw. He had been living with his Chiricahua band on the Fort

Bowie reservation, where they had agreed to live under terms of a peace treaty made with General Oliver O. Howard. At first, Howard had seen to it that the tribe was given every provision stipulated by the treaty. The federal government, however, soon began "reinterpreting" the agreement. When Geronimo uncovered a scheme to relocate his tribe, he led a band of Chiricahuas off the Fort Bowie reservation to join his friend Victoria, chief of the Cheyenne Apaches. But after a year of constant chasing and hiding, Geronimo and Victoria surrendered themselves to agent John P. Clum.

For the next two years the Apaches lived peacefully on the San Carlos Reservation. Then, hearing a rumor that federal officers at San Carlos were planning to incarcerate the "savages," Geronimo again fled the reservation. "We thought it more manly to die on the warpath," he said, "than to be killed in prison."

A year later a cavalry regiment led by General George Crook, one of the most impressive Apache trackers of all time, caught up with Geronimo's band and convinced them to return to the reservation. Geronimo showed up some days later steering a herd of stolen cattle and horses: if the whites placed such importance on riches, the warrior explained, he was going to join the white world well-supplied. The army, of course, had no intention of permitting Geronimo to raid livestock as he saw fit, and his property was confiscated.

It wasn't long before Geronimo, suffering the sting of this latest insult to his Apache sense of decorum, again abandoned the reservation. He had coaxed two other Indian chiefs to join his band by claiming that they were about to be arrested for the murder of a third chief—a murder which had not actually occurred. When the chiefs discovered the deception, they tried to kill him, and Geronimo once more set out on the run. But after an exhausting and hopeless dash, in which he managed to elude both federal troops and Mexican bandits, he again gave himself up to Crook. "Two or three words are enough," he told the General " . . . Do with me what you please. I surrender. Once I moved about like the wind. Now I surrender to you and that is all."

Geronimo nevertheless yearned to be free. Eventually, when his distrust of the white man had once again been piqued, he slipped away from the reservation for the final time. After agreeing to scout for an Army tracking expedition, Geronimo turned aside when the company was about a half mile from camp, said "Adios, Señores," with a salute—and began to scale a nearby mountain. Crook, his troops unable to follow Geronimo's trail, resigned his post; he had lost his biggest catch. Years later, when he heard that Crook had died, Geronimo said, "I think that General Crook's death was sent by the Almighty as a punishment for the many evil deeds he committed."

General Nelson A. Miles replaced Crook and immediately sent a large pursuit force after the rebels with orders to kill or capture Geronimo—preferably the former. Geronimo remembered the desperation he and his band felt at the time: "We had become reckless of our lives because we felt every man's hand was against us . . . [So] we gave no quarter to anyone and asked no favors."

After five months of battling both Mexicans and federal troops, the warriors' spirits were finally broken. On September 4, 1886, Geronimo surrendered for the last time, marching to Skeleton Canyon to place himself in the custody of General Miles. A few days later, he found himself aboard a train headed for Florida, where for two years he was kept at hard labor. [The terms of the surrender have since been hotly disputed. It appears, however, to have been largely unconditional, except for the guarantee that Geronimo and his band would be reunited unharmed with their families. Geronimo himself, until the day he died, swore that the accord had been directly violated more than once.]

In the spring of 1887, the Apache rebels and their families were sent to Alabama. With no property on which to build houses or raise livestock, they suffered horribly. Finally they were transported West—not to the ancestral lands promised them but to Fort Sill, Oklahoma, where Geronimo remained a prisoner.

Geronimo ends his narrative with an impassioned plea to President Roosevelt to return him and his people to their Arizona homeland: "It is my land, my home, my father's land, to which I now ask to return. I want to spend my last days there, and be buried among those mountains. If this could be I might die in peace, feeling that my people, placed in their native homes, would increase in numbers, rather than diminish as at present, and that our name would not become extinct."

Commentary:

Before Geronimo was eventually subdued, he fought one of the greatest wars of liberation in the histories of dispossessed peoples. His love of freedom, his skillful leadership, and his fierce attachment to his homeland enabled him to avoid final defeat for over a decade. But these years were filled with violence, treachery, and broken promises on both sides.

The Apaches' circumstances became desperate. Here was a group of people whose attachment to their land was so enduring that they were willing to pay for it with their lifeblood; running the wheels of "progress" over them was another group whose only tie to the land was, from Geronimo's perspective, "what they could rape out of it."

Encouragingly, Americans today have adopted a more balanced, judicious alliance with the earth. For Geronimo, however, change was too late in coming. He died in a military hospital in Fort Sill on February 17, 1909—a tragically ironic and uncelebrated death: After getting drunk, he died of exposure after falling from his buggy and lying out all night in the freezing rain. His behest that his body be returned to his homeland was sadly forgotten; he died a prisoner of war and was ignominiously buried in foreign soil.

FREDERICK DOUGLASS

by William S. McFeely, W.W. Norton & Company, New York, N.Y., 1991

As a man who was born a slave and who would later advise presidents, Frederick Douglass was a true American hero. He was one of the greatest orators of the 19th century and probably did more than any other individual to abolish slavery, an amazing feat considering his humble beginnings.

William McFeely's biography is an excellent study both of the early struggle for racial equality and of the troubled times in which Douglass lived. Despite opposition, Douglass worked to achieve his goals. *Except to run free, Frederick Douglass never ran away from anything.*

McFeely relies heavily on Douglass' three autobiographies but also consults a vast number of other sources. The resulting Frederick Douglass is thus often portrayed as human (vain, impatient and stubborn)—but no less brilliant or powerful.

✧ ◆ ✧

In February of 1818, near the eastern shore of the Chesapeake Bay, Frederick Augustus Washington Bailey was born to a Maryland slave mother and an unknown white father. The child was raised by his grandmother, Betsey Bailey, in her small and overcrowded cabin. *With the resilience and wonder of a bright child, Frederick explored the world he had entered.* When the boy was six, he was taken into the homes of other relatives, one of whom was Aaron Anthony, the "absentee master" who managed the grand estate at Wye House for the wealthy Lloyd family.

Frederick soon caught the attention of Lucretia and Thomas Auld, Anthony's daughter and son-in-law. When their father lost his position, the two arranged to send Frederick to Baltimore to live with Thomas' brother, Hugh Auld, his wife Sofia, and their two-year-old son. He would stay with the Aulds for nearly six years.

Sophia initiated Frederick's formal education. Just as the boy was beginning to learn to read, however, Hugh put a stop to the lessons, warning that "learning would spoil the best nigger in the world. . . . It would forever unfit him for the duties of a slave." But Frederick had by then mastered enough skills to continue teaching himself, and in his studies he developed an intense interest in the subject of slavery: "I was eager to hear any one speak of slavery. Every little while, I could hear something about the abolitionists." At twelve he began attending Sabbath school, and at fourteen he was made a teacher in the school. Then in March of 1833, Frederick was sent back to live with Thomas Auld.

After less than a year, Frederick was hired out to Edward Covey, a well-known "nigger breaker." For the next six months *there were regular beatings and regular labor, plowing and tending the fields.* A few days after receiving a savage whipping, Frederick fought back. After nearly two hours of grappling with Covey, neither man

was able to gain the upper hand and the fight ended. Now Frederick was more determined than ever to escape slavery.

The next year, 1835, Frederick was transferred to William Freeland's farm—a much more congenial workplace, at least when compared to Covey's estate—where he worked the fields alongside four other slaves. There he spent his Sundays teaching his fellow slaves to read. Word got around, and he soon held school for 20 or 30 slaves from nearby farms. The talk at the meetings would often turn to slavery—and escaping. Before long a small group of them had hatched a plan to make their break, but, before it could be carried out, they were betrayed from within. However, due to a lack of evidence, all of the slaves involved were returned to their masters.

Frederick was sent back to Baltimore to live in the home of Hugh and Sophia, there to apprentice out in the ship-caulking trade. Baltimore accommodated a large free black community, and Frederick eagerly involved himself in its churches and intellectual organizations. It was while engaged in these interests that he met and courted Anna Murray, a free woman working as a domestic servant.

Though a slave, the industrious young man soon enjoyed considerable independence. He was allowed to live apart from the Aulds, upon the stipulation that he report to Hugh each week and pay the man three dollars of his earnings. But when Frederick was late in making a payment, he was ordered to move back in with the family and give up all of his earnings. He obeyed, but *the Auld brothers had lifted the lid of their slave's hopes too widely ever to get it shut again. Now he—with Anna—would run away.*

Dressed as a sailor and carrying a packet of seaman's papers acquired from a free man, Frederick Bailey left Baltimore on September 3, 1838. Traveling by road, river and rail through Delaware and Philadelphia, after being recognized but not betrayed and having his papers demanded but not scrutinized, Frederick reached his destination: New York City. Once Anna had made her way there, too, the couple was married and set off for New England, settling down in New Bedford, Massachusetts.

To avoid capture, Frederick dropped his two middle names and changed his last name to Douglass. He found good work caulking ships at the New Bedford shipyard, but the other men refused to work with him because of his color. He found solace, however, as an active member of the local African Methodist Episcopal Zion congregation: "The days I spent in little Zion, New Bedford, in the several capacities of sexton steward, class leader, clerk, and local preacher . . . [were] among the happiest days of my life."

At a meeting on March 12, 1839, the runaway slave spoke out against colonization (the proposal to return slaves to Africa) and told of his experiences. A notice of his speech subsequently appeared in the Liberator, published by William Lloyd Garrison, who had been instrumental in founding both the Massachusetts and the New England Anti-Slavery Societies. In the spring of 1841, the wealthy abolitionist, William C. Coffin, heard Douglass speak and "thought that a good many people ought to hear what the beautifully spoken, earnest young black man had to say."

At a prominent anti-slavery conference later that year, Douglass was invited to take the stage. The sermon, based on his own life story, inspired his listeners. *He paid no attention to Parker Pillsbury's advice that it was "better [to] have a little of the plantation" in his speech and [ignored] Garrison's [warning] that he should not sound too "learned" lest people not "believe you were ever a slave." At the convention's close, he was invited to become an agent of the Massachusetts Anti-Slavery Society and go out on the lecture circuit to tell the world of his experiences as a slave.*

In 1843, Douglass took to the road, leaving his wife and children sometimes for months at a time to speak out against slavery's evils. Nearly 100 audiences—some dominated by pro-slavery advocates or, worse yet, angry mobsters—heard the soaring voice of the orator.

Indeed, the anti-slavery movement included many different factions whose leaders often disagreed on which course to follow. Accused by some of being an agitator, Douglass had by this time distanced himself from the Anti-Slavery Society, and, as early as 1844, he was becoming a leader in his own right.

In 1845, when he published his first autobiography, *Narrative of the Life of Frederick Douglass,* Douglass crossed the Atlantic for a tour of the United Kingdom. His visits in Scotland and England went so well that he considered settling in Edinburgh. A British friend, Ellen Richardson, began a campaign to collect donations to buy their friend's freedom from Auld and, early in 1847, Frederick Douglass returned to the United States as a free man.

While in England, Douglass had also accepted contributions to embark on publishing his newspaper, a project opposed by the Anti-Slavery Society's leaders, who felt Douglass could be more productive as a lecturer than as an editor. Nevertheless, the first issue of his *North Star* was published on December 3, 1847.

Following Douglass' formal break with the American Anti-Slavery Society in 1851—a split precipitated by his persistence in citing the U.S. Constitution to achieve emancipation—the *North Star's* name was changed to Frederick Douglass' Paper, a politically charged weekly.

Shortly after Douglass had completed his second book, *My Bondage and My Freedom* (an expanded version of his autobiography, of which a third volume, *Life and Times of Frederick Douglass,* would appear in 1881), bloody skirmishes erupted in Kansas after the 1855 passage of the Kansas-Nebraska Act. This time those *antislavery leaders who had been pacific, in action if not always in rhetoric—Henry Ward Beecher, Gerrit Smith, and Douglass himself . . . —now called on their followers to send guns to the Kansas abolition-*

ists. On October 16, 1859, John Brown, along with 22 fellow abolitionists, attacked and seized the Harpers Ferry arsenal; their victory was short-lived, as all were soon captured or killed.

By 1860 *more and more militancy was in the air. Black Americans were as despondent as they had ever been. Efforts to end slavery seemed to have been frustrated on every side.*

When Abraham Lincoln assumed the Presidency in 1861, Douglass did all he could to convince the President that emancipation of the slaves should be the main objective of the Civil War that was just underway. Finally, the President had heard enough. *Lincoln did announce that on January 1, 1863, he would issue a proclamation freeing the slaves in the rebellious states.* Sensing that history was in the making, Douglass urged young black males to support the Union cause. As thousands of black volunteers swelled Union ranks, Douglass believed it would not only bring ultimate victory but also bring about the respect of their white neighbors. Despite his assertions that Lincoln moved too slowly on black issues, the two developed a good working relationship—which was cut short by the President's assassination on April 14, 1865, just five days after Lee surrendered to Grant at Appomattox.

The end of slavery meant anything but the end of Douglass' public life. He protested President Andrew Johnson's retrograde policies and fought even more vigorously against racism and segregation practices. Douglass' new crusade was aimed at winning for blacks the right to vote. Upon ratification of the Fifteenth Amendment in 1870, however, the power behind the movement was immediately weakened, as long-time allies were forced to choose between black causes or those of American women—who would be denied voting and other basic human rights for another half century.

Douglass spent his later years waiting for a presidential appointment. He also continued to lend his strong voice to black rights. Paul Laurence Dunbar, a poet and aspiring journalist, described a speech Douglass read, consisting of his essay "The Race Problem in America," on "Colored People's Day," August 25, 1893: *As he read his paper . . . Douglass was interrupted by jeers and catcalls from white men in the rear of the crowd . . . The old man tried to go on, but the mocking persisted. His hand shook . . . the great orator's voice faltered. Then to his fellow abolitionists' delight and to his enemies' dismay, his voice came again drowning out the catcalls as an organ would a penny whistle.* "Men talk of the Negro problem," Douglass roared. "There is no Negro problem. The problem is whether the American people have loyalty enough, honor enough, patriotism enough, to live up to their Constitution." On he went for an hour: " . . . We Negroes love our country. We fought for it. We ask only that we be treated as well as those who fought against it." *Thunderous applause followed. He had won the day and the hearts of many.*

The legacy of Frederick Douglass' fight for black rights lives on long after his death, which came on February 20, 1895.

GORBACHEV

by Gerd Ruge (translated from German by Peter Tegel), Chatto & Windus, London 1991

Gerd Ruge's highly acclaimed biography *Gorbachev* recounts how a man of humble origins ultimately rose to lead the Soviet Party, dominating and altering Soviet policy so radically that his name will forever be remembered in the annals of world history.

The Birth of a Reformer

On March 2, 1931, in the small Russian farming village of Privolnoye, Mikhail Sergeyevich Gorbachev was born. Perhaps his village's name, which translates to "Freedom," in some way influenced the extraordinary changes Gorbachev would someday effect. Indeed, he would make more freedom available to Soviet citizens than anyone could ever recall or imagine.

Gorbachev's independent turn of mind may actually have been inherited from his Cossack ancestors: *A love of freedom and independence was central to [Cossacks'] lives and nowhere in Russia was there a stronger feeling for equality before the law and democracy.* Gorbachev's maternal grandfather Panteli Gopalko exemplified Cossack independence. Gopalko was one of the first post-Revolutionary Russians to organize peasants into a co-operative where they could both farm their own land and work together to improve farming methods. Gopalko was highly respected and his approach to co-operative farming was widely copied before collectivism replaced it.

In addition to caring for her young son, Mikhail, Gopalko's daughter, Maria, also worked on the co-operative. Her husband, Sergei Gorbachev, drove tractors and maintained and repaired agricultural implements. The parents worked hard and lived quietly during Mikhail's childhood—until the advent of Stalin's enforced collectivism and political purges. Stalin's purges resulted in the arrest of three-fourths of the regional Stravropol Party cadres, and persecution of the peasants soon followed. The purges, of course, had a profound influence on Mikhail: *Although he was still a young child, he saw what was happening to the people around him. To the simple, honest people who had made the Revolution, who had fought in the Civil War, who had founded the collective farms. They had all suffered, though they were innocent. Naturally he didn't accept this.*

When Mikhail was ten, the terror finally subsided. However, shortly thereafter his country was invaded by the Germans. Throughout most of World War II, the Germans occupied Privolnoye. Mikhail's father served in the Soviet army for four years, while his mother worked long hours loading trains in a neighboring region.

When the town was finally liberated, normal life resumed and school classes opened up once more. For a period of time, however, Mikhail was unable to attend because he had no clothes to wear. When the boy was finally able to return to class, his father promised him that he would never again be forced to interrupt his studies.

In 1950, when Mikhail was accepted to the Moscow University of Law, he quickly perceived the extent to which he was considered an outsider. But in spite of his ill-fitting clothes, he gradually established some close friendships. He soon moved into a room with five other young intellectuals. They dubbed it the "open room," because it was here that they freely exchanged their ideas.

Despite his outspokenness—which at the time certainly was not a valued trait—Gorbachev joined and rose quickly through the ranks of the Young Communist League. "What I liked about him was that he achieved what he did on his own," a friend remembers. "He had no influential relatives or friends, he wasn't even from Moscow. He got there on his own merits."

Gorbachev became a full member of the Communist Party in 1952. The following year, Stalin died, inaugurating a period of open debate known as "The Thaw." Muscovite students and intellectuals cautiously addressed the problems and controversies facing the Soviet Union. In the ensuing months, the citizens of Moscow demanded elections and a genuine political party, not the bureaucratic chaos they had recently endured. The pressure for political restructuring taking place in Moscow during the 1950s aroused Gorbachev's mind and heart; 30 years later, similar ideas would resurface in his politics.

It was also during this period that Gorbachev met the slim, haughty, and seemingly unattainable Raisa Titarenko, also a young intellectual. The couple later married and, after their graduation, they moved to Stravopol, the capital of Gorbachev's home region. While Gorbachev worked for the Young Communists, Raisa became a university lecturer. In 1957, she gave birth to their daughter, Irina.

The Rise of a Political Leader

Although he disagreed with many policies of new Soviet leader Nikita Khrushchev, Gorbachev continued to advance within the Party. By October 1964, he had been promoted to a department leader in the Regional Party Committee. In this capacity, Gorbachev was constantly forced to grapple with the shortcomings of worker productivity and agricultural technology. To better equip himself to confront these problems, Gorbachev enrolled as a student of economics at Stravopol Agricultural College.

In 1978, Gorbachev was elevated to the position of Agricultural Secretary of the Central Committee. One of his fellow Committee members later remarked, "This was one of the rare moments in Soviet history when a man's personal qualities brought about his rise. Gorbachev was young and energetic, he had made a name for himself in the Central Committee with his speeches on agriculture, but he belonged to no clan and no one was afraid of him or jealous of him."

Gorbachev worked hard to build and maintain his reputation as a *diligent* Party member rather than a *well-connected* Party member. Indeed, he "did not simply follow instructions from party headquarters. He made changes on his own initiative, which entailed a certain amount of risk." Moreover, Gorbachev abhorred fellow Party members' corruption and nepotism, and took every measure to avoid their hunting parties and drinking binges. He also took pains to ensure that Irina was not treated as a typical Party brat, who usually spent summers abroad. Instead, Irina stayed in Privolnoye for the holidays, working in the garden with her grandmother. She wore no fur coats or diamonds, and was treated like any other young Soviet student.

Gorbachev soon was promoted to Secretary of the Central Committee and the following year was made a member of the Politburo: Mikhail Gorbachev was now one of the 14 most powerful men in the Soviet Union.

At the death of Soviet leader Leonid Brezhnev in 1982, Gorbachev's succession to the highest ranks of Soviet power seemed all but assured when his close friend Yuri Andropov was named as Party chief. However, neither Andropov nor his aged successor, Konstantin Chernenko, were to lead the country for very long; both died shortly after taking power. Thus, in 1985, the Party deputies elected Gorbachev as the new Communist Party Leader—he was now the most powerful man in the Soviet Union.

On the Road to Freedom

Gorbachev, subtly at first, began piloting the Soviet Union in a new direction. Being careful only to make changes within the established bureaucracy, Gorbachev's first two goals were *uskorehiye,* the acceleration of modernization based on technical development, and *povorot,* a change of focus. To facilitate his new goals, Gorbachev began slowly to replace the old faces of the Party with new, liberal thinkers—reformers in his own mold.

He quickly gained allies, especially from outside the Soviet Union. Though initially hesitant, Western leaders soon gained confidence in Gorbachev and were thrilled to see a new Soviet order beginning to emerge. *The astonished Western world had discovered a Soviet leader with a new style—a dynamic man, quite unlike his senile predecessors, who already seemed to stand for a new Soviet Union.* After Gorbachev visited Great Britain, Margaret Thatcher referred to him as a man "with whom one could do business."

Back home in the Soviet Union, meanwhile, Gorbachev grappled with severe problems; increased shortages of food and supplies had beget millions of impatient, angry workers. Realizing that in order to bring reform to the country he would have to allow citizens the right to speak freely against the Party, Gorbachev called for an open dialogue. He asked questions, seeking answers from the villager, the factory worker, the businessman engaged in foreign trade. His people were astonished that he expected truthful answers—that he encouraged freedom of expression. *Glasnost* had begun.

For the first time since "The Thaw," Soviet citizens now began to speak and write openly about the problems of their country. They accused the parliament of being falsely elected, and called for election by the people. The average Soviets citizen began to demand rights accorded him under the constitution—a situation unheard of before Gorbachev assumed power.

For most Soviets, *perestroika*—Gorbachev's plan for economic and political reform—seemed a beneficent philosophy that promised a better life. Indeed, Soviet workers merely wanted a better standard of living, not a Westernized government. Few, however, were prepared to accept the time it would take to exact reforms and to establish a market-driven economy. Both democracy and a better standard of living would not come all at once.

Gorbachev moved slowly, patiently, cautiously, working and making compromises within the system. Other officials, however, like Boris Yeltsin, whom Gorbachev had brought to Moscow as Party Secretary, preferred a more accelerated pace. Speaking on behalf of reform and against corruption, Yeltsin endorsed many of the same principles as Gorbachev, but completely disagreed with his strategies.

Once many of the older and more conservative members had retired from Congress—announcing that they were simply too old to wage the new battles that would have to be fought—the people elected in 1989 young radicals such as Yeltsin to serve in Congress—and to begin the democratic debate.

After the elections, Congress appointed Gorbachev as both General Secretary of the Party and the State President, making him more powerful than even Stalin had been. Second in power was Boris Yeltsin, the newly elected President of the Russian Federation.

Now that Moscow was moving toward a multi-party system, political and special interest groups were formed. Clearly policy had to change and develop as quickly as the people generated new, reform-minded ideas. Unfortunately, Gorbachev could not keep pace.

On November 9, 1989, the Berlin Wall came down and the tangible barrier between East and West was removed. The world now recognized Gorbachev's role in the sudden liberation of millions of people. In recognition of and appreciation for his efforts, he was awarded the Nobel Peace Prize.

Gorbachev was a hero—everywhere but in the Soviet Union. As fall turned to winter, food lines began to lengthen. Nevertheless, the Supreme Soviet retained its confidence in Gorbachev and elected him in May 1990 to the new office of Soviet President.

Within six months of the election, five of the Soviet Republics declared themselves independent, and another six announced their sovereignty within a disintegrating Union. Clearly Gorbachev's presidency was in crisis. Yeltsin, in fact, soon led movements to help win independence for the Russian Republic. Because an independent Russia would end the Communist Party, Gorbachev was forced to exercise his executive powers to repeal Russia's independence.

In an effort to retain power, Gorbachev turned to supporters on the far right, allying himself with those *opposed* to reform and attempting to stifle *glasnost* by controlling the media.

On January 13, 1991 Soviet tanks and troops surged into Lithuania to crush a provincial uprising. It was evident that Gorbachev was losing the battle. Finally on Christmas Day 1991, Gorbachev resigned his presidency of the collapsed Soviet empire. The next day, Boris Yeltsin assumed the Kremlin office. The once-powerful union now was reduced to an indistinct group of independent states struggling for economic, political and social stability.

Gorbachev had managed, nevertheless, to create a new future for his country and for the world, and to guarantee himself a prominent pedestal in the annals of history.

THE IRON LADY

A Biography of Margaret Thatcher
by Hugo Young, Farrar Straus Giroux, New York, N.Y., 1989

The Iron Lady not only mirrors political events but delves into the *meaning* behind those events. Considered an outstanding example of British political journalism, Hugo Young's moving biography of a woman who "has intrigued the world more than any of her predecessors since Churchill" is, in the words of Kirkus Reviews, "as definitive as a biography can be of a life still in progress."

◇ ♦ ◇

Margaret was born on October 13, 1925 in Grantham, Lincolnshire, England, the youngest daughter of Alderman Alfred Roberts. Raised under strict Victorian values of "hard work, self-help, rigorous budgeting and a firm belief in the immorality of extravagance," she applied the teachings of her father: "He taught me that you first sort out what you believe in . . . then apply it. You don't compromise on things that matter." And as Prime Minister, Margaret Thatcher held to her beliefs: "Some say I preach merely the homilies of housekeeping or the parables of the parlour . . . but, I do not repent. Those parables would have saved many a financier from failure and many a country from crisis."

Margaret's entrance into Oxford University in 1943 marked the "beginning of a lifetime's dedication to Conservative politics." She earned her degree in chemistry, a discipline she plied throughout her political career. In December 1984, for example, while discussing "Star Wars" (defensive space technology) with U.S. President Ronald Reagan, she reputedly told the president in a "moment of exasperation: But, I'm a chemist. I *know* it won't work."

Being a natural-born leader and a strong woman with a mind of her own, Thatcher impressed many in the Conservative Party. Her political future was "crucially facilitated" by her marriage to the wealthy Denis Thatcher in 1945. Their marriage produced twins, Mark and Carol, and provided her with the financial freedom to pursue her political career with "undistracted single-mindedness."

At 32, Thatcher won the parliamentary seat at Finchley, with a Conservative majority of 12,000. The Finchley Press summarized her achievement in a single ecstatic sentence: *Speaking without notes, stabbing home points with impressive hands, Mrs. Thatcher launched fluently into a clear-cut appraisal of the Middle East situation, weighed up Russia's propagandist moves with the skill of a housewife measuring the ingredients in a familiar recipe . . . switched swiftly to Britain's domestic problems (showing a keen grasp of wage and trade union issues), then swept her breathless audience into a confident preview of Conservatism's dazzling future.* With the cementing of "valuable" political friendships and her own political ideologies, Thatcher rose to parliamentary prominence.

Later, the 1964 election in which Harold Macmillan was deposed and Edward Heath came into power heralded the beginning of a "new era." Heath did as he had promised, freeing up international trade, modernizing antiquated factories, and slaughtering other of government's "sacred cows." During this time Thatcher moved through junior positions that provided her little political glory but immeasurable experience for the years to come.

Heath was reelected in 1970. Viewing Margaret as a "diligent, reliable . . . fit colleague," he appointed her to the Department of Education and Science. This formative experience taught her "both the limits . . . and huge potential of a minister's power."

After sailing through the 1974 election, Heath appointed Thatcher to a housing policy committee. It was during this time that she began a "cautious break with Heathism" and emerged "a singularly 'political' politician . . . well able to depart, where necessary, from what she personally believed to be right."

Under the tutelage of Airey Neave, who viewed her as a political genius, Thatcher won the nomination for Prime Minister of the newly formed National Coalition Government, taking control at a time when the party was ready for a return to fundamentalist Conservatism. Cautiously, she established "a philosophy most people could understand," while economist and political ally Joseph Keith drove home the message of the new "Thatcherism." She reiterated these philosophies whenever she spoke: Britain and socialism were not the same. The British inheritance—the right of every man to enjoy the rewards of his own labor—was the very essence of a free country.

To fulfill the British inheritance, she empowered a number of men and women—some highly controversial choices—to iron out, among other things, the regulations on the economy, inflation, public spending, trade union law reform, public sector pay, and public sector fights.

During her first six months in office as Prime Minister, Thatcher established her dominance and educated herself in the intricacies of foreign affairs. Expounding on her deep-rooted abhorrence of Communism, she called for European unity and common defense. In doing so, she introduced her new "international personality" during a speech in January 1976. "The Russians . . . put guns before butter," she declared. "[They are] a super power only . . . in the military sense . . . a failure in human and economic terms." Her voice reverberating, she then urged Britain to meet the challenge of unity or "end up on the scrap heap of history."

"The Iron Lady" forcefully established her iron-willed reputation. Recognizing her own shortcomings, she commissioned leaders who would compensate for her lack of skill in certain areas, and who would accept her authoritarian style of leadership. One of these was Lord Carrington, a foreign advisor chosen as her first

Foreign Secretary. Of utmost importance on Carrington's agenda was the issue of Rhodesia, which had been torn by civil war for the previous seven years. After many months of seeking Rhodesian control through the ballot box, Thatcher finally saw no other option but to seize control of the former colony, a decision that led to the formal transfer of power to an independent Zimbabwe on April 17, 1980. *The Zambia Times* applauded the action, expressing that Thatcher had "left a ray of hope on a dark horizon" and that "inside the iron casing is a soft heart." She won the praise of Britons and Rhodesians alike as a champion of human rights.

Initially, positive popular opinion followed Thatcher into the war to reclaim the Falkland Islands from Argentinean occupation. "However, as soon as the war was over, the obvious question had to be addressed; that is, why had it occurred?" The report of the Franks Committee, however, found her not guilty of negligence or of failing to provide protection for the islands before seizure had occurred. Consequently, Thatcher won a second term.

Now, for the first time, the Prime Minister succeeded in filling the three most senior positions in the cabinet with partisan ministers. Despite inside support, Thatcher's second term was torn with problems. The nation remained in dire straits in terms of employment, health care, and defense spending. Personal scandals involving key cabinet members, the American invasion of Grenada—about which she had not been forewarned—and the imminent arrival of Cruise missiles in Britain further distressed Prime Minister Thatcher. As a result, she "began to experience what most other British leaders had learned to suffer much sooner in their time." Friends, disillusioned, turned away; the press, which had compared her performance during her first term "to that of the gigantic and leonine spirit of Winston Churchill," now censured her. Her failure to accompany the Americans into Grenada was touted as a "huge failure of judgment." Still, "the quality which distinguishes politicians from most other people, is resilience," and, unlike some of her predecessors, Thatcher wasn't prone to despair. She declared, "I am in politics because of the conflict between good and evil, and I believe that in the end, good will triumph."

Thatcher set to work stripping the powerful monopoly unions of their power and bringing the budget under control. She also increased defense spending and modernized the British nuclear deterrent. The Soviets were "not to be trusted," Mrs. Thatcher explained, but negotiations would continue.

About this time she visited Hungary, a trip that eventually led her to a meeting with Mikhail Gorbachev. In December 1984, the Soviet leader brought a large delegation to London: *It proved to be a most providential occasion. Within three months, Chernenko was dead and Gorbachev had succeeded him.*

Gorbachev made a powerful impression on Thatcher, who, she said, shared two great goals: first, to stimulate effective disarmament talks and, second, to further trade and cultural exchange. Gorbachev also acknowledged a personal warmth for "his new found friend," a relationship which later enabled Thatcher to act as an interlocutor between the super powers of Russia and the United States.

While Gorbachev was still in London, Thatcher set off on a six-day world tour. On a stop-over in Beijing, she undertook one of the "most momentous pieces of bilateral treaty-making [of] her time"—the surrender of the lease on Hong Kong. The last leg of her tour took her to Washington, where, only *a week after her brilliant conversations with the greatest enemy of Star Wars (Gorbachev), she would be sitting . . . with its most determined friend . . . Camp David might not have stopped the Star Warriors in their tracks, but it provided a frame of reference for a later address to Congress where she supported the President's continued research in nuclear deterrence—the Strategic Defense Initiative.*

Thatcher finally managed to sway public opinion back to her side: *For want of an organized, politically credible alternative, the intellectual argument in favour of Thatcherite economics had carried the day . . .* Further determining her success was the perception among Conservative Britons of a vibrant economy, in which even the unemployed "felt better off"; privatization had made positive inroads, and monopolies no longer held sway. In fact, the burgeoning economy became a headline story, and, by the time of the election, British optimism was at an all-time high.

Consequently, Thatcher's third term cleared the way *for the pursuit of a brand of Conservatism which no longer had quite the same need to answer to the customary hazards of democratic existence. It was in place, as it seemed unchallengeable. And so with question, was its leader: confirmed in her luxuriant conviction that she had carried Britain, by the only honest policies available, towards the destiny her people desired and the world would strive to emulate . . . However, this populism . . . was marked by a disabling paradox:* her strong, sometimes abrasive personality soon began to wear thin on Britons; many disliked her, few loved her. What was worse, she did not seem to like them. Over-anxious to have Britain succeed and run on sound economic principles, she would not tolerate less than precision among her staff. Here she was, a populist who had lost her popularity: *She was one of us . . . arguably our supreme representative, the complete personification of what we were. And yet, after ten years, she remained different. In an important sense, she wasn't "one of us" at all. She was altogether too superior.*

To the end, Thatcher remained the ultimate, irrepressible fighter; as she often described herself, she "was made of sterner stuff." And, in the final outcome, though loved and hated at once, Thatcher was always respected. "I hang on," she once told an interviewer after nine years as Prime Minister, "until I believe there are people who can take the banner forward with the same commitment, belief, vision, strength and singleness of purpose."

TRUMAN

by David McCullough, Simon and Schuster, New York, N.Y., 1992

"I am just a common everyday man whose instincts are to be ornery, who's anxious to be right . . . " Thus did Harry Truman describe himself, and for good or ill, this is how most Americans perceive their 33rd President—as a "common man," a man of the people. But David McCullough, in his exhaustive, Pulitzer Prize-winning biography *Truman,* leaves us with a vivid, three-dimensional portrait of an *uncommon* man—and of the dramatic times he lived through and helped shape.

Harry S Truman (the middle S, in true Truman style, is an independent entity, not an initial) was born in Lamar, Missouri on May 8th, 1884 to John and Martha Truman, and grew up on his grandfather Solomon Young's Blue Ridge farm in Jackson County, Missouri. Young Harry's eyesight was notably bad; he was, in his own words, "blind as a mole." As a consequence he avoided most sports, preferring to stay home and read, play the piano or spend time with his mother, whom he adored. "I was kind of a sissy," he later admitted; but boyhood friends claimed they respected his seriousness and intelligence.

After graduating with honors from high school, Truman went to work first for a newspaper, then a railroad, and then a bank, until his father asked him to stay home and work with the family farm. *The family came first. If Harry harbored any regrets or resentment, he never let on . . . Everything now revolved around the farm . . . Everyone worked, "and woe to the loafer,"* as Harry remembered.

Truman stayed on the farm for more than a decade, and took it over entirely after his father died in 1914. Then, in 1917, when America entered World War I, the 33-year-old farmer joined the National Guard and was sent to France, where he attained the rank of captain and commanded a battery of 194 men and four artillery guns. He was soon recognized for displaying "fierce courage under fire," and won the lifelong loyalty of his men.

When he returned to Missouri in 1918, Truman was a changed man; he had discovered he could lead. And just as important, in the Army Truman had made the acquaintance of Jim Pendergast, whose father Michael headed a powerful political organization in Kansas City.

In 1919 Truman married Bess Wallace, whom he had loved since childhood, and opened a Kansas City haberdashery. Times were tough in Missouri and the store eventually failed; but as fate would have it, that same year the Pendergasts asked him to run for Jackson County judge. "Mike Pendergast picked me up and put me into politics and I've been lucky," he later wrote.

The neophyte campaigner won the judgeship, and twelve years later, in 1934, the Pendergast political machine endorsed him for the United States Senate. Again Truman won the race, but it was said that he had obtained his new post "under a cloud" because of his Pendergast connections. Nevertheless, Truman remained loyal to his benefactors.

In 1940, Lloyd C. Stark, a former governor of Missouri, challenged Truman for his Senate seat. Few people, including President Roosevelt—who favored Truman, because of his support for the New Deal—thought the incumbent had much of a chance to win without Pendergast backing. But Truman refused to give up. He campaigned all across the state, and pulled off a stunning political upset.

Not long afterwards, with World War II raging in Europe, Senator Truman chaired what became known as the *Truman Committee,* established to investigate waste and inefficiency in the awarding of defense contracts. The committee did such capable work that "often a threat to 'take everything to the Truman Committee' [was] sufficient to force a cure of abuses."

Because President Roosevelt's health was deteriorating and Democratic Party bosses cringed at the thought of "liberal pacifist" Vice President Henry Wallace assuming the Presidency, Roosevelt was pressured to pick the reluctant Truman as his fourth-term running mate. The choice was not without detractors: Truman's selection was labeled "the Missouri Compromise"; *Time* magazine, which only the summer before had lauded the Senator's committee work, now portrayed him as a "drab mediocrity [and] 'the mousy little man from Missouri'."

Roosevelt and Truman narrowly defeated Dewey. But although the victory seemed to have rejuvenated the President, he died only 82 days after taking office. Truman felt totally overwhelmed. "Boys," he pleaded with a group of reporters, "if you ever pray, pray for me now. I don't know whether you fellows ever had a load of hay fall on you, but when they told me yesterday what had happened, I felt like the moon, the stars, and all the planets had fallen on me." Truman's critics, meanwhile, were aghast; they saw him as shallow and naive, an unsophisticated farmer with a good heart. "If Harry Truman can be President," jeered one, "so could my next-door neighbor."

On May 7, 1945, only three weeks after Truman had taken the Presidential oath, Germany surrendered to the Allied forces. As Russian troops scurried to occupy most of Eastern Europe, Secretary of War Henry Stimson kept Truman abreast of advances in the Manhattan Project, the top-secret development of the atomic bomb.

In July of 1945, Truman, Churchill, and Stalin, the leaders of the "Big Three" Allied nations, held meetings in Potsdam, Germany. It was there that Truman received momentous news: the first atomic bomb had been successfully detonated in New Mexico. The President gave much consideration to the precedent that would be set if he introduced atomic weapons to the world. Nevertheless, continuing heavy American losses in the Pacific eventually convinced him to give the go-ahead to use the weapon against Japan.

On August 6th, 1945, an atomic bomb was dropped on Hiroshima, annihilating much of the city; four days later a second bomb devastated the city of Nagasaki. Then, with Japan reeling in shock, Truman mercifully ordered a cease-fire. "The thought of wiping out another city was too horrible," he said. Japan surrendered on August 14, eventually bringing World War II to an end.

As Truman struggled to help the nation convert to a peacetime economy, he was beset by problems: his liberal domestic programs drew immediate Congressional opposition; a series of labor strikes crippled the nation; a succession of cabinet resignations and firings became fodder for the press; and he was criticized for bringing his inexperienced Missouri "cronies" into the White House. Even his now-famous relationship with his mother became a target of ridicule. He was depicted by the media as "indecisive," "vacillating," and "disorganized," and one newsman cited Truman's "curious reluctance or even inability to think of himself as President . . . "

The Republicans swept the 1946 elections in both houses of Congress—losses which some interpreted as a referendum on Truman's lackluster administration; now he was viewed by most as not only an "ordinary" man but as one "sadly miscast" in his role.

Others, however, took a wider view. Winston Churchill, who had coined the term "Iron Curtain" just one year earlier, admired Truman's firm stand against the Russians. Undersecretary of State Dean Acheson labeled Truman "the captain with the mighty heart." Clark Clifford remained staunchly loyal; he had worked in the Truman White House during the era that produced both the Truman Doctrine—a policy which provided economic and military aid to countries threatened by interference from other states, most notably the Soviet Union—and the Marshall Plan, a program of massive economic aid to rebuild European nations. "Harry Truman and the United States saved the free world," Clifford declared categorically.

Republicans often accused the Truman administration of being "soft on Communism." This was one of the charges which led Truman in exasperation to declare that "no man in his right mind would ever wish to be President if he knew what it entailed." Nevertheless, in 1948 he decided to run for election in his own right, saying that he relished the "prospect of taking on the Republicans in an all-out, full-scale championship fight."

As usual, most observers didn't give Truman much of a chance. In addition to his other political problems, he had adopted a civil-rights stance, thereby alienating Southern Democrats and dividing his party. Many of the New Dealers in Truman's own party wanted to dump the President and nominate Dwight Eisenhower, the most popular man in the country, as the Democratic candidate. The press became openly contemptuous, labeling the President as "inept and pathetic." Truman's approval rating dipped to an all-time low.

Even before the Democratic Convention, Truman was rated so far behind Republican nominee Thomas E. Dewey that some pollsters predicted Truman could not possibly win. But when Truman named the much respected Alben Barkley as his running mate and promised a Democratic victory, he brought the convention to its feet.

Then the never-say-die Missourian traveled the country by train, covering 21,928 miles in his now famous "Whistle-stop Campaign." Grinning, he promised, "I'm going to give 'em hell." At each stop, huge crowds gathered to hear Truman speak. Detractors claimed that people came only out of curiosity, but if so, Truman confounded their expectations. His potent message struck a responsive chord nationwide. He tore into the Republican Congress, calling its leaders "gluttons of privilege," and "cold . . . cunning men [who] had stuck a pitchfork in the farmer's back." One correspondent later characterized the energetic though grueling Truman campaign as "sharp speeches fairly criticizing Republican policy and defending New Deal liberalism mixed with sophistry, bunkum piled higher than haystacks, and demagoguery tooting merrily down the track."

Meanwhile, Truman's aides were growing more and more despondent—and with good reason: newspapers were already loudly proclaiming Dewey as the next President. But to the media's mammoth chagrin, on November 2, 1948, Truman defeated Dewey in the biggest upset in the history of presidential elections. "Not one polling organization had been correct in its forecast," notes McCullough. "Every expert had been proven wrong, [and] 'a great roar of laughter arose from the land.'"

Although the late forties and the fifties were a time of unequaled wealth and prosperity for Americans, controversy surrounded Truman's second term. The most debated issue was the President's decision to commit American troops to armed conflict in Korea. Some argued that the military intervention was nothing less than an undeclared war—in which many American lives were lost and no real objectives were achieved. Others insisted that Truman's firmness and resolve had saved South Korea from a Communist takeover.

In one of the most questionable decisions of the war, Truman revoked the command of a much decorated general, Douglas MacArthur. A nationwide storm of almost hysterical protest ensued. Many in Congress called for the President's impeachment. But to Truman, the decision boiled down to a Constitutional issue: the President—acting as civilian Commander-in-Chief—should have authority over all military leaders.

Truman declined to run for reelection in 1952, despite the fact that he knew no other Democrat had a chance of defeating Dwight Eisenhower—who had changed affiliations to run on the Republican ticket. The President's reason for stepping down, writes McCullough, was simple: *For as far back nearly as he could remember, Truman had held to the ideal of the mythical Roman hero Cincinnatus, the patriot farmer who assumes command in his country's hour of peril, then returns to the plow.*

In 1953 Truman and his wife Bess, who never was comfortable living in Washington, moved back to Independence, Missouri. For the next twenty years the retired President devoted his time to working on his memoirs and organizing the Harry Truman Library, where his papers would be preserved. "I tried never to forget who I was," Truman said, "and where I'd come from and where I was going back to."

Harry S Truman died on December 26, 1972. In summing up the meaning of his Presidency to American history, McCullough quotes Eric Severeid: *"I am not sure he was right about the atomic bomb, or even Korea. But remembering him reminds people what a man in office ought to be like. It's character, just character. He stands like a rock in memory now."*

MY LIFE

by Golda Meir, G. P. Putnam's Sons, New York, N. Y., 1975

Golda Meir's childhood in Russia passed with few happy memories. Her most vivid impressions, she said, were marked by fear. "I didn't know then . . . " she wrote, "what a pogrom was, but I knew it had something to do with being Jewish and with the rabble that used to surge through town, brandishing knives and huge sticks, screaming 'Christ killers' as they looked for the Jews, and who were now going to do terrible things to me and to my family." To escape persecution, Golda's father immigrated with his family to "the golden country of America," where he—and thousands of other Jews—hoped to find safety and prosperity.

The Meirs settled in Milwaukee and Golda's father quickly set out to fashion his family into "Americans." This transformation included wearing American clothes, speaking English instead of Yiddish, and attending school. For Golda, her family's new freedom was best characterized by a Labor Day parade in which her father marched alongside mounted police, who, instead of shooting the marchers, as the Cossacks had so often done, escorted them down the route.

Not all the Meirs, however, were happy in America. Golda's older sister Sheyna found only loneliness in their new home. She argued constantly with her parents and several times attempted to move out on her own. Sheyna broke with her parents finally when she contracted TB and had to be sent to a Jewish sanatorium in Denver. There, against the will of her parents, she married a Russian socialist who had escaped prison and made his way to America.

Afterwards, family pressures mounted on Golda as well. First, her mother tried to arrange a marriage for her. Golda, however, who was only fourteen, rejected her mother's plans. Then, thinking Golda had all the education a girl needed, her parents refused to send her to high school. Unable to bear such treatment, Golda escaped to Denver to live with her sister and continue her education there—a move which proved to be a turning point in her life.

In Russia, Golda had often listened to Sheyna and her friends discuss liberal politics, and in Denver the independent young woman again found herself in company of her sister's circle of intellectuals—many of whom were Labor Zionists. Not only did these discussions prove to form the political ideals Golda would practice for the rest of her life, but while taking part in them she also met her future husband Morris Meyerson.

Shortly after Golda's seventeenth birthday, an urgent letter from her father drew her back to Milwaukee. This time her parents were less strict with her; they could see that she had matured and would no doubt move on to college in preparation to become a teacher. Her parents, especially her father, had also become involved in the local Labor Zionist movement, the same movement through which Golda had met many of the great pioneers of Zionism, who

had already begun their struggle for a Jewish homeland in Palestine.

Morris, who later joined her in Milwaukee, was less enthusiastic about Golda's increasing political involvement in Labor Zionism. After organizing a successful march protesting an outbreak of anti-Semitic pogroms in Eastern Europe, Golda, dissatisfied with the breadth of her efforts, decided once and for all to unite with her fellow Zionists in Palestine. Morris understood her decision, but it took several long months of deliberation before he decided that he, too, would accompany her. In 1909 the two of them were married; Golda became Mrs. Meyerson—which later, while serving as a minister in the Israeli cabinet, she changed to its Hebrew equivalent "Meir."

Golda and her husband were joined by Sheyna and together they sailed to Egypt. When they reached Tel Aviv, however, the newest Jewish community outside of Jaffa, they were unimpressed. After lodging there temporarily, Golda and Morris joined a kibbutz at Mehavia. It was there that Golda found a way of life "more likely than any other to offer us a channel for expressing ourselves as Zionists, as Jews and as human beings."

Golda adapted quite quickly to the stark, demanding lifestyle—and soon took up a position of leadership. Morris, however, could not adjust to the lack of privacy and artistic opportunities. When he became ill, Golda was forced to leave the kibbutz. After he recovered, Golda briefly returned to the kibbutz, but because Morris refused to join her, Golda resigned herself to living in Jerusalem.

The ensuing four years were the most miserable of Golda's life. More than the struggle against deprivation, she felt trapped by the anxiety of providing for a family that now included two children, Sarah and Menachem. She also longed for the sense of purpose she had felt in the kibbutz. Thus, when she was asked to join the leadership of the Histadrut, a major Jewish labor union, she jumped at the chance. Morris understood—as Golda would also come to understand—that her political interests had driven an ever-widening wedge between them. Eventually Golda moved with the children to Tel Aviv, and Morris visited them on weekends.

During her first years with the Histadrut, Golda served on the Executive Committee, and there met the people who would later bring about Israel's statehood: David Ben-Gurion, the father of modern Israel; Levi Eshkol, Israel's third prime minister; and Berl Katznelson, the unofficial "father figure" of the Labor Zionists. Her political work on the committee also taught her the value of "pragmatic socialism"—which would form the root of her public service for the rest of her life.

While relations between Arabs and Jews had often been tenuous, in 1936 Arab "disturbances" exacerbated existing tensions. The colonial British government quickly established the

Peel Commission, which was to suggest partitioning Palestine into Jewish and Arab sectors. The Arabs rejected the proposal, and, with little international sponsorship for Zionism, the British closed Jewish immigration.

The British upheld their exclusive policies throughout the long, bitter years of the holocaust. To Golda it was inexplicable that a government which fought so valiantly against Hitler could, at the same time, actively oppose Jewish immigration to Palestine. Ironically, when the British Labor Party—which had vocally supported Zionism—came to power, they pursued a policy that blocked or turned back from Palestine "illegal" ships filled with Holocaust survivors. It seemed that the gateway to the Jewish promised land would forever be closed.

Then, finally, the British government, caught in an escalating conflict between Jews and Arabs, appealed to the United Nations, which proposed a partition plan much like that of the Peel Commission. This time, despite Arab opposition, the U.N.'s affirmative vote sanctioned Israeli autonomy.

Golda cried like a child when she and other Zionist leaders signed the official Israeli Scroll of Independence. She was soon dispatched to the U.S. to lobby American Jews to arm the infant state against the Arab militias massed at its borders.

As the War of Independence unfolded, Golda witnessed little of the early action. Shortly after returning to Israel, she was sent to Moscow as first Israeli minister to Russia. Back in the country of her birth, she saw again firsthand the anti-Semitism which had so shattered her childhood.

Her stay in Moscow lasted only seven months. Ben-Gurion, Israel's first Prime Minister, called Golda home to serve as Minister of Labor in his cabinet. For seven years Golda dealt with the waves of Jewish immigrants. She oversaw the construction of immigrant camps, the development of language and work skills programs, and the construction of houses and communities to permanently settle the expanding populace.

During this busy period, Morris died. Though the couple had long been separated, they had always loved each other, and she privately grieved over his death.

In 1956, other sorrows took center stage in Golda's life. The Arab states continued to arm themselves against the Jewish nation. Serving as Foreign Minister, Golda was well aware of the dangers and was one of few who knew beforehand about the Sinai Offensive, an attack in which Israeli troops, in a few short days, swept across the Sinai Peninsula and Gaza Strip. Though the offensive freed the Israelis from exposure to the terrorist bases, the U.N. demanded that the Israelis withdraw and cede the territory to a peace-keeping force. As Golda attempted to negotiate a peace settlement, she realized that the international community had never understood the Israeli people or the complex nature of the Middle East conflict. "We were the firstborn of the United Nations," she admitted, "but we were being treated like unwanted stepchildren, and I must admit that it hurt."

In her duties as Foreign Minister, Golda headed numerous outreach programs to developing African and Asian countries. Israel's enormous pool of trained specialists, however, soon gave way to Arab pressure. The ensuing Yom Kippur War forced most of these partner countries to break ties with Israel, and, once again, the Jewish state learned that "One can count on no one but oneself." This bitter lesson was only reinforced by the international indifference to Egyptian and Syrian rhetoric—and further Arab readiness to launch another attack on Israel. In the end, the world did not resist when Egypt's Nasser ordered U.N. forces out of the Sinai Peninsula. Once again Israel stood on its own—and once again, with American support, it swiftly routed its foes.

Golda, after decades of government service, observed this war from retirement. Within a short few months, however, the Labor Party called on her to head a delegation with the mission of unifying its three factions.

When her work was done, Golda hoped to return to private life. One night, however, she received a phone call: Eshkol, the Prime Minister, had died of a heart attack. As "manager" of the unified Labor Party, she was asked to supervise the interim government until formal elections could be held. In the fall of 1969, at the age of seventy, she was elected Prime Minister of Israel.

Her five years in office began and ended with war. Israel was determined to hold the territories gained during the Six-Day War until a permanent peace agreement could be signed. The Arabs, on the other hand, were just as adamant that Israel return the occupied lands. The result was a War of Attrition, in which Egypt, with Soviet backing, made consistent attacks on Israeli holdings. Golda, knowing that another full-scale assault would soon commence, did all she could both to initiate peace talks with Arab leaders and secure arms for her country. After several visits to Washington, she finally won U.S. assurances of continued support.

In 1973, on Yom Kippur—or sacred "Day of Atonement"—Egypt and Syria suddenly launched a two-front attack. Caught off guard, the Israelis initially gave up ground. For Golda Meir, every decision became a harrowing dilemma in which Israeli lives were at stake. Not until a few weeks into the war, with U.S. military aid on its way, did the tide turn.

In November of the same year, a cease-fire agreement was signed, but the "Yom Kippur War" had taken its toll, both on the nation and its aged Prime Minister. Exhausted, Golda resigned in June of the following year.

Golda Meir's vision of Israel, a homeland for her people, has endured. Until her death at age 80 in 1978, she continued to dream of a strong and peaceful nation where her grandchildren would "grow up as free Jews in a country that is their own."

PROFILES IN COURAGE

by John F. Kennedy, Harper & Brothers, New York, N.Y., 1955

This is a book about that most admirable of human virtues—courage . . . These are the stories of the pressures experienced by eight United States Senators and the grace with which they endured them—the risks to their careers, the unpopularity of their courses, the defamation of their characters, and sometimes, but sadly only sometimes, the vindication of their reputations and their principles.

The eight political heroes spotlighted in John F. Kennedy's Pulitzer Prize-winning *Profiles in Courage* truly exemplify the philosophy made famous by its author: *Ask not what your country can do for you—ask what you can do for your country.*

All eight men—John Quincy Adams, Daniel Webster, Thomas Hart Benton, Sam Houston, Edmund G. Ross, Congressman Lucius Quintus Cincinnatus Lamar, George Norris, and Robert A. Taft—refused to sacrifice their principles despite the most crushing opposition. Each also bucked the will of his political party, an important matter to Kennedy, who believed that politicians must sometimes rise above partisan considerations.

Four of Kennedy's heroic profiles are featured here. The idea they embody—that individuals can be a force for liberty and justice by following their convictions in the face of popular opposition—still appeals to Americans' noblest qualities.

❖ ♦ ❖

John Quincy Adams was the son of the second U.S. President, John Adams, and was eventually to assume the mantle of the Presidency himself. *Harsh and intractable . . . he had a tenacity of purpose, a lofty and inflexible courage, an unbending will, which never qualified or flinched before human antagonist, or before exile, torture, or death.* Unfortunately, these qualities did not serve him well in the political arena. "A politician in this country must be the man of a party," he explained. "I would fain be the man of my whole country."

Elected to the Massachusetts State Senate in 1803, Adams immediately infuriated his own Federalist party by sanctioning the views of Republican President Thomas Jefferson, who argued for individual rights over government intervention. Although ostracized by the Federalists and ignored by colleagues and constituents, he stuck to his ideals: *His guiding star was the principle . . . his father had laid down many years before: "The magistrate is the servant not of his own desires, not even of the people, but of his God."*

In 1807 Adams supported an embargo bill designed to retaliate against "British aggressions upon American ships." The embargo hit New England, including his home state, harder than any other section of the country. Newspapers attacked him as "a party scavenger . . . one of those ambitious politicians who lives on both land and water, and occasionally resorts to each, but who finally settles down in mud." The criticism didn't surprise Adams; early on he confided to a fellow supporter of the embargo that "This measure will cost you and me our seats . . ."

As Adams predicted, the Massachusetts legislature voted to replace him at the end of his term, and instructed the state's Senators to vote for repeal of the embargo. Out of deference to his constituents' wishes, Adams straightway resigned rather than serve out his term. Eventually, his political fortunes rose again. He went on to serve a "politically independent term" as United States President, then closed out his political career in the House of Representatives.

"Far from regretting any one of those acts for which I have suffered," he said looking back, "I would do them over again . . . at the hazard of ten times as much slander, unpopularity, and displacement."

❖ ♦ ❖

On March 7th, 1850, a Massachusetts Senator delivered a speech that postponed the outbreak of civil war in the United States for eleven more years. That "7th of March" speech, however, ruined him politically, bringing on vicious criticism which continued even after his death.

Daniel Webster was, in the words of contemporaries, "a compound of strength and weakness, dust and divinity . . . a great man with a small ambition." He was also probably the greatest orator the Congress has ever seen.

In 1850 many Southern leaders were threatening secession over the Northern states' refusal to allow the expansion of slavery into the Western territories. Virginia Senator Henry Clay asked the gifted Webster for his support on a compromise bill that would allow slave states to remain as such. A fervent abolitionist, Webster regarded slavery "as a great moral and political evil," but he was also a Union man, long famous for his impassioned cry, "Liberty and Union, now and forever, one and inseparable!" He believed that secession would lead to bloodshed and was convinced that Clay's compromise was the country's only salvation.

On the appointed day, Webster stood before a packed Senate chamber and said, "I wish to speak today, not as a Massachusetts man, nor as a Northern man, but as an American and a Member of the Senate . . ." The three-hour speech that followed literally "disarmed and quieted the South." One newspaper later reported: *Webster did more than any other man in the whole country, and at a greater hazard of personal popularity, to stem and roll back the torrent of sectionalism which . . . threatened to overthrow the pillars of the Constitution and the Union.*

But at the time Northern abolitionists were outraged at what they regarded as Webster's betrayal. He was labeled a "traitor to the cause of freedom." Educator Horace Mann called him "a fallen star! Lucifer descending from Heaven!"— and he lost any chance for the Presidential nomination that he had long coveted.

Webster died in 1852, "disappointed and discouraged" but true to the Union to the end. " . . . No man can suffer too much, and no man can fall too soon," he proclaimed some weeks before his death, "if he suffer or if he fall in defense of the liberties and Constitution of his country."

❖ ♦ ❖

Thomas Hart Benton, who served the people of Missouri in the Senate for thirty consecutive years, loved a good fight. Once he warned an opponent, "I never quarrel, sir. But sometimes I fight, sir; and whenever I fight, sir, a funeral follows, sir." But his last great fight—waged against secessionists in the South, including voters from his own state—resulted in the Democratic Senator's own political funeral.

As a long-time champion of Westward expansion, Benton was enormously popular among his fellow Missourians throughout his first four Senate terms; but by the early 1840s, Missouri, as a slave state, had begun to identify strongly with its Southern neighbors. Benton, holding to his Union ideals, suffered a steep decline in popularity and was barely elected to his fifth term in 1844. Despite the close election, however, he insisted on going against his party and his constituents by opposing the annexation of Texas—which would have upset the ration of slave to free states. South Carolina Senator John C. Calhoun, a pro-slavery advocate, denounced Benton as "false to the South," and the Missouri legislature agreed, pushing through resolutions that instructed all its national representatives to vote for annexation. Benton refused, calling the resolutions "the speckled progeny of a vile conjunction, redolent with lurking treason to the Union." This intransigent refusal cost him his Senate seat.

But in the end, Benton triumphed—even in death. At the outbreak of the Civil War, four years after he had surrendered to his ultimate adversary, throat cancer, Missouri declined to secede with the other Southern states, in part inspired by Benton's memory. The faith he had displayed in his last Senate report to his constituency was finally borne out: "I sometimes had to act against the preconceived opinions and first impressions of my constituents; but always with full reliance upon their intelligence to understand me and their equity to do me justice—and I have never been disappointed."

❖ ◆ ❖

Edmund G. Ross, "the man who saved a President," may actually have saved the institution of the Presidency itself by casting a courageous vote that completely destroyed his own political career. One historian called this vote "the most heroic act in American history, incomparably more difficult than any deed of valor upon the field of battle."

In 1868 the "Radical Republicans," who dominated the Congress by a count of 42 to 12, sought to remove their one-time Senatorial colleague the stubborn Tennessee-born Andrew Johnson from the Presidency because he resisted the vengeful Reconstruction policies imposed on the South during the post-Civil War period. According to the Articles of Impeachment they needed only a two-thirds majority (36 votes) to convict Johnson of official misconduct.

It soon became clear that the Prosecution could produce little, if any, evidence of presidential wrongdoing. Six Republicans stood up to say that, without proper evidence, they would vote for acquittal. The Radicals knew that they could not afford to lose even one of the 36 remaining Republican votes, or they would lose their necessary two-thirds majority. But at the caucus, Senator Ross, a solid Republican from Kansas who disliked the President, said his vote was still "undecided."

The Radicals were offended. Sputtered one Republican leader, "I did not think that a Kansas man could quibble against his country." As the one undecided Republican senator, Ross now received "the full brunt" of his party's pressure tactics.

" . . . So far as I am concerned, though a Republican and opposed to Mr. Johnson and his policy," Ross told an associate as the trial for impeachment got under way, "he shall have as fair a trial as an accused man ever had on this earth." Mail poured in from the Senator's home state, demanding Johnson's conviction. He received scores of dire warnings, even threats of assassination if he did not vote for impeachment. *Ten minutes before the vote . . . [Ross'] Kansas colleague warned him . . . that a vote for acquittal would mean trumped up charges and his political death.*

"I almost literally looked down into my open grave," Ross later recalled. "Friendships, position, fortune, everything that makes life desirable to an ambitious man were about to be swept away by the breath of my mouth, perhaps forever." Still, Ross voted not guilty.

The President and the Presidency were saved; but newspapers across the country assailed the man who had "sold himself and betrayed his constituents . . . basely lied to his friends, shamefully violated his solemn pledge [and] signed the death warrant of his country's liberty . . . "

Ross served out the whole of his six-year term, all the while referred to as "traitor Ross." His fellow senators shunned him as if he were a leper. Finally, upon leaving the Senate in 1871, he moved with his family back to Kansas, there to suffer "social ostracism, physical attack, and near poverty." Only late in his life did national opinion vindicate Ross' actions. It was finally recognized that, in supporting the President, the Senator from Kansas had "saved the country from . . . a strain that would have wrecked any other form of government [and a] calamity greater than war . . . "

❖ ◆ ❖

Reflecting on the lives of these great patriots, Kennedy writes, . . . *Without belittling the courage with which men have died, we should not forget those acts of courage with which men . . . have lived . . .*

Endnote: *A Profile of the Author*

Born in 1917, John F. Kennedy served his country heroically during World War II, receiving the Navy and Marine Corps Medal and a purple heart. He also served three times as a U.S. Representative from Massachusetts, and in 1952 successfully ran for the U.S. Senate. It was while recuperating from back surgery during his term as a Senator that he wrote *Profiles in Courage.*

In 1960 he was elected President of the United States. In 1963, while riding in a Dallas motorcade, he fell victim to an assassin's bullet—an incident that devastated a nation and shattered the "American Camelot" that characterized Kennedy's brief term in office.

COMPACT
Classics ®

LIBRARY #6: Thought Collections
moods and musings for the moment

Thought Collections is organized, not by topic, but by mood and voice—the various moods and voices of human nature. Each separate gourmet selection of quotes and anecdotes is designed to be tasted, savored, and re-savored—for escape, entertainment, or insight—according to your wants and needs of the moment.

If you feel you need to recharge the wells of your inspiration and motivation—or want to help recharge the wells of others—perhaps items under the headings "The Religious Voice" or "Lights to Live By" will help. If you want to infuse a little spice or controversy into your conversation, check out entries under "The Human Condition" or "Point/Counterpoint," or ponder on a few quotes from "Maxims and Mottos," or maybe "Deep Ideas." And to renew your appreciation of life—or just to bring a smile to your lips—turn to the "Wisecracks and Witticisms" or "Tutorial Tales" sections.

Uplifting, informative, refining, faith- and confidence-building...the fruits we reap from others' pungent perceptions can leave fertile new furrows within our own hearts and minds to nurture the seeds of our own individual wisdom.

MAXIMS AND MOTTOS

(Piercing Insights and Uncommon-Sense Advice)

Never give advice. Look at Socrates, a noted Greek philosopher, who went around giving good advice . . . and they poisoned him.
- Anonymous

You cannot plow a field by turning it over in your mind.
You have to get off your butt and do something!
- Dail C. West

And now here is my secret, a very simple secret: It is only with the heart that one can see rightly; what is essential is invisible to the eye.
- Antoine de Saint-Exupery

It is sometimes necessary to step backward in order to go forward.
- French saying

The shoe that fits one person pinches another; there is no recipe for living that suits all cases.-
- Carl Jung

The only ones . . . who will be really happy are those who have sought and found how to serve.
- Albert Schweitzer

People are lonely because they build walls instead of bridges.
- Joseph Fort Newton

The dog barks but the caravan moves on.
- Arabic proverb

It is better to die on your feet than live on your knees.
- Dolores Ibarruri

My duty is to obey orders.
- Stonewall Jackson

One can acquire everything in solitude—except character.
- Stendhal

The tragedy of love is indifference.
- W. Sommerset Maugham

Draw your salary before spending it.
- George Ade

Neither a borrower nor a lender be.
- William Shakespeare, Hamlet

If we don't change direction, we will arrive at where we are going.
-Richard L. Evans

News is the first draft of history.
-Benjamin Bradlee

Ideas shape the course of history.
-John Maynard Keynes

History is bunk.
-Henry Ford

History . . . is a nightmare from which I am trying to awake.
-James Joyce, Ulysses

Of course everything has been said that needs to be said—but since no one was listening it has to be said again.
-Author Unknown

There can be no freedom or beauty about a home life that depends on borrowing and debt.
- Henrik Ibsen, A Doll's House

Whatever you have, spend less.
- Samuel Johnson

There is no substitute for hard work.
- Thomas Edison

I'm curious about jumping off a cliff, and I won't do that either.
- Herschel Walker, on why he wasn't curious about taking a drink

Don't blame the mirror if your face is faulty.
- Nikolai Gogol

Statistics are no substitute for judgment.
- Henry Clay

It is easier to resist at the beginning than at the end.
- Leonardo da Vinci

A small daily task, if it be really daily, will beat the labors of a spasmodic Hercules.
- Anthony Trollope

Being entirely honest with oneself is a good exercise.
- Sigmund Freud

Nothing great was ever achieved without enthusiasm.
- Ralph Waldo Emerson

You can't get spoiled if you do your own ironing.
- Meryl Streep

To be able to say how much you love is to love but little.
- Petrarch

Honor is not the exclusive property of any political party.
- Herbert Hoover

Always be sure you're right, then go ahead.
- Davey Crockett

Chill out, folks. You can't shake hands with a clenched fist.
- Ann Landers (from I. Gandhi)

Work keeps us from three great evils—boredom, vice and need.
- Voltaire

He who has begun has half done. Dare to be wise; begin!

- Horace, c. 65 BC

When eating bamboo sprouts, remember the man who planted them.

- Chinese Proverb

Nothing is worth more than this day.

- Johann Goethe

Those who have the most to do and are willing to work will find the most time.

- Samuel Smiles

Failure is an event, never a person.

- William D. Brown

Cleverness is not wisdom.

- Euripides

Do what you can, with what you have, where you are.

- Theodore Roosevelt

Leadership is action, not position.

- Donald H. McGannon

Act well at the moment and you have performed a good action to all eternity.

- Johann Kaspar Lavater

A teacher affects eternity; he can never tell where his influence stops.

- Henry Adams

Good manners and soft words have brought many a difficult thing to pass.

- Aesop

The man who insists on seeing with perfect clearness before he decides, never decides.

- Henri Frederic Amiel

Ask thyself, daily, to how many ill-minded persons thou has shown a kind disposition.

- Marcus Antoninus

A fool may be known by six things: anger without cause; speech without profit; change without progress; inquiry without object; putting trust in a stranger; and mistaking foes for friends.

- Arab Proverb

Rest is not idleness, and to lie sometimes on the grass under the trees, listening to the murmur of the water, or watching the clouds float across the blue sky, is by no means a waste of time.

- Lord Avebury

A wise man will make more opportunities than he finds.

- Francis Bacon

The ants find kingdoms in a foot of ground.

- William Rose Benet

Charity should begin at home, but it should not stay there.

- Phillips Brooks

Because half a dozen grasshoppers under a fern make the field ring with their importunate chirps, do not imagine that they are the only inhabitants of the field.

- John Bunyan

He who loses wealth loses much; he who loses a friend loses more; but he who loses courage loses all.

- Miguel de Cervantes

A single conversation across the table with a wise man is worth a month's study of books.

- Chinese Proverb

Better guide well the young than reclaim them when they are old.

- Joseph Malin

Make it a rule of life never to regret and never to look back. Regret is an appalling waste of energy.

- Katherine Mansfield

We should learn, by reflecting on the misfortunes of others, that there is nothing singular in those which befall ourselves.

- William Melmoth

Obstacles are those frightful things you see when you take your eyes off the goal.

- Hannah Moore

Every man goes down to his death bearing in his hands only that which he has given away.

- Persian Proverb

It is with our judgments as with our watches; no two go alike, yet each believes his own.

- Alexander Pope

We have no more right to consume happiness without producing it than to consume wealth without producing it.

- George Bernard Shaw

It is not enough to be industrious—so are the ants. What are you industrious about?

- Henry David Thoreau

Happy is he who has been able to learn the causes of things.

- Virgil

Keep your face toward the sunshine and the shadows will fall behind you.

- Walt Whitman

Perhaps someday it will be pleasant to remember even this.

- Virgil, c. 20 BC

Sometimes a person has to go a very long distance out of his way to come back a short distance correctly.

- Edward Albee, Zoo Story

To live for some future goal is shallow. It's the sides of the mountain that sustain life, not the top.

- Robert M. Pirsing

No man is justified in doing evil on the grounds of expediency.
- *Theodore Roosevelt*

Words are easy, like the wind; faithful friends are hard to find.
- *Richard Barnfield*

The ladder of life is full of splinters, but they always prick the hardest when we are sliding down.
- *William L. Brownell*

One vice worn out makes us wiser than fifty tutors.
- *Edward G. Bulwer-Lytton*

Only your real friends will tell you when your face is dirty.
- *Sicilian proverb*

There never was a day that did not bring its own opportunity for doing good that never could have been done before, and never can be done again.
- *William Burleigh*

An idle man is like a house that hath no walls; the devils may enter on every side.
- *Geoffrey Chaucer*

Never give in, never give in—never—in nothing, great or small, large or petty— never give in except to convictions of honour and good sense.
- *Winston Churchill*

The best place to find helping hands is at the end of your own arms.
- *Confucius*

Hope is the dream of a waking man.
- *Diogenes*

It's not how old you are, but how you are old.
- *Marie Dressler*

The measure of success is not whether you had a tough problem to deal with, but whether it's the same problem you had last year.
- *John Foster Dulles*

In everything consider the end.
- *French proverb*

It is a bad plan that admits of no modification.
- *Publilius Syrus*

Bad habits are as infectious by example as the plague itself is by contact.
- *Henry Fielding*

To acquire self-discipline and self-control, you start with a single step: you decide that you can do it.
- *Norman Vincent Peale*

As land is improved by sowing it with various seeds, so is the mind by exercising it with different studies.
- *Pliny the Elder*

Before we passionately desire anything which another possesses, we should examine as to the happiness of the possessor.
- *Francois Rochefoucauld*

To consider oneself different from ordinary men is wrong, but it is right to hope that one will not remain like ordinary men.
- *Publilius Syrus*

It is better to shoot for the stars and miss than aim at the gutter and hit it.
- *Anonymous*

You won't find a solution by saying there is no problem.
- *William Rostler*

When you read a classic, you do not see more in the book than you did before; you see more in you than there was before.
- *Clifton Fadiman*

Trust because you are willing to accept the risk, not because it's safe or certain.
- *Stephen C. Paul*

If you want to earn more than you get, you need to be worth more than you are paid.
- *Author Unknown*

I never did anything worth doing by accident, nor did any of my inventions come by accident. They came be work.
- *Thomas A. Edison*

Our faults irritate us most when we see them in others.
- *Pennsylvania Dutch Proverb*

Even a single hair casts its shadow.
- *Publilius Syrus*

You never really lose until you quit trying.
- *Mike Ditka*

One can pay back the loan of gold, but one dies forever in debt to those who are kind.
- *Malay Proverb*

Common sense is not common.
- *Will Rogers*

He who can take advice is sometimes superior to him who can give it.
- *Karl von Knebel*

A rattlesnake that doesn't bite teaches you nothing.
- *Jessamyn West, The Life I Really Lived*

If you can't stand the heat, get out of the kitchen.
- *Harry S Truman*

The best thing to do behind a person's back is pat it.
- *Franklin P. Jones*

Dig the well before you are thirsty.
- *Chinese proverb*

A mule dressed in a tuxedo is still a mule. If a man calleth thee a donkey, pay him no mind. If two men calleth thee a donkey, get thee a saddle.
- *Yiddish proverb*

You get out of life just what you put into it—minus taxes.
- *Al Lerrera*

Do not free a camel of the burden of his hump. You may be freeing him from being a camel.
- *G.K. Chesterton*

The porcupine, whom one must handle gloved, may be respected, but is never loved.
- *Arthur Guiterman*

He is educated who knows how to find out what he doesn't know.
- *George Simmel*

Everyone must row with the oars he has.
- *English proverb*

He that is everywhere is nowhere.
- *Thomas Fuller*

Lose an hour in the morning, and you will be all day hunting for it.
- *Richard Whately*

This above all: to thine own self be true,
And it must follow, as the night the day,
Thou canst not then be false to any man.
- *William Shakespeare, Hamlet*

Don't look back. Something might be gaining on you.
- *Leroy "Satchel" Paige*

Stopping at third base adds nothing to the score.

The middle of the road is where the white line is—and that's the worst place to drive.
- *Robert Frost*

That lucky rabbit's foot didn't work for the rabbit.

Watch the little things; a small leak will sink a great ship.
- *Benjamin Franklin*

Plan ahead . . . It wasn't raining when Noah built the ark.

Behold the turtle: He only makes progress when he sticks his neck out.
- *James B. Conant*

Every man is a damn fool for at least five minutes every day; wisdom consists in not exceeding the limit.
- *Elbert Hubbard*

The reverse side also has a reverse side.
- *Japanese proverb*

Be as smart as you can, but remember that it's always better to be wise than to be smart. And don't be upset that it takes a long, long time to find wisdom. Like a rare virus, wisdom tends to break out at unexpected times, and it's mostly people with compassion and understanding who are susceptible to it.
- *Alan Alda*

Chronic remorse is a most undesirable sentiment . . . Rolling in the mud is not the best way of getting clean.
- *Aldous Huxley*

Here's a good rule of thumb:
Too clever is dumb.
- *Ogden Nash*

We should not be like misers who never enjoy what they have but only bewail what they lose.
- *Plutarch*

Many receive advice, few profit by it.
- *Publilius Syrus*

Be bold and courageous. When you look back on your life, you'll regret the things you didn't do more than the ones you did.

Don't say you don't have enough time. You have exactly the same number of hours per day that were give to Pasteur, Michelangelo, Mother Teresa, Helen Keller, Leonardo da Vinci, Thomas Jefferson, and Albert Einstein.
- *H. Jackson Brown Jr.*

Be excellent to each other.
- *Bill and Ted's Excellent Adventure*

Little drops of water wear down big stones.
- *Russian proverb*

Men show their characters in what they think laughable.
- *Goethe*

The best of blessings—a contented mind.
- *Latin proverb*

It is better to walk than to run; it is better to stand than to walk; it is better to sit than to stand; it is better to lie than to sit.
- *Hindu proverb*

Misfortune does not always come to injure.
- *Italian proverb*

Remember that thou art mortal.
- *Greek proverb*

If Heaven creates a man, there must be some use for him.
- *Chinese proverb*

The more stupid, the happier.
- *Chinese proverb*

If you are afraid of being lonely, don't try to be right.
- *Jules Renard*

Let your children go if you want to keep them.
- *Malcolm Forbes*

He who seizes the right moment is the right man.
- *Goethe*

Cruelties should be committed all at once.
- *Machiavelli*

Granting our wish one of Fate's saddest jokes is!

— *James Russell Lowell*

A good intention clothes itself with power.

— *Ralph Waldo Emerson*

Beware of all enterprises that require new clothes.

— *Henry David Thoreau*

Keep thy hook always baited, for a fish lurks even in the most unlikely waters.

— *Ovid*

There's small choice in rotten apples.

— *William Shakespeare*

The blow of a whip raises a welt, but a blow of the tongue crushes bones.

— *Ecclesiasticus*

We should take care not to make the intellect our god; it has, of course, powerful muscles, but no personality.

— *Albert Einstein*

You cannot endow even the best machine with initiative; the jolliest steamroller will not plant flowers.

— *Walter Lippmann*

We lie loudest when we lie to ourselves.

— *Eric Hoffer*

Once the toothpaste is out of the tube, it is awfully hard to get it back in.

— *H.R. Haldeman*

Teach thy tongue to say "I do not know."

— *Maimonides*

Beware of the man of one book.

— *St. Thomas Aquinas*

No man sees far, the most see no farther than their noses.

— *Thomas Carlyle*

Avoid as you would a pestilence—two things: fear and anger. Scientific investigation has proven that these two excesses engender poisons in the body that destroy its health and break down its efficiency.

— *Anonymous*

Whom the gods would destroy they first make mad.

— *Dryden*

Fear not that thy life shall come to an end, but rather fear that it shall never have a beginning.

— *Cardinal Newman*

Worry is a misuse of the imagination. It is assuming responsibility that God never intended you to have. It brings sorrow and saps the day of its strength.

— *Alfred A. Montapert*

Life is a journey. Not a camp.

— *Anonymous*

When men speak ill of thee, live so nobody will believe them.

— *Plato*

Even on the most exalted throne in the world we are only sitting on our own bottom.

— *Michel Eyquem De Montaigne*

Worry is as useless as sawing sawdust.

— *Anonymous*

Never get so busy making a living that you forget to make a life.

— *Anonymous*

. . . Behold, the fear of the Lord, that is wisdom; and to depart from evil is understanding.

— *Holy Bible Job 28:28*

Forbidden fruit is responsible for many bad jams.

— *Anonymous*

Men occasionally stumble over the truth, but most of them pick themselves up and hurry off as if nothing had happened.

— *Sir Winston Churchill*

Many a man thinks he has an open mind when it's merely vacant.

— *Anonymous*

Hell is truth seen too late.

— *Anonymous*

You can usually judge the caliber of a man by the size of the things that get his goat.

— *Anonymous*

Time is a dressmaker specializing in alterations.

— *Faith Baldwin*

I dance to the tune that is played.

— *Spanish Proverb*

The dog barks, but the caravan moves on.

— *Arabic Proverb*

Great souls have wills; feeble ones have only wishes.

— *Chinese proverb*

Most of us swim in the ocean of the commonplace.

— *Pio Baroja*

You can avoid having ulcers by adapting to the situation: if you fall in the mud puddle, check your pockets for fish.

— *Anonymous*

Past experience should be a guide post, not a hitching post.

— *Anonymous*

The past is a bucket of ashes, so live not in your yesterdays, nor just for tomorrow, but in here and now. Keep moving and forget the post mortems. And remember, no one can get the jump on the future.

— *Victor Hugo*

Know the difference between success and fame. Success is Mother Teresa. Fame is Madonna.

- Erma Bombeck

Whenever you're sitting across from some important person, always picture him sitting there in a suit of long underwear. That's the way I always operated in business.

- Joseph P. Kennedy

Are these things, then, necessities? Then let us meet them like necessities.

- William Shakespeare, King Henry IV

We do not remember days, we remember moments.

- Cesare Pavese

Never bend your head. Always hold it high. Look the world straight in the eye.

- Helen Keller

When you betray somebody else, you also betray yourself.

- Isaac Bashevis Singer

Never make a promise in haste.

- Mahatma Gandhi

The brightest things you ever say
Are those you think about next day.

- Arnold Glasow

The man who says just what he thinks should think.

- Author Unknown

What would be the use of immortality to a person who cannot use well a half hour.

- Ralph Waldo Emerson

I beseech you . . . , think it possible that you may be mistaken.

- Oliver Cromwell

There is no dishonor in rethinking a problem.

- The Royal Bank of Canada Monthly Letter

My mind is a chest of drawers. When I wish to deal with a subject, I shut all the drawers but the one in which the subject is to be found. When I am wearied, I shut all the drawers and go to sleep.

- Napoleon Bonaparte

It is a wise father who throws away his old report cards.

- Author Unknown

There are times when if you are not feeling like yourself, it is quite an improvement.

- Author Unknown

One must separate from anything that forces one to repeat "No" again and again.

- Friedrich Nietzsche

If you draw your thread too fine it will break.

- Petrarca

It's pretty hard to tell what does bring happiness. Poverty an' wealth have both failed.

- Kin Hubbard

When a man has not a good reason for doing a thing, he has one good reason for letting it alone.

- Thomas Scott

You win the victory when you yield to friends.

- Sophocles

The most important thing in a man is not what he knows, but what he is.

- Narciso Yepes

The perpetual obstacle to human advancement is custom.

- John Stuart Mill

He that jokes confesses.

- Italian proverb

Do not give, as many rich men do, like a hen that lays an egg, and then cackle.

- Henry Ward Beecher

If you want a thing done, go—if not, send.

- Benjamin Franklin

The go between wears out a thousand sandals.

- Japanese proverb

Consider the little mouse, how sagacious an animal it is which never entrust its life to one hold only.

- Plautus

It is fine to aim high if we have developed the ability to accomplish our aims, but there is no use aiming unless the gun is loaded.

- William Ross

I don't want the cheese, I just want to get out of the trap.

- Latin American Proverb

Ambition destroys its possessor.

- The Talmud

He that hath a head of wax must not walk in the sun.

- George Herbert

If we had no faults, we should not take so much pleasure in noting those of others.

- La Rochefoucauld

Almost all our faults are more pardonable than the methods we think up to hide them.

- La Rochefoucauld

Know thyself. Don't accept your dog's admiration as conclusive.

- Mayes

The proverb warns that, "You should not bite the hand that feeds you." But maybe you should, if it prevents you from feeding yourself.

- Thomas Szasz

Be thine own palace, or the world's thy jail.

- John Donne

It is our responsibilities, not ourselves, that we should take seriously.
> *- Peter Ustinov*

Keep out of ruts; a rut is something which
If traveled in too much, becomes a ditch.
> *- Arthur Guiterman*

Go to bed. Whatever you're staying up late for isn't worth it.
> *- Andrew A. Rooney*

I learned certain things about wasting energy. It hit me the hardest after the French [Open]. The important thing is to learn a lesson every time you lose. Life is a learning process and you have to try to learn what's best for you. Let me tell you, life is not fun when you're banging your head against a brick wall all the time.
> *- John McEnroe*

Straighten up your room first, then the world.
> *- Jeff Jordan*

More than any other time in history, mankind faces a crossroad. One path leads to despair and utter hopelessness. The other, to total extinction. Let us pray we have the wisdom to choose correctly . . . Summing up, it is clear the future holds great opportunities. It also holds pitfalls. The trick will be to avoid the pitfalls, seize the opportunities and get back home by six o'clock.
> *- Woody Allen, "My Speech to the Graduates"*

Trust, but verify.
> *- Old Russian proverb*

Be not afraid of life. Believe that life *is* worth living and your belief will help create the fact.
> *- William James*

You have to believe in happiness or happiness never comes.
> *- Douglas Malloch*

Now if you are going to win any battle you have to do one thing. You have to make the mind run the body. Never let the body tell the mind what to do. The body will always give up. It is always tired morning, noon, and night. But the body is never tired if the mind is not tired. When you were younger the mind could make you dance all night, and the body was never tired . . . .You've always got to make the mind take over and keep going.
> *- George S. Patton*

Do not get excited over the noise you have made.
> *- Desiderius Erasmus*

Let us satisfy our own consciences, and trouble not ourselves by looking for fame. If we deserve it, we shall attain it; if we deserve it not, we cannot force it.
> *- Seneca*

If it's working, keep doing it.
If it's not working, stop doing it.
If you don't know what to do, don't do anything.
> *- Medical school advice*

Beware of fishing for compliments—you might come up with a boot.
> *- Carol Weston*

Don't ask questions of fairy tales.
> *- Jewish proverb*

When things go wrong—don't go with them.
> *- Anonymous*

Don't change your plans too often. One sometimes meets destiny on the road he took to avoid it.
> *- Quoted by Ann Landers*

Don't talk about yourself, it will be done when you leave.
> *- Addison Mizner*

I think we consider too much the good luck of the early bird, and not enough of the bad luck of the early worm.
> *- Franklin D. Roosevelt*

Stumbling is not falling.
> *- Portuguese proverb*

The problem when solved will be simple.
> *- Sign on the wall of a General Motors research laboratory*

Where there is no vision, the people perish . . .
> *- Proverbs 29:18*

Victory—a matter of staying power.
> *- Elbert Hubbard*

Don't be afraid to take a big step if one is indicated. You can't cross a chasm in two small jumps.
> *- David Lloyd George*

He who is above the conscience of the community is as likely to be slain as he who is below.
> *- Harold Cooke Phillips*

Do not speak of secret matters in a field that is full of little hills.
> *- Hebrew proverb*

He that conquereth himself is greater than he that taketh a city.
> *- Proverbs*

Your plan for work and happiness should be big, imaginative and daring. Strike out boldly for the things you honestly want more than anything else in the world. The mistake is to put your sights too low, not to raise them too high. The definite, faraway goal will supercharge your whole body and spirit; it will awaken your mind and spirit; it will awaken your mind and creative imagination, and put meaning into otherwise lowly step-by-step tasks you must go through in order to attain your final success.
> *- Henry J. Kaiser*

There is more adventure alive in the world today than there ever was, plenty of unexplored places. Adventure is there waiting for any man with the courage to go and find it. but you'll never discover it by looking at the calendar—and counting yourself to death.

- Louis L'Amour

It's the hardest thing in the world to accept a pinch of success and leave it that way.

- Marlon Brando

What you do for yourself may start you up in the world. But from there on up, it's what you do for others.

- Burton Hillis

Lost battles do not lose a war, if our cause is just and our spirit strong . . . Defeat isn't bitter if you don't swallow it.

- Ben K. O'Dell

The bigger your head gets son, The easier it'll be to fill your shoes.

- James J. O'Reilly, Your Life

Patience accomplishes its objective, while hurry speeds to its ruin.

- Sa'di

A patronizing disposition always has its meaner side.

- George Eliot, Adam Bede

The noblest grace that sweetens life is charity borne with selflessness.

- Author unknown

Expect nothing; live frugally on surprise.

- Alice Walker

I have a real belief that life takes care of itself. And it's usually much better than what I imagine.

- Dana Delany

Blot out vain pomp; check impulse; quench appetite; keep reason under its own control.

- Marcus Aurelius

Be aware that a halo has to fall only a few inches to be a noose.

- Dan McKinnon

Never look down on anybody unless you're helping him up.

- The Rev. Jesse Jackson

The only thing to know is how to use your neuroses.

- Arthur Adamov

If we are not our brother's keeper, let us at least not be his executioner.

- Marlon Brando

The wise man in the storm prays to God, not for safety from danger, but for deliverance from fear.

- Ralph Waldo Emerson

We must not think our world is the only one. There are worlds outside our experience. "Call that a sunset?" said the lady to Turner as she stood before the artist's picture. "I never saw a sunset like that." "No, madam," said Turner. "Don't you wish you had?" Perhaps your world and mine is only mean because we are near-sighted. Perhaps we missed the vision not because the vision is not there, but because we darken the window.

- "Alpha of the Plough"

The essence of life: fight as if there were no death.

- Guy de Rothschild

Confessions come in pairs.

- Sparrow

People ask for criticism, but they only want praise.

- Somerset Maugham

You can't have everything. Where would you put it?

- Steven Wright

Striving for excellence motivates you; striving for perfection is demoralizing.

- Harriet Braiker, The Type E Woman

Fifty-one percent of being smart is knowing what you are dumb about.

- Ann Landers

We must not be innocents abroad in a world that is not innocent.

- Ronald Reagan

THE HUMAN CONDITION

Every man carries the entire form of human condition.
> *- Michel de Montaigne*

The world is still deceiv'd with ornament . . . In religion, what damned error but some sober brow will bless it, and approve it with a text, hiding the grossness with fair ornament? There is novice so simple but assumes some mark of virtue on his outward parts. How many cowards, whose hearts are all as false as stairs of sand, wear yet upon their chins the beards of Hercules and frowning Mars; who inward searched, have livers white as milk?
> *- William Shakespeare, The Merchant of Venice*

We must not let our passion destroy our dreams.
> *- King Arthur from Camelot*

I think society has changed tremendously in the last 25 years. Today, everybody talks about their rights and privileges. Twenty-five years ago, everybody talked about their obligations and responsibilities.
> *- Lou Holtz*

Whenever God erects a house of prayer
The Devil always builds a chapel there.
And twill be found, upon examination,
The latter has the largest congregation.
> *- Daniel Defoe*

If the profession you have chosen has some unexpected inconveniences, console yourself that no profession is without them . . . and that all the perplexities of business are softness compared with the vacancy . . . of idleness.
> *- Samuel Johnson*

We are all worms, but I do believe I am a glowworm.
> *- Winston Churchill*

The great companies did not know that the line between hunger and anger is a thin line.
> *- John Steinbeck*

America is an enormous frosted cupcake in the middle of millions of starving people.
> *- Gloria Steinem*

Endeavor to be always patient of the faults and imperfections of others, for thou hast many faults and imperfections of thy own that require a reciprocation and forbearance. If thou art not able to make thyself that which thou wishest to be, how canst thou expect to mold another in conformity to thy will?
> *- Thomas Kempis*

As a painter I shall never signify anything of importance. I feel it absolutely.
> *- Vincent van Gogh*

If I'm such a legend, why am I so lonely?
> *- Judy Garland*

A tremendous flash of light cut across the sky . . . Under [a] dust cloud, the day grew darker and darker.
> *- John Hersey, Hiroshima*

The world is full of suffering; it is also full of the overcoming of it.
> *- Helen Keller*

Music . . . can name the un-nameable and communicate the unknowable.
> *- Leonard Bernstein*

Music expresses that which cannot be put into words and that which cannot remain silent.
> *- Victor Hugo*

You can't say that civilizations don't advance . . . For every war they kill you in a new way.
> *- Will Rogers*

. . . Even when you lack self confidence, keep in mind that if you want a woman to think you're a prince, you should treat her like a queen.
> *-Marilyn vos Savant*

In the beginning, our Creator gave all the races of mankind the same songs and the same drums to keep in touch with Him, to keep faith. But people kept forgetting. In the fullness of time, the spiritual traditions of all the peoples—they are the same—will be united again in a great gathering of their secret leaders. And they will gain power to remake the world.
> *- Mohawk prophecy, told by Tom Porter*

Wherever they burn books, they will also, in the end, burn human beings.
> *- Heinrich Heine*

Careful the things you say,
Children will listen.
Careful the things you do,
Children will see.
And learn.

Children may not obey,
But children will listen.
Children will look to you
For which way to turn,
To learn what to be.
Careful before you say,
"Listen to me."
Children will listen.
> *- Stephen Sondheim, Into the Woods*

A friend loves you for your intelligence, a mistress for your charm, but your family's love is unreasoning; you were born into it and are of its flesh and blood. Nevertheless it can irritate you more than any group of people in the world.

- André Maurois

Rare is the person who can weigh the faults of others without putting his thumb on the scales.

- Byron J. Langenfield

All who have meditated upon the art of governing mankind have been convinced that the fate of empires depends on the education of youth.

- Aristotle

Decency is quiet, but it lasts.

- Anonymous

Artists can color the sky red because they know it's blue. Those of us who aren't artists must color things the way they really are or people might think we're stupid.

- Jule Feiffer

What is destructive is impatience, haste, expecting too much too fast.

- May Sarton, Journal of a Solitude

To consider oneself different from ordinary men is wrong, but it is right to hope that one will not remain like ordinary men.

- Anonymous

The basic difference between an ordinary man and a warrior is that a warrior takes everything as a challenge, while an ordinary man takes everything either as a blessing or as a curse.

- Don Juan

There are no great people. Rather, there are great challenges that ordinary people are forced to meet.

- Anonymous

The fear of death keeps us from living, not from dying.

- Paul C. Roud, Making Miracles

Don't look . . . you might see.
Don't listen . . . you might hear.
Don't think . . . you might learn.
Don't walk . . . you might stumble.
Don't run . . . you might fall.
Don't make a decision . . . you might be wrong.
Don't live . . . you might die.

- Anonymous

Be sure you gurgle [laugh] three times a day for your own well-being. And if you can get other people to join you in your laughter, you may help keep this shaky boat afloat. When people are laughing, they're generally not killing one another.

- Alan Alda

It must be the aim of education to teach the citizen that he must first of all rule himself.

- Winthrop Aldrich

There is a foolish corner even in the brain of a sage.

- Aristotle

The life of every man is a diary in which he means to write one story, and writes another; and his humblest hour is when he compares the volume as it is with what he hoped to make it.

- James Barrie

I have learned silence from the talkative, tolerance from the intolerant, and kindness from the unkind; yet strangely, I am ungrateful to these teachers.

- Khalil Gibran

The heart has reasons which reason itself does not understand.

- Jacques Bossuet

Even when we fancy that we have grown wiser, it may be only that new prejudices have displaced old ones.

- Christian Bovee

Education makes a people easy to lead, but difficult to drive; easy to govern, but impossible to enslave.

- Lord Brougham

Character is what you are in the dark.

- Dwight L. Moody

They say, best men are molded out of faults; and for the most become much more better for being a little bad.

- William Shakespeare, Measure for Measure

We can easily forgive a child who is afraid of the dark; the real tragedy of life is when men are afraid of the light.

- Plato

The one who will be found in trial capable of great acts of love is ever the one who is always doing considerate small ones.

- Frederick William Robertson

If you were going to die soon and had only one phone call you could make, who would you call and what would you say? And why are you waiting?

- Stephen Levine

Life is like an onion; you peel it off one layer at a time, and sometimes you weep.

- Carl Sandberg

I shall never permit myself to stoop so low as to hate another man.

- Booker T. Washington

I hope that I shall always possess firmness and virtue enough to maintain what I consider the most enviable of all titles, the character of an honest man.

- George Washington

If there is light in the soul,
There will be beauty in the person.
If there is beauty in the person,
There will be harmony in the house.
If there is harmony in the house,
There will be order in the nation.
If there is order in the nation,
There will be peace in the world.

- Chinese Proverb

Whatever women do they must do twice as well as men to be thought of as half as good.

- Ella Wheeler Wilcox

America does not consist of groups. A man who thinks of himself as belonging to a particular national group in America has not yet become an American.

- Woodrow Wilson

Strength and struggle go together. The supreme reward of struggle is strength. Life is a battle and the greatest joy is to overcome. The pursuit of easy things makes men weak. Do not equip yourselves with superior power and hope to escape the responsibility and work. It cannot be done. It is following the lines of least resistance that makes rivers and men crooked.

- Ralph Parlette

Pain nourishes courage. You can't be brave if you've only had wonderful things happen to you.

- Mary Tyler Moore

Many hands and hearts and minds generally contribute to anyone's notable achievements.

- Walt Disney

Thou shalt have justice, more than thou desir'st.

- William Shakespeare,
The Merchant of Venice

It is far more impressive when others discover your good qualities without your help.

- Judith Martin

Valor would cease to be a virtue if there were no injustice.

- Agesilaus

Unfortunately large numbers of people all over the world have been specifically taught in childhood not to think, because thinking would lead to questioning the certainties of the elders, and this has not been allowed in most cultures.

- Brock Chisholm

Unblessed is the son who does not honor his parents; but if reverent and obedient to them, he will receive the same from his own children.

- Euripides

There are some people who have to do, in order to make their mark. They have to perform, they have to contribute. And there are some people who only have to be.

- F. Scott Fitzgerald

The human being who lives only for himself finally reaps nothing but unhappiness. Selfishness corrodes. Unselfishness enables, satisfies. Don't put off the joy derivable from doing helpful, kindly things for others.

- B.C. Forbes

Not to be able to bar poverty is a shameful thing; but not to know how to chase it away by work is a more shameful thing yet.

- Pericles

There is only one kind of love, but there are a thousand imitations.

- Francois Rochefoucauld

Everybody can be great . . . because anybody can serve. You don't have to have a collage degree to serve. You don't have to make your subject and verb agree to serve. You only need a heart full of grace. A soul generated by love.

- Martin Luther King, Jr.

I've never been poor, only broke. Being poor is a frame of mind. Being broke is only a temporary situation.

- Michael Todd

There are only two ways of getting on in this world: by one's own industry, or by the weakness of others.

- Jean de La Bruyere

Everybody wants sympathy, but nobody wants people feeling sorry for them.

- Beryl Pitzer

Aging is not "lost youth" but a new stage of opportunity and strength . . . The way you define yourself makes such a difference.

- Betty Friedan

Cocaine is God's way of telling you you've got too much money.

- Sting (British rock star)

A generation ago, most people finished a day's work and needed a rest. Now they need exercise.

- Anonymous

If people were more concerned with being reconciled than with being right, the world would be a better place.

- Judith Martin

The proper function of Man is to live, not to exist. I shall not waste my days in trying to prolong them. I shall use my time.

- Jack London

Life is either a daring adventure or nothing.
- Helen Keller

Worry, self-doubt, fear, and anxiety—these are some of the culprits that bow the head and break the spirit.

- Anonymous

Man is the animal that intends to shoot himself out into interplanetary space, after having given up on the problem of an efficient way to get himself five miles or so to work and back each day.

- Bill Vaughan

No one can harm you except yourself.

- Ghandi

Character is the sum total of all our every-day choices.

- Margaret Jensen, A Nail in a Sure Place

I find, by experience, that the mind and the body are more than married,
For they are most intimately united;
And when the one suffers, the other sympathizes.

- Lord Chesterfield, Philip D. Stanhope

A strange thing about life. I am always looking for something to do.

- Robert E. Lee

Who hears music feels his solitude peopled at once.

- Robert Browning

Human nature is eternally hungry for recognition. The perfect food for this hunger is credit, written or spoken, acknowledgement of service rendered. Give the credit—all the credit—to the other person—when giving credit is second nature, you will take your place among the world's bigger people, for that is the way of bigness the world over.

- James T. Mangan

It's a complex world. I hope you'll learn to make distinctions. A peach is not its fuzz, a toad is not its warts, a person is not his or her crankiness. If we can make distinctions, we can be tolerant, and we can get to the heart of our problems instead of wrestling endlessly with the gross exteriors . . . Your assumptions are your windows on the world. Scrub them off every once in a while, or the light won't come in.

- Alan Alda, at his daughter's commencement address

It is hard to fight against impulsive desire; whatever it wants it will buy at the cost of the soul.

- Heraclitus

Education is an admirable thing, but it is well to remember from time to time that nothing that is worth knowing can be taught.

- Oscar Wilde

Apart from the wheel [opium] is man's only discovery.

- Pablo Picasso

What sets the world in motion is the interplay of differences, their attractions and repulsions.

- Octavio Paz

Youth is not a time of life—it is a state of mind, a product of the imagination, a vigor of the emotions a predominance of courage over timidity, an appetite for adventure.

- Anonymous

No one is so eager to gain new experience as he who doesn't know how to make use of the old ones.

- Marie Von Ebner-Eschenbach

Nobody grows old by living a given number of years. Years wrinkle the skin, but to give up enthusiasm wrinkles the soul.

- Author unknown

It does no harm just once in a while to acknowledge that the whole country isn't in flames, that there are people in the country besides politicians, entertainers and criminals.

- Charles Kuralt

One cannot be too extreme in dealing with social ills: besides, the extreme thing is generally the true thing.

- Emma Goldman, Anarchism

Dreaming permits each and every one of us to be safely insane every night of the week.

- Dr. William Charles Dement

Life is what happens when you are making other plans.

- John Lennon

In this world there are only two tragedies. One is not getting what one wants, and the other is getting it.

- Oscar Wilde

First the elms will die. Then the maples. Then the fish will go belly-up in poison waters. The strawberries will no longer bear fruit, and then our world will be close to dying.

- Tom Porter, A Bear Clan chief and spiritual leader of the Mohawks, regarding the end of the world

If a problem causes many meetings, the meetings eventually become more important than the problem.

- Anonymous

I see no hope for the future of our people if they are dependent on the frivolous youth of today, for certainly all youth are reckless beyond words . . . When I was a boy, we were taught to be discreet and respectful of elders, but the present youth are exceedingly wise and impatient of restraint."

- Hesiod, 8th century B.C.

Love and work are the cornerstones of our humanness.

- Sigmund Freud

The gem cannot be polished without friction nor man without trials.

- Confucius

The people who can do you the most damage are the ones who are closest to you.
- Robert Mitchum

I smoked pot once in my life. I thought it smelled like dirty socks and I never did it again.
- Dick Booth

. . . they praise me, and make an ass of me; now my foes tell me plainly I am an ass; so that by my foes, sir, I profit in the knowledge of myself, and by my friends I am abused.
- William Shakespeare, Twelfth Night

In an age contorted by violence, I have no doubt whatever that people are born to kindness as a wind is born to movement. After all, if tenderness were rare instead of normal, wouldn't the newspapers give it headlines? MOTHER CHERISHES FAMILY—BLIND PERSON HELPED ACROSS STREET—PRISONERS VISITED—DESPERATE PEOPLE CARED FOR—BOY SHARES HIS LUNCH WITH PUPPY . . . and on and on. But such events are not news; they are as common and as beautiful as dandelions.
- Neil Millar

Everyone is a moon, and has a dark side which he never shows to anybody.
- Mark Twain

I am glad every day for all the reckless things we did. If we had waited till we could afford them, now it would be too late.
- Anonymous

In the coldest February, as in every other month of every other year, the best thing to hold on to in this world is each other.
- Linda Ellerbee, Move On: Adventures in the Real World

But ah! Think what you do when you run in debt: You give to another power over your liberty.
- Benjamin Franklin

It was not I that sinned the sin
The ruthless body dragged me in
Though long I strove courageously,
The body was too much for me.
- Walt Whitman

An honest man is one who knows that he can't consume more than he
has produced.
- Ayn Rand, Atlas Shrugged

People of character don't allow the environment to dictate their style.
- Lucille Kallen, The Tanglewood Murder

Virtue is its own revenge.
- E.Y. Harburg

[Anger] builds nothing but can destroy everything.
- L. Douglas Wilder

Imagination is only intelligence having fun.
- George Scialabbe

One must ask children and birds how cherries and strawberries taste.
- Johann Wolfgang Von Goethe

One moment of a man's life is a fact so stupendous as to take the lustre out of all fiction.
- Ralph Waldo Emerson

The song I came to sing remains unsung. I have spent my life stringing and unstringing my instrument.
- Rabindranath Tagore

We shall cut down God knows how many trees so that we can have one edition of this book.
- R.D. Laing

I can think of nothing less pleasurable than a life devoted to pleasure.
- John D. Rockefeller

We don't read and write poetry because it's cute; we read and write poetry because we are members of the human race, and the human race is filled with passion.
- Robin Williams, Dead Poets Society

They sicken of the calm, who know the storm.
- Dorothy Parker

The majority of us lead quiet, unheralded lives as we pass through this world. There will most likely be no ticker-tape parades for us, no monuments created in our honor. But that does not lessen our possible impact, for there are scores of people waiting for someone just like us to come along . . . someone who will live a happier life merely because we took the time to share what we have to give. Too often we underestimate the power of a touch, a smile, a kind word . . . .all of which have the potential to turn a life around. It's overwhelming to consider the continuous opportunities there are to make our love felt.
- Leo Buscaglia

Insanity is doing the same thing over and over again, but expecting different results.
- Rita Mae Brown, Sudden Death

Seek always to do some good, somewhere. Every man has to seek in his own way to realize his true worth. You must give some time to your fellow man.. For remember, you don't live in a world all your own. Your brothers are here too.
- Albert Schweitzer

What you think in the egotism of anger you will pay for in the humiliation of saner moments.
- Crane

Most of us will do anything to be good, except change our way of living.
- Anonymous

I would rather be one mile from hell going in the opposite direction, than to be one thousand miles from hell going straight to it.

- Wilford Hinkson

The notion of the "war on gangs" being successful is as realistic as the People's Republic of China telling Americans to stop being American. When gang members stop their wars and find that there is no longer a need for their sets to exist, banging will cease. But until then, all attempts by law enforcement to seriously curtail its forward motion will be in vain.

- Kody Scott, Monster, An autobiography of an L.A. gang member

God give us men, the time demands
strong minds, great hearts, true faith and ready hands;
Men whom the lust of office does not kill;
Men whom the spills of office cannot buy;
Men who possess opinions and a will;
Men who have honor; men who will not lie;
Men who can stand before a demagogue
and damn his treacherous flatteries without winking;
Tall men, sun crowned, who live above the fog
In public duty and in private thinking!
For while the rabble with their thumb-worn creeds,
Their large professions and their little deeds.
Mingle in selfish strife; lo! Freedom weeps!
Wrong rules the land, and waiting justice sleeps!

- J.G. Holland

I am extraordinarily patient provided I get my own way in the end.

- Margaret Thatcher

I wouldn't swap one wrinkle of my face for all the elixirs of youth. All of these wrinkles represent a smile, a grimace of pain and disappointment . . . some part of being fully alive.

- Helen Hayes

The tragedy of life is what dies inside a man while he lives.

- Albert Schweitzer

A straight line is the shortest in morals as in geometry.

- Joseph L. Baron

Perhaps the straight and narrow path would be wider if more people used it.

- Kay Ingram

"Hush, don't say that—you'll lose some of your friends." My answer is simple and final: If I don't say it, I'll lose my own soul.

- E. Stanley Jones

We all find it in ourselves to do what we have to do. People are capable of an awful lot when they have no choice . . . Courage is when you have choices.

- Terry Anderson, the longest-held American hostage

Formerly, when religion was strong and science weak, men mistook magic for medicine, now when science is strong and religion is weak, men mistake medicine for magic.

- Thomas Szasz

Our National Anthem

. . . In the media glare
like a deer we just stare
losing sight of what counts
as our heads fill with air.
In a land where high tech shows us
endless sordid tales from bad to worse,
we have all become voyeurs
peeking at the perverse

- Horsey, "Seattle Post Intelligencer"

And often times excusing a fault doth make the fault worse by excuse,—as patches set upon a little breach discredit more in hiding of the fault than did the fault before it was so patched.

- William Shakespeare, King John

We are more inclined to hate one another for points on which we differ, than to love one another for points on which we agree.

- Charles Caleb Colton

The world is quickly bored by the recital of misfortune, willingly avoids the sight of distress.

- W. Somerset Maugham

The happiness of others is never bearable for very long.

- Francoise Sagan

Evil is the stone on which the good sharpens itself.

- Dorothy Auchterlonie

We neither get better or worse as we get older, but more like ourselves.

- Robert Anthony

The opportunities of man are limited only by his imagination. But so few have imagination that there are ten thousand fiddlers to one composer.

- Charles F. Kettering

Be not angry . . .
that you cannot make others
as you wish them to be . . .
since you cannot even make YOURSELF
as you wish to be.

- Thomas a Kempis

Per year, gangs in South Central [LA] recruit more people than the four branches of the U.S. Armed Forces do. Crack dealers employ more people in South Central than AT&T, IBM, and Xerox combined.

- Kody Scott, Monster, An autobiography of an L.A. gang member

We crucify ourselves between two thieves;
Regret for yesterday and fear of tomorrow.
- *Fulton Oursler*

Peace can come only as a consequence of freedom.
- *Ernest L. Wilkinson*

It was not the apple on the tree, but the pair on the ground, I believe, that caused the trouble in the garden.
- *M.D. O'Connor*

There is something curiously boring about somebody else's happiness.
- *Aldous Huxley*

In any contest between power and patience bet on patience.
- *W.B. Prescott*

The man who views the world at 50 the same as he did at 20 has wasted 30 years of his life.
- *Muhammad Ali*

So much is pressing on humans today that no one has time to stand still long enough to evaluate it. They gulp life and taste nothing! They eat life and have no savor.
- *Geraldine Farrar*

Pretty much all the honest truth telling there is in the world is done by children.
- *Oliver Wendell Holmes, Sr.*

Our strength is often composed of the weakness that we're damned if we're going to show.
- *Mignon McLaughlin, The Second Neurotic's Notebook*

I have never seen greater monster or miracle in the world than myself.
- *Michel De Montaigne*

Lord, what fools these mortals be!
- *William Shakespeare*

There is nobody so irritating as somebody with less intelligence and more sense than we have.
- *Don Herold*

Let Wall Street have a nightmare and the whole country has to help get them back in bed again.
- *Will Rogers*

. . . that is what learning is. You suddenly understand something you've understood all your life, but in a new way.
- *Doris Lessing*

It doesn't take a hero to order men into battle. It takes a hero to be one of those men who goes into battle.
- *General H. Normann Schwarzkopf*

In a consumer society there are inevitably two kinds of slaves; the prisoners of addiction and the prisoners of envy.
- *Ivan Illich*

How would I have felt standing naked in front of an armed SS officer being forced to dig a pit that I knew would be my grave? Empathy is a required element of morality . . . That emotion needs to be cultivated among our children and ourselves.
- *Steven Spielberg*

Five basic reasons for the *Decline and Fall of the Roman Empire* from Edward Gibbon's book by the same title, published in 1788

1) The undermining of the dignity and sanctity of the home, which is the basis for human society.
2) Higher and higher taxes: the spending of public money for free bread and circuses for the populace.
3) The mad craze for pleasure, with sports and plays becoming more exciting, more brutal, and more immoral.
4) The building of great armaments when the real enemy was within—decay of individual responsibility.
5) The decay of religion, whose leaders lost touch with life and their power to guide.

And I beseech you to treasure up in your hearts these my parting words: Be ashamed to die till you have won some victory for humanity.
- *Horace Mann, his last baccalaureate sermon at Antioch College*

A proposal that every citizen should be required to appear at reasonable intervals before a properly qualified jury to justify his existence. If he could not justify it, his existence would be swiftly and efficiently terminated.
- *George Bernard Shaw*

Age does not protect you from love but love to some extent protects you from age.
- *Jeanne Moreau*

My children say all hippies became yuppies—except me.
- *Sundra Allen*

Self-fulfillment presupposes that you have a self worth fulfilling.
- *James Q. Wilson*

Bravery is the capacity to perform properly even when scared half to death.
- *Omar Bradley*

I reckon there's as much human nature in some folks as there is in others, if not more.
- *Edward Noyes Westcott*

If only there were evil people somewhere, insidiously committing evil deeds, and it were necessary only to separate them from the rest of us and destroy them. But the line dividing good and evil cuts through the heart of every human being. And who is willing to destroy a piece of his own heart.
- *Aleksandr Solzhenitsyn*

Do not lose faith in humanity: there are over a hundred million people in America who have never played you a single nasty trick.

- Hubbard

Hatred paralyzes life; love releases it. Hatred confuses life; love harmonizes it. Hatred darkens life; love illumines it.

- Martin Luther King, Jr.

My sense now of age is that it's a new period in life, as yet mostly unknown and untested, which has to be seen in its own terms.

- Betty Friedan

He worked like hell in the country so he could live in the city where he worked like hell so he could live in the country.

- Don Marquis

Violence is not strength, and compassion is not weakness.

- Camelot

The world is a beautiful place
to be born into
if you don't mind some people dying
all the time
or maybe only starving
some of the time
which isn't half so bad
if it isn't you.

- Laurence Ferlinghetti

It is not the ape, nor the tiger in man that I fear, it is the donkey.

- William Temple

Every human being is your counterpart. Every other human being possesses and embodies aspects of yourself: your dreams, your sorrows, your hopes . . . For each of us there was a time when the world was young, a springtime of spirit that was later tested by the winters of discontent; and in the midst of each of our lives lies the haunting shadow of death.

Therefore we are all quite alike; indeed at the core we are all one, all lost—and all found—in the same mysterious enterprise that is life. Hold this in your heart as you go about your day, and the world will cease to be inhabited by strangers, and the burden of life itself will no longer be a process of loneliness.

- Daphne Rose Kingma

Whatever you have received more than others—in health, in talents, in ability, in success—all this you must not take to yourself as a matter of course. In gratitude for your good fortune, you must render in return some sacrifice.

- Albert Schweitzer

I cannot believe that the purpose of life is to be "happy." I think the purpose of life is to be useful, to be responsible, to be honorable, to be compassionate. It is, above all, to matter, to count, to stand for something, to have made some difference that you lived at all.

- Leo C. Rosten

We live very close together. So, our prime purpose in this life is to help others. And if you can't help them at least don't hurt them.

- The Dalai Lama

As a rule a man's a fool;
When it's hot he wants it cool;
When it's cool he wants it hot.
Always wanting what is not.

- Anonymous

It has been said that man is the only animal who laughs, and the only one who weeps; the only one who prays; the only one who walks fully erect; the only one who makes fires; the only one who guides his own destiny; the only one who is penitent; and the only one who needs to be.

- David Elton Fineblood, Philosophy of Religion

So far as is known, no bird ever tried to build more nests than its neighbors; and no fox ever fretted because he had only one hole in the earth in which to hide; and no squirrel ever died in anxiety lest he should not lay up enough nuts for two winters instead of one; and no dog ever lost sleep over the fact that he did not have enough bones buried in the ground for his declining years.

- Religious Telescope

The terrible crisis we face may be nothing less than God's call to us to reach a new level of humanity.

- Samuel H. Miller

At bottom every man knows well enough that he is a unique being . . . and by no extraordinary chance will such a marvelously picturesque piece of diversity in unity as he is, ever be put together a second time.

- Friedrich Nietzsche

There is scarcely any man sufficiently clever to appreciate all the evils he does.

- La Rochefoucauld

THE RELIGIOUS VOICE

(Words that Kindle Faith, Hope and Charity)

God may not always come when we need Him, but He will always be on time.
- Alex Haley

Live in such a way that those who know you but don't know God will come to know God because they know you.
- Anonymous

Will is to grace as the horse is to the rider.
- St. Augustine

My atheism, like that of Spinoza, is true piety towards the universe and denies only gods fashioned by men in their own image to be servants of their human interests.
- George Santayana

To claim to be a Christian or Jew who loves God and neighbor and not to take an active part in the formation of social policies affecting those neighbors would seem to deny complete fulfillment of one's faith.
- Ruben Askew

There can be no surer sign of decay in a country than to see the rites of religion held in contempt.
- Niccolo Machiavelli, c. 1500

Rabbi Zusya said that on that day of judgment, God would not ask him, why he had not been Moses, but why he had not been Zusya.
- Walter Kaufmann

I shall tell you a secret, my friend. Do not wait for the last judgment, it takes place every day.
- Albert Camus

Time is so fleeting that if we do not remember God in our youth, age may find us incapable of thinking about Him.
- Hans Christian Anderson

Seven days without prayer makes one weak.
- Allen E. Bartlett

Every day people are straying away from the church and going back to God.
- Lenny Bruce

There's not much practical Christianity in the man who lives on better terms with angels and seraphs than with his children, servants and neighbors.
- Henry Ward Beecher

He who merely knows right principles is not equal to him who loves them.
- Confucius

I think you will understand me when I say that I have never known a thinking man who did not believe in God.
- Robert Andrews Millikan

Riches are not from an abundance of worldly goods, but from a contented mind.
- Mohammed

If we acknowledge God in all our ways, He has promised safely to direct our steps, and in our experience we shall find the promise fulfilled.
- Edward Payson

Practice in life what you pray for and God will give it to you more abundantly.
- Edward R. Pusey

If thou neglecteth thy love to thy neighbor, in vain thou professeth thy love to God.
- Francis Quarles

In Christianity there can be no divorce of religion from morality.
- Milton Valentine

God has two dwellings; one in heaven, and the other in a meek and thankful heart.
- Izaak Walton

Grant that I may not so much seek to be consoled as to console,
To be understood as to understand;
To be loved as to love.
For it is in giving that we receive.
- St. Francis of Assisi

O lord, wilt thou not shut the gates of thy righteousness before me, that I may walk in the path of the low valley and that I may be strict in the plain road.
- The Book of Mormon

An honest man is the noblest work of God.
- Alexander Pope

It was pride that changed angels into devils; it is humility that makes men as angels.
- St. Augustine

Prayer is not conquering God's reluctance but taking hold of God's willingness.
- Phillips Brooks

A man should first direct himself in the way he should go. Only then should he instruct others.
- Buddha

Christianity is not a theory or speculation, but a life; not a philosophy of life, but a live and living process.
- Samuel Taylor Coleridge

If you believe in the Lord he will do half the work, but the last half. He helps those who help themselves.
- Cyrus K. Curtis

Do not wish to be anything but what you are, and try to be that perfectly.
- St. Francis De Sales

It is good to be children sometimes, and never better than at Christmas time, when its mighty founder was a child Himself.

- Charles Dickens

The whole meaning of the presence of the Child in the manger rests on our accepting the wonderful fact that God has come to be with us, as man and woman, and as we are. Of course the child cried, and I expect that God continues to cry over what we do to one another. How could it be otherwise? The one who has loved us to the point of degrading himself to be with us on humanly terms also must laugh a great deal. How could it be otherwise?

- Jeff Smith

Nothing sets a person so much out of the devil's reach as humility.

- Jonathon Edwards

Fear knocked at the door. Faith answered. No one was there.

- English Proverb

Show me the man who would go to heaven alone, and I will show you one who will never be admitted there.

- Owen Feltham

The worship most acceptable to God comes from a thankful and cheerful heart.

- Plutarch

What can I give Him, poor as I am?
If I were a shepherd I would give him a lamb.
If I were a wise man I would do my part,
Yet what can I give Him: Give my heart.

- Christina Rossetti

What shall I say when I see God?

- Sister Madelva Wolff

God says to me with kind of a smile,
"Hey how would you like to be God awhile
and steer the world?"
"Okay," says I, "I'll give it a try.
Where do I set?
How much do I get?
What time is lunch?
When can I quit?"
"Gimme back that wheel," says God,
I don't think you're quite ready yet."

- Unknown

Eternity is not something that begins after you are dead. It is going on all the time. We are in it now.

- Charlotte Perkins Gillman, The Forerunner

When God conceived the world, that was poetry; He formed it, and that was sculpture; He varied and colored it, and that was painting; and then, crowning all, He peopled it with living beings, and that was the grand divine, eternal drama.

- Charlotte Cushman

A synagogue or church that admitted only saints would be like a hospital that admitted only healthy people. It would be a lot easier to run, and a more pleasant place to be, but I'm not sure it would be doing the job it is here to do.

- Harold Kushner, Who Needs God

Puritanism—The haunting fear that someone, somewhere, may be happy.

- H.L. Mencken

. . . I said to the man who stood at the gate of the year:
"Give me a light, that I may tread safely into the unknown!"
And he replied:
"Go out into the darkness and put your hand into the Hand of God.
That shall be to you better than light and safer than a known way."

- M. Louis Haskins

This must be what God sees.

- Frank Borman, Apollo 8 astronaut, of the dwindling globe below him

We should at every opportunity ask ourselves, "What would Jesus do?" and then be more courageous to act upon the answer . . . We must be about his work as he was about his Father's.

- Howard W. Hunter

For every soul, there is a guardian watching it.

- The Koran

In a world in which we are overwhelmed with a blizzard of messages, we can easily lose sight of which messages are really important. But, realistically there is only one message that can never be ignored. It is the message of God, the one message which gives meaning to all others. Read the Bible and encourage others to do so. It's got a message for each of us.

- William M. Ellinghous, president AT&T

We are most deeply asleep at the switch when we fancy we control any switches at all.

- Annie Dillard, Holy the Firm

If you're not closer to the Lord today than you were yesterday . . . guess who moved.

- Author Unknown

The same loving hand that has created you has created me. If He is your Father He must be my Father also. We all belong to the same family . . . Naturally I would like to give them the joy of what I believe but that I cannot do; only God Can. Faith is a gift of God but God does not force Himself.

- Mother Teresa

Christians, Muslims, Hindus, believers and nonbelievers have the opportunity with us to do works of love, have the opportunity with us to share the joy of loving and come to realize God's presence.

Hindus become better Hindus. Catholics become better Catholics. Muslims become better Muslims.
- Mother Teresa

O Lord, thou hast searched me out, and known me; thou knowest my down-sitting, and mine up-rising; thou understandest my thoughts long before.
- Prayer Book

O God, the Creator and Preserver of all mankind, we humbly beseech thee for all sorts and conditions of men.
- Prayer Book

I will give thanks unto thee, for I am fearfully and wonderfully made.
- Prayer Book

The glory of Christianity is to conquer by forgiveness.
- William Blake

The Lord works from the inside out. The world works from the outside in. The world would take people out of the slums. Christ takes the slums out of the people, and then they take themselves out of the slums. The world would mold men by changing their environment. Christ changes men, who then change their environment. The world would shape human behavior, but Christ can change human nature.
- Ezra Taft Benson

Show me the way—
Not to fortune or fame,
Not how to win laurels
Or praise for my name—
But show me the way
To spread the Great Story
That *"Thine is the Kingdom
and Power and Glory."*
- Author Unknown

We are born for a higher destiny than earth.
- Bulwer

Educate men without religion and you make them but clever devils.
- Duke of Wellington

Morality without religion is a tree without roots; a stream without any spring to feed it; a house built on the sand; a pleasant place to live in till the heavens grow dark, and the storm begins to beat.
- J.B. Shaw

Religion presents few difficulties to the humble; many to the proud; insuperable ones to the vain.
- Hare

In the last analysis everything operates by the will of God.
- W.R. Whitney

The better we understand the intricacies of the atomic structure, the nature of life, or the master plan for the galaxies, the more reason we have found to marvel at the wonder of God's creation.
- Wernher Von Braun

Christ has no hands but our hands
To do His work today;
He has no feet but our feet
To lead men in His way.
He has no tongue but our tongues
To tell men how He died;
He has no help but our help
To bring them to His side.
- Annie Johnson Flint

Great Spirit, help me never to judge another until I have walked in my brothers moccasins two weeks.
-Indian Prayer

Lord, when we are wrong, make us willing to change, and when we are right, make us easy to live with.
- Peter Marshall

Do not pray for tasks equal to your powers. Pray for powers equal to your tasks. Then the doing of your work will be no miracle, but you shall be the miracle.
- Phillip Brooks

I sought to hear the voice of God,
and climbed the topmost steeple
But God declared: "Go down again,
I dwell among the people."
- Lewis Newman

The higher we are placed, the more humbly should we walk.
- Cicero

The New Testament never simply says "remember Jesus Christ." That is a half-finished sentence. It says "remember Jesus Christ is risen from the dead."
- Robert Runcie, Archbishop of Canterbury

The value of persistent prayer is not that he will hear us . . . but that we will finally hear him.
- William McGill

Prayer doesn't use up artificial energy, doesn't burn up any fossil fuel, doesn't pollute.
- Margaret Mead

If men wish to draw near to God, they must seek Him in the hearts of men.
- Abu Sa'id Ibn Abi Khayr

A little child of God . . . God's last, best and so far as we know, final expression of Himself.
- W.S. Rainsford, The Story of a Varied Life

A miracle cannot prove what is impossible; it is useful only to confirm what is possible.
- Maimonides

I could not say I believe. I know! I have had the experience of being gripped by something that is stronger than myself, something that people call God.
- Carl Jung

The glory of Christianity is to conquer by forgiveness.

- William Blake

How flowers become thee
And almost match thy beauty.
Oh, to be a gardener
To work the soil and plant the seed
That brings forth such beauty.

In my mind there is another garden
That grows incessantly, day and night.
In this hidden garden of the mind
I grow roses overnight
Make gingkos flourish in a trice.

What other trees do I cultivate there
In a space no larger than a melon?
How many trees
How many flowers
Are there in this wide world?

Near the center of this vast garden of the mind's eye
There grows a tree, most majestic.
It's called the tree of knowledge of good and evil.
I have tasted its fruit, both bitter and sweet.
Oh, curious is me!

I hear a whisper that there is another tree
More beautiful and the fruit thereof
More delicious than any I have ever tasted.
They say its name is the tree of life
Or is it called the tree of paradise?

The fruit is so everlastingly sweet
That almost I forgot the other trees,
The Gingko—the Rose
And almost thee.

I,
A gardener would be!
And make a paradise
Of this tangled wilderness
Betwixt me and thee.

God, be thou my gardener
Help me make a paradise
of the wilderness of my soul.

- Dean W. Bitter

Would to God that we might spend a single day really well.

- Thomas A Kempis, Imitation of Christ

You don't mess around with the Bible.

- Dr. Lawrence Shoen

The name of God is Truth.

- Hindu Proverb

Oh God, help us to be master of ourselves that we may be the servants of others.

- Sir Alec Paterson

Nobody ever outgrows Scripture; the book widens and deepens with our years.

- Charles Haddon Spurgeon

Did not God
Sometimes withhold in mercy what we ask,
We should be ruined at our own request.

- Hannah More

I asked Jesus "How much do you love me?"
"This much," He answered.
Then He stretched out his arms and He died . . .

- Author unknown

All I have seen teaches me to trust the Creator for all I have not seen.

- Ralph Waldo Emerson

I know this world is ruled by Infinite Intelligence. It required Infinite Intelligence to create it and it requires Infinite Intelligence to keep it on its course . . . It is mathematical in its precision.

- Thomas A. Edison

The more I try to unravel the mysteries of the world we live in, the more I come to the conception of a single overruling power— God.

- Henry Eyring

God is the silent partner in all great enterprises.

- Abraham Lincoln

A mighty fortress is our God,
A tower of strength ne'er failing.
A helper mighty is our God,
O'er ills of life prevailing.
He overcometh all.
He saveth from the fall.
His might and pow'r are great.
He all things did create,
And he shall reign forever more.

- Martin Luther

We act in faith, and miracles occur.

- Dag Hammerskjold

Certain thoughts are prayers. There are moments when, whatever the attitude of the body, the soul is on its knees.

- Victor Hugo

There is no brotherhood of man without the fatherhood of God.

- Henry Martyn Field

Behind everything stands God. . . . Do not avoid, but seek, the great, deep, simple things of faith.

- Phillips Brooks

I would not lift my little finger to defend the western world against communism if I thought that man were just a machine with no spark of divinity in him.

- Dwight D. Eisenhower

He who has ceased to pray has lost a great friendship.

- Richard L. Evans

I would rather walk with God in the dark than go alone in the light.

- Mary Gardiner Brainard

We are perishing for want of wonder, not for want of wonders.

- Gilbert Keith Chesterton

Nothing in life is more wonderful than faith—the one great moving force which we can neither weigh in the balance nor test in the crucible.

- Sir William Osler

We don't know what water is. We don't know what electricity is. We don't know what heat is. We have a lot of hypotheses about these things, but that is all. But we do not let our ignorance about these things deprive us of their use.

- Thomas A. Edison

In all my perplexities and distresses, the Bible has never failed to give me light and strength.

- Robert E. Lee

It made me shiver, and I about made up my mind to pray and see if I couldn't try to quit bein' the kind of boy I was and be better. So I kneeled down. But the words wouldn't come. Why wouldn't they? It weren't no use to try and hide it from Him . . . I knowed very well why they wouldn't come. It was because my heart wasn't right; it was because I was playin' double. I was lettin' on to give up sin, but way inside of me I was holdin' on to the biggest one of all. I was tryin' to make my mouth say I would do the right thing and the clean thing, but deep down in me I knowed it was a lie and He knowed it. You can't pray a lie. I found that out.

- Mark Twain, from the words of Huckleberry Finn

The existence of the Bible, as a Book for the people, is the greatest benefit which the human race has ever experienced.

- Immanuel Kant

I have lived, seen God's hand through a lifetime, and all was for the best.

- Robert Browning

If radio's slim fingers can pluck a melody
From night—and toss it over a continent or sea;
If the petaled white notes of a violin
Are blown across the mountains or the city's din;
If songs, like crimson roses, are culled from thin blue air—
Why should mortals wonder if God hears prayer?

- Ethel Romig Fuller

It is not permitted us to know everything.

- Horace

The disease with which the human mind now labors is want of faith.

- Ralph Waldo Emerson

A perfect faith would lift us absolutely above fear.

- George MacDonald

I read in a book that a man called Christ went about doing good. It is most disconcerting to me to find that I am so easily content with just going about.

- Toyohiko Kagawa

God's in his heaven—
All's right with the world!

- Robert Browning

When thou prayest, rather let thy heart be without words than thy words be without heart.

- John Bunyan

When you pray don't insult God's intelligence by asking Him to do something which would be unworthy of even you, a mortal.

- Mme Chiang Kai-shek, I Confess My Faith

For God hath made you able to create worlds in your own mind which are more precious to Him than those which He created.

- Thomas Traherne, Centuries of Meditations

Self-discipline never means giving up everything, for giving up is a loss. Our Lord did not ask us to give up the things of earth, but to exchange them for better things.

- Fulton J. Sheen

To believe only possibilities is not faith, but mere philosophy.

- Sir Thomas Browne

God had so much love in him he had to make us to get some love out.

- Rachel, age 9

Life is an adventure in forgiveness.

- Norman Cousins

All good moral philosophy is but a handmaid to religion.

- Francis Bacon

To seek God means first of all to let yourself be found by Him.

- Brakkenstein Community of Blessed Sacrament Fathers

The Indian sees no need for setting apart one day in seven as holy day, since to him all days are God's.

- Charles E. Eastman, The Soul of the Indian

If mountains can be moved by faith, is there less power in love?

- Frederick W. Faber

He [Christ] carried our sin, our captivity and our suffering, and he did not carry it in vain. He CARRIED IT AWAY.

- Karl Barth

Be simple; take our Lord's hand and walk through things.

- Fr. Andrew

Religion is not proficiency in the fine art of spiritual knowledge, but just the love of God and our neighbour.

- Fr. Andrew SDC

Some people think reconciliation is a soft option, that it means papering over the cracks. But the biblical meaning means looking facts in the face and it can be very costly; it cost God the death of his own son.

- Archbishop Desmond Tuto

We shall match your capacity to inflict suffering with our capacity to endure suffering. Do to us what you will and we shall continue to love you.

- Martin Luther King

God warms his hands at man's heart when he prays.

- John Masefield

I shall seek to develop the perfection of generosity, virtue, doing without, wisdom, energy, forbearance, truthfulness, resolution, love, serenity.

- The Ten Perfections ,
Buddhist spirituality

Lord, make me according to thy heart.

- Br Lawrence

I find the doing of the will of God leaves me no time for disputing about His plans.

- George MacDonald

If men were only a little more aware of what they are all doing together this very moment, they would feel as if they were in church, singing in a chorus. How they all love one another without knowing it, and how beautiful it would be if they knew! If only they could do consciously what they now do unawares!

- Paul Claudel

Let me not pray to be sheltered from dangers but to be fearless in facing them.
Let me not beg for the stilling of my pain but for the heart to conquer it.
Let me not look for allies in life's battlefield but to my own strength.
Let me not crave in anxious fear to be saved but hope for the patience
to win my freedom.
Grant me that I may not be a coward, feeling your mercy in my success
alone; but let me find the grasp of your hand in my failure.

- Rabindranath Tagore

God obligeth no man more than he hath given him ability to perform.

- Koran

That money will be more profitable to you . . . if you so give it to a poor man that you actually bestow it on Christ.

- St. Ambrose

No man is a true Christian who does not think constantly of how he can lift his brother, how he can assist his friend, how he can enlighten mankind, how he can make virtue the rule of conduct in the circle in which he lives.

- Woodrow Wilson

If thou wilt gladly bear the cross, it shall bear thee, and bring thee to the end that thou desirest, where thou shalt never have anything to suffer.

- Thomas A. Kempis

It is impossible for the mind which is not totally destitute of piety, to behold the sublime, the awful, the amazing works of creation and Providence, the heavens with their luminaries, the mountains, the oceans, the storm, the earthquake, the volcano, the circuit of the seasons, and the revolutions of empire—without marking in them all, the mighty hand of God, and feeling strong emotions and reverence toward the Author of these stupendous works.

- Timothy Dwight

Creation means the transformation of an otherwise chaotic world into a thing of order and beauty. It is the shaping of an indifferent matter into a world of value.

- J.E. Boodin

Experience of the spiritual world is not only possible in special moments of ecstasy but is waiting for us within every experience, however ordinary.

- A. Victor Murray

All those who journey,
soon or late,
Must pass within the
garden's gate;
must kneel alone in
darkness there,
And battle with some
fierce despair.
God pity those who
cannot say:
"Not mine but thine";
who only pray:
"Let this cup pass,"
and cannot see
The purpose in Gethsemane.

- Ella Wheeler Wilcox

What a piece of work is man, how noble in reason, how infinite in faculty, in form and moving how like an angel, in appearance HOW LIKE A GOD.

- William Shakespeare

I believe we are free, within limits, and yet there is an unseen hand, a guiding angel, that somehow, like a submerged propeller, drives us on.

- Rabindranath Tagore

Everyone, no matter how humble he may be, has angels to watch over him. They are heavenly, pure and splendid and yet they have been given us to keep us company on our way; they have been given the task of keeping careful watch over you, so that you do not become separated from Christ, their Lord.

And not only do they want to protect you from the dangers which waylay you throughout your journey: they are actually by your side, helping your soul as you strive to go ever higher in your union with God through Christ.

- Pope Pius XII

All of our great political leaders believed in God. The most beautiful music, the finest art, the greatest writings and the most advanced political systems were all produced by those who believed in God.

- Wilford Hinkson

We hold these truths to be self-evident, that all men are created equal, that they are endowed by their Creator with certain unalienable rights, that among these are Life, Liberty and the pursuit of Happiness.

- Thomas Jefferson

Through the thick gloom of the present, I see the brightness of the future as the sun in heaven. We shall make this a glorious, an immortal day. When we are in our graves, our children will honor it. They will celebrate it with thanksgiving, with festivity, with bonfires, and illuminations . . .

Before God, I believe the hour is come. My judgment approves this measure, and my whole heart is in it. All that I have, and all that I am, and all that I hope, in this life, I am now ready here to stake upon it . . . It is my living sentiment, and by the blessing of God it shall be my dying sentiment. Independence now, and Independence forever.

- John Adams

I have now disposed of all my property to my family. There is one thing more I wish I could give them, and that is the Christian religion. If they had that, and I had not given them one shilling, they would have been rich; and if they had not that, and I had given them all the world, they would be poor.

- Patrick Henry

Pray for our country—quietly and silently—each in his own way.
Where there is hate, let me sow love;
Where there is injury, pardon;
Where there is doubt, faith;
Where there is despair, hope;
Where there is darkness, light.

- St. Francis of Assisi

There is a God! The herbs of the valley, the cedars of the mountains, bless Him. The insect sports in His beam; the bird sings Him in the foliage; the thunder proclaims Him in the heavens; the ocean declares His immensity; man alone has said, "There is no God!"

- Anonymous

. . . Where there is a plan, there is intelligence, and an orderly, unfolding universe testifies to the truth of the most majestic statement ever uttered—"In the beginning—God."

- Arthur H. Compton

There are no facts yet wrested from the intriguing mysteries of this strange, onrushing cosmos which can in any degree disprove the existence and intelligent activities of an unconditioned, personal God.

. . . For science is indeed "watching God work."

- Morritt Stanley Congdon

Man, himself, is the crowning wonder of creation; the study of his nature the noblest study the world affords.

- William Gladstone

The destiny of mankind is not decided by material computation. When great causes are on the move in the world . . . we learn that we are spirits, not animals . . .

- Winston Churchill

There is no burden of the spirit but is lightened by kneeling under it. Little by little, the bitterest feelings are sweetened by the mention of them in prayer.

- William Mountford

Ye call me Master,
And obey me not;
Ye call me light,
And seek me not;
Ye call me life,
And desire me not;
Ye call me wise,
And follow me not;
Ye call me fair,
And love me not;
Ye call me rich,
And ask me not;
Ye call me eternal,
And seek me not;
Ye call me gracious,
And trust me not;
Ye call me noble,
And serve me not;
Ye call me mighty,
And honor me not;
Ye call me just,
And fear me not;
If I condemn you,
Blame me not.

- Inscription in the cathedral at Tubeck, Germany

. . . We would stop in at the church very often because I wanted [our children] to know that church was something for every day in the week, it wasn't just for Sunday, just for a special day or special hour; that you could pray or that you could talk to God any time and He would be there, He would listen to you. He would give you advice or sympathy or whatever it was you felt you needed.

- Rose Kennedy

I like to speak of prayer as listening. We live in a culture that is terribly afraid to listen. We'd prefer to remain deaf. The Latin root word of the word "deaf is "absurd." Prayer means moving from absurdity to obedience. Let the words descend from your head to your heart so you can begin to know God. In prayer, you become who you are meant to be.

- Henri Nouwen

People who pray for miracles usually don't get miracles . . . But people who pray for courage, for strength to bear the unbearable, for the grace to remember what they have left instead of what they have lost, very often find their prayers answered . . . Their prayers helped them tap hidden reserves of faith and courage which were not available to them before.

- Harold S. Kushner

All that troubles is but for a moment.
That only is important which is eternal.

*- Inscription over the door
of the Milan Cathedral*

I am here to be truly helpful. I am here to represent Him who sent me. I do not have to worry about what to say or what to do, because He who sent me will direct me. I am content to be wherever He wishes, knowing He goes there with me. I will be healed as I let Him teach me to heal.

- Foundation for Inner Peace

The Touch of the Master's Hand

'Twas battered and scarred, and the auctioneer
Thought it scarcely worth his while
To waste much time on the old violin,
But held it up with a smile.
"What am I bidden, good folks," he cried,
"Who'll start the bidding for me?"
"A dollar, a dollar," then, two! Only two?
"Two dollars, and who'll make it three?
"Three dollars, once; three dollars, twice;
Going for three..." But no,
From the room, far back, a grey-haired man
Came forward and picked up the bow;
Then, wiping the dust from the old violin,
And tightening the loose strings,
He played a melody pure and sweet
As a caroling angel sings.

The music ceased, and the auctioneer,
With a voice that was quiet and low,
Said: "What am I bid for the old violin?"

And he held it up with the bow.
"A thousand dollars, and who'll make it two?
Two thousand! And who'll make it three?
Three thousand, once; three thousand, twice;
And going and gone," said he.
The people cheered, but some of them cried,
"We do not quite understand
What changed its worth?" Swift came the reply:
"The touch of a master's hand."

And many a man with life out of tune,
And battered and scarred with sin,
Is auctioned cheap to the thoughtless crowd,
Much like the old violin.
A "mess of potage," a glass of wine;
A game - and he travels on.
He is "going" once, and "going" twice,
He's "going" and almost "gone."
But the Master comes and the foolish crowd
Never can quite understand
The worth of a soul and the change that's wrought
By the touch of the Master's hand.

- Myra B. Welch

LIGHTS TO LIVE BY

(Words that Encourage and Enliven)

Thee lift me, and I lift thee, and together we ascend.
- *John Greenleaf Whittier*

Somewhere beyond the cortex is a small voice whose mere whisper can silence an army of arguments. It stands alone in final judgment as to whether we have demanded enough of ourselves and, by that example, have inspired the best in those around us.
- *The New York Times*

People tell me "don't"—I do. They say "can't"—I prove I can.
- *Lily Havey, Japanese internment survivor*

Think of all the beauty still left around you and be happy.
- *Anne Frank, Diary of a Young Girl*

Only he who attempts the ridiculous can achieve the impossible.
- *Will Henry*

The people who get on in this world are the people who get up and look for the circumstances they want, and, if they can't find them, make them.
- *George Bernard Shaw*

You're a good man, Charlie Brown.
- *Charles M Schulz, Peanuts comic strip*

Move out, man! Life is fleeting by.
Do something worthwhile, before you die.
Leave behind a work sublime,
that will outlive you, and time!
- *Alfred A. Montapert*

Anyone who says something is impossible, is always being interrupted by someone doing it.
- *Anonymous*

What do we live for, if it is not to make life less difficult for each other?
- *George Eliot*

Necessity can set me helpless on my back, but she can't keep me there; nor can four walls limit my vision.
- *Margaret Fairless Barbar*

Occasionally in life there are those moments of unutterable fulfillment which cannot be completely explained by those symbols called words. Their meanings can only be articulated by the inaudible language of the heart.
- *Martin Luther King Jr.*

The happiness of life is made up of minute fractions—the little, soon-forgotten charities of a kiss or smile, a kind look, a heartfelt compliment—countless infentesimals of pleasurable and genial feeling.
- *Samuel Taylor Coleridge*

He drew a circle that shut me out—
Heretic, rebel, a thing to flout.
But love and I had the wit to win:
We drew a circle that took him in.
- *Edwin Markham*

Obstacles are those frightful things you see when you take your eyes off your goal.
- *Henry Ford*

They conquer who believe they can. He has not learned the first lesson of life who does not every day surmount a fear.
- *Ralph Waldo Emerson*

Discovery consists in seeing what everybody has seen and thinking what nobody has thought.
- *Albert Szent-Gyorgyi*

You're on the road to success when you realize that failure is merely a detour.
- *William G. Milnes, Jr.*

A mediocre idea that generates enthusiasm will go further than a great idea that inspires no one.
- *Mary Kay Ash*

According to the theory of aerodynamics, as may be readily demonstrated through wind tunnel experiments, the bumblebee is unable to fly. This is because the size, weight and shape of his body in relation to the total wing-spread makes flying impossible. The bumblebee, being ignorant of these scientific truths, goes ahead and flies anyway and makes a little honey each day.
- *Anonymous*

We need to be motivated by a new Spirit from within. Stir us out of our apathy and put the fire of love and goodness in us to move and motivate us to bigger and better days.
- *Supreme Philosophy of Man*

If we are intended for great purposes, we are expected to overcome great trails.
- *Alfred A. Montapert*

God created memory so that we might have roses in December.
- *Italo Svevo*

LIVE so enthusiastically you cannot fail.
- *Dorthea Brande*

Give me men with fire in their bowels.
- *Oliver Cromwell*

Creativity inspires more creativity.

Saints are sinners who kept on trying.

If you're feeling low, don't despair. The sun has a sinking spell every night, but it comes back up every morning.

© 1994, Compact Classics, Inc.

The way I see it, if you want the rainbow, you gotta put up with the rain.

- Dolly Parton

Our world was not designed to be fair. If you demand it, and use that unanswered demand to excuse a lack of drive, you'll be miserable and unsuccessful . . . so don't ask for fairness and don't let your limitations hold you back. Take what you have and get what you want with it. Being happy is your own personal duty.

Don't listen to those who say, "It's not done that way." Maybe it's not, but maybe you'll do it anyway. Don't listen to those who say, "You're taking too big a chance." Michelangelo would have painted the Sistine floor, and it would surely be rubbed out by today . . .

I firmly believe that if you follow a path that interests you, not to the exclusion of love, sensitivity, and cooperation with others, but with the strength of conviction that you can move others by your own efforts, and do not make success or failure the criteria by which you live, the chances are you'll be a person worthy of your own respect.

- Neil Simon

Together, hand in hand, with our matches and our necklaces, we shall liberate this country.

- Winnie Mandela

Attempt the impossible in order to improve your work.

- Bette Davis

Your task, to build a better world,
God said, I answered, How?
This world is such a large, vast place, so complicated now,
And I so small and useless am,
There's nothing I can do. But God in all his wisdom said,
Just build a better you . . .
You must do the thing you think you cannot do.

- Eleanor Roosevelt

There are defeats more triumphant than victories.

- Michel De Montaigne

The game was to just find something about everything to be glad about—no matter what 'twas . . . You see, when you're hunting for the glad things, you sort of forget the other kind.

- Eleanor H. Porter, Pollyanna

We must view young people not as empty bottles to be filled, but as candles to be lit.

- Robert H. Shaffer

Our business in life is not to get ahead of others, but to get ahead of ourselves—to break our own records, to outstrip our yesterday by our today.

- Stewart B. Johnson

You gotta walk that lonesome valley,
You gotta walk it by yourself,
Ain't nobody else gonna walk it for you.

- William H. Armstrong, Sounder

Nothing is worth more than this day.

- Goethe

1. Know yourself . . . Socrates
2. Control yourself . . . Cicero
3. Give yourself . . . Christ

- Dr. Darrell Hyde

. . . Courage must come from the world within,
The man must furnish the will to win.
So figure it out for yourself, my lad,
You were born with all that the great have had,
With your equipment they all began.
Get hold of yourself, and say: "I can."

- Edgar A. Guest

And the world will be better for this,
That one man, scorned and covered with scars,
Still strove, with his last ounce of courage,
To reach the unreachable star.

- Joe Darion, Man of La Mancha

Whoever is happy will make others happy too. He who has courage and faith will never perish in misery.

- Ann Frank

The tree that never had to fight
For sun and sky and air and light,
But stood out in the open plain
and always got its share of rain,
Never became a forest king
But lived and died a scrubby thing.

The man who never had to toil
to gain and farm his patch of soil,
Who never had to win his share
Of sun and sky and light and air,
never became a manly man
But lived and died as he began.

Good timber does not grow with ease,
The stronger wind, the stronger trees.
The further sky, the greater length.
The more the storm, the more the strength.
by sun and cold, by rain and snow,
In trees and men good timbers grow.

Where thickest lies the forest growth
We find the patriarchs of both.
And they hold counsel with the stars
Whose broken branches show the scars
Of many winds and much of strife.
This is the common law of life.

- Douglas Malloch

The soul would have no rainbow had the eyes no tears.

- John Vance Cheney

They never told me I couldn't.

- Tom Dempsey

Everyone suddenly burst out singing.

- Siegfried Sassoon

Don't wait for your ship to come in; swim out to it.

- Anonymous

Be bold—and might forces will come to your aid.

- Basil King

If a door slams shut it means that God is pointing to an open door further on down.

- Anna Delaney Peale

There ain't nothing from the outside can lick any of us.

- Margaret Mitchell, Gone with the Wind

Roy has a great asset—20 percent vision. He wears thick glasses with an extra strong lens. So he never sees an obstacle in his path and goes on to success.

- John Tigrett on publisher Roy Thomson

The second mile of hard work is what makes the difference between the exhilaration of achievement and the acceptance of mediocrity.

- F. David Stanley

Here and there, and now and then, God makes a giant among men . . . It is not the critic who counts, nor the man who points out how the strong man stumbled or where the doer of deeds could have done better. The credit belongs to the man who is actually in the arena; whose face is marred by dust and sweat and blood; who strives valiantly; who errs and comes short again and again; . . . who, at the best, knows in the end the triumph of high achievement; and who, at the worst, if he fails, at least fails while daring greatly, so that his place shall never be with those cold and timid souls who know neither victory nor defeat.

- Theodore Roosevelt

The day will come when, after harnessing space, the winds, the tides and gravitation, we shall harness for God the energies of love. And on that day, for the second time in the history of the world, we shall have discovered fire.

- Tielhard de Chardin

Nothing can stop the man with the right mental attitude from achieving his goal; nothing on earth can help the man with the wrong mental attitude.

- Thomas Jefferson

"Brave Adm'r'l, say but one good word;
What shall we do when hope is gone?"
The words leapt like a leaping sword;
"Sail on! sail on! sail on! and on!"

- Joaquin Miller

It is invariably the tree that has been stressed and challenged surviving in a high windy place, that yields the wood I value most.

- Harry Nohr, World Class Wood Designer

In the city, a road with no exit is marked Dead End. In the country, we call these roads lanes. I always think that it is sad to label anything a dead end. No one wants to explore it then. But walking down a lane is romantic and exciting. I hesitate to venture down a dead-end road, but I look for lanes to explore with a favorite friend. An unexpected building, a rare flower, a quiet peace all wait for me on country lanes.

- Kathleen S. Abrams

. . . I live the way I wish. There are always people who will object. If you're short, tall people diminish you. If you're tall, shorter people don't like you. If you're alive, people wish you were dead. I do the best I can for the most I can . . .

- Robert Mitchum

The difference between a lady and a flower girl is not how she behaves, but how she is treated. I shall always be a flower girl to Professor Higgins because he always treats me as a flower girl and always will. But I know that I shall always be a lady to Colonel Pickering because he always treats me as a lady and always will.

- Eliza Doolittle from My Fair Lady

Forgiveness is the fragrance of the violet that clings fast to the heel that crushed it.

- Unknown

To be astonished at anything is the first movement of the mind toward discovery.

- Louis Pasteur

We are not interested in the possibility of defeat.

- Victoria, Queen of Great Britain (1819-1901)

If I have seen farther than other men, it is by standing on the shoulders of giants.

- Sir Isaac Newton

All we are given is possibilities—to make ourselves one thing or another.

- Ortegay Gasset

Commitment is the stuff character is made of; the power to change the face of things. It is the daily triumph of integrity over skepticism.

- Shearson/Lehman Bros.

I have used all my doubt as energy, and created with it. I have used all my pain as energy, and created with it. I have used all my anxiety as energy, and created with it. I plan to use my death as energy, and create with it . . .

- Stymean Karlen

Seize the day! Make your lives extraordinary.

- from Dead Poets Society

Every day someone does something that couldn't be done.

- Anon.

Not failure, but low aim, is crime.

- Lowell

Did you tackle that trouble that came your way
With a resolute heart and cheerful?
Or hide your face from the light of day
With a craven soul and fearful?
Oh, a trouble's a ton, or a trouble's an ounce,
Or a trouble is what you make it.
And it isn't the fact that you're hurt that counts,
But only how did you take it?

You are beaten to earth? Well, well, what's that?
Come up with a smiling face.
It's nothing against you to fall down flat,
But to lie there—that's disgrace.
The harder you're thrown, why the higher you bounce.
Be proud of your blackened eye!
It isn't the fact that you're licked that counts.
It's how did you fight and why? . . .

- Edmund Vance Cooke

For all the trials and tears of time,
For every hill I have to climb,
My heart sings but a greatful song . . .
These are the things that make me strong.

- Anonymous

If I can stop one heart from breaking,
I shall not live in vain;
If I can ease one life the aching,
Or cool one pain,
Or help one fainting robin
Unto his nest again,
I shall not live in vain.

- Emily Dickinson

On a garden wall in Peking, China, was a brass plate about two feet long with these words:
Enjoy yourself.
It is later than you think!
Well, maybe it is later than you think; why don't you do something about it?

- Charles W. Miller

I'd look at one of my stonecutters hammering away at a rock, perhaps a hundred times without as much as a crack showing in it. Yet, at the hundred and first blow it would split in two, and I knew it was not that blow that did it, but all that had gone before.

- Jacob A. Riis

Two men bearing each a heavy load
Met one day in a narrow road.
The bully blurted loud, abusive, cruel:
"I don't back up for any fool."
Said the other in kindly spirit true:
"I feel very much the same as you—
Except I do."

- E.L.M.

You cannot dream yourself into a character.
You must hammer and forge yourself one.

- Froude

Sir Andrew Barton said, I'm hurt,
I'm hurt, but I'm not slain.
I will lay me down and bleed awhile,
then rise and fight again.

- Anonymous

Happiness is excitement that has found a settling down place, but there is always a little corner that keeps flapping around.
- E.L. Konigsburg, From the Mixed-Up Files of Mrs. Basil E. Frankweiler

No star is ever lost we once have seen,
We always may be what we might have been.

- Adalaide A. Proctor

The Beatitudes of the Aged
Blessed are they who understand my faltering step and palsied hand
Blessed are they who know that my ears today must strain to catch the things they say
Blessed are they who seem to know that my eyes are dim and my wits are slow
Blessed are they who looked away when coffee spilled at the table today
Blessed are they with a cheery smile who stopped to chat for a little while
Blessed are they who never say you've told that story twice today
Blessed are they who know the ways to bring back memories of yesterdays
Blessed are those who ease the days on my journey home in loving ways
Blessed are they who make it known that I'm loved respected and not alone.
Blessed are they who know I'm at a loss to find the strength to carry the cross

- Victor Hugo

I don't want to get to the end of my life and find that I just lived the length of it. I want to have lived the width of it as well.

- Diane Ackerman

Life loves to be taken by the lapel and told:
"I am with you kid. Let's go."

- Maya Angelou

Vision is the art of seeing things invisible.

- Jonathan Swift

. . . Our doubts are traitors, and make us lose the good we oft might win by fearing to attempt.
- William Shakespeare, Measure for Measure

I was raised by two sick people who taught me insanity and fear and hatred. I was raised in hell, chaos felt like home. Result: I learned to land on my feet in any situation. I can stand face to face with the cruelest of ogres.

- Steven J. Wolin, The Resilient Self

We are face to face with our destiny and we must meet it with a high and resolute courage. For us is the life of action, of strenuous performance of duty; let us live in the harness, striving mightily; let us rather run the risk of wearing out than rusting out.

- Theodore Roosevelt

Somebody said that it couldn't be done,
But he with a chuckle replied
That "maybe it couldn't,"
but he would be one
Who wouldn't say so till he'd tried.
So he buckled right in with a trace of a grin
On his face. If he worried he hid it.
He started to sing as he tackled the thing
That couldn't be done, and he did it.

- Edgar A. Guest

Ah, but a man's reach should exceed his grasp,
Or what's a heaven for?

- Robert Browning

The most welcomed people of the world are never those who continually look back upon the trials, the sorrows, the failures, the bitter frustrations of yesterday, but those who cast their eyes forward with faith, hope . . . courage, happy curiosity.

- James Francis Cooke

By perseverance the snail reached the Ark.

- Charles Hadon Spurgeon

If a man is called to be a street sweeper he should sweep streets even as Michelangelo painted, or Beethoven composed music. He should sweep streets so well that all the host of heaven and earth will pause and say, here lived a great sweeper who did his job well.

- Martin Luther King

I know of no higher fortitude than stubbornness in the face of overwhelming odds.

- Louis Nizer

A winner is someone who recognizes his God given talents, works his tail off to develop them into skills, and uses these skills to accomplish his goals.

- Larry Bird

When things go wrong as they sometimes will,
When the road you're treading seems all up hill,
When the funds are low and debts are high,
And you want to smile, but have to sigh,
When care is pressing you down a bit,
Rest—if you must—but don't you quit.

Life is queer with its twists and turns,
As every one of us sometimes learns,
And many a failure turns about
When he might have won had he stuck it out.
Don't give up, though the pace seems slow—
You might succeed with another blow.

Often the goal is nearer than
It seems to a faint and faltering man,
Often the struggler has given up
When he might have captured the victor's cup.
And he learned too late, when the night slipped
down,
How close he was to the golden crown.

Success is failure turned inside out—
The silver tint of the clouds of doubt—
And you never can tell how close you are,
It may be near when it seems afar;
So stick to the fight when you're hardest hit—
It's when things seem worst that you mustn't quit.

- Anonymous

Just Do It!

- Advertisement for Nike

The ninety and nine are with dreams content;
But the hope of a world made new
Is the hundredth man who is grimly bent
On making that dream come true.

- Anonymous

Nothing in the world can take the place of persistence.
Talent will not; nothing is more common than unsuccessful men with talent. Genius will not; unrewarded genius is almost a proverb. Education will not; the world is full of educated derelicts. Persistence and determination alone are omnipotent. The slogan "Press on" has solved and always will solve the problems of the human race.

- Calvin Coolidge

Every friend represents a world in us, a world possibly not born until they arrive, and it is only by this meeting that a new world is born.

- Anais Nin

Courage is not limited to the battlefield or the Indianapolis 500 or bravely catching a thief in your house. The real tests of courage are much deeper and much quieter. They are the inner tests, like remaining faithful when nobody's looking, like enduring pain when the room is empty, like standing alone when you're misunderstood.

- Charles R. Swidoll

Courage is not the absence of fear but the ability to carry on with dignity in spite of it.

- Scott Turow, The Burden of Proof

It is said the one machine can do the work of fifty ordinary men. No machine, however, can do the work of one extraordinary man.

- Tehyi Hsieh

From the biographies of the world's celebrities:

Thurlow Weed walked two miles through the snow with pieces of rag carpet about his feet for shoes, that he might borrow a book.

Milton wrote "Paradise Lost" in a world he could not see, and then sold it for fifteen pounds.

John Bunyan wrote "Pilgrim's Progress" in prison, at the behest of conscience and in disregard of the edict of his accusers.

Carlyle, after lending the manuscript of the "French Revolution" to a friend, whose servant carelessly used it to kindle a fire, calmly went to work and rewrote it.

Handel practiced on his harpsichord in secret, until every key was hollowed by his fingers to resemble the bowl of a spoon.

- From Leaders of Men

Tenderness toward those weaker than ourselves strengthens the heart toward life itself. The moment we understand and feel sorry for the next man and forgive him, we wash ourselves, and it is a cleaner world.

- Albert Schweitzer

The power that makes grass grow, fruit ripen, and guides the bird in flight is in us all.

- Anizia Yezierska, Red Ribbon on a White Horse

Triumph is a great word, but it is the first syllable that counts. Who ever found any meaning in "Umph"?

- Anonymous

There are three rules for success. The first is: Go on. The second is: Go on. And the third is: Go on.

- Crane

The nerve which never relaxes—the eye which never blanches—the thought which never wanders—the purpose that never wavers—these are the masters of victory.

- Burke

He who has struggled in the dark best knows the radiance of the light.

- Anonymous

Out of suffering have emerged the strongest souls.

- E. H. Chapin

Spread love everywhere you go: first of all in your own house. Give love to your children, to your wife or husband, to a next door neighbor . . . Let no one ever come to you without leaving better and happier. Be the living expression of God's kindness; kindness in your face, kindness in your eyes, kindness in your smile, kindness in your warm greeting.

- Mother Teresa of Calcutta

I have found the paradox that if I love until it hurts, then there is no hurt, but only more love.

- Mother Teresa

Believe that you have it, and you have it.

- Desiderius Erasmus

A Ship ought not to be held by one anchor, nor life by a single hope.

- Epictetus

You cannot run away from weakness; you must sometimes fight it out or perish; and if that be so, why not now, and where you stand?

If it is to be, it is up to me.

- E. Wilford Edmar

If you want to lift yourself up, lift up someone else.

- Booker T. Washington

The great pleasure in life is doing what people say you cannot do.

- Walter Bagehot

Eagles: When they walk, they stumble. They are not what one would call graceful. They were not designed to walk. They fly, and when they fly, oh, how they fly, so free, so graceful. They see from the sky what we never see.

- Dr. Thomas C. Lee, Georgetown University Medical School, inscription given with a painting of an eagle to a paraplegic medical student

Far away there in the sunshine are my highest aspirations. I may not reach them, but I can look up and see their beauty, believe in them and try to follow where they lead.

- Louisa May Alcott

He has achieved success who has lived well, laughed often and loved much; who has enjoyed the trust of pure women, the respect of intelligent men and the love of little children; who has filled his niche and accomplished his task; who has left the world better than he found it, whether by an improved poppy, a perfect poem or a rescued soul; who has never lacked appreciation of earth's beauty or failed to express it; who has always looked for the best in others and given the best he had; whose life was an inspiration; whose memory a benediction.

- Bessie Anderson Stanley

Expect trouble as an inevitable part of life, and when it comes, hold your head high, look it squarely in the eye and say, "I will be bigger than you. You cannot defeat me." Then repeat to yourself the most comforting of all words, "This too shall pass." Maintaining self-respect in the face of a devastating experience is of prime importance.

- Ann Landers

In the long run men hit only what they aim at. Therefore, though they should fail immediately, they had better aim at something high.

- Henry David Thoreau

Don't be afraid to give up the good to go for the great.

- Kenny Rogers

Let's climb up to the top of our ivory tower, right up to the last step, close to the heavens!

- Gustave Flaubert

If you would attain to what you are not yet, you must always be displeased by what you are. For where you were pleased with yourself there you have remained. But once you have said, "It is enough" you are lost. Keep adding, keep walking, keep advancing; do not stop, do not turn back, do not turn from the straight road.

- St. Augustine

Don't bunt, aim out of the ball park. Aim for the company of the immortals.

- David Ogilvy

If you cannot win, you must win.

- Reb Menshim Mendl of Kotsk

If we are ever to enjoy life, now is the time—not tomorrow, nor next year, nor in some future life after we have died. The best preparation for a better life next year is a full, complete, harmonious, joyous life this year. Today should always be our most wonderful day.

- Thomas Dreier

This is the beginning of a new day. God has given me this day to use as I will. I can waste it—or use it for good, but what I do today is important, because I am exchanging a day of my life for it! When tomorrow comes, this day will be gone forever, leaving in its place something that I have traded for it. I want it to be gain, and not loss; good, and not evil; success, and not failure; in order that I shall not regret the price that I have paid for it.

- W. Heartsill Wilson

It was a little thing for the janitor to leave a lamp swinging in the cathedral at Pisa, but in that steady swaying motion the boy Galileo saw the pendulum, and conceived the idea of thus measuring time.

- Author unknown

Teach only love, for that is what you are.

- A Course In Miracles

Let miracles replace all grievances.

- Foundation for Inner Peace

Any song that moves you to joy or tears has greatness. Everything in life should be enjoyed for what it is.

- Marguerite Piazza, Metropolitan Opera

And you're in the trap called here. But you can get out of it. You can get there from here. The goal, the objective—the dream!—they are all attainable. The first step is to take the first step—raise one foot off dead center. You're not compelled to achieve your aspiration by one soaring flight, not even by giant steps, only one foot at a time. After the first footstep, the second is easier, the third is surer, the fourth is faster. Suddenly the miracle happens. Your mind is off the footsteps and only on the dream. Only you're not dreaming the dream anymore—you're living it. Winning. Getting the best of yourself.

- Katherine Nash

Some folks are natural born kickers. They can always find a way to turn disaster into butter.

- Katherine Paterson, Lyddi

Nothing ever built arose to touch the skies unless some man dreamed that it should, some man believed that it could, and some man willed that it must.

- Charles F. Kettering

If you can imagine it,
You can achieve it;
If you can dream it,
You can become it.

- William Ward

When I was a cub in Milwaukee I had a city editor who'd stroll over and read across a guy's shoulder when he was writing a lead. Sometimes he would approve, sometimes he'd say gently, "Try again," and walk away. My best advice is, try again. And then again. If you're for this racket, and not many really are, then you've got an eternity of sweat and tears ahead. I don't just mean you. I mean anybody.

- Red Smith

You win some, you lose some, and some get rained out, but you gotta suit up for them all.

- J. Askenberg

When you come to the end of your rope, tie a knot and hang on.

- Franklin D. Roosevelt

As long as you're going to be thinking anyway, think big.

- Donald Trump

It's not what happens to us, but what happens in us that supremely counts.

Whenever we conquer our fears, whenever we do with love and courage the things we have to do, then no matter what the results may seem to be at the time, we are victorious and we are counted as those who have been a success.

- Dale E. Turner

It's such a good feeling to know you're
alive
It's such a happy feeling you're growing
inside
And when you wake up ready to say
It's gonna be a snappy new day
It's such a good feeling, a very good feeling
A feeling to know that we're friends.
   - Fred Rogers, Mr. Rogers Neighborhood

. . . Because I'm good enough
I'm smart enough
And doggone it, people like me.
                  - Al Franken as Stuart Smalley,
                       Saturday Night Live

POINT/COUNTERPOINT

(Controversy and Persuasion)

You're right from your side, I'm right from mine.
- *Bob Dylan, "One Too Many Mornings"*

No race has a monopoly on vice or virtue . . .
- *Whitney Young*

And if any mischief follow, then thou shalt give life for life. Eye for eye, tooth for tooth, hand for hand, foot for foot, burning for burning, wound for wound, stripe for stripe.
- *The Bible, Exodus 21:23-25.*

[Capital Punishment] . . . tells our children that it is OK to meet violence with violence.
- *Mario Cuomo*

. . . the loathsome practice of Church and State.
- *Thomas Jefferson*

. . . the fatal theory of the separation of Church and State.
- *Pope Leo XIII*

It is conceivable that religion may be morally useful without being intellectually sustainable.
- *John Stuart Mill*

The fact that a believer is happier than a skeptic is no more to the point than the fact that a drunken man is happier than a sober one.
- *George Bernard Shaw*

There are many people who have the gift, or failing, of never understanding themselves. I have been unlucky enough, or perhaps fortunate enough to have received the opposite gift.
- *Charles de Talleyrand*

Only the shallow know themselves.
- *Oscar Wilde*

I consider myself a Christian, Hindu, Moslem, Jew, Buddhist, and Confucian.
- *Mohandas Ghandi*

The equal toleration of all religions . . . is the same thing as atheism.
- *Pope Leo XIII*

I don't see much future for the Americans .. Everything about the behavior of American society reveals that it's half judaized and half negrefied. How can one expect a state like that to hold together?
- *Adolf Hitler*

Satan is indeed loose in the world—and he is racism.
- *Elie Weisel*

What's right about America is that although we have a mess of problems, we have the great capacity - intellect and resources -to do something about them.
- *Henry Ford II*

Whoever kindles the flames of intolerance in America is lighting a fire underneath his own home.
- *Harold E. Stassen*

Capitalism did not arise because capitalists stole the land . . . but because it was more efficient than feudalism. It will perish because it is not merely less efficient than socialism, but actually self-destructive.
- *J. B. S. Haldane*

Socialism is only workable in heaven where it isn't needed and hell where they've got it.
- *Cecil Palmer*

Under capitalism man exploits man; under socialism the reverse is true.
- *Polish Proverb*

Tobacco, divine, rare, superexcellent tobacco, which goes far beyond all the panaceas, potable gold and philosopher's stones, a sovereign remedy to all disease.
- *Robert Burton, c. 1600*

Cigarettes dull the faculties, stunt and retard the physical development, unsettle the mind, and rob the persistent user of will power and the ability to concentrate.
- *Dick Merriwell*

. . . All faiths do harm. We may define faith as a firm belief in something for which there is no evidence. When there is evidence, no one speaks of faith. We do not speak of our faith that two and two are four or that the earth is round. We only speak of faith when we wish to substitute emotion for evidence.

We are told that faith could remove mountains, but no one believed it; we are now told that the atomic bomb can remove mountains, and everyone believes it.
- *Bertrand Russell*

If the work of God could be comprehended by reason, it would be no longer wonderful, and faith would have no merit if reason provided proof.
- *Pope Gregory I, c. 600*

When you have read the Bible, you will know that it is the word of God, because you will have found it the key to your own heart, your own happiness and your own duty.
- *Woodrow Wilson*

There can be no doubt that the Bible . . . became a stumbling block in the path of progress, scientific, social and even moral. It was quoted against Copernicus as it was against Darwin.
- *Preserved Smith*

No woman can call herself free who does not own and control her body. No woman can call herself free until she can choose consciously whether she will or will not be a mother.

- Margaret Sanger

Any use whatsoever of matrimony exercised in such a way that the act is deliberately frustrated in its natural power to generate life is an offense against the law of God and of nature, and those who indulge in such are branded with the guilt of a grave sin.

- Pope Pius XI

This country was formed for the white, not the black man. And looking upon African slavery from the same viewpoint held by the noble framers of our constitution, I for one have ever considered it one of the greatest blessings (for both themselves and us) that God ever has bestowed upon a favored nation.

- John Wilkes Booth

I have a dream that one day in the red hills of Georgia, the sons of former slaves and the sons of former slave owners will be able to sit together at the table of brotherhood . . . that one day even the State of Mississippi, a state sweltering with the heat of injustice, sweltering with the heat of oppression, will be transformed into an oasis of freedom and justice . . . that my four little children will one day live in a nation where they will not be judged by the color of their skin but by the content of their character.

- Martin Luther King

. . . That peculiar disease of intellectuals, that infatuation with ideas at the expense of experience that compels experience to conform to bookish preconceptions.

- Archibald MacLeish

A book is the only place in which you can examine a fragile thought without breaking it, or explore an explosive idea without fear that it will go off in your face . . . It is one of the few havens remaining where a man's mind can get both provocation and privacy.

- Edward P. Morgan

The growth of a large business is merely the survival of the fittest . . . The American beauty rose can be produced in the splendor and fragrance which bring cheer to its beholder only by sacrificing the early buds which grow up around it.

- John D. Rockefeller

God must love the common man, he made so many of them.

- Abraham Lincoln

God must hate the common man, he made him so common.

- Philip Wylie

I think every woman wants to look up to a man, if she has any sense.

- Katharine Hepburn

When you want anything said, ask a man. If you want anything done, ask a woman.

- Margaret Thatcher

I don't agree with you, But I'd fight to the death to protect your right to say it.

- Unknown

It's a great pity the right to free speech isn't based on the obligation to say something sensible.

- Unknown

What mother wouldn't go to jail to help her suffering child?

- Mildred Kaitz, who received a summons for growing marijuana to help her son who has multiple sclerosis

Marijuana cases damaged brain cells and respiratory systems, decreased hormone production in both sexes, acute memory loss, lower immune systems, miscarriages and stillbirths.

- Stephen Greene, deputy administrator, Drug Enforcement Administration

The blood lust by the DA against marijuana users is being used to justify an abuse of civil rights.

- William F. Buckley Jr.

I will fight with all the vigor God has given me, any step that would expand the opportunities for people to self-destruct.

-U.S. Rep. Charles Rangel

Here we are, we're alone in the universe, there's no God, it just seems that it all began by something as simple as sunlight striking on a piece of rock. And here we are. We've only got ourselves. Somehow, we've just got to make a go of it. We've only ourselves.

- Jean, The Entertainer, by John Osborne

But if from thence thou shalt seek the Lord thy God, thou shalt find him, if you seek him with all thy heart and with all thy soul.

- The Bible, Deuteronomy 4:29

Son, we live in a world that has walls, and those walls have to be guarded with guns . . . because deep down in places you don't talk about at parties, you want me on that wall—you need me on that wall. I have neither the time nor the inclination to explain myself to a man who rises and sleeps under the blanket of freedom I provide and then questions the manner in which I provide it . . . I would rather you just say thank you.

- Jack Nicholson, A Few Good Men

Every gun that is fired, every warship launched, every rocket fired, signifies, in the final sense, a theft from those who hunger and are not fed, those who are cold and are not clothed. The world in arms is

not spending money alone. It is spending the sweat of its laborers, the genius of its scientists, the hopes of its children.
- *Dwight David Eisenhower*

Nothing could have been more obvious to the people of the early twentieth century than the rapidity with which war was becoming impossible. And so certainly they did not see it. They did not see it until the atomic bombs burst in their fumbling hands.
- *H. G. Wells*

The emotional security and political stability in this country entitles us to be a nuclear power.
- *Sir. Ronald Mason*

They have taken sin and made it as mediocre as non-sin. Gambling is no longer a vice, it's just play. Pretty soon they will have people convinced that gambling is doing God's work.
- *Vicki Abt, sociologist*

We are simply following the demographics. We did not put arcade games in for the purpose of addicting children and we have not hired Joe Camel as our spokesman.
- *Larry Wolf, CEO, MGM Grand*

We declare henceforth that all animals shall enjoy these inalienable rights: The right to freedom from fear, pain and suffering—whether in the name of science or sport, fashion or food, exhibition or service. The right, if they are wild, to roam free, unharried by hunters, trappers or slaughterers . . . And finally the right, at the end, to a decent death—not by a club, by a trap, by harpoon, cruel poison or mass extermination chamber. We have only one creed—to speak for those who can't.
- *The Fund for Animals, Inc.*

The only people with a right to complain about what I do for a living are vegetarian nudists.
- *Ken Bates, one of California's 700 licensed fur trappers*

If someone was unhappy being tall, would those same people call for sawing off his legs?
- *Anonymous response*

And God blessed them, saying, Be fruitful, and multiply . . .
- *Genesis 1:22*

Man tends to increase at a greater rate than his means of subsistence; consequently he is occasionally subjected to a severe struggle for existence.
- *Charles Darwin*

I am the Lord thy God . . . Thou shalt have no other gods before me.
- *Exodus 20:2-3*

Congress shall make no law respecting an establishment of religion, or prohibiting the free exercise thereof . . .
- *The United States Constitution, Amendment 1*

My child is an honor student.
- *Bumper sticker*

My kid beat up your honor student.
- *Bumper sticker*

The highest result of education is tolerance.
- *Helen Keller*

What are schools for if not indoctrination against Communism?
- *Richard Nixon*

Absence makes the heart grow fonder.
- *Thomas Haynes Bayly*

Out of sight, out of mind.
- *Proverb*

We are going to monitor every minute of your broadcast news, and if this kind of bias continues . . . you just might find yourself having a little trouble getting some of your licenses renewed.
- *Frank Shakespeare*

They can't censor the gleam in my eyes.
- *Charles Laughton*

It is true that liberty is precious—so precious that it must be rationed.
- *V.I. Lenin*

Those who deny freedom to others, deserve it not for themselves.
- *Abraham Lincoln*

Never does nature say one thing and wisdom another.
- *Juvenal*

Nature is usually wrong.
- *James Whistler*

Our rocket has bypassed the moon. It is nearing the sun, and we have not discovered God.
- *From a 1960 Moscow radio broadcast*

There are no facts yet wrested from the intriguing mysteries of this strange, onrushing cosmos which can in any degree disprove the existence and intelligent activities of an unconditioned, personal God. For science is indeed "watching God work."
- *Morritt Stanley Congdon*

A violently active, dominating, intrepid, brutal youth—that is what I am after.
- *Adolf Hitler*

Social justice cannot be attained by violence. Violence kills what it intends to create.
- *Unknown*

It's called jury duty, not jury inconvenience. It is an obligation, not an interruption.
- *Newsweek, public service advertisement*

Jury: A group of twelve men who, having lied to the judge about their hearing, health and business engagements, have failed to fool him.

- H.L. Mencken

You know what I think about violence. For me it is profoundly moral, more moral than compromises and transactions.

- Benito Mussolini

Democracy cannot sustain itself amid a high degree of violence.

- Mary Ritter Beard in Nancy F. Cott,
A Woman Making History

Guns are neat little things, aren't they? They can kill extraordinary people with very little effort.

- John W. Hinckley Jr., President Ronald
Reagan's attempted assassin

In 1988, handguns killed
7 people in Great Britain
19 in Sweden
53 in Switzerland
25 in Israel
13 in Australia
8 in Canada
and 8,915 in the United States
God Bless America

- Poster by Center to Prevent Handgun
Violence

We don't have to be what you want us to be.

- Bill Russell

When in Rome do as the Romans do.

- Billy Joel, Storm Front

The hottest place in hell is reserved for those who in the time of great moral crisis maintain their neutrality.

- Dante Alighieri

I don't know, I don't care, and it doesn't make any difference.

- Jack Kerouac

Fear of losing is what makes competitors so great. Show me a gracious loser and I'll show you a permanent loser.

- O.J. Simpson

Every man's got to figure to get beat sometime.

- Joe Louis

Freedom of the press is not an end in itself but a means to the end of a free society.

- Felix Frankfurter

A free press can, of course, be good or bad, but, most certainly, without freedom it will never be anything but bad.

- Albert Camus

If the 1st Amendment means anything, it means that a state has no business telling a man, sitting alone in his own house, what books he may read or what films he may watch.

- Thurgood Marshall, unanimous opinion
that the 1st Amendment guarantees the
right to possess in one's home material that
might be regarded as obscene in public.

Nobody, including the Supreme Court, knows what obscenity is.

- Norman Dorsen

People keep writing songs about how rock 'n' roll will never die. Well, rock 'n' roll died a long time ago. It never even made it into the '60s. A certain joy went out of rock-'n'roll, and what was left was militancy—which I guess makes sense because of the times.

- Joni Mitchell

That is, rock'n'roll is only rock'n'roll if it's not safe . . . the real thing is always brash. Violence and energy—that's really what rock'n'roll is all about.

- Mick Jagger

What joy in that light cloud!

- Ermanno Wolf-Ferrari

I want all hellions to quit puffing that hell fume into God's clean air.

- Carrie Nation

There is nothing so aggravating as a fresh boy who is too old to ignore and too young to kick.

- Kin Hubbard

Children love and want to be loved and they very much prefer the joy of accomplishment to the triumph of hateful failure. Do not mistake a child for his symptom.

- Dr. Erik Erikson

Oh, call back yesterday, bid time return.

- William Shakespeare, Richard II

What's done is done.

- Shakespeare, Macbeth

Women are not men's equals in anything except responsibility. We are not their inferiors, either, or even their superiors. We are quite simply different races.

- Phyllis McGinley

There is only one sex . . . A man and a woman are so entirely the same thing that one can scarcely understand the subtle reasons for sex distinction with which our minds are filled.

- George Sand

To curse is to pray to the Devil.

- German proverb

Grant me some wild expressions, Heavens, or I shall burst.

- George Farquhar

I tremble for my country when I reflect that God is just.

- Thomas Jefferson

Sometimes a nation abolishes God, but fortunately God is more tolerant.

- Anonymous

Art is meant to disturb. Science reassures.

- Georges Braque

We especially need imagination in science. It is not all mathematics, nor all logic, but it is somewhat beauty and poetry.

- Maria Mitchell

The individual who commits violence in the name of peace is already on the road to becoming that which he hates.

- Lawrence J. Peter, The Peter Program

There's no question in my mind but that rights are never won unless people are willing to fight for them.

- Eleanor Smeal

The proliferation of guns must be stopped . . . We must also stop glorifying the materialism that drives people to violence.

- Marian Wright Edelman

A bit of shooting takes your mind off your troubles—it makes you forget the cost of living.

- Brendan Behan

When a nation's young men are conservative, its funeral bell is already rung.

- Henry Ward Beecher

There are no more liberals . . . They've all been mugged.

- James Q. Wilson

Better that we should die fighting than be outraged and dishonored . . . Better to die than to live in slavery.

- Emmeline Pankhurst

Better Red than dead.

- Anonymous

When even despair ceases to serve any creative purpose, then surely we are justified in suicide.

- Cyril Connolly

Often the test of courage is not to die but to live.

- Vittorio Alfieri

The first thing we do, let's kill all the lawyers.

- William Shakespeare, King Henry VI

Thou shalt not avenge.

- The Bible, Leviticus 19:18

Open thine heart not to every man, lest he requite thee with a shrewd turn.

- The Bible, Ecclesiastics 8:19

"Come into my parlor," said the spider to the fly.
"'Tis the prettiest sight you ever did spy."

- Mary Howitt

Men can know more than their ancestors did if they start with a knowledge of what their ancestors had already learned. This is why a society can progress only if it conserves its traditions, then refines and builds.

- Distilled Wisdom

Is it progress if a cannibal uses knife and fork?

- Stanislaw J. Lec

We are a religious people whose institutions presuppose a Supreme Being.

- William O Douglas

I believe in an America where the separation of church and state is absolute . . .

- John F. Kennedy

No country without an atom bomb could properly consider itself independent.

- Charles De Gualle

The Atomic Age is here to stay—but are we?

- Bennett Cerf

Everything according to reason.

- Cardinal Richelieu

Pure logic is the ruin of the spirit.

- Antoine De Saint-Exupery

Whatever choice Elizabeth Bouvia may ultimately make, I can only hope that her courage, persistence and example will cause our society to deal realistically with the plight of those unfortunate individuals to whom death beckons as a welcome respite from suffering.

- Lynn Compton

Euthanasia is a long, smooth-sounding word, and it conceals its danger as long, smooth words do, but the danger is there, nevertheless.

- Pearl Buck, The Child Who Never Grew

The next time someone you love becomes afflicted with an incurable illness and the situation is hopeless and filled with suffering, just remember the "cure" may have been gassed in Auschwitz or burned in the crematoria of Buchenwald. We all pay in one way or another for man's inhumanity to man.

- M.P., (Ann Landers, July 1994)

Another improvement . . . was that we built our gas chambers to accommodate two thousand people at one time.

- Rudolph Hess

In all my years of public life I have never obstructed justice.

- Richard M. Nixon

Give the investigators an hors d'oeuvre and maybe they won't come back for the main course.

- Richard M. Nixon

Madam, we took you in order to have children, not to get advice.
- *Charles XI*

But if God had wanted us to think with our wombs, why did he give us a brain?
- *Clare Boothe Luce*

A society that views graphic violence as entertainment . . . should not be surprised when senseless violence shatters the dreams of its youngest and brightest . . .
- *Deseret News*

It's cool seeing people being blown up, shot, squished, and chopped.
- *Boy, age 8 from Misti Snow, Take Time To Play Checkers*

Our goal is not the conquest of Iraq—it is the liberation of Kuwait. It is my hope that somehow the Iraqi people can, even now, convince their dictator that he must lay down his arms, leave Kuwait, and let Iraq itself rejoin the family of peace-loving nations . . .
- *George Bush, speech to nation, January 1991*

We're Going To War To Defend People Who Won't Let Women Drive?
- *Button*

When you buy a pill and buy peace with it you get conditioned to cheap solutions instead of deep ones.
- *Max Lerner*

God is still the best medicine that we physicians can ever prescribe. But He expects us to team up with Him and utilize our wits, plus all the available drugs and other techniques that scientists have developed.
- *Dr. George W. Crane*

How many deaths will it take 'til he knows that too many people have died?
- *Bob Dylan, "Blowin' in the Wind"*

Troops are made to let themselves be killed.
- *Napoleon Bonaparte*

Greed is good! Greed is right! Greed works! Greed will save the U.S.A.!
- *Michael Douglas, Wall Street*

Big mouthfuls often choke.
- *Italian Proverb*

When the European settlers landed on these wonderful shores they . . . could not even have lasted that first winter had it not been for the kindness of the Native American. The Native American kept us Europeans alive because he felt it was his duty . . . The Native American gave us food and taught us how to use these foods because he felt he should, and now he is very sorry. He is tragically sorry.
- *Jeff Smith*

I don't feel we did wrong in taking this great country away from them. There were great numbers of people who needed new land, and the Indians were selfishly trying to keep it for themselves.
- *John Wayne*

Politicians—especially state legislators—are disinclined to do anything constructive like spend more money on schools for fear it might become a precedent and send society down the primrose path of spending enough money on schools.
- *Bill Hall*

Movements born in hatred very quickly take on the characteristics of the thing they oppose.
- *J.S. Habgood*

It's not that I want to be ungracious. I am flattered at being invited to dinner at the White House. Sort of. Maybe. Actually, I'm not at all flattered, since I know it is a political game.
- *Mike Royko, syndicated columnist*

Unemployment and despair can lead to desperation. But most people will not commit desperate acts if they have been taught that dignity, honesty and integrity are more important than revenge or rage; if they understand that respect and kindness ultimately give one a better chance at success . . .
- *Deseret News*

To knock a thing down, especially if it is cocked at an arrogant angle, is a deep delight to the blood.
- *George Santayana*

One more such victory and we are lost.
- *Plutarch, Pyrrhus*

This place needs a laxative.
- *Bob Geldof, Irish rock singer of EEC bureaucracy*

When I was born
I was Black
When I grew up
I was Black
When I go out in
The sun
I am Black
But you!
When you were born
You were pink
When you grow up
You are white
When you get sick
You are green
When you go out in
The sun
You are red
When you get cold
You are blue
And when you die
You are purple
And you call me
Colored!
- *Anonymous African-American child*

You have put me in here a cub, but I will come out roaring like a lion, and I will make all hell howl!
- *Carry Nation, on her imprisonment*

It [Ku Klux Klan] gathers under its hood the mentally ill, the haters who have forgot what it is they hate or who dare not harm their real hate object, and also the bored and confused and ignorant. The Klan is made up of ghosts on the search for ghosts who have haunted the southern soul too long.
- *Lillian Smith, Killers of the Dream*

A defendant on trail for a specific crime is entitled to his day in court, not in a stadium or a city or nationwide arena.
- *Tom C. Clark*

There's no greater gap between our good intentions and our misguided consequences than you see in the welfare system.
- *Bill Clinton*

This is classic Clinton: overpromise, under-deliver, and then try to fudge the difference.
- *William Bennett*

We look forward to the time when the power of love will replace the love of power. Then will our world know the blessings of peace.
- *William Gladstone*

Let him who desires peace prepare for war.
- *Vegetius (4th century A.D.)*

Nationalized health care would have: The compassion of the IRS, the efficiency of the Postal Service, the failure rate of government schools, the enforcement tactics of the Bureau of Alcohol, Tobacco and Firearms, and all at Pentagon prices!
- *Albert V. Burns*

God may pardon you, but I never can.
- *Elizabeth I, Queen of England*

I, the Lord will forgive whom I will forgive, but of you it is required to forgive all men.
- *Doctrine & Covenants 64:10*

I'm sick of hearing about twelve-step programs for healing and recovery. What we need are fewer twelve-step programs and more twelve-gauge shotguns.
- *Name withheld by request*

It is men, not women, who have promoted the cult of brutal masculinity; and because men admire muscle and physical force, they assume that we do too.
- *Elizabeth Gould Davis*

One fifth of the people are against everything all the time.
- *Robert F. Kennedy*

The mining West . . . the timber, the grazing, and the homestead West were raided, not settled . . . by different breeds of raiders.
- *Wallace Stegner*

The most dreadful thing of all is that millions of people in the poor countries are going to starve to death before our eyes . . . upon our television sets.
- *C.P. Snow*

When Hitler attacked the Jews . . . I was not a Jew, therefore, I was not concerned. And when Hitler attacked the Catholics, I was not a Catholic, and therefore, I was not concerned. And when Hitler attacked the unions and the industrialists, I was not a member of the unions and I was not concerned. Then, Hitler attacked me and the Protestant church—and there was nobody left to be concerned.
- *Martin Niemoller*

I think Hitler was too moderate.
- *J.B. Stoner*

My sacred beliefs have been made pencils, names of cities, gas stations.
My knee is wounded so badly that I limp constantly
Anger is my crutch. I hold myself upright with it.
- *Chrystos, This Bridge Called My Back*

We must stand together; if we don't there will be no victory for any one of us.
- *Mother Jones*

If the Church makes outcasts of people with Aids then it has no right to exist for that particular community. Love is the only answer and for the Christian anything less will simply not do.
- *Fr. John Michael*

We're all going to go crazy, living this epidemic every minute, while the rest of the world goes on out there, all around us, as if nothing is happening, going on with their own lives and not knowing what it's like, what we're going through. We're living through war, but where they're living it's peacetime, and we're all in the same country.
- *Larry Kramer*

Do we fear our enemies more than we love our children?
- *Bumper Sticker*

And who was wrong?
And who was right?
And did it matter in the thick of the fight?
- *Billy Joel, The Nylon Curtain*

Sink or swim, live or die, survive or perish, I give my hand and my heart to this vote . . . You and I, indeed, may rue it. We may not live to see the time when this Declaration shall be made good. We may die; die Colonists, die slaves, die, it may be, ignominiously and on the scaffold.

Be it so. Be it so.

If it be the pleasure of Heaven that my country shall require the poor offering of my life, the victim shall be ready . . . But while I do live, let me have a country, or at least the hope of a country, and that a free country.

But whatever may be our fate, be assured . . . that this Declaration will stand. It may cost treasure, and it may cost blood, but it will stand and it will richly compensate for both.

- John Adams, attributed
by Daniel Webster

On behalf of the people of the United States, I extend sincere condolences to the people of North Korea on the death of President Kim Il Sung. We appreciate his leadership in resuming the talks between our governments. We hope they will continue as appropriate.

- Statement issued by President Bill
Clinton on the death of Kim

I'm at a loss to understand his statement extending "sincere condolences" to the people of North Korea on "behalf of the people of the United States." Perhaps President Clinton has forgotten that Kim Il Sung was responsible for the war that caused the loss of more than 54,000 American lives and 100,000 Americans wounded.

- Senator Bob Dole, July 9, 1994

I got a mama who joined the Peace Corps when she was sixty-eight, I got one sister who's a Holy Roller preacher. Another wears a helmet and rides a motorcycle. And my brother thinks he's going to be President. So that makes me the only sane one in the family.

- Billy Carter

I might say, first of all, I don't have any control over what my brother says or what he does . . .

- Jimmy Carter

There were some judgment mistakes made [at the White House] . . . [But] if being dumb was a criminal offense, half these senators would be in prison.

- Senator Ben Nighthore Campbell

It is seldom that liberty of any kind is lost all at once. The "why" is easy. Tyrants know they'd meet stronger resistance that way. When you're trying to get something over on somebody, it pays to do it in degrees.

- David Hume

To survive it is often necessary to fight, and to fight you have to dirty yourself.

- George Orwell

Are you not ashamed of heaping up the greatest amount of money and honor and reputation, and caring so little about wisdom and truth and the greatest improvement of the soul?

- Socrates

The more I read him, the less I wonder that they poisoned him.

- Thomas Macaulay, about Socrates

He would not blow his nose without moralizing on conditions in the handkerchief industry.

- Cyril Connolly, on George Orwell

To have a reason to get up in the morning, it is necessary to possess a guiding principle. A belief of some kind. A bumper sticker if you will.

- Judith Guest, "Ordinary People"

There's a difference between a philosophy and a bumper sticker.

- Charles M. Schulz

Technology—the knack of so arranging the world that we don't have to experience it.

- Max Frisch

I'm not convinced that the world is in any worse shape than it ever was. It's just that in this stage of almost instantaneous communication, we bear the weight of problems our forefathers only read about after they were solved.

- Burton Hillis

The American reading his Sunday paper in a state of lazy collapse is perhaps the most perfect symbol of the triumph of quantity over quality . . . Whole forests are being ground into pulp daily to minister to our triviality.

- Irving Babbitt

DEEP IDEAS

(Penetrating Thoughts and Reflections)

Statistically, the probability of any one of us being here is so small that you'd think the mere fact of existing would keep us all in contented dazzlement of surprise.
- *Lewis Thomas, The Lives of A Cell: Notes of A Biology Watcher*

As long as there are sovereign nations possessing great power, war is inevitable.
- *Albert Einstein*

[People] take the images outside them for reality and never allow the world within to assert itself.
- *Hermann Hesse*

Science without religion is lame, religion without science is blind.
- *Albert Einstein*

People who say it cannot be done should not interrupt those who are doing it.
- *Anonymous*

I know well what I am fleeing from, but not what I am in search of.
- *Michel de Montaigne, c. 1550*

The acts of this life are the destiny of the next.
- *Persian Proverb*

To see things in the seed, that is genius.
- *Lao-tzu*

Why should we be in such desperate haste to succeed, and in such desperate enterprises? If a man does not keep pace with his companions, perhaps it is because he hears a different drummer.
- *Henry David Thoreau*

It is impossible to escape the impression that people commonly use false standards of measurement - that they seek power, success, and wealth for themselves and admire them in others, and that they underestimate what is of true value in life.
- *Sigmund Freud*

Everything intercepts us from ourselves.
- *Ralph Waldo Emerson*

It's an abnormal world I live in. I don't belong anywhere. It's like I'm floating down the middle. I'm never quite sure where I am.
- *Arthur Ashe*

A speech is a solemn responsibility. The man who makes a bad thirty minute speech to two hundred people wastes only a half hour of his own time. But he wastes one hundred hours of the audiences time—more than four days—which should be a hanging offense.
- *Jenkin Lloyd Jones*

If you would convince a man that he does wrong, do right. Men will believe what they see. Let them see.
- *Henry David Thoreau*

The world is a looking glass, and gives back to every man the reflection of his own face.
- *William Makepeace Thackery*

Let us lament as over stomachs, minds who do not eat. If there is anything more poignant than a body agonizing for want of bread, it is a soul which is dying of hunger for light.
- *Victor Hugo, Les Miserables*

In the midst of winter, I finally learned that there was in me an invincible summer.
- *Camus*

A day . . . is a miniature eternity.
- *Ralph Waldo Emerson*

So few of us really think. What we do is rearrange our prejudices.
- *George Vincent*

Being a philosopher, I have a problem for every solution.
- *Robert Zend*

Pity the meek, for they shall inherit the earth.
- *Don Marquis*

On second thought, when the meek eventually inherit the earth it will probably be in such a condition that nobody would have it.
- *Laurence J. Peter*

You give but little when you give of your possessions. It is when you give of yourself that you truly give.
- *Kahlil Gibran*

He who would find a friend without faults will be without friends.
- *Author Unknown*

Perhaps any of us could get along with perfect people. But our task is to get along with imperfect people.
- *Richard L. Evans*

Those who know the truth are not equal to those who love it, and those who love it are not equal to those who live it.
- *Confucius*

Would there be this eternal seeking if the found existed?
- *Antonio Porchia*

A woman, in her sleep, dreamt Life stood before her, and held in each hand a gift—in the one Love, in the other Freedom. And she said to the woman, "Choose!" And the woman waited long; and she said, "Freedom!" and Life said, "Thou has well chosen. If thou hadst said, 'Love' I would have given thee that thou didst ask for; and I would have returned to thee no more. Now the day will come when I shall return. In that day I shall bear both gifts in one hand." The woman, in her sleep, laughed.
- *Olive Schreiner*

We are such stuff
As dreams are made on, and our little life
Is rounded with a sleep.
- *William Shakespeare*

If we could be twice young and twice old, we could correct all our mistakes.
- *Euripides*

To be seventy years young is sometimes far more cheerful and hopeful than to be forty years old.
- *Oliver Wendell Holmes*

Lots of people want to ride with you in the limo, but what you want is someone who will take the bus with you when the limo breaks down.

- Oprah Winfrey

The comfort of having a friend may be taken away, but not that of having had one.

- Seneca

The glory of friendship is not the outstretched hand, nor the kindly smile nor the joy of companionship; it is the spirited inspiration that comes to one when he discovers that someone else believes in him and is willing to trust him.

- Ralph Waldo Emerson

The supreme happiness of life is the conviction of being loved for yourself, or, more correctly, being loved in spite of yourself.

- Victor Hugo

Sometimes, it's like a hair across your cheek. You can't see it, you can't find it with your fingers, but you keep brushing at it because the feel of it is irritating.

- Marian Anderson

All the beautiful sentiments in the world weigh less than a single lovely action.

- James Russell Lowell

I am content with what I have, little be it, or much.

- John Bunyan

If all mankind minus one were of one opinion, and only one person were of the contrary opinion, mankind would be no more justified in silencing that one person than he, if he had the power, would be justified in silencing mankind.

- John Stuart Mill

Public opinion in this country is everything.

- Abraham Lincoln

We cannot solve life's problems except by solving them.

- M. Scott Peck

The friend who can be *silent* with us in a moment of despair or confusion, who can stay with us in an hour of grief and bereavement, who can tolerate not-knowing, not-curing, not-healing, and face with us the reality of our powerlessness—that is the friend who cares.

- Henri Nouwen, Out of Solitude

Two may talk together under the same roof for many years, yet never really meet; and two others at first speech are old friends.

- Mary Catherwood "Marianson"
Mackinac and Lake Stories

I would rather be a superb meteor, every atom of me in magnificent glow, than a sleepy and permanent planet.

- Jack London

We cannot put off living until we are ready. The most salient characteristic of life is its coerciveness; it is always urgent, "here and now," without any possible postponement. Life is fired at us point blank.

- Ortega y Gasset

I like trees because they seem more resigned to the way they have to live than other things do.

- Willa Cather

If an ass goes traveling, he will not come home a horse.

- Thomas Fuller

Life is absurd and meaningless—unless *you* bring meaning to it, unless *you* make something of it. It is up to us to create our own existence.

- Alan Alda

You're not like me. When you lose, it's all over. When I lose, I get invited to more countries. What did the man say? Loser and still champion.

- Muhammad Ali

This people draws its origin from Abraham, our father in faith . . . The very people that received from God the commandment "Thou shalt not kill" itself experienced in a special measure what is meant by killing. It is not permissible for anyone to pass by this inscription with indifference.

- Pope John Paul II on visiting
Auschwitz concentration camp

What separates the enlightened man from the savage? Is civilization a thing distinct, or is it an advanced stage of barbarism?

- Herman Melville

Believe nothing, no matter where you read it, or who said it—even if I have said it—unless it agrees with your own reason and your own common sense.

- Guatama Buddha

To know what you are, you must first investigate and know what you are not . . . The clearer you understand that on the level of mind you can be described in negative terms only, the quicker will you come to the end of your search and realize that you are the limitless being.

- Sri Nisargadatta Maharaj

What struck me most was the silence. It was a great silence, unlike any I have encountered on Earth, so vast and deep that I began to hear my own body; my heart beating, my blood vessels pulsing, even the rustle of my muscles moving over each other seemed audible.

- Aleksei Leonov, first man to walk in space

Nothing is inevitable until it happens.

- A.J.P. Taylor

Everyone believes in something. It might be God or no God, manifest greed for money or power, a career or a friends, science, a principle—*something.* Remember, whatever it is we place before ourselves is what we run toward. When we commit to high ideals, we succeed before the outcome is known. Your life is worth a noble motive.

- Walter Anderson

The life of these Indians is nothing but a continuous religious experience. To them, the essence of religion is the "spirit of wonder," the recognition of power as a mysterious concentrated form of nonmaterial energy, of something loose in the world and contained in a more or less condensed degree by every object.

- Jaime de Angulo, of the Pit River Indians

It is man's destiny to ponder on the riddle of existence and, as a by-product of his wonderment, to create a new life on this earth.

- Charles F. Kettering

God made the world round so we would never be able to see too far down the road.

— *Isak Dinesen*

Why do you climb philosophical hills? Because they are worth climbing . . . There are no hills to go down unless you start from the top.

— *Margaret Thatcher*

We will be better and braver if we engage and inquire than if we indulge in the idle fancy that we already know—or that it is of no use seeking to know what we do not know.

— *Plato*

The unrecorded past is none other than our old friend, the tree in the primeval forest which fell without being heard.

— *Barbara Tuchman*

One is sorry one could not have taken both branches of the road. But we were not allotted multiple selves.

— *Gore Vidal*

In God's economy, nothing is wasted. Through failure, we learn a lesson in humility which is probably needed, painful though it is.

— *Bill Wilson, co-founder, Alcoholics Anonymous*

Trying to define yourself is like trying to bite your own teeth.

— *Alan Watts*

Dog scientists, hoping to make life better for their species, struggle to understand the principle of the doorknob.

— *Gary Larson*

Nothing is interesting if you're not interested.

— *Anonymous*

What you are to be you are now becoming.

— *Cameron Beck*

The fundamental law of nature is that all force must be kept in balance. When any force goes off on a tangent, there is a smash.

— *Thomas Edison*

Change occurs when you become what you are, not when you try to become what you are not . . . Change seems to happen when you have abandoned the chase after what you want to be (or think you should be) and have accepted—and fully experienced—what you are.

— *Janette Rainwater*

There is a period near the beginning of every man's life when he has little to cling to except his unmanageable dream, little to support him except good health, and nowhere to go but all over the place.

— *E.B. White*

Humor [is] something that thrives between man's aspirations and his limitations. There is more logic in humor than in anything else. Because, you see, humor is truth.

— *Victor Borge*

The one thing that can be safely predicted about life is that it is unpredictable . . . there is nothing on earth that in the twinkling of an eye is not subject to change.

— *Richard L. Evans*

Man himself is a visitor who does not remain.

— *Anonymous*

Don't think! Thinking is the enemy of creativity. It's self-conscious, and anything self-conscious is lousy. You can't try to do things; you simply must do them.

— *Ray Bradbury*

Hell is yourself [and the only redemption is] when a person puts himself aside to feel deeply for another person.

— *Tennessee Williams*

The opposite of love is not hate, it's indifference. The opposite of art is not ugliness, it's indifference. The opposite of faith is not heresy, it's indifference. And the opposite of life is not death, it's indifference.

— *Eli Wiesel*

We are all refugees of a future that never happened.

— *Lee Weiner*

We have confused the free with the free and easy.

— *Adlai E. Stevenson*

Cosmic upheaval is not so moving as a little child pondering the death of a sparrow in the corner of a barn.

— *Thomas Savage*

Life does not accommodate you, it shatters you. It is meant to, and it couldn't do it better. Every seed destroys its container or else there would be no fruitation.

— *Florida Scott-Maxwell*

The true joy of life [is] being used for a purpose recognized by yourself as a mighty one . . . being thoroughly worn out before you are thrown to the scrap heap . . . being a force of nature instead of a feverish, selfish clod of ailments and grievances.

— *George Bernard Shaw*

The analysis of character is the highest human entertainment.

— *Isaac Bshevis Singer*

Civilization is hideously fragile [and] there's not much between us and the horrors underneath, just about a coat of varnish.

— *C.R. Smith*

When a friend speaks to me, whatever he says is interesting.

— *Jean Renoir*

There is really nothing more to say—except why. But since why is difficult to handle, one must take refuge in how.

— *Toni Morrison*

People change and they forget to tell each other.

— *Lillian Hellman*

The thing that makes you exceptional, if you are at all, is inevitably that which must also make you lonely.

— *Lorraine Hansberry*

The significance of man is that he is that part of the universe that asks the question—what is the significance of man?

— *Cal Lotus Becker*

There's only one thing that I know how to do well and I've often been told that you only can do what you know how to do well, and that's be you, be what you're like, be like yourself. And so I'm hav-

ing a wonderful time. But I'd rather be whistling in the dark.
- *They Might Be Giants, from the album Flood*

We don't believe in rheumatism and true love until after the first attack.
- *Marie Von Ebner-Eschenbach*

What difference does it make if the thing you are scared of is real or not?
- *Toni Morrison, Song of Solomon*

To be sure, the dog is loyal. But why, on that account, should we take him as an example? He is loyal to men, not to other dogs.
- *Karl Kraus*

To treat your facts with imagination is one thing, but to imagine your facts is another.
- *John Burroughs*

The least of things with a meaning is worth more in life than the greatest of things without it.
- *Carl Jung*

There is nothing so well-known as that we should not expect something for nothing—but we all do and call it Hope.
- *Edgar Watson Howe*

Every reform movement has a lunatic fringe.
- *Theodore Roosevelt*

Of course everything has been said that needs to be said—but since no one was listening it has to be said again.
- *Author Unknown*

If we don't change direction, we will arrive at where we are going.
- *Richard L. Evans*

If a bomb falls in the desert and our audio doesn't pick it up, does it still make a sound?
- *Daniel Golden, Boston Globe*

Things don't change. You change your way of looking, that's all.
- *Carlos Castaneda*

The quizzical expression of the monkey at the zoo comes from his wondering whether he is his brother's keeper, or his keeper's brother.
- *Evan Esar*

You never conquer a mountain. You stand on the summit a few moments; then the wind blows your footprints away.
- *Arlene Blum, Annapurna*

Where does the white go when the snow melts? I would like to know because I'm very curious . . . and it seems like a mystery.
- *Rachel, age 8*

Men imagine that thought can be kept secret, but it can not; it rapidly crystallizes into habit, and habit solidifies into circumstance.
- *James Allen*

What makes life dreary is the want of motive.
- *George Eliot, Daniel Deronda*

Nothing is more desirable than to be released from affliction, but nothing is more frightening than to be deprived of a crutch.
- *James Baldwin*

To be able to say how much love, is to love but little.
- *Petrarch*

Each person's only hope for improving his lot rests on his recognizing the true nature of his basic personality, surrendering to it, and becoming who he is.
- *Sheldon Kopp*

The malignant disease of the "what-ifs."
- *Dr. Robert L. DuPont*

What is destructive is impatience, haste, expecting too much too fast.
- *May Sarton, Journal of a Solitude*

The price one pays for pursuing any profession, or calling, is an intimate knowledge of its ugly side.
- *James Baldwin*

If only no one had told them I was mad. Then I wouldn't be.
- *Kate Millett, The Looney-Bin Trip*

There is no moral virtue in being endowed with genius rather than talent: It is a gift of the gods or the luck of the genes.
- *Dorothy Auchterlonie*

The great corrupter of public man is the ego . . . Looking at the mirror distracts one's attention from the problem.
- *Dean Acheson*

The trouble with dreams is that they're just synaptic meanderings—*gossamer* mind fiction—so that one minute everything is *perfect* and this thing you've been chasing is so CLOSE you can almost inhale it, and the next, *WHAM*. It's gone, and you're back in reality because no matter how wonderful a dream is, it's never really *real*.
- *Advertisement for the Oldsmobile Aurora*

Often men can see farther through a tear than through a telescope.
- *Leo J. Muir*

Who is not afraid of pure space—that breath-taking empty space of an open door? But despite fear, one goes through to the room beyond.
- *Anne Morrow Lindbergh*

People often say that this or that person has not yet found himself. But the self is not something that one finds. It is something that one creates.
- *Thomas Szasz*

Order is the shape upon which beauty depends.
- *Pearl Buck*

Take heed how you disguise yourself and copy others. Stick to nature if you desire to please, for whatever is fictitious and affected, is always insipid and distasteful.
- *Charles Palmer*

If you would understand your own age, read the works of fiction produced in it. People in disguise speak freely.
- *Arthur Helps*

The dead of midnight is the noon of thought.
- *Anna Letitia Barbauld*

We tend to think things are new because we've just discovered them.
- *Madeleine L'Engle, A Wind in the Door*

Almost the whole world is asleep—everybody you know, everybody you see, everybody you talk to . . . only a few people are awake and they live in a state of constant total amazement.
- *Meg Ryan, Joe vs the Volcano*

The hardest thing to explain is the glaringly evident which everybody has decided not to see.
- *Ayn Rand, The Fountainhead*

I know not what the world will think of my labors, but to myself it seems that I have been but as a child playing on the seashore; now finding some prettier pebble or more beautiful shell than my companions, while the unbounded ocean of truth lay undiscovered before me.
- *Sir Isaac Newton*

A hundred times every day I remind myself that my inner and outer life depends on the labors of other men, living and dead, and that I must exert myself in order to give in the measure as I have received and am still receiving.
- *Albert Einstein*

Nobody dast blame this man. You don't understand; Willy was a salesman, there is no rock bottom to the life. He don't put a bolt to a nut, he don't tell you the law or give you medicine. He's a man way out there in the blue, riding on a smile and a shoeshine. And when they start not smiling back— that's an earthquake. And then you get yourself a couple of spots on your hat, and you're finished. Nobody dast blame this man. A salesman is got to dream, boy. It comes with the territory.
- *Arthur Miller, Death of a Salesman*

I'm very healthy. And I have an eternal curiosity. Then, I think I'm not dependent on any person. I love people, I love my family, my children . . . But inside myself is a place where I live all alone and that's where you renew your springs that never dry up.
- *Pearl Buck*

Science, freedom, beauty, adventure. What more could you ask of life? Aviation combined all the elements I loved . . . I began to feel that I lived on a higher plane than the skeptics of the ground; one that was richer because of its very association with the element of danger they dreaded, because it was freer of the earth to which they were bound. In flying I tasted the wine of the gods of which they could know nothing . . .
- *Charles A. Lindbergh*

In the last analysis, it is our conception of death which decides our answers to all the questions that life puts to us.
- *Dag Hammarskjold*

To go fishing is the chance to wash one's soul with pure air, with the rush of the brook or the serenity of a lake, and the shimmer of the sun on blue water. It brings meekness and inspiration from the decency of nature, charity toward tackle-makers, patience toward fish, a mockery of profits and egos, a quieting of hate, a rejoicing that you do not have to decide a darned thing until next week. And it is discipline in the equality of men—for all men are equal before fish.
- *Herbert Hoover*

The sense of obligation to continue is present in all of us. A duty to strive is the duty of us all. I felt a call to that duty.
- *Abraham Lincoln*

The barriers are not yet erected which shall say to aspiring talent, thus far and no farther.
- *Ludwig van Beethoven*

If you can't have faith in what is held up to you for faith, you must find things to believe in yourself, for a life without faith in something is too narrow a space to live.
- *George E. Woodbury*

I think we are well advised to keep on nodding terms with the people we used to be, whether we find them attractive company or not. Otherwise they turn up unannounced and surprise us, come hammering on the mind's door at 4 a.m. of a bad night and demand to know who deserted them, who betrayed them, who is going to make amends.
- *Joan Didion*

If only we'd stop trying to be happy, we could have a pretty good time.
- *Edith Wharton*

The psychic task which a person can and must set for himself is not to feel secure but to be able to tolerate insecurity.
- *Erich Fromm*

Creative minds always have been known to survive any kind of bad training.
- *Anna Freud*

You can no more win a war than you can win an earthquake.
- *Jeanette Rankin*

Talent is a question of quantity. Talent does not write one page— it writes three hundred.
- *Jules Renard*

It is often the scientist's experience that he senses the nearness of truth when . . . connections are envisioned. A connection is a step toward simplification, unification. Simplicity is indeed often the sign of truth and a criterion of beauty.
- *Mahlon Hoagland*

By his very success in inventing labor-saving devices, modern man has manufactured an abyss of boredom that only privileged classes in earlier civilizations have ever fathomed.
- *Lewis Mumford*

We Americans cannot save the world. Even Christ failed at that. We Americans have our hands full trying to save ourselves.
- *Edward Abbey*

No trumpets sound when the important decisions of our life are made. Destiny is made known silently.
- *Agnes De Mille*

I am secretly afraid of animals—of all animals except dogs, and even of some dogs. I think it is because of the us-ness in their eyes, with the underlying not-usness which belies it.
- *Edith Wharton*

I'll appreciate my gift of choice today and linger in the past only as it benefits the better part of the present.
- *Author Unknown*

I am a Pilgrim on the edge,
on the edge of my perception.
We are travelers at the edge,
We are always at the edge of our perception.
- *Scott Mutter*

Each honest calling, each walk of life, has its own elite, its own aristocracy based upon excellence of performance.
- *James Bryant Conant*

Children begin by loving their parents; as they grow older they judge them; sometimes they forgive them.
- *Oscar Wilde, The Picture of Dorian Gray*

In philosophy, it is not the attainment of the goal that matters; it is the things that are met with by the way.
- *Havelock Ellis*

All things are possible until they are impossible— and even the impossible may only be so as of now.
- *Pearl Buck*

The wrong way always seems the more reasonable.
- *George Moore*

Peace is not a passive but an active condition, not a negation but an affirmation. It is a gesture as strong as war.
- *Mary Roberts Rinehart*

The destruction of the past is perhaps the greatest of all crimes.
- *Simone Weil, The Need for Roots*

Opposition may become sweet to a man when he has christened it persecution.
- *George Eliot, Janet's Repentance*

Without feeling, a work does not have soul. If you feel it before you do it, then it will be right.
- *John Prazen*

We possess nothing in the world—a mere chance can strip us of everything—except the power to say "I."
- *Simone Weil, Gravity and Grace*

The real voyage of discovery consists not in seeking new landscapes but in having new eyes.
- *Marcel Proust*

Power can be taken, but not given. The process of the taking is empowerment in itself.
- *Gloria Steinem, Outrageous Acts and Everyday Rebellions*

Not to engage in the pursuit of ideas is to live like ants instead of like men.
- *Martimer Adler*

This great misfortune—to be incapable of solitude.
- *Jean De La Bruyere*

We told that boy when he marched away that he was fighting a war to end all wars. He fell, believing.
- *Bruce Barton*

There are things that are worth dying for—the honor of one's country, the sanctity of the home, the virtue of women, and the safety of little children. But, if they are worth dying for, they are worth living for!
- *George W. Truett*

Peace is more than the absence of aggression. It is the creation of a world community in which every nation can follow its own course without fear of its neighbors.
- *Lyndon B. Johnson*

History fades into fable; fact becomes clouded with doubt and controversy; the inscription molders from the tablet; the statue falls from the pedestal. Columns, arches, pyramids, what are they but heaps of sand; and their epitaphs, but characters written in the dust?
- *Washington Irving*

The universe is a stairway leading nowhere unless man is immortal.
- *E.Y. Mullins*

The mind is no match with the heart in persuasion; constitutionality is no match with compassion.
- *Everett M. Dirksen*

Modern man worships at the temple of science, but science tells him only what is possible, not what is right.
- *Milton S. Eisenhower*

The stairway of time ever echoes with the wooden shoe going up and the polished boot coming down.
- *Jack London*

We sleep, but the loom of life never stops and the pattern which was weaving when the sun went down is weaving when it comes up tomorrow.
- *Henry Ward Beecher*

Perhaps the only true dignity of man is his capacity to despise himself.
- *George Santayana*

Society is frivolous, and shred its day into scraps, its conversations into ceremonies and escapes.
- *Ralph Waldo Emerson*

Yes, we did produce a near perfect Republic. But will they keep it? Or will they in the enjoyment of plenty lose the memory of Freedom? Material abundance without character is the surest way to destruction.
- *Thomas Jefferson*

Last, but by no means least, courage—moral courage, the courage of one's convictions, the courage to see things through. The world is in a constant conspiracy against the brave. It's the age-old struggle—the roar of the crowd on one side and the voice of your conscience on the other.
- *Douglas MacArthur*

For, on this shrunken globe, men can no longer live as strangers. Men can war against each other as hostile neighbors, as we are determined not to do; or they can coexist in frigid isolation, as we are doing. But our prayer is that men everywhere will learn, finally, to live as brothers.
- *Adlai E. Stevenson*

In the final analysis, our most basic common link is that we all inhabit this small planet. We all breathe the same air. We all cherish our children's future. And we are all mortal.
- *John F. Kennedy*

Miracles occur naturally as expressions of love. The real miracle is the love that inspires them. In this sense everything that comes from love is a miracle.
- *Marianne Williamson, A Return To Love*

WISECRACKS AND WITTICISMS

(Ticklish Facts and Fictions)

If you want to be witty, work on your character and say what you think on every occasion.
- *Stendhal*

A little nonsense now and then is relished by the wisest men.
- *Anonymous*

The goodness of a pun is proportional to its intolerableness.
- *Edgar Allan Poe*

Beware of jokes [from which] we go away hollow and ashamed.
- *Ralph Waldo Emerson*

Man is distinguished from all other creatures by the faculty of laughter.
- *Joseph Addison*

There's nothing funnier than the Human Animal.
- *Walt Disney*

It's like saying she's a beautiful girl except for her face.
- *J. D. Salinger*

If my doctor told me that I had only six minutes to live . . . I'd type a little faster.
- *Isaac Asimov*

Anyone who thinks the way to a man's heart is through his stomach must have flunked anatomy.
- *Anonymous*

I don't know anything about music. In my line you don't have to.
- *Elvis Presley*

I feel safer on a racetrack . . . than I do on Houston expressways.
- *A. J. Foyt*

The most important thing in acting is honesty. If you can fake that, you've got it made.
- *George Burns*

Married at haste, we may repent in leisure.
- *William Congreve*

Dr. Livingstone, I presume?
- *Henry Stanley to missing explorer David Livingstone*

On the whole, I'd rather be in Philadelphia.
- *W. C. Fields, his own epitaph*

It took me 17 years to get 3,000 hits in baseball. I did it in one afternoon on the golf course.
- *Hank Aaron*

I adore life, but I don't fear death. I just prefer to die as late as possible.
- *Georges Simenon*

I've got a tooth that's driving me to extraction.
- *Edgar Bergen as Charlie McCarthy*

One loss is good for the soul. Too many losses are not good for the coach.
- *Knute Rockne*

All pro athletes are bilingual. They speak English and profanity.
- *Gordie Howe*

If I'd known how much packing I'd have to do, I'd have run again.
- *Harry S Truman, on leaving office*

My problem lies in reconciling my gross habits with my net income.
- *Errol Flynn*

I became an actor because I did poorly on law school exams.
- *Fred Grandy, Actor and US Congressman*

If you gotta' ask, you'll never know.
- *Louis Armstrong , when asked what Jazz is*

Age is a question of mind over matter. If you don't mind, it doesn't matter.
- *Satchel Paige*

I never graduated from Iowa. I was only there for two terms -
Truman's and Eisenhower's.
- *Alex Karras*

A verbal contract isn't worth the paper it's written on.
- *Samuel Goldwyn*

Why do grandparents and grandchildren get along so well? They have the same enemy - the mother.
- *Claudette Colbert*

Eighty percent of success is showing up.
- *Woody Allen*

In this world of sin and sorrow there is always something to be thankful for; as for me, I rejoice that I am not a Republican.
- *H. L. Mencken*

When your husband comes home with cockleburs in the cuffs of his pants, don't ask him what his score was.
- *Sam Sneed, advice to golf widows*

Always acknowledge a fault frankly. This will throw those in authority off guard and allow you opportunity to commit more.
- *Mark Twain*

It is a sad fact that fifty percent of marriages in this country end in divorce. But, hey, the other half end in death. You could be one of the lucky ones.
- *Richard Jeni*

The only mystery in life is why the kamikaze pilots wore helmets.
- *Al McGuire, former coach*

My wife and I were happy for twenty years. Then we met.

- Rodney Dangerfield

My mother says I didn't open my eyes for eight days after I was born, but when I did, the first thing I saw was an engagement ring. I was hooked.

- Elizabeth Taylor

Getting married, like getting hanged, is a great deal less dreadful than it has been made out.

- H. L. Mencken

A converted cannibal is one who, on Friday, eats only fishermen.

- Emily Lotney

My greatest strength as a consultant is to be ignorant and ask a few questions.

- Peter Drucker

In the country of the blind the one-eyed king can still goof up.

- Laurence J. Peter

Old people love to give good advice. It compensates them for their inability to set a bad example.

- Duc de La Rochefoucauld, c. 1650

An atheist is a guy who watches a Notre Dame - SMU football game and doesn't care who wins.

- Dwight D. Eisenhower

America is the country where you buy a lifetime supply of aspirin for one dollar, and use it up in two weeks.

- John Barrymore

How prophetic L'Enfnet was when he laid out Washington as a city that goes around in circles.

- John Mason Brown

We pay for the mistakes of our ancestors, and it seems only fair that they should leave us the money to pay with.

- Don Marquis

The guy who marries the boss's daughter just winds up with two bosses.

- Ethel Merman

Most people would rather die than think. In fact, some do.

- Bertrand Russell

There are three kinds of lies: lies, damned lies, and statistics.

- Benjamin Disraeli

There are two times in a man's life when he shouldn't speculate: When he can't afford it, and when he can.

- Mark Twain

The more you speak of yourself, the more you are likely to lie.

- Johann Zimmermann

When I watch captain Picard on "Star Trek: The Next Generation," I get really depressed. Hundreds of years have passed and they still don't have a cure for baldness.

- Erma Bombeck

The best way to convince a fool that he is wrong is to let him have his own way.

- Josh Billings

Husbands are awkward things to deal with; even keeping them in hot water will not make them tender.

- Mary Buckle

Man who stumble over the same rock twice deserve to break neck.

- Chinese Proverb

A fanatic is one who can't change his mind and won't change the subject.

- Winston Churchill

Men will confess to treason, murder, arson, false teeth, or a wig. How many of them will own up to a lack of humor.

- Frank Colby

Few people blame themselves until they have exhausted all other possibilities.

- Francis Duffy

Man once subscribed to the theory of male superiority - then woman cancelled his subscription.

- Shannon Fife

Success, I shall tell you out of the wisdom of my years, is a toy balloon among children armed with sharp pins.

- Gene Fowler

The best reply to an atheist is to give him a good dinner an ask him if he believes there is a cook.

- Louis Nizer

When a man is wrapped up in himself, he makes a pretty small package.

- John Ruskin

If the Republicans will stop telling lies about the Democrats, we will stop telling the truth about them.

- Adlai Stevenson

Get your facts first, and then you can distort them as much as you please.

- Mark Twain

We have not lost faith, but we have transferred it from God to the medical profession.

- George Bernard Shaw

When you have no basis for an argument, abuse the plaintiff.

- Marcus Tullius Cicero, c. 100 BC

Abstract Art: A product of the untalented, sold by the unprincipled to the utterly confused.

- Al Capp

You loan a hard-covered book to a friend and when he doesn't return it you get mad at him. It makes you mean and petty. But twenty-five cent books are different.
- *John Steinbeck*

A statesman is a politician who's been dead for ten or fifteen years.
- *Harry S. Truman*

The closest to perfection a person ever comes is when he fills out a job application.
- *Stanley J. Randall*

Actually, I'm an overnight success. But it took me twenty years.
- *Monty Hall*

The handwriting on the wall may be a forgery.
- *Ralph Hodgson*

I know only two tunes: one of them is "Yankee Doodle," and the other isn't.
- *Ulysses S. Grant*

Opera in English is, in the main, just about as sensible as baseball in Italian.
- *H.L. Mencken*

There's a difference between a philosophy and a bumper sticker.
- *Charles M. Schultz*

Maybe death and taxes are inevitable, but death doesn't get worse every time Congress meets.
- *Joan I. Welsh*

Advice to speakers:
If you don't strike oil in twenty minutes stop boring.
- *Adam S. Bennion*

Procrastination is the art of keeping up with yesterday.
- *Don Marquis*

Please, dear God, make my words today sweet and tender, for tomorrow I may have to eat them.
- *Author Unknown*

Money talks - but credit has an echo.
- *Bob Thaves, Newspaper Enterprise Assn.*

If you want to stand in the shortest line in the world, fall in behind those who think they're overpaid.
- *Bill Vaughan*

Some folks never exaggerate - they just remember big.
- *Audrey Snead*

How often are we offended by not being offered something we do not really want.
- *Eric Hoffer*

Television has raised writing to a new low.
- *Sam Goldwyn*

Too bad that all the people who know how to run the country are busy driving taxi cabs and cutting hair.
- *George Burns*

Don't be humble. You're not that great.
- *Golda Meir*

The recipe for a good speech includes some shortening.
- *Gene Yasenak*

Egotism is that special something which enables a man who's in a rut to think he's in a groove.
- *Unknown*

I don't care to belong to any social organization which would accept me as a member.
- *Groucho Marx*

If you love something, set it free. If it comes back, you treasure it. If it doesn't, hunt the sucker down and kill it.
- *Anonymous*

The taxpayer - that's someone who works for the federal government but doesn't have to take a civil service exam.
- *Ronald Reagan*

There may be luck in getting a job, but there's no luck in keeping it.
- *J. Ogden Armour*

Advertising is the art of making whole lies out of half truths.
- *Edgar A. Shoaff*

Fish and visitors stink after three days.
- *Unknown*

Names are not always what they seem. The common Welsh name Bzjxxllwcp is pronounced Jackson.
- *Mark Twain*

If you're parents didn't have any children, there's a good chance that you won't have any.
- *Clarence Day*

You know you're getting old when the candles cost more than the cake.
- *Bob Hope*

You've heard of the three ages of man: youth, middle age, and "you're looking wonderful!"
- *Francis Cardinal Spellman*

Henry James was one of the nicest old ladies I ever met.
- *William Faulkner*

Drive carefully. It's not only cars that can be recalled by their maker.
- *Anonymous*

Television is an invention that permits you to be entertained in your living room by people you would not have in your home.
- *David Frost*

Being a child isn't what it used to be. Huck Finn is a delinquent. Tom Sawyer isn't working up to capacity, and Heidi is in foster care. Jim Hawkins is too young to be a cabin boy, and whoever would let Alice just sit there doing nothing at all but dream through a summer afternoon?

- Anonymous

Basically my wife was immature. I'd be at home in the bath and she'd come in a and sink my boats.

- Woody Allen

Men don't care what's on TV. They only care what else is on TV.

- Jerry Seinfeld

It took a genius to develop an aspirin bottle that couldn't be opened by a child capable of operating a VCR.

- Doug Larson

If your yearning for the good old days, just turn off the air conditioning.

- Griff Niblack

In spite of the cost of living, it's still popular.

- Kathleen Norris

Three things in life are hard to do: climb a forward-leaning fence, kiss a backward-leaning woman, and say something clever when accepting a trophy.

- Josh Pons

Everything is changing. People are taking their comedians seriously and the politicians as a joke.

- Will Rogers

Some guy hit my fender the other day, and I said unto him, "be fruitful and multiply." But not in those words.

- Woody Allen

A loser is a window washer on the 44th floor who steps back to admire his work.

- Unknown

I have friends who are short and it has always struck me as a ridiculous way to live. People laugh at you and you have trouble getting things out of cupboards.

- Bill Hall

Sir: My secretary, being a lady, cannot take down, in short hand, what I would like to say to you; I, being a gentleman, cannot think it; but you, being neither, can easily guess my thoughts.

- Anonymous

If your feeling really good about life . . . Don't worry, it will pass.

- Anonymous

If you are going to wear a hat at all, be decisive and go the whole hat. In making a courageous choice of millinery, you have nothing to lose but your head.

- The Bedside Guardian

Baseball: A game which consists of tapping a ball with a piece of wood, then running like a lunatic.

- H. J. Dubiel

The fishing rod: A stick with a hook at one end and a fool at the other.

- Samuel Johnson

If your going to do something wrong, at least enjoy it.

- Leo Rosten

In response to one critics scornful accusation, "Mr. Churchill, you are drunk," Churchill replied, "And you madam, are ugly, but I shall be sober tomorrow."

Seize the moment. Remember all those women on the *Titanic* who waved off the dessert cart.

- Erma Bombeck

When your wearing a short skirt and walking past a crew of construction workers, always pick your nose. It acts as a deterrent to catcalls.

- Amy Wallace

A closed mouth gathers no feet.

- Bob Cooke

Red light: The place where you catch up with the motorist who passed you at 60 m.p.h. a mile back.

- Robert M. Lewis

Never learn to do anything. If you don't learn, you will always find someone else to do it for you.

- Mark Twain

An expert is someone called in at the last minute to share the blame.

- Sam Ewing

A person who buries his head in the sand offers an engaging target.

- Mabel A. Keenan

I like a woman with a head on her shoulders. I hate necks.

- Steve Martin

Science has not yet found a cure for the pun.

- Robert Byrne

Always forgive your enemies—nothing annoys them so much.

- Oscar Wilde

[When] high school seniors graduate . . . some will seek further expansion of knowledge through a higher education. Others will go to college.

- Unknown

What bothers me about TV is that it tends to take our minds off our minds.

- Author unknown

Such is the human race. Often it does seem such a pity that Noah . . . didn't miss the boat.

- Mark Twain

Stay in college, get the knowledge.
And stay there until you're through.
If they can make penicillin out of moldy bread,
they can sure make something out of you!
- *Muhammad Ali*

Reality is a temporary illusion brought on by an absence of beer.
- *Author unknown*

I think, therefore I'm single.
- *Liz Winston*

In certain situations, it pays to be open, honest, and direct, and to express your true feelings. But dating is not one of those situations.
- *Gibson Greetings, Inc.*

I thought I told you to wait in the car.
- *Tallulah Bankhead on seeing a former lover for the first time in years.*

Do you have any problems other than that you're unemployed, a moron, and a dork?
- *John McEnroe to a fan*

I believe that sex is the most beautiful, natural, and wholesome thing that money can buy.
- *Steve Martin*

Just because I have rice in my clothing doesn't mean I've been to a wedding. A Chinese person threw up on me.
- *Phyllis Diller*

I told my mother-in-law that my house was her house, and she said, "Get the hell off my property."
- *Joan Rivers*

My wife wanted to call our daughter Sue, but I felt that in our family that was usually a verb.
- *Dennis Wolfberg*

School is where you go between when your parents can't take you and industry can't take you.
- *John Updike*

The same time that women came up with PMS, men came up with ESPN.
- *Blake Clark*

The imaginary friends I had as a kid dropped me because their friends thought I didn't exist.
- *Aaron Machado*

Ever have one of those nights when you didn't want to go out but your hair looked too good to stay home?
- *Jack Simmons*

My wife has never suffered from stress, but she's a carrier.
- *Blake Clark*

If you don't show up to a party, people will assume you're fat.
- *Newhart*

. . . Hell, I even thought I was dead, 'till I found out it was just that I was in Nebraska.
- *Lil' Bill (Gene Hackman) in The Unforgiven*

I don't jog. It makes the ice jump right out of my glass.
- *Martin Mull*

Everybody lies, but it doesn't matter because nobody listens.
- *Nick Diamos*

The living are the dead on vacation.
- *Maurice de Maeterlinck*

Blame someone else and get on with your life.
- *Alan Woods*

I tend to live in the past because most of my life is there.
- *Herb Caen*

How many more bathroom-window curtains must die needlessly to clothe golfers?
- *Mike Lough*

When buying a used car, punch the buttons on the radio. If all the stations are rock and roll, there's a good chance that the transmission is shot.
- *Larry Lujack*

I'm pleased that television is now showing murder stories, because it brings murder back into its rightful setting—the home.
- *Alfred Hitchcock*

When I coached at Niagara, we gave recruits a piece of caramel candy. If they took the wrapper off before eating it, they got a basketball scholarship; otherwise, they got a football scholarship.
- *Frank Layden*

Don't worry about people stealing your ideas. If your ideas are any good, you'll have to ram them down people's throats.
- *Howard Aiken*

We live in an age when pizza gets to your home before the police.
- *Jeff Marder*

The world would not be in such a snarl
Had Marx been Groucho instead of Karl.
- *Irving Berlin*

Somebody has to do something, and it's just incredibly pathetic that it has to be us.
- *Jerry Garcia of the Grateful Dead*

Democracy means that anyone can grow up to be president, and anyone who doesn't grow up can be vice president.
- *Johnny Carson*

George Bush will lead us out of this recovery.
- *Dan Quayle*

Why does the Air Force need expensive new bombers? Have the people we've been bombing over the years been complaining?
- George Wallace

I was born with a priceless gift, the ability to laugh at the misfortunes of others.
- Dame Edna Everage

It's time to open your parachute when cars look as big as ants. If ants look as big as cars, you've waited too long.
- Ernst Luposchainsky III

It's amazing that the amount of news that happens in the world every day always just exactly fits the newspaper.
- Jerry Seinfeld

Societies that don't eat people are fascinated by those who do.
- Ronald Wright

When are you going to realize that if it doesn't apply to me it doesn't matter?
- Murphy Brown (Candice Bergen)

Comedy may be big business, but it isn't pretty.
- Steve Martin

Comedy is tragedy plus time.
- Carol Burnett

I've always wanted to be somebody but I see now I should have been more specific.
- Lily Tomlin

The only gracious way to except an insult is to ignore it. If you can't ignore it, top it. If you can't top it, laugh at it. If you can't laugh at it, it's probably deserved.
- Russell Lynes

A weed is a plant that has mastered every survival skill except learning how to grow in rows.
- Doug Larson

The object of most prayers is to wangle an advance on good intentions.
- Robert Brault

Witty and Wise definitions

Coward: One who in a perilous emergency thinks with his legs.
- Ambrose Bierce

Desk: A waste basket with drawers.
- Wall Street Journal

Justice: A decision in your favor.
- Harry Kaufman

Corporation: an ingenious device for obtaining profit without individual responsibility.
- Ambrose Bierce

Middle age: When you begin to exchange your emotions for symptoms.
- Irvin S. Cobb

War: A passion play performed by idiots.
- Bill Corum

Wretched: How you pronounce Richard in the South.
- Anonymous

Your worst humiliation is only someone elses momentary entertainment.
- Karen Crockett

If Moses had been a committee the Israelites would still be in Egypt.
- J.B. Hughes

I would like to share with you folks a pleasant surprise I had this morning. I woke up.
- Richard F. Carter, 74-year-old comedian

I had never had a piece of toast
Particularly long and wide,
But fell upon the sanded floor,
And always on the buttered side.
- James Payne

Mother, food, love, and career are the four major guilt groups.
- Cathy Guisewite

Welcome to hell. Here's your accordion.
- Gary Larson

Asthma doesn't seem to bother me any more unless I'm around cigars or dogs. The thing that would bother me most would be a dog smoking a cigar.
- Steve Allen

Don't cross this field unless you can do it in 9.9 seconds. The bull can do it in 10.
- Sign on a bison range

To be rich is no longer a sin; it's a miracle.
- Anonymous

Most rock journalism is people who can't write interviewing people who can't talk for people who can't read.
- Frank Zappa

When I was a kid my parents moved a lot— but I always found them.
-Rodney Dangerfield

A word to the wise ain't necessary—it's the stupid ones who need the advice.
- Bill Cosby

I like long walks, especially when they are taken by people who annoy me.
- Fred Allen

It is not that the U.S. government is an entirely comic matter; but to deal in power, ambition, and the people driven by both, a fine madness and sense of humor are handy things to have.
- Barbara Howar, Laughing All the Way

The doctor calls the patient, "I have bad news and worse news. The bad news is that you have 24 hours to live, and the worse news is that I forgot to call you yesterday."
- Unknown

A new study suggests TV may contribute to clinical depression. It's what's known in scientific language as going down the tube.
- *Bill Tammeus, Kansas City Star*

Dear Sir, Your profession has, as usual, destroyed your brain.
- *George Bernard Shaw,*
letter to a journalist

I would venture to guess that Anon, who wrote so many poems without signing them, was a woman.
- *Virginia Woolf*

When women are depressed they either eat or go shopping. Men invade another country. It's a whole different way of thinking.
- *Elayne Boosler*

I have long thought that the aging process could be slowed down if it had to work its way through Congress.
- *George Bush's gag writers*

I would never die for my beliefs because I might be wrong.
- *Bertrand Russell*

Alzhiemers has its own advantages. You meet new people every day. There's no such thing as a rerun on television, and you can hide your own Easter eggs.
- *Richard F. Carter*

What I look forward to is continued immaturity followed by death.
- *Dave Barry*

God in His wisdom made the fly
And then forgot to tell us why.
- *Ogden Nash*

We hope that, when the insects take over the world, they will remember with gratitude how we took them along on all our picnics.
- *Bill Vaughan*

If there's one major cause for the spread of mass illiteracy, it's the fact that everybody can read and write.
- *Peter De Vries*

Can't anything be done about that klunky phrase *male bonding*?
What kind of people invent phrases like *male bonding*?
- *Russell Baker*

A pat on the back is only a few vertebrae away from a kick in the pants.
- *Dennis Crocket*

Plant and your spouse plants with you, weed and you weed alone.
- *Dennis Breeze*

To keep your marriage brimming
with love in a loving cup
Whenever your wrong admit it
Whenever your right shut up
- *Ogden Nash*

If you're hanging around with nothing to do and the zoo is closed, come over to the Senate. You'll get the same kind of feeling and you won't have to pay.
- *Robert J. Dole*

The people I'm furious with are the women's liberationists. They keep getting up on soapboxes and proclaiming women are brighter than men. That's true, but it should be kept quiet or it ruins the whole racket.
- *Anita Loos*

Too often, the opportunity knocks, but by the time you push back the chain, push back the bolt, unhook the two locks and shut off the burglar alarm, it's too late.
- *Rita Coolidge*

A vasectomy is never having to say you're sorry.
- *Rubin Carson*

This recipe is certainly silly. It says to separate eggs, but it doesn't say how far to separate them.
- *Gracie Allen, The George Burns and*
Gracie Allen Show

Well, I certainly don't believe God's a woman, because if He were, men would be the ones walking around wearing high heels, taking Midol, and having their upper lips waxed.
- *Dixie Carter*

One morning I shot an elephant in my pajamas. How he got into my pajamas I'll never know.
- *Groucho Marx*

I suggest we give him ten years in Leavenworth or eleven years in Twelveworth.
I tell you what I'll do. I'll take five and ten in Woolworth.
- *Groucho Marx and Chico Marx,*

If at first you don't succeed, try looking in the wastebasket for the instructions.
- *Ann Landers*

The scientific theory I like best is that the rings of Saturn are composed entirely of lost airline luggage.
- *Mark Russell*

When primitive man screamed and beat the ground with sticks, they called it "witchcraft." When modern man does the same thing, they call it "golf."
- *Ann Landers*

There's a new telephone service that lets you test your I.Q over the phone. It costs $3.95 a minute. If you make the call at all, you're a moron. If you're on the line for three minutes, you're a complete idiot.
- *Jay Leno*

The best substitute for experience is being sixteen.
- *Raymond Duncan*

Parenthood: That state of being better chaperoned than you were before marriage.
- *Marcelene Cox*

A neighborhood is where, when you get out of it, you get beat up.
- *Murray Kempton*

Ours seems to be the only nation on earth that asks its teenagers what to do about world affairs and tells its golden-agers to go out and play.
- *Julian F. Grow*

Somebody's boring me. I think it's me.
- *Dylan Thomas*

Never run after your hat—others will be delighted to do it; why spoil their fun?
- *Mark Twain*

If you couldn't read, you couldn't look up what was on television.
- *From "Leave It to Beaver"*

Anybody who watches three games of football in a row should be declared brain dead.
- *Erma Bombeck*

A lawyer with a briefcase can steal more than a thousand men with guns.
- *Mario Puzo*

The reason there is so little crime in Germany is that it's against the law.
- *Alex Levin*

A decision is what a man makes when he can't find anybody to serve on a committee.
- *Fletcher Knebel*

I want my data back, scumbag, and I want it back now!
- *Secretary overheard conversing with her computer*

Communism doesn't work because people like to own stuff.
- *Frank Zappa*

The surest sign that intelligent life exists elsewhere in the universe is that it has never tried to contact us.
- *Calvin and Hobbes, comic by Bill Watterson*

I hate being a bureaucrat and will resign as soon as I know the proper procedure.
- *Hector Breeze*

The reason there are two senators for each state is so that one can be the designated driver.
- *Jay Leno*

It doesn't make any difference what temperature a room is, it's always room temperature.
- *Steven Wright*

Life is too short for traffic.
- *Dan Bellack*

Until you've lost your reputation, you never realize what a burden it was.
- *Margaret Mitchell*

Man is the only animal that fears children.
- *Sparrow*

My dog is worried about the economy because Alpo is up to .99 cents a can. That's almost $7.00 in dog money.
- *Joe Weinstein*

Walking like a dork is popular among people who used to jog for their health but can no longer afford orthopedic surgery.
- *David Barry*

How is it possible to find meaning in a finite world, given my waist and shirt size?
- *Woody Allen*

Lead us not into temptation. Just tell us where it is; we'll find it.
- *Sam Levenson*

Don't bother discussing sex with small children. They rarely have anything to add.
- *Fran Lebowitz*

Never accept an invitation from a stranger unless he offers you candy.
- *Linda Festa*

Why do they put the Gideon Bibles only in the bedrooms, where it's usually too late?
- *Christopher Darlington Morley*

He who dies with the most toys—still dies.
- *T-shirt*

This life is a test; it is only a test. If it were a real life, you would receive instructions on where to go and what to do.
- *Unknown*

TUTORIAL TALES

(Anecdotes with a Message)

When Thomas Edison was working on improving his first electric light bulb, the story goes, he handed the finished bulb to a young helper, who nervously carried it upstairs, step by step. At the last possible moment, the boy dropped it—requiring the whole team to work another 24 hours to make a second bulb.

When it was finished, Edison looked around, then handed it to the same boy. The gesture probably changed the boy's life. Edison knew that more than a bulb was at stake.

- James D. Newton

Rule 6 in golf is the Ten Commandments packed into one. It means you cannot lie, cheat or steal. You cannot conceal the truth or spread disinformation . . .

The best example of Rule 6 at work occurred in 1968, when Roberto De Vicenzo of Argentina signed for a score that was one stroke higher than he actually deserved and thereby lost the chance to play off for the Masters. When the mistake was brought to his attention, he didn't blame the scorekeeper or the tournament officials. And he didn't hire a lawyer.

His comment will live for as long as golf is played. In the ultimate demonstration of sportsmanship he said: "What a stupid I am."

In life, too few of us are ever willing to admit it.

- Jerry Tarde, Golf Digest

A visitor was admiring a painting in the studio of Renoir, who was noted for the voluptuousness of his nudes. "How do you achieve such realistic flesh tints?" he asked. "Who can say?" shrugged the French impressionist. "I keep adding a stroke here and a stroke there until I am satisfied that everything is right."

"But how do you know when it is exactly right?" prodded the visitor. Confided Renoir, "When I feel like pinching."

President Grover Cleveland was a draft dodger. He hired someone else to enter the service in his place, for which he was ridiculed by his political opponent, James G. Blaine. It was soon discovered, however, that Blaine had done the same thing himself.

On July 20, 1969, the day man first walked on the moon, one of the sisters in Mother Teresa's home for the destitute in Calcutta asked her, "Do you think you will ever go to the moon?" She wasted no time in replying, "If there are poor and unwanted people on the moon, I will surely take my sisters there."

Kim Woo-Choong, founder of the Korean-based Daewoo Group, a conglomerate with sales of $25 billion in 1991—more than Coca-Cola or Nabisco, forged his determination as a young refugee in wartime Korea:

When Kim was 14-years-old, his father was kidnapped by North Koreans and the young boy was thrown into the sober responsibility of feeding his family. He sold newspapers from a makeshift shack along a river, which was forced to close during inclement weather.

Following one storm he had only a few coins to give the family for the day's meals. When he arrived home, his mother said, "We've already eaten. You must be hungry, so eat." In truth, there had been only one bowl of rice, and his brothers had all been put to bed hungry. "I thought I would cry," said Kim. "I had a bowl of noodles on the way home," he lied. "You should eat."

I had learned a valuable lesson," he recalls, "You must be generous with others, but severe with yourself.

Until he reached middle age, French artist Paul Cezanne lived a hand-to-mouth existence. Then a Paris dealer held an exhibition of his paintings, and overnight he caught on.

During his first visit to the exhibition, he was touched by the warmth of the reception accorded him. But something else impressed him more. He pointed at the canvases on the walls and whispered to a friend: "Look, they're framed!"

- E. E. Edgar

Henri Dunant, a 30-year-old wealthy Swiss banker and financier was sent by his government to propose a business deal to Napoleon III. He found Napoleon on the plain of Solferino, seconds away from entering a battle with the Austrians. Dunant sat and watched the battle transfixed—entranced by the horror taking place below him. After the battle had ended, Dunant entered the small town. Driven by the compassion and sympathy at the suffering he witnessed, he declared that the world should abolish the barbarous act of war.

When Dunant returned to Switzerland he became a fanatic on the subject of peace—preaching it everywhere. His business suffered and he eventually went broke. But he persisted.

At the first Geneva Conference he carried his one-man assault against war. As a result, the first international law against war was passed. In 1901, he was awarded the first Nobel Peace prize. Despite his nearly hopeless financial state, he donated all his prize money to the worldwide movement he had founded. Despite the fact he died almost totally forgotten by the world, he needed no monument to mark his grave—except the symbol of the organization he founded—the everlasting monument of the Red Cross.

Some time ago a 10-year-old boy entered a coffee shop and sat down. When approached by the waitress he asked, "How much is an ice cream sundae?"

"Fifty cents," she replied.

The boy studied the number of coins in his hand and then asked, "How much is a dish of plain ice cream?"

The waitress, becoming impatient, replied brusquely, "Thirty-five cents."

The boy looked at the coins again and ordered the plain ice-cream.

The waitress brought his order, and put the bill on the table next to it. When the boy finished, he paid the cashier and left. When the waitress returned to pick up his empty plate, she paused and swallowed hard. There, placed neatly beside the empty dish, were two nickels and five pennies as her tip.

When Dr. Robert J. Oppenheimer, supervisor of the creation of the first atomic bomb, was asked by a congressional committee if there was any defense against the weapon, he quickly responded, "Certainly."

"And that is . . ." they inquired.

Dr. Oppenheimer looked over the hushed, expectant audience and subtly whispered, "Peace."

Oliver Wendell Holmes once attended a meeting in which he was the shortest man present. "Dr. Holmes," quipped a friend, "I should think you'd feel rather small among us big fellows."

"I do," retorted Holmes. "I feel like a dime among a lot of pennies."

Once, Napoleon suddenly appeared at one of his camps at Boulogne-sur-Mer. His first words to Marshal Soult on arrival were, "How much time do you require to be able to embark? Three days, sire." "I can only give you one," replied Napoleon. "That's impossible," said the Marshal. 'Impossible' is not a word in my dictionary. Erase it from yours,' commanded Napoleon.

The challenge that awaits reminds me of the ancient coat of arms of the royal family of Spain. Before Columbus set sail to cross the Atlantic, it was believed that the world ended out there somewhere past Gibraltar. To the Spanish, one of their real glories was that they were the last outpost of the world, and that their country fronted right on the great beyond. Therefore the royal coat of arms showed the Pillars of Hercules, the great columns guarding the Strait of Gibraltar, and the royal motto said plainly Ne Plus Ultra, meaning, roughly, "there is no more beyond here."

But then, when Columbus returned, he had actually discovered a whole new world out there. The ancient motto was now meaningless. In this crisis someone at Court made a noble and thrifty suggestion, which was immediately adopted by Queen Isabella. It was simply that the first word, Ne, be deleted. Now the motto on the coat of arms read—and has read ever since—just two words: Plus Ultra— "There is plenty more beyond."

Jacques Lipchitz, the sculptor, spent his youth in Paris, where he was a close friend of Soutine,

Modigliani, and Chagall. One day a friend complained that he was dissatisfied with the light he painted on his canvases, and went off to Morocco, seeking a change in light. He found, however, that the light in his Moroccan canvases was no different. Lipchitz then advised him, "An artist's light comes from within, not from without."

Before Lou Little became the most successful football coach in Columbia University history, he coached for Georgetown University. There was one boy on his team who, although not a great football player, served as a great morale booster for the team. Little was fond of the boy and even let him play on occasion.

One day, about a week before the big finale game of the season, the boy's mother called coach Little with bad news—the boy's father had died that morning. The boy used to go arm-in-arm around the campus with his father. Little knew he would take the news hard. Little broke the news to the boy, who immediately left for home—only to return three days later to ask the coach if he could start in the big game. "I think it's what my father would have liked most," he said. After a brief hesitation, Little agreed, provided the boy only stay in a play or two.

True to his word, Little started the boy—but never took him out. For sixty jarring minutes the boy played inspired football, running, blocking, and tackling like an All-American, and sparking the team to victory. After the game Little threw his arms around the boy and asked him what got into him.

The boy answered, "Remember how my father and I used to go about arm-in-arm? There was something about him very few people knew. Dad was blind. And I knew today would be the first time he would ever see me play."

Upon being dismissed from his government job in the custom house, Nathaniel Hawthorne arrived home in deep despair. With his head hung he told his tale with all hopelessness to his wife who didn't waste a minute before she set pen and ink on the table, lit the fireplace, and sat him down. Putting her arms around his shoulders she said, "Now you will be able to write your novel." Which of course he did; dramatically proving the statement that "out of breakdown comes possibility."

One day, Count Leo Tolstoy was stopped on the street by a beggar who appeared emaciated and weak. The author searched his pockets for a coin to give the starving man and discovered that he did not carrying a single penny. Taking the worn hands of the beggar's between his own he said, "Do not be angry with me, my brother; I have nothing with me." The sunken face of the beggar immediately became illuminated as he replied, "But you called me brother—that was a great gift."

After Michelangelo completed the statue of Moses, the Renaissance sculptor stared at his work, scrupulously studying it for a long time, and then suddenly struck the knee of the masterpiece in anger crying, "Why dost thou not speak?"

Michelangelo's eternal search for divine perfection was the very fuel for his compulsive artistic drive.

Life is a succession of lessons which must be lived to be understood.

- Emerson

Many years ago in the city of Hamburg, the saintly philosopher Moses Mendelssohn fell in love with a charming woman named Fruntje. He approached her father, Guggenheim, to inform him of his love for her. Guggenheim, referring to Mendelssohn's hunched back, the result of a curvature of the spine, replied "Well, you are a philosopher and a wise man, so you will not take it amiss. The girl said she became frightened when she saw you because of your appearance."

This did not surprise Mendelssohn, and he immediately asked to speak with Fruntje. Although she avoided looking at him throughout the conversation, Mendelssohn was able to lead the conversation to the subject that was on his mind. Timidly, Fruntje asked if he too, believed in marriages that were made in heaven. Mendelssohn said that yes he did, and then went on to relate an unusual story: "As you know, they call out in Heaven at the birth of a boy, 'This one will get that girl for a wife.' When I was born, my future wife was also thus announced, but it was added, 'She will, alas, have a terrible hump.' I shouted, 'Oh, Lord, a girl who is humpbacked will very easily become bitter and hard. A girl should be beautiful. Good Lord, give the hump to me, and let her be handsome and well formed!'"

Fruntje immediately accepted his proposal and soon became the faithful and devoted wife of Mendelssohn.

It was the year 1870, and the Methodists were having their annual conference in Indiana. The presiding Bishop was asking the group for an interpretation of current events, when the president of the college where the conference was being held volunteered his input: "I think we are in a very exciting age."

The Bishop asked him to expound. The president continued, "I believe we are coming into a time when we will see, for example, wonderful inventions. I believe men will fly through the air like birds."

The Bishop Wright, visibly disturbed by this scientifically based comment proclaimed, "This is heresy, this is blasphemy; I read in my Bible that flight is reserved for the angels. We will not have such talk here in my area." And he returned home to his two young sons, Orville and Wilbur.

Some time ago, a young mother took her baby and embarked on a journey over the hills of South Wales during a terrible blizzard. However, overtaken by the relentless freezing snow, she was never able to arrive at her destination. A search party later located her frozen body beneath the snow.

As the search party dug her body out, they were surprised to find that she had no outer clothes on. But as they lifted her body, they learned why.

The selfless mother had taken them off to wrap around her baby. When they unwrapped the child, they found him still alive and in amazingly good condition.

The son was David Lloyd George, who grew up to be the prime minister of Great Britain during World War I. He was known as one of England's greatest statesmen. The vital sacrifice his mother had made, was a noted contribution to all of humanity.

- B. Charles Hostetter, Christian Life

In his forty-two year career as coach of the University of Chicago, Amos Alonzo Stagg was the idol of students and graduates alike. He was especially noted for his uncompromising honesty.

This honesty was illustrated on one specific occasion when Stagg's champion baseball team was defending its college title. It was the final play, the batter had singled, and one of Stagg's players was racing home with the winning run. "Get back to third base," Stagg yelled to his man, "You cut it by a yard!"

"But the umpire didn't see me!" cried the runner.

"That doesn't make any difference!" Stagg yelled, "Get back!"

The game was lost, but a character battle was won.

In the year 1884, a young American man died while visiting Europe. His parents were heartbroken, the boy had had his whole life ahead of him. Rather than erect an ornate grave, they began to consider some kind of living memorial to their son, one that would help other young men like him. Thus, they arranged to meet with Charles Eliot, the president of Harvard University.

When the ordinary, unpretentious couple arrived in his office and explained about their son and their intention of establishing a memorial, such as a building or the likes, Eliot crisply responded with a suggestion of aristocratic disdain, " . . . What you suggest costs a great deal of money." He obviously didn't think this ordinary couple capable of such a donation.

The woman paused and rose slowly. "Mr. Eliot," she said, "what did this entire university cost?"

Eliot muttered a figure amounting to several million dollars.

"Oh, we can do better than that," she said. And the plain, unpretentious couple contributed $26 million for a memorial to their son—to be named Leland Stanford, Jr. University.

It was somewhere around the year 635 when St.

Aidan, bishop of Northumbria, was given a fine horse by his good friend King Oswin, ruler of the former British province of Deira. Upon meeting a beggar down the road, the bishop immediately dismounted his horse and gave the fine animal, including all its costly trappings, to the poor man. When the king heard of this, he summoned Aidan, "Why did you give away the horse that we specially chose for your personal use when we knew that you had need of one for your journeys? We have many less valuable horses that would have been suitable for beggars."

Aidan replied, "Is this foal of a mare more valuable to you than a child of God?" The king thought for a minute and suddenly cast his sword aside to kneel at Aidan's feet and beg his forgiveness. Of course he was immediately forgiven. And as Aidan watched the king go, he became very sad. When his chaplain asked why, he replied, "I know that the king will not live long, for I have never seen a king so humble as he is. He will be taken from us as the country is not worthy to have such a king."

A few years later, King Oswin was treacherously killed by his northern neighbor, King Oswy.

When Leonardo da Vinci was working on the face of Jesus in his painting "The Last Supper," he became angry with a certain man and lost his temper with him—lashing out at him with bitter words and threats. When he returned to his canvas, he attempted to continue his work but found himself unable to do so. Thus, he lay down his tools and searched for the man to ask his forgiveness. The man accepted his apology and Leonardo returned to his workshop and finished painting the face of Jesus.

William Allen White, the man responsible for establishing the Emporia Gazette as a national newspaper, generously gave fifty acres of parkland to his home town. When asked to explain his action, he replied, "This is the last kick in a fistful of dollars I am getting rid of. I have tried to teach people that there are three kicks in every dollar: one, when you make it—and how I love to make a dollar; two, when you have it—and I have the Yankee lust for saving. The third kick is when you give it away—and it is the biggest kick of all."

In 1825 Pope Leo XII went on a visit to the jail of the Papal States. Upon arriving, he insisted on questioning each of the prisoners as to how they had ended up there. Every man, with the exception of one, begged their innocence. The one man who did not humbly admitted that he was both a forger and a thief. Turning to the prison warden, Pope Leo sternly commanded: "Release this rascal at once. I do not wish that his presence should corrupt all these noble gentlemen here!"

— Leaves from the Garden of St. Bernard

A few years ago, a man decided to visit a fellow member of his church, since he had not seen him there for a while. When asked where he had been, the man responded "Christianity makes too many demands. It is always asking for money or time or something. "You know," the visitor said, "twenty-five years ago a son was born to me. From the moment he came into this world, he took my time and energy and he cost me plenty of money—first the hospital bills, then the toys and food, then shoes, books, and lessons. I had to haul him from dances and to Boy Scouts. And then one day, just as he was about to graduate from college, my son was infected with a terrible disease and he died." Attempting to hold back the tears, he continued, "Since that time, my boy has not taken one minute of my time, nor cost me one cent—not one cent."

When eight-year-old Joey's little sister underwent a necessary operation, it turned out she had lost so much blood she was in need of an immediate transfusion. Joey's blood type was the same as his little sister's.

"Will you give your sister some of your blood?" asked the doctor.

Joey paused for a long time before he agreed.

The boy tried to be brave as the blood was being drawn from his veins, but the doctor noticed that he was growing paler and paler. When the draw was complete, Joey looked up at the doctor and timidly asked, "I was just wondering how long it will be before I die?" The doctor looked down at Joey and said, "Do you think people die when they give blood?"

"Well, yes sir," replied Joey.

"And you were willing to die for your sister?"

"Yes, sir," he said quietly.

As the great sculptor, Phidias was carving the statue of Diana to be placed in the Acropolis, he seemed to be taking an unusually long time on the back side of the head. He was meticulously bringing out every strand of hair as far as possible, when someone remarked, "That figure is to stand a hundred feet high, with its back to the marble wall. Who will ever know what details you are putting there?"

Phidias replied, "I will know." And he continued with his painstaking detail.

At the bedside of H.G. Wells, who was in his last illness, an old friend attempted to get a conversation going by recalling incidents of years gone by. Wells, however, evinced little interest.

"I have no time to dwell on where I have been," he finally said. "I am too busy thinking of where I am going."

— E.E. Edgar

During World War II Jimmy Durante was doing a tour of veterans' hospitals under the supervision of Ed Sullivan. At one rehabilitation center on Long Island, Ed warned Jimmy that they were on a tight schedule and there would be no time for encores or they would miss their plane. But when the time came for them to leave, there was Durante—doing an encore. Sullivan frantically motioned from behind the curtain for Durante to come off stage. Jimmy quickly walked over to Ed and said, "Look, Ed, plane or no plane, I can't leave—look at the pair of soldiers clapping in the second row." Ed looked over and spotted the two one-armed veterans—clapping together with their good arms. The fact that they missed their plane suddenly became inconsequential.

One evening at the White House, during the William Howard Taft presidential administration, an incident occurred that sought to inspire parents in sustaining their relentless duty of discipline.

The President and his family were at the dinner table when Taft's youngest son made a surprisingly disrespectful remark to his father. The table was suddenly quiet. Finally, the first lady addressed her husband, "Well," she said, "aren't you going to punish him?"

Taft thought for a minute and then responded, "If the remark was addressed to me as his father, he certainly will be punished. However," he added, "if it was addressed to the President of the United States, that is his constitutional privilege."

It was the celebration of the brilliant conductor, Arturo Toscanini's eightieth birthday. Groups of people were standing around the room talking when someone asked Toscanini's son what his father ranked as his most important achievement. "For him there can be no such thing," replied the son. "Whatever he happens to be doing at the moment is the biggest thing in his life, whether it is conducting a symphony or peeling an orange."

It was the first week of October in 1843. A certain man was attending the ceremonies of the new Athenaeum at Manchester, when he felt a sudden inspiration to write a story that would arouse the people's awareness of the need to improve conditions of the poor. One week later he returned to London and started his composition.

As the story began to take form, he fell under its spell, laughing and weeping in turn with his characters. For seven weeks he labored relentlessly on the manuscript. Finally, on December 18, 1843, his masterpiece was completed, and the first edition of six thousand copies appeared on the bookstalls of London. Unaware that he had written a classic, Charles Dickens was astonished when he learned that the entire six thousand copies of A Christmas Carol had sold out within twenty-four hours.

The harvest of 1783 was a poor one, but the bailiffs of the estates at Chavaniac owned by Marquis de Lafayette, the French general and politician who helped to found the revolutionary National Assembly, had managed to fill the barns with wheat anyway. "The bad harvest has raised the price of wheat," said the bailiff. "This is the time to sell." Lafayette thought about the hungry peasants in the surrounding villages. "No," he replied, "this is the time to give."

When the French scientist Louis Pasteur was stricken with a cerebral thrombosis, during the construction of a laboratory that the government was building for him; his condition seemed so hopeless that the government ordered the construction to be stopped. When Pasteur heard of this news his condition began to rapidly decline. His friends, aware of what was happening, appealed to Emperor Napoleon III, who responded to their plea and ordered construction resumed. Pasteur suddenly began an amazingly rapid recovery. And in the completed laboratory he conquered rabies and several other diseases.

- Tom Mahoney, American Legion Magazine

Several years ago, an American woman journalist had been sent to China to cover a story. While there she witnessed a frail Catholic Sister cleansing the gangrenous sores of wounded soldiers. "I wouldn't do that for a million dollars!" she informed the Sister. Without pausing from her work, the Sister humbly replied, "Neither would I."

- Catholic Digest

At a banquet honoring a leading actor, the actor was asked to recite something for the pleasure of his guests. He consented and asked if there was anything special that anyone in the audience would like to hear.

After a moment's pause, an old clergyman asked, "Could you, sir, recite the Twenty-third Psalm?"

The actor was puzzled but agreed to this request upon one condition, that after he had recited it, that the clergyman do the same.

Initially, the clergyman protested, arguing that he was not an elocutionist. However, seeing that this was the only way the actor would grant his request, he finally agreed.

The actor began the psalm, holding the audience spellbound from start to finish—after which there was a great burst of applause from the guests.

Then it was the clergyman's turn. The psalm was recited, and when it was done, there was not a single ripple of applause from the audience, but every guest had their head bowed and not one was dried eyed.

The actor then put his hand on the shoulder of the old clergyman, and with a trembling voice exclaimed, "I reached your eyes and ears, my friends; this man reached your hearts. I know the Twenty-third Psalm; this man knows the Shepherd."

It was a sleety and slushy day in New York. Pedestrians were hurrying along Forty-second Street with their coat collars pressed around their ears, scarcely looking up to glance at passers-by. A young black man, carrying a heavy valise in one hand and huge suitcase in the other, was rushing toward Grand Central Station slipping and skidding along the walk as he went. Suddenly, a hand reached out and took the valise, and a pleasant voice said, "Let me take one, brother! Bad weather to have to carry things." The black man was a little reluctant, but the other man insisted that it was on his way and it was no trouble. All the way to the station the two chatted like old friends.

Years later, Booker T. Washington told his story. "That was my first introduction to Theodore Roosevelt," he said.

- Maeanna Chesterton-Mongle,
Sunshine Magazine

When an American soldier in France won the Croix de Guerre, he refused to wear it. When asked why he did not wear it proudly as he should, the soldier explained, "I was no good back home. I let my sister and my widowed mother support me. I was a deadbeat. And now they have given me the Croix de Guerre for something I did at the front. I am not going to put it on. I am going back home first. I am going to win out there. I am going to show my mother that I can make good at home. Then I will put on the Croix de Guerre."

He is not the first to have discovered that being heroic in a crisis is sometimes even easier than being useful at home.

- Harry Emerson Fosdick

One day a not-so-well-known painter asked Albert Einstein to sit for a portrait. The famous mathematician replied, "No, no, no, I do not have time."

But when the painter confessed that he desperately needed the money he would get for the picture, Einstein replied, "Well, that's another story. Of course I'll sit."

Alexander the Great noticed Diogenes, the great philosopher, staring attentively at a large collection of human bones and asked what he was looking for.

"I am searching for the bones of your father," said the philosopher, "but I cannot distinguish them from those of his slaves."

Turner, the famous artist, once invited Charles Kingsley into his studio to see a picture of a storm at sea. Kingsley was full of admiration for the reality of the painting. "How did you do it, Turner?" he asked.

The artist's answer was indeed inspiring: "I wished to paint a storm at sea, so I went to the coast of Holland, and engaged a fisherman to take me out in his boat in the next storm. The storm was brewing, and I went down to his boat and asked him to bind me to its mast. Then he drove the boat out into the teeth of the storm. The storm was so furious that I longed to lie down in the bottom of the boat and allow it to blow over me. But I could not: I was bound to the mast. Not only did I see that storm and feel it, but it blew itself into me, till I became part of the storm. And then I came back and painted that picture."

Poet Vachel Lindsay told of an experience that happened to him one night when he was very tired and hungry. He stopped at a farmhouse and asked to stay overnight. He had no money, but offered to pay for his lodging by reciting original poetry. The housewife was not interested in poetry and replied, "We cannot keep you, but those people there may," and she pointed across the field to a small house.

Lindsay went to the house where the man welcomed him and invited him in saying, "You may stay if you are willing to put up with what we have." The house consisted of two very small rooms. There was no rug on the floor, no window shades, and not a piece of furniture worth more than two dollars. There was only a rickety old table, surrounded by a few broken chairs, a small bed and an old stove.

When Lindsay left the next morning, he was inspired. "That man had nothing," he told a friend, "and gave me half, and we both had abundance."

One day the Baron de Rothschild was approached by a man who needed a loan of $1,000. The Baron agreed to grant the loan, if the client would provide an endorser. The man could not think of a single person who would accept that responsibility. Finally, nearly ready to give up, he told the Baron that the only person who trusted him was God Almighty. The Baron looked thoughtful for a moment and then replied, "He will be fine. I'll accept Him as an endorser." He asked the man to sign the note, and on the back he wrote, "Endorsed by God Almighty."

Six months later, the client returned to pay back his note, but the Baron refused payment. The man looked confused and asked the Baron to explain why. The Baron replied with a smile, "My dear friend, the Endorser has already repaid the loan."

After the death of Chaim Weizman, Ben-Zvi was called to the presidency of Israel. On the first day of his presidency, he returned home at night and found a sentry marching up and down in front of his residence. He asked the soldier what he was doing there. The young officer replied that he was sent by the Chief of Staff as an honor guard before the home of the President. Ben-Zvi was amazed. He entered his home and within a few minutes came out again into the cold, wintry, night air.

"Look here," he said to the soldier, "It's cold outside. Come in and have a cup of hot tea."

The soldier informed him that he was not allowed to leave his post.

The President went inside once again and asked his wife to make some hot tea. Once again he walked out and addressing the sentry said, "Look, I have an idea. You go in and have a cup of tea. I will stand outside with your gun and take your post."

<u>*Personal Notes:*</u>

COMPACT

Classics®

LIBRARY #7: Fantastic Facts
inquiries, curiosities, oddities, and particulars

In the grand tradition of our Trivia to Learn By sections from Volumes I and II, **Fantastic Facts** offers you another all-new, all-fun collection of eye-opening facts and intriguing questions. But this library also boasts two major changes:
(1) A grand total of 47 specific, custom-tailored category headings to help armchair experts delve faster and more selectively into the topics that engage them; and
(2) A "Did You Know That..." sampling of "fast facts" tucked handily under every heading, to be used for warm-up and easy reference.

So check out our "Rest and Relaxation" section before planning your next vacation. And on the road you can impress your spouse and kids (or your parents) with tidbits from "Arachnids and Angiosperms."

Meanwhile, for free fun and enlightenment anytime, anywhere, you have more than forty other categories at your fingertips. So learn on. And enjoy.

FANTASTIC FACTS

Inquiries, Curiosities, Oddities, and Particulars

BON APPETIT!
Did You Know That . . .

. . . The FDA allows an average of 30 or more insect fragments and one or more rodent hairs per 100 grams of peanut butter?

. . . Diet product spending was down $309 million in 1993, while non-diet product purchases ballooned by $1.6 billion?

. . . Women burn fat more slowly than men, by a rate of about 50 calories—about one chocolate-chip cookie's worth—per day?

. . . Americans spent an estimated $267 billion dining out in 1993?

. . . In ancient China and certain parts of India mice are considered a great delicacy?

. . . A 16-cup tub of buttered movie theater popcorn has more grams of fat in it than a bacon and egg breakfast, a Big Mac with fries, and a full steak dinner *combined* (at least before modifications were made by the theaters in mid-1994)?

. . . The name "pretzel" was derived from the early Latin word "brachiatus," meaning "having branch-like arms," because its shape resembles a pair of folded arms?

. . . The "57" in Heinz '57 sauce refers to the "nearly three-score" varieties of the product; in 1923, Heinz offered flavors that included "grape jelly," "peanut butter," "cherry preserves," and "cream of pea soup"?

Curious Cuisines of the Galloping Gourmet

• The "science of dining" or "the art of eating well" is known as _____; and one who is an expert in this field—a "connoisseur of good food"—goes by what name(s)?	Gastronomy; gastronome (gastronomer, gastronomist), gourmet, or epicure
• Devoured at the rate of about 1.2 billion pounds a year, what is America's favorite snack food?	Potato chips
• What is the pasta noodle whose name means "tongues" in Italian?	Linguine
• What dessert is traditionally served to fans at the Wimbledon tennis tournament each year?	Strawberries and cream
• Which "shade" of turkey meat contains the most fat and calories, white or dark?	Dark
• What sounds do Rice Krispies make in Dutch-speaking countries, comparable to our English "snap, crackle, and pop"?	"Pif, paf, pof"
• What is the English translation for the popular Italian dish, "pie"?	Pizza
• With over 6 billion sold each year, what is the world's best-selling brand of cookie?	Nabisco's *Oreo*
• Name, in order of preference, the three most popular ice cream flavors in America.	Vanilla, chocolate and butter pecan
• Who was the Baby Ruth candy bar named after? (Hint: No, it wasn't baseball player Babe Ruth.)	Ruth Cleveland, daughter of President Grover Cleveland and the first baby girl ever born in the White House
• What is the name of a breakfast product made up of edible letters?	Alphabits
• Food names can range from the whimsical to the tantalizingly oblique. Fill in the blanks below with the correct terms:	
- "Albany beef" is actually a fish known as _____.	Sturgeon

© 1994, Compact Classics, Inc.

- The "Barbary Fig," "India Fig," or "Indian Pearl" is more commonly known in North America as the _____ _____.	Prickly pear
- A "tenderloin trout" is really a _____.	Catfish
- The dried-fruit pastries known as "funeral pies" are usually filled with _____.	Raisins
- The common cornmeal "hoecake" or "johnny-cake" was originally known as _____cake because itinerant preachers could pack it away for months without fear of mold or spoilage.	"Journey"
- "Indian snacks"—dried, salted and cured strips of beef—are known by the Quechua derivative _____.	Jerky
- "Farmer" cheese is also known as _____ cheese.	Cottage
- "Cherrystones" are a delicacy found near the sea; usually they are known as _____.	Clams
- The deep-sea anglerfish—a popular restaurant menu item—is commonly known as the _____.	Monkfish

• In the Middle Ages, what soup was believed to be an aphrodisiac?   Chicken soup

• Give the city, nationality or place-name popularly associated with each of these foods:

- Baked beans	Boston
- Sourdough bread	San Francisco
- Rye bread	New York
- Clam chowder	New England or Manhattan
- Fried chicken	Kentucky
- Oven cooking	Dutch
- Waffles	Belgian

• What tropical fruit serves as the traditional garnish for ham?   Pineapple

• In 1955, Quaker Oats made an unusual offer: free in each box of cereal was a folded paper. What did it award the bearer?   Lawful deed to one square inch of land in Canada's Yukon Territory

• What major "Flintstone" character is missing in a bottle of children's Flintstone Chewable Vitamin tablets?   Betty Rubble

• What are the external buds on a potato called?   Eyes

• What are the blue veins in blue cheese?   Mold

• The following products originally went by different names. Give the more current name that replaced the original.

- "Little Short-Cake Fingers"	Twinkies
- "Kandy Kake"	Baby Ruth candy
- "Fairy Fluff"	Cotton candy
- "Brad's Drink"	Pepsi-Cola
- "Fruit smack flavored syrup" (before being marketed in its dehydrated form)	Kool-Aid

• What percentage of fat is saved by opting for a margarine spread over butter?   None—both are 100 percent fat

• According to 172-pound Larry Coker (who formerly weighed 750 pounds), of the 70-million Americans who try to lose weight annually, what is the rate of permanent success?	Two percent
• How many boxes of Girl Scout cookies did Americans purchase in 1993?	172 million
• A submarine sandwich is known by several different names, depending on which region of the country in which you order. Give the regional English word for this oblong sandwich in each of the following areas:	
- Philadelphia	"Hoagie"
- Upstate New York	"Bomber"
- New York City	"Wedge"
- Boston	"Grinder"
- Miami	"Cuban sandwich"
- Kansas City	"Italian"

ONE FOR THE MONEY
Did You Know That . . .

. . . When your bank deducts $15.00 or $20.00 from your account as compensation for a bounced check, the bank only expends about one dollar and 15 cents' worth of manpower, computer power, overhead, and mailing costs to process the matter?

. . . Live pigs recently replaced money as a form of payment at a steel spring manufacturing plant in Belgrade, Yugoslavia?

. . . Inner-city Los Angeles families spend on the average 36 percent of their income on food, while their suburbanite counterparts spent only 12 percent?

. . . The I.R.S. allows taxpayers to take thousands of dollars in deductions for vanity surgery such as facelifts, breast enlargements, and nose jobs, if business related, but health club fees and weight-reducing programs are not deductible?

. . . Typical hospital expenses for a child struck by gunfire total more than $14,000—the same as a full-year's tuition at an average private college?

. . . According to Alex Haley's TV miniseries "Roots," Kunta Kinte was bought by his first master John Reynolds for $155, whereas in Haley's book Reynolds paid the more accurate price of $850?

. . . If people in their 30s invested the $25.00 a month usually spent on credit card interest they'd have more than $57,200 by the time they reached age 65?

. . . In the 1992 U.S. Presidential election campaign, candidate Ross Perot spent $3.08 per vote received, compared to Bush's $2.95 and Clinton's $2.50?

. . . Credit-card fraud costs consumers $6.74 per year for each card they carry? (The total cost of fraud to issuers in 1993 was one billion dollars.)

. . . Americans spend approximately $25 billion each year on beer? (This amount, incidentally, could prevent the yearly deaths of over four million impoverished children around the world.)

. . . By 1995 the average annual outlay per student for room, board, fees and tuition is projected to exceed $26,000 at Yale, Harvard, Sarah Lawrence, and many other prestigious private universities?

Fascinating Finances

• In 1993, what was the average salary, *per game*, of a major-league baseball player?	$42,000
• About how much money is consumed on military purposes every 13 days by the armed nations of the world?	About $25 billion (again, an incredible amount, considering how it could better be used)

• In 1969, how much did comedian Eddie Murphy pay for a flowered headband worn by rock star Jimi Henrix?	$19,500
• What is the estimated annual cost to U.S. taxpayers for keeping secret government documents classified?	$20 billion a year ($6 billion more than NASA's total budget)
• Per person, how much did it cost the U.S. Census Bureau to conduct the 1990 census?	$10 (for a total of $2.51 billion)
• In 1993, an average-size tube of Colgate toothpaste sold for less than two dollars. How much would buying Colgate—or about any other toothpaste brand—set you back in the small west-African country of Cameroon? What about China?	$6.05; $5.39
• What was the annual rate of inflation in Brazil for 1993?	2,500 percent
• What is the meaning of the words *Annuit Coeptis,* printed on the $1 bill? What do the eye and the pyramid represent?	"He (God) has favored our undertakings"; the all-seeing deity and strength
• From what source is the Nobel Peace Prize money derived?	Interest earned on the $9.2 million bequeathed for that purpose by Alfred Nobel at the time of his death in 1896
• Currently, what is the largest denomination of U.S. currency being issued?	The one-hundred-dollar bill
• What is the average life span of a $1 bill?	18 months
• The one-dollar bill, of course, is the most circulated denomination of U.S. currency. What is the second most used denomination?	The $20 bill
• How much money was Gennifer Flowers paid by the tabloid *Star* Magazine to reveal the story of her alleged sexual escapades with Bill Clinton?	$175,000
• What was the 1993 "capital punishment" cost for execution by lethal injection? The cost for an execution by firing squad?	$46,000; $7,000

DRIVIN' IN MY CAR
Did You Know That . . .

. . . Each year consumers burn enough gas in bumper-to-bumper traffic to drive to the sun and back more than 300 times?

. . . Driving with the air-conditioner on reduces gas mileage by approximately 2.5 miles per gallon?

. . . The "Father of Traffic Safety," William Phelps Engo—the man who originated modern traffic regulations—never drove a car? (He relied on a chauffeur.)

. . . It is an estimated 62 times safer to travel by plane than by highway, according to per-mile fatality rates?

. . . A combustion engine puts out more power at lower altitude than at higher altitude—due to greater air pressure and oxygen density?

. . . John and Horace Dodge had built an auto empire that, by 1920, was cranking out 1000 cars a day—and that both of these extraordinary men were illiterate?

. . . Most American automobile horns give off the musical note F?

On the Road Again

• How many cow hides does it take to make the leather interior for one Lexus GS300?	Five
• If, on cue, every person in the United States were to climb into a car, how many, on average, would be in each car? If everyone in the country of Ecuador did the same thing, how crowded would the average car be?	In the U.S. there would be 1.7 persons per car; in Ecuador, 132 would be in each car

• What name did the Nissan company originally go by?	Datsun
• What company manufactures the Corvette Stingray?	General Motors
• What do the initials of the Fiat Automobile stand for?	"Fabrica Italiana Automobile Tovino"
• What does the "GTO" in the 1964 Pontiac GTO stand for?	"Gran Turismo Omologato" (loosely translated, "Grand Award Sedan")
• What type of car was featured as the *General Lee* on CBS's 1979 "Dukes of Hazard" series?	A 1967 Dodge Charger
• What was the name of the classic car featuring a pop-up shield used by James Bond to defy bullets in the 1967 movie "Thunderball"? What was the name of the car that turned into a submarine in his 1977 movie "The Spy Who Loved Me"?	An Austin Martin; a Lotus Esprit
• What did Grandpa Munster of TV's "The Munsters" series call his 160-mph coffin-on-wheels?	*Dracula*
• Name the vehicle used by Luke Skywalker to cover the desert terrain of his home planet of Tatooine in the 1977 film "Star Wars."	The *Landspeeder*
• What does "MSRP" stand for in automobile commercials?	"Manufacturer's Suggested Retail Price"
• What German auto proudly advertised itself as the only car that would float on water? (Though it will definitely float, it won't float indefinitely.)	The Volkswagen Beetle
• Name the car that goes with each of these advertising mottos.	
- "A car ahead"	Honda
- "We are driving excitement."	Pontiac
- "It just feels right."	Mazda
- "I love what you do for me."	Toyota
- "The relentless pursuit of perfection"	Lexus
- "Quality is job one."	Ford
- "Cars that make sense"	Hyundai
- "A different *Kind* of Company. A Different *Kind* of Car."	Saturn
• What automobile company's logo consists of an emblem with a three-pointed star?	Mercedes Benz
• When a hot-rod brandishes "Snowballs," what feature is it showing off?	White-wall tires
• What is a CBer referring to when he talks about a "pregnant roller skate?"	A Volkswagen Beetle
• What automobile model—famous as a dismal market failure—was named after Henry Ford's only child?	The Edsel
• How are "Vince" and "Larry" employed by the U.S. Department of Transportation?	As the famous pair of crash-test dummies
• What device made its debut in Cleveland, Ohio, August 5, 1914, on the corner of Euclid Avenue and East 105th Street?	The traffic light
• What is a "self-canceling trafficator"?	The British term for a turn signal
• Name the make of automobile associated with each of the following number codes:	
- 3000GT	Mitsubishi

- 240SX	Nissan
- 900SE	Saab
- 456GT	Ferrari
- RX7	Mazda
- Z28	Chevy

• What was the most popular car ever made?

The Volkswagen Beetle (In the U.S. sales reached five million between 1949 and 1981—when U.S. production stopped—and total world-wide sales reached 21 million by 1992)

• According to DuPont Automotive, what were America's top five colors of choice for vehicles in 1993?

White, at 20%, followed by green (15%), medium red (10.5%), bright red (8.8%), and black (7.2%)

• Name the consumer activist whose book, *Unsafe at Any Speed* (1965), led to the passage of the 1966 National Traffic and Motor Vehicle Safety Act.

Ralph Nader

• According to oddsmaker William Hill in London, what are the odds that Britain will switch to driving on the right-hand side of the street before the year 2005?

250 to 1

—— ◇ ◆✧◆ ◇ ——

THE MEASURE OF ALL THINGS
Did You Know That . . .

. . . The base of the Great Pyramid of Egypt is large enough to cover ten football fields?

. . . Atomic clocks are accurate to a few millionths of a second a year?

. . . If you piled a billion one-dollar bills one on top of another, the pile would be 70 miles high?

. . . Disneyland sells enough soft drinks every year to fill a five-acre lake?

. . . New York City has 230 miles of subway track?

. . . The distance required for an average-length freight train (carrying about 100 cars and weighing about 12 million pounds) to come from a speed of 60 miles per hour to a complete stop is a full mile?

. . . Basketball Hall-of-Famer Bob Lanier wore a size 22 shoe?

Get Out Your Gauges

• Why is a manhole round?

If it were any other shape, its cover could conceivably be turned so that it could fall through the hole.

• Both the English and metric systems of measuring temperature use the "degree" as their units. The English system is measured in degrees "fahrenheit." What is the temperature scale for the metric system called? And, for each scale, at what temperatures does water freeze and boil?

Centigrade (or celsius); 0 and 100 degrees centigrade, 32 and 212 degrees fahrenheit

• In circular measures, if 90 degrees equals one "quadrant," what does 30 degrees equal?

One "sign"—originally named for the 12 signs of the Zodiac (which occur at 30-degree intervals along the astrological circle)

• What are the common dimensions of a credit card?

3 3/8 by 2 1/8 inches

• One "sidereal" (or "astral") day—the time it takes for Earth to revolve once around its axis in relation to the background stars—is short of the 24-hour solar day by about how many minutes?

Four minutes

- *Centennial* is to 100 years as _____ is to 1,000 years. | Millennial

- The prefix *deci* is to a tenth as the prefix *nano* is to a _____. | Billionth

- The states of Washington, California, Nevada, and most of Oregon lie in what time zone? | Pacific

- Of what significance is the date Jan. 1, 2001? | It is technically the first day of the 21st century

- How long is the Statue of Liberty's nose? How wide is her mouth? | 4 feet long; 3 feet wide

- On average, how many trips to the bathroom does an American make on a daily basis? How much time does this add up to throughout a lifetime? | Six trips, for a total of 47 minutes daily, which adds up to 2-1/2 "bathroom years" in an average lifetime

- How long is the average duration of a yawn? | Six seconds

- How long did it take the estimated 400,000 men who worked on it to complete the construction of the Great Pyramid of Egypt? | 20 years

- About how long would it take to walk once around the Pentagon? | 20 minutes

- What unit is used to assess the weight of precious stones and gems? What is the term used to express the purity of gold? | "Carat"; "karat"

- If Barbie—the long-legged, big-busted, shiny-blonde-haired doll—were a real five-foot-nine model, what would her actual measurements be? What would be the measurements of Popeye's 29-year-old girlfriend Olive Oyl? | She would have a 36-inch bust, a 17-inch waist, and 32-inch hips; 19-19-19

- How many seconds are there in a day? | 86,400

- What unit is used for measuring the height of horses? | A "hand"—which is equal to 4 inches

- What is a "Branock device" used to measure? | Shoe size

- What fraction of an iceberg shows above water? | One-ninth

- Name the brand of stopwatch used on the TV series "60 Minutes." | Heuver

- In the fairy tale, how long did Sleeping Beauty sleep? | 100 years

NUMEROUS NUMBERS
Did You Know That . . .

. . . The average number of letters used in a movie title is seventeen?

. . . There are 1575 steps from the ground floor to the top of the Empire State Building?

. . . According to the Library of Congress, of their 16.4 million books 300,000 of them are officially overdue?

. . . The parking lot at Bloomington, Minnesota's massive Mall of America has 13,000 parking spaces—a fact that led to some 2,000 shoppers requesting help to find their cars in 1993?

Let Me Count the Ways

- What do the numbers 11, 69, and 88 all have in common? | They read the same right-side up and upside down

- What IQ score is considered to mark the beginning of the genius level? | 140

- If you are a U.S. citizen, what is the breakdown of the "mysterious code" represented by the numbers on your social security card?

The first three digits show what part of the country you applied from, the next two signify the year you applied—again, conveyed in code—and the last four digits denote your "citizen's number," kept on file by the government

- "When you're torn between two of these, the best rule is to choose the lesser." What are the items in question?

Two evils

- In what sort of work are you most likely to use "Mach" numbers?

Test pilot

- Each of the following sets of three items forms a part of a larger group involving a number. Identify the group:

     - Anger, envy, pride

The Seven Deadly Sins

     - Frogs, locusts, hail

The ten Biblical plagues of Egypt

     - John, Thomas, Simon

Jesus' Twelve Apostles

     - Carpenter, Cooper, Shepard

The seven original U.S. astronauts

     - Capitoline, Esquiline, Palatine

The seven hills of Rome

     - Jane, Anne, Catherine

Wives of Henry VIII

- According to Robert Louis Stevenson's novel, *Treasure Island*, how many men are there on a dead man's chest?

15

- What is Fred and Wilma Flintstone's home telephone number?

BC 1234

- What renowned Parisian courtiere, when she died in 1971, left a legacy of perfume named by number?

Coco Chanel

- Which directions do you travel on odd-numbered highways in the United States? On even-numbered highways?

North and south; east and west

- How many days constitutes a "fortnight"?

14

- What was Sergeant Joe Friday's badge number in the popular television series "Dragnet"?

714

- How many holes (or indentations) are there on a Chinese Checker board?

121

- What are the last four digits of the IRS agency's toll-free telephone number?

1040

- How many times can the digit 9 be found in the numbers between 1 and 100?

20

- How many times does the word "One" appear on the face side of a one-dollar bill? How about on the reverse side? And how about the isolated *digit* "1" on the face and reverse sides?

"One" appears twice on the face and six times on the back; "1" appears four times on the face and four times on the back—for a grand total of sixteen "big ones."

- What is the number commonly used in journalism to signify the end of a newspaper story?

30

- How many steps lead up to a gallows? How many loops are tied in a hangman's noose?

In both cases, 13

- What is the number of herbs and spices in the mixture that coats Colonel Sanders' Kentucky Fried Chicken?

11

——— ◇ ◆ ✧ ◆ ◇ ———

FUN AND GAMES
Did You Know That . . .

. . . The craze of swallowing goldfish was initiated during a 1939 bull session at Harvard

University's Holworthy Hall by freshman Lothrop Withington Jr., son of a prominent Boston lawyer—and soon everyone was following suit?

. . . The biggest-selling toy of the year 1957 was the Hula Hoop?

. . . The Slinky, a loosely coiled spring toy, made its debut in November 1945—and has been crawling down America's stairways ever since?

. . . "Patience," "Canfield," "Klondike" and "Spider" are all variations of the card game Solitaire?

. . . When it was first introduced on Mississippi riverboats in the 1800s, the game of poker originally went by the name "Bluff"?

Games People Play

• In the game of Chess, what is the maximum number of squares a king can move in any given direction? A queen?

Only one; eight

• Which color always moves first in a Chess game?

White

• What aromatic World Championship contest takes place annually in Beaver, Oklahoma?

The World Championship Cow Chip Throwing Contest

• Gambling has been legalized in all but two U.S. states. As of 1994, which two states still do not allow any form of organized gaming?

Hawaii and Utah

• In 1978, Bob Speca Jr. had 100,000 of these standing at one time before they all toppled with the help of a klutzy ABC-TV cameraman. What were they?

Dominoes

• What are the playing tiles commonly called in the game of Dominoes?

Bones

• "Art & Literature," "Science & Nature," and "Sports & Leisure" are three of the six categories in the classic Trivial Pursuit board game. Name the other three categories.

"Geography," "Entertain-ment," and "History"

• What Chinese parlor game, first popularized as early as 500 B.C., became a fad among upper-class Americans during the 1920s?

Mah-Jongg

• What suspect in the game of Clue has the same name as a popular condiment?

Colonel Mustard

• How many flat colored squares are there on a Rubik's Cube?

54

• In the game of Backgammon, how many playing pieces does each player start with?

15

• Exceeding 80 million sales since its invention in 1935, what is the world's all-time best-selling board game?

Monopoly

• Answer these other questions about the game of Monopoly:

- What household item—often associated with a sometimes tedious chore—is used as a token in Monopoly?

An iron

- What articles of clothing are used as tokens?

A hat and a shoe

- What property, according to Monopoly aficionados, is landed on most often?

Illinois Avenue

- What is the rent for Boardwalk with a hotel?

$2,000

- How many total properties are there on a Monopoly board?

28

• In what game does the word fudgies mean "mistakes"?

Marbles

• What toy can let you "walk the dog," go all the way "around the world," and then come home to "sleep?"

The yo-yo

• What is the stretchable, bouncing, viscous toy that is packaged and sold in plastic eggs?

Silly Putty

• What was the high-bouncing, hard rubber sphere sold to Wham-O by Norman Stingley in 1965?	The Super Ball
• What is the common name for an alabaster marble?	An "alley"
• What category of adrenaline-inducing mechanical contraptions includes heavy-duty performers like the "Texas Cyclone" and "Mister Twister"?	Roller Coasters
• What kind of footwear, first fabricated in 1760 by Belgium's Joseph Merlin, exploded into an international craze in the late 1970s and early 1980s?	Roller skates
• Another roller craze was sparked by Jan and Dean in their 1965 hit "Sidewalk Surfing." Name the still-popular vehicle that this duo celebrated in song.	The skateboard
• These skates, featuring wheels arranged in a straight-line and used in sports like "asphalt hockey," are known as what?	Rollerblades
• What is the measurement used in Frisbee tournaments to determine how long a Frisbee remains airborne?	"Maximum Time Aloft"
• What game, from the Japanese word *Paka* (meaning "to eat"), gobbled up a generous share of the six-billion-dollar video-game business during 1982?	Pac-Man
• Name the gravity-defying thrill that took America by storm in 1991.	Bungee jumping

• Take a gamble and match the gambling terms listed in the left column with the definitions on the right.

- Another name for Blackjack	Twenty-one
- Gambling's "ivories"	Dice
- "Doped Cards"	A marked deck
- A "Fruit Machine"	A slot machine
- The three colors on a roulette wheel	Red, green and black
- Roulette's country of origin	France
- The "suicide king"	The king of hearts

——— ⋄ ♦ ✧ ♦ ⋄ ———

CRIME AND CORRUPTION
Did You Know That ...

. . . By the time a child finishes elementary school she will have witnessed 8,000 murders and 100,000 acts of violence on television?

. . . Though not one "witch" was burned in the early days of Salem, Massachussets, 19 women and young girls were hanged on the town's barren "Gallows Hill"?

. . . Between 1979 and 1991, close to 50,000 children were killed by guns in the U.S.—a figure roughly equivalent to the number of Americans killed in the Vietnam War?

. . . Arrests for violent crimes perpetrated by American youths under the age of 18 jumped from 54,596 in 1970 to 104,137 in 1992—a 91% hike?

. . . Elliot Ness, a real-life FBI agent, was instrumental in locking up mobster Al Capone, cleaning up corrupt cops, instituting The Cleveland Police Academy, and in founding Cleveland's Boys Town?

. . . According to the Jan. 1994 issue of *U.S. News & World Report*, the annual cost of crime in the United States exceeds $674 billion? (Another independent source estimates the cost of crime in the U.S. at $1.3 million *per minute*.)

. . . Some 3,862 prisoners were executed in the U.S. between 1930 and 1980?

. . . Nationwide, a woman is beaten ever 15 seconds?

. . . Statistics from the Bureau of Justice indicate that, in 1992, about 2,600 U.S. prisoners were on death row, while 31 were executed?

. . . In 1991, James Campbell, a chemist at Virginia Tech, was caught manufacturing methamphetamines in a university laboratory, yet was acquitted on the legal defense that he had only tried it after watching the TV program "48 Hours" and hearing correspondent Dan Rather explain the process for making speed?

On the Wrong Side of the Law

• Someone who pulls fraudulent or deceptive "deals" may be called a "con"—an expert at evoking and then abusing the trust of his target. What is con short for?

Confidence, as in "confidence man"

• In 1978, Dan White, a former policeman, shot and killed San Francisco's mayor George Moscone. White's attorney brought in a battery of psychiatrists to testify in his behalf. What was one especially peculiar testimony?

It was claimed that White's addiction to Twinkies, Coca-Cola and potato chips resulted in extreme blood-sugar level variations exacerbating his manic depression which, in turn, led to his psychopathic behavior.

• What popular soul singer was arrested for brandishing a shotgun in his office building while demanding to know who had used his private toilet?

James Brown

• On April 4, 1993, police in Charles City, Virginia apprehended a runaway drug dealer without breaking into a sweat. What was the suspect wearing that made it so easy to spot him?

L.A. Gear's Light Gears—battery powered sneakers that flash red lights when the heels hit the ground

• What earth-shaking event occurred on February 26, 1993 in New York City, causing the death of six people and injuring 1000 more?

The bombing of the World Trade Center

• Mohammed Salemeh was arrested as a suspect in the World Trade Center bombing. How was he caught?

He appeared at a rental center to reclaim his $400 deposit on the van he had used in the bombing

• On his way to the electric chair, what did James Donald French helpfully submit as a possible headline for the next morning's newspaper?

"French Fries"

• Gifted con-artist Victor "The Count" Lustig devoted his entire life to carrying out various scams. However, in 1922 one con game in particular made him the most infamous cheat of all time. What was it?

He sold the Eiffel Tower to a scrap-metal dealer for $50,000

• What bit of religious advice did Victor Lustig give for dealing with a potential con victim?

Wait for the mark to reveal his religious affiliation, and then become a member of the same church.

• Gangster Al "Scarface" Capone claimed he had received his scar in World War I. However, Capone never served in World War I. Where did his scar actually come from?

He was knifed in Brooklyn—in a fight over a woman—while working as a bouncer in a saloon

• Al Capone's nickname was "Scarface." His brother, Ralph, was assigned the primary duty of intimidating prospective customers into buying Al's liquor. What was Ralph's nickname?

"Bottles"

• What was Charlie "Lucky" Luciano's real first name? What other three infamous gangsters linked up with him in 1917?

Salvatore; Luciano was joined by Frank Costello, Benny "Bugsy" Siegel, and Meyer Lansky

• What Mafia leader's nickname was "Teflon Don" before he was sentenced to life in prison on July 23, 1992 after being found guilty on 44 counts of racketeering and murder? Who finally ripped away the criminal cover of this mob kingpin?

John Gotti; he was betrayed by his lieutenant, Salvatore "Sammy the Bull" Gravano

- In 1934, police arrested a carpenter and charged him with the 1932 murder of Charles and Anne Lindbergh's 20-month-old son Charles Augustus, Jr. What is the name of this man who was convicted and executed in 1936 for the crime? Also, what law was subsequently passed by Congress making it a federal offense to transport a kidnap victim across state lines?

Bruno Richard Hauptmann; the "Lindbergh law"

- What event in Chicago on June 20, 1993, led to a rampage that resulted in nearly 700 arrests?

The Chicago Bulls basketball team won its third consecutive NBA title

- Recently, the doodles of a judge triggered an appeal from a death-row inmate. What did the judge draw on the letter setting the date for this inmate's execution?

A smiley face

- Buying event tickets at regular prices and selling them at inflated prices is commonly known as _____.

Scalping

- Name "The Rock" that became known as "America's Devil's Island"—a prison characterized by maximum security, minimum privilege, and a rule of silence? Also, what was its unofficial "slogan"?

Alcatraz (it was finally closed in 1963 amid protests against its "cruel methods" of punishment); it was jokingly referred to as "A Super Prison for Super Prisoners"

- Name the young Massachusetts woman who allegedly killed her father and stepmother with an ax in 1892, but was acquitted largely due to her exemplary charitable and religious activities?

Lizzie Borden

- Who was the former heavyweight champion sentenced in 1992 to six years in prison for date rape?

Mike Tyson

- Give the correct definition for the following slang crime terms:

    - "Air dance"

Execution by hanging

    - "Black act"

Picking a lock in the dark

    - "Meat-eater"

A policeman or politician who accepts a bribe

    - "Chicago overcoat"

A 1920s underworld term for coffin

    - "State chemists"; "state electricians"

Executioners who kill condemned prisoners by lethal injection or electric chair, respectively

- What was the sentence received by James Earl Ray for killing Martin Luther King, Jr. in 1968?

He was sentenced to 99 years in prison on March 12, 1969

- What criminal mastermind, said to have played a role in fixing the 1919 World Series, was nicknamed, among other things, "Mr. Big," the "Brain," and the "Fixer"?

Arnold Rothstein

- What are "Saturday night specials"?

Inexpensive handguns

- In 1925, John T. Scopes, a young biology teacher from Dayton Tennessee, was convicted for breaking a state law. What was his crime?

He was teaching the theory of evolution

- Who "takes the cake" in rate of shoplifting convictions—men or women?

Women outnumber men by four or five to one for this crime

- What were the real names of Butch Cassidy and the Sundance Kid?

Cassidy was born Robert Leroy Parker on April 1, 1866 in Circleville, Utah; the Sundance Kid was born Harry Longbaugh in Phoenixville, Pennsylvania in 1870

• As of 1990, what is the estimated number of guns that can be found in the U.S.?	201 million
• What are the three basic symbolic concepts in Chinese philosophy that represent the "Triads"—Chinese secret societies which function as crime syndicates?	Heaven, Earth, and Man

HAIL TO THE CHIEF
Did You Know That . . .

. . . John Quincy Adams (1825-1829) frequently went out "skinny-dipping" in the Potomac River before sunrise?

. . . As the nation's "largest-ever" President, Grover Cleveland stood over six feet tall and weighed over 300 pounds while in office? (A few weeks after his birth, his mother said of him, "He is very large for his age and grows fat every day.")

. . . Richard M. Nixon's nickname in college was "Iron Butt"—and in law-school he was dubbed "Gloomy Gus"?

. . . President William H. Harrison served the shortest term in office, dying of pneumonia in 1841 just 31 days after taking the presidential oath? (He probably contracted the illness after walking in the rain, having refused to ride during his inaugural parade.)

. . . President Franklin D. Roosevelt served a total of 12 years, 1 month and 8 days in the White House—and, in 1939, was the first President to speak on television?

. . . Upon the death of President William H. Harrison, John Tyler was the first Vice President to serve as unelected President?

White House Goings-on

• Which U.S. President never won election to either the office of the Vice President or President?	Gerald Ford
• Since President James Buchanan was not married, who acted as First Lady during his term in office?	His niece, Harriet Lane
• Name the President who appears on the $500 bill. What about the $1,000 and $5,000 bills?	William McKinley ($500); Grover Cleveland ($1,000) and James Madison ($5,000)
• Who were the only grandfather and grandson to have both served as President?	William H. (1841) and Benjamin Harrison (1889-1893)
• Who were the only father and son to serve as President?	John Adams (1797- 1801) and John Quincy Adams (1825-1829)
• What former First Lady purportedly administered a professional judo flip to a New York news photographer for taking pictures of her outside a movie house in 1969?	Jacqueline Kennedy Onassis
• Which President seemed to enjoy showing off his gallbladder scar after his operation?	Lyndon B. Johnson
• How many of his eight years in office did George Washington live in the White House?	Zero—the White House was completed during Washington's successor, John Adams' term
• Which President had the most children?	John Tyler, with 15
• Who was the U.S. Presidential retreat Camp David named after?	David Eisenhower II, grandson of Dwight D. Eisenhower
• Before President Eisenhower changed the name of the retreat, what name was it known by?	Shangri-La
• Alexander Hamilton was killed in 1804 while engaged in a duel with whom?	Thomas Jefferson's Vice President, Aaron Burr
• Name the first U.S. President ever to visit the former Soviet Union.	Richard Nixon

- What two former presidents died on the same day? On what "select" day of 1826 did they die?

John Adams (at age 90) and Thomas Jefferson (83); July 4 (By a remarkable coincidence, John Adams' last words were, "Thomas Jefferson still survives.")

- Who was the only former Vice President to later be elected President but did not succeed the President under whom he served?

Richard Nixon

- When most of the White House gardeners were drafted to fight in WWI, what creative substitute did President Woodrow Wilson use to mow the lawn?

A small flock of sheep

- Besides Washington, Jefferson, Van Buren, and Lincoln, name the other five U.S. Presidents who did not attend college.

Taylor, Fillmore, Andrew Johnson, Cleveland, and Truman

- George Washington, Dwight D. Eisenhower, Ulysses S. Grant and Zachary Taylor all served in what post before assuming the Presidency?

General in the United States Army

- Shortly after President Ronald Reagan was shot in 1981, what cabinet member declared, "I'm in control"?

Secretary of State Alexander Haig

- What special orders did the press receive after Franklin Roosevelt was crippled by in 1921—eleven years before he assumed the Presidency?

There were to be no pictures taken of him that showed his legs

- Which President was the first to grow a beard in office?

Abraham Lincoln

- What celebrated poet performed a reading at President John F. Kennedy's inauguration?

Robert Frost

- Most people believe that JFK, at 43 years old, was the youngest President ever elected to office. Actually, he was second youngest. Who, at age 42, held this distinction among Presidents?

Theodore Roosevelt

- Most Americans know that Kennedy was the first and only Roman Catholic to serve as President, and that the Presidency has been filled by a number of Methodists (Polk, A. Johnson, Grant, McKinley . . .), Presbyterians (Jackson, Lincoln, Wilson, Eisenhower . . .), Unitarians (both Adamses, Jefferson, Taft . . .) and Episcopalians (Washington, Madison, Monroe, FDR, Ford, Bush . . .). Name the Presidents affiliated with the following religions:

  - Disciples of Christ

James Garfield, LBJ and Reagan

  - Baptist

Warren G. Harding and Bill Clinton

  - Congregationalist

Calvin Coolidge

  - Friend (Quaker)

Herbert Hoover and Richard Nixon

- Which President was known as a "genius for inactivity"—averaging 10 hours of sleep a day and another 10 of loafing—leaving four hours for work?

Calvin Coolidge

- Name the former U.S. President who admitted to shooting his sister in the rear end with a BB gun when he was 15.

Jimmy Carter

- Only one president served two non-consecutive terms. Who was this President, and who was elected to take over the reigns of office between his terms?

Grover Cleveland; Benjamin Harrison (1889-1893)

- Which former U.S. President appeared on a 1942 cover of Cosmopolitan magazine dressed in a Navy uniform?

Gerald Ford

- As of 1993, what is the annual salary for the President of the United States?

$200,000

- Name the limited right that the President may invoke to withhold information from Congress.

Executive privilege

- Who were the only two men elected to Congress after serving as President?

John Quincy Adams (1831-1848) and Andrew Johnson (1874-1875)

- Who is the only U.S. President known to have reported sighting a UFO?

Jimmy Carter

- What six Presidents have shared the common name of "James"?

Madison, Buchanan, Monroe, Garfield, Polk and Carter

- What was the title of the play President Lincoln was viewing at Ford's Theater on the evening of April 14, 1865, the night of his assassination?

"Our American Cousin," written by Tom Taylor

- What was Gerald R. Ford's recorded birth name before he was adopted as an infant by his mother's new husband, Gerald R. Ford, Sr.?

Leslie Lynch King, Jr.

- Name the five offices, in order, that are in line of succession to the Presidency.

The Vice-President, Speaker of the House of Representatives, President Pro Tempore of the Senate, Secretary of State, and, if all else fails, the Secretary of the Treasury will, in turn, succeed the President

- Which President was sworn into office on an airplane?

Lyndon B. Johnson, following Kennedy's assassination in 1963

WORLD LEADERS
Did You Know That . . .

. . . Ivan IV Vasilievich, the unifier and first Czar of Russia, best known as Ivan the Terrible, was dubbed with this infamous title after ordering thousands of political executions among his subjects, and, in a fit of rage, murdering his own heir—his eldest son?

. . . Famed physicist Albert Einstein was once offered—but turned down—the presidency of Israel?

Kings, Commanders, Governors and Czars

- Name the Mongolian sovereign whose territorial conquests between A.D. 1206 and 1227 (4,860,000 square miles of tribal control, including much of present-day Russia and China) exceeded the total combined conquests of Alexander the Great, Attila the Hun and Napoleon Bonaparte (4,350,000 square miles).

Genghis Khan

- What common bond do the terms Ming, Shang, Tang, Sung, Han and Ch'ing all share?

They all refer to Chinese dynasties

- French Emperor Napoleon Bonaparte exhibited a zeal for conquest and control; but what small, feeble creatures could allegedly make this great man shake, sweat, scream, and cry for help?

Kittens

- What 1953 female graduate of Mt. St. Vincent College in New York City went on to become a world leader from 1986-1992?

Corazon Aquino— President of the Philippines

- During the 480-odd years between 1068 and 1547 eight King Henrys ruled over England. Which Henry was responsible for each of the following?

    - In connection with his famed attraction to women, he is remembered for his break with papist Rome, which resulted in the creation of the Church of England.

Henry VIII

- This King's argument with Thomas Becket, the Archbishop of Canterbury, eventually led to Becket's murder.	Henry II
- Also known as Henry of Lancaster, this ruler became king after seizing the throne from Richard II. He left the crown with a huge debt.	Henry IV
- Also known as Henry Tudor, he instituted the Court of the Star Chamber simply to curb the power of the nobles.	Henry VII
- While his brother, the rightful monarch, was abroad, he generously crowned himself king.	Henry I
- As a ruler during the War of the Roses, he suffered from acute periods of insanity and was eventually sent to prison—where he was murdered.	Henry VI
- This incompetent sovereign survived in power for an eternal and intolerable forty-five years; in his old age he relinquished most of his power to his son Edward.	Henry III
- He was actually recognized by the French as heir to the throne of France.	Henry V

• Between 1239 and 1972, Great Britain also boasted eight King Edwards. Identify each Edward from the following descriptions:

- He expelled the Jews from England in 1290.	Edward I
- The eldest son of Queen Victoria, he brought international goodwill to England and was a highly popular king.	Edward VII
- According to the widely accepted story told by Sir Thomas More, this boy-king was suffocated in the Tower of London upon the order of Richard III.	Edward V
- The brief rule of this frail young son of King Henry VIII was dominated by relatives and advisors. Protestantism was established in England during his reign.	Edward VI
- He abdicated after less than one year to marry an American-born divorcee.	Edward VIII

• Name the Zimbabwian president who passed a law in 1983 declaring it a crime to make fun of his name.	President Canaan Banana
• A decisive battle that took place on December 2, 1805 is known as the Battle of the Three Emperors. Who are the three emperors referred to?	Napoleon I of France, Alexander I of Russia, and Francis I of Austria
• Which English king, born June 4, 1738, is best known in the U.S. for losing the American colonies?	King George III (Coincidentally, his visit to Eton College in England is still celebrated annually on July 4, the day Americans celebrate their independence.)

• Name the world leaders who went by the following nicknames:

- This South American leader (1783-1830), known as "The Liberator," made his whole life a quest for his continent's independence.	Simon Bolivar
- Also known as "The Liberator," this Irish nationalist leader served in the British House of Commons from 1775 to 1847.	Daniel O'Connell

- This Frankish ruler (688-c.741), whose surname literally means "The Hammer," finally halted the Muslim invasion of Europe.	Charles Martel
- Commonly surtitled "The Upright," this direct successor of Mohammed became the first Muslim caliph.	Abu Bakr
- Known as "Mr. Republican" (1889-1953), this "party patriot" was a U.S. Senator from Ohio and son of a former U.S. President.	Robert Alphonso Taft
• What did Emperor Menlik II of Abyssinia (now Ethiopia) do with the electric chair he ordered from the U.S.?	He used the chair as a throne (When he made the order, electricity was not yet available in his country to power the "electric" chair.)
• What enigmatic world leader has made cameo appearances in several Hollywood films? (Hint: He's an avowed socialist.)	Fidel Castro
• By a former marriage, actress Sophia Loren is sister-in-law to the son of a well-known world ruler. Who was this most loathed dictator?	Benito Mussolini
• According to the Bible, who was the first king of Israel?	Saul
• Who were the four King Herods, and which of them was in power when Jesus was born? Who ruled at the time of Jesus' crucifixion?	Herod the Great was in power at Jesus' birth; his sons—Herod Archelaus and Herod Antipas—followed; and his grandson, Herod Agrippa I ruled at the time of Jesus' death.

THE '60s AND '70s
Did You Know That . . .

. . . The "pass/fail" grading system took hold in colleges and universities across the nation during the mid-sixties when it became clear to a sympathetic faculty that low grades could send students on a long trip to Vietnam?

. . . In 1963 the Zone Improvement Plan (ZIP Codes) was implemented by the U.S. Post Office, carving the nation into 43,000 parts—and dramatically improving mail sorting efficiency?

Those Were the Days?

• What colorful food additive did the Food and Drug Administration approve in 1962 that would be declared carcinogenic 16 years later?	Red Dye #2
• What popular mid-sixties fashion trend, originated by fashion designer Mary Quant, was often worn with knee-high boots?	The mini skirt
• Former First Lady Jackie Kennedy became a trendsetter when she "wrapped" two of her best-known features in mystery with one of these articles designed in 1961 for a Madison Avenue store called Purdy. What were they?	Wrap-around sunglasses
• The Scott Paper Company put out a special line of easy-to-care-for dresses for $1.25 each in 1966 and advertised them as "flexible, fire-resistant and reinforced by rayon scrim." What were the dresses actually made of?	Paper
• In 1964, a new beachwear item left Bob Hope saying, "Instead of *Playboy*, the guys will be buying *Ladies Home Journal*." He added that "It leaves nothing to the imagination, and at my age it's good to have an imagination." Phyllis Diller, however, quipped, "When I wore one, everyone thought I was Albert Schweitzer." What were Hope and Diller talking about?	The topless bathing suit

• What was the name of the hairdo made popular by Olympic gold-medal figure skater Dorothy Hamill in 1976?	The wedge
• What was the title of the 1969 movie that became the first and only X-rated production to win the Academy Award for Best Picture?	"Midnight Cowboy" (Its rating has since been lowered to R)
• For two years during the '70s Mattel put out a doll called "Growing Up Skipper." What happened to this doll when her arm was turned?	Her breasts grew
• When this series debuted in 1964, it was immediately panned as one of the dumbest, most cliche-infested television sitcoms in history. Nevertheless, it did become a smash hit—with syndicated reruns still popular even into the nineties. What is the series?	"Gilligan's Island"
• What highly-rated 1968-to-1970 comedy show featured the classic one-liners "You bet your bippy," "Here comes the judge," and "Sock it to me! Sock it to me!"?	"Rowan and Martin's Laugh-In"
• In 1962, the Mashed Potato, the Loco-Motion, the Frug, the Monkey and the Funky Chicken were all in vogue. What were they?	Dances
• What historic musical event commenced August 15, 1969 on Max Yasgur's Bethel, New York dairy farm? How long did the event last?	The Woodstock Music Festival (originally scheduled for Woodstock, N.Y.); three days
• What 1960s fad, dubbed as America's "exotic dance and party rouser," had kids bending over backwards?	The Limbo
• What popular campus activity, practiced primarily by sororities and fraternities in the 1960s, was rejuvenated by the 1978 movie premier of "National Lampoon's Animal House"?	Toga parties
• Name the "sport" that had college students of the 1960s trying to see how many bodies would fit into a common curbside compartment.	Phonebooth packing
• Name the district in San Francisco associated in the 1960s with "hippies" and other segments of the "counter culture."	Haight-Ashbury
• In 1975, these trademarked items were cared for, nurtured, and treated like pampered dogs. What were they?	Pet Rocks
• What requirement was enacted as a law by LBJ in 1965 in response to evidence linking a common consumer product to significant health hazards?	Manufacturers must put health warnings on cigarette packs
• What round yellow 1970s fad accessories were inscribed with thin black lines and often accompanied by the words, "Have a Nice Day?"	Smile buttons
• In 1975, one-time stockbroker Josh Reynolds bolstered his assets by creating a temperature-sensitive juju which he claimed could reveal the wearer's state of mind. What was the name of this trinket?	The trademarked "Mood Ring"
• Name the landmark 1973 U.S. Supreme Court case that barred states from preventing abortion in the first six months of pregnancy.	Roe vs. Wade
• What term became famous—or infamous—as a designation for the wholesale firing that took place in the midst of the Watergate Scandal on the evening of October 20, 1973?	The Saturday Night Massacre
• Name the teenage heiress who was dragged screaming from her apartment in a kidnapping by the Symbionese Liberation Army on February 4, 1974—and then after being apprehended months later by FBI agents, was accused of adopting her captors' radical beliefs and convicted of bank robbery?	Patty Hearst
• Name the tall, leafy, herbaceous annual plant known in the Latin as "cannabis sativa."	Marijuana

- On November 22, 1963, the CBS daytime soap-opera "As the World Turns" was interrupted by the somber voice of "the most trusted man in America" announcing the assassination of President John Kennedy. Who was this eminent announcer?

CBS newsman Walter Cronkite

- What Monday-evening ABC television program debuted in the Fall of 1970 and became an immediate and permanent success?

"Monday Night Football"

- Name the type of light that guided the mid-1970s into an era of "dark illumination," as kids decorated their rooms with glowing black velvet posters.

Ultraviolet, or "black" light

MYSTERIES OF MYTH

Did You Know That . . .

 . . . Roman men once used a type of sacred thong—a "februa," which became a symbol of Juno, Roman goddess of marriage and fertility—as an "instrument of purification"? (They believed that striking a woman with this thong during the month of February would ensure her fertility.)

 . . . Aphrodite, Greek goddess of love and beauty, was born from the foam that bubbled about the severed genitals of her recently castrated father, Uranus?

For the Love of Zeus!

- What 9800-foot mountain peak, straddling the border of Thessaly and Macedonia, is professed to be the home of the Greek gods?

Mt. Olympus

- What ore, a primary source of atomic energy, is named after the primeval Greek sky god who became the grandfather of the classic Olympian gods?

Uranium (after the god Uranus)

- What flower sporting varied and striking colors was named for the Greek goddess of the rainbow?

The *iris*

- Name the poor nymph whose unsettling love for Narcissus caused her to pine away until nothing but her voice remained.

Echo

- What common English word is derived from the name of a Greek god who had a human torso combined with the horns, ears, and legs of a goat—enabling him to arouse terror in lonely places?

Panic—from the Greek shepherd god Pan

- According to Greek mythology, who had "the face that launched a thousand ships . . ."? What was the result of this beauty's abduction?

Helen, wife of King Menelaus of Argos; her abduction by Paris, a Trojan prince, brought on the Trojan War

- Name the two ravens that perched on the shoulder of the Nordic god, Odin, to inform him of worldly secrets.

Thought and Memory

- What English verb is derived from the name of a king in Greek mythology whom Zeus punished by hanging fine fruit just above his head—which rose out of reach when he tried to eat it?

Tantalize—from the Greek king Tantalus

- In Norse mythology, Asgard is the home of the gods. What is Asgard also believed to be?

The center of the universe

- What day of the week was named after the Norse god of thunder and storm who was also the protector of mankind?

Thursday, from the Norse god Thor

- What was unique about the birth of Athena, the Greek goddess of war, wisdom and handicrafts?

She was born fully armed from the head of her sky-god father Zeus, the supreme ruler of Olympus

• What was the punishment that Sisyphus was sentenced to in Hades for having cheated death?	He was forced to eternally roll a stone up a hill every morning, only to have it roll back down every night
• Who are the three "Graces" in Greek mythology?	The collective title of the three daughters of Zeus, all goddesses of fertility and named for the pleasing appearance of fertile gardens and fields
• In Greek mythology, who is the goddess of victory?	Nike—sometimes portrayed as an "aspect" of Athena
• What insect-eating plant was named for the Roman goddess of love?	The Venus flytrap
• What English word for a soft, gentle breeze comes from the name of the Greek god of the West Wind?	Zephyr
• In Greek mythology, what name refers to the "primal void" that gave birth to Earth, the infernal regions, Love, Darkness, and Night?	Chaos
• What month was named for the Roman god of war? (Hint: Most soldiers did not look forward to marching to war in the middle of winter.)	March (from the Roman god Mars)
• In Greek mythology, who lost a foot race because she couldn't ignore the golden apples dropped in her path by Hippomenes, her suitor?	Atalanta
• Three Greek beings—Clotho, who spins the thread of our life, Lachesis, who determines its length, and Atropos, who cuts it off—present each mortal at birth with both good and evil gifts. By what name do these providence-providers go by?	The three "Fates"
• Queen Jocasta hanged herself when she found out that her husband was also her son. Who was her unfortunate consort—given a new shot at fame in the twentieth century when Freud linked his name to his theory of childhood development?	Oedipus
• What mythological mother of fourteen sons and fourteen daughters was punished for her arrogance by being changed to a column of stone, whose face remained forever wet with tears over her slain children?	Niobe
• Who were the winged dragon-like creatures with writhing snakes for hair whose looks turned men to stone?	The Gorgons

———— ◇ ◆ ✧ ◆ ◇ ————

AT THE MOVIES
Did You Know That ...

... Sales of undershirts plummeted 40 percent shortly after Clark Gable opened his shirt to reveal a bare chest in 1934's "It Happened One Night"?

... It took John Hughes only four days to write the script for the 1983 comedy film "National Lampoon's Vacation"?

... The little-known 1966 movie "The Persecution and Assassination of Jean-Paul Marat as Performed by the Inmates of the Asylum of Charenton Under the Direction of the Marquis de Sade" is the longest-titled film in history?

That's a Wrap!

• What was German war-leader Adolph Hitler's favorite movie?	"King Kong"

• Actor William Pratt was once considered a hopeless cause by producers and directors because of his lisp. However, after answering an agent's advertisement in *Billboard* magazine, this 23-year-old became world famous for his contributions to Universal Studio's "Frankenstein." What is William Pratt's stage name?

Boris Karloff

• A hot new trend in movies was launched with the 1986 release of the Academy Award-winning feature "Platoon." Similar movies, such as "Full Metal Jacket" and "Hamburger Hill," followed one on top of the other. What was the fad behind their success?

The craze for realistic and ultra-violent Vietnam War movies

• What 1981 Academy Award-winning movie, starring Mary Tyler Moore, Donald Sutherland, and Timothy Hutton, marked Robert Redford's directorial debut?

"Ordinary People"

• Bing Crosby and Bob Hope starred in a series of movies that featured the word "road" in each title. What was their first "Road" movie called?

"The Road to Singapore"

• The year 1939 marked an apex in movie making. Answer these questions from that splendidly memorable year:

- Shot in 1939, what was the name of Humphrey Bogart's one-and-only horror film? What was Bogart's role?

"Return of Dr. X"; he played Maurice Xavier, a child killer

- What famous Southern-belle role did Bette Davis turn down in 1939 because she thought her leading man would be Errol Flynn, whom she refused to work with? What actress was pushed into stardom after landing the role Davis had declined?

Scarlet O'Hara of "Gone With the Wind"; Vivian Leigh

- Who was first offered the male lead in "Gone With the Wind" but turned it down, saying, "I'm glad it'll be Clark Gable who's falling flat on his face . . ."?

Gary Cooper

- In 1939 W.C. Fields was offered $75,000 to play an ultimately wise and good-hearted con-man in an epic fantasy motion picture. What was the role, and why—even though it was written with Fields in mind—did he decline it?

"The Wizard of Oz"; he wanted $100,000

• Name the irreverent underground animator who produced the first landmark X-rated cartoon, "Fritz the Cat" (1972), and then went on to make a feature-length animated movie of J.R.R. Tolkien's G-rated classic "The Lord of the Rings" (1978).

Ralph Bakshi

• What is the name of the famous trademark lion for Metro Goldwyn Mayer (MGM) studios?

Leo

• What 1987 Steve Martin movie was actually a modern-day remake of Edmond Rostand's classic "Cyrano de Bergerac"?

"Roxanne"

• What 1930 German "cabaret" film kicked off the acting career of Marlene Dietrich?

"The Blue Angel"

• What two common "eat-it-it's-good-for-you" items were combined to create Linda Blair's realistic looking "vomit" in the 1973 film "The Exorcist"?

Split-pea-soup and oatmeal

• What was used for the blood in the infamous black-and-white shower scene from Alfred Hitchcock's 1960 thriller-classic "Psycho"?

Chocolate sauce

• Alfred Hitchcock always made a brief "cameo" appearance in each of his films; however, in the 1944 movie "Lifeboat," the entire storyline was set in a lifeboat out at sea and there was no opportunity for "Hitch" to dip in and out of the action. What was the ingenious solution that ensured his appearance in this film?

He placed a photo of himself in a newspaper that is read on camera by one of the characters. (He is the "before" specimen in a before-and-after ad for a diet product.)

• What two well-known Hollywood actors both turned down the part of young Corleone in "The Godfather" (1972), leaving Al Pacino to play the role?

Robert Redford and Warren Beatty

• Brian de Palma's 1984 film "Scarface" holds the dubious distinction of using the four-letter F-word a record number of times. How many times was this word spoken during the film?

206 (an average of once every 29 seconds)

• While viewing daily film takes from the 1937 Humphrey Bogart gangster movie "Marked Woman," producer Hal Wallis objected to a puny-looking extra standing among the tough guys. When he asked the director why he had used this actor, what was the response?

It wasn't an actor; the insignificant little man was an actual member of the Lucky Luciano gang who had been cast to add realism

• The high-grossing 1989 Spielberg film "Indiana Jones and the Last Crusade" is cherished by blunder buffs for record number of mistakes found in a single movie. What is wrong with the following scenes?

- The beginning of the film shows young Indy crossing the Atlantic in 1938 by airliner and, later, embarking for the return journey by airship (blimp).

Transatlantic passenger air service didn't *begin* until 1939, one year later; and transatlantic airship services had *ceased* in 1937—the year before Indy is shown using the service

- In the airport lounge in Berlin, two passengers are shown reading identical German newspapers.

The papers are dated 1918, 20 years before the year in which the film is set

- An intertitle reading "The *Republic* of Hatay" is immediately followed by a scene in which the ruler is addressed as "Your Royal Highness."

A republic, by definition, has no royal rulers

• And before leaving the same subject, how old was Sean Connery when he played the father of 46-year-old Harrison Ford (Indiana Jones) "The Last Crusade"?

58

• What physical characteristic would have prevented actor Tom Cruise, who played the lead role in "Top Gun," from actually becoming a naval pilot in real life?

The Navy requires that officers be 5 feet 10 inches tall—and Cruise is only 5'9"

• Legendary movie mogul Samuel Goldwyn was notorious for his frequent abuse of the English language. Fill in the blanks to complete the following classic "Goldwynisms":

- "Our comedies are not to be _____ at."

Laughed

- "I don't think anybody should write his autobiography until after he's _____."

Dead

- "We've passed a lot of _____ since then."

Water

- "I would be sticking my head in a _____."

Moose

- "I can't make it, but I hope you'll give me a _____."

Raincoat

- To a supposedly valuable employee who was leaving the studio: "It always makes me very unhappy to say good-bye to a _____ in my machine."

Clog

- After a sculptor commented on the beauty of Mrs. Goldwyn's hands: "Go ahead, make a _____ of them."

Bust

• What famous director broke his own 1982 record for the all-time top-grossing film with another blockbuster in 1993? What were the names of the two record-smashers in question?

Steven Spielberg, with his 1993 film "Jurassic Park" and 1982 classic "E.T."

TELEVISION TIDBITS
Did You Know That ...

... Ninety-eight percent of U.S. households own at least one television set—for a grand total of some 93,100,000 households?

... Some viewers of "Gilligan's Island" actually sent letters to the U.S. Coast Guard asking them to rescue the castaways?

... Jack Nicholson guest-starred in two episodes of "The Andy Griffith Show"?

... Comedian David Letterman was first to perform the sticky stunt of "velcro wall-jumping" before a national audience in the mid 1980s, which brought about an immediate increase in popularity in his late-night television show?

... Producers of "Saturday Night Live" had their doubts about hiring John Belushi? (They were afraid he was not disciplined enough for live TV.)

... The characters in the sitcom "Barney Miller"—Captain Miller, Inspector Luger, Wojo, Fish, and Lt. Scanlon—were made honorary detectives by the New York Police Department?

Tuning In To the Tube

• A cable television company serving Columbia, South Carolina needed to occupy a vacant channel while awaiting the start-up of their new Science-Fiction channel. In the interim they chose a fairly innocuous—some might even say "monotonous"—scene to occupy the vacant channel's screen. When the channel finally began regular broadcasting, however, complaints were so numerous that the company had to acquire another channel on which to resume running their temporary picture. What was this soothing scene?

A camera aimed full time at an aquarium

• What is the first name of Andy Griffith's character in the TV series "Matlock"?

Benjamin

• Name the 1960s TV spy spoof immortalized by its star, Don Adams. Also, what apologetic phrase did Adams employ in every episode after botching an assignment or committing some other blunder?

"Get Smart"; "Sorry 'bout that, Chief"

• Another TV star known for his bungling ways was Don Knotts. What two series did he appear in?

"The Andy Griffith Show" and "Three's Company"

• Match these TV/movie superheroes with their secret identities:

- Superman
- The Shadow
- Spiderman
- The Incredible Hulk
- Wonder Woman

Clark Kent
Lamont Cranston
Peter Parker
Dr. David Banner
Diana Prince

• Johnny Carson took over the reins of the Tonight Show from Jack Parr 31 years ago; who did he pass them to when he "dismounted" in 1992?

Jay Leno

• Name the mellifluous-voiced British-born American who hosted Masterpiece Theatre for the Public Broadcasting Service from 1971 until his death in 1992.

Alistair Cooke

• Who succeeded musician Doc Severinson when Jay Leno became host of "The Tonight Show"?

Branford Marsalis

• Who was the voice of "Charlie" on the television series "Charlie's Angels"?

John Forsythe

• Who made his acting debut as Mickey in "The Little Rascals," then grew up to portray a tough street cop named "Baretta"?

Robert Blake

- Name the TV military sitcoms that go with the settings described below:

- A World-War-II German POW camp known as Stalag 13	"Hogan's Heroes"
- An Old West military outpost (the perfect location for this "comedy of arrows")	"F Troop"
- An Army surgical hospital camp during the Korean War	"M*A*S*H"
- A basic-training boot camp for the United States Marine Corps	"Gomer Pyle, USMC"
- A World-War-II P.T. boat under the command of actor Ernest Borgnine	"McHale's Navy"

- Name the four shows that were direct spin-offs of the series "All In The Family." — "Maude," "The Jeffersons," "Archie Bunker's Place," and "Gloria"

- "Corey," "Jeff" and "Timmy" have all been owners of what famous TV and movie canine? — Lassie

- Name the plush purple reptile who teaches children to love everyone—and who became the PBS TV craze of 1993. — Barney the Dinosaur

- What TV sitcom took an uncouth family from the backwoods of the Ozarks and introduced them to the glamours of California? — "The Beverly Hillbillies"

- What two classic horror-spoof sitcoms first ran between 1964 and 1966 on national TV? — "The Munsters" and "The Addams Family"

- Who composed the opening music for the TV game show "Jeopardy"? — The show's creator, Merv Griffin

- Like today's Vanna White, Jay Silverheels was a TV "sidekick." Who was he sidekick to, and what was his television name? — The Lone Ranger; Tonto

- What was the occupation of Jack Tripper, Jack Ritter's character in "Three's Company"? — Chef

- What was the name of the professor on "Gilligan's Island"? — Roy Hinkley

- What does the T. stand for as the initial in Captain James T. Kirk's name from the Television series "Star Trek"? — Tiberius

- Name the leading TV character played by the indicated actor from each series below:

- "The Man from U.N.C.L.E" (Robert Vaughn)	Napoleon Solo
- "The Fugitive" (David Janssen)	Richard Kimble
- "Batman" (Adam West)	Bruce Wayne

- The Six Million Dollar Man" (Lee Majors) — Col. Steve Austin

- What were the full names of the characters Starsky and Hutch in the TV series that went by the same title? — Dave Starsky and Ken Hutchison

- Supply the name of the actor who portrays the enigmatic character Larry "Bud" Melman on "Late Night With David Letterman"? — Calvert de Forest

- Who "did" the voice for Magnum P.I.'s heard-but-not-seen boss on the show? — Orson Welles

- What famous late Chinese martial arts icon guest-starred in a two-part episode of "Batman" as the Green Hornet's right-hand-man, Kato? — Bruce Lee

- What body parts were "bionic" on the "Six Million Dollar Man" and the "Bionic Woman" characters? — His left eye, right arm, and both legs; her right ear, right arm, and both legs

- Name the three original "Charlie's Angels" of the 1970s. — Kate Jackson, Farrah Fawcett and Jaclyn Smith

• In April, 1970, a few days after the riot trial on the "Chicago 8" had ended, radical Abbie Hoffman appeared on the Merv Griffin Show. Censors, however, never allowed Hoffman's shirt to be seen by the public. What symbol was his shirt fashioned to represent?	The American flag
• What were the names of Tom and Joan Bradford's eight children in the 1977-1981 comedy-drama "Eight Is Enough"?	Mary, Joanie, Nancy, Elizabeth, Susan, David, Tommy, and Nicholas

OPENING THE BIBLE
Did You Know That . . .

. . . Abraham wasn't the only Old Testament father to face the prospect of sacrificing a child? (Centuries later, a homeward-bound Gileadite general named Jephthah in the book of Judges vowed to sacrifice "whatever shall first come out . . . of my house to meet me" in thanksgiving for his victorious return from Mizpah. When he was greeted by his "only child," Adah, the father, heartsick, cried out, "Alas, my daughter!" Nevertheless, with Adah's determined blessing, he eventually carried out his vow. See Judges 11:34-40)

. . . Scholars estimate that the 66 books of the King James version of the Bible were written by some 50 different authors?

. . . "Lucifer"—literally meaning "Lightbearer" or "Full of light"—our best-known name for the Devil, is mentioned only once in the Old Testament (Isaiah 14:12), and not at all in the New Testament?

. . . The word *Maher-shalal-hash-baz* (See Isaiah 8:1 and 3), meaning "To speed to the spoil, he hasteneth the prey," is the longest word in the Old Testament?

. . . According to legend the names of the two thieves crucified at Jesus' right and left were named Disma and Gestas, and that after ordering the crucifixion of Jesus Pontius Pilate supposedly went and killed himself?

. . . The respective traditional symbols of Matthew, Mark, Luke and John as the Four Evangelists are a man, a lion, an ox, and an eagle?

It's In the Book!

• An early English Bible, published in 1560, was given a nickname for its rendition of a verse from Genesis that has Adam and Eve sewing fig leaves together to make themselves a certain type of clothing. What is the nickname that honors this Edenic garb?	The Breeches Bible
• Who asked, "Am I my brother's keeper?"	Cain, speaking to the Lord after slaying his brother Abel
• What Old Testament characters used these other well-known lines—and to whom is each speaking?	
- "It is not good for the man to be alone . . . " (Gen. 2:18)	The Lord God, speaking to no one in particular
- "Ye shall not surely die . . . Ye shall be as gods, knowing good and evil." (Gen. 3:4-5)	The serpent in the Garden of Eden, speaking to Eve
- "God hath made me to laugh . . . " (Gen. 21:6)	Sarah, speaking to no one in particular about the birth of her and Abraham's son, Isaac
- "Get thee from me . . . see my face no more; for in that day thou seest my face thou shalt die." (Exodus 10:28)	Pharaoh to Moses
- "Speak; for thy servant heareth." (I Sam. 3:10)	The boy Samuel, to the Lord
- "Come to me, and I will give thy flesh unto the fowls of the air, and to the beasts of the field." (I Sam. 17:44)	The Philistine giant Goliath, to young David
- "And though after my skin worms destroy this body, yet in my flesh shall I see God." (Job 19:26)	Job, to Bildad the Shuhite

- "Did we not cast three men bound into the midst of the fire? . . . Lo, I see four men loose, walking . . . and they have no hurt . . . "

King Nebuchadnezzar, to his councellors concerning the casting of Shadrach, Meshach, and Abed-nego into the fiery furnace

• What was—and is—the name of the city where Samson brought down the pillars, killing over 3,000 Philistines, including himself?

Gaza

• According to the book of Genesis, how old was Noah when he died?

950 years old

• What were the only two animals on Noah's arc mentioned specifically by the Bible?

A raven and a dove

• Name the Four Horsemen of the Apocalypse as mentioned in the book of Revelations. What different items does each one carry with him?

Pestilence (conveys a bow and a crown); War (wields the "great sword"); Famine (carries balancing scales); and Death (brings Hell along)

• According to the Old Testament, whom did God tell Abraham to sacrifice on the altar?

His and Sarah's son, Isaac (Muslim tradition insists that it was Ishmael, the son of Abraham and Hagar—and the "father" of the Arabic peoples.)

• What group of people did the giant Goliath represent in his fight with the boy David?

The Philistines—or, as we call them today, the Palestinians

• What feathered black long-distance flightmasters brought meat and bread to Elijah as he hid by the brook east of Jordan?

Ravens (See I Kings 17:6)

• What name does the Bible assign to Noah's wife?

"Noah's wife"

• How many people were aboard Noah's ark during the time of the Great Flood?

Eight (Noah, his wife, their three sons, and their son's wives)

• What were the names of Noah's three sons?

Shem, Ham and Japheth

• What happened to Lot's wife when she disobeyed God's commandment and looked back toward the sinful cities of Sodom and Gomorrah as she and her family fled before the holocaust sent by God to consume them?

She was turned into a pillar of salt

• What is the shortest verse in the Bible?

"Jesus wept." (John 11:35)

• Who was given custody of Jesus' body after he was crucified?

Joseph of Arimathea

• In what form did God first appear to instruct Moses?

A burning bush

• Name the Old Testament book that contains the famous chapter beginning, "To every thing there is a season . . . "

Ecclesiastes

• What is the fifth of the Ten Commandments?

"Honour thy father and thy mother . . . "

• According to the gospel of St. Matthew, what did Judas Iscariot, the apostle who betrayed Jesus, accept from the chief priests in return for identifying his master with a kiss? What did he ultimately do with his reward? What did the chief priests then do with this "blood money"?

Thirty pieces of silver; he went and cast it on the floor of the temple; they bought a potter's field, called "the field of blood," for the burial of paupers and strangers

• At whose request was John the Baptist beheaded?

Salome, the stepdaughter of Herod Antipas

• What was Lazarus' claim to fame in the New Testament?

Jesus raised him from the dead

• Which of the four New Testament gospels—often referred to as the "Gospel of the Word"—is generally considered to be most concerned with spiritual discourse, and is often vaguest on historical narrative?

St. John

• Which gospel, regarded as the most complete account of Jesus' sayings, is referred to as the "Gospel of the Son of David"?	Matthew
• Who authored the Acts of the Apostles, as well as one of the four gospels referred to as the "Gospel of the Saviour"?	St. Luke
• Name the Old Testament book that tells the remarkable story of the love between a Moabite woman and her Israelite mother-in-law. Also, name these two women.	Ruth; Ruth and Naomi
• Name the Canaanite fertility god whose worship became synonymous with evil among the Israelites—in part because, like many other Near-Eastern divinities, he required human sacrifice.	Baal
• Give the dimensions of Noah's Ark, according to Genesis.	It was 300 by 50 by 30 cubits (one cubit equals about 18 inches)
• Coverdale's Bible of 1535 was nicknamed the "Bug Bible" because it translated Psalm 91:5 as "Thou shalt not need to be afrayed for eny bugges by night." What is the more modern translation that replaces the word "bugges" in the King James Version?	"Terrors" ("Bugges" related to the bogeymen and bugaboos that still "haunt" current English usage; it once did refer to all scary notions and elusive phenomena, and not just to insects.)
• What was the name of the wooden chest that contained the stone tablets inscribed with the Ten Commandments?	The Ark of the Covenant
• According to Genesis, why did Cain have a mark placed on him after he killed his brother?	To protect him from anyone who might want to kill him in retaliation for his murder of Abel
• John's book of Revelation—as well as several Old Testament books—refers to a last great battle between good and evil in which Christ will triumph. What is the name of this decisive conflict fought at the Lord's second coming?	Armageddon
• Name the two women Jacob, father of the "twelve tribes," married. Which was his favorite? What was their relationship to each other?	Leah and Rachel; Jacob "loved Rachel"; the wives were sisters
• King Ahaziah, along with 102 of his soldiers, was executed by fire for trying to capture what great prophet of Israel?	Elijah "the Tishbite"
• How were Korah, Dathan, Abiram, and their families punished for rejecting Moses' authority and founding their own congregation?	They were swallowed by the earth

—— ⬦ ◆✧◆ ⬦ ——

REST AND RELAXATION
Did You Know That . . .

. . . According to "Harper's Magazine Index," a staggering—or "only," depending on how you see the statistic—six percent of Americans say they find life "dull"?

. . . Britain's Queen Elizabeth II took a course when she was 18 to acquire skills to help with the war effort and enjoyed the class so much that she took it on as a hobby? And what did this course cover? Heavy mechanics, of course; she learned to strip and service engines.

. . . In 1985 men and women averaged between 40 and 41 hours of free time each week, compared to only 34 "spare" hours in 1965?

. . . More Americans visit zoos each year than go to all sporting events combined?

. . . Former President Ronald Reagan spent 24 percent of his time in office on vacation or at Camp David compared to the 10 percent vacation-time taken by his predecessor President Jimmy Carter?

. . . Renowned U.S. attorney Clarence Darrow, an avid crossword puzzle fan, once tried in embarrassment to hide the crossword he was working on from H.G. Wells, who replied, "Don't be foolish. I work two of them every day of my life"?

. . . Over half of an "average" American teen's spare time is filled watching television or listening to music?

. . . "Food" was listed as the number-one worry for those planning and carrying out a social event?

Don't Worry, Be Happy!

• What is the preferred reading material for the 66 percent of Americans who admit to reading in the bathroom?

"Reader's Digest"

• As a husband, Austrian psychoanalyst Sigmund Freud often engaged in "collective" competitions with his family. What did the Freuds collect?

Mushrooms

• What former athlete and entertainer adopted needlepoint as a hobby and has, in fact, written a book on needlepoint for men?

Rosey Grier, former professional football lineman and actor

• What does Palestinian political leader Yasir Arafat do to relax?

He watches cartoons

• Name the miniatures, distributed by Joshua L. Cowen, that hit an all-time sales high in 1941. Also, what company distributed these favorite collectables? (Hint: Gomez Addams of the Addams Family loved to crash them to "ease his mind.")

Electric trains; the Lionel Corporation

• Almost any kind of leisure activity can become a hobby. Name the four general, overlapping categories that most hobbies fall under.

The arts, collecting, handicrafts, and games and sports

• Identify the type of hobbyist that matches each of these scientific designations:

- Deltiologist

Post-card collector

- Spelunker

Cave explorer

- Philatelist

Stamp collector

- Lepidopterist

Moth and butterfly collector

- Pugilist

Boxer

- Notaphile

A banknote collector

- Bandophile

A cigar band collector

• What are you doing if you interlace a "warp" and "weft"?

Weaving

• A "kiln" and a "kick wheel" are used in what hobby?

Pottery-making

• The terms "yarn over," "popcorn," and "cast on" belong to what creative diversion?

Knitting

• What activity does a "piscatologist" participate in?

Fishing

• What soothing sport uses "plugs" and "leaders"?

Also fishing

• The "rough terrain" bicycles of the 1990s more commonly go by what name?

Mountain bikes

• The sport of climbing mountains with as little equipment as possible is called what?

Rock climbing

• What is another name for a "natatorium"?

A swimming pool

• What are a "bucket hitch" and a "fisherman's bend"?

Types of knots

• What type of hobbyist might be interested in "first-day-issues"?

A stamp or magazine collector

• What is the common term for three consecutive strikes in bowling?

A turkey

• What is the name of the area located immediately behind the pins in bowling?

The pit

• What is the most popular participant sport in the U.S.?

Fishing

• What are the three general classifications of skis?

Downhill, jumping, and cross country

• In horseshoes, what is the distance between the stakes?	40 feet
• What novel sports competition, held during the 1992 Labor Day weekend in Grayslake, Illinois, sparked a controversial complaint from members of the Outdoor Power Equipment Institute?	The first national lawnmower racing championship (Participants were chastised for failing to promote safe and effective use of outdoor equipment.)

LET'S WATCH CARTOONS
Did You Know That . . .

. . . Bugs Bunny, the smart-alecky "wascally wabbit" created by Warner Brothers animator Chuck Jones, first appeared as a hare in "Porky's Hare Hunt" (1938)? (He was changed into a smart rabbit for later films.)

. . . Pat Sullivan's creation Felix the Cat, after making his debut in 1923 and having his animated short-films shown to children during afternoon matinees, was the first cartoon character to gain superstardom?

Characters and Comic Strips

• What is the name of Batman's butler?	Alfred
• What are the names of Dagwood and Blondie Bumstead's two children?	Alexander and Cookie
• In the comic strip "Beetle Bailey," what is the name of the camp he and his fellow soldiers are stationed at?	Camp Swampy
• What is "Mr. Magoo's" first name?	Quincy
• Give the name of these "Dennis the Menace" characters:	
- Dennis' easily-riled next-door neighbor and his more easy-going wife	George and Martha Wilson
- Dennis' father and mother	Henry and Alice Mitchell
- The local librarian	Miss Davis
- Dennis' best friend	Joey
- Dennis' self-proclaimed "girlfriend"—actually, the bane of his existence	Margaret Wade
• What satirical comic book, created in the 1950s, gave us coverman Alfred E. Neuman with his "What, me worry?" smile?	MADD magazine
• What is Mr. Dither's wife's name in the comic strip "Blondie"?	Cora
• What was the first cartoon series ever to be broadcast during prime time?	"The Flintstones"
• What DC Comics hero died in 1992 during a battle with an invader named Doomsday who came from another dimension?	Superman
• What is Doonesbury's first name?	Michael
• Name the first feature-length animated film, released by Disney Studios in 1937.	"Snow White and the Seven Dwarfs"
• In the Popeye comics, who was Popeye's formidable 372-pound enemy? What was his name in the Popeye films and TV shorts that followed?	Brutus; Bluto
• Name the cartoon character that brought to life each of these famous lines:	
- "Shhh, I'm hunting wabbits."	Elmer Fudd
- "Hello, all you happy people!"	Droopy the dog
- "Oh, my darlin', oh, my darlin', oh, my darlin' Clementine."	Huckleberry Hound

- "Ah, what's up, doc?"	Bugs Bunny
- "You're dethhhpicable!"	Daffy Duck
- "Ablee, ablee, ablee, ablee—that's all folks!"	Porky Pig
- "Thufferin' thuccotash!"	Sylvester the Cat
- "Exit, stage left."	Snagglepuss the Lion
- "El kabong!"	Quick Draw McGraw
- "I tawt I taw a puddy tat."	Tweety bird
- "Yabba-dabba-doo!"	Fred Flintstone

• Name the creative production team that brought America both "The Flintstones" and "The Jetsons." — William Hanna and Joseph Barbera

• Who were the original members of the "Fantastic Four" super-hero pack? — Mr. Fantastic, Invisible Girl, The Human Torch, and The Thing

• Creator Jim Davis called his popular tubby character "A little bit of Archie Bunker and Morris the Cat tossed together." To whom was he referring? — Garfield the Cat

• Name the editor of Clark Kent's "The Daily Planet" newspaper in Metropolis? Who portrayed him in the celebrated Superman movies of the 1980s? — Perry White; Jackie Cooper

• What is the last name of Linus and Lucy in the "Peanuts" comic strip? — Van Pelt

A WOMAN'S WORLD
Did You Know That . . .

. . . In 1958 Julia Child was the first woman to be "christened" a full-fledged "Chef," a title traditionally held only by men in this profession?

. . . Women represent 63 percent of all persons over the age of 18 living below the poverty level?

. . . Los Angeles resident Alice Wells was sworn in as the first policewoman in the United States on September 12, 1910?

. . . According to a survey conducted in 1991 by a research firm and Cornell University, female executives receive a promotion an average of every 2.6 years, while their male colleagues must wait an average of 3.3 years?

. . . The number of woman-owned businesses increased a dramatic 57 percent toward the end of the 1980s?

. . . Recent statistics show that women with master's degrees, working year round and full time, earn only about the same amount as men with associate degrees?

. . . French dancer and notorious World War I German spy Mata Hari (born Margaretha Geertruida Zeele), after being arrested in a Paris hotel in 1917, was said to have smiled and winked at the firing squad as they raised their rifles to shoot her?

It's a Women's World, Too

• In 1992, what nation had the highest percentage of women in their legislature? — Finland, with 38.5%

• In 1853, who founded the Una, the first women's rights magazine? — Paulina Wright Davis (1813-1876)

• In 1939, an acclaimed black female contralto was barred from singing in Washington's Constitutional Hall because of her race. Who was she? — Marian Anderson

• After allowing current title holder Nicole Dunsdon to complete her reign in October 1992, what country successfully lobbied to have its national beauty contest canceled, claiming that it was degrading to women? — Canada

- In 1959, Anita Bryant—who later became the spokeswoman for Florida orange juice—represented what state in the Miss America Beauty pageant?

Oklahoma

- What woman was rejected by 29 medical schools before finally gaining admission, and went on to become the first licensed woman doctor in the U.S.?

Elizabeth Blackwell

- What well-known women's activist was arrested and convicted of attempting to vote in the 1872 U.S. national election?

Susan B. Anthony

- In 1853, Antoinette Brown Blackwell became the first formally educated woman minister. What church did she belong to?

The Congregationalist Church

- Who was the first first lady ever to obtain a college education?

Lucy Hayes, wife of Rutherford B.

- What military-leader "Maid of Orleans" was condemned for heresy and burned at the stake?

Joan of Arc

- Aside from the fictional, idealistic representations of "Justice" and "Liberty," name the three females who have appeared on U.S. currency.

Martha Washington, Pocahontas, and Susan B. Anthony

- Who was the notorious Wild West character who was said to have had 12 husbands, who dressed, cursed and shot like a man, and was buried beside Wild Bill Hickock in Deadwood, South Dakota?

Martha Jane Canary, a.k.a. Calamity Jane

- What revolutionary woman educator served as president of the National College Equal Suffrage League from 1908-1917 and as president of Bryn Mawr College, Pennsylvania from 1894-1922?

Martha Carey Thomas

- Former British Prime Minister Margaret Thatcher was nicknamed _____.

"The Iron Lady"

- Who were the first two women to head the two major political parties in the U.S.?

Jean Westwood headed the Democratic party in 1972; Mary Louise Smith, in 1974, was first to lead the Republicans

- Who was the first woman to run for President of the United States, and in what year?

Victoria Woodhull of Homer, Ohio, in 1872

- In 1933, Frances Perkins, serving under F.D. Roosevelt, became the first female cabinet member. What "semi-ironic" position did she hold?

Secretary of Labor

- What little-known woman worked alongside Eli Whitney to invent the cotton gin?

Catherine Greene

- What American social worker and founder of Chicago's Hull House won the 1931 Nobel Peace Prize for her work in the Women's International League for Peace and Freedom?

Jane Addams

- Since 1969, the number of women serving in state legislatures has increased fivefold. As of 1994, which state has the highest percentage of women legislators? Which state has the lowest percentage?

Washington (39.5 percent); Kentucky (5.1 percent)

- What gracious woman was founder of the Special Olympics?

Eunice Kennedy Shriver

- Name the woman who is the current president of the Newspaper Association of America.

Cathleen Black

- Who was the first woman to appear on a U.S. postage stamp?

Queen Isabella of Spain in 1893

- Also in the year 1893, what nation of the world became the first to grant women the right to vote? When—and with what Amendment to the Constitution—did the U.S. grant this right?

New Zealand; 1920 with the 19th Amendment

• Martha Mitchell, wife of former Nixon Attorney General John Mitchell, earned a nickname for her often outrageous comments on liberals, protesters and reporters. What was this tongue-in-cheek nickname?	"The Mouth That Roared"
• Of the 2200 persons quoted in the current edition of "Bartlett's Familiar Quotations," how many are women?	Only 164
• Who was the only female to win the U.S. Medal of Honor? What services did she render during the Civil War to merit this award?	Mary Walker; she served as a surgeon in the 52nd Ohio Regiment
• The actress who played opposite John Wayne in the 1970 film "Rio Lobo" became 20th Century-Fox's president of production 10 years later. What is her name?	Sherry Lansing
• Noted for her studies of the cultures of the Pacific Islands, the United States, and Russia, who was born Dec. 16, 1901?	Anthropologist Margaret Mead
• What "loose-trousered" fashion item did woman's rights activist Amelia Bloomer popularize?	Bloomers
• What is the name of the Hollywood stunt woman and race-car driver who set 22 records in various racing sports—and, incidentally, was born deaf?	Kitty O'Neil
• Hired in 1973 by Frontier Airlines, who was the first female commercial airline pilot in the U.S.?	Emily Warner

ROMANCE AND MARRIAGE
Did You Know That . . .

. . . According to *Longevity* magazine over 50 percent of married men and women do not consider their spouse their best-ever lover?

. . . A study done by *McCall's* magazine reported that the divorce rate is 23-percent lower in cities with Major League baseball teams than in those without a team?

. . . Women who complete 16 or more years of school are less likely to divorce their first husbands?

Love Makes the World Go 'Round

• How many years of marriage are celebrated on the Crystal Anniversary?	15
• If you were to receive a gift made of leather this year on your anniversary, how many years of marriage would you be celebrating?	9
• Monogamy—being married to one spouse—is the most common form of marriage in our modern society. How many other known forms of marriage are there? Name them.	There are three others: Polygyny—one husband several wives; Polyandry—one wife, several husbands; and Group marriage—several husbands and wives
• How many wives did early Mormon leader/colonizer Brigham Young have?	27
• What Old Testament prophet had 700 wives and 300 concubines?	Solomon (I Kings 11:3)
• Mongkut of Siam—the king represented in the famous play "The King and I"—was the most married person in history. How many wives did he have?	He was known to have a total of 9,000 wives and concubines.
• Adolf Hitler's lifelong mistress was never allowed to appear with him in public. Who was this woman, and did the two ever marry?	Eva Braun and Adolf Hitler were married on April 30, 1945—the eve of their joint suicide.

- Name the famous person who made each of the following rollicking statements about marriage:

  - "A man may be a fool and not know it—but not if he is married." → H.L. Mencken

  - "I've only slept with the men I've been married to. How many women can make that claim?" → Elizabeth Taylor

  - "I don't think I'll get married again. I'll just find a woman I don't like and buy her a house." → Lewis Grizzard

  - "We would have broken up except for the children. Who were the children? Well, she and I were." → Mort Sahl

  - "Gettin' married's a lot like getting into a tub of hot water. After you get used to it, it ain't so hot." → Minnie Pearl

  - "Sex in marriage is like medicine. Three times a day for the first week. Then once a day for another week. Then once every three or four days until the condition clears up." → Peter De Vries

- What is the name of Barbie doll's boyfriend? → Ken

- Provide the names of the spouses who divorced and later remarried each of these celebrities:

  - Elizabeth Taylor (actress) → Richard Burton

  - William Saroyan (writer) → Carol Marcus

  - Milton Berle (comedian) → Joyce Matthews

  - Billy Rose (showman) → Joyce Matthews

  - Dorothy Parker (writer) → Alan Campbell

  - Robert Wagner (actor) → Natalie Wood

  - Jayne Wyman (actress) → Fred Karger

  - Elliot Gould (actor) → Jenny Bogart

- What surname do discreet unmarried American couples most commonly use when signing in at a motel or hotel? → Smith

- According to a 1994 opinion poll, British women would rather give up having sex than having to abstain from what gastronomical delight? → Chocolate

- Besides a number of friends and relatives, what two large and unusual guests were present at the second wedding of Elizabeth Taylor and Richard Burton? → A couple of hippopotami

- What is the significance of wearing an engagement ring on the fourth or "ring" finger of the left hand? → Traditional belief held that a delicate nerve ran from that finger directly to the heart

- By what nickname did Ronald Reagan refer to his former wife, Jane Wyman? → "Button Nose"

- Name the pioneering pair of sex therapists who filed for divorce in 1992. → William H. *Masters* and Virginia E. *Johnson*

- What couple exchanged marriage vows on Johnny Carson's "Tonight Show" on the evening of December 17, 1969? → Tiny Tim and his bride Miss Vickie

- Who was Xanthippe's husband? (Hint: He was a famed Greek philosopher.) → Socrates

THE MEDIA JUNGLE
Did You Know That . . .

. . . CBS News anchor Dan Rather used to invent and give play-by-play accounts of fictitious football games while walking to his elementary school in Wharton, Texas?

. . . Pop singer Madonna's name was mentioned over 4,300 times in major newspapers during the year 1992?

. . . According to *Harper's* magazine, contributions made to the Sam Donaldson Hairpiece Replacement Fund totalled a prodigious ninety dollars in 1992?

. . . Although Horace Greeley has always been given credit, it was actually John Soule who, in an 1851 article for the "Terre Haute Express," coined the phrase "Go west, young man . . . "?

. . . Playing on the rivalry of the "yellow kid" comic strip that appeared in 1895, two newspapers, "The New York World" and "The New York Journal," coined the phrase "yellow journalism"?

The "New York World" and "New York Journal" . . . The powerful media moguls that owned the above-mentioned papers were, respectively, William Randolph Hearst and Joseph Pulitzer?

. . . The first male to appear on the cover of *Playboy* magazine was comedian-actor Peter Sellers in 1964?

The Fourth Estate

• Name the magazine that corresponds to the mottos or "mission statements" given below:

- "The magazine for men" — *Esquire*

- "The humor magazine" — *National Lampoon*

- "The weekly news magazine" — *Time*

- "The magazine of news significance" — *Newsweek*

• On February 9, 1993, "Dateline NBC" was forced to publicly apologize for a scandal which caused new NBC president Michael Gartner to resign. What was the scandal? — "Dateline" rigged a GM truck with explosives to simulate a "scientific" crash-test demo

• What controversial political figure was named *Time* magazine's "Man of the Year" for 1979? — Ayatollah Ruhollah Khomeini

• Who was the first woman to anchor a nightly television network newscast? — Barbara Walters

• What radioactive extremely tall Japanese movie star once made appearances on the covers of *Time* and *Newsweek* magazines? And, how tall was he? — Godzilla; 164 feet tall

• When King Kong's giant mechanical hand was pictured on *Time* magazine's cover in 1976, who was it clutching in its grasp? — Newcomer Jessica Lange

• What was journalist Nellie Bly's real name? What stunt did this tough newswoman pull off in 1889 that put her name in the record books? — Elizabeth Cochrane (Seaman); she traveled around the world in 72, not 80, days

• Name the editorial columnist and TV personality who founded and still edits *The National Review*? — William F. Buckley, Jr.

• The cover of August 1991's *Vanity Fair* magazine sported a controversial photo of actress Demi Moore. What two startling factors sparked the controversy? — Moore was both nude and in her last trimester of pregnancy

• In 1871 "The New York Herald" sent journalist Sir Henry Morton Stanley to Africa to find a Scottish missionary-explorer. What was this explorer's name and what was he looking for when Stanley met him? — David Livingstone; he was attempting to trace the source of the Nile River

• What current (1994) U.S. Senator was both editor and publisher of "The Troy Tribune" at the age of 19?	Paul Simon
• While serving in the U.S. Army during World War II, what future CBS-TV "60 Minutes" reporter penned a brilliant and cynical novel of young love titled *Tell Me About Women?*	Harry Reasoner
• After establishing Christian Science and the Church of Christ Scientist, what woman, at the ripe old age of 87, founded the magazine *The Christian Science Monitor?*	Mary Baker Eddy
• Name the A.P. correspondent who was the last U.S. hostage to be released from Lebanon in December 1991.	Terry Anderson

CHEERS, AND BOTTOMS UP!

Did You Know That . . .

. . . "Huffcup," "mad dog," "Father Whoreson," "Angel's Food," "dragon's milk" and "left leg" were all common terms for beer in Elizabethan England?

. . . It took the Nestle Company eight years to develop the first instant coffee?

. . . Bordeaux wine is usually aged in casks made of oak?

. . . Fifty percent of Americans start their day with a cup of coffee?

Raise a Glass

• What thirst-quenching drink is sometimes referred to as "Adam's Ale"?	Water
• Name the rum, sugar, and lime cocktail that takes its name from a town in Cuba.	Daiquiri
• Name the "Englishman's Drink."	"The Bloody Mary"
• What drink was called "Tonsil Paint" in the Old West?	Whiskey
• Name the alcoholic drink that matches each of the following descriptions:	
- Sweet vermouth mixed with whiskey.	A Manhattan
- Rum, mixed with pineapple and coconut milk.	"Pina Colada"
- Red wine laced with fresh fruit.	Sangria
- Ginger ale, a cherry, and grenadine.	A Shirley Temple
- Whiskey chased by beer.	A Boiler Maker
- Tequila, triple sec, and lime juice.	A Margarita
• In the year 800, sheep from Ethiopian flocks got a caffeine buzz from eating coffee leaves and berries; humans soon picked up the habit. Answer the following questions about this bean-made brew:	
- What type of coffee has the highest caffeine content?	Perked (with 108 mg per five-ounce serving)
- On average, how many cups of coffee does an American coffee-drinker consume per day?	In 1993, 3.58 cups
- "Specialty" coffees—usually pre-flavored with nuts and powders—are growing in popularity in the U.S. Name the top-selling five flavors for 1993.	Vanilla Nut, Irish Cream, Chocolate, Vanilla and Macadamia Nut
• The fragrance of a coffee bean is called its "aroma." Fill in the blanks of these other coffee terms:	
- _____ refers to the sense of heaviness, richness and thickness one tastes when drinking the warm beverage.	Body

© 1994, Compact Classics, Inc.

- Deriving its name from its foam or "cap," which resembles the hooded robes of a certain class of Italian friars, _____ is a concoction of espresso and steamed, foamed milk.	Cappuccino
- _____ coffee is made from very strong black beans, ground extra fine and brewed by mechanically forcing hot water through the grounds.	Espresso
• What was Ludwig Roselius' motivation when he decided to "decaffeinate" coffee in 1900?	He believed that the death of his father, a coffee taster, was caused by too much caffeine
• As first spoken in Old-English pubs, what did it mean to mind one's *p*s and *q*s?	To keep an accounting of a customer's consumption by *pints* and *quarts*
• How many bottles make up a "magnum" of champagne?	Two
• Burgundy wine comes in large bottles. What is the name of this bottle, equivalent in size to eight standard bottles?	A Methusaleh

ACROSS THE U.S.A.
Did You Know That . . .

. . . Boca Grande, Florida boasts a trio of streets named "Damn If I Know," "Damn If I Care," and "Damn If I Will"?

. . . The American people adopted "In God We Trust" as their national credo in 1956?

. . . Chicago boasts the largest variety of ethnic groups in the entire Great Lakes region?

O See Can You Say . . .

• What two states have never adopted Daylight Saving Time?	Arizona and Hawaii
• What is the only U.S. state that does not have a motto?	Alaska
• But for the flip of a coin, what Oregon city was nearly named Boston?	Portland
• What exclusive part of Boston, Massachusetts was once called both Mount Whoredom and "Satan's Seat," due not only to the several hundred prostitutes that plied their trade there but also to the countless taverns that occupied the area?	Beacon Hill
• Who designed the American flag? (Hint: It was not Betsy Ross.)	Francis Hopkinson, a naval flag designer
• What is the "treasure state," which every year turns out hundreds of pounds of flawless sapphires?	Montana
• What Michigan city did Kellogg's Cereal adopt as its world "breakfast city?"	Battle Creek
• Name the U.S. city associated with the following well-known descriptions:	
- "The Rubber Capital of the World"	Akron, Ohio
- "Pittsburgh of the South"	Birmingham, Alabama
- "Celery City"	Kalamazoo, Michigan
- "Pretzel City"	Reading, Pennsylvania
- "Insurance City"	Hartford, Connecticut
- "Cement City"	Allentown, Pennsylvania
• The windy city of Chicago actually ranks 16th on the list of all-time windiest American cities. With average wind speeds of 13.1 miles per hour, what, in truth, is the windiest city in America?	Great Falls, Montana

- Name the U.S. state with the most national park sites.

- Name these national park sites by these summaries of their most prominent features:

    - A one-mile-deep canyon.

    - Boasts the highest point on the Atlantic coast of the U.S.; rugged coastlines and sandy beaches.

    - The world's greatest geyser area; forests, waterfalls, and a wide variety of wildlife.

    - Two active volcanoes; rare plants and animals.

    - High mountains; large hardwood and evergreen forests.

    - Giant rock arches, windows, and towers formed by erosion.

    - Huge underground caves and strange rock formations.

    - The greatest single-peak glacier system in the United States.

    - A subtropical wilderness with plentiful wildlife.

- Which state has the greatest number of hazardous waste sites?

- Name the U.S. city (actual or created) made famous by each of the following characters:

    - Wyatt Earp

    - Batman

    - Dick Tracy

    - Dirty Harry

    - Robocop

- In what state is the Greater Cincinnati International Airport located?

- A tiny, disease-transmitting tick was named after the Connecticut town in which the illness was first reported. Name the town.

- Identify the following Manhattan sites:

    - This educational institution was originally known as Kings College.

    - *Sports Illustrated* magazine is published here.

    - NBC studios are located here.

    - This complex includes twin towers.

    - This is the world's largest Gothic cathedral.

    - These are New York's two major train stations.

    - It's known as the "Showplace of the Nation."

    - It's David Letterman's new "really big sheeew" place.

    - This museum is noted for its contemporary art collection and original architecture.

    - It's the famous structure that earned the state its nickname.

Alaska, with eight

Arizona's Grand Canyon

Maine's Acadia

Wyoming's Yellowstone

Hawaii Volcanoes National Park

North Carolina's Great Smoky Mountains

Utah's Arches

New Mexico's Carlsbad Caverns

Washington's Mount Rainier

Florida's Everglades

New Jersey, with 96

Tombstone, AZ

Gotham City

Anytown America

San Francisco, CA

Detroit, Michigan

Kentucky

Lyme

Columbia University

Time-Life Building

The G.E. Building

The World Trade Center

Church of St. John the Divine

Grand Central and Pennsylvania stations

Radio City Music Hall

The Ed Sullivan Theater

The Guggenheim Museum

The Empire State Building

• Which state's residents, in median age, are the youngest? The oldest?	Utah, with a median age of 26.3 years; Florida, with a median age of 37.2 years
• What are the only two states whose names include the letter "X"?	New Mexico and Texas
• What state name is the only one to contain the letter "Z"?	Arizona
• What is the only state with the letter "J" in its name?	New Jersey
• There is only one letter of the alphabet that is not in a state name. What is the letter?	"Q"
• With one exception, the name of every state in the Union contains two or more syllables. Which is the exception?	Maine
• What does the word *Nevada* mean in Spanish?	"Snow-clad"
• The motto of Kansas is "Ad Astra Per Aspera." What is the English translation?	"To the stars through difficulties"

WORLD TRAVELS
Did You Know That . . .

. . . China's illustrious Beijing Duck Restaurant can seat 9000 people at a time?

. . . Eighty-two percent of airline pilots rate Washington, D.C.'s National Airport the country's most challenging airport at which to land?

. . . The world's largest musical instrument can be found in Atlantic City, N.J.'s Municipal Auditorium? (The impressive organ has 33,112 pipes that range from one quarter of an inch to 64 feet in length.)

. . . Aberdeen, Maryland boasts the world's only tank museum?

Jetlag in the Global Village

• What nation do more tourists visit than any other?	France
• What is the most frequent trip-spoiling ailment travelers experience, especially when visiting less-developed countries? What is it most commonly caused by?	Diarrhea; water (including ice cubes)
• According to travel guidebooks, what can a traveler do to avoid experiencing the above-mentioned "unmentionable" ailment?	Use bottled water for both drinking and brushing teeth
• The second most common travelers' affliction is frequently contracted in Africa, Central and South America, Asia and in some South Pacific islands. It can be prevented by taking medication and using an insect repellent. Name this deadly disease.	Malaria
• Another bit of travelers' advice includes avoiding food from street vendors, since a certain disease can be transmitted through water, food, and generally unsanitary conditions. What is this disease?	Hepatitis A
• What are the three official languages of Switzerland?	French, German and Italian
• Name the group of Pacific islands, located off the coast of Ecuador, in which unusual animals such as Giant tortoises, marine iguanas, and tool-using finches can be spotted.	The Galapagos Islands
• In what U.S. state can travelers enjoy the Zydeco, the accordion-based music of French-speaking Creoles?	Louisiana
• What is the name of Israel's counterpart to the U.S. dollar?	The shekel
• The *rand,* named from a prosperous gold-mining region in Africa, is the official currency of what country?	South Africa
• Travelers have often said of this city that "you can die after you see it." Name this most beautiful city.	Naples, Italy

• What zoo boasts the largest collection of animals in the world?	The San Diego Zoo in California
• Copenhagen's most famous landmark is a statue that greets ships arriving in Copenhagen harbor. What does this statue depict, and what Dane inspired it?	*The Little Mermaid,* from Hans Christian Andersen's fairy tale
• Name the country in which you can visit King Solomon's Mines.	Israel
• Both athletes and spectators from all over the world traveled to the capital of Bosnia for the 1984 Winter Olympics. Name this city.	Sarajevo
• What city in China is home to the Temple of Heaven landmark?	Beijing
• What is unique about the Ayres Rock located in Australia's Mount Olga National Park?	Its circumference measures over five miles
• What two New York structures—one built in 1883 and one in 1931—were, at their respective completions, each labeled "the eighth wonder of the world"?	The Brooklyn Bridge and the Empire State Building
• Name the romanticized vehicles that glide up and down the canals of Venice.	Gondolas
• Where can you go to longingly view a hundred $10,000 bills on display? (What's the total amount of cash on display?)	Blinton's Horseshoe Club in Las Vegas, Nevada; a million dollars
• Which U.S. city is home to a voodoo museum?	New Orleans, Louisiana
• A famous bridge built in Lima, Peru in 1610 is still used today. Its mortar, however, was mixed using a singular viscous liquid in place of water. As reflected by the bridge's name, what liquid was used?	Egg whites from 10,000 eggs; The Bridge of Eggs
• Give the name of the island that lies among the southern edge of a major U.S. city and where you can take a walk down a three-mile boardwalk, watch sharks and beluga whales at the aquarium, and experience the thrill of the "Cyclone." (Hint: It was once home to countless rabbits.)	Coney Island
• What romance-thriller topped the air as the number one movie shown on airlines worldwide in 1993?	"The Bodyguard"
• If you visited Liverpool, England, what would you call its residents?	Liverpuddlians

CELEBRITY SHOWDOWN
Did You Know That . . .

. . . In his earlier years as a bachelor actor Tom Selleck appeared twice on TV's "The Dating Game"—and lost out to other contestants both times?

. . . Russian President Boris Yeltsin rises every morning at 5:00, reads contemporary authors for two hours, and then exercises before leaving for his office?

. . . Mattel's billionaire Barbie doll's full name is Barbie Millicent Roberts?

. . . In April, 1994 pop singer Madonna made an appearance on the David Letterman show, treating viewers to as many as 13 obscene utterances that had to be bleeped?

. . . On that same Letterman show Madonna not only smoked a cigar but refused to leave the set until the show was over, despite the army of stagehands waving her off?

. . . At the height of his fame Fred Astaire's feet were insured for $650,000?

. . . After comic actor Groucho Marx lost $240,000 in the 1929 two-day stock market crash, his insomnia became so bad that he often would call people in the middle of the night just to insult them?

. . . When preeminent cartoonist Charles Schulz was in high school the yearbook staff turned down his offer to include a few of his comic strips? (His work now appears in over

© 1994, Compact Classics, Inc.

2,000 newspapers in 68 different countries.)

. . . Actress Tallulah Bankhead commonly hired young homosexual "caddies" to hold her hand until she drifted off to sleep?

. . . Famed German composer Ludwig van Beethoven sometimes poured ice water over his head in an effort to stimulate his brain?

. . . When another musical genius, Wolfgang Amadeus Mozart, was just two years old he correctly picked out a pig's squeal as a "G-sharp"?

Little-Known Facts About Well-Known People

• What popular network newscaster was a high school drop-out?	ABC's Peter Jennings
• What world-famous pediatrician was once arrested at Cape Canaveral, Florida at the age of 83 for demonstrating on behalf of world peace?	Dr. Benjamin Spock
• Statesman Winston Churchill suffered a lifelong inability to enunciate one particular letter of the alphabet; thus, he wrote all his speeches with this terminal letter carefully eliminated. What letter was it?	"S"
• What naturalist, plagued by a lifetime of nervous disorders, turned to science because his stutter precluded him from becoming a minister? (Hint: In a bit of irony, ministers were later to be counted among his most ardent detractors.)	Charles Darwin, the father of the theory of evolution
• In their early years, Sir Winston Churchill, Thomas Edison, Albert Einstein, Henry Ford and Sir Isaac Newton were all once considered what?	Incorrigible students and failures in school
• What did Michelangelo, Leonardo da Vinci and Jack the Ripper each have in common?	They were left-handers
• After all his narrow escapes, what was the cause of Harry Houdini's ultimate demise? On what U.S. holiday did he die?	Acute appendicitis overtook him on Halloween day, 1926
• What was the color of actress Jayne Mansfield's house and automobile?	Pink (her favorite color)
• Who holds the still-standing record for the most fan mail ever received?	Mickey Mouse (as of 1993 he had received several *hundred-million* letters)
• What good-luck object does Opera singer Luciano Pavarotti carry in his pocket whenever he sings?	A bent nail
• Carol Burnett signaled her grandmother every week at the end of her show to let her know everything was all right. What was this trademark signal?	She would tug slightly on her left earlobe
• What Academy Award-winning actor often registers at hotels under the name of Lord Greystoke?	Marlon Brando
• Swordsman D'Artagnan was the captain of what famous French trio?	The Three Musketeers
• Born in Hot Springs, Iowa, her measurements—according to her late creator—are 70-30-32. Name her.	Miss Piggy
• Just days after the death of film star Rudolph Valentino, an anonymous woman mysteriously placed 13 roses on his grave. By what nickname was this legendary figure later known?	"The Lady in Black"
• Dick Wilson, a one-time movie actor, did not gain his fame from his movie work, but rather as what grocery clerk? What product did he tout, and what famous line did he commonly recite as this character?	Mr. Whipple; toilet tissue; "Don't squeeze the Charmin"
• What rock star was once elected homecoming queen by his alma mater, the University of Houston?	Alice Cooper
• Upon what comedian did columnist Walter Winchell confer the nickname "Thief of Bad Gags"?	Milton Berle

• The play/movie "Amadeus" fancifully attributes Mozart's murder to a jealous fellow composer, the intellectual Antonio Salieri, who openly questioned why God would give such a wondrous gift to a 35-year-old brat. According to some historians, how did Salieri carry out his plan? In fact, what was the probable cause of Mozart's death?	He poisoned his rival; he likely died of overwork and typhus
• What celebrity was once sentenced to six months behind bars for attacking television executive Sheldon Saltman with a baseball bat?	Motorcycle stunt rider Evil Knievel
• What commercial product did both rock musician Dr. John and model/actress Brooke Shields pose for as babies?	Ivory soap
• The birth name of this comedian/actor is Albert Einstein. What is his stage name?	Albert Brooks
• Singer Neil Diamond won a scholarship to New York University, where he majored in biology in hopes of becoming a doctor. In what sport did he win his scholarship?	Fencing
• Among his many accomplishments, football star Joe Namath will forever be remembered for modeling what product for a television commercial?	Beautymist pantyhose
• This country singer, who also took the lead role in several movies, was a Rhodes scholar in his youth. Name him.	Kris Kristofferson
• What actress/model held the title of "Miss Pro Tennis" in 1968?	Farrah Fawcett

GOOD CHEMISTRY
Did You Know That . . .

. . . Every time you breath in, you inhale at least one or two of the same molecules you inhaled as a baby with the first breath you took?

. . . The chemical compound carbon dioxide, which makes up less than one percent of dry air, can suffocate plants and animals if administered in levels that are too concentrated?

. . . Albert Einstein was denied security clearance from the U.S. government when he first arrived to work on the atom bomb prior to World War II?

. . . The colorless material called celluloid—often used in the manufacturing of toys, toilet articles, and film—was the result of attempts to produce better billiard balls?

Proton and Electron Soup

• Decompression sickness—known by pilots as "altitude sickness" and by deep sea divers as "the bends"—is linked to a release of gas bubbles into body tissues, resulting in pain, shock, or even death. Name this most abundant gas. (Hint: It makes up about 70 percent of the air you breathe.)	Nitrogen
• What element was observed through a spectroscope for the first time in 1868? During what event was it observed?	Helium; during a solar eclipse
• Name the inert gas that fills the lighted tubes of advertising signs and Las Vegas casinos.	Neon
• What pungent, water-soluble gas was first produced by camel dung near Egypt's Temple of Ammon—the place from which the gas derived its name?	Ammonia
• Give the name of the unstable gas that accounts for the sharp, fresh odor that is sometimes present in the air after a lightning storm.	Ozone
• Nitrous oxide can cause feelings of euphoria if inhaled. What is the name of this mirth-producing compound, and who developed it—a man who, incidentally, later committed suicide.	"Laughing gas"; Horace Wells

• What essential ingredient, common to many expensive cosmetics, is, in its native form, a foul-smelling tar-like substance extracted from the fleece of sheep?

Lanolin

• The atoms in this chemical compound are a chain in the form H-O-O-H (two hydrogen atoms connected by two oxygen atoms), and is sometimes used for bleaching hair. What is this chemical?

Hydrogen Peroxide

• What type of substance turns blue litmus paper red? Conversely, what substance will turn a red piece of litmus blue?

An acid; a base

• Given the reputation of Italy's Lucrezia Borgia, Duchess of Ferrara during the early sixteenth century, which of the following would she have found most handy to have around: calcium chloride, sodium carbonate, strychnine, or pizza?

Strychnine, a poison (calcium chloride is the compound making up common table salt, and sodium carbonate is the gas in soda pop—which can wash down your pizza!)

• Cement, mixed with sand and water, turns to what over time?

Concrete

• When water is frozen to create ice, what chemical changes occur?

The chemical composition (H_2O) of its molecules remains the same (only the structure— how the molecules themselves are "stacked"—is changed upon freezing)

• What would you most likely do with the compound $MgSO_4$: power a car with it, use it to blow up a building, add it to water and soak one's feet, or use it to fertilize a lawn?

Soak one's feet—it is the formula for Epsom salt

—— ◇ ◆✧◆ ◇ ——

ALL I WANT FOR CHRISTMAS . . .
Did You Know That . . .

. . . Swedish men have been known to wrap themselves up in huge boxes and have themselves delivered to a girlfriend's homes at Christmastime?

. . . Cartoonist Thomas Nast was first to depict Santa Claus in today's modern, red-suited image?

. . . In 1890 James Edgar became the first department-store Santa Claus, dressing up for the Boston store in Brockton, Massachusetts?

. . . Each year over three billion Christmas cards are sent throughout the world?

. . . In the countries of South America, setting off fireworks is a common way to celebrate Christmas?

Fa-la-la-la-la!

• If your true love gave you all of the gifts described in the song "The Twelve Days of Christmas," how many total birds would be fluttering about your home?

23 (1 partridge, 2 turtle doves, 3 French hens, 4 "calling birds," 6 geese ('a laying), and 7 swans ('a swimming)

• In the Charles Dickens' classic, "A Christmas Carol," what was the name of Ebenezer Scrooge's dead partner?

Jacob Marley

• Where did the "X" in the abbreviation *X-mas* come from?

From the Greek word for "Christ," which begins with the letter *X*.

• In medieval England, who was the mythical leader of Christmas revelries?

The Lord of Misrule

• According to both French and Pennsylvania Dutch tradition, what is the name of Santa's brother?

Bells Nichols

• What are the names of Santa's eight "basic line-up" Reindeer? And when is the ninth, lead reindeer Rudolph added?	Blitzen, Comet, Cupid, Dancer, Dasher, Donner, Prancer, Vixen; when inclement weather is forecast
• What are the last five words of "A Christmas Carol," and which character are they credited to?	"God Bless us, Every One!"; Tiny Tim
• What is the name of the legal holiday celebrated in Britain and Canada that refers to the custom of giving gift boxes to faithful employees on the day after Christmas?	Boxing Day
• In what Christmas song are the ages 1 and 92 mentioned?	"Chestnuts Roasting on an Open Fire"
• What did the billboard at Times Square, paid for by John Lennon on Christmas of 1969, read?	"War Is Over! If You Want It—Happy Christmas from John and Yoko"
• What parasitic plant, grown in the branches of trees, is hailed by lovers at Christmas time?	Mistletoe
• St. Nicholas is patron saint of what country?	Russia
• Give the name of the fairy-tale opera—often performed at Christmastime—composed by Englebert Humperdinck and based on a story from the Brothers Grimm.	"Hansel and Gretel"
• In what year did Christmas became a national holiday in the United States? What state already had declared it a state holiday as early as 1836?	1890; Alabama
• How many recordings of "White Christmas" have been purchased since its release in 1942? In what film did the song debut?	165 million; "Holiday Inn"
• What is the English title for the Latin Christmas carol "Adeste Fidelis"?	"Oh Come All Ye Faithful"
• Word for word, what is the last line of Clement Clarke Moore's poem "A Visit from St. Nicholas," published in 1823?	"Happy Christmas to all and to all a good night."
• How many times is Santa Claus mentioned in Clement Moore's "A Visit From St. Nicholas"?	The name "Santa Claus" is not mentioned at all.

KIDS' LIT. 101
Did You Know That . . .

. . . Comedian Dom DeLuise wrote a children's book about an ugly caterpillar who is transformed into a butterfly titled "Charlie the Caterpillar"?

. . . In 1985 London education officials removed the classic novel *The Adventures of Tom Sawyer* from school libraries because they deemed it both "racist" and "sexist"?

"Once Upon a Time . . ."

• Who is the carrot-topped 9-year-old who bears the unique middle name of "Provisionia Gaberdina Dandeliona Ephraimsdaughter," and lives in the villa Villekula with her purple spotted horse?	Pippi Longstocking
• What were the names of Cinderella's two ugly stepsisters?	Anastasia and Drizella
• Three animals refused to help make the bread—but later were most eager to eat it—in the tale of "The Little Red Hen." Name them. Who finally did help the exasperated mother with the bread-making?	Cat, Duck and Pig; her children
• What Dr. Seuss character stole Christmas?	The Grinch
• Name the title book character who was born in a flower and slept in a cradle made out of a walnut shell.	Thumbelina

- What nationality was Aladdin of "Aladdin and the Magic Lamp" fame?

Chinese

- Where did *The Wonderful Wizard of Oz* author L. Frank Baum allegedly obtain the name of his magical kingdom?

From a tag on one of his filing cabinets labeled "O-Z"

- Give the title of Dr. Seuss' first book, which was rejected by 28 different publishers before one finally decided to give it a chance. What was the birth name of this creator of delightfully nonsensical verse?

"And to Think That I Saw It on Mulberry Street"; Theodor Seuss Geisel

- As a young girl, an imaginative and widely read children's author sewed flowers onto her father's sweater, named her doll after a tractor, and was in the lowest reading group in her first-grade class. Who is this author of children's works?

Beverly Cleary

- What were Cinderella's slippers originally made of before a translation error transformed them to "glass" in the 1600s?

Fur (the word *glauser* was used to describe the "shine" of the slippers' fur)

- What was Lewis Carroll's birth name and every-day profession?

Rev. Charles Lutwidge Dodgson was a lecturer on mathematics at Christ Church, Oxford

- Identify the "Jacks" in the following nursery rhymes:

    - He tried to raise his cholesterol level.

Jack Sprat

    - He suffered a pretty serious head trauma.

Jack, from "Jack and Jill"

    - He was nice to cats.

Jack Stout

    - His table manners left something to be desired.

Jack Horner

- This tale of the Arabian Nights begins with the command "Open sesame." Name the tale.

"Ali Baba and the Forty Thieves"

- *Anthropomorphism* is the assigning of human attributes to things that are not human. Give the name of each of the following anthropomorphic works of fiction:

    - The classical English work about Mr. Toad, Rat and Mole.

The Wind in the Willows

    - The Watty Piper story about a persistent "coupled" character.

"The Little Engine That Could"

    - A story about a mongoose and a cobra.

"Rickki-tikki-tavi"

    - The medieval beast epic about the lion, the wolf, the bear, and the fox.

"Reynard the Fox"

- In the story "Pinocchio," what is the name of:

    - Geppetto's cat and goldfish?

Figaro and Cleo

    - Pinocchio's friend and "conscience"?

Jiminy Cricket

    - The bully who coaxes Pinocchio to spend his "father's" money on candy?

Lampwick

    - The puppetmaster who captures Pinocchio?

Stromboli

    - The whale who swallows both Geppetto and Pinocchio?

Monstro

- What is the favorite food of the Hobbits, created J.R. Tolkien?

Mushrooms

- What Raymond Briggs book was removed in 1979 from elementary classrooms in Holland, Michigan due to several parental complaints about the book portraying Santa Claus as having a negative attitude toward Christmas?

Father Christmas

- What book, written by Claire H. Bishop and Kurt Wise, describes the exploits of a boy who could swallow the sea, his brother with an iron neck, still a third brother who could stretch and stretch his legs, a fourth who could not be burned, and a fifth brother who could hold his breath indefinitely?

"The Five Chinese Brothers"

• Name the animal that Lewis Carroll describes as "frumious" in his poem "Jabberwocky."	The Bandersnatch
• Jacob and Wilhelm are the first names of what two storytelling brothers?	The Brothers Grimm
• By what pen name is the author Elizabeth Forest better known?	Mother Goose
• What well known writer of adult spy novels authored the children's story titled *Chitty Chitty Bang Bang*?	Ian Fleming
• What basic reader series of books for young children was written by Zerna A. Sharp?	Dick and Jane
• In *The Phantom Tollbooth*, a novel by Norton Juster, what is the rival city of the city Dictionopolis?	Digitopolis

OLYMPIC GOLD
Did You Know That . . .

. . . The early Olympic Games (c. 1400 B.C. to A.D. 394, when conquering Roman Emperor Theodosius ordered them ended) played an important part of Greek religious festivals? (The exciting athletic contests were regarded as pleasing to the spirits of the dead.)

. . . The ancient Games permitted competition only between male athletes?

. . . Norwegian-born American Anders Haugen garnered fourth place in the large hill ski jump during the 1924 Winter Olympics in France, but 50 years later, when Anders was 83, was awarded the bronze medal when a scoring error was discovered?

. . . Tons of snow had to be shipped in from Canada in order to hold the 1980 Winter Olympics at Lake Placid, New York?

Faster, Higher, Farther

• After winning the women's 100-meter dash against favored Stella Walsh of Poland in the 1936 Berlin Olympics, Missouri's Helen Stephens was accused by the screaming crowd of being a man. How did Olympic officials solve the problem?	They insisted that Stephens disrobe in front of the crowd.
• What notorious state leader was Head of Ceremonies at these same 1936 Berlin Games?	Dictator Adolph Hitler
• Fill in the following blanks in these statements about the Olympics (and identify the Olympic event to which each statement applies):	
- The rapid-fire pistol target holds a resemblance to a small _____ _____.	Human figure (shooting)
- The first perfect "10" score to be awarded in this event went to _____ _____ at the 1976 Olympics.	Nadia Comaneci (gymnastics)
- A pool is required to contain a minimum of 8 _____, each 7 to 9 feet wide.	Lanes (swimming)
- The _____ is considered by many to be the ultimate test to determine the best all-around athlete.	Decathlon (track and field)
- In this event, running at top speed the men approach the _____ from one end, while the women approach it from the side.	Horse (gymnastics)
- Water temperature is required to be within a two-degree range between _____ and _____ degrees Fahrenheit.	78 and 80 (swimming)
- The _____ _____ measures 16 feet, 3 inches long by 4 inches wide, and stands nearly 4 feet off the floor.	Balance Beam (gymnastics)

- The only track-and-field event in which a world record has never been set in the Olympics is the _____ .

• Name the 10 track-and-field events that make up the Decathlon. Which of these ten is generally run last?

• Athletes competing from countries in the Southern Hemisphere have won a grand total of one Winter Olympics medal. In the 1992 Albertville games, who won the Silver Medal in slalom skiing, and what "down-under" country is she from?

• The "iron-man" triathlon—an event requiring its entrants to swim 2.4 miles, immediately move to a 112-mile bike race, and end with a 26.2-mile marathon run—has been an Olympic event for how many years?

• What is the only Olympic sport that is timed to the one thousandth of a second?

• What twin brothers won the Gold and Silver medals in the 1984 Winter Olympics men's slalom?

• What were the original five events of the pentathlon in ancient Greece?

• Name the two Olympic decathlon champions that each appeared on the front of Wheaties breakfast cereal boxes.

• What two sites have hosted the Olympic Winter games twice?

• What great athlete was an Olympic gold medalist in track and field, and later went on to win ten major golf titles?

• What well-known pediatrician was an oarsman for the Yale crew that won the 1924 Olympic Gold Medal in Paris?

• What country's delegation is the only one that refuses to dip its flag during the opening-day Olympic parade?

• The athletes from what country are always *first* to march in the Olympic parade at the opening-day ceremonies? What country is always the *last* to receive the accolades of the crowd?

• Canada won the Winter Olympics gold medal in hockey every year until 1936. What country finally broke their stranglehold on Olympic hockey titles?

• Rudi Ball was the only one of "these" to play hockey for the German squad in the 1936 Winter Olympics. What distinguished Ball from his teammates?

• What was the first non-European site to host the Winter Olympics?

• Give the names of the three Winter Olympic game sites that end with the letter O.

• Polish Olympic Gold Medal track star Stella Walsh became the first female to run 100 yards in less than 11 seconds. What startling bit of information about her was discovered upon her death several decades later?

• In 1952, Emil and Dana Zatopek became the first married couple each to win a Gold Medal at an Olympics. In which two events did they prevail?

• The first American ever to participate in the modern Olympic Pentathlon in 1912 later became a famed U.S. Army general. Name him.

Discus

100-meter run, 400-meter run, 1500-meter run, 110-meter hurdles, high jump, long jump, javelin throw, pole vault, shot put, and discus throw; the 1500-meter run is run last

Annelise Coberger; New Zealand

It is not an event sponsored by the Olympics

The luge

Phil and Steve Mahre

Leaping, running, wrestling, and throwing the discus and the spear

Bob Mathis and Bruce Jenner

Lake Placid, New York and St. Moritz, Switzerland

Babe Dridrikson (Zaharias)

Dr. Benjamin Spock

The United States

Greece; the host country

Great Britain

He was the only Jewish member of the German team

Lake Placid, New York

Oslo, Sarejevo and Sapporo

"She" was actually a "he"

Emil won the men's marathon and Dana the women's javelin throw.

General George S. Patton

WAR AND PEACE
Did You Know That . . .

. . . As of 1993, the United States had provided 128 billion dollars' worth of military assistance and weapons to more than 125 countries?

. . . Applicants seeking routine jobs at the atomic bomb development "Manhattan Project" facilities near Los Alamos, New Mexico between 1942 and 1945 were automatically disqualified if they were literate?

. . . Leo Tolstoy's famed Russian novel *War and Peace,* set during the Napoleonic War, is jammed with over 500 characters?

Wars and Weaponry

• What war has been referred to as "The War of Faulty Communications," since it might have been avoided entirely had telegraphic communications existed then? (Hint: Two days before war was declared, Britain had agreed to repeal the laws that were the chief excuse for fighting. However, the news did not reach President Madison in time to avert war.)

The War of 1812

• What important front-line capacity did late movie mogul Walt Disney hold during World War I?

He was an ambulance driver for the allies

• In the Nazi army of the 1940s, the "Brownshirts" were ordinary foot soldiers. By contrast, who were the "Blackshirts"?

They were elite troopers chosen as bodyguards for high-ranking officials

• The son of a famed foreign leader was captured by Germany during World War II. Instead of accepting an offer to exchange prisoners, the leader allowed his son to die in a prison camp. Who was this infamously ruthless man?

Joseph Stalin

• Today the initials CD most commonly refer to Compact Disc. What did these same initials represent for the average U.S. citizen during the 1940s?

Civil Defense

• As of 1993, what eight countries were suspected or known to have nuclear weapons?

The United States, Russia (and possibly one or two of its former satellites), the United Kingdom, China, India, France, Israel, and South Africa

• This American Civil War hero, known as Frank Thompson, fought at Bull Run in 1861 and Fredericksburg in 1862; he also spied behind Confederate lines disguised as a female. What was particularly unusual about Thompson?

"He" was actually Sarah Edmonds, who had initially disguised herself as a man

• Name the Civil War Confederate general who was accidentally shot and killed by one of his own men.

Stonewall Jackson

• During the Persian Gulf War, the U.S. Defense Department substituted euphemisms for many common sites, situations, and events. What does each of these more politically-accepted euphemisms refer to?

- "Airborne Sanitation"

Shooting down enemy planes

- "An Armed Situation"

War

- "Collateral Damage"

Killing innocent victims

- "Suppression of Assets"

Bombing key buildings

- "Effort"

A bombing attack

- "Security Review"

Censorship

- "Servicing the Target"

Killing the enemy

- "Weapons Systems"

Bombs

• What was the result of the first bomb dropped by the German Luftwaffe on the Russian city of Leningrad during World War II?	It killed the only elephant in the city's zoo
• Which type of explosive device derived its name from the tropical pomegranate fruit?	The grenade
• Upon its refinement in 1862, what weapon of war was deemed so horrible that it was said no war could ever be fought again? Who was responsible for this death-instrument's development?	The machine gun; Richard Gatling
• What did the Germans name the large cannon they used to bombard Paris during World War I?	Big Bertha
• What Italian soldier and patriot, whose conquest paved the way for his country's unification, extended the unusual recruiting statement, "I offer thirst, forced marches, battles and death"—subsequently drawing thousands of 19th-century Italians to defend the banner?	Giuseppe Garibaldi
• What term, interpreted to mean "divine wind," was used in World War II to describe the actions of Japanese air force fliers crashing their bomb-laden planes into enemy targets?	Kamikaze
• Name the Union Army cavalry commander, labeled "Little Phil" during the Civil War, who offended many loyal Texans in his district with the words, "If I owned Texas and Hell, I would rent out Texas and live in Hell."	Philip Sheridan
• The building located at Prinsengracht 263—one of the most well-known addresses to emerge from World War II—is a major tourist attraction today. What is the significance of this structure?	It the annex above which Jewish diarist Anne Frank and her family lived for two years while hiding from the Nazis
• What was classical Greek inventor/mathematician Archimedes' fatal "death-ray"? (Hint: Legend has it that it was used to set fire to an attacking fleet of Roman ships.)	Sunlight reflected by mirrors

THE BUSINESS OF BUSINESS
Did You Know That ...

. . . On one occasion the Coca-Cola Company was presented an offer to buy out the bankrupt Pepsi-Cola Company for $1,000, but— confident that they would continue to monopolize soft-drink sales—corporate executives refused the offer, missing the opportunity to strangle the very company that would soon become its arch-rival?

. . . New York businessman Richard Charles Drew conceived of and opened the first blood bank back in 1940? (Unfortunately, because Drew was black, he was not allowed to contribute blood to his own bank.)

. . . The largest industrial complex in the world—occupying a whopping 204.3 acres of floor space—is the Nizhiny Tagil Railroad Car and Tank Plant located near Moscow, Russia?

. . . Back in 1956 two men named Henry and Richard established a company called H & R Block to assist people with the odious task of preparing their taxes?

. . . Ford Motor Company president Ernest Breech, when asked if Ford would be interested in manufacturing the Volkswagen after the war, decided it was "not worth a damn" and instead chose to produce the Edsel, which proved a $350 million failure?

. . . Eli Whitney, inventor of the cotton gin, did not strike it rich with his invention, but made the majority of his money as a New England gun manufacturer, acquiring lucrative contracts from the government?

. . . Chain stores account for 72% of all grocery sales in the U.S.?

Buying, Selling and Industry-Making

• What successful businessman has an ice-cream-cone-shaped swimming pool in the back yard of his California home?	Irvin Robbins (Burton Baskin's partner)

• What do the three *M*'s stand for in the 3M company?

Minnesota Mining and Manufacturing

• What do the *M*'s stand for in M&M's candy?

Victor Mars and his associate Mr. Merrie, who developed the candy in 1941

• My Little Pony, GI Joe, and Mr. Potato Head are all toys marketed by what company?

Hasbro

• What product corresponds with each of the following inauspicious foreign brand names and descriptions:

- In Japan, *Green Piles* can be found in many lawn and garden centers.

Fertilizer

- In China, *Pansy* is certainly not a fresh scented flower; in fact, it is a brand of _____ _____.

Men's underwear

- In Spain, *Colon Plus* is not a breakfast cereal, but rather a _____ _____.

Liquid detergent

- In Greece, this *Zit* could, in principle, be "popped," since it is a _____-_____ _____ _____.

Lemon-lime soft drink

- In Sweden, *Krapp* is a fitting name for this brand of _____ _____.

Toilet tissue

- In Japan, *Mucus* is something you may want to sample after all.

A soft drink

- In Sweden, a big *Plopp* would be a welcome energy boost after work.

Chocolate bar

• In the 1993, there were 172 million of these boxes purchased in the United States. What are in these popular boxes?

Girl Scout cookies

• What automobile manufacturer produced the Gremlin—and, in 1976, promptly *reduced* its price by 7.8 percent to $2995?

American Motors

• In 1992, the Pro-Line Cap Company in Fort Worth, Texas was cited by the Occupational Safety and Health Administration for not having adequate restroom facilities for its female employees. How did the company solve the problem?

They fired all 30 of their female employees

• What was the first home appliance introduced by Sunbeam?

The iron

• What is the name of the chubby little man made of Michelin tires who can be seen on the covers of Michelin travel guides?

Bibendum

• What do the *BVD* initials stand for in the brand of men's underwear? (Hint: It does not stand for "Baby"s Ventilated Diapers.")

The company's founders, Bradley, Voorhees, and Day

• The name of a popular skin cream—originally called "Dr. Bunting's Sunburn Remedy"—was changed because it soon became fashionably known as the concoction that "knocks eczema"?

Noxzema

• Jules Lederer, husband of advice columnist Ann Landers, borrowed $5,000 and turned it into a $10 million business. Name the company.

Budget Rent-A-Car

• What distinctive marketing gimmick—a strategy with respect to dollars-and-cents merchandise pricing which is still widely used today—did Melville E. Stone introduce in 1875?

He subtracted a penny from an item's price, making it appear to be cheaper (i.e. $1.99 instead of $2.00)

• What is the name of the fictional company that supplies "The Road Runner" cartoon's Wile E. Coyote with explosives and other devices used in his attempt to capture his rival?

Acme

• In 1951, Topps became the first manufacturer of this product and continues to hold its #1 spot in the market today. Name this collectable commodity. | Baseball cards

ALL TOO HUMAN
Did You Know That . . .

. . . Even if the stomach, the spleen, 75 percent of the liver, 80 percent of the intestines, one kidney, one lung, and virtually every organ from the pelvic and groin area were removed, the human body could still function quite normally?

. . . Tears which are incited by air-borne irritants (i.e. when cutting onions or when getting a whiff of ammonia) differ in composition from those tears shed out of emotion?

. . . By the time you turn 70, your heart will have beat some two-and-a-half billion times (figuring on an average of 70 beats per minute)?

. . . The human sense of smell is so keen that it can detect the odors of certain substances even when they are diluted to 1 part in 30 billion?

. . . A full one-half to three-fourth of the heat produced by the body is lost through the head?

. . . The lens of the eye continues to grow throughout a person's life?

. . . More than a century ago, Darwin claimed that facial expressions could actually intensify emotions, thus, people could really be happier if they forced themselves to smile? (Support for this theory is now high; scientists have noticed that an increase in a chemical hormone called serotonin brings on heightened feelings of well-being, and that smiling accelerates the manufacture of this "natural narcotic.")

How's a Body To Know?

• If you climbed to an elevation of 63,000 feet above sea level, what would your blood do? | At normal body temperature, your blood would boil

• In what part of the body does a stroke occur? | The brain

• How many muscles does it take to smile? To frown? | Seventeen; 43

• What part of the throat is actually a projection of the thyroid cartilage of the larynx? (Hint: It's named after a prominent Bible character.) | The Adam's apple

• How many linear feet of nerve fiber are contained in one square inch of skin from the human hand? | Approximately 72 feet

• When you sit in a tub of water for an hour or so, the skin on your hands and feet become wrinkled. Why is this? | These thicker layers of skin expand due to water retention.

• What is the location of the "20 moons" that grace the human body? | The base of the finger nails and toe nails

• What is the medical explanation for someone turning white from fear? | When frightened, the blood vessels constrict, pressing blood away from the skin to the center of the body

• What is the *gluteus maximus'* claim to fame—besides the fact that you can sit on it? | It is the largest muscle in the body.

• What "piliferous" growth on the human body cannot be destroyed by cold, change in climate, water or other natural forces, is resistant to many kinds of acids and corrosive chemicals—and therefore is hated by all amateur plumbers? | Hair (Aside from its vulnerability to fire, human hair is nearly impossible to destroy)

• Statistically, what percentage of men in the U.S. are sexually impotent? | One out of ten men admit to the affliction

• Where on the human body is the *philtrum* located? | It is the indentation in the middle of the area between the nose and the upper lip.

• If hit by lightening, which of the five senses is most likely to be lost?	Hearing
• If you eat too much, what temporarily happens to your sense of hearing?	It becomes duller
• As you descend into a deep underground mine shaft, what happens to your body weight?	It decreases ever so slightly
• Which lung in the human body is larger, the left or the right?	The right
• What part of the human body receives no supply of blood, and therefore must obtain its oxygen from the air?	The cornea of the eye

AUTHOR! AUTHOR!
Did You Know That . . .

. . . William Faulkner's name was originally spelled with no letter "U"? (When the error was made by the typesetter on his first novel, he decided to leave it rather than create a hassle.)

. . . The Encylopaedia Britannica was banned and pulped in Turkey in 1986 amid accusations that it spread "separatist propaganda"?

. . . The FBI has a voluminous thousand-page file on writer Dorothy Parker? (Although she never proved to be member of the Communist Party, her record does show that she was a member of the League of Women Shoppers.)

The Power of the Pen

• Three writers—Lewis Carroll (best-known for his *Alice's Adventures in Wonderland*), Thomas Jefferson (drafter of the Declaration of Independence) and Ernest Hemingway (author of *For Whom the Bell Tolls*)—each shared a particular writing habit. What was it?	They all wrote while standing up
• Samuel Clemens (Mark Twain) once compiled a 1-through-27 list of people and things to be rescued from a burning boarding house. What was the first item on the list? The last thing to be rescued?	Fiancees; Mothers-in-law
• What English Dame is the world's top-selling fiction writer, having penned a total of 78 novels that have sold an estimated two billion copies worldwide?	Agatha Christie
• What American poet always used lowercase letters when signing or printing his poetry? What did the initials used in his literary signature stand for?	e.e. cummings; Edward Estlin
• What is the title of the Abbie Hoffman book which can only be checked out by members of Congress?	*Steal This Book*
• Who was the author of *The Autobiography of Alice B. Toklas?*	Gertrude Stein
• What 19th-century Russian medical doctor wrote a number of short stories and plays, which have currently gained popularity in translation.	Anton Chekhov
• Who were Scarlet's twin admirers in Margaret Mitchell's *Gone With the Wind?*	Stuart and Brent Tarleton
• Name the book that was author Joyce Jillson's response to *Real Men Don't Eat Quiche.*	*Real Women Don't Pump Gas*
• What acclaimed female author had a habit of smoking big black cigars?	Amy Lowell
• What novel did Charles Dickens leave unfinished at his death?	*The Mystery of Edwin Drood*
• What author waged an unsuccessful campaign to become Mayor of New York City in 1969?	Norman Mailer

- Name the Russian writer who compared Stalin's mustaches to cockroaches and, as a result, was sent to a death camp.

  Osip Mandelstam

- What plumed gratuity did T.S. Eliot once release under his chair at a staid London restaurant?

  A live pigeon

- What is the subject of the do-it-yourself guides that are annual bestsellers—and whose sales in the U.S. are especially brisk in late March and early to mid-April?

  Income tax guidebooks

- What Daniel Defoe work of fiction was based on the real-life adventures of Alexander Selkirk?

  Robinson Crusoe

- Name the novel written by English author Anthony Burgess in which the title is based on a mechanical citrus fruit.

  "Clockwork Orange"

- Who was the real Poor Richard who authored the Almanacs?

  Benjamin Franklin

- Identify the famous writer who, due to his tallness, was known to use the top of his refrigerator as a table to write his books.

  Thomas Wolfe

- In which direction of the compass did Charles Dickens always face when writing—and aimed his head when sleeping?

  North

- What did author Timothy Dexter do in response to criticism over the lack of punctuation in his book *A Pickle for the Knowing Ones?*

  In the book's second edition he published an entire page of nothing but punctuation marks

- What is the pen-name that contemporary mystery novelist Evan Hunter writes under?

  Ed McBain

- What is the Feb. 2, 1905 birthplace of novelist Ayn Rand, author of the acclaimed *The Fountainhead* (1943) and *Atlas Shrugged* (1957)?

  St. Petersburg (Leningrad), Russia

- Name the mystery writer who suddenly disappeared in 1926 for a period of eleven days—an event she expressly left unexplained.

  Agatha Christie

- Which of the Apollo XI astronauts did *not* write a book?

  Neil Armstrong

- Give the name of the Stephen King novel about a burial ground used for reincarnation—and, harder still, spell it correctly.

  Pet Sematary

20,000 LEAGUES UNDER THE SEA
Did You Know That . . .

. . . The tropical sea anenome willingly provides shelters to a colony of damselfish, but if approached by damselfish outside its colony it will sting them to death?

. . . The aggressively fierce walking catfish—originally imported from Asia as an aquarium fish—escaped from Florida breeding tanks in the 1970s, is able to breath and crawl on land, and can eat other fish up to seven inches long?

. . . A tuna can traverse a hundred miles of ocean in a single day?

. . . Most fish do not sleep, though their constant motion is marked by periods of reduced activity? (A few fish have been found to "sleep" in coral reefs by leaning against rocks or standing on their tails.)

. . . As a result of the "stress" of swimming in small tanks, nearly 10 percent of the bluefin and yellowfin tuna in the Tokyo Sea Life Park aquarium are reported to have developed bumpy, deformed faces and/or dislodged eyes?

. . . The elephant seal, the largest seal known to man, can grow as long as 20 feet and weigh some 8000 pounds?

. . . The four-eyed tropical *anableps* fish can browse underwater with one set of eyes while scanning above water with the other pair?

. . . The *Johnsonia Eriomma* is more commonly called the "bigeye fish" because its eyes are a full one-fifth as long as its body?

. . . A blue whale's heart weighs upwards of 1200 pounds?

. . . Biologists from Cornell University recently found that families of spermwhales, separated geographically from one another, develop radically different vocal repertoires?

. . . The Nile perch, known as the "elephant of the water," has proven to be a severely misguided ecological experiment, having devoured most of the 300 other fish species in Africa's Lake Victoria since its introduction in 1960?

THAR SHE BLOWS!

• At 188 decibels, more shrill than a pneumatic drill, what is believed to be the loudest sound produced by any living animal?

The whistle of the blue whale

• What creature could look at you with 35 large blue eyes?

The scallop

• Imported to the United States as a food source in the 1870s, what giant cousin of the goldfish paves its muddy way by uprooting aquatic plants, often rendering its environment unhabitable for other species?

Carp

• What female fish stores her eggs in the abdominal pouch of her mate?

The sea horse

• Depending on which of the over 200 species you are referring to, this sea animal's tentacles vary in number from just a few to more than 800; some tentacles are less than an inch long, while others trail 120 feet (about ten stories) down into the water. What kind of sea creature are we talking about?

The jellyfish

• Name the jellyfish that is capable of inducing a sting more lethal than an entire nest-full of wasps?

A Portuguese Man-of-War

• Name the four stages of growth that the salmon fish passes through.

Fry, pan, smelt, and grilse

• Where is the most likely place to catch a sardine?

There is no such fish as a "sardine"—canned sardines generally contain young herring or pilchard

• What happens to goldfish when they either go without adequate illumination or are placed in a body of running water?

They lose their color

• If you cut open a lobster, what color would its blood be?

Blue

• What starfish, commonly associated with the Pacific Ocean, is known for the damage it has done to many of the world's coral reefs?

The crown-of-thorns starfish

• What flatfish is born with two eyes, one on each side of its head, but eventually ends up with both eyes moving to the top of its head?

The turbot

• What sea creature is made up of 98 percent water and will virtually disappear if washed up to shore and allowed to dry?

The jellyfish

• Name the luminous fish whose male species eventually attaches itself to the female, becoming completely connected.

The Anglerfish (All the male angler's internal organs—with the exception of the reproductive system—are fused to its female companion)

• For what purpose were Goldfish originally bred by the Chinese?

Strictly culinary

• What two eight-legged sea animals also have two kidneys and three hearts?

Octopus and squid

© 1994, Compact Classics, Inc.

• When threatened, what fish will engorge itself with with water and display its sharp spines, often frightening away enemies as large and formidable as the tiger shark?	The porcupine fish
• What is the strainer in a certain class of whale's mouth referred to?	The baleen
• Provided it's not caught and eaten, what is the lifespan of a trout?	Four years
• What was the intimidating promotional line used to advertise the 1978 movie "Jaws II"?	"Just when you thought it was safe to go back in the water . . . "

RAINING CATS AND DOGS
Did You Know That . . .

. . . According to the American Animal Hospital Association, over 65 percent of cat owners admitted that if their pet needed emergency medical treatment, they would treat the pet before themselves?

. . . The only dogs that bark regularly are those that come in contact with humans or other domesticated dogs? (Dogs in the wild rarely if ever bark.)

. . . Despite the long-time domestication factor, there is no genetic barrier between dogs and wolves?

. . . A skilled tracker dog can easily distinguish between individual scents, but fails only when it comes to the scent of identical twins?

. . . In 1885, the English banned as inhumane the use of dogs for hauling carts?

Canines vs. Felines

• What is the most popular cat derivation in the United States?	The Siamese
• All dogs have a normal body temperature of between 100 and 102 degrees Fahrenheit with the exception of one. What dog has a body temperature that reaches upwards of 104 degrees? (Hint: It needs to conserve all the warmth it can.)	Mexican Hairless
• What hunting/guard dog derived its name from a German tax collector, who, aware of the unpopularity of his job and bent on protecting his person, developed this exceptionally fierce breed?	Doberman pinscher
• What was the penalty for killing a cat in Egypt 4000 years ago?	Death
• According to a 27-year-old New York City study, what breed of dog is known to bite the most? The least?	German police dog; the golden retriever
• Name the wild dog largely associated with the Australian continent.	The dingo
• Compared to a human's five million scent-sensitive cells, how many smell cells does a German shepherd dog have?	220 million
• Give the dog terms that match each of the following definitions:	
- The bulldog's drooping lip.	The chops
- The part of the body located in front of the chest.	The brisket
- A spotted nose.	A butterfly nose
- Where the tip of the ear falls over the orifice, covering it.	A button ear
- A pointed or pricked ear.	A tulip ear
- A short round foot with high, well developed knuckles.	A cat foot

- Pendulous folds of skin under the throat.	The dewlap
- The tops of the hip joints.	Hucklebones
• In which country did the French poodle originate?	Germany
• Each day in the U.S., animal shelters are forced to destroy how many dogs and cats?	30,000
• What are the three most commonly used names for dogs in the U.S.?	Rover, Spot and Max
• The cat referred to in Lewis Carroll's *Alice's Adventures In Wonderland* is of what breed?	There is no such breed as "Cheshire"
• Cats seem to talk or send messages with their tails. Interpret what a cat is saying by the following tail positions:	
- Straight up in the air.	He likes you
- Slightly raised and curved outward.	She's curious
- Fluffed out and lowered.	He's afraid
- A twitching tip.	She's irritated
- Arched back, bristled tail.	He's ready to fight

LIKE A ROLLING STONE
Did You Know That . . .

. . . Bette Midler, Barry Manilow and many other famous vocalists got their start in a club in New York City called The Continental Baths, located in the basement of the Ansonia Hotel?

. . . Comedian Peter Sellers had "In the Mood" played at his funeral as an inside joke?

. . . On Jan 1, 1960 country singer Johnny Cash gave his first free concert at California's San Quentin Prison? (Coincidentally, Merle Haggard was in the audience during Cash's performance.) . . . Rock artists Jim Morrison, Jimi Hendrix, and Janis Joplin each died at the tender young age of 27?

. . . Australian-based rock group Men At Work got their inspiration for their name from a road sign?

The Beat Goes On

• What do the famous rock groups The Doors, The Who, The Rolling Stones, The Beach Boys, and The Grateful Dead all have in common?	None of the groups ever won a Grammy Award
• Given the artist and the year, identify each Grammy-winning "Best Record" title:	
- Eric Clapton, 1992	"Tears in Heaven"
- Bobby McFerrin, 1988	"Don't Worry, Be Happy"
- Natalie Cole, with Nat "King" Cole, 1991	"Unforgettable"
- USA for Africa, 1985	"We Are the World"
- Bette Middler, 1989	"Wind Beneath My Wings"
- Christopher Cross, 1980	"Sailing"
- Michael Jackson, 1983	"Beat It"
- Phil Collins, 1990	"Another Day in Paradise"
- The 5th Dimension, 1969	"Aquarius" ("Let the Sun Shine")
- Roberta Flack, 1973	"Killing Me Softly With His Song"
- Frank Sinatra, 1966	"Strangers in the Night"
- Tina Turner, 1984	"What's Love Got to Do With It?"

• What comedian/singer recorded his first song in a bathroom across the hall from the radio station where he worked? What was the name of the song?	"Weird Al" Yankovic; "My Bologna"
• What physical feature does country-western singer Dolly Parton share with rock 'n roll singer Pat Benatar?	They both stand only five feet tall
• At the group's first major show, what popular rock band made its entrance by skydiving from a plane into Anaheim Stadium?	Van Halen
• Who wrote "Leaving on a Jet Plane," made famous by Peter, Paul and Mary?	John Denver
• What did Grace Slick, lead singer of Jefferson Airplane (or Starship), name her daughter?	god (with a lower case g)
• What song, crooned by Ernie of "Sesame Street," topped the charts in 1970?	"Rubber Duckie"
• Elvis Presley's loyal following of friends, bodyguards and musicians were referred to by what nickname?	The "Memphis Mafia"
• What is the most widely sung tune in the English-speaking world?	"Happy Birthday to You"

• Identify the famous pop/rock music groups that once went by these names:

- The Paramours	The Righteous Brothers
- Caesar and Cleo	Sonny and Cher
- Johnny and the Moondogs	The Beatles
- Carl and the Passions	The Beach Boys
- Big Thing	Chicago
- The Golden Gate Rhythm Section	Journey
- Sparrow	Steppenwolf
- Earth	Black Sabbath

• What group is ranked as having the highest grossing concert act in America, having pulled in upwards of $47 million a year from concerts?	The Greatful Dead
• Actor Dustin Hoffman once challenged Paul McCartney to compose a ballad based on the haunting last words of artist Pablo Picasso. McCartney took the dare, and as a result recorded what song with his group, Wings?	"Drink to Me . . . "
• What animal appears on the cover of many of Pink Floyd's albums?	A pig
• What Captain and Tenille song examines the intricacies of rodent romance? For what song did the duo receive a Grammy in 1975?	"Muskrat Love"; "Love Will Keep Us Together"
• What punk rocker died of an overdose before he could be brought to trial for the murder of his girlfriend, Nancy Spungen, who was found dead in New York City's Chelsea Hotel on October 17, 1978?	Sid Vicious
• Carly Simon's 1972 hit "You're So Vain" was said to have been inspired by the actions of what actor?	Warren Beatty

• What pop/rock 'n roll feature artist(s) gave us each of these "trademark" titles?

- "Sad Songs"	Elton John
- "Born in the U.S.A."	Bruce Springsteen
- "Piano Man"	Billy Joel
- "Tapestry"	Carole King
- "You've Got a Friend"	James Taylor
- "U Can't Touch This"	M.C. Hammer

- "Hotel California"	The Eagles
- "Every Breath You Take"	The Police
- "Monday, Monday"	The Mamas and the Papas
- "Bridge Over Troubled Water"	Simon and Garfunkel
- "Stayin' Alive"	The Bee Gees
- "Stop! In the Name of Love"	The Supremes
- "I Heard It Through the Grapevine"	Marvin Gaye
- "Oh Pretty Woman"	Roy Orbison
- "My Girl"	The Temptations
- "The Dock of the Bay"	Otis Redding
- "Breaking Up is Hard to Do"	Neil Sedaka
- "Jump"	Van Halen

• Who is considered by most musical "in-the-knows" to be the most successful family in music history?

The Jacksons

• What does the slogan on folk singer Woody Guthrie's guitar read?

This Machine Kills Fascists

• Name the rock group most closely associated with each of the following performers:

- Robert Plant	Led Zepplin
- Jerry Garcia	The Grateful Dead
- Brian Jones	The Rolling Stones
- Roger Daltry	The Who
- Belinda Carlisle	The Go-Go's
- David Lee Roth	Van Halen
- Fred Mercury	Queen
- Jim Morrison	The Doors

• What popular rock band became the first group to have two video games designed after them?

Journey

• Coincidentally, what song were the Rolling Stones playing during their famous Altamont Speedway free concert when one of the Hell's Angles security force members knifed a member of the audience (an act that was captured on film)?

"Under My Thumb"

THE ANIMAL FAIR
Did You Know That . . .

. . . Bulls are colorblind? (Thus, the traditional red cape used by bullfighters is primarily for aesthetic purposes; it is the movement the bull is attracted to.)

. . . Once the female lays its single egg, the male penguin takes over the job of incubating it for the next two months? (During this period the male does not eat, and will lose up to 40 percent of its body weight.)

. . . The quills of a newborn porcupine are soft enough to touch, but within about four hours they turn into the sharp, prickly needles for which these animals are notorious?

. . . The average male Alaskan brown bear weighs 250 pounds compared to the 487 pounds for the Pennsylvanian brown bear?

. . . A skunk will not bite and throw its scent at the same time?

. . . The human nose can detect a skunk's smell up to one mile away?

. . . The only known animal that will eat a skunk is the great horned owl?

It's a Wild World Out There!

- What one characteristic differs in twin calves born of the opposite sex compared to those born of the same gender?

Opposite-sexed calves are sterile

- Appropriately enough, what is the middle name of George Grinnel, who, in 1886, founded the Audubon Society, named in honor of naturalist John James Audubon?

Bird

- What is the color in the name of the largest living Rhino?

White

- Compared to humans, how many cervical vertebrae does a giraffe's neck contain? (Hint: You and the giraffe have the same number.)

Seven

- What is the name of the *female* offspring of a mule?

Mules are sterile—they have no offspring

- What animal, besides humans, can get a sunburn?

A pig

- What common trait does the hummingbird, the loon, the swift, the kingfisher, and the grebe share?

They are all birds that cannot walk

- What was likely the earliest animal domesticated by man? (Hint: The answer is not the dog.)

The reindeer

- About how many hours a day do each of the following animals sleep?

    - The sloth

20 hours

    - The elephant

2 1/2 hours

    - The horse

5 hours

    - The shrew

It does not sleep at all

    - The squirrel

14 hours

    - The koala

18 hours

    - The rat

13 hours

- What rodent, long prized for its extraordinarily soft fur, is native to the Andes Mountains of South America?

The Chinchilla

- What two kinds of dairy cows are named after the British islands in which their breeds originated?

Guernseys and Jerseys

- Which arctic animal has traditionally held an important role in the lifestyle and economy of the Lapp peoples? Where are these herders found?

Reindeer; in the extreme northern climes of Norway

- Provide the name of the animal that completes the following phrases:

    - To keep the _____ from the door is to ward off hunger.

Wolf

    - In the lap of luxury, one is said to live high on the _____.

Hog

    - A carefree person is said to be happy as a _____ at high tide.

Clam

    - If you're looking to escape responsibility, you're trying to _____ out of it.

Weasel

- Why would it be said of the Great Auk, the Dodo, the Labrador duck, the Carolina parakeet, and the Passenger pigeon that they have only a past but no future?

They are extinct

- What are the names of the two huge lions that guard the entrance to the New York Public Library's central research branch in Manhattan?

Patience and Fortitude

- What do camels store in their humps that, when combined with oxygen molecules from inhaled air, forms water?

Fat

- What two animals describe the up-and-down action of the stock market?

Bull and Bear

• What animal appears on the Izod Lacoste polo shirt? (Hint: It's not an alligator.)	It's a crocodile
• In most species of songbirds, only the males sing. What two primary purposes does this action serve?	To protect territory and to attract a mate
• What is the other name for a wildebeest, a type of wild African cattle?	The gnu
• What kind of an animal does "hog wool" come from?	A year-old sheep
• What kind of archaic animals are the Diplodocus and the Pteranodon?	They are dinosaurs
• Give the name of the "repetitive" bird that deposits its egg in the nests of other birds.	The cuckoo
• Speaking of eggs, identify the following egg-laying animals by their descriptions:	
- This waddling bird lays but one egg per year.	The penguin
- This insect queen lays 30,000 eggs daily.	The termite
- This huge flyer lays only one egg every two years.	The California condor
- This bi-valve mollusk produces some 500 million eggs per year.	The oyster

ARACHNIDS AND ANGIOSPERMS
Did You Know That . . .

. . . Birds avoid eating the colorful Monarch butterfly because its diet of leaves from the poisonous milkweed plant gives it a bad taste?

. . . Only one-half of the people who live in areas where poison ivy grows actually become allergic to it?

. . . The notorious germ-carrying housefly can transport bacteria as far away as 15 miles from the original source of contamination?

. . . When more than one threat is present, a fly's central nervous system will overload, causing immobilization?

. . . Only full-grown male crickets can chirp?

. . . The part of the mushroom that is picked and eaten represents only 10 percent of the entire fungus?

. . . A tarantula spider can live a full two years without food—but when it catches its food, it can devour it quickly? (A tarantula can ingest an entire mouse—including the bones—in only a day and a half.)

. . . According to the U.S. Forest Service, approximately 1,100 types of trees are native to the United States?

. . . If it ever escaped into the wild, a single slug of the Giant African Snail species could conceivably reproduce itself 16 quadrillion times over a five year period?

Bugs and Vegetation—"Creepy" and Otherwise

• What is the only state in the U.S. where houseflies cannot live and breed?	Alaska
• What incestuous insect creates her own husband from scratch and then copulates with her sons within a few days of laying the eggs—after which her sons immediately die?	The female mite
• What plant is the source of the drug digitalis, used to treat heart disease?	The Foxglove
• Name the insect that is roasted and eaten by the handful by many native South African tribes. (Hint: These same "party snacks" once could have eaten the natives out of house and home.)	Termites

• What effect does hard rock music, played to colonies of termites, have on the insects?	With accompaniment, they chew through wood at twice the normal rate.
• So effective is this animal's self-produced protective "foot film" that it can crawl along the cutting edge of a razor without injuring itself. What is it?	A snail
• What is the only species a queen bee will use her stinger on?	Another queen bee
• What are "cooties"?	A type of body lice
• The world's largest living plant is said to be a 3,500-year-old tree that stands 272 feet tall. What is the name of this giant and where is it located?	The General Sherman Tree is a giant sequoia in Sequoia National Park, California
• What insect kills more people world-wide than do all the poisonous snakes combined.	Honeybees
• What is the most widely cultivated plant, and on which continents is it grown?	Wheat; it is cultivated extensively on every continent except Antarctica
• What is the origin of the killer bee that is now making its way north into regions of the United States?	It escaped from an experimental breeding colony in Brazil 35 years after it was introduced.
• What insect seriously damaged the fruit, nut, and vegetable crops of California in the 1980s?	The Mediterranean fruit fly
• In proportion to its size, what insect has the largest brain of any living creature on Earth?	The ant
• In ancient Egypt, this plant's roots were used as fuel, its innards were eaten, and its stems—when torn into strips, plaited together and crushed—provided writing material. Name the plant.	Papyrus
• What sinister flying insect injects her eggs into a host's body—paralyzing its victim without killing it—and then tortures its prey after the eggs hatch by eating its fatty deposits and digestive organs before eating the heart.	The ichneiumon wasp
• What pesky insect has been found by researchers to be the perfect lab specimen since it resists disease, can survive radical surgery, and, if beheaded, dies, not from decapitation, but rather from starvation?	The roach
• What is known as the hardiest of all the world's insects—feeling equally at home at the frigid North Pole as in the steamiest equatorial jungle?	The mosquito
• What tall perennial plant yields a strong fiber used for making rope and the drug cannabis?	Hemp

THE GRIM REAPER—AND HIS HIRELINGS
Did You Know That . . .

. . . A majority of fire-related deaths are due to smoke inhalation rather than burns?

. . . Teenagers are 50 percent more susceptible to catching a cold than people over 50?

. . . Ninety percent of teenagers suffer from some form of acne?

. . . Men commit suicide three times more frequently than women do—but women *attempt* suicide two to three times more often than men?

. . . Over 80 percent of professional boxers have suffered brain damage?

. . . Fewer than ten people were present at "founder of Communism" Karl Marx's funeral in 1883?

. . . In 1888, the worst hailstorm ever recorded hit Moradabad India, killing 246 people?

. . . The world's deadliest famine, which killed an estimated 30 million people in China between 1959 and 1961, was not revealed to the rest of the world until 20 years later?

. . . Amnesty International worldwide organization for the defense of human rights estimates that there are about 500,000 prisoners of conscience throughout the world, and many others who have been summarily executed by governments?

. . . According to a recent study, nearly half of all deaths occur within three months *after* a person's birthday, while only eight percent die during the three-month period *preceding* a birthday? (Researchers hypothesize that the period following a birthday is anticlimactic, whereas the period before is viewed as a psychological goal to be achieved.)

Death, Disease and Injury

- Which of the following is currently the least likely to cause death: smoking, nuclear power, home appliances, or hand guns?

Nuclear power, by far (as far as we know)

- Death is known as one of life's two inevitable misfortunes. Name the other.

Taxes

- In the United States, how many years does it take before a missing person can be declared legally dead?

Seven years

- How many young men were killed in college football games during the 1905 season?

18 (Today, with improvements in equipment, the number of annual football-related deaths can be counted on one hand)

- Name the form of cancer that involves the uncontrolled growth of white blood cells (leukocytes).

Leukemia

- What is the highly transmittable disease that is often referred to as "the kissing disease?"

Mononucleosis

- The symptoms of this common disease are usually brought about as a result either of allergic reactions or exercise, which precipitate a narrowing of the bronchial tubes. What is the name for this disease?

Asthma

- Which of the following sources expose Americans to the largest amount of radiation: buildings, television sets, medical diagnoses, nuclear reactors?

Medical diagnoses

- If you have Verruca Vulgaris, what are you suffering from?

Warts

- What is the virus that causes AIDS?

Human Immunodeficiency Virus (HIV)

- What necessary substance secreted by the pancreas lowers the body's blood sugar levels, and, if not produced in sufficient quantities, can cause diabetes?

Insulin

- Throughout history, what dreaded "bad air" disease has been carried by anopheles mosquitoes?

Malaria

- Name the condition that often afflicts the elderly which is characterized by painful, inflamed and fragile joints.

Arthritis

- When 16-year-old Anissa Ayala of California was diagnosed with leukemia in 1993, what well-publicized—and, according to some, ethically questionable—action did her parents take to successfully save her life?

They conceived a baby to serve as a bone marrow donor for their older daughter

- Roman emperor Augustus Caesar suffered from this "black" phobia. What couldn't Caesar bring himself to do?

Sit in the dark (he had Achluophobia)

- Millionaire businessman Howard Hughes suffered from a fear of public places (agoraphobia). What other phobia did he have?

Mysophobia—fear of germs

- British Queen Elizabeth I suffered from anthophobia. What was she afraid of?

Roses

- Comedian Sid Caesar was known to have tonsurphobia—a fear of _____.

Having his hair cut

- Novelist John Cheever had gephyrophobia, or fear of _____.

Crossing bridges

- On February 26, 1992, Beijing worker Xu Denghai was hospitalized with a "twisted intestine." In fact, Xu was the third such case in several weeks since this craze had swept China. What was the cause of these mysterious injuries? | Excessive play with a Hula Hoop

- The Consumer Product Safety Commission recently found at least 11 brands of these to be a health threat to children because they contain lead. What are they? | Crayons

- Give the common term used to describe the disruption of our circadian rhythm as the result of a lengthy airplane flight. | Jet lag

- What is the only thing that can sober up a liquor-intoxicated person? | Time

- Give the name of the psychiatric disorder that corresponds with the following definitions:

    - People who suffer from this disease mistrust everyone and cannot abandon constant suspicions that someone is "out to get them." | Paranoia

    - Self-love is healthy, to a certain degree. However, this illness is manifested by excessive love of self, including delusions of grandeur and a constant need for attention. | Narcissism

    - People who survive a trauma may have painful recollections or nightmares, and, during an "episode" may in fact behave as if they were reliving the trauma. | Post-Traumatic Stress Disorder

    - Primary symptoms of this illness include delusional thinking, usually accompanied by auditory or visual hallucinations. It seems there is an inherited vulnerability to this disease. | Schizophrenia

    - This disease is characterized by establishment of two or more separate identities that seem to be responsible for a specific feeling or act of the individual. | Multiple Personality Disorder (Split personalities)

- What percentage of the U.S. population seeks mental health treatment each year? | About eleven percent

- What injury is a first-time snow skier most likely to sustain? | Sunburn

- What animal's skin can be successfully grafted onto the human body to repair burns? | A pig's

- According to German researchers, on what day of the week is the risk of heart attack greatest? | Monday (nearly 50 percent greater than on any other day)

- In the Excedrin pain reliever commercials, what was the cause of Excedrin Headache Number 1040? | A tax audit

- What is the name of the bizarre neurological disorder in which one hand acts independently of the other and against the body's wishes—sometimes pinching, slapping, or striking its owner? | The Dr. Strangelove Syndrome

———— ◇ ◆ ✧ ◆ ◇ ————

GOOD ADVICE
Did You Know That . . .

. . . A woman walking past a crew of construction workers can keep herself from being hassled by picking her nose—an act that creates an immediate deterrent?

. . . Since bees are infuriated by the gas that comes out of our mouths when we breath, the best way to avoid a bee sting is to hold your breath?

. . . Mark Twain once made the wise suggestion that "It is better to keep your mouth shut and appear stupid than to open it and remove all doubt"?

. . . If everyone who owned a fax machine switched to half-page cover sheets rather than full-page, it would save nearly two million miles of unrecyclable fax paper a year?

. . . The first of syndicated humor columnist and author Erma Bombeck's "10 Rules to Live By" is "Never have more children than you have car windows"?

Mother Knows Best

• What is the best way to escape an attack by killer bees?

Run in a zigzag motion

• In 1846 a group of 87 pioneers left Illinois on a wagon migration to California. In accordance with Lansford Warren Hastings' authoritative guidebook *Emigrant's Guide to Oregon and California*, they took a new route around the southern tip of the Great Salt Lake and became snowbound in the Sierra Nevada Mountains. Forced to camp for four months, the 47 survivors eventually resorted to cannibalism to ward off starvation. What was the name of this ill-fated company?

The Donner Party, led by George Donner

• The following are statistically documented ways to stretch life expectancy. Guess the amount of time a person can expect to add or subtract from her life by following these bits of advice:

- Install a smoke detector in your home.

Add nine days

- Drink tall glasses of chlorinated swimming-pool water.

Slice off half-a-day

- Drive a sedan rather than a compact car.

Add 70 days

- Always wear a seat belt.

Tack on 69 days

- Try to come in contact with snakes and bees as often as possible.

Subtract 12 hours for each bite or sting

• "Remain still until you are floating, then slowly turn to a horizontal position and roll yourself onto firm ground." What are you doing if you're following this advice?

Extracting yourself from quicksand

• According to the King James Version of The Holy Bible, which commandment advises us against "keeping up with the Joneses"?

The 10th: "Thou shalt not covet thy neighbor's house . . . wife . . . nor any thing that is thy neighbor's"

• When Bob Hope met night club singer Anthony Dominick Benedetto, he advised him to change his name—which he did. What did he change it to?

Tony Bennett

• What was the staunch Miss Post advising against when she recommended the following restrictions: "Certainly not in church, or during recitation periods in school . . . And certainly not when wearing formal clothes"?

Against chewing gum in public

• To combat the problem of misplacing your keys or locking them in your car, Shell Oil offers a list of suggestions. Identify the advice that corresponds with each clue:

- It may be more cumbersome to lug around, but this item is easier to find when you are in a hurry.

Carry an extra-large key ring.

- Instead of using your car's automatic door-lock system, _____.

Always lock your door from the outside using the key.

- If you follow this piece of advice, you will always be able to enter your vehicle, since most people generally carry this around with them.

Carry an extra key in your purse or billfold.

- Many of these offer an emergency service which may pay for or reimburse members for locksmith charges.

Join an auto club.

- By doing this, entrance into your car may just be a phone call away.

Give an extra key to a spouse or friend.

• According to Benjamin Franklin's "Poor Richard's Almanac," what else besides fish "begins to stink in three days"?	House guests (visitors)
• From the same source ("Poor Richard's Almanac"), what is the best way to learn the value of money?	Try to borrow some
• If a grizzly bear begins to attack you, what is the best way to respond?	Curl up in a ball and play dead
• What three well-known historical characters might give you the following bits of advice: "Know yourself . . . ," "Control yourself . . . ," and "Give yourself . . . "?	Socrates, Cicero, and Jesus

WIDE WORLD OF SPORTS
Did You Know That . . .

. . . Seventy percent of all the hats sold each year in the U.S. are baseball caps?

. . . Until the 1870s, baseball games were played without the use of gloves?

. . . Lyrist Jack Northwood, who wrote "Take Me Out To the Ball Game," did not actually attend his first game until 34 years after writing the song?

. . . Tennis star Tracy Austin appeared on the cover of *World Tennis* magazine at age four and *Sports Illustrated* at age 13?

. . . In Thailand, teams of soldiers play tug-of-war against a team of elephants, who wear T-shirts to identify themselves as the opposing team?

C'mon, Be a Sport!

• What is listed as the most dangerous sport by American insurance companies?	Football
• In what high-school sport are the most injuries reported?	Each year, 62% of participants in girls' cross country report an injury
• What is the name marathon runners attach to the physiological phenomenon that typically effects them after 20 miles, caused by the loss of glycogen to the muscles and often resulting in severe cramps and fever?	"Hitting the Wall"
• What notoriously confident tennis player said, "My greatest strength is that I have no weakness"?	John McEnroe
• Why was American football nearly banned in 1905? Who finally stepped in to save the sport?	18 players were killed during games that year; President Theodore Roosevelt took steps to make the game safer
• What basketball squad, organized in Chicago by Abe Saperstein in 1926, remains one of the few professional teams without a home court.	The Harlem Globetrotters

• For the following universities and colleges, give the rather feeble name chosen for their sports-team mascot:

- Whitman College (Washington)	Missionaries
- St. Bonaventure College (New York)	Bonnies
- Centenary College (Louisiana)	Gentlemen
- Whittier College (California)	Poets
- New York University	Violets
- University of Pennsylvania	Quakers
- Heidelberg College (Ohio)	Student Princes
- University of New England (Maine)	Pilgrims

• Often presumed to be ice hockey, what is actually the official national sport of Canada?	Lacrosse

• What purpose do the dimples on a golf ball serve?	They allow the ball to travel faster and farther
• What do the initials in former Buffalo Bills great running back O.J. Simpson's name stand for?	Orenthal James
• In 1915 the Indianapolis 500 was won by Ralph DePalma. However, DePalma did not drive across the finish line; he didn't even finish the race inside his Mercedes. How did he win?	He pushed his car the last mile and a half
• Organized in 1845, the New York Knickerbockers became the first professional team in what sport?	Baseball
• What color of uniform is the home team required to wear in basketball?	White or light colored
• What is China's fast-paced national sport?	Table Tennis (Ping-Pong)
• Name the three sporting events that are won by moving backwards.	Tug of war, the back-stroke (in swimming), and sculling (rowing)
• Prior to the year 1875, when one of its lawns was set aside for a tennis game, for what sport was England's famed Wimbledon Tennis complex designed?	It was the home of the All England Croquet Club
• What TV sports announcer was forced to apologize on national television because the week before he had referred to Richard Nixon as "Tricky Dick"?	ABC Monday Night Football analyst "Dandy" Don Meredith
• Give the name of the real-life sports figures portrayed in the following films:	
- "The Pride of the Yankees"	Lou Gehrig
- "Raging Bull"	Jake LaMotta
- "Fear Strikes Out"	Jimmy Piersall
- "The Pride of St. Louis"	Dizzy Dean
- "Field of Dreams"	"Shoeless" Joe Jackson
• Name the sport originally known as *sphairistike*.	Tennis

SUPERSTITIONS AND FOLKLORE
Did You Know That . . .

. . . In 1969, an estimated 20 million Americans spent more than $150 million on personal horoscopes?

. . . According to Old-English folklore, if a rabbit or a hare crosses the road in front of you, you must take off your hat, spit on it, and put it back on your head?

. . . Standing in front of a latrine and inhaling the stench, being in the presence of pigs, and applying the entrails of a young pigeon or newborn puppy to the forehead were all anti-plague remedies prescribed throughout fourteenth-century Europe?

. . . For centuries wearing a blue shirt or dress has been believed to ward off witches, who, apparently, were thought to abhor the color?

. . . Of gypsies, peasants and gamblers, three groups considered by many to be three of the most superstitious in the world, gamblers are regarded as *the* most superstitious?

Charmed, I'm Sure

• A superstition is a traditional belief that a certain action or event can cause or foretell an apparently unrelated event. Many superstitions deal with important life passages, such as birth, marriage, pregnancy, and death. A *causal* superstition involves taking a deliberate action to ensure good luck or avoid bad luck. Identify what the alleged result will be for each of the following actions or events:

    - A newborn child is carried upstairs before being carried down a flight of stairs.　　He or she will rise to success in the world

- A child is born on a Sunday.	He or she will enjoy good luck
- You drop a knife or fork on the floor.	Company is coming
- A young woman pins a four-leaf clover to her door.	She will marry the first bachelor who comes through the door
- Knocking on wood.	You will avoid bad luck
- A bride and groom see one another on their wedding day prior to the ceremony.	They will have bad luck
- At a wedding, the guests throw rice at the newlyweds.	The marriage will result in many children
- When a person dies, the doors and windows of the room are left open.	The spirit of the departed can leave in peace
- A person always carries a silver dollar with him.	He will carry good luck
- A pregnant woman eats unhealthy foods.	Her child will bear an unwanted birthmark

• Some superstitions likely derived from a practical origin. For example, besides any supernatural effects, what might be the practical result of hanging a bag of garlic around a child's neck to ward off disease?

Its smell keeps away other children—including those carrying any contagious virus

• Similarly, many people believe that lighting cigarettes for three persons from a single match will bring bad luck. For what practical reason may this superstition have started? (Hint: It may have originated among soldiers during World War I.)

At night, a match that stayed lit long enough to light three cigarettes provided an easy target for the enemy

• Name the lucky object that is both looked over in song— and most often overlooked in our everyday travels.

A four-leaf clover

• In fact, finding a four-leaf clover or a horseshoe is said to bring good luck, and is an example of a *sign* superstition. Sign superstitions foretell an event without any conscious action by the person involved. Breaking a mirror or spilling salt, for instance, brings bad luck. What do each of these signs supposedly mean?

- You hear a dog howling in the night.	Death is near
- You meet a person with red hair.	He or she has a quick temper
- You see a ring around the moon.	Rain is on its way

• What other animal, besides black cats, brings bad fortune (since, it is said, witches often transform themselves into this animal)?

Hares

• According to Japanese belief, a sick person should not be given cut flowers, which soon wither and die. What would be a more appropriate gift, representing hope for the patient's recovery?

A potted plant

• Similarly, what would one include inside a gift of a purse or wallet to ensure that the recipient will always be blessed with sufficient money?

Money

• What is teratology?

The study of monsters

• What is tasseography?

Tealeaf reading

• Millions of people place great importance in—and base critical decisions on—the position of the sun, moon, planets and stars. What is this the name of this study?

Astrology

• What would be a proper meal for a fairy?

Milk, cream, and butter

• According to legend, the gift of eloquence can be obtained by kissing the Blarney Stone. However, the stone must be kissed in a specific way to obtain this gift. How must it be kissed—and where is the stone located?

With the head hanging downward; in Blarney Castle near Cork, Ireland

• Considered an omen of bad luck, what is the name of the legendary ghost ship—the subject of one of Wagner's operas—which is said to wander forever off the Cape of Good Hope?	The Flying Dutchman
• What number did musical composer Frederic Chopin fear so intensely that he refused to compose music on this day of the month, and would not live in a house with that number anywhere on it?	Seven
• Complete the following well-known superstitions—most often espoused by con men—by filling in the following blanks:	
- If your _____ _____ itches, rub it on the seat of your pants.	Left hand
- Giving money to a _____ will bring you good luck.	Stranger
- In order to ensure that a police officer won't harass you, always _____ over your left shoulder when you see one.	Spit
- Never _____ on rainy days.	Work
- Never take advantage of anyone with a _____.	Harelip
• If a *lycanthrope* looked in the mirror, what might his reflection show?	A werewolf
• Upon the death of a professional magician, what does tradition stipulate that a colleague do with the deceased's magic wand?	Break it over the casket
• To a folkorist, what is "The Greateful Dead"? (Hint: It is not a rock group.)	It is a tale in which a young man buries a corpse at great personal risk to himself and then obtains a bride with the help of the appreciative deceased
• Induced sneezing, jumping up and down, and swallowing dead bees in honey were all techniques used by both men and women throughout the centuries to prevent what?	Conception of a child

NINE MONTHS TO GO
Did You Know That . . .

. . . A screaming baby can produce a sound level of 90 decibels, five decibels higher than the level that will cause permanent hearing loss?

. . . Several recent studies have proven that preschoolers whose mothers smoked 10 or more cigarettes per day during pregnancy have significantly lower IQs than children of nonsmokers?

. . . Prenatal and infant deaths are significantly higher among males than females?

. . . A fetus reacts to sound as early as the fourth month from conception, and, as a newborn, will most likely turn toward a female voice in preference to that of a male?

Heavy With Child

• What does a human embryo develop into after about eight weeks?	A fetus
• What part of a newborn baby accounts for one-quarter of its entire weight?	Its head
• A gamete is a functional sex cell—either an egg or a sperm—which can unite with a gamete of the opposite sex. What results in the fusion of two gametes?	A zygote

• In the U.S., what are the odds of having twins?	1 in 90
• What blood type is the father sure not to have if a mother with O-type has a B-type baby?	O-type
• How many children did the average married American woman give birth to in the 1600s?	Thirteen
• In the year 1900, what were the most popular first names given to boy and girl American babies?	John and Mary
• What is the synthetic hormone that is used intravenously to either initiate contractions or speed up the progress of labor?	Pitocin
• This approach to childbirth, pioneered by the doctor it was named for, relies on intensive training and practice to substitute useful responses to the stimulus of labor contractions in place of counterproductive ones. What is this method called?	Lamaze
• What is the process in which eggs are fertilized in a test tube and then implanted into the uterus?	In-vitro fertilization
• The fertilization of two ovum results in what type of twins? What is the result of a single egg cell that is fertilized, which then divides into two equal parts?	Fraternal; identical twins
• Which parent's chromosome determines the sex of the baby?	The father's
• What is another name for "pregnancy-induced hypertension"?	Toxemia, or preeclampsia
• Name the yellowish liquid which is excreted from the mammary gland as a precursor to breast milk.	Colostrum
• Uterine contractions occur early in pregnancy but are not usually felt until the last trimester. These mild contractions, often perceived as a moderate hardening of the uterus, are not strong enough to deliver a baby. What are they referred to?	"Braxton Hicks"
• After how many weeks of pregnancy is a miscarriage considered a "premature birth" rather than a "spontaneous abortion"?	20 weeks
• Doctors once believed that a pregnant woman should limit her weight-gain to about 15 pounds. What is considered an acceptable weight-gain during pregnancy now?	Between 25 and 35 pounds
• If both expectant birth parents have three brothers and no sisters, what sex is their baby likely to be?	There is a fifty-fifty chance of having either a boy or a girl. (Gender has not been proven to be genetically determined.)
• According to the National Center for Health Statistics, in what month of the year are most babies born? What is the top birth day?	September; Tuesday

"IN CHURCH"
Did You Know That . . .

. . . Hindus in Nepal worship a personal living goddess (their own *Kumari Devi*) who is chosen at the age of three and must be without any physical blemish? (When the child reaches puberty, his or her *Kumari Devi* is released and replaced by a new goddess.)

. . . According to a survey conducted by the National Opinion Research Center, nine out of ten Americans believe in God, and approximately 40 percent attend church at least two or three times a month?

. . . According to Mohammed, only four perfect women ever lived on the earth: Asia, wife of Pharaoh who raised Moses; Mary, daughter of Imram; Khadijah, Mohammed's first wife; and Fatima, Mohammed's daughter?

. . . Most religious authorities believe the Jews borrowed their belief that Heaven and Hell await humans in the afterlife and that a Messiah will one day bring peace and happiness to the earth from Zoroastrianism?

Praises Unto God

• Name the country that was created in 1929 by an agreement between the Roman Catholic Church and the government of Italy.	Vatican City
• K'ung Fu-tzu, once a Minister of Crime, has inspired some 400 million adherents throughout the world—including Protestants, Buddhists, Taoists and Catholics—through his sacred teachings. By what name is he better known?	Confucius
• What is Siddhartha's First Law of Life—which he discovered while sitting under a bo tree for forty-nine days—that enabled him to become Buddha (the Enlightened One)?	"From good must come good, and from evil must come evil."
• According to the *Koran*, what was the forbidden fruit eaten by Adam and Eve in the Garden of Eden?	A banana
• Who was the founder of Methodism? Where did it begin?	John Wesley; Oxford University
• What religion affirms a belief in the universal brotherhood of man yet rejects the idea of the Trinity (the Christian "Godhead"—Father, Son and Holy Ghost), holding that God is a single being?	Unitarianism
• Who is eligible for election to the papacy?	Any Roman Catholic male who has been baptized
• What have been the three most popular names for popes?	There have been 23 Johns (and 2 John Pauls), 16 Gregorys, and 15 Benedicts
• What celibate religious sect founded the town of Canterbury, New Hampshire?	The Shakers
• The first day of Lent is referred to as what?	Ash Wednesday
• This religion's founder nailed his 95 theses on the Wittenberg Church doors in 1517. Name the religion and the founder.	Lutheranism; Martin Luther
• Give the name of the religion founded by each of the following individuals:	
- Charles Tazel Russell	Jehovah's Witness
- George Fox	The Society of Friends, or Quakers
- Ann Lee	The Shakers
- Margaret and Kate Fox	The Spiritualist Movement
- Emanuel Swedenborg	The Church of the New Jerusalem
- William Miller	The Adventists
- Thomas Campbell	The Disciples of Christ
• Consider these questions about Judaism:	
- What is the name of the four-sided top used for children's play during the Jewish festival of Hanukkah?	The dreidel
- What is the miracle remembered at Hanukkah?	The Maccabeean lamp that burned for eight days without exhausting its oil
- In what book are Jewish religious and civil laws contained?	The *Talmud*
- At what age does a Jewish male celebrate his bar mitzvah?	13 years

- What does the seven-stemmed candelabrum, one of the most famous Jewish emblems, commemorate?

The seven lamps of Solomon's Temple

- Who is considered Judaism's founder?

Abraham

- What is the collective name by which the first five books of the Old Testament are known?

The Pentateuch

- What process involves cutting all religious, social and business ties to a Jewish person who is considered dangerous to the community?

Herem (the Hebrew word for excommunication)

- Give the name of the ceremonial feast which begins the Passover celebration.

Seder

• During the Jewish Seder, most of the foods served are symbolic in nature. Identify each food by its description:

- Symbolizes the haste with which the Jews had to leave Egypt.

Matzah (unleavened bread)

- Represents rebirth.

A hard-boiled egg

- Eaten in remembrance of the sacrificial lamb whose blood was smeared on the doors of Israelites so the angel of death would pass over them.

Roasted shank bone

- Symbolizes the suffering of the Israelites in slavery.

Bitter herbs

- Denotes the tears shed by the slaves.

Salt water

- The "cup of Elijah," symbolizing the Jews' yearning for the coming of the Messiah.

Wine

• Who called religion "the opium of the people"?

Karl Marx

• What Protestant sect is based on the Calvinist creed affirming that salvation is predestined?

Presbyterianism

• Who was the founder of Methodism?

John Wesley

• Muslims are urged to journey to a certain city at least once in their lives, and are always required to face toward it while praying. What is this holy city?

Mecca, Saudi Arabia

• What famous Islamic prophet was born in Mecca?

Mohammed

• What is the literal Arabic translation of word *Muslim*?

"One who surrenders"

• What is the collective name for the basic goals of Hinduism?

The "ends of man"

• When a Hindu is finally released from the cycle of rebirth (reincarnation), he or she returns to the ultimate unchanging reality known as what?

Brahman

• What is the name of Islam's supreme being?

Allah (Arabic for "the Lord")

• What is the state of bliss to which Buddhists aspire?

Nirvana

• What Japanese ritual contains strict rules for preparing and serving a certain beverage as an expression of Zen Buddhism?

A sacred tea ceremony

• On what date does the ancient Islamic calender begin? What is the significance of this date?

September 13, 622; the date on which Mohammed traveled from Mecca to Medina

• Name the collection of works in which the Hindu tenets are set forth.

The Veda

• In what work is it mentioned that one should enter the clean part of a house with the right foot first, and an unclean place with the left foot first (the bathroom, for example)?

The Sharia—the Muslim handbook for living an ideal life

• What do Moslems call the month in which they observe a dawn-to-dusk fast?

Ramadan

WORLD AFFAIRS AND POLITICS
Did You Know That . . .

. . . The last time the United States could boast a national budget surplus was in 1835-36?

. . . After former press secretary James Brady had been shot in the head in the assassination attempt of President Reagan, the President insisted that Brady keep his title as press secretary—despite the fact that he could no longer function as one—and that his successors be referred to as White House "spokesmen"?

. . . There are seven obvious, yet perplexing coincidences about former U.S. Presidents Abraham Lincoln and John F. Kennedy: (1) both were assassinated, (2) both were shot in the head from behind, (3) both were shot on a Friday (4) both had their wives present at the time, (5) Lincoln's assassin (John Wilkes Booth) was born in 1839 while Kennedy's (Lee Harvey Oswald) was born in 1939, (6) Lincoln's personal secretary was surnamed Kennedy while Kennedy's was surnamed Lincoln, and (7) Lincoln was elected in 1860—Kennedy in 1960?

Political Platforms

• During World War II, what American became the first to receive Hitler's Supreme Order of the German Eagle? (Hint: Each kept a framed photograph of the other on his desk.)	Henry Ford
• As of 1994, what were Tamil separatists fighting for on the island of Sri Lanka off the coast of India?	An independent homeland
• What modern-day technologically advanced nation at one time voluntarily gave up guns for more than 200 years?	Japan (1637-1853)
• Name the country that at one time required foreign visitors to wade through a trough of disinfectant upon entering its borders.	Albania
• Hailing a new era of freedom and cooperation, what country finally had its first all-race election in 1994?	South Africa
• What famous film star took time out of his career to serve two years as mayor of the small town of Carmel, California?	Clint Eastwood
• During the 1940 U.S. presidential election campaign, the Democratic and Republican parties were joined by a third party. What was the name of this party, and who ran for president on its ticket?	The Surprise Party; Comedienne Gracie Allen (George Burns' wife)
• What political party, founded by dime novelist Ned Buntline in the 1850s, is today known as the American Party? (Hint: Since this party's adherents were opposed to U.S. immigration policies—especially of allowing Irish-Catholic immigrants—they each took an oath of secrecy.)	The Know Nothing Party
• In its 2,500-year history, which country had never held an election until 1987? What percentage of the population voted that year?	Ethiopia (Abyssinia); 96 percent
• Name the country in which 75 percent of the citizens are still illiterate and make the equivalent of only $80 per capita income a year.	Tibet—currently controlled and occupied by Chinese Communists
• What more common term has been replaced by these more politically correct—perhaps "politically comical"—terms?	
- Differently interesting; charm-free	Boring
- Uniquely coordinated	Clumsy
- Terminally inconvenienced	Dead
- Morally different; ethically disoriented	Dishonest
- Sobriety deprived	Drunk
- A previously recounted humorous narrative	An old joke
- An unaffiliated applicant for private-sector funding	A panhandler

- A nontraditional shopper	A shoplifter
- Melanin impoverished	White
- A directionally impoverished person	A vagrant
• Who is the British version of the United States' Uncle Sam?	John Bull
• On which continent have most of the countries gained their independence only during the last 30 years?	Africa
• What country houses more than a dozen of the world's largest banks in terms of total assets?	Japan
• According to the Population Crisis Committee, what nation has the highest human suffering index? The lowest?	Mozambique; Denmark

THOSE AMAZING PEOPLE
Did You Know That . . .

. . . In 1972 a student skydiver dropped 3,300 feet without his parachute opening, landed on his face, and a few minutes later got up and walked away with only a broken nose and a few missing teeth?

. . . In 1985 a 14-year-old boy in perfect health heard of his girlfriend's desperate need for a heart transplant and publicly vowed that he would give his life if he could save hers? A few days later, the boy collapsed due to a blood clot in the brain and was pronounced brain-dead. His heart was donated to his girlfriend, who recovered completely.

. . . In September 1954, Mrs. Hewlett Holdges of Sylacuaga, Alabama was napping in her living room when a meteorite crashed through her roof and hit her? (She was only slightly injured.)

. . . Two retarded brothers named George and Charles, known as the Bronx Calendar Twins and featured in a 1966 edition of *Life* magazine, can, in just seconds, calculate the day of the week for any date over a period of 80,000 years?

You May Not Believe It, But . . .

• Already a double-leg amputee when shot down and captured by the Nazis, Douglas Bader, one of England's greatest fighter pilots, persistently tried to escape from his POW camp. What did the German guards finally do to stop his escape efforts?	They confiscated one of his artificial legs
• In 1901, Anna Edson Taylor was the first person to take the 186-foot plunge off Niagara Falls. After being helped from the cushioned barrel in which she was enclosed, what fact did she admit that made her feat even more audacious?	She could not swim
• Chang and Eng, a set of twins born in 1811 to Chinese parents living in Siam (now Thailand), worked for P.T. Barnum's circus, after which they married and fathered 22 children. On the same day in 1874, they died. What was extraordinary about these twin boys?	They were conjoined at the hip (thus the name "Siamese Twins") and remained fused throughout their lives
• What was the name of the retired park ranger from Virginia who survived seven direct lightning strikes, making him the most lightning-struck—perhaps most "revolting"—person on record?	Roy C. Sullivan (struck in 1942, '69, '70, '72, '73, '76 and '77)
• On December 13, 1982, this well-known sports figure, while out jogging, saved the life of 67-year old Jessie Dye by freeing her from a burning automobile—after which he continued his jog. Who is this heroic athlete?	Former Heisman Trophy winner and professional running-back Herschel Walker
• After losing both hands in a dynamite explosion, what actor wrote his 1949 autobiography titled *Victory in My Hands*?	Harold Russell
• What autistic mathematical savant, currently residing in Salt Lake City, Utah, was the inspiration for the character played by actor Dustin Hoffman in the Academy Award-winning movie "Rain Man"?	Kim Peake

- This amazing couple has been around since the 1300s and is still going strong. They take the place of anyone whose true identity is unknown—and their names can be found on death certificates, birth certificates and legal documents. Who are they?

John and Jane Doe

- Born in 1674 in Germany, Matthew Buchinger played 12 musical instruments, danced the hornpipe, was an expert with a pistol, excelled in bowling, calligraphy, and magic. Besides these amazing accomplishments, what physical characteristics made this man even more remarkable?

He was only 28 inches tall and had no arms or legs

- The subject of the Emmy-winning film "The Woman Who Willed a Miracle," this prodigious savant is blind, and yet she possesses an extraordinary memory and is able to sing and play the piano with amazing talent. Who is she?

Leslie Lemke

- During the Revolutionary War, an exhausted army messenger nearly collapsed at a Connecticut home—unable to ride any farther. A 16-year-old girl finished the messenger's mission, riding the remaining 40 miles—at night, on horseback—to summon the needed reinforcements. A statue in Carmel, New York commemorates her act. What is this heroine's name?

Sybil Ludington

- In 1983, when 11-year-old Samantha Smith of Maine wrote a letter to Soviet leader Yuri Andropov pleading with him to stop the nuclear arms race. What was Andropov's response? Also, what tragedy occurred two years later?

Samantha was invited to visit him at the Kremlin—which she did; She and her father were killed in a plane crash

—— ◇ ◆✧◆ ◇ ——

WORD SOUND-ALIKES

- The answer to each of the following riddles is a pair of sound-alike—but not spelled-alike—words. Identify the words:

   - I rent a home on the boundary between two countries.

Boarder and border

   - This happens when two female deer take naps.

Does doze

   - Seven rather feeble days.

A weak week

   - How would you tell an item of footwear to go away?

Shoo, shoe!

   - When a large, powerful African animal joins a band of fighters that hide in trees, ambush the enemy, and go on sudden raids, what do you call him?

A guerrilla gorilla

   - This is the money the government collects on the sale of tiny nails.

A tacks tax

   - When Mr. Cornseed finally achieved the status of a high-ranking army officer, what was he called?

Colonel Kernel

   - This year's fashionable country lodging is the _____ _____.

In Inn

   - What is immovable writing paper called?

Stationary stationery

   - What award could you win for sticking your nose into other people's business?

A Meddle Medal

- Identify the sound-alike pairs or triplets for the following set of definitions:

   - To modify or change; an elevated table upon which religious services may be performed.

Alter; altar

   - Inactive or unemployed; one that is adored; an event of rural simplicity.

Idle; idol; idyll

- A line formed by sewing two pieces of material together; to give the impression of being.	Seam; seem
- Entirely; having several perforations; associated with divine power.	Wholly; holey; holy
- To have measured a certain amount; to walk in water.	Weighed; wade
- A portion or element; freedom from disagreement.	Piece; peace
- Most important; a long, thick growth of hair down the neck.	Main; mane
- In the direction of; a cardinal number; in addition.	To; two; too
- To prefer above others; masticates.	Choose; chews
- To have rented for a specified period of time; lowest in importance or rank.	Leased; least
- Of recent origin; either of two large African antelopes; having apprehended with clarity.	New; gnu; knew

• Homographs are words that are spelled alike but pronounced differently. Find the single word to fit each set of dual definitions below:

- The *tiny sixty seconds* passed swiftly.	Minute
- He'll *give* the *gift* after dinner.	Present
- He looked *sickly* in his *pointed* hat.	Peaked
- I suggest you *get back to* typing your *summary of job qualifications*.	Resume(e`)
- The professor *exposes* us to endless lectures on boring *topics*.	Subjects
- He'll *speak closely* with the people who *live and work together*.	Commune
- It will *enrage* him to smell the pleasant *burning aroma*.	Incense
- Her opinions *differ* from his in this *struggle*.	Conflict

TREASURES OF THE EARTH
Did You Know That . . .

. . . It takes about the same amount of energy to make 20 cans from recycled aluminum as it does to make one can from the the raw mineral ore?

. . . Each American expends an average of ten tons of rock and mineral products every year?

. . . It takes 42 different minerals/metals to construct a telephone handset, and the most unadorned TV set contains at least 35?

. . . The gold coating found on the face masks worn by astronauts is what protects them from the sun's fierce radiation?

Can You Dig It?

• Roman soldiers were paid in part with a salt ration called "sarium argentum," which is where the modern term _____ comes from.	"Salary"
• The presence of particular metals serves what purpose in a fireworks display?	The metals are the source of the varied brilliant colors
• Give the name of the mineral that assists in each of the following bodily functions:	
- Essential for manufacturing red blood cells.	Iron

- Required for bone and cell growth and for normal functioning of the nervous system.	Manganese
- Maintains fluid and mineral balance; assists nerves and muscles, and helps the heart function normally.	Potassium
- Aids the body in producing healthy blood cells.	Zinc
- Assists in maintaining healthy muscles, red blood cells and proteins in the hair and nails.	Selenium
- Builds strong bones and teeth; helps nerve function and blood clotting.	Calcium
• What metal is derived from the German "kobold," meaning "goblin"?	Cobalt
• What is carbon-14 primarily used for?	To date objects

• Give the mineral/metal used for each of the following products:

- Jewelry, electrical conductors, and heat shields	Gold
- Thermometers, mercury vapor lamps, electric switches	Mercury
- Batteries, radioactive shields, bullets, and fishing weights	Lead
- Pottery, china, and bricks	Clay
- Glass, computers, lubricants, and water repellents	Silica
- Cement, mortar, and building stone	Limestone
- Mirrors, photographic film, utensils, and coins	Silver
- Fertilizers and animal feed	Phosphates
- Electrical cable and pennies (before 1982)	Copper
- The inside of all pennies minted *after* 1982	Zinc
- Steel girders, nails, tools, and magnets	Iron
- Beverage containers and airplane bodies	Aluminum
- Plaster, wallboard, and alabaster	Gypsum
• The French expression "puvoir hydrogen" means "hydrogen power." How is this term more commonly expressed?	The pH level
• What metallic element—the least dense of any metal—is used as an antidepressant in medicines?	Lithium
• Of the 109 identified elements, only eight make up 98 percent of the Earth's crust, name them.	Oxygen, silicon, aluminum, iron, calcium, sodium, potassium, and magnesium
• What color is diamond dust?	Black
• A diamond will not dissolve in acid. What is the only thing that can destroy it?	Intense heat

—— ◇ ◆✧◆ ◇ ——

NOBODY ASKED, BUT . . .
Did You Know That . . .

. . . A person walks the equivalent of twice around the world in an average lifetime?

. . . More than half the people in the U.S. are technophobic (afraid to familiarize themselves with modern points of technology)?

. . . When you put a shell next to your ear the sound you hear is not that of the ocean, but rather the sounds around you and those coming from inside your ear (amplified by the vibration of air molecules bumping into each other)?

. . . According to *Glamour* magazine, more than 40 percent of American women are now a size 14 or larger, compared to the women's fashion-industry standard, size 8?

. . . As of 1990, 3.6 pounds of toxins had been released from manufacturing plants across the United States?

. . . Before buttons became a common suit coat-cuff adornment, they were first sewn on the cuffs of midshipmen to keep them from wiping their noses with their sleeves?

. . . Gardiner Greene Hubbard, appointed to be the first president of the National Geographic Society in 1888, was also Alexander Graham Bell's father-in-law?

. . . The visible lightning bolt you see during a thunderstorm is not coming from the sky but actually traveling upward from the ground?

. . . During a severe hailstorm in Mississippi on May 11, 1894 an eight-inch-long gopher turtle, completely encased in ice, fell to the ground?

Well, You're Still Reading, So . . .

• What letter of the alphabet is located at the top of an optomestrist's eye chart?	"E"
• How many times a month does the average American male cry? The average female?	1.5; over 5
• On a standard cube, how many more corners than sides are there?	Two (eight corners, six sides)
• According to a recent Dell Computer Corp. survey, how many Americans have never programmed a VCR to record a television show?	25 percent
• How many words is a regular lead pencil capable of writing?	About 50,000
• What letter is to the left of "V" on a computer keyboard?	"C"
• According to custom which side of a cow would you sit on during milking time?	The left
• Name the annual award which is presented by the National Council of Teachers of English to a specific public figure or agency who uses the most deceptive, evasive and confusing language?	The Doublespeak Award
• What Patuxet/Wampanoag Indian achieved fame for helping the Pilgrims survive their first winter in America?	Squanto
• What percent of U.S. taxpayers typically mail in their returns on the last possible day (April 15)?	33 percent
• Of the 25 highest mountains on Earth, in what single area can you find 19 of them?	The Himalayas (in Tibet)
• What do veteran sailor term a comrade who has not yet crossed the equator?	A Polliwog
• According to the book *52 Ways to Live a Long and Healthy Life*, what percentage of Americans are happy with their physical appearance?	Four percent
• What is still the most popular Halloween mask purchased by adults?	The Richard Nixon mask
• How many *non-adult* U.S. residents own their own television sets?	50 percent
• What inspired Leo Gerstenzag to invent Q-Tips cotton swabs in 1923?	He saw his wife use cotton on the end of a toothpick to clean their baby's ears
• What couple created the first "Barbie" doll in their basement in 1959? Who is the doll named after?	Elliot and Ruth Handler; their only daughter
• What is the name of the large sea monster that represents the forces of evil in the Old Testament?	Leviathan
• How long would it take a lightly-clothed person to freeze to death in the Antarctica—or, for that matter, anywhere else—at a temperature of -70 degrees Fahrenheit?	Only about 60 seconds

• Give the *kn-* word that matches each of these quasi-definitions:

- One nautical mile an hour.	A knot
- A "treasured" fort.	Knox
- *Casting on* a needle.	Knitting
- An benevolent international organization of Roman Catholic men.	Knights of Columbus
- Probably the most useful of all the common tools used by people.	The knife
- A bag worn on the back during hikes.	A knapsack
- To strike with a hard blow.	Knock
- The *patella*	The kneecap
- A small rounded hill.	A knoll
- To ring or sound a bell (especially for a funeral).	Knell
- Understanding gained through experience or study (as in the phrase, "_____ is swell").	Knowledge

★ ★ ★ ★ ★
What Readers Are Doing With The Book

One reader (who had already purchased a copy for himself) picked up another copy of the Bathroom Book for a friend who was turning 40. He wrapped it up, complete with a package of stool softener, and presented it at the surprise party. He came back the next day and said it got the best laugh of the night. Other readers report having friends walk out of the bathroom saying "Where did you get this?" Then they've turned around and headed straight for the store. One woman wrapped it up in toilet paper and gave it as a house warming present. She called the publisher to report it was "a hit!" and ordered four more copies. A scout master came in to one store and purchased 10 copies for all the young men in his troop. "Wish I'd had one of these when I was in school," was his comment.

★ ★ ★ ★ ★
The Story Behind the Book

The story behind this book is just as fun as the cover and the contents. The Great American Bathroom Book was conceived by Lan England, an entrepreneur, on a long cross-country flight. (Lan hates to read novels. He just wants the facts.) On the flight, he started wishing he had short summaries of all the classics he'd heard about. He wanted to know what was inside those great books, but he didn't have time to read them.

Lan decided he wasn't the only one who would like this, so he hired an editor, Stevens Anderson, who hired college professors and other bookworms who loved to read. A list of classics was compiled. Great books—from many different categories and genres—were read and reviewed. Stevens edited each summary for consistency and flow and put together the book Lan wanted. (At his office, the staff likes to tease Lan—he still hasn't finished reading the whole book. He just grins. He now has reading material for long flights for the rest of his life, with two more volumes now available.)

The original version was titled Compact Classics, but, so many of Lan's customers mentioned they were reading Compact Classics in the bathroom...the unofficial "library" in many homes...that he couldn't resist retitling Compact Classics as The Great American Bathroom Book. The rest is publishing history. The retitling of this book may have made Shakespeare rethink his adage that "a rose by any other name would smell as sweet." Compact Classics has sold modestly, but The Great American Bathroom Book is breaking all kinds of records.

Whether you're intrigued by the title, the contents, the idea behind the book, or its repackaging history, it's well worth reading. Check with your local bookstore. If they don't have it, call 1-800-755-9777. Then, wherever you like to read, whether it's in the tub, on a plane, or at the office, lean back and enjoy one great book after another.

ORDER FORM

Complete Satisfaction Guaranteed! 30-Day Money-Back Guarantee

❏ New Customer

Name_____

Address_____

City_____ State_____ Zip_____

Phone (   )_____

Method of Payment: Check One (To avoid delay, payment must accompany order)

❏ Check enclosed payable to Compact Classics
❏ Money Order (enclosed) Sorry, no C.O.D.'s or Cash
❏ VISA   ❏ MasterCard   ❏ Discover

Acct# _____ Exp. Dt. _____

Signature _____

Mail this form today, or for faster service call: TOLL-FREE 1-800-755-9777, 7 AM-5 PM (MST) Mon. - Fri.

		Qty.	Price	Total
VOLUME 1				
The Great American Bathroom Book	(1-880184-04-4)		19.95	
Compact Classics Library Edition	(1-880184-01-X)		19.95	
Compact Classics Planner Edition	(1-880184-00-1)		39.95	
Compact Classics Leather Bound	(1-880184-15-X)		49.95	
CD-ROM w/ book G.A.B.B.	(1-880184-45-1)		39.95	
CD-ROM only G.A.B.B.	(1-880184-49-4)		29.95	
Floppy Disc w/book G.A.B.B.	(1-880184-47-8)		39.95	
Floppy Disc only G.A.B.B.	(1-880184-51-6)		29.95	
VOLUME 2				
The Great American Bathroom Book	(1-880184-10-9)		19.95	
Compact Classics Library Edition	(1-880184-11-7)		19.95	
Compact Classics Planner Edition	(1-880184-12-5)		39.95	
Compact Classics Leather Bound	(1-880184-14-1)		49.95	
CD-ROM w/ book G.A.B.B.	(1-880184-46-X)		39.95	
CD-ROM only G.A.B.B.	(1-880184-50-8)		29.95	
Floppy Disc w/book G.A.B.B.	(1-880184-48-6)		39.95	
Floppy Disc only G.A.B.B.	(1-880184-52-4)		29.95	
VOLUME 3				
The Great American Bathroom Book	(1-880184-26-5)		19.95	
Compact Classics Library Edition	(1-880184-25-7)		19.95	
Compact Classics Planner Edition	(1-880184-27-3)		39.95	
Compact Classics Leather Bound	(1-880184-28-1)		49.95	
3 VOLUME SETS				
The Great American Bathroom Book	(1-880184-29-X)		56.95	
Compact Classics Library Edition	(1-880184-30-3)		56.95	
NEW SIZE! 8 1/2" X 11" VOLUME 1 ONLY				
The Great American Bathroom Book	(1-880184-41-9)		24.95	
Compact Classics Library Edition	(1-880184-31-1)		24.95	
THE GREAT CANADIAN BATHROOM BOOK		U.S. Currency Only		
Volume 1	(1-880184-06-0)		19.95	
Volume 2	(1-880184-13-3)		19.95	
Volume 3	(1-880184-32-X)		Coming Soon	
Also available in many fine bookstores.		Shipping & handling (Utah residents add 6.25% sales tax) Continental U.S. only	$3.00	$3.00
			TOTAL	

COMPACT CLASSICS INC.
P.O. BOX 526145
SALT LAKE CITY, UTAH 84152-6145

FROM: